REFERENCE

Holidays and Anniversaries of the World

Holidays and Anniversaries of the World

A Comprehensive Catalogue Containing Detailed Information
on Every Month and Day of the Year, with Extensive Coverage of
Holidays, Anniversaries, Fasts and Feasts, Holy Days, Days of the Saints,
the Blesseds, and Other Days of Heortological Significance,
Birthdays of the Famous, Important Dates in History, and Special
Events and Their Sponsors, with an Introduction on the Development
of Our Modern Calendar That Includes Notes of Interest on the
Egyptian, Babylonian, Hebrew, Roman, and Gregorian Calendars,
a Perpetual Calendar for the Years 1753-2100, a Projection
of Major Movable Feasts through 1990, As Well As a Glossary of
Time Words, the Text Arranged in Calendar Order and Supplemented
by an Index of All Listed Names and Events

FIRST EDITION

Laurence Urdang, Editorial Director

Christine N. Donohue, Editor

Frank R. Abate, Managing Editor

GALE RESEARCH COMPANY ● BOOK TOWER ● DETROIT, MICHIGAN 48226

Editorial Staff:

Editorial Director: Laurence Urdang
Editor: Christine N. Donohue
Managing Editor: Frank R. Abate
Glossary Editor: Ethel Olicker

Editorial Associates: Peter M. Gross,
   Linda M. D. Legassie, Charles F. Ruhe

Editorial Assistants: Pamela Korsmeyer,
   Emily Mitchell

Research Assistants: Joan W. Allingham, Julie
   Battersby, Patricia Bunker, Laura Devine, Barbara
   Ann Kipfer, Carolyn Kolwicz, Dorothy H.
   McCaughtry, J. Inka Perczerski, Mary P. Savage,
   Martha Smart

Keyboarding: Jean Hankins

Consultants:

The Rev. Harvey Blaise, Bethany Lutheran Church,
   West Hartford, Connecticut
The Rev. Douglas T. Cooke, Archdiocese of Hartford,
   Connecticut
Jean Dudley, Astronomer, U.S. Naval Observatory,
   Washington, D.C.
Dr. Wadi Z. Haddad, Hartford Seminary Foundation,
   Hartford, Connecticut
Peter Knapp, Head of Reference, Library, Trinity
   College, Hartford, Connecticut
Dr. David Menke, Director, Copernican Observatory,
   Central Connecticut State University, New Britian,
   Connecticut
Renae P. Reese, Yale-China Association, New Haven,
   Connecticut

Gale Research Company:

Publisher: Frederick G. Ruffner
Executive Vice-President/Editorial: James M. Ethridge
Editorial Director: Dedria Bryfonski
Director, Indexes and Dictionaries Division: Ellen T.
   Crowley

Production Director: Carol Blanchard
Production Associate: Dorothy Kalleberg
Art Director: Arthur Chartow

Library of Congress Cataloging in Publication Data

Main entry under title:

Holidays & anniversaries of the world.

   Includes index.
   1. Holidays. 2. Chronology, Historical. 3. Calendar.
I. Urdang, Laurence. II. Donohue, Christine N.
III. Abate, Frank R. IV. Title: Holidays and anniver-
saries of the world.
GT3930.H65 1985   394.2′6   85-10350
ISBN 0-8103-1546-7

Typographic and Systems Design by Laurence Urdang
Data Processing, Composition, and Paste-up by Alexander Typesetting Inc., Indianapolis, Indiana

Printed in the United States of America

Contents

Foreword

For thousands of years, man has needed calendars, in the earliest times to enable him to predict the most propitious times for planting and harvesting, later on, to schedule religious observances that might not have coincided, as they had before, with agricultural needs. It is to the need for calendars that the development of astronomy can be traced, for men determined that the regularity of the positioning of the heavenly bodies would enable them to predict, with some accuracy, the seasons of the year. Early calculations were based on the moon, partly because its changes were viewed as magical, partly because it offered a readily observable, regular object on which to base observations. Most of the religions of the world developed calendars for holy days based on the moon's positions and the frequency of appearance of its several phases.

Despite the replacement of the lunar calendars in everyday life by more predictable solar, then astronomical, calendars, religions today still calculate many major holidays on the old "lunar month"—a term that is redundant, at least etymologically. Hence, it has become difficult for the layman to determine when Easter, Ramadan, or Yom Kippur falls without some help, as these movable holidays, unlike Christmas, Bastille Day, and the Fourth of July, are not tied to a particular date in the modern calendar.

In more recent times, and especially since the beginning of the Christian Era, holy days have traditionally been linked with dates in the civil calendar, and most of the information offered in *Holidays & Anniversaries of the World* is organized in keeping with the January 1–December 31 year, which is recognized everywhere today and observed in most countries.

This book, though arranged in chronological sequence, is provided with a comprehensive index that enables the user to look up any particular event or name he may be seeking for reference to the date or dates of occurrence or significance. Saints' days, Blesseds' days, days of major events in world history, holidays and anniversaries of all major—and many minor—nations are included, together with the birth dates of well-known people from every area of human endeavor. The user is thus enabled to look up a given day—say, his birthday—and learn the important events that took place on that day throughout history as well as the famous people born on that day.

For the practical, a given date can be checked to determine whether it is a bank holiday in Scotland, a national holiday in The Gambia, or a religious fast day in Saudi Arabia.

For businesses and institutions that attend to the many and various "Days," "Weeks," or "Months" such as have been established for promotional purposes, such Special Events are detailed in the pages at the beginning of a given month, along with the names and addresses of their sponsors. These, too, are included in the index. In addition, certain days, like Mother's Day and Election Day, are listed in the months when they occur, with information about how they are established—e.g., "the first Sunday," "the first Tuesday after the first Monday," etc.

Historians, historical novelists, and science-fiction writers will find useful the Perpetual Calendar, which allows for the ready calculation of the day of every date (or the date of every day) for every year from 1753 through 2100. For those unable to recall it, the day of the week on which they were born can easily be determined.

Within the realm of practicality, every religious and civil observance in modern times has been documented, making *Holidays & Anniversaries of the World* an invaluable work of reference, the most complete book of its kind available today. During the course of the compilation and editing of *Holidays & Anniversaries of the World*, many thousands of facts, dates, and names have been laboriously checked for accuracy. Still, the editors realize that there will be unfortunate omissions and the need for corrections, so we welcome the comments and suggestions of all who use the book. It is hoped that in a subsequent edition we may then be able not only to update the book but to enhance its accuracy and usefulness.

Laurence Urdang

Essex, Connecticut

Introduction

Holidays & Anniversaries of the World is really a book about time, at least, absolute time and the arbitrary standards that have been used to measure and mark it. The concentration in the text is upon people and events of all periods, ancient and modern, with the approach and structure provided by the familiar (to most) and widely utilized Gregorian calendar system. All manner of significant and curious people, events, and dates are herein recorded in order from January through December.

For each of the 366 days of the Gregorian year are listed regional, national, and international holidays and anniversaries: both civil and religious, fixed and movable; birthdates of renowned individuals: political and religious leaders, artists, inventors, entrepreneurs, celebrities, etc., who have influenced history or culture; and finally historical events of significance or interest. In addition, every month is treated individually, with a brief note on its history, name, and associations, as well as a list of special holidays, commemorations, and events celebrated, observed, or sponsored during that month in places around the world. Whether for serious research or casual browsing, there is quick and convenient reference to pertinent information on each and every day and month of the year. This vast array of material is also conveniently accessible through the detailed index that follows the text.

To supplement the text and enhance the overall usefulness of *Holidays & Anniversaries*, several additional features have been included in this Introduction, viz.:

1. A historical presentation of the development of our modern calendar, wherein are discussed the Babylonian, Egyptian, and Hebrew calendars, as well as the early Roman, Julian, and, finally, Gregorian systems.

2. A projection of major movable holidays for the years 1985 through 1990.

3. An easy-to-use perpetual calendar covering the years 1753 through 2100.

4. A glossary of time words, compiled by Ethel Olicker, including tables that present and explain common abbreviations and references to time that are the subject of frequent questions.

The Development of Our Modern Calendar

The Egyptian Calendar

The earliest calendar known, that of the Egyptians, was lunar-based, i.e., dependent upon observation of one cycle of the moon's phases, say from one new moon to the next. One cycle is a lunar month, about 29.5 days in length (by solar reckoning). Although the observations required for lunar reckoning are fairly simple, reliance upon lunar months eventually leads to a problem: a lunar year, based upon 12 lunations (complete lunar cycles), is only 354 days, shorter than the solar year by more than 11 days. In any agricultural society (such as ancient Egypt), the solar-based seasons of the year are vitally important, as they are the most reliable guide for knowing when to plow, plant, harvest, store, etc. Hence the discrepancy between the lunar and solar year must somehow be addressed.

The Egyptian solution was to rely on a solar calendar to govern civil affairs and agriculture; this was put in place around the third millennium B.C. This calendar observed the same new year's day as the older lunar one, which for the Egyptians was the day, about July 3, of the heliacal rising (i.e., appearance on the horizon just before sunrise) of the star Sirius, the "Dog Star," called Sothis by the Egyptians. This event was significant for the Egyptians, for it was nearly coincidental with the annual flooding of the Nile, the key to their agricultural prosperity. The new Egyptian solar calendar also retained the division of days into months, although they were no longer based on lunar cycles. The Egyptian year in the reformed calendar contained 12 months of 30 days, with 5 intercalated days, bringing the total number of days to 365, only a fraction of a day different from the length of the solar year as determined by modern scientific means.

The Sumerian Calendar

Like the early Egyptian calendar, the ancient Sumerian calendar, developed around the 27th century B.C., was lunar. To the Sumerians, however, the lunar cycles apparently had greater significance, for they retained lunar months and a 354-day year, making alignment with the seasons by means of intercalation, i.e., the addition of extra days outside the regular calendar, added as necessary to reconcile the lunar with the solar year. The calendar of the sacred city of Nippur, which became the Sumerian standard in the 18th century B.C., assigned names to the months, with the intercalary month designated by royal decree. (See also below.)

The Seven-day Week

The ancient Babylonians, a Sumerian people, are thought to be the first people to observe a seven-day week. The concept apparently was based upon the periods between the distinct phases of the moon, which roughly correspond to seven days. They also regarded the number seven as sacred, probably because of the fact that the Babylonians, in their highly developed astronomy, knew of seven principal heavenly bodies. The Babylonians saw supernatural significance in the movements of the seven: Sun, Moon, Mars, Mercury, Jupiter, Venus, and Saturn. They referred to them as *bibbu* 'wild sheep' because of their irregular movements against a backdrop of fixed stars. The days of the week were named for these principal heavenly bodies, one assigned to each day according to which governed the first hour of that day. (See also below.)

In addition to their lunar calendar, the Babylonians also devised a solar calendar based upon the points at which the sun rises in relation to the constellations. This calendar is the basis for the zodiac system, the key to astrology.

From the Babylonians, the ancient Hebrews are believed to have adopted the practices of intercalation and observance of a seven-day week, probably during the time of Jewish captivity in Babylon beginning in 586 B.C. Babylonian influence may also have suggested or at least encouraged the practice of observing every seventh day as special—the Jewish concept of a Sabbath. It should be mentioned, however, that evidence for an earlier Jewish calendar (from at least the 12th century B.C.) does exist, so the observance of a Sabbath may well antedate Babylonian influence. In any event, it is clear that the tradition of the seven-day week, as well as the retention of the concept of months, has much to do with the Western inheritance of Jewish calendar practices. (See also **The Hebrew Calendar**, below.)

The seven-day week as we know it today was carried into Christian use in the 1st century A.D. and was officially adopted by the Roman emperor Constantine in the 4th century. It is also worth noting that the English names for the days and their Romance equivalents still reflect, etymologically, their origin in the references to the seven principal heavenly bodies of the ancient Babylonian astronomy:

Sunday
Old English *Sunnan daeg*, a translation of Latin *dies solis* 'day of the sun.'

Monday
Old English *Monan daeg*, a translation of Latin *lunae dies* 'day of the moon'; cf. French *lundi*.

Tuesday
Old English *Tiwes daeg* 'day of Tiw,' an adaptation of Latin *dies Martis* 'day of Mars' (the god Tiw being identified with the Roman Mars); cf. French *mardi*.

Wednesday
Old English *Wodnes daeg* 'Woden's Day,' an adaptation of Latin *Mercurii dies* 'day of Mercury' (the god Woden being identified with the Roman Mercury); cf. French *mercredi*.

Thursday
Old English *Thunres daeg* 'Thunor's day' or 'Thor's day,' an adaptation of the Latin *dies Jovis* 'day of Jove' (the god Thor being identified with the Roman Jove); cf. French *jeudi*.

Friday
Old English *Friȝe daeg* 'Freya's Day,' an adaptation of the Latin *dies Veneris* 'day of Venus' (the goddess Freya being identified with the Roman Venus); cf. French *vendredi*.

Saturday
Old English *Saetern(es) daeg*, derived from the Latin *Saturni Dies* 'day of Saturn.'

The Hebrew Calendar

Little is known of the Hebrew calendar prior to the Exodus from Egypt (c. 1250 B.C.) except that it appears to have contained four single and four double months called *yereah*. The early Hebrews apparently did not study the heavens and timekeeping as did their Sumerian and Egyptian neighbors. In fact, it was only after the period of Babylonian Exile (586–516 B.C.) that a more fully developed method of timekeeping was adopted to modify the ancient practices. After their return from captivity, the Hebrews employed a calendar very similar to that of the Babylonians, intercalating months into the lunar calendar to keep it in correspondence with the solar year. However, despite the Babylonian practice of marking the beginning of the new year in the spring, the Hebrews retained the custom of recognizing the new year in the autumn, the time of their principal religious festivals of Rosh Hashanah (New Year), Yom Kippur, and Sukkoth, all falling in the month of Tishri (September/October). Still, similarities of the Jewish to the Babylonian calendar are clear from a comparison of the names used in each system for the months:

The Names of the Months in the Babylonian and Jewish Calendar Systems:

Babylonian	Jewish	equivalent
Nisanu	*Nisan*	March/April
Aiaru	*Iyar*	April/May
Simanu	*Sivan*	May/June
Du'uzu	*Tammuz*	June/July
Abu	*Ab*	July/August
Ululu	*Elul*	August/September
Tashritu	*Tishri*	September/October
Arahsamnu	*Heshvan*	October/November
Kislimu	*Kislev*	November/December
Tebetu	*Tebet*	December/January
Shabatu	*Shebat*	January/February
Adaru I	*Adar*	February/March
Adaru II	*Veadar*	(intercalary)

Thus, the year in the Jewish (and Babylonian) calendar consists of 12 lunar months, with the addition of the intercalary month, as necessary, to synchronize with the solar year. The months contain alternately 29 or 30 days; the beginning of each originally was marked by the appearance of the new moon, but with the use of intercalation this correspondence no longer obtained.

The Hebrew week ends with observation of the Sabbath, lasting from sunset Friday to sunset Saturday, a day to rest and pay homage to God. The use of weeks and observation of a day of rest are primarily contributions from Jewish tradition to our present-day calendar. (See also **The Seven-day Week**, above.)

The Jewish Era, designated *A.M.* (for Latin *anno mundi* 'year of the world'), begins with the supposed date of Creation, which tradition sets at 3761 B.C.

After more than two thousand years, devout Jews still observe essentially the same calendar for religious purposes, although they follow other calendars for their business and social life. With its Mosaic roots and later, though still ancient, modifications, the Hebrew calendar has remained a primary binding force of tradition and continuity throughout the long and varied history of the Jewish people.

The Early Roman Calendar

Another source of significant influence in the development of our modern method of reckoning time was ancient Rome. The earliest known Roman calendar, created, according to legend, by the city's eponymous founder, Romulus, in the 8th century B.C., had 10 months totalling 304 days—6 months of 30 days and 4 months of 31 days. The new year began in March, the time when agricultural activities were revived and new military campaigns were initiated, and ended with December, which was followed by a winter gap that was used for intercalation. The Etruscan king Numa Pompilius (reigned 715–673 B.C.) reformed the primitive calendar of Romulus, instituting a lunar year of 12 months. The two new months, following December, were named *Januarius* and *Februarius*, and were respectively assigned 29 and 28 days.

While this reform was a clear improvement, it was set aside at Rome after the expulsion of the kings in about 510 B.C.. Still, its advantages were remembered, and in 153 B.C. the calendar of Numa Pompilius was once again adopted. At the same time the beginning of the Roman civil year was changed to January 1, which became the day that newly elected consuls assumed office.

Days of the Roman Month

The Romans had no serial method of numbering the days of their months. They did, however, establish three fixed points from which other days could be reckoned. These three designations were: 1) *Kalends*, the first day of the month (ancestor of English *calendar*); 2) *Nones*, the ninth day (reckoned inclusively) before 3) *Ides*, originally the day of the full moon of the lunar month. In months of 31 days (March, May, July, October) the Nones were the seventh day and the Ides the fifteenth, while in the shorter months the Nones fell on the fifth and the Ides on the thirteenth day.

The Romans also recognized a market day, called *nundinae*, which occurred every eighth day. This established a cycle for agriculture in which the farmer worked for seven days in his field and brought his produce to the city on the eighth for sale.

The Julian Calendar

It was not until the mid-first century B.C., by which time the reformed lunar calendar had shifted eight weeks out of phase with the seasons, that Julius

Caesar took it upon himself to effect a truly long-term and scientific reform of the calendar. In order to accomplish this, he enlisted the aid of the Alexandrian astronomer Sosigenes to devise a new calendar. The solar year was reckoned quite accurately at 365.25, and the calendar provided for years of 365 days with an additional day in February every fourth year. In 46 B.C. a total of 90 days were intercalated into the year, bringing the calendar back into phase with the seasons. As a result, what would have been March 1, 45 B.C. was, in the new system, referred to as January 1, 45 B.C. Thus 46 B.C. was a long year, containing 445 days, and was referred to by the Romans as *ultimus annus confusionis* 'the last year of the muddled reckoning.'

In 10 B.C. it was found that the priests in charge of administering the new Roman calendar had wrongly intercalated the extra day every third year rather than every fourth. In order to rectify the situation, the emperor Augustus declared that no 366-day years should be observed for the next 12 years, and made certain that future intercalation would be properly conducted. With this minor adjustment, the Julian calendar was fully in place, so to remain for the next 1626 years.

The Gregorian Calendar

Since the Julian calendar year of 365.25 days (averaging in the leap-year day) was slightly longer than the actual length of a solar year, 365.242199 days, over time even this system proved wanting, growing out of phase by about three days every four centuries. By the time of Pope Gregory XIII in the late 16th century, the difference between the calendar and the seasons had grown to 10 days; the vernal equinox of 1582 occurred on March 11. Left without change, the Julian calendar would have resulted in fixed holy days occurring in the "wrong" season, which bewil-dered church officials. Moreover, certain fixed holy days were also used to determine when to plant and harvest crops. Pope Gregory's reform, enunciated in the papal bull of February 24, 1582, consisted of deleting 10 days from the year (the day following October 5 was designated as October 15) and declaring that three out of every four "century" years (1700, 1800, etc.) would not be leap years; if a century year, such as 1600, were divisible by 400, it would be a leap year. These modifications established the form of our present calendar.

In spite of its superior accuracy, the Gregorian calendar met with resistance in various parts of the world, and was not utilized until the 18th century in Protestant Europe and the American colonies, and even later still in areas under strong Byzantine influence:

Dates of Adoption of the Gregorian Calendar

Countries	Date of Adoption
Italy, France, Spain, Portugal, Luxembourg	1582
Germany (Protestant areas), Sweden, Norway	1700
Great Britain & colonies	1752
Japan	1873
Egypt	1876
Turkey	1908
China	1912
Bulgaria	1915
Russia, Finland	1918
Rumania	1919
Greece	1923

Although the Gregorian calendar measures out a year that is slightly longer than the solar year (differing by about 25 seconds a year, or 3 days in every 10,000 years) its general workability and accuracy have led to its use world-wide for nearly all non-religious purposes.

Projection of Movable Holidays 1985–1990

The holidays listed below are not fixed to particular dates on the Gregorian calendar, owing to their dependence upon a lunar-based calendar. Each is given with its date of incidence according to the Gregorian calendar for the years shown.

Principal Christian Holidays

Ash Wednesday
1985 February 20
1986 February 12
1987 March 4
1988 February 17
1989 February 8
1990 February 28

Ascension Thursday
1985 May 15
1986 May 8
1987 May 28
1988 May 12
1989 May 4
1990 May 24

Trinity Sunday
1985 June 2
1986 May 25
1987 June 2
1988 May 29
1989 May 21
1990 June 10

Easter Sunday
1985 April 7
1986 March 30
1987 April 19
1988 April 3
1989 March 26
1990 April 15

Pentecost Sunday
1985 May 26
1986 May 18
1987 June 7
1988 May 22
1989 May 14
1990 June 3

Beginning of Advent
1985 December 1
1986 November 30
1987 November 29
1988 November 27
1989 December 3
1990 December 2

Principal Jewish Holidays

Purim
1985 March 7
1986 March 25
1987 March 15
1988 March 3
1989 March 21
1990 March 11

Tish Ab B'ab
1985 July 27
1986 August 14
1987 August 4
1988 July 23
1989 August 10
1990 July 31

Shemini Atzereth
1985 October 7
1986 October 25
1987 October 15
1988 October 3
1989 October 21
1990 October 11

Passover
1985 April 6
1986 April 24
1987 April 14
1988 April 2
1989 April 20
1990 April 10

Rosh Hashanah
1985 September 16
1986 October 4
1987 September 24
1988 September 12
1989 September 30
1990 September 20

Simhath Torah
1985 October 8
1986 October 26
1987 October 16
1988 October 4
1989 October 22
1990 October 12

Yom Ha' Azma'ut
1985 April 25
1986 May 14
1987 May 5
1988 April 21
1989 May 10
1990 April 30

Yom Kippur
1985 September 25
1986 October 13
1987 October 3
1988 September 21
1989 October 9
1990 September 28

Hanukkah
1985 December 8
1986 December 27
1987 December 16
1988 December 4
1989 December 23
1990 December 12

Shavuoth
1985 May 26
1986 June 13
1987 June 3
1988 May 22
1989 June 9
1990 May 30

Sukkoth
1985 September 30
1986 October 18
1987 October 8
1988 September 26
1989 October 14
1990 October 4

Principal Islamic Holidays

N.B.: The dates shown are only approximations, since the months in the Islamic calendar do not begin until there has been a verified, visual sighting of the new moon.

1 Ramadan

1985	May 21
1986	May 11
1987	April 30
1988	April 19
1989	April 8
1990	March 29

10 Dhu'l Hijjah

1985	August 28
1986	August 17
1987	August 6
1988	July 26
1989	July 15
1990	July 5

1 Muharram

1985	September 16
1986	September 6
1987	August 26
1988	August 14
1989	August 4
1990	July 24

10 Muharram

1985	September 25
1986	September 15
1987	September 4
1988	August 23
1989	August 13
1990	August 2

12 Rabi Al-Awal

1985	November 26
1986	November 15
1987	November 5
1988	October 24
1989	October 14
1990	October 3

Chinese New Year

Date		**Chinese Year**
1985	February 22	Yi Chou (Ox)
1986	February 9	Bing Yin (Tiger)
1987	January 30	Ding Mao (Hare)
1988	February 17	Wu Chen (Dragon)
1989	February 6	Ji Si (Snake)
1990	January 27	Kang Wu (Horse)

Perpetual Calendar: 1753–2100

To find the calendar in use for any month or year from 1753 (the year in which Great Britain and its possessions adopted the Gregorian calendar) to 2100, simply select the desired year from the table at right, read the number next to it, and refer to the calendar so numbered.

For example, to find the day of the week on which *July 4, 1776*, occurred, look up *1776* in the table, take the number given there, *9*, refer to calendar number 9, and find that *July 4* was on a Thursday that year.

Calendar 1

```
January                  February                 March                    April
S  M  T  W  T  F  S      S  M  T  W  T  F  S      S  M  T  W  T  F  S      S  M  T  W  T  F  S
      1  2  3  4  5  6  7              1  2  3  4              1  2  3  4                          1
 8  9 10 11 12 13 14      5  6  7  8  9 10 11      5  6  7  8  9 10 11      2  3  4  5  6  7  8
15 16 17 18 19 20 21     12 13 14 15 16 17 18     12 13 14 15 16 17 18      9 10 11 12 13 14 15
22 23 24 25 26 27 28     19 20 21 22 23 24 25     19 20 21 22 23 24 25     16 17 18 19 20 21 22
29 30 31                 26 27 28                 26 27 28 29 30 31        23 24 25 26 27 28 29
                                                                           30

May                      June                     July                     August
S  M  T  W  T  F  S      S  M  T  W  T  F  S      S  M  T  W  T  F  S      S  M  T  W  T  F  S
      1  2  3  4  5  6              1  2  3                          1          1  2  3  4  5
 7  8  9 10 11 12 13      4  5  6  7  8  9 10      2  3  4  5  6  7  8      6  7  8  9 10 11 12
14 15 16 17 18 19 20     11 12 13 14 15 16 17      9 10 11 12 13 14 15     13 14 15 16 17 18 19
21 22 23 24 25 26 27     18 19 20 21 22 23 24     16 17 18 19 20 21 22     20 21 22 23 24 25 26
28 29 30 31              25 26 27 28 29 30        23 24 25 26 27 28 29     27 28 29 30 31
                                                  30 31

September                October                  November                 December
S  M  T  W  T  F  S      S  M  T  W  T  F  S      S  M  T  W  T  F  S      S  M  T  W  T  F  S
            1  2          1  2  3  4  5  6  7              1  2  3  4                    1  2
 3  4  5  6  7  8  9      8  9 10 11 12 13 14      5  6  7  8  9 10 11      3  4  5  6  7  8  9
10 11 12 13 14 15 16     15 16 17 18 19 20 21     12 13 14 15 16 17 18     10 11 12 13 14 15 16
17 18 19 20 21 22 23     22 23 24 25 26 27 28     19 20 21 22 23 24 25     17 18 19 20 21 22 23
24 25 26 27 28 29 30     29 30 31                 26 27 28 29 30           24 25 26 27 28 29 30
                                                                           31
```

Calendar 2

```
January                  February                 March                    April
S  M  T  W  T  F  S      S  M  T  W  T  F  S      S  M  T  W  T  F  S      S  M  T  W  T  F  S
    1  2  3  4  5  6              1  2  3                    1  2  3      1  2  3  4  5  6  7
 7  8  9 10 11 12 13      4  5  6  7  8  9 10      4  5  6  7  8  9 10      8  9 10 11 12 13 14
14 15 16 17 18 19 20     11 12 13 14 15 16 17     11 12 13 14 15 16 17     15 16 17 18 19 20 21
21 22 23 24 25 26 27     18 19 20 21 22 23 24     18 19 20 21 22 23 24     22 23 24 25 26 27 28
28 29 30 31              25 26 27 28              25 26 27 28 29 30 31     29 30

May                      June                     July                     August
S  M  T  W  T  F  S      S  M  T  W  T  F  S      S  M  T  W  T  F  S      S  M  T  W  T  F  S
      1  2  3  4  5                    1  2      1  2  3  4  5  6  7                1  2  3  4
 6  7  8  9 10 11 12      3  4  5  6  7  8  9      8  9 10 11 12 13 14      5  6  7  8  9 10 11
13 14 15 16 17 18 19     10 11 12 13 14 15 16     15 16 17 18 19 20 21     12 13 14 15 16 17 18
20 21 22 23 24 25 26     17 18 19 20 21 22 23     22 23 24 25 26 27 28     19 20 21 22 23 24 25
27 28 29 30 31           24 25 26 27 28 29 30     29 30 31                 26 27 28 29 30 31

September                October                  November                 December
S  M  T  W  T  F  S      S  M  T  W  T  F  S      S  M  T  W  T  F  S      S  M  T  W  T  F  S
                  1          1  2  3  4  5  6                1  2  3                          1
 2  3  4  5  6  7  8      7  8  9 10 11 12 13      4  5  6  7  8  9 10      2  3  4  5  6  7  8
 9 10 11 12 13 14 15     14 15 16 17 18 19 20     11 12 13 14 15 16 17      9 10 11 12 13 14 15
16 17 18 19 20 21 22     21 22 23 24 25 26 27     18 19 20 21 22 23 24     16 17 18 19 20 21 22
23 24 25 26 27 28 29     28 29 30 31              25 26 27 28 29 30        23 24 25 26 27 28 29
30                                                                         30 31
```

Calendar 3

```
January                  February                 March                    April
S  M  T  W  T  F  S      S  M  T  W  T  F  S      S  M  T  W  T  F  S      S  M  T  W  T  F  S
      1  2  3  4  5                    1  2                    1  2      1  2  3  4  5  6
 6  7  8  9 10 11 12      3  4  5  6  7  8  9      3  4  5  6  7  8  9      7  8  9 10 11 12 13
13 14 15 16 17 18 19     10 11 12 13 14 15 16     10 11 12 13 14 15 16     14 15 16 17 18 19 20
20 21 22 23 24 25 26     17 18 19 20 21 22 23     17 18 19 20 21 22 23     21 22 23 24 25 26 27
27 28 29 30 31           24 25 26 27 28           24 25 26 27 28 29 30     28 29 30
                                                  31

May                      June                     July                     August
S  M  T  W  T  F  S      S  M  T  W  T  F  S      S  M  T  W  T  F  S      S  M  T  W  T  F  S
         1  2  3  4                          1      1  2  3  4  5  6                  1  2  3
 5  6  7  8  9 10 11      2  3  4  5  6  7  8      7  8  9 10 11 12 13      4  5  6  7  8  9 10
12 13 14 15 16 17 18      9 10 11 12 13 14 15     14 15 16 17 18 19 20     11 12 13 14 15 16 17
19 20 21 22 23 24 25     16 17 18 19 20 21 22     21 22 23 24 25 26 27     18 19 20 21 22 23 24
26 27 28 29 30 31        23 24 25 26 27 28 29     28 29 30 31              25 26 27 28 29 30 31
                         30

September                October                  November                 December
S  M  T  W  T  F  S      S  M  T  W  T  F  S      S  M  T  W  T  F  S      S  M  T  W  T  F  S
 1  2  3  4  5  6  7            1  2  3  4  5                    1  2      1  2  3  4  5  6  7
 8  9 10 11 12 13 14      6  7  8  9 10 11 12      3  4  5  6  7  8  9      8  9 10 11 12 13 14
15 16 17 18 19 20 21     13 14 15 16 17 18 19     10 11 12 13 14 15 16     15 16 17 18 19 20 21
22 23 24 25 26 27 28     20 21 22 23 24 25 26     17 18 19 20 21 22 23     22 23 24 25 26 27 28
29 30                    27 28 29 30 31           24 25 26 27 28 29 30     29 30 31
```

Calendar 4

```
January                  February                 March                    April
S  M  T  W  T  F  S      S  M  T  W  T  F  S      S  M  T  W  T  F  S      S  M  T  W  T  F  S
      1  2  3  4                          1                          1      1  2  3  4  5  6
 5  6  7  8  9 10 11      2  3  4  5  6  7  8      2  3  4  5  6  7  8      7  8  9 10 11 12 13
12 13 14 15 16 17 18      9 10 11 12 13 14 15      9 10 11 12 13 14 15     14 15 16 17 18 19 20
19 20 21 22 23 24 25     16 17 18 19 20 21 22     16 17 18 19 20 21 22     21 22 23 24 25 26 27
26 27 28 29 30 31        23 24 25 26 27 28        23 24 25 26 27 28 29     28 29 30
                                                  30 31

May                      June                     July                     August
S  M  T  W  T  F  S      S  M  T  W  T  F  S      S  M  T  W  T  F  S      S  M  T  W  T  F  S
            1  2  3      1  2  3  4  5  6  7            1  2  3  4  5                    1  2
 4  5  6  7  8  9 10      8  9 10 11 12 13 14      6  7  8  9 10 11 12      3  4  5  6  7  8  9
11 12 13 14 15 16 17     15 16 17 18 19 20 21     13 14 15 16 17 18 19     10 11 12 13 14 15 16
18 19 20 21 22 23 24     22 23 24 25 26 27 28     20 21 22 23 24 25 26     17 18 19 20 21 22 23
25 26 27 28 29 30 31     29 30                    27 28 29 30 31           24 25 26 27 28 29 30
                                                                           31

September                October                  November                 December
S  M  T  W  T  F  S      S  M  T  W  T  F  S      S  M  T  W  T  F  S      S  M  T  W  T  F  S
 1  2  3  4  5  6            1  2  3  4                          1      1  2  3  4  5  6
 7  8  9 10 11 12 13      5  6  7  8  9 10 11      2  3  4  5  6  7  8      7  8  9 10 11 12 13
14 15 16 17 18 19 20     12 13 14 15 16 17 18      9 10 11 12 13 14 15     14 15 16 17 18 19 20
21 22 23 24 25 26 27     19 20 21 22 23 24 25     16 17 18 19 20 21 22     21 22 23 24 25 26 27
28 29 30                 26 27 28 29 30 31        23 24 25 26 27 28 29     28 29 30 31
                                                  30
```

Calendar 5

```
January                  February                 March                    April
S  M  T  W  T  F  S      S  M  T  W  T  F  S      S  M  T  W  T  F  S      S  M  T  W  T  F  S
            1  2  3      1  2  3  4  5  6  7      1  2  3  4  5  6  7            1  2  3  4
 4  5  6  7  8  9 10      8  9 10 11 12 13 14      8  9 10 11 12 13 14      5  6  7  8  9 10 11
11 12 13 14 15 16 17     15 16 17 18 19 20 21     15 16 17 18 19 20 21     12 13 14 15 16 17 18
18 19 20 21 22 23 24     22 23 24 25 26 27 28     22 23 24 25 26 27 28     19 20 21 22 23 24 25
25 26 27 28 29 30 31                             29 30 31                 26 27 28 29 30

May                      June                     July                     August
S  M  T  W  T  F  S      S  M  T  W  T  F  S      S  M  T  W  T  F  S      S  M  T  W  T  F  S
               1  2          1  2  3  4  5  6            1  2  3  4                          1
 3  4  5  6  7  8  9      7  8  9 10 11 12 13      5  6  7  8  9 10 11      2  3  4  5  6  7  8
10 11 12 13 14 15 16     14 15 16 17 18 19 20     12 13 14 15 16 17 18      9 10 11 12 13 14 15
17 18 19 20 21 22 23     21 22 23 24 25 26 27     19 20 21 22 23 24 25     16 17 18 19 20 21 22
24 25 26 27 28 29 30     28 29 30                 26 27 28 29 30 31        23 24 25 26 27 28 29
31                                                                         30 31

September                October                  November                 December
S  M  T  W  T  F  S      S  M  T  W  T  F  S      S  M  T  W  T  F  S      S  M  T  W  T  F  S
      1  2  3  4  5                1  2  3      1  2  3  4  5  6  7            1  2  3  4  5
 6  7  8  9 10 11 12      4  5  6  7  8  9 10      8  9 10 11 12 13 14      6  7  8  9 10 11 12
13 14 15 16 17 18 19     11 12 13 14 15 16 17     15 16 17 18 19 20 21     13 14 15 16 17 18 19
20 21 22 23 24 25 26     18 19 20 21 22 23 24     22 23 24 25 26 27 28     20 21 22 23 24 25 26
27 28 29 30              25 26 27 28 29 30 31     29 30                    27 28 29 30 31
```

Calendar 6

```
January                  February                 March                    April
S  M  T  W  T  F         S  M  T  W  T  F  S      S  M  T  W  T  F  S      S  M  T  W  T  F  S
            1  2                    1  2  3  4                    1  2  3            1  2  3
 3  4  5  6  7  8  9      5  6  7  8  9 10 11      4  5  6  7  8  9 10      4  5  6  7  8  9 10
10 11 12 13 14 15 16     12 13 14 15 16 17 18     11 12 13 14 15 16 17     11 12 13 14 15 16 17
17 18 19 20 21 22 23     19 20 21 22 23 24 25     18 19 20 21 22 23 24     18 19 20 21 22 23 24
24 25 26 27 28 29 30     26 27 28                 25 26 27 28 29 30 31     25 26 27 28 29 30
31

May                      June                     July                     August
S  M  T  W  T  F  S      S  M  T  W  T  F  S      S  M  T  W  T  F  S      S  M  T  W  T  F  S
                  1          1  2  3  4  5            1  2  3  4  5  6  7      1  2  3  4  5  6  7
 2  3  4  5  6  7  8      6  7  8  9 10 11 12      4  5  6  7  8  9 10      8  9 10 11 12 13 14
 9 10 11 12 13 14 15     13 14 15 16 17 18 19     11 12 13 14 15 16 17     15 16 17 18 19 20 21
16 17 18 19 20 21 22     20 21 22 23 24 25 26     18 19 20 21 22 23 24     22 23 24 25 26 27 28
23 24 25 26 27 28 29     27 28 29 30              25 26 27 28 29 30 31     29 30 31
30 31

September                October                  November                 December
S  M  T  W  T  F  S      S  M  T  W  T  F  S      S  M  T  W  T  F  S      S  M  T  W  T  F  S
            1  2  3  4                1  2      1  2  3  4  5  6            1  2  3  4
 5  6  7  8  9 10 11      3  4  5  6  7  8  9      7  8  9 10 11 12 13      5  6  7  8  9 10 11
12 13 14 15 16 17 18     10 11 12 13 14 15 16     14 15 16 17 18 19 20     12 13 14 15 16 17 18
19 20 21 22 23 24 25     17 18 19 20 21 22 23     21 22 23 24 25 26 27     19 20 21 22 23 24 25
26 27 28 29 30           24 25 26 27 28 29 30     28 29 30                 26 27 28 29 30 31
                         31
```

Calendar 7

```
January                  February                 March                    April
S  M  T  W  T  F  S      S  M  T  W  T  F         S  M  T  W  T  F  S      S  M  T  W  T  F  S
                  1          1  2  3  4  5                1  2  3  4  5                1  2
 2  3  4  5  6  7  8      6  7  8  9 10 11 12      6  7  8  9 10 11 12      3  4  5  6  7  8  9
 9 10 11 12 13 14 15     13 14 15 16 17 18 19     13 14 15 16 17 18 19     10 11 12 13 14 15 16
16 17 18 19 20 21 22     20 21 22 23 24 25 26     20 21 22 23 24 25 26     17 18 19 20 21 22 23
23 24 25 26 27 28 29     27 28                    27 28 29 30 31           24 25 26 27 28 29 30
30 31

May                      June                     July                     August
S  M  T  W  T  F  S      S  M  T  W  T  F  S      S  M  T  W  T  F  S      S  M  T  W  T  F  S
 1  2  3  4  5  6  7                1  2  3  4                    1  2      1  2  3  4  5  6
 8  9 10 11 12 13 14      5  6  7  8  9 10 11      3  4  5  6  7  8  9      7  8  9 10 11 12 13
15 16 17 18 19 20 21     12 13 14 15 16 17 18     10 11 12 13 14 15 16     14 15 16 17 18 19 20
22 23 24 25 26 27 28     19 20 21 22 23 24 25     17 18 19 20 21 22 23     21 22 23 24 25 26 27
29 30 31                 26 27 28 29 30           24 25 26 27 28 29 30     28 29 30 31
                                                  31

September                October                  November                 December
S  M  T  W  T  F  S      S  M  T  W  T  F  S      S  M  T  W  T  F  S      S  M  T  W  T  F  S
            1  2  3                      1      1  2  3  4  5                    1  2  3
 4  5  6  7  8  9 10      2  3  4  5  6  7  8      6  7  8  9 10 11 12      4  5  6  7  8  9 10
11 12 13 14 15 16 17      9 10 11 12 13 14 15     13 14 15 16 17 18 19     11 12 13 14 15 16 17
18 19 20 21 22 23 24     16 17 18 19 20 21 22     20 21 22 23 24 25 26     18 19 20 21 22 23 24
25 26 27 28 29 30        23 24 25 26 27 28 29     27 28 29 30              25 26 27 28 29 30 31
                         30 31
```

Calendar 8

```
January                  February                 March                    April
S  M  T  W  T  F  S      S  M  T  W  T  F         S  M  T  W  T  F  S      S  M  T  W  T  F  S
 1  2  3  4  5  6  7              1  2  3  4                    1  2  3      1  2  3  4  5  6  7
 8  9 10 11 12 13 14      5  6  7  8  9 10 11      4  5  6  7  8  9 10      8  9 10 11 12 13 14
15 16 17 18 19 20 21     12 13 14 15 16 17 18     11 12 13 14 15 16 17     15 16 17 18 19 20 21
22 23 24 25 26 27 28     19 20 21 22 23 24 25     18 19 20 21 22 23 24     22 23 24 25 26 27 28
29 30 31                 26 27 28 29              25 26 27 28 29 30 31     29 30

May                      June                     July                     August
S  M  T  W  T  F  S      S  M  T  W  T  F  S      S  M  T  W  T  F  S      S  M  T  W  T  F  S
      1  2  3  4  5                    1  2      1  2  3  4  5  6  7                1  2  3  4
 6  7  8  9 10 11 12      3  4  5  6  7  8  9      8  9 10 11 12 13 14      5  6  7  8  9 10 11
13 14 15 16 17 18 19     10 11 12 13 14 15 16     15 16 17 18 19 20 21     12 13 14 15 16 17 18
20 21 22 23 24 25 26     17 18 19 20 21 22 23     22 23 24 25 26 27 28     19 20 21 22 23 24 25
27 28 29 30 31           24 25 26 27 28 29 30     29 30 31                 26 27 28 29 30 31

September                October                  November                 December
S  M  T  W  T  F  S      S  M  T  W  T  F  S      S  M  T  W  T  F  S      S  M  T  W  T  F  S
                  1          1  2  3  4  5  6                1  2  3                          1
 2  3  4  5  6  7  8      7  8  9 10 11 12 13      4  5  6  7  8  9 10      2  3  4  5  6  7  8
 9 10 11 12 13 14 15     14 15 16 17 18 19 20     11 12 13 14 15 16 17      9 10 11 12 13 14 15
16 17 18 19 20 21 22     21 22 23 24 25 26 27     18 19 20 21 22 23 24     16 17 18 19 20 21 22
23 24 25 26 27 28 29     28 29 30 31              25 26 27 28 29 30        23 24 25 26 27 28 29
30                                                                         30 31
```

1753 2	1792 8	1831 7	1870 7	1909 6	1948 12	1987 5	2026 5	2065 5
1754 3	1793 3	1832 8	1871 1	1910 7	1949 7	1988 13	2027 6	2066 6
1755 4	1794 4	1833 3	1872 9	1911 1	1950 1	1989 1	2028 14	2067 7
1756 12	1795 5	1834 4	1873 4	1912 9	1951 2	1990 2	2029 2	2068 8
1757 7	1796 13	1835 5	1874 5	1913 4	1952 10	1991 3	2030 3	2069 3
1758 1	1797 1	1836 13	1875 6	1914 5	1953 5	1992 11	2031 4	2070 4
1759 2	1798 2	1837 1	1876 14	1915 6	1954 6	1993 6	2032 12	2071 5
1760 10	1799 3	1838 2	1877 2	1916 14	1955 7	1994 7	2033 7	2072 13
1761 5	**1800** 4	1839 3	1878 3	1917 2	1956 8	1995 1	2034 1	2073 1
1762 6	1801 5	1840 11	1879 4	1918 3	1957 3	1996 9	2035 2	2074 2
1763 7	1802 6	1841 6	1880 12	1919 4	1958 4	1997 4	2036 10	2075 3
1764 8	1803 7	1842 7	1881 7	1920 12	1959 5	1998 5	2037 5	2076 11
1765 3	1804 8	1843 1	1882 1	1921 7	1960 13	1999 6	2038 6	2077 6
1766 4	1805 3	1844 9	1883 2	1922 1	**1961** 1	**2000** 14	2039 7	2078 7
1767 5	1806 4	1845 4	1884 10	1923 2	1962 2	2001 2	2040 8	2079 1
1768 13	1807 5	1846 5	1885 5	1924 10	1963 3	2002 3	2041 3	2080 9
1769 1	1808 13	1847 6	1886 6	1925 5	1964 11	2003 4	2042 4	2081 4
1770 2	1809 1	1848 14	1887 7	1926 6	1965 6	2004 12	2043 5	2082 5
1771 3	1810 2	1849 2	1888 8	1927 7	1966 7	2005 7	2044 13	2083 6
1772 11	1811 3	1850 3	1889 3	1928 8	1967 1	2006 1	2045 1	2084 14
1773 6	1812 11	1851 4	1890 4	1929 3	1968 9	2007 2	2046 2	2085 2
1774 7	1813 6	1852 12	1891 5	1930 4	1969 4	2008 10	2047 3	2086 3
1775 8	1814 7	1853 7	1892 13	1931 5	1970 5	2009 5	2048 11	2087 4
1776 9	1815 1	1854 1	1893 1	1932 13	1971 6	2010 6	2049 6	2088 12
1777 4	1816 9	1855 2	1894 2	1933 1	1972 14	2011 7	2050 7	2089 7
1778 5	1817 4	1856 10	1895 3	1934 2	1973 2	2012 8	2051 1	2090 1
1779 6	1818 5	1857 5	1896 11	1935 3	1974 3	2013 3	2052 9	2091 2
1780 14	1819 6	1858 6	1897 6	1936 11	1975 4	2014 4	2053 4	2092 10
1781 2	1820 14	1859 7	1898 7	1937 6	1976 12	2015 5	2054 5	2093 5
1782 3	1821 2	1860 8	1899 1	1938 7	1977 7	2016 13	2055 6	2094 6
1783 4	1822 3	1861 3	**1900** 2	1939 1	1978 1	2017 1	2056 14	2095 7
1784 12	1823 4	1862 4	1901 3	1940 9	1979 2	2018 2	2057 2	2096 8
1785 7	1824 12	1863 5	1902 4	1941 4	1980 10	2019 3	2058 3	2097 3
1786 1	1825 7	1864 13	1903 5	1942 5	1981 5	2020 11	2059 4	2098 4
1787 2	1826 1	1865 1	1904 13	1943 6	1982 6	2021 6	2060 12	2099 5
1788 10	1827 2	1866 2	1905 1	1944 14	1983 7	2022 7	2061 7	2100 13
1789 5	1828 10	1867 3	1906 2	1945 2	1984 8	2023 1	2062 1	
1790 6	1829 5	1868 11	1907 3	1946 3	1985 3	2024 9	2063 2	
1791 7	1830 6	1869 6	1908 11	1947 4	1986 4	2025 4	2064 10	

Calendar 9

January — S M T W T F S
```
          1  2  3  4  5  6
 7  8  9 10 11 12 13
14 15 16 17 18 19 20
21 22 23 24 25 26 27
28 29 30 31
```
February — S M T W T F S
```
             1  2  3
 4  5  6  7  8  9 10
11 12 13 14 15 16 17
18 19 20 21 22 23 24
25 26 27 28 29
```
March — S M T W T F S
```
                1  2
 3  4  5  6  7  8  9
10 11 12 13 14 15 16
17 18 19 20 21 22 23
24 25 26 27 28 29 30
31
```
April — S M T W T F S
```
    1  2  3  4  5  6
 7  8  9 10 11 12 13
14 15 16 17 18 19 20
21 22 23 24 25 26 27
28 29 30
```
May — S M T W T F S
```
          1  2  3  4
 5  6  7  8  9 10 11
12 13 14 15 16 17 18
19 20 21 22 23 24 25
26 27 28 29 30 31
```
June — S M T W T F S
```
                   1
 2  3  4  5  6  7  8
 9 10 11 12 13 14 15
16 17 18 19 20 21 22
23 24 25 26 27 28 29
30
```
July — S M T W T F S
```
    1  2  3  4  5  6
 7  8  9 10 11 12 13
14 15 16 17 18 19 20
21 22 23 24 25 26 27
28 29 30 31
```
August — S M T W T F S
```
             1  2  3
 4  5  6  7  8  9 10
11 12 13 14 15 16 17
18 19 20 21 22 23 24
25 26 27 28 29 30 31
```
September — S M T W T F S
```
 1  2  3  4  5  6  7
 8  9 10 11 12 13 14
15 16 17 18 19 20 21
22 23 24 25 26 27 28
29 30
```
October — S M T W T F S
```
          1  2  3  4  5
 6  7  8  9 10 11 12
13 14 15 16 17 18 19
20 21 22 23 24 25 26
27 28 29 30 31
```
November — S M T W T F S
```
                1  2
 3  4  5  6  7  8  9
10 11 12 13 14 15 16
17 18 19 20 21 22 23
24 25 26 27 28 29 30
```
December — S M T W T F S
```
 1  2  3  4  5  6  7
 8  9 10 11 12 13 14
15 16 17 18 19 20 21
22 23 24 25 26 27 28
29 30 31
```

Calendar 10

January — S M T W T F S
```
          1  2  3  4  5
 6  7  8  9 10 11 12
13 14 15 16 17 18 19
20 21 22 23 24 25 26
27 28 29 30 31
```
February — S M T W T F S
```
                1  2
 3  4  5  6  7  8  9
10 11 12 13 14 15 16
17 18 19 20 21 22 23
24 25 26 27 28 29
```
March — S M T W T F S
```
                   1
 2  3  4  5  6  7  8
 9 10 11 12 13 14 15
16 17 18 19 20 21 22
23 24 25 26 27 28 29
30 31
```
April — S M T W T F S
```
          1  2  3  4  5
 6  7  8  9 10 11 12
13 14 15 16 17 18 19
20 21 22 23 24 25 26
27 28 29 30
```
May — S M T W T F S
```
             1  2  3
 4  5  6  7  8  9 10
11 12 13 14 15 16 17
18 19 20 21 22 23 24
25 26 27 28 29 30 31
```
June — S M T W R S
```
 1  2  3  4  5  6  7
 8  9 10 11 12 13 14
15 16 17 18 19 20 21
22 23 24 25 26 27 28
29 30
```
July — S M T W T F S
```
          1  2  3  4  5
 6  7  8  9 10 11 12
13 14 15 16 17 18 19
20 21 22 23 24 25 26
27 28 29 30 31
```
August — S M T W T F S
```
                1  2
 3  4  5  6  7  8  9
10 11 12 13 14 15 16
17 18 19 20 21 22 23
24 25 26 27 28 29 30
31
```
September — S M T W T F S
```
       1  2  3  4  5  6
 7  8  9 10 11 12 13
14 15 16 17 18 19 20
21 22 23 24 25 26 27
28 29 30
```
October — S M T W T F S
```
             1  2  3  4
 5  6  7  8  9 10 11
12 13 14 15 16 17 18
19 20 21 22 23 24 25
26 27 28 29 30 31
```
November — S M T W T F S
```
                   1
 2  3  4  5  6  7  8
 9 10 11 12 13 14 15
16 17 18 19 20 21 22
23 24 25 26 27 28 29
30
```
December — S M T W T F S
```
       1  2  3  4  5  6
 7  8  9 10 11 12 13
14 15 16 17 18 19 20
21 22 23 24 25 26 27
28 29 30 31
```

Calendar 11

January — S M T W T F S
```
             1  2  3  4
 5  6  7  8  9 10 11
12 13 14 15 16 17 18
19 20 21 22 23 24 25
26 27 28 29 30 31
```
February — S M T W T F S
```
                   1
 2  3  4  5  6  7  8
 9 10 11 12 13 14 15
16 17 18 19 20 21 22
23 24 25 26 27 28 29
```
March — S M T W T F S
```
 1  2  3  4  5  6  7
 8  9 10 11 12 13 14
15 16 17 18 19 20 21
22 23 24 25 26 27 28
29 30 31
```
April — S M T W T F S
```
             1  2  3  4
 5  6  7  8  9 10 11
12 13 14 15 16 17 18
19 20 21 22 23 24 25
26 27 28 29 30
```
May — S M T W T F S
```
                1  2
 3  4  5  6  7  8  9
10 11 12 13 14 15 16
17 18 19 20 21 22 23
24 25 26 27 28 29 30
31
```
June — S M T W R S
```
       1  2  3  4  5  6
 7  8  9 10 11 12 13
14 15 16 17 18 19 20
21 22 23 24 25 26 27
28 29 30
```
July — S M T W T F S
```
             1  2  3  4
 5  6  7  8  9 10 11
12 13 14 15 16 17 18
19 20 21 22 23 24 25
26 27 28 29 30 31
```
August — S M T W T F S
```
                   1
 2  3  4  5  6  7  8
 9 10 11 12 13 14 15
16 17 18 19 20 21 22
23 24 25 26 27 28 29
30 31
```
September — S M T W T F S
```
          1  2  3  4  5
 6  7  8  9 10 11 12
13 14 15 16 17 18 19
20 21 22 23 24 25 26
27 28 29 30
```
October — S M T W T F S
```
                1  2  3
 4  5  6  7  8  9 10
11 12 13 14 15 16 17
18 19 20 21 22 23 24
25 26 27 28 29 30 31
```
November — S M T W T F S
```
 1  2  3  4  5  6  7
 8  9 10 11 12 13 14
15 16 17 18 19 20 21
22 23 24 25 26 27 28
29 30
```
December — S M T W T F S
```
          1  2  3  4  5
 6  7  8  9 10 11 12
13 14 15 16 17 18 19
20 21 22 23 24 25 26
27 28 29 30 31
```

Calendar 12

January — S M T W T F S
```
             1  2  3
 4  5  6  7  8  9 10
11 12 13 14 15 16 17
18 19 20 21 22 23 24
25 26 27 28 29 30 31
```
February — S M T W T F S
```
 1  2  3  4  5  6  7
 8  9 10 11 12 13 14
15 16 17 18 19 20 21
22 23 24 25 26 27 28
29
```
March — S M T W T F S
```
          1  2  3  4  5  6
 7  8  9 10 11 12 13
14 15 16 17 18 19 20
21 22 23 24 25 26 27
28 29 30 31
```
April — S M T W T F S
```
             1  2  3
 4  5  6  7  8  9 10
11 12 13 14 15 16 17
18 19 20 21 22 23 24
25 26 27 28 29 30
```
May — S M T W T F S
```
                   1
 2  3  4  5  6  7  8
 9 10 11 12 13 14 15
16 17 18 19 20 21 22
23 24 25 26 27 28 29
30 31
```
June — S M T W T F S
```
          1  2  3  4  5
 6  7  8  9 10 11 12
13 14 15 16 17 18 19
20 21 22 23 24 25 26
27 28 29 30
```
July — S M T W T F S
```
             1  2  3
 4  5  6  7  8  9 10
11 12 13 14 15 16 17
18 19 20 21 22 23 24
25 26 27 28 29 30 31
```
August — S M T W T F S
```
 1  2  3  4  5  6  7
 8  9 10 11 12 13 14
15 16 17 18 19 20 21
22 23 24 25 26 27 28
29 30 31
```
September — S M T W T F S
```
          1  2  3  4
 5  6  7  8  9 10 11
12 13 14 15 16 17 18
19 20 21 22 23 24 25
26 27 28 29 30
```
October — S M T W T F S
```
                1  2
 3  4  5  6  7  8  9
10 11 12 13 14 15 16
17 18 19 20 21 22 23
24 25 26 27 28 29 30
31
```
November — S M T W T F S
```
       1  2  3  4  5  6
 7  8  9 10 11 12 13
14 15 16 17 18 19 20
21 22 23 24 25 26 27
28 29 30
```
December — S M T W T F S
```
             1  2  3  4
 5  6  7  8  9 10 11
12 13 14 15 16 17 18
19 20 21 22 23 24 25
26 27 28 29 30 31
```

Calendar 13

January — S M T W T F S
```
                1  2
 3  4  5  6  7  8  9
10 11 12 13 14 15 16
17 18 19 20 21 22 23
24 25 26 27 28 29 30
31
```
February — S M T W T F S
```
          1  2  3  4  5  6
 7  8  9 10 11 12 13
14 15 16 17 18 19 20
21 22 23 24 25 26 27
28
```
March — S M T W T F S
```
                1  2  3  4  5
 6  7  8  9 10 11 12
13 14 15 16 17 18 19
20 21 22 23 24 25 26
27 28 29 30 31
```
April — S M T W T F S
```
                1  2
 3  4  5  6  7  8  9
10 11 12 13 14 15 16
17 18 19 20 21 22 23
24 25 26 27 28 29 30
```
May — S M T W R S
```
 1  2  3  4  5  6  7
 8  9 10 11 12 13 14
15 16 17 18 19 20 21
22 23 24 25 26 27 28
29 30 31
```
June — S M T W T F S
```
          1  2  3  4
 5  6  7  8  9 10 11
12 13 14 15 16 17 18
19 20 21 22 23 24 25
26 27 28 29 30
```
July — S M T W T F S
```
                1  2
 3  4  5  6  7  8  9
10 11 12 13 14 15 16
17 18 19 20 21 22 23
24 25 26 27 28 29 30
31
```
August — S M T W T F S
```
          1  2  3  4  5  6
 7  8  9 10 11 12 13
14 15 16 17 18 19 20
21 22 23 24 25 26 27
28 29 30 31
```
September — S M T W T F S
```
             1  2  3
 4  5  6  7  8  9 10
11 12 13 14 15 16 17
18 19 20 21 22 23 24
25 26 27 28 29 30
```
October — S M T W T F S
```
                   1
 2  3  4  5  6  7  8
 9 10 11 12 13 14 15
16 17 18 19 20 21 22
23 24 25 26 27 28 29
30 31
```
November — S M T W T F S
```
                1  2  3  4  5
 6  7  8  9 10 11 12
13 14 15 16 17 18 19
20 21 22 23 24 25 26
27 28 29 30
```
December — S M T W T F S
```
             1  2  3
 4  5  6  7  8  9 10
11 12 13 14 15 16 17
18 19 20 21 22 23 24
25 26 27 28 29 30 31
```

Calendar 14

January — S M T W T F S
```
                   1
 2  3  4  5  6  7  8
 9 10 11 12 13 14 15
16 17 18 19 20 21 22
23 24 25 26 27 28 29
30 31
```
February — S M T W T F S
```
          1  2  3  4  5
 6  7  8  9 10 11 12
13 14 15 16 17 18 19
20 21 22 23 24 25 26
27 28 29
```
March — S M T W T F S
```
             1  2  3  4
 5  6  7  8  9 10 11
12 13 14 15 16 17 18
19 20 21 22 23 24 25
26 27 28 29 30 31
```
April — S M T W T F S
```
                   1
 2  3  4  5  6  7  8
 9 10 11 12 13 14 15
16 17 18 19 20 21 22
23 24 25 26 27 28 29
30
```
May — S M T W R S
```
       1  2  3  4  5  6
 7  8  9 10 11 12 13
14 15 16 17 18 19 20
21 22 23 24 25 26 27
28 29 30 31
```
June — S M T W T F S
```
             1  2  3
 4  5  6  7  8  9 10
11 12 13 14 15 16 17
18 19 20 21 22 23 24
25 26 27 28 29 30
```
July — S M T W T F S
```
                   1
 2  3  4  5  6  7  8
 9 10 11 12 13 14 15
16 17 18 19 20 21 22
23 24 25 26 27 28 29
30 31
```
August — S M T W T F S
```
          1  2  3  4  5
 6  7  8  9 10 11 12
13 14 15 16 17 18 19
20 21 22 23 24 25 26
27 28 29 30 31
```
September — S M T W T F S
```
                1  2
 3  4  5  6  7  8  9
10 11 12 13 14 15 16
17 18 19 20 21 22 23
24 25 26 27 28 29 30
```
October — S M T W T F S
```
 1  2  3  4  5  6  7
 8  9 10 11 12 13 14
15 16 17 18 19 20 21
22 23 24 25 26 27 28
29 30 31
```
November — S M T W T F S
```
             1  2  3  4
 5  6  7  8  9 10 11
12 13 14 15 16 17 18
19 20 21 22 23 24 25
26 27 28 29 30
```
December — S M T W T F S
```
                1  2
 3  4  5  6  7  8  9
10 11 12 13 14 15 16
17 18 19 20 21 22 23
24 25 26 27 28 29 30
31
```

Glossary of Time Words

by

Ethel Olicker

In this glossary are definitions for more than 200 time period terms, such as:

—*semiweekly* and *fortnightly*, terms that indicate recurrence

—*aeon* and *age*, terms that take the measure of a block of time

—A.H. and C.E., abbreviations that fix a year in a particular calendar

—*sesquicentennial* and *jubilee*, terms that mark particular anniversaries

—*ab initio*, *circa*, and *pro tempore*, Latin terms for relations of time

—terms that relate to specific fields, like *trecento* to art or *olympiad* to sports.

Most of the terms have unambiguous definitions and are presented in this glossary for the convenience of the user. However, for many of the time period terms presented herein there is uncertainty regarding precise meaning. The meaning of *monthly* is fairly clear and consistently applied, but what about *bimonthly*? A word such as *annual* poses little difficulty, but *biannual* (or should it be *biennial?*) is used in two senses. Prior to and during the year 1976 in the United States, the popular use of the term *bicentennial* grew dramatically, and its meaning was quite clear, but other, similar terms are elusive. The word *triannual*, for example, does not appear in most dictionaries, yet it is used by publishers and others. Many of the time period terms that begin with *bi-* or *tri-* have two definitions, with the first having a meaning that is the "inverse" of the second. To compound the problem, dictionaries do not always agree as to which is the standard or which the second definition.

Thus, to present a single definition as standard does not accurately describe the general use of many terms.

Books on usage discuss this matter and make recommendations; this glossary has attempted to address the problem by presenting, as the first meaning for certain ambiguous terms, the standard definition used by publishers in reference to periodicals and serials. The planning and revenues of the publishing industry are based upon the assumption of conventionally accepted meanings for frequency-of-issue terms. If an issue is promised every two months, all scheduling and costs are so predicated; the term *bimonthly*, for publishers, has a single meaning: 'once in (every) two months.' Applying, then, the standards of publishing, this glossary defines ambiguous terms with the first meaning according to this convention and any other meanings following.

Most of the terms in the glossary are general, with application to the periodicity of events, publications, and divers temporal relations. A few items were drawn from specialized fields such as medicine, law, and art. In addition, various terms, abbreviations, and other temporal references that are the subject of frequent questions are conveniently presented in the tables that follow the glossary itself. Time-related subjects, such as relativity and clock time, which are (better) treated in special studies and encyclopedia articles, were mentioned as necessary, but without detailed coverage.

If other terms that may fit into the scope of this glossary are known or discovered by the reader, the editors would welcome being informed of them.

Glossary

ab init., abbreviation for *ab initio (Latin)*, 'from the beginning.'

absolute time, *n*. Newton's concept that time flows equally without relation to anything external, independent of all particular events and processes. This concept was shown to be inadequate and modified by Einstein's concepts of relativity of time and space-time in his Special and General Theories of Relativity.

A.D., abbreviation for *Anno Domini* (Latin), 'in the year of our Lord'; in reference to the count of years measured from the birth of Christ, arbitrarily fixed as A.D. 1. Properly, A.D. should precede references to a specific year, as A.D. *395*, although it regularly follows words such as *century*, as in the *fourth century A.D.* When neither *B.C.* nor *A.D.* accompanies a date, it is usually understood that the year is part of our present calendar. Dating by A.D. was adopted in 525 by Christendom. See also **B.C.; C.E.; Table 1.**

ad inf., abbreviation for *ad infinitum (Latin)*, 'to infinity, endlessly, without limit.'

ad init., abbreviation for *ad initium (Latin)*, 'at the beginning.'

ad int., abbreviation for *ad interim (Latin)*, 'in the meantime.'

aeon, *n*. Also **eon. 1.** an indefinitely long period of time. **2.** *Geology*. the longest period of geologic time, comprising two or more eras. See also **Table 4. —aeonian, eonian,** *adj*.

aet., aetat. See **anno aetatis suae.**

age, *n*. **1.** the length of time during which a being or thing has existed. **2.** a particular period of history as distinguished from others; a historical epoch. **3.** a long, indeterminate span of time. **4.** *Geology*. a period of time shorter than an epoch during which one particular stage of rock formation takes place.

A.H.[1], abbreviation for *Anno Hejirae (Latin)*, 'in the year of the Hegira,' i.e., A.D. 622, the year of the flight of Muhammad from Mecca, subsequently established as the first year of the Muslim era. See also **Table 1.**

A.H.[2], abbreviation for *Anno Hebraico (Latin)*, 'in the Hebrew year,' i.e., based upon the Hebrew reckoning of the year of creation as 3761 B.C. See also **Table 1.**

A.L. See **Anno Lucis.**

almanac, *n*. an annual publication that contains information on weather, tides, astronomy, events, and anniversaries for the coming year, and fre-quently gives useful information about the past year, as well as agricultural data, vital statistics, maps, prizes and awards in many fields, etc.

a.m., A.M., 1. abbreviation for *ante meridiem (Latin)*, 'before noon.' **2.** The period from 12 midnight to 12 noon, especially in reference to the daylight hours before noon.

A.M. See **Anno Mundi.**

anniversary, *n*. **1.** the yearly recurrence of the date of a past event; the commemoration or celebration of an event on its recurring date. —*adj*. **2.** pertaining to an anniversary, as *an anniversary dinner.*

anno aetatis suae, *Latin*. 'in the year of his (or her) life,' used in reference to an individual's age, as on gravestones. Abbreviated **aet., aetat.**

Anno Domini. *See* **A.D.**

Anno Lucis, *Latin*. 'in the year of light.' Abbreviated **A.L.** Used by Freemasons to indicate the number of years elapsed since 4000 B.C.; A.D. 1985 is A.L. 5984. See also **Table 1.**

Anno Mundi, *Latin*. 'in the year of the world,' used in reference to time since the date of creation in the chronology of Bishop Usher, i.e., 4004 B.C. Abbreviated **A.M.** See also **Table 1.**

Anno Regni, *Latin*. 'in the year of the reign,' used to designate the year in the reign of a king or queen, as A.R. *Victoriae Reginae vicesimo secundo*, 'in the 22nd year of the reign of Queen Victoria.' Abbreviated **A.R.** See also **Table 1.**

annual, *n*. **1.** a publication issued once a year. **2.** a plant that grows from seed to maturity in one growing season or year. —*adj*. **3.** of, for, or pertaining to a year; occurring or returning once a year; happening during one year. —**annually,** *adv*.

ante meridiem. See **a.m., A.M.**

A.R. See **Anno Regni.**

atomic second, *n*. a standard for time measurement, defined in 1967 by the 13th General Conference on Weights and Measures, to replace reckoning based on astronomical measurements. The second is equal to 9,192,631,770 cycles or vibrations within a hyperfine electron level of the cesium atom. The accuracy of this cesium-based second is about one part in ten billion.

B.C. abbreviation for *before Christ.* Used in referring to dates before A.D. 1. *B.C.* follows the year, as in *1,000,000 B.C.*, as contrasted with A.D., which properly precedes. Use of *B.C.* was introduced in the 17th century. Dates followed by *B.C.* are reckoned from A.D. 1, the year set as that for the birth of Christ. The first century B.C. extends from 1 B.C. to 100 B.C.; the second century B.C. goes from 101 B.C. to 200 B.C., and so on. It is useful to note that, since there was no year *O*, intervals that span from B.C. to A.D. are one year less than standard arithmetic would suggest: someone born in 4 B.C. would be seven years old on his birthday in A.D. 4. See also **A.D.; B.C.E.; Table 1.**

B.C.E. abbreviation for *before the Common Era* or *before the Christian Era*. Used instead of *B.C.* as a secular date reference. See also **Table 1.**

bi- prefix meaning 'twice' or 'once every two.'
   Usage: The confusion about the part played by the prefix *bi-* in words like *biweekly, bimonthly,* and *biyearly,* stems from the fact that its derivation can be tied to either of two related yet subtly different Latin words, the adjective *bini* 'two at a time, two together' and the adverb *bis* 'twice, two times.' Unfortunately, their similarity has led to confusion over the meaning of *bi-,* and the problem has affected English usage, where the question has not been consistently resolved. It has been the practice of some dictionaries to give both possible meanings, the first in a "standard definition," followed by a "loose" meaning which differs from the first. Another source of confusion is the fact that the established, "standard" sense of *bi-* in words such as *biannual* and *biquarterly* is 'twice per ——,' and in other words like *biennial* and *bimonthly* it is 'once every two ——.'

biannual, *adj.* occurring, appearing, being made, done, or acted upon twice a year, but not necessarily six months apart. Biannual exams, for instance, may be given in separate terms of a school year, but four or five months apart. —**biannually,** *adv.*

bicentenary, *n. Chiefly British.* bicentennial.

bicentennial, *n.* **1.** a 200th anniversary or the celebration of such an anniversary. Also **bicentenary, bicentennium.** —*adj.* **2.** pertaining to or acknowledging a 200th anniversary; consisting of or lasting 200 years; occurring every 200 years. —**bicentenially,** *adv.*

bicentennium. See **bicentennial.**

biennial, *n.* **1.** an event, act, or publication with a frequency of once every two years. **2.** a plant that takes two years to develop and mature; lasting or living for two years. —*adj.* **3.** happening every two years. Also **biyearly.** —**biennially,** *adv.*

biennium, *n. (pl. -iums, -ia)* a period of two years.

bihourly, *adj.* occurring every two hours, as *a bihourly medical bulletin.*

bimester, *n.* a two-month period. —**bimestrial,** *adj.*

bimillenary, *n.* **1.** a 2000-year period. **2.** an anniversary or celebration of an event that occurred 2000 years earlier. Also **bimillennial; bimillennium.**

bimillennial, *n.* **1.** bimillenary. —*adj.* **2.** of or relating to a 2000-year period or its celebration.

bimillennium. See **bimillenary.**

bimonthly, *n.* **1.** an act, event, or publication with a frequency of once every two months; a period of two months. Cf. **semimonthly.** —*adj.* **2.** of or pertaining to a two-month period. —*adv.* **3.** every two months.

biquarterly, *adj.* occurring twice every three months.

biweekly, *n.* **1.** a publication appearing once every two weeks; an event that takes place or lasts over a two week period. —*adj.* **2.** occurring every two weeks. —*adv.* **3.** every two weeks. Also **fortnightly.** Cf. **semiweekly.**

biyearly, *adj.* **1.** of or pertaining to a two-year period. Also **biennial.** —*adv.* **2.** every two years; biennially.

c, common abbreviation for *circa*. Also written **c., ca, ca., cir., circ.**

C.E. abbreviation for *Common Era* or *Christian Era*, a secular reference used in place of *A.D.* See also **Table 1.**

centenarian, *n.* **1.** one who has lived to the age of 100 years. —*adj.* **2.** pertaining to or having lived 100 years or longer.

centenary, *n.* **1.** a period of 100 years. **2.** *esp. Brit.* a commemoration 100 years after an event. Also **centennial, centennium, century.** —*adj.* **3.** of or pertaining to a period of 100 years. Also **centennial.**

centennial, *n.* **1.** a 100th anniversary or its celebration; centenary. Also **centennium.** —*adj.* **2.** pertaining to a period of 100 years; lasting or aged 100 years. —**centennially,** *adv.*

centennium. See **centenary, centennial.**

centurial, *adj.* relating to 100 years; marking or beginning a century, as the centurial years of 1600 and 1700.

centuriate, *adj.* of or relating to, or divided in hundreds or centuries.

century, *n.* a period of 100 years. The first century included the years 1 to 100; 101 to 200 was the second century, etc. The twentieth century, which began in 1901, will technically end at the end of the year 2000.

Christian Era. See **C.E.**

cinquecento, *n.* the 16th century or 1500s, esp. with reference to art and literature in Italy [for Italian *mil cinque cento,* '1500']. —**cinquecentist,** *adj.*

circa, *prep., adv. Latin.* 'about, around' used especially in referring to approximate dates, as *circa 1850.* Abbreviated **c, c., ca, ca., cir., circ.**

circadian, *adj.* **1.** pertaining to a biological cycle that repeats itself at 24-hour intervals. —*n.* **2.** a daily, 24-hour rhythm inherent in living organisms, with optimum times for waking, sleeping, and other activities.

Common Era. See **C.E.**

cycle of indiction, a recurring 15-year period in the Roman calendar, used as a basis for the revaluation of property.

daily, *n.* **1.** an event or publication that occurs or appears everyday. —*adj.* **2.** of, done, occurring, or appearing each day, or on each weekday. Also **diurnal.** —*adv.* **3.** on each day.

de die in diem, *Latin.* 'from day to day.'

decade, *n.* any period of ten years. Specific decades are usually thought to begin with the year ending in *0*, as the Fifties ran from 1950-59. Also **decennary, decennial, decennium.**

decennary, *n.* **1.** a period of ten years. Also **decade, decennial, decennium.** —*adj.* **2.** pertaining to a ten-year span.

decennial, *n.* **1.** a ten-year anniversary or its celebration. Also **decade, decennary, decennium.** —*adj.* **2.** of or pertaining to ten years; occurring every ten years.

decennium, *n.* *(pl.* **-iums; -ia)** a period of ten years. Also **decade, decennary, decennial.**

demi-, *prefix.* **1.** half. **2.** shortened.

diurnal, *adj.* **1.** of, belonging to, or occurring each day; daily. **2.** of or occurring during the daytime; not nocturnal. **3.** opening during the day, closing at night (of flowers and leaves of some plants). See **nocturnal.**

dominical letter, a letter from A–G assigned in church calendars to designate the Sundays of the liturgical year as an aid in determining the date for Easter Sunday.

duecento, the 13th century or 1200s, esp. with reference to art and literature in Italy [for Italian *mil due cento* '1200']. —**duecentist,** *adj.*

eon. See **aeon.**

epact, *n.* **1.** the difference in days between a lunar and a solar year. **2.** a period added to harmonize the lunar with the solar calendar. **3.** the number of days since the new moon at the beginning of the calendar year.

epoch, *n.* **1.** a characteristic, remarkable, or memorable period of time. **2.** the beginning of such a new period in time. **3.** *Geology.* A unit of time shorter than a period, but longer than an age. See also **Table 4. 4.** a period of time during which a particular culture is dominant.

equinox, the time at which the sun crosses the plane of the earth's equator, so that day and night are of equal duration. The equinoxes occur approximately on March 21 (**vernal equinox**) and September 22 (**autumnal equinox**). —**equinoctial,** *adj.*

era, *n.* **1.** a period of time that utilizes a specific point in history as the basis of its chronology. **2.** a period of time notable because of its memorable aspects, events, or personalities. **3.** *Geology.* The longest period of named time. See also **Table 4.**

femtosecond, *n.* one quadrillionth of a second, i.e., 10^{-15} sec., used in measuring the briefest events known to physical science. Abbrev. **fsec.**

fin de siècle, *French.* 'end of the century,' esp. in reference to the end of the 19th century. Also **fin-de-siècle.**

fortnight, *n.* fourteen continuous days and nights; two weeks.

fortnightly, *n.* **1.** a periodical or publication appearing once every two weeks or fourteen days. —*adj.* **2.** occurring or appearing once every two weeks. —*adv.* **3.** once in two weeks. Also **biweekly.**

generation, *n.* **1.** the period between the birth of parents and that of their children, for humans, usually reckoned as 25 or 30 years. **2.** a single step in natural descent.

Gregorian calendar, a calendar in use worldwide for civil, commercial, and political purposes, named for Pope Gregory XIII, who promulgated its use in 1582 to replace the Julian calendar. It differs from the Julian calendar in that no centennial year (e.g., 1800, 1900) is a leap year unless it is divisible by 400. See also **Julian calendar; leap year.**

hebdomad, *n.* **1.** a group of seven. **2.** a period of seven days; a week.

hebdomadal, *adj.* **1.** taking place, coming together, or published once every seven days. Also **weekly. 2.** lasting seven days. —**hebdomadally,** *adv.*

hebdomadary, *adj.* occurring every seven days; weekly.

heliacal rising, the rising of a particular celestial object most nearly coincident with the rising of the sun.

hemi-, *prefix.* half.

horal, *adj.* relating to hours; hourly.

horary, *adj.* pertaining to, noting the hours; continuing or occurring hourly.

in pr., abbreviation for *in principio* (Latin), 'in the first place; in the beginning.'

instant, *n.* **1.** an infinitesimal space of time; a moment. **2.** the present or current month.

intercalate, to insert an extra period of time into a calendar.

isochronal, *adj.* of equal duration; occurring in, characterized by, or recurring in equal intervals of time; performed in equal intervals of time. —**isochronally,** *adv.*

jubilee, *n.* **1.** the celebration of special anniversaries, such as the 25th (silver jubilee), 50th (golden jubilee), or 60th and 75th (diamond jubilee). See also **Table 7. 2.** any time of rejoicing and celebration. **3.** *Hebrew law.* a year of celebration observed by Jews once every 50 years. **4.** *Roman Catholic law.* a period of time proclaimed by the pope every 25 years as a time of rejoicing.

Julian calendar, a calendar in use in the Roman Empire and much of Europe from 45 B.C. until the 16th century or later, named after Julius Caesar, who established its use. Caesar consulted the Greek astronomer, Sosigenes, who drew up the calendar and based it on the Egyptian solar calendar with 365 days per year plus 1 extra day every fourth year. See also **Gregorian calendar.**

leap year, a year in which an extra day is inserted in order to precisely coordinate the calendar year with the solar-based seasons. In the Gregorian calendar, every fourth year is a leap year, with an extra day inserted at the end of February, except for centennial years (e.g., 1800, 1900) whose number is not divisible by 400.

lunar calendar, a system of reckoning the passing of the year based on the recurrence of the phases of the moon.

lunar year, n. a period of 12 complete lunations or revolutions of the moon around the earth; a period of roughly 354 days or 12 lunar months, each equaling 29.531 days.

lustrum, n. **1.** Roman history. a ceremonial purification of the people, performed every five years, after the taking of the census. **2.** any five-year period.

m., abbreviation for meridies (Latin), 'noon.'

Metonic Cycle, a cycle of 235 synodic months, very nearly 19 years, after which the new moon occurs on the same day as it had at the beginning of the cycle [After Meton, 5th-century B.C. Greek astronomer who discovered the cycle.]. See also **synodic month.**

microsecond, one millionth of a second. Abbreviated μsec.

millenarian, adj. **1.** of or pertaining to a thousand years, especially to the thousand years of the prophesied Millennium. —n. **2.** a believer in the millennium. See also **millenium,** def. 2.

millenary, n. **1.** an aggregate of a thousand; millennium. **2.** a 1000th anniversary or celebration. —adj. **3.** consisting of or pertaining to a thousand, especially a thousand years.

millennium, n. (pl. **-iums; -ia**) **1.** a period of a thousand years; an anniversary of an event that occurred a thousand years earlier. **2.** usu. **The Millennium,** the predicted period of a thousand years during which Christ will reign on earth; a period of general righteousness and happiness. —**millennial,** adj.

millisecond, n. one thousandth of a second. Abbreviated **msec.**

monthly, n. **1.** a periodical published once a month. **2.** any event which occurs once a month. —adj. **3.** done, happening, appearing once a month, or continuing or lasting a month. —adv. **4.** by the month; once a month.

musical time. See **Table 6.**

myriad, n. **1.** an immense number of persons or things. **2.** ten thousand. —adj. **3.** of an indefinitely great number; countless.

nanosecond, n. one billionth of a second. Abbreviated **nsec.**

Nippur calendar, the standard calendar of the ancient Babylonians during the age of Hammurabi (late 18th century B.C.)

nocturnal, n. **1.** of, belonging to, or occurring each night; nightly. **2.** of or occurring during the nighttime; not diurnal. **3.** active at night, as a nocturnal predator. see **diurnal.**

nonage, n. **1.** the period of legal minority. **2.** the condition of not being of legal age to partake in certain activities. **3.** any period of immaturity.

nonagenarian, n. **1.** someone who has reached the age of 90 years, but is not yet 100. —adj. **2.** between the ages of 90 and 100.

notes, musical. See **Table 6.**

novendial, adj. Rare. **1.** lasting nine days. **2.** on the ninth day after an event.

novena, n. Roman Catholicism. a prayer service lasting nine consecutive days.

novennial, adj. occurring every ninth year.

nychthemeron, n. **1.** (pl. **-ra**) a full period of a night and a day; 24 hours. —adj. **2.** pertaining to a 24-hour period. Also **nycthemeron.**

octennial, adj. **1.** happening every eighth year. **2.** lasting for an eight-year period.

octogenarian, n. **1.** someone who has reached the age of 80 years, but is not yet 90. —adj. **2.** between the ages of 80 and 90 years.

olympiad, n. **1.** a period of four years reckoned from one celebration of the Olympic Games to the next, by which the ancient Greeks computed time from 776 B.C. **2.** a quadrennial celebration of the modern Olympic Games, as in 1976, 1980, 1984, etc.

pentad, n. a period of five years. Also **quinquenniad, quinquennial, quinquennium.**

per annum, by the year; yearly [from Latin]. Often used in stating a yearly basis in accounting, as $20,000 per annum. Abbreviated **p.a., per an.**

per diem, **1.** by the day; daily. **2.** a daily allowance for living expenses. [from Latin]

perennial, n. **1.** something that is continuing or recurrent for an indefinite number of years. **2.** Botany. a plant that renews its top growth every growing season and lives more than two years; trees, bushes, and plants such as chrysanthemums and strawberries are perennials. Cf. **annual; biennial.** —adj. **3.** continuing or lasting for an indefinitely long time. **4.** enduring, present all through the year; perpetual; recurrent. —**perennially,** adv.

period, *n.* **1.** a division or unit of time marked by a beginning, a duration, and an end; a specified division or portion of time. **2.** the duration of a cyclic occurrence. **3.** an interval in time that can be characterized by certain conditions, events, technology, development, culture, or ideology. **4.** *Geology.* The unit of time comprising several epochs and included with other periods in an era. See **Table 4.** —**periodic,** *adj.*

periodical, *n.* **1.** a magazine or other publication whose issues appear at regular intervals, more often than once a year. **2.** periodic.

photoperiodism, *n.* the biological responses of an organism such as a bird, flower, or animal to the period of daylight.

picosecond, *n.* one trillionth of a second. Abbreviated **psec.**

Platonic Year, the period of about 26,000 years that equals the time for one complete revolution of the equinoxes. See also **precession of the equinoxes.**

p.m., abbreviation for *post meridiem* (Latin), 'after noon,' in reference to the hours from 12 noon until midnight. Also written **P.M.**

precession of the equinoxes, the progressively earlier occurrence of the equinoxes each year caused by the gravitational force of the sun, moon, and planets on the earth's orbit. A cycle of gradually shifting equinoxes (and seasons) takes approximately 26,000 years. See also **Platonic Year.**

pro tem, abbreviation for *pro tempore,* Latin 'for the time being,' i.e., temporary, or, *adverbially,* temporarily.

proximo, *adv.* in, of, or during the next or following month; occurring next month; e.g., in April, the *6th proximo* is the 6th of May. See also **ultimo.**

quadragenarian, *n.* **1.** someone who has reached the age of 40 years, but is not yet 50. —*adj.* **2.** Also **quadragenarious.** between the ages of 40 and 50.

Quadragesima or **Quadragesima Sunday,** *n. Christian calendar.* the first Sunday in Lent, its name referring to the forty days (excepting Sundays) from Ash Wednesday to Easter.

Quadragesimal, *adj. Christian religion.* **1.** of, pertaining to, or suitable for Lent; Lenten. **2.** lasting 40 days, as the period of Lent.

quadrennial, *n.* **1.** a fourth anniversary or its celebration. **2.** an event occurring every four years. —*adj.* **3.** occurring every four years, as *a quadrennial election.* —*adv.* **quadrennially.**

quadrennium, *n.* a period of four years.

Quadrennium Utile, *n. Scots Law.* a period of four years after reaching one's majority, during which a person is within his rights to avoid carrying out certain contracts and other obligations.

quadricentennial, *n.* **1.** a 400th anniversary or its celebration. —*adj.* **2.** of, pertaining to, or marking the completion of a 400-year period.

quartan, *n.* **1.** a fever that recurs every fourth day. **2.** something that is fourth after three others.

quattrocento, *n.* **1.** the 15th century or 1400s, esp. with reference to art and literature in Italy [for Italian *mil quattro cento,* '1400']. —**quattrocentist,** *adj.*

quincentenary, *adj.* of or relating to a 500th anniversary. Also **quincentenary.**

quincentennial, *n.* **1.** a 500th anniversary or its celebration. —*adj.* **2.** of or relating to a 500th anniversary or to a 500-year period. Also **quincentenary.**

quindecennial, *n.* **1.** a fifteenth anniversary. —*adj.* **2.** of or pertaining to a period of 15 years or the 15th occurrence of a series, as an anniversary.

quinquagenarian, *n.* **1.** someone who has reached the age of 50, but is not yet 60. —*adj.* **2.** between the ages of 50 and 60 years.

quinquagenary, *n.* **1.** a 50th anniversary or its celebration. —*adj.* **2.** consisting of or containing 50 (years).

Quinquagesima or **Quinquagesima Sunday,** *n. Christian calendar.* the Sunday before Lent, approximately fifty days before Easter. Also called **Shrove Sunday.**

quinquagesimal, *adj.* occurring in a season of 50 days; consisting of 50 days.

quinquennial, *n.* **1.** something that occurs every five years. **2.** a five-year term of office. **3.** a fifth anniversary. **4.** Also **quinquennium, pentad, quinquenniad.** a period of five years. —*adj.* **5.** of or for five years; lasting five years. **6.** occurring every five years. —*adv.* **quinquennially.**

quinquenniad. See **quinquennial.**

quinquennium. See **quinquennial.**

quintan, *n.* **1.** a fever that recurs every fifth day. **2.** something that is the fifth after four others.

quotidian, *n.* **1.** something occurring daily, like a report or fever. —*adj.* **2.** daily. **3.** everyday. **4.** ordinary.

regnal year, a year calculated within the reign of a sovereign.

saros, the period of 223 synodic months, equalling about 18 years, after which eclipses repeat their cycle, but shifted 120° west.

score, *n.* a count, group, or set of 20, frequency referring to years, as in *four score and seven years ago.*

seicento, the 17th century or 1600s, esp. with reference to art and literature in Italy [for Italian *mil sei cento* '1600']. —**seicentist,** *adj.*

semester, *n.* **1.** a term comprising half of an academic year, lasting from 15 to 18 weeks. **2.** (in semestral

German universities) an academic term lasting about six months including holidays.

semestral, *adj.* **1.** of or pertaining to a semester. **2.** of or pertaining to a six-month period. Also **semestrial**.

semi-, *prefix.* **1.** half. **2.** half of or occurring halfway through a time period.

semiannual, *n.* **1.** a publication that is issued every six months or twice a year. **2.** *Botany.* a plant that lives for half a year. Also **semiyearly.** —*adj.* **3.** occurring, done, or published every six months or twice a year; lasting for half a year. —**semiannually,** *adv.*

semicentenary. See **semicentennial**.

semicentennial, *n.* **1.** a 50th anniversary or its celebration. Also, *Chiefly Brit.* **semicentenary.** —*adj.* **2.** of or pertaining to the 50th year after an event.

semimonthly, *n.* **1.** something that occurs twice a month. Cf. **bimonthly.** —*adj.* **2.** made, done, occurring, or published twice a month. —*adv.* **3.** twice a month.

semiweekly, *n.* **1.** something which takes place twice a week, as a publication. —*adj.* **2.** occurring, done, appearing, or being published twice a week. —*adv.* **3.** twice a week.

semiyearly, *adj.* **1.** occurring, done, or appearing every half year or twice a year. Also **semiannual.** —*adv.* **2.** twice a year. Also **semiannually.**

septenary, *n.* **1.** a group or set of seven. **2.** a period of seven years. Also **septennate; septennial; septennium.** —*adj.* **3.** of or pertaining to the number seven or forming a group of seven. Also **septennial.**

septennate, *n.* a seven-year term of office; a period of seven years. Also **septenary; septennial; septennium.**

septennial, *n.* **1.** something that occurs every seven years; a period of seven years. Also **septenary; septennate; septennium.** —*adj.* **2.** occurring every seven years; of or for seven years. Also **septenary.** —*adv.* **septennially.**

septennium, *n.* (*pl.* **-ia**) a period of seven years. Also **septenary; septennate; septennial.**

septicentennial, *n.* a 700th anniversary or its celebration.

septuagenarian, *n.* **1.** someone who has reached the age of 70 years, but is not yet 80. —*adj.* **2.** between the ages of 70 and 80 years. Also **septuagenary.**

Septuagesima or **Septuagesima Sunday,** *n. Christian calendar.* The third Sunday before Lent or the ninth Sunday before Easter, roughly seventy days before Easter.

sesquicentenary. See **sesquicentennial**.

sesquicentennial, *n.* **1.** a 150th year anniversary or its celebration. —*adj.* **2.** of or pertaining to or marking the completion of a period of 150 years. Also **sesquicentenary.** —**sesquicentennially,** *adv.*

sesquimillennium, *n.* **1.** a period of 1500 years or 15 centuries; the anniversary or celebration of such a span of time. —*adj.* **2.** of or pertaining to a period of 1500 years.

sexagenarian, *n.* **1.** someone who has reached the age of 60 years, but is not yet 70. —*adj.* **2.** between the ages of 60 to 70 years. Also **sexagenary.**

Sexagesima or **Sexagesima Sunday,** *n. Christian calendar.* the second Sunday before Lent and the eighth before Easter, approximately sixty days before Easter.

sexcentenary, *n.* **1.** a 600th anniversary or its celebration. —*adj.* **2.** pertaining to the number *600* or a period of 600 years; marking the completion of 600 years.

sexennial, *adj.* **1.** pertaining to six years or a period of six years; occurring every six years. **2.** continuing or lasting for six years. —**sexennially,** *adv.*

ship's bells, *n.* a signal of the half-hour aboard a ship. There are six four-hour watches in one 24-hour day; at the end of the first half-hour of a watch, one bell is struck; at the the end of the first hour, two bells, and so on to eight bells at the end of the watch. Watches begin at 8 p.m., midnight, 4 a.m., etc.

sidereal year, *n.* the time in which the earth completes one revolution in its orbit around the sun, measured with respect to the fixed stars: 365 days, 6 hours, 9 minutes, and 9.54 seconds of solar time.

sine die, *Latin.* 'without a day,' i.e., no time fixed for future action or meeting; indefinite. Abbreviated **s.d.** See **Table 2.**

solar calendar, a calendar based on the movement of the sun. Measured from equinox to equinox or solstice to solstice.

solar cycle, *n.* a period of 28 years, at the end of which the days of the month return to the same days of the week.

solar day, the 24-hour interval from one midnight to the next.

solar year, *n.* a division of time equal to the interval between one vernal equinox and the next, equal to 365 days, 5 hours, 48 minutes, and 46 seconds. Also **astronomical year, equinoctial year, tropical year.**

solstice, the time at which the sun is at its greatest distance north (about June 21, the **summer solstice**) or south (about December 22, the **winter solstice**) of the plane of the earth's equator. —**solstitial,** *adj.*

sub anno, *Latin.* 'under a year,' i.e., within the span of a given year. Abbreviated **s.a.** See **Table 2.**

synodic month, period between two successive new moons, equal to 29.531 days. See also **Metonic cycle.**

tercentenary, *n.* a 300th anniversary or its celebration. —*adj.* **2.** pertaining to a 300th anniversary or its celebration. Also **tercentennial, tricentenary, tricentennial.**

tercentennial, *adj.* or *n.* See **tercentenary.**

tertian, *n.* **1.** a fever with paroxysms every other day. —*adj.* **2.** recurring at approximately 48-hour intervals; recurring every third day.

trecento, *n.* **1.** the 14th century or 1300s, esp. with reference to art and literature in Italy [for Italian *mil tre cento* '1300']. —**trecentist,** *adj.*

triannual, *adj.* an event or publication that occurs or appears three times a year. —**triannually,** *adj.*

tricenary, *adj.* of or pertaining to thirty days or a month; containing or lasting thirty days.

tricennial, *n.* **1.** a 30-year celebration. **2.** a 30th anniversary or its celebration. —*adj.* **3.** of or pertaining to thirty years; taking place every thirty years.

tricentenary. See **tercentenary.**

tricentennial. See **tercentenary.**

triennial, *n.* **1.** a three-year period. **2.** a third anniversary; something that occurs once in three years. Also **triennium.** —*adj.* **3.** consisting of or lasting for three years. **4.** being done or occurring once every three years. —**triennially,** *adv.*

triennium, *n.* (*pl.* **-iums; -ia**) a period of three years. Also **triennial.**

trimester, *n.* **1.** a period of three months. **2.** one of the three terms into which an academic year may be divided. —**trimestral, trimestrial,** *adj.*

trimonthly, *n.* **1.** a publication or event appearing or occurring once every three months. —*adj.* **2.** occurring, appearing, being made, done, or acted upon every three months.

triweekly, *n.* **1.** a publication that is issued three times a week. **2.** a publication that is issued every three weeks. —*adj.* **3.** occurring or appearing three times a week. —*adv.* **4.** three times a week.

tropical year. See **sidereal year.**

twenty-four-hour time, *n.* system of clock-time used by the military, airlines, and continental Europe. The first two digits stand for the hour, the next two for the minutes. The last minute of the day is 2359; 0000 is midnight; 0001 is the first minute of the new day.

ultimo, *adv.* in, of, or during the preceding month, e.g., in October, the *5th ultimo* is the 5th of September. See also **proximo.**

vicennial, *adj.* **1.** of or for twenty years. **2.** occurring once every twenty years.

weekly, *n.* **1.** a periodical or event appearing or occurring once a week. —*adj.* **2.** being made, done, acted upon or appearing every week. Also **hebdomadal.** —*adv.* **3.** once a week, by the week. Also **hebdomadally.**

yearly, *n.* **1.** a publication appearing or an event occurring once a year; an annual. —*adj.* **2.** reckoned by the year; occurring or recurring every year. Also **annual.** —*adv.* **3.** from year to year; once a year; annually.

(Tables 1–7 begin on the next page.)

Table 1
Date References

Abbreviation	Full Term	Translation
A.D.	*Anno Domini* (Latin)	in the year of our Lord (Christ)
aet. or aetat.	*anno aetatis suae* ˜ (Latin)	in the ˜ year of his (or her) age
A.C.	*Anno Christi* (Latin)	in the year of Christ
A.H.	*Anno Hebraico* (Latin)	in the Hebrew year (i.e., since 3761 B.C.)
A.H.	*Anno Hegirae* or *Hejirae* (Latin)	in the year of the Hegira (A.D. 622)
A.H.S	*Anno Humanae Salutis* (Latin)	in the year of man's redemption (= A.D.)
A.L.	*Anno Lucis* (Latin)	in the year of light (i.e., since 4000 B.C.)
A.M.	*Anno Mundi* (Latin)	in the year of the world (i.e., since 4004 B.C.)
A.N.C.	*Ante Nativitatem Christi* (Latin)	before the birth of Christ (= B.C.)
A.P.C.N.	*Anno Post Christum Natum* (Latin)	in the year after the birth of Christ
A.P.R.C.	*Anno Post Roman Conditam* (Latin)	in the year after the founding of Rome (which took place 753 B.C.)
A.R.	*Anno Regni* (Latin)	in the year of the reign (of king, queen)
A.S.	*Anno Salutis* (Latin)	in the year of salvation (= A.D.)
A.U.C.	*Ab Urbe Condita* or *Anno Urbis Conditae* (Latin)	in the year of the founding of Rome (753 B.C.)
B.C.	Before Christ	
B.C.E.	Before the Common Era	
B.P.	Before the Present	
C.E.	Common Era	

Table 2
Latin Terms of Time

Abbreviation	Latin	Translation
ab init.	*ab initio*	from the beginning
ad an.	*ad annum*	up to the year
ad ex.	*ad extremum*	to the extreme, to the end
ad inf.	*ad infinitum*	to infinity, endlessly, no end
ad init.	*ad initium*	at the beginning
ad int.	*ad interim*	in the meantime
ca.	*circa*	about, approximately
in pr.	*in principio*	in the beginning
pro tem.	*pro tempore*	for the time being
prox.	*proximo*	of next month
s.a.	*sine anno*	without year or date
s.a.	*sub anno*	under the year
s.d.	*sine die*	without fixing a date for future action or future meeting
ult.	*ultimo*	of last month

Table 3
Clock Time

Abbreviation	Latin	Translation
a.m./A.M.	*ante meridiem*	before noon
m./M.	*meridies*	noon, meridian
p.m./P.M.	*post meridiem*	after noon

Table 4
Geologic Time

The succession of eras, periods, and epochs as considered in historical geology pertaining to the physical history and age of the earth.

(B = billion years; M = million years)

Years Ago	Era	Period	Epoch
5 B to 1-1/2 B	Precambrian-Archeozoic		
1-1/2 B to 600 M	Precambrian-Proterozoic		
600 M to 500 M		Cambrian	
500 M to 440 M		Ordovician	
440 M to 400 M		Silurian	
400 M to 350 M		Devonian	
350 M to 300 M	Paleozoic	Mississippian/ Carboniferous, Lower	
300 M to 270 M		Pennsylvanian/ Carboniferous, Upper	
270 M to 220 M		Permian	
220 M to 180 M		Triassic	
180 M to 135 M	Mesozoic	Jurassic	
135 M to 70 M		Cretaceous	
70 M to 60 M		Tertiary/Paleogene	Paleocene
60 M to 40 M			Eocene
40 M to 25 M			Oligocene
25 M to 10 M	Cenozoic	Tertiary/Neogene	Miocene
10 M to 1 M			Pliocene
1 M to 10,000		Quaternary	Pleistocene
10,000 to present			Holocene

Table 5
Prescription Abbreviations Referring to Time

Abbreviation	Expanded Form (Latin)	Meaning
a.c.	*ante cibos*	before meals
ad lib.	*ad libitum*	at pleasure
alt. hor.	*alternis horis*	every other hour
b.	*bis*	twice
b.i.d.	*bis in die*	twice a day
C	*centum*	a hundred
cito disp!	*cito dispensetur!*	let it be dispensed quickly!
d.	*dies*	day
dieb. alt.	*diebus alternis*	on alternate days
dieb. secund.	*diebus secundis*	every second day
h.s.	*hora somni*	at the hour of sleep, at bedtime
i.c.	*inter cibos*	between meals
m.	*mane*	in the morning
n. et m.	*nocte et mane*	night and morning
noct.	*nocte*	at night
non rep.	*non repetatur*	do not repeat
omn. hor.	*omni hora*	at every hour
omn. man.	*omni mane*	on every morning
p.c.	*post cibos*	after meals
p.r.n.	*pro re nata*	as occasion arises, as needed
pt.	*perstetur*	let it be continued
q., qq.	*quisque* (and related forms)	each, every
q.i.d.	*quater in die*	four times a day
qq. hor.	*quaque hora*	at every hour
quot. op. sit	*quoties opus sit*	as often as necessary
ren. sem.	*renovetur semel*	shall be renewed (only) once
rept.	*repetatur*	let it be repeated
sesquih.	*sesquihora*	an hour and a half
s.o.s.	*si opus sit*	if there is need
ss.	*semis*	one half
stat.	*statim*	immediately
t.i.d.	*ter in die*	three times a day
ult.	*ultime*	lastly
vesp.	*vespera*	in the evening

Table 6
Time of Notes in Music

breve   twice as long as a whole note.
whole note   the standard measure; also **semibreve.**
half note   half the time of a whole note; also **minim.**
quarter note   one-quarter the time of whole note; also **crotchet.**
eighth note   one-eighth the time of whole note; also **quaver.**
sixteenth note   one-sixteenth the time of a whole note; also **semiquaver.**
thirty-second note   one thirty-second of a whole note; also **demisemiquaver.**
sixty-fourth note   one sixty-fourth of a whole note; also **hemidemisemiquaver.**

Table 7
Anniversaries and Suggested Gifts

Year	Traditional Gift	Modern Gift
1st	Paper	Clock
2nd	Cotton	China
3rd	Leather	Crystal or Glass
4th	Fruit or Flowers	Appliances
5th	Wood	Silverware
6th	Candy or Ironware	Wood
7th	Copper or Wool	Pens, Pencils, Desk Sets
8th	Pottery or Bronze	Linens or Laces
9th	Pottery or Willow	Leather
10th	Aluminum or Tin	Diamond Jewelry
11th	Steel	Fashion Jewelry and Accessories
12th	Silk or Linen	Pearls or Colored Gems
13th	Lace	Textiles or Furs
14th	Ivory	Gold Jewelry
15th	Crystal	Watches
16th		Silver Hollow Ware
17th		Furniture
18th		Porcelain
19th		Bronze
20th	China	Platinum
25th (Jubilee)	Silver	Silver
30th	Pearl	Diamond
35th	Coral	Jade
40th	Ruby	Ruby
45th	Sapphire	Sapphire
50th (Jubilee)	Gold	Gold
55th	Emerald	Emerald
60th (Jubilee)	Diamond	Diamond
75th (Jubilee)	Diamond	Diamond

Holidays and Anniversaries of the World

January

January is the first month of the Gregorian calendar and has 31 days. The early Roman calendar, discussed in the Introduction, was organized on the basis of ten months, with a winter gap occurring between December, the tenth month, and March, then the first month; January and February did not exist as months. During the reign of the Roman king Numa Pompilius (715–673 B.C.), the calendar was expanded from ten to twelve months, and *Januarius* and *Februarius* were the names given to the new months.

During the period of the Etruscan kings at Rome (616–510 B.C.), the beginning of the year was moved to January 1. With the expulsion of the kings in 510 B.C., the beginning of the year reverted to March 1, and so it remained through much of the Roman Republican period.

In 153 B.C., January 1 was officially set as the beginning of the new civil year at Rome, i.e., the day that newly elected consuls took office, and it has retained that position through both the Julian and Gregorian calendar reforms. However, popular usage long continued to regard March as the beginning of the year, primarily owing to the occurrence of the vernal equinox in that month, marking the beginning of a new agricultural season (see also at **March**).

January (Latin *Januarius*) is derived from the name of the ancient Roman deity, *Janus*, the god of gates and doors and, hence, all beginnings, whose image is of two faces, one looking forward and one back. Janus was also regarded as the protector of ships and trade, apparently as a sort of providential deity. January, the month which looked both to the past and the future, came to be important in Roman ritual and was consecrated by offerings of wine, salt, meal, and frankincense. On the first day of January, Romans exchanged gifts of small coins bearing the image of Janus on one side and a ship on the other.

In the astrological calendar, January spans the zodiacal signs of Capricorn, the Goat (December 22–January 19) and Aquarius, the Water Bearer (January 20–February 18).

The birthstone for January is the garnet, and the flower is the carnation or snowdrop.

State, National, and International Holidays

New Year's Day
January 1

George Washington Carver Day
(United States)
January 5

Three Kings' Day
(Puerto Rico)
January 6

Battle of New Orleans Day
(Louisiana)
January 8

DeHostos' Birthday
(Puerto Rico)
January 11

Feast of Christ of Esquipulas
or the **Black Christ Festival**
(Guatemala)
January 15

Teacher's Day
(Venezuela)
January 15

Confederate Heroes' Day
(Texas)
January 19

Franklin D. Roosevelt's Birthday
(Kentucky)
January 30

Handsel Monday
(Scotland)
First Monday

Maitlisunntig
(Switzerland)
Second Sunday

Martin Luther King, Jr.'s Birthday
(United States)
Third Monday;
an official national
holiday beginning in 1986

Robert E. Lee's Birthday
(Alabama, Mississippi)
Third Monday

(Arkansas, Florida, Georgia, Kentucky, Louisiana, South Carolina)
January 19

Lee-Jackson Day
(Virginia)
Third Monday

Australia Day
(Australia)
Last Monday

Special Events and Their Sponsors

Stamp Collector's Month
Franklin D. Roosevelt Philatelic Society
154 Laguna Court
St. Augustine Shores, Florida 32084

Weeks' Week
First Week
Richard R. Falk Associates
1472 Broadway
New York, New York 10036

Man Watchers' Week
Second Week
Man Watchers, Inc.
8033 Sunset Boulevard
Suite 363
Los Angeles, California 90046

International Printing Week
Third Week
International Association
of Printing House Craftsmen
7599 Kenwood Road
Cincinnati, Ohio 45236

Printing Ink Day
Tuesday of International Printing Week, above
National Association
of Printing Ink Manufacturers
550 Mamaroneck Avenue
Harrison, New York 10528

National Jaycees Week
Third Week
United States Jaycees
Public Relations Department
Box 7
Four West 21st Street
Tulsa, Oklahoma 74121

World-wide Kiwanis Week
Third Week
Kiwanis International
3636 Woodview Trace
Indianapolis, Indiana 46268

Graphics Communication Week
Week of January 17
International Graphic Arts
   Education Association, Inc.
4615 Forbes Avenue
Pittsburgh, Pennsylvania 15213

Junior Achievement Week
Final Week
Junior Achievement Inc.
550 Summer Street
Stamford, Connecticut 06901

Trivia Day
January 4
Puns Corp.
c/o Robert L. Birch
Box 2364
Falls Church, Virginia 22042

Benjamin Franklin's Birthday
January 17

Philately Day
January 20

Franklin D. Roosevelt's Birthday Anniversary
January 30
Franklin D. Roosevelt
   Philatelic Society
154 Laguna Court
St. Augustine Shores, Florida 32084

Handwriting Day
January 23
Writing Instrument
   Manufacturers Association
1625 I Street, N.W.
Washington, D.C. 20006

Special Days—Other Calendars

	Chinese New Year
1987	January 30
1990	January 27

Holidays

New Year's Day
Observed in all countries of the world that follow the Gregorian calendar.

Cuba   **Liberation Day** or **Anniversary of the Triumph of the Revolution**
Commemorates the overthrow of the Batista government by Fidel Castro, 1959.

Haiti   **Independence Day**
Commemorates the declaration of independence of the island by Jean Jacques Dessalines, 1804. Also called **Heroes Day, Ancestors Day,** or **The Day of the Glorification of the Heroes of Independence.**

January 1

Birthdates

1449   **Lorenzo de Medici,** Florentine statesman, merchant prince, patron of the arts. [d. April 8, 1492]

1484   **Huldrych (Ulrich) Zwingli,** Swiss Protestant reformer; leader of the Protestant Reformation. [d. October 11, 1531]

1618   **Bartolomé Esteban Murillo,** Spanish baroque religious painter. [d. April 13, 1682]

1697   **Joseph Dupleix,** Governor-General of French possessions in India, 1742–54. [d. November 10, 1763]

1735   **Paul Revere,** American patriot, silversmith; his famous ride (April 18, 1775) to warn the colonists of the arrival of the British made him a legend in American history. [d. May 10, 1818]

1745   **Anthony (*Mad Anthony*) Wayne,** American Revolutionary general; his capture of the fortress at **Stony Point, New York,** provided great inspiration for the colonial cause. [d. December 15, 1796]

1750   **Frederick Augustus Conrad Muhlenberg,** U.S. statesman, Lutheran clergyman; first president, **Muhlenberg College,** Pennsylvania, 1867–76. [d. June 4, 1801]

1752   **(Elizabeth) Betsy Ross,** American colonial patriot; reputed to have sewn the first American flag. [d. January 30, 1836]

1823   **Sandor Petofi (Petrovics),** Hungarian poet and revolutionary; among the first of Hungary's lyric poets; his lyrics for revolutionary patriotic songs won him recognition as the **national poet of Hungary.** [d. July 31, 1849]

1834   **Ludovic Halévy,** French dramatist, novelist, born in Turkey; known for his theory that the Sumerian people never existed and that their writings were merely secret codes of the Babylonian priesthood. [d. May 8, 1908]

1854   **Sir James George Frazer,** Scottish anthropologist, classicist; best known as the author of *The Golden Bough.* [d. May 7, 1941]

1859   **Michael J. Owens,** U.S. inventor of the automatic **bottle-making machine**; a founder of the **Libbey-Owens Sheet Glass Co.,** 1916. [d. December 27, 1923]

1863   **Pierre Coubertin,** French sportsman; revived **Olympic Games** in 1894; President of the International Olympic Committee, 1894–1925. [d. September 1, 1937]

1864   **Alfred Stieglitz,** U.S. photographer; known as the *Father of Modern Photography.* [d. July 13, 1946]

1879   **E(dward) M(organ) Forster,** British novelist, critic. [d. June 7, 1970]

      William Fox, U.S. film executive; founder of **Twentieth-Century Fox.** [d. 1952]

Somali Democratic Republic	Bank Holiday
Sudan	**Independence Day** Celebrates Sudan's treaty of independence with Great Britain, 1956.
Taiwan	**Founding of Republic of China** Celebrates the establishment of the Republic by Chiang Kai-shek, 1949.

Religious Calendar

Solemnities

Octave of Christmas Commemorates the **Circumcision of Christ.**

Solemnity of Mary, Mother of God Sometimes called the **Birthday of Mary**; honors the divine motherhood of Mary. Celebrated on December 26 in the Byzantine and Syrian churches; on January 16 in the Coptic rite.

The Saints

St. Concordius, martyr. Also called **Concord.** [d. c. 178]

St. Almachius, martyr. Also called **Telemachus.** [d. c. 400]

St. Euphrosyne, virgin. Called *Our Mother* by the Greeks. [d. c. fifth century]

St. Eugendus, Abbot of the Monastery of Condat (Saint-Oyend). Also called **Oyend.** [d. c. 510]

St. Fulgentius, Bishop of Ruspe. [d. 533]

St. Felix of Bourges, bishop. [d. c. 580]

St. Clarus, Abbot of the Monastery of St. Marcellus at Vienne in Dauphine. First monk in the Abbey of St. Ferreol. [d. c. 660]

Ernest Jones, British psychoanalyst; popularizer, translator and biographer of Sigmund Freud. [d. February 11, 1958]

1883 **Roy Wilson Howard,** U.S. newspaperman; a founder of the **Scripps-Howard** newspaper chain. [d. November 20, 1964]

William Joseph (*Wild Bill*) Donovan, U.S. Army general, lawyer, public official; World War I hero; Congressional Medal of Honor; World War II Head of Office of Strategic Services, 1942–45. [d. February 8, 1959]

1887 **Wilhelm Franz Canaris,** German admiral; chief of military intelligence, anti-Hitler conspirator. [d. April 9, 1945]

1888 **John Cantius Garand,** U.S. rifle inventor, designer; designer of the **M-1 rifle,** the basic weapon of U.S. infantry during World War II. [d. February 16, 1974]

1892 **Manuel Roxas y Acuna,** Philippine statesman, first president of the Philippines, 1946–48. [d. April 15, 1948]

Martin Niemöller, German priest; open opponent of Hitler in the 1930s; President of the World Council of Churches. [d. March 6, 1984]

1895 **J(ohn) Edgar Hoover,** U.S. government official, lawyer, criminologist; director of F.B.I., 1924–72. [d. May 1, 1972]

Red Allen, U.S. musician; Dixieland-jazz trumpet player. [d. April 17, 1967]

1909 **Barry (Morris) Goldwater,** U.S. Senator, 1969– .

1911 **Hank Greenberg,** U.S. baseball player; elected to Baseball Hall of Fame, 1956.

1912 **Harold (*Kim*) Philby,** Soviet master-spy in British intelligence, 1933–63; defected and escaped to Soviet Union.

1913 **Eliot Janeway,** U.S. economist, author.

1919 **J(erome) D(avid) Salinger,** U.S. novelist, short-story writer; author of *Catcher in the Rye, Frannie and Zooey.*

1930 **Goafar Mohammed Nimeiri,** Sudanese political leader; President, 1969– ; Prime Minister, 1977– .

1957 **Nancy Lopez,** U.S. golfer; named Rookie of the Year and Player of the year, 1978; set record (of $153,336) for rookie earnings.

Historical Events

1515 **Louis XII** of France dies and is succeeded by **Francis I.**

1519 **Ulrich Zwingli,** Swiss religious reformer, is ordained at Zurich.

1531 **Rio de Janeiro (*River of January*),** in Brazil, is discovered by Portuguese navigators.

1547 **Michelangelo** is appointed chief architect of St. Peter's by **Pope Paul III.**

1596 The first Dutch colonists land on **Sumatra,** Indonesia, an ancient trade center.

January 1 Continued

St. Peter of Atroa, abbot. [d. 837]

St. William of Saint Benignus, abbot; advocate of Cluniac reform. [d. 1031]

St. Odilo, abbot of the monastery at Cluny; instituted the annual commemoration of all the faithful departed on November 2, or All Souls' Day. Also called **Alou, Olon.** [d. 1049]

The Beatified

Blessed Zdislava, matron. Founded the Dominican priory of St. Laurence. [d. 1252]

Blessed Hugolino of Gualdo, abbot. [d. 1260]

Blessed Joseph Tommasi, Cardinal of the Holy Roman Church. Called the *Prince of Liturgists.* [d. 1713]

1651 **King Charles II** is crowned King of Scotland, marking the last coronation at Scone.

1673 Dutch capture **St. Helena Island,** in the South Atlantic, from the British.

1776 First U.S. flag, *The Great Union,* is displayed by **George Washington**; it becomes the unofficial national flag, preceding the 13-star, 13-stripe version.

1801 Legislative Union of Great Britain with Ireland under the name of **United Kingdom** becomes effective.

1804 **Haiti** declares its independence from France.

1808 **Sierra Leone** becomes a crown colony of Great Britain.

1833 Great Britain gains sovereignty over the **Falkland Islands.**

1840 First recorded **ten-pin bowling match** is played at **Knickerbocker Alleys,** New York City.

1863 The **Emancipation Proclamation** becomes law, marking the end of legalized slavery in the U.S.

1871 **Church of Ireland** is established.

1873 Japan adopts the **Gregorian calendar.**

1876 Egypt adopts the **Gregorian calendar.**

1877 **Queen Victoria** is proclaimed Empress of Egypt and India.

1886 **Upper Burma** is annexed by the British.

1889 State of New York introduces use of the **electric chair** for capital punishment.

1890 Italian possessions on the Red Sea in **Eritrea** are united as a colony.

1898 The five boroughs of New York are joined to form greater **New York.**

1900 **Upper Nigeria, Lower Nigeria,** and **Lagos** are proclaimed protectorates of Great Britain.

1901 The **Commonwealth of Australia** is proclaimed, consisting of New South Wales, Victoria, Queensland, South Australia, Western Australia, and Tasmania.

1902 First **Rose Bowl** football game is played at Pasadena, California.

1903 **King Edward VII** of Great Britain is proclaimed Emperor of India.

1908 **Gustav Mahler** makes his first American appearance, conducting the Metropolitan Opera in *Tristan und Isolde.*

1912 The **Chinese Republic** is declared; **Dr. Sun Yat-sen** is sworn in as provisional president.

1913 **U.S. Parcel Post** begins.

1914 The Colony and Protectorate of **Nigeria** is formed from ten old British protectorates of Southern and Northern Nigeria.

1915 The British battleship *Formidable* is sunk in the English Channel by a German submarine with the loss of 600 lives (**World War I**).

1917 **Rasputin's** body is taken from the Neva River in St. Petersburg, Russia, following his assassination by Russian noblemen.

1920 The **eight-hour workday** becomes law in Sweden.

1921 New **Elementary Education Act** goes into effect in the **Netherlands.**

Mauritania becomes a separate French colony.

1922   French and Flemish are declared official languages in **Belgium.**

1923   **Union of Soviet Socialist Republics** is proclaimed.

1925   **Christiana,** the capital of Norway, resumes the name **Oslo.**

       Damascus and **Aleppo** are united to form the state of **Syria** by decree of the French government.

1927   The **metric system** of weights and measures is adopted by the U.S.S.R.

1930   The **Indian National Congress** votes for complete independence.

1942   **Atlantic Charter** officially proclaimed.

       The Allied nations begin their **East Indies Campaign (World War II).**

1945   **British 14th Army** offensive in Burma begins **(World War II).**

1947   **Great Britain** nationalizes its coal mines and communications.

1948   **Great Britain** nationalizes its railways.

1956   **Sudan** gains independence from Great Britain and Egypt.

1958   **European Economic Community,** referred to as the **Common Market,** is formed.

1960   **Cameroon** becomes independent of France.

1962   **Western Samoa** becomes independent.

1965   **Intermall,** an international steel trust made up of the U.S.S.R. and five Eastern European nations, begins operations from headquarters in Budapest, Hungary.

1966   **Col. Jean-Bedel Bokassa** assumes power in the Central African Republic after a coup d'état.

1968   **C(ecil) Day Lewis** is named Poet Laureate of Great Britain, succeeding John Masefield.

1969   New **Czechoslovak federal government** is inaugurated, marking the beginning of a massive Communist Party reorganization in that country.

1973   United Kingdom, Ireland, and Denmark become members of the **European Economic Community** or **Common Market.**

1975   **John Ehrlichman, H. R. Haldeman,** and **John Mitchell** are found guilty of obstructing justice in the **Watergate Incident.**

1977   **Episcopal Church of U.S.** ordains its first woman priest.

1979   The **People's Republic of China** and the U.S. establish full diplomatic relations as the U.S. simultaneously severs diplomatic relations with Chinese Nationalists in Taiwan.

1981   **Premier Abdou Diouf** is named President of **Senegal.**

       Greece officially becomes the tenth member of the **European Economic Community** (Common Market).

January 2

Holidays

Botswana	Public holiday
Haiti	Ancestry Day
St. Lucia	Public holiday
Switzerland	Berchtoldstag or Berchtold's Day.

Honors the 12th century **Duke Berchtold V,** who founded the City of **Berne.**

Religious Calendar

Solemnities

Feast of the Holy Name of Jesus Celebrated January 2 when there is no Sunday between January 1 and January 6. Otherwise, a moveable feast falling on

Birthdates

1647 **Nathaniel Bacon,** American colonial leader, pioneer; leader of **Bacon's Rebellion** against the Indians in Virginia, 1676. [d. October 1676]

1721 **John Manners,** Marquis of Granby, British military commander; commander in chief of English forces during the **Seven Years' War.** [d. October 18, 1770]

1727 **James Wolfe,** British army general; led the British expedition against Quebec, 1759; completed British conquest of North America. [d. September 13, 1759]

1751 **Ferdinand IV,** King of Naples; also, **Ferdinand III,** King of Sicily; **Ferdinand I,** King of the Two Sicilies, 1816–20. [d. January 4, 1825]

1752 **Philip Morin Freneau,** American poet, journalist; known as the *Poet of the American Revolution.* [d. December 19, 1832]

1831 **Justin Winsor,** U.S. historian; librarian of Boston Public Library, 1866–77; and of Harvard College, 1877–97; a founder and first president of the **American Library Association,** 1876–88. [d. October 22, 1897]

1857 **Martha Carey Thomas,** U.S. educator, suffragist; President of **Bryn Mawr College,** 1894–1922. [d. December 2, 1935]

1866 **(George) Gilbert Murray,** British classical scholar, translator; recognized as a guiding force in the creation of the **League of Nations.** [d. May 20, 1957]

1895 **Count Folke Bernadotte,** Swedish statesman, Red Cross official; UN mediator in Palestine during the partition of Palestine after British withdrawal. Assassinated by Israeli extremists. [d. September 17, 1948]

1904 **Sally Rand (Helen Beck),** U.S. fan dancer. [d. August 31, 1979]

1920 **Isaac Asimov,** U.S. biochemist, author born in Russia; noted for his prolific work and clear style of writing on extremely complicated subjects.

1922 **Renata Tebaldi,** Italian operatic lyric soprano.

Historical Events

1492 Moors surrender **Granada** to Spain.

1788 **Georgia** ratifies **U.S. Constitution.**

1799 **Napoleon Bonaparte** advances into **Syria.**

1861 **Frederick William IV** of Prussia dies and is succeeded by **William I.**

1896 Men of the **Jameson Raid,** including **Starr Jameson,** are captured by the Boers at Doornkop, South African Republic (**Boer War**).

1901 First municipal crematorium opens in England, at **Hull.**

1905 Russians are defeated at **Port Arthur** by the Japanese (**Russo-Japanese War**).

1915 Turks are defeated by the Russians in the **Battle of Sarikamish** in the Caucasus (**World War I**).

1922 **Ukraine** signs treaty with Turkey recognizing independence of the Ukraine.

the Sunday between January 1, the Circumcision, and January 6, the Epiphany. Suppressed 1970.

The Saints

St. Basil the Great, Archbishop of Caesarea, Doctor of the Church, and patriarch of Eastern monks; founder of the Order of Basilicans. Feast formerly June 14. [d. 379] Obligatory Memorial.

St. Gregory Nazianzen, Bishop of Constantinople and Doctor of the Church; one of the very earliest of Christian poets. Surnamed the *Theologian*; also called **Nazianzus.** Feast formerly May 9. [d. 390] Obligatory Memorial.

St. Macarius of Alexandria, monk; called the *Younger*; patron saint of pastry cooks and confectioners. [d. 394]

St. Munchin, bishop. Called the *Wise*. Principal patron saint of the Diocese of Limerick. Feast celebrated throughout Ireland. [d. 7th century]

St. Vincentian. [d. c. 672]

St. Adalhard, abbot; cousin to Emperor **Charlemagne.** Founder of Monastery of New Corbie, or Corwey. Also called **Adalard, Adelard, Alard.** [d. 827]

St. Caspar del Bufalo, priest; founder of the Missioners of the Precious Blood. [d. 1837]

The Beatified

Blessed Ayrald, Bishop of Maurienne. [d. c. 1146]

Blessed Stephana Quinzani, virgin; founder of the Convent at Soncino. [d. 1530]

1926	**Royal Academy of Italy** is created.
1942	Japanese invade and occupy **Manila** and the **Philippines** after successful attack on **Pearl Harbor.**
1946	**King Zog** of Albania is deposed *in absentia*.
1955	**José Antonio Remón,** President of Panama 1951–1955, is assassinated.
1959	**Fidel Castro** and his followers capture **Santiago, Cuba; Fulgencio Batista** goes into exile.
	Luna I, first Soviet moon probe, is launched.
1962	**King Hassan II of Morocco** signs decree creating a free zone in the port of **Tangier.**
1963	General **Lyman L. Lemnitzer** becomes the supreme commander of NATO.
1968	**Robert Clark** is seated as first black legislator in **Mississippi** in 74 years.
1968	**Philip Blaiberg** becomes the third recipient of a transplanted heart.
1975	**Elizabeth Domitien** is named the first woman premier in Africa by the President of the **Central African Republic,** Jean-Bedel Bokassa.

January 3

Holidays

Japan	**Genshi-Sai** or **First Beginning** One of the four great holidays of the Emperor and his family; observed by the reading of the Imperial Proclamations.
U.S. (Alaska)	**Admission Day** Celebrates Alaska's admission to the Union as the 49th state.
Upper Volta	**Revolution Day**

Birthdates

1698 **Pietro Antonio Domenico Buonaventura Metastasio,** Italian poet, dramatist; celebrated librettist. [d. April 12, 1782]

1793 **Lucretia (Coffin) Mott,** U.S. abolitionist, feminist, Quaker minister; with Elizabeth Cady Stanton (November 12) founded the women's rights movement in the U.S. [d. November 11, 1880]

1823 **Robert Whitehead,** British engineer; inventor of the **naval torpedo.** [d. November 14, 1905]

1835 **Larkin Goldsmith Mead,** U.S. sculptor; among his works are the statue of *Ethan Allen*, Montpelier, Vermont, and *Abraham Lincoln*, Springfield, Illinois. [d. October 15, 1910]

1840 **Joseph Damie de Veuster (Father Damien),** Belgian priest; known for his missionary work in the leper colony in Molokai, Hawaii. [d. April 15, 1889]

1876 **Wilhelm Pieck,** German Communist leader, President of German Democratic Republic (East Germany), 1949–60. [d. September 1960]

1883 **Clement (Richard) Attlee,** Viscount Prestwood, British politician; Prime Minister, 1945–52. [d. October 8, 1967]

1886 **Raymond Ames Spruance,** U.S. admiral; Ambassador to the Philippines, 1951–55. [d. December 13, 1969]

1892 **J(ohn) R(onald) R(euel) Tolkien,** British philologist, writer; known for his fantasy novels including *The Hobbit* and *The Lord of the Rings.* [d. September 2, 1973]

1898 **T(ubal) Claude Ryan,** U.S. aircraft manufacturer; established first year-round passenger air service in U.S.; responsible for design and construction of Charles A. Lindbergh's *Spirit of St. Louis.* [d. September 11, 1982]

1901 **Ngo Dinh Diem,** Vietnamese leader; President of the Republic of Vietnam, 1954–63. [d. November 2, 1963]

1909 **Victor Borge,** Danish-American pianist, comedian.

1926 **W(erner) Michael Blumenthal,** U.S. economist, businessman; U.S. Secretary of the Treasury, 1977–79.

Historical Events

1322 **Philip V** of France dies and is succeeded by **Charles IV.**

1399 **Timur (Tamerlane)** and his Mongols, at the height of their power in Asia, defeat **Emperor Mahmud** of India and gain control of Delhi.

1521 **Martin Luther** is formally excommunicated from the Roman Catholic Church by **Pope Leo X.**

1661 In England, **female actresses** appear on stage for the first time.

1777 General **George Washington** defeats the British under **Lord Cornwallis** at the **Battle of Princeton.**

1847 **Yerba Buena,** a U.S. town of 200 people, is renamed **San Francisco.**

1857 **Archbishop Sebour** of Paris is assassinated by **Verger,** a priest.

1868 The **Emperor of Japan** assumes direct control of the government, precipitating civil war with forces of the shogunate.

1870 Construction begins on the **Brooklyn Bridge.**

1888 Waxed paper **drinking straws** are patented in the United States.

Religious Calendar

The Saints

St. Antherus, Pope and martyr. Elected Bishop of Rome 235. Also called **Anterus.** [d. 236]

St. Peter Balsam, martyr. [d. 311]

St. Geneviève, virgin. Patroness of Paris, secretaries, actors, lawyers, and the Woman's Army Corps. Invoked against fever. Also called **Genoveia, Genoveffa.** [d. c. 500]

St. Bertilia of Mareuil, widow. [d. 8th century]

The Beatified

Blessed Alanus de Solminihac. [beatified 1981]

1895	*An Ideal Husband,* by **Oscar Wilde,** premieres at the Haymarket Theatre, London.
1903	**Shanghai** is evacuated by last detachment of German troops (**Boxer Rebellion**).
1921	First parliament in India meets.
1928	**Leon Trotsky** and thirty other members of the opposition are banished to the provinces of the Soviet Union.
1938	**March of Dimes** anti-polio campaign is organized in the U.S.
1941	**Sergei Rachmaninoff's** suite, *Symphonic Dances,* premieres in Philadelphia; it is performed by the Philadelphia Orchestra, Eugene Ormandy conducting.
1946	**William Joyce,** nicknamed *Lord Haw-Haw,* British broadcaster of propaganda from Nazi Germany during World War II, is hanged in Great Britain for treason.
1951	U.S. President **Harry S. Truman** creates the **Defense Production Administration,** headed by William H. Harrison, to centralize various emergency production agencies.
1959	**Alaska** is admitted to the Union as the 49th state.
1960	**Moscow State Symphony,** performs in New York City, becoming the first Russian orchestra to perform in the U.S.
1961	U.S. breaks diplomatic relations with **Cuba.**
1967	**Jack Ruby,** who shot **Lee Harvey Oswald,** alleged assassin of U.S. President **J. F. Kennedy,** dies in a Dallas hospital.
1970	**People's Republic of the Congo** is formed under a new constitution.
1972	**William Tolbert, Jr.,** is inaugurated as President of **Liberia.**
1974	Spain's new premier, **Carlos Arias Navarro,** forms a new cabinet, following the assassination of **Luis Carrero Blanco.**
	The **Socialist Republic of the Union of Burma** is proclaimed.
1975	**Lopez Rega** becomes the most powerful man in Argentine government when President **Isabel Perón** gives him special powers.

January 4

Holidays

Burma	**Independence Day**
	Commemorates achievement of independence from Great Britain, 1948.
U.S. (Utah)	**Admission Day**
	Commemorates Utah's entry into the Union, 1896.
Zaire	**Martyrs of Independence**

Birthdates

1581 **James Ussher,** Irish scholar, prelate of Ireland; Archbishop of Armagh, 1625; known for his scheme of Biblical chronology which dated creation at 4004 B.C. [d. March 21, 1656]

1643 **Sir Isaac Newton,** English physicist, mathematician; leader of 17th century scientific revolution. [d. March 20, 1727]

1710 **Giovanni Pergolesi,** Italian composer; noted for his influence in the development of comic opera. [d. March 16, 1736]

1785 **Jacob Grimm,** German philologist, folklorist, scholar, fairy-tale collector; with his brother Wilhelm (February 20) edited numerous collections of folk and fairy tales. [d. September 20, 1863]

1809 **Louis Braille,** French musician, teacher; inventor of **Braille system** used by the blind. [d. January 6, 1852]

1813 **Sir Isaac Pitman,** British printer, publisher; inventor of **shorthand.** [d. January 12, 1897]

1858 **Carter Glass,** U.S. politician; Secretary of the Treasury, 1918–20; U.S. Senator, 1920–46. [d. May 28, 1946]

1874 **Thornton W. Burgess,** U.S. author of children's books; noted for nature stories and animal tales. [d. June 6, 1965]

1887 **Edwin Emil Witte,** U.S. economist; author of **U.S. Social Security Act of 1935.** [d. May 20, 1960]

1895 **Leroy Randle Grumman,** U.S. aircraft manufacturer. [d. October 4, 1982]

1896 **Everett McKinley Dirksen,** U.S. public official; U.S. Senator, 1950–69. [d. September 7, 1969]

1905 **Sterling Holloway,** U.S. actor; known for his parts as the voice of many **Walt Disney** animated characters.

1935 **Floyd Patterson,** U.S. boxer; world heavyweight champion, 1956-59.

1940 **Brian David Josephson,** British physicist; Nobel Prize in physics for research on the occurrence of **superconductivity** (with L. Esaki and I. Giaever), 1973.

Historical Events

1717 **Triple alliance** is signed between England, France, and Holland.

1762 England declares war on Spain and Naples (**Seven Years' War**).

1805 Spain enters the **War of the Third Coalition** on the side of Napoleon and against the British and their allies.

1896 **Utah** is admitted to the Union as the 45th state.

1908 **Mulai Hafid** is proclaimed **Sultan of Morocco.**

1916 British make the first attempt to raise the Turkish siege of **Kut-el-Amara** (**World War I**).

1919 **Riga, Latvia,** is captured by the Bolsheviks (**Russian Revolution**).

1920 Polish troops capture **Dvinsk.**

1932 **Mahatma Gandhi** is arrested and begins a fast unto death to win suffrage for the untouchables.

1945 Allies bomb **Brenner Pass** in the Alps to prevent retreat of German troops (**World War II**).

1948 **Burma** becomes independent of Great Britain; Thakin Nu is appointed Prime Minister.

1951 **Seoul** is captured by Chinese Communists and North Koreans (**Korean War**).

1960 Countries outside the Common Market form the **European Free Trade Association.**

Religious Calendar

The Saints

St. Gregory, Bishop of Langes. [d. 539]

St. Pharaïldis, virgin. Invoked by mothers who are anxious about their children's health. Also called **Varelde, Veerle, Verylde.** [d. c. 740]

St. Rigobert, Archbishop of Rheims. Also called **Robert.** [d. c. 745]

St. Elizabeth Ann Seton, nun; founder of the American Sisters of Charity. First native-born American citizen to be canonized. [d. 1821]

The Beatified

Blessed Roger of Ellant, founder of Monastery of Ellant in Diocese of Rheims. [d. 1160]

Blessed Oringa, virgin. [d. 1310]

1962 Council of **Organization of American States** lifts all diplomatic and economic sanctions against the **Dominican Republic.**

1965 President **Lyndon B. Johnson,** in his State of the Union message, outlines a sweeping program to move U.S. toward the *Great Society.*

1966 Reconstruction work begins on the ancient **Abu Simbel** temples in Egypt, salvaged during construction of **Aswan High Dam.**

1967 **Swahili** is designated as the official language of **Tanzania.**

January 5

England   **Twelfth Night**
The last or 12th night of the Christmas season according to the Gregorian or New Style calendar; or
Wassail Eve, reflecting the tradition celebrating the good health of friends and neighbors by drinking a spicy wine or ale from what is commonly referred to as the *loving cup*; or
Eve of Epiphany, being the evening before the **Epiphany** or **Manifestation of God** or the **Feast of the Three Kings.**

Birthdates

1592   **Shah Jahan (Prince Khurram),** fifth Emperor of Hindustan, 1628–58; ruler of India during the golden age of Mohammedan architecture; builder of the **Taj Mahal.** [d. January 22, 1666]

1744   **Gaspar Melchor de Jovellanos,** Spanish statesman and writer; Chief Justice of the Spanish Court, 1778. [d. July 29, 1811]

1745   **Benjamin Rush,** U.S. physician, medical educator, patriot, reformer; established first free dispensary in America, 1786; Treasurer of the Mint of the U.S., 1797–1813; author of the first systematic treatment of the subject of mental illness in the U.S., 1812. [d. April 19, 1813]

1779   **Zebulon Montgomery Pike,** U.S. army officer, explorer; famous for his explorations of the American southwest; produced the first English language account of the region. **Pike's Peak** is named for him; killed while leading victorious attack on Toronto (War of 1812). [d. April 27, 1813]

Stephen Decatur, U.S. naval commodore; led one of the greatest naval victories of the War of 1812, capturing the British frigate *Macedonian.* Issued the famous quote, "Our country! In her intercourse with foreign nations may she always be in the right; but our country, right or wrong." [d. March 22, 1820]

1789   **Thomas Pringle,** Scottish-South African traveller, poet; funder of parent publication of *Blackwood's Magazine.* [d. December 5, 1834]

1846   **Rudolph Christoph Eucken,** German philosopher; Nobel Prize in literature, 1908. [d. September 14, 1926]

1855   **King C. Gillette,** U.S. inventor of **safety razor**; founder and head of Gillette Safety Razor Company, 1901–32. [d. July 9, 1932]

1864   **Byron Bancroft Johnson,** U.S. sportsman; organizer and first president of **American Baseball League.** [d. October 4, 1902]

1874   **Joseph Erlanger,** U.S. physiologist; Nobel Prize in physiology or medicine for study of functions of nerve fibers (with H. S. Gasser), 1944. [d. December 5, 1965]

1876   **Konrad Adenauer,** German statesman; first chancellor of the **Federal Republic of Germany,** 1949–63. [d. April 19, l967]

1882   **Herbert Bayard Swope,** U.S. journalist; Pulitzer Prize in reporting, 1917. [d. June 20, 1958]

1887   **Courtney Hicks Hodges,** U.S. army general; commander of Third and First Armies, World War II. [d. January 16, 1966]

1913   **Kemmons Wilson,** U.S. hotelier, founder of Holiday Inn chain.

Jean-Pierre Aumont (Jean-Pierre Salomons), French actor, in U.S. since 1941.

1921   **Friedrich Durrenmatt,** Swiss playwright, novelist.

Grand Duke Jean, Head of State, Grand Duchy of Luxembourg, 1964– .

Religious Calendar

The Saints

St. Telesphorus, Pope and martyr. Elected 7th bishop of Rome, A.D. 125. [d. c. 136]

St. Apollinaris, virgin. [death date unknown]

St. Syncletica, virgin. Also called **Syncletia.** [d. c. 400]

St. Simon the Stylite, founder of an order of solitary devotees called *pillar-saints.* [d. 459]

St. Convoyon, founder and abbot of the Monastery of Saint Savior in Brittany. [d. 868]

St. Dorotheus the Younger, abbot. Also called *Dorotheus of Khiliokomos.* [d. 11th century]

St. Gerlac, hermit. [d. c. 1170]

St. John Nepomucen Neumann, Bishop of Philadelphia; organized Catholic schools into diocesan system. [d. 1860]

The Beatified

Blessed Maria Repetto. [beatified 1981]

1926 **William Dewitt Snodgrass,** U.S. poet; Pulitzer Prize in poetry, 1960.

1928 **Walter (Frederick) Mondale,** U.S. politician, lawyer; U.S. Senator; Vice-President, 1977–81; Democratic Party nominee for President, 1984.

1931 **Alvin Ailey,** U.S. dancer, choreographer.

1938 **Juan Carlos I de Borbon y Borbon,** King of Spain, 1975– .

Historical Events

1340 **Edward III** of England assumes title of King of France. (**Hundred Years' War**)

1371 **Pierre Roger de Beaufort** is crowned **Pope Gregory XI.**

1537 **Alessandro de' Medici,** Duke of Florence and last male of elder branch of his family, is assassinated.

1762 **Elizabeth of Russia** dies and is succeeded by **Peter III.**

1887 First library school in the U.S. opens at **Columbia University.**

1905 **National Association of Audubon Societies** is incorporated.

1911 **Monaco** promulgates its constitution.

1919 **National Socialist (German Workers) Party** is founded.

Bolsheviks capture **Vilna (Russian Revolution).**

1925 **Nellie Taylor Ross** of Wyoming becomes first woman governor in American history.

1929 **King Alexander I** of Yugoslavia proclaims a dictatorship.

1940 Frequency modulation (**FM**) radio is successfully demonstrated by **Edwin H. Armstrong,** near Worcester, Massachusetts.

1962 **El Salvador** promulgates a new constitution, replacing that of 1950.

1964 **Pope Paul VI** and **Athenagoras I,** ecumenical patriarch of Constantinople, meet in Jerusalem in the first meeting of leaders of the Roman Catholic and Orthodox churches since 1439.

1967 U.S. President **Lyndon B. Johnson** signs executive order cutting off virtually all trade between the U.S. and **Rhodesia.**

1968 **Alexander Dubček** succeeds **Antonin Novotny** as First Secretary of the Czechoslovak Communist Party.

1970 United Mine Workers official **Joseph A. Yablonski** and his wife and daughters are found slain in their Clarksville, Pennsylvania, home.

1971 **Chile** establishes diplomatic relations with **People's Republic of China.**

1972 U.S. President Nixon orders **National Aeronautics and Space Administration (NASA)** to begin work on a manned space shuttle.

1976 **Kumpuchea (Cambodia)** becomes a Communist people's republic.

1982 **Dr. Roberto Suazo Córdova** is inaugurated as President of Honduras.

January 6

Holidays

Cyprus	**Epiphany Day**
Ethiopia	**Christmas**
	Marks the Nativity of Christ according to the Eastern Orthodox Church.
Iraq	**Army Day**
U.S. (New Mexico)	**Admission Day**
	Commemorates New Mexico's admission as the 47th state, 1912.

Religious Calendar

Solemnities

The Epiphany. Also called **The Adoration of the Magi** or **The Manifestation of God.** In the Christian Church in the East this day has long been recog-

Birthdates

1367 **Richard II of Great Britain.** [d. February 1400]

1799 **Jedediah Strong Smith,** U.S. explorer and fur trader; the first American explorer to enter **California** from the east, the first to explore the northern California-Oregon coast by land, the first to cross the Sierra Nevada from west to east. [d. May 27, 1831]

1811 **Charles Sumner,** U.S. politician, abolitionist; uncompromising in his opposition to slavery; U.S. Senator, 1851–74. [d. March 11, 1874]

1822 **Heinrich Schliemann,** German archaeologist; discovered the ruins of **Troy.** [d. December 26, 1890]

1842 **Clarence King,** U.S. geologist; founder of the **U.S. Geological Survey.** [d. December 24, 1901]

1878 **Carl Sandburg,** U.S. poet, historian, folklorist; Pulitzer Prize in poetry, 1918, 1951; Pulitzer Prize in biography, 1940. [d. July 22, 1967]

1880 **Tom Mix (Thomas Edwin Mix),** U.S. actor; leading box office attraction of the 1920s, starred in over 100 silent films. [d. October 12, 1940]

1882 **Sam Taliaferro Rayburn (*Mr. Sam*),** U.S. politician, lawyer; U.S. Congressman, 1912–61; Speaker of the House of Representatives, 1940–47; 1949–53; 1955–61. [d. November 16, 1961]

1883 **Khalil Gibran,** Syrian-American Symbolist poet. [d. April 10, 1931]

1913 **Edward Gierek,** Polish communist leader; First Secretary of Central Committee, 1975–80.

1915 **Alan (Wilson) Watts,** British-American writer, lecturer, philosopher known for his study of Zen Buddhism. [d. November 16, 1973]

1931 **E(dgar) L(awrence) Doctorow,** U.S. novelist, editor; author of *Ragtime.*

Historical Events

871 **Battle of Ashdown** is fought between Saxons and Danes.

1066 **Harold II** is crowned King of England.

1099 **Henry V** is elected King of Germany.

1169 Peace is established between **Henry II** of England and **Louis VII** of France.

1540 **Henry VIII** of England marries **Anne of Cleves.**

1622 **Sir Edward Coke** is sent to prison by **James I** of England for championing common law in face of royal prerogative.

1797 **Albany** is designated the permanent capital of New York State.

1821 **Indianapolis** is designated as the capital of the State of Indiana.

1838 **S. F. B. Morse** demonstrates his completed **telegraph** at the Speedwell Iron Works.

nized as the celebration of the Nativity of Our Lord. In the fourth century, December 25, the date of the Feast in the Western Christian Church, was adopted. It is believed that this early change in dates gave rise to the tradition of the **12 Days of Christmas.** In some records, Christmas and Epiphany were referred to as the first and second nativity; the second being Christ's manifestation to the world. Specifically, in present usage, the Epiphany celebrates four distinct events: 1) the nativity of Christ; 2) the manifestation of Christ to the Magi; 3) Christ's baptism by John the Baptist in the River Jordan; and 4) the miracle at Cana, in which Christ changed water into wine at the wedding feast.

The Saints

St. Wiltrudis, widow and abbess. [d. c. 986]

St. Erminold, Abbot of the Monastery of Prufening. [d. 1121]

St. Guarinus, Bishop of Sion. Also called **Guerin.** [d. 1150]

St. John De Ribera, Archbishop of Valencia. Founded and endowed the College of Corpus Christi. [d. 1611]

St. Carol Melchiori, priest. [d. 1670]

St. Raphaela Mary, virgin and founder of the Handmaids of the Sacred Heart, and **St. Corde Jesu,** virgin. [d. 1925]

The Beatified

Blessed Gertrude of Delft, virgin and mystic. Called *van Oosten.* [d. 1358]

Blessed Maria Angela Astorch. [beatified 1982]

Blessed Andrew Bessette. [beatified 1982]

1857 **Marthinius Pretorius** is inaugurated as first president of the **South African Republic (Transvaal).**

1871 **Henry M. Stanley,** *New York Herald* journalist, arrives in Zanzibar to begin his search for **Dr. David Livingstone,** missing since 1867.

1883 **Pendleton Act** reforms **U.S. civil service,** initiating competitive examinations for placement.

1896 **Cecil Rhodes** resigns as Prime Minister of the **Cape Colony** following accusations of complicity in the **Jameson Raid** into Transvaal.

1912 **New Mexico** is admitted to the Union as the 47th state.

1916 British parliament passes its first compulsory **military service bill** despite much opposition **(World War I).**

1931 New **Sadler's Wells Theatre** opens in London.

1942 First around-the-world commercial flight is completed by Pan American Airways.

1946 **Poland** nationalizes basic industries.

1950 **Great Britain** gives official recognition to the **People's Republic of China.**

1967 U.S. and South Vietnamese troops launch a major offensive against the **Viet Cong** stronghold in the **Mekong River delta,** the first direct commitment of U.S. troops to combat in that area **(Vietnam War).**

Angostura Bridge over the **Orinoco River,** the longest suspension bridge in Latin America, is opened by President **Raul Leoni** of Venezuela.

1971 **Human growth hormone** is synthesized by University of California Medical Center scientists.

1977 Czechoslovak intellectuals issue a manifesto demanding human rights as spelled out in the **Helsinki Agreement** of 1975.

1978 U.S. Secretary of State **Cyrus Vance** turns over the **Crown of St. Stephen** to Hungarian officials in Budapest.

January 7

Holidays

Liberia | Pioneers' Day
Commemorates the black pioneers, mostly freed slaves from the U.S. who settled there, the oldest of Africa's independent republics, 1820.

Religious Calendar

The Saints
St. Lucian of Antioch, priest and martyr. [d. 312]
St. Valentine, Bishop of Rhaetia. [d. c. 440]

Birthdates

1502 **Pope Gregory XIII,** Pope, 1572–85; issued the reformed (Gregorian) calendar. [d. 1585]

1718 **Israel Putnam,** American Revolutionary general; known for his heroic and sometimes mythical exploits; a hero of the **Battle of Bunker Hill.** [d. May 29, 1790]

1745 **Jacques Etienne Montgolfier,** French inventor and balloonist; with his brother, Joseph Michel (August 26), developed the first practical hot air balloon, 1783. [d. August 2, 1799]

1768 **Joseph Bonaparte,** King of Naples, 1806–08, King of Spain, 1808–13; brother of Napoleon Bonaparte. [d. July 28, 1844]

1794 **Eilhardt Mitscherlich,** German chemist; noted for experiments in chemical geology; produced artificial minerals. [d. August 28, 1863]

1800 **Millard Fillmore,** U.S. lawyer, politician; 13th president of the United States. [d. March 8, 1874]

1830 **Albert Bierstadt,** German-U.S. landscape painter of the **Hudson River School.** [d. February 18, 1902]

1844 **Bernadette (Marie Bernarde Soubirous** or **Soubiroux),** French nun; her visions of the Virgin Mary resulted in **Lourdes** becoming a major Marian shrine; canonized, 1933. [d. April 16, 1879]

1845 **King Louis III,** last King of Bavaria; reigned 1913–18; abdicated. [d. October 18, 1921]

1863 **Konstantin Stanislavsky,** Russian actor, director; co-founder and director of Moscow Art Theater, 1898–1938; developed a system of dramatic training now called "method acting." [d. August 7, 1938]

1873 **Charles Peguy,** French poet, philosopher, socialist; known for his studies of Joan of Arc, Victor Hugo, and Henri Bergson. Killed at the Battle of the Marne, World War I. [d. September 5, 1914]

Adolph Zukor, U.S. film executive born in Hungary; founder of Famous Players Film Co., 1912; Chairman of the Board, Paramount Pictures, 1935–76. [d. June 10, 1976]

1899 **Francis Poulenc,** French composer; member of *The Six,* ultramodern school of music in Paris. [d. January 30, 1963]

1910 **Orval Faubus,** U.S. politician, teacher, editor; as Governor of Arkansas, led resistance to Supreme Court-mandated desegregation of educational institutions.

Baron Alain de Rothschild, French banker; a leading member of the French banking family; president of the Representative Council of Jewish groups, 1957–82; member of the Legion of Honor. [d. October 20, 1982]

1912 **Charles (Samuel) Addams,** U.S. cartoonist; noted for his cartoons in *New Yorker* magazine from 1935.

1922 **Jean-Pierre Louis Rampal,** French flautist.

1925 **Gerald Durrell,** British author, naturalist; noted for his contributions to magazines, lectures, and television series on wildlife; brother of Lawrence Durrell (February 27).

Historical Events

1450 **University of Glasgow** is founded.

St. Tillo, priest. Also called **Theau, Thillo** in France, **Tilloine** or **Tilman** in Flanders, **Hillonius** in Germany. [d. c. 702]

St. Kentigerna, matron and anchoress. Also called **Caentigern, Quentigerna.** [d. 734]

St. Aldric, Bishop of Le Mans. [d. 856]

St. Reinold, monk and martyr. Honored in some places as patron of stone masons. [d. c. 960]

St. Canute Lavard, martyr. Also called **Knud Lavard,** *the Lord.* [d. 1131]

St. Raymond of Peñafort, Dominican friar. Also called **Raymund of Pennafort.** Feast formerly January 23. [d. 1275]

The Beatified

Blessed Edward Waterson, priest and martyr. [d. 1593]

1558	**Calais,** last English possession in France, is regained by the French.
1610	Major satellites of **Jupiter** are first seen by **Galileo.**
1714	First **typewriter** patent is issued in England.
1761	The **Mogul** rule in India ends.
1782	**Bank of North America,** first commercial bank in the U.S., opens in Philadelphia.
1785	**François Blanchard** and **John Jeffries** cross the English Channel from Dover to Calais by hot-air balloon; the first crossing of the Channel by air.
1789	First U.S. **presidential election** is held; **George Washington** is elected.
1807	British blockade the French coast (**Napoleonic Wars**).
1841	The British seize ten forts at Chuenpi, China, in the first of the **Opium Wars.**
1857	**London General Omnibus Company** begins operation.
1865	Indians attempt to ambush Cavalry of Iowa Volunteers at **Julesburg, Colorado.**
1888	*The Players,* a club for New York theatrical people, is founded.
1895	**Korea** declares its independence from China.
1902	The imperial Chinese court returns to Peking from its exile during the foreign occupation (**Boxer Rebellion**).
1920	The capital of the Don Cossacks, Novo 'Tcherksk, is taken by Soviet forces (**Russian Revolution**).
1927	**Transatlantic telephone service** begins between New York and London.
1933	Louis Gruenberg's opera *The Emperor Jones* is produced at the Metropolitan Opera House in New York.
1964	New constitution initiates self-government in the **Bahama Islands.**
1968	*Surveyor VII* lands on the moon, the last flight of the U.S. *Surveyor* series, and begins transmitting data and photographs.
1969	**France** bars the sale of military equipment to **Israel.**
1977	A 347.5 per cent cost of living rise is reported during 1976 in **Argentina.**
1979	**Phnom Penh,** capital of Cambodia, falls to United Front insurgents.

January 8

Holidays

U.S.
(Louisiana)

Battle of New Orleans Day
Commemorates U.S. troops, under General Andrew Jackson, and the defeat of the British at New Orleans, 1815.

Birthdates

1081   **Henry V, Holy Roman Emperor** and King of Germany, 1106–25; last of the Franconian dynasty. [d. 1125]

1682   **Jonathan Belcher,** American merchant; colonial governor of Massachusetts, New Hampshire, and New Jersey. [d. August 31, 1757]

1735   **John Carroll,** U.S. clergyman; first Roman Catholic bishop in the U.S.; founded **Georgetown University.** [d. December 3, 1815]

1786   **Nicholas Biddle,** U.S. financier, lawyer, diplomat, publisher; director of the Bank of the United States, 1822–36. [d. February 27, 1844]

1791   **Jacob Collamer,** U.S. public official; U.S. Congressman, 1843–49; U.S. Senator, 1855–65; U.S. Postmaster General, 1849. [d. 1865]

1792   **Lowell Mason,** U.S. educator, hymn writer; known for his efforts to introduce musical education into U.S. public schools. [d. August 11, 1872]

1821   **James Longstreet,** Confederate general during U.S. Civil War; ill-reputed for his lack of aggressiveness during several major battles, resulting in Confederate defeats. [d. January 2, 1904]

1823   **Alfred Russel Wallace,** British naturalist, explorer; simultaneously theorized on **natural selection,** publishing his findings jointly with **Charles Darwin** (February 12). [d. November 7, 1913]

1824   **(William) Wilkie Collins,** British novelist; collaborated with Charles Dickens (February 7). [d. September 23, 1889]

1825   **Henri Giffard,** French aeronaut, inventor; the first to build and fly a steerable airship. [d. April 15, 1882]

1862   **Frank Nelson Doubleday,** U.S. publisher and editor; founder of Doubleday & Co., 1897. [d. January 30, 1934]

1867   **Emily Green Balch,** U.S. economist, social scientist, pacifist; Nobel Peace Prize (with J. R. Mott), 1946. [d. January 9, 1961]

1871   **Viscount Craigavon (James Craig),** Irish statesman; first Prime Minister of Northern Ireland, 1921–40. [d. November 24, 1940]

1881   **William Thomas Piper,** U.S. aircraft manufacturer. [d. January 15, 1970]

1885   **John Curtin,** Australian editor, statesman; Prime Minister, 1941–45. [d. July 5, 1945]

1891   **William Kiplinger,** U.S. journalist; founder of *Kiplinger Washington Letters.* [d. August 6, 1967]

     Walther Wilhelm Georg Franz Bothe, German physicist; Nobel Prize in physics for development of coincidence method of time-telling (with Max Born), 1954. [d. February 8, 1957]

1902   **Georgi Maximilianovich Malenkov,** Russian leader; Premier of U.S.S.R., 1953–55; expelled from Communist Party, 1964.

1904   **Peter Arno (Curtis Arnoux Peters),** U.S. cartoonist, writer; known for his frequent cartoon contributions to *New Yorker* magazine. [d. February 22, 1968]

1910   **Galina Sergeyevna Ulanova,** Soviet prima ballerina.

1912   **José Ferrer (José Vincente Ferrer y Centron),** Puerto Rican actor, director, producer.

1914   **John Thomas Watson, Jr.,** U.S. business executive; Ambassador to U.S.S.R., 1979–81.

1935   **Elvis (Aron) Presley,** U.S. popular singer, actor; leader in the American and eventually the international **rock and roll** revolution. [d. August 16, 1977]

Religious Calendar

The Saints

St. Apollinaris, Bishop of Hieropolis. Called the *Apologist.* [d. c. 179]

St. Lucian of Beauvais, martyr. [d. c. 290]

St. Severinus of Noricum, missionary to Austria. [d. c. 480]

St. Severinus, Bishop of Septempeda; brother of **St. Victorinus.** [d. c. 550]

St. Erhard, Bishop of Ratisbon. [d. c. 686]

St. Gudula, virgin. Patron saint of Brussels. Also called **Ergoule, Gedula, Goelen, Goule.** [d. c. 712]

St. Pega, virgin, hermit; sister of **St. Guthlac.** [d. c. 719]

St. Wulsin, Bishop of Sherborne. Also called **Vulsin.** [d. 1005]

St. Thorfinn, Bishop of Hamar. [d. 1285]

1942   **Stephen Hawking,** British scientist; called by many the greatest theoretical physicist since Einstein.

Historical Events

1107   **Alexander I of Scotland** accedes to the throne.

1790   First State of the Union message is delivered by **President George Washington.**

1798   The **11th Amendment** of the U.S. Constitution, modifying the power of the Supreme Court, is ratified.

1800   First **soup kitchens** are opened in London for the relief of the poor.

1806   British occupy the **Cape of Good Hope.**

1815   Andrew Jackson defeats the British at the **Battle of New Orleans (War of 1812).**

1904   **Pope Pius X** sanctions the **cantus tradionalis** in preference to the reformed **Gregorian chant.**

1915   Turkish forces occupy **Tabriz,** northern Persia, after the Russians evacuate (**World War I**).

       The **Battle of Soissons** breaks out along the Western Front (**World War I**).

1926   **Ibn Saud** is proclaimed King of the **Hijaz** and sultan of **Nejd** (**Saudi Arabia**).

1952   **Jordan** promulgates a new constitution.

1959   **General Charles de Gaulle** becomes President of the Fifth Republic of France.

1961   **U.S. Civil War centennial** officially opens with ceremonies in New York City and in Lexington, Virginia.

1962   **El Salvador** promulgates a constitution.

1966   **Stephen Cardinal Wyszynski,** Roman Catholic primate of Poland, is barred by the Polish government from attending the Vatican celebration of the thousandth anniversary of Christianity in Poland.

1976   Countries of the **International Monetary Fund** agree to a monetary reform that would permit currencies to "float" in the world market.

January 9

Holidays

Panama   **National-Mourning Day** or **Martyrs' Day**

Religious Calendar

The Saints

St. Marciana, virgin, martyr. [d. c. 303]

SS. Julian and **Basilissa,** companions, martyrs. Julian and Basilissa were man and wife; St. Julian is regarded as the patron of hospitality and hotelkeepers. [d. c. 304]

Birthdates

1554   **Pope Gregory XV,** pope, 1621–23. [d. July 8, 1623]

1735   **John Jervis,** Earl of St. Vincent, English admiral; First Lord of the Admiralty, 1801–04. [d. 1823]

1839   **John Knowles Paine,** U.S. composer; first professor of music in an American university, at Harvard, 1875–1906. [d. April 25, 1906]

1859   **Carrie Chapman Catt,** U.S. women's rights leader; founder of **National League of Women Voters,** 1919. [d. March 9, 1947]

1873   **Hayyim Nahman Bialik,** Hebrew writer, poet; strong supporter of Zionism; influenced revival of Hebrew. [d. July 4, 1934]

1878   **John Broadus Watson,** U.S. psychologist; founder of **behaviorist school** of psychology. [d. September 25, 1958]

   Humbert I, King of Italy, 1844–1900. [assassinated July 29, 1900]

1900   **Richard Halliburton,** U.S. traveler, author; traced routes of numerous great explorers, including Hannibal, Alexander the Great; lost at sea trying to sail a Chinese junk from Hong Kong to San Francisco. [d. March 23 or 24, 1939]

1902   **Sir Rudolph Bing,** Anglo-Austrian impresario; general manager, Metropolitan Opera, New York, 1950–72.

1904   **George Balanchine** (Georgy Melitonovich Balanchivadze), Russian-American choreographer; director, New York City Ballet Co., 1948–1983. [d. April 30, 1983]

1908   **Simone de Beauvoir,** French novelist, essayist, existentialist; front runner in the movement toward equal rights for women.

1913   **Richard Milhous Nixon,** U.S. lawyer, politician; 37th president of U.S.; first president to resign office.

1914   **Gypsy Rose Lee (Rose Louise Hovick),** U.S. entertainer, author; burlesque dancer; perfected the art of the striptease. [d. April 26, 1970]

1922   **Har Gobind Khorana,** U.S. chemist; Nobel Prize in physiology or medicine for research on the role of enzymes in genetic development (with M. W. Nirenberg and R. W. Holley), 1968.

1941   **Joan Baez,** U.S. singer, political activist.

Historical Events

1493   **Vladislav II** of Poland grants Polish noblemen **Habeas Corpus Constitution** of Cracow.

1570   **Ivan the Terrible** of Russia, suspecting a revolt in the city of Novgorod, captures city and executes many of its inhabitants.

1788   **Connecticut** becomes the fifth state to ratify the U.S. Constitution.

1792   **Peace of Jassy** between Russia and Turkey is signed; Russia obtains the coast of the Black Sea, including the Crimea.

1793   First successful U.S. balloon flight is completed in Philadelphia, Pennsylvania, by **François Blanchard.**

1809   U.S. issues **Non-Intercourse Act** against British commerce.

1861   **Mississippi** secedes from the Union (**U.S. Civil War**).

1867   **Emperor Mutsuhito (Meiji)** assumes throne as the Emperor of Japan, leading the nation into the modern period.

St. Peter, Bishop of Sebastea. Parents were **St. Basil the Elder** and **St. Emmelia.** Brother of **St. Basil, St. Gregory of Nyssa,** and **St. Macrina.** [d. 391]

St. Waningus. Assisted **St. Wandrille** in founding the **Abbey at Fontenelle.** Also called **Vaneng.** [d. c. 683]

St. Adrian, abbot of Canterbury. Abbot of the monastery of SS. Peter and Paul (afterwards called St. Augustine's), at Canterbury. [d. 710]

St. Berhtwald, Archbishop of Canterbury. Also called **Berctuald, Brithwald.** [d. 731]

The Beatified

Blessed Alix Le Clercq, virgin, cofounder of the **Augustinian Canonesses Regular of the Congregation of Our Lady.** [d. 1622]

1875	**Alfonso XII** lands at Barcelona and is recognized as King of Spain.
1878	**Victor Emmanuel** of Italy dies and is succeeded by **Humbert I.**
1912	Russian troops begin to expel Chinese from Mongolia.
1917	The last Turkish troops are driven back across the Egyptian frontier (**World War I**).
1945	U.S. forces invade Luzon, Philippines (**World War II**).
1957	British Prime Minister, **Anthony Eden,** resigns from office.
1960	**Aswan High Dam** construction is initiated in ceremonies at Aswan, Egypt.
1962	U.S. and Japan conclude a formal agreement for the final settlement of U.S. postwar economic assistance to Japan.
1968	U.S. spacecraft *Surveyor VII* makes a successful landing on the moon.
1969	*Concorde,* a supersonic jetliner, is tested for the first time at Bristol, England.
1970	**Cuba** and **Soviet Union** sign technical assistance agreement for installation of a satellite communications station in Cuba.
1972	The *Queen Elizabeth,* luxury ocean liner, is gutted by fire in Hong Kong harbor.

January 10

Religious Calendar

The Saints
St. Marcian. [d. 471]

St. Saethrith, abbess of Faremoutier-en-Brie. Also called Saethryda. [d. 7th century]

St. John the Good, Bishop of Milan. [d. 660]

St. Agatho, Pope. Elected Bishop of Rome 678. [d. 681]

Birthdates

1738 **Ethan Allen,** American patriot; best known for his leadership of the **Green Mountain Boys,** who fought for the independence and integrity of Vermont; performed heroically during American Revolution. [d. February 12, 1789]

1769 **Michel Ney,** Napoleonic military commander; commanded the Old Guard at the **Battle of Waterloo**; tried and condemned for treason, 1815. [d. December 7, 1815]

1834 **John Emerich Edward Dalberg-Acton, First Baron Acton,** British historian; planned *Cambridge Modern History.* [d. June 19, 1902]

1850 **John Wellborn Root,** U.S. architect; with his partner, Daniel H. Burnham (September 4), led the emergence of the **Chicago School** of American architecture, which was marked by design based on function. [d. January 15, 1892]

1880 **Grock (Adrien Wettach),** Swiss clown, entertainer. [d. July 14, 1959]

1882 **Aleksei Nikolaevich Tolstoi,** Russian novelist and short-story writer. [d. February 23, 1945]

1883 **Francis X(avier) Bushman,** U.S. silent-screen actor; considered the greatest leading man of the silent film era. [d. August 23, 1966]

1887 **(John) Robinson Jeffers,** U.S. poet; Pulitzer Prize for poetry, 1954. [d. January 20, 1962]

1893 **Vicente Huidobro,** Chilean poet, novelist, literary theorist. [d. January 2, 1948]

1898 **Katharine Burr Blodgett,** U.S. physicist, chemist; first woman research scientist at General Electric Corp.; invented **non-reflecting (invisible) glass** used in optical equipment. [d. October 12, 1979]

1913 **Gustáv Husák,** Czechoslovak communist leader; First Secretary, Committee of Presidium, 1969–71; General Secretary, 1971–75; President, 1945– .

Mehmet Shehu, Albanian statesman; Premier of Albania, 1978–81; committed suicide. [d. December 17, 1981]

1915 **Dean Dixon,** U.S. musician; first black and youngest musician ever to conduct **New York Philharmonic Orchestra.** [d. November 4, 1976]

1935 **Sherrill Eustace Milnes,** U.S. operatic baritone; most recorded American opera singer.

1936 **Robert Wilson,** U.S. physicist; Nobel Prize in physics for discovery of cosmic radiation that validates **Big Bang Theory.** (with A. A. Penzias and P. Kapitsa), 1978.

1949 **George Foreman,** U.S. boxer; world heavyweight champion, 1973–74.

Historical Events

1356 **Charles IV, Holy Roman Emperor,** issues **Golden Bull** at Nuremberg, settling procedure for election of German king and creating a constitution for the Empire.

1429 The **Order of the Golden Fleece,** famous chivalric order, is founded by Duke Philip the Good of Burgundy.

1757 Holy Roman Empire declares war on Prussia; Russia, Poland and Sweden also oppose Prussia (**Seven Years' War**).

1776 American **Thomas Paine** publishes his *Common Sense,* a pamphlet calling for independence from England.

1840 **Penny postage** begins in Great Britain.

1861 **Florida** secedes from the Union (**U.S. Civil War**).

1863 London's underground transportation system is inaugurated.

St. Dermot Diarmaid, abbot; founder of the monastery on the island of Inchcleraun in Lough Ree. [d. 6th century]

St. Peter Orseolo, monk. Also called **Peter Urseolus.** [d. 987]

St. William, Archbishop of Bourges. [d. 1209]

The Beatified

Blessed Gregory X, pope. [d. 1276]

1870	**Standard Oil Company** is incorporated at Cleveland, Ohio.
1883	**Arabi Pasha** and other Egyptian rebels are exiled to Ceylon.
1900	Field-Marshal **Lord Roberts** and **Lord Kitchener** arrive at Cape Town to take command of British troops (**Boer War**).
1902	*Spindletop,* the first great Texas oil strike, is made.
1915	German airplanes bomb Dunkirk, France, and raid the east coast of England (**World War I**).
1918	Cossacks declare the independence of the **Republic of Don** with General Kaledin as president (**Russian Revolution**).
1919	Rumania annexes Transylvania.
1920	**League of Nations** is founded.
	British mandate over German East Africa (Tanganyika) goes into effect.
1921	War trials begin in Leipzig, Germany, before the German Supreme Court.
1923	Burton Lane's musical *Finian's Rainbow* opens in New York.
	Juan de la Cierva demonstrates the first **autogyro,** in Spain.
1946	**League of Nations** is dissolved.
	First **United Nations General Assembly** meets in London.
	World's first communication through space occurs as radar pulses from Fort Monmouth, New Jersey, are echoed from the moon.
1957	**Harold Macmillan** becomes Prime Minister of Great Britain after the resignation of **Anthony Eden.**
	Tunisia and the **People's Republic of China** establish diplomatic relations.
1969	Sweden extends full diplomatic recognition to **North Vietnam.**

Saturday Evening Post announces suspension of publication effective in early fall of the year.

January 11

Holidays

Albania   **Proclamation of the Republic Day**
Commemorates establishment of Albanian Republic, 1946.

Chad   **Independence Day**
Celebration of independence of Chad, August 11, 1960. Official observation is held in January to avoid the August rainy season.

Birthdates

1503   **Francesco Mazzola** (*Il Parmigiano*), Italian Mannerist painter. [d. 1540]

1755   **Alexander Hamilton,** U.S. statesman, lawyer, author; first U.S. Secretary of the Treasury. [d. July 12, 1804]

1807   **Ezra Cornell,** U.S. capitalist and philanthropist; founder of **Cornell University.** [d. December 9, 1894]

1808   **Jean Gilbert Fialin Persigny,** French statesman; ardent Bonapartist; Minister of Interior, 1852–54; 1860–63; Ambassador to Great Britain, 1855–58; 1859–60. [d. January 11, 1872]

1815   **Sir John Macdonald,** Canadian statesman, first Prime Minister, 1867–73, 1878–91; regarded as the organizer of Canada as a Dominion. [d. June 6, 1891]

1839   **Eugenio Maria De Hostos,** Puerto Rican philosopher, educator, patriot. [d. August 11, 1903]

1842   **William James,** U.S. philosopher, teacher, psychologist; founder of **pragmatism.** [d. August 26, 1910]

1859   **George Nathaniel Curzon,** First Baron and First Marquis Curzon of Kedleston, British statesman; Viceroy of India, 1899–1905; Secretary of State for Foreign Affairs, 1919–24; leader of House of Lords, 1919–24. [d. March 20, 1925]

1864   **Harry Gordon Selfridge,** U.S.-British merchant; partner in Marshall Field & Co.; founded Selfridge & Co., Ltd., London, in 1909. [d. May 8, 1947]

1885   **Alice Paul,** U.S. feminist, lawyer, leader of the Equal Rights Amendment movement. [d. July 9, 1977]

1889   **Calvin Blackman Bridges,** U.S. geneticist. [d. December 17, 1938].

1897   **Bernard A. De Voto,** U.S. editor, critic, historian, novelist; editor, *Saturday Review of Literature,* 1936–38; Pulitzer Prize in history, 1947; one of the most widely read critics and historians of his time. [d. November 13, 1955]

1903   **Alan Stewart Paton,** South African novelist, political activist; author of *Cry, the Beloved Country.*

1905   **Manfred B. Lee,** U.S. mystery writer; with his cousin Frederic Dannay (October 20) wrote over 40 **Ellery Queen** novels, which became the most widely read mystery novels in the world, selling over 100 million copies by the 1950s. [d. September 3, 1982]

1907   **Pierre Mendes-France,** French political leader, economist; Premier, 1954–55. [d. October 18, 1982]

1911   **Zenko Suzuki,** Japanese statesman; Prime Minister, 1980–83.

1924   **Roger Guillemin,** U.S. physiologist; Nobel Prize in physiology or medicine for research on the pituitary hormone (with A. Schally and R. S. Yalow), 1977.

Historical Events

1360   **Treaty of Guillon** between **Edward III** of England and **Philip of Burgundy** of France is signed, in which the English renounce all claims to the French crown in exchange for Aquitaine (**Hundred Years' War**).

1851   The **Taiping Rebellion,** led by Hung Hsiu-Ch'uan, attempts to overthrow Manchu Dynasty.

1861   **Alabama** secedes from the Union (**U.S. Civil War**).

Nepal	**National Unity Day**	
	Celebration dedicated to King Prithvinarayan, Shah 1773–75, who established this, the only Hindu kingdom in the world.	
Puerto Rico	**De Hostos' Birthday**	
	Celebrates the birth of the philosopher and patriot, Eugenio Maria De Hostos, 1839.	

Religious Calendar

The Saints

St. Hyginus, Pope. Elected Bishop of Rome c. 138. [d. c. 142]

St. Theodosius the Cenobiarch. Appointed head of all Cenobites, or men living in community, throughout Palestine. [d. 529]

St. Salvius, Bishop of Amiens. Also called **Sauve.** [d. c. 625]

1864   **Charing Cross Railway Station** opens in London.

1904   The **Hereros** of South-West Africa begin a bloody and costly uprising against their German colonizers.

1916   The Russians begin a general offensive against the Turks in Armenia (**World War I**).

The French seize the Greek island of **Corfu** as a base for the Serbian army.

1925   *Symphony* by **Aaron Copland** is performed by the New York Symphony.

1940   **Sergei Prokofiev's** ballet *Romeo and Juliet* opens in Leningrad.

1970   Owerri in **Biafra** is taken by federal Nigerian troops; the Biafran leader **General Ojukwu** leaves the country.

January 12

Holidays

Tanzania   **Zanzibar Revolution Day**
Commemorates People's
Revolution of 1964.

Birthdates

1580   **Jan Baptist van Helmont,** Belgian chemist, physiologist, physician; the first to differentiate gas as a distinct form; conducted early research in digestive process of humans. [d. December 30, 1644]

1628   **Charles Perrault,** French writer, especially known for his fairy tales. [d. May 16, 1703]

1729   **Edmund Burke,** British statesman, political writer, conservative political theorist; advocate of liberal treatment of American colonies. [d. July 9, 1797]

      Lazzaro Spallanzani, Italian physiologist; noted for his experiments on human digestive process; disproved theory of spontaneous generation. [d. February 11, 1799]

1737   **John Hancock,** American Revolutionary leader; famed signer of the Declaration of Independence; first governor of state of Massachusetts. [d. October 8, 1793]

1746   **Johann H. Pestalozzi,** Swiss educator, reformer; his emphasis on the concrete approach to education strongly influenced elementary education throughout Europe and the U.S. [d. February 17, 1827]

1751   **Jakob Michael Reinhold Lenz,** German dramatist, poet, critic; a member of circle of writers who followed Johann Von Goethe (August 28). [d. May 24, 1792]

1810   **Ferdinand II,** King of the Two Sicilies, 1830–59. [d. May 22, 1859]

1852   **Joseph Jacques Joffre,** Commander in Chief of French armies, World War I; a hero of the Battle of the Marne, 1914. [d. January 3, 1931]

1856   **John Singer Sargent,** U.S. artist; noted especially for his portraiture; also known for his decorative work, especially in the Boston Public Library and the Boston Museum of Fine Arts. [d. April 25, 1925]

1860   **Sir Charles Oman,** British military historian; noted for his exhaustive histories of military events in Europe from the fifth century through 1930. [d. 1946]

1873   **Frank Gerber,** U.S. manufacturer; founder of Gerber Products, 1917; his son, Daniel Gerber (May 6), introduced the strained baby food which ultimately made the company famous. [d. October 7, 1952]

1876   **Jack London,** U.S. novelist, short-story writer; well-known for his adventure stories which displayed a preoccupation with primitive strength, violence, and exciting action. [d. November 22, 1916]

1893   **Hermann Wilhelm Göring,** prominent German Nazi leader; headed *Luftwaffe*; jailed for his activities after World War II; committed suicide. [d. October 15, 1946]

1899   **Paul Müller,** Swiss chemist; Nobel Prize in physiology or medicine for research in DDT, 1948. [d. October 12, 1965]

1899   **Herbert Orin Crisler (Fritz),** U.S. football coach; one of most innovative coaches in early football history; devised the platoon system. [d. August 19, 1982]

1902   **Joe E. Lewis,** U.S. comedian. [d. June 4, 1971]

1907   **Tex Ritter (Woodward Maurice Ritter),** U.S. cowboy songwriter, singer; starred in over 60 early American Western films; father of actor **John Ritter** (September 17). [d. January 2, 1974]

1908   **José Arcadio Limón,** Mexican-U.S. modern dancer, choreographer, teacher. [d. December 2, 1972]

1920   **James Leonard Farmer,** U.S. civil rights activist, union organizer, lecturer; a founder of the **Congress of Racial Equality (CORE),** 1942.

1942   **Bernadine Rae Dohrn,** U.S. radical activist; leader of **Weatherman** faction of

Religious Calendar

The Saints

St. Arcadius, martyr. [d. c. 304]

SS. Tigrius, priest, and **Eutropius,** a reader, both martyrs. [d. 404]

St. Caesaria, virgin, abbess. Sister of **St. Caesarius.** [d. c. 529]

St. Victorian, abbot of Asan in Aragon. [d. 558]

St. Benedict, abbot of Wearmouth and Jarrow. Also called **Benet, Bennet, Biscop.** [d. 690]

The Beatified

Blessed Margaret Bourgeoys.

Blessed Anthony Pucci, priest. [d. 1892]

Students for a Democratic Society (SDS). Disappeared, 1970.

1952 **John Walker,** New Zealand runner; Olympic gold medalist in 1,500 meter race, 1976.

Historical Events

1701 The **Gregorian calendar** is adopted by Swiss Protestants.

1773 First museum in America is organized in **Charlestown, South Carolina**.

1777 **Mission Santa Clara de Asis** in California is established.

1816 Family of **Bonaparte** is excluded from France forever.

1848 Revolution against **Ferdinand II,** King of the Two Sicilies begins.

1866 **Aeronautical Society of Great Britain** is formed in London.

1875 **Kwang-su** becomes Emperor of China.

1879 **Zulu War** begins between the British of the Cape Colony and the natives of Zululand.

1907 *Histoires Naturelles* by **Maurice Ravel** premieres at a concert of Société Nationale de Musique in Paris.

1918 **Latvia** declares its independence from Russia.

1950 Restoration of the death penalty in the U.S.S.R. for treason, espionage, and sabotage is decreed by Presidium of the Supreme Council.

1954 Parliament in **New Zealand** is opened by **Queen Elizabeth II**; the first time the parliament is opened by a reigning monarch.

1962 U.S. State Department denies passports to **American Communist Party** members.

1964 African rebels overthrow the predominantly Arab government of **Zanzibar** and proclaim a republic.

1965 Prime ministers of 13 **Arab nations** announce agreement on a unified policy against foreign countries that have established relations with Israel.

1970 **Biafra** capitulates to the federal Nigerian government, ending the 31-month-old civil war.

Boeing 747 lands at Heathrow Airport in London after its first trans-atlantic proving flight from New York.

January 13

Ghana   **Redemption Day**
Commemorates military
government takeover, 1972.

Norway   **Tyvendedagen**
The official end of Yuletide in
Norway.

Sweden   **Canutes (Knute's) Day**
Swedish occasion for
dismantling Christmas trees
and celebrating the end of the
Christmas season.

Togo   **Liberation Day**
Commemorates the overthrow
of the **Grunitzky** government
by **General Gnassingbé
Eyadéma**, 1967.

Birthdates

1749 **Friedrich Müller** (called **Maler**), German
poet, painter, and engraver. [d. April 23,
1825]

1808 **Salmon Portland Chase,** U.S. jurist, lawyer, teacher; U.S. Secretary of the Treasury,
1861–64; Chief Justice of U.S., 1864–73. [d.
May 7, 1873]

1867 **Francis Everett Townsend,** U.S. physician, social reformer; originator and head
of Old-Age Revolving Pensions, Inc., the
controversial forerunner to the Social Security Act of 1935. [d. September 1, 1960]

1870 **Ross Granville Harrison,** U.S. zoologist;
discovered technique for culturing tissue
cells outside of the body. [d. September 30,
1959]

1884 **Sophie Tucker (Sophia Abuza),** U.S. singer, vaudeville star. [d. February 10, 1966]

1885 **Carl Alfred Fuller,** U.S. manufacturer;
founder of Fuller Brush Co. [d. December
4, 1973]

1905 **Kay Francis (Katherine Gibbs),** U.S. actress. [d. August 26, 1968]

1924 **Sir Brian Barratt Boyes,** New Zealand
heart surgeon.

1925 **Gwen Verdon (Gwyneth Evelyn Verdon),**
U.S. dancer, actress, musical performer.

1931 **Charles Nelson Reilly,** U.S. comedic actor,
director.

Historical Events

1842 A British force is massacred in the **Khyber
Pass** by the Afghans.

1846 American troops are ordered into disputed
territory between the Nueces and Rio
Grande River, precipitating the **Mexican-
American War.**

1864 The **Zemstous,** or provincial assemblies,
are formed in Russia.

1874 Conscription is introduced in Russia.

1886 **Gold Coast of Africa** is divided into the
two separate colonies of **Lagos** and the
Gold Coast by British charter.

1893 **Independent Labour Party** is formed in
Great Britain under the auspices of **Keir
Hardie.**

1898 Emile Zola's **J'accuse,** about the **Dreyfus
case,** first appears in a French newspaper.

1904 **Kossuth,** first truly symphonic work by
Béla Bartók, is first performed in Budapest.

1916 Flooding of northern Holland occurs when
the dikes of the **Zuider Zee** collapse.
Greek government refuses to permit Allied
occupation of **Corfu (World War I).**

1919 **Medina** is surrendered to **King Hussein** of
the Hejaz.

1930 The **Mawson Antarctic Expedition** lands
on **Proclamation Island,** reaffirming British possession.

U.S.   **Stephen Foster Memorial Day**
Commemorates the death of
the composer of numerous
popular romantic songs of the
American South.

Religious Calendar

The Saints

St. Agrecius, Bishop of Trier. Also called **Agritius.**
[d. c. 329]

St. Hilary, Bishop of Poitiers and Doctor of the
Church. Feast formerly January 14. [d. c. 368]

St. Berno, first Abbot of Cluny and founder of Abbey
og Gigny. [d. 927]

The Beatified

Blessed Godfrey of Kappenberg, Count of Kappenberg. [d. 1127]

Blessed Jutta of Huy, widow and mystic. Also
called **Juetta.** [d. 1228]

Blessed Veronica of Binasco, virgin. [d. 1497]

1959	**Inter-Governmental Maritime Commission** is established as an agency of the United Nations.
	President **Sukarno** of Indonesia dissolves all opposition parties.
1961	**Brazil** and the U.S. sign their first extradition treaty.
1963	Military insurgents seize power in **Togo** after assassinating President **Sylvanus Olympio** and arresting most of his ministers; **Nikolas Grunitzky** is named president.
1964	U.S. and Canadian negotiators reach agreement on the **Columbia River** hydraulic and flood-control project.
1966	**Robert C. Weaver,** the first black ever nominated to the U.S. Cabinet, is named Secretary of the new **Department of Housing and Urban Development.**
1967	Army Chief of Staff Lt. Col. **Etienne Eyadéma** overthrows Grunitzky government of **Togo** and establishes the **Third Togalese Republic.**
1971	U.S. Department of the Interior approves construction of **Alaska pipeline.**
1977	The London Court of Appeals rules that mere possession of **cannabis leaves** is not an offense under English law.
1982	Air Florida plane crashes into a Washington, D.C. bridge, killing 78 people.

January 14

Religious Calendar

The Saints

St. Sava, Archbishop of the Serbs. Patron saint of Serbia. Orthodox Serbians consider him the founder of their national church. Also called **Savas.** [d. 123]

St. Felix of Nola. Invoked against perjury. [d. c. 260]

St. Macrina the Elder, widow. [d. c. 340]

St. Barbasymas, Bishop of Seleucia and Ctesiphon, and his companions, martyrs. Also called **Barbasceminus, Barbashemin, Barba'shmin.** [d. 346]

The Martyrs of Mount Sinai. [d. 4th century]

Birthdates

1131 **Waldemar I,** King of Denmark (called *the Great*); reigned 1157–82. [d. May 12, 1182]

1730 **William Whipple,** American Revolutionary leader; member of Continental Congress, 1776–77; a signer of the Declaration of Independence. [d. November 28, 1785]

1741 **Benedict Arnold,** American Revolutionary War general and traitor. [d. June 14, 1801]

1798 **Jan Rudolf de Thorbecke,** Dutch statesman; Premier, 1849–53; 1862–66; 1871–72. [d. June 4, 1872]

1806 **Matthew Fontaine Maury,** U.S. oceanographer, meteorologist; first to publish a work defined as contemporary **oceanography.** [d. February 1, 1873]

1831 **William Drew Washburn,** U.S. manufacturer; government official; U.S. Congressman 1879–85; U.S. Senator, 1889–95. [d. July 29, 1912]

1841 **Berthe Morisot,** French Impressionist painter; sister-in-law of Edouard Manet (January 23). [d. March 2, 1895]

1875 **Albert Schweitzer,** Alsatian physician, missionary, philosopher, musician; Nobel Peace Prize, 1952. [d. September 4, 1965]

1882 **Hendrik Van Loon,** Dutch-American author, lecturer, historian. [d. March 11, 1944]

1886 **Hugh Lofting,** British-American writer of children's stories; best known for the *Dr. Doolittle* series. [d. September 26, 1947]

1892 **Hal Roach,** U.S. film director and producer.

1896 **John (Roderigo) Dos Passos,** U.S. novelist, journalist. [d. September 18, 1970]

1904 **Cecil (Walter Hardy) Beaton,** British photographer, theatrical designer, writer. [d. January 18, 1980]

1905 **Takeo Fukuda,** Japanese politician; Prime Minister, 1976–78.

1906 **William Bendix,** U.S. actor. [d. December 14, 1964]

1919 **Giulio Andreotti,** Italian politician, journalist, editor; Prime Minister, 1972–73; 1976–78.

1925 **Yukio Mishima (Kimitake Hiraoka),** Japanese novelist; noted for his novels relating the conflict between the older military traditions and the modern trends in Japan. [d. by seppuku (ritual suicide), November 25, 1970]

1926 **Thomas Tryon,** U.S. author and actor; known especially for his novels dealing with the supernatural.

1932 **Loretta Lynn (Loretta Webb),** U.S. country-and-western singer.

1940 **Julian Bond,** U.S. politician, poet, television commentator; gained national attention while challenging the Georgia delegation to the Democratic National Convention, 1968.

Historical Events

1604 The **Hampton Court Conference** begins in England to discuss Puritan requests for changes in the Church of England.

1639 **The Fundamental Orders of Connecticut** is ratified; considered the first constitution written in America.

1784 **Continental Congress** ratifies **Treaty of Paris** at the Maryland State House.

1797 **Napoleon Bonaparte** defeats Austrians at **Rivoli (Napoleonic Wars).**

St. **Datius,** Bishop of Milan. [d. 552]

St. **Kentigern,** Bishop of Strathclyde. Patron of Glasgow. Feast kept throughout Scotland and also in the dioceses of Liverpool, Salford, Lancaster, and Menevia. Also called **Mungo.** [d. 603]

St. **Anthony Pucci,** priest. [d. 1892]

The Beatified

Blessed **Odo of Novara,** Carthusian monk. [d. 1200]

Blessed **Roger of Todi,** monk. Also called **Ruggiero.** [d. 1237]

Blessed **Odoric of Pordenone,** monk. [d. 1331]

Blessed **Giles of Lorenzana,** lay-brother. [d. 1518]

Blessed **Maria Rivier.**

Blessed **Peter Donders.**

1814	Norway is ceded to the King of Sweden by the King of Denmark (**Treaty of Kiel**).
1858	In France, Orsini's attempted assassination of **Napoleon III** fails.
1866	**Peru** declares war on **Spain**.
1868	*Boston Weekly Journal* is printed on paper derived from wood-pulp; first recorded instance of a U.S. newspaper's using the material.
1875	**Alfonso XII** is proclaimed king of Spain; reigned 1875–85.
1878	W. H. Preece first demonstrates A. G. Bell's **telephone** to Queen Victoria.
1900	*Tosca* by **Giacomo Puccini** has its world premiere at the Costanzi Theatre in Rome.
1902	Imperial Chinese edicts are issued protecting missionaries and native Christians.
1915	The **Battle of Soissons** is ended with the Germans gaining a bridgehead on the **Aisne (World War I).**
1922	The **Irish Free State** is established.
1929	**King Amanulla** of Afghanistan is forced to abdicate; his brother **Inayatullah** is named successor.
1943	**Casablanca Conference** begins; Allies agree on military strategy and demand for unconditional surrender of Axis nations.
1950	U.S. recalls all consular personnel from People's Republic of China.
1961	U.S. President **Dwight D. Eisenhower** issues prohibition against holding of **gold** abroad by U.S. citizens and corporations.
1965	The Prime Ministers of **Northern Ireland** and the **Irish Republic** meet for the first time since the partition of Ireland in 1921.
1969	The *Enterprise*, a U.S. nuclear-powered aircraft carrier, suffers several explosions off the coast of Hawaii.
1972	Formation of a new government in the Yugoslav republic of **Croatia** is announced in a continuing purge of nationalism begun in 1971.

January 15

Holidays

Japan	**Adults' Day**
	Day of tribute to young men and women who have reached adulthood.
Jordan	**Arbor Day**
U.S. and Virgin Islands	**Martin Luther King's Birthday** Commemorates the birth of the U.S. civil rights leader, assassinated in 1968.

Birthdates

1716 **Philip Livingston,** American patriot, merchant, signer of Declaration of Independence. [d. June 12, 1778]

1785 **William Prout,** English chemist; discovered presence of **hydrochloric acid** in the stomach. [d. April 9, 1850]

1795 **Aleksandr Sergeievich Griboedov,** Russian poet; known for his satirical comedy discrediting the struggle between generations, *Woe from Wit.* [d. February 11, 1829]

1809 **Pierre Proudhon,** French socialist, anarchist, writer; called the *Father of Anarchism.* [d. January 19, 1865]

1812 **Peter Christen Asbjörnsen,** Norwegian folklorist. [d. January 1, 1885]

1842 **Josef Breuer,** Austrian physician, physiologist; known for his studies of the ear; with Sigmund Freud wrote work on hysteria. [d. June 20, 1925]

1845 **Ella Flagg Young,** U.S. educator; associated with Jane Addams (September 6) in **settlement house movement**. [d. October 26, 1918]

1859 **Nathaniel Lord Britton,** U.S. botanist; long-time director of the New York Botanical Garden. [d. June 25, 1934]

1866 **Nathan Söderblom,** Swedish theologian; Nobel Peace Prize, 1930. [d. July 12, 1931]

1870 **Pierre Samuel Du Pont,** U.S. industrialist; President and Chairman of the Board, E. I. Du Pont de Nemours, 1915–40. [d. April 5, 1954]

1877 **Lewis Madison Terman,** U.S. psychologist; creator of the **I.Q. test,** 1916; advocate of superior educational opportunities for gifted children. [d. December 21, 1956]

1895 **Artturi I. Virtanen,** Finnish biochemist; Nobel Prize in chemistry for research into plant synthesis of nitrogen compounds, conservation of fodder, 1945. [d. November 11, 1973]

1899 **Goodman Ace,** U.S. radio performer, humorist; co-starred with his wife Jane in 1930s radio comedy show, *Easy Aces.* [d. March 25, 1982]

1902 **Saud, King of Saudi Arabia,** 1953–64; deposed by Crown Prince Faisal in 1964. [d. February 23, 1969]

1908 **Edward Teller,** U.S. physicist, born in Hungary; known as the *Father of the Hydrogen Bomb.*

1909 **Gene Krupa,** U.S. drummer, bandleader. [d. October 16, 1973]

1912 **Leonid Kantorovich,** Russian mathematician; Nobel Prize in economics for development of theory of optimum allocation of resources, 1975.

1918 **João Baptista de Oliveira Figueiredo,** President of Brazil, 1979–

Gamal Abdel Nasser, President of Egypt, 1956–59; President of United Arab Republic 1958–70. [d. September 28, 1970]

1926 **Chuck Berry (Charles Edward Anderson Berry),** U.S. singer, songwriter; one of earliest **rock and roll** stars.

1929 **Martin Luther King, Jr.,** U.S. civil rights leader; Nobel Peace Prize, 1964. [d. April 4, 1968]

1937 **Margaret O'Brien (Angela Maxine O'Brien),** U.S. actress.

Religious Calendar

The Saints

St. Paul, first Christian hermit; patron saint of clothing industry workers, weavers. [d. 342]

St. Macarius the Elder, anchorite. One of the fathers of Egyptian monasticism. [d. 390]

St. Isidore of Alexandria, priest and hospitaler. [d. 404]

St. John Calybites. [d. c. 450]

St. Ita, abbess and virgin. Also called **Ida, Ide, Mida.** [d. c. 570]

St. Bonitus, Bishop of Clermont. Also called **Bonet, Bont.** [d. 706]

St. Ceolwulf, Northumbrian king and monk. [d. 1208]

The Beatified

Blessed Peter of Castelnau, martyr and monk. [d. 1208]

Blessed Francis de Capillas, priest and martyr. First beatified martyr in China. [d. 1648]

Blessed Arnold Janssen, priest. [d. 1909]

Historical Events

1535 The **Act of Supremacy** is passed in England.

1549 **Uniformity Act** is issued in England, demanding consistency in order of divine worship.

1552 **Treaty of Chambord** is signed by **Henry II** of France and German Protestants, who cede Metz, Toul, and Verdun to France.

1559 Queen **Elizabeth I** of England is crowned.

1582 Peace of **Jam-Zapolski** between Russia and Poland is signed. Russia is cut off from Baltic Sea (**Livonian War**).

1701 **Prussia** is proclaimed a kingdom.

1759 **British Museum** opens in London.

1777 **Vermont** declares its independence as a republic called **New Connecticut.**

1844 **University of Notre Dame,** South Bend, Indiana, is founded.

1858 **Alexander II** of Russia begins emancipation of serfs.

1859 **National Portrait Gallery** opens in London.

1863 Confederate cruiser *Florida* leaves Mobile, Alabama, to begin its raids on Union shipping (**U.S. Civil War**).

1895 *Swan Lake,* Tchaikovsky's ballet, opens in St. Petersburg, Russia.

1910 The name of the **French Congo** is changed to **French Equatorial Africa.**

1925 **Leon Trotsky** is relieved of his duties as chairman of the Revolutionary War Council by the Central Executive Committee of the Russian Communist Party.

1936 **Ford Foundation** is incorporated to administer funds for scientific, educational, and charitable purposes.

1939 First **Pro Bowl** game in **National Football League** history is played at Los Angeles.

1943 **Pentagon Building** in Washington, D.C., is completed.

U.S. troops force the Japanese off **Guadalcanal (World War II).**

1951 U.S. Supreme Court rules invalid a New York City ordinance requiring police permits for preachers to hold religious services on city streets.

1969 Denmark, Finland, Norway, and Sweden propose a **Nordic Economic Union.**

General Gowan of Nigeria accepts unconditional surrender from Biafran commanders and officers.

1971 **Aswan High Dam**, in Egypt, is formally dedicated.

1972 **Margrethe II** is proclaimed Queen of Denmark, following the death of her father, **King Frederick IX.**

1973 President **Richard Nixon** orders all offensive military operations against North Vietnam halted (**Vietnam War**).

Israeli Prime Minister **Golda Meir** and **Pope Paul VI** meet at the Vatican.

January 16

Holidays

Benin   Martyrs' Day

Religious Calendar

The Saints
St. Priscilla, matron. [d. c. 98 A.D.]
St. Marcellus I, Pope and martyr. Elected Bishop of Rome 309. [d. 309]

Birthdates

1697   **Richard Savage,** English poet, satirist; friend and biographer of Samuel Johnson (September 18). [d. August 1, 1743]

1749   **Count Vittorio Alfieri,** Italian dramatic poet; his poetry is said to have inspired the revival of the Italian national spirit. [d. October 8, 1803]

1757   **Samuel McIntire,** U.S. architect and woodcarver; called the *architect of Salem*; best known for the exquisite detail of his carvings in the *Sheraton style*. [d. February 6, 1811]

1815   **Henry Wager Halleck,** U.S. military officer, Union Army; known for the brilliance of his administrative abilities during the U.S Civil War. [d. January 9, 1872]

1845   **Charles Dwight Sigsbee,** U.S. admiral during Spanish-American War; commander of U.S. battleship *Maine* when it was sunk in Havana, 1898. [d. July 19, 1923]

1853   **Andre Michelin,** French industrialist; developed the **pneumatic tire** for use on automobiles. [d. April 4, 1931]

1874   **Robert W. Service,** Canadian poet; best known for his poems about travels in the subarctic region. [d. September 11, 1958]

1901   **Fulgencio Batista y Zaldivar,** Cuban dictator, 1934–59; overthrown by **Fidel Castro.** [d. August 6, 1973]

1909   **Ethel Merman (Ethel Zimmerman),** U.S. singer, actress; regarded as the *First Lady of American Musical Comedy.* [d. February 15, 1984]

1911   **Eduard Frei,** Chilean politician; President of Chile, 1964–70. [d. Janury 22, 1982]

   Dizzy Dean (Jerome Dean), U.S. baseball player, radio broadcaster. [d. July 17, 1974]

1934   **Marilyn Horne,** U.S. operatic mezzo-soprano.

1935   **A(nthony) J(ames) Foyt,** U.S. auto racer; three-time winner of Indianapolis 500, 1961, 1967, 1977; seven-time U.S. Auto Club National Champion.

Historical Events

1547   **Ivan IV** of Russia is crowned; first Russian leader to assume title of Tsar officially.

1556   **Charles V, Holy Roman Emperor,** resigns Spain to his son, **Philip II.**

1756   **Treaty of Westminster** between England and Prussia is signed, declaring England's neutrality (**Seven Years' War**).

1883   **Pendleton Act** is passed in the U.S., providing for competitive examinations for civil service.

1915   Germany refuses to give up **submarine warfare** against Allied merchant ships (**World War I**).

1920   **Prohibition** goes into effect in the U.S. one year after ratification of the **18th Amendment.**

1945   **Battle of the Bulge,** the final German offensive of **World War II** ends in allied victory.

1967   All-black cabinet headed by Prime Minister **Lynden O. Pindling** takes office in the **Bahama Islands.**

1969   Two Soviet **Soyuz spacecrafts** dock in orbit, accomplishing the first transfer of men from one space vehicle to another.

   Jan Palach, a Czech student, burns himself to death publicly in Prague to protest the Soviet occupation of **Czechoslovakia.**

   Swiss Ambassador to Brazil, **Giovanni Enrico Bucher,** is released 40 days after being kidnapped by Brazilian terrorists.

1979   **Shah Mohammad Reza Pahlavi** leaves Iran, ending his 37-year reign.

St. Honoratus, Archbishop of Arles. Founded Monastery of Lerins. Also called **Honaratus.** [d. 429]

St. Fursey, abbot. Also called **Fursa.** [d. c. 648]

St. Henry of Cocket, hermit. [d. 1127]

St. Berard and his companions, friars and martyrs. First martyrs of the Franciscan order. Berard also called **Berardus** or **Bernard.** Companions: **Adjutus**; **Odo** or **Otto**; **Peter.** [d. 1220]

The Beatified

Blessed Ferreolus, Bishop of Grenoble, martyr. [d. c. 670]

Blessed Gonsalo of Amarante, Dominican friar. Also called **Gundisalvus.** [d. c. 1259]

1973   ***Lunokhod 2,*** unmanned Soviet lunar vehicle, lands on the moon.

January 17

Religious Calendar

The Saints

SS. Speusippus, Eleusippus, and **Meleusippus,** martyrs. [d. c. 155]

St. Genulf, bishop. Also called **Genou, Gundulphus.** [d. c. 250]

St. Anthony the Abbot, hermit. Founder of monasticism. Patron saint of Italy, butchers, brushmakers, domestic animals, and cemetery workers. Invoked against the disease St. Antony's Fire. Also called **Antony, Antonius.** [d. 356] Feast celebrated by the Coptic, Syrian and Byzantine Rites. Obligatory Memorial.

Birthdates

1501   **Leonhard Fuchs,** German physician, botanist; the plant genus **fuchsia** is named for him. [d. May 10, 1566]

1504   **Pope St. Pius V,** ascetic and reformer; Pope, 1566–72; opponent of Queen Elizabeth I of England. [d. May 1, 1572]

1600   **Pedro Calderon de la Barca,** Spanish dramatist, priest; author of over 120 comedies. [d. May 25, 1681]

1612   **Thomas Fairfax, Third Baron Fairfax,** British nobleman and military leader; Commander in Chief of Parliamentary Army, 1645 (English Civil War). [d. November 12, 1671]

1706   **Benjamin Franklin** (b. January 6, Old Style), American statesman, inventor, diplomat, journalist; established first **subscription library** in America; founder of the **American Philosophical Society;** published *Poor Richard's Almanac,* the most popular publication in the colonies; invented the **Franklin stove;** proposed theories of **electricity;** organized the **U.S. Postal system;** invented **bifocals;** served as American delegate to France during American Revolution; described as "an harmonious human multitude" by his biographer, Carl Van Doren. [d. April 17, 1790]

1732   **Stanislas II** of Poland, last king of independent Poland, 1764–95. [d. February 12, 1798]

1761   **Sir James Hall,** Scottish scientist; founder of **experimental geology.** [d. June 23, 1832]

1820   **Anne Brontë,** English novelist, poet; author of *Agnes Grey;* sister of Emily Brontë (July 30) and Charlotte Brontë (April 21). [d. May 28, 1849]

1834   **August Weismann,** German biologist; a pioneer in **embryology;** one of the founders of science of **genetics.** [d. November 5, 1914]

1860   **Anton (Pavlovich) Chekhov,** Russian playwright; author of *The Sea Gull, The Cherry Orchard.* [d. July 2, 1904]

       Douglas Hyde, known as *An Craoibhin Aoibhinn* or *The Fair Branch,* Irish scholar, statesman; first president of Ireland, 1938–45. [d. July 12, 1949]

1863   **David Lloyd George,** British statesman; Prime Minister, 1916–22. [d. March 26, 1945]

1867   **Carl Laemmle,** German-American motion picture producer; founder of Universal Picture Corporation; produced first full-length photoplay, 1912, first million dollar movie, 1922. [d. September 24, 1939]

1871   **David, Earl Beatty, First Earl of the Northsea and of Brooksby,** first Sea Lord of the Admiralty, 1919–27. [d. 1936]

1880   **Mack Sennett,** Canadian film comedian and producer; produced first American feature length comedy film; creator of **Keystone Kops;** prime promotor of such film greats as Charlie Chaplin, W. C. Fields, Buster Keaton. [d. November 5, 1960]

1886   **Glenn Luther Martin,** U.S. aviation pioneer, manufacturer; beginning as a barnstorming pilot, became a pioneer in Ameri-

St. Julian Sabas, hermit. [d. 377]

St. Sabinus, Bishop of Piacenza. [d. 420]

St. Sulpicius II, Bishop of Bourges. Also called **Pius, Sulpice.** [d. 647]

St Mildgyth, abbess of Eastry. [d. 7th century]

St. Richimir, abbot. Founder of the monastery at Saint-Rigomer-des-Bois. [d. c. 715]

The Beatified

Blessed Roseline, virgin and prioress. [d. 1329]

can aviation industry; early advocate of military use of aircraft; many of his planes played significant roles in World Wars I and II; designed **Martin flying boats,** the first transoceanic clippers. [d. December 4, 1955]

1899 **Nevil Shute (Nevil Shute Norway),** British novelist, aeronautical engineer; author of *On the Beach.* [d. January 12, 1960]

Alphonse (*Scarface Al***) Capone,** U.S. gangster; one of the most notorious figures in America's gangland era. [d. January 25, 1947]

1922 **Luis Echeverria Alvarez,** Mexican leader; President, 1970–76.

1926 **Moira Shearer,** Scottish ballerina.

1931 **James Earl Jones,** U.S. actor.

1934 **Shari Lewis (Shari Hurwitz),** U.S. entertainer, ventriloquist, puppeteer.

Historical Events

1328 **Louis IV, the Bavarian,** is crowned Holy Roman Emperor at Rome.

1377 **Pope Gregory XI** returns to Rome, signalling the end of the **Avignonese papacy.**

1562 **Edict of St. Germain** formally recognizes French Protestantism.

1601 **Treaty of Lyons** between France and Savoy is signed; France gains Bresse, Bugey, Gex, and Valromey.

1781 **Daniel Morgan** and his sharpshooters are victorious over British at **Cowpens, South Carolina.** (**American Revolution**).

1837 The second party of Boers in the Great Trek from the British Cape Colony reaches the land of Zulu chief Mosilikatze and defeats him in battle.

1852 **Sand River Convention** is agreed upon, in which the British government recognizes the independence of the **Transvaal,** South Africa.

1912 **Robert Scott's** expedition reaches the **South Pole.**

1917 The **Original Dixieland Jazz Band,** first ensemble to call themselves a *jazz* band, opens at Reisenweber's Restaurant in New York City.

Virgin Islands are formally purchased from Denmark by United States.

1919 **Ignace Paderewski** becomes Premier of Poland, the first musician to become head of a modern state.

1929 **Bacha-i-Saquao** captures Kabul and proclaims himself king as **Amir Habibullah Ghazi** of Afghanistan.

1977 Capital punishment is reinstated in U.S. when **Gary Gilmore** is executed at Utah State Prison.

Catholic schools in South Africa defy racial segregation by admitting black and colored (mixed-race) students.

January 18

Holidays

Tunisia   **National Revolution Day**
Honors nationalist movements
of the 1930s and 1940s;
independence in 1956, and
abolition of monarchy in 1957.

Religious Calendar

Feasts

Confession of St. Peter the Apostle [major holy
day, Episcopal Church; minor feast day, Lutheran
Church]

Birthdates

1689   **Charles Louis de Secondat, Baron de La
Brède et Montesquieu.** French lawyer,
philosopher; author of *Lettres Persanes*, a
criticism of French society of his day, and
of *L'Esprit des Lois*, which greatly in-
fuenced political thought on the Continent
and in America. [d. February 10, 1755]

1779   **Peter Mark Roget,** English physician, author; creator of *Thesaurus of English Words
and Phrases*, 1852. [d. September 12, 1869]

1782   **Daniel Webster,** U.S. statesman, lawyer,
orator; a leader of the Whig Party, 1832–52;
U.S. Secretary of State, 1841–43; 1850–52. [d.
October 24, 1852]

1813   **Joseph Farwell Glidden,** U.S. farmer, inventor; inventor of **barbed wire. [d. October 9, 1906]**

1825   **Edward Frankland,** British chemist; discovered **helium** in the sun. [d. August 9,
1899]

1858   **Daniel Hale Williams,** U.S. surgeon; pioneer in **open heart surgery,** performing
first successful repair of a wound of the
heart. [d. August 4, 1931]

1867   **Rubén Dario (Félix Rubén García-
Sarmiento),** Nicaraguan poet, government
official; Nicaraguan Minister to Brazil, 1904;
Minister to Madrid, 1908–11. [d. February 6,
1916]

1882   **A(lan) A(lexander) Milne,** British author,
poet, playwright; best known as the creator
of *Winnie the Pooh.* [d. January 31, 1956]

1888   **Sir Thomas Sopwith,** British aircraft designer; World War I aircraft the **Sopwith
Camel** named for him.

1892   **Oliver Hardy,** U.S. comedian; with his
partner, Stan Laurel (June 16), comprised
one of the great American comedy teams
of all time; the team starred in over 200
films between 1926 and 1951. [d. August 7,
1957]

1904   **Cary Grant (Archibald Leach),** British-
American actor.

1913   **Danny Kaye (David Daniel Kaminsky),**
U.S. actor, comedian.

1931   **Chun Doo Hwan,** Korean political leader;
President of the Repubic of Korea, 1980– .

1942   **Muhammad Ali (Cassius Clay),** U.S. boxer;
World Heavyweight Champion, 1964–67;
1974–78; 1978–79.

Historical Events

1074   Imperial charter is issued for the **City of
Worms.**

1401   **Poland** and **Lithuania** are formally united.

1562   *Gorboduc*, by **Thomas Norton** and
Thomas Sackville, the first real English
tragedy, is presented before Queen Elizabeth I.

1701   **Frederick of Brandenburg** is crowned
King of Prussia, as **Frederick I.**

1871   **William I of Prussia** is proclaimed Emper-
or of Germany.

1919   The opening session of the Peace Conference ending **World War I** is held in Paris
with **Georges Clemenceau** of France presiding.

1928   Norway annexes **Bounet Island.**

1963   British colony of **Aden** joins the Federation
of **Saudi Arabia.**

The Saints

St. Volusian, Bishop of Tours. [d. 496]

St. Deicolus, abbot. Founder of Abbey of Lure. Also called **Deel, Desle.** [d. c. 625]

St. Bathan, bishop. Also called **Baithan, Bothanus.** [death date unknown]

St. Prisca, virgin and martyr. Also called **Priscian, Priscilla.** [death date unknown]

The Beatified

Blessed Beatrice D'Este of Ferrara, widow. [d. 1262]

Blessed Christina of Aquila, virgin. [d. 1543]

Brazil and **International Telephone and Telegraph Corporation** sign an agreement whereby Brazil will compensate the company for property expropriated by Brazil in February 1962.

1974   Disengagement agreement is reached on the **Suez Canal** between Egypt and Israel.

1977   Cause of **Legionnaires' Disease** is identified as a hitherto unknown bacterium.

Prime Minister **Indira Gandhi** calls for national elections in India, also freeing some of her imprisoned political opponents.

1982   Four members of the **U.S. Air Force Thunderbirds** flying team die while practicing aerial stunts over the Nevada desert.

January 19

Holidays

Cyprus	**Name Day of Archbishop Makarios**
Ethiopia	**Timket** (Eastern Orthodox Epiphany)
Guyana	**Youman Nabi**
U.S. (Texas)	**Confederate Heroes Day** Honors **Robert E. Lee,** Civil War leader; also honors **Jefferson Davis** and other Confederate heroes.

Birthdates

1544 **Francis II,** King of France. [d. December 5, 1560]

1736 **James Watt,** Scottish mechanical engineer, inventor; invented modern **condensing steam engine**; originated the word **horsepower**; the **watt** is named for him. [d. August 25, 1819]

1737 **Jacques Henri Bernardin de Saint-Pierre,** French novelist, naturalist; precursor of Romantic Movement in France. [d. January 21, 1814]

1747 **Johann Elert Bode,** German astronomer; catalogued over 12,000 stars; **Bode's Law** for expressing planets' relative distance from the sun is named for him. [d. November 23, 1826]

1798 **(Isidore) Auguste (Marie François) Comte,** French philosopher; founder of **positivism.** [d. September 5, 1857]

1807 **Robert E(dward) Lee,** Confederate Army general during U.S. Civil War; the outstanding military leader of the Confederacy. [d. October 12, 1870]

1809 **Edgar Allan Poe,** U.S. poet, short-story writer, critic; best known for his mystery stories and poems of a supernatural bent. [d. October 7, 1849]

1837 **William Williams Keen,** U.S. surgeon; a pioneer in **neurosurgery.** [d. June 7, 1932]

1839 **Paul Cezanne,** French painter; a leader in the Post-Impressionistic era. [d. October 11, 1906]

1851 **David Starr Jordan,** U.S. biologist, educator, philosopher; leading U.S. biologist; world renowned ichthyologist; first president of **Stanford University.** [d. September 19, 1931]

1887 **Alexander Woollcott,** U.S. journalist, critic, author; leading personality in literary circles; member of the literary *Round Table* at the New York Algonquin Hotel; exerted great influence on American culture. [d. January 23, 1943]

1905 **Ovetta Culp Hobby,** U.S. government official, newspaper publisher; Director, U.S. Women's (Auxiliary) Army Corps, 1942–45; Editor and Chairman of the Board, Houston Post Co., 1965– .

1918 **John Johnson,** U.S. publisher; founder and President, Johnson Publishing Co., Inc.; member of the board of a number of major U.S. corporations.

1943 **Janis Joplin,** U.S. singer. [d. October 4, 1970]

1946 **Dolly Parton,** U.S. country-and-western singer.

Historical Events

1419 Rouen in France capitulates to **Henry V** of England (**Hundred Years' War**).

1479 **Union of Aragon and Castile** is established under **Ferdinand the Catholic** and **Isabella.**

Religious Calendar

The Saints

St. Germanicus, martyr. [d. c. 155]

SS. Marius, Martha, Audifax, and **Abachum,** martyrs. Marius also called **Maris.** [d. c. 260] Suppressed 1970.

St. Nathalan, bishop. [d. 678]

St. Albert of Cashel, bishop. [d. 7th century]

St. Fillan, abbot. Also called **Felan, Fillian, Foelan.** [d. 8th century]

St. Canute of Denmark. King and patron saint of Denmark. Also called **Cnut, Knut.** [d. 1086]

St. Wulfstan, Bishop of Worcester. Also called **Wulstan.** [d. 1095]

St. Henry, Bishop of Uppsala, martyr. Patron saint of Finland. [d. c. 1156]

St. Charles of Sezze, Franciscan Lay-Brother of the Observance. [d. 1670]

The Beatified

Blessed Andrew of Peschiera, missionary. [d. 1485]

Blessed Bernard of Corleone, Capuchin lay-brother. [d. 1667]

Blessed Margaret Bourgeoys, virgin, founder of the Congregation of Notre Dame of Montreal. First schoolmistress of Montreal. [d. 1700]

Blessed Thomas of Cori, Franciscan priest. [d. 1729]

1493   **Peace of Barcelona** between France and Spain is signed, by which France cedes **Roussillon** and **Cerdagne.**

1904   A serious anti-European uprising breaks out in the British protectorate of **Southern Nigeria.**

1915   The first major German air raid over England occurs with attacks on Yarmouth, Kings Lynn, and other Norfolk County towns **(World War I).**

1921   **Pact of Union** is signed between **Costa Rica, Guatemala, Honduras,** and **Salvador** (dissolved in 1922).

1929   Communist leader **Leon Trotsky** is exiled from Russia.

1951   Viet-Minh Communist offensive in Indochina is defeated by French forces.

1961   U.S. Federal Communications Commission authorizes first space **satellite communications** link between U.S. and Europe on an experimental basis.

1962   Canadian Immigration Minister **Ellen Fairclough** announces new **immigration regulations** abolishing discrimination based on race, color, or religion.

1966   **Indira Gandhi,** daughter of **Jawaharlal Nehru,** is elected India's third prime minister.

1968   Great Britain and Russia sign agreement to cooperate in the fields of applied science and technology.

1970   U.S. Supreme Court rules that the **Selective Service System** lacks authority to accelerate the induction of persons violating **draft regulations.**

India's first (and Asia's largest) **nuclear power plant** at Tarapur is dedicated by Prime Minister **Indira Gandhi.**

1975   **Papua** New Guinea is declared a **Papua Republic** with an interim government by separatists who pledge to seize control of the island.

China publishes a new state constitution embodying the basic ideas of **Mao Tse-tung.**

1977   President Gerald Ford pardons **Iva Toguri D'Aquino,** known as *Tokyo Rose* to U.S. servicemen during World War II.

Radio astronomers at the **Max Planck Institute** in West Germany report discovery of water molecules outside earth's galaxy.

January 20

Holidays

Brazil (Rio de Janeiro)	St. Sebastian Day
Cape Verde Islands	National Heroes Day
Great Britain	St. Agnes Eve Traditionally believed to be the night during which a maid dreams of her future spouse.
Guinea-Bissau	National Heroes Day
Republic of Mali	Army Day

Birthdates

1716   **Charles III,** King of Spain, 1757–88. [d. December 14, 1788]

1724   **John Goddard,** U.S cabinetmaker; considered one of the finest furniture craftsmen that America has produced. [d. July 16, 1785]

1732   **Richard Henry Lee,** American Revolutionary patriot, lawyer, signer of the Declaration of Independence; first Senator from Virginia. [d. June 19, 1794]

1734   **Robert Morris,** American merchant, public official; signer of the Declaration of Independence; established the **Bank of North America.** [d. May 9, 1806]

1763   **Theobald Wolfe Tone,** Irish nationalist; persuaded French military to help overthrow English rule in Ireland. [d. November 19, 1798]

1812   **Sir William Fox,** New Zealand author, statesman; Prime Minister, 1856; 1861–62; 1869–72; 1873. [d. June 23, 1893]

1814   **Jean-François Millet,** French painter. [d. January 20, 1875]

1873   **Johannes Jensen,** Danish poet, novelist; Nobel Prize in literature, 1944. [d. November 25, 1950]

1879   **Ruth St. Denis,** U.S. dancer, choreographer; noted for her innovative dance concepts, based on cultures of the Far East; considered one of the great women of American dance. [d. July 21, 1968]

1889   **Huddie (*Leadbelly*) Ledbetter,** U.S. blues singer, guitarist; noted for his folk songs and stories, which he not only performed but also helped gather for the Library of Congress. [d. December 6, 1949]

1894   **Walter Piston,** U.S. composer, teacher; Pulitzer Prize in music, 1947, 1960. [d. November 12, 1976]

1896   **George Burns (Nathan Birnbaum),** U.S. comedian, actor; an institution in American comedy for over 70 years.

1906   **Aristotle Socrates Onassis,** Greek shipping magnate; married Jacqueline Kennedy, widow of U.S. President John F. Kennedy. [d. March 15, 1975]

1920   **Federico Fellini,** Italian screenwriter and film director; world renowned for such films as *La Dolce Vita* and *8 1/2.*

        Joy (Friederike Victoria) Adamson, Austrian wildlife conservationist; best known as author of *Born Free,* an account of her life in Kenya. [d. January 3, 1980]

1926   **Patricia Neal,** U.S. actress.

1930   **Edwin Eugene (*Buzz*) Aldrin, Jr.,** U.S. astronaut; crew member of *Apollo 11,* first manned spacecraft to land on the moon.

1937   **Dorothy Provine,** U.S. actress.

Historical Events

1301   In England, **Parliament of Lincoln** rejects papal claims on Scotland.

1320   **Wladyslaw I,** known as the *Short,* is crowned King of Poland.

1327   **Edward II** of England resigns throne and is succeeded by **Edward III.**

1558   French, under the **Duke of Guise,** take **Calais,** the last English possession in France.

1612   **Rudolf II,** Holy Roman Emperor, dies, and is succeeded by **Matthias.**

U.S. **Inauguration Day**
Twentieth Amendment to the U.S. Constitution declares that the term of newly elected President and Vice-President begin at noon on this day.

Religious Calendar

The Saints

St. Fabian, Pope and martyr; elected Bishop of Rome, 236. [d. 250] Optional Memorial.

St. Sebastian, martyr; patron saint of Portugal, archers, soldiers, pinmakers, and athletes; invoked against plague. [d. c. 288] Optional Memorial.

St. Euthymius the Great, abbot. [d. 473]

St. Fechin, abbot. [d. 665]

The Beatified

Blessed Benedict of Coltiboni. [d. c. 1107]

Blessed Desiderius, Bishop of Thèrouanne. Also called **Didier.** [d. 1194]

1801	The **War of the Oranges** breaks out between Spain and Portugal.
1841	**Hong Kong** is ceded by China to the British.
1848	**Christian VIII** of Denmark dies and is succeeded by **Frederick VII.**
1874	**The Treaty of Pangkor** gives the British a protectorate over Perak in the Malay Peninsula.
1885	**Mersey Tunnel** between Birkenhead and Liverpool, England, opens.
1887	U.S. gains exclusive right to establish a fortified naval base at **Pearl Harbor** in Hawaii.
1892	First game of **basketball** is played at YMCA gym in Springfield, Massachusetts, with peach baskets nailed to balconies at each end of room.
1918	The *Breslau,* a German-Turkish cruiser, is sunk in the Dardanelles; the *Goeben* is beached in an action with British warships **(World War I).**
1921	**Mustapha Kemal** issues the Fundamental Law providing for a parliament and responsible ministry, a president, and manhood suffrage for Turkey.
1924	The first **Kuo Min Tang National Congress** opens at Canton, China; **Sun Yat-sen** is elected president.
1936	King **George V** of Great Britain dies and is succeeded by his son, **Edward VIII.**
1949	**Harry S. Truman** is inaugurated as 33rd president of the U.S.; **Alben W. Barkley** is sworn in as vice-president.
1953	**Dwight David Eisenhower** is first inaugurated as 34th president of the U.S.; **Richard Nixon** is sworn in as vice-president.
1960	**William V. S. Tubman** is inaugurated for a fourth 4-year term as president of Liberia.
1961	**John Fitzgerald Kennedy** is inaugurated as 35th president of the U.S.; **Lyndon B. Johnson** takes the oath as vice-president.
1965	**Lyndon Baines Johnson** and **Hubert H. Humphrey** are inaugurated as president and vice-president of the U.S.
1969	**Richard Milhous Nixon** is first inaugurated as 37th president of the U.S.; **Spiro Agnew** is sworn in as vice-president.
1971	United Kingdom postal workers begin the first nationwide postal strike in the nation's history.
1977	**Jimmy Carter** is inaugurated as 39th president of the U.S.; **Walter Mondale** is sworn in as vice-president.
1981	The 52 **American hostages** in Iran are freed after 444 days in captivity and are flown to a U.S. Air Force base in Wiesbaden, West Germany.
	Ronald Wilson Reagan is inaugurated as the 40th president of the U.S.; **George Bush** is sworn in as vice-president.

January 21

Holidays

Dominican Republic   **Altagracia Day**
Celebrated with processions to the shrine of St. Altagracia.

Religious Calendar

The Saints

St. Fructuosus, Bishop of Tarragona and martyr. [d. 259]

Birthdates

1337   **Charles V,** King of France (called the *Wise*); reigned, 1364–80. [d. September 16, 1380]

1721   **James Murray,** English soldier; Governor of Quebec, 1760; Governor of Canada, 1763–66. [d. June 18, 1794]

1743   **John Fitch,** U.S. inventor; an early pioneer in the development of steam-powered boats. [d. July 2, 1798]

1813   **John Charles Frémont,** U.S. explorer, public official, Union general, mapmaker; Republican presidential candidate; Territorial Governor of Arizona, 1878–81. [d. July 13, 1890]

1815   **Horace Wells,** U.S. dentist; one of the first to use **ether** and **nitrous oxide** as **anesthetic** in dental surgery. [d. January 24, 1848]

1821   **John Cabell Breckinridge,** U.S. politician, lawyer, railroad executive; Confederate Army general during U.S. Civil War, 1864–65. [d. May 17, 1875]

1823   **Imré Madách,** Hungarian poet, dramatist; author of *The Tragedy of Man*, a dramatic poem dealing with the fall of the human race. [d. October 5, 1864]

1824   **Thomas Jonathan (*Stonewall*) Jackson,** Confederate Army general during U.S. Civil War; known as a master of military tactics and a great military leader. [d. May 10, 1863]

1829   **Oscar II,** King of Sweden and Norway; reigned over both countries until Norway became independent in 1905. [d. December 8, 1907]

1884   **Roger Nash Baldwin,** U.S. social reformer; founder of **American Civil Liberties Union.** [d. August 26, 1981]

1887   **Wolfgang Köhler,** German-U.S. *Gestalt* psychologist; known especially for experiments in **animal psychology.** [d. June 11, 1967]

1895   **Cristobal Balenciaga,** Spanish fashion designer. [d. March 24, 1972]

1900   **J. Carroll Naish,** U.S. character actor. [d. January 24, 1973]

1905   **Christian Dior,** French fashion designer. [d. October 24, 1957]

1906   **Igor Alexandrovich Moiseyev,** Russian ballet dancer, choreographer, director; Ballet Master, Bolshoi Theater, 1924–39.

1912   **Konrad Emil Bloch,** U.S. biochemist; Nobel Prize in physiology or medicine for research on **cholesterol metabolism** (with F. Lynen), 1964.

1922   **Barney Clark,** U.S. dentist; the first human to receive a permanent **artificial heart.** [d. March 23, 1983]

1922   **Paul Scofield,** British stage and film actor.

1927   **Telly Savalas (Aristotle Savalas),** U.S. actor.

1928   **Reynaldo Benito Antonio,** Argentine statesman; President of Argentina, 1982– .

1940   **Jack Nicklaus,** U.S. golfer; won more major tournaments than any golfer in history.

1941   **Plácido Domingo,** Spanish operatic tenor.

Historical Events

1528   England declares war on **Holy Roman Emperor Charles V.**

1645   In England, **Sir Thomas Fairfax** is appointed head of the Parliamentary army, opposing **Charles I (English Civil War).**

St. Patroclus, martyr. [d. c. 259]

St. Agnes, virgin and martyr. Patron of purity, virginity, young girls, girl scouts, and Cumana, Venezuela. [d. c. 304] Obligatory Memorial.

St. Epiphanius, Bishop of Pavia; called the *Peacemaker, the Glory of Italy, the Light of Bishops,* and also *Papa.* [d. 496]

St. Meinrad, hermit and martyr; patron of the Abbey of Einsiedeln in Switzerland; also called **Meginrat.** [d. 861]

St. Alban Roe, priest and martyr. [d. 1642]

The Beatified

Blessed Edward Stransham, priest and martyr. [d. 1586]

Blessed Thomas Reynolds, priest and martyr. [d. 1642]

Blessed Josepha of Beniganim, virgin and nun. [d. 1696]

1793   **Louis XVI** of France is beheaded (**French Revolution**).

1896   **Dr. Starr Jameson** and those arrested with him for the raid into the Transvaal, leave Durban, South Africa, for trial in Britain.

1899   **Lord Kitchener** is appointed governor-general of the Sudan.

1908   New York City's **Sullivan Ordinance** makes it illegal for woman to smoke in public.

1911   **National Progressive Republican League,** led by **Robert La Follette,** is organized in U.S.

1915   **Kiwanis International** is founded in Detroit, Michigan.

1925   **Albania** is proclaimed a republic.

1929   **Leon Trotsky** is deported by **Josef Stalin** from the U.S.S.R. and goes to Istanbul, Turkey.

1930   **London Naval Conference** opens with Japan, the United States, Great Britain, France, and Italy attempting to reach agreement on naval limitations.

1950   Treaty of friendship, commerce, and navigation between the U.S. and the **Republic of Ireland** is signed in Dublin.

       Alger Hiss is found guilty of perjury by a U.S. federal jury in denying that he had passed confidential U.S. documents to **Whittaker Chambers.**

1954   *U.S.S. Nautilus,* world's first nuclear- powered submarine, is launched.

1965   **Indonesia** withdraws from the UN.

1970   North Vietnam refuses to publish the names of captured U.S. pilots, branding them criminals, not prisoners of war.

1977   **President Carter** issues a pardon for U.S. draft evaders.

1979   **Pittsburgh Steelers** become the first football team to win three Super Bowls.

January 22

Holidays

St. Vincent   Discovery Day

Religious Calendar

The Saints

St. Vincent of Saragossa, martyr; patron of the wine industry. [d. 304] Optional Memorial.

Birthdates

1440 **Ivan III** (the *Great*), Grand Duke of Muskovy; ruler of Russia, 1462–1505; regarded as founder of the **Russian empire.** [d. October 27, 1505]

1561 **Sir Francis Bacon,** Baron Verulam, Viscount St. Albans, English philosopher, essayist, statesman; deveoped a new system of analysis of knowledge, designed to replace Aristotle's logic, published in Latin as *Novum Organum,* 1620. [d. April 9, 1626]

1592 **Pierre Gassendi,** French physicist, philosopher; opposed to Aristotelian philosophy; revived **Epicurean doctrine.** [d. October 24, 1655]

1729 **Gotthold Ephraim Lessing,** German critic, dramatist; author of the first German tragedy of middle-class life, *Miss Sara Sampson.* [d. February 15, 1781]

1783 **Henri Joseph Paixhans,** French artillery expert; inventor of one of the earliest shell-guns, the *Paixhans Gun,* 1837. [d. August 19, 1854]

1788 **George Gordon, Sixth Baron Byron (Lord Byron),** British Romantic poet, satirist; known for *Childe Harold's Pilgrimage, The Corsair,* and other romantic works; joined Greek struggle for independence; died of malaria. [d. April 19, 1824]

1802 **Richard Upjohn,** U.S. architect; known especially for his church designs; a founder and first president of **American Institute of Architects.** [d. August 17, 1878]

1849 **(Johan) August Strindberg,** Swedish playwright, novelist, short story writer; sometimes called the *Shakespeare of Sweden.* [d. May 14, 1912]

1850 **Robert Somers Brookings,** U.S. manufacturer, philanthropist; President of **Washington University,** 1897–1916; helped establish the **Brookings Institution,** famed research center named for him. [d. November 15, 1932]

1858 **Beatrice (Potter) Webb,** British socialist, economist; with her husband, Sidney Webb (July 13), founded the **London School of Economics.** [d. April 30, 1943]

1875 **D(avid) W(ark) Griffith,** U.S. film producer, director; renowned for his pioneering film epics *Birth of a Nation* and *Intolerance.* [d. July 23, 1948]

1877 **Hjalmar Schacht,** German financier; Minister of Economics under the Third Reich, 1934–37; acquitted of war crimes after participation in Reparations Commission deliberations. [d. June 4, 1970]

1882 **Louis Pergaud,** French novelist, short-story writer; best known for his animal stories. [d. April 8, 1915]

1890 **Frederick Moore Vinson,** U.S. politician, jurist; Director, Office of Stabilization, 1939–45; Chief Justice of U.S. Supreme Court, 1946–53. [d. September 8, 1953]

1897 **Rosa Melba Ponselle,** U.S. operatic soprano. [d. May 25, 1981]

1908 **Lev Davidovitch Landau,** Russian physicist; Nobel Prize in physics for studies on condensed gas, 1962. [d. April 1, 1968]

1909 **U Thant,** Burmese diplomat; Secretary-General of UN, 1962–72. [d. November 25, 1974]

1911 **Bruno Kreisky,** Austrian political leader; Federal Chancelior of Austria, 1970- .

1912 **Ann Sothern (Harriette Lake),** U.S. comedic actress.

1928 **Birch (Evans) Bayh,** U.S. politician, lawyer, farmer; U.S. Senator, 1963–80.

St. Blesilla, widow. [d. 383]

St. Anastasius the Persian, martyr. [d. 628]

St. Dominic of Sora, abbot; invoked against thunderstorms. [d. 1031]

St. Berhtwald, Bishop of Ramsbury. [d. 1045]

St. Vincent Pallotti, founder of the Society of Catholic Apostolate, the Pallottine Fathers. [d. 1850]

The Beatified

Blessed William Patenson, priest and martyr. [d. 1592]

Blessed Joseph Freinademetz, priest. [d. 1908]

1937   **Joseph Wambaugh,** U.S. novelist; author of *The Onion Field, The Choir Boys.*

1945   **William Harris,** head of the **Symbionese Liberation Army,** responsible for the kidnapping of newspaper heiress Patricia Hearst.

     Michael Christofer (Michael Anthony Procaccino), U.S. playwright, actor; Pulitzer Prize in drama, 1977.

Historical Events

1760   The French are defeated in the **Battle of Wandiwash,** India, by the British.

1771   Spain cedes the **Falkland Islands** to Great Britain.

1840   First British colonists in New Zealand land at **Port Nicholson.**

1901   **Queen Victoria** of Great Britain dies after the longest reign of any British monarch (63 years, 7 months), and is succeeded by her son, **Edward VII.**

1905   **Bloody Sunday** begins in St. Petersburg, Russia (**Revolution of 1905**).

1907   Richard Strauss' *Salome* has its American premiere in New York, outraging the moralistic American audience.

1917   U.S. President **Woodrow Wilson** makes his *peace without victory* address to the Senate, favoring establishment of a **League of Nations.**

1924   First Labour Cabinet gains power in Great Britain under **Ramsey MacDonald.**

1936   Paul Hindemith first performs his *Funeral Music* in memory of the death of King **George V** of Great Britain.

1964   Canada and the U.S. sign agreements for the development of the **Columbia River** basin and for establishment of an international park at the former summer home of Franklin D. Roosevelt, Campobello Island.

     Kenneth D. Kaunda is sworn in as first prime minister of Northern Rhodesia (Zambia).

1967   **Brazil** adopts a new constitution.

1968   U.S. B-52 bomber carrying four unarmed hydrogen bombs crashes near **Thule, Greenland.**

1970   The first regularly scheduled commercial flight of the **Boeing 747** jumbo jet arrives in London.

1973   **George Foreman** knocks out **Joe Frazier** for world heavyweight boxing title.

     Former U.S. President **Lyndon B. Johnson** dies of a heart attack.

     U.S. Supreme Court rules that states may not prevent a woman from obtaining an **abortion** during the first six months of pregnancy.

January 23

Holidays

Liechtenstein   National Holiday
Celebrates the formation of the principality, 1719.

Religious Calendar

The Saints
St. Asclas, martyr. [d. c. 3rd century]
St. Emerentiana, virgin and martyr. [d. c. 304]

Birthdates

1688   **Ulrika Eleonora,** Queen of Sweden, reigned 1718–20; abdicated in favor of her husband who became **King Frederick I.** [d. November 24, 1741]

1730   **Joseph Hewes,** U.S. merchant; signer of Declaration of Independence. [d. November 10, 1779]

1783   **Stendahl (Marie Henri Beyle),** French novelist; author of biographies of Haydn, Rossini, and Napoleon; best known for his novels *Le Rouge et le Noir,* and *La Chartreuse de Parme.* [d. March 23, 1842]

1813   **Camilla Collett,** Norwegian novelist; a leader of the feminist movement in Norway. [d. March 6, 1895]

1832   **Edouard Manet,** French painter, printmaker; originator and leader of French Impressionism. [d. April 30, 1883]

1876   **Otto Paul Hermann Diels,** German chemist; Nobel Prize in chemistry for studies in synthesizing of organic compound (with K. Adler), 1950. [d. March 7, 1954]

1903   **Randolph Scott (Randolph Crance),** U.S. actor.

1907   **Hideki Yukawa,** Japanese physicist; Nobel Prize in physics for theory of existence of **mesons,** 1949. [d. September 8, 1981]

1915   **Sir W. Arthur Lewis,** British agricultural economist; Nobel Prize in economics, 1979.

Potter Stewart, U.S. jurist, lawyer; Associate Justice, U.S. Supreme Court, 1958– .

Historical Events

1516   **Ferdinand of Aragon** dies and is succeeded by **Charles V,** his grandson.

1668   **Alliance of the Hague,** a triple alliance of England, Holland, and Sweden against France, is signed.

1719   Principality of **Liechtenstein** is formed.

1793   Second partition of **Poland** by Russia and Prussia takes place.

1911   **International Oceanographic Institute** opens in Paris.

1913   A coup d'état of the **Young Turks** overthrows the Turkish Ministry of Kemal Pasha as a triumvirate of Enver, Talaat, and Jemal seizes power.

1916   Austrians seize **Scutaria, Albania,** and **Podgorica, Montenegro (World War I).**

1920   Holland refuses to bow to pressures to surrender the exiled **Kaiser Wilhelm** of Germany.

1924   Polish decree introduces a new national currency, the **zloty.**

1960   U.S. Navy bathyscape **Trieste** breaks all records by descending to a depth of 35,800 feet in the Pacific Ocean off Guam.

1961   **Venezuela** adopts a new constitution providing for a strong central government.

1968   **U.S.S. Pueblo,** a U.S. Navy intelligence ship, is seized off the Korean coast by North Korean patrol boats.

1973   **Eldfell Volcano** in Iceland, dormant for thousands of years, erupts, forcing the evacuation of the town of **Vestmannaeyjax.**

SS. Clement and Agathangelus, martyrs. [d. c. 308]

St. John the Almsgiver, Patriarch of Alexandria; patron of the Order of St. John at Jerusalem, the Knights of Malta. [d. c. 619]

St. Ildephonsus, Archbishop of Toledo. Also called **Alfonso, Alphonsus, Alonzo, Hildephonsus, Ildefonsus.** [d. 667]

St. Bernard, Archbishop of Vienne. Also called **Barnard.** [d. 842]

St. Lufthildis, virgin. Also called **Leuchteldis, Liuthild, Lufthold.** [d. c. 850]

St. Maimbod, missionary and martyr. Also called **Mainboeuf.** [d. c. 880]

The Beatified

Blessed Margaret of Ravenna, virgin. [d. 1505]

January 24

Religious Calendar

The Saints

St. Babylas, Bishop of Antioch and martyr. First martyr of whom a translation of relics is recorded. [d. c. 250]

Birthdates

1670 **William Congreve,** English dramatist; known for his wit and refined dialogue; best known for *The Way of the World.* [d. January 19, 1729]

1712 **Frederick II** (*the Great*), King of Prussia, 1740–86. [d. August 17, 1786]

1732 **Pierre Augustin Caron de Beaumarchais,** French dramatist; author of *Le Barbier de Sèville* and *Le Mariage de Figaro,* later inspiring operas by Rossini and Mozart. [d. May 18, 1799]

1746 **Gustavus III,** King of Sweden; his reign was known as the **Gustavian Enlightenment.** [d. March 29, 1792]

1749 **Charles James Fox,** English statesman, orator; major parliamentary opponent of King George III. [d. September 13, 1806]

1776 **Ernst Theodor Hoffmann,** German writer, composer, caricaturist; his novels are among the finest produced during the German Romantic movement. [d. June 25, 1822]

1800 **Sir Edwin Chadwick,** British social reformer; laid the foundation for the **government inspection** system. [d. July 6, 1890]

1828 **Ferdinand Julius Cohn,** Polish botanist; called the *Father of Bacteriology.* [d. June 25, 1898]

1836 **Nikolai Dobrolyubov,** Russian radical, critic; looked upon as a founder of the revolutionary movement in Russia. [d. November 17, 1861]

1855 **Charles Henry Niehaus,** U.S. sculptor; responsible for numerous sculptures in rotunda of national capitol, Washington, D.C., as well as statues of many American heroes in various state capitols throughout the country. [d. June 19, 1935]

1860 **Bernard Henry Kroger,** U.S. grocer. [d. July 21, 1938]

1862 **Edith (Newbold) Wharton,** U.S. novelist, short-story writer; Pulitzer Prize in fiction, 1921. [d. August 11, 1937]

1885 **Umberto Nobile,** Italian aeronautical engineer; pioneer in Arctic aviation; flew with Amundsen and Ellsworth across the North Pole, 1926. [d. July 29, 1978]

1888 **Vicki Baum,** Austrian-American novelist, dramatist; author of *Grand Hotel.* [d. August 29, 1960]

1917 **Ernest Borgnine (Ermes Borgnino),** U.S. actor.

1918 **(Granville) Oral Roberts,** U.S. evangelist.

1919 **Leon Kirchner,** U.S. composer, pianist; Pulitzer Prize in music, 1967.

1925 **Maria Tallchief,** U.S. ballerina; former wife of George Balanchine.

1941 **Neil Diamond,** U.S. singer, songwriter.

1947 **Giorgio Chinaglia,** Italian soccer player.

1950 **John Belushi,** U.S. actor, comedian. [d. March 5, 1982]

Historical Events

661 **Caliph Ali of Arabia,** son-in-law of Muhammad, is murdered by anti-Shiite faction.

1076 **Synod of Worms** is held; German bishops challenge **Pope Gregory VII,** who dethrones and excommunicates **Henry IV** of Germany.

1446 **Pope Eugene IV** deposes archbishops of Cologne and Trier for their opposition to **Frederick III** of Germany.

St. Felician, Bishop of Foligno and martyr; patron of Foligno, Italy. Original Apostle of Umbria. [d. c. 254]

St. Macedonius, ascetic. [d. c. 430]

St. Francis de Sales, Bishop of Geneva and Doctor of the Church. Co-founder of the Order of the Visitation. Feast formerly January 29. [d. 1622] Obligatory Memorial.

St. Timothy, pastor and confessor. [minor Lutheran festival]

The Beatified

Blessed Marcolino of Forlì, Dominican monk. [d. 1397]

1742	**Charles Albert,** Elector of Bavaria, is elected Holy Roman Emperor; he becomes **Charles VII.**
1848	Gold is discovered at **Sutter's Mill,** in the San Joaquin Valley of California, marking the beginning of the great **California Gold Rush.**
1857	**University of Calcutta** in India is established.
1867	**Schleswig** and **Holstein** are incorporated into **Prussia.**
1915	German cruiser *Blücher* is sunk by the British in the **Battle of Dogger Bank (World War I).**
1919	The **Catalonian Union** meets at Barcelona, Spain, drawing up a program for home rule.
1943	**Tripoli** falls to British Eighth Army (**World War II).**
1960	**General Maurice Challe,** Supreme French Commander in Algeria, declares a state of siege in **Algiers.**
1965	**Sir Winston Churchill,** British statesman and author, dies in London.
1966	**Indira Gandhi,** daughter of **Jawaharlal Nehru,** is sworn in as the third prime minister of India, following the January 11 death of Prime Minister **Lal Bahadun Shastri.**
1969	**Italy** recognizes the **People's Republic of China.**
1972	U.S.S.R. becomes the first major world power to recognize the newly formed nation of **Bangladesh.**
	Japanese Army Sergeant **Shoichi Yokoi,** unaware that the war had ended in 1945, is found in the jungles of Guam where he has lived in hiding since U.S. troops seized the island in **World War II.**
1978	Fragments of Soviet reconnaissance satellite *Cosmos 954* land in a remote area of Canada's Northwest Territory.

January 25

Religious Calendar

Feasts

The Conversion of St. Paul, apostle of the Gentiles. Baptism and conversion took place in 34 A.D. [major holy day, Episcopal Church; minor festival, Lutheran Church]

Birthdates

1627 **Robert Boyle,** Anglo-Irish physicist, chemist; noted for his early research in chemistry and natural philosophy; a founding member of England's **Royal Society.** [d. December 30, 1691]

1736 **Joseph Louis Lagrange,** French mathematician, astronomer; developer of the **calculus of variations.** [d. April 10, 1813]

1746 **Stéphanie Félicité du Crest de Saint Aubin, Comtesse de Genlis,** French novelist, educator; governess of the children of the **Duchesse de Chartres.** [d. December 31, 1830]

1759 **Robert Burns,** Scottish poet; the national poet of Scotland; renowned throughout the world for his ballads and songs. [d. July 21, 1796]

1783 **William Colgate,** U.S. manufacturer, philanthropist; founder of the Colgate Soap Company, 1804; founder of **Colgate University,** which is named for him. [d. March 25, 1857]

1813 **James Marion Sims,** U.S. surgeon. [d. November 13, 1883]

1825 **George Edward Pickett,** Confederate army general in U.S. Civil War; led **Pickett's Charge,** one of the most celebrated military actions in U.S. history. [d. July 30, 1875]

1851 **Arne Evenson Garborg,** Norwegian novelist, poet, playwright, essayist; proponent of **Landsmaal,** a Norwegian literary language based on peasant dialect. [d. January 14, 1924]

1860 **Charles Curtis,** U.S. politician, lawyer; U.S. Vice President, 1929–33. [d. February 8, 1936]

1874 **W(illiam) Somerset Maugham,** British novelist, short-story writer, playwright; known for the realism of his novels, and his depiction of the essential tragedies and victories of human life. [d. December 16, 1965]

1878 **Ernst Frederick Werner Alexanderson,** U.S. electrical engineer; with the General Electric Company, received over 300 patents for developments in electrical equipment; with Radio Corporation of America, did pioneer work in radio and television. [d. May 14, 1975]

1882 **(Adeline) Virginia Woolf,** British novelist, short-story writer, playwright, screen-writer; master of the stream of consciousness style of writing. [d. March 18, 1941]

1891 **William Christian Bullitt,** U.S. diplomat; first U.S. Ambassador to the U.S.S.R., 1933–36; U.S. Ambassador to France, 1936–42. [d. February 15, 1967]

1899 **Paul Henri Spaak,** Belgian statesman; Premier, 1938–39, 1946; first President of UN General Assembly, 1946. [d. July 31, 1972]

1917 **Ilya Prigogine,** Belgian chemist; Nobel Prize in chemistry for explanation of contradictory biological processes, 1977.

1919 **Edwin (Harold) Newman,** U.S. news commentator, author.

1935 **Antonio dos Santos Ramalho Eanes,** Portuguese statesman; President, 1976– .

Historical Events

1327 **Edward III** of England seizes the throne of England.

1502 **Margaret,** daughter of **Henry VII** of England, marries **James IV** of Scotland.

1533 **Henry VIII** of England and **Anne Boleyn** are secretly married, he for the second time.

1909 *Elektra,* by Richard Strauss, premieres at the Dresden Royal Opera House.

The Saints

SS. **Juventinus** and **Maximinus,** soldiers and martyrs. [d. 363]

St. Publius, abbot. [d. c. 380]

St. Apollo, abbot. [d. c. 395]

St. Dwyn, virgin and nun; Welsh patron of lovers. Invoked to cure sick animals. Also called **Donwen, Donwenna, Dunwen, Dwynwen.** [d. 5th–6th century]

St. Praejectus, Bishop of Clermont and martyr. Also called **Prelis, Prest, Priest, Prix.** [d. 676]

St. Poppo, abbot. [d. 1048]

St. Artemas, martyr. [death date unknown]

1915   First **transcontinental telephone call** is made, between New York and San Francisco; Alexander Graham Bell and Dr. Thomas A. Watson exchange greetings.

1919   The Peace Conference of World War I adopts President Wilson's resolution for the creation of a **League of Nations** as part of the peace agreement.

1970   The Vatican refuses to accredit a West German diplomat, Mrs. **Elisabeth Mueller,** because she is a woman.

1971   General **Idi Amin Dada** creates the **Second Republic of Uganda** after a military coup.

1975   Prime Minister **Sheikh Mujiur Rahman** of **Bangladesh** is inaugurated as President.

1980   **Abolhassan Bani-Sadr** is elected President of the **Islamic Republic of Iran.**

January 26

Holidays

Dominican Republic   **Duarte's Birthday** Commemorates the birth of **Juan Pablo Duarte,** a founder of the Republic and leader in the fight for freedom from Haiti.

India   **Basant Pancami** or **Independence Day** Celebrates the proclamation of the Republic, 1950.

U.S. (Arkansas)   **Douglas MacArthur Day**

U.S. (Michigan)   **Admission Day** Commemorates Michigan's admission to the Union, 1837.

Birthdates

1468   **Guillaume Budé** or **Budaeus,** French humanist; responsible for laying foundation of **Bibliothèque National.** [d. August 23, 1540]

1715   **Claude Adrien Helvetius,** French philosopher; exponent of **sensationalism** or **sensualism.** [d. December 26, 1771]

1763   **Charles XIV John (Jean Baptiste Jules Bernadotte),** French soldier and King of Sweden and Norway, 1818–44. [d. March 8, 1844]

1810   **Joseph Brown,** U.S. inventor; designed the first universal **milling machine,** a breakthrough in machinery, 1862; also devised precision **measuring instruments** (calipers, protractors). [d. July 23, 1876]

1831   **Mary Elizabeth Dodge (Mary Elizabeth Mapes),** U.S. editor, author of children's books; author of *Hans Brinker or The Silver Skates*; pre-eminent figure in U.S. children's literature, 1864–84. [d. August 21, 1905]

1880   **Douglas MacArthur,** U.S. Army officer; one of the greatest but most controversial military leaders in U.S. history; U.S. Army Chief of Staff, 1930–35; Supreme Commander of Allied Forces in Southwest Pacific, 1942–45; 1950–51; relieved of duty after conflict with U.S. President Harry Truman. [d. April 5, 1964]

1904   **Sean MacBride,** Irish international civil servant; Nobel Peace Prize, 1974; Lenin Peace Prize, 1977.

1905   **Maria Augusta von Trapp,** Austrian-American musician; of the world famous **Trapp Family Singers**; the subject of *The Sound of Music.*

1911   **Polykarp Kusch,** U.S. physicist; Nobel Prize in physics for measurement of electromagnetic properties of electrons, 1955.

1913   **Jimmy Van Heusen (Edward Chester Babcock),** U.S. composer; known for his compositions, *Swinging on a Star, High Hopes,* and *The Second Time Around.*

1918   **Nicolae Ceauşescu,** Rumanian political leader; first president of Socialist Republic of Rumania, 1974– .

1923   **Anne Jeffreys,** U.S. actress.

1925   **Paul Newman,** U.S. actor.

1928   **Eartha Kitt,** U.S. singer, actress.

(Plemmianikov) Roger Vadim, French film director; credited with discovery of **Brigitte Bardot** (September 28).

1929   **Jules Feiffer,** U.S. cartoonist, writer.

1936   **Samuel Chao Chung Ting,** U.S. physicist; Nobel Prize in physics for discovery of subatomic particle known as *psi* or *J particle* (with B. Richter), 1976.

1944   **Angela (Yvonne) Davis,** U.S. black militant; Communist activist.

Historical Events

1699   The **Treaty of Karlowitz** is signed with the Turks giving up most of Hungary, Transylvania, Croatia, and Slavonia to Austria; Venice and Poland also receive territory.

Religious Calendar

The Saints

St. Timothy, bishop and martyr. Disciple of the Apostle Paul. Patron of stomach patients. Feast formerly January 24. [d. c. 97] Obligatory Memorial.

St. Titus, Bishop in Crete. Feast formerly February 6. [d. 1st century] Obligatory Memorial. [minor Lutheran festival]

St. Paula, widow. [d. 404]

St. Conan, Bishop of Man. Also called **Conon.** [d. 7th century]

St. Alberic, Abbot of Citeaux; co-founder of the Cistercian Order. Also called **Aubrey.** [d. 1109]

St. Eystein, Archbishop of Nidaros. [d. 1188]

St. Margaret of Hungary, virgin and Dominican nun; daughter of Bela IV, King of Hungary. [d. 1270]

1788 First settlers, including 717 convicts, arrive at **Sydney, Australia.**

1827 **Peru** secedes from Colombia.

1837 **Michigan** is admitted as the 26th state of the Union.

1885 **Khartoum,** the Sudan, falls to the Mahdi who massacre **General Gordon** and the Egyptian garrison.

1911 *Der Rosenkavalier* by Richard Strauss premieres at the Dresden Opera.

1915 Turkish forces led by Germans begin their advance across the Sinai towards the **Suez Canal (World War I).**

Russians open a counter-offensive against the Austrians in the **Battles of the Carpathian Passes (World War I).**

1920 The U.S. recognizes the **Armenian Republic.**

1930 **Wireless telegraph service** is opened between Japan and London.

1931 The British release **Mahatma Gandhi** from prison after the second campaign of civil disobedience.

1936 **Barcelona** is captured by General Francisco Franco's troops **(Spanish Civil War).**

1942 First U.S. Expeditionary Force to Europe in **World War II** reaches Northern Ireland.

1950 **India** becomes an independent republic; **Rajendra Prasad** is inaugurated as first president.

1960 **Cameroon** is admitted to the UN as the 83rd member.

1965 Military leaders of **South Vietnam** oust the civilian government of Premier **Tran Van Huong** and name Lieut. Gen. Hguyen Khanh to deal with the crisis caused by anti-government demonstrations.

Hindi is designated the official language of India, replacing English; the declaration results in riots in the southern part of the country; shortly afterwards, the Official Languages Act of 1963 is amended to confirm English as the "associate language."

1970 Poor Richard's Universal Life Church, a tax-exempt atheist church, is founded by **Madalyn Murray O'Hair.**

1975 **Thailand** holds its first parliamentary elections since 1957.

1977 The Spanish government bans public demonstrations.

1978 Tunisian workers rise against President **Habib Bourguiba** in worst civil violence in decades.

1983 The *W particle,* a new subatomic particle, is discovered by Swiss physicists.

January 27

Holidays

Monaco   St. Devote
              Commemorates the patron
              saint of Monte Carlo.

Religious Calendar

The Saints

St. Marius, abbot. Also called Maurus, May. [d. c. 555]

Birthdates

1756 **Wolfgang Amadeus (Johannes Chrysostomus Wolfgangus Theophilus) Mozart,** Austrian composer; one of the universal geniuses of music; composed over 600 pieces, including *Idomeneo*, said to have revolutionized lyrical drama, and *Don Giovanni* and *The Magic Flute*, which were the beginnings of romantic opera. [d. December 5, 1791]

1775 **Friedrich Wilhelm Joseph von Schelling,** German romantic philosopher; espoused theory recognizing *purpose* as the guiding principle of the universe. [d. August 20, 1854]

1814 **Giovanni Prati,** Italian poet, patriot; ardent advocate of Italian unity. [d. May 9, 1884]

1832 **Lewis Carroll (Charles Lutwidge Dodgson),** British author of children's books, mathematician; best known as author of *Alice's Adventures in Wonderland* and *Through the Looking Glass*. [d. January 14, 1898]

1836 **Leopold von Sacher-Masoch,** Austrian short-story writer, novelist, dramatist; term *masochism* was created to describe the abnormal behavior portrayed in his novels. [d. March 9, 1895]

1859 **William II, (Kaiser Wilhelm),** Emperor of Germany and King of Prussia, 1888–1918; led Germany in World War I; abdicated, 1918. [d. June 4, 1941]

1885 **Jerome (David) Kern,** U.S. composer; widely acclaimed for his show music; composed 50 scores during his career. [d. November 11, 1945]

1900 **Hyman George Rickover,** U.S. naval officer, born in Russia; responsible for design and development of the *Nautilus*, the world's first nuclear-powered submarine; established nuclear power educational facilities for the U.S. Navy; known for his outspokenness, especially his criticism of American education.

1903 **Sir John Carew Eccles,** Australian physiologist; Nobel Prize in physiology or medicine for research on electrical charges and their passage through nerve membranes (with A. L. Hodgkin and A. F. Huxley), 1963.

1921 **Donna Reed (Donna Mullenger),** U.S. actress; received Academy Award in 1953.

1929 **Ingrid Thulin,** Swedish actress; appeared in *Wild Strawberries* and *Cries and Whispers*.

1944 **Mairead Corrigan,** Irish pacifist; established the **Northern Ireland Peace Movement;** Nobel Peace Prize, 1976.

Historical Dates

1186 **Henry VI** of Germany marries Constance, heiress of Sicily, and assumes title of Caesar.

1822 **Greece** proclaims its independence from Turkey, setting off over a decade of conflict.

1943 First U.S. air attack on Germany is staged by the Eighth Air Force on the docks of Wilhemshaven (**World War II**).

1950 **Somaliland** is declared a UN trust territory.

1961 **Georgia** legislature repeals the state's public school **segregation laws.**

1962 Soviet government confirms the removal of all place names in the U.S.S.R. designated **Molotov, Voroshilov, Kaganovich,** and **Malenkov.**

St. Vitalian, Pope. Elected Bishop of Rome, 657. [d. 672]

St. Angela Merici, [d. 1540] Optional Memorial.

St. Julian, Bishop of Le Mans. [death date unknown]

The Beatified

Blessed John of Warneton, Bishop of Thérouanne. [d. 1130]

Blessed Henry de Osso y Cervello. [beatified 1979]

1964   France recognizes the **People's Republic of China** and establishes diplomatic relations.

1967   Representatives of 60 nations including the U.S. and U.S.S.R. sign a UN treaty providing for the peaceful uses of outer space and banning weapons of mass destruction in space.

Three U.S. astronauts die in a flash fire at Cape Kennedy, Florida, while training for the first launch of the *Apollo* spacecraft.

1973   **Vietnam War Cease-Fire** is signed in Paris, ending U.S. combat role in **Vietnam.**

January 28

Holidays

Rwanda   Democracy Day

Religious Calendar

The Saints

St. John Reomay, abbot. [d. c. 544]

St. Paulinus, Patriarch of Aquileia. [d. 804]

St. John the Sage. [d. 11th century]

St. Amadeus, Bishop of Lausanne. [d. 1159]

Birthdates

1457 **Henry VII,** King of England, founder of the Tudor dynasty; brought an end to the War of the Roses; father of Henry VIII. [d. April 21, 1509]

1600 **Pope Clement IX**; pope, 1667–69; credited with writing first comic opera. [d. December 9, 1669]

1608 **Giovanni Borelli,** Italian physiologist, physicist, mathematician, astronomer. [d. December 31, 1679]

1768 **Frederick VI,** King of Denmark, 1808–39, and of Norway, 1808–14. [d. December 3, 1839]

1822 **Alexander Mackenzie,** Canadian statesman, first Liberal premier of Canada, 1873–78. [d. April 17, 1892]

1833 **Charles George Gordon** (**Chinese Gordon** or **Gordon Pasha**), British officer sent to rescue Egyptian garrison before British abandoned the region; trapped at **Khartoum** by the Mahdi; defended the position for ten months before being killed when the city fell. [d. January 26, 1885]

1841 **Henry Morton Stanley (John Rowlands),** British-American journalist; best known for his expedition in search of African explorer **David Livingstone**; led several other expeditions in which he discovered **Lake Edward,** circumnavigated **Lake Victoria,** and surveyed **Lake Tanganyika.** Published several accounts of his travels and explorations. [d. May 10, 1904]

1853 **José Marti,** Cuban poet, patriot; leader in struggle for Cuban independence. [d. May 19, 1895]

1855 **William Seward Burroughs,** U.S. inventor; developed first successful recording **adding machine,** 1888. [d. September 15, 1898]

1861 **Daniel Willard,** U.S. railroad executive; President of Baltimore and Ohio Railroad, 1910–42; Chairman of U.S. War Industries Board, 1917–18. [d. July 6, 1942]

1864 **Charles William Nash,** U.S. manufacturer, automobile pioneer; developed the Nash Motor Co., 1916; President of the merged Nash-Kelvinator Corporation, 1937–48. [d. June 6, 1948]

1873 **Colette (Sidonie Gabrielle Colette),** French novelist; known for her fictional romances built around an autobiographical character, Claudine. [d. August 3, 1954]

1884 **Auguste Piccard,** Swiss physicist; made balloon ascents into stratosphere in 1930s; made observations about **cosmic rays.** [d. March 24, 1962]

1887 **Arthur Rubinstein,** U.S. concert pianist, born in Poland; considered one of the towering musical figures of the 20th century. [d. December 20, 1982]

1912 **(Paul) Jackson Pollock,** U.S. painter; a founder of the **Abstract Expressionist** school. [d. August 11, 1956]

1922 **Robert William Holley,** U.S. chemist; Nobel Prize in physiology or medicine for studies in role of **enzymes** in genetic development (with H. G. Khorana and M. W. Nirenberg), 1968.

1933 **Susan Sontag,** U.S. critic, essayist, novelist.

1936 **Alan Alda,** U.S. actor.

1948 **Mikhail Baryshnikov,** Soviet-American ballet dancer; Artistic Director, American Ballet Theater, 1980– .

Historical Events

1077 **Henry IV,** King of Germany and Holy Roman Emperor, excommunicated by **Pope**

St. Peter Nolasco, founder of the Order of Our Lady of Ransom or Mercedarians; patron of midwives. [d. 1258]

St. Thomas Aquinas, Doctor of the Church; patron of Naples and of all universities, colleges, and schools. Invoked against thunderstorms and sudden death. Feast formerly March 7. [d. 1274] Obligatory Memorial.

St. Peter Thomas, titular patriarch of Constantinople, martyr. [d. 1366]

The Beatified

Blessed Charlemagne, first Holy Roman Emperor. [d. 814]

Blessed James, the *Almsgiver.* [d. 1304]

Blessed Antony of Amandola, Augustinian friar. [d. 1350]

Blessed Mary of Pisa, widow. [d. 1431]

Blessed Julian Maunoir, priest. [d. 1683]

Gregory VII over the issue of lay investiture, makes his pilgrimage to Canossa where he stands for three days, bareheaded and barefooted, awaiting an audience with the Pope.

1547 **Henry VIII** of England dies and is succeeded by **Edward VI.**

1871 Paris capitulates to Prussia (**Franco-Prussian War**).

1915 The *William P. Frye,* a U.S. merchant ship, is sunk in the Atlantic by the German *Prince Eitel Friedrich.*

United States Coast Guard is established by Congress, combining the **Life Saving Service** and the **Revenue Cutter Service.**

1918 The **Ukraine** proclaims itself independent of Russia.

1932 Japanese troops seize **Shanghai** to force an end to intensive Chinese boycott of Japanese goods.

1941 Aaron Copland's instrumental suite, *Quiet City,* premieres in New York.

1944 **Leonard Bernstein** conducts the premiere of his first symphony *Jeremiah,* at Pittsburgh, Pennsylvania.

1951 **Shah Mohammad Riza Pahlavi** of Iran orders sale to peasants on favorable terms of all land he had inherited from his father.

1963 Black student **Harvey Gantt** enters Clemson College in South Carolina, thus breaking the barrier in the last state to hold out against **integration.**

1970 **Arthur Ashe,** U.S. black tennis star, is denied a visa to South Africa.

January 29

Birthdates

1688 **Emanuel Swedenborg,** Swedish scientist, mystic, philosopher, theologian; known for his voluminous works of interpretations of the Bible; his followers, who founded the **New Jerusalem Church,** are called **Swedenborgians.** [d. March 29, 1772]

1737 **Thomas Paine,** American colonial political philosopher; patriot; pamphleteer; author of *Common Sense,* pamphlet calling for independence from England. [d. June 8, 1809]

1749 **Christian VII, King of Denmark and Norway,** 1766–1808. [d. March 13, 1808]

1759 **Henry (*Light-Horse Harry*) Lee,** American Revolutionary cavalry officer, public official; Governor of Virginia, 1791–95. [d. March 25, 1818]

1761 **Albert Gallatin,** U.S. politician, banker, farmer; U.S. Secretary of the Treasury, 1801–14, U.S. Minister to France, 1816–23, and Great Britain, 1826–27. [d. August 12, 1849]

1773 **Friedrich Mohs,** German mineralogist; developed the **scale of hardness** still used in mineralogy. [d. September 29, 1839]

1838 **Edward Williams Morley,** U.S. chemist, physicist; renowned for his experiment, (known as the **Michelson-Morley experiment**) with Albert Michelson (December 19), on the behavior of light waves, an experiment which was used to test Einstein's contention, in his **special theory of relativity** that light rays are bent by gravitational force when passing near a heavenly body. [d. February 24, 1923]

1843 **William McKinley,** U.S. lawyer, politician; 25th President of the United States, 1897–1901; assassinated. [d. September 14, 1901]

1864 **Whitney Warren,** U.S. architect; known for his designs of **Grand Central Terminal,** New York City; the **Ritz-Carlton Hotel,** New York City; and the **Louvain Library,** Belgium. [d. January 24, 1943]

1866 **Romain Rolland,** French novelist, dramatist, biographer, essayist; Nobel Prize in literature, 1914. [d. December 30, 1944]

1867 **Vincente Blasco Ibáñez,** Spanish novelist; best known internationally for his *Four Horsemen of the Apocalypse.* [d. January 28, 1928]

1874 **John Davison Rockefeller, Jr.,** U.S. industrialist, philanthropist. [d. May 11, 1960]

1880 **W. C. Fields (William Claude Dukenfield),** U.S. comedian, film actor. [d. December 25, 1946]

1892 **Reinhard Johannes Sorge,** German dramatist; a member of the ultramodern expressionist school. [d. July 20, 1916]

1895 **Adolf Augustus Berle,** U.S. lawyer, economist; an early expert in the study of the concentration of wealth in industry; a member of President Franklin D. Roosevelt's *Brain Trust*; Assistant Secretary of State, 1938–44; U.S. Ambassador to Brazil, 1945–46. [d. February 17, 1971]

1905 **Barnett Newman,** U.S. abstract expressionist painter. [d. July 3, 1970]

1916 **Victor Mature,** U.S. actor.

1923 **Paddy Chayefsky,** U.S. playwright; wrote screenplays for *Altered States* and *Network*; best-known television play, later a film, was *Marty.* [d. August 1, 1981]

1926 **Abdus Salam,** Pakistani scientist; Nobel Prize in physics for studies in electromagnetism as it relates to the weak force in subatomic particles, 1979.

1943 **Katharine Ross,** U.S. actress.

Historical Events

1635 **Cardinal Richelieu** founds **Académie Française.**

1820 **George III** of Great Britain dies and is succeeded by **George IV.**

1850 **Slave trade** is abolished in the District of Columbia.

Religious Calendar

The Saints
St. Gildas the Wise, abbot. [d. c. 570]

St. Sulpicius, Bishop of Bourges. Also called Severus. [d. 591]
St. Sabian, martyr.

1857   Order of the **Victoria Cross** is instituted to reward persons of all ranks in the British army and navy.

1861   **Kansas** is admitted to the Union as the 34th state.

1896   U.S. physician **Emil H. Grube** becomes the first to use **X-ray treatment** for **breast cancer.**

1900   **American Baseball League** is formed in Chicago.

1914   **Academy of International Law** is founded at The Hague.

1932   George Gershwin's ***Second Rhapsody,*** for piano and orchestra, premieres at Boston.

1936   **Baseball Hall of Fame** is established at Cooperstown, New York, to honor distinguished players.

1950   The Indochinese states of **Vietnam, Laos,** and **Cambodia** become independent states within the French union.

1960   French President **Charles de Gaulle** calls on the French army to restore order in **Algeria,** marking the final struggle for Algerian independence, finally achieved in 1962.

1967   **Pope Paul VI** and Soviet President **Podgorny** confer at the Vatican in the first meeting between the Roman Catholic pontiff and the head of a Communist state.

1968   **Nauru** adopts a constitution in preparation for its independence from Great Britain.

January 30

Holidays

Mauritius   Cavadee

Religious Calendar

Feasts

Holy Day of the Three Hierarchs Honors SS. Basil, Gregory, and John Chrysostomos. Celebrated in the Eastern Orthodox Churches.

Birthdates

1775 **Walter Savage Landor,** British poet, writer; a quarrelsome and temperamental artist who lived in a storm of controversy most of his life. [d. September 17, 1864]

1816 **Nathaniel Prentiss Banks,** Union Army general during U.S. Civil War; U.S. Congressman, 1852–88; Governor of Massachusetts, 1858--61. [d. September 1, 1894]

1862 **Walter J(ohannes) Damrosch,** U.S. conductor, composer, born in Prussia; one of the greatest American conductors; Director of New York Symphony Orchestra, 1885–1927; conducted the first symphony to be broadcast by radio, 1925; introduced many new works by old composers; son of Leopold Damrosch (October 22). [d. December 22, 1950]

1882 **Franklin Delano Roosevelt,** U.S. politician, statesman; 32nd President of the United States, 1933–45; led the U.S. out of the **Great Depression** and through **World War II.** [d. April 12, 1945]

1894 **Boris III, King of Bulgaria**; reigned 1918–43; attempted to steer a neutral course for Bulgaria during World War II. [d. August 28, 1943]

1899 **Max Theiler,** U.S. microbiologist; Nobel Prize in physiology or medicine for discovery of a **yellow fever vaccine,** 1951. [d. August 11, 1972]

1909 **Saul (David) Alinsky,** U.S. social activist; renowned for his adamant striving for political and social equality; established the **Industrial Areas Foundation** to support organizations in communities. [d. June 12, 1972]

1912 **Barbara Tuchman (Wertheim),** U.S. historian; Pulitzer Prize in history, 1963, 1972.

1928 **Harold Stern Prince,** U.S. producer, director.

1931 **Gene Hackman,** U.S. actor.

1937 **Vanessa Redgrave,** British actress, political activist.

Boris Spassky, Soviet chessmaster; world champion, 1969–72.

1939 **Eleanor Cutri Smeal,** U.S. feminist; President of National Organization of Women (NOW), 1977–83.

Historical Events

1648 Peace is concluded between Spain and Netherlands, ending the **30 Years' War.**

1649 Charles I of Great Britain is beheaded; **Oliver Cromwell** takes control of the government.

1889 **Archduke Rudolph,** heir to the Austrian throne, commits suicide with his mistress, **Marie Vetsera,** at Mayerling.

1902 Great Britain and Japan sign treaty recognizing independence of **China** and **Korea.**

1915 The Russians take **Tabriz, Persia** (Iran) from the Turks (**World War I**).

1920 The White Russian government of General **Rozanov** at Vladivostok is overthrown by the Bolsheviks (**Russian Revolution**).

1933 *The Lone Ranger* makes its radio debut.

Adolf Hitler becomes Chancellor of Germany.

1948 **Mahatma Gandhi,** Indian spiritual leader, is assassinated by a young Hindu extremist, Nathuram Godse.

1962 U.S. President **John F. Kennedy** and **Aleksei I. Adzhubei,** editor of *Izvestia*, principal Russian newspaper, hold conversations at the White House.

The Saints

St. Bersimaeus, Bishop of Edessa. [d. c. 250]

St. Bathildis, widow, queen of France. Also called **Baldechilde, Baldhild, Barthild, Barthildis, Bathildas, Bathildes, Bauteur.** [d. 680]

St. Aldegundis, virgin. Also called **Aldegondes.** [d. 684]

St. Adelemus, abbot. Also called **Aleaume.** [d. c. 1100]

St. Hyacintha Mariscotti, virgin and nun. Also called **Giacinta.** [d. 1640]

St. Martina, virgin and martyr. Patron of Rome.

The Beatified

Blessed Sebastian Valfrè, priest. [d. 1710]

1965 Government of **Burundi** breaks diplomatic relations with the **People's Republic of China.**

1970 Prime Minister Chief **Leabua Jonathan** declares a state of emergency in **Lesotho** and orders the arrest of his political opponent, **Ntsu Mokhehle.**

1972 **Pakistan** becomes independent of Great Britain.

January 31

Holidays

Nauru   Independence Day

Religious Calendar

The Saints

SS. Cyrus and John, martyrs. [d. c. 303]

St. Marcella, widow. Organized a religious sister-hood, the beginnings of St. Jerome's famous follow-ing of cultivated ladies. [d. 410]

Birthdates

1734 **Robert Morris,** U.S. financier, Revolution-ary patriot. [d. May 8, 1806]

1735 **Michael-Guillaume-Jean de Crèvecoeur** (Hector Saint-John de Crèvecoeur, J. Hec-tor St. John, Agricola), French-American writer, naturalist. [d. November 12, 1813]

1752 **Gouverneur Morris,** American Revolu-tionary patriot, government official, dele-gate to Continental Congress, 1777–78, U.S. Minister of Finance, 1781–85, Senator, 1800–03. [d. November 6, 1816]

1785 **Charles Green,** British balloonist. [d. March 26, 1870]

1797 **Franz Peter Schubert,** Austrian compos-er. [d. November 19, 1828]

1812 **William Hepburn Russell,** U.S. business-man; founded **Pony Express** [d. Septem-ber 10, 1872]

1830 **Victor-Henri Rochefort, Marquis de Rochefort-Luçay,** French polemical jour-nalist, politician. [d. June 30, 1913]

  James Gillespie Blaine, U.S. politician, newspaper editor. [d. January 27, 1893]

1831 **Rudolph Wurlitzer,** U.S. manufacturer. [d. January 14, 1914]

1848 **Nathan Straus,** U.S. merchant. [d. January 11, 1931]

1868 **Theodore William Richards,** U.S. chem-ist. Nobel Prize in chemistry, 1914. [d. April 2, 1928]

1872 **Zane Grey,** U.S. novelist. [d. October 23, 1939]

1881 **Irving Langmuir,** U.S. chemist; Nobel Prize in chemistry, 1932. [d. 1957]

1892 **Eddy Cantor (Edward Israel Iskowitz),** U.S. comedian, song-and-dance man. [d. October 10, 1964]

1903 **Tallulah (Brockman) Bankhead,** U.S. ac-tress. [d. December 12, 1968]

1905 **John Henry O'Hara,** U.S. short-story writ-er, novelist. [d. April 11, 1970]

1913 **Don Hutson,** U.S. football player.

1914 **Jersey Joe Walcott (Arnold Raymond Cream),** U.S. boxer, world heavyweight champion, 1951–52.

1915 **Bobby Hackett,** U.S. cornetist. [d. June 7, 1976]

  Garry Moore (Thomas Garrison Morfit), U.S. television personality.

1919 **Rudolf Ludwig Mössbauer,** German physicist; Nobel Prize in physics for dis-covery of the phenomenon known as the **Mössbauer effect** (with **R. Hofstadter**), 1961.

  Jack(ie) Roosevelt Robinson, U.S. base-ball player and civil-rights activist; first black to enter major leagues, with the Brooklyn Dodgers, 1947; Hall of Fame, 1962. [d. October 24, 1972]

1920 **Stewart Lee Udall,** U.S. politician.

  Paul Culliton Warnke, U.S. government of-ficial, lawyer.

1921 **Mario Lanza (Alfredo Arnold Cocozza),** U.S. singer, actor. [d. October 7, 1959]

1923 **Carol Channing,** U.S. actress, singer.

  Joanne Dru (Joanne La Cock), U.S. ac-tress.

  Norman Mailer, U.S. novelist, journalist; Pulitzer Prize in general nonfiction, 1969.

1929 **Jean Simmons,** British actress.

1931 **Ernie Banks,** U.S. baseball player; Baseball Hall of Fame, 1977.

1934 **James Franciscus,** U.S. actor.

1937 **Suzanne Pleshette,** U.S. actress.

St. Aidan of Ferns, Bishop. Founded a monastery at Ferns in County Wexford and became the first bishop. Also called **Aidar, Aidus, Aiduus, Edan, Maedhog, Maedoc, Maidoc, Mogue, Maodhog.** [d. 626]

St. Adamnan of Coldingham, monk. Also called **Eunan.** [d. c. 680]

St. Ulphia, virgin and hermit. Also called **Olfe, Wulfe.** [d. c. 750]

St. Eusebius, martyr and hermit. [d. 884]

St. Nicetas, Bishop of Novgorod. Also called **Nikita.** [d. 1107]

St. Francis Xavier Bianchi, priest. [d. 1815]

St. John Bosco, founder of the Salesians of Don Bosco and the Daughters of Our Lady, Help of Christians. [d. 1888]

The Beatified

Blessed Paula Gambara-Costa, matron. [d. 1515]

1947   **(Lynn) Nolan Ryan,** U.S. baseball player.

Historical Events

1850   New Prussian constitution is promulgated.

1910   Slavery is abolished in China.

1915   A German air raid over England hits the industrial centers in the midland counties **(World War I).**

1917   The German government informs U.S. that unrestricted submarine warfare will begin on February 1, 1917 **(World War I).**

1918   The **Gregorian calendar** replaces the Julian in Russia.

1926   Italian law is enacted giving the prime minister the power to issue decrees with the force of law.

1946   **Yugoslavia** adopts its constitution and officially becomes a *people's republic.*

1950   President Truman directs **U.S. Atomic Energy Commission** to continue work on all forms of atomic weapons.

1958   *Explorer I,* first U.S. satellite, is launched.

1961   Ham, a male chimpanzee, is recovered alive in the Caribbean after being carried to a height of 155 miles in a U.S. space capsule launched from Cape Canaveral, Florida.

1962   Foreign ministers of the OAS, meeting at Punta del Este, vote to expel Cuba from participation in inter-American affairs.

1964   French President **Charles de Gaulle** in cooperation with the People's Republic of China, proposes the neutralization of Cambodia, Laos, and Vietnam.

1965   **Iraq** abolishes military tribunals and martial law and enacts a new public security regulation.

1967   **National Traffic Safety Agency** issues the first set of U.S. federal safety standards for vehicle safety.

1968   South Pacific island of **Nauru,** a former UN trust territory, becomes an independent republic.

   West Germany and **Yugoslavia** resume diplomatic relations after a 10-year break.

   Kenya and **Somalia** resume diplomatic relations.

1971   Telephone service between **East and West Berlin** is re-established for the first time in 19 years.

   Apollo 14 manned spacecraft is launched.

1972   King **Mahendra of Nepal** dies and is succeeded by his oldest son, Birendra.

1975   **Angola** adopts a transitional government.

February

February, the second month of the Gregorian calendar, has 28 days in the ordinary year of 365 days, and 29 days in every fourth year (leap year) of 366 days. Like January, February did not exist in the early Roman calendar, but was added as the twelfth month in approximately 700 B.C. under the calendar reform of the Etruscan King at Rome, Numa Pompilius. The Etruscan calendar reforms were abandoned at Rome for a time, but eventually a 12-month year, including February, was permanently adopted. (See also at **January**.)

The Latin name *Februarius* is thought to be derived from the word *februa*, which means *rites of purification*. As the last month of the year in the early Roman calendar, it was dedicated to acts of purification in preparation for the coming of the new year in March. During the Feast of Lupercalia, February 15, women would be ritually struck with strips of skin from sacrificial goats, a ceremony honoring the god Faunus and thought to assure fertility and an easy delivery.

In the astrological calendar, February spans the zodiac sign of Aquarius, the Water Bearer (January 20–February 18), and Pisces, the Fishes (February 19–March 20).

The birthstone for February is the amethyst, and the flower is the violet or primrose.

State, National, and International Holidays

Lincoln's Birthday
(Delaware, Oregon)
First Monday

Lincoln Day
(Arizona)
Second Monday

Washington's Birthday
(United States)
Third Monday

Washington Day
(Arizona)
Third Monday

Presidents' Day
(Hawaii, Nebraska, Pennsylvania, South Dakota)
Third Monday

Washington-Lincoln Day
(Ohio, Wisconsin, Wyoming)
Third Monday

Pageant of Light
(Florida)
near Thomas Edison's Birthday
(February 11)

Race Relations Sunday
(United States)
Sunday nearest Lincoln's Birthday

Independence Day
(St. Lucia)
Third Monday

Hamstrom
(Switzerland)
First Sunday

Bean-throwing Festival or Setsubun
(Japan)
February 3

Special Events and Their Sponsors

American History Month
National Society
Daughters of the American Revolution
Administration Building
1776 D Street, N.W.
Washington, D.C. 20006

National Afro-American (Black) History Month
Association for the Study of Afro-American Life
    and History, Inc.
1401 14th Street
Washington, D.C. 20005

World Understanding Month
World Understanding and Peace Day
February 23
Rotary International
1600 Ridge Ave.
Evanston, Ill. 60201

Party Time is Pickle Time
Pickle Packers International, Inc.
P.O. Box 31
One Pickle & Pepper Plaza
St. Charles, Ill. 60174

International Friendship Month
Franklin D. Roosevelt Philatelic Society
154 Laguna Court
St. Augustine Shores, Florida 32084

National Cherry Month
National Red Cherry Institute
Riverview Center
678 Front Street, N.W.
Grand Rapids, Michigan 49504

National Hobby Month
Hobby Industry of America
319 E. 54th Street
Elmwood Park, New Jersey 07407

National Children's Dental Health Month
American Dental Health Association
211 E. Chicago Avenue
Chicago, Illinois 60611

Potato Lover's Month
National Potato Promotion Board
1385 South Colorado Boulevard
Suite 512
Denver, Colorado 80222

National Crime Prevention Week
Week of Lincoln's Birthday
National Exchange Club
3050 Central Avenue
Toledo, Ohio 43606

Engineer's Week
Week of Washington's Birthday
National Society of Professional Engineers
2029 K Street N.W.
Washington, D.C. 20006

National Kraut & Frankfurter Week
Week containing February 14
National Kraut Packers Association
One Sauerkraut Plaza
P.O. Box 31
St. Charles, Illinois 60174

National Pay Your Bills Week
First Full Week
American Collectors Association
4040 W. 70th Street
Minneapolis, Minnesota 55435

Brotherhood-Sisterhood Week
Week of Washington's Birthday
National Conference of Christians and Jews
43 W. 57th Street
New York, New York 10019

Scouting Anniversary
Week containing February 8
Boy Scouts of America
1325 Walnut Hill Lane
Irving, Texas 75060

National FFA Week
Week containing Washington's Birthday
Future Farmers of America
National FFA Center
Box 15160
Alexandria, Virginia 22309

FHA/HERO Week
(Future Homemakers of America/
Home Economics Related Occupation)
Second Full Week
Future Homemakers of America
2010 Massachusetts Avenue, N.W.
Washington, D.C. 20036

National Safety Sabbath
Second Weekend
National Safety Council
444 N. Michigan Avenue
Chicago, Illinois 60611

USO Anniversary
February 4
United Services Organization
World Headquarters
1146 19th Street, N.W.
Washington, D.C. 20036

Special Days—Other Calendars

	Ash Wednesday	Chinese New Year
1985	20 February	22 February
1986	12 February	9 February
1987		
1988	17 February	17 February
1989	8 February	6 February
1990	28 February	

February 1

Holidays

Australia	**Australia Day**
Malaysia	**Federal Territory Day**
Nicaragua	**Air Force Day**
	Honors the achievements of the nation's airmen.
United States	**National Freedom Day**
	Commemorates the ratification of the Thirteenth Amendment to the U.S. Constitution by

Birthdates

1552   **Sir Edward Coke,** English jurist, defender of the supremacy of the common law. [d. September 3, 1634]

1757   **John Philip Kemble,** English Shakespearean actor; director of **Drury Lane Theater,** 1783–1802. [d. February 26, 1823]

1797   **John Bell,** U.S. politician, lawyer; conservative Southern politician who supported the Union during the **U.S. Civil War.** [d. September 10, 1869]

1801   **Thomas Cole,** U.S. romantic landscape painter; a founder of the **Hudson River school** of painters. [d. February 8, 1848]

        (Maximilien Paul) Emile Littré, French lexicographer and philosopher; successor to Auguste Comte as head of positivist school. [d. June 2, 1881]

1805   **Louis Auguste Blanqui,** French Revolutionary socialist; prominent activist in the revolutions of 1839, 1848, 1871. First advocate of a dictatorship of the proletariat. [d. January 1, 1881]

1828   **Meyer Guggenheim,** U.S. industrialist; known for his mining operations in Central and South America, from which he amassed a considerable fortune. [d. March 15, 1905]

1831   **Henry McNear Turner,** U.S. Methodist Episcopal bishop, government worker; advocate of return of blacks to Africa. [d. May 8, 1915]

1844   **Granville Stanley Hall,** U.S. psychologist; the first president of the **American Psychological Association.** [d. April 24, 1924]

1859   **Edward Aloysius Cudahy,** U.S. meat packer; partner, Armour & Co., 1875–87; founder of Cudahy Packing Co., 1890. [d. October 18, 1941]

        Victor Herbert, U.S. virtuoso cellist, conductor, composer born in Ireland. [d. May 26, 1924]

1874   **Hugo von Hofmannsthal,** Austrian dramatist, poet. [d. July 15, 1919]

1878   **Hattie Wyatt Caraway,** U.S. politician, teacher; the first woman elected to the U.S. Senate. [d. December 21, 1950]

1882   **Louis Stephen St. Laurent,** Canadian lawyer and statesman; Prime Minister, 1948–57. [d. July 25, 1973]

1887   **Harry Scherman,** Canadian-American writer; originator of **Book-of-the-Month Club.** [d. November 12, 1969]

        Charles Bernard Nordhoff, U.S. travel and adventure writer. [d. April 11, 1947]

1895   **John Ford (Sean O'Feeney),** U.S. film director. [d. August 31, 1973]

1896   **Nat Holman,** U.S. basketball player, coach.

        Anastasio Somoza, Nicaraguan leader; President, 1937–47, 1950–56. [d. April 13, 1967]

1901   **(William) Clark Gable,** U.S. actor. [d. November 16, 1960]

1902   **(James) Langston Hughes,** U.S. poet. [d. May 22, 1967]

1904   **S(idney) J(oseph) Perelman,** U.S. author, humorist. [d. October 17, 1979]

1905   **Emilio Segrè,** U.S. physicist born in Italy; Nobel Prize in physics for discovery of the **antiproton** (with O. Chamberlain), 1959.

1906   **Hildegarde (Loretta Sell),** U.S. cabaret singer.

1918   **(Sarah) Muriel Spark,** Scottish novelist, critic, poet; author of *The Prime of Miss Jean Brodie,* 1961.

1923   **Stansfield Turner,** U.S. admiral; Commander in Chief of Allied Naval Forces in Southern Europe, 1975–77. Director of U.S. Central Intelligence Agency, 1977–80.

President Abraham Lincoln, abolishing slavery.

Religious Calendar

The Saints

St. Pionius, martyr. [d. c. 250]

St. Seiriol, abbot; founder of Penman church; patron of Anglesey. [d. 6th century]

St. Brigid, virgin, abbess of Kildare; patron of Ireland, Wales, Australia, and New Zealand, all Irish women, Irish nuns and dairy workers. Also called **Bride, the Mary of the Gael.** [d. c. 525]

St. Sigebert (King Sigebert III of Austrasia). [d. 656]

St. John of the Grating, Bishop of Saint-Malo. [d. c. 1170]

The Beatified

Blessed Antony the Pilgrim. [d. 1267]

Historical Events

772   **Adrian I** is elected Pope; reigned 772–795.

1328   **Charles IV** of France, last of the Capets, dies and is succeeded by **Philip VI** of Valois.

1440   Frederick, Duke of Styria, is elected **Frederick III** of Germany.

1539   **Treaty of Toledo** between **Holy Roman Emperor Charles V** and **Francis I** of France is signed, temporarily halting the **Hapsburg-Valois Wars.**

1642   Holland signs the first treaties with chiefs of the **Gold Coast of Africa** for purchase of land.

1790   First meeting is held of the **U.S. Supreme Court,** Chief Justice **John Jay** presiding.

1793   **France** declares war on England, Holland, and Spain (**French Revolutionary period**).

1864   **Ferdinand de Lesseps** begins French effort to construct **Panama Canal.**

1884   First section of *Oxford English Dictionary* is published.

1896   *La Bohème,* by Giacomo Puccini, premieres in Turin, Italy.

1898   First **automobile insurance policy** is issued to Dr. Truman J. Martin of Buffalo, N.Y., protecting his automobile from damage caused by frightened horses.

1904   **Enrico Caruso** makes his first phonograph recording in America.

1908   **Carlos I** of Portugal and his eldest son are assassinated.

1914   The railroad from Dar-es-Salaam to Lake Tanganyika is completed.

1915   A German offensive renews the **Battle of Champagne** on the Western Front (**World War I**).

1917   Germany begins unrestricted **submarine warfare** on all neutral and belligerent shipping (**World War I**).

1924   Great Britain recognizes the **Bolshevik regime** in Russia.

1940   First official network **television broadcast** in the U.S. is aired.

1941   **British Air Training Corps** is founded.

1942   **Vidkun Quisling,** whose name became synonymous with traitor, is named Premier of Norway. His collaboration with the Germans during **World War II** led to his arrest and execution.

1957   First **turbo-prop** airliner enters into scheduled service in Great Britain.

1958   Egypt and Syria unite to form the **United Arab Republic.**

1961   First U.S. **Intercontinental Ballistic Missile,** the **Minuteman,** is successfully fired from Cape Canaveral, Florida.

1963   **Hastings Banda** is sworn in as the first Prime Minister of **Nyasaland** (formerly **Malawi**).

1969   U.S.S.R. and Peru reestablish diplomatic relations following the overthrow of the **Fernando Belaúnde Terry** government.

1970   **Pope Paul VI** reiterates teaching of priestly celibacy as a fundamental principle of the Roman Catholic Church.

1979   **Ayatollah Ruhollah Khomeini** returns to Iran after 15 years' exile in France to direct a revolution against the Iranian government and the overthrow of the Shah.

1982   The African nations of **Senegal** and **The Gambia** form a confederation, **Senegambia,** but they retain their sovereignties.

February 2

Holidays

Canada	**Groundhog Day** Same as in the U.S. (see below); however, sometimes a bear is looked for instead of the groundhog.
Liechtenstein	**Candlemas**
Mexico	**Dia de la Candelaria** Candlemas Day celebration in Mexico and other Latin American countries.
Scotland	**Scottish Quarter Day** Fortieth day of Christmas.
U.S.	**Groundhog Day** Traditionally, the day on which the groundhog appears from

Birthdates

1208 **James I, the Conqueror,** King of Aragon. [d. 1276]

1649 **Pope Benedict XIII,** Pope 1724–30. [d. February 21, 1730]

1650 **Nell Gwyn (Eleanor Gwyn),** English actress; mistress of **Charles II.** [d. November 13, 1687]

1754 **Charles Maurice de Talleyrand-Périgord, Prince de Bénévet,** French statesman, diplomat, politician. [d. May 17, 1838]

1859 **(Henry) Havelock Ellis,** British scientist, man of letters; early advocate of sex education; pioneer in the study of the psychology of sex. [d. July 8, 1939]

1875 **Fritz Kreisler,** Austrian-American violin virtuoso. [d. January 29, 1962]

1882 **James Joyce,** Irish novelist, author of *Ulysses.* [d. January 13, 1941]

1886 **William Rose Benét,** U.S. poet, editor. [d. May 4, 1950]

1890 **Charles Correll,** U.S. comedic actor; best known as *Andy* in radio show *Amos 'n Andy.* [d. September 26, 1972]

1895 **George Halas,** U.S. football player, coach, executive; founder and coach of the **Chicago Bears** and one of founders of the **National Football League.** [d. October 31, 1983]

1901 **Jascha Heifetz,** Russian-American violin virtuoso.

1905 **Ayn Rand,** U.S. novelist born in Russia; noted for her political and philosophical conservatism; originator of a doctrine called *Objectivism.* [d. March 6, 1982]

1911 **Jussi Bjørling (Johan Jonaton Bjørling),** Swedish operatic tenor. [d. September 9, 1960]

1914 **Renato Dulbecco,** Italian-American molecular biologist; Nobel Prize in physiology or medicine for study of interaction between tumor viruses and genetic material (with D. Baltimore and H. Temin), 1975.

1919 **Anne Fogarty,** U.S. fashion designer; noted for her feminine designs during the early 1950s. [d. January 15, 1980]

1926 **Valéry Giscard D'Estaing,** French political leader; President, 1974–81.

1931 **Andreas van Agt,** Dutch politician; Prime Minister of the Netherlands, 1977– .

Historical Events

962 **Otto I** is crowned **Holy Roman Emperor** at Rome.

1074 **Peace of Gerstungen** between **Henry IV** of Germany and the Saxons is promulgated.

1509 The Portuguese, under **Francisco de Almeida,** defeat Moslem fleet in the **Battle of Diu,** establishing Portuguese control of Indian waters.

1522 **Pope Leo X** bestows title *Defender of the Faith* on **Henry VIII** of England.

1775 British House of Commons declares **Massachusetts** to be in a state of rebellion.

his hibernation. If he sees his shadow, it indicates another six weeks of winter are forthcoming. (Especially significant in Punxsutawney, Pa., where *the* groundhog is said to reside.)

Religious Calendar

Feasts

Presentation of the Lord or
Candlemas or
Christ's Presentation or
Dia de la Candelaria or
Holiday of St. Simeon or

Purification of the Blessed Virgin Mary or
The Wives' Feast Celebration of the presentation of the Child Jesus to St. Simeon, and the Purification of Mary. Observed by Roman Catholics, Anglicans, and various Protestant churches.

The Saints

St. Adalbald of Ostrevant, martyr. [d. 652]
The Martyrs of Ebsdorf. [d. 880]
St. Joan de Lestonnac, widow and founder of the Religious of Notre Dame of Bordeaux. [d. 1640]

The Beatified

Blessed Maria Catherine Kasper. [beatified 1979]

1801 First parliament of the **United Kingdom of England and Ireland** meets.

1848 **Treaty of Guadalupe Hidalgo** ends the war with Mexico and provides for the cession of Texas, New Mexico, and California to the U.S. (**Mexican War**).

1872 The Netherlands cedes the **Gold Coast of Africa** to Great Britain.

1882 The **Knights of Columbus** are organized at New Haven, Connecticut.

1884 **Basutoland (Lesotho)** becomes a British Crown Colony.

1901 **Army Nurse Corps** is organized as a branch of the U.S. Army.

1916 British test armored motor cars, called *tanks*, for the first time (**World War I**).

1920 **Estonia** gains independence from Russia with the signing of the **Treaty of Dorpat.**

1922 *Ulysses* by **James Joyce** is published in Paris.

1932 **U.S. Reconstruction Finance Corporation** is established as a depression-relief measure.

1943 Last German troops surrender in Stalingrad pocket, completing Russian victory at **Stalingrad (World War II).**

1959 **Virginia schools** are desegregated, following Virginia State Supreme Court decision.

1960 Sit-in demonstrations begin in **Greensboro, N.C.,** to protest storekeepers' refusals to serve blacks.

1964 U.S. lunar probe *Ranger 6* effects lunar landing and begins transmission of the first close-up photographs of the moon.

1967 **General Anastasio Somoza Debayle,** candidate of the ruling Nationalist Liberal Party, is elected president of **Nicaragua.**

American Basketball Association, the second major American league, is formed.

1971 Major-General **Idi Amin** declares himself absolute ruler in Uganda and maintains control until his government is overthrown in 1979.

1973 **Philippine President Ferdinand E. Marcos** offers amnesty to Communists and other "subversives" but not to their leaders.

Pope Paul VI nominates thirty new cardinals, bringing membership of the College of Cardinals to 145.

1974 A new **Cultural Revolution** begins in the **Peoples' Republic of China,** including an anti-Confucius campaign.

1982 Photographs transmitted by U.S. space probe *Voyager 2* reveal four to six previously undiscovered moons orbiting **Saturn.**

February 3

Holidays

Mozambique	**Heroes' Day**
Paraguay	**St. Blas**
Puerto Rico	**Fiesta St. Blas** Feast of St. Blaise, patron of harvests.
São Tome and **Principe**	**Day of Martyrs** and **Liberation**
U.S.	**Four Chaplains Memorial Day** Honors Chaplains **Alexander Goode** (Jewish), **John P. Washington** (Roman Catholic), **George L. Fox** and **Clark V. Poling** (Protestant) who gave their life jackets to others and perished when the *Dorchester*, U.S. troopship, was sunk off the coast of Greenland, 1943.

Birthdates

590   **Pope St. Gregory I, the Great;** Pope, 590–604; responsible for sending St. Augustine to convert the Anglo-Saxons. [d. 604]

1735   **Count Ignacy Krasicki,** Polish poet and man of letters; a favorite of Frederick the Great. [d. March 14, 1801]

1793   **José Antonio de Sucre,** Venezuelan general and South American liberator; first President of Bolivia, 1826–28. [d. June 4, 1830]

1809   **Felix Mendelssohn (Jacob Ludwig Felix Mendelssohn-Bartholdy),** German composer, pianist; founder of the **Leipzig Conservatory of Music,** 1843. [d. November 4, 1847]

1811   **Horace Greeley,** U.S. journalist, editor, and politician; Congressman, 1848–52; nominated for president, 1872. [d. November 29, 1872]

1821   **Elizabeth Blackwell,** U.S. physician born in England; first woman in U.S. to gain an M.D. degree, 1849. [d. May 31, 1910]

1830   **Lord Robert Cecil, Third Marquess of Salisbury;** British Prime Minister, 1885–86, 1886–92, 1895–1902. [d. August 22, 1903]

1842   **Sidney Lanier,** U.S. poet, musician, and critic. [d. September 7, 1881]

1853   **Hudson Maxim,** U.S. inventor and explosives expert; developed and patented various powerful, increasingly stable explosive powders, which allowed for improvements in firearms and torpedoes. [d. May 6, 1927]

1873   **Hugh Montague Trenchard,** 1st Viscount Trenchard, British air marshal; principal organizer of the **Royal Air Force.** [d. February 10, 1956]

1874   **Gertrude Stein,** U.S. author, poet, novelist, critic; patron of the arts. [d. July 27, 1946]

1894   **Norman Rockwell,** U.S. illustrator, painter; known for his sentimental, realistic illustrations of American life. [d. November 8, 1978]

1895   **Carl Richard Soderbert,** Swedish-American engineer and educator; developer of the turbine engine. [d. October 17, 1979]

1897   **William White,** U.S. railroad executive. [d. April 6, 1967]

1898   **(Hugo) Alvar (Henrick) Aalto,** Finnish-American architect, city planner, furniture designer, and educator. [d. May 11, 1976]

1907   **James A(lbert) Michener,** U.S. novelist; Pulitzer Prize in fiction, 1947.

1909   **Simone Weil,** French mystic, social philosopher; an activist in French resistance during World War II. [d. August 24, 1943]

Historical Events

1014   **Sweyn Forkbeard, King of the Danes,** dies and is succeeded by **Canute II (the Great),** his son.

1194   **Henry VI** of Germany releases King **Rich-**

74

Religious Calendar

The Saints

St. Blaise, Bishop of Sebastea and martyr; patron of wool combers, wild animals, and all who suffer from afflictions of the throat. Also called **Blaize, Blase, Blasius.** [d. c. 316] (Optional Memorial)

St. Ia, virgin. [d. 6th century]

St. Laurence, Bishop of Spoleto. Also called The Enlightener. [d. 576]

St. Laurence, second Archbishop of Canterbury. [d. 619]

St. Werburga, virgin and abbess; patron of Chester. Daughter of King Wulfhere of Mercia. Also called **Werburgh, Wereburge, Wereburg.** [d. c. 700]

St. Anskar, Archbishop of Hamburg and Bremen. First missionary to northwestern Europe; patron of Norway, Sweden, and Denmark. Also called **Anscharius, Ansgar, Auscharius.** [d. 865] (Optional Memorial)

St. Margaret of England, virgin. [d. 1192]

The Beatified

Blessed Simon of Cascia, Augustinian friar. [d. 1348]

Blessed John Nelson, Jesuit priest and martyr. [d. 1578]

Blessed Stephen Bellesini, priest. [d. 1840]

Blessed Richard Pampuri. [beatified, 1981]

Blessed Maria Rivier. [beatified, 1982]

---

ard I of England, captured while on the Third Crusade.

1388   **Merciless Parliament** in England meets in opposition to King **Richard II.**

1488   **Bartholomeu Dias,** Portuguese navigator, lands at **Mossal Bay, Cape of Good Hope.**

1518   **Pope Leo X** imposes silence on Augustinian monks.

1521   **Magellan** discovers **Shark Island** in the Pacific.

1766   **Benjamin Franklin** begins testifying to House of Commons in London on unenforceability of the **Stamp Act.**

1777   **Felipe de Neve,** Spanish governor, arrives at Monterey, designating it the capital of the **Californias.**

1831   **Louis Charles, Duc de Nemours,** third son of Louis-Philippe of France, is elected King of the Belgians.

       U.S. copyright law is amended, making term of copyright twenty-eight years, with right of renewal for fourteen more. (This second term extension was increased to 47 years in 1976.)

1855   **Calcutta Railway** is opened.

1867   **Prince Mutsuhito** becomes Emperor of Japan at the age of 15 and reigns until 1912.

1915   Defeat of the last Boer rebels in South Africa brings an end to the **Boer War.**

1917   *S.S. Housatonic* is sunk by a German submarine, resulting in severing of diplomatic relations between Germany and the U.S. **(World War I).**

1925   The first **electric railway** in India opens in Bombay.

1954   **Battle of Dien Bien Phu** begins in French Indochina.

1958   **Benelux Economic Union** formally establishes the customs union of Belgium, Luxembourg, and the Netherlands, begun in 1948.

1960   British Prime Minister **Harold Macmillan** makes *Winds of Change* speech in Cape Town, South Africa, condemning apartheid.

1962   U.S. President **John F. Kennedy** orders a ban on nearly all U.S. trade with **Cuba.**

1966   Soviet spacecraft *Luna 9* lands successfully on the moon and begins relaying signals.

1972   **XI Winter Olympics** open in **Sapporo,** Japan.

1977   Ethiopian chief of state, Brigadier General **Teferi Bante,** is assassinated. Lieutenant Colonel **Mengistu Haile-Mariam** becomes the new government leader.

1978   China and the **European Economic Community** sign a five-year bilateral trade agreement.

February 4

Holidays

USO Anniversary
Sponsored by United Services Organization.

Angola **Commencement of the Armed Struggle**
Celebrates the beginning of the struggle for freedom from Portugal, 1961.

Sri Lanka **Independence Commemoration Day**
Celebrates independence from Great Britain, 1948.

Religious Calendar

The Saints

St. Phileas, Bishop of Thmuis and martyr. [d. 304]

St. Isidore of Pelusium, abbot. [d. c. 450]

St. Modan, abbot; titular saint of the High Church at Stirling, Scotland. [d. c. 550]

Birthdates

1746 **Thaddeus Kosciusko (Tadeusz Andrzej Bonawentura Kościuszko),** Polish general and national hero. [d. October 15, 1817]

1778 **Augustine Pyrame Candolle,** Swiss botanist, taxonomist; developed system of plant classification. [d. September 9, 1841]

1792 **James Gillespie Birney,** U.S. author, abolitionist; presidential candidate of the Liberty Party, 1840, 1844. [d. November 25, 1857]

1802 **Mark Hopkins,** U.S. educator, philosopher; chief proponent of the **gospel of wealth,** which stressed individualism and pursuit of wealth. [d. June 17, 1887]

1848 **Francis Wayland Ayer,** U.S. advertising pioneer; standardized contract relations with clients; first to use **market research;** Ayer's *American Annual Newspaper Directory* is a product of his procedure. [d. March 5, 1923]

1871 **Friedrich Ebert,** first President of German Reich, 1919–25. [d. February 28, 1925]

1875 **Ludwig Prandtl,** German physicist; the *Father of Aerodynamics.* [d. August 15, 1953]

1881 **Kliment Efremovich Voroshilov,** Russian Army marshal and political leader; directed operations that broke German siege of Leningrad, 1943; President of U.S.S.R., 1953–60. [d. December 3, 1969]

Fernand Leger, French Cubist painter. [d. August 17, 1955]

1895 **Nigel Bruce,** British actor. [d. October 8, 1953]

1897 **Ludwig Erhard,** German statesman, economist; Chancellor of West Germany, 1963–66. [d. May 5, 1977]

1902 **Charles (Augustus) Lindbergh,** (*The Lone Eagle*), U.S. aviator; Pulitzer Prize for his autobiography, *The Spirit of St. Louis,* 1953. [d. August 26, 1974]

1904 **McKinlay Kantor,** U.S. novelist; Pulitzer Prize in fiction, 1955. [d. October 11, 1977]

1912 **Erich Leinsdorf,** U.S. conductor, born in Austria; conductor of the Metropolitan Opera Co., 1939–43; 1957–61; musical director of the Boston Symphony, 1962–68.

1917 **Agha Muhammad Yahya Khan,** Pakistani statesman; President, 1969–71; responsible for first nation-wide elections based on universal suffrage, 1970. [d. August 8, 1980]

1918 **Ida Lupino,** British-born U.S. actress, director, producer.

1921 **Betty Friedan (Naomi Goldstein),** U.S. feminist and writer; founder of the **National Organization of Women (NOW),** a civil rights group dedicated to equality of opportunity for women.

Historical Events

900 **Louis, the Child,** is crowned King of Germany.

1111 **Treaty of Sutri** is signed, in which Holy Roman Emperor **Henry V** renounces investiture of **Pope Paschal II.**

1629 Monopoly of trade in the **St. Lawrence River** and Gulf is granted to **Sir William Alexander** and his partners.

1787 **Daniel Shays'** forces, in rebellion against the government of Massachusetts, are routed in Petersham, Massachusetts (**Shays' Rebellion**).

1789 **George Washington** is elected the first President of the several states, with **John Adams** as Vice-President.

St. Aldate, bishop and martyr. [d. c. 577]

St. Nicholas Studites, abbot. [d. 863]

St. Rembert, Archbishop of Hamburg and Bremen. Also called **Rimbert.** [d. 888]

St. Andrew Corsini, Bishop of Fiesole. Invoked to settle quarrels and discords. [d. 1373]

St. Gilbert of Sempringham, founder of the Gilbertine's, only medieval order of English origin. [d. 1189]

St. Joan of France, matron; founder of the Annonciades of Bourges. Daughter of Louis IX of France. Also called **Joan of Valois.** [d. 1505]

St. Joseph of Leonessa, Capuchin friar. [d. 1612]

St. John de Britto, Jesuit priest and martyr; missionary to India. [d. 1693]

St. Theophilus the Penitent. [death date unknown]

The Beatified

Blessed Rabanus Maurus, Bishop of Mainz. [d. 856]

Blessed Thomas Plumtree, martyr. [d. 1570]

1830	Britain, France, and Russia formally recognize Greek independence under British protection (**Conference of London**).
1861	**Confederate States of America,** of Alabama, Georgia, Florida, Louisiana, Mississippi, and South Carolina, are organized.
1870	**Museum of Fine Arts** in Boston is incorporated.
1874	**Battle of Kumasi** ends the **Ashanti War** between Ghana and Britain.
1887	**Interstate Commerce Act** is passed by the U.S. Congress.
1899	The **Philippines** rebel against U.S. control.
1904	Japan lays siege to **Port Arthur** on the outbreak of the **Russo-Japanese War.**
1913	**National Institute of Arts & Letters** is incorporated to further the cause of literature and fine arts in the U.S.
1915	**Battle of Masuria** frees East Prussia from the Russians (**World War I**).
	Germany announces that the waters around Great Britain are a war zone and that after February 18, 1915, enemy vessels will be destroyed without regard to safety of passengers or crew (**World War I**).
1919	The French government passes a law granting citizenship to select Algerian natives.
	Washington Conference delegates sign a treaty agreeing to respect China's sovereignty and maintain the *Open Door Policy*.
1924	British officials release **Mahatma Gandhi** from prison after two years.
1929	**Col. Charles A. Lindbergh** opens air mail service to Central America, carrying mail from Miami to Havana and to Belize, British Honduras.
1938	**Adolf Hitler** becomes German War Minister; von Ribbentrop appointed Foreign Minister.

1941	**United Service Organizations** is founded, to serve the social, educational, and religious needs of U.S. armed forces.
1945	**Yalta Conference** begins; President Franklin D. Roosevelt, Prime Minister Winston Churchill, and Premier Joseph Stalin meet to discuss post-war diplomacy.
1948	**Sri Lanka** (formerly Ceylon) becomes an independent member of the British Commonwealth of Nations.
1952	**United Nations Disarmament Commission** meets for the first time.
1962	**Francisco José Orlich Bolmarcich** is elected President of Costa Rica.
1964	**London *Times*** issues its first color Sunday supplement.
	24th Amendment to U.S. Constitution is adopted, abolishing the poll tax.
1971	**Rolls-Royce, Ltd.** of Great Britain declares bankruptcy.
1972	**Bangladesh** is officially recognized by Great Britain and seeks Commonwealth membership.
1974	**Grenada,** West Indies, gains independent status within the British Commonwealth.
	Symbionese Liberation Army kidnaps **Patricia Hearst,** granddaughter of newspaper publisher William Randolph Hearst.
1976	Earthquake in **Guatemala** kills 23,000.
	XII Winter Olympic Games open in Innsbruck, Austria.
1978	**Sri Lanka** modifies its government to a presidential system. **Junius Richard Jay Awardene** is sworn in as the first president.
1981	**Gro Harlem Brundtland** becomes the first woman premier of Norway.

February 5

Holidays

Finland	**Runeberg's Day**
	Celebration of birthday of Johan Ludvig Runeberg, national poet of Finland.
Mauritius	**Spring Festival**
Mexico	**Constitution Day**
	Celebrates anniversaries of Constitutions of 1857 and 1917.
San Marino	**Anniversary of the Liberation of the Republic.**
Tanzania	**Chama Cha Mapenduzi (CCM Day)**
	Commemorates the foundation of the Chama Cha Mapenduzi Party, 1976.

Birthdates

1534   **Giovanni de' Bardi,** Italian scholar and music patron; creator of **Florentine camerata,** which eventually developed into **opera.** [d. 1612]

1723   **John Witherspoon,** Scottish-American Presbyterian clergyman; President of the College of New Jersey (later **Princeton University**), 1768–94; a signer of the Declaration of Independence. [d. November 15, 1794]

1725   **James Otis,** American Revolutionary leader; best known for his oratory skills and his pamphleteering. [d. May 23, 1783]

1744   **John Jeffries,** American physician, scientist; a pioneer in aerial scientific observations (balloons). [d. September 16, 1819]

1770   **Alexandre Brongniart,** French scientist; the first to arrange the geological formations of the Tertiary Period in chronological order. [d. October 7, 1847]

1788   **Sir Robert Peel,** British statesman; Prime Minister, 1834–35; founder of London **Metropolitan Police Force** (hence police referred to as *bobbies*.) [d. July 2, 1850]

1799   **Dr. John Lindley,** botanist; pioneer in the development of classification system for plants. [d. November 1, 1865]

1837   **Dwight Lyman Moody,** U.S. evangelist; built the first YMCA building in America, in Chicago. Founded **Chicago Bible Institute,** now known as the **Moody Bible Institute.** [d. December 22, 1899]

1840   **John Boyd Dunlop,** Scottish veterinary surgeon; developer of the **pneumatic rubber tire.** [d. 1921]

Sir Hiram Stevens Maxim, British inventor born in U.S.; known for the invention of the recoil-operated **machine gun.** [d. November 24, 1916]

1848   **Joris Karl Huysmans (Charles Marie George Huysmans),** French novelist. [d. May 12, 1907]

Belle Starr (Myra Belle Shirley), U.S. outlaw. [d. February 3, 1889]

1888   **Cleveland Dodge,** U.S. businessman, philanthropist; Vice-President of Phelps Dodge Corporation, 1924–61. [d. November 24, 1982]

Bruce Austin Fraser, 1st Baron Fraser of North Cape, British naval officer; commander in chief of the Home Fleet, World War II; responsible for countering German U-boat attacks against Great Britain; First Sea Lord and Chief of Naval Staff, 1948–51 [d. February 12, 1981]

1898   **Ralph E. McGill,** U.S. journalist, spokesman for **Southern Progressive** position in politics; Pulitzer Prize in journalism, 1958. [d. February 3, 1969]

1900   **Adlai E(wing) Stevenson,** U.S. statesman and politician; Governor of Illinois, 1948–52; Democratic presidential candidate, 1951; 1956. [d. July 14, 1965]

1903   **Joan Whitney Payson,** U.S. philanthropist, sportswoman. [d. October 4, 1975]

U.S.   **Roger Williams Day**
Observed by American Baptists to celebrate the arrival of Roger Williams, their American founder, on the North American continent, 1631.

Martyrs of Japan 26 martyrs killed by Emperor Tagosama. [d. 1597]

St. Agatha, virgin, martyr; patron of Catania, Sicily, nurses, and bell-makers. Invoked against breast disease and any outbreak of fire. [death date unknown] Obligatory Memorial.

Religious Calendar

The Saints

St. Avitus, Bishop of Vienne. [d. c. 525]

St. Bertulf. Also called **Bertoul.** [d. c. 705]

SS. Indractus and Dominica, martyrs. Dominica also called **Drusa.** [d. c. 710]

St. Vodalus. Also called **Voel.** [d. c. 720]

St. Adelaide of Bellich, virgin, abbess. Also called **Alice.** [d. 1015]

1914   **William (Seward) Burroughs,** U.S. author; noted for his picaresque, avante-garde, and science-fiction novels which were widely distributed in the U.S. literary underground long before they achieved popular recognition.

         Sir Alan Lloyd Hodgkin, British physiologist; Nobel Prize in physiology or medicine for research on nerve cells and the sodium-potassium exchange (with A. F. Huxley and J. C. Eccles), 1963.

1915   **Robert Hofstadter,** U.S. physicist; Nobel Prize in physics for research on subatomic particles (with R. L. Mossbauer), 1961.

Historical Events

1265   **Pope Clement IV** is elected.

1556   **Truce of Vaucelles** between **Henry II** of France and **Philip II** of Spain ends the **Hapsburg-Valois Wars.**

1725   **Bering Expedition** sets out from St. Petersburg, Russia.

1811   The insanity of **George III** of England leads to the **Regency Act** and the Prince of Wales (later George IV) becomes the Prince Regent.

1818   **Marshall Bernadotte** becomes King of Sweden as **Charles John XIV.**

1884   **Grolier Club** of New York book lovers is founded.

1885   Belgium settles the frontiers of the French and **Belgian Congo.**

1917   **Mexican Constitution** is adopted.

1918   Formal separation of church and state goes into effect in **Russia.**

1919   **League of Nations** meets for the first time in Paris, with U.S. President Woodrow Wilson as chairman.

1945   U.S. troops under the command of **General Douglas MacArthur** enter Manila **(World War II).**

1960   **Felipe Herrera** of Chile is elected first president of the Inter-American Development Bank.

1965   People's Republic of China forms a patriotic front to overthrow the **Thailand** government, forcing Thailand's withdrawal from SEATO.

1975   U.S. cuts off military aid to **Turkey** as a result of the Cyprus dispute.

February 6

Holidays

New Zealand   **Waitangi Day** or **New Zealand Day**
Commemorates the signing of the Waitangi Treaty between the European leaders and Maori tribesmen, 1840.

U.S. (Arizona)   **Arbor Day**

Birthdates

1665   **Anne, Queen of England,** 1702–14. [d. August 1, 1714]

1756   **Aaron Burr,** U.S. politician; killed Alexander Hamilton in duel; known for his controversial attempts to establish an independent nation in the American West as well as other schemes to solicit foreign interest in the western lands and Mexico. [d. September 14, 1836]

1802   **Sir Charles Wheatstone,** British physician; developer of the **Wheatstone bridge,** a device for precision measurement of electrical resistance. [d. October 19, 1875]

1820   **Thomas Clark Durant,** U.S. railroad magnate; one of the prime movers behind the completion of the **Union Pacific Railroad;** with Leland Stanford (March 9), drove the golden spike linking the Union Pacific with the Central Pacific at Promontory Point, Utah. [d. October 5, 1885]

1833   **James (*Jeb*) Ewell Brown Stuart,** Confederate cavalry commander in U.S. Civil War. [d. May 12, 1864]

1845   **Isidor Straus,** U.S. merchant born in Germany; became partner and eventually half-owner of Macy's Department Store in New York City. With his wife, perished on the *Titanic.* [d. April 15, 1912]

1878   **Walter Boughton Pitkin,** U.S. psychologist, journalist, editor; best known for his book, *Life Begins at Forty.* [d. January 25, 1953]

1887   **Ernest Gruening,** U.S. politician, journalist, editor; Governor of Alaska, 1939–53; U.S. Senator, 1959–69. [d. June 26, 1974]

1892   **William P. Murphy,** U.S. physician; Nobel Prize in physiology or medicine for discovery of liver therapies against **anemia** (with G. H. Whipple and G. R. Minot), 1934.

1894   **Eric (Honeywood) Partridge,** British lexicographer, author; known for his *Dictionary of Slang and Unconventional Usage.* [d. June 1, 1979]

1895   **George Herman (Babe) Ruth,** U.S. baseball player; elected to Hall of Fame, 1936. [d. August 16, 1948]

Robert Marion La Follette, Jr., U.S. politician, publishing and broadcasting executive; Governor of Wisconsin, 1900–06; U.S. Senator, 1906–53. [d. February 24, 1953]

1902   **Louis Nizer,** U.S. lawyer, author, born in England; best known for his legal defense of American celebrities.

1903   **Claudio Arrau,** Chilean-American concert pianist; a child prodigy.

1905   **Wladyslaw Gomulka,** Polish political leader; First Secretary of Polish Communist Party, 1956. [d. September 1, 1982]

1911   **Ronald (Wilson) Reagan,** U.S. actor, politician; Governor of California, 1967–1975; President of the United States, 1981– .

1912   **Eva Braun,** mistress of Adolf Hitler. [d. April 30, 1945]

1913   **Mary Leakey,** British archaeologist; with her husband, Louis S(eymour) B(azett) Leakey (August 7), made significant discoveries in the Olduvai Gorge, Africa, of fossil evidence for early hominids.

1919   **Zsa Zsa Gabor (Sari Gabor),** Hungarian-American actress.

1931   **(Maria Estela) Isabel (Martinez) de Perón,** Argentine dancer, political leader; succeeded her husband, Juan Perón (October 8), as President of Argentina, 1974–76.

1932   **François Truffaut,** French filmmaker, producer, director, writer, actor.

Religious Calendar

The Saints

St. Dorothy, virgin, martyr; patron of gardeners and florists. Also called **Dorothea.** [d. c. 303]

SS. Mel and **Melchu,** bishops. [d. 488]

St. Vedast, Bishop of Arras; patron of children who are slow to walk. Also called **Gaston, Vaast.** [d. 539]

St. Aumand, missionary and bishop; father of monasticism in ancient Belgium; one of the most imposing figures of the Merovingian epoch. Also called **Amand.** [d. c. 679]

St. Guarinus, Cardinal-Bishop of Palestrina. [d. 1159]

St. Hildegund, widow and prioress. [d. 1183]

St. Paul Miki and his companions, first martyrs of the Far East. Obligatory Memorial.

The Beatified

Blessed Raymund of Fitero, abbot. Founded the military order of the Knights of Calatrava. [d. 1163]

Blessed Angelo of Furcio. [d. 1327]

Historical Events

46 B.C. **Gaius Julius Caesar** gains victory at Thapsus, in North Africa, over the adherents of Pompey under Cato, Metellus Scipio, and King Juba II.

337 **Julius I** is elected Pope.

1682 **Sieur de La Salle** sights the Mississippi River.

1685 **Charles II** of Great Britain dies and is succeeded by **James I.**

1778 **Britain** declares war on France.

France and the U.S. form an offensive and defensive alliance (**American Revolution**).

1788 **Massachusetts** ratifies the Constitution and joins the Union as the sixth state.

1838 Zulu warriors massacre Dutch settlers in **Natal, South Africa.**

1840 **Treaty of Waitangi** is signed, granting Queen Victoria sovereignty over New Zealand.

1862 **Battle of Fort Henry** (Kentucky) results in an early victory for Union troops under **General Ulysses S. Grant (U.S. Civil War).**

1865 **General Robert E. Lee** is appointed Commander in Chief of the Confederate armies (**U.S. Civil War**).

1897 Union with Greece is proclaimed by **Crete.**

1899 U.S. Congress ratifies peace treaty ending the **Spanish-American War.**

1915 The British Cunard liner *Lusitania* flies the American flag as protection against German attack during its passage through the declared war zone of British waters (**World War I**).

1922 **Washington Conference,** with delegates from Japan, England, France, Italy, and U.S. ends after fixing the ratio of naval armaments and restricting **poison gas** and **submarine warfare.**

1933 **The 20th Amendment** to the U.S. Constitution is ratified, moving Inauguration Day from March 4 to January 20 and establishing rules of succession in the event of the death of the president.

1943 **General Dwight D. Eisenhower** is appointed Commander in Chief of all Allied forces in North Africa (**World War II**).

1950 President Harry S. Truman invokes national emergency provisions of the **Taft-Hartley Act** and appoints a fact-finding board to report to him in the soft-coal dispute.

85 persons are killed and about 500 injured when a railroad train plunges from a temporary wooden overpass in Woodbridge, New Jersey.

1952 **King George VI** of Great Britain dies and is succeeded by his daughter, **Elizabeth II.**

1956 First black student is enrolled in the **University of Alabama.**

1969 Peruvian President **Juan Velasco Alvarado** announces the seizure of all the assets of the **International Petroleum Co.**

1970 **European Economic Community** and **Yugoslavia** sign their first full-scale trade pact, the first such agreement between the EEC and an Eastern European nation.

1974 U.S. House of Representatives approves an **impeachment** inquiry against President **Richard M. Nixon** by the House Judiciary Committee.

Grenada proclaims its independence from Great Britain.

1977 **Queen Elizabeth II** observes the 25th anniversary of her accession to the throne of Great Britain.

February 7

Holidays

Grenada   **Independence Day**
Commemorates the achievement of independence from Great Britain, 1974.

Religious Calendar

The Saints

St. Adaucus, martyr. Also called **Adauctus.** [d. 303]
St. Moses, bishop. Apostle of the Saracens, nomad tribes of the Syro-Arabian Desert. [d. c. 372]

Birthdates

1478   **Sir Thomas More,** English statesman, humanist; well-known for his treatise *Utopia*, a description of a communal lifestyle that allowed equality for all members. Beheaded for treason, 1478, on order of King Henry VIII. Canonized, 1935. [d. July 6, 1535]

1693   **Anna, Empress of Russia,** 1730–40. [d. October 28, 1740]

1804   **John Deere,** U.S. manufacturer; introduced the **steel plow** in the U.S., 1837; founder of Deere & Co., 1868. [d. May 17, 1886]

1812   **Charles (John Huffon) (*Boz*) Dickens,** British novelist; noted for his graphic depiction of life of the poor in Engand; author of *Oliver Twist* and *David Copperfield*, among many others. [d. June 9, 1870]

1814   **George Palmer Putnam,** U.S. publisher. [d. December 20, 1872]

1824   **Sir William Huggins,** British astronomer; first to elucidate the similarity in structure between the sun and the stars. [d. May 12, 1910]

1834   **Dmitri Ivanovich Mendeleev,** Russian chemist; stimulated extensive use of the **periodic table of elements.** [d. February 2, 1907]

1837   **Sir James Augustus Murray,** Scottish lexicographer, philologist; chief work of his life was the **Oxford English Dictionary,** which he planned and edited, based on materials collected over many years. [d. July 26, 1915]

1867   **Laura Ingalls Wilder,** U.S. author of fiction for juveniles; best known for her stories of the pioneer life in the American West. [d. January 10, 1957]

1870   **Alfred Adler,** Austrian psychiatrist; advanced theories of **inferiority complex** as cause of psychopathic behavior. [d. May 28, 1937]

1883   **Eubie Blake,** U.S. pianist, singer, vaudeville performer; awarded Presidential Medal of Freedom, 1981. [d. February 12, 1983]

1885   **(Harry) Sinclair Lewis,** U.S. novelist; first American to win Nobel Prize in literature, 1930. [d. January 10, 1951]

1889   **H(aroldson) L(afayette) Hunt,** U.S. businessman; with **J. Paul Getty** (December 15), considered one of the richest men in U.S. history. [d. February 17, 1974]

1899   **Arvid Y. Pelshe,** Russian military officer, statesman; last member of the Soviet leadership who took part in the Bolshevik Revolution of 1917. [d. June 1, 1983?]

1905   **Ulf Svante von Euler,** Swedish physiologist; Nobel Prize in physiology or medicine for investigations into substances found at the end of nerve fibers (with B. Katz and J. Axelrod), 1970. [d. March 10, 1983]

1909   **Buster Crabbe (Clarence Linden Crabbe),** U.S. athlete, actor; Olympic gold medalist, 1932; star of numerous movie series in the 1930s and 1940s including *Flash Gordon* and *Buck Rogers*. [d. April 23, 1983]

Historical Events

1807   Napoleon engages Russians and Prussians at Battle of Eylau (**War of the Third Coalition.**)

St. Richard, King of the West Saxons. [d. 720]

St. Luke the Younger. Surnamed **Thaumaturgus** or the Wonderworker. [d. c. 946]

St. Ronan, Bishop of Kilmaronen. [death date unknown]

St. Theodore of Heraclea, martyr. Surnamed **Stratelates,** General of the Army. Also called **Theodorus.** [death date unknown]

The Beatified

Blessed Rizzerio, Franciscan friar. [d. 1236]

Blessed Antony of Stroncone, lay-brother. [d. 1461]

Blessed Thomas Sherwood, martyr. [d. 1578]

Blessed James Sales, Jesuit priest, and **Blessed William Saultemouche,** Jesuit lay-brother, martyrs. [d. 1593]

Blessed Giles Mary. Also called **Giles Mary-of-St.-Joseph.** [d. 1812]

Blessed Eugenia Smet, founder of the Helpers of the Holy Souls. Also called **Mother Mary of Providence.** [d. 1871]

1865 **Hampton Roads Conference** takes place aboard the *River Queen*; Lincoln meets with Confederate peace commissioners.

1868 **Shinto** is officially adopted as the state religion of Japan.

1883 First meeting of **Irish Nationalist League.**

John L. Sullivan defeats **Paddy Ryan** in a bare knuckles contest to win the American heavyweight championship.

1904 Fire in **Baltimore** destroys 2600 buildings; it is the largest fire in the U.S. since the Chicago fire of 1871.

1924 The **Tangiers Convention** is signed by Britain, France, and Spain, providing for permanent neutralization of the **Tangier Zone** and government by international commission.

1925 Chinese delegates withdraw from the second **Opium Conference** at Geneva.

1940 Great Britain nationalizes its railroads.

1941 British capture **Benghazi (World War II).**

1945 **General Douglas MacArthur** enters **Manila** more than three years after he had been forced out by the Japanese (**World War II**).

1950 Great Britain and the U.S. recognize the governments of **Laos** and **Cambodia** and the Vietnam government headed by Bao Dai in **French Indochina.**

1968 All ten Canadian provincial premieres approve Prime Minister Lester Pearson's proposal to give the French language equal status with English throughout Canada.

Six Latin-American nations sign a convention at Bogotá, Colombia, establishing the **Andean Development Corporation.**

1969 **Diana Crump** becomes first woman jockey to race at a U.S. pari-mutuel track.

1970 Roman Catholic marchers in ten **Northern Ireland** cities defy the two-day-old **Public Order Act,** establishing conditions for demonstrations.

1971 Swiss voters approve a referendum giving women the right to vote in federal elections and to hold office.

1981 Fire sweeps through 20 floors of the **Las Vegas Hilton** hotel, killing eight and injuring at least 200.

1982 **Luis Alberto Monage Alvarez** is elected President of Costa Rica.

February 8

Holidays

Iraq	**Eighth of February Revolution**
Norway	**Narvik Sun Pageant**
	Celebrates the return of the sun after its winter absence.

Religious Calendar

The Saints

St. Kew, virgin; patron of St. Kew, Cornwall. Also called **Ciwa, Kuet,** or **Kywere.** [d. c. 5th cent.]

St. Nicetius, Bishop of Besancon. Also called **Nizier.** [d. c. 611]

Birthdates

1577 **Robert Burton,** (Democritus Junior), English clergyman and author; noted for his writings on melancholy, its causes and cures. [d. January 25, 1640]

1819 **John Ruskin,** British writer, art critic, reformer; noted for his writings on art and society. [d. January 20, 1900]

1820 **William Tecumseh Sherman,** Union Army general in U.S. Civil War. [d. February 14, 1891]

1825 **Henry Walter Bates,** British naturalist, South American traveler; known for his expeditions and recovery of unknown species in the Amazon. [d. February 16, 1892]

1828 **Jules Verne,** French writer; known especially for his science fiction. Légion d'Honneur, 1892. [d. March 24, 1905]

1851 **Kate O'Flaherty Chopin,** U.S. novelist, short-story writer. [d. August 22, 1904]

1878 **Martin Buber,** Austrian-Jewish philosopher and theologian; best known for his espousal of *I-Thou* relationships. [d. June 13, 1965]

1886 **Charles Ruggles,** U.S. comedic character actor of the 1930s and 1940s. [d. December 23, 1970]

1888 **Dame Edith Evans,** British stage and film actress. [d. October 14, 1976]

1906 **Chester Carlson,** U.S. physicist; inventor of **xerography,** 1937. [d. September 19, 1968]

1920 **Lana Turner,** U.S. actress.

1925 **Jack Lemmon,** U.S. actor.

1931 **James Dean (James Byron),** U.S. actor. [d. September 30, 1955]

1932 **John Williams,** U.S. conductor, composer; composer of numerous film scores, including that for *Star Wars*; conductor of Boston Pops Orchestra, 1980– .

Historical Events

1587 **Mary, Queen of Scots,** is beheaded at Fotheringay Castle in England.

1690 French and Indians attack **Schenectady,** New York. (**French and Indian Wars**)

1693 **College of William and Mary,** the second oldest in the U.S., is chartered.

1725 **Peter the Great** of Russia dies and is succeeded by **Catherine I,** his Empress.

1849 **Roman National Assembly** divests the Pope of all governing power and proclaims a republic.

1861 **Jefferson Davis** is chosen president and **Alexander H. Stephens** vice-president of the **Confederate States of America.**

1862 Union forces take **Roanoke Island, N.C.,** from the Confederacy (**U.S. Civil War**).

1863 Prussia allies with Russia to suppress Polish insurrection (**Alvensleben Convention**).

1887 **Interstate Commerce Act** is passed in the U.S., chiefly to regulate railways.

1908 **Sergei Rachmaninoff** conducts premiere of his *Second Symphony in E Minor* with the orchestra of Moscow Philharmonic Society.

1910 **Boy Scouts of America** are incorporated.

1915 *Birth of a Nation,* one of the most celebrated films of its time, is first shown at Clune's Auditorium in Los Angeles.

St. Elfleda, virgin and abbess of Whitby; daughter of Oswy, King of Northumbria. Also called **Aelbfled, Aelfflaed.** [d. 714]

St. Cuthman. [d. c. 900]

St. Meingold, martyr; patron of bakers and millers. [d. c. 892]

St. Stephen of Muret, abbot. Sometimes called **Stephen of Grandmont.** [d. 1124]

St. John of Matha, priest; co-founder of the Order of the Most Holy Trinity; also called the Trinitarian Order for the Redemption of Captives. [d. 1213]

St. Jerome Emiliani, founder of the Somaschi; patron saint of orphans and abandoned children.

Also called **Jerom Miliani.** Feast formerly July 20. [d. 1537] Optional Memorial.

The Beatified

Blessed Peter Igneus, Cardinal-Bishop of Albano. [d. 1089]

Blessed Isaiah of Cracow, Augustinian friar. [d. 1471]

1920	Odessa is taken by Bolshevik forces (**Russian Revolution**).
1937	**General Francisco Franco** captures **Malaga** with Italian support (**Spanish Civil War**).
1949	**Cardinal Mindszenty,** Primate of Hungary, is convicted of treason and espionage and sentenced to life imprisonment.
1950	**U.S. War Claims Commission** rules that 120,000 former U.S. prisoners of war of Germany and Japan will receive $1 for each day of imprisonment because of substandard rations.
1962	**Argentina** breaks diplomatic relations with **Cuba.**
1965	South Vietnamese Air Force planes, accompanied by U.S. jet fighters, bomb and strafe a military communications center in **North Vietnam.**
1966	**Declaration of Honolulu** is issued by U.S. President Lyndon Johnson and South Vietnamese Premier Ky outlining both nations' political and military policies in **South Vietnam.**
	Vatican office charged with the censure of books is abolished.
1969	*The Saturday Evening Post* publishes its last issue, ending its 148-year history.
1974	*Skylab 4* crew returns to earth after a record 84 days, 1 hour, 16 minutes in space.
1977	**Larry C. Flynt,** publisher of *Hustler* magazine, is convicted in a test case of obscenity pandering.
1979	U.S. severs military ties with **Nicaragua.**

February 9

Holidays

Lebanon   **St. Maron's Day**
Commemorates massacres of
Maronite Christians by Druzes.

Religious Calendar

The Saints

St. Apollonia, virgin and martyr; patron of dentists.
Invoked against toothache and dental diseases. [d.
249]

Birthdates

1773 **William Henry Harrison,** U.S. politician,
statesman; President for only 32 days,
March 4–April 4, 1841. First U.S. president
to die in office. [d. April 4, 1841]

1814 **Samuel Jones Tilden,** U.S. politician, lawyer; best known for his participation in the
overthrow of the Tweed Ring; U.S. presidential candidate, 1876 (lost the election
by one electoral vote to Rutherford B.
Hayes). [d. August 4, 1886]

1819 **Lydia Estes Pinkham,** U.S. patent-medi-
cine manufacturer; creator of **Mrs. Lydia
E. Pinkham's Vegetable Compound,** an
advertising phenomenon of the time. [d.
May 17, 1883]

1853 **Sir Leander Starr Jameson (Doctor
Jameson),** Scottish physician, statesman
in South Africa; leader of the Jameson Raid
during the **Boer War** in South Africa;
Prime Minister of Cape Colony, 1904–08. [d.
November 26, 1917]

1865 **Mrs. Patrick Campbell (Beatrice Stella
Tanner),** British stage actress, for whom
George Bernard Shaw created the part of
Eliza Doolittle in *Pygmalion.* [d. April 9,
1940]

1866 **George Ade,** U.S. humorist, playwright;
noted for his short, humorous fables of the
common man. [d. May 16, 1944]

1874 **Amy (Lawrence) Lowell,** U.S. poet, critic;
Pulitzer Prize in poetry, 1925. [d. May 12,
1925]

1891 **Ronald Colman,** British actor. [d. May 19,
1958]

Pietro Nenni, Italian political leader; head
of Italian Socialist Party, 1949–69. [d. January 1, 1980]

1909 **Dean Rusk,** U.S. government official; Secretary of State, 1961–69.

1910 **Jacques Lucien Monod,** French biochemist; Nobel Prize in physiology or medicine for research in genetic control of enzymes, (with F. Jacob and A. M. Lwoff),
1965. [d. May 31, 1976]

1923 **Brendan (Francis) Behan,** Irish playwright. [d. March 20, 1964]

Kathryn Grayson (Zelma Hendrick), U.S.
singer, actress.

1928 **Roger Mudd,** U.S. television newsman.

Historical Events

1555 **Bishop John Hooper,** English prelate and
martyr, is burned at the stake.

1674 **Treaty of Westminster** ends the war between Holland and Great Britain.

1798 France dissolves the **Swiss Confederation**
and decrees the establishment of a **Helvetic Republic** in its place.

1801 **Peace of Lunéville** between France and
Austria is signed, signalling the end of the
Holy Roman Empire.

1849 Giuseppe Mazzini proclaims a Republic in
Rome.

1861 Constitution of **Confederate States of
America** is promulgated.

1870 **U.S. Weather Bureau** is established by
Congress as part of **Signal Corps.**

1904 Russian cruisers *Variag* and *Korietz* are
sunk off Korea by the Japanese (**Russo-
Japanese War**).

1909 The Franco-German agreement over **Morocco** is signed, with Germany recognizing France's special position in Morocco in
return for economic concessions.

St. Sabinus, Bishop of Canosa. [d. c. 566]

St. Ansbert, Bishop of Rouen. [d. c. 695]

St. Alto, abbot. [d. c. 760]

St. Teilo, bishop. [d. 6th cent.]

St. Nicephorus, martyr and layman. [death date unknown]

The Beatified

Blessed Marianus Scotus. [d. 1088]

1926	The Viceroy of India announces the creation of the **Royal Indian Navy** and reconstruction of the **Indian Mercantile Marine.**
1929	The **Litvinov Protocol,** an eastern pact for renunciation of war, is signed at Moscow by Russia, Poland, Romania, Estonia, and Latvia.
1934	**Balkan Pact** between Greece, Romania, Turkey, and Yugoslavia is signed.
1941	German troops cross to North Africa under command of **Marshal Erwin Rommel (World War II).**
1942	France's *Normandie* burns at the pier in New York City.
1943	The Japanese evacuate **Guadalcanal Island (World War II).**
1970	Forty-one persons are killed in an avalanche in **Val d'Isere**, France.
1971	Worst **earthquake** since 1933 strikes southern California, measuring 6.5 on the Richter scale; 60 lives are lost and several hundred people are injured.
1977	The dramatization of Alex Haley's *Roots* sets new television viewing records in the U.S.
1978	**Canada** expels 11 Soviet diplomats for operating a highly sophisticated spy ring.
1981	Polish Premier **Josef Pinkowski** is replaced by **Gen. Wojciech Jaruzelski** in the face of continuing labor unrest.

February 10

Holidays

Malta **St. Paul's Shipwreck**
Commemorates wreck of the
Christian apostle St. Paul off the
coast of Malta in A.D. 60

Religious Calendar

The Saints

St. Soteris, virgin and martyr. Also called **Coteris.**
[d. 304]

Birthdates

1775 **Charles Lamb,** British essayist, critic; active in British literary circles during the late 18th century; close friend of S. T. Coleridge (October 21). [d. December 27, 1834]

1824 **Samuel Plimsall,** British social reformer leader of shipping reform; known as *The Sailors' Friend. Plimsall's mark,* the load line allowed by law on ships, is named for him. [d. 1898]

1846 **Ira Remsen,** U.S. chemist; discovered **saccharin.** [d. March 4, 1927]

1859 **Etienne Alexandre Mitterand,** French statesman; President of the French Republic, 1920–24. [d. April 6, 1943]

1868 **William Allen White** (*the Sage of Emporia*), U.S. journalist, editor; Pulitzer Prize in editorial writing, 1923; in biography (posthumously), 1947. [d. January 29, 1944]

1890 **Boris (Leonidovich) Pasternak,** Russian poet, novelist; Nobel Prize in literature, 1958 (refused). [d. May 30, 1960]

1892 **Ivo Andrić,** Yugoslav novelist, short-story writer, poet; Nobel Prize in literature, 1961. [d. March 13, 1975]

1893 **Jimmy Durante,** U.S. comedian, vaudeville performer. [d. January 29, 1980]

1894 **Harold Macmillan,** British statesman; Prime Minister, 1957–63.

1897 **John Franklin Enders,** U.S. microbiologist; Nobel Prize in physiology or medicine for research on polio virus (with T. H. Weller and F. C. Robbins), 1954.

1898 **Dame Judith Anderson,** Australian actress.

Bertolt Brecht, German dramatist, poet. [d. August 11, 1956]

1900 **Cevdet Sunay,** Turkish statesman, political leader; President of Turkish Republic, 1960–66. [d. May 22, 1982]

1902 **Walter Houser Brattain,** U.S. physicist; Nobel Prize in physics for the development of the **electronic transistor** (with W. Shockley and J. Bardeen), 1956.

1913 **(Albert) Merriam Smith,** U.S. journalist; called the *Dean of the White House Correspondents;* Pulitzer Prize in national reporting, 1964. [d. April 13, 1970]

1927 **Leontyne Price,** U.S. operatic soprano.

1950 **Mark Spitz,** U.S. Olympic swimmer; first athlete to win seven gold medals in a single Olympic Games, 1972.

Historical Events

1364 **Treaty of Brünn,** a family pact of succession between the **Luxemburgs** and the **Hapsburgs,** is signed.

1495 **Aberdeen University** in Scotland is founded.

1567 **Lord Darnley** dies in a gunpowder explosion; his wife, **Mary, Queen of Scots,** is suspected of murder.

1763 France cedes **Canada** to England at the **Treaty of Paris,** ending the **French and Indian War.**

The Seven Years' War between Great Britain and Spain ends with the signing of the **Treaty of Paris.**

1840 **Queen Victoria** of England marries **Prince Albert** of Saxe-Coburg-Gotha.

Upper and Lower Canada are united.

1846 The **Mormon exodus** to the American West begins.

St. Scholastica, virgin; sister of **St. Benedict,** and first Benedictine nun. Patron of Benedictine nuns and nunneries, and of children in convulsions. Invoked against storms. [d. 543] Obligatory Memorial.

St. Trumwin, Bishop of the Picts. [d. c. 690]

St. Austreberta, virgin. Also called **Eustreberta.** [d. 704]

St. Merewenna, Abbess of Romsey. [d. 10th cent.]

St. William of Maleval. [d. 1157]

The Beatified

Blessed Hugh of Fosses. [d. 1164]

Blessed Clare of Rimini, widow. [d. 1346]

1899	The use of the **Revised Version of the Bible** in church services is authorized by the Church of England.
1916	German government informs the U.S. that after March 1, 1916, armed merchantmen will be treated as warships and attacked without warning (**World War I**).
1926	A treaty designed to control the smuggling of liquor is signed by the U.S. and Spain.
1944	**PAYE (pay-as-you-earn) system of income tax** is introduced in Britain.
1950	**Klaus E. J. Fuchs,** British atomic scientist, confesses to revealing atomic secrets to the Soviets.
1960	French President Charles de Gaulle dissolves the **Algerian Home Guard.**
1962	Soviets release U.S. U-2 pilot **Francis Gary Powers** in Berlin in exchange for convicted Soviet agent **Rudolf Abel.**
1963	**Third Afro-Asian People's Solidarity Conference,** at Moshi, Tanganyika, approves resolutions for the use of violence to end **apartheid** in South Africa and an economic boycott of Portugal.
1964	**Nationalist China** severs diplomatic relations with France.
1967	The **25th Amendment** to the U.S. Constitution is ratified, providing a contingency plan for **presidential succession.**
1970	**Arab terrorists** kill one Israeli and wound 11 persons in an attack at a **Munich**, West Germany, airport.
1974	British coal miners begin a strike which causes Prime Minister **Edward Heath** to dissolve Parliament and call for a general election.
1975	**The Eritrean Liberation Front** launches new offensives in northern Ethiopia.
	National Awami (Opposition) **Party** is banned in Pakistan.
1977	Soviet dissident **Yuri Orlov** is arrested in the Soviet Union.
1978	**The National Organization of Cypriot Struggle** is dissolved.

February 11

Holidays

Cameroon	**Youth Day**
	Dedicated to children and young people of the nation.
Iran	**Revolution Day**
Japan	**Empire Day** or **National Foundation Day**
	Commemorates founding of the nation in 660 B.C. by the first emperor, Jimmu Tenno.
Liberia	**Armed Forces Day**
	Public holiday honoring professional army, navy, and militia.
U.S.	**National Inventors Day**
U.S. (Michigan)	**White Shirt Day**
	Observed as a day of recognition of the dignity of work and the anniversary of the

Birthdates

1535 **Pope Gregory XIV,** pope 1590–91. [d. October 16, 1591]

1800 **William Talbot,** British physicist; first to produce **paper positives,** a landmark discovery in **photography,** 1841. [d. September 17, 1877]

1812 **Alexander Hamilton Stephens,** U.S. political leader, lawyer; Vice-President of the Confederacy during U.S. Civil War., 1861–65. [d. March 4, 1883]

1833 **Melville Weston Fuller,** U.S. lawyer; eighth Chief Justice of the U.S. Supreme Court. [d. July 4, 1910]

1839 **Josiah Willard Gibbs,** U.S. physicist; considered to be the greatest American theoretical scientist up to his time. [d. April 28, 1903]

1847 **Thomas Alva Edison** U.S. inventor; with over 1000 patents to his credit, including the electric light bulb, the phonograph, and an early version of the movie camera, he is the archetypical inventor. [d. October 18, 1931]

1863 **John Fitzgerald** (*Honey Fitz*), U.S. newspaper publisher, banker, insurance broker. [d. October 2, 1950]

1898 **Leo Szilard,** U.S. physicist; developed first method of separating isotopes of radioactive elements. [d. May 30, 1964]

1907 **William Jaird Levitt,** U.S. building executive; developer of Levittown, N.Y.

1909 **Joseph Leo Mankiewicz,** U.S. writer, film director; director of *Cleopatra* and *Sleuth.*

1912 **Rudolf Firkusny,** Czech-American pianist; a child prodigy, noted especially for his interpretation of Beethoven.

1920 **Faruk I** (or **Farouk**), King of Egypt, 1936–52; abdicated after a coup led by **Gamal Abdel Nasser.** [d. March 18, 1965]

1921 **Lloyd Millard Bentsen, Jr.,** U.S. politician, businessman; U.S. Senator, 1971– .

1926 **Leslie Nielsen,** U.S. actor.

1934 **Mary Quant,** British fashion designer.

1936 **Burt Reynolds,** U.S. actor, director.

1941 **Sergio Mendes,** Brazilian musician.

1947 **Emily Harris,** U.S. revolutionary; member of the **Symbionese Liberation Army.**

Historical Events

1573 **Sir Francis Drake** of England first views the Pacific Ocean.

1730 **Peter II** of Russia dies and is succeeded by Anna, daughter of Ivan V.

1755 **Severndroog** and other strongholds on the coast of India are taken by British forces, providing for the establishment of the British Empire in **India.**

	1937 sit-down strike in Flint, Michigan.	**St. Caedmon,** monk. *The Father of English Sacred Poetry.* [d. c. 680]
Vatican City State	**Anniversary of Lateranensi** Commemorates the independence of the State of Vatican City and the recognition of the sovereignty of the Holy See, established by the Lateran Treaty, 1929.	**St. Benedict of Aniane,** abbot. [d. 821] **St. Paschal I,** Pope; elected Bishop of Rome 817. [d. 824] **Feast of the Appearing of Our Lady at Lourdes,** celebrating the appearances of the Virgin to Bernadette Soubirous, her sister, and a friend at a grotto in Lourdes, France, 1858. Optional Memorial.

Religious Calendar

The Saints

St. Saturninus, priest, **St. Dativus,** senator, and other martyrs. [d. 304]

St. Lucius, Bishop of Adrianople and martyr. [d. 350]

St. Lazarus, Bishop of Milan. [d. c. 450]

St. Gobnet, virgin. [d. 5th cent.]

St. Severinus, abbot. [d. 507]

1768 **Massachusetts Circular Letter** is sent to assemblies of 12 other American colonies denouncing the **Townshend Acts** of Great Britain.

1809 **Robert Fulton** receives a patent for his **steamboat** invention.

1810 **Napoleon** marries **Maria-Luisa of Austria.**

1826 **London University** is chartered.

1873 **King Amadeo I** of Spain abdicates and Spain is declared a republic.

1922 **Honduras** is declared an independent republic.

1929 **Lateran Treaty** between Italy and the Holy See is made, establishing Vatican City as a separate, independent Papal state.

1945 **Yalta Conference** ends (see February 4).

1965 People's Republic of China and Algeria sign an agreement providing for Chinese military aid to **Algeria.**

1975 **Margaret Thatcher** becomes head of Great Britain's Conservative Party, the first woman to ever head a political party in Britain.

Col. **Richard Ratsimandrava,** President of the **Malagasy Republic,** is assassinated in the capital city of Tananarive.

1976 **Popular Movement for the Liberation of Angola** is recognized by the **Organization for African Unity.**

February 12

Holidays

Burma	**Union Day** Commemorates formation of Union of Burma, 1947.
U.S. (Georgia)	**Georgia Day** or **Oglethorpe Day** Legal holiday commemorating the landing of James Edward Oglethorpe and his colonists at Savannah, 1733.
U.S.	**Lincoln's Birthday** Commemorates the birth of U.S. President Abraham Lincoln. Observed as a legal holiday in some states. First celebrated in 1866 as a memorial service to the assassinated president. (See additional information in *Introduction to February*)

Birthdates

1567 **Thomas Campion,** British poet, composer, and physician; noted for his musical lyrics; wrote *Cherry Ripe.* [d. March 1, 1620]

1663 **Cotton Mather,** American colonial clergyman; active in the promotion of the founding of Yale College; author of over 400 separate works on theology and science; some of his writings provoked the witchcraft trials at Salem, Massachusetts. [d. February 13, 1728]

1768 **Francis II, Holy Roman Emperor**, 1792–1806; forced to abdicate; his daughter, Maria Luisa, married Napoleon of France, 1810. [d. March 2, 1835]

1785 **Pierre-Louis Dulong,** French chemist physicist; contributor to early **atomic theory.** [d. July 18, 1838]

1791 **Peter Cooper,** U.S. inventor, manufacturer, philanthropist; designed and constructed the first U.S. steam locomotive, the *Tom Thumb,* 1830. [d. April 4, 1883]

1809 **Abraham Lincoln,** U.S. lawyer, politician; 16th President of the U.S., 1860–65; led the Union through the Civil War; assassinated. [d. April 15, 1865]

Charles Robert Darwin, British naturalist; famed for his studies in **evolution** and **natural selection.** [d. April 19, 1882]

1828 **George Meredith,** British novelist, poet. [d. May 18, 1909]

1850 **William Morris Davis,** U.S. geographer, geologist; a principal founder of the science of **geomorphology.** [d. February 5, 1934]

1870 **Marie Lloyd (Matalida Alice Wood),** British musical entertainer; known for her impersonations of low-comedy characters. [d. October 7, 1922]

1880 **John L(lewellyn) Lewis,** U.S. labor leader; President of the **United Mine Workers,** 1920–60; first president of the **Congress of Industrial Organization,** 1935–41. [d. June 11, 1969]

1884 **Alice Lee Roosevelt Longworth,** U.S. socialite; daughter of U.S. President Theodore Roosevelt. [d. February 20, 1980]

1893 **Omar Nelson Bradley,** U.S. army general; Commander of 12th Army Group, the largest unit to serve under a single American field commander; first chairman of the Joint Chiefs of Staff, 1949–53. [d. April 18, 1981]

1898 **David K(ilpatrick) E(stes) Bruce,** U.S. diplomat; Ambassador to France, 1949–52; to West Germany, 1957–59; to Great Britain, 1961–69. [d. December 4, 1977]

1918 **Julian Seymour Schwinger,** U.S. physicist; Nobel Prize in physics for research in **quantum electrodynamics** (with R. P. Feynman and S. I. Tomonaga), 1965.

1923 **Franco Zeffirelli,** Italian stage, opera director and designer.

Religious Calendar

The Saints

St. Meletius, Archbishop of Antioch. [d. 381]

St. Ethelwald, Bishop of Lindisfarne. [d. c. 740]

St. Anthony Kausleas, Patriarch of Constantinople. [d. 901]

St. Ludan. [d. c. 1202]

The Seven Founders of the Servite Order. Also called **Servants of Mary.** [d. 13th cent.]

St. Julian the Hospitaller; patron of innkeepers, travelers, boatmen, violinists, jugglers, clowns, shepherds, pilgrims, and ferrymen. [death date unknown]

St. Marina, monk and virgin (her sex was not detected until her death). [death date unknown]

The Beatified

Blessed Thomas Hemerford and his companions, priests and martyrs. [d. 1584]

Historical Events

881   **Charles III** is crowned Holy Roman Emperor.

1111   **Henry V,** Holy Roman Emperor, imprisons **Pope Paschal II.**

1531   English clergy are ordered henceforth to regard the ruler of England as head of the Church.

1554   **Lady Jane Grey,** considered a rival for the English throne, is beheaded under orders of **Queen Mary I.**

1733   **James Oglethorpe** founds Savannah, Georgia.

1818   **Chile** declares independence from Spain after seven years of war.

1832   Ecuador annexes the **Galapagos Islands.**

1877   First public demonstration of Alexander Graham Bell's articulating **telephone** is made.

1895   Japanese destroy the Chinese army and navy and end the **Sino-Japanese War** in the **Battle of Weihaiwei.**

1909   **National Association for the Advancement of Colored People** is formed in the U.S.

1912   **Emperor Pu-Yi** of China abdicates, ending the rule of the **Manchu Dynasty; China** becomes a republic.

1915   Protocol of **Opium Convention of 1912** is signed at The Hague by China, the U.S., and the Netherlands.

1922   Indian Nationalist campaign of mass civil disobedience led by **Mahatma Gandhi** is suspended because of murders at **Chauri Chaura.**

1924   **Tutankhamen's sarcophagus** is opened, disclosing three sumptuously ornamented coffins. (See also February 16, 1923.)

George Gershwin is piano soloist in the premiere of his *Rhapsody in Blue* in New York.

1947   First launching of a **guided missile** from a submarine takes place off Ft. Mugo, California.

1961   Tribesmen kill **Patrice Lumumba,** Prime Minister of the **Republic of the Congo,** and two companions.

1970   **Israel** bombs a **U.A.R.** steel plant, killing or wounding Egyptian civilian workers.

1973   First group of U.S. prisoners of war are freed by North Vietnam and flown from Hanoi to Clark Air Force Base in the Philippines (**Vietnam War**).

1978   The **Sandinista National Liberation Front,** a Nicaraguan guerilla organization, declares war on the **Somoza** government.

February 13

Holidays

U.S. (Florida)   **Fiesta de Menéndez**
Observed to honor the birthday of the founder of St. Augustine, Pedro Menéndez de Avilés.

Religious Calendar

The Saints

St. Polyeuctus, martyr. [d. 259]

St. Stephen of Rieti, abbot. [d. c. 560]

St. Modomnoc. Also called **Dominic, Dominick,**

Birthdates

1599   **Pope Alexander VII,** Pope, 1655–67. [d. May 22, 1667]

1793   **Philipp Veit,** German painter; founder of the **Nazarenes.** [d. December 18, 1877]

1849   **Lord Randolph (Henry Spencer) Churchill,** British politician; developed a school of progressive conservatives called Tory Democrats; father of **Winston Churchill** (November 30). [d. January 24, 1895]

1873   **Fyodor Ivanovich Chaliapin,** Russian-French operatic bass; best known for popularization of *The Song of the Volga Boatmen.* [d. April 12, 1938]

1885   **Bess Truman,** U.S. First Lady; wife of President Harry S. Truman. [d. October 18, 1982]

1892   **Robert Houghwout Jackson,** U.S. jurist, lawyer; Associate Justice of the U.S. Supreme Court, 1941–45; 1946–54. [d. October 9, 1954]

   Grant Wood, U.S. painter; best known for his painting *American Gothic.* [d. February 12, 1942]

1910   **William Bradford Shockley,** U.S. physicist; Nobel Prize in physics for development of the **transistor** (with J. Bardeen and W. H. Brattain), 1956.

1919   *Tennessee* **Ernie Ford (Ernest Jennings Ford),** U.S. country singer.

1920   **Eileen Farrell,** U.S. operatic soprano.

1929   **Omar Torrijos-Herrera,** Panamanian leader, soldier; Chief of Government, 1972–78. [d. August 1, 1981]

1938   **(Robert) Oliver Reed,** British actor.

Historical Events

1498   **Maximilian I,** Holy Roman Emperor, establishes the Imperial Council, Chancery, and Chamber.

1542   **Catherine Howard,** fifth wife of **Henry VIII** of England, is beheaded.

1566   **St. Augustine, Florida,** is founded.

1635   First **public school** in America, **Boston Latin School,** is opened.

1668   Spain recognizes the independence of **Portugal.**

1689   **William and Mary** are proclaimed joint rulers of Great Britain and reign together until December 27, 1694.

1692   **Glencoe Massacre** occurs in the Scottish Highlands; 38 members of Clan MacDonald are murdered by opposing clan leaders.

1706   **Charles XII** of Sweden defeats the Russians and Saxons at **Altranstädt.**

1779   **Captain James Cook,** English explorer, is murdered by Hawaiian natives in a scuffle over a stolen boat.

1788   The trial of **Warren Hastings,** former governor of Bengal, for high crimes and misdemeanors, begins in England. His trial, in which Edmund Burke (January 12) and Richard Brinsley Sheridan (November 4) were among prosecuting counsel, achieved wide public attention and resulted in Hastings' acquittal, 1795.

1793   Coalition against France is formed by Prussia, Austria, Holland, Britain, Sardinia, and Spain (**French Revolutionary period**).

1795   **The University of North Carolina,** the first state university in the U.S., opens.

Medomnoc, Modomnoe. [d. 6th cent.]

St. Licinius, Bishop of Angers. Also called **Lésin.** [d. c. 616]

St. Huna, priest and monk. [d. 7th cent.]

St. Ermengild, Abbess of Ely and widow; daughter of King Ercombert of Kent. Also called **Ermenilda.** [d. 703]

St. Catherine dei Ricci, virgin, prioress, and mystic. Also called **Katherine dei Ricci.** [d. 1590]

St. Martinian the Hermit. Also called **Martinianus.** [death date unknown]

The Beatified

Blessed Beatrice of Ornacieu, virgin, Carthusian nun. [d. 309]

Blessed Christina of Spoleto. [d. 1458]

Blessed Eustochium of Padua, virgin and nun. [d. 1469]

Blessed Archangela Girlani, virgin and prioress. [d. 1494]

1858   **Sir Richard Burton** and **Captain John Speke,** British explorers, discover **Lake Tanganyika** in East Africa.

1886   Afghanistan gives **Penjdeh** up to Russia.

1895   **Louis Jean** and **Auguste Lumière** receive a French patent on their **motion-picture projector.**

1904   **Panama** adopts a constitution.

1906   **Lockhart Medical College** at Peking, China, opens.

1914   **The American Society of Composers, Authors, and Publishers (ASCAP)** is established.

1918   Cossack rebels marching on Moscow are defeated by the Bolshevik forces, and General Aleksei Kaledin, the Cossack leader, commits suicide **(Russian Revolution).**

1920   The **Declaration of London** of the Council of the League of Nations recognizes the perpetual neutrality of **Switzerland.**

1953   The Catholic Church in **Poland** is placed under state control.

1960   U.S. District Court in Tulsa, Oklahoma, acquits 29 large oil companies accused of conspiring to fix crude oil prices.

1967   **National Student Association** confirms that since 1952 it has received more than $3 million in secret funds from the U.S. **Central Intelligence Agency.**

1969   **U.S.S.R.** and **Japan** sign an agreement allowing commercial Japanese planes to fly across Siberia.

1970   World Jewish leaders and officials of the **World Council of Churches** announce the beginning of regular meetings.

1974   **Alexander Solzhenitsyn,** Nobel Prize winning novelist, is expelled from Russia.

1975   **Turkish Cypriots** proclaim the northern 40 per cent of the island of **Cyprus** to be a separate state.

Holidays

St. Valentine's Day
Celebrates the two 3rd-century martyrs of this name. Also believed to be a continuation of the Roman festival of *Lupercalia.* Observed by the exchange of love messages and greetings.

Bulgaria **Viticulturists' Day** or **Trifon Zarenzan**
Celebration of the viticulturists' art; based on ancient cult rituals honoring Dionysius.

Denmark **Fjartende Februar** (Fourteenth of February)
Day for exchange of tokens and gifts among Danish school children.

Liberia **Literacy Day**
Established to honor worldwide campaign to eliminate illiteracy and encourage adult education.

February 14

Birthdates

1401 **Leon Battista Alberti,** Italian architect, scholar, art theorist, moral philosopher, mathematician. [d. April 25, 1472]

1760 **Richard Allen,** U.S. clergyman; founder and first bishop of **African Methodist Church.** [d. March 26, 1831]

1763 **Jean Victor Marie Moreau,** French Revolutionary general; bitter opponent of Napoleon. [d. September 2, 1813]

1766 **Thomas (Robert) Malthus,** British political economist; known for his theory of the ratio of population increase to the means of subsistence. [d. December 29, 1834]

1819 **Christopher Latham Sholes,** U.S. inventor; patented first practical **typewriter.** [d. February 17, 1890]

1824 **Winfield Scott Hancock,** U.S. army general; with the Union Army during the U.S. Civil War. [d. February 9, 1886]

1847 **Anna Howard Shaw,** U.S. suffrage leader, physician, cleric; first woman ordained in the Methodist Church. [d. July 2, 1919]

1856 **Frank Harris (James Thomas Harris),** Irish-American editor, journalist, biographer; known for his frank biography of **Oscar Wilde.** [d. August 26, 1931]

1858 **Joseph Thomson,** Scottish geologist and naturalist; conducted explorations into Africa, which led to great discoveries of its natural life and geology. [d. August 2, 1895]

1869 **Charles T. R. Wilson,** British physicist; Nobel Prize in physics for experiments with **x rays** (with A. H. Compton), 1927. [d. November 15, 1959]

1882 **George Jean Nathan,** U.S. editor, critic; known as the most influential drama critic in America, 1906–58; with H. L. Mencken (September 12) founded *The American Mercury.* [d. April 8, 1958]

1894 **Jack Benny (Benjamin Kubelsky),** U.S. comedian. [d. December 26, 1974]

1896 **Andrei Alexandrovich Zhdanov,** Soviet government Communist Party official; a close associate of Joseph Stalin. [d. August 31, 1948]

1898 **Fritz Zwicky,** Swiss physicist in the U.S.; known for investigations of **cosmic rays.** [d. February 8, 1974]

1905 **Thelma Ritter,** U.S. character actress. [d. February 5, 1969]

1913 **James R(iddle) Hoffa,** U.S. labor leader; President of the Teamsters Union, 1957–71

Mexico	Day of National Mourning
	Commemorates the death of **Vincente Guerrero,** revolutionary war hero.
U.S. (Arizona)	**Admission Day**
	Commemorates Arizona's admission to the Union, 1912.
U.S. (Oregon)	**Admission Day**
	Commemorates the admission of Oregon, 1859.

Religious Calendar

The Saints

St. Valentine, priest and martyr; patron of engaged couples. Invoked against plague, epilepsy, and fainting. [d. c. 269]

St. Abraham, Bishop of Carrhae. Also called **Abraames.** [d. c. 422]

St. Maro, abbot; patriarch of Maronites. [d. 433]

St. Auxentius, hermit. Also called **Augentius.** [d. 473]

St. Conran, bishop. [d. 6th cent.]

St. Antoninus of Sorrento, abbot; patron of Sorrento. [d. 830]

St. Cyril and **St. Methodius,** Archbishop of Sirmium, missionaries; apostles of the Slavs. St. Cyril developed an alphabet for the Slavs. Feast formerly July 7. [d. 869, 885] Obligatory Memorial.

St. Adolf, Bishop of Osnabrück. [d. 1224]

The Beatified

Blessed Conrad of Bavaria. [d. 1154]

Blessed Nicholas Paglia, prior. [d. 1255]

Blessed Angelo of Gualdo, solitary. [d. 1325]

Blessed John Baptist of Almodovar, founder. Founded the Barefooted, Reformed or Displaced Trinitarians. [d. 1613]

[disappeared July 30, 1975; presumed dead]

(James) Albert Pike, U.S. Episcopal priest, lawyer. [d. September 7, 1969]

1944 **Carl Bernstein,** U.S. journalist, author; best known as a member of the *Washington Post's* reporting team during the **Watergate Incident.**

Historical Events

1014 **Henry II,** *the Saint,* is crowned **Holy Roman Emperor.**

1130 **Innocent II** elected pope; reigns 1130–43.

1400 **Richard II** of England is murdered.

1674 **John III Sobieski** is crowned King of Poland.

1764 A patent on **spinning and carding machinery** is granted to **James Davenport.**

1859 **Oregon** is admitted to the Union as the 33rd state.

1903 **U.S. Department of Labor and Commerce** is established by Congress.

1912 **Arizona** is admitted to the Union as the 48th state.

1917 Sweden, Norway, and Denmark refuse to recognize the German submarine blockade **(World War I).**

1918 *Swanee,* by **George Gershwin,** premieres in New York.

1929 Seven die in a gangland massacre in **Chicago (St. Valentine's Day Massacre).**

Puerto Rico's legislature meets for the first time.

1939 German warship **Bismarck** is launched.

1949 **Chaim Weizmann** is elected first president of **Israel.**

1956 The **Twentieth Communist Party Congress** begins.

1958 The **Arab Federation of Iraq and Jordan** is proclaimed.

1962 Council of **Organization of American States** formally excludes Cuba from participation in any organizational activities.

1969 Longest dock strike in **New York** history ends after 57 days.

1970 Indian Prime Minister **Indira Gandhi** renationalizes private banks.

1979 U.S. Ambassador to Afghanistan, **Adolph Dubs,** is assassinated in Kabul by Muslim extremists.

February 15

U.S. **Susan B. Anthony Day**
Celebrates the birthday of the pioneer crusader for women's rights, 1820.

U.S. (Maine and Massachusetts) **Maine Memorial Day**
Commemorates sinking of U.S.S. *Maine* and beginning of the **Spanish-American War.**

Religious Calendar

The Saints

St. Walfrid, abbot. Also called **Galfrido della Gherardesca.** [d. c. 765]

Birthdates

1368 **Sigismund, King of Hungary,** 1387–1437, Holy Roman Emperor, 1410. [d. December 9, 1437]

1497 **Philipp Melanchthon,** German theologian, Protestant reformer, educator; collaborator with Martin Luther in the Protestant Reformation. [d. April 19, 1560]

1519 **Pedro Menéndez de Avilés,** Spanish soldier, navigator; settled Florida as a Spanish colony. [d. September 17, 1574]

1564 **Galileo Galilei,** Italian physicist, astronomer; pioneered the use of the telescope for astronomical study; put forth the theory of **heliocentricity** of the universe; tried by the Inquisition for his teachings. [d. January 8, 1642]

1571 **Michael Praetorius (Schutheiss),** German composer, music historian [d. February 15, 1621]

1710 **Louis XV, King of France.** [d. May 10, 1774]

1748 **Jeremy Bentham,** English Utilitarian economist; proposed the theory that man makes ethical decisions on the basis of pleasure and pain. [d. June 6, 1831]

1782 **William Miller,** U.S. Protestant revivalist; founder of the **Millerites,** the forerunners of the Seventh-Day Adventists. [d. December 20, 1849]

1797 **Henry Engelhard Steinway,** German-U.S. piano manufacturer; founder of Steinway and Sons. [d. February 7, 1871]

1803 **John Augustus Sutter,** U.S. pioneer; his discovery of gold precipitated the California gold rush. [d. June 18, 1880]

1809 **Cyrus Hall McCormick,** U.S. inventor of farm machinery; founder of International Harvester Co. [d. May 13, 1884]

1812 **Charles Lewis Tiffany,** U.S. merchant; founder of Tiffany and Co., jewelers. [d. February 18, 1902]

1817 **Charles François Daubigny,** French landscape painter; leader of the **Barbizon School.** [d. February 19, 1878]

1820 **Susan B(rownell) Anthony,** U.S. social reformer; a pioneer crusader for women's suffrage. [d. March 13, 1906]

1845 **Elihu Root,** U.S. Secretary of War, 1899–1904; U.S. Secretary of State, 1905–1909; awarded Nobel Peace Prize, 1912. [d. February 7, 1937]

1861 **Charles Edouard Guillaume,** Swiss-French physicist; Nobel Prize in physics for discovery of anomalies in nickel-steel alloys, 1920. [d. June 13, 1938]

Alfred North Whitehead, British mathematician, philosopher. [d. December 30, 1947]

1873 **Hans Karl August Simon Euler-Chelpin,** Swedish chemist born in Germany; Nobel Prize in chemistry for investigation into fermentation process (with A. Harden), 1929. [d. November 6, 1964]

1882 **John Barrymore,** U.S. actor; younger brother of Ethel and Lionel Barrymore; his

St. Tanco, Bishop of Verden and martyr. Also called **Tatta,** or **Tatto.** [d. 808]

St. Sigfrid, Bishop of Växjö; the Apostle of Sweden. Also called **Sigefride.** [d. c. 1045]

St. Agape, virgin and martyr; patron of Terni in Umbria. [death date unknown]

SS. Faustinus and Jovita, martyrs; patrons of Brescia. [death date unknown]

The Beatified

Blessed Jordan of Saxony, second master general of the Dominicans; the first university chaplain. [d. 1237]

Blessed Angelo of Borgo San Sepolcro, Augustinian hermit. [d. c. 1306]

Blessed Julia of Certaldo, virgin and anchoress. [d. 1367]

Blessed Claud la Colombière, Jesuit priest. [d. 1682]

---

portrayal of Hamlet is considered one of the best of all time. [d. May 29, 1942]

1892 **James Vincent Forrestal,** U.S. government official; first U.S. Secretary of Defense. [d. May 22, 1949]

1911 **Leonard (Freel) Woodcock,** U.S. government and labor union official; President of United Automobile Workers, 1970–77.

1916 **Ian Keith Ballantine,** U.S. publishing executive.

1922 **John Bayard Anderson,** U.S. politician; third-party presidential candidate, 1980.

1929 **James Rodney Schlesinger,** U.S. government official and economist; U.S. Secretary of Defense, 1973–75.

1931 **Claire Bloom (Claire Blume),** British actress.

1935 **Roger Chaffee,** U.S. astronaut; one of astronauts killed aboard *Apollo I.* [d. January 27, 1967]

Historical Events

44 B.C. **Julius Caesar** is offered the diadem of kingship by Antony and refuses it.

1637 **Ferdinand II, Holy Roman Emperor,** dies and is succeeded by **Ferdinand III.**

1763 **Treaty of Hubertusburg** between Prussia and Austria is signed. Prussia retains Silesia and emerges as a great military power.

1764 City of **St. Louis, Missouri** is founded by **Auguste Chouteau** under the direction of **Pierre Laclède.**

1876 U.S. patent is issued for the manufacture of **barbed wire.**

1898 ***U.S.S. Maine*** is mysteriously blown up in Havana harbor, leading U.S. to declare war on Spain (**Spanish-American War**).

1905 **Rimsky-Korsakov, Rachmaninoff, Taneyev, Gretchaninoff, Glière, Chaliapin, Siloti,** and 25 others sign a declaration protesting the political repression of the government of Czar Nicholas II.

1912 **Yüan Shih-kai** replaces **Sun Yat-sen** as provisional president of China.

1922 The **Permanent Court of International Justice** opens at The Hague.

1933 Assassin **Giuseppe Zangara** fires at President-elect Franklin Roosevelt's party in Miami, Florida, missing Roosevelt but fatally wounding Chicago Mayor **Anton Cermak.**

1938 Rebel forces under General Francisco Franco take **Teruel** (**Spanish Civil War**).

1942 **Singapore** is surrendered to the Japanese army (**World War II**).

1944 Allies bomb **Monte Cassino** monastery (**World War II**).

1965 **Canada** officially adopts a new flag; the Red Maple Leaf becomes the new symbol, replacing the Union Jack.

1971 **Britain** adopts the **decimal currency** system after 1200 years of a system based on 12-penny shillings.

1975 The government of **Ethiopia** declares a state of emergency in the northern province of **Eritrea** where fighting between the government and Eritrean secessionists has been going on for 13 years.

February 16

Holidays

U.S.
(Lithuanian Community)

Lithuanian Independence Day
Commemorates proclamation of independence, 1918.

Religious Calendar

The Saints

St. Onesimus, martyr. [d. 1st cent.]

St. Juliana, virgin and martyr. [d. c. 305]

Birthdates

1740   **Giambattista Bodoni,** Italian printer and type designer. [d. November 29, 1813]

1812   **Henry Wilson,** U.S. politician; leader in the anti-slavery movement. [d. November 22, 1875]

1821   **Heinrich Barth,** German explorer and scholar; considered one of the greatest African explorers. [d. November 25, 1865]

1822   **Sir Francis Galton,** British anthropologist; founder of the science of **eugenics**; devised system for **fingerprint identification.** [d. January 17, 1911]

1831   **Nikolai Semyanovich Leskov,** Russian novelist. [d. March 5, 1895]

1834   **Ernst Heinrich Haeckel,** German biologist, philosopher; first German advocate of **organic evolution.** [d. August 9, 1919]

1838   **Henry Brooks Adams,** U.S. historian, novelist. [d. March 27, 1918]

1843   **Henry Martyn Leland,** U.S. manufacturer, auto-industry pioneer. [d. March 26, 1932]

1848   **Hugo Marie De Vries,** Dutch botanist; one of chief elucidators of Gregor Mendel's law of inheritance of characteristics. [d. May 21, 1935]

1886   **Van Wyck Brooks,** U.S. literary critic, cultural historian; Pulitzer Prize in history, 1937. [d. May 2, 1963]

1893   **Katherine Cornell,** U.S. stage actress. [d. June 8, 1974]

1903   **Edgar Bergen (John Edgar Bergren),** U.S. ventriloquist, actor; with his dummy, **Charlie McCarthy,** set a standard for American comedy during the 1930s and 1940s. Upon Bergen's death, McCarthy was placed in the Smithsonian Institution. [d. September 30, 1978]

1904   **George Frost Kennan,** U.S. diplomat, historian; Pulitzer Prize in history, 1957; Pulitzer Prize in biography, 1968.

1907   **Alec Wilder,** U.S. composer; composed hundreds of popular songs, as well as operas, operettas, and chamber music. [d. December 24, 1980]

1926   **Vera-Ellen (Rohe),** U.S. actress, dancer; one of the most renowned dancers of the 1940s. [d. August 30, 1981]

Historical Events

1486   **Maximilian I** is elected King of Germany; ruled, 1486-1519.

1801   **William Pitt** resigns as Prime Minister of Great Britain.

1804   The U.S. frigate *Philadelphia,* captured by Tripolitans, is destroyed by an American party led by **Stephen Decatur.**

1808   France invades Spain (**Peninsular War).**

1862   Confederates surrender **Fort Donelson** in Tennessee to General **Ulysses S. Grant (U.S. Civil War).**

1868   **Benevolent and Protective Order of Elks** is founded in New York City.

1915   After small German gains, the French open a counter-offensive in the continuing **Battle of Champagne** on the Western Front (**World War I).**

1916   The Russian army, under Grand Duke Nicholas, seizes **Erzerum,** the strongest fortified city in Asiatic Turkey, from the Turks (**World War I).** The Allies (Great Britain, France, Russia, Serbia, and Italy) pledge to continue World War I until Belgium is restored to independence.

SS. Elias, Jeremy, Isaias, Samuel, and **Daniel,** martyrs. [d. 309]

The Beatified

Blessed Philippa Mareri, virgin and anchoress. [d. 1236]

Blessed Verdiana, virgin and recluse. Also called **Veridiana,** or **Viridiana.** [d. c. 1240]

Blessed Eustochium of Messina, virgin and abbess. [d. 1468]

Blessed Bernard Scammacca. [d. 1486]

1923	**Bessie Smith** makes her first recording, *Downhearted Blues*, for Columbia Records.
	British archaeologist **Howard Carter** opens **Tutankhamen's sepulchral chamber.** (See also February 12, 1924.)
1927	The first **railway** service between India and Nepal begins.
1944	Japanese naval base at **Truk** is raided by U.S. aircraft which destroy 201 enemy planes **(World War II).**
1945	**Corregidor** in Manila Bay is bombarded by Allies **(World War II).**
1959	**Fidel Castro** becomes Prime Minister of **Cuba.**
1965	Giant winged satellite called *Pegasus*, designed to measure the potential hazards of meteoroids to astronauts and spacecraft, is launched from Cape Kennedy, Florida.
1967	Legislation is enacted to give the British colonies of **Antigua, Dominica, Grenada, St. Kitts-Nevis** and **Anguilla,** and **St. Lucia** the status of states associated with the United Kingdom.
1970	**Joe Frazier** knocks out **Jimmy Ellis** in five rounds for world heavyweight boxing title.
1971	Highway between **West Pakistan** and **China** is formally opened.
1972	U.S. Census Bureau issues report showing steep decline in **U.S. birthrate.**

February 17

Religious Calendar

Seven Founders of the Servite Order. Formerly February 12. Optional Memorial.

The Saints

SS. Theodulus and **Julian,** martyrs. [d. 309]

St. Loman, Bishop of Trim. Also called **Luman.** [d. c. 450]

St. Fintan of Cloneenagh, abbot. [d. 603]

Birthdates

1653 **Arcangelo Corelli,** Italian composer and violinist; considered the creator of the *concerto grosso.* [d. January 8, 1713]

1740 **Horace de Saussure,** Swiss geologist; first scientific explorer of the Alps. [d. January 22, 1799]

1781 **René Laënnec,** French physician; inventor of the **stethoscope.** [d. August 13, 1826]

1844 **Montgomery Ward,** founder of Montgomery Ward & Co., first U.S. mail-order house. [d. December 7, 1913]

1856 **Frederich Eugene Ives,** U.S. inventor; perfected **half-tone printing process.** [d. May 27, 1937]

1874 **Thomas John Watson,** U.S. industrialist; introduced **printing tabulator, electric typewriter, electronic calculator.** [d. June 19, 1956]

1877 **André Maginot,** French statesman; responsible for construction of **Maginot Line,** a defensive barrier along the eastern border of France prior to World War II. [d. January 7, 1932]

1879 **Dorothy Canfield Fisher,** U.S. novelist; dealt especially with stories of Vermont life. [d. November 9, 1958]

1888 **Otto Stern,** U.S. physicist born in Germany; Nobel Prize in physics for studies in the **magnetic properties of atoms,** 1943. [d. August 17, 1969]

1890 **Ronald A. Fisher,** British biologist; the first to demonstrate that Darwinian **evolution** was compatible with **genetics.** [d. July 29, 1962]

1902 **Marian Anderson,** U.S. contralto, concert artist.

1907 **Marjorie Lawrence,** Australian operatic soprano; known especially for her interpretation of Wagner. [d. January 13, 1979]

1929 **Chaim Potok,** U.S. novelist.

1942 **Huey P. Newton,** U.S. militant; founder of the **Black Panther Party.**

Historical Events

1461 Queen Margaret of England defeats Warwick at **St. Albans (War of the Roses).**

1854 **Convention of Bloemfontein** constitutes the **Orange Free State** as the British government withdraws.

1864 First successful submarine attack takes place, in which Confederate ship *Hunley* sinks Union *Housatonic* with charge of gunpowder (**U.S. Civil War**).

1865 **Columbia,** South Carolina, is burned by Union Army (**U.S. Civil War**).

1880 An explosion rips through the dining room of the Winter Palace, St. Petersburg, Russia, during an attempt to assassinate **Czar Alexander II**; the Czar escapes injury because he and his family are late for dinner.

1897 **National Congress of Parents and Teachers** is founded in Washington, D.C.

1904 World premiere of *Madame Butterfly* by **Giacomo Puccini** takes place at the Teatro alla Scala in Milan.

1905 **Grand Duke Serge,** uncle of Czar Nicholas II, is killed when a bomb is thrown under his carriage in Moscow.

1915 German forces reoccupy Memel, pushing back the Russians in the **Battle of Masuria (World War I).**

1916 The Allied forces occupy **Chios** in the Aegean Sea (**World War I**).

1933 *Newsweek* magazine begins publication.

1934 **Albert I** of Belgium dies and is succeeded by **Leopold III.**

1936 Military revolt leads to overthrow of Paraguayan president **Eligio Ayala.**

St. Finan, Bishop of Lindisfarne. [d. 661]

St. Silvin, bishop. [d. c. 720]

St. Evermod, Bishop of Ratzeburg; Apostle of the Wends. [d. 1178]

The Beatified

Blessed Reginald of Orleans. [d. 1220]

Blessed Luke Belludi, Franciscan friar. [d. c. 1285]

Blessed Andrew of Anagni, friar minor. Also called **Andrea dei Conti du Segni (Andrew of the Counts of Segni), Andreas de Comitibus.** [d. 1302]

Blessed Peter of Treia, Franciscan. [d. 1304]

Blessed William Richardson, priest and martyr; last martyr to suffer death for his religion during the reign of Queen Elizabeth I. [d. 1603]

The Martyrs of China. [d. 19th cent.]

1965	**English language** is declared an associate official language in India after weeks of language riots in southern India.
1966	Pope Paul VI announces major liberalizing changes in the rules of **fasting and abstinence** for Roman Catholics.
1972	President **Richard M. Nixon** leaves Washington for his historic trip to China.
1976	President **Gerald Ford** announces a reorganization of U.S. intelligence agencies, the first since 1947.
1979	Chinese troops invade **Vietnam** as a punishment for Vietnam's intrusion into Cambodia and alleged violations of Chinese territory.

February 18

Holidays

The Gambia   **Republic Day**
Commemorates day on which The Gambia became self-governing nation within British Commonwealth, 1965.

Nepal   **Democracy Day**
Celebration of anniversary of 1952 Constitution.

Religious Calendar

Feasts

Martin Luther, Doctor and Confessor. [Lutheran Minor Festival].

Birthdates

1516   **Mary I of England** (*Bloody Mary*), first English queen to rule in her own right; persecuted Protestants in an attempt to restore Roman Catholicism in England. [d. November 17, 1558]

1609   **Edward Hyde,** 1st Earl of Clarendon, British statesman, historian; brought Oliver Cromwell to power after English Civil War. [d. December 9, 1674]

1745   **Conte Alessandro Giuseppe Volta,** Italian physicist; invented the **electric battery.** [d. March 5, 1827]

1790   **Marshall Hall,** British physician, physiologist; discovered **reflex action.** [d. August 11, 1857]

1795   **George Peabody,** U.S. merchant, philanthropist; donated the **Peabody Museum** at Yale and at Harvard. Peabody, Massachusetts, is named for him. [d. November 4, 1869]

1836   **Ramakrishna,** Hindu teacher, writer, religious reformer; looked upon as a sainted wise man by the Hindus. [d. August 16, 1886]

1838   **Ernst Mach,** Austrian physicist, psychologist; noted for his research into the physiology and psychology of the senses; developed method of measuring movement in terms of the speed of sound, (i.e. Mach number). [d. February 19, 1916]

1848   **Louis Comfort Tiffany,** U.S. painter, craftsman, designer, glassmaker, and philanthropist; internationally known for his stained glass creations. [d. January 17, 1933]

1853   **August Belmont,** U.S. banker; **Belmont Stakes** and **Belmont Racetrack** named in his family's honor. [d. December 10, 1924]

1859   **Sholem Aleichem (Solomon J. Rabinowitz),** Ukranian-Yiddish writer; known as the *Yiddish Mark Twain.* [d. May 13, 1916]

1862   **Charles Michael Schwab,** U.S. manufacturer, considered the *Boy Wonder* of the American steel industry. [d. September 18, 1939]

1890   **Adolphe Menjou,** U.S. actor. [d. October 29, 1963]

1892   **Wendell Lewis Willkie,** U.S. politician, business executive, lawyer; Republican presidential candidate, 1940. [d. October 8, 1944]

1894   **Andrés Segovia,** Spanish classical-guitar virtuoso.

1896   **André Breton,** French poet, essayist, critic; one of the founders of the **Surrealist movement.** [d. September 28, 1966]

1898   **Luis Muñoz Marín,** Puerto Rican statesman; first governor of **Commonwealth of Puerto Rico.** [d. April 30, 1980]

1903   **Nikolai Viktorovich Podgorny,** Russian politician; President of U.S.S.R., 1965–1977. [d. January 11, 1983]

1922   **Helen Gurley Brown,** U.S. author, editor.

Historical Events

1248   Lombards defeat **Frederick II** of Germany, at Parma.

The Saints

St. Simeon, Bishop of Jerusalem and martyr; cousin of Jesus. Also called **Simon.** [d. c. 107]

St. Flavian, patriarch of Constantinople, martyr. [d. 449]

St. Helladius, Archbishop of Toledo. [d. 633]

St. Colman, Bishop of Lindisfarne. [d. 676]

St. Angilbert, abbot. [d. 814]

St. Theotonius, Abbot of the Monastery of the Holy Cross. [d. 1166]

St. Leo and **St. Paregorius,** martyrs. [death date unknown]

The Beatified

Blessed William Harrington, priest, martyr. [d. 1594]

Blessed John Pibush, priest, martyr. [d. 1601]

1405   **Timur Lenk (Tamerlane),** Mongul ruler, dies and is succeeded by **Shah Rokh.**

1678   *Pilgrim's Progress* by **John Bunyan** is published.

1861   The first **Italian parliament** meets.

1865   **Charleston,** South Carolina is taken by the Union fleet (**U.S. Civil War**).

1876   Direct **telegraphic line** between London and New Zealand is established.

1884   **Gen. Charles Gordon** arrives at **Khartoum** to suppress the rebellion led by the Mahdi in the Sudan against the Egyptian ruler.

1915   The Germans begin their **submarine blockade** of British waters (**World War I**).

1916   The Germans in **Cameroon** surrender to the Allies, ending that African campaign and German control of the Colony of Cameroon (**World War I**).

1918   Bolshevik forces capture **Kiev,** the capital of the newly-proclaimed **Republic of the Ukraine (Russian Revolution).**

1930   Planet **Pluto** is discovered by **Clyde Tombaugh** at Lowell Observatory in Flagstaff, Arizona.

1932   Japan establishes the independent nation of **Manchukuo** from seized Manchurian territory.

1943   **Carl Orff's** *Die Kluge* opens in Frankfurt, Germany.

1960   Foreign ministers of **Argentina, Brazil, Chile, Mexico, Paraguay, Peru,** and **Uruguay** sign a treaty providing for a free-trade zone linking the economies of their nations.

     VIII Winter Olympic Games open at **Squaw Valley,** California.

1963   **U.S. Supreme Court** declares unconstitutional two acts of Congress depriving Americans of citizenship for leaving the country to avoid the draft.

1965   **The Gambia** becomes an independent state within the British Commonwealth.

1970   All defendants in the **Chicago Seven** trial are acquitted of charges of conspiring to incite a riot during the 1968 Democratic National Convention.

February 19

Holidays

U.S.   **Robert E. Lee Day**
(Kentucky)

Religious Calendar

The Saints

St. Mesrop, bishop. Principal colleague of St. Isaac the Great in developing the Armenian church. Also called **Mesrop the Teacher,** or **Mashtots.** [d. 441]

Birthdates

1473 **Nicolaus Copernicus,** Polish astronomer; developed the mathematics and was first to propose the heliocentric solar system. [d. May 24, 1543]

1717 **David Garrick,** British actor, theatrical manager. [d. January 20, 1779]

1743 **Luigi Boccherini,** Italian composer, cellist; developed concept of string quartets and quintets. [d. May 28, 1805]

1792 **Roderick Impey Murchison,** Scottish geologist; developed **Silurian system of geology.** [d. October 27, 1871]

1817 **William III of the Netherlands,** ruled 1849–90. [d. November 23, 1890]

1833 **Elie Ducommun,** Swiss journalist, pacifist; led organization of **International League of Peace and Freedom.** Nobel Peace Prize (with C. A. Gobat), 1902. [d. December 7, 1906]

1859 **Svante August Arrhenius,** Swedish chemist; Nobel Prize in chemistry for development of the theory of **ionization,** 1903. [d. October 2, 1927]

1863 **Augusto Bernardino Leguía y Salcedo,** Peruvian politician; President 1908–13; dictator 1919–30. [d. February 6, 1932]

1865 **Sven Anders Hedin,** Swedish scientist and explorer of central and east Asia; explorations determined the source of the **Indus River.** [d. November 26, 1952]

1880 **Alvaro Obregón,** Mexican revolutionary and reformer; President of Mexico, 1920–24. [d. July 17, 1928]

1893 **Sir Cedric Hardwicke,** British actor. [d. August 6, 1964]

1911 **Merle Oberon,** British actress; especially noted for her leading roles in the 1930s and 1940s. [d. November 23, 1979]

1912 **Stan Kenton,** U.S. musician, arranger. [d. August 25, 1979]

Anton Buttigieg, President of Malta, 1976–82.

1916 **Eddie Arcaro,** U.S. jockey; winner of 4,779 races, including five Kentucky Derbies.

1917 **Carson McCullers,** U.S. author and playwright; author of *The Heart Is a Lonely Hunter.* [d. September 29, 1967]

1924 **Lee Marvin,** U.S. actor.

1960 **Prince Andrew Albert Christian Edward,** second son of **Queen Elizabeth II** of England.

Historical Events

1800 **Napoleon** centralizes French administration; establishes himself in the Tuileries as First Consul.

1864 **Knights of Pythias** are founded.

1878 Patent for first **gramophone** is awarded to **Thomas Alva Edison.**

1915 A combined British-French fleet begins the naval bombardment of the **Dardanelles (World War I).**

1918 Nationalization of all land, farm buildings, machinery, and livestock is announced in Russia.

1923 **Jean Sibelius** conducts the premiere of his *Sixth Symphony,* op. 104, in Helsinki.

1929 The entire artillery corps of the **Spanish army** is disbanded by royal decree following riots and mutiny of artillery garrisons.

1945 U.S. Marines invade **Iwo Jima. (World War II)**

1962 **U.S. Senator Carl Hayden** completes fifty years of service in the U.S. Congress—the longest term in U.S. history.

Talks with France on ending the 7 1/2-year

St. Barbatus, Bishop of Benevento; patron of Benevento. Also called **Barbas.** [d. 682]

St. Beatus of Liebana, priest. [d. c. 798]

St. Boniface, Bishop of Lausanne. [d. 1260]

St. Conrad of Piacenza, anchoret; invoked against ruptures. [d. 1351]

The Beatified

Blessed Alvarez of Cordova, Dominican friar. [d. c. 1430]

rebellion in **Algeria** conclude with full agreement on a cease-fire and accords on a provisional government.

1964   Detection of **omega-minus sub-atomic particle,** providing confirmation of a new theory of binding forces in the atomic nucleus, is announced.

1972   Five U.S. airmen, allegedly captured during intensive bombing raids of February 16–17, are publicly displayed in **Hanoi (Vietnam War).**

1976   **Iceland** severs diplomatic relations with Britain in dispute over fishing limits in Icelandic waters.

1977   **Lady Spencer-Churchill,** the 91-year-old widow of Britain's wartime leader Sir Winston Churchill, begins selling items of great sentimental value, citing serious financial difficulties.

February 20

Holidays

Bangladesh   **Shaheed Day** or **Martyrs' Day** or **National Mourning Day.**

Religious Calendar

The Saints

SS. **Tyrannio,** Bishop of Tyre, **Zenobius,** priest and physician, and other martyrs. [d. 304 and 310]

Birthdates

1726   **William Prescott,** American Revolutionary officer, hero of the **Battle of Bunker Hill,** 1775. [d. October 13, 1775]

1791   **Karl Czerny,** Austrian pianist, composer. [d. July 15, 1857]

1805   **Angelina Emily Grimké,** U.S. reformer, abolitionist; woman's rights advocate. [d. October 26, 1879]

1844   **Ludwig Boltzmann,** Austrian physicist; made great contributions to the development of **statistical mechanics.** [d. September 5, 1906]

1887   **Vincent Massey,** Canadian statesman; first native-born Canadian to become governor-general of Canada, 1952–59. [d. December 30, 1967]

1898   **Enzo Ferrari,** Italian auto manufacturer.

1901   **René Dubos,** U.S. microbiologist, environmentalist, educator, author; primarily concerned with environmental issues during his lengthy career. [d. February 20, 1982]

1902   **Ansel Adams,** U.S. landscape photographer; recognized as one of the foremost photographic artists in America. [d. April 24, 1984]

1904   **Alexei Nikolaevich Kosygin,** Russian communist leader; Russian premier, 1964–80. Led Soviet effort at economic modernization in 1960s. [d. December 18, 1980]

1912   **Pierre François Marie-Louis Boulle,** French novelist; best known for *Bridge over the River Kwai* and *Planet of the Apes.*

1923   **Linden Forbes Burnham,** Guyanan politician; President, 1964– .

1925   **Robert Altman,** U.S. film producer, director.

1927   **Sidney Poitier,** U.S. actor; first black male to win Academy Award as Best Actor.

1934   **Bobby Unser,** U.S. auto racer; three-time winner of Indianapolis 500 Auto Race.

Historical Events

1437   **James I** of Scotland is murdered by **Sir Robert Graham** at Perth.

1471   **James III** of Scotland annexes **Orkney** and **Shetland Islands.**

1547   **Edward VI** of England ascends the throne.

1790   **Joseph II,** Holy Roman Emperor, dies and is succeeded by Leopold II.

1815   U.S. frigate **Constitution** captures the British **Cyane** and **Levant** (War of 1812).

1862   **William Wallace Lincoln,** the son of U.S. President Abraham Lincoln, dies in the White House.

1864   **Battle of Olustee** or **Ocean Pond,** Florida, results in a Confederate victory. (**U.S. Civil War**).

1915   **Liquid fire (flamethrower)** is first used as a weapon by the Germans in attacks against the French in the **Argonne (World War I).**

1916   **Battle of Verdun** begins (**World War I**).

1928   Treaty with Great Britain is signed providing for autonomous government in Trans-Jordan (now primarily **Jordan**).

1960   Cuban cabinet approves a new law bringing all private enterprise in **Cuba** under control of a **Central Planning Board** headed by Premier **Fidel Castro.**

1962   U.S. astronaut **John Glenn** becomes first American to orbit the earth, in spaceship *Friendship VII.*

1965   U.S. spacecraft **Ranger 8** relays to earth 7,000 pictures of the moon before crashing into an area known as the **Sea of Tranquillity.**

1970   **Chile** agrees to sell $11 million worth of foodstuffs to **Cuba** despite the embargo imposed by members of the Organization of American States in 1964.

St. Sadoth, Bishop of Seleucia-Ctesiphon, and martyr. Also called **Sadosh, Schiadurte, Shadost, Shahdost,** or **Shiadustes.** [d. c. 342]

St. Eleutherius, first Bishop of Tournai. [d. 532]

St. Eucherius, Bishop of Orleans. [d. 743]

St. Wulfric, anchoret. Also called **Ulric, Ulrich,** or **Ulrick.** [d. 1154]

The Beatified

Blessed Elizabeth of Mantua, virgin. [d. 1468]

Construction begins on 5,118 foot **Bosporus Bridge,** linking Istanbul in Europe to Uskudar in Asia.

February 21

Holidays

Norway   Crown Prince Harald's
                Birthday

Religious Calendar

The Saints

St. Severian, Bishop of Scythopolis and martyr. [d. 453]

Birthdates

1728 **Peter III, Emperor of Russia,** 1761–62; deposed in favor of his consort, **Catherine the Great.** [d. July 17, 1762]

1794 **Antonio Lopez de Santa Anna,** Mexican statesman and army officer; President of Mexico, 1833–36, 1846–47. [d. June 21, 1876]

1801 **St. John (Henry) Newman,** British Catholic cardinal, theologian, and writer. Canonized 1980. [d. August 11, 1890]

1821 **Charles Scribner,** U.S. publisher; publisher and founder *Scribner's Monthly*; also with Issac D. Baker founder of Baker & Scribner, publishers, 1846 (later Charles Scribner's Sons). [d. August 26, 1871]

1855 **Alice (Elvira) Freeman Palmer,** U.S. educator; president of Wellesley College, 1882–88; co-founder of the Association of Collegiate Alumnae (later the **American Association of University Women**); first dean of women at the **University of Chicago,** 1892–95. [d. December 6, 1902]

1863 **Rudolph Jay Schaefer,** U.S. brewery executive; introduced first **bottled beer** in U.S., 1891; founder of F. M. Schaefer Brewing Co., 1882. [d. November 9, 1923]

1866 **August von Wasserman,** German bacteriologist; developed the diagnostic test for **syphilis,** 1906. [d. March 15, 1925]

1867 **Otto Hermann Kahn,** U.S. banker, philanthropist; noted patron of the arts. [d. March 29, 1934]

1876 **Constantin Brancusi,** Rumanian-French sculptor; noted for his sculpture of abstract figures. [d. March 16, 1957]

1895 **Henrik C. P. Dam,** Danish biochemist; Nobel Prize in physiology or medicine for discovery of **Vitamin K,** 1943. [d. April 1976]

1903 **Anaïs Nin,** French-U.S. diarist, novelist, short-story writer; well-known for her diaries, especially those recounting bohemian life in war-torn Europe. [d. January 14, 1977]

1907 **W(ystan) H(ugh) Auden,** British-U.S. poet, dramatist, editor; Pulitzer Prize in poetry, 1947. [d. September 18, 1973]

1914 **Zachary Scott,** U.S. actor. [d. October 3, 1965]

1924 **Robert Mugabe,** Prime Minister of newly independent state of **Zimbabwe,** 1980– .

1925 **(David) Sam(uel) Peckinpah,** U.S. film director; known for his artistic but violent films.

1927 **Erma Bombeck,** U.S. newspaper columnist, author; known for her witty writings about the American domestic scene.

Hubert de Givenchy, French fashion designer.

1936 **Barbara Jordan,** U.S. politician, orator; the first black woman to serve in the Texas legislature.

1940 **John (Robert) Lewis,** U.S. black activist civil rights organizer.

Historical Events

891 **Wido of Spoleto** is crowned Holy Roman Emperor and King of Italy.

1613 **Michael Romanov** is elected Tsar of Russia, marking the beginning of the reign of the Romanovs, which lasted until 1917.

1849 British forces crush the Sikh army in the **Battle of Gujarat,** leading to annexation of the **Punjab (Second Sikh War).**

1885 **Washington Monument,** designed by **Robert Mills,** is dedicated in Washington, D.C.

1911 Treaty between U.S. and Japan is signed, affirming the Gentlemen's Agreement for Japanese restriction of labor emigration to the U.S.

St. Germanus of Granfel, abbot and martyr. Also called **German.** [d. c. 677]

St. George, Bishop of Amastris. [d. c. 825]

St. Peter Damian [d. 1072] Optional Memorial.

The Beatified

Blessed Pepin of Landen, mayor of the palace to Kings Clotaire II, Dagobert I, and Sigebert III of France. [d. 646]

Blessed Noel Pinot, priest and martyr. [d. 1794]

1918   British troops capture **Jericho** as the Turks retreat beyond the Jordan (**World War I**).

1921   **Reza Khan,** an army officer, seizes Teheran, overthrowing the Persian government of the Kajars and marking the beginning of the **Pahlavi** dynasty.

1943   Allied Forces in North Africa are placed under the supreme command of **General Dwight D. Eisenhower (World War II).**

1950   U.S. Justice Department files a civil antitrust suit against **Lee and Jacob J. Shubert,** charging them with monopolizing the legitimate theater in the U.S.

1961   The constitution of **Gabon** is promulgated.

1965   **Malcolm X (Malcolm Little),** U.S. black nationalist leader, is assassinated in New York City as he addresses the **Afro-American Unity Organization.**

1971   Brazilian diplomat **Aloysio Dias Gomide** is released by Uruguayan rebels almost seven months after his kidnapping.

1972   U.S. President **Richard M. Nixon** becomes the first U.S. President to visit the **People's Republic of China.**

1975   **John Ehrlichman, H. R. Haldeman,** and **John Mitchell** are sentenced for their participation in the **Watergate Incident.**

1976   Former president **Richard M. Nixon** begins an eight-day visit to the **People's Republic of China** at the invitation of the Chinese government.

1979   **St. Lucia,** a tiny island in the Caribbean, gains independence from Great Britain.

February 22

Holidays

Egypt — **Unity Day**
Celebrates the cooperation among Arab states.

India — **Mothers' Day**
Established as a memorial to **Mrs. Mahatma K. Gandhi,** wife of the Hindu religious leader, nationalist, and social reformer.

Mexico — **Day of Mourning**
Commemorates the death of **Francisco I. Madero,** leader of the campaign to overthrow the dictatorship of **Porfiro Díaz.**

Birthdates

1403   **Charles VII** of France. [d. July 22, 1461]

1440   **Ladislas V,** King of Hungary, 1444–57 posthumous son of Albert II. [d. November 23, 1457]

1732   **George Washington,** first president of the United States, 1789–97; commander-in-chief of the Continental Army. [d. December 14, 1799]

1788   **Arthur Schopenhauer,** German philosopher. [d. September 21, 1860]

1796   **(Lambert) Adolphe Quetelet,** Belgian mathematician; a founder of the **London Statistical Society;** formulated the theory of the **average man.** [d. February 17, 1874]

1810   **Frédéric François Chopin,** Polish-French composer and pianist; noted for his lyric compositions; intimate of **George Sand** (July 1); (some sources give his birthdate as March 1). [d. October 17, 1849]

1819   **James Russell Lowell,** U.S. poet, critic, editor; co-founder of the *Atlantic Monthly;* a key figure in the New England literary renaissance; U.S. Minister to Great Britain, 1880–85. [d. August 12, 1891]

1857   **Robert (Stephenson Smyth) Baden-Powell,** First Baron Baden-Powell of Gilwell; British founder of the **Boy Scouts.** [d. January 8, 1941]

      Heinrich Rudolf Hertz, German physicist; his theories of **electromagnetism** led to the discovery of **wireless telegraphy; Hertzian waves** are named for him. [d. January 1, 1894]

1882   **(Arthur) Eric Gill,** British sculptor, type designer. [d. November 17, 1940.]

1886   **Hugo Ball,** German poet, theatrical producer, Catholic theologian; a founder of **Dadaism.** [d. September 14, 1927]

1892   **David Dubinsky,** U.S. labor leader, born in Poland; President of International Ladies Garment Workers Union (ILGWU), 1932–66. [d. September 17, 1982]

      Edna St. Vincent Millay, U.S. poet, dramatist; Pulitzer Prize in poetry, 1923. [d. October 19, 1950]

1900   **Luis Buñuel,** Spanish film director, working in France, 1920s–30s; in Mexico, 1945–60. [d. July 29, 1983]

      Sean O'Faolain (Sean Whelan), Irish short-story writer, novelist, essayist, biographer.

1907   **Robert Young,** U.S. actor.

1908   **Romulo Betancourt,** Venezuelan statesman; President, 1945–47, 1959–63. [d. September 28, 1981]

      Eddie Albert (Edward Albert Heimberger), U.S. actor.

      Sir John Mills, British actor.

1912   **Henry S. Reuss,** U.S. politician, lawyer; U.S. Congressman, 1954–82.

1932   **Edward M(oore) Kennedy,** U.S. politician, U.S. Senator, 1963– ; brother of President John F. Kennedy (May 29) and Robert F. Kennedy (November 20).

Historical Events

1370   **Robert II** of Scotland accedes to the throne.

Syria	**Unity Day**	
	Celebrates the cooperation among Arab states.	
U.S.	**George Washington's Birthday**	
	Commemorates birthday of the commander-in-chief of the Continental Army and the first president of the U.S.	

Religious Calendar

Feasts

Chair of Peter Commemorates the founding of the See of Antioch by St. Peter. [1st century A.D.]

The Saints

St. Thalassius and **St. Limnaeus**, anchorets. [d. c. 450]

St. Baradates, anchoret. [d. c. 460]

St. Margaret of Cortona, penitent and founder of the Congregation of the Poverelle and the Confraternity of Our Lady of Mercy. [d. 1297]

1418	**Pope Martin V** condemns the doctrines of **John Wycliffe** and **John Hus.**
1785	The merchant ship *Empress of China* leaves New York, inaugurating U.S. trade with the Orient.
1787	The first black settlers, freed slaves, sail from Portsmouth, England, to settle in **Sierra Leone,** Africa.
1819	Treaty between Spain and the U.S. is signed, in which Spain cedes **Florida** to the U.S.; the western boundaries of the **Louisiana Purchase** are fixed.
1847	**Battle of Buena Vista** begins in which Americans under **Zachary Taylor** defeat Mexicans led by **Santa Anna (Mexican War).**
1892	The **People's Party** (Populist Party) is organized at St. Louis, Missouri.
1912	**J. Vedrines,** a Frenchman, becomes the first man to fly over 100 m.p.h.
1913	Mexican President **Francisco I. Madero** is assassinated.
1966	**Prime Minister Milton Obote** of **Uganda** seizes all governmental power and arrests five cabinet members.
1967	A force of over 25,000 U.S. and South Vietnamese troops launch *Operation Junction City,* the largest offensive of the **Vietnam War.**
	Donald B. Sangster is sworn in as Prime Minister of Jamaica.
1972	Irish Republican Army kills seven people at **Aldershot.**

Jean-Bédel Bokassa is named President for Life of the **Central African Republic.**

1980	Martial law is declared in **Afghanistan** as Soviet army attempts to curb civilian unrest.
1983	U.S. government offers to buy all homes and businesses in **Times Beach, Mo.,** which was evacuated because of **dioxin** contamination.

February 23

Holidays

Guyana **Republic Day**
Commemorates Guyana's becoming a republic, 1970.

USSR **Soviet Army and Navy Day**

Religious Calendar

The Saints

St. Polycarp, Bishop of Smyrna and martyr. Most famous of the Apostolic Fathers, the immediate dis-

Birthdates

1417 **Pope Paul II,** Pope from 1464–71. [d. July 26, 1471]

1633 **Samuel Pepys,** English diarist, Secretary to the Admiralty, 1673; 1684–89; his diary offers a unique picture of life in England, 1660–69. [d. May 26, 1703]

1680 **Jean-Baptiste Le Moyne sieur de Bienville,** French-Canadian explorer and colonizer; founder of **New Orleans.** [d. March 7, 1767]

1685 **George Frederick Handel,** British composer born in Germany; noted for his oratorios, especially his *Messiah.* [d. April 14, 1759]

1743 **Meyer Rothschild,** German banker, financier; founder of the **House of Rothschild** financial dynasty. [d. September 19, 1812]

1787 **Emma (Hart) Willard,** U.S. educator; established **Emma Willard School,** Troy, New York, 1821. [d. April 15, 1870]

1817 **George Frederic Watts,** British painter and sculptor; used grand allegorical themes in his work; noted for his fresco *George and the Dragon* in the British Parliament Hall of Poets; executed over 300 portraits of distinguished contemporaries. [d. July 1, 1904]

1832 **John Heyl Vincent,** U.S. Methodist bishop; noted for his development of the **Chatauqua** concept of training Methodist Sunday school teachers. [d. May 9, 1920]

1856 **George Cave,** British judge, political leader; Lord Chancellor, 1922–28. [d. March 29, 1928]

1868 **W(illiam) E(dward) B(urghardt) Dubois,** U.S. historian, reformer; a founder of the **Niagara Movement,** which eventually merged with the National Association for the Advancement of Colored People; editor of numerous books on the black experience; joined the Communist party, 1961; emigrated to Africa where he became a citizen of Ghana, 1962. [d. August 27, 1963]

1879 **Norman Lindsay,** Australian artist and novelist. [d. November 29, 1969]

1883 **Karl Theodor Jaspers,** German philosopher, existentialist. [d. February 26, 1969]

1904 **William (Lawrence) Shirer,** U.S. journalist; author of *Berlin Diary,* 1941, *The Rise and Fall of the Third Reich,* 1960.

1907 **Constantine Karamanlis,** President of Greece, 1980–81.

1924 **Allan MacLeod Cormack,** U.S. physicist. Nobel Prize in physiology or medicine for development of **CAT (computerized axial tomography) scanning x-ray** technique (with G. N. Hounsfield), 1979.

Historical Events

1660 **Charles X** of Sweden dies and is succeeded by **Charles XI.**

1820 **Cato Street Conspiracy** to murder members of the British Cabinet is uncovered in London.

1841 Hostilities between Britain and China resume in the **First Opium War.**

1854 Great Britain recognizes the independence of the **Orange Free State** in South Africa.

1863 Captains **John Speke** and **Richard Burton** publish the news of their discovery of the source of the **Nile River** in Lake Victoria.

1866 **King Alexander Cuza** of Rumania is dethroned and is succeeded by **Charles, Prince of Hohenzollern.**

ciples of the Apostles. Feast formerly January 26. [d. c. 155] Obligatory Memorial

St. Serenus the Gardener, ascetic and martyr. Also called **Cerneulf.** [d. 302]

St. Alexander Akimetes, monk. Instituted a form of choral service which was carried on night and day without interruption. [d. c. 430]

St. Dositheus, monk. [d. c. 530]

St. Milburga, abbess of Wenlock and virgin; founder of the nunnery of Wenlock in Shropshire. Invoked for the protection of crops against the ravages of birds. Also called **Milburge, Mildburga, Mildburh, Mildgytha,** or **Milgithe.**

St. Willigis, Archbishop of Mainz. [d. 1011]

St. Peter Damian, Cardinal-Bishop of Ostia and Doctor of the Church. One of the chief forerunners of the Hildebrandine reform in the Church. Patron of Faenza. [d. 1072]

1905	**Rotary Club International** is founded.
1915	The island of **Lemnos** in the Aegean Sea is seized by the British as a base in their attack on the **Dardanelles,** arousing the protests of the Greek government (**World War I**).
1921	Anti-Bolshevik mutiny by Russian sailors at **Kronstadt** naval base is crushed.
1942	First enemy attack on the U.S. mainland in **World War II** occurs when a Japanese submarine shells an oil refinery near Santa Barbara, California.
1945	U.S. flag is raised on **Mt. Suribachi, Iwo Jima.**
1961	U.S. **National Council of Churches** approves the use of artificial methods for birth control in family planning.
1964	**Libya** announces cessation of U.S. leases for military bases.
	The revolutionary government of **Zanzibar** is officially recognized by the United Kingdom.
1966	Syrian premier Salah al-Bitar's moderate **Baath Party** government is overthrown by left-wing militants in a bloody coup.
1967	Council of the **Organization of American States** unanimously approves the admission of **Trinidad and Tobago.**
1970	**Guyana** formally ends over 150 years of British rule by declaring itself an independent republic.
1971	**Rolls-Royce Ltd.** aircraft and marine divisions are nationalized.
1976	**Daniel Schorr,** U.S. television news correspondent, is suspended from his job at

CBS News for disclosing a secret report of the House Select Committee on Intelligence.

February 24

Holidays

Mexico   **Flag Day**
Anniversary of proclamation of
the *Plan of Iguala*, a proposal
for independence from Spain.

Birthdates

1440   **Matthias I,** of Hungary, 1458–90; brought the Renaissance to eastern Europe. [d. April 6, 1490]

1500   **Charles V,** Holy Roman Emperor, 1519–56, and (as Charles I), King of Spain, 1516–56. [d. September 21, 1558]

1536   **Pope Clement VIII,** pope 1592–1605. [d. March 5, 1605]

1619   **Charles Le Brun,** French painter; first to be appointed painter to the king. Responsible for decoration of **Palace of Versailles.** [d. February 12, 1690]

1709   **Jacques de Vaucanson,** French inventor; created early robot devices of significance for modern industry; noted for contributions to silk-weaving industry. [d. November 21, 1782]

1786   **Wilhelm Carl Grimm,** German philologist, folklorist, lexicographer; with his brother Jacob (January 4) authored the famous *Grimm's Fairy Tales.* [d. December 16, 1859]

1836   **Winslow Homer,** U.S. Romantic painter. [d. September 29, 1910]

1842   **Arrigo Boito,** Italian composer, librettist, poet; known chiefly for his opera *Mefistofele,* which marks a major transition in Italian opera. [d. June 10, 1918]

1852   **George Moore,** Irish novelist, dramatist, critic; with William Butler Yeats (June 13) created a revival in Irish literature. [d. January 21, 1933]

1885   **Chester William Nimitz,** U.S. admiral; commanded U.S. fleet in the Pacific during World War II, 1941–45. [d. February 20, 1966]

Historical Events

1389   Danes defeat **Albert** of Sweden at **Falköping,** paving way for union of Sweden, Denmark, and Norway.

1525   Germans and Spaniards defeat French and Swiss at Paris; **Francis I** of France is taken prisoner **(Hapsburg-Valois Wars).**

1582   **Pope Gregory XIII** issues a papal bull correcting the **Julian Calendar.** His new calendar, the **Gregarian Calendar** still in use today, became effective October 4, 1582.

1664   Confederation of Hamburg, Bremen, and Lübeck is formed as part of the **Hanseatic League.**

1777   **Joseph I** of Portugal dies and is succeeded by **Maria I.**

1785   **John Adams** is appointed the first U.S. Minister to Great Britain.

1848   Revolution in Paris succeeds; **Louis Philippe** abdicates, and the **Republic of France** is proclaimed.

1917   The Germans begin a strategic withdrawal along the Western Front to the fortified **Hindenburg Line (World War I).**

1967   Malaysia, Indonesia, Thailand, Singapore, and the Philippines form the **Association of Southeast Asian Nations (ASEAN)** to promote economic progress and stability in Southeast Asia.

1970   Hawaii state legislature approves a bill legalizing **abortions** on demand.

1971   French oil companies and natural gas facilities are nationalized in **Algeria.**

1972   Rumania and Hungary sign a new 20-year friendship treaty proclaiming their independence and disregard of the **Brezhnev Doctrine.**

1974   Pakistan officially recognizes the nation of **Bangladesh** (formerly **East Pakistan**).

1976   U.S. Secretary of State **Henry Kissinger** signs a foreign policy agreement with Brazil, the first such agreement with a Latin American country.

Religious Calendar

The Saints

SS. Montanus, Lucius, and their companions, martyrs. [d. 259]

St. Praetextatus, Bishop of Rouen and martyr. Also called Pretextatus, or Prix. [d. 586]

St. Matthias the Apostle. [Major Episcopal Holy Day; Minor Lutheran Feast Day]

February 25

Holidays

Kuwait   **National Day**
                Celebrates the accession of
                **Shaykh Sir 'Ab-dallah Al-Salim
                al-Sabah.**

Religious Calendar

The Saints

SS. Victorinus and his companions, martyrs. [d.
284]

Birthdates

1682   **Giovanni Battista Morgagni,** Italian anatomist; the *Father of Medical Pathology.* [d.
December 6, 1771]

1707   **Carlo Goldoni,** Italian dramatist; the father of modern Italian comedy. [d. Februa-
ry 6, 1793]

1746   **Charles Cotesworth Pinckney,** U.S.
statesman, diplomat; a prominent soldier
in the American Revolution. [d. August 16,
1825]

1778   **José de San Martín,** South American
statesman, soldier; with **Simon Bolivar**
(July 24) was one of the leaders in the
South American liberation movement. [d.
August 17, 1850]

1823   **Li Hung-Chang,** leading 19th-century Chinese statesman; advocated modernization
of China. [d. November 7, 1901]

1841   **Pierre Auguste Renoir,** French painter;
one of the founders of **French Impressionism.** [d. December 3, 1919]

1848   **Edward Henry Harriman,** U.S. railroad
magnate; one of the prime movers in the
revitalization of the Union Pacific, the
Southern Pacific, and the Central Pacific
Railroads. [d. September 9, 1909]

1856   **Charles Lang Freer,** U.S. industrialist,
philanthropist; made his fortune manufacturing railroad cars. [d. September 25, 1919]

1866   **Benedetto Croce,** Italian idealist philosopher, author, statesman, critic. [d. Novem-
ber 20, 1952]

1873   **Enrico Caruso,** Italian operatic lyric ten-
or; one of the all-time stars of the Metropolitan Opera, New York. [d. August 2,
1921]

1888   **John Foster Dulles,** U.S. government official, diplomat, lawyer; U.S. Secretary of
State, 1953–59. [d. May 24, 1959]

1901   **Herbert (*Zeppo*) Marx,** U.S. comedian;
with his brothers Harpo (November 21),
Groucho (October 2), Chico (March 26),
and Gummo (date unknown), performed
as an extremely popular vaudeville team.
[d. November 30, 1979]

1904   **(Daisie) Adelle Davis,** U.S. nutritionist, author, natural-foods crusader. [d. May 31,
1974]

1917   **Anthony Burgess,** British novelist, critic;
known for his bizarre novels, usually with
a linguistic twist; author of *Clockwork Orange.*

1943   **George Harrison,** British rock performer;
member of the *Beatles,* 1963–70.

Historical Events

1225   Third re-issue is made of the **Magna
Carta,** this time in its final form.

1308   **Edward II** of England ascends the throne.

1455   The **Italian League** is formed under the
protection of **Pope Nicholas V.**

1570   **Elizabeth I** of England is excommunicated
by **Pope Pius V** for her severe persecution
of Roman Catholics in England.

1803   **Diet of Ratisbon** reconstructs Germany,
abolishing most ecclesiastical princedoms
and imperial cities.

1863   **National Banking Act** is passed in the U.S.,
strengthening the national fiscal system.

1871   The Netherlands cedes all Dutch forts and
towns on the **Gold Coast of Africa** to
Great Britain in exchange for recognition of
Dutch claims in the Far East.

St. Caesarius of Nazianzus, physician. [d. 369]

St. Ethelbert, first Christian king of Kent. Also called **Albert.** [d. 616]

St. Walburga, virgin and abbess of Heidenheim. Also called **Falbourg, Gauburge, Vaubourg, Walburg, Waldburg, Walpurgis, Warpurg,** or **Wilburga.** [d. 779]

St. Gerland, Bishop of Girgenti. [d. 1100]

St. Tarasius, Patriarch of Constantinople. [d. 806]

The Beatified

Blessed Robert of Arbrissel, abbot of Fontevrault. [d. 1117]

Blessed Avertanus, Carmelite lay-brother, and **Romaeus.** [d. 1380]

Blessed Constantius of Fabriano. [d. 1481]

Blessed Sebastian Aparicio, friar. [d. 1600]

1885	Germany annexes **Tanganyika** and **Zanzibar.**
1913	**Sixteenth Amendment** to U.S. Constitution is adopted, providing for an income tax.
1922	*Carnaval des Animaux* by **Camille Saint-Saëns** premieres in Paris.
1933	*U.S.S. Ranger,* the first true aircraft carrier, is commissioned.
1951	**The 22nd Amendment** to the U.S. Constitution is ratified, providing for a maximum of two consecutive presidential terms.
1972	A one-party state is announced in **Zambia.** *Luna 20*, unmanned Soviet probe, returns to earth with samples from the moon's surface.

February 26

Religious Calendar

The Saints

St. Nestor, Bishop of Magydus, martyr. [d. 251]

St. Alexander, Bishop of Alexandria. [d. 328]

Birthdates

1564 **Christopher Marlowe,** baptized on this date, English playwright; author of *Tamburlaine the Great* and *The Tragedy of Dr. Faustus.* [d. 1593]

1786 **François Arago,** French physicist; the first to work out the fundamental laws of **light waves.** [d. October 2, 1853]

1802 **Victor Hugo,** French poet, novelist, dramatist, politician; a leader in the Romantic movement in France. [d. May 22, 1885]

1808 **Honoré Daumier,** French caricaturist, painter, sculptor; known for his satirical cartoons. [d. February 11, 1879]

1846 **William Frederick Cody (Buffalo Bill),** U.S. buffalo hunter, Army scout, Indian fighter, showman. [d. January 10, 1917]

1852 **John Harvey Kellogg,** U.S. physician; his experiments with health foods and dry breakfast cereals inspired brother **Will Kellogg** to found the Kellogg Cereal Co., 1906. [d. December 14, 1943]

1861 **Ferdinand I** of Bulgaria; first king of modern **Bulgaria.** [d. September 10, 1948]

1866 **Herbert Henry Dow,** U.S. chemist; founder of the Dow Chemical Co., 1897. [d. October 15, 1930]

1882 **Husband Edward Kimmel,** U.S. naval officer; commander of **Pearl Harbor** naval base at the time of the Japanese attack, 1941. [d. May 14, 1968]

1887 **Sir Bengal Narsing Rau,** Indian jurist, diplomat; head of United Nations Security Council, 1950. [d. November 29, 1953]

1898 **Shields Warren,** U.S. pathologist; noted for his studies of the effects of radiation on humans. [d. July 1, 1980]

1903 **Giulio Natta,** Italian chemist; Nobel Prize in chemistry for the development of methods for converting simple hydrocarbons into complex polymeric structures (with K. Ziegler), 1963.

Orde Charles Wingate, British Army general; led *Chindits,* or *Wingate's Raiders,* against Japanese Army in northern Burma during World War II. [d. March 24, 1944]

1905 **Umberto Remano,** U.S. artist born in Italy; noted for his portraits of such famous figures as Albert Einstein, Martin Luther King Jr., and John F. Kennedy. [d. September 27, 1982]

1916 **Jackie Gleason,** U.S. comedian, actor.

1932 **Johnny Cash,** U.S. country singer.

Historical Events

1443 **Alfonso V** of Aragon invades Naples.

1797 One-pound and two-pound bank notes are first used in England.

1876 **Korea** is opened to Japanese trade by the signing of a Korean-Japanese Treaty.

1913 *Deux Images* by **Béla Bartók** premieres in Budapest.

1919 **Grand Canyon National Park** in Arizona is established.

1929 **Grand Teton National Park** in Wyoming is established.

1935 *First Symphony* by **Georges Bizet** premieres in Basel, Switzerland.

1961 **Crown Prince Mulay Hassan** is proclaimed King of Morocco.

1962 **Irish Republican Army** announces the end of its campaign of violence against the partition of Ireland with the laying down of its arms and disbanding of its volunteers.

1963 Data from Venus probe *Mariner II,* made public by NASA, indicates that the temperature of **Venus** is about 800 degrees Fahrenheit.

1965 **European Social Charter** comes into force, with Ireland, Norway, Sweden, the United Kingdom, and West Germany as initial parties.

1972 Agreement ending 26 years of civil war in **Sudan** is reached in Addis Ababa.

1980 **Egypt** and **Israel** exchange diplomatic ambassadors for the first time.

St. Porphyry, Bishop of Gaza. Also called **Porphyrius.** [d. 420]

St. Victor the Hermit, priest. Also called **Vittré.** [d. c. 610]

The Beatified

Blessed Leo of Saint-Bertin, abbot. [d. 1163]

Blessed Isabel of France, princess and virgin; daughter of Louis VIII. Founded the monastery of the Humility of the Blessed Virgin Mary. [d. 1270]

February 27

Birthdates

1807 **Henry Wadsworth Longfellow,** U.S. poet; the best-loved and best-known poet of his time; the first American to be honored with a memorial bust in Poets' Corner, Westminster Abbey. [d. March 24, 1882]

1847 **Dame Ellen Alice Terry,** British stage actress; famous for paper courtship with **George Bernard Shaw.** [d. July 21, 1928]

1850 **Henry Edwards Huntington,** U.S. capitalist; organized and financed the Los Angeles transit system and **Pacific Light & Power Co.** [d. May 23, 1927]

Laura Elizabeth Richards, U.S. novelist, short-story writer; Pulitzer Prize in biography, 1917. [d. January 14, 1943]

1861 **Rudolph Steiner,** Austrian educator, writer, social philosopher; founder of movement called **anthroposophy.** [d. March 30, 1925]

1863 **Joaquin Sorolla y Bastida,** Spanish painter; considered one of the foremost modern Impressionists. [d. August 11, 1923]

1881 **Sveinn Björnsson,** first President of Iceland upon its becoming a republic, in 1944. [d. January 25, 1952]

1882 **Burton K. Wheeler,** U.S. politician, lawyer; U.S. Senator, 1923–47; Progressive Party vice-presidential candidate, 1924. [d. January 7, 1975]

1886 **Hugo Lafayette Black,** U.S. jurist, lawyer; U.S. Senator, 1927–37. [d. September 24, 1971]

1891 **David Sarnoff,** U.S. communications executive; President of Radio Corporation of America, 1930–49; Chairman of the Board, 1947–70. [d. December 12, 1971]

1896 **Arthur William Radford,** U.S. admiral; engaged in campaigns in Gilbert and Marshall Islands (World War II). [d. August 17, 1973]

1902 **John (Ernst) Steinbeck,** U.S. novelist; Nobel Prize in literature, 1962. [d. December 20, 1968]

1904 **James Thomas Farrell,** U.S. novelist; author of *Studs Lonigan.* [d. August 22, 1979]

1912 **Lawrence (George) Durrell,** British novelist, poet, playwright, travel writer; author of *Alexandria Quartet.*

1913 **Irwin Shaw,** U.S. novelist, short-story writer. [d. May 16, 1984]

1917 **John Bowden Connally,** U.S. politician, lawyer; Governor of Texas, 1963–69.

1930 **Joanne (Gignilliat) Woodward,** U.S. actress.

1932 **Elizabeth Taylor,** British-U.S. actress.

1934 **Ralph Nader,** U.S. lawyer, consumer advocate, author.

Historical Events

380 **Emperor Theodosius** issues edict regarding the Catholic faith, suppressing **Arianism,** and promoting unity.

1386 Death of **Charles III** of Naples sets off war of succession between his son, **Ladislaus,** and **Louis II** of Anjou.

1844 **Dominican Republic** gains independence from Haiti.

1915 The **Battle of Przasnyz** in northern Poland ends in a Russian victory over the Germans (**World War I**).

1939 France and Britain recognize the government of **General Francisco Franco** in Spain.

1950 U.S. and Canada sign a 50-year treaty designed to increase the power output of

The Saints

SS. Julian, Cronion, and **Besas,** martyrs. Cronion also called **Chronion.** [d. 250]

St. Thalelaeus the Hermit, surnamed **Epiklautos;** also called **Thaliloeus,** or **Thalelaeus the Cilician.** [d. c. 450]

St. Leander, Bishop of Seville. Honored in Spain as a Doctor of the Church. [d. 596]

St. Baldomerus, subdeacon; patron of locksmiths. Also called **Galmier.** [d. c. 660]

St. Alnoth, hermit. [d. c. 700]

St. John of Gorze, abbot. [d. 974]

St. Gabriel Possenti, priest. Also called **Gabriel-of-our-Lady-of-Sorrows.** [d. 1862]

The Beatified

Blessed Mark Barkworth, priest and martyr. Also called **Lambert.** [d. 1601]

---

the **Niagara River** and to protect the beauty of **Niagara Falls.**

1963 **Juan Bosch** takes office as the first constitutionally elected president of the **Dominican Republic** since 1924.

1967 **Antigua** in the Caribbean becomes an associated state within the United Kingdom.

1973 **Wounded Knee,** on the **Oglala Sioux** reservation in South Dakota, is occupied by members of the **American Indian Movement,** who demand an investigation of federal treatment of Indians.

1974 A new constitution is promulgated in **Sweden.**

1976 **Polisario Republic (Saharan Arab Democratic Republic,** formerly the **Spanish Sahara)** is proclaimed.

February 28

Holidays

Finland   **Kalevala Day**
National holiday dedicated to
epic poem **Kalevala.**

Religious Calendar

Feasts

Feast of the Martyrs in the Plague of Alexandria.
[d. 261]

The Saints

St. Proterius, Patriarch of Alexandria and martyr.
[d. 457]

Birthdates

1533   **Michel Eyquem de Montaigne,** French essayist; the founder of a new style in French literature. [d. September 13, 1592]

1683   **René A. F. de Réaumur,** French scientist, entomologist; devised the **thermometric scale**; wrote first technical treatise on iron. [d. October 17, 1757]

1712   **Louis Joseph Montcalm,** French army general; Commander in Chief of French forces in Canada, 1756–59. [d. September 14, 1759]

1797   **Mary Lyon,** U.S. educator; founder of **Mt. Holyoke College,** the first women's college in the U.S., 1837. [d. March 5, 1849]

1820   **Sir John Tenniel,** British cartoonist, artist; illustrated *Alice's Adventures in Wonderland*; cartoonist for *Punch* magazine. [d. February 25, 1914]

1823   **(Joseph) Ernest Renan,** French theologian, religious writer; author of *Life of Jesus,* 1863. [d. October 2, 1892]

1824   **Charles Blondin,** (Jean-François Gravelet), French tightrope walker; crossed above Niagara Falls many times. [d. February 19, 1897]

1833   **Alfred Graf von Schlieffen,** German army field marshal; Chief of General Staff, 1891–1905. [d. January 4, 1913]

1865   **Sir Wilfred Grenfell,** British medical missionary in Labrador; fitted out first hospital ship to serve fishermen in the North Sea; founder of **King George V Seamen's Institute.** [d. October 9, 1940]

1877   **Abbé Henri Edouard-Prosper Breuil,** French priest, archaeologist; authority on **paleolithic art.** [d. August 14, 1961]

1894   **Ben Hecht,** U.S. journalist, playwright, novelist, short-story writer; author of *The Front Page, The Scoundrel.* [d. April 18, 1964]

1896   **Philip Showalter,** U.S. physician; Nobel Prize in physiology or medicine for discovery of **cortisone** (with E. C. Kendall and T. Reichstein), 1950. [d. March 31, 1965]

1901   **Linus Carl Pauling,** U.S. chemist; Nobel Prize in chemistry for studies of molecular bonding, 1954; Nobel Peace Prize, 1962.

1909   **Stephen (Harold) Spender,** British poet, critic.

1915   **Peter Brian Medawar,** British biologist; Nobel Prize in physiology or medicine for discovery of acquired immunity (with F. M. Burnet), 1960.

1924   **Christopher Columbus Kraft,** U.S. aeronautical engineer; flight director of U.S. manned space-flight program, 1959–70.

1930   **Leon N. Cooper,** U.S. physicist; Nobel Prize in physics for work in the field of superconductors (with J. Bardeen and J. R. Schrieffer), 1972.

Historical Events

1474   **Peace of Utrecht** is signed between Hanseatic League and England.

1704   **Abenaki Indians** destroy **Deerfield, Massachusetts.**

1803   Swiss **Act of Mediation** is promulgated under Napoleon, establishing a centralized

St. Hilarus, pope. [d. 468]

SS. Romanus and **Lupicinus,** brothers and abbots; founders of the monasteries of Condat and Leuconne. Romanus is invoked for cure of insanity and protection from drowning. Lupicinus is commemorated separately on March 21. [d. c. 460 and 480]

St. Oswald of Worcester, Archbishop of York. [d. 992]

The Beatified

Blessed Angela of Foligno, widow and mystic. [d. 1309]

Blessed Villana of Florence, matron. [d. 1360]

Blessed Hedwig of Poland, matron. Also called **Jadwiga.** [d. 1399]

Blessed Antonia of Florence, widow and abbess. [d. 1472]

Blessed Louisa Albertoni, widow and nun. Also called **Lodovica.** [d. 1533]

structure for the **Helvetic Republic** (Switzerland).

1825   Treaty between Britain and Russia is signed settling boundaries between Canada and Alaska.

1900   British forces under **Redvers Buller** raise the siege of **Ladysmith,** driving the Boers back **(Boer War).**

1921   Treaty of friendship between **Russia** and **Afghanistan** providing financial and political aid for the Afghans is signed.

1922   **Egypt** is declared independent, ending a seven-year British protectorate. **Fuad I** is recognized as ruler.

1952   **Vincent Massey** becomes the first Canadian-born Governor-General of Canada.

1971   Male voters in **Liechtenstein** defeat a referendum granting women voting rights.

1979   White minority rule in **Rhodesia** comes to an end with the adjournment of the country's parliament.

February 29

Birthdates

1468 **Pope Paul III,** Bishop of Rome, 1534–40; excommunicated Henry VIII of England. [d. November 10, 1549]

1736 **Ann Lee,** English religious leader; founder of American sect of Shakers. [d. September 8, 1784]

1792 **Karl Ernst von Baer,** Russian naturalist, embryologist; discovered the **human ovum.** [d. November 28, 1876]

Gioacchino Antonio Rossini, Italian opera composer; one of the last masters of *opera buffa.* [d. November 13, 1868]

1840 **John Philip Holland,** U.S. inventor born in Ireland; a pioneer in the development of the modern submarine. [d. August 12, 1914]

1904 **Jimmy Dorsey,** U.S. musician; a key figure during the **Big Band** era. [d. June 12, 1957]

1924 **David Stuart Beattie,** New Zealand politician; Governor-General, 1980– .

Historical Events

1720 **Ulrica Eleanor, Queen of Sweden**; abdicated in favor of her husband, **Frederick I.**

1868 British Prime Minister **Benjamin Disraeli** begins his first ministry.

1880 **Gotthard Railway Tunnel** connecting Switzerland and Italy is completed.

1956 **Islamic Republic** is proclaimed in **Pakistan.**

1968 Discovery of the first **pulsar** is announced at Cambridge, England.

March

March, the third month in the Gregorian calendar, has 31 days. In the early Roman civil calendar March marked the beginning of the new year, since it corresponded with the revival of agriculture and of military campaigning. It was named *Martius* in honor of the Roman god of war, Mars.

In 153 B.C., January 1 was adopted as the day the Roman consuls assumed office and as the beginning of the new year, and March was then accepted as the third month for civil purposes. Nevertheless, popular sentiment still viewed March as the first month, so that even in medieval Europe the Christian feast of the Annunciation on March 25 was regarded as the beginning of the year. It was not until after 1582, with the Gregorian calendar reform, that January generally came to be accepted as the start of the year. It is also the month of the vernal equinox (occuring about March 21), after which daylight is longer than darkness. This fact, too, may have contributed to the persistence of regarding March as the first month.

In the astrological calendar, March spans the zodiac signs of Pisces, the Fishes (February 19–March 20) and Aries, the Ram (March 21–April 19).

The birthstone for March is the bloodstone or aquamarine, and the flower is the jonquil or daffodil.

State, National, and International Holidays

St. Patrick's Day
(especially in Ireland)
March 17
Feast of St. Joseph
(Spain)
around March 19
Afghan New Year
(Afghanistan)
Day of vernal equinox
Vernal Equinox Day
(Japan)
usually March 21 or 22
Commonwealth Day
(Swaziland)
First Monday

Town Meeting Day
(Vermont)
First Tuesday
Youth Day
(Zambia)
Second Saturday
Tree Planting Day
(Lesotho)
during Third Week
Youth Day
(Taiwan)
Fourth Monday
Transfer Day
(Virgin Islands)
Final Monday

Seward's Day
(Alaska)
Final Monday
Decoration Day
(Liberia)
during Second Week
Youth Day
(Oklahoma)
First Day of Spring
Prince Johan Kuhio Kalanianaole Day
(Hawaii)
on or near March 26

Special Events and Their Sponsors

National Nutrition Time
American Dietetic Association
Lock Box 99209
Chicago, Illinois 60693
Parents Without Partners Founder's Month
Parents Without Partners
7910 Woodmont Avenue
Bethesda, Maryland 20814
National Peanut Month
National Peanut Council
1000 16th Street, N.W.
Suite 700
Washington, D.C. 20036
Philatelic Literature Month
Franklin D. Roosevelt Philatelic Society
154 Laguna Court
St. Augustine Shores, Florida 32084
National Youth Art Month
The Art and Craft Materials Institute, Inc.
715 Boylston Street
Boston, Massachusetts 02116
National Foreign Language Week
First Week
Alpha Mu Gamma
Los Angeles City College
855 North Vermont Avenue
Los Angeles, California 90029

National Procrastination Week
First Week
Procrastinators' Club
111 Broad-Locust Building
Philadelphia, Pennsylvania 19102
National Save Your Vision Week
First Week
American Optometric Association
243 North Lindbergh Boulevard
St. Louis, Missouri 63141
Volunteers of America Week
First Week
Volunteers of America
3939 North Causeway Boulevard
Metairie, Louisiana 70002
Camp Fire Birthday Week
Second Week
Camp Fire, Inc.
4601 Madison Avenue
Kansas City, Missouri 64112
Girl Scout Week
Second Week
Girl Scouts of the U.S.A.
830 Third Avenue
New York, New York 10022
Music in our Schools Week
Second or Third Week
Music Education National Conference
1902 Association Drive
Reston, Virginia 22091

National Poison Prevention Week
Third Week
Poison Prevention Week Council
P.O. Box 1543
Washington, D.C. 20013

National Wildlife Week
Third Week
National Wildlife Association
1412 16th Street N.W.
Washington, D.C. 20036

Art Week
Final Week
Richard R. Falk Associates
1472 Broadway
New York, New York 10036

International Women's Day
March 8

World Maritime Day
March 17

World Meteorological Day
March 23
United Nations
New York, New York 10017

Fireside Chat Anniversary Day
March 12
Franklin D. Roosevelt Philatelic Society
154 Laguna Court
St. Augustine Shores, Florida 32084

Girl Scout Birthday
March 12

Girl Scouts of the U.S.A.
830 Third Avenue
New York, New York 10022

St. Urho's Day
March 16
Sauna Society of America
1001 Connecticut Avenue, N.W.
Washington, D.C. 20036

Camp Fire Founder's Day
March 17
Camp Fire, Inc.
4601 Madison Avenue
Kansas City, Missouri 64112

Agriculture Day
March 21 or 22
Agriculture Council of America
Suite 708
1625 I Street, N.W.
Washington, D.C. 20006

Memory Day
March 21
Puns Corp.
c/o Robert L. Birch
Box 2364
Falls Church, Virginia 22042

Doctor's Day
March 30
McLaren Hospital
Barrow City, Georgia

Special Days--Other Calendars

	1 Ramadan	Purim	Ash Wednesday	Easter Sunday
1986		March 25		March 30
1987		March 15	March 4	
1988		March 3		
1989		March 21		March 26
1990	March 29	March 11		

March 1

Holidays

Korea	**Independence Movement Day** Anniversary of passive revolution against Japan, 1919.
Paraguay	**Heroes' Day** or **National Defense Day**

Religious Calendar

The Saints
St. Felix II (III), pope. Elected 483. [d. 492]
St. Albinus, Bishop of Angers. Also called **Aubin.** [d. c. 550]

Birthdates

1456 **Ladislas II, King of Bohemia,** 1490–1516; his rule was contested by the Hungarian king, **Matthias Corvinus.** [d. March 13, 1516]

1701 **Johann Jakob Breitinger,** Swiss critic, literary theorist; his anti-rationalism won him the recognition of Goethe and Schiller. [d. December 13, 1776]

1747 **Sir Samuel Romilly,** English lawyer, reformer; opposed harsh and irrational laws; agitated against slavery. [d. November 2, 1818]

1782 **Thomas Hart Benton,** U.S. politician, lawyer, teacher, editor, author; U.S. Senator, 1821–51. [d. April 10, 1858]

1810 **Frédéric François Chopin,** Polish-French composer, pianist; one of the foremost composers of all time; an intimate of George Sand (July 1); some sources give his birthdate as February 22. [d. October 17, 1849]

1812 **Augustus Welby Pugin,** British Victorian Gothic architect; made detail drawings for **Houses of Parliament.** [d. September 14, 1852]

1837 **William Dean Howells,** U.S. novelist, editor, critic; was commonly acknowledged as the *Dean of American Letters.* [d. May 11, 1928]

Georg Moritz Ebers, German Egyptologist, novelist; known for his acquisition of the 16th-century B.C. papyrus henceforth called the **Ebers papyrus.** [d. August 7, 1898]

1841 **Blanche Kelso Bruce,** first black to serve full term as U.S. Senator. [d. March 17, 1898]

1848 **Augustus Saint-Gaudens,** U.S. sculptor, born in Ireland; known for his sculptures of *Abraham Lincoln,* in Chicago, and *General Sherman,* New York City. [d. August 3, 1907]

1880 **(Giles) Lytton Strachey,** British biographer. [d. January 21, 1932]

1886 **Oskar Kokoschka,** Austrian expressionist artist; noted for his use of expressive distortion; condemned by the Nazis, 1937. [d. February 22, 1980]

1896 **Dimitri Mitropoulos,** U.S. symphony conductor; known for interpretations of twentieth-century music. [d. November 2, 1960]

1904 **Glenn Miller,** U.S. bandleader, trombonist. [d. December 16, 1944]

1906 **Joseph Edwin Curran,** U.S. labor leader. [d. August 14, 1981]

1910 **Archer John Porter Martin,** British biochemist; Nobel Prize in chemistry for **paper partition chromatography** (with Richard L. M. Synge), 1952.

David Niven, British actor; known for his roles as a sophisticated and debonair man-about-town. [d. July 29, 1983]

1914 **Ralph Waldo Ellison,** U.S. novelist; author of *The Invisible Man.*

1917 **Robert Traill Spence Lowell,** U.S. poet; Pulitzer Prize in poetry, 1947. [d. September 12, 1977]

St. David, Bishop of Mynyw. Patron of Wales and of poets. Surnamed **The Waterman.** Also called **Dewi.** [d. c. 589]

St. Swithbert, bishop and missionary. Joint patron of St. Peter's Kaiserswerth. Also called **Suidbert, Swibert, Swidbert,** or **Swithbert the Elder.** [d. 713]

St. Rudesind, Bishop of Dumium and abbot. Founded monastery at Celanova. Also called **Rosendo.** [d. 977]

The Beatified

Blessed Roger Le Fort, Archbishop of Bourges. [d. 1367]

Blessed Bonavita, Franciscan tertiary. [d. 1375]

Blessed Christopher of Milan, Apostle of Liguria. [d. 1484]

Blessed Peter René Roque, priest and martyr. [d. 1796]

1920   **Howard Nemerov,** U.S. poet, critic, novelist, teacher; author of *The Salt Garden* and *Mirrors and Windows.*

1921   **Dinah Shore (Frances Rose Shore),** U.S. singer, talkshow hostess.

       Richard Purdy Wilbur, U.S. poet; Pulitzer Prize in poetry, 1956.

1927   **Harry Belafonte,** U.S. singer, actor.

Historical Events

1498   **Vasco da Gama** arrives at **Mozambique,** Africa, on his voyage to India.

1562   Massacre of French Protestants at Vassy begins **Huguenot Wars.**

1692   **Salem Witch Trials** begin in Massachusetts with the conviction of West Indian slave, **Tituba,** for witchcraft.

1790   First **U.S. census** begins.

1792   Holy Roman Emperor **Leopold II** dies and is succeeded by his brother, **Francis II.**

1797   The **Jesuits** are expelled from Spain by **King Charles III.**

1803   **Ohio** is admitted to the Union as the 17th state.

1811   **Mohammed Ali,** Turkish governor of Egypt, massacres the **Mameluke** leaders, breaking their power and seizing supreme power for himself.

1815   **Georgetown College** is chartered, becoming the first Catholic college established in the U.S.

       Napoleon returns to France from Elba.

1836   **Texas** declares its independence from Mexico.

1845   **Texas** is annexed to the U.S. by joint resolution of Congress.

1862   **Kingdom of Italy** is recognized by Prussia.

1865   Telegraph service between Europe and India begins.

1867   **Nebraska** is admitted to the Union as the 37th state.

1871   **Napoleon III** of France is deposed. The French people revolt against his dictatorial rule and unwise empire-building policies.

1872   **Yellowstone National Park,** first of the great U.S. national parks, is established.

1896   **Battle of Aduwa** is fought in which the Abyssinians under Menelik defeat Italians decisively, forcing Italy's withdrawal from the country.

1897   **Japan** adopts the gold standard.

1907   Debussy's *La Mer* premieres in Boston.

1915   The British naval blockade of German East Africa begins (**World War I**).

1917   **February Revolution** in Russia ends.

1919   The new colony of **Upper Volta** is formed by the French.

1921   The first imperial census of Japan is published.

1929   French Chamber of Deputies ratifies **Paris Peace Pact.**

1941   **Bulgaria** permits German troops to enter the country (**World War II**).

1947   **International Monetary Fund** begins operation.

1949   **Joe Louis,** undefeated heavyweight boxing champion, retires.

March 1, cont.

1950 Generalissimo **Chiang Kai-shek** resumes presidency of the Chinese Nationalist government.

1961 President John F. Kennedy establishes the **Peace Corps,** composed of U.S. men and women volunteers for service in underdeveloped foreign countries.

1962 **Benedicto Kiwanuka** takes office as the first prime minister of Uganda, marking the beginning of self-government.

Pakistani President **Mohammed Ayub Khan** announces the adoption of a new constitution providing for a strong presidential form of government.

1965 Remains of **Sir Roger Casement,** Irish patriot hanged in England for treason in 1916, are reburied with state honors in Dublin.

1965 **Indonesia** temporarily withdraws from the United Nations.

1966 Russian spacecraft **Venus 3,** launched November 16, 1965, crashes on Venus, the first man-made object to reach another planet.

Ghanaian National Liberation Council orders the expulsion of Soviet, East German, and Communist Chinese technicians and teachers from the country.

1967 **Oscar Diego Gestido** is inaugurated as President of Uruguay.

U.S. House of Representatives votes to exclude **Rep. Adam Clayton Powell, Jr.,** from the 90th Congress and declares his Harlem seat vacant.

1974 Seven former White House and Nixon campaign officials are indicted by a grand jury investigating the **Watergate Incident.**

1975 A fact-finding delegation of the U.S. Congress visits **South Vietnam** and **Cambodia** at request of U.S. President **Gerald Ford** to determine whether Saigon and Phnom Penh require additional military aid.

1979 The Unión Centro Democrático, headed by **Premier Adolfo Suárez González,** is victorious in the first parliamentary elections held in Spain since the adoption of a new constitution in December 1978.

In a national referendum, Wales and Scotland reject home rule. British **Prime Minister James Callaghan** suffers a political setback because of his strong support of the proposal.

U.S. spacecraft **Voyager 1** begins relaying information as it approaches **Jupiter.**

March 2

Holidays

Burma	**Peasants Day**
Ethiopia	**Victory of Aduwa Day**
	Celebrates Aduwa victory of 1896, which saved country from becoming possession of Italy.
U.S. (Texas)	**Independence Day**
	Commemorates the signing of a declaration of independence from Mexico, 1836.

Birthdates

1316 **Robert II, King of Scotland,** 1371–90, grandson of **Robert Bruce**; called **The Steward**; first of the so-called Stuart line. [d. April 19, 1390]

1459 **Pope Adrian VI,** the only Dutch Pope; reigned 1522–23. [d. September 14, 1523]

1705 **William Murray,** 1st Earl of Mansfield, English jurist; authority on **commercial law.** [d. March 20, 1793]

1769 **Dewitt Clinton,** U.S. political leader, lawyer, historian; Mayor of New York City, 1803–15; Governor of New York, 1817–21, 1825–28. [d. February 11, 1828]

1793 **Sam(uel) Houston,** U.S. politician, soldier, lawyer; U.S. Senator, 1846–59; chief military figure in Texas' fight for independence from Mexico; Governor of Texas, 1859–61. [d. July 26, 1863]

1810 **Pope Leo XIII**; reigned 1878–1903; known for willingness to compromise with civil governments; considered one of the most notable pontiffs in Church history for his constant efforts to achieve world peace. [d. July 20, 1903]

1817 **János Arany,** Hungarian poet; known for his *Toldi* trilology and his epic poem, *King Buda's Death.* [d. October 22, 1882]

1820 **Eduard Douwes Dekker** (*Multatuli*), Dutch novelist, essayist, satirist; wrote works protesting Dutch colonial policies. [d. February 19, 1887]

1824 **Bedřich Smetana,** Czech composer; known as the *Father of Modern Czechoslovak Music.* [d. May 12, 1884]

1829 **Carl Schurz,** U.S. statesman, orator, writer, lawyer, reformer; U.S. Senator, 1869–75, U.S. Secretary of the Interior, 1877–81. [d. May 14, 1906]

1876 **Pius XII,** reigned 1939–58; proclaimed the dogma of the **Assumption of the Virgin Mary,** 1950. [d. October 9, 1958]

1880 **Ivar Kreuger,** Swedish financier, industrialist, swindler; known for his vast international match monopoly; after his empire collapsed, he committed suicide. [d. March 12, 1932]

1897 **William Miles (Webster) Thomas, Baron Thomas,** British industrialist; President, International Air Transport Association, 1951–52; Chairman, Monsanto Chemicals, Ltd., 1956–63. [d. February 9, 1980]

1900 **Kurt Weill,** German composer; wrote *Threepenny Opera*; husband of Lotte Lenya (October 18). [d. April 3, 1950]

1902 **A(lmer) S(tilwell) Monroney,** U.S. journalist, politician; U.S. Congressman, 1939–50; U.S. Senator, 1951–68. [d. February 13, 1980]

1904 **Theodore Seuss Geisel (*Dr. Seuss*),** U.S. author and illustrator of children's books.

1909 **Mel(vin Thomas) Ott,** U.S. baseball player; inducted into Baseball Hall of Fame, 1951. [d. November 21, 1958]

1931 **Tom Wolfe (Thomas Kennerly Wolfe, Jr.),** U.S. journalist; leader in the **New Journalism** movement in the U.S.; author of *Kandy-Kolored Tangerine-Flake Streamline Baby, The Electric Kool-Aid Acid Test*, and *The Right Stuff.*

1942 **John Irving,** U.S. novelist; author of *The World According to Garp*, and *The Hotel New Hampshire.*

Historical Events

1476 The Swiss Confederacy defeats **Charles the Bold** of Burgandy at the **Battle of Granson**.

The Saints

St. Joavan, monk and bishop. [d. c. 562]

St. Chad, Bishop of Lichfield; patron saint of medicinal springs. Also called **Caedda, Ceada,** or **Ceadda.** [d. 672]

The Martyrs under the Lombards. [d. c. 579]

The Beatified

Blessed Charles the Good, Count of Flanders and Amiens, and martyr. Also called **the Dane.** [d. 1127]

Blessed Fulco of Neuilly, priest and missionary. [d. 1201]

Blessed Agnes of Bohemia, virgin and founder of first establishment of Poor Clares north of the Alps. Also called **Agnes of Prague.** [d. 1282]

Blessed Henry Suso, Dominican prior. [d. 1365]

Blessed Angela de la Cruz Guerrero Gonzalez. [beatified, 1982]

1765 **Stamp Act** is passed by the English Parliament, requiring American colonists to buy and affix British-issued stamps to most documents.

1801 Spain declares war on Portugal (**War of the Oranges**).

1835 **Francis I** of Austria dies and is succeeded by **Ferdinand I.**

1855 **Nicholas I** of Russia dies and is succeeded by **Alexander II.**

1865 First message by cable from Calcutta to London is sent.

1867 U.S. Congress passes **Reconstruction Act,** setting up conditions for reintegration of Southern states into the Union.

1877 **Rutherford B. Hayes** is declared U.S. President by a special Electoral Commission in the disputed election of 1876.

1887 **Hatch Act** providing for the promotion of U.S. agricultural science by creating **state agricultural experiment stations** becomes law.

1917 **Puerto Rico** becomes U.S. territory and its inhabitants become U.S. citizens.

Hamadan is captured by the Russians in a new drive against the Turks in Persia (Iran) (**World War I**).

1939 **Pius XII** is elected pope.

1943 **Battle of Bismarck Sea** begins, resulting in major victory by U.S. over Japanese shipping and aircraft (**World War II**).

1949 U.S. Air Force Captain **James Gallagher** and 13 crew members complete the first round-the-world non-stop flight in a Boeing B-50 Superfortress, *Lucky Lady II*.

1956 **Morocco** gains independence from France.

1958 First crossing of **Antarctica** by land is made by **Sir Vivian Fuchs.**

1961 French troops complete the evacuation of all their military bases in Morocco.

1962 Coup d'état in **Burma** replaces the U Nu government with a military government.

1969 Soviet and Chinese border forces engage in heavy fighting over **Damansky (Chanpao) Island,** a disputed territory in the Ussuri River.

1970 **Rhodesia** declares itself a republic, dissolving its last ties with Great Britain.

1972 *Pioneer 10*, unmanned U.S. interplanetary probe, is launched from Cape Kennedy, Florida.

1973 Representatives of 80 countries agree to a treaty outlawing trade in 375 **endangered wildlife species.**

1974 Military rule ends in **Burma** with the adoption of a new constitution; U Ne Win is declared President.

1977 U.S. House of Representatives approves stringent **code of ethics** for itself.

March 3

Holidays

Bulgaria   **Liberation Day**
Commemorates Bulgaria's release from Ottoman Rule, 1878.

Japan   **Hina Matsuri** or **Dolls' Day** or **Peach Festival**
A day on which ceremonial dolls are displayed throughout the country by young girls. The dolls are decorated with peach blossoms, the symbols of mildness and peacefulness, qualities the girls hope to achieve before marriage.

Malawi   **Martyrs' Day**
Honors the nation's heroes.

Birthdates

1606   **Edmund Waller,** English poet; political activist; popularized the **heroic couplet.** [d. October 21, 1687]

1756   **William Godwin,** English philosopher; a noted proponent of English radicalism. [d. April 7, 1836]

1793   **Charles Sealsfield (Karl Anton Postl),** Austrian novelist, short-story writer. [d. May 26, 1864]

William Charles Macready, English actor. theatrical manager; known for Shakespearean roles. [d. April 27, 1873]

1826   **Joseph Wharton,** U.S. metals producer; developed process for making pure malleable nickel; a founder of **Swarthmore College**; **Wharton School of Business and Commerce** at University of Pennsylvania is named for him. [d. January 11, 1909]

1831   **George Mortimer Pullman,** U.S. manufacturer, inventor; developed first **Pullman railroad car.** [d. October 19, 1897]

1841   **John Murray,** Canadian scientist; one of the pioneers of **oceanography.** [d. March 16, 1914]

1845   **Georg Cantor,** German mathematician; founded **theory of sets** and **theory of irrational numbers.** [d. January 6, 1918]

1847   **Alexander Graham Bell,** U.S. inventor, born in Scotland; the first to patent and commercialize the **telephone.** [d. August 2, 1922]

1869   **Sir Henry Joseph Wood,** British conductor, composer; conductor of Queen's Hall Symphony (**London Symphony**), 1897–1944. [d. August 19, 1944]

1873   **William Green,** U.S. labor leader; President of American Federation of Labor, 1924–52. [d. November 21, 1952]

1883   **Clifford Milburn Holland,** U.S. civil engineer; **Holland Tunnel** in New York City is named for him. [d. October 27, 1924]

1895   **Ragnar Frisch,** Norwegian economist; Nobel Prize in economics for contributions to study of business cycles, 1969. [d. January 31, 1973]

Matthew Bunker Ridgway, U.S. Army general; Supreme Commander, Allied Forces in Europe, 1952–53; U.S. Army Chief of Staff, 1953–55.

1899   **Alfred M. Gruenther,** U.S. Army general; gifted staff officer and administrator; remembered for his work with the North Atlantic Treaty Organization (NATO). [d. 1966]

1911   **Jean Harlow (Harlean Carpentier),** U.S. actress. [d. June 7, 1937]

1918   **Arthur Kornberg,** U.S. physician; Nobel Prize in physiology or medicine for discoveries concerning **DNA,** 1959.

| Morocco | **Feast of the Throne** or **Morocco National Day** or **Fête du Trône** Marks accession to throne of **King Hassan II**, 1961. |
| Sudan | **National Unity Day** Honors cooperation among Arab nations. |

Religious Calendar

The Saints

SS. Marinus and **Astyrius,** martyrs. Also called **Asterius** and **Marnan.** [d. c. 262]

SS. Emeterius and Chelidonius, soldiers and martyrs. Patrons of Santander, Spain. Emeterius also called **Madir.** [d. 304]

St. Arthelais, virgin. [d. c. 560]

St. Non. Also called **Nonnita.** [d. 6th century]

St. Winwaloe, abbot. Also called **Galnutius, Gué-** nolé, **Guignolé, Guingalois, Guinvaloeus, Wingalotus,** or **Winwalocus.** [d. 6th century]

St. Anselm of Nonantola, abbot. [d. 803]

St. Cunegund, Empress of Rome and widow. Also called **Cunegunda,** or **Cunegundes.** [d. 1033]

St. Gervinus, Abbot of Saint-Riquier. Also called the **Holy Abbot.** [d. 1075]

St. Aelred, Abbot of Rievaulx. Also called **Ailred.** [d. 1167]

The Beatified

Blessed Serlo, Abbot of Gloucester. [d. 1104]

Blessed Jacopino of Canepaci, Carmelite lay-brother. [d. 1508]

Blessed Teresa Verzeri, virgin and founder of the Daughters of the Sacred Heart. [d. 1852]

Blessed Innocent of Berzo, priest and Capuchin Friar Minor. [d. 1890]

Historical Events

1812 First **U.S. foreign aid bill** authorizes $50,000 for relief of victims of an earthquake in Venezuela.

1815 U.S. declares war on **Algiers.**

1819 U.S. Congress authorizes war on pirates in Gulf of Mexico.

1820 **Missouri Compromise** is passed by U.S. Congress, admitting **Maine** as a free state and **Missouri** as a slave state.

1845 **Florida** is admitted to the Union as 27th state.

1861 Serfs are emancipated in Russia.

1875 *Carmen,* by **Georges Bizet,** premieres in Paris.

1878 Russia signs treaty of peace with the Turks at **San Stefano,** ending the **Russo-Turkish War; Serbia** gains its independence.

1879 **Belva Anna Bennett Lockwood** becomes first woman to try a case before the **U.S. Supreme Court.**

1886 Peace is established between Bulgaria and Serbia with the signing of **Treaty of Bucharest.**

1918 **Treaty of Brest-Litovsk** is signed by Russia and the Central Powers, ending World War I.

1921 **Crown Prince Hirohito** begins the first world tour by any member of the Japanese imperial family.

1924 **Turkish Caliphate** is abolished.

1931 *The Star-Spangled Banner* is officially designated **U.S. national anthem.**

1960 **Pope John XXIII** names seven new cardinals of the Roman Catholic Church; among them the first Japanese, Filipino, and black cardinals.

1962 **George Borg Olivier** is sworn in as **Malta's** first prime minister under a constitution extending self-rule to the British colony.

1963 **Senegal** adopts a new constitution.

1964 **George C. Price** is sworn in as the first prime minister of **British Honduras** under a constitution providing internal self-government.

1967 Caribbean island of **Grenada** is granted internal self-government.

1969 *Apollo 9* spacecraft is launched from Cape Kennedy.

March 4

Holidays

| U.S. | **Constitution Day** Celebration of the day when the U.S. Constitution came into effect, March 4, 1789. |
| U.S. (Vermont) | **Admission Day** Celebrates Vermont's admission to the Union, 1791. |

Religious Calendar

The Saints

St. Lucius, pope; reigned 253–254; elected Bishop of Rome 253. Patron of Copenhagen. [d. 254]

Birthdates

1394 **Prince Henry the Navigator,** Portuguese prince; sponsored voyages of discovery leading to foundation of the Portuguese Empire. [d. November 13, 1460]

1678 **Antonio Vivaldi,** Italian composer, violin virtuoso. [d. July 28, 1741]

1747 **Count Casimir Pulaski,** Polish cavalry general in the American Revolution. [d. October 11, 1779]

1754 **Benjamin Waterhouse,** U.S. physician; promoted scientific approach to **vaccination** in U.S. [d. October 2, 1846]

1782 **Johann Rudolf Wyss,** Swiss folklorist; edited his father's story, *Swiss Family Robinson.* [d. March 21, 1830]

1798 **Sigurdur Eirikson Breidfjord,** Icelandic poet. [d. July 21, 1846]

1826 **John Buford,** Union Army general during U.S. Civil War; known for his brilliant command of Union infantry. [d. December 16, 1863]

1888 **Knute (Kenneth) Rockne,** U.S. football coach; famous for leadership in sport; best known for development of *Fighting Irish* of Notre Dame. [d. March 31, 1931]

1901 **Charles Henry Goren,** U.S. bridge expert, lawyer.

1904 **George Gamow,** U.S.-Russian physicist; known for research in **stellar evolution.** [d. August 19, 1968]

1913 **John Garfield (Julius Garfinkle),** U.S. actor. [d. May 21, 1952]

1928 **Alan Sillitoe,** British novelist.

1932 **Miriam Makeba,** South African singer.

Historical Events

1152 **Frederick I Barbarossa** is elected King of Germany.

1193 **Saladin of Damascus,** sultan and Muslim hero, one of the chief opponents of the Crusades, dies.

1461 **Henry VI** of England is deposed; succeeded by **Edward IV.**

1493 **Christopher Columbus** lands at Lisbon after completing his first voyage to the New World.

1510 **Afonso de Albuquerque,** Portuguese navigator, annexes **Goa,** on Indian subcontinent, for Portugal.

1681 **William Penn** is given a charter for lands in the New World by **King Charles II.**

1789 First meeting of **U.S. Congress** under the Constitution takes place.

1791 **Vermont** is admitted to the Union as the 14th state.

1793 **George Washington** is inaugurated for a second term as President of the United States, in Philadelphia; **John Adams** is Vice-President.

1794 **Eli Whitney** is granted a patent for his **cotton gin.**

1797 **John Adams** is inaugurated as the second President of the United States; **Thomas Jefferson** becomes Vice-President.

1801 **Thomas Jefferson** becomes the first president to be inaugurated in the new U.S. capital of **Washington, D.C.; Aaron Burr** becomes Vice-President.

St. Adrian, missionary bishop, and his companions, martyrs. [d. c. 875]

St. Peter of Cava, first bishop of Policastro. [d. 1123]

St. Casimir of Poland, prince. Patron of Poland. Son of Casimir IV, King of Poland. Also called the **Peacemaker.** [d. 1484] Optional Memorial.

The Beatified

Blessed Humbert III of Savoy, count. [d. 1188]

Blessed Christopher Bales, priest and martyr. Also called **Bayles.** [d. 1590]

Blessed Placida Viel, virgin and second superior general of the Sisters of the Christian Schools. [d. 1877]

1809   **James Madison** is inaugurated as fourth President of the United States; **Elbridge Gerry** is Vice-President.

1817   **James Monroe** is inaugurated as fifth President of the United States; **Daniel D. Tompkins** is Vice-President.

1825   **John Quincy Adams** is inaugurated as sixth President of the United States; **John C. Calhoun** is Vice-President.

1828   The **Baltimore & Ohio Railroad** is begun; it is the first public railroad in the U.S.

1829   **Andrew Jackson** is inaugurated as the seventh President of the United States; **John C. Calhoun** is Vice-President.

1837   **Martin Van Buren** is inaugurated as eighth President of the United States; **Richard M. Johnson** is Vice-President.

1841   **William H. Harrison** is inaugurated as ninth President of the United States; on his death a month later, the Vice-President, **John Tyler,** becomes the tenth President.

1845   **James Polk** is inaugurated as the 11th President of the United States; **George M. Dallas** is Vice-President.

1849   **Zachary Taylor** is inaugurated as the 12th President of the United States; **Millard Fillmore,** the Vice-President, becomes the 13th President following Taylor's death in 1850.

1853   **Franklin Pierce** is inaugurated as the 14th President of the United States; **William R. King** is Vice-President.

1857   **James Buchanan** is inaugurated as the 15th President of the U.S.; **John C. Breckinridge** is Vice-President.

1861   **Abraham Lincoln** is inaugurated as 16th President of the United States; **Hannibal Hamlin** is Vice-President.

U.S. Government Printing Office is established.

1865   **Abraham Lincoln** is inaugurated for a second term; his Vice-President, **Andrew Johnson,** becomes 17th President following Lincoln's assassination.

1869   **Ulysses S. Grant** is inaugurated as 18th President of the United States; **Henry Wilson** is Vice-President.

1871   **U.S. Civil Service Commission** is established by U.S. President **Ulysses S. Grant.**

1876   **Don Carlos,** pretender to the Spanish throne and leader of the **Carlist** forces, arrives in England, having given up his fight in Spain.

1877   **Rutherford B. Hayes** is inaugurated as 19th President of the United States; **William A. Wheeler** is Vice-President.

1878   **Pope Leo XIII** revives Roman Catholic hierarchy in Scotland.

1881   **James Garfield** is inaugurated as 20th President of the United States; **Chester A. Arthur,** Vice-President, becomes 21st President following Garfield's assassination.

1885   **Grover Cleveland** is inaugurated as 22nd President of the United States; **Thomas A. Hendricks** is Vice-President.

1889   **Benjamin Harrison** is inaugurated as 23rd President of the United States; **Levi P. Morton** is Vice-President.

1893   **Grover Cleveland** is inaugurated for a second term as 24th President of the

March 4, cont.

United States; **Adlai E. Stevenson** is Vice-President.

1897 **William McKinley** is inaugurated as the 25th President of the United States; **Garret A. Hobart** is Vice-President.

1901 **William McKinley** is inaugurated for a second term as President of the United States; **Theodore Roosevelt**, his Vice-President, becomes 26th President following McKinley's assassination.

1905 **Theodore Roosevelt** is inaugurated after being elected President; **Charles Warren Fairbanks** is Vice-President.

1909 **William Howard Taft** is inaugurated as the 27th President of the United States; **James S. Sherman** is Vice-President.

1913 **(Thomas) Woodrow Wilson** is inaugurated as the 28th President of the United States; **Thomas R. Marshall** is Vice-President.

1915 Railroad passenger service across the Lower Ganges opens in India.

1917 **(Thomas) Woodrow Wilson** is inaugurated for a second term as President of the United States; **Thomas R. Marshall** remains his Vice-President.

1921 **Warren G. Harding** is inaugurated as 29th President of the United States; **Calvin Coolidge** is Vice-President.

1925 **Calvin Coolidge** is inaugurated as the 30th President of the United States; **Charles G. Dawes** is Vice-President.

1927 The rush for the **Grosfontein diamond field** in South Africa opens with about 25,000 runners participating.

1929 **Herbert C. Hoover** is inaugurated as the 31st President of the United States; **Charles Curtis** is Vice-President.

1931 Indian leader **Mahatma Gandhi** ends second **civil disobedience** campaign as British release nonviolent political prisoners.

1933 **Franklin Delano Roosevelt** is inaugurated as the 32nd President of the United States; **John Nance Garner** is Vice-President.

1942 U.S. Air Force strikes **Marcus Island,** 1200 miles southeast of Tokyo (**World War II).**

1958 The *Nautilus,* U.S. atomic submarine, passes under the polar ice cap.

1962 U.S. Atomic Energy Commission announces that the first **atomic power plant** in Antarctica is in operation at **McMurdo Sound.**

1964 **James R. Hoffa,** President of the International Brotherhood of Teamsters, is found guilty in Chattanooga, Tennessee, of tampering with a federal jury in 1962.

1975 The government of Rhodesia arrests Methodist clergyman **Ndabaningi Sithole,** President of the militant **Zimbabwe African National Union,** on charges of plotting to murder black rivals.

1977 Earthquake destroys parts of **Bucharest, Rumania,** and nearby area, leaving 1,500 dead.

March 5

Religious Calendar

The Saints
SS. Adrian and Eubulus, martyrs. [d. 309]
St. Eusebius of Cremona. [d. c. 423]

Birthdates

1326 **Louis I, King of Hungary,** reigned 1342–82. Joint ruler of Poland with **Casimir III.** [d. September 10, 1382]

1512 **Gerardus Mercator** (Gerhard Kremer), Flemish geographer; Mercator projection, used in cartography, is named for him. [d. December 5, 1594]

1658 **Antoine de la Mothe Cadillac,** French fur trader, explorer; founded the city of **Detroit, Michigan,** 1701. [d. October 15, 1730]

1824 **James Merritt Ives,** U.S. painter, lithographer; with his partner, Nathaniel Currier (March 27), founded the firm **Currier & Ives,** which produced art prints extremely popular in the U.S. and in Europe, 1857–95. [d. January 3, 1895]

Elisha Harris, U.S. physician; pioneer in **public health** field in U.S. [d. January 31, 1884]

1830 **Charles Wyville Thomson,** British naturalist; led early oceanographic voyage, which circumnavigated the globe; described his findings in *The Voyage of the Challenge.* [d. March 10, 1882]

1836 **William Steinway,** U.S. piano manufacturer. [d. November 30, 1896]

1852 **Lady Isabella Gregory,** Irish writer, playwright; contributed greatly to the renaissance of **Irish literature** in the late 19th century. [d. May 22, 1932]

1853 **Howard Pyle,** U.S. illustrator, painter, author; noted for his highly popular children's books, usually dealing with medieval themes; also recognized for his renderings of American historical scenes; among his students were **Maxfield Parrish** (July 25) and **N. C. Wyeth** (October 22). [d. November 9, 1911]

1870 **(Benjamin) Franklin Norris,** U.S. novelist. [d. October 25, 1902]

1879 **William Henry Beveridge,** British economist; wrote *Beveridge Report* on social services in post-war Great Britain. [d. March 16, 1963]

1887 **Hector Villa-Lobos,** Brazilian composer, music educator; composed 12 symphonies; known for his espousal of nationalistic themes in his music. [d. November 17, 1959]

1936 **Cannan Banana,** Zimbabwean statesman; President, 1980– .

Historical Events

493 **Odoacer,** leader of German tribe, is defeated at **Ravenna** by **Theodoric** and his Ostrogoths.

1460 **Christian I** of Denmark becomes Duke of **Schlesvig and Holstein,** which are declared forever indivisible.

1496 **Henry VII** of England gives his patronage to **John Cabot** for his voyages of exploration and discovery to **North America.**

1770 **Boston Massacre** occurs as a result of the American colonists' resentment of having British troops quartered in the city; several are killed as British troops fire into a mob.

1904 *String Quartet in F* by **Maurice Ravel** premieres in Paris.

1907 First **radio broadcast** of a musical composition takes place when **Lee De Forest** transmits a performance of Rossini's *William Tell Overture* from Telharmonic Hall in New York to the Brooklyn Navy Yard.

1916 **General Jan Smuts** of the **Union of South Africa** begins an advance on **Kilimanjaro,** German East Africa (**World War I**).

1920 **Norway** joins **League of Nations.**

1923 **Montana** and **Nevada** enact the first old-age pensions in the U.S.

The first **Workmen's Compensation Act** is passed in India.

1924 **Sweden** officially recognizes the government of **Soviet Russia.**

1928 A passive resistance strike begins in India against the **East Indian Railway.**

1931 The **Delhi Pact** between **Mahatma Gandhi** and **Edward Wood, Viceroy Irwin,** brings a halt to the **civil disobedience** campaign with Gandhi accepting the federal constitution plan adopted by the conference in return for British efforts to lessen repression.

1960 Indonesian President **Sukarno** suspends the Indonesian parliament.

Guinea becomes the first nation outside the Communist bloc to recognize **East Germany.**

1967 UN Secretary General **U Thant,** returning to New York from Burma, declares that "Peace is not yet in sight" in Vietnam, and predicts a "prolonged and bloody" conflict unless the U.S. halts bombing raids on **North Vietnam.**

1976 **Spain** moves towards democracy by allowing free political parties, except terrorists, anarchists, separatists, or Communists.

1977 In an unprecedented two-hour radio broadcast, U.S. President **Jimmy Carter** speaks over the telephone with 42 callers from 26 states.

1979 *Voyager 1* relays data from **Jupiter,** including photographs of its four largest moons.

China begins withdrawal of its troops from **Vietnam.**

March 6

Holidays

Ghana   **Independence Day**
Honors establishment of sovereignty of Ghana, 1957.

Guam   **Discovery Day** or **Magellan Day**
Commemorates discovery of island by Magellan on this date, 1521.

Religious Calendar

The Saints
St. Chrodegang, Bishop of Metz. [d. 766]

Birthdates

1475   **Michelangelo (surnamed Buonarroti),** Italian painter, sculptor, architect, poet; the consummate creative genius; known throughout the world for his mastery of several different art forms. [d. February 18, 1564]

1483   **Francesco Guicciardini,** Italian historian and statesman; prominent in the affairs of Florence. [d. May 22, 1540]

1492   **Juan Luis Vives,** Spanish humanist, philosopher; known especially as a proponent of induction as a philosophical method; *De Anima et Vita*, his chief work, is the first work dealing with psychology. [d. May 6, 1540]

1619   **(Savinien de) Cyrano de Bergerac,** French novelist, playwright; noted duelist. [d. July 28, 1655]

1787   **Joseph von Fraunhofer,** German astronomer; the first to chart lines of **solar spectrum,** naming the principal ones. [d. June 7, 1826]

1806   **Elizabeth Barrett Browning,** English poet; best known for her *Sonnets from the Portuguese*; wife of Robert Browning (May 7). [d. June 29, 1861]

1812   **Aaron Lufkin Dennison,** U.S. watch manufacturer; dubbed *Father of the Watch Industry* in the U.S. [d. January 9, 1895]

1831   **Philip Henry Sheridan,** Union Army general during U.S. Civil War; known more for his aggressiveness and ability to inspire confidence in his troops than for his skill in military strategy; Commander-in-Chief of U.S. Army, 1883–88. [d. August 5, 1888]

1844   **Nicolai Rimski-Korsakov,** Russian composer, teacher; composed numerous operas; among his most popular symphonic poems is *Scheherazade*. [d. June 21, 1908]

1885   **Ring(old) Lardner,** U.S. humorist, short-story writer. [d. September 25, 1933]

1906   **Lou Costello (Louis Cristillo),** U.S. comedian; partner of Bud Abbott (October 2); made numerous comedy films in 1940s and 1950s. [d. March 3, 1959]

Lawrence (Lovell) Schoonover, U.S. author; wrote dozens of historical novels based on carefully researched fact; author of *The Burnished Blade*. [d. January 8, 1980]

1909   **Obafemi Awolowo,** Nigerian politician, writer; Chancellor of **University of Ife,** 1967– ; leader of **Unity Party of Nigeria,** 1979– .

1927   **Leroy Gordon Cooper,** U.S. astronaut; commander pilot of *Gemini 5* spacecraft, 1965.

1930   **Lorin Maazel,** U.S. conductor, violinist.

1937   **Valentina Vladimirovna Tereshkova,** Russian cosmonaut; the first woman to travel into space, 1963.

1941   **Willie Stargell,** U.S. baseball player.

1947   **Dick Fosbury,** U.S. high jumper; originator of the *Fosbury Flop*; won Olympic gold medal, 1968.

Historical Events

1480   **Treaty of Toledo** is signed, in which Spain recognizes conquest of **Morocco** by Portugal and Portugal cedes claims to **Canary Islands.**

144

St. Fridolin, abbot. Also called the **Traveller, Viator.** [d. c. 6th century]

SS. Cyneburga, abbess, **Cyneswide,** abbess, and **Tibba,** hermitess. Cyneburga founded the Convent of Cyneburgecester, or Castor. [d. 7th century]

St. Cadroe, abbot. Also called **Cadroc,** or **Cadroel.** [d. 976]

SS. Balred and **Bilfrid,** hermits. Balred also called **Baldrede,** or **Balther.** [d. 8th century]

St. Ollegarius, Archbishop of Tarragona. Also called **Olaguer,** or **Oldegar.** [d. 1137]

St. Cyril, Patriarch of Constantinople and prior-general of the Carmelites. Also called **Cyrillus.** [d. c. 1235]

St. Colette, virgin and superior of all convents of Minoresses. [d. 1447]

The Beatified

Blessed Jordan of Pisa, Dominican priest. [d. 1311]

1629 **Edict of Restitution** orders all church property secularized in Germany since 1552 to be restored to the Roman Church.

1714 **Peace of Rastatt** between France and Holy Roman Emperor, **Charles VI,** is signed; France recognizes Italian possessions of the Hapsburgs; Electors of Bavaria and Cologne are restored; Spain relinquishes possessions in Flanders, Luxembourg, and Italy.

1819 U.S. Supreme Court hands down landmark *M'Culloch v. Maryland* decision; Justice Marshall states doctrine of loose construction of U.S. Constitution.

1834 The city of **Toronto, Canada** is incorporated; William Lyon Mackenzie is its first mayor.

1836 Mexican troops under **Santa Anna** capture the **Alamo** and massacre the American garrison defending it, including **Davy Crockett** and **James Bowie.**

1882 **Milan IV** is proclaimed king of an independent **Serbia** by the Serbian assembly.

1889 **Milan, King of Serbia,** abdicates in favor of his young son **Alexander;** a liberal regency is established.

1898 **Sino-German Convention** is signed, giving Germany a 99-year lease on **Kiaochow Bay** and railway and mining privileges in **Shantung.**

1912 The first use of **dirigibles** in warfare takes place in an Italian action against the Turks in **Tripoli** (**First Balkan War**).

1916 The **Battle of Verdun** is renewed with German attacks on both sides of the Meuse River (**World War I**).

1933 A four-day **national bank holiday** begins in the U.S., marking the start of the administration of U.S. President **Franklin D. Roosevelt.**

1943 U.S. cruisers and destroyers bombard **Vila** and **Munda** in the **Solomon Islands** (**World War II**).

1944 In an Allied air offensive, 600 U.S. planes bomb **Berlin** (**World War II**).

1945 Allied troops capture **Cologne** (**World War II**).

1947 U.S. Supreme Court upholds a fine against **John L. Lewis,** President of **United Mine Workers,** for a strike called in November 1946 in defiance of an injunction.

1962 U.S. pledges itself to defend **Thailand** without waiting for prior agreement on action by the Southeast Asia Treaty Organization.

1964 Crown Prince **Constantine** is proclaimed King of Greece following the death of his father, **Paul I.**

1967 **Svetlana Alliluyeva,** daughter of the late Soviet dictator **Joseph Stalin,** seeks asylum at the U.S. Embassy in New Delhi, India.

March 7

Religious Calendar

The Saints

SS. **Perpetua, Felicity, Revocatus, Saturninus, Saturus,** and **Secundulus,** martyrs. Felicity patron

Birthdates

1693   **Pope Clement XIII,** reigned 1758–69. [d. February 2, 1769]

1707   **Stephen Hopkins,** American patriot, farmer, merchant, signer of the Declaration of Independence; Governor of Rhode Island. [d. July 13, 1785]

1765   **Joseph Nicéphore Niepce,** French physicist, inventor; pioneer in development of **photography.** [d. July 5, 1833]

1785   **Alessandro (Francesco Tommaso Antonio de) Manzoni,** Italian novelist, poet; best known for his novel *I Promessi Sposi* (*The Betrothed*), a model of modern Italian prose. [d. April 28, 1873]

1792   **Sir John Frederick Herschel,** English astronomer; son of **Sir William Herschel** (November 15); continued his father's experiments and studies; discovered solvent powers of sodium hyposulfite, later used in **photography;** first to use terms **positive** and **negative** in photographic experiments. [d. May 11, 1871]

1814   **Kamehameha III (Kauikeaouli),** Hawaiian King, responsible for giving Hawaii a constitution, 1840; revised, 1852. [d. December 15, 1854]

1837   **Henry Draper,** U.S. astronomer, physician; noted for his pioneering experiments in **celestial photography** and **spectroscopy.** [d. November 20, 1882]

1849   **Luther Burbank,** U.S. botanist, horiculturist; known for his numerous experiments in hybridizing new species of hundreds of different vegetables and flowers. [d. April 11, 1926]

1850   **Champ Clark (James Beauchamp Clark),** U.S. politician; U.S. Congressman, 1892–1920; Speaker of the House of Representatives, 1911–19. [d. March 3, 1921]

     Thomáš Garrigue Masaryk, Czech statesman, philosopher; member of Austrian Parliament, 1891–93, 1907–14; first President of the Czechoslovak Republic, 1918–35. [d. September 14, 1937]

1857   **Julius Wagner von Jauregg,** Austrian scientist; Nobel Prize in physiology or medicine for treatment of paralysis by **malarial therapy,** 1927. [d. September 17, 1940]

1872   **Pieter Cornelis Mondrian (Mondriaan),** Dutch artist; representative of **ultramodern school.** [d. February 1, 1944]

1875   **Maurice Joseph Ravel,** French impressionist composer, best known for his *Boléro.* [d. December 28, 1937]

1904   **Reinhard Heydrich,** German Nazi official; deputy chief of Gestapo and administrator of Nazi **concentration camps.** [d. June 4, 1942]

1908   **Anna Magnani,** Italian actress. [d. September 26, 1973]

1938   **David Baltimore,** U.S. microbiologist; Nobel Prize in physiology or medicine for research on **tumor viruses** (with R. Dulbecco and H. Temin), 1975.

     Janet Guthrie, U.S. auto racer; the first woman to qualify for and race in the **Indianapolis 500.**

Historical Events

1080   **Pope Gregory VII** excommunicates **Henry IV** of Germany for the second time over the issue of **lay investiture.**

1138   **Conrad III** is elected King of Germany.

1645   Swedes defeat army of Holy Roman Empire at **Jankau (Thirty Years' War).**

1792   French National Assembly adopts the **guillotine** as method of execution throughout France (**French Revolution**).

1793   France declares war on Spain (**French Revolution**).

1857   U.S. Supreme Court issues the **Dred Scott decision,** declaring that the **Missouri Compromise** is unconstitutional.

1876   **Alexander Graham Bell** is awarded patent for the **telephone.**

of young children. [d. 203] Feast formerly March 6. Obligatory Memorial.

St. Paul the Simple, hermit. [d. c. 339]

St. Drausius, Bishop of Soissons. Also called **Drausin.** [d. c. 674]

St. Esterwine, Abbot of Wearmouth. Also called **Eosterwine.** [d. 686]

St. Ardo, priest. [d. 843]

St. Theophylact, Bishop of Nicomedia. [d. 845]

1917 World's first **jazz recording** is issued by the Victor Company, including *Livery Stable Blues* and *Dixieland Jazz Band One Step.*

1936 Germany denounces the **Locarno Pacts** of 1925 and reoccupies the Rhineland.

1945 U.S. troops capture the key **Remagen Bridge** across the **Rhine (World War II).**

1951 Premier **Ali Razmara** of Iran is assassinated by a religious fanatic in a mosque in Teheran.

U.S. **House Un-American Activities Committee** releases a list of subversive organizations and publications.

1965 **Pope Paul VI** celebrates mass in a parish church in Rome mainly in Italian instead of Latin, and facing the congregation, thus implementing the decisions of the **Ecumenical Council.**

1970 **Malaysia** and **Thailand** sign an agreement permitting their troops to combat Communist guerrillas in each other's territory.

March 8

Holidays

Afghanistan	Women's Day
British Virgin Islands	Commonwealth Day
Cape Verde Islands	Women's Day
Guinea-Bissau	Women's Day
Libya	National Day
Mauretania	Women's Day
Nepal	Women's Day
Swaziland	Commonwealth Day
Syria	Revolution Day
	Commemorates the coming to power of the National Council of Revolution, 1963.
U.S.S.R.	Revolution Day

Birthdates

1714   **Karl Philipp Emanuel Bach,** German composer; the most gifted of **Johann Sebastian Bach's** 11 sons. [d. December 14, 1788]

1726   **Richard Howe, Earl Howe,** British admiral; commander of British forces in North America, 1776–78. [d. August 5, 1799]

1830   **João de Deus Ramos,** Portuguese lyric poet; the foremost poet of his time in Portugal. [d. January 11, 1896]

1841   **Oliver Wendell Holmes, Jr.** U.S. jurist; son of Oliver Wendell Holmes (August 29), U.S. poet; known as the *Great Dissenter.* [d. March 6, 1935]

1859   **Kenneth Grahame,** British author of children's books; known especially for *Wind in the Willows.* [d. July 6, 1932]

1865   **Frederic William Gaudy,** U.S. type designer, printer; known as the designer of a number of new type faces, several of which bear his name, *Gaudy, Gaudy Old Style.* [d. May 11, 1947]

1879   **Otto Hahn,** German chemist; Nobel Prize in chemistry for discovery of **fission of heavy atomic nuclei,** 1944. [d. July 28, 1968]

1886   **Edward Calvin Kendall,** U.S. biochemist; Nobel Prize in physiology or medicine for discovery of **cortisone** (with P. Hench and T. Reichstein), 1950. [d. May 4, 1972]

1890   **George Magoffin Humphrey,** U.S. manufacturer, government official; Secretary of the Treasury, 1953–57. [d. January 20, 1970]

1900   **Howard Hathaway Aiken,** U.S. mathematician, inventor; developed first large-scale **computer,** *Mark I.* [d. March 14, 1973]

1909   **Claire Trevor (Claire Wemlinger),** U.S. actress.

1917   **Leslie Fiedler,** U.S. literary critic, professor of English; known for his application of theories of Freud and Jung to contemporary literature.

1923   **Cyd Charisse,** U.S. dancer.

1927   **Stanislaw Kania,** Polish politician; head of Polish Communist Party, 1980– .

1937   **Juvenal Habyarimana,** Rwandan statesman; President, Republic of Rwanda, 1973–

Historical Events

1198   **Philip, Duke of Swabia,** and brother of **Emperor Henry VI,** is elected King of Germany.

1702   **William III** of Great Britain dies and is succeeded by **Queen Anne.**

1844   **Charles XIV John, King of Sweden and Norway,** dies and is succeeded by his son, **Oscar I.**

1862   Confederate ironclad frigate *Merrimac* sinks the Union *Cumberland* at **Hampton Roads,** Virginia (**U.S. Civil War**).

UN Member Countries	**International Women's Day** This day is recognized in many socialist countries as the counterpart to **Mother's Day.** Official greetings are conveyed by way of red and white banners hung from buildings and press, radio, and television messages.

Religious Calendar

The Saints

St. Dontius. [d. 260]

SS. Philemon and **Apollonius,** martyrs. [d. c. 305]

St. Senan of Scattery Island, bishop. [d. 560]

St. Felix of Dunwich, Bishop and Apostle of the East Angles. [d. 648]

St. Julian, Archbishop of Toledo. [d. 690]

St. Humphrey, Bishop of Thérouanne. Also called **Hunfrid.** [d. 871]

St. Duthac, Bishop of Ross. Also called **Duthak.** [d. c. 1065]

St. Veremund, Abbot of Hyrache. [d. 1092]

St. Stephen of Obazine, abbot. [d. 1154]

St. John of God, founder of the Brothers Hospitallers; patron of all hospitals, sick people, nurses, and book and print sellers. [d. 1550] Optional Memorial.

The Beatified

Blessed Vincent, Bishop of Cracow. First Polish chronicler. [d. 1223]

1917 Food riots break out in Petrograd (formerly St. Petersburg), Russia (**Russian Revolution**).

1920 **Switzerland** and **Denmark** join the **League of Nations.**

1921 Spanish Prime Minister **Eduardo Dato** is assassinated.

1922 **Wireless telephone service** is inaugurated between Peking and Tientsin.

1924 **Greece** officially recognizes the Soviet government of Russia.

1948 U.S. Supreme Court rules in *McCollum v. Board of Education* that religious instruction in public schools is unconstitutional.

1950 British government withholds recognition of **Seretse Khama** as tribal chief in **Bechuanaland** because of his marriage to a white woman.

1963 Pro-Nasser military elements seize control of the Syrian government in that country's third revolution in 18 months.

1971 U.S. army Captain **Ernest L. Medina** is ordered court-martialed on murder charges in connection with the **My-Lai incident** of March 1968 (**Vietnam War**).

Muhammad Ali (Cassius Clay) is defeated by **Joe Frazier** in what is dubbed *The Fight of the Century* at Madison Square Garden. Frazier becomes undisputed world heavyweight boxing champion.

1973 **Northern Ireland** referendum favors maintenance of ties with the **United Kingdom.**

1976 **Meteorites** fall in northeastern China, with the largest fragment weighing about 3,900 pounds, perhaps largest in recorded history.

March 9

Holidays

Belize   **Baron Bliss Day**
Commemorates the birth of
Baron Bliss, who left his fortune
to Belize.

Religious Calendar

The Saints
St. Pacian, Bishop of Barcelona. [d. c. 390]

Birthdates

1749   **Gabriel Honoré Rigueti Mirabeau,**
French orator, statesman; considered one
of most significant figures in early French
Revolutionary period; President of French
National Assembly, 1791. [d. April 2, 1791]

1773   **Isaac Hull,** U.S. naval commodore; commander of *U.S.S. Constitution* during War
of 1812; under his command, the ship
earned its nickname, *Old Ironsides.* [d.
February 13, 1843]

1791   **George Hayward,** U.S. surgeon; credited
with being first surgeon to perform major
surgery using **ether** as an **anesthetic.** [d.
1863]

1806   **Edwin Forrest,** U.S. actor; famous for his
Shakespearean roles. [d. December 12,
1872]

1814   **Taras Grigorievich Shevchenko,** Russian
poet, artist; considered the *Father of
Ukrainian National Literature.* [d. March 10,
1861]

1824   **A(masa) Leland Stanford,** U.S. financier,
philanthropist, major California pioneer;
Governor of California, 1861–63; U.S. Senator, 1885–93. **Stanford University** was
founded in memory of his son, Leland
Stanford, Jr., who died in 1884 at the age of
15. [d. June 21, 1893]

1857   **Eddie Foy (Edward Fitzgerald),** U.S.
vaudeville entertainer; known for his
vaudeville act with his children, billed as
The Seven Little Foys, 1913–20. [d. February
16, 1928]

1881   **Ernest Bevin,** British statesman, labor
leader; Minister of Labour, 1940–45; Foreign Minister, 1945–51. [d. April 14, 1951]

1890   **Vyacheslav Mikhailovich Molotov (V. M.
Skryabin),** Soviet communist leader;
Chairman, Council of People's Commis-
sars, 1930–41.

1892   **Victoria Mary Sackville-West,** British novelist, poet, critic. [d. June 2, 1962]

1902   **Will Geer,** U.S. character actor. [d. April 22,
1978]

Edward Durell Stone, U.S. architect;
known for his use of traditional elements
in contemporary designs; early works are
classified as prime examples of the **International Style.** [d. August 6, 1978]

1910   **Samuel Barber,** U.S. composer; Pulitzer
Prize in music, 1958, 1963. [d. January 23,
1981]

1918   **Mickey Spillane (Frank Morrison Spillane),** U.S. author; known for his detective
novels.

1922   **Floyd (Bizler) McKissick,** U.S. civil rights
activist, lawyer; National Director of **Congress of Racial Equality,** 1966–68; developer of **Soul City, North Carolina.**

1925   **G(eorge) William Miller,** U.S. government
official, lawyer, business executive; Chairman of Federal Reserve Board, 1978–79;
U.S. Secretary of the Treasury, 1979–81.

1930   **Thomas Schippers,** U.S. conductor; conductor of Metropolitan Opera, 1955–77. [d.
December 16, 1977]

1934   **Yuri Alekseyevich Gagarin,** Soviet cosmonaut; first man to travel into space, April
12, 1961. [d. March 27, 1968]

1943   **Robert James (Bobby) Fischer,** U.S.
chess player; the first American to hold the
world chess title (at age 15).

Historical Events

1074   All **married priests** are excommunicated
from Roman Catholic Church.

St. Gregory, Bishop of Nyssa. Also called *Father of the Fathers.* [d. c. 395]

St. Bosa, Bishop of York. [d. 705]

St. Frances of Rome, widow and founder of the Oblates of Tor de' Specchi. Also called **Francesca Romana** or **Frances the Roman.** [d. 1440] Optional Memorial.

St. Catherine of Bologna, virgin and Abbess of Corpo di Cristo. Patron of artists. Also called **Katherine of Bologna.** [d. 1463]

St. Dominic Savio. [d. 1857]

1551 Hapsburg family declares **Philip II** of Spain the sole heir of **Charles V,** Holy Roman Emperor.

1796 **Napoleon Bonaparte** marries **Josephine de Beauharnais.**

1846 **Kashmir** is ceded to the **British East India Company** by the **Treaty of Lahore,** ending the **First Sikh War.**

1858 The rule of the Mogul emperors ends in India with the banishment of **Bahadur Shah II** by the British for his part in the **Sepoy Mutiny.**

1864 **Ulysses S. Grant** is appointed commander-in-chief of the U.S. Union armies (**U.S. Civil War**).

1869 Great Britain buys the territories of the **Hudson Bay Company.**

1888 **Emperor William I** of Germany dies and is succeeded by **Frederick III.**

1916 Germany declares war on Portugal as a result of Portugal's seizing German and Austrian shipping in Portuguese harbors (**World War I**).

1917 Capital of Russia is moved from **Leningrad** (**St. Petersburg, Petrograd**) to **Moscow.**

1920 **Sweden** and the **Netherlands** join the **League of Nations.**

1933 **Emergency Banking Relief Act** is passed by U.S. Congress, giving the President broad discretionary fiscal powers.

1942 Japanese complete conquest of **Java** (**World War II**).

1961 Radio Moscow announces that U.S.S.R. has orbited and recovered a spaceship carrying a dog and other live biological specimens.

1962 U.S. Department of State confirms that U.S. pilots are flying combat training missions with South Vietnamese airmen over guerrilla-held areas.

1975 Work begins on the 789-mile **Alaskan oil pipeline,** the largest private construction project in U.S. history.

1978 Korean businessman **Park Tong Sun** testifies before the House Ethics Committee pertaining to allegations of South Korean influence-buying on Capitol Hill.

1983 **Anne M. Burford** is forced to resign her post as head of the U.S. **Environmental Protection Agency** (**EPA**) following a dispute with Congress over the agency's enforcement of toxic waste regulations.

March 10

Holidays

Korea   Labor Day

Religious Calendar

The Saints

St. Codratus and his companions, martyrs. [d. c. 258]

The Forty Martyrs of Sebastea, Roman soldiers of The Thundering Legion. [d. 320]

Birthdates

1452 **Ferdinand V** of Castile (Ferdinand II of Aragon). King of Aragon who unified Spain by his marriage to **Isabella I,** Queen of Castile. [d. January 25, 1516]

1503 **Ferdinand I, King of Bohemia** 1526 and Hungary 1527; Holy Roman Emperor, 1558–64. [d. July 25, 1564]

1628 **Marcello Malpighi,** Italian physiologist; called *Founder of Microscopic Anatomy.* [d. November 30, 1694]

1748 **John Playfair,** Scottish geologist, mathematician; promoted and popularized theory of **uniformitarianism.** [d. July 20, 1819]

1772 **Friedrich von Schlegel,** German critic, orientalist, poet. [d. January 12, 1829]

1787 **Francisco Martinez de la Rosa,** Spanish writer, statesman; Premier of Spain, 1820–23; 1834; Spanish Ambassador to France, 1847–51. [d. February 7, 1862]

1788 **Joseph Karl Eichendorff,** German poet; member of the Romantic religious group of poets including Friederich von Schlegel (above, 1772). [d. November 26, 1857]

1791 **Angel Saavedra (Ramírez de Baquedano),** Spanish poet, dramatist; the outstanding figure of **Spanish romanticism.** [d. June 22, 1865]

1810 **John McCloskey,** U.S. Roman Catholic clergyman; first president of **St. John's College (Fordham University**), 1841; first U.S. Roman Catholic cardinal, 1875. [d. October 10, 1885]

1833 **Pedro Antonio de Alarcón,** Spanish novelist, journalist; known especially for his short stories, sketches of rustic Spanish life. [d. July 20, 1891]

1845 **Alexander III, Emperor of Russia,** 1881–94; supporter of Russian nationalism; interfered in politics of Balkan States; formed close alliance with France. [d. November 1, 1894]

1867 **Lillian D. Wald,** U.S. social worker, public health nurse; responsible for establishment of first municipally sponsored **public school nursing program** in the world. [d. September 1, 1940]

1886 **Frederic Waller,** U.S. manufacturer, inventor; developed the **Cinerama** process, 1938. [d. May 18, 1954]

1888 **Barry Fitzgerald (William Joseph Shields),** Irish character actor. [d. January 4, 1961]

1891 **Shih-Chieh Wang,** Chinese government official, diplomat, educator; Minister of Foreign Affairs, 1945–48; one of Chiang Kai-shek's most valued and trusted advisers. [d. April, 1981]

1892 **Arthur Oscar Honegger,** French composer; identified as leader of **The Six,** an ultramodern school of music. [d. November 27, 1955]

1903 **Leon Bismarck (Bix) Beiderbecke,** U.S. jazz cornetist, composer; one of leaders in world of jazz; strongly influenced style of later musicians. [d. August 7, 1931]

Historical Events

1528 **Hubmaier,** leader of Austrian Anabaptists, is burned at the stake in Vienna.

1624 England declares war on France (**Thirty Years' War**).

1839 Imperial Commissioner **Lin Tse-hsu** arrives in Canton and is forced to surrender and burn opium shipments (**First Opium War**).

1862 Great Britain and France recognize the independence of **Zanzibar.**

St. Macarius, Bishop of Jerusalem. [d. c. 335]

St. Simplicius, pope. Elected 468. [d. 483]

St. Droctoveus, abbot. Also called **Drotté.** [d. c. 580]

St. Kessog, bishop and martyr; patron of Lennox, Scotland. Also called **Mackessog,** or **Mackessoge.** [d. 6th century]

St. Attalas, abbot. [d. 627]

St. Himelin, priest [d. c. 750]

St. John Ogilvie, Jesuit priest and martyr. [d. 1615]

St. Anastasia Patricia, virgin and hermit. Also called **Anastasius the Eunuch.** [death date unknown]

The Beatified

Blessed Andrew of Strumi, Abbot of San Fedele. [d. 1097]

Blessed John of Vallombrosa, monk and hermit. Also called the **Hermit of the Cells.** [d. c. 1380]

Blessed Peter Geremia, Dominican priest. [d. 1452]

1863 The Prince of Wales (later **Edward VII** of England) is married to Princess Alexandra of Denmark.

1876 **Alexander Graham Bell** transmits first complete intelligible sentence by **telephone.**

1893 The name of the **Rivières du Sud** colony is changed to **French Guinea.**

The **Ivory Coast** is constituted as a French colony.

1900 A definitive treaty is signed between **Uganda** and **Great Britain** regulating the form of government in Uganda.

1911 France adopts **Greenwich time** as legal standard.

1912 **Yüan Shih-K'ai** is installed as first President of the **Republic of China,** ending two millenia of monarchy and empire.

1914 Militant suffragists mutilate Velásquez's *Venus with the Mirror* in National Gallery, London.

1915 The British launch a vigorous attack on the Germans in the start of the **Battle of Neuve Chapelle (World War I).**

1917 The **Second Battle of Monastir** opens in Serbian Macedonia with an Allied offensive **(World War I).**

A general mutiny of Russian troops occurs in the capital of St. Petersburg (**Russian Revolution**).

1922 **Mahatma Gandhi** is arrested by the British government of India for sedition.

1952 **Fulgencio Batista** executes a coup d'état in **Cuba,** preventing popular elections and assuming military control of the country.

1966 Violent clashes among Hindus, Punjabi-speaking Sikhs, and police, break out following a decision by India's ruling Congress Party to create a Punjabi-speaking state within the existing state of Punjab.

1969 **James Earl Ray** pleads guilty to the assassination of the Rev. Martin Luther King, Jr., and is sentenced to 99 years in prison.

1972 Morocco promulgates its Constitution.

1976 Critics of the South Korean government of President **Park Chung Hee** are arrested.

Former U.S. President **Richard M. Nixon** testifies that he ordered wiretapping in 1969 and that **Henry Kissinger** selected those to be tapped.

March 11

Religious Calendar

The Saints

St. Constantine, King of Cornwall, Abbot of Govan, and first martyr of Scotland. [d. 6th century]

St. Sophronius, Patriarch of Jerusalem. Surnamed the **Sophist.** [d. c. 638]

St. Vindician, Bishop of Cambrai. [d. 712]

St. Benedict, Archbishop of Milan. [d. 725]

Birthdates

1544 **Torquato Tasso,** Italian poet; best known for his heroic epic poem, *Jerusalem Delivered.* [d. April 25, 1595]

1731 **Robert Treat Paine,** American public official, judge; signer of the Declaration of Independence. [d. May 11, 1814]

1811 **Urbain Le Verrier,** French astronomer; one of the first to predict existence of planet **Neptune.** [d. September 23, 1877]

1885 **Sir Malcolm Campbell,** British businessman, race-car driver; established numerous early speed records. [d. December 31, 1948]

1890 **Vannevar Bush,** U.S. electrical engineer; headed U.S. scientific war effort and early research on the **atomic bomb.** [d. June 28, 1974]

1892 **Thomas T(roy) Handy,** U.S. Army general; after World War II, was commander of all American forces in Europe. [d. April 14, 1982]

1897 **Henry Dixon Cowell,** U.S. composer; a pioneer in **experimental music;** developed the **rhythmica,** an early electronic musical instrument. [d. December 10, 1965]

1898 **Dorothy Gish (Dorothy de Guiche),** U.S. silent-screen actress. [d. June 4, 1968]

1899 **Frederick IX, King of Denmark,** 1947–72; encouraged Danish resistance to the Nazi occupation during World War II. [d. January 14, 1972]

1903 **Lawrence Welk,** U.S. bandleader, television host.

1916 **Sir (James) Harold Wilson,** British statesman, economist; Prime Minister, 1964–76.

1926 **Ralph Abernathy,** U.S. civil rights leader, clergyman; President of **Southern Christian Leadership Conference.**

Historical Events

1824 The **Bureau of Indian Affairs** is created in the U.S. War Department.

1898 The British reopen the **Khyber Pass** after quelling the **Afridi uprising.**

1915 The Germans begin a new offensive against the Russians near Przasnyz, Poland (**World War I**).

1917 **Baghdad** is captured by British forces (**World War I**).

1918 **Universal suffrage** is decreed in Portugal.

1920 **Faisal I** is proclaimed **King of Syria** by the Syrian National Congress.

1925 *No No Nanette* by Vincent Youmans opens in London.

1936 Rafael Franco proclaims a totalitarian state in **Paraguay.**

1941 U.S. Congress maintains neutrality but passes **Lend-Lease Act** enabling England to borrow aircraft, weapons, and merchant ships.

1960 *Pioneer V,* U.S. planetoid, is launched from Cape Canaveral, Florida, into orbit around the sun.

1964 **South Africa** withdraws from the International Labour Organization.

1968 Major riots occur in **Poland** as tens of thousands of Poles protest government inference in cultural affairs.

1970 **Iraq** recognizes the autonomy of the **Kurdish people,** ending over eight years of warfare.

Brazilian revolutionaries kidnap **Nobuo Okuchi,** Japanese consul general in São Paulo.

1973 Peronista presidential candidate **Héctor J. Cámpora** is the victor in the first Argentine election since 1965.

1976 The **Dow Jones** industrial stock average passes the 1,000 mark.

St. Oengus, abbot and bishop. Also called Aengus, Culdee or Kele-De [d. c. 824]

St. Eulogius of Córdova, priest and martyr; patron of carpenters. Wrote *The Memorial of the Saints*, a 7-year chronicle of the suffering of other martyrs. [d. 859]

St. Aurea, virgin and nun. [d. c. 1100]

St. Teresa Margaret Redi, virgin and Carmelite nun. Also called Teresa-Margaret-of-the-Sacred-Heart. [d. 1770]

The Beatified

Blessed John Larke, Jermyn Gardiner and John Ireland, martyrs. Jermyn also called German Gardiner. [d. 1544]

Blessed Christopher Macassoli, Franciscan priest. [d. 1485]

Blessed John Baptist of Fabriano, priest. [d. 1539]

1981   General Augusto Pinochet declares himself President of Chile for an 8-year term.

1982   U.S. Senator Harrison Williams resigns his Senate seat as a result of being charged with misconduct; he is the first Senator to do so in over 60 years.

March 12

Holidays

Gabon Republic	**Anniversary of Renewal** or **Renovation Day**
Lesotho	**Moshoeshoe's Day** Honors the tribal leader who consolidated the **Bosotho** nation, now Lesotho, in the 19th century.
Mauritius	**Independence Day** Commemorates the attainment of independence from Great Britain, 1968.

Birthdates

1613 **André LeNôtre,** French landscape gardener; called *Gardener of Kings and King of Gardeners.* [d. September 15, 1700]

1626 **John Aubrey,** English antiquary and author; known for his biographical sketches of Milton, Raleigh, and Hobbes, among others. [d. June 1697]

1685 **George Berkeley,** Irish philosopher, Anglican bishop; known for development of philosophy of **subjective idealism.** [d. January 14, 1753]

1710 **Thomas Augustine Arne,** English composer; composed *Rule Britannia.* [d. March 5, 1778]

1831 **Clement Studebaker,** U.S. wagon, carriage, and auto manufacturer; founder of Studebaker Corporation, 1902. [d. November 27, 1901]

1832 **Charles Cunningham Boycott,** British land-estate manager; became subject of economic and social isolation practices of **Irish Land League** agitators. The term *boycott* comes from his name. [d. June 19, 1897]

1835 **Simon Newcomb,** U.S. astronomer, mathematician. Revised motion theories and position tables for all the major celestial reference objects; responsible for adoption of universal system of **astronomical constants;** a founder and first president of the **American Astronomical Society.** [d. July 11, 1909]

1838 **Sir William Henry Perkin,** British chemist; discovered and produced **mauve,** the first of the synthetic aniline dyes. [d. July 14, 1907]

1858 **Adolph Simon Ochs,** Publisher of the *New York Times,* 1896–1935; responsible for funding publication of the *Dictionary of American Biography.* [d. April 8, 1935]

1862 **Jane Delano,** U.S. nurse; organized **Red Cross Nursing Service,** 1911. [d. 1919]

1863 **Gabriele d'Annunzio,** Italian author, political leader, soldier; a popular hero of World War I; known for his voluminous output of poetry, short stories, and novels. [d. March 1, 1938]

1864 **William Halse Rivers,** British physiologist, anthropologist; founder of **Cambridge School of Experimental Psychology.** [d. June 4, 1922]

1880 **Kemal Atatürk,** Turkish military leader; first President of the Turkish Republic, 1923–38. [d. November 10, 1938]

1890 **Vaslav Nijinsky,** Russian ballet dancer; member of Diaghilev's **Ballet Russe;** became insane during later life and was committed to an asylum. [d. April 8, 1950]

1910 **Masayoshi Ohira,** Japanese politician; Prime Minister, 1978–80. [d. June 12, 1980]

1922 **Jack Kerouac,** U.S. author; associated with the beat generation. [d. October 21, 1969]

(Joseph) Lane Kirkland, U.S. labor leader; President of AFL-CIO, 1979– .

1923 **Walter Marty Schirra, Jr.,** U.S. astronaut; participated in Mercury *Sigma* 7 space flight, 1962; commanded *Gemini* 6, 1965, and *Apollo* 7, 1968, space flights.

1925 **Leo Esaki,** Japanese physicist; Nobel Prize in physics for research on **superconduc-**

| Taiwan | Arbor Day |
| | The death of Dr. Sun Yat-Sen on this day in 1925 is commemorated by the planting of trees. |

St. Mura, abbot; founder of the monastery of Fahan. Also called **Muranus** or **Muru.** [d. 7th century]

St. Theophanes the Chronicler, Abbot of Mount Sigriana. [d. 817]

St. Alphege, Bishop of Winchester. Also called the **Bald Elder.** [d. 951]

St. Bernard of Capua, Bishop of Caleno. [d. 1109]

St. Fina, virgin. Also called **Seraphina.** [d. 1253]

Religious Calendar

The Saints

St. Maximilian, martyr. [d. 295]

SS. Peter, Gorgonius, and **Dorotheus**, martyrs. [d. 303]

St. Paul Aurelian, Bishop of Léon. Also called **Paulinus**, or **Pol de Léon.** [d. c. 573]

The Beatified

Blessed Justina of Arezzo, virgin and anchoress. [d. 1319]

Blessed Aloisius Orione. [beatified, 1980]

---

tors (with I. Giaever and B. D. Josephson), 1973.

1928 Edward Franklin Albee, U.S. dramatist; Pulitzer Prize in drama, 1967, 1975.

1932 Andrew Young, U.S. politician, clergyman; the first black to win a Democratic nomination for Congress from the South in over 100 years.

1946 Liza Minnelli, U.S. singer, actress.

1948 James Taylor, U.S. folk-rock singer, guitarist, composer.

Historical Events

1799 Austria declares war on France (**War of the Second Coalition**).

1814 Duke of Wellington takes Bordeaux (**Peninsular War**).

1849 Sikhs surrender to the British at Rawalpindi.

1854 Great Britain, France, and Turkey form an alliance against Russia (**Crimean War**).

1868 Basutoland is annexed by British Cape Colony.

1888 The Great Blizzard of '88 hits the northeastern United States, paralyzing all major cities and causing the deaths of more than 400 people.

1912 First patrol of **Girl Guides**, forerunner of **Girl Scouts**, is formed by **Juliet Low.**

1917 The **Petrograd Soviet of Workers and Soldiers Deputies** is organized as part of the continuing revolutionary unrest in Russia.

1922 Armenia, Azerbaijan, and Georgia establish the **Trans-Caucasian Soviet Socialist Republic.**

First transatlantic radio broadcast is made.

1930 Indian leader **Mahatma Gandhi** begins his second **civil disobedience** campaign to protest the British government's salt tax.

1933 U.S. President **Franklin D. Roosevelt** delivers his first **fireside chat**, a nationwide radio address.

1934 **Konstantin Paets,** aided by the military, sets up a virtual dictatorship in **Estonia.**

1938 Germany invades and annexes **Austria (World War II).**

1940 **Russo-Finnish War** ends with significant territorial gains by the U.S.S.R.

1962 British ministries of Health and Education start a drive to inform the British public of the dangers of **cigarette smoking.**

1965 U.S. Marines in South Vietnam engage in their first skirmish with Viet Cong forces (**Vietnam War**).

1968 **Mauritius** achieves independence from Great Britain.

1970 U.S. lowers voting age to 18 years.

1971 Syrian Premier **Hafez al-Assad** is elected President of Syria in a national referendum.

1973 Syrian electorate approves a new permanent constitution.

1979 **Luis Herrera Campins** is inaugurated as President of Venezuela.

March 13

Holidays

Grenada   National Day
            Commemorates Grenada
            Revolution, 1979.
Liberia   Decoration Day

Religious Calendar

The Saints
St. Euphrasia, virgin and nun. Also called
Eupraxia. [d. c. 420]

Birthdates

1615   **Pope Innocent XII,** reigned 1691–1700. [d. September 17, 1700]

1720   **Charles Bonnet,** Swiss naturalist, philosopher; discovered **parthenogenesis.** [d. May 20, 1793]

1733   **Joseph Priestley,** English chemist, clergyman, political radical; research resulted in discovery of **oxygen, ammonia, sulfur dioxide, hydrogen chloride.** [d. February 6, 1804]

1741   **Josef II, King of Germany** and Holy Roman Emperor, 1765–90, one of the **enlightened despots** of 18th-century Europe. [d. February 20, 1790]

1764   **Charles Grey,** Second Earl Grey, English statesman; Foreign Secretary, 1806–07, Prime Minister, 1830–34. [d. July 17, 1845]

1813   **Lorenzo Delmonico,** U.S. restaurateur, born in Switzerland; dubbed *Father of American Restaurants*; owner and operator of the first and largest restaurant in America, 1832–81. [d. September 13, 1881]

1855   **Percival Lowell,** U.S. astronomer; known for research on planet **Mars**; postulated the existence of a planet beyond **Neptune** which ultimately led to the discovery of **Pluto**; brother of the poet Amy Lowell. [d. November 12, 1916]

1857   **Herbert Charles Onslow Plumer,** 1st Viscount Plumer, British army field marshal; Governor of Malta, 1919–25. [d. July 16, 1932]

1860   **Hugo Wolf,** Austrian composer; a disciple of Wagner. [d. February 22, 1903]

1869   **Ramón Menéndez Pidal,** Spanish literary historian, linguist. [d. November 14, 1968]

1872   **Oswald Garrison Villard,** U.S. editor, journalist; founder of *The Nation*, a journal of social protest. [d. October 1, 1949]

1887   **Alexander Archer Vandegrift,** U.S. Marine Corps general; in charge of troop landing at **Guadalcanal,** 1942. [d. May 8, 1973]

1892   **Janet Flanner,** U.S. journalist, correspondent for *The New Yorker* for nearly 50 years. [d. November 7, 1978]

1899   **John Hasbrouck Van Vleck,** U.S. physicist; Nobel Prize in physics for contributions to development of **solid state circuitry** (with N. F. Mott and P. W. Anderson), 1977.

1900   **Giorgos Seferis (Giorgos Sefiriades),** Greek poet; Nobel Prize in literature, 1963. [d. September 20, 1971]

1911   **L(afayette) Ron(ald) Hubbard,** U.S. science fiction writer, religious leader; founder of **Scientology.**

1913   **Sammy Kaye,** U.S. bandleader.

1914   **Edward Henry O'Hare,** U.S. Navy officer, aviator. Chicago's **O'Hare Airport** is named for him. [d. November 27, 1943]

1939   **Neil Sedaka,** U.S. singer, songwriter.

Historical Events

1470   Yorkists defeat Lancastrians at **Battle of Stamford.**

1781   **Sir William Herschel,** English astronomer, discovers planet **Georgium Sidres,** later named **Uranus.**

1806   **Gustavus IV** of Sweden is deposed, and the crown is assumed by his uncle, who becomes **Charles XIII.**

St. Mochoemoc, abbot. [d. 7th century]

St. Gerald of Mayo, abbot. [d. 732]

St. Nicephorus, Patriarch of Constantinople. [d. 828]

St. Ansovinus, Bishop of Camerino; patron saint and protector of crops. [d. 840]

St. Heldrad, abbot. [d. c. 842]

SS. Roderic and **Solomon,** martyrs. [d. 857]

The Beatified

Blessed Agnello of Pisa, founder of the English Franciscan province. [d. 1236]

1813 Sweden joins the **Grand Alliance** against Napoleon's France and its allies.

1848 **Prince Clemens Metternich** of Austria resigns under pressure of a mob in Vienna; the ruler of Austria since 1809, he maintained unprecedented stability there by repressing liberal ideas.

1861 Richard Wagner's opera, *Tannhäuser,* premieres in Paris.

1865 Confederate Congress agrees to the recruitment of **slaves** into the army (**U.S. Civil War).**

1881 **Czar Alexander II** of Russia dies in the explosion of a bomb thrown at him as he rides through the streets of St. Petersburg.

1884 **Somali Coast, Nigeria,** and **New Guinea** become British protectorates.

1900 **Bloemfontein,** the Orange Free State, surrenders to Lord Frederick Roberts in the **Boer War** and the government of the Free State retires to Kroonstad.

1904 *Christ of the Andes,* a bronze statue of Christ on the Argentine-Chile border, is dedicated.

1907 **New York stock market** drop sets off **Panic of 1907.**

1915 The **Battle of Neuve Chapelle** ends as a limited British victory (**World War I).**

The Swedish vessel *Hana* becomes the first neutral ship to be sunk by a German submarine in World War I.

1917 Russian revolutionaries seize the **Winter Palace** in Petrograd (St. Petersburg).

1938 Hitler takes formal possession of Vienna (**World War II).**

Léon Blum forms the **Popular Front** Ministry in France.

1947 Frederick Loewe's musical fantasy *Brigadoon* premieres in New York.

1954 The **Viet-Minh** begin a successful siege of the French-held **Dien Bien Phu** in Vietnam.

1961 **Floyd Patterson** defeats **Ingemar Johansson** in professional heavyweight championship bout.

1963 Soviets establish **Supreme Council of National Economy** to coordinate national economic planning.

1969 U.S. *Apollo 9* spacecraft splashes down in the Atlantic Ocean after a ten-day flight testing the **lunar module.**

1972 United Kingdom and People's Republic of China establish diplomatic relations at the ambassadorial level.

Clifford Irving and his wife, Edith, plead guilty to conspiring to defraud **McGraw-Hill** by selling it a fake autobiography of **Howard Hughes.**

1979 The **Common Market** officially inaugurates the new **European Monetary System** (EMS).

Sir Eric Gairy is ousted as Prime Minister of **Grenada. Maurice Bishop,** leader of the **New Jewel Movement,** takes power.

March 14

Holidays

Zambia   Youth Day

Religious Calendar

The Saints
St. Leobinus, Bishop of Chartres. Also called Lubin. [d. c. 558]

Birthdates

1681 **Georg Philipp Telemann,** German baroque composer; composed over 600 overtures and 40 operas. [d. June 25, 1767]

1750 **Caroline Lucretia Herschel,** English astronomer; discovered seven comets; sister of Sir William Herschel. [d. January 9, 1848]

1782 **Thomas Hart Benton,** U.S. politician; U.S. Senator, 1820–50; U.S. Representative, 1852–54; strongly opposed to the abolition of slavery. [d. April 10, 1858]

1800 **James Bogardus,** U.S. inventor; designed the world's first **cast-iron construction,** in New York City. [d. April 13, 1874]

1804 **Johann Strauss, the Elder,** Austrian composer, conductor; composed over 150 waltzes, 19 marches. [d. September 24, 1849]

1816 **William Marsh Rice,** U.S. merchant, philanthropist; bequeathed his fortune for founding of **Rice Institute,** Houston, Texas. [d. September 23, 1900]

1820 **Victor Emmanuel II,** first king of modern, united **Italy,** 1871–78. [d. January 9, 1878]

1835 **Giovanni Virginio Schiaparelli,** Italian astronomer, the discoverer of the canals on Mars. [d. July 4, 1910]

1837 **Charles Ammi Cutter,** U.S. librarian; devised **Cutter system** of book labeling by alphanumeric code. [d. September 6, 1903]

1844 **Sir Thomas Lauder Brunton,** Scottish pharmacologist, physician; best known for his research on **circulation.** [d. September 16, 1916]

1854 **Paul Ehrlich,** German bacteriologist; Nobel Prize in physiology or medicine for work in **immunology** (with E. Metchnikoff), 1908. [d. August 20, 1915]

Thomas Riley Marshall, U.S. politician; Governor of Indiana, 1909–13; U.S. Vice-President, 1913–21. [d. June 1, 1925]

1862 **Vilhelm F. K. Bjerknes,** Norwegian physicist; proposed theory of **electric resonance,** which aided development of **wireless telegraphy.** [d. April 9, 1951]

1864 **John Luther (Casey) Jones,** U.S. railroad engineer memorialized in *Ballad of Casey Jones.* [d. April 30, 1900]

1875 **Isadore Gilbert Mudge,** U.S. librarian, author, bibliographer; an award for distinguished service in bibliography is given in her name annually by the American Library Association. [d. May 17, 1957]

1879 **Albert Einstein,** German-American physicist; one of the foremost scientists of all time, responsible for the **theory of relativity**; Nobel Prize in physics for his explanation of the photoelectric effect, which verified the quantum theory proposed by Max Planck, 1921. [d. April 18, 1955]

1923 **Diane Arbus,** U.S. photographer. [Suicide July 26, 1971]

1928 **Frank Borman,** U.S. astronaut, piloted first manned flight around the moon, 1968; currently Chairman of the Board of Eastern Airlines.

Michael Caine (Maurice Micklewhite), British actor.

Historical Events

1369 **Peter of Castile** is defeated at **Monteil (Hundred Years' War).**

1489 **Catherine Cornaro, Queen of Cyprus,** cedes her kingdom to Venice.

1558 **Ferdinand I** assumes title of **Holy Roman Emperor,** the first to do so without being crowned by the Pope.

1590 **Henry IV, King of Navarre (Henry III** of France), defeats the Catholic League at Ivry (Ypres).

St. Eutychius, martyr. Also called Eustathius. [d. 741]

St. Matilda, Queen of Germany and widow. Also called Mathilda, Mathildis, or Maud. [d. 968]

The Beatified

Blessed James, Archbishop of Naples. [d. 1308]

1647   Treaty of neutrality between Bavaria, France, and Sweden, is signed at Ulm (Thirty Years' War).

Frederick Henry, Dutch stadholder, dies and is succeeded by William II as Dutch ruler.

1794   Eli Whitney patents the cotton gin.

1849   The Sikhs surrender unconditionally to the British in India (Second Sikh War).

1864   Sir Samuel White Baker discovers Lake Albert Nyanza in East Africa.

1872   Sir Henry Morton Stanley leaves David Livingstone at Unyamwize in Central Africa, bringing away his diary and other documents.

1885   *The Mikado,* a comic opera by Gilbert and Sullivan, premieres in London.

1888   Sino-American treaty is signed, allowing Chinese immigration to the U.S. for twenty years.

1891   The first submarine telephone line is put into place across the English channel.

1900   U.S. Congress adopts gold standard.

1904   The anti-European rebellion led by the native society, the Silent Ones, in Southern Nigeria is suppressed by the British.

1915   German cruiser *Dresden* is sunk (World War I).

1917   Germany begins retreat to Hindenburg Line (World War I).

The czar's train is stopped at Pskov, Russia, by revolutionaries, and Czar Nicholas II is placed under arrest.

1951   Seoul, capital of South Korea, is recaptured without opposition by UN forces (Korean War).

1964   Jack Ruby is found guilty in Dallas of the murder of Lee Harvey Oswald, accused assassin of U.S. President John F. Kennedy, and is sentenced to death.

1965   Israel establishes diplomatic relations with West Germany.

1968   U.S. command in Saigon reports that the number of U.S. casualties in Vietnam has exceeded those in the Korean War.

1970   Japanese World Exposition, *Expo 70,* opens in Osaka.

1974   Kurdish rebels seize a large area on the Iraqi border with Turkey.

1978   By a unanimous vote, the UN Security Council rejects as illegal and unacceptable Rhodesia's plan for black majority rule. Great Britain, U.S., Canada, France, and West Germany abstain from voting.

1983   In an effort to stabilize world oil markets, the 13 members of the Organization of Petroleum Exporting Countries (OPEC) agree to cut prices.

March 15

Holidays

Ides of March
Day on which Julius Caesar was assassinated, 44 B.C.

Liberia   **J. J. Roberts' Birthday**
Honors Liberia's first president, born on this day, 1809.

U.S. (Maine)   **Admission Day**
Commemorates Maine's admission to the Union, 1820.

Religious Calendar

The Saints

St. Longinus, martyr. [d. 1st century]

Birthdates

1767   **Andrew Jackson,** U.S. soldier, lawyer, military hero of the War of 1812; seventh President of the United States. [d. June 8, 1845]

1779   **William Lamb,** 2nd Viscount Melbourne, British statesman; Prime Minister, 1835–41; political advisor to Queen Victoria. [d. November 24, 1848]

1794   **Friedrich Christian Diez,** German linguist; called *Founder of Romance linguistics.* [d. May 29, 1876]

1830   **Paul Johann Ludwig von Heyse,** German short-story writer, novelist, poet; Nobel Prize in literature, 1910. [d. April 2, 1914]

1838   **Alice Cunningham Fletcher,** U.S. ethnologist, author; pioneer in the study of American Indian music. [d. May 22, 1932]

1842   **Robert C. Delarge,** U.S. Congressman, 1871–73. [d. 1874]

1854   **Emil von Behring,** German physician, immunologist; discoverer of **diphtheria antitoxin** and **bovovaccine**; Nobel Prize in physiology or medicine for research in serum therapy, 1901. [d. March 31, 1917]

1858   **Liberty Hyde Bailey,** U.S. botanist, horticulturist; organized first college department of horticulture in U.S., 1884. [d. December 25, 1954]

1900   **Luigi Longo,** Italian political leader; Secretary General of Italian Communist Party, 1964–72; a founder of the party, 1921; recognized as a major anti-Mussolini force in World War II. [d. October 16, 1980]

1907   **Jimmy McPartland (James Dulgald McPartland),** U.S. jazz cornetist.

1912   **Sam (*Lightnin'*) Hopkins,** U.S. songwriter, blues singer. [d. January 30, 1982]

1915   **David Franz Schoenbrun,** U.S. journalist.

1916   **Harry James,** U.S. trumpeter, bandleader. [d. July 5, 1983]

1926   **Norm Van Brocklin,** U.S. football player, coach. [d. May 2, 1983]

1932   **Alan L. Bean,** U.S. astronaut; with *Apollo 12*, landed in **Sea of Storms** on moon's surface in Lunar Module (with C. Conrad, Jr.). Flew *Skylab 3* mission, July 28, 1973.

1933   **Philippe Claude Alex de Broca,** French film director, producer.

Historical Events

44 B.C.   **Ides of March; Julius Caesar** is assassinated by Brutus, Cassius, and others.

1077   Diet of **Forchheim** deposes **Henry IV, King of Germany and Holy Roman Emperor; Rudolf, Duke of Swabia,** is elected Emperor.

1341   Alliance is signed between Holy Roman Emperor **Louis IV** and **Philip VI** of France (**Hundred Years' War**).

1744   France declares war on England (**War of the Austrian Succession**).

1781   British army, under Lord Cornwallis, wins **Battle at Guilford Courthouse,** North Carolina (**American Revolution**).

1808   **U.S. Embargo Act** is repealed under pressure by New England states.

1815   **Joachim, King of Naples,** declares war on Austria.

St. Zachary, pope. Elected 741. [d. 752]

St. Leocritia, virgin and martyr. Also called **Lucretia.** [d. 859]

St. Louisa de Marillac, widow and cofounder of the Vincentian Sisters of Charity. Also called **Louise de Marillac.** [d. 1660]

St. Clement Hoïbauer, priest; founder of the Redemptorists. [d. 1820]

St. Matrona, virgin and martyr. [death date unknown]

The Beatified
Blessed William Hart, martyr. [d. 1583]

Blessed Placid Riccardi, Benedictine monk. [d. 1915]

1820	**Maine** is admitted to the Union as the 23rd state.
1915	A British order prohibits all traffic to and from Germany (**World War I**).
	The German offensive in Poland is checked by a Russian victory at the **Battle of Augustovo Forest** near Przasnysz (**World War I**).
1916	Austria-Hungary declares war on Portugal (**World War I**).
	U.S. troops enter Mexico in futile search for revolutionary bandit **Pancho Villa.**
1917	**Czar Nicholas II** of Russia abdicates for himself and his son in favor of his brother, **Grand Duke Michael.**
1922	The **Sultan of Egypt** is proclaimed king of the newly sovereign state of **Egypt** as **Fuad I.**
1924	The first parliament of an independent **Egypt** is opened by **King Fuad.**
1927	The British formally hand over their concessions at **Hankow** and **Kiukiang** to the Nationalist Chinese.
1939	Germany occupies **Bohemia** and **Moravia**; Slovakia remains nominally independent; Czech state becomes extinct (**World War II**).
	Hungary occupies and annexes the **Carpatho-Ukraine** region (**World War II**).
1951	U.S. warships bombard **Wonsan,** killing 8,000 enemy troops (**Korean War**).
	Iranian national assembly votes to nationalize the oil industry.
1955	Lerner and Loewe's *My Fair Lady* premieres in New York.
1960	**Syngman Rhee** is elected to a fourth consecutive four-year term as President of South Korea.
	National Observatory at **Kitt Peak,** Arizona, site of the world's largest **solar telescope,** is dedicated.
	Police in Orangeburg, South Carolina, arrest more than 350 blacks as **sit-in demonstrations** and sporadic racial violence spread throughout the South.
1971	U.S. government lifts restrictions on travel to **China** by U.S. citizens.
1975	The **High Council of the Revolution** in Portugal nationalizes the country's banks and insurance companies.
	Brazil grants asylum to ex-President **António de Spinola** of Portugal.
1979	**Gen. João Baptista da Figueiredo** assumes the office of President of Brazil.
	An agreement in Kano, Nigeria, ends civil war in **Chad**; France withdraws its troops.

March 16

Holidays

U.S.   St. Urho's Day   FINNS
Sponsored by the Sauna Society
of America, Washington, D.C.

Religious Calendar

The Saints
St. Finnian Lobhar, abbot. Also called the Leper.
[d. c. 560]

Birthdates

1581 **Pieter (Corneliszoon) Hooft,** Dutch poet, humanist; leader of the Dutch Renaissance. [d. May 21, 1647]

1739 **George Clymer,** American merchant; signer of the Declaration of Independence and of the U.S. Constitution. [d. January 24, 1813]

1751 **James Madison,** U.S. lawyer; fourth President of the U.S.; known as the *Father of the U.S. Constitution.* [d. June 28, 1836]

1774 **Jethrow Wood,** U.S. inventor; developer of **cast-iron plow,** 1819. [d. September 18, 1834]

1787 **George Simon Ohm,** German physicist, pioneer in electricity; developed the unit for measurement of **electrical resistance, the ohm,** which is named for him. [d. July 7, 1854]

1803 **Nikolay Yazykov,** Russian poet. [d. January 7, 1846]

1822 **Rosa Bonheur,** French artist and painter of animals. [d. May 25, 1899]

John Pope, U.S. Union Army general during Civil War. [d. September 23, 1892]

1825 **Camillo Castello Branco,** Portuguese novelist. [d. June 1, 1890]

1839 **Sully Prudhomme (René François Armand Prudhomme),** French poet; Nobel Prize in literature, 1901. [d. September 7, 1907]

1868 **Maksim Gorki (Aleksei Maksimovich Peshkov),** Russian writer. [d. June 14, 1936]

1878 **Emile Cammaerts,** Belgian poet, writer, patriot. [d. November 2, 1953]

1896 **Conrad Nagel,** U.S. character actor. [d. February 24, 1970]

1903 **Michael (Mike) Joseph Mansfield,** U.S. politician, diplomat, engineer; Senate Majority Leader, 1961–76; U.S. Ambassador to Japan, 1977– .

1908 **Robert Rossen,** U.S. screen writer, producer, director. [d. February 18, 1966]

1926 **Jerry Lewis (Joseph Levitch),** U.S. comedian, actor.

1927 **Daniel Patrick Moynihan,** U.S. politician, professor; U.S. Ambassador to India, 1973–74, U.S. Senator, 1977– .

1928 **Christa Ludwig,** Austrian operatic mezzo-soprano.

1940 **Bernardo Bertolucci,** Italian film director; directed *Last Tango in Paris*, 1972.

Historical Events

1322 **Edward II** of England defeats rebellious **Thomas of Lancaster** at **Boroughbridge.**

1517 The **Fifth Lateran Council** of the Roman Catholic Church ends after forbidding the printing of books without ecclesiastical authority.

1792 Count Ankerström assassinates **Gustavus III** of Sweden.

1802 U.S. Military Academy is founded at **West Point,** New York.

1827 *Freedom Journal,* the first black newspaper in the U.S., is printed in New York City.

1843 **Molly Maguire,** a secret society, is formed in Ireland.

1851 A concordat is signed between the papacy and Spain recognizing the **Roman Catholic** faith as the only authorized religion of **Spain** and giving the Church total control of education and censorship.

1881 The **Barnum and Bailey Circus** makes its debut in New York City.

St. Abraham Kidunaia, hermit. [d. 6th century]

St. Eusebia, abbess. [d. c. 680]

St. Gregory Makar, Bishop of Nicopolis and recluse. [d. c. 1010]

St. Heribert, Archbishop of Cologne. Invoked for rain. Also called **Herbert.** [d. 1021]

St. Julian of Antioch, martyr. [death date unknown]

The Beatified

Blessed John, Bishop of Vicenza and martyr. [d. 1183]

Blessed Torello, hermit. [d. 1282]

Blessed John Amias and **Robert Dalby,** priests and martyrs. [d. 1589]

1910 Foundation stone of **Hong Kong University** is laid.

1916 **Admiral Alfred von Tirpitz,** conductor of Germany's submarine campaign, resigns in disagreement over German policy (**World War I**).

1918 The Soviet Congress ratifies the **Treaty of Brest-Litovsk.**

1926 U.S. scientist **Robert Goddard** launches the first successful **liquid-fuel rocket,** at Worcester, Massachusetts.

1968 **My-Lai** and **My-Khe** villagers are killed by American troops in Vietnam (**Vietnam War**).

1978 Former Italian premier **Aldo Moro** is kidnapped in Rome by the **Red Brigade**; his five bodyguards are killed.

Two Russian cosmonauts return to earth in their *Soyuz 27* capsule after setting a new endurance record in space of 96 days.

1979 **Ayatollah Khomeini** orders a halt to the secret trials and summary executions by the **Revolutionary Council of Iran.**

March 17

Holidays

Ireland and many other countries in the West

St. Patrick's Day
Honors the patron saint of Ireland.

Special Events

U.S.

Camp Fire Founders Day
Sponsored by Camp Fire, Inc. Kansas City, Missouri

U.N. Member Countries

World Maritime Day

Birthdates

1473 **James IV, King of Scotland,** 1489–1513; his marriage to the daughter of **Henry VII** of England led ultimately to the union of Scotland and England. [d. September 9, 1513]

1628 **François Girardon,** French baroque sculptor; under Charles Le Brun, decorated Palace at Versailles; executed the tomb of **Cardinal Richelieu** at the Sorbonne. [d. September 1, 1715]

1777 **Roger Brooke Taney,** U.S. jurist, lawyer; Chief Justice of U.S. Supreme Court, 1836–64. [d. October 12, 1864]

1780 **Thomas Chalmers,** Scottish Presbyterian clergyman; a leader of the **Free Church of Scotland.** [d. May 31, 1837]

1787 **Edmund Kean,** English actor; the leading tragic actor of his day; best known for his portrayal of **Shylock** in Shakespeare's *Merchant of Venice*. [d. May 15, 1833]

1804 **James Bridger,** U.S. fur trapper, scout; the first white man to view the Great Salt Lake in Utah. [d. July 17, 1881]

1817 **Pasquale Stanislao Mancini,** Italian statesman, jurist; Minister of Justice, 1876–78; Minister of Foreign Affairs, 1881–85; responsible for Italian occupation of **Eritrea.** [d. December 26, 1888]

1834 **Gottlieb Wilhelm Daimler,** German inventor; developed high speed, gasoline burning **internal combustion engine.** [d. March 6, 1900]

1846 **(Catherine) Kate Greenaway,** British painter, illustrator; noted for her illustrations of children's books. [d. November 6, 1901]

1849 **Charles Francis Brush,** U.S. scientist, inventor; made numerous contributions to modern electrical engineering, including the **electric arc light** and a **storage battery.** [d. June 15, 1928]

1866 **Pierce Butler,** U.S. jurist; Associate Justice, U.S. Supreme Court, 1923–39. [d. November 16, 1939]

1873 **Margaret Grace Bondfield,** British labor leader; first woman minister in the British cabinet. [d. June 16, 1953]

1874 **Stephen Samuel Wise,** U.S. reform rabbi, Jewish leader; founder of **Zionist Organization of America,** 1906; a major anti-Hitler spokesman in the 1930s. [d. April 19, 1949]

1881 **Walter Hess,** Swiss physiologist; Nobel Prize in physiology or medicine for studies of the brain (with E. Moniz), 1949. [d. 1973]

1884 **Frank (Howard) Buck,** U.S. jungle explorer, adventurer, animal collector; author of *Bring 'em Back Alive*; idol of American men and boys during 1930s. [d. March 25, 1950]

1898 **Ella Winter,** U.S. journalist, social activist born in Australia; known for her writings on the post-revolutionary Russia; intimate of Donald Ogden Stewart, the black-listed Hollywood writer. [d. August 5, 1980]

1903 **Marquis William Childs,** U.S. journalist; Pulitzer Prize in commentary, 1969.

1910 **Bayard Rustin,** U.S. civil-rights activist; organized early freedom rides in U.S.

1919 **Nat (King) Cole (Nathaniel Adams Coles),** U.S. singer, pianist. [d. February 15, 1965].

Religious Calendar

Popularly regarded in the Middle Ages as the day **Noah** entered the Ark.

The Saints

St. Joseph of Arimathea, disciple who obtained the body of Jesus and buried it in his own tomb. [d. 1st century]

The Martyrs of the Serapeum. [d. 390]

St. Patrick, Archbishop of Armagh and Apostle of Ireland. Patron of Ireland. Also called **Patricius.** [d. 461] Optional Memorial.

St. Agricola, Bishop of Chalon-sur-Saône. Also called **Arègle.** [d. 580]

St. Gertrude of Nivelles, virgin and abbess. Patron of travelers and of souls on their journey from this world to the next. Invoked against mice and rats, for good quarters on a journey, and for gardens. [d. 659]

St. Paul of Cyprus, martyr. [d. c. 760]

The Beatified

Blessed John Sarkander, priest and martyr. [d. 1620]

1938 **Rudolph (Hametovich) Nureyev,** Soviet-British ballet dancer; defected from Russia, 1962.

Historical Events

45 B.C. **Caesar** defeats Pompey's supporters at **Munda.**

1776 British, threatened by American artillery in **Dorchester Heights,** evacuate Boston **(American Revolution).**

1860 **Maori War** begins in New Zealand.

1861 **Kingdom of Italy** is proclaimed by the first Italian parliament, with **Victor Emmanuel** as first king.

1910 **Camp Fire Girls** are established in the United States.

1915 The first **Battle of Champagne** on the Western Front ends, with small gains by the French **(World War I).**

1917 **Nicholas II** of Russia abdicates; Russia becomes a republic **(Russian Revolution).**

1918 **Oliver Plunkett,** Archbishop of Armagh, Ireland, is beatified.

1921 **Lenin** inaugurates the New Economic Policy in Russia.

1929 The **University of Madrid** is closed by royal decree because of rioting by students and opposition to the government by intellectuals.

1941 **National Gallery of Art** opens in Washington, D.C.

1945 Battle of **Iwo Jima** ends with U.S. victory **(World War II).**

1948 **Brussels Pact,** a 50-year military alliance, is signed between Great Britain, France, Belgium, the Netherlands, and Luxembourg.

1950 **Californium,** a new element, is identified by researchers at the University of California at Berkeley.

1951 Vatican excommunicates all persons connected with the persecution of the Roman Catholic Church in **Czechoslovakia.**

1958 *Vanguard I* spacecraft is launched by U.S. at Cape Canaveral.

1960 U.N. conference on the **Law of the Sea** opens at Geneva, Switzerland.

1963 **Mother Elizabeth Ann Bayley Seton,** U.S. founder of the **Sisters of Charity of St. Joseph,** is beatified by Pope John XXIII in Rome.

1968 Violent anti-Vietnam demonstrations outside U.S. embassy in London result in over 300 arrests.

1969 **Golda Meir** is sworn in as Israel's fourth Prime Minister.

1978 One of worst **oil spills** in history occurs when supertanker *Amoco Cadiz* breaks in two off the Brittany Coast in France, dumping more than 1.3 million barrels of crude oil into the sea.

Bolivian government severs diplomatic relations with Chile because of a dispute over giving **Bolivia** an outlet to the Pacific Ocean.

March 18

Religious Calendar

The Saints

St. Alexander, Bishop of Jerusalem and martyr. [d. 251]

St. Cyril, Archbishop of Jerusalem and Doctor of the Church. [d. 386] Optional Memorial.

St. Frigidian, Bishop of Lucca. Patron of Lucca, Italy. Also called **Erigdian, Frediano, Fridian, Frigdian.** [d. c. 588]

Birthdates

1578 **Adam Elsheimer,** German painter. [d. December 1610]

1609 **Frederick III, King of Denmark and Norway,** 1648–70; established the absolute monarchy maintained in Denmark until 1848. [d. February 9, 1670]

1733 **Christoph Friedrich Nicolai,** German critic, novelist, publisher; champion of the Enlightenment in Germany. [d. January 1, 1811]

1782 **John (Caldwell) Calhoun,** U.S. statesman, proponent of slavery; U.S. Secretary of War, 1817–24; U.S. Vice-President, 1824–28; U.S. Secretary of State, 1844–45. [d. March 31, 1850]

1827 **Pierre Eugene Marcelin Berthelot,** French chemist; noted for his research in **thermochemistry**; Foreign Minister, 1895–96; Secretary of French Academy, 1886–87. [d. March 18, 1902]

1830 **Numa Denis Fustel de Coulanges,** French historian; known for his studies of ancient and medieval history. [d. September 12, 1889]

1837 **(Stephen) Grover Cleveland,** U.S. attorney, politician; 22nd and 24th President of the U.S., 1885–89, 1893–97. [d. June 24, 1908]

1838 **Sir William Randal Cremer,** British jurist; Nobel Peace Prize for advocating international arbitration, 1903. [d. July 22, 1908]

1842 **Stéphane Mallarmé,** French poet, essayist, translator; member of **Symbolist School** of poets. [d. September 9, 1898]

1858 **Rudolf Diesel,** German mechanical engineer; inventor of the **diesel engine** (1897). [d. September 30, 1913]

1869 **Neville Chamberlain,** British statesman; Prime Minister, 1937–40. [d. November 9, 1940]

1875 **Lee Shubert,** U. S. theatrical producer; with his brother Jacob (August 15) controlled the most powerful monopoly of theaters in the U.S. [d. December 25, 1953]

1892 **(Robert Peter) Tristram Coffin,** U.S. writer; Pulitzer Prize in poetry, 1935. [d. January 20, 1955]

1893 **Wilfred Owen,** British poet; wrote most of his poetry during World War I. [d. November 4, 1918]

1897 **Ray H(oward) Jenkins,** U.S. lawyer; acted as special counsel during U.S. Senate hearings of Senator Joseph McCarthy's accusations against the U.S. Army. [d. December 26, 1980]

1899 **Lavrenti Pavlovich Beriya,** Russian secret-police chief under Stalin. [d. December 23, 1953]

1905 **Robert Donat,** British actor. [d. June 9, 1958]

Mollie Parnis, U.S. fashion designer.

1910 **Chiang Ching-Kuo,** Chinese statesman; Head of State, Republic of China (Taiwan), 1978– .

1915 **Hamilton Shirley Amerasinghe,** Sri Lankan diplomat, statesman; chief delegate to UN General Assembly, 1967–80; President of General Assembly, 1967. [d. December 4, 1980]

1915 **Richard Condon,** U.S. novelist.

1932 **John (Hoyer) Updike,** U.S. novelist, short-story writer, poet.

1956 **Ingemar Stenmark,** Swedish skier; winner of several World Cup championships and Olympic events.

St. Edward the Martyr, King of England. [d. 979]

St. Anselm, Bishop of Lucca. Patron of Mantua. [d. 1086]

St. Salvator of Horta, Franciscan friar. [d. 1567]

St. Finan of Aberdeen. [death date unknown]

The Beatified

Blessed Christian, Abbot of Mellifont, the first Cistercian monastery in Ireland. Also called **Christian O'Conarchy, Giolla Criost Ua Condoirche.** [d. 1186]

Historical Events

979   **King Edward the Martyr** of England is murdered by his stepmother; **Ethelred II,** the Unready, succeeds to throne.

1123   The First **Lateran Council** of the Roman Catholic Church begins.

1229   **Frederick II, Holy Roman Emperor,** crowns himself **King of Jerusalem** during the **Sixth Crusade.**

1438   **Albert of Austria** is elected King of Germany.

1766   British Parliament repeals the **Stamp Act** because of widespread opposition to it in America.

1848   Revolution breaks out in **Milan.**

1861   Widespread revolts and continued attacks from Haiti lead President **Pedro Santana** of **Santo Domingo** to place his country under Spanish rule.

1871   Commune uprising in **Paris** starts the brief rule of the socialist government.

1890   **Prince Bismarck** of Germany resigns offices of premier and foreign minister after frequent clashes with the new emperor, **William II.**

1891   Telephone communication between London and Paris is established.

1897   **Crete** proclaims union with **Greece.**

1913   **King George I** of Greece is assassinated at Solonika and is succeeded by his son, **Constantine I.**

1915   The **Russians** retake Memel, East Prussia, in their continuing counter-offensive against Germany on the Eastern Front **(World War I).**

1916   Dutch ship *Palembang* is sunk by a German torpedo **(World War I).**

The **Battle of Narock** marks the beginning of a Russian offensive against the Germans on the Eastern Front **(World War I).**

1919   British Parliament passes **Rowlatt Acts,** drastically curbing civil liberties in India.

1921   **Treaty of Riga** concludes Russian-Polish war and defines frontiers.

1922   **Mahatma Gandhi** is sentenced to six years in jail after his first **civil disobedience** campaign against British rule in India.

1938   Mexican government expropriates properties of British and U.S. oil companies valued at $450 million.

1945   U.S. naval task force conducts carrier strike against military targets on **Kyushu, Japan (World War II).**

1965   Russian cosmonaut **Aleksei A. Leonov** becomes the first man to float freely in space, on a lifeline attached to Soviet spacecraft *Voskhod 2.*

1966   Fourteen **NATO** members (all except France) express their support for the North Atlantic Treaty and the principle of military integration.

1967   The tanker *Torrey Canyon* is wrecked near Cornwall, England, and discharges more than 30,000 tons of crude oil.

1969   *Apollo 10* spacecraft is launched from Cape Kennedy.

1974   Arab oil companies, except Libya and Syria, end oil embargo against U.S.

1977   **Maj. Marien Ngouabi,** President of the **Congo,** is shot and killed in Brazzaville.

1978   Former Pakistani Prime Minister **Zulfikar Ali Bhutto,** removed from power by a military coup in July 1977, is convicted and sentenced to death; he is hanged April 4.

March 19

Holidays

Andorra,   St. Joseph's Day
Colombia,
Costa Rica,
Lichten-
stein, San
Marino,
Spain,
Vatican City,
Venezuela

Birthdates

1519 **Henry II, King of France**; husband of **Catherine de' Médicis.** [d. July 10, 1559]

1589 **William Bradford,** American colonial leader; Governor of **Plymouth Colony** for thirty years; author of *History of Plymouth Plantation.* [d. May 9, 1657]

1601 **Alonso Cano (El Granadino)**, Spanish painter, sculptor, architect; chief architect of **Granada Cathedral.** [d. October 5, 1667]

1721 **Tobias George Smollett,** Scottish novelist; author of several picaresque novels; edited a *Universal History*; translated Voltaire's works. [d. September 17, 1771]

1727 **Ferdinand Berthoud,** Swiss-French watchmaker, marine clockmaker, writer on horological subjects. [d. June 20, 1807]

1813 **David Livingstone,** British missionary, physician, explorer. [d. May 1, 1873]

1821 **Sir Richard Francis Burton,** British scholar, explorer; explored Somaliland, Lake Tanganyika region, and Gold Coast; published translations of *Arabian Nights.* [d. October 20, 1890]

1847 **Albert Pinkham Ryder,** U.S. painter; known for landscapes, marines; his *Toilers of the Sea* hangs in the Metropolitan Museum of Art, New York City. [d. March 28, 1917]

1848 **Wyatt Earp,** U.S. law officer, gunfighter; most famous for his participation at the gunfight at O.K. Corral. [d. January 13, 1929]

1849 **Alfred von Tirpitz,** German admiral; Secretary of the Navy, 1897–1916. [d. March 6, 1930]

1858 **K'ang Yu-wei,** Chinese scholar, reformer; known as the *Rousseau of China.* [d. March 31, 1927]

1860 **William Jennings Bryan,** U.S. politician, orator, lawyer, editor; Democratic presidential nominee, 1896, 1900, 1908; U.S. Secretary of State, 1912–13. [d. July 26, 1925]

1872 **Sergei Pavlovich Diaghilev,** Russian ballet master, theatrical impresario; revitalized ballet by integrating ideals of other art forms. [d. August 19, 1929]

1876 **Sir John Hubert Marshall,** British archaeologist; discoverer of the **Indus Valley civilization.** [d. August 17, 1958]

1883 **Sir Walter N. Haworth,** British chemist; Nobel Prize in chemistry for determining chemical structures of carbohydrates (with P. Karrer), 1937. [d. March 19, 1950]

Joseph Warren Stilwell (*Vinegar Joe*), U.S. Army general; commanded U.S. forces in the China-Burma-India theater during **World War II.** [d. October 12, 1946]

1891 **Earl Warren,** U.S. lawyer, jurist; Governor of California, 1943–53; 14th Chief Justice of U.S. Supreme Court, 1953–69. [d. July 9, 1974]

1900 **Jean Frédéric Joliot-Curie** (originally Joliot), French nuclear physicist; Nobel Prize in chemistry for synthesis of new **radioactive elements** (with wife Irène, the daughter of Marie and Pierre Curie), 1935. [d. August 14, 1958]

1901 **Jo Mielziner,** U.S. stage designer. [d. March 15, 1976]

1904 **John J(oseph) Sirica,** Chief Judge of U.S. District Court, District of Columbia, 1971–74; presided over the Watergate trials, 1972–74.

1905 **Albert Speer,** German architect; confidante of Hitler; sentenced at Nuremburg trials and imprisoned 1945–1966. [d. September 1, 1981]

U.S.
(California)

Swallow Day
The day on which the swallows traditionally return to the Mission of San Juan Capistrano.

Religious Calendar

Solemnities

St. Joseph, husband of the Virgin Mary; step-father of Christ; Patron of the Universal Church, also of carpenters, wheelwrights, and combatants against Communism. [d. 1st century]

The Saints

St. John of Panaca, abbot. [d. 6th century]
St. Landoald, [d. c. 668]
St. Alcmund, martyr. [d. c. 800]

The Beatified

Blessed Andrew of Siena, founder of the Society of Mercy. [d. 1251]

1906 **(Karl) Adolf Eichmann,** German Nazi official held responsible for the execution of millions of Jews during World War II. [executed May 31, 1962]

1916 **Irving Wallace,** U.S. novelist.

1928 **Hans Küng,** Swiss-German liberal Roman Catholic theologian, author; censured by Catholic Church in 1979.

1930 **Ornette Coleman,** U.S. jazz saxophonist.

1933 **Philip Roth,** U.S. writer; author of *Goodbye Columbus* and *Portnoy's Complaint.*

1936 **Ursula Andress,** Swiss actress.

Historical Events

72 The first **lunar eclipse** recorded in history is observed by the Babylonians (according to Ptolemy).

1284 The **Statute of Wales** is enacted making that land part of the Kingdom of England.

1286 **Margaret, Maid of Norway,** becomes Queen of Scotland under six guardians upon the death of her husband, **Alexander III** of Scotland.

1452 **Frederick III** is crowned Holy Roman Emperor.

1563 **Edict of Amboise** grants French Huguenots some freedom, ending first **Huguenot War.**

1782 English Prime Minister, **Lord North,** resigns and is replaced as by **Charles Watson-Wentworth, Marquis of Rockingham.**

1799 **Napoleon** lays siege to **Acre.**

1808 **Charles IV** of Spain abdicates in favor of his son, **Ferdinand.**

1853 The **Taiping rebels** seize **Nanking** and make it their capital (**Taiping Rebellion**).

1861 The **Maori insurrection** ends in New Zealand with surrender of the Maori.

1896 **Horatio Kitchener** begins an advance up the Nile with British troops to check the activity of the dervishes and to relieve **Kasala** in the Sudan.

1920 The U.S. Senate rejects the **Versailles Treaty.**

1921 **Georgia** proclaimed a Soviet Republic.

1942 **Netherlands East Indies** formally surrenders to Japan (**World War II**).

1964 **Great St. Bernard Tunnel,** 3.4 miles long, between Italy and Switzerland in the Alps, is officially opened to automobile traffic.

1968 President Johnson signs into law a bill eliminating the requirement that 25 per cent of U.S. currency be backed by **gold.**

1970 East German Premier Stoph and West German Chancellor Brandt confer in Erfurt, East Germany, at the first meeting of the heads of the **postwar German states.**

1972 **India** and **Bangladesh** sign a 25-year treaty of friendship and mutual defense in Dacca.

March 20

Holidays

Tunisia   **Independence Day**
Commemorates the signing by the French of the March 20, 1956, treaty recognizing Tunisian autonomy.

Religious Calendar

The Saints
St. Martin, Archbishop of Braga. [d. 579]
St. Cuthbert, Bishop of Lindisfarne. [d. 687]

Birthdates

43 B.C. **Publius Ovidius Naso,** Latin poet, known as **Ovid.** [d. c. A.D. 17]

1741 **Jean Antoine Houdon,** French neoclassical sculptor; known for his sculptures of such renowned figures as **Voltaire, George Washington,** and **Thomas Jefferson.** [d. July 15, 1828]

1770 **Johann Friedrich Hölderlin,** German poet. [d. June 7, 1843]

1796 **Edward Gibbon Wakefield,** British colonizer of **South Australia** and **New Zealand.** [d. May 16, 1862]

1811 **George Caleb Bingham,** U.S. painter; best known for his works portraying river scenes, frontier life, and historical events in the Missouri River Valley. [d. July 7, 1879]

1823 **Ned Buntline (Edward Zane Carroll Judson),** U.S. novelist, adventurer; organized the **Know-Nothing Party,** 1850s. [d. July 16, 1886]

1828 **Henrik Ibsen,** Norwegian poet and playwright: author of *Hedda Gabler, A Doll's House,* and *The Wild Duck.* [d. May 23, 1906]

Prince Frederick Charles, the *Red Prince* of Prussia. [d. January 15, 1885]

1834 **Charles William Eliot,** U.S. educator; President, Harvard University, 1869–1909; a founder of **Radcliffe College.** [d. August 22, 1926]

1856 **Frederick Winslow Taylor,** U.S. engineer; particularly known for his **time and motion studies** which revolutionized production techniques and industrial management in the U.S. [d. March 21, 1915]

1890 **Beniamino Gigli,** Italian opera tenor. [d. November 30, 1957]

Lauritz (Lebrecht Hommel) Melchior, U.S. operatic tenor, born in Denmark; known for his Wagnerian roles. [d. March 18, 1973]

1892 **Max Brand (Frederick Faust),** U.S. novelist, screenwriter; under various pseudonyms, created such classic stories as *Destry Rides Again* and the *Dr. Kildare* series of the 1930s. Known as the *King of the Pulp Writers,* it is estimated that he produced more than 500 full-length novels before his death at the Battle of Santa Maria Infante in Italy during World War II. [d. May 16, 1944]

1897 **Frank (Joseph) Sheed,** U.S. publisher, lecturer, lay theologian; founder of Sheed and Ward publishing house. 1926; author of *Theology and Sanity,* 1953. [d. November 20, 1981]

1904 **B(urrhus) F(rederic) Skinner,** U.S. behavioral psychologist; known as the *Father of Programmed Instruction;* espoused principles of **behavioral engineering.**

1908 **Sir Michael Redgrave,** British actor; father of Vanessa and Lynn Redgrave.

Frank (Nicholas) Stanton, U.S. communications executive; Director, CBS Inc., 1945–78.

1909 **Kathryn Forbes (Kathryn Anderson McLean),** U.S. short-story writer; well known for her collection of stories which were dramatized as *I Remember Mama.* [d. May 15, 1966]

1915 **Rudolf Kirchschlaeger,** Austrian statesman; President, 1970– .

1920 **Marian Margaret McPartland,** U.S. jazz pianist and composer, born in England.

St. Herbert, anchoret and priest. [d. 687]

St. Wulfram, Archbishop of Sens. [d. c. 703]

The Martyrs of Mar Saba, monks. [d. 796]

St. Photina and her companions, martyrs. [death date unknown]

The Beatified

Blessed Evangelist and **Peregrine,** hermits. [d. c. 1250]

Blessed Ambrose of Siena, Dominican friar. [d. 1286]

Blessed John of Parma, seventh minister general of the Franciscans. [d. 1289]

Blessed Maurice of Hungary, friar. [d. 1336]

Blessed Mark of Montegallo, Franciscan friar. [d. 1497]

Blessed Baptist of Mantua, prior general of the Carmelite Order. Surnamed **Spagnuolo,** the **Spaniard.** [d. 1516]

Blessed Hippolytus Galantini, founder of the Institute of Christian Doctrine or the Vanchetoni. [d. 1619]

1922 **Ray (Walter) Goulding,** U.S. comedian; with partner Bob Elliott formed the popular radio comedy team of *Bob and Ray.*

1925 **John D(aniel) Ehrlichman,** U.S. government official, lawyer; played a major role in the **Watergate Incident.** Convicted, 1975; released, 1978.

Historical Events

1239 **Pope Gregory IX** excommunicates **Holy Roman Emperor Frederick II.**

1602 **Dutch East India Company** is established.

1604 **Charles IX** assumes title of King of Sweden.

1751 **Frederick, Prince of Wales,** son of **George II** of Great Britain, dies, leaving a son who becomes **George III.**

1806 The foundation stone of **Dartmoor Prison** in England is laid.

1815 The independence and perpetual neutrality of **Switzerland** is secured by acts of the **Congress of Vienna.**

Napoleon arrives at Fontainebleau, the beginning of **The Hundred Days** in France.

1819 The **Burlington Arcade** is opened in London.

1848 **Ludwig I, King of Bavaria,** resigns.

1890 **General Federation of Women's Clubs** is founded in U.S.

1915 **Great Britain, France,** and **Russia** sign a secret agreement granting Constantinople (Istanbul) and the Dardanelles to Russia, and Persia (Iran) to Great Britain (**World War I).**

General Botha defeats German forces at Pforteberg, South Africa (**World War I).**

1919 **Wireless telephone service** is established between Ireland and Canada.

1920 The first successful flight across Africa, from Cairo to Cape Town, is completed by Col. H. A. van Rejneveld and Maj. C. J. Brand of the South African Air Force.

1922 First **U.S. aircraft carrier,** *U.S.S. Langley,* is commissioned.

1952 The peace treaty restoring Japanese sovereignty is ratified, ending American occupation of Japan.

1953 **Nikita Khrushchev** succeeds Malenkov as First Secretary of the Communist Party's Central Committee.

1956 **Tunisia** gains full independence from France.

March 21

Iraq	**Spring Day** or **Nairuz**
Mexico	**Juárez Birthday**
	Honors the national hero and former president Benito Juárez
U.S.	**Memory Day**
	Sponsored by Puns Corporation Falls Church, Virginia.
U.S.	**Fragrance Day**
	Sponsored by Richard R. Falk Associates
UN Member Countries	**International Day for the Elimination of Racial Discrimination** in memory of victims of racial discrimination at Sharpeville, South Africa, and in other parts of the world.

Birthdates

1685 **Johann Sebastian Bach,** German composer; founder of a musical dynasty; internationally renowned as a master of **keyboard compositions**. [d. July 28, 1750]

1713 **Francis Lewis,** American merchant; signer of Declaration of Independence. [d. December 31, 1802]

1763 **Jean Paul Friedrich Richter (Jean Paul),** German novelist. [d. November 14, 1825]

1768 **Joseph Jean Baptiste Fourier,** French mathematician; first conceived mathematic theory of **heat conduction**. [d. May 16, 1830]

1806 **Benito Juárez,** Mexican leader, revolutionary hero; President, 1858–59, 1861–63, 1867–72. [d. July 18, 1872]

1831 **Dorothea Beale,** British educator; a founder of **St. Hilda's Hall** at Oxford. [d. November 9, 1906]

1839 **Modest Petrovich Mussorgsky,** Russian composer; composed *Boris Godunov*. [d. March 28, 1881]

1869 **Albert Kahn,** U.S. architect; noted for his design of office and factory buildings. [d. December 8, 1942]

Florenz Ziegfeld, U.S. producer, particularly known for extravagant stage shows, *Ziegfeld Follies*. [d. July 22, 1932]

1882 **Gilbert (*Bronco Billy*) Anderson (Max Aronson),** U.S. producer; star of silent western movies.

1884 **George David Birkoff,** U.S. mathematician; renowned for his research in theoretical mathematics; developed the **ergodic theorem** of the kinetic theory of gases; expanded on Einstein's theory of relativity; Dean of Harvard Faculty of Arts and Sciences, 1935–39. [d. November 12, 1944]

1889 **Frederick (Henry) Osborn,** U.S. demographer, author; known for his efforts on behalf of atomic energy control; Chairman of Population Council, 1930–68. [d. January 5, 1981]

1900 **Eugenie Leontovich,** Russian-U.S. actress, dramatic coach; founder of **Actors's Workshop,** 1953.

1905 **Phyllis McGinley,** U.S. poet; Pulitzer Prize in poetry, 1960. [d. February 22, 1978]

1920 **Eric Rohmer (Jean-Marie Maurice Schere),** French director; directed *Claire's Knee, Chloe in the Afternoon.*

1921 **Terence James Cooke,** U.S. Roman Catholic cardinal; Archbishop of New York, 1969–1983. [d. October 6, 1983].

1925 **Peter Brook,** British director; co-director of the Royal Shakespeare Theatre; N.Y. Drama Critics Award for the Best Director 1965–6; founded the Centre International de Créations Théâtrales, Paris, 1971.

1927 **Claurène duGran,** British author.

Religious Calendar

The Saints

St. Serapion, Bishop of Thmuis. Surnamed the **Scholastic** or **Sindonite.** Also called **Sarapion.** [d. c. 370]

St. Enda, abbot, and **St. Fanchea**, virgin. Enda also called **Enna**, or **Endeus.** Fanchea also called **Faenche,** or **Faine.** [d. c. 530]

The Beatified

Blessed Santuccia, matron. [d. 1305]

Historical Events

1098 Monastery at **Cîteaux** is founded.

1413 **Henry IV** of England dies and is succeeded by **Henry V** who ruled through August 31, 1422.

1556 **Thomas Cranmer,** Archbishop of Canterbury and supporter of Henry VIII, is burned at the stake under orders of Mary Tudor.

1791 **Bangalore,** India, is seized by the British under Lord Cornwallis in the **Third Mysore War.**

1847 **Union of Central American Republics** is formed.

1859 The **Scottish National Gallery** opens.

1871 The first **Reichstag** officially opens.

Sir Henry Morton Stanley embarks on African expedition to find **Dr. David Livingstone.**

1917 The provisional Russian government restores the Finnish Constitution and declares **Finland** a free and independent state in the Russian federation.

Czar Nicholas II and his wife, Alexandra, are ordered imprisoned at their residence by the provisional Russian government.

1918 The great **Somme offensive** begins as the Germans pierce British lines (**World War I).**

1919 The **Rowlatt Acts** is passed in India giving the government far-reaching and arbitrary anti-sedition powers.

1927 **Shanghai** is taken by the Nationalist Chinese forces of Chiang Kai-shek.

1935 Persia is renamed **Iran.**

1946 U.S. Air Force establishes the **Strategic Air Command** and the **Tactical Air Command.**

1960 **Sharpeville Massacre** takes place in South Africa when blacks besiege Johannesburg police station protesting law requiring all blacks to carry papers (**Pass Law**).

1968 Israelis capture **Karameh** in major assault on Jordan.

1983 **Barney Clark,** first human to receive a permanent artificial heart, dies 112 days after the operation from circulatroy collapse and multiorgan failure.

March 22

Holidays

Arab League Countries	**Arab League Day** — A holiday for all signatories in the March 22, 1945, formation of the Arab League.
Lesotho	**National Tree Planting Day**
Puerto Rico	**Emancipation Day** or **Abolition Day** — Commemorates the abolition of slavery on the island on March 22, 1873.

Birthdates

1459 **Maximilian I, Holy Roman Emperor,** 1493–1519. [d. January 12, 1519]

1599 **Sir Anthony Van Dyke,** Flemish artist; court painter under **Charles I** of England; his style influenced English art for more than 100 years. [d. December 9, 1641]

1785 **Adam Sedgwick,** English geologist; introduced term *Devonian*. [d. January 27, 1873]

1797 **Emperor William I** of Prussia (Kaiser Wilhelm I), 1871. [d. March 9, 1888]

1817 **Braxton Bragg,** Confederate Army general during the U.S. Civil War; responsible for Confederate victory at **Shiloh.** [d. September 27, 1876]

1846 **Randolph Caldecott,** British artist; illustrator; annual U.S. award for outstanding illustration in juvenile literature is presented in his honor (**Caldecott Award**). [d. February 12, 1886]

1857 **Paul Doumer,** French statesman; 13th President of the Third Republic, 1931–32; assassinated by **Paul Gorgoulov.** [d. May 7, 1932]

1868 **Robert Andrews Millikan,** U.S. physicist; Nobel Prize in physics for research on **photoelectricity,** 1923. [d. December 19, 1953]

1884 **Arthur Hendrick Vandenberg,** U.S. politician, editor, U.S. senator; played significant role in formation of **United Nations, NATO,** and the **Marshall Plan.** [d. April 18, 1951]

1907 **James Maurice Gavin,** U.S. army general, diplomat; Ambassador to France, 1960–62.

1908 **Maurice Hubert Stans,** U.S. government official; Secretary of Commerce, 1969–72; a leading figure in **Watergate Incident.**

1913 **Karl Malden (Maiden Sekulovich),** U.S. actor.

1914 **William E. Miller,** U.S. politician; unsuccessful Republican nominee for vice-president, 1964.

1923 **Marcel Marceau,** French mime.

1930 **Stephen (Joshua) Sondheim,** U.S. composer, lyricist.

1931 **Burton Richter,** U.S. physicist; Nobel Prize in physics for discovery of **subatomic particle** *J*, with S. C. C. Ting, 1976.

1933 **Abolhassan Bani-Sadr,** Iranian political leader; first President of the Islamic Republic of Iran, 1980–81.

Historical Events

1312 **Pope Clement V** abolishes **Order of Templars.**

1673 In England, the **Test Act** excludes Roman Catholics and dissenters from holding office.

1830 Richard and John Lander, British explorers, begin exploration of the **Niger River** establishing that its outlet is at the Bight of Benim.

1847 The first meeting of **Young Men's Hebrew Association** is held in New York.

1848 **Venetian Republic** proclaims its independence.

1915 Russians capture Austrians' fortress camp of **Przemyśl, Galicia,** taking 119,000 prisoners, the greatest number ever to surrender in war time (**World War I**).

1917 The U.S., Great Britain, France, Italy, Rumania, and Switzerland recognize the provisional government of **Russia.**

Religious Calendar

The Saints

St. Paul of Narbonne, missionary. [d. c. 290]

St. Basil of Ancyra, priest and martyr. [d. 362]

St. Deogratias, Bishop of Carthage. [d. 457]

St. Benvenuto, Bishop of Osimo. [d. 1282]

St. Nicholas von Flüe, layman and hermit. Also called **Brother Klaus,** or **Bruder Klaus.** [d. 1487]

The Beatified

Blessed Isnardo of Chiampo, Dominican priest. [d. 1244]

Blessed Hugolino of Cortona, Augustinian hermit. [d. c. 1470]

1919 A Bolshevik coup headed by **Béla Kun** overthrows the republican government of **Hungary.**

1929 **King Alexander of Yugoslavia** orders the replacement of the Cyrillic alphabet with the Latin alphabet in Yugoslavia.

1944 German troops occupy Hungary and set up a pro-German régime (**World War II**).

1946 First U.S. **rocket** to leave the earth's atmosphere, launched from White Sands, New Mexico, attains a height of 50 miles.

Great Britain announces the independence of **Transjordan.**

1966 Congolese President **Joseph D. Mobutu** abolishes Parliament's functions and assumes all national legislative powers.

1971 Argentine President **Roberto Marcelo Levingston** is deposed in a bloodless coup.

1972 U.S. Senate passes **Equal Rights Amendment** subject to ratification by the fifty states.

1979 British ambassador to the Netherlands, **Sir Richard Sykes,** is assassinated at The Hague.

1982 U.S. space shuttle *Columbia* lifts off for its third voyage into outer space.

March 23

Holidays

Japan	**Spring Imperial Festival** or **Shunki-Koreisan** A day on which the Emperor pays special respect to his ancestors.
Pakistan	**Pakistan Republic Day** Commemorates the establishment of Pakistan Republic on March 23, 1956.
UN Member Countries	**World Meteorological Day**

Birthdates

1430 **Margaret of Anjou, Queen of England;** wife of Henry VI. [d. August 25, 1482]

1699 **John Bartram,** American botanist; called the *Greatest Contemporary Botanist* by Carolus Linnaeus; later recognized as the *Father of Botany in U.S.* [d. September 22, 1777]

1749 **Pierre Simon, Marquis de Laplace,** French astronomer, mathematician; noted for discovery of **invariability of planetary mean motions,** 1773. [d. March 5, 1827]

1760 **William Smith,** English geologist; founder of **stratigraphical geology.** [d. August 28, 1839]

1780 **Count Karl Robert Nesselrode,** Russian statesman; Chancellor of Russia, 1845–56. [d. 1862]

1823 **Schuyler Colfax,** U.S. politician, newspaper editor; U.S. Congressman, 1854–69; U.S. Vice-President, 1868–72. [d. January 13, 1885]

1855 **Franklin Henry Giddings,** U.S. sociologist; author of *The Principles of Sociology.* [d. June 11, 1931]

1857 **Fannie (Merritt) Farmer,** U.S. cookery expert; noted for her standardization of measurements in recipes and the publication of her *Boston Cooking School Cookbook,* still a classic in its revised form as *Fannie Farmer Cookbook.* [d. January 15, 1915]

1858 **Ludwig Quidde,** German peace activist; Nobel Peace Prize (with F. E. Buisson), 1927. [d. March 5, 1941]

1872 **Michael Joseph Savage,** first Labour Prime Minister of New Zealand, 1935–40. [d. March 27, 1940]

1873 **Barron Gift Collier,** U.S. business executive, financier. [d. March 13, 1939]

1881 **Hermann Staudinger,** German chemist; Nobel Prize in chemistry for work on **giant molecules** and contributions to the development of **plastics,** 1953. [d. September 8, 1965]

Roger Martin du Gard, French novelist, dramatist; Nobel Prize in literature, 1937. [d. August 22, 1958]

1884 **Florence Ellinwood Allen,** U.S. jurist; first woman to be named to U.S. Circuit Court of Appeals, 1934. [d. September 12, 1966]

1887 **Juan Gris,** Spanish cubist painter. [d. 1927]

Sidney Hillman, U.S. labor leader, born in Lithuania; a founder and president of **Amalgamated Clothing Workers of America,** 1915–46. [d. July 10, 1946]

1899 **Louis Adamic,** U.S. author, born in Yugoslavia; known for his expression of immigrants' ideals. [d. September 4, 1951]

1900 **Erich Fromm,** U.S. psychoanalyst, born in Germany; author of *The Art of Loving.* [d. March 18, 1980]

1907 **Daniel Bovet,** Swiss-Italian pharmacologist; Nobel Prize in physiology or medicine for development of **muscle-relaxing drugs,** 1957.

1908 **Joan Crawford (Lucille Le Sueur),** U.S. actress. [d. February 14, 1977]

1910 **Akira Kurosawa,** Japanese movie director.

1912 **Werner (Magnus Maximilian) von Braun,** German-U.S. engineer; pioneer of rocketry; responsible for German develop-

Religious Calendar

The Saints

St. Victorian and his companions, martyrs. [d. 484]

St. Benedict the Hermit. [d. c. 550]

St. Ethelwald the Hermit. Also called **Edelwald, Ethelwold, Oidilwald.** [d. 699]

St. Turibius of Mongrovejo. [d. 1606] Optional Memorial.

St. Joseph Oriol, priest. [d. 1702]

St. Gwinear, missionary; patron of Gwinear, Cornwall. Also called **Fingar, Guigner.** [death date unknown]

The Beatified

Blessed Peter of Gubbio, Augustinian hermit. [d. c. 1250]

Blessed Sibyllina of Pavia, virgin and recluse. [d. 1367]

---

ment of **V-2 rockets**; the *Father of U.S. Space Exploration.* [d. June 16, 1977]

1929 **Roger Bannister,** British athlete, physician; first to run a mile in under four minutes, May 6, 1954.

1938 **Maynard Jackson,** U.S. politician, lawyer.

Historical Events

1324 **Pope John XXII** excommunicates **Louis IV** of Germany.

1509 **League of Cambrai** is formed, allying the Papacy, Holy Roman Empire, France, and Aragon against Venice.

1752 The first known example of printing in Canada, the *Halifax Gazette,* is produced by **John Bushell** in Nova Scotia.

1765 British Parliament passes the **Stamp Act,** imposing duties on the 13 American colonies.

1775 To encourage the arming of Virginia militia, **Patrick Henry** delivers *Give me liberty or give me death* speech to the second Virginia convention.

1801 **Paul I, Czar of Russia** is assassinated in the course of a palace revolution and succeeded by **Alexander I.**

1848 First officially organized settlers of New Zealand land at Dunedin.

1849 **Charles Albert, King of Sardinia,** abdicates in favor of his son, **Victor Emmanuel.**

1861 First tram cars in London begin operation at Bayside.

1877 **Mormon Bishop John D. Lee** is executed by a firing squad in Utah for his part in the September, 1857, **Mountain Meadow Mas-**

sacre of 120 emigrants bound for California.

1889 Lord Rosebery opens the **free steam ferry** at Woolwich in London.

1903 **Irish Bank Holiday** bill is passed, establishing **St. Patrick's Day** as bank holiday.

1918 The **German bombardment of Paris** by long-range guns begins from a distance of 75 miles (**World War I**).

1919 **Benito Mussolini** founds the Fascist movement, *Fasci del Combattimento,* in Milan.

1933 **Adolf Hitler,** as Reich Chancellor and leader of the Nazi party, is formally given dictatorial powers by German Reichstag.

1935 The U.S.S.R. sells its share of the **Chinese Eastern Railway** to Manchuria, then ruled by Japan.

1950 **World Meteorological Organization** is established by United Nations to facilitate an international system of coordinating weather data and observation.

1962 The world's first nuclear-powered merchant vessel, the *Savannah,* is launched at Camden, New Jersey.

1965 Maj. **Virgil I. Grissom** and Lieut. Comdr. **John Young** of the U.S. orbit the earth three times in a *Gemini* spacecraft and then land in the Atlantic off Grand Turk Island.

1966 **Arthur Michael Ramsey, Archbishop of Canterbury,** exchanges public greetings with **Pope Paul VI** in the first official visit to a Roman Catholic pontiff by a head of the Anglican Church in 400 years.

March 24

Religious Calendar

The Saints

St. Irenaeus, Bishop of Sirmium and martyr. [d. 304]

St. Dunchad, Abbot of Iona; patron of sailors in Ireland. [d. 716]

St. Aldemar, abbot. Surnamed the **Wise.** [d. c. 1080]

St. Catherine of Vadstena, virgin and abbess. Invoked against miscarriages. Also called **Catherine of Sweden, Karin, Katherine.** [d. 1381]

Birthdates

1494 **Georgius Agricola (Georg Bauer),** German mineralogist, physician; called the *Father of Mineralogy.* [d. November 21, 1555]

1607 **Michiel Adriaanszoon de Ruyter,** Dutch naval commander, hero in Dutch-English Wars. [d. 1676]

1754 **Joel Barlow,** U.S. poet, statesman; one of the *Hartford Wits.* [d. December 24, 1812]

1755 **Rufus King,** U.S. politician, diplomat, lawyer. U.S. senator, 1789–96 and 1813–25. [d. April 27, 1827]

1809 **Mariano José de Larra y Sanchez de Castro,** Spanish writer; considered one of the greatest Spanish satirists of the 19th century. [d. February 13, 1837]

1822 **Henry Murger,** French journalist, poet; known for his sketches of Bohemian life in Paris. [d. January 28, 1861]

1834 **William Morris,** British poet, artist; his work exerted great influence on decorating taste of Victorian England; considered a leader of the modern romantic school of English art. [d. October 1, 1896]

John Wesley Powell, U.S. geologist, ethnologist; explored **Grand Canyon**; an early director of the U.S. Geological Survey, 1881–94. [d. September 23, 1902]

1855 **Andrew William Mellon,** U.S. financier, government official, philanthropist; U.S. Secretary of the Treasury, 1921–32. [d. August 26, 1937]

1874 **Harry Houdini (Ehrich Weiss),** U.S. magician, escape artist, born in Hungary; renowned for his spectacular magic and escape tricks. [d. October 31, 1926]

1884 **Peter J. W. Debye,** Dutch chemist; Nobel Prize in chemistry for his investigations of dipole moments, 1936. [d. November 2, 1966]

1886 **Edward Weston,** U.S. photographer; known for his exceptional artistry as a nature photographer. [d. January 1, 1958]

1887 **Fatty Arbuckle (Roscoe Conkling Arbuckle),** U.S. film comedian. [d. June 29, 1953]

1893 **George Sisler,** U.S. baseball player. Baseball Hall of Fame, 1939. [d. March 26, 1973]

1902 **Thomas E(dmund) Dewey,** U.S. politician, lawyer; Governor of New York, 1943–55; Republican candidate for President, 1944 and 1948. [d. March 16, 1971]

1903 **Adolf Friedrich Johann Butenandt,** German chemist; Nobel Prize in chemistry for studies of **sex hormones** (with L. Ruzicka), 1939.

1906 **Dwight MacDonald,** U.S. writer, critic; known for his sardonic wit and relentless standards in discussions of social issues; staff writer for *New Yorker,* and *Esquire.* [d. December 19, 1982]

1907 **Lauris Norstad,** U.S. Air Force general; Commander-in-Chief of U.S. Air Forces in Europe, 1951–56; Supreme Allied Commander in Europe, 1956–62.

1909 **Clyde Barrow,** U.S. outlaw, robber, murderer; companion of Bonnie Parker (October 1). [d. May 23, 1934]

1917 **John C. Kendrew,** British scientist; Nobel Prize in chemistry for determining the structure of the muscle protein **myoglobin** (with M. F. Perutz), 1962.

1919 **Lawrence (Monsanto) Ferlinghetti,** U.S. poet, publisher.

1930 **Steve McQueen,** U.S. actor. [d. November 7, 1980]

SS. Simon of Trent, infant, and **William of Norwich,** martyrs. Simon also called **Simeon.** [d. 1475, 1144]

St. Gabriel the Archangel, the angel of the annunciation to Mary. Patron of postal, telegraph, and telephone workers.

The Beatified

Blessed Didacus of Cadiz, Franciscan priest; called the **Apostle of the Holy Trinity.** Also called **Diego.** [d. 1801]

Historical Events

1267	**Saint Louis of France** calls his knights to Paris to prepare for his **Second Crusade.**
1401	**Timur Lenk (Tamerlane),** Mongol ruler, conquers **Damascus.**
1449	English break truce, capturing **Fougères,** France, in **Hundred Years' War.**
1603	**Elizabeth I** of England dies and is succeeded by **James VI** of Scotland who is proclaimed **James I, King of England, Ireland, Scotland, and France.**
1644	A charter is granted to **Roger Williams** for the colony of **Rhode Island.**
1927	**Nationalist Chinese** troops seize Nanking.
1934	The U.S. adopts the **Tydings-McDuffie Act** providing for eventual independence for the **Philippines.**
1941	German General **Erwin Rommel** begins North African offensive (**World War II**).
	Yugoslavia capitulates and signs pact with Germany (**World War II**).
1944	U.S. President **Franklin D. Roosevelt** issues statement appealing to Hungarians to help the Jews escape from Nazis (**World War II**).
1965	U.S. spacecraft *Ranger 9* crash-lands precisely on target in the Alphonsus crater of the moon after transmitting to earth 5,814 photographs of the crater region.
1976	The government of **Argentine President Isabel Perón** is overthrown by armed forces lead by Lt. General **Jorge Rafaél Videla.**
1977	**Morarji R. Desai** is sworn in as India's fourth prime minister, replacing **Indira Gandhi.**
1982	Military coup in **Bangladesh** results in suspension of the constitution and imposition of martial law.

March 25

Holidays

Great Britain   **Lady Day** or **Quarter Day**
A day marking the end of the first quarter of the year (calculated from Christmas); also commemorates the appearance of the Angel Gabriel to the Virgin Mary announcing that she would be the mother of Christ.

Greece   **Independence Day**
Commemorates the day when the Greek flag was first raised in revolt against Ottoman domination, 1821.

San Marino   **Universal Vote Day**

Birthdates

1252   **Conradin** (also called **Conrad V**), Holy Roman Emperor; King of Jerusalem and Sicily, 1266–68; last of the German Hohenstaufen dynasty; executed. [d. October 29, 1268]

1767   **Joachim Murat,** French cavalry leader; marshal with **Napoleon**; King of Naples, 1808–15; known as the *Dandy King*. [d. October 13, 1815]

1797   **John Winebrenner,** U.S. clergyman; founder of the **Church of God** denomination. [d. September 12, 1860]

1839   **William Bell Wait,** U.S. educator; devised an embossing machine for printing books for the blind. [d. October 25, 1916]

1862   **William Eugene Johnson (*Pussyfoot Johnson*),** U.S. reformer; militant Prohibitionist. [d. February 2, 1945]

1863   **Simon Flexner,** U.S. pathologist, bacteriologist; discoverer of the serum to treat **meningitis.** [d. May 2, 1946]

1867   **Arturo Toscanini,** U.S. conductor, born in Italy; one of the best known modern conductors. [d. January 16, 1957]

1871   **Gutzon Borglum (John Gutson de la Mothe Borglum),** U.S. sculptor; famed for his presidential sculptures on **Mt. Rushmore,** South Dakota. [d. March 6, 1941]

1881   **Béla Bartók,** Hungarian composer, pianist; recognized as the father of contemporary Hungarian music. [d. September 26, 1945]

1887   **Raymond Gram Swing,** U.S. radio commentator. [d. December 22, 1968]

1891   **Byron Price,** U.S. journalist, public official; U.S. Director of Censorship, 1941–45; Assistant Secretary General of UN, 1947–54. [d. August 6, 1981]

1914   **Norman E. Borlaug,** U.S. agronomist; Nobel Peace Prize for his work in developing new varieties of **high-yield cereals,** 1970; U.S. Medal of Freedom, 1970.

1920   **Howard Cosell (Howard William Cohen),** U.S. sportscaster.

1921   **Simone Signoret (Simone-Henriette-Charlotte Kaminker),** French actress.

1925   **(Mary) Flannery O'Connor,** U.S. short-story writer, novelist. [d. August 3, 1964]

1928   **James Arthur Lovell Jr.,** U.S. astronaut; aboard *Gemini 12* space mission.

1934   **Gloria Steinem,** U.S. feminist, writer, lecturer; founder and editor of *Ms.* magazine.

Historical Events

1306   **Robert Bruce** is crowned **Robert I, King of Scotland.**

1634   Lord Baltimore's settlers arrive in **Maryland,** establishing the foundation of the new colony.

1799   Austrians defeat French at **Stokach** in **War of the Second Coalition.**

1821   Uprising occurs in the **Greek Peloponnesus,** initiating a decade of revolution against the Turks and civil war in Greece.

U.S.
(Maryland)

Maryland Day
Commemorates the landing of Lord Baltimore and the first colonists on St. Clement's Island, 1634.

Religious Calendar

Solemnities

The Annunciation of Our Lord to the Blessed Virgin Mary. [Also major Episcopal Holy Day; minor Lutheran festival.]

The Saints

The Good Thief, the thief who was crucified with Christ; patron of thieves. Also called **Dismas, Gestas,** or **Titus.** [d. 29 A.D.]

St. Barontius, monk and hermit. [d. c. 695]
St. Hermenland, abbot. [d. c. 720]
St. Alřwold, Bishop of Sherborne. [d. c. 1058]
St. Lucy Filippini, virgin. [d. 1732]
St. Ermelandus, abbot. [death date unknown]

The Beatified

Blessed Thomasius, hermit. Also called **Thomas.** [d. 1337]
Blessed James Bird, layman and martyr. [d. 1593]

1900   Warfare breaks out anew between the **Ashantis** of West Africa and the British when the British seize the *Golden Stool,* a symbol of Ashanti royalty.

1904   *Armida,* the last opera of **Antonin Dvořák,** premieres in Prague.

1911   Fire in the Triangle Shirtwaist Co., near Washington Square, New York City, kills more than 150 persons, mostly young seamstresses who are unable to escape; the tragedy awakens New Yorkers to the misery and dangers of the **sweatshop** system.

1919   The Peace Conference of World War I is reduced to a **Council of Four** for decision making: Clemenceau of France, Lloyd George of Britain, President Wilson of the U.S., and Orlando of Italy.

1935   **Paul Van Zeeland** becomes premier of Belgium and is given decree powers for one year to cope with the nation's desperate financial situation.

1957   The **Treaty of Rome** is signed, establishing the **European Economic Community (Common Market).** Members are Belgium, France, West Germany, Italy, Luxembourg, and the Netherlands.

1965   About 25,000 **civil rights demonstrators** end a five-day march from Selma, to Montgomery, Alabama, with a rally demanding equal rights for blacks.

1972   Agreement to coordinate efforts to control the trade in **narcotic drugs** is signed by 36 countries in Geneva.

1975   **King Faisal** of Saudi Arabia is assassinated in Riyadh by his nephew, Prince Faisal ibn Musad, who is subsequently beheaded publicly. **Crown Prince Khalid,** brother of the king, succeeds to the throne.

March 26

Holidays

Bangladesh   **Independence Day**
Commemorates the proclamation establishing Bangladesh, 1971.

Spain   **Fiesta del Arbol** or **Arbor Day**
Celebrated since 1895 when **King Alfonso XIII** planted a pine sapling at a ceremony near Madrid.

U.S. (Hawaii)   **Prince Jonah Kuhio Kalanianaole Day** or **Regatta Day**. Commemorates the birth of the Prince.

Birthdates

1516   **Konrad von Gesner,** Swiss naturalist; his *Historiae Animalium* is considered the basis of modern zoology. [d. December 13, 1565]

1749   **William Blount,** U.S. politician; one of first two senators of Tennessee; expelled from the Senate for attempting a conspiracy to increase illegally the value of western land. [d. March 21, 1800]

1753   **Sir Benjamin Thompson, Count Rumford,** American-English physicist; responsible for bringing Watt's steam engine into general use. [d. August 21, 1814]

1773   **Nathaniel Bowditch,** U.S. mathematician, navigator, astronomer. [d. March 16, 1838]

1819   **Louise Otto,** German writer; founder of the feminist movement in Germany. [d. March 13, 1895]

1840   **George Smith,** British Assyriologist; deciphered many cuneiform scripts. [d. August 19, 1876]

1850   **Edward Bellamy,** U.S. author; wrote *Looking Backward*, a utopian novel which gave rise to **Nationalist Clubs** throughout the U.S. devoted to achieving the ideals expressed in the novel. [d. May 22, 1899]

1859   **A(lfred) E(dward) Housman,** British poet, classical scholar. [d. April 30, 1936]

1868   **Ahmed Fuad Pasha, Fuad I, King of Egypt,** 1922–1936. [d. June 1936]

1873   **Sir Gerald du Maurier,** British theatrical manager and actor; father of novelist Daphne du Maurier. [d. April 11, 1934]

1874   **Robert Frost,** U.S. poet; Pulitzer Prize in poetry, 1921, 1924, 1937, 1943. [d. January 29, 1963]

   Condé Nast, U.S. magazine publisher. [d. September 19, 1942]

1879   **Othmar H. Ammann,** U.S. engineer, bridge builder; designed the **George Washington**, **Golden Gate,** and **Mackinac** Bridges. [d. September 22, 1965]

1880   **Duncan Hines,** U.S. gourmet. [d. March 15, 1959]

1884   **Wilhelm Backhaus,** Swiss pianist; exponent of classical German music; professor of piano at Manchester Royal College. [d. July 5, 1969]

1891   **Leonard (*Chico*), Marx** U.S. comedian, member of the **Marx Brothers.** [d. October 11, 1961]

1892   **Paul Howard Douglas,** U.S. politician, educator; U.S. Senator, 1948–66. [d. September 24, 1976]

1893   **James Bryant Conant,** U.S. educator, diplomat; President of Harvard University, 1933–53; U.S. Ambassador to West Germany, 1955–57.

   Palmiro Togliatti, Italian political leader; Vice-Premier of Italy, 1945. [d. April 21, 1964]

1909   **Héctor José Cámpora,** Argentinian government official; President of Chamber of Deputies, 1946–55; ardent supporter of Juan D. Perón; President of Argentina for seven weeks (May–July, 1973) as stand-in for Perón who was in exile. [d. December 19, 1980]

The Saints

St. Castulus, martyr. Also called **Castalus.** [d. 286]

St. Felix, Bishop of Trier. [d. c. 400]

St. Macartan, bishop. [d. c. 505]

St. Govan, hermit. Also called **Gowan.** [d. 6th century]

St. Braulio, Bishop of Saragossa; patron of Aragon; one of the most famous of the Spanish saints. [d. 651]

St. Ludger, Bishop of Münster; founder of the Monastery of Werden. Also called **Liudger.** [d. 809]

St. Basil the Younger, hermit. [d. 952]

1911   **Sir Bernard Katz,** British physiologist; Nobel Prize in physiology or medicine for discoveries of nature of substances found at the end of **nerve fibers** (with J. Axelrod and U. S. Von Euler), 1970.

Tennessee Williams (Thomas Lanier Williams), U.S. dramatist; Pulitzer Prize in drama, 1947, 1955. [d. February 25, 1983]

1914   **William Childs Westmoreland,** U.S. army general; commanded U.S. forces in Vietnam, 1964–68.

1916   **Christian Boehmer Anfinsen,** U.S. biochemist; Nobel Prize in chemistry (with S. Moore and W. H. Stein) for research on structure of **ribonuclease,** 1972.

1925   **Pierre Boulez,** French conductor, composer of abstract constructivist music.

1930   **Sandra Day O'Connor,** U.S. jurist; first woman U.S. Supreme Court justice.

1942   **Erica (Mann) Jong,** U.S. novelist, poet.

1943   **Robert (Upshur) Woodward,** U.S. journalist; with colleague Carl Bernstein (February 14) reported on the **Watergate Incident.**

Historical Events

1027   **Conrad II** is crowned Holy Roman Emperor.

1780   The first British Sunday newspaper, ***The British Gazette and Sunday Monitor,*** is published.

1793   The Holy Roman Empire formally declares war on France.

1825   The **Republic of Mexico** is proclaimed at Monterey, California.

1871   The **Paris Commune,** the socialistic government of Paris which ruled until May 27, is formally established.

1913   Bulgarians take Adrianople in Turkey (**Balkan War**).

1917   The first **Battle of Gaza** begins (**World War I**).

1934   The **British Road Traffic Act** requires **driving tests** for car owners.

1943   **Battle of Komandorskie Islands** is fought in Bering Sea (**World War II**).

1960   **Malagasy Republic (Madagascar)** becomes independent of France.

1964   The seven men accused in the **Great Train Robbery** are convicted in London.

1971   Shaikh Mujibur Rahman declares East Pakistan independent as **Bangladesh.**

1975   North Vietnamese take **Hué (Vietnam War).**

1979   President **Anwar el-Sadat** of Egypt and Prime Minister **Menachem Begin** of Israel sign a peace treaty ending more than 30 years of hostility between their nations.

1982   Groundbreaking takes place in Washington, D.C., for a memorial to honor American soldiers killed in **Vietnam.**

March 27

Holidays

Burma
    Resistance Day
Honors the movement of
guerrilla forces to oppose
invaders during World War II.

U.S.S.R.
    International Theater Day

Birthdates

1676   **Ferenc Rákóczy II** Hungarian patriot; led insurrection in Hungary, 1703; defeated by Austrians, 1708. [d. April 8, 1735]

1753   **Andrew Bell,** Scottish educator, clergyman; introduced **Bell** or **monitorial system** of education. [d. January 27, 1832]

1785   **Louis XVII,** (Louis Charles) titular King of France, 1793–95. [d. June 8, 1795]

1797   **Alfred Victor, Comte de Vigny (Alfred de Vigny),** French poet, playwright, novelist; author of *Cinq-Mars*, 1826; elected to the French Academy, 1845. [d. September 17, 1863]

1809   **Georges Eugène Haussmann,** French architect; responsible for the replanning of **Paris.** [d. January 11, 1891]

1813   **Nathaniel Currier,** U.S. lithographer; partner with James Merritt Ives (March 5) in **Currier and Ives.** [d. November 20, 1888]

1844   **Adolphus Washington Greely,** U.S. Arctic explorer, soldier; supervised one of first successful meteorological expeditions to the Arctic; chief of U.S. Signal Service, responsible for laying thousands of miles of telephone and telegraph cables, 1886–1906; [d. October 20, 1935]

1845   **Wilhelm Konrad Röntgen,** German scientist; Nobel Prize in physics for discovery of **x rays,** 1901. [d. February 10, 1923]

1847   **Otto Wallach,** German organic chemist; Nobel Prize in chemistry for discovery of **alicyclic compounds,** 1910. [d. February 26, 1931]

1851   **Vincent d'Indy,** French composer; founder of *Schola Cantorum*; a leader in the radical modern school of French music. [d. December 1, 1931]

1857   **Karl Pearson,** British mathematician; developed **standard deviation theory,** 1893. [d. April 27, 1936]

1863   **Sir Frederick Henry Royce,** British automaker; with his partner C. S. Rolls founded Rolls Royce Ltd., 1904. [d. April 22, 1933]

1879   **Miller Huggins,** U.S. baseball manager; Baseball Hall of Fame, 1964. [d. December 25, 1929]

Edward Steichen, U.S. photographer; created such classics as *The Family of Man.* [d. March 25, 1973]

1880   **James Wares Bryce,** U.S. inventor; responsible for early developments in electronics and business machines; leader in development of visual display monitors for computers. [d. March 27, 1949]

1886   **(Ludwig) Mies van der Rohe,** prominent modern architect; Director of the Bauhaus 1930–1937. [d. August 17, 1969]

1892   **Ferde Grofé (Ferdinand Rudolph von Grofé),** U.S. composer and arranger; best known for *Grand Canyon Suite* and his arrangement of Gershwin's *Rhapsody in Blue.* [d. April 3, 1972]

1893   **Draža Mihajlović (or Mikhailovitch),** Serbian soldier; organizer of guerrilla warfare against German and Italian armies (**World War II**). [d. July 17, 1946]

1899   **Gloria (May Josephine) Swanson,** U.S. actress. [d. April 4, 1983]

1901   **Eisako Sato,** Japanese statesman; Prime Minister, 1964–72; Nobel Peace Prize (with S. MacBride), 1974.

1906   **Pee Wee Russell (Charles Ellsworth Russell),** U.S. jazz clarinetist. [d. February 15, 1969]

1912   **(Leonard) James Callaghan,** British politician; Prime Minister, 1976–79.

1914   **Budd Schulberg,** U.S. writer, scriptwriter; author of *What Makes Sammy Run?*

1917   **Cyrus (Robert) Vance,** U.S. government official; U.S. Secretary of State, 1977–80.

1923   **Louis Simpson,** U.S. poet, teacher; Pulitzer Prize in poetry, 1963.

1924   **Sarah (Lou) Vaughan,** U.S. jazz vocalist.

1927   **Anthony Lewis,** U.S. journalist; Pulitzer Prize in national reporting, 1955.

Mstislav Rostropovich, Russian–U.S. cello virtuoso, conductor; Music Director, National Symphony Orchestra, Washington, D.C., 1977– .

1930 **David Janssen (David Meyer),** U.S. actor. [d. February 13, 1980]

1942 **Michael York (Michael York-Johnson),** British actor.

1953 **Annemarie Proell,** Austrian skier; World Cup champion, 1971–75, 1979.

1964 **Anchorage, Alaska** is devastated by an earthquake which kills 114 people and generates waves that sweep U.S. Pacific coast.

1977 Two jumbo jets collide in **Tenerife,** Canary Islands, in the worst air disaster in history, killing 582 persons.

1980 **Mount St. Helens,** a volcano in Washington, dormant for 123 years, begins to erupt.

Historical Events

1625 **James I** of Great Britain dies and is succeeded by **Charles I.**

1794 U.S. President George Washington signs act officially establishing the **United States Navy.**

1802 England and France sign **Peace of Amiens** by which England receives **Trinidad** and **Ceylon.**

1854 France declares war on Russia (**Crimean War**).

1884 The first inter-city telephone link in the U.S. is put into service between New York City and Boston.

1890 Spain adopts **universal suffrage.**

1899 First signals of **wireless telegraph** are sent across English Channel.

1917 The Russian grand dukes and royal princes renounce their hereditary rights and privileges (**Russian Revolution**).

1927 80,000 young Italian men are inducted into **Fascist party** and declared members of Fascist militia in Italy.

1945 U.S. troops land on **Caballo Island** in the Philippines (**World War II**).

1962 Archbishop Joseph Francis Rummel orders all Roman Catholic schools in the New Orleans diocese to end **segregation.**

March 28

Holidays

Czechoslova-kia   **Teachers' Day**
Commemorates birth of John Komenský, 17th century Moravian educational reformer, 1592.

Birthdates

1475   **Fra Bartolommeo (Baccio della Porta; Bartolommeo di Pagolo del Fattorino),** Italian painter; associated with Raphael, Bellini, and Giorgione; known for his *Apparition of the Virgin to St. Bernard.* [d. October 31, 1517]

1483   **Raphael (Raffaello Sanzio** or **Santi),** Italian painter; chief architect of St. Peter's in Rome; one of the great painters of the Italian Renaissance. [d. April 6, 1520]

1515   **Teresa of Avila (Teresa de Cepeda y Ahumda),** Spanish reformer, author; Carmelite nun famous for her mystical visions. [d. October 4, 1582]

1592   **Jan Amos Komenský (Johannes Amos Comenius),** Czech philosopher, educator; known for his innovations in education; devised the first textbook adapted for teaching children. [d. November 4, 1670]

1652   **Samuel Sewall,** American colonial jurist; presided over the **Salem witchcraft trials,** 1692. [d. January 1, 1730]

1660   **George I, King of Great Britain and Ireland,** 1714–27. [d. June 11, 1727]

1702   **Ignacio de Luzán,** Spanish critic, poet; known for his strict adherence to classical rules in composition. [d. May 19, 1754]

1750   **Francisco Antonio Gabriel Miranda,** Venezuelan revolutionary; led patriot army in Venezuela; dictator of Venezuela when it gained independence, 1811; forced to sign a treaty with Royalists, 1812. [d. July 14, 1816]

1811   **St. John Nepomucene Neumann,** U.S. Roman Catholic bishop; first male Roman Catholic saint from the U.S.; canonized, 1977. [d. January 5, 1860]

1817   **Francesco De Sanctis,** Italian critic; dubbed the *Father of Modern Literary Criticism in Italy.* [d. December 19, 1883]

1818   **Wade Hampton,** Confederate cavalry general during U.S. Civil War; Governor of South Carolina, 1876–79; U.S. Senator, 1879–91. [d. April 11, 1902]

1819   **Sir Joseph William Bazalgette,** British civil engineer; responsible for construction of London's main drainage system. [d. March 15, 1891]

1862   **Aristide Briand,** French statesman; prime minister seven times, 1909–32; Nobel Peace Prize (with G. Stresemann), 1926. [d. March 7, 1932]

1869   **William Allen Neilson,** U.S. educator, editor, author; President of **Smith College,** 1917–39. [d. February 13, 1946]

1871   **Willem Mengelberg,** Dutch orchestra conductor, pianist, composer; upon his suggestion the National Symphony Orchestra of New York merged with the New York Philharmonic Society to form the **New York Philharmonic-Symphony Orchestra.** [d. March 21, 1951]

1891   **Paul (Samuel) Whiteman,** U.S. musician, bandleader. [d. December 29, 1967]

1892   **Corneille J. F. Heymans,** Belgian physiologist; Nobel Prize in physiology or medicine for work on **respiration of sensory organs,** 1938. [d. July 18, 1968]

1895   **Christian Archibald Herter,** U.S. diplomat, journalist, politician; U.S. Secretary of State, 1959–61. [d. December 30, 1966]

1903   **Rudolf Serkin,** Austrian-U.S. pianist.

1909   **Nelson Algren,** U.S. novelist; author of *The Man with the Golden Arm* and *A Walk on the Wild Side.* [d. May 9, 1981]

1914   **Edmund (Sixtus) Muskie,** U.S. politician, lawyer; Democratic vice-presidential candidate, 1968; U.S. Secretary of State, 1980–81.

1921   **Dirk Bogarde (Derek van den Bogaerd),** British actor, author.

1928   **Zbigniew Brzezinski,** U.S. government official, political scientist, born in Poland; as-

Commemorates the withdrawal of British troops and the end of Allied occupation after World War II, 1951.

Religious Calendar

The Saints

St. Guntramnus, King of Burgundy. Also called **Gontran.** [d. 592]

St. Tutilo, Benedictine monk. [d. c. 915]

sistant to the U.S. president for national security affairs 1977–1981.

Historical Events

1774   British pass **Coercive Acts** against Massachusetts, one of the immediate causes of the **American Revolution.**

1849   **Frederick William IV** of Prussia is elected **Emperor of the Germans** by the German National Assembly.

1854   Great Britain declares war on Russia and France (**Crimean War.**)

1891   First world **weight-lifting** championship match is held in London.

1930   **Constantinople** is officially renamed **Istanbul, Angora** is renamed **Ankara,** and other Greek names are changed to Turkish ones by the government of Turkey.

1939   **Spanish Civil War** ends with the surrender of Madrid and Valencia to rebel forces under General **Francisco Franco.**

1942   British commandos raid **St. Nazaire** on the French coast (**World War II**).

1951   U.S. and United Nations officials sign agreement permitting the United Nations to issue its own postage stamps.

1960   **Pope John XXIII** creates ten new cardinals in a secret consistory, increasing the number of cardinals to a record 88.

1969   Czechoslovak victory over a Russian team in the world championship hockey tournament in Stockholm touches off anti-Soviet demonstrations in Czechoslovak cities.

      Earthquake in Kutahya, Turkey, kills over 1000 and causes devastating damage.

1972   **Sir Dawda Jawara** is elected to a five-year term as president in The Gambia's first parliamentary elections.

1973   Egyptian President **Anwar el-Sadat** proclaims himself military governor-general of Egypt and assumes the duties of prime minister.

1974   Rumanian Communist Party leader **Nicolae Ceauşescu** is elected to the newly created post of President of Rumania.

1979   **Three Mile Island** nuclear power plant in southeastern Pennsylvania seriously malfunctions, raising fears of a meltdown of the reactor's core, causing the evacuation of thousands, and creating widespread concern about the safety of such facilities.

      British Labour government falls when, for the first time in 55 years, the British House of Commons votes "no confidence" in Her Majesty's government.

March 29

Holidays

Central African Republic	**Boganda Day** Anniversary of the death of **Barthelemy Boganda,** the nation's first president, 1959.
Malagasy Republic	**Memorial Day** Commemorates the martyrs of the Malagasy Revolution of 1947.
Nationalist China (Taiwan)	**Youth and Martyrs' Day**
U.S.	**Vietnam Veterans' Day** Commemorates the withdrawal

Birthdates

1769 **Nicolas Jean de Dieu Soult,** Duke of Dalmatia; Marshal of France under Napoleon. [d. November 26, 1851]

1790 **John Tyler,** U.S. lawyer, politician; tenth President of the U.S.; first vice-president to succeed to the presidency in U.S. history, upon the death of William Henry Harrison, 1841. [d. January 18, 1862]

1815 **Sir Henry Bartle Frere,** British statesman; colonial administrator; responsible for precipitating the **Zulu War.** [d. May 29, 1884]

1819 **Edwin Laurentine Drake,** U.S. oil-industry pioneer; drilled the first oil well in the world at Titusville, Pennsylvania. [d. November 8, 1880]

Isaac Mayer Wise, German-U.S. rabbi; the *Father of Reformed Judaism* in America. [d. March 26, 1900]

1853 **Elihu Thomson,** U.S. inventor; discovered alternating current (AC) repulsion phenomenon. [d. March 13, 1937]

1859 **Oscar Ferdinand Mayer,** U.S. businessman; founder of Oscar Mayer Co., meatpackers, 1888. [d. March 11, 1955]

1867 **Cy Young (Denton True Young),** U.S. baseball pitcher; Baseball Hall of Fame, 1937; annual award to outstanding pitcher in each major league named for him. [d. November 4, 1955]

1869 **Sir Edwin Landseer Lutyens,** British architect, artist; President of Royal Academy of Great Britain, 1938–44. [d. January 1, 1944]

Aleš Hrdlihčka, Bohemian-U.S. anthropologist, author; curator of physical anthropology department of the U.S. National Museum, Washington, D.C., 1910–43. [d. September 5, 1943]

1889 **Howard Lindsay,** U.S. playwright; Pulitzer Prize in drama, 1946. [d. 1968]

1892 **Joseph (Jozsef Pehm) Mindszenty,** Hungarian Roman Catholic cardinal; known throughout the world for his adamant anti-Communist stand; imprisoned by Polish Communists, 1949–56. [d. May 6, 1975]

1902 **Sir William Walton,** British composer; first important work was *Façade* written to accompany poems by his patron, **Edith Sitwell.** [d. May 8, 1983]

1906 **E(dward George) Power Biggs,** British-U.S. organist; authority on J. S. Bach; popularized baroque organ music. [d. March 10, 1977]

1916 **Eugene McCarthy,** U.S. politician, Senator; contender for Democratic presidential nomination, 1968.

1918 **Pearl (Mae) Bailey,** U.S. singer.

1956 **Kurt Thomas,** U.S. gymnast; first U.S. male to win gold medal in world competition for gymnastics.

Historical Events

1461 **Edward IV** of York defeats former **King Henry VI** of Lancaster at Towton (**War of the Roses**).

of U.S. troops from Vietnam, 1973.

U.S. (Delaware) **Swedish Colonial Day** Celebrates the establishment of the first Swedish settlement in Delaware, 1638.

Religious Calendar

The Saints

SS. Jonas and **Barachisius,** monks and martyrs. [d. 327]

SS. Mark, Bishop of Arethusa, and **Cyril,** deacon and martyr. [d. c. 365]

SS. Armogastes, Archinimus, and **Saturus,** martyrs. [d. c. 455]

SS. Gundleus, chieftain, and **Gwladys,** his wife. Gundleus also called **Gwynllyw,** or **Woolo.** [d. 6th century]

St. Rupert, Bishop of Salzburg; evangelized the Germans. [d. c. 710]

St. Berthold, priest, hermit; first superior of the Carmelite order. [d. c. 1195]

St. Ludolf, Bishop of Ratzeburg and martyr. [d. 1250]

The Beatified

Blessed Diemoda, virgin, nun, and recluse. Also called **Diemux.** [d. c. 1130]

1632 **Treaty of St. Germain-en-Laye**; England restores North American possessions of **Acadia** and the **St. Lawrence** to France **(Thirty Years' War).**

1638 The first Swedish colonists in America establish a Lutheran settlement at **Fort Christiana, Delaware.**

1792 **Gustavus III** of Sweden dies of gunshot wounds suffered 13 days earlier and is succeeded by **Gustavus IV.**

1804 Thousands of whites are massacred in **Haiti** as a result of a proclamation by **Jean Jacques Dessalines.**

1809 **Gustavus IV** of Sweden is forced to abdicate and is succeeded by **Charles XIII.**

1847 **Vera Cruz** is besieged by U.S. troops and surrenders (**Mexican War**).

1849 The **British** formally annex the **Punjab** after the defeat of the Sikhs in India.

1871 Queen Victoria opens the **Royal Albert Hall** in London.

1882 **The Knights of Columbus** fraternal benefit society of Catholic men is chartered.

1923 A customs union is concluded between **Switzerland** and **Liechtenstein** under which Switzerland will operate postal and telegraph services and protect the foreign interests of Liechtenstein.

1925 **Japan** passes a universal **male suffrage** law.

1936 **Nazi** candidates win elections in Germany with **Adolf Hitler** receiving 99 per cent of the vote.

1959 **Barthelemy Boganda,** first President of the **Central African Republic,** is killed in a plane crash.

1961 The **23rd Amendment** to the U.S. Constitution, giving District of Columbia residents the right to vote in presidential elections, is ratified.

1963 United Kingdom grants **Northern Rhodesia** the right to secede from the **Federation of Rhodesia and Nyasaland.**

1967 *Le Redoutable,* France's first nuclear-powered submarine, is launched.

1971 U.S. army court-martial finds 1st Lieut. **William L. Calley, Jr.,** guilty of the premeditated murder of at least 22 South Vietnamese civilians at **My-Lai** in March 1968.

1973 Last U.S. prisoners of war held by Communist forces in **Vietnam** are released and the last U.S. troops withdrawn from **South Vietnam.**

1976 Argentinian Lt. General **Jorge Rafaél Videla** takes oath of office as president of Argentina five days after overthrow of the government of **Isabel Perón.**

1982 **El Chínchon** volcano in **Mexico** begins series of eruptions, killing and injuring hundreds.

March 30

Holidays

U.S. (Georgia)   **Doctor's Day**
Sponsored by McLaren General Hospital, Barrow County, Georgia

Religious Calendar

The Saints

St. Regulus, first bishop of Senlis, France. Patron of the City and Diocese of Senlis. Also called **Rieul.** [d. c. 250]

Birthdates

1135   **Moses Maimonides,** Spanish rabbi, physician, Arabic scholar, and Jewish philosopher; attempted to reconcile Judaism with Aristotelian philosophy. [d. December 13, 1204]

1746   **Goya, (Francisco José de Goya y Lucientas),** Spanish painter, etcher; known as the master of 18th-century Spanish school of art. [d. April 16, 1828]

1840   **Charles Booth,** British shipowner, sociologist, statistician, and reformer; known for efforts to obtain passage of **Old Age Pension Act.** [d. November 23, 1916]

1844   **Paul Verlaine,** French symbolist poet; recognized as the leader of the **Symbolist School** of French poetry. [d. January 8, 1896]

1853   **Vincent van Gogh,** Dutch painter; associated with **Post-Impressionist School.** [d. July 29, 1890]

1876   **Clifford Whittingham Beers,** U.S. mental hygienist; dubbed *Father of the Mental Hygiene Movement* in the U.S. [d. July 9, 1943]

1880   **Sean O'Casey (John O'Casey),** Irish dramatist. [d. September 18, 1964]

1883   **Jo Davidson,** U.S. sculptor; known for his portraits and sculptures of many of the leading figures of his time. [d. January 2, 1952]

1919   **McGeorge Bundy,** U.S. educator, government official; Dean, Faculty of Arts and Sciences, Harvard University, 1953–61; Special Assistant for National Security Affairs, 1961–66; President, Ford Foundation, 1966–79.

1938   **Warren Beatty,** U.S. actor, director, screenwriter.

Historical Events

1406   **James I** of Scotland is captured near **Flamborough Head** by the English and is imprisoned by **Henry IV** of England.

1492   The Jews are expelled from Spain by Inquisitor-General Tomás de Torquemada (**Spanish Inquisition**).

1806   **Joseph Bonaparte** is declared **King of Naples.**

1856   The **Crimean War** ends with the signing of the **Treaty of Paris.**

1863   **William, Prince of Denmark,** assumes the throne as king of **Greece.**

1867   U.S. purchases **Alaska** from Russia for $7,200,000. The purchase is referred to as *Seward's Folly.*

1869   **The 15th Amendment** to the U.S. Constitution is ratified, forbidding voting discrimination based on race, color, or previous condition of servitude.

1917   The independence of **Poland** is proclaimed by the Russian provisional government.

All imperial lands and lands belonging to monasteries are confiscated by the Russian provisional government.

1919   **Mahatma Gandhi** begins organized defiance of British government after passage of the **Rowlatt Acts** with a general strike and a campaign of peaceful **civil disobedience.**

1941   U.S. takes possession of all German, Italian, and Danish ships in the U.S. (**World War II**).

1951   Rodgers and Hammerstein's *The King and I* premieres in New York.

St. John Climacus, hermit and Abbot of Mt. Sinai. Wrote the *Ladder to Perfection*. Also called **John the Scholastic.** [d. c. 649]

St. Zosimus, Bishop of Syracuse. Also called **Zozimus.** [d. c. 660]

St. Osburga, virgin and first abbess of Coventry. [d. c. 1016]

The Beatified

Blessed Dodo, solitary. [d. 1231]

Blessed Amadeus IX of Savoy, duke. [d. 1472]

1972	**Great Britain** imposes direct rule on **Northern Ireland.**
1975	North Vietnamese capture **Da Nang,** South Vietnam.
1981	U.S. President **Ronald Reagan** is shot during an assassination attempt by **John W. Hinckley, Jr.**

March 31

Holidays

Malta   **National Day** or **Freedom Day**
Commemorates Maltese
achievement of independence
from Great Britain, 1964.

Religious Calendar

The Saints

St. Acacius, bishop. Also called **Achates,** or **Achatius.** [d. 3rd century]

St. Benjamin, deacon and martyr. [d. c. 421]

St. Guy of Pomposa, abbot. Also called **Guido, Guion, Wido, Wit,** or **Witen.** [d. 1046]

St. Balbina, virgin. [death date unknown]

Birthdates

1499   **Pope Pius IV,** pope 1560–65. [d. December 9, 1565]

1596   **René Descartes,** French philosopher, mathematician, scientist; founder of **Rationalism**; his philosophy, **Cartesianism,** espoused the possibility of mathematical certitude in metaphysical issues. [d. February 1, 1650]

1675   **Pope Benedict XIV,** pope 1740–58. [d. May 3, 1758]

1723   **Frederick V, King of Denmark and Norway,** 1746–66. [d. January 14, 1766]

1732   **(Franz) Joseph Haydn,** Austrian composer. [d. May 31, 1809]

1809   **Edward Fitzgerald,** British poet, translator; especially noted for his translation of works of **Omar Khayyám.** [d. June 14, 1883]

        Nikolai Vasilyevich Gogol, Russian short-story writer, novelist, dramatist. [d. February 21, 1852]

1811   **Robert Wilhelm Bunsen,** German chemist, inventor. [d. August 16, 1899]

1835   **John La Farge,** U.S. landscape and figure painter. [d. November 14, 1910]

1837   **Robert Ross McBurney,** U.S. YMCA leader; responsible for centralized system of leadership in **YMCA.** [d. December 27, 1898]

1838   **Léon Dierx,** French poet. [d. June 11, 1912]

1844   **Andrew Lang,** Scottish author, translator. [d. July 20, 1912]

1857   **Edouard Rod,** Swiss novelist, critic. [d. January 29, 1910]

1878   **Jack Johnson,** U.S. boxer; first black to hold world heavyweight title, 1908–15. [d. June 10, 1946]

1887   **St. John Perse (Marie René Auguste Alexis Léger),** French poet, diplomat; Nobel Prize in literature, 1960. [d. September 20, 1975]

1890   **Sir William Lawrence Bragg,** Australian-British physicist; Nobel Prize in physics (with W. H. Bragg), 1915; the youngest man ever to win a Nobel Prize. [d. July 1, 1971]

1906   **Sin-Itiro Tomonaga,** Japanese physicist; Nobel Prize in physics (with J. S. Schwinger and R. P. Feynman), 1965.

1908   **Red Norvo,** U.S. musician.

1912   **William (Julius) Lederer,** U.S. novelist, non-fiction writer.

1914   **Octavio Paz,** Mexican poet, critic, social philosopher.

1926   **John Fowles,** British novelist.

1927   **Cesar Estrada Chavez,** U.S. labor union organizer.

Historical Events

1084   **Clement III** (antipope) crowns **Henry IV** Holy Roman Emperor.

1146   **St. Bernard of Clairvaux** preaches the **Second Crusade** at Vezelay.

1282   A bloody uprising of the Sicilians against the French (Angevin) rule takes place;

The Beatified

Blessed Joan of Toulouse, virgin; founder of the Carmelite Tertiary Order. [d. 14th century]

Blessed Bonaventure of Forli, Vicar General of the Order of Servites. [d. 1491]

called the **Sicilian Vespers** because it breaks out at the hour of vespers.

1495 **Holy League,** consisting of Holy Roman Emperor Maximilian I, Pope Alexander VI, Spain, Venice, and Milan, is formed against **Charles VIII** of France who is forced to leave Italy.

1547 **Francis I** of France dies and is succeeded by **Henry II.**

1621 **Philip III** of Spain dies and is succeeded by **Philip IV.**

1657 **Humble Petition and Advice** offers title of King of England to **Oliver Cromwell.**

1814 **Paris** surrenders to Alliance of Austria, Russia, and Prussia (**Napoleonic Wars**).

1854 U.S. Commodore **Matthew Perry** signs **Treaty of Kanagawa,** the first treaty between Japan and the U.S., opening two Japanese ports and permitting regulated trade.

1861 Great Britain recognizes Italy as a kingdom under **Victor Emmanuel II.**

1901 A British proclamation outlaws **slave trade** in the Nigerian protectorates.

1917 **Danish West Indies** (Virgin Islands, St. Thomas, St. Croix, and St. John) purchased from Denmark by U.S. for $25 million.

1918 **Daylight Saving Time** first goes into effect in the U.S.

1933 **Civilian Conservation Corps** is established under the **Unemployment Relief Act** in U.S. to provide work for more than 3 million unemployed American men.

1943 Rodgers and Hammerstein's *Oklahoma!* premieres in New York.

1947 **Dodecanese Islands,** held by Italy from 1912 to 1943, are transferred to Greece.

1949 **Newfoundland** joins Canadian Federation as the tenth province.

1959 The **Dalai Lama,** fleeing Chinese occupation of Tibet, is given political asylum by India.

1967 **NATO Supreme Military Headquarters** formally opens in Casteau, Belgium.

1968 U.S. President **Lyndon B. Johnson** announces that he will neither seek nor accept another term as president.

1970 **Lesotho** Prime Minister **Leabua Jonathan** orders **King Moshoeshoe II** into exile.

1971 U.S. army jury sentences Lt. **William Calley** to life imprisonment for murder of South Vietnamese civilians at **My Lai** in 1968.

1976 The New Jersey Supreme Court rules that a mechanical life sustaining system may be removed from **Karen Ann Quinlan.**

April

April is the fourth month in the Gregorian calendar and has 30 days. Prior to the reform of the calendar in 153 B.C., April was the second month of the Roman civil calendar. The Roman name for the month, *Aprilis*, is thought to be derived from the Latin verb aperire 'to open (as buds do)'; the precise etymology, however, is very uncertain.

The Roman emperor Nero (ruled 54–68) attempted unsuccessfully to have the name *Neronius* adopted for this month. In the time of Charlemagne April was referred to as the "Grass Month," one indication of its strong associations with the beginning of Spring and blossoming. The principal Christian and Jewish feasts, Easter and Passover, respectively, usually fall in April, and this parallels the celebration at this time of Spring festivals in many religions throughout history.

April spans the zodiac signs of Aries, the Ram (March 21–April 20) and Taurus, the Bull (April 20-May 20).

The birthstone for April is the diamond, and the flower is the sweet pea or daisy.

State, National, and International Holidays

Fast and Prayer Day
(Lesotho)
Second Friday
Patriot's Day
(Maine, Massachusetts)
Third Monday
Oklahoma Day
(Oklahoma)
April 22

Arbor Day
(Nebraska, Delaware)
April 22

(Wyoming)
Final Monday

(Utah)
Final Friday

Confederate Memorial Day
(Alabama, Mississippi)
Final Monday
(Florida, Georgia)
April 26
Geologists' Day
(U.S.S.R.)
First Sunday
World Sister Cities Day
(U.S.S.R.)
Final Sunday

Special Events and Their Sponsors

Boost Your Home Town Month
Fraternal Order of Eagles
2401 West Wisconsin Avenue
Milwaukee, Wisconsin 53233
Correct Posture Month
American Chiropractic Association
1916 Wilson Boulevard
Arlington, Virginia 22201
Freedom Shrine Month
National Exchange Club
3050 Central Avenue
Toledo, Ohio 43606
Glaucoma Alert Month
Society to Prevent Blindness
79 Madison Avenue
New York, New York 10016
Philatelic Societies' Month
Franklin D. Roosevelt Philatelic Society
154 Laguna Court
St. Augustine Shores, Florida 32084
Red Cross Month
American Red Cross
17th and D Streets, N.W.
Washington, D.C. 20006
National Drafting Week
First Week
American Institute for Design and Drafting
102 North Elm Place
Suite F
Broken Arrow, Oklahoma 74012
Publicity Stunt Week
First Week
Richard R. Falk Associates
1472 Broadway
New York, New York 10036

Week of the Young Child
First Week
National Association for the Education of Young Children
1834 Connecticut Avenue, N.W.
Washington, D.C. 20009
National Bike Safety Week
Third Week
National Safety Council
444 North Michigan Avenue
Chicago, Illinois 60611
Keep America Beautiful Week
Third Week
Keep America Beautiful, Inc.
99 Park Avenue
New York, New York 10016
National Library Week
Third Week
American Library Association
50 East Huron Street
Chicago, Illinois 60611
National Victims' Rights Week
Third Week
National Organization for Victim Assistance
1757 Park Road, N.W.
Washington, D.C. 20010
General Federation of Womens' Clubs Week
Week containing April 24
General Federation of Womens' Clubs
1734 N Street, N.W.
Washington, D.C. 20036
Canada-U.S. Goodwill Week
Final Week
Kiwanis International
3636 Woodview Trace
Indianapolis, Indiana 46268

Jewish Heritage Week
Final Week
Jewish Community Relations Council of New York
Suite 2600
111 West 40th Street
New York, New York 10018

National YWCA Week
Final Week
National Board of the YWCA of the U.S.A.
135 West 50th Street
New York, New York 10018

Professional Secretaries' Week
Final Full Week
Professional Secretaries International
2440 Pershing Road
Crown Center G10
Kansas City, Missouri 64108

Grange Week
Final Full Week
The National Grange
1616 H Street. N.W.
Washington, D.C. 20006

Lion's Journey for Sight
Second Weekend
Lion's Club
300 22nd Street
Oak Brook, Illinois 60570

Death Anniversary of Franklin D. Roosevelt
April 12
Franklin D. Roosevelt Philatelic Society
154 Laguna Court
St. Augustine Shores, Florida 32084

Arbor Day
April 22
National Arbor Day Foundation
Arbor Lodge 100
Nebraska City, Nebraska 68410

Earth Day
April 22
Environmental Action, Inc.
1346 Connecticut Avenue, N.W.
Suite 731
Washington, D.C. 20036

General Federation of Womens' Clubs Day
April 24
General Federation of Womens' Clubs
1734 N Street, N.W.
Washington, D.C. 20036

World YWCA Day
Final Wednesday
National Board of the YWCA of the U.S.A.
135 West 50th Street
New York, New York 10018

World Day of Prayer for Vocations
Final Sunday (or First Sunday in May)
National Catholic Vocation Council
1307 South Wabash Avenue
Suite 350
Chicago, Illinois 60605

Special Days—Other Calendars

	Easter Sunday	Passover	Yom Ha'Azma'ut	1 Ramadan
1985	April 7	April 6	April 25	
1986		April 24		
1987	April 19	April 14		April 30
1988	April 3	April 2	April 21	April 19
1989		April 20		April 8
1990	April 15	April 10	April 30	

April 1

	April Fools' Day or **All Fools' Day** A day of practical jokes, intended to make fools of unsuspecting people.
Popular Republic of Benin	**Youth Day** and **Abdoulaye Issa Day**
Iran	**Islamic Republic Day**
San Marino	**National Day** or **Captain Regents Day** The traditional date for the installation of **Capitani Regginti** or government officials.

Birthdates

1578 **William Harvey,** English physician; *Father of Modern Physiology*; discovered that blood circulates. [d. June 3, 1657]

1616 **Charles de Marguetel de Saint-Denis, Sieur de Saint-Evremond,** French courtier, writer; exiled to England; an intimate of Hortense Mancini, Duchess of Mazarin. [d. September 20, 1703]

1697 **Antoine François Prévost** (*Abbé Prévost* or *Prévost d'Exiles*), French novelist, journalist; spent his life in travel and adventure. [d. December 23, 1763]

1730 **Salomon Gessner,** Swiss writer, painter, and etcher; wrote *Der Tod Abels*, which was translated into most European languages. [d. March 2, 1788]

1753 **Joseph Marie de Maistre,** French statesman, writer, and philosopher; opponent of the French Revolution. [d. February 26, 1821]

1755 **Anthelme Brillat-Savarin,** French politician, writer; best known for his *Physiologie du Goût*, a literary work on gastronomy. [d. 1825]

1815 **Otto von Bismarck** (*The Iron Chancellor*), German statesman; founder and first chancellor of the German Empire. Unified the German states into one empire under Prussian leadership. [d. July 20, 1898]

1823 **Simon Bolivar Buckner,** Confederate Army general during U.S. Civil War; Governor of Kentucky, 1887–91. [d. January 8, 1914]

1852 **Edwin Austin Abbey,** U.S. artist, illustrator.

1865 **Richard Adolf Zsigmondy,** German chemist; Nobel Prize in chemistry for research on **colloid solutions,** 1925. [d. September 23, 1929]

1866 **Sophonisba Breckinridge,** U.S. social reformer, social worker, educator; prominent activist for woman suffrage, child welfare, prison reform, labor legislation, and international peace. [d. July 30, 1948]

Ferruccio Benvenuto Busoni, Italian composer, transcriber, pianist, conductor. [d. July 27, 1924]

1868 **Edmond Rostand,** French dramatist; best known for his play, *Cyrano de Bergerac*. [d. December 2, 1918]

1873 **Sergei (Wassilievitch) Rachmaninoff,** U.S. piano virtuoso, composer, born in Russia. [d. March 28, 1943]

1881 **Wallace Beery,** U.S. character actor. [d. April 15, 1949]

1883 **Lon Chaney,** U.S. silent-screen actor; known as the *Man of a Thousand Faces*. [d. August 26, 1930]

1885 **Eli Lilly,** U.S. drug manufacturer, philanthropist; President and Chairman of the Board, Eli Lilly & Co. [d. January 24, 1977]

1887 **Leonard Bloomfield,** U.S. linguistic scholar, educator. [d. April 18, 1949]

1901 **(Jay David) Whittaker Chambers,** U.S. journalist; His testimony accusing **Alger Hiss** of espionage led to the latter's conviction for perjury in a *cause célèbre* of 1949–1950. [d. July 9, 1961]

Religious Calendar

The Saints

St. Melito, Bishop of Sardis. [d. c. 180]

St. Walaricus, Abbot of Leuconaus and missionary. Also called **Valéry.** [d. c. 620]

St. Agilbert, Bishop of Paris. Also Bishop of Dorchester-on-Thames. [d. c. 690]

St. Tewdric, prince and hermit. Also called **Theodoric.** [d. 5th–6th centuries]

St. Macarius the Wonder-worker, Abbot of Constantinople. [d. c. 830]

St. Hugh, Bishop of Grenoble. [d. 1132]

St. Gilbert of Caithness, bishop. [d. 1245]

St. Catherine of Palma, virgin. [d. 1574]

The Beatified

Blessed Ludovic Pavoni, founder of the Sons of Mary Immaculate of Brescia. [d. 1849]

1909   **Eddy Duchin (Edwin Frank Duchin),** U.S. pianist. [d. February 9, 1951]

1920   **Toshiro Mifune,** Japanese actor, director.

1922   **William Manchester,** U.S. novelist, biographer; author of *The Death of a President,* 1967.

1929   **Jane Powell (Suzanne Burce),** U.S. actress, singer; a leading lady in 1940s–1950s films.

Historical Events

1406   **Robert III, of Scotland,** dies and is succeeded by his younger brother, **Robert Stewart,** Duke of Albany.

1810   **Napoleon** marries Archduchess **Marie Louise,** daughter of Francis I of Austria.

1865   The **Battle of Five Forks** proves to be the final and decisive battle of the **U.S. Civil War** as General Robert E. Lee's forces are defeated by the Union Army.

1906   Parliamentary elections for the first **Duma** (official assembly) are held in St. Petersburg, Russia, and result in a sweeping victory for the constitutional democrats.

1912   **Metric system** of weights and measures is adopted in **Denmark.**

        Royal Flying Corps (later called the **Royal Air Force**) is established in Great Britain.

1924   The **Bank of Poland** is established.

1925   **Lord Balfour** dedicates **Hebrew University** at Jerusalem.

1929   The **Iraqi Army** is established.

1930   The **Child Marriage Act** prohibiting marriages of boys under 18 and girls under 14 comes into effect in India.

1933   An official **Anti-Semitic Day** is held in Germany as systematic persecution of German Jews begins.

1939   The United States recognizes Spanish rebel government of **Francisco Franco (Spanish Civil War).**

1945   U.S. invasion of **Okinawa** begins (**World War II**).

1950   **Indian government** centralizes control of post office, telegraph, customs, excise and income taxes, and armed forces.

1954   The **U.S. Air Force Academy** is established.

1960   *Tiros I,* first U.S. satellite designed to provide detailed photos of the earth's weather, is launched into orbit.

April 2

Holidays

U.S. (Florida)   Pascua Florida Day

Religious Calendar

The Saints

SS. Apphian of Palestine, and Theodosia, martyrs. Apphian also called Apian. [d. 306]

St. Mary of Egypt, penitent; patron of penitent women who formerly lived in sin. Also called Mary Egyptica. [d. c. 5th century]

Birthdates

742   **Charlemagne (Charles the Great, Charles I),** French ruler; King of the Franks, 768–814; conquered and united almost all of the Christian lands of western Europe and ruled as emperor 800–814. [d. 814]

1725   **Giovanni Casanova de Seingalt (*Casanova*),** Italian writer; adventurer whose name has become synonymous with roguery and romantic exploits. [d. June 4, 1798]

1798   **August Heinrich Hoffmann von Fallersleben,** German poet, scholar; author of *Deutschland, Deutschland über Alles,* adopted as national hymn, 1922. [d. January 19, 1874]

1805   **Hans Christian Andersen,** Danish fairy-tale writer, poet, novelist. [d. August 4, 1875]

1814   **Erastus Brigham Bigelow,** U.S. textile manufacturer; inventor of several types of looms for specialty work (particularly carpets). Founded Bigelow Carpet Mills, 1850. A founder of **Massachusetts Institute of Technology.** [d. December 6, 1879]

1827   **(William) Holman Hunt,** British painter; one of the founders of **Pre-Raphaelite Brotherhood,** 1848. [d. September 7, 1910]

1834   **Frédéric-Auguste Bartholdi,** French-Italian sculptor; designer of **Statue of Liberty.** [d. October 4, 1904]

1838   **Léon Gambetta,** French political leader; one of the chief founders of the Third Republic. [d. December 31, 1882]

1840   **Émile Zola,** French novelist, critic; considered one of the great leaders of the naturalistic movement in French literature. [d. September 1902]

1862   **Nicholas Murray Butler,** U.S. educator; president of Columbia University; Nobel Peace Prize, 1931. [d. December 7, 1947]

1875   **Walter Percy Chrysler,** U.S. industrialist; developer of the six-cylinder auto engine; founder of Chrysler Corporation; responsible for construction of **Chrysler Building** in New York City. [d. August 18, 1940]

1891   **Max Ernst,** German expressionist-surrealist painter, sculptor; chief exponent of **Dadaism** in Germany.

1893   **Harold Lloyd,** U.S. comedian, actor; highest paid film star of the 1920s. [d. March 8, 1971]

1914   **Sir Alec Guinness,** British actor; received Tony award for Best Actor, 1964, and Academy Award for Best Actor, 1957.

1920   **Jack Webb,** U.S. actor, producer; prominent in *Dragnet* television series. [d. December 23, 1982]

1926   **Sir John Arthur Brabham,** Australian auto racer, auto builder; Grand Prix champion, 1959–60, 1960–61, 1966.

1927   **Kenneth (Peacock) Tynan,** British drama critic; noted for his provocative criticism; leader in the acceptance of *new realism* in the British theater. [d. July 26, 1980]

Historical Events

1513   **Juan Ponce de León** discovers **Florida** and claims it for the King of Spain.

1792   **U.S. Mint** is established.

1801   **Lord Nelson** of England destroys the Danish fleet off Copenhagen.

1832   **Dom Pedro** proclaims himself regent of **Portugal.**

1849   Great Britain annexes the **Punjab** in India.

St. Nicetius, Bishop of Lyons. Also called **Nizier.** [d. 573]

St. Francis of Paola. Founded the Minim Friars; patron saint of sailors. [d. 1507] Optional Memorial.

St. Leopold of Gaiche, priest. [d. 1815]

The Beatified

Blessed Francis Coll. [beatified, 1979]

1860   First **Italian Parliament** meets at Turin.

1895   **The East India Railway** is opened by the lieutenant governor of Bengal.

1917   The Russian provisional government repeals all laws abridging religious freedom.

1921   **Armenian Soviet Socialist Republic** is proclaimed.

1945   U.S. troops land on **Sanga Sanga** and **Bangao Islands,** Philippines (World War II).

1951   **United Nations Food and Agriculture Organization** opens its new headquarters in Rome.

1960   **France** and **U.S.S.R.** sign agreements on trade, scientific and cultural exchanges, and peaceful uses of atomic energy.

1970   U.S. grand jury in Chicago indicts 12 members of the **Weatherman** faction of the **Students for a Democratic Society** on charges of conspiring to incite riot in October 1969.

       Massachusetts Governor **Francis W. Sargent** signs a bill providing that servicemen from that state do not have to fight in an undeclared war.

1982   Argentina seizes the **Falkland Islands,** held by Great Britain since 1833.

April 3

Religious Calendar

The Saints

St. Pancras, first bishop of Taormina and martyr. Also called Pancratius. [d. c. 90 A.D.]

St. Sixtus I, pope and martyr. Elected pope c. 119. Also called Xistus, or Xystus. [d. c. 127]

Birthdates

1245   **Philip III,** also called **Philip the Bold,** King of France, 1270–85. [d. October 5, 1285]

1367   **Henry IV,** King of England, (surnamed *Bolingbroke*) 1399–1413. [d. March 21, 1413]

1593   **George Herbert,** English clergyman, poet; best known for his poem *The Temple.* [d. March 1, 1633]

1715   **John Hanson,** U.S. farmer, politician; first president under the Articles of Confederation, 1781–82. Considered by some as the first president of the U.S. [d. November 15, 1783]

1737   **Arthur St. Clair,** American Revolutionary general, public official; president of Continental Congress, 1787. [d. August 31, 1818]

1783   **Washington Irving,** U.S. essayist, historian, and "spinner of tales," his most notable works are *Legend of Sleepy Hollow* and *Rip Van Winkle.* [d. November 28, 1859]

1798   **Charles Wilkes,** U.S. naval officer, explorer; led round-the-world expedition that explored Antarctic area now known as **Wilkes Land,** 1838–42. [d. February 8, 1877]

1822   **Edward Everett Hale,** U.S. clergyman; author of *The Man Without a Country.* [d. June 10, 1909]

1823   **William Marcy (*Boss*) Tweed,** U.S. politician; Democratic political boss. [d. April 12, 1878]

1837   **John Burroughs,** U.S. essayist, naturalist. [d. March 29, 1921]

1866   **James Barry Munnik Hertzog,** Afrikaans nationalist; Prime Minister of South Africa, 1924–39. [d. 1942]

1881   **Alcide de Gasperi,** Italian politician; as Prime Minister, 1945–53, led the reconstruction of Italy after World War II. [d. August 19, 1954]

1893   **Leslie Howard (Leslie Stainer),** British actor. [d. June 1, 1943]

1898   **George Jessel,** U.S. vaudevillian entertainer. [d. May 24, 1981]

       Henry Robinson Luce, U.S. editor and publisher; founded *Time, Fortune,* and *Life* magazines. [d. February 28, 1967]

1923   **Jan Sterling (Jane Sterling Adriance),** U.S. actress.

1924   **Marlon Brando,** U.S. actor; known for his *method acting* in dramatic roles.

       Doris Day (Doris von Kappelhoff), U.S. singer, dancer, actress.

1925   **Tony Benn,** British political leader, cabinet minister; head of Labour Party, 1971–72.

1926   **Virgil Ivan (Gus) Grissom,** U.S. astronaut, killed in *Apollo I* when fire broke out during a simulation exercise. [d. January 27, 1967]

1934   **Jane Goodall (Baroness Jane Van Lawick-Goodall),** British ethologist; noted for studies on chimpanzees.

1942   **Marsha Mason,** U.S. actress.

Historical Events

1189   **Peace of Strasbourg** is signed, effecting a reconciliation between **Emperor Frederick Barbarossa** of Germany and **Pope Clement III.**

1559   The **Treaty of Cateau-Cambrésis** ends **Hapsburg-Valois Wars** between France and Spain; reaffirms Spanish possession of its Italian states and the **Franche-Conté** and France's ownership of **Saluzzo.**

1696   **Sir John Friend** and **Sir William Parkyns** are executed for attempted assassination of **William III** of England.

1860   The first **Pony Express** leaves St. Joseph, Missouri, bound for Sacramento, California, with the U.S. mail.

SS. Agape, Chionia, and **Irene,** virgins and martyrs. [d. 304]

St. Burgondofara, virgin and abbess; founder of Benedictine Abbey of Faremoutiers. Also called **Fare.** [d. 657]

St. Nicetas, abbot and martyr. [d. 824]

St. Richard of Wyche, Bishop of Chichester, ascetic. Also called **Richard of Burford.** [d. 1253]

The Beatified

Blessed Gandulf of Binasco, Franciscan friar. [d. 1260]

Blessed John of Penna, Franciscan friar. [d. 1271]

1861   **Czar Alexander II** of Russia issues the **Emancipation Edict,** liberating the Russian serfs.

1865   **Richmond, Virginia,** the capital of the U.S. Southern Confederacy, is surrendered to the Army of the Potomac under General Ulysses S. Grant (**U.S. Civil War**).

1903   U.S. President **Theodore Roosevelt** inaugurates East Room musicales in the **White House** with a special concert given by **Ignace Paderewski.**

1930   **Ras Tafari** is proclaimed Emperor of Ethiopia under the throne-name **Haile Selassie I.**

1941   German forces under General Wavell capture **Benghazi, Libya** (**World War II**).

1948   U.S. Congress passes **Marshall Plan,** authorizing spending over $17 billion in economic aid to 16 European countries.

1949   **Israel** and **Transjordan** sign armistice; Transjordan gains control of West Bank and part of Jerusalem.

1962   U.S. Department of Defense orders full and effective **racial integration** in military reserve units exclusive of National Guard.

1964   **U.S.** and **Panama** sign a joint declaration providing for immediate resumption of diplomatic relations.

1966   Soviet spacecraft *Luna 10* becomes the first man-made object to achieve a lunar orbit.

1970   U.S. President Richard Nixon signs the **Water Quality Improvement Act of 1970.**

1974   Some 350 persons are killed as **tornadoes** sweep from Georgia in the U.S. to Ontario Province in Canada; nearly 1,200 are injured and property damage is set at $1 billion.

1979   **Wilfried Martens,** Chairman of the Social Christian Party, becomes Prime Minister of Belgium following six months of political crisis.

April 4

Holidays

Hungary	**Liberation Day** Commemorates the day when the last German soldier was driven from Hungarian soil, 1945.
Senegal	**National Day** Commemorates completion of agreements with France giving sovereignty to Senegal, 1960.

Birthdates

1648 **Grinling Gibbons,** English woodcarver, sculptor; under **Sir Christopher Wren,** carved stalls in **St. Paul's Cathedral,** London. [d. 1720]

1752 **Nicola Antonio Zingarelli,** Italian composer; *maestro di cappella,* St. Peter's, Rome, 1804–11. [d. 1837]

1780 **Edward Hicks,** U.S. folk painter; painted *Peaceable Kingdom.* [d. August 23, 1849]

1792 **Thaddeus Stevens,** U.S. statesman; a radical anti-slavery spokesman in Congress, 1849–53, 1859–68. [d. August 11, 1868]

1793 **Jean François Casimir Delavigne,** French poet and dramatist. [d. December 11, 1843]

1802 **Dorothea (Lynde) Dix,** U.S. social reformer; pioneer in the movement for specialized treatment of the insane. [d. July 17, 1887]

1809 **Benjamin Peirce,** U.S. mathematician, astronomer; active in U.S. Coast Survey; a founding member of **Smithsonian Institution.** [d. October 6, 1880]

1819 **Maria II (da Gloria),** Queen of Portugal, 1834–53. [d. November 15, 1853]

1823 **Sir William Siemens (Wilhelm Siemens),** British inventor, industrialist; a steel-making process is named after him. [d. November 18, 1883]

1826 **Zénobe Théophile Gramme,** Belgian engineer; developer of the first practical dynamo. [d. January 20, 1901]

1843 **Hans Richter,** Hungarian conductor. [d. November 21, 1916]

1846 **Le Comte de Lautréamont (Isidore Lucien Ducasse),** French prose-poet, born in Uruguay; recognized as precursor of surrealism. [d. November 24, 1870]

1863 **Samuel Shannon Childs**, U.S. restaurateur; founder of Childs Restaurant chain in U.S. [d. March 17, 1925]

1866 **George Pierce Baker,** U.S. teacher of playwrighting; founded **47 Workshop** at Harvard, 1905; students included Eugene O'Neill, Philip Barry, Thomas Wolfe, and John Dos Passos. Founded **Yale Drama School.** [d. January 6, 1935]

1875 **Pierre Monteux,** U.S. orchestra conductor born in France; conductor of Metropolitan Opera, 1917–19; Boston Symphony Orchestra, 1919–24; Paris Symphony Orchestra, 1930–38; San Francisco Symphony Orchestra, 1935–64. [d. July 1, 1964]

1877 **Georg Kolbe,** German sculptor. [d. November 21, 1947]

1884 **Isoroku Yamamoto,** Japanese admiral; planned and led attack on **Pearl Harbor,** 1941. [d. April 18, 1943]

1888 **Tris(tram) Speaker,** U.S. baseball player. [d. December 8, 1958]

1895 **Arthur Murray,** U.S. dancing teacher; founded the **Arthur Murray School of Dancing.**

1896 **Robert Sherwood,** U.S. dramatist; winner of four Pulitzer Prizes, 1936, 1939, 1941, 1949. [d. November 14, 1955]

1906 **John Cameron Swayze, Sr.,** U.S. news correspondent.

1913 **Jules Léger,** Canadian statesman; Governor-General of Canada, 1974–79. [d. November 22, 1980]

1914 **Marguerite (Donnadieu) Duras,** French novelist, playwright, screenwriter.

1922 **Elmer Bernstein,** U.S. composer.

1924 **Gil(bert Raymond) Hodges,** U.S. baseball player, manager. [d. April 2, 1972]

Religious Calendar

The Saints

SS. **Agathopus** and **Theodulus,** martyrs. [d. 303]

St. **Tigernach,** bishop. Also called **Tierney.** [d. 549]

St. **Isidore,** Bishop of Seville and Doctor of the Church. [d. 636] Optional Memorial.

St. **Plato,** abbot. [d. 814]

St. **Benedict the Black,** Franciscan lay brother; patron saint of North American blacks and the town of Palermo. [d. 1589]

The Beatified

Blessed Peter, Bishop of Poitiers. [d. 1115]

1932 **Anthony Perkins,** U.S. actor.

1938 **A(ngelo) Bartlett Giamatti,** U.S. educator; President of Yale University, 1978– .

Historical Events

1406 **James I of Scotland** officially accedes to the throne although not crowned until May 21, 1424.

1541 **Ignatius Loyola** is elected first General of **Jesuit Order.**

1581 **Elizabeth I** of England confers knighthood on **Francis Drake,** first Englishman to circumnavigate the globe.

1611 **Denmark** declares war on **Sweden.**

1841 **William Henry Harrison,** U.S. President, dies after only one month in office; he is succeeded by his Vice-President, **John Tyler.**

1884 **Bolivia** cedes her coast to **Chile.**

1892 Anarchist plot to blow up the royal palace and the Chamber of Deputies is discovered in **Spain.**

1905 A severe **earthquake** hits northern **India;** 20,000 people are believed killed.

1911 The **Masai** sign a treaty with Great Britain, giving up their lands in **Laikipia,** East Africa, to European colonization.

1917 **Union of Polish Falcons Societies** votes to form *Army of Kosciuszko* to fight with U.S. for liberty and independence of Poland.

1928 **Mussolini's** ten commandments are promulgated to govern activities of **Fascists** abroad.

1939 **Faisal II** becomes child-king of Iraq on the death of his father, **King Ghazi I.**

1942 Japanese naval task force enters Bay of Bengal and strikes **Ceylon** (**World War II**).

1949 **North Atlantic Treaty** is signed; U.S., Canada, and Western European powers agree on common defense.

1960 **France** and **Mali Federation** sign accords granting independence to the Federation's two constituent republics, **Senegal** and **Sudan.**

1968 U.S. civil rights leader Rev. **Martin Luther King, Jr.** is shot and killed by a sniper in Memphis, Tennessee.

1969 The world's first totally artificial heart is implanted in a human by U.S. surgeon Dr. **Denton A. Cooley.** The patient, **Haskell Karp,** lives only 38 hours, dying of pneumonia and kidney failure.

1975 Prime Minister **Ian Smith** of Rhodesia releases the Rev. **Ndabaningi Sithole,** Zimbabwe African National Union leader accused of plotting the murder of black leaders in Rhodesia.

1978 Cuban troops lead Angolan attack on pro-western **National Union for the Total Independence of Angola.**

1979 Former Pakistani Prime Minister **Zulfikar Ali Bhutto** is hanged on charges of conspiring to murder a political opponent.

1983 **U.S. Space Shuttle** *Challenger* is launched into orbit for a five-day mission which includes the deploying of a tracking and data relay satellite, the world's largest communications satellite, and a **space walk** by two of the four astronauts aboard.

April 5

Holidays

Korea   Arbor Day

Religious Calendar

The Saints

St. Derfel Gadarn, monk and warrior. [d. 6th century]

St. Ethelburga, Abbess of Lyminge and matron. Daughter of King Ethelbert of Kent, who did much

Birthdates

1588   **Thomas Hobbes,** English philosopher; exiled to France for his political convictions; known for his theory of **social contracts.** [d. December 4, 1679]

1684   **Catherine I,** Empress of Russia, 1725– 27; widow of Peter the Great; she ruled in her own right for two years. [d. 1727]

1732   **Jean-Honoré Fragonard,** French painter, engraver. [d. August 22, 1806]

1784   **Louis Spohr,** German violin virtuoso, composer. [d. 1859]

1795   **Sir Henry Havelock,** British colonial officer in India; distinguished himself during **Sepoy Mutiny.** [d. 1857]

1801   **Vincenzo Gioberti,** Italian patriot, author, philosopher; Premier of Sardinia, 1848–49; Ambassador at Paris, 1849–51. [d. October 26, 1852]

1804   **Matthias Schleiden,** German biologist, botanist; evolved an important theory concerning **origin of plant cells.** [d. June 23, 1881]

1811   **Jules Dupré,** French landscape painter; regarded as one of the founders of modern French school of landscape painting. [d. October 6, 1889]

1821   **Linus Yale,** U.S. inventor and lock manufacturer. [d. December 25, 1868]

1827   **Joseph Lister, Baron Lister of Lyme Regis,** British surgeon; responsible for practice of **antiseptic medicine.** [d. February 10, 1912]

1832   **Jules François Camille Ferry,** French statesman; Premier, 1880–81, 1883–85. [d. March 16, 1893]

1835   **Vítezslav Hálek,** Czech poet, novelist, dramatist; considered the *Father of Modern Czech Poetry.* [d. October 8, 1874]

1837   **Algernon Charles Swinburne,** British poet and critic; a leader in lyric poetry. [d. April 10, 1909]

1839   **Robert Smalls,** U.S. Congressman, 1875–79, 1881–87; only black naval captain during U.S. Civil War. [d. 1916]

1856   **Booker (Taliaferro) Washington,** U.S. educator, social reformer; founder of **Tuskegee Institute,** 1881. [d. November 14, 1915]

1858   **W(ashington) Atlee Burpee,** U.S. seed-products executive, born in Canada; founded first successful mail-order seed business. [d. November 26, 1915]

1893   **David Burpee,** U.S. horticulturist; president of world's largest mail order seed company; son of W. Atlee Burpee (see above). [d. June 24, 1980]

1900   **Spencer Tracy,** U.S. actor. [d. June 10, 1967]

1901   **Chester Bowles,** U.S. diplomat, advertising executive; Governor of Connecticut, 1949–51.

        Melvyn Douglas (Melvyn Hesselberg), U.S. actor. [d. August 4, 1981]

1904   **Richard Ghormley Eberhart,** U.S. poet; Pulitzer Prize in poetry, 1966.

        Bette (Ruth Elizabeth) Davis, U.S. actress; one of the foremost dramatic actresses in film history.

        Herbert von Karajan, Austrian orchestral and operatic conductor.

1916   **Gregory Peck,** U.S. actor; Hollywood leading man for more than 30 years.

1929   **Ivar Giaevar,** U.S. physicist born in Norway; Nobel Prize in physics for research in **semi-conductor and superconductor**

to convert her husband, King Edwin, and his realm, Northumbria, to Christianity. Also called **Tata.** [d. c. 647]

St. Gerald of Sauve-Majeure, abbot. [d. 1095]

St. Albert, Bishop of Montecorvino in Apulia. [d. 1127]

St. Vincent Ferrer, Dominican preacher, missionary; patron of brick and tile manufacturers, plumbers, and pavement workers. [d. 1419] Optional Memorial.

The Beatified

Blessed Juliana of Mount Cornillon, virgin. Responsible for introducing the Feast of Corpus Christi. [d. 1258]

Blessed Crescentia of Kaufbeuren, virgin. [d. 1744]

---

electronics (with L. Esaki and B. D. Josephson), 1973.

Historical Events

1355 **Charles IV** is crowned Holy Roman Emperor at Rome.

1513 **Treaty of Mechlin** between **Maximilian I,** Holy Roman Emperor, **Henry VIII** of England, **Ferdinand** of Aragon, and **Pope Leo X** is signed.

1614 **Pocahontas,** daughter of Indian chief **Powhatan,** marries **John Rolfe,** English colonist at Virginia.

1873 The **Ashanti War** breaks out between African natives and the British along the **Gold Coast.**

1879 **Chile** declares war on **Bolivia** and **Peru,** beginning what is called the *Saltpetre War* in which Chile hopes to acquire the saltpeter mines in Bolivia and Peru.

1881 The **Treaty of Pretoria** ends the rebellion of the Transvaal Boers; the South African Republic attains independence under British suzerainty (**Boer War**).

1897 The **Czech language** is granted equal status with the German language in **Bohemia.**

1915 **Jess Willard** knocks out **Jack Johnson** to win world heavyweight boxing title.

1917 The German strategic retreat along the Western Front to the **Hindenburg Line** is completed (**World War I**).

1919 **Eamon de Valera** is named President of Ireland's **Sinn Fein.**

1951 **Julius and Ethel Rosenberg** are sentenced to death by U.S. federal court after being found guilty of treason in passing **atomic bomb** secrets to Soviet agents.

1960 **U Nu** succeeds Gen. Ne Win as Premier of **Burma.**

1963 **J. Robert Oppenheimer,** U.S. physicist, declared a security risk in 1954, is named winner of the Atomic Energy Commission's Fermi award.

1964 **Jigme Dorji,** Prime Minister of **Bhutan,** is assassinated.

1968 Czechoslovakia's Communist Party Secretary **Alexander Dubček** issues liberal reform program.

1970 Count **Karl von Spreti,** West German Ambassador to Guatemala, is found slain after the Guatemalan government refuses to grant demands of his kidnappers.

1973 **American Indian Movement** leaders and representatives of the U.S. government agree to a cease-fire in the 37-day siege of **Wounded Knee,** South Dakota.

1974 A coalition government is formed in **Laos;** Prince Souvana Phouma continues as premier.

1976 Foreign Secretary **James Callaghan** becomes the new Prime Minister of Great Britain, succeeding Harold Wilson.

April 6

Holidays

Republic of South Africa	**Van Riebeeck Day** or **Founders Day** Honors Dutch explorer Jan van Riebeeck, who founded Cape Town, South Africa, 1652.
Thailand	**Chakri Memorial Day** Commemorates the founding of the ruling dynasty by King Rama I, 1782.

Birthdates

1671   **Jean-Baptiste Rousseau,** French poet, dramatist; exiled because of satires aimed at prominent political and literary figures. [d. March 17, 1741]

1773   **James Mill,** Scottish economist, historian, philosopher in England; father of **John Stuart Mill.** [d. June 23, 1836]

1818   **Aasmund Olavssen Vinje,** Norwegian poet, essayist, journalist; active in **Landsmaal** movement. [d. July 30, 1870]

1826   **Gustave Moreau,** French painter; donated his home to the city of Paris (Musée Gustave Moreau). [d. 1898]

1852   **Timothy Cole,** U.S. wood engraver, born in England; known for his engravings of the old masters. [d. May 17, 1931]

1866   **(Joseph) Lincoln Steffens,** U.S. journalist; one of the foremost **muckraking** journalists of the early 20th century. [d. August 9, 1936]

1869   **Louis Raemaekers,** Dutch political cartoonist, artist; known for his anti-German cartoons during World War I. [d. 1956]

1870   **Oscar Straus,** Austrian composer; widely known for his comic operas and operettas; wrote *Der Tapfere Soldat.* [d. 1954]

1884   **Walter Huston (Walter Houghston),** Canadian character actor. [d. April 7, 1950]

1890   **Anthony Herman Gerard Fokker,** Dutch airplane designer, builder; manufacturer of German pursuit planes during World War I. [d. December 23, 1939]

1892   **Donald Willis Douglas,** U.S. aircraft manufacturer; founded Douglas Aircraft, 1920. [d. February 1, 1981]

     Lowell (Jackson) Thomas, U.S. traveler, author, radio news commentator. [d. August 29, 1981]

1906   **Sir John Betjeman,** British poet; named Poet Laureate of England, 1972.

1910   **Olin E(arl) Teague,** U.S. politician; Congressman, 1946–77; frequently identified with issues related to American veterans. [d. January 23, 1981]

1911   **Feodor Lynen,** German biochemist; Nobel Prize in physiology or medicine for work on the metabolism of **cholesterol and fatty acids** (with K. E. Bloch), 1964. [d. 1979]

1918   **Alfredo Ovanda Candia,** Bolivian statesman; President of Bolivia, 1966; 1969–70; Led military campaign against Cuban-backed guerrillas in which **Che Guevara** was killed; his government overthrown, 1970. [d. January 24, 1982]

1927   **Gerry Mulligan,** U.S. jazz musician.

1928   **James Dewey Watson,** U.S. biochemist; Nobel Prize in physiology or medicine for discovery of molecular structure of **DNA** (with F. H. C. Crick and M. H. F. Wilkins), 1962.

1929   **André Previn,** U.S. composer, conductor.

Historical Events

6 B.C.   Day believed by some scientists to be the real date of the Nativity of Jesus Christ.

1199   **Richard I of England** dies in battle; succeeded by his brother, **John Lackland.**

1490   **Matthias Corvinus, King** of Hungary, dies; succeeded by **Ladislas II** of Bohemia, the son of **Casimir IV** of Poland.

1652   A Dutch East India Company expedition, led by **Jan van Riebeeck,** reaches Table Bay and establishes the **Cape Colony,** first permanent European settlement in South Africa.

Religious Calendar

The Saints

120 Persian martyrs put to death for refusing to worship the sun. [d. 345]

St. Marcellinus, martyr. [d. 413]

St. Celestine I, pope. Elected 422. [d. 432]

St. Eutychius, Patriarch of Constantinople. [d. 582]

St. Prudentius, Bishop of Troyes. [d. 861]

St. Elstan, Bishop of Ramsbury. Also called **Elfstan.** [d. 981]

St. William of Eskill, abbot. [d. 1203]

St. Brychan, Welsh king. [death date unknown]

The Beatified

Blessed Notker Balbulus, monk, poet, and musician. [d. 912]

Blessed Catherine of Pallanza, virgin. [d. 1478]

1793 **Committee of Public Safety** assumes dictatorial powers in France (**French Revolution**).

1830 The **Mormon Church** is organized by **Joseph C. Smith** and **Oliver Crowdy** at Fayette, New York.

1862 The **Battle of Shiloh** begins at Pittsburg Landing, Tennessee, with the Union Army under General U. S. Grant and the Confederate forces under Generals Albert Johnston and Pierre Beauregard (**U.S. Civil War**).

1868 **Brigham Young, Mormon Church** leader, marries his 27th and last wife.

Emperor Meiji proclaims the **Charter Oath,** promising **Japan** a deliberative assembly and an open attitude to the West.

1896 The first modern **Olympic Games** begin at **Athens, Greece.**

1909 Expedition of **Admiral Robert Peary** reaches the **North Pole.**

1917 The U.S. declares war on Germany (**World War I**).

George M. Cohan composes *Over There* as U.S. declares war on Germany; the song is copyrighted on June 1, 1917.

1918 The **First Battle of the Somme** ends with the German offensive stopped after driving 40 miles into the British lines (**World War I**).

1929 The *City of Glasgow* arrives in Karachi, opening weekly air mail service between Great Britain and India.

1930 **Mahatma Gandhi** and his followers begin taking salt from the sea in defiance of the British monopoly on salt production.

1941 Germany invades Greece and Yugoslavia (**World War II**).

1945 First heavy attack by Japanese Kamikaze planes damages U.S. ships at **Okinawa (World War II).**

1951 **Oscar Collazo,** Puerto Rican nationalist, is sentenced to death after being found guilty of murdering a White House guard in an attempt to assassinate President **Harry S. Truman** on November 1, 1950.

1955 **Sir Anthony Eden** becomes Prime Minister of Great Britain.

1965 *Early Bird,* the world's first commercial **communications satellite**, is launched from Cape Kennedy, Florida.

1968 Canadian Justice Minister **Pierre Elliott Trudeau** is elected to succeed Prime Minister Pearson as leader of the Liberal Party.

1972 **Egypt** severs diplomatic relations with **Jordan.**

1973 **Sweden** becomes the first Western nation to recognize **North Korea.**

1977 U.S. President **Jimmy Carter** signs legislation that restores to the White House authority for government reorganization.

1978 U.S. President **Jimmy Carter** signs into law legislation raising **mandatory retirement age** from 65 to 70 for private industry and eliminating it for most federal workers.

April 7

World Health Day
Marks the anniversary of the establishment of the World Health Organization, 1948. Sponsored by the United Nations.

People's Republic of Mozambique — **Women's Day**

U.S. (New York) — **Verrazano Day**
Celebrates the discovery of New York Harbor by Giovanni da Verrazano, 1524.

Yugoslavia — **Yugoslav Republic Day**
Anniversary of formation of Socialist Federal Republic of Yugoslavia, 1963.

Birthdates

1506 **Saint Francis Xavier (Francisco Javier),** Spanish Jesuit missionary to the Orient. [d. 1552]

1652 **Clement XII,** pope 1730–40. [d. February 6, 1740]

1770 **William Wordsworth,** English poet; leader of the English Romantic movement. [d. April 23, 1850]

1772 **François Marie Fourier,** French philosopher, social reformer; developed cooperative society concept called **Fourierism,** of which **Brook Farm** in the U.S. is an example. [d. October 10, 1837]

1780 **William Ellery Channing,** U.S. religious leader; founder of American Unitarianism. [d. October 2, 1842]

1859 **Jacques Loeb,** U.S. physiologist and experimental biologist, born in Germany; known for his rigorously scientific studies of **reproduction** and **regeneration.** [d. February 11, 1924]

1860 **Will Keith Kellogg,** U.S. food-products manufacturer; founded W. K. Kellogg Co. [d. October 6, 1951]

1873 **John Joseph McGraw** (*Little Napoleon*), U.S. baseball player, manager; coach of the New York Giants, 1902–32. [d. February 25, 1934]

1884 **Bronislaw Kasper Malinowski,** Polish social anthropologist; known for his studies of the societies of the western Pacific islands. [d. May 16, 1942]

1889 **Gabriela Mistral (Lucila Godoy Alcayaga),** Chilean poet; first Latin-American woman to win Nobel Prize in literature, 1945. [d. January 10, 1957]

1891 **Sir David Alexander Cecil Low,** British political cartoonist, caricaturist; created character **Colonel Blimp.** [d. September 19, 1963]

1893 **Irene Castle,** U.S. dancer; formed popular dance team with her husband, Vernon. Created *Turkey Trot* and *Castle Walk.* [d. January 25, 1969]

Allen Dulles, U.S. government official, diplomat, lawyer; brother of **John Foster Dulles** (February 25). [d. January 29, 1959]

1897 **Walter Winchell,** U.S. journalist, syndicated columnist. [d. February 20, 1972]

1899 **Robert Casadesus,** French concert pianist, composer. [d. September 19, 1972]

1908 **Frank Fitzsimmons,** U.S. labor leader; President of Teamsters Union in U.S., 1971–81. [d. May 6, 1981]

1915 **Billie Holiday** (*Lady Day*), U.S. jazz singer. [d. July 17, 1959]

1920 **Ravi Shankar,** Indian musician, sitar player.

1928 **James Garner (James Baumgardner),** U.S. actor.

Religious Calendar

The Saints

St. Hegesippus, church historian. [d. c. 180]

St. Aphraates. [d. c. 345]

St. George the Younger, Bishop of Mitylene, Greece. [d. c. 816]

St. Celsus, Archbishop of Armagh. Also called **Ceallach.** [d. 1129]

St. Aybert. Also called **Aibert, Albert.** [d. 1140]

St. John Baptist de La Salle, founder of the Brothers of the Christian Schools for the training of teachers. [d. 1719]. Feast formerly May 15. Obligatory Memorial.

St. Goran, hermit; patron of Gorran, Cornwall. Also called **Goron,** or **Gorran.** [death date unknown]

The Beatified

Blessed Herman Joseph, mystic. [d. 1241]

Blessed Ursulina, virgin. [d. 1410]

Blessed William of Scicli, Franciscan tertiary. [d. 1411]

Blessed Alexander Rawlins and **Henry Walpole,** martyrs. [d. 1595]

Blessed Edward Oldcorne and **Ralph Ashley,** martyrs. [d. 1606]

Blessed Mary Assunta Pallotta, religious of the Franciscan Missionaries of Mary. [d. 1905]

1931 **Donald Barthelme,** U.S. novelist, short-story writer.

1939 **Francis Ford Coppola,** U.S. film director, producer, writer; directed *The Godfather*, 1971.

David (Parradine) Frost, British television personality.

Historical Events

1118 **Pope Gelasius II** excommunicates **Henry V,** Holy Roman Emperor.

1348 **Prague University** (Czechoslovakia) is founded by Holy Roman Emperor **Charles IV.**

1763 **George, Lord Grenville,** succeeds John Stuart, Earl of Bute, as British prime minister.

1823 War between France and Spain begins as 100,000 **Sons of St. Louis** invade Spain.

1831 **Pedro I** of Brazil abdicates in favor of his son, **Pedro II.**

1862 Union forces under General **Ulysses S. Grant** win **Battle of Shiloh** in **U.S. Civil War** (see April 6).

1907 Provincial government is instituted in **Manchuria** by China.

1921 **Sun Yat-sen** is elected president of China by the rebel parliament at Canton.

1934 **Mahatma Gandhi** of India suspends his civil disobedience campaign.

1936 **President Niceto Alcalá Zamora y Torres** of Spain is deposed (**Spanish Civil War**).

1939 Italians bombard **Albania** and overrun the country (**World War II**).

1945 In South China Sea, U.S. carrier-based planes sink the Japanese battleship *Yamato,* one of the largest enemy ships sunk during World War II.

1948 The **World Health Organization** is established by the United Nations.

1949 **Rodgers and Hammerstein's** musical, *South Pacific,* premieres in New York City.

1951 Vietnamese Communist leader **Ho Chi Minh** orders his forces to revert to guerrilla warfare (**French-Indo-Chinese War**).

1963 By proclamation the Socialist Federal Republic of **Yugoslavia** is established, and **Marshal Tito** becomes president for life.

1978 Philippine President **Ferdinand E. Marcos** permits the first national elections since his imposition of martial law on September 23, 1972.

1980 U.S. breaks diplomatic ties with **Iran** over the seizure of Americans as hostages at the U.S. embassy in Tehran.

1983 Scientists at the **Smithsonian Institution** detail the discovery, in 1982, in Egypt, of a human skeleton 60–80,000 years old, a significant link in the study of human evolution.

April 8

Holidays

Japan	Hana Matsuri or **Flower Festival**, **Buddha's Birthday** Commemorates the birth of the founder of Buddhism, Gautama Buddha.
Korea	**Buddha's Birthday**

Birthdates

c. 563 B.C. **Gautama Buddha,** Indian religious leader, philosopher; founder of Buddhism. [d. c. 483 B.C.]

1605 **Philip IV,** King of Spain, 1621–65, during its decline as a great world power. [d. September 17, 1665]

1726 **Lewis Morris,** American colonist; member of Continental Congress; signer of the Declaration of Independence. [d. January 22, 1798]

1783 **John Claudius Loudon,** Scottish horticulturist, writer. [d. 1843]

1798 **Dionysius Solomos,** Greek poet; author of *Hymn to Liberty*, from which come words to Greek National Anthem. [d. February 21, 1857]

1817 **Charles Edouard Brown-Séquard,** French physiologist, physician; known for experiments in life-prolonging injections of serum extracted from sheep. [d. April 2, 1894]

1818 **Christian IX** of Denmark. [d. January 29, 1906]

August Wilhelm von Hofmann, German organic chemist; noted for work on coaltar products. [d. 1892]

1850 **William Henry Welch,** U.S. physician, bacteriologist, teacher; developed first pathology laboratory in U.S., 1879; influential in founding of **Johns Hopkins University.** [d. April 30, 1934]

1859 **Edmund Husserl,** German philosopher; founder of **phenomenology.** [d. April 26, 1938]

1869 **Harvey Williams Cushing,** U.S. neuro-surgeon, a specialist on the pituitary gland; introduced **blood pressure** determination in U.S. [d. October 7, 1939]

1875 **Albert I,** of Belgium, acceded to throne 1909; led the Belgian Army during World War I and guided his country's economic recovery afterwards. [d. February 17, 1934]

1889 **Sir Adrian Cedric Boult,** British conductor; knighted, 1937; known for his persistence in broadcasting BBC Symphonies throughout World War II, in spite of air raids and other disruptions. [d. February 23, 1983]

1893 **Mary Pickford (Gladys Marie Smith),** U.S. actress; leading lady of the silent screen, then talkies. Helped establish United Artists Co. with her husband, Douglas Fairbanks, and Charlie Chaplin and D. W. Griffith. [d. May 29, 1979]

1896 **E(dgar) Y. (*Yip*) Harburg,** U.S. lyricist, librettist; wrote lyrics for Broadway musicals and films. [d. March 5, 1981]

Lansing Peter Shield, U.S. business executive; President of Grand Union, 1947–60. [d. January 6, 1960]

1897 **Louis Skidmore,** U.S. architect; partner in Skidmore, Owings, and Merrill, an architectural firm that pioneered in commercial and institutional design and structure. [d. September 27, 1962]

1904 **Sir John R. Hicks,** British economist; Nobel Prize in economics for contributions to general equilibrium (with K. J. Arrow), 1972.

1908 **Donald Ford Whitehead,** U.S. journalist; known for coverage of the major battles of World War II in Europe and North Africa; Pulitzer Prize in international reporting, 1951. [d. January 12, 1981]

1912 **Sonja Henie,** U.S. figure skater, born in Norway; Olympic gold medalist, 1928, 1932, and 1936. [d. October 12, 1969]

1919 **Ian (Douglas) Smith,** Rhodesian political leader; led Rhodesian move to independence from Great Britain; opponent of black equality in **Rhodesia** (Zimbabwe).

Religious Calendar

The Saints
St. Dionysius, Bishop of Corinth. [d. c. 180]

St. Perpetuus, Bishop of Tours. [d. c. 494]

St. Walter of Pontoise, abbot. [d. 1095]

The Beatified
Blessed Clement of Osimo, Augustinian prior. [d. 1291]

Blessed Julian of St. Augustine, Franciscan monk. [d. 1606]

Blessed Julia Billiart, virgin and cofounder of the Institute of Notre Dame of Namur. [d. 1816]

1921   **Franco Corelli,** Italian operatic tenor.

1929   **Jacques Brel,** Belgian composer, singer. [d. Oct. 9, 1978]

Historical Events

1341   **Francesco Petrarch,** Italian lawyer and diplomat, is crowned poet laureate in Rome.

1364   **John II** of France dies in England and is succeeded by **Charles V.**

1838   The *Great Western*, British passenger steamer, leaves Bristol, England, on its maiden trans-Atlantic voyage to New York.

1904   *Entente Cordiale* between Great Britain and France settles colonial disputes over Egypt and Moroccan interests.

1913   Convocation of the first elected parliament of the **Chinese Republic** is held at Peking.

1915   Turkish government begins the deportation and massacre of **Armenians** accused of aiding the Russians in the Caucasus (**World War I**).

1917   **Austria-Hungary** severs diplomatic relations with the U.S. (**World War I**).

1926   **Benito Mussolini** embarks on visit to **Tripoli**; first visit of Italian premier to African colonies.

1934   U.S. Congress enacts the **Emergency Relief Appropriation Act,** which leads to the **Works Progress Administration.**

1939   **King Zog of Albania** abdicates the day after Mussolini's forces seize Albania (**World War II**).

1974   Baseball's **Hank Aaron** surpasses Babe Ruth's career home run record of 714.

1977   Israeli Prime Minister **Yitzak Rabin** plunges the country into political turmoil when he admits violating Israeli currency laws; Defense Minister **Shimon Peres** takes over the government.

April 9

Holidays

Bolivia	**National Day** Commemorates popular uprising and reestablishment of National Revolutionary Movement, 1952.
Tunisia	**Martyrs' Day**

Birthdates

1798 **Giuditta Pasta,** Italian operatic soprano. [d. April 1, 1865]

1802 **Elias Lönnrot,** Finnish folklorist, philologist, and physician. [d. March 19, 1884]

1806 **Isambard Kingdom Brunel,** British engineer; designer and builder of bridges, railroads, and steamships. [d. 1859]

1815 **Alphonse Beau de Rochas,** French engineer; developed early **internal combustion engine.** [d. March 27, 1893]

1821 **Charles Baudelaire,** French poet, critic, translator; much of his work was banned during his lifetime; known for his decadent, bohemian lifestyle. [d. August 31, 1867]

1830 **Eadweard (Edward) Muybridge,** U.S. motion picture pioneer born in England; known for developments in **rapid sequence photography.** [d. May 8, 1904]

1835 **Leopold II, of Belgium,** 1865–1909; leader of first European efforts to develop Africa's Congo Basin, which was annexed in 1908 as the **Belgian Congo.** [d. December 17, 1909]

1848 **Helene Lange,** German feminist educator, author, and editor. [d. May 13, 1930]

1864 **William George Stuber,** U.S. business executive; succeeded George Eastman as president of Eastman Kodak Co., 1925–34. [d. June 17, 1959]

1865 **Erich Friedrich Wilhelm Ludendorff,** German Army general; launched unlimited **submarine warfare** that drew U.S. into World War I. [d. December 20, 1937]

Charles Proteus Steinmetz (Karl August Rudolf Steinmetz), U.S. electrical engineer born in Germany; established the mathematical methods of **electrical engineering.** [d. October 26, 1923]

1870 **Nikolai Lenin (Vladimir Ilich Ulyanov),** Russian Communist leader; Premier of Russia, 1918–24. [d. January 21, 1924]

1872 **Léon Blum,** French socialist statesman; Premier, 1936–37; provisional President, 1946. [d. 1950]

1887 **Frank (Earl) Adair,** U.S. surgeon; a leader in research in cancer of the breast; led in the development of the clinical section of Sloan-Kettering Institute for Cancer Research. [d. December 31, 1981]

1888 **Sol(omon) Hurok,** U.S. impresario born in Russia; considered one of most influential figures in development of knowledge and appreciation of music and dance in the U.S. [d. March 5, 1974]

1889 **Efrem Zimbalist,** Russian violinist, composer.

1898 **Curly Lambeau (Earl Louis Lambeau),** U.S. football coach; founder of **Green Bay Packers.** [d. June 1, 1965]

Paul (Bustill) Robeson, U.S. dramatic actor, singer. [d. Jan. 23, 1976]

1903 **Ward Bond,** U.S. character actor; appeared in many Westerns in movies and on TV. [d. November 5, 1960]

Gregory Pincus, U.S. biologist; responsible for development of the **birth control pill.** [d. August 22, 1967]

1905 **William Fulbright,** U.S. politician, lawyer, teacher; U.S. Senator, 1942–74; founded the **Fulbright Scholarship Program.**

1906 **Antal Dorati,** U.S. composer, conductor born in Hungary; Music Director, Washington National Symphony Orchestra, 1970–77; Principal Conductor, Royal Philharmonic Orchestra, 1975–78; Conductor Laureate, 1978– .

1910 **Abraham A. Ribicoff,** U.S. politician; Congressman, 1948–52; Governor of Connecticut, 1954–61; Secretary of U.S. Dept. of Health, Education and Welfare, 1961–62; U.S. Senator, 1962–80.

1925 **Frank Joseph Shakespeare, Jr.,** U.S. government official, broadcast executive; Pres-

Religious Calendar

The Saints

St. Mary of Cleophas, matron. [d. 1st century]

St. Waldetrudis, widow; patron of Mons, Belgium. Also called **Vaudru, Vautrude, Waltrude,** or **Waudru.** [d. c. 688]

St. Hugh, Bishop of Rouen. [d. 730]

St. Gaucherius, abbot. Also called **Gaucher, Gautier.** [d. 1140]

The Beatified

Blessed Ubald of Florence. [d. 1315]

Blessed Thomas of Tolentino, martyr and missionary. [d. 1321]

Blessed Anthony Pavoni, martyr. [d. 1374]

ident, CBS Television Service Division, 1967–69; Head, U.S. Information Agency, 1969–73; President, RKO General, 1975– .

1926 **Hugh Hefner,** U.S. editor; publisher of *Playboy.*

1933 **Jean-Paul Belmondo,** French actor.

1957 **Severiano Ballesteros,** Spanish golfer.

Historical Events

1241 Mongols defeat Polish princes under **Batu** at **Liegnitz,** Silesia; **Henryk II, Duke of Silesia,** is killed.

1454 **Peace of Lodi** is signed between Venice and Milan; Venice secures Brescia, Bergamo, Crema, and Treviglio.

1483 **Edward V** of England accedes to throne on death of Edward IV.

1609 **Truce of Antwerp** grants independence of the United Provinces (**Netherlands**).

1682 **Sieur de La Salle,** French explorer, claims vast interior of North America for France, naming it **Louisiana.**

1865 Confederate general **Robert E. Lee** surrenders to Union general **Ulysses S. Grant** at **Appomattox Court House,** ending **U.S. Civil War.**

1891 **Pan-German League** is formed.

1909 **Lee De Forest** engineers first wireless transmission of the human voice singing, of **Enrico Caruso** in the Metropolitan Opera House in New York.

1917 Canadians storm **Vimy Ridge** in northern France (**World War I**).

1918 Germans break through Allied lines in **Flanders** but are halted by British and French reenforcements (**World War I**).

The **Moldavian Republic (Bessarabia)** proclaims its union with **Rumania.**

1928 **Turkey** ends legal status of **Islam** as the state religion.

1938 Civil disobedience campaign begins in **Tunisia,** organized by **Habib Bourguiba.**

1940 German troops invade Denmark and Norway by sea and air (**World War II**).

1941 The Professional Golfers Association establishes the **Golf Hall of Fame** in U.S.

1942 **Bataan** in the Philippines falls to the Japanese after more than three months of siege (**World War II**).

1952 **Victor Paz Estenssoro** seizes power in Bolivian revolution, reestablishing the **National Revolutionary Movement.**

1963 **Sir Winston Churchill** is proclaimed an honorary U.S. citizen in ceremony televised internationally from the White House.

1974 **India, Pakistan,** and **Bangladesh** sign Indian subcontinent accord in New Delhi.

1977 Communist Party is legalized in **Spain** after a 38-year ban.

April 10

Religious Calendar

The Saints

St. Bademus, abbot. [d. 376]

The Martyrs under the Danes, Anglo-Saxon monks. [d. c. 870]

Birthdates

1512   **James V** of Scotland, 1513–42; upheld Roman Catholicism and allied his country with France against England. [d. December 24, 1542]

1583   **Hugo Grotius,** Dutch theologian, jurist; called the *Father of Modern International Law.* [d. August 28, 1645]

1755   **Samuel Christian Friedrich Hahnemann,** German physician; the founder of **homeopathy.** [d. July 2, 1843]

1778   **William Hazlitt,** English critic, essayist. [d. September 18, 1830]

1794   **Matthew Calbraith Perry,** U.S. Navy commodore; negotiated **Treaty of Kanagawa,** which opened U.S. trade with Japan. [d. March 4, 1858]

1827   **Lew(is) Wallace,** U.S. soldier, lawyer, diplomat, novelist; *Ben Hur.* [d. February 15, 1905]

1829   **William Booth,** British social reformer; founder of the **Salvation Army.** [d. August 20, 1912]

1835   **Henry Villard (Ferdinand Heinrich Gustav Hilgard),** U.S. journalist, railroad magnate, born in Germany; President of Northern Pacific Railroad, 1881–84. [d. November 12, 1900]

1847   **Joseph Pulitzer,** U.S. newspaper publisher; called the *Father of Modern American Journalism.* Established and endowed the School of Journalism at Columbia University and the **Pulitzer Prize,** which is awarded for excellence in journalism, letters, and music. [d. October 29, 1911]

1857   **Lucien Lévy-Bruhl,** French philosopher, sociologist, anthropologist. [d. March 13, 1939]

1862   **Wilbur Lucius Cross,** U.S. educator, politician; Governor of Connecticut, 1931–39. [d. October 5, 1948]

1864   **Eugen Francis Charles d'Albert,** German-French pianist, composer, born in Scotland; best known for his operas. [d. March 3, 1932]

1868   **George Arliss (Augustus George Andrews),** British actor. [d. February 5, 1946]

1882   **Frances Perkins,** U.S. Secretary of Labor, 1933–45; first woman to serve in a presidential cabinet. [d. May 14, 1965]

1885   **Bernard Feustman Gimbel,** U.S. retailer; president of Gimbel Brothers, 1927–53. [d. September 29, 1966]

1887   **Bernardo Alberto Houssay,** Argentine physiologist; Nobel Prize in physiology or medicine for research on **pituitary hormone** (with C. F. and G. T. Cori), 1947. [d. September 21, 1971]

1894   **Ben Nicholson,** British artist; known especially for his all-white reliefs of *absolute form* executed in the 1930s.

1897   **Eric Mowbray Knight,** British-U.S. writer; best known for his children's classic, *Lassie Come Home.* [d. January 21, 1943]

1903   **Claire Boothe Luce,** U.S. author, journalist, politician, diplomat; congresswoman, 1943–47; U.S. Ambassador to Italy, 1953–56.

1906   **Thomas S(overeign) Gates, Jr.,** U.S. businessman, politician; U.S. Secretary of the Navy, 1957–59; U.S. Secretary of Defense, 1959–60. [d. March 25, 1983]

1917   **Robert Burns Woodward,** U.S. chemist; Nobel Prize in chemistry for work in chemical synthesis, particularly of **chlorophyll,** 1965. [d. July 8, 1979]

1923   **Marshall Warren Nirenberg,** U.S. biochemist; Nobel Prize in physiology or medicine for research in **genetic development** (with H. G. Khorana and R. W. Holley), 1968.

1929   **Max (Carl Adolf) von Sydow,** Swedish actor.

1932   **Omar Sharif (Michel Shalhouz),** Egyptian actor.

1941   **Paul Theroux,** U.S. novelist.

St. Macarius of Ghent. Invoked against epidemic diseases. Also called **Macaire.** [d. 1012]

St. Fulbert, Bishop of Chartres. [d. 1029]

St. Paternus of Abdinghof. [d. 1058]

St. Michael de Sanctis, priest and convent superior. [d. 1625]

The Beatified

Blessed Antony Neyrot, martyr. [d. 1460]

Blessed Mark Fantucci, Franciscan monk and missionary. [d. 1479]

Historical Events

1302 First meeting of the **French States-General.**

1606 First **Charter of Virginia** is issued to London and Plymouth Companies by **James I** of England.

1741 **Frederick II** of Prussia defeats Austrians at **Mollwitz** and conquers **Silesia.**

1854 The constitution of the **Orange Free State** is adopted.

1861 Confederates demand evacuation of **Fort Sumter** in Charleston, S.C., leading to outbreak of the **U.S. Civil War.**

1864 Archduke **Maximilian of Austria,** supported by the French army, accepts the Mexican crown.

1866 **American Society for the Prevention of Cruelty to Animals** is founded.

1922 The **Genoa Conference** opens to discuss reconstruction of Europe following World War I; it marks the first international involvement with Communist Russia since the war.

1930 **London Naval Conference Treaty** is signed between Great Britain, U.S., France, Italy, and Japan, regulating submarine warfare and tonnage on all classes of ships.

1932 **Paul von Hindenburg** defeats **Adolf Hitler** in German presidential election.

1963 *U.S.S. Thresher,* nuclear-powered submarine, is lost in the Atlantic with 129 men on board.

Papal encyclical *Pacem in Terris,* devoted to world peace and addressed to all men of good will, is issued by **Pope John XXIII.**

1968 **Algeria, Mali, Mauritania,** and the **Congo** resume diplomatic ties with **Great Britain,** broken during the dispute over **Rhodesia** in December 1965.

1972 A treaty prohibiting the stockpiling of **biological weapons** is signed by more than 70 nations in ceremonies in Washington, London, and Moscow.

1974 **Golda Meir** resigns as Israeli prime minister.

1977 **Zaire,** under invasion from neighboring Angola, receives military aid from Morocco, France, and the U.S.

1978 The United Nation's highest-ranking Russian official, **Arkady N. Shevchenko,** renounces his Russian citizenship and applies for political asylum in the U.S.

April 11

Birthdates

1492   **Margaret of Navarre (Margaret of Angoulême),** outstanding figure of French Renaissance; active in politics, supporter of Protestantism. [d. December 21, 1549]

1770   **George Canning,** English statesman; Foreign Secretary; Prime Minister, 1822–27. [d. August 8, 1827]

1794   **Edward Everett,** U.S. statesman, orator; President of Harvard College, 1846–49; the speaker who immediately preceded Abraham Lincoln at the dedication of the National Cemetery at **Gettysburg.** [d. January 15, 1865]

1825   **Ferdinand Lassalle,** German socialist leader; founder of **German Social Democratic Party.** [d. August 31, 1864]

1862   **William Wallace Campbell,** U.S. astronomer; President, University of California, 1923–30; President, National Academy of Sciences, 1931–35. [d. June 14, 1938]

    Charles Evans Hughes, U.S. jurist, lawyer; Governor of New York, 1907–10; Republican presidential nominee, 1916; U.S. Secretary of State, 1921–25; Chief Justice, U.S. Supreme Court, 1930–41. [d. August 27, 1948]

1879   **Clarence Cannon,** U.S. politician, lawyer, history professor; a noted parliamentarian. [d. May 12, 1964]

1893   **Dean G. Acheson,** U.S. lawyer, statesman; Secretary of State, 1949–53; the principal creator of the U.S. foreign policy aimed at containment of Communist expansion after World War II. [d. October 12, 1971]

1899   **Percy Lavon Julian,** U.S. chemist and steroid researcher; most noted for development of **steroids** used in treatment of **arthritis.** [d. April 19, 1975]

1907   **Paul Douglas,** U.S. actor. [d. September 11, 1959]

1910   **António de Spinola,** Portuguese leader, army officer; provisional President of Portugal, May-September, 1974.

1911   **Stella Walsh (Stanisława Walasiewicz),** U.S. athlete, born in Poland; won over 40 U.S. track-and-field titles and set many world records.

1917   **Morton Sobell,** U.S. spy; co-defendant with **Julius** and **Ethel Rosenberg** in U.S. atomic secrets spy trial, 1951. Found guilty and sentenced to thirty years in prison; released, 1969.

1919   **Hugh (Leo) Carey,** U.S. politician, lawyer; U.S. Congressman, 1960–75; Governor of New York, 1975–82.

1932   **Joel Grey (Joe Katz),** U.S. actor.

Historical Events

1512   The French are defeated in the **Battle of Ravenna** and are expelled from Italy.

1677   In Dutch war with France, **William of Orange** is defeated at **Cassel.**

1713   **Peace of Utrecht** between France and Prussia ends **War of the Spanish Succession.**

1764   Treaty is signed between **Russia** and **Prussia** to control **Poland.**

1805   Russia joins Great Britain, Austria, and Sweden in the **Third Coalition** against France and its leader, **Napoleon.**

1814   Defeated by the English, **Napoleon** abdicates and is banished to **Elba.**

St. Godeberta, virgin. Invoked against all kinds of calamities, especially drought and epidemics. [d. c. 700]

St. Guthlac, hermit. Also called **Guthlake.** [d. 714]

St. Stanislaus, Bishop of Cracow and martyr; patron of Poland. [d. 1079] Feast formerly May 7. Optional Memorial.

St. Gemma Galgani, virgin and laywoman. [d. 1903]

The Beatified

Blessed Waltman, abbot. [d. 1138]

Blessed Rainerius Inclusus of Osnabruck, recluse. Also called **Rayner.** [d. 1237]

Blessed George Gervase, priest and martyr. Also called **Jervis.** [d. 1608]

Blessed Helen Guerra, founder of the Congregation of St. Rita, later called the Oblates of the Holy Spirit. [d. 1914]

1894   **Uganda** is declared a British protectorate.

1900   The U.S. Navy buys its first submarine, the *U.S.S. Holland.*

1905   The **Victoria Falls Bridge** over the Zambezi River, 2,875 feet above sea level, is completed, providing a link in the Cape to Cairo Railway.

1919   **Geneva,** Switzerland, is chosen as the headquarters of the **League of Nations.**

1939   Under German pressure, **Hungary** withdraws from the **League of Nations.**

1951   U.S. General **Douglas MacArthur** is relieved of command in the Korean conflict by President **Harry Truman** after a dispute over the former's exercise of authority.

1958   U.S. pianist **Van Cliburn** wins the Tchaikovsky International Piano and Violin Competition held in Moscow.

1961   Trial of **Adolf Eichmann** begins in an Israeli court in Jerusalem.

1963   British government rejects the request of the all-white government of **Southern Rhodesia's** for early independence.

1968   U.S. President Lyndon B. Johnson signs a **civil rights bill** prohibiting racial discrimination in the sale or rental of U.S. housing.

1970   *Apollo 13* is launched, manned by astronauts James A. Lovell, Jr., John L. Swipert, and Fred W. Haise, Jr.

1979   **Kampala,** the capital of Uganda, is captured by Tanzanians and rebellious Ugandans.

1982   British explorers **Charles Burton** and **Sir Ranulph Fiennes** become the first to cross both poles in a single journey around the earth.

April 12

Holidays

U.S. (North Carolina)	Anniversary of the Signing of the **Halifax Resolves**
U.S.	**Franklin Delano Roosevelt** Death Anniversary Sponsored by Franklin D. Roosevelt Philatelic Society, St. Augustine Shores, Florida
U.S.S.R.	**Cosmonautics Day**

Birthdates

1539 **Garcilaso de la Vega,** *El Inca,* Peruvian historian. [d. 1616]

1577 **Christian IV** of Denmark and Norway; led his country into the **Thirty Years' War.** [d. February 28, 1648]

1777 **Henry Clay,** U.S. statesman; known as *The Great Compromiser.* [d. June 29, 1852]

1791 **Francis Preston Blair,** U.S. journalist, politician. [d. October 18, 1876]

1823 **Alexander Nikolaevich Ostrovsky,** [O.S., March 31] Russian playwright; considered the greatest representative of Russian realism. [d. June 14 [O.S., June 2], 1886]

1825 **Richard Harvey Cain,** U.S. Congressman, 1873–75, 1877–79. [d. 1887]

1831 **Constantin Emile Meunier,** Belgian painter, sculptor; known for his paintings of mines and factories. [d. April 4, 1905]

1838 **John Shaw Billings,** U.S. Army surgeon, librarian; responsible for organization of **New York Public Library** system. [d. March 11, 1913]

1871 **Johannes Metaxas,** Greek statesman, general; dictator of Greece, 1936–41. [d. January 29, 1941]

1879 **Frederick G. Melcher,** U.S. book publisher, editor; founder of **Children's Book Week,** 1919. [d. March 9, 1963]

1883 **Imogen Cunningham,** U.S. photographer. [d. June 24, 1976]

1884 **Otto F. Meyerhof,** German biochemist; Nobel Prize in physiology or medicine for research on the chemical reactions of metabolism in the muscle (with A. V. Hill), 1922. [d. October 6, 1951]

1903 **Jan Tinbergen,** Dutch economist; Nobel Prize in economics for developing mathematical models to measure economic change (with R. Frisch), 1969.

1905 **Warren G. Magnuson,** U.S. politician, lawyer; U.S. Senator, 1944–82.

1913 **Lionel Hampton,** U.S. jazz musician, bandleader.

1923 **Ann Miller (Lucille Ann Collier),** U.S. dancer.

1924 **Raymond Barre,** French politician; Vice-President of Commission of European Communities, 1967–72.

1933 **Montserrat Caballe,** Spanish operatic soprano.

1939 **Alan Ayckbourn,** British dramatist.

Historical Events

1204 Crusaders capture **Constantinople** and establish the Latin Empire (**Fourth Crusade**).

1500 **Peace of Basel** establishes Swiss independence from Holy Roman Empire.

1533 **Thomas Cromwell** is appointed Privy Councillor and Secretary of State of England.

1654 Scotland and Ireland are united with **England** by the **Ordinance of Union.**

1859 First U.S. **billiards** championships match is played in Detroit, Michigan, between **Michael Phelan** and **John Seereiter**; Phelan is the winner.

1861 The **U.S. Civil War** begins with an attack on **Fort Sumter** by South Carolina forces (see also April 10).

1877 Great Britain annexes the Boer South African Republic as the **Transvaal.**

1907 A new **Swiss Army** bill passes, reorganizing military forces and designating the army as a standing militia with required training biennially.

Religious Calendar

The Saints

St. Julius I, pope. Elected 337. Fixed December 25 as the date of the birth of Jesus Christ. [d. 352]

St. Zeno, Bishop of Verona. [d. 371]

St. Sabas the Goth, martyr. [d. 372]

St. Alferius, Abbot of La Cava; founder of the Abbey of La Cava. [d. 13th century]

The Beatified

Blessed Andrew of Montereale. [d. 1480]

Blessed Angelo of Chivasso, priest and evangelical. [d. 1495]

1915	The **Battle of Shaiba** begins with a Turkish attack on British positions in Mesopotamia (**World War I**).
1929	The **Trades Disputes Act** and the **Public Safety Act** are enacted in India.
1945	U.S. President **Franklin D. Roosevelt** dies and is succeeded by his vice-president, **Harry S. Truman.**
1961	**Yuri Gagarin,** Russian astronaut, is first man in space, orbiting the earth in *Vostok I.*
1971	**East Pakistan** declares its independence as **Bangladesh.**
1978	Transitional government of **Rhodesia** replaces its cabinet with an 18-member Council of Ministers; Prime Minister Ian D. Smith is the only white on the four-man Executive Council.
1980	**Samuel K. Doe** and the **People's Redemption Party** oust Liberian president **William Tolbert.**
1981	*Columbia*, U.S. **space shuttle**, is first launched from Kennedy Space Center in Florida.
1983	**Harold Washington** is elected mayor of Chicago, the first black to win that office.
	U.S. embassy in **Beirut, Lebanon** is destroyed by a car bomb. 17 Americans are among the 63 people killed by the blast, for which a pro-Iranian terrorist group, the **Islamic Jihad Organization**, claims responsibility.

April 13

Holidays

U.S. (Alabama,   Thomas Jefferson's Birthday
Oklahoma,
Virginia)

Religious Calendar

The Saints

SS. Carpus, Papylus, and **Agathonice,** martyrs. Carpus, bishop from Lydia; Papylus, deacon from Thyateria; and Agathonice, matron. [d. c. 170]

Birthdates

1519   **Catherine de Medici,** queen consort of Henry II of France; regent of France, 1560–63. [d. January 5, 1589]

1593   **Sir Thomas Wentworth, 1st Earl of Strafford,** English statesman; supporter of **Charles I**; Lord Deputy of Ireland, 1632–38. [d. May 11, 1641]

1732   **Frederick North, 2nd Earl of Guilford,** English statesman; Prime Minister, 1770–82; his policies led to the **American Revolution** and British loss of the American colonies. [d. August 5, 1792]

1739   **Christian Friedrich Daniel Schubart,** German poet; under patronage of **Frederick the Great.** [d. October 10, 1791]

1743   **Thomas Jefferson,** U.S. politician, educator, architect; third President of the U.S.; a principal intellectual force behind the founding of the American republic. [d. July 4, 1826]

1748   **Joseph Bramah,** English machinist; inventor of the modern **toilet.** [d. December 9, 1814]

1769   **Sir Thomas Lawrence,** English portrait painter; principal painter to the King of England after Sir Joshua Reynolds (July 16). [d. January 7, 1830]

1771   **Richard Trevithick,** English engineer; built first **steam locomotive** to be tried on a railway, 1804. [d. April 22, 1833]

1795   **James Harper,** U.S. publisher; with his brother John (January 22), founded **Harper's Monthly, Harper's Weekly,** and **Harper's Bazaar.** Founded J. J. Harper Co. publishers (later Harper & Row). [d. March 27, 1869]

1852   **Frank Winfield Woolworth,** U.S. merchant; founder of F. W. Woolworth Co., 1879. [d. August 8, 1919]

1869   **Tully Marshall (William Phillips),** U.S. silent film actor. [d. 1943]

1892   **Sir Robert Alexander Watson-Watt,** Scottish physicist; responsible for development of U.S. and British **radar systems.** [d. December 5, 1973]

1901   **Robert Lee Dennison,** U.S. naval officer; naval aide to U.S. President Harry S. Truman, 1948–53; Commander-in-Chief, U.S. Atlantic Fleet and Supreme Allied Commander of the Atlantic forces for NATO, 1960–63. [d. March 14, 1980]

1906   **Samuel Beckett,** British-French playwright, novelist; Nobel Prize in literature, 1969.

1907   **Harold Edward Stassen,** U.S. lawyer, politician; Governor of Minnesota, 1938–45.

1909   **Eudora Welty,** U.S. short-story writer, novelist.

1917   **Robert Orville Anderson,** U.S. oil industry executive; Chairman of the Board of Atlantic Richfield Co., 1965– .

1919   **Madalyn (Mays) O'Hair,** U.S. lawyer; well-known for atheist beliefs. As Madalyn Murray, filed suit that resulted in Supreme Court ruling (1963) for the removal of Bible reading and prayer recitation in public schools.

Historical Events

1059   **Pope Nicholas II** decrees that future popes will be elected by cardinals only.

1111   **Henry V** is crowned Holy Roman Emperor at Rome.

St. Martius, Abbot of Clermont. Also called **Mars.** [d. c. 530]

St. Hermenegild, martyr. [d. 585]

St. Martin I, pope and martyr. Elected 649. [d. 655] Feast formerly November 12. Optional Memorial.

St. Guinoch, counsellor of King Kenneth. Also called **Guinochus.** [d. 838]

The Beatified

Blessed Ida of Boulogne, widow; founded the Monastery of Saint-Wulmer at Boulogne and Vasconvilliers. [d. 1113]

Blessed James of Certaldo, abbot. [d. 1292]

Blessed Ida of Louvain, virgin. [d. c. 1300]

Blessed Margaret of Cittæa-di-Castello, virgin. [d. 1320]

Blessed John Lockwood and **Blessed Edmund Catherick,** priests and martyrs. [d. 1642]

1346 Pope **Clement VI** excommunicates and dethrones **Holy Roman Emperor Louis IV.**

1598 **Henry IV** of France promulgates the **Edict of Nantes,** granting toleration to **Huguenots.**

1640 **Short Parliament** is convened by **Charles I** of England.

1742 Handel's *Messiah* premieres in Dublin, Ireland.

1749 **Radcliffe Library, Oxford University,** is opened.

1752 **Philadelphia Contributionship,** the first **fire insurance company** in colonial America, is established.

1848 **Sicily** declares itself independent of Naples.

1862 **Treaty of Saigon** between France and Annam is signed; France annexes **Cochin-China.**

1870 The **Metropolitan Museum of Art** is incorporated in New York City.

1913 An attempt on the life of **King Alfonso XIII** of Spain by the Catalonian anarchist, S. Alegre, fails.

1919 The **Amritsar Massacre** occurs in India, as a British commander orders his troops to fire on an unarmed assembly, killing 379 and wounding 1200.

1932 German government under Chancellor **Heinrich Brüning** imposes ban on Nazi storm troops.

1945 Nearly five square miles of **Tokyo** are destroyed in attacks by Allied bombers (**World War II**).

1960 *Transit I-B*, 265-pound U.S. experimental **space lighthouse,** designed as an aid to navigation, is placed in orbit from Cape Canaveral, Florida.

1962 **Ahti Karjalainen** becomes Finland's youngest prime minister at the age of 39.

1964 **Ian D. Smith** is named Prime Minister of Southern Rhodesia, succeeding Winston J. Field.

1968 Tanzania becomes the first country to grant recognition to the Nigerian secessionist state of **Biafra.**

1972 First players' strike in the history of **baseball** ends in its thirteenth day, forcing delay of the opening of the season until April 15.

1975 **President François Tombalbaye** of **Chad** is assassinated and his regime is overthrown by the army.

April 14

Holidays

Pan American Day
Commemorates the first International Conference of American States, 1890.

Chad **Independence Day**
Commemorates the promulgation of the nation's constitution, 1962.

Religious Calendar

The Saints
St. Ardalion, martyr. [d. c. 300]
St. Lambert, Archbishop of Lyons. [d. 688]

Birthdates

1527 **Ortelius (Abraham Oertel),** Flemish geographer, cartographer, and engraver. [d. 1598]

1578 **Philip III** of Spain, 1598–21; his reign was characterized by a peaceful foreign policy in western Europe. [d. March 31, 1621]

1629 **Christian Huygens,** Dutch physicist, mathematician, astronomer; developed many improvements in production of telescopes, including a new method of grinding lenses, negative eyepieces; also discovered a satellite and a ring of **Saturn**; with his brother was first to use pendulum to regulate clock movements. [d. June 8, 1695]

1812 **Sir George Grey,** British Colonial Governor of New Zealand, 1845–54, 1861–67. [d. September 20, 1898]

1813 **Junius Spencer Morgan,** U.S. merchant, philanthropist. [d. April 8, 1890]

1842 **Adna Chaffee,** U.S. Army Chief of Staff, 1904–06. [d. November 1, 1914]

1866 **Anne Sullivan (Macy),** U.S. teacher; best known for her work with **Helen Keller.** [d. October 20, 1936]

1868 **Peter Behrens,** German architect, artist; an early proponent of the use of steel and glass; developed modern industrial architectural style. [d. March 2, 1940]

1878 **George Malvin Holley,** U.S. industrialist; manufacturer of first practical **motorcycle,** 1899. [d. June 26, 1963]

1879 **James Branch Cabell,** U.S. novelist; wrote about first families of Virginia. [d. May 5, 1958]

1886 **Edward Chace Tolman,** U.S. psychologist; a leader in the **behaviorist** movement. [d. November 19, 1959]

1889 **Arnold Toynbee,** British historian; analyzed cyclical development and decline of civilizations. [d. October 22, 1975]

1892 **Vere Gordon Childe,** Australian archaeologist. [d. 1957]

1896 **Arthur Bartlett Homer,** U.S. industrialist, Bethlehem Steel Corporation's president and chief executive officer. [d. June 18, 1972]

1904 **Sir John Gielgud,** British actor, director; particularly distinguished as a Shakespearean actor.

1906 **Hastings Kamuzu Banda,** Malawian statesman; President, Republic of Malawi, 1966– .

1907 **François Duvalier (*Papa Doc*),** Haitian leader; President, 1957–71. [d. April 21, 1971]

1914 **Richard Salant,** U.S. communications executive.

1925 **Rod Steiger,** U.S. actor.

Abel Mozorewa, Zimbabwean statesman; Prime Minister of Zimbabwe, 1979–80; the first black to occupy the position.

1929 **Chadli Bendjedid,** Algerian leader; President, 1979– .

1935 **Erich von Däniken,** Swiss author.

St. Bernard of Tiron, abbot. Also called **Bernard of Abbeville.** [d. 1117]

St. Caradoc, hermit. [d. 1124]

St. Bénezet; one of the patrons of Avignon. Also called **Benedict, Little Benedict the Bridge Builder.** [d. 1184] SS. **John, Antony,** and **Eustace,** martyrs. [d. 1342] SS. **Tiburtius, Valerius,** and **Maximus,** martyrs. [death date unknown]

The Beatified

Blessed Lanvinus, Carthusian monk. [d. 1120]

Blessed Peter Gonzalez; patron of mariners. Also called **St. Elm, Elmo, Telm, Telmo.** [d. 1246]

Blessed Lydwina of Schiedam, virgin; patron of those who lead lives of intense suffering to expiate others' sins. Also called **Lidwina, Lydwid.** [d. 1433]

Historical Events

979   **Ethelred II** is crowned King of England.

1028   **Henry III** is elected King of Germany.

1191   **Henry VI** is crowned Holy Roman Emperor.

1471   In England the rebellious **Warwick** is defeated and killed by **Edward IV** at Barnet (**War of the Roses**).

1528   **Pánfilo de Narváez,** Spanish soldier, lands near **Tampa, Florida,** with group of 400 colonists.

1800   **Banque de France** is founded.

1828   **Noah Webster** obtains copyright for the first edition of his *American Dictionary of the English Language.*

1849   **Hungary** declares itself independent of **Austria.**

1865   U.S. President **Abraham Lincoln** is assassinated at Ford's Theater in Washington by **John Wilkes Booth.**

1879   An attempt to assassinate Russian **Czar Alexander II** is made by **Alexander Solovieff.**

1915   The **Battle of Shaiba** in Mesopotamia ends when British forces repel and rout a Turkish attack (**World War I**).

1929   Nationalist Chinese take control of **Manchuria.**

1930   **Jawarhalal Nehru** is arrested by the British government of India for abetting the manufacture of contraband salt.

1931   The **Republic of Spain** is established.

1937   **Richard Rodgers'** Musical comedy, *Babes in Arms,* with lyrics by **Lorenz Hart,** premieres in New York.

1959   **Taft Memorial Bell Tower** is dedicated in Washington, D.C., in memory of Robert Alphonso Taft, son of President **William Howard Taft.**

1962   **Georges Pompidou** is named Premier of France by President **Charles de Gaulle.**

       Chad promulgates its constitution.

1979   Liberian demonstration over food prices ends in rioting and granting of emergency powers to President **William R. Tolbert** for one year.

1981   U.S. **space shuttle** *Columbia* lands safely after a 36-orbit mission, its first.

April 15

Holidays

Bangladesh   **Bengali New Year**
Niger   Assumption of Power by the
   Supreme Military Council, 1974.

Religious Calendar

The Saints
SS. **Basilissa** and **Anastasia,** martyrs. [d. c. 65 A.D.]
St. **Padarn,** Bishop in Ceredigion; missionary and

Birthdates

1452 **Leonardo da Vinci,** Italian artist, architect, musician, scientist; considered one of the most versatile talents of all time, the ultimate Renaissance man. [d. May 2, 1519]

1469 **Nanak,** founder of **Sikhism,** an Indian religious sect. [d. 1538]

1646 **Christian V** of Denmark and Norway. [d. August 25, 1699]

1672 **Etienne (Geoffroy) Saint-Hilaire,** French naturalist; published first table of chemical affinities, 1718. [d. June 19, 1744]

1707 **Leonhard Euler,** Swiss mathematician; established many of the mathematical notations used today. [d. September 18, 1783]

1741 **Charles Wilson Peale,** U.S. painter; best known for portraits of American Revolutionary figures. [d. February 22, 1827]

1793 **Friedrich Georg Wilson von Struve,** German-Russian astronomer; pioneer in the study of **binary stars.** [d. November 23, 1864]

1797 **Louis Adolphe Thiers,** French statesman, historian; a founder and the first president of the Third Republic, 1871–73. [d. September 3, 1877]

1800 **Sir James Clark Ross,** British polar explorer; the first to explore **Antarctica,** 1839. [d. April 3, 1862]

1801 **Edouard Armand Isidore Hippolyte Lartet,** French paleontologist; regarded as one of the founders of **paleontology.** [d. January 28, 1871]

1809 **Hermann Günther Grassmann,** German mathematician, Sanskritist; laid foundation of modern **vector analysis.** [d. September 26, 1877]

1817 **Benjamin Jowett,** British theologian, classical scholar, and educational reformer; renowned for his translations of Plato and Aristotle. [d. October 1, 1893]

1820 **Mariano Melgarejo,** Bolivian ruler; President of Bolivia, 1864–71. [d. November 23, 1872]

1832 **Wilhelm Busch,** German poet, painter; originator of the **comic strip.** [d. January 9, 1908]

1843 **Henry James,** U.S.-British novelist, renowned for his prose style; became naturalized British citizen, 1915. [d. February 28, 1916]

1856 **Jean Moréas (Ioannes Papadiamanto-poulos),** French symbolist poet, born in Greece; organized **École Romane.** [d. March 30, 1910]

1858 **Émile Durkheim,** French sociologist; one of founders of modern sociology. [d. November 15, 1917]

1874 **Johannes Stark,** German physicist; Nobel Prize in physics for discoveries concerning electricity and light, 1919. [d. June 21, 1957]

1889 **Thomas Hart Benton,** U.S. painter, muralist; created an American artistic style called *Regionalism.* [d. January 19, 1975]

Asa Philip Randolph, U.S. labor leader; a pioneer in the unionization of blacks in America. [d. May 16, 1979]

1890 **Wallace Reid,** U.S. actor; leading man in silent films. [d. January 18, 1923]

1894 **Bessie Smith** (*The Empress of the Blues*), U.S. singer; legendary blues singer of 1920s–1930s. [d. September 26, 1937]

monastery founder. Also called **Patern.** [d. c. 5th-6th centuries]

St. Ruadan of Lothra, abbot, monastery founder; one of the Apostles of Ireland. Also called **Ruadhan.** [d. c. 584]

St. Hunna, matron. Also called the *Holy Washerwoman,* **Huva.** [d. c. 679]

1896　**Nikolay Nikolaevich Semenov,** Russian physical chemist; Nobel Prize in chemistry for study of kinetics of chemical reactions (with C. N. Hinshelwood), 1956.

1903　**Waverley L(ewis) Root,** U.S. writer, journalist; best known as author of *The Foods of France,* 1958, and *Contemporary French Cooking,* 1962. [d. October 31, 1982]

1907　**Nikolaas Tinbergen,** British ethologist; Nobel Prize in physiology or medicine for research in ethology (with K. Z. Lorenz and K. von Frisch), 1973.

1912　**Kim Il-Sung,** Korean political leader; organized Korean People's Revolutionary Army in Korean struggle against Japan.

1924　**Neville Marriner,** British conductor, musician.

1930　**Vigdís Finnbogadóttir,** Icelandic politician; President of Iceland, 1980– ; first woman to hold that position.

Historical Events

1450　French defeat English at **Formigny (Hundred Years' War).**

1861　U.S. President **Abraham Lincoln** calls for 75,000 volunteers to serve for three months in the Union Army (**U.S. Civil War**).

1891　**Katanga Company** is formed in Brussels to develop and settle the Katanga area in Central Africa.

1912　*Titanic,* largest passenger liner afloat, supposedly unsinkable, strikes an iceberg and sinks on its maiden voyage; over 1500 drown.

　　　Albert Einstein, during a lecture at Columbia University on his theory of relativity, speaks of *time* as the Fourth Dimension.

1927　**Chiang Kai-Shek** and conservative members of the Kuomintang split with the Communists at Hankow.

1938　Gen. Francisco Franco's forces capture **Vinaroz (Spanish Civil War).**

1942　The entire population of **Malta** is awarded the George Cross of Great Britain for gallantry under heavy fire (**World War II**).

1945　Prisoners of war in **Belsen,** a German concentration camp, are liberated by the British Second Army.

1963　About 70,000 persons participate in a **Ban the Bomb** rally in London, during which the British government's secret emergency plan is circulated.

1967　Peace demonstrators numbering over 100,000 march through the streets of New York City and assemble before the United Nations in protest against the **Vietnam War.**

1968　Two unmanned Russian satellites in earth orbit find each other by radar, maneuver together, and dock automatically.

1971　Yugoslav Ambassador to Sweden **Vladimir Lolovic** dies of gunshot wounds received a week earlier in an attack by Croatian separatists.

1974　**Hamani Diori,** President of Niger, is deposed.

April 16

Holidays

Denmark   **Queen Margrethe's Birthday**
Celebrates the queen's birth, 1940.

Puerto Rico   **de Diego's Birthday**
Commemorates the birthday of José de Diego, poet and statesman, 1867.

Religious Calendar

The Saints

SS. Optatus and his companions, and **St. Encratis,** virgin, martyrs. St. Encratis also called **Engratia.** [d. 304]

Birthdates

1319   **John II (the Good)** of France, acceded to the throne 1350. [d. April 8, 1364]

1646   **Jules Hardouin-Mansart,** French architect; designed the **Galerie de Glaces** at **Versailles.** Building superintendent and architect of Louis XIV. [d. May 11, 1708]

1660   **Sir Hans Sloane,** English physician, naturalist; his museum and library formed the nucleus of the **British Museum.** [d. 1753]

1661   **Charles Montagu, 1st Earl of Halifax,** English politician and poet; first Lord of Treasury and Prime Minister. [d. 1715]

1728   **Joseph Black,** Scottish chemist; evolved theory of **latent heat.** [d. December 6, 1799]

1786   **Sir John Franklin,** English naval officer, explorer; lost in the Arctic while searching for the **Northwest Passage.** [d. June 11, 1847]

1821   **Ford Madox Brown,** British romantic painter; teacher of **Dante Gabriel Rossetti.** [d. October 11, 1893]

1838   **Ernest Solvay,** Belgian industrial chemist; patented the **Solvay ammonia process** for the manufacture of sodium carbonate, 1861. [d. May 26, 1922]

1844   **Anatole France (Jacques Anatole Thibault),** French novelist, poet, critic; Nobel Prize in literature, 1921. [d. October 13, 1924]

1850   **Herbert Baxter Adams,** U.S. historian; a founder and first secretary of **American Historical Association.** [d. July 30, 1901]

1854   **Jacob Sechler Coxey,** U.S. reformer; leader of the 1894 march of the unemployed on Washington, D.C. called *Coxey's Army.* [d. May 18, 1951]

1856   **Albert Blake Dick,** U.S. inventor of **mimeograph process** and machines; founder of A. B. Dick Co. [d. August 15, 1934]

1867   **Wilbur Wright,** U.S. aviation pioneer; with his brother Orville (August 19) made first powered, controlled, sustained airplane flight on December 17, 1903, at **Kitty Hawk, North Carolina.** [d. May 30, 1912]

1871   **John Millington Synge,** Irish dramatist, poet; noted for his portrayal of primitive life. [d. March 24, 1909]

1881   **Edward Wood, Earl of Halifax,** British statesman, diplomat; Viceroy of India, 1925–31; British Foreign Secretary, 1938–40. [d. December 23, 1959]

1889   **Charlie (Sir Charles Spencer) Chaplin,** English comedian, producer, director; the beloved *Little Tramp* of the silent-film era. [d. December 25, 1977]

1904   **Lily Pons (Alice Josephine Pons),** U.S. operatic soprano. [d. February 13, 1976]

1915   **Walter Washington,** U.S. politician, lawyer; Mayor of Washington, D.C., 1975–80.

1921   **Peter (Alexander) Ustinov,** British actor, producer, writer.

1922   **Kingsley Amis,** British author.

1924   **Henry Mancini,** U.S. composer.

1930   **Herbie Mann (Herbert Jay Solomon),** U.S. jazz musician.

St. **Turibius,** Bishop of Astorga. [d. c. 450]

St. **Paternus,** Bishop of Avranches. Also called **Pair.** [d. 564]

St. **Fructuosus,** Archbishop of Braga. [d. 665]

St. **Magnus of Orkney,** martyr. Son of king of Orkneys. Patron saint of fishmongers. Also called **Mans.** [d. 1116]

St. **Drogo.** Patron of shepherds. Invoked against ruptures, hernias, and unpleasant births. Also called **Drugo, Druon.** [d. 1189]

St. **Contardo,** the pilgrim. [d. 1249]

St. **Benedict Joseph Labre,** mendicant. Patron of displaced persons. Also called the *Beggar of Rome.* [d. 1783]

St. **Bernadette,** virgin and visionary. [d. 1879]

The Beatified

Blessed Joachim of Siena. [d. 1305]

Blessed William of Polizzi, mendicant religious; patron of Castelbuono. [d. c. 1317]

Blessed Archangelo of Bologna. [d. 1513]

1940   **Margrethe II** of Denmark; acceded to throne January 14, 1972; first woman to rule Denmark.

Historical Events

1175   **Treaty of Montebello** is signed between **Frederick I, Holy Roman Emperor,** and the Lombard League.

1712   The **Peace of Constantinople** ends war between Russia and the Ottoman Empire.

1746   **Battle of Culloden,** in Scotland, results in final defeat of Jacobites by the English.

1853   The first **Indian railway,** from Bombay to Tannah, is opened.

1883   **Paul Kruger,** Boer leader, is elected President of the **South African Republic.**

1912   **Harriet Quimby** becomes first woman to fly across the English Channel.

1917   The **Second Battle of the Aisne** opens between Soissons and Reims (**World War I**).

1922   The **Treaty of Rapallo** is signed by Germany and the Soviet Union resulting in resumption of diplomatic relations and renunciation of reparations for World War I.

1941   German raider *Atlantis* attacks and sinks an Egyptian passenger liner with 138 Americans aboard, arousing great anti-German sentiment in the U.S. (**World War II**).

1945   U.S. troops land on Ie Shima in Ryuku Islands (**World War II**).

1972   Two giant pandas, given to the U.S. by China in return for a pair of musk oxen, arrive at the National Zoo in Washington, D.C.

April 17

Holidays

American Samoa	**Flag Day** Commemorates signing of Instrument of Cession, 1900, and establishment of Samoan constitutional government, 1960.
Japan	**Children's Protection Day** Commemorates passage of laws protecting juveniles.
Syria	**Evacuation Day** or **Independence Day** Commemorates withdrawal of French troops, 1946.
Zimbabwe	**Independence Day** Commemorates the achievement of independence from Great Britain, 1980.

Birthdates

1586 **John Ford,** English playwright. [death date unknown]

1622 **Henry Vaughan,** Welsh mystic poet, translator. [d. 1695]

1676 **Frederick I** of Sweden, 1720–51; his rule superseded by a powerful parliament. [d. March 25, 1751]

1741 **Samuel Chase,** U.S. jurist, lawyer; signer of the Declaration of Independence; U.S. Supreme Court Justice, 1796–1811. [d. June 19, 1811]

1806 **William Gilmore Simms,** U.S. poet; wrote numerous histories of the American South. [d. June 11, 1870]

1837 **John Pierpont Morgan,** U.S. financier, philanthropist; controlled one of the most prosperous and powerful financial empires in the world. [d. March 31, 1913]

1842 **Charles Henry Parkhurst,** U.S. clergyman; remembered for denunciation of crime in New York City government. President of **Society for the Prevention of Crime.** [d. September 8, 1933]

1845 **Isabel Barrows,** U.S. editor; early penologist. [d. October 25, 1913]

1851 **(Adrian) Cap Anson,** pioneer U.S. baseball player. [d. April 14, 1922]

1859 **Walter (Chauncey) Camp,** U.S. football player, coach, athletic director; called the Father of American Football. [d. March 14, 1925]

1866 **Ernest Henry Starling,** British physiologist; with W. M. Bayliss, discovered hormone **secretin,** 1902. [d. May 2, 1927]

1874 **Charles Hungerford Mackay,** U.S. financier, art patron. [d. November 12, 1938]

1880 **Sir Charles Leonard Woolley,** British archaeologist; excavated **Ur of the Chaldees.** [d. 1960]

1894 **Nikita Khrushchev,** Russian Communist leader; Premier of the Soviet Union, 1958–64. [d. September 11, 1971]

1897 **Thornton (Niven) Wilder,** U.S. playwright, and novelist. [d. December 7, 1975]

1915 **Rebekah (West) Harkness,** U.S. philanthropist, patron of dance; President and Director of William Hale Harkness Foundation; supported Robert Joffrey Ballet and Jerome Robbins Ballet; President and Artistic Director, Harkness Ballet, 1970–75. [d. June 17, 1982]

1916 **Sirimavo Bandaranaike,** Ceylonese stateswoman; first woman to hold position of Prime Minister, 1960–65, 1970–77.

1918 **William Holden (William Beedle),** U.S. actor. [d. November 16, 1981]

1923 **Harry Reasoner,** U.S. television news correspondent.

Religious Calendar

The Saints

St. Anicetus, pope and martyr. Elected 155. [d. c. 165]

SS. Mappalicus and his companions, martyrs. [d. c. 250]

St. Innocent, Bishop of Tortona. [d. c. 350]

SS. Donnan and his companions, monks and martyrs. [d. 618]

St. Robert of Chaise-Dieu, abbot; founder of Benedictine abbey in Auvergne. Also called **Robert de Turlande.** [d. 1067]

St. Stephen Harding, Abbot of Cîteaux; co-founder of Cistercian Order. [d. 1134]

The Beatified

Blessed Eberhard of Marchthal, abbot. [d. 1178]

Blessed James of Cerqueto, Augustinian monk. [d. 1367]

Blessed Clare of Pisa, widow and prioress. [d. 1419]

Blessed Kateri Tekakwitha. [beatified 1980]

Historical Events

1194 Second coronation of **Richard I** of England takes place upon his return from the **Third Crusade.**

1492 **Christopher Columbus** receives his commission from the Spanish monarchy to explore the western ocean.

1521 **Martin Luther** is excommunicated by **Diet of Worms.**

1555 Spaniards capture **Siena** and sell it to **Cosimo de Medici.**

1711 **Josef I, Holy Roman Emperor,** dies and is succeeded by **Charles VI.**

1895 The Sino-Japanese **Treaty of Shimonoseki** is signed, ending warfare and recognizing the independence of **Korea.**

1922 **Dom Miguel of Portugal** renounces succession in favor of **Dom Duarte Nuna.**

1941 Yugoslavian army surrenders to invading Germans (**World War II**).

1946 **Syria** gains independence.

1961 **Bay of Pigs,** attempted invasion of **Cuba** by American-backed troops, begins.

1969 **Sirhan Bishara Sirhan** is convicted by a Los Angeles jury of first-degree murder for the slaying of Senator **Robert F. Kennedy.**

1974 Nigerian army, under Chief of Staff Lt. Col. **Seyni Kountché,** takes power in Niger, ousting President **Hamani Diori.**

1975 War in **Cambodia** ends with the takeover of **Phnom Penh** by **Khmer Rouge** troops.

1977 Women vote in **Liechtenstein** for the first time.

1980 **Zimbabwe,** formerly **Rhodesia,** gains its independence.

1982 Queen Elizabeth II proclaims **Constitution Act,** supplanting British North America Act of 1867 and bringing **Canada** solely under its own jurisdiction.

April 18

Holidays

Religious Calendar

The Saints
St. Apollonius, the Apologist, martyr. [d. c. 185]
St. Laserian, Bishop of Leighlin. Also called Laisren, Molaisre, or Molaisse. [d. 639]

Birthdates

1480 **Lucrezia Borgia,** Duchess of Ferrara, Italian noblewoman; her name, long associated with vice and crime, has recently been vindicated. [d. June 24, 1519]

1740 **Sir Francis Baring,** English banker, merchant; director of **East India Company.** [d. 1810]

1759 **Thomas Thorild,** Swedish poet, critic, and philosopher; sympathizer with revolutionary leaders in France. [d. October 1, 1808]

1789 **John Young Mason,** U.S. politician, jurist, diplomat; U.S. Congressman, 1831–37; U.S. Secretary of the Navy, 1844–45; 1846–49; U.S. Attorney General, 1845–46. [d. October 3, 1859]

1817 **George Henry Lewes,** British critic, philosopher; associated with **Marian Evans (George Eliot).** [d. November 28, 1878]

1842 **Antero de Quental,** Portuguese poet, philosopher; known for his extremely pessimistic works. [d. September 11, 1891]

1857 **Clarence (Seward) Darrow,** U.S. labor and criminal lawyer; served as defense counsel in many notable trials. [d. March 13, 1938]

1864 **Richard Harding Davis,** U.S. author, journalist; best-known and most influential U.S. reporter of his era. [d. April 11, 1916]

1882 **Leopold Stokowski,** British-U.S. conductor. [d. September 13, 1977]

1902 **Giuseppe Pella,** Italian economist, legislator; Prime Minister of Italy, 1953–54 (for five months); his administration marked by crisis with Yugoslavia over Trieste. [d. May 31, 1981]

1907 **Rául Roa y García,** Cuban government official, lawyer; responsible for strengthening Cuban ties with the Soviet Union. [d. July 6, 1982]

1911 **Maurice Goldhaber,** Austrian-U.S. physicist; responsible for breakthroughs in study of **neutron physics** and nuclear reactor technology.

1918 **Frederika (Louise),** consort of **Paul I,** King of the Hellenes, mother of former King Constantine of Greece and Queen Sofia of Spain. [d. February 6, 1981]

1934 **George Shirley,** U.S. operatic tenor.

Historical Events

1328 **Holy Roman Emperor Louis IV** of Bavaria deposes **Pope John XXII** for heresy and lese majesty.

1775 **Paul Revere,** American patriot, makes his famous midnight ride to warn colonists of advance of British troops.

1847 U.S. General **Winfield Scott** wins **Battle of Cerro Gordo (Mexican War).**

1897 **Greece** declares war on **Turkey.**

1906 **San Francisco** is destroyed by the most devastating **earthquake** in U.S. history.

1909 **Joan of Arc** is beatified in ceremony held at St. Peter's in Rome.

1916 Russians capture port of **Trebizond** on the Black Sea from the Turks (**World War I**).

1922 **Vilna** is incorporated into Poland.

1923 **Yankee Stadium** opens in New York City.

1927 **Chiang Kai-shek** inaugurates moderate Nationalist government of China at Nanking.

1942 Sixteen American bombers under the command of **Col. James Doolittle** successfully attack **Tokyo, Yokohama,** and **Nagoya (World War II).**

1945 **League of Nations** votes to dissolve, transferring its material property to the **United Nations.**

1951 France, West Germany, Italy, Belgium, the Netherlands, and Luxembourg sign a trea-

St. Deicola, Abbot of Bosham. Also called **Dicuill, Dicul.** [d. 7th century]

St. Idesbald, Abbot of Our Lady of the Dunes Abbey, in France. [d. 1167]

St. Galdinus, Archbishop of Milan and Cardinal; patron of **Milan.** [d. 1176]

SS. Eleutherius and his companions, martyrs. [death date unknown]

ty establishing a single market for coal and steel; this constitutes an important first step in the direction of **European economic union.**

1960 **Tangier** is reintegrated financially and economically with **Morocco.**

1963 Successful **transplants of human nerves** are reported by **James B. Campbell** of the New York University Medical Center.

1975 U.S. President Gerald Ford initiates the **American Revolution Bicentennial,** a nationwide celebration, on the 200th anniversary of Paul Revere's famous ride.

1978 U.S. Senate ratifies second **Panama Canal Treaty** providing for operation and defense of the canal until 1999.

April 19

Holidays

Sierra Leone	**Republic Anniversary Day** Commemorates the founding of the Republic, 1971.
Uruguay	**Landing of the 33 Orientales,** or **33 Immortals** Commemorates landing of 33 patriotic exiles in 1825, an event that ultimately resulted in independence of Uruguay from Brazil.
Venezuela	**Independence Day** Commemorates the birth of the Republic, 1830.

Birthdates

1721 **Roger Sherman,** U.S. statesman, lawyer, surveyor; signer of the Declaration of Independence, the Articles of Association, the Articles of Confederation, and the Constitution; the only person who signed all four documents. [d. July 23, 1793]

1772 **David Ricardo,** English political economist; founder of the classical school of economics. [d. September 11, 1823]

1793 **Ferdinand I,** Emperor of Austria. [d. June 29, 1875]

1795 **Christian Ehrenberg,** German naturalist; founder of **protozoology.** [d. 1876]

1832 **José Echegaray y Eizaguirre,** Spanish dramatist, mathematician; Nobel Prize in literature, 1904. [d. September 14, 1916]

1865 **May Robson (Mary Robison),** U.S. character actress. [d. October 20, 1942]

1877 **Gertrude Vanderbilt Whitney,** U.S. sculptor; conceived and financed **Whitney Museum of American Art,** 1931. [d. April 18, 1942]

1883 **Getulio Dorneles Vargas,** Brazilian leader; President, 1930–45, 1951–54. [d. August 24, 1954]

1900 **Richard Hughes,** British novelist.

1901 **Edith (Clara) Summerskill, Baroness Summerskill,** British politician, physician; a founder of the **Socialist Medical Association,** which led to the establishment of the National Health Service, 1948. [d. February 4, 1980]

1903 **Eliot Ness,** U.S. government agent; headed investigation of **Al Capone,** notorious Chicago gangster, 1929–32. [d. May 7, 1957]

1912 **Glenn T. Seaborg,** U.S. nuclear chemist, physicist; Nobel Prize in chemistry for isolating and identifying elements heavier than uranium (with E. M. McMillan), 1951.

1921 **Yitzhak Navon,** Israeli statesman; President, 1978–83.

Historical Events

1012 In England, Danes murder **Archbishop Elfheah** and are bought off by **King Ethelred.**

1428 **Peace of Ferrara** is signed, in which Milan cedes **Brescia** and **Bergamo** to Venice.

1539 **Truce of Frankfort** between **Holy Roman Emperor Charles V** and his rebellious Protestant subjects is signed.

1587 **Sir Francis Drake** of England attacks **Cadiz,** destroying 33 Spanish vessels and escaping unscathed.

1713 **Charles VI, Holy Roman Emperor,** issues **Pragmatic Sanction,** giving females the right of succession in Hapsburg possessions.

1770 **Captain James Cook** sights the eastern coast of **Australia.**

1775 The **American Revolution** begins with the battles of **Lexington** and **Concord.**

1839 **Treaty of London** is signed, establishing recognition of **Kingdom of Belgium** by all the states of Europe.

1850 **Clayton-Bulwer Treaty** between U.S. and Great Britain is signed, providing that neither country may obtain exclusive con-

Religious Calendar

The Saints

St. Ursmar, abbot and bishop. [d. 713]

St. Geroldus, recluse. [d. 978]

St. Alphege, Archbishop of Canterbury and martyr. Also called **Aelfheah,** or **Elphege.** [d. 1012]

St. Leo IX, pope. Elected 1049. Originator of the Crusades. [d. 1054]

The Beatified

Blessed Bernard the Penitent. [d. 1181]

Blessed Conrad of Ascoli, Franciscan and papal legate. [d. 1289]

Blessed James Duckett, martyr. Patron of booksellers and publishers. [d. 1602]

trol over proposed interoceanic canal in Central America.

1853 Russia claims protectorate over Turkey in a prelude to the **Crimean War.**

1861 Blockade of Confederate ports is proclaimed by Union forces (**U.S. Civil War**).

1917 The **Second Battle of Gaza** ends in British failure to dislodge the Turks (**World War I**).

The first American shot of **World War I** is fired from the steamer *Mongolia* in repulsing a German submarine attack.

1919 **Jozef Pilsudski** and Polish army drive Bolsheviks out of **Vilna.**

1928 *Oxford English Dictionary* is completed.

1932 The U.S. officially abandons the **gold standard.**

1945 **Rodgers' and Hammerstein's** *Carousel* premieres in New York.

1961 U.S. soldiers officially assume positions as advisors to **Laotian army.**

1971 **Sierra Leone** declares itself a republic within the British Commonwealth.

April 20

The Saints

St. Marcellinus, first bishop of Embrun. [d. c. 374]

St. Marcian, monk. Also called **Marian.** [d. c. 488]

St. Caedwalla, King of the West Saxons. [d. 689]

Birthdates

121   **Marcus Aurelius,** Roman Emperor. [d. A.D. 180]

1492   **Pietro Aretino,** Italian man of letters, notorious libertine. [d. October 21, 1556]

1745   **Philippe Pinel,** French physician; primary founder of **psychiatry**; first to call insanity a disease rather than result of possession by demons. [d. October 26, 1826]

1786   **Marc Séguin,** French engineer; inventor of the wire-cable **suspension bridge** and the tubular steam-engine boiler. [d. February 24, 1875]

1807   **Louis Jacques Napoleon Bertrand (*Aloysius*),** French writer of prose poems. [d. April 29, 1841]

1808   **Napoleon III (*Louis Napoleon*),** Emperor of France, 1852–70. [d. January 9, 1873]

1839   **Carol I,** first king of Romania; ruled 1866–1914. [d. October 10, 1914]

1850   **Daniel Chester French,** U.S. sculptor; created statue of Lincoln in the **Lincoln Memorial.** [d. October 7, 1931]

1868   **Charles Maurras,** French writer, philosopher; founder of **Action Française.** [d. 1952]

1880   **Sol Harry Goldberg,** U.S. manufacturer. [d. June 4, 1940]

1882   **Holland McTyeire (*Howlin' Mad*) Smith,** U.S. Marine Corps general during World War II. [d. January 12, 1967]

1889   **Adolf Hitler,** German politician; leader of the National Socialist Workers' (Nazi) Party, 1921–45; dictator of Germany, 1933–45. [d. April 30, 1945]

1893   **Joan Miró,** Spanish Surrealist painter. [d. December 25, 1983]

1900   **Norman Norell,** U.S. clothing designer. [d. October 25, 1972]

1903   **Gregor Piatigorsky,** U.S. cello virtuoso born in Russia. [d. August 6, 1976]

1904   **Edward Louis Bartlett,** U.S. politician, gold miner, newspaperman. [d. December 11, 1968]

1905   **Harold Stanley Marcus,** U.S. retailer; President of Nieman-Marcus Co., 1950–72.

1910   **Robert (Ferdinand) Wagner, Jr.,** U.S. politician, diplomat; Mayor of New York City, 1954–66.

1920   **John Paul Stevens,** U.S. jurist; Associate Justice of Supreme Court, 1975– .

1924   **Nina Foch,** Dutch actress.

Historical Events

1534   **Jacques Cartier,** French explorer, reaches **Labrador.**

1653   In England, **Oliver Cromwell** expels **Long Parliament** for attempting to pass **Perpetuation Bill** which would have kept parliament in the hands of only a few members.

1657   Spanish West Indian fleet is destroyed by the English under Admiral **Robert Blake** in the harbor of **Santa Cruz de Tenerife.**

1792   **France** declares war on Austria, Prussia, and Sardinia.

1890   The **Haka Road** connecting Burma and India is completed.

1911   Decree for separation of church and state in **Portugal** is issued.

1915   The **Armenians** revolt against Turkish atrocities and seize the fortress at **Van** in the Caucasus (**World War I**).

1916   The French counter-attack German positions on the east bank of the Meuse at the **Battle of Verdun** (**World War I**).

     Sir Roger Casement lands in Ireland to incite rebellion against British involvement in **World War I;** subsequently, he is hanged as a traitor.

1920   **Montenegro** becomes part of **Yugoslavia.**

1941   German troops occupy **Belgrade,** Yugoslavia (**World War II**).

St. Hildegund, virgin. [d. 1188]

St. Agnes of Montepulciano, virgin and founder of Dominican nunnery at Montepulciano. [d. 1317]

The Beatified

Blessed Hugh of Anzy, prior. [d. c. 930]

Blessed Simon of Todi, Augustinian prior. [d. 1322]

Blessed James Bell and **Blessed John Finch,** martyrs. [d. 1584]

Blessed Robert Watkinson and **Blessed Francis Page,** priests and martyrs. [d. 1602]

1943   Germans massacre Jews in **Warsaw ghetto.**

1947   **King Christian X** of Denmark dies and is succeeded by his son, **Frederick IX.**

1961   **Fidel Castro** proclaims a victory after last of the Cuban rebel invaders are captured at **Playa Giron** near the original landing point of the **Bay of Pigs** invasion.

1969   Terrorists attack nine post offices and a bus station in a weekend of violence among Roman Catholics, Protestants, and police in **Northern Ireland.**

1978   A South Korean Boeing 707 is shot down, killing two persons and injuring 13, when the plane strays into Russian territory.

1979   **Palace of the Senators** on Capitoline Hill in Rome is bombed by a neo-Fascist organization and a previously unknown group, the **Italian Popular Movement.**

1982   Spain reopens its border with British-owned **Gibraltar** after a lapse of 12 years.

April 21

Holidays

Brazil   **Independence Hero Tiradentes (Tiradentes Day)**
Commemorates the execution of Joaquim José de Silva Xavier, conspirator in revolt against Portugal, 1789.

Indonesia   **Kartini Day**
A day of tribute to Baden Adjeng Kartini, leader in the emancipation of Indonesian women.

Birthdates

1488   **Ulrich von Hutten,** German author, humanist, and soldier. [d. September 1523]

1555   **Ludovico Carracci,** Italian painter; a pioneer of Italian baroque painting. [d. November 13, 1619]

1634   **Jan van Riebeeck,** Dutch surgeon; founder of **Cape Town, South Africa.**

1729   **Catherine the Great (Catherine II),** Empress of Russia. [d. November 6, 1796]

1816   **Charlotte (Currer Bell) Brontë (Mrs. A. B. Nicholls),** British novelist, poet; best known as the author of *Jane Eyre*; sister of Ann (January 17) and Emily Brontë (July 30). [d. March 31, 1855]

1828   **Hippolyte Adolphe Taine,** French literary critic, historian, positivist philosopher. [d. March 5, 1893]

1837   **Fredrik Bajer,** Danish statesman, writer; Nobel Peace Prize for his work in helping found the International Peace Bureau, 1908. [d. January 22, 1922]

1838   **John Muir,** U.S. naturalist; primary force behind U.S. **land conservation** movement. [d. December 24, 1914]

1843   **Walther Flemming,** German anatomist; discovered **chromosomes** and process of **mitosis.** [d. August 5, 1905]

1864   **Max Weber,** German sociologist; founder of modern **sociology.** [d. June 14, 1920]

1865   **Frederick Albert Cook,** U.S. physician, Arctic explorer; claimed to have been the first person to reach the **North Pole.** [d. August 5, 1940]

1872   **Friedrich Wilhelm Froebel,** German educator; founder of the **kindergarten system.** [d. June 21, 1952]

1882   **Percy Williams Bridgman,** U.S. physicist; philosopher of science; Nobel Prize in physics for development of high pressure chambers for study of matter at extreme pressure, 1946. [d. August 20, 1961]

1889   **Paul Karrer,** Swiss chemist; Nobel Prize in chemistry for investigations into chemistry of **carotenoids, flavins,** and **Vitamins A and B$_2$,** 1937. [d. June 18, 1971]

1905   **(Edmund Gerald) Pat Brown,** U.S. politician, lawyer; Governor of California, 1958–66. Father of Edmund G. (Gerry) Brown, Jr. (July 7).

1911   **Leonard Warren (Leonard Vaarenov),** U.S. operatic baritone. [d. March 4, 1960]

1915   **Anthony (Rudolph) Quinn,** U.S. actor; a specialist in ethnic roles.

1926   **Elizabeth II,** Queen of Great Britain and Northern Ireland, 1952– .

Historical Events

1408   **Ladislaus, King of Naples,** seizes Rome for the first time in attempt to conquer Italy.

1509   **Henry VII** of England dies and is succeeded by **Henry VIII.**

1538   **John Calvin,** Protestant religious reformer, is banished from Geneva, Switzerland.

1836   Texans under General **Sam Houston** defeat the Mexican forces of **Santa Anna** at **San Jacinto.**

1912   **Tibet** becomes a province of China.

1914   U.S. Marines occupy port of **Veracruz, Mexico** in effort to prevent German ship from unloading munitions there. The inci-

U.S. (Texas)   San Jacinto Day
                 Commemorates the Battle of
                 San Jacinto, 1836.

Religious Calendar

The Saints

SS. Simeon Barsabae, Bishop of Seleucia-Ctesiphon, and his companions, martyrs. [d. 341]

St. Anastasius I, Patriarch of Antioch. [d. 599]

St. Beuno, Abbot of Clynnog. Also called **Beunor.** [d. c. 640]

St. Malrubius, abbot. Also called **Maelrubha.** [d. 722]

St. Anselm, Archbishop of Canterbury and Doctor of the Church. Also called **Anselem,** *Father of Scholasticism.* [d. 1109] Optional Memorial.

St. Conrad of Parzham, Capuchin lay-brother. [d. 1894]

dent nearly causes war between Mexico and the U.S.

1918 **Manfred von Richthofen, the *Red Baron*** German air ace, dies in battle over France (**World War I**).

1922 Civil war begins in **China** between the War Lord of Manchuria and the War Lord of the Yangtze.

1927 **Fascist Charter of Labor** is promulgated by **Benito Mussolini** of Italy.

1960 **Brasilia,** the new city in Brazil's interior, is proclaimed the national capitol.

1963 **Bruno M. Pontecorvo,** atomic scientist who defected from Britain to the U.S.S.R. in 1950, is named a winner of the Lenin Prize in science.

1966 Opening of the **British Parliament** is telecast for the first time.

1967 **George Papadopoulos** stages a coup d'état, gaining control of the government of Greece.

1970 **Bruno Kreisky** is sworn in as Chancellor of Austria.

1972 U.S. *Apollo 16* astronauts **Charles M. Duke, Jr.** and **John W. Young** walk on surface of moon and collect 214 pounds of lunar rocks and soil.

1975 South Vietnamese president **Nguyen Van Thieu** resigns after ten years in office.

1979 **United African National Council** wins Rhodesia's first universal suffrage elections; **Bishop Abel Muzorewa** is elected prime minister.

April 22

Holidays

Spain	**Queen Isabella Day** Honors the birth of the Spanish queen who sponsored Christopher Columbus's voyage to the New World.
U.S. (Delaware, Nebraska)	**Arbor Day** Commemorates birthday of J. Sterling Morton, Nebraska politician and agriculturist.
U.S. (Oklahoma)	**Oklahoma Day** Commemorates the opening of the Oklahoma Territory for settlement, 1889.

Birthdates

1451   **Isabella I,** Queen of Castile, 1474–1504; patron of **Christopher Columbus.** [d. November 26, 1504]

1707   **Henry Fielding,** English novelist, playwright; among his best known works are *Tom Jones* and *Joseph Andrews.* [d. October 8, 1754]

1711   **Eleazar Wheelock,** U.S. educator; founder of **Hanover, New Hampshire,** and of **Dartmouth College;** first president of Dartmouth, 1770–79. [d. April 24, 1779]

1724   **Immanuel Kant,** German philosopher; one of foremost thinkers of the Enlightenment. [d. February 12, 1804]

1766   **Anne Louise Germaine,** Baroness of Staël-Holstein (**Madame de Staël**), French novelist, critic; an enemy of Napoleon; exiled during French Revolution. [d. July 14, 1817]

1832   **Julius Sterling Morton,** U.S. politician, agriculturist; responsible for establishment of **Arbor Day** in several U.S. states.

1854   **Henri La Fontaine,** Belgian lawyer, politician; Nobel Peace Prize for establishing **Permanent Court of International Justice,** 1913. [d. May 14, 1943]

1861   **Count Nobuaki Makino,** Japanese statesman; Japanese representative at Paris Peace Conference, 1919. [d. January 25, 1949]

1874   **Ellen Glasgow,** U.S. novelist. [d. November 21, 1945]

1876   **Robert Bárány,** Austrian otologist; Nobel Prize in physiology or medicine for his work on the physiology and pathology of the inner ear, 1914. [d. April 8, 1936]

O(le) E(dvart) Rolvaag, U.S. novelist, educator, born in Norway; author of *Giants in the Earth.* [d. November 5, 1931]

1881   **Aleksandr Feodorovich Kerenski,** Russian revolutionary leader; prime minister of post-revolutionary Russia; overthrown by Bolsheviks. [d. June 11, 1970]

1887   **James Hall,** U.S. novelist, short-story writer; collaborator with C. B. Nordhoff (February 1) on *Mutiny on the Bounty* and *Pitcairn's Island.* [d. July 5, 1951]

1891   **Nicola Sacco,** U.S. radical, factory worker; with Bartolomeo Vanzetti (July 11), was tried, convicted, and executed for a 1920 robbery and shooting; became martyrs representing an aggrieved Italian-American community. They were pardoned in 1977 by proclamation of the Governor of Massachusetts. [d. by electrocution August 23, 1927]

1899   **Vladimir Nabokov,** U.S. novelist, short-story writer, born in Russia; gained international attention with his 1950s novel *Lolita.* [d. July 2, 1977]

1904   **J. Robert Oppenheimer,** U.S. physicist; headed Los Alamos, New Mexico laboratories during development of first **atomic bombs.** [d. February 18, 1967]

1916   **Yehudi Menuhin,** U.S. violin virtuoso.

1922   **Charles Mingus,** U.S. jazz musician; a major figure in jazz of the 1950s and 1960s. [d. January 12, 1979]

1938   **Glen Campbell,** U.S. country-rock singer.

1939   **Jason Miller,** U.S. playwright, actor.

U.S.S.R.	**V. I. Lenin Memorial Day**
	Commemorates the leader of the revolutionary movement in Russia.
U.S.	**Earth Day**
	Sponsored by Environmental Action, Inc., Washington, D.C.

Religious Calendar

The Saints

SS. Soter and **Caius,** popes and martyrs. Elected, respectively, c. 173 and 283. Caius also called **Gaius.** [d. 174 and 296]

SS. Epipodius and **Alexander,** martyrs. [d. 178]

St. Leonides, martyr. [d. 202]

St. Agapitus I, pope. Elected 535. Also called **Agapetus.** [d. 536]

St. Theodore of Sykeon, Bishop of Anastasiopolis. [d. 613]

St. Opportuna, virgin and abbess. [d. c. 770]

The Beatified

Blessed Wolfhelm, abbot. [d. 1091]

Blessed Francis of Fabriano, Franciscan friar. First Franciscan to form a library. [d. c. 1322]

Blessed Bartholomew of Cervere, martyr. [d. 1466]

Historical Events

1124 **Alexander I** of Scotland dies and is succeeded by **David I.**

1500 **Pedro Alvarez Cabral** reaches the coast of **Brazil** and claims the territory for Portugal.

1529 **Treaty of Saragossa** defines Spanish-Portuguese frontier in Pacific; Spain gives up **Molucca Islands.**

1793 **George Washington,** U.S. president, issues proclamation of neutrality in effort to keep the U.S. from becoming embroiled in war between Britain and France.

1834 The **Quadruple Alliance** is formed between Great Britain, France, Portugal, and Spain, supporting **Isabella II** of Spain against the pretender, Don Carlos.

The island of **Saint Helena** is placed under the direct administration of the British government.

1884 The U.S. becomes the first nation to recognize the **International Association of the Congo** as a federal state.

1889 Unoccupied land in **Oklahoma,** formerly in Indian hands, is opened to white settlers.

1900 French are victorious over the Muslims in the battle for control of **Chad.**

1915 The first use of **poison gas** (chlorine) as a battle weapon is instituted by the Germans against French colonial troops in the **Second Battle of Ypres (World War I).**

1918 Women in **Denmark** vote for the first time.

1920 **Leningrad** becomes the new name of **Petrograd** (formerly **St. Petersburg**).

1960 **American Lutheran Church** is formed in Minneapolis by the merger of three major Lutheran denominations–Evangelical Lutheran, American Lutheran, and United Evangelical Lutheran churches.

1970 **Earth Day** observances focus attention on environmental problems in communities throughout the U.S.

1971 Death of Haitian President **François Duvalier** is announced; his son Jean-Claude is sworn in as President for Life.

1975 A bloodless military coup d'état ousts Honduran chief of state General **Oswaldo López Arellano.**

April 23

Holidays

Bermuda   **Peppercorn Day**
Commemorates payment of one peppercorn to Bermuda governor for use of Old State House by Masonic Lodge, 1816.

England   **St. George's Day**
Celebrates St. George, patron saint of England.

Turkey   **National Sovereignty Day**
Commemorates inauguration of Grand National Assembly, 1923.

Birthdates

1484 **Julius Caesar Scaliger,** Italian-French literary critic. [d. October 21, 1558]

1697 **George Anson,** English admiral; effected reforms in naval administration, raising navy to high efficiency. [d. June 6, 1762]

1720 **Elijah Ben Solomon,** Hebrew religious writer born in Lithuania. [d. October 17, 1797]

1775 **J(oseph) M(allard) W(illiam) Turner,** English romantic painter; best known for impressionistic landscapes and seascapes. [d. December 19, 1851]

1791 **James Buchanan,** U.S. lawyer; 15th President of the United States, 1857–61; the only bachelor president. [d. June 1, 1868]

1804 **Maria Taglioni,** Italian ballet dancer born in Sweden; popularized dancing *sur les pointes.* [d. April 24, 1884]

1813 **Stephen (Arnold) Douglas,** U.S. politician, lawyer; a distinguished orator noted for his debates with Abraham Lincoln during the 1858 Senate campaign. [d. June 3, 1861]

1839 **James Bartlett Hammond,** U.S. inventor; developed the modern **typewriter keyboard**, patented 1880. [d. January 27, 1913]

1844 **Sanford Ballard Dole,** U.S. lawyer, political leader; President, Republic of Hawaii, 1894–1900; Governor, Territory of Hawaii, 1900–03. [d. June 9, 1926]

1852 **Edwin Charles Markham,** U.S. poet, lecturer; known for his poem *Man with the Hoe,* which became a standard statement of exploitation of the working classes. [d. March 7, 1940]

1853 **Alphonse Bertillon,** French criminologist; founded a system for identifying people through bodily measurements (**anthropometry**). [d. February 13, 1914]

1856 **Arthur Twining Hadley,** U.S. economist, educator; President of Yale University, 1899–1921. [d. March 6, 1930]

1858 **Max (Karl Ernst Ludwig) Planck,** German physicist; Nobel Prize in physics for development of **quantum theory**, 1918. [d. October 3, 1947]

1861 **Edmund Henry Hynman Allenby, 1st Viscount Allenby of Megiddo,** British field marshal; led Egyptian Expeditionary Force in World War I. [d. May 14, 1936]

1867 **Johannes A. G. Fibiger,** Danish pathologist; Nobel Prize in physiology or medicine for his work in cancer research, 1926. [d. January 20, 1928]

1891 **Serge Prokofiev,** Russian composer; known especially for *Peter and the Wolf.* [d. March 5, 1953]

1897 **Lucius Clay,** U.S. army general; Commander in Chief of U.S. Forces in Germany, 1945–49; administered Berlin airlift, 1948–49. [d. April 16, 1978]

Lester (Bowles) Pearson, Canadian statesman, diplomat; president of U.N. General Assembly; Nobel Peace Prize for his role in settlement of the **Suez Crisis,** 1957. [d. December 27, 1972]

1899 **Dame Ngaio Marsh,** New Zealand novelist; known especially for mysteries featuring **Inspector Roderick Alleyn of Scotland Yard.** [d. February 18, 1982]

1921 **Warren Spahn,** U.S. baseball player.

1926 **J(ames) P(atrick) Donleavy,** U.S.-Irish novelist.

Religious Calendar

The Saints

SS. **Felix, Fortunatus,** and **Achilleus,** martyrs. [d. 212]

St. George, martyr. Protector of the Kingdom of England; patron of Portugal, soldiers, and Boy Scouts. Invoked against skin diseases. [d. c. 303] Optional Memorial.

St. Ibar, Bishop of Beggery. Also called **Ivor.** [d. 5th century]

St. Gerard, Bishop of Toul. [d. 994]

St. Adalbert, Bishop of Prague, martyr and founder of the Abbey of Brevnov in Prague. [d. c. 997]

The Beatified

Blessed Giles of Assisi, Franciscan and companion to St. Francis of Assisi. [d. 1262]

Blessed Helen of Udine, widow. [d. 1458]

1928	**Shirley Temple Black,** U.S. actress, diplomat; child film star; U.S. representative to the United Nations, 1969–70; Ambassador to Ghana, 1974–76.
1932	**(Roy) Halston (Frowick),** U.S. fashion designer.
1936	**Roy Orbison,** U.S. country-rock musician, singer.
1947	**Bernadette (Josephine) Devlin (McAliskey),** Irish civil rights leader; youngest woman ever elected to **British Parliament.**

Historical Events

1014	**Brian Borormke,** King of Ireland, defeats Danes at **Clantarf** but is himself slain.
1348	**Order of the Garter,** oldest and most famous order of British knighthood, is established by **Edward III.**
1616	**William Shakespeare** dies.
1625	**Maurice of Nassau** dies and is succeeded by **Frederick Henry** as *stadholder* (ruler of the Netherlands).
1633	**League of Heilbronn** is established, creating a union of South German Protestants with Sweden and France.
1661	**Charles II** of England, (the *Merry Monarch*), is crowned.
1795	**Warren Hastings** is acquitted of charges of high crimes and misdemeanors during his term as governor of Bengal.
1850	**Alfred Lord Tennyson** becomes British poet laureate.
1860	**Savoy** is annexed to France by its own vote.
1895	**Tongoland** is annexed by Great Britain.
1896	The first **motion picture** to be commercially exhibited is shown in New York City.
1904	**American Academy of Arts and Letters** is founded by **National Institute of Arts and Letters,** with membership limited to 50 chosen from among members of the Institute.
1909	Villages of **Benevente** and **Samora** in Portugal are destroyed by an **earthquake.** **Theodore Roosevelt** sails for Africa on a scientific expedition under the auspices of the Smithsonian Institution.
1910	**Mount Etna,** on the island of Sicily, erupts.
1923	The **Second Lausanne Conference** opens between the Allied Powers and Turkey to settle disputes in the Mid-East and Turkey.
1941	Greek army surrenders to Germany (**World War II**).
1945	U.S. uses **guided missiles** for only time in **World War II** as two BAT missiles are released at Balikiapen, Borneo.
1950	**Hainan Island** is abandoned to Chinese Communist troops by Nationalist forces.
1964	Official celebration of the four hundredth anniversary of **William Shakespeare's birth** begins at Stratford-on-Avon, England, his birthplace.
1969	**Sirhan Beshara Sirhan** is sentenced to death in the gas chamber for the murder of **Robert F. Kennedy.**
1970	**The Gambia** is proclaimed a republic within the British Commonwealth.

April 24

Birthdates

216   **Manes (Mani, Manichaeus),** Persian religious leader; founder of Manichaean sect. [d. c. 274]

1533   **William I, *the Silent*,** Prince of Orange and Count of Nassau; founder of the Dutch Republic which proclaimed its independence in 1581. [d. July 1584]

1703   **José Francisco Isla,** Spanish novelist, satirist; known for his scathing satires on pulpit oratory; his works were banned by the Inquisition. [d. November 2, 1781]

1719   **Giuseppe Marc'antonio Baretti,** Italian writer, critic, lexicographer; intimate of Dr. Johnson, Burke, and Garrick in England. [d. May 5, 1789]

1743   **Edmund Cartwright,** English clergyman; invented the **power loom,** 1785. [d. October 30, 1823]

1815   **Anthony Trollope,** British novelist; known for his novels of Victorian life. [d. December 6, 1882]

1845   **Carl Friedrich George Spitteler** (*Felix Tandem*), Swiss poet, novelist; Nobel Prize in literature, 1919. [d. December 29, 1924]

1856   **Henri (Philippe Omer) Pétain,** French army marshal, chief of state; his defense of Verdun in 1916 made him a national hero; Premier of unoccupied France, 1940–44; later convicted of conspiring with the enemy; sentence commuted from death to life imprisonment. [d. July 23, 1951]

1876   **Erich Raeder,** German admiral; Naval Commander-in-Chief, 1928–43. [d. November 6, 1960]

1882   **Hugh Caswall Tremenheere Dowding, 1st Baron Dowding,** British general; head of Royal Air Force fighter command, 1936–40. [d. February 13, 1970]

1902   **Halldor Kiljan Laxness,** Icelandic novelist, poet, playwright; a major figure in Icelandic literature.

1905   **Robert Penn Warren,** U.S. novelist, poet, critic, educator; Pulitzer Prize in fiction, 1947; Pulitzer Prize in poetry, 1958, 1979.

1934   **Shirley Maclaine (Shirley Beaty),** U.S. dancer, actress, author.

1942   **Barbra (Joan) Streisand,** U.S. actress, singer.

Historical Events

1558   **Mary, Queen of Scots** marries Dauphin Francis of France.

1704   The *Boston News-Letter* begins publication, the first successful newspaper in the American colonies.

1800   U.S. **Library of Congress** is established.

1898   Spain declares war on U.S. (**Spanish-American War**).

1916   **Sinn Fein** rebellion (**Great Easter Rebellion**) begins in **Ireland,** with rebels declaring the establishment of a republic.

1921   The **Tyrol** region votes for union with Germany.

1945   **Dachau,** German concentration camp, is liberated by Allies (**World War II**).

Russian troops enter **Berlin** (**World War II**).

1950   The state of **Jordan** is formed by union of Jordanian-occupied Palestine and the Kingdom of Transjordan.

Religious Calendar

The Saints

St. Mellitus, Archbishop of Canterbury. Built St. Mary's Church at Canterbury. [d. 624]

St. Egbert, bishop. [d. 729]

St. William Firmatus of Tours, hermit. [d. c. 1090]

St. Fidelis of Sigmaringen, martyr. [d. 1622] Optional Memorial.

St. Mary Euphrasia Pelletier, virgin and founder of the Institute of Our Lady of Charity of the Good Shepherd. [d. 1868]

St. Ivo, bishop; patron of lawyers, civilians, and of St. Ive, England. Also called **Ive, Ivia,** or **Yves.** [death date unknown]

1960	Riots break out in **Biloxi, Mississippi** after blacks attempt to swim at city's beaches.
1965	All foreign-owned enterprises in **Indonesia** are seized by the Sukarno government.
1970	**The Gambia** Constitution is promulgated. **China** launches its first earth satellite.
1971	*Soyuz 10,* Soviet spacecraft carrying three cosmonauts, docks in space with *Salyut,* a previously launched space station.
1975	Terrorists attack the West German embassy in Stockholm, killing the military attaché and demanding the release of 26 anarchists in West Germany.
1980	U.S. attempt to rescue its hostages in **Iran** is aborted because of malfunctioning helicopters.

April 25

Holidays

Australia, New Zealand, Samoa, Tonga	**ANZAC Day** (Australia, New Zealand Army Corps) Marks the day on which the combined Army Corps landed at Gallipoli during World War I, 1915.
Italy	**Liberation Day** Celebrates the Allied Victory of World War II, 1945.
Papua New Guinea	**Remembrance Day**

Birthdates

1214   **Louis IX (Saint Louis)** of France. [d. August 25, 1270]

1228   **Conrad IV, Holy Roman Emperor,** 1250–54; lost lower Italy to **Charles of Anjou.** [d. May 21, 1254]

1284   **Edward II** of England, 1307–27; lost power to baronial committee; overthrown and imprisoned by **Roger de Mortimer,** protégé of **Queen Isabella;** forced to resign throne, 1327; murdered. [d. September 1327]

1599   **Oliver Cromwell,** English statesman, soldier; led the parliamentary forces in the English Civil War; installed as Lord Protector of England, Scotland, and Ireland, 1653–58. [d. September 3, 1658]

1769   **Sir Marc Isambard Brunel,** U.S. engineer, inventor born in France; solved the problem of **underwater tunnelling** with his invention of the cast iron tunnel shield, 1818. [d. December 12, 1849]

1825   **Sebastián Lerdo de Tejada,** Mexican lawyer, statesman; President of Mexico, 1872–76. [d. April 21, 1889]

1873   **Walter de la Mare,** British poet. [d. June 23, 1956]

1874   **Guglielmo Marconi,** Italian physicist; inventor of the **radio.** [d. July 20, 1937]

1900   **Wolfgang Pauli,** U.S. physicist born in Austria; Nobel Prize in physics for explaining the behavior of a class of atomic particles, 1945. [d. December 15, 1958]

1906   **William Joseph Brennan, Jr.,** U.S. jurist, lawyer; Associate Justice of U.S. Supreme Court, 1956– .

1918   **Ella Fitzgerald,** U.S. jazz singer.

1923   **Melissa Hayden (Mildred Herman),** Canadian ballerina.

        Arnold Ray Miller, U.S. labor leader.

1925   **Alhaji Shehu Shagari,** Nigerian statesman; President of Nigeria, 1979– .

1930   **Paul Mazursky,** U.S. director, writer.

1940   **Al Pacino,** U.S. actor.

1946   **Talia Shire,** U.S. actress.

Historical Events

1284   **Edward Plantagenet** (later **King Edward II**), son of **Edward I** of England, is born at Caernarvon Castle, Wales and is proclaimed the first **Prince of Wales.**

1792   **Guillotine** is first used in France (**French Revolution**).

1859   Work is started on the **Suez Canal.**

1867   Edo (**Tokyo**) is opened to foreign trade by **Japan.**

1903   First stone of new **Campanile** at Venice is laid.

1905   **Jean Sibelius** conducts the premiere performance of chamber-orchestra version of *Valse Triste.*

1915   **Australian-New Zealand** troops make first invasion of Turkey, beginning **Gallipoli Campaign (World War I).**

1920   The Supreme Council of the Paris Peace Conference mandates **Syria** to France and **Iraq** and **Palestine** to Great Britain.

Portugal	**Portugal Day** or **Liberty Day** Commemorates seizing of power by Portuguese Armed Forces and establishment of provisional military government, 1974.
Swaziland	**National Flag Day**

The Saints

St. Anianus, Bishop of Alexandria. [d. 1st century]

St. Heribald, Bishop of Auxerre. [d. c. 857]

The Beatified

Blessed Robert Anderton and **Blessed William Marsden,** priests and martyrs. [d. 1586]

Blessed Peter de Betancur. [beatified 1980]

Religious Calendar

Feasts

St. Mark, evangelist and martyr; patron of Venice, lawyers, and glaziers. Invoked against sudden and unexpected death. [d. c. 74] [minor festival, Lutheran church; major holy day, Episcopal Church]

1926   **Reza Shah Pahlavi** is crowned Shah of Persia at Teheran.

1950   U.S. government orders **Rumania** to close its commercial attaché office in New York City.

1953   **DNA** (deoxyribose nucleic acid) structure is first presented in the British publication *Nature* in an article by U.S. scientist **James Dewey Watson** and British geneticist **Francis H. C. Crick.**

1961   U.S. and West Germany exchange notes effecting a $587 million partial settlement of Germany's post-World War II debt to the U.S.

1974   In military coup in Portugal, Dr. **Marcelo Caetano** is overthrown and **General Antonio de Spinola** becomes president.

1975   **Prince Norodom Sihanouk,** head of a government-in-exile since 1970, is named chief of state for life by the Khmer Rouge's Royal Government of National Union of **Cambodia.**

1976   New constitution of **Portugal** goes into effect.

Vietnamese elect joint National Assembly to seal the reunification of the two **Vietnams** into one country.

1980   **Liberia** is taken over by a 17-member **People's Redemptive Council,** and the constitution is suspended.

1982   Israel returns the **Sinai,** captured in 1967, to Egypt as part of the 1979 **Camp David agreement.**

British troops retake **South Georgia Island** from Argentina in first military action in battle over **Falkland Islands.**

1983   Portugal's Social Democrat Party, led by former Prime Minister **Mario Soares,** wins national elections.

Pioneer 10, U.S. space probe launched on March 2, 1972, hurtles past the orbit of the planet **Pluto,** becoming the first man-made object to reach such a distance from the earth.

April 26

Holidays

Tanzania   **Union Day**
Commemorates the unification of **Zanzibar** and **Tanganyika**, 1964.

U.S. (Florida)   **Confederate Memorial Day**

Religous Calendar

The Saints

SS. Cletus and **Marcellinus,** popes and martyrs. Cletus, elected 76. Marcellinus elected 296. Cletus

Birthdates

1564   Christening date of **William Shakespeare,** England's most renowned playwright. [d. April 23, 1616]

1711   **David Hume,** Scottish philosopher; developed philosophy of **skepticism.** [d. August 25, 1776]

1718   **Esek Hopkins,** American Revolutionary naval commander; first Commander-in-Chief of **American Navy.** [d. February 26, 1802]

1774   **Leopold von Buch,** German geologist, geographer; noted for early research on **volcanic processes.** [d. March 4, 1853]

1785   **John James Audubon (Jean Rabine),** U.S. naturalist, painter, born in Santo Domingo; renowned for his ornithological illustrations. [d. January 27, 1851]

1798   **Eugene Delacroix,** French Romantic painter; recognized as a leader in the development of Romanticism in France. [d. August 13, 1863]

1812   **Alfred Krupp,** German armaments manufacturer; considered the *Father of Modern Armaments.* [d. July 14, 1887]

1822   **Frederick Law Olmsted** (or Olmstead), U.S. landscape architect; designer of New York's **Central Park.** [d. August 28, 1903]

1828   **Martha Finley,** U.S. novelist; wrote novels for young girls, including the *Elsie Dinsmore* stories. [d. January 30, 1909]

1834   **Charles Farrar Browne (Artemus Ward),** U.S. humorist, lecturer. [d. March 6, 1867]

1868   **Harold Sidney Harmsworth, Viscount Rothmere,** Irish newspaper publisher; founded British newspaper empire. [d. November 26, 1940]

1875   **Syngman Rhee,** Korean statesman; President of Korean provisional government in exile, 1919–39; first president of the **Republic of Korea** (South Korea). [d. July 19, 1965]

1879   **Sir Owen Willans Richardson,** British physicist; Nobel Prize in physics for study of electron emissions from heated bodies, 1928. [d. February 15, 1959]

1880   **Michel Fokine,** U.S. dancer, choreographer, born in Russia; called the *Father of Modern Ballet.* [d. August 22, 1942]

      Ma Rainey (Gertrude Melissa Nix Pridgett), U.S. musician, jazz singer. [d. December 22, 1939]

1886   **William L. Dawson,** U.S. Congressman, 1943–70. [d. November 9, 1970]

1889   **Ludwig Josef Johann Wittgenstein,** British philosopher, born in Austria; early student of logical positivism; known for studies of philosophical significance of ordinary language. [d. April 19, 1951]

1893   **Anita Loos,** U.S. screenwriter, novelist; author of *Gentlemen Prefer Blondes.* [d. August 18, 1981]

1894   **(Walther Richard) Rudolf Hess,** German Nazi official; Hitler's deputy and second in line of succession to Hitler, until his defection in 1941; imprisoned for life after World War II.

1896   **Jules (Caesar) Stein,** U.S. businessman; founder and president of Music Corporation of America, 1924–46; fought for creation of **National Eye Institute.** [d. April 29, 1981]

also called **Anacletus,** or **Anencletus.** [d. c. 91 and 304]

St. Peter, Bishop of Braga; patron of Braga, Portugal. [d. c. 350]

St. Richarius, abbot. Also called **Riquier.** [d. c. 645]

St. Paschasius Radbertus, Abbot of Corbie. [d. c. 860]

St. Franca of Piacenza, virgin and abbess. [d. 1218]

St. Stephen, Bishop of Perm; linguist; translated the liturgy and scriptures into Russian. [d. 1396]

The Beatified

Blessed John I, Bishop of Valenca. [d. 1146]

Blessed Dominic and **Blessed Gregory,** Dominican missionaries. [d. 1300]

Blessed Alda, widow and visionary. Also called **Aldobrandesca.** [d. 1309]

1897 **Cass Canfield,** U.S. publishing executive; Senior Editor, Harper & Row, 1967– .

1898 **Vicente Aleixandre,** Spanish poet; Nobel Prize in literature, 1977.

1900 **Charles Francis Richter,** U.S. seismologist; developed method of measuring earthquake intensity; the **Richter scale** is named for him.

1902 **Jonathan (Worth) Daniels,** U.S. journalist, author, government official; member of U.S. President Franklin D. Roosevelt's administration; later wrote biographies of Roosevelt, disclosing his love affair with **Lucy Page Mercer.** [d. November 6, 1981]

1914 **Bernard Malamud,** U.S. novelist, short-story writer; Pulitzer Prize in fiction, 1966.

1916 **Morris (Langlo) West,** Australian novelist; author of *The Naked Country* and *The Shoes of the Fisherman.*

1917 **I(eoh) M(ing) Pei,** U.S. architect, born in China; known for innovative modernist structures.

1930 **Bruce Friedman,** U.S. novelist, short-story writer, playwright; author of *Steambath.*

1933 **Arno Allan Penzias,** U.S. physicist; Nobel Prize in physics for discovery of **cosmic microwave background radiation,** lending support to Big Bang theory (with R. W. Wilson), 1978.

1936 **Carol Burnett,** U.S. comedienne.

Historical Events

1798 **Geneva, Switzerland** is annexed by France.

1849 **Civita Vecchia** is occupied by French forces.

1865 **John Wilkes Booth,** assassin of Abraham Lincoln, is shot by federal troops at a farmhouse near Washington, D.C.

1915 **Italy** signs a secret treaty with the Allies in London, gaining territorial concessions at the expense of Austria-Hungary and Turkey and joining the Allies (**World War I**).

1922 The U.S. recognizes the newly independent state of **Egypt.**

1943 U.S. task force bombards Japanese installations at **Attu** in the Aleutians (**World War II**).

1962 First **international satellite,** carrying British experiments and propelled aloft by a U.S. rocket, is launched from Cape Canaveral.

1964 Tanganyika and Zanzibar unite to form the **United Republic of Tanganyika and Zanzibar**; it is renamed **Tanzania** on October 29, 1964.

1966 *Aleksandr Pushkin,* the first Soviet transatlantic liner, arrives in Quebec on her maiden voyage.

1977 **Tanzanian Constitution** is promulgated.

April 27

Holidays

Afghanistan	**Saur Revolution Day** Commemorates the creation of the People's Republic upon the upset of the government by Marxist rebels, 1978.
Sierra Leone	**Independence Day** Commemorates achievement of independence from Great Britain, 1961.
Togo	**Independence Day** Commemorates establishment of Togo as a sovereign nation, 1960.

Birthdates

1733 **Josef Gottlieb Kölreuter,** German botanist; a pioneer in field of **hybridization.** [d. November 12, 1806]

1737 **Edward Gibbon,** British historian; best known for his classic *The History of the Decline and Fall of the Roman Empire.* [d. January 16, 1794]

1744 **Nikolay Ivanovich Novikov,** Russian writer, publisher; attempted to popularize good literature by publishing inexpensive volumes of classics. [d. July 31, 1818]

1748 **Adamantios Koraës,** Greek physician, philologist, patriot, educator; contributed to purification of Greek language in contemporary literature. [d. April 6, 1833]

1759 **Mary (Wollstonecraft) Godwin,** English writer, feminist; an early advocate of women's rights; mother of Mary Shelley (August 30). [d. September 10, 1797]

1791 **Samuel F(inley) B(reese) Morse,** U.S. inventor; invented first practical **telegraph.** Devised **Morse Code** for use in telegraph communications. [d. April 2, 1872]

1818 **Amasa Stone,** U.S. philanthropist, railroad tycoon; built Cleveland, Columbus, and Cincinnati Railroad, 1846; Chicago and Milwaukee Railroad, 1858. [d. May 11, 1883]

1820 **Herbert Spencer,** British naturalist philosopher; a primary formulator of **Social Darwinism.** Popularized idea of *survival of the fittest.* [d. December 8, 1903]

1822 **Ulysses S(impson) Grant,** U.S. army general for the Union, 18th President of United States; his presidential administration was characterized by corruption and bitter partisan politics. [d. July 23, 1885]

1855 **Benjamin Newton Duke,** U.S. tobacco-products manufacturer, philanthropist; with his brother, James Buchanan (December 23), founded American Tobacco Company and Imperial Tobacco Company. **Duke University** is named for the two brothers. [d. January 8, 1929]

1893 **Norman Bel Geddes,** U.S. theatrical and industrial designer; noted for stage designs and airplane, train, and automobile interiors. [d. May 8, 1958]

1896 **Wallace Hume Carothers,** U.S. chemist; invented first form of **nylon** and **neoprene** (synthetic rubber), 1931. [d. April 29, 1937]

Rogers Hornsby (*The Rajah*), U.S. baseball player; elected to Baseball Hall of Fame, 1942. [d. January 5, 1963]

1898 **Ludwig Bemelmans,** U.S. writer, illustrator, born in Austria. [d. October 1, 1962]

1904 **Arthur Burns,** U.S. government official, economist; Chairman, Federal Reserve Board, 1950–78.

C(ecil) Day Lewis (Nicholas Blake), British poet; Poet Laureate of England, 1967–72. [d. May 22, 1972]

1927 **Coretta (Scott) King,** U.S. civil rights leader, lecturer, writer, concert singer; widow of **Martin Luther King, Jr.**

1932 **Anouk Aimee (Françoise Sorya),** French actress; leading lady in 1960s films.

Religious Calendar

The Saints

St. Anthimus, Bishop of Nicomedia. [d. 303]

St. Asicus, Bishop of Elphin; patron of **Elphin** in County Roscommon, Ireland. Also called **Tassach.** [d. c. 470]

St. Maughold, Bishop of Man. Also called **Macallius, Maccul,** or **Macul.** [d. c. 498]

St. Floribert, Bishop of Liège. [d. 746]

St. Stephen Pechersky, Bishop of Vladimir. [d. 1094]

St. Zita, virgin; patron of domestic workers. [d. 1278]

St. Turibius, Archbishop of Lima and missionary. First saint of the New World; founded college at Lima, first seminary for training clergy in the Americas. [d. 1606]

The Beatified

Blessed Peter Armengol. [d. 1304]

Blessed Antony of Siena, hermit. [d. 1311]

Blessed James of Bitetto, lay-brother of Observant Franciscan Friars. [d. c. 1485]

Blessed Osanna of Cattaro, virgin and anchoress. [d. 1565]

1967   **Prince Willem-Alexander Claus** of the Netherlands, oldest son of Queen Beatrix.

Historical Events

1124   **David I** (*the Saint*) of Scotland accedes to the throne.

1296   **Edward II** of England defeats the Scots at the **Battle of Dunbar.**

1521   **Ferdinand Magellan** is killed by natives of the Philippine Islands during his circumnavigation of the globe.

1773   **Tea Act** is passed by British Parliament, setting stage for conflict with Americans over the tea tax; leads to **Boston Tea Party** of December 16.

1784   *Le Mariage de Figaro* by Beaumarchais premieres in Paris.

1805   U.S. naval forces capture **Derne, Tripoli,** in a combined land-sea assault, and raise U.S. flag over foreign soil for the first time.

1914   Sino-Tibetan convention is signed recognizing independence of **Tibet** under Chinese suzerainty.

1916   The **University of Capetown, Stellenbosch University,** and the **University of South Africa** are established by the Union of South Africa.

1919   **Korean nationalists** declare a republic and begin rebellion against Japan.

1935   **U.S. Soil Conservation Service** is established by Congress.

1939   British government begins **conscription (World War II).**

1941   German troops enter **Athens** and raise the Swastika over the Acropolis (**World War II**).

1950   The state of **Israel** is recognized by the British government.

1960   United Nations trust territory of **Togoland** becomes the independent **Republic of Togo.**

1961   **Sierra Leone** gains independence from Great Britain.

1965   Soviet communications satellite *Molniya 1* is first used for a scheduled telecast.

1969   Bolivian President **René Barrientos** is killed in a helicopter crash; Vice-President **Luis Adolfo Siles Salinas** succeeds him.

1972   *Apollo 16* spacecraft comes down in the Pacific after a successful mission during which U.S. astronauts **John Young** and **Charles Duke** spend a record 71 hours and 2 minutes on the moon.

1973   **L. Patrick Gray** resigns as acting director of the **F.B.I.** (**Watergate Incident**).

1978   President **Sardar Mohammad Daud Khan** of Afghanistan is killed in a military coup.

April 28

Religious Calendar

The Saints
SS. **Vitalis** and **Valeria**, martyrs. [d. c. second century]
St. **Pollio**, martyr. [d. 304]
SS. **Theodora** and **Didymus**, martyrs. [d. c. 304]
St. **Cronan of Roscrea**, abbot. [d. c. 626]

Birthdates

1442   **Edward IV** of England, a major participant in the **War of the Roses.** [d. April 9, 1483]

1630   **Charles Cotton,** English poet, burlesque writer; completed a second part to Walton's *Compleat Angler,* 1676; produced standard translation of Montaigne's *Essays.* [d. February 16, 1687]

1665   **Pier Iacopo Martello** (Martelli), Italian poet, man of letters; attempted to create classical Italian tragedy. [d. May 10, 1727]

1758   **James Monroe,** U.S. politician, diplomat; fifth President of the United States; established the **Monroe Doctrine.** [d. July 4, 1831]

1795   **Charles Stuart,** English explorer in Australia; responsible for much early knowledge of the interior of the continent. [d. June 16, 1869]

1838   **Tobias M. C. Asser,** Dutch jurist; Nobel Peace Prize for helping form the **Permanent Court of Arbitration** at the first Hague peace conference, 1911. [d. July 29, 1913]

1869   **Bertram Grosvenor Goodhue,** U.S. architect; best known for his Gothic revival designs. [d. April 23, 1924]

1874   **Sidney Toler,** U.S. character actor. [d. February 12, 1947]

1878   **Lionel Barrymore,** U.S. actor; leading character actor, often in sentimental roles. [d. November 15, 1954]

1889   **António de Oliveira Salazar,** Portuguese dictatorial leader, 1932–68. [d. July 27, 1970]

1892   **Walter Nathan Rothschild,** U.S. merchant; President of Abraham & Straus department store, 1937–55. [d. October 8, 1960]

      John Jacob Niles, U.S. folk singer, folklorist; collected American folk songs, ballads; composed musical accompaniment to the poems of Trappist monk Thomas Merton. [d. May 1, 1980]

1900   **Jan Hendrik Oort,** Dutch astronomer; President, International Astronomical Union, 1959–61.

1924   **Kenneth David Kaunda,** Zambian leader; President of Zambia, 1964–81.

1926   **(Nelle) Harper Lee,** U.S. novelist; author of *To Kill a Mockingbird.*

1937   **Saddam Hussein,** Iraqi statesman; President, 1979– .

      Jack Nicholson, U.S. actor.

1941   **Ann-Margret (Ann Margret Olsson),** U.S. dancer, singer, actress.

Historical Events

1521   **Ferdinand,** brother of **Holy Roman Emperor Charles V,** obtains Austrian dominions of the Hapsburgs.

1770   **Captain James Cook** lands at Cape Everard, Botany Bay, **Australia,** and claims possession for Great Britain.

1788   **Maryland** becomes seventh state to ratify U.S. Constitution.

1789   Crew members of the English ship *H.M.S. Bounty* stage a mutiny against **Captain William Bligh.**

1864   **Ionian Islands** are turned over to Greece by England.

1915   The great Austro-German offensive begins under the command of **Gen. von Machensen** against the Russian army in **Galicia (World War I).**

      The *U.S.S. Cushing* is bombed by German planes in the North Sea (**World War I**).

1919   The Covenant of the **League of Nations** is adopted by the Peace Conference at Paris (**World War I**).

St. Pamphilus, Bishop of Sumona. [d. c. 700]

St. Cyril, Bishop of Turov, Biblical scholar. Considered one of outstanding figures in early Russian Christian culture. [d. 1182]

St. Louis Mary of Montfort, founder of the Company of Mary and of the Daughters of Wisdom. [d. 1716]

St. Peter Mary Chanel, missionary and martyr. First martyr in the South Seas. [d. 1841] Optional Memorial.

The Beatified

Blessed Luchesio, the first Franciscan tertiary of Italy. [d. 1260]

1936   **King Fuad I of Egypt** dies and is succeeded by **Farouk I.**

1945   **Benito Mussolini,** Italian dictator, is captured and killed by Italian partisans (**World War II**).

1950   **Frédéric Joliot-Curie,** Nobel Prize winner and well-known French Communist, is dismissed as High Commissioner for Atomic Energy by French cabinet.

1964   Japan becomes the 21st full member of the **Organization for Economic Cooperation and Development.**

       Yemeni government promulgates a new constitution declaring **Yemen** to be an Islamic Arab state.

1969   French President **Charles de Gaulle** resigns; Senate president **Alain Poher** becomes interim president.

1977   U.S. Secretary of Health, Education, and Welfare, **Joseph A. Califano,** signs regulations prohibiting discrimination against the **handicapped** in institutions receiving federal support.

April 29

Holidays

Japan   **Emperor's Birthday**
Honors the birth of Emperor
Hirohito, 1901.

Religious Calendar

The Saints

St. Endellion, virgin. Also called **Endelient.** [d. c.
6th century]

Birthdates

1745   **Oliver Ellsworth,** U.S. jurist; third Chief
Justice of the U.S. Supreme Court. [d. November 26, 1807]

1818   **Alexander II,** Emperor of Russia, 1855– 81.
[d. March 13, 1881]

1854   **Jules Henri Poincaré,** French mathematician; made significant contributions in
areas of probability, calculus, and analytics. [d. July 17, 1912]

1860   **Lorado Taft,** U.S. sculptor; known for his
monumentalal sculptures, including *Fountain of Time* in Chicago. [d. October 30,
1936]

1863   **William Randolph Hearst,** U.S. editor,
publisher; creator of **Hearst Newspapers,**
one of largest newspaper chains in U.S. [d.
August 14, 1951]

1879   **Sir Thomas Beecham,** British conductor;
founder of the **London Philharmonic
Orchestra,** 1932. [d. March 8, 1961]

1885   **Frank Jack Fletcher,** U.S. admiral; led U.S.
naval forces in Pacific in World War II. [d.
April 25, 1973]

1893   **Harold Clayton Urey,** U.S. chemist; Nobel
Prize in chemistry for discovery of **heavy
hydrogen (deuterium),** 1934. [d. January
5, 1981]

1899   **Duke Ellington (Edward Kennedy Ellington),** U.S. musician, bandleader. [d.
May 24, 1974]

1901   **Hirohito,** Emperor of Japan, 1926– .

1907   **Fred Zinnemann,** U.S. film director; established Neo-Realist movement in U.S. cinema.

1919   **Celeste Holm,** U.S. actress.

1936   **Zubin Mehta,** U.S. conductor, born in India; Music Director, New York Philharmonic, 1978–

1938   **Rod McKuen,** U.S. poet.

Historical Events

1091   **Alexius I Comnenus,** Byzantine Emperor,
defeats the invading Patzinaks and
Kumans by the River Leburnium.

1916   The British garrison of 10,000 at **Kut-el-
Amara** surrenders to the Turks after repeated failures to lift the siege (**World War
I**).

1930   The world's largest lock, at the point where
North Sea channel cuts across North Holland, is opened.

1942   Japanese forces capture **Lashio** and cut
the **Burma Road,** the only viable route between India and China (**World War II**).

1944   Aircraft from 12 U.S. carriers bomb **Truk** in
the Caroline Islands (**World War II**).

1965   **Malta** becomes the 18th member of the
Council of Europe.

1975   U.S. presence in **Vietnam** comes to an end;
thousands of Vietnamese and Americans
are evacuated.

1979   **Jaime Roldós Aquilera,** of the Concentración de Fuerzas Populares party, is elected
President of **Ecuador**; he rules until his
death in a plane crash, May 24, 1981.

St. Wilfrid the Younger, Bishop of York. [d. c. 744]

St. Hugh the Great, Abbot of Cluny; advisor to nine popes. Invoked against fevers. [d. 1109]

St. Robert of Molesmes, abbot; a founder of the Cistercian Order. [d. 1110]

St. Peter of Verona, martyr. [d. 1252]

St. Catherine of Siena, virgin, papal advisor, and Doctor of the Church. Patron of Italian nurses. [d. 1380] Feast formerly April 30. Obligatory Memorial.

St. Joseph Cottolengo, founder of the Societies of the Little House of Divine Providence. [d. 1842]

April 30

Holidays

Germany and Scandinavian Countries

Walpurgis Night
Ancient rituals for warding off witches and evil spirits are traditionally performed on this night, particularly in the Harz Mountains of Germany.

Netherlands and Netherlands Antilles

Queen's Birthday
Commemorates the birthday of Queen Juliana, 1909.

Birthdates

1309 **Casimir III (*the Great*),** King of Poland, 1333–70. [d. November 5, 1370]

1651 **Jean Baptiste de La Salle,** French educator, Roman Catholic saint; feast day celebrated April 7. [d. April 7, 1719]

1770 **David Thompson,** Canadian explorer, geographer, born in England; the first European to explore the Columbia River; head of British Commission for demarcating borders between Canada and U.S., 1816–26. [d. February 10, 1857]

1771 **Hosea Ballou,** U.S. preacher, an early leader of the Universalists. [d. June 7, 1852]

1777 **Karl Friedrich Gauss (Johann Friedrich Karl Gauss),** German mathematician; developed concept of complex numbers and proved the fundamental algebraic theorems; considered one of the greatest mathematicians of all time. [d. February 23, 1855]

1870 **Franz Lehár,** Hungarian composer; best known for his operetta, *The Merry Widow*. [d. October 24, 1948]

1883 **Jaroslav Hašek,** Czech novelist, short-story writer; known for his satire *The Good Soldier Schweik*. [d. January 3, 1923]

1888 **John Crowe Ransom,** U.S. poet, critic; founder of *Kenyon Review* and proponent of **New Criticism,** which focused on close textual reading of poetry. [d. July 3, 1974]

1893 **Joachim von Ribbentrop,** German diplomat; Ambassador to Great Britain, 1936–38; played key role in German attack on Poland which started **World War II.** [d. October 16, 1946]

1901 **Simon Kuznets,** U.S. economist; Nobel Prize in economics for extensive research on the economic growth of nations, 1971.

1902 **Theodore W. Schultz,** U.S. economist; Nobel Prize in economics for his work in agricultural economics, 1979.

1909 **Juliana,** Queen of the Netherlands, 1948–80; abdicated in favor of her daughter, Beatrix.

1916 **Claude Elwood Shannon,** U.S. mathematician.

1946 **Carl XVI Gustaf,** King of Sweden, 1973– .

Historical Events

1789 **George Washington** is inaugurated at New York City as the first U.S. president under the Constitution.

1803 U.S. purchases **Louisiana Territory** from France, more than doubling the size of the country.

1812 **Louisiana** is admitted to the Union as the 18th state.

1815 Central provinces are designated **Kingdom of Poland** under Alexander of Russia.

1900 U.S. railroad engineer **Casey Jones** dies at the throttle, slowing down his crashing **Cannonball** to save his passengers' lives.

1902 Debussy's opera ***Pelléas et Mélisande*** premieres at the Opéra-Comique in Paris.

1934 New constitution in Austria sets up a dictatorship under **Engelbert Dollfuss.**

1945 **Adolf Hitler** commits suicide in Berlin as Russian troops capture the city.

Women are given the right to vote in **France.**

1961 Cuban Prime Minister **Fidel Castro** is awarded the 1960 **Lenin Peace Prize.**

1965 **Basutoland (Lesotho)** attains internal self-government.

Religious Calendar

The Saints

St. Maximus, martyr. [d. 250]

SS. Marian and James, martyrs. [d. 259]

St. Eutropius, Bishop of Saintes and martyr. [d. 3rd century]

St. Forannan, Abbot of Waulsort in France. [d. 982]

St. Gualfardus, hermit-monk. Also called **Wolfhard.** [d. 1127]

St. Pius V, pope. Elected 1565. [d. 1572] Feast formerly May 5. Optional Memorial.

The Beatified

Blessed Hildegard, matron and wife of Charlemagne. [d. 783]

Blessed Francis Dickenson and **Blessed Miles Gerard,** priests and martyrs. [d. 1590]

Blessed Benedict of Urbino, friar. [d. 1625]

1973 U.S. Attorney General **Kleindienst** and presidential advisors **H. R. Haldeman** and **John Ehrlichman** resign; **John Dean,** presidential counsel, is dismissed (**Watergate Incident**).

1975 **Saigon,** Vietnam, is renamed **Ho Chi Minh City.**

1980 Iranian embassy in London is seized by five armed **Iranian dissidents.**

Juliana, Queen of the Netherlands, abdicates in favor of her daughter, **Beatrix.**

May

May is the fifth month of the Gregorian calendar and has 31 days. In the early Roman calendar, May was the third month of the year.

The name has two possible origins: from the Greek goddess Maia, the mother of Hermes, or from the Italian goddess of spring, Maia Maiesta, to whom sacrifices were made to insure the growth of crops.

The "merry month of May" has traditionally been associated with dancing, singing, love, and general rejoicing over the return of spring. During early Roman times, the month was regarded as being under the protection of the god Apollo, and Romans celebrated by gathering boughs and blossoms to adorn temples, statues, or sweethearts' homes, continuing the spirit of the Floralia, honoring Flora, goddess of flowers, whose festival commenced at the end of April. The Druids instituted sacrificial May bonfires to assure successful planting and rich harvests. In medieval England, May poles and May queens reflected a spirit similar to that of the Romans' Floralia.

In the astrological calendar, May spans the signs of Taurus, the Bull (April 20–May 20) and Gemini, the Twins (May 21–June 21).

The birthstone for May is the emerald, and the flower is the lily of the valley or hawthorn.

State, National, and International Holidays

May Day
May 1

Loyalty Day
(United States)
May 1

Independence Day
(Rhode Island)
May 4

Bird Day
(Oklahoma)
May 1

Truman Day
(Missouri)
May 8

Minnesota Day
(Minnesota)
May 11

Mecklenburg Independence Day
(North Carolina)
May 20

National Maritime Day
(United States)
May 22

Constitution Day
(Japan)
First Monday

King's Birthday
(Lesotho)
First Monday

Prayer Day
(Denmark)
First or Second Saturday

Simbra Oilor at Oas
(Romania)
First Sunday

Mother's Day
(United States)
Second Sunday

Discovery Day
(Cayman Islands)
Third Monday

Battle of Las Piedras
(Uruguay)
Third Monday

Primary Election Day
(Pennsylvania)
Third Tuesday
(Indiana)
First Tuesday after First Monday

Armed Forces Day
(United States)
Third Saturday

Confederate Memorial Day
(North Carolina, South Carolina)
May 10
(Virginia)
May 30

Commonwealth Day
(Belize)
Fourth Monday

Victoria Day
(Scotland)
Fourth Monday
(Canada)
Monday before May 25

Memorial Day
(most of the United States)
Final Monday

except:

(New Mexico)
May 25

(Puerto Rico)
May 28

(Delaware, Illinois,
    Maryland, New Hampshire
    South Dakota, Vermont)
May 30

Mothers' Day
(Central African Republic)
Final Saturday

Chemists' Day
(U.S.S.R)
Final Sunday

Carnival in Valletta
(Malta)
Second Weekend

Windmill Day
(The Netherlands)
Second Saturday

Gabrovo's Biannual Comedic Extravaganza
(Bulgaria)
mid-May (odd years)

Special Events and Their Sponsors

Arthritis Month
Arthritis Foundation
3400 Peachtree Road
Atlanta, Georgia 30326

Better Hearing and Speech Month
Council for Better Hearing and Speech
1081 Rockville Pike
Rockville, Maryland 20852

National Barbecue Month
Barbecue Industry Association
710 East Ogden Avenue
Suite 114
Naperville, Illinois 60540

Bike Safety Month
National Safety Council
444 North Michigan Avenue
Chicago, Illinois 60611

National Home Decorating Month
National Decorating Products Association
1050 North Lindbergh Boulevard
St. Louis, Missouri 63132

National Hope Chest Month
National Multiple Sclerosis Society
205 East 42nd Street
New York, New York 10017

Older Americans Month
National Safety Council
444 North Michigan Avenue
Chicago, Illinois 60611

National Mental Health Month
National Mental Health Association
1800 North Kent Street
Arlington, Virginia 22209

Philatelic Exhibitions Month
The Philatelic Journalist
154 Laguna Court
St. Augustine Shores, Florida 32084

Touring Theater Month
Richard R. Falk Associates
1472 Broadway
New York, New York 10036

Be Kind to Animals Week
First Week
American Humane Society
P.O. Box 1266
Denver, Colorado 80201

International Classified Advertising Week
First Week
Association of Newspaper Classified Advertising
    Managers, Inc.
P.O. Box 223
Danville, Illinois 61832

National Extension Homemaker Council Week
First Week
National Extension Homemakers Council
522 Madison Street
Stanley, Wisconsin 54768

National Pet Week
First Week
Auxiliary to the American Veterinary
    Medical Association
227 South Wind Place
Manhattan, Kansas 66502

National Girls Club Week
Second Week
Girls Clubs of America
205 Lexington Avenue
New York, New York 10016

National Historic Preservation Week
Second Week
National Trust for Historic Preservation
1785 Massachusetts Avenue, N.W.
Washington, D.C. 20036

National Nursing Home Week
Second Week
American Health Care Association
1200 15th Street, N.W.
Washington, D.C. 20005

National Salvation Army Week
Second Week
The Salvation Army
799 Bloomfield Avenue
Verona, New Jersey 07044

National White Cane Week
Third Week
National Federation of the Blind
1800 Johnson Street
Baltimore, Maryland 21230

Pickle Weeks
Final Two Weeks
Pickle Packers International, Inc.
One Pickle and Pepper Plaza
P.O. Box 31
St. Charles, Illinois 60174

Public Relations Week
Final Full Week
Richard R. Falk Associates
1472 Broadway
New York, New York 10036

Law Day
May 1
American Bar Association
1155 East 60th Street
Chicago, Illinois 60637

Anniversary of the First Postage Stamp
May 6
The Philatelic Journalist
154 Laguna Court
St. Augustine Shores, Florida 32084

Birthday Anniversary of Jean Henri Dunant
May 8
Franklin D. Roosevelt Philatelic Society
154 Laguna Court
St. Augustine Shores, Florida 32084

World Day of Prayer for Vocations
First Sunday (or last Sunday in April)
National Catholic Vocation Council
1307 South Wabash Avenue
Suite 350
Chicago, Illinois 60605

Special Days—Other Calendars

	Ascension Thursday	Pentecost Sunday	Trinity Sunday	1 Ramadan	Yom Ha'Azma'ut	Shavuoth
1985	May 16	May 26		May 21		May 26
1986	May 8	May 18	May 25	May 11	May 14	
1987	May 28				May 5	
1988	May 12	May 22	May 29			May 22
1989	May 4	May 14	May 21		May 10	
1990	May 24					May 30

May 1

Labor Day (except U.S. and Canada)
Recognizes the alliance of working people in most nations of the world. Recognized as a workers' holiday in most socialist countries.

May Day
Traditionally a day of flower festivals; celebrated with hanging of May Baskets and dancing around May Poles in England and some sections of U.S.

Mongolia	**International Solidarity Day**
Turkey	**Spring Day**

Birthdates

1218   **Rudolf I,** founder of the **Hapsburg Dynasty**; became King of Germany, 1273. [d. July 1291]

1672   **Joseph Addison,** English poet, essayist, critic, playwright. [d. June 17, 1719]

1764   **Benjamin Henry,** U.S. architect. [d. September 3, 1820]

1769   **Arthur Wellesley, 1st Duke of Wellington,** British Army field marshal, public official; defeated Napoleon at **Waterloo.** British Prime Minister, 1829–30. [d. September 14, 1852]

1824   **Alexander William Williamson,** British chemist; first to describe principle of dynamic equilibrium and function of catalyst in chemical reaction. [d. May 6, 1904]

1825   **George Inness,** U.S. painter; landscapist of the **Hudson River School.** [d. August 3, 1894]

1827   **Jules Adolphe Breton,** French painter. [d. July 4, 1906]

1828   **Adelardo López de Ayala y Herrera,** Spanish dramatist, politician; President, Chamber of Deputies, 1878. [d. December 30, 1879]

1830   **Mary Jones (*Mother Jones*),** U.S. labor leader; famous as an agitator in behalf of Appalachian coal miners. [d. November 30, 1930]

1839   **Louis Marie Chardonnet,** French chemist; invented **rayon,** the first common artificial fiber. [d. March 12, 1924]

1852   **Santiago Ramón y Cajal,** Spanish histologist; Nobel Prize in physiology or medicine for work establishing the neuron as the basic unit of the nervous system (with C. Golgi), 1906. [d. October 17, 1934]

1852   **Martha Jane Burke (*Calamity Jane*),** U.S. frontier adventuress, legendary dance-hall girl and Indian fighter. [d. August 1, 1903]

1880   **Albert Davis Lasker,** U.S. advertising executive; created ads telling consumers why to buy products. [d. May 30, 1952]

1881   **Pierre Teilhard de Chardin,** French Roman Catholic priest, paleontologist, philosopher; synthesized theories of Christianity and evolution. [d. April 10, 1955]

1896   **Mark Wayne Clark,** U.S. army general; commanded United Nations forces in Korea, 1952–53. [d. April 17, 1984]

1909   **Kate Smith,** U.S. singer.

1916   **Glenn Ford (Gwyllyn Ford),** U.S. actor, born in Canada.

1923   **Joseph Heller,** U.S. novelist; author of *Catch 22.*

1925   **(Malcolm) Scott Carpenter,** U.S. astronaut, oceanographer.

Historical Events

1429   **Joan of Arc,** inspiring loyal French troops, raises siege of Orléans, driving back the English and Burgundian attackers.

1703   **Charles XII of Sweden** defeats **Peter the Great of Russia** at Pultusk.

U.S.	Law Day
	Established to enhance citizen awareness of the benefits of law and order.
Oklahoma	**Bird Day**
U.S.S.R.	**International Workers' Solidarity Day**
Vatican City	**St. Joseph the Worker Day**
Yemen	**Workers' Day**

Religious Calendar

Feasts

SS. Philip and **James,** apostles. Philip is considered the first of Christ's disciples. James is also called **Minor,** or **The Less,** [d. 1st century] [Major holy day, Episcopal Church; minor festival, Lutheran Church.] (Transferred to May 11.)

The Saints

St. Amator, Bishop of Auxerre. Also called **Amatre.** [d. 418]

St. Sigismund of Burgundy, King of Burgundy. [d. 524]

St. Marculf. Invoked to cure skin diseases. Also called **Marcon, Marcoul, Marculfus.** [d. c. 558]

St. Brieuc, abbot of monastery in Brittany. Also called **Briocus.** [d. 6th century]

St. Corentin, first bishop of Cornouaille. Also called **Cury.** [d. 6th century]

St. Theodard, Archbishop of Narbonne. Also called **Audard.** [d. 893]

St. Peregrine Laziosi, Servite friar. [d. 1345]

1707 Union of **England** and **Scotland** under the name of **Great Britain** becomes effective.

1808 **Napoleon** forces both **Charles IV of Spain** and his son **Ferdinand** to relinquish the Spanish crown in his favor.

1809 **Napoleon** annexes **Papal States**; Pope **Pius VII** is held prisoner at Savona.

1851 First **Great Exhibition** of industries of all nations opens in Hyde Park, London.

1862 **New Orleans** falls to Union troops after naval bombardment by **Admiral Farragut (U.S. Civil War).**

1876 **Queen Victoria** of Great Britain is proclaimed Empress of India.

1893 **Columbian Exhibition** opens in Chicago.

1898 **Battle of Manila Bay** ends with destruction of Spanish fleet by U.S. Navy commanded by Admiral **George Dewey** (**Spanish-American War**).

1911 U.S. Supreme Court, acting under the **Sherman Anti-Trust Act,** orders dissolution of **Standard Oil Co.** and **American Tobacco Co.**

1915 The American merchant ship, the tanker *Gulflight,* is first to be torpedoed and sunk by a German submarine (**World War I**).

1920 Longest major league baseball game, 26 innings, ends in a tie, called because of darkness (Brooklyn 1, Boston 1).

1922 The first **National Labor Congress of China** opens in Canton.

1924 **Greece** is proclaimed a republic after overthrow of **King George II.**

1931 The **Empire State Building,** then the world's tallest building, is dedicated in New York.

1960 U.S. **U-2 reconnaissance plane** is shot down near Sverdlovsk, central U.S.S.R., and pilot **Francis Gary Powers** is captured.

1961 Cuban Prime Minister **Fidel Castro** declares **Cuba** to be a socialist nation.

Tanganyika, British protectorate, achieves full internal self-government; **Julius Nyerere** becomes first prime minister.

1971 **Amtrak** (National Railroad Passenger Corporation) takes over operation of most U.S. passenger trains.

1975 Communist victory in **South Vietnam** is completed.

1981 Japan voluntarily limits its automobile exports to the U.S. for two years.

New Jersey Senator **Harrison Williams** is convicted of criminal charges related to the **Abscam investigation.**

May 2

Religious Calendar

The Saints

SS. Exsuperius and Zoë, husband and wife, martyrs. [d. c. 135]

St. Athanasius, Archbishop of Alexandria and Doctor of the Church. [d. 373] Obligatory Memorial.

St. Waldebert, Abbot of Luxeuil. Also called Gaubert, Walbert. [d. c. 665]

Birthdates

1551 **William Camden,** English antiquary, historian. [d. November 9, 1623]

1660 **Alessandro Scarlatti,** Italian composer; considered the *Father of Modern Opera.* [d. October 24, 1725]

1729 **Catherine II, the Great,** (Sophia Augusta Frederika), Empress of Russia, 1762–96. [d. November 17, 1796]

1750 **John André,** British army officer; conspired with Benedict Arnold for surrender of West Point during American Revolution. [d. October 2, 1780]

1837 **Henry Martyn Robert,** U.S. military engineer, parliamentarian; author of *Robert's Rules of Order,* the standard work on parliamentary procedure. [d. May 11, 1923]

1851 **Graham Taylor,** U.S. clergyman, sociologist; founder of forerunner of **University of Chicago School of Social Work.** [d. September 26, 1938]

1860 **Theodor Herzl,** Austrian Jewish writer born in Hungary; founder of modern **Zionism.** [d. July 3, 1904]

Sir William Maddock Bayliss, British physiologist; discovered (with E. H. Starling) hormone **secretin** manufactured by glands on wall of small intestine. [d. August 27, 1924]

1866 **Jesse William Lazear,** U.S. bacteriologist, army surgeon; served with Walter Reed on Yellow Fever Commission, 1900. [d. September 25, 1900]

1879 **James Francis Byrnes,** U.S. politician, lawyer, editor; U.S. Senator, 1931–41; Associate Justice of U.S. Supreme Court, 1941–42; Director, Office of Economic Stability, 1941–42; Director, Office of War Mobilization 1943–45; U.S. Secretary of State, 1945–47; Governor of South Carolina, 1951–55. [d. April 9, 1972]

1887 **Vernon Castle (Vernon Castle Blythe),** U.S. dancer; with wife **Irene Castle** formed famous dancing team in period before World War I. [d. February 15, 1918]

1892 **Manfred (Freiherr) von Richthofen (*The Red Baron*),** German aviator, World War I fighter ace. [d. April 21, 1918]

1895 **Lorenz (Milton) Hart,** U.S. lyricist; collaborator with Richard Rodgers (June 28) on musical scores for numerous plays. [d. November 22, 1943]

1902 **Brian (Delacy) Aherne,** U.S. actor.

1903 **Benjamin (McLane) Spock,** U.S. pediatrician; major influence on modern U.S. child-rearing practices and health care.

Bing Crosby (Harry Lillis Crosby), U.S. singer, actor; leading crooner of the 1930s and 1940s. [d. October 14, 1977]

1923 **Patrick J. Hillery,** Irish statesman; President, Irish Republic, 1976– .

1938 **Moshoeshoe II, King of Lesotho,** 1960– .

Historical Events

1316 **Edward Bruce,** brother of the Scottish king, is crowned King of Ireland.

1322 **Parliament of York** declares that all legislation must be approved by both the king and parliament.

1670 **Hudson Bay Company** receives a charter from English crown and is given a monopoly of the trade in Hudson Bay region.

1885 **Congo Free State** is established with Belgian king **Leopold II** as sovereign.

1913 **Republic of China** is recognized by the United States and Mexico.

1915 The **Battle of Gorlice-Tarnow** begins **(World War I).**

1936 **Prokofiev's** *Peter and the Wolf* premieres at a children's concert in Moscow.

St. Ultan, Abbot of Fosses. Also called **Ultain.** [d. 686]

St. Wiborada, virgin, recluse, and martyr. Also called **Guiborat, Weibrath.** [d. 926]

St. Mafalda, princess and nun. Also called **Matilda.** [d. 1252]

The Beatified

Blessed Conrad of Seldenbüren, founder of Benedictine Abbey of Engelberg. [d. 1126]

1945   **Berlin** falls to the Allied armies (**World War II**).

German forces in Italy surrender to the Allies (**World War II**).

1951   **German Federal Republic** becomes a full member of the **Council of Europe.**

Iran nationalizes its oil industry.

1965   *Early Bird*, the world's first commercial satellite, begins transmission.

1974   Former U.S. Vice-President **Spiro Agnew** is barred from practicing law in Maryland, the only state where he was licensed.

May 3

Holidays

Japan	**Constitution Memorial Day**
Poland	**Constitution Day**

Commemorates the adoption of Poland's first constitution, ratified on this day in 1794.

Birthdates

1469   **Niccolò di Machiavelli,** Italian statesman, author; one of the outstanding figures of the Renaissance; best known for *The Prince*, a pragmatic guide to the use and furtherance of political power. [d. June 21, 1527]

1748   **Emmanuel Joseph Sieyès (Abbé Sieyès),** French Revolutionary leader; one of chief figures in Napoleon's rise to power. [d. June 20, 1836]

1791   **Count Henryk Rzewuski (*J. Bejla*),** Polish novelist. [d. February 28, 1866]

1826   **Charles XV, King of Sweden and Norway,** 1859–72. [d. September 18, 1872]

1827   **John Hanning Speke,** British African explorer; confirmed theory that Lake Victoria is one source of the Nile. [d. September 15, 1864]

1844   **(Richard) D'Oyly Carte,** British operatic impresario; founded the Savoy Theatre, home of **Gilbert and Sullivan** productions. [d. April 3, 1901]

1848   **Francisco Teixeira de Queiroz,** Portuguese short-story writer, novelist. [d. 1919]

1849   **Jacob August Riis,** U.S. journalist, reformer, author; a crusader for urban reforms. [d. May 26, 1914]

Prince Bernhard von Bulow, German statesman; Chancellor of Germany, 1900–09. [d. October 28, 1929]

1874   **François Coty,** French industrialist, newspaper owner, parfumier. [d. 1934]

1892   **Sir George Paget Thomson,** British physicist; Nobel Prize in physics for discovery of diffraction of electrons by crystals (with C. J. Davisson), 1937. [d. September 10, 1975]

1898   **Golda Meir,** Israeli stateswoman; first woman premier of Israel, 1969–74. [d. December 8, 1978]

1902   **Alfred Kastler,** French physicist; Nobel Prize in physics for research in atomic structure, 1966. [d. January 9, 1984]

Walter Slezak, U.S. actor. [d. April 22, 1983]

1906   **Roberto Rossellini,** Italian film director.

1907   **Earl Wilson,** U.S. syndicated columnist.

1912   **Virgil (Keel) Fox,** U.S. organist; known for his flamboyant, popular presentation style. [d. October 25, 1980]

1913   **William Motter Inge,** U.S. playwright. [d. June 10, 1973]

1919   **Pete Seeger,** U.S. folksinger, composer.

1920   **(*Sugar*) Ray Robinson (Walker Smith),** U.S. boxer; five-time middleweight champion, 1951–60.

1933   **Steven Weinberg,** U.S. physicist; Nobel Prize in physics for formulating theory concerning interaction of elementary particles (with S. L. Glashow), 1979.

Historical Events

1616   **Treaty of Loudun** ends second civil war in France and rebellion of Henry, Prince de Condé.

1660   **John II Casimir of Poland** signs the **Treaty of Oliva,** abandoning his claim to the throne of Sweden and ending the **Northern War.**

1841   **New Zealand** becomes a British colony.

1859   France, under **Napoleon III,** declares war on Austria.

1895   The name of **Rhodesia** is given to the territories of the British South Africa Company.

1915   The Austrian army under Archduke Josef Ferdinand takes **Tarnow** as the Russians fall back from the Austro-German offensive in Galicia (**World War I**).

1939   Drastic anti-Jewish laws are introduced in **Hungary.**

1945   U.S. troops land at **Santa Cruz, Philippines. (World War II)**

Religious Calendar

Feasts

The Saints

SS. Alexander, Eventius, and **Theodolus,** martyrs. [d. c. 113]

SS. Timothy and **Maura,** martyrs. [d. c. 286]

St. Juvenal, Bishop of Narni. [d. c. 376]

St. Philip of Zell, priest and recluse. [d. 8th century]

St. Glywys, monk; patron of St. Gluvias, Cornwall. Also called **Gluvias.** [death date unknown]

1947   **Japan** promulgates its constitution.

1960   **Cyrus Eaton,** U.S. industrialist, is awarded the Lenin Peace Prize.

1965   **Cambodia** severs diplomatic relations with U.S.

1968   South African House of Assembly votes to abolish parliamentary representation for the country's blacks.

1971   **Erich Honecker** becomes First Secretary of the East German Communist Party.

1972   U.S. Assistant Attorney General, **L. Patrick Gray III**, is named acting director of the FBI, succeeding J. Edgar Hoover, who died May 2.

1979   **Margaret Thatcher,** the 53-year old head of the Conservative Party, becomes the first woman Prime Minister of Great Britain.

Headquarters of the ruling Christian Democrats in Rome are bombed by the terrorist **Red Brigade**.

May 4

Holidays

Tonga   **Birthday of Crown Prince Tupouto'a**

U.S. (Rhode Island)   **Independence Day** Commemorates day on which Rhode Island proclaimed its independence from Great Britain, 1776.

Religious Calendar

The Saints

St. Cyriacus, bishop; principal patron of Ancona. Also called **Judas Quiriacus.** Believed to have aided

Birthdates

1654   **K'ang-hsi,** second emperor of the **Manchu Dynasty.** [d. December 20, 1722]

1655   **Bartolommeo Cristofori,** Italian maker of harpsichords; credited with development of hammer action later used in modern pianos. [d. 1731]

1796   **Horace Mann,** U.S. educator, public official; established model for U.S. public education system. [d. August 2, 1859]

1806   **William F. Cooke,** British technician; with Charles Wheatstone, patented a **telegraph,** 1837.

1825   **Thomas Henry Huxley,** British philosopher, biologist. [d. June 29, 1895]

       Henry Browne Blackwell, U.S. social reformer. [d. September 7, 1909]

1826   **Frederick Edwin Church,** U.S. painter. [d. April 7, 1900]

1866   **William Ellis Corey,** U.S. industrialist; second president of U.S. Steel Corp. [d. May 11, 1934]

1870   **Vladimir Ilyich Lenin** (original surname, Ulyanov), Russian Communist leader; founder of **Bolshevism;** architect of first Soviet state. [d. January 21, 1924]

1889   **Francis Joseph Spellman,** U.S. Roman Catholic Cardinal; Archbishop of New York, 1939–67. [d. December 2, 1967]

1896   **(Edward William) Alton Ochsner,** U.S. physician; one of first to present evidence that cigarette smoking is a major cause of lung cancer; founder of the **Alton Ochsner Clinic** at Tulane University. [d. September 24, 1981]

       Mary Ellis (Opdycke) Peltz, U.S. journalist, author, editor; first editor of *Opera News,* 1936–57; author of several books on the history of opera in America. [d. October 24, 1981]

1918   **Kakuei Tanaka,** Japanese statesman; Prime Minister, 1972–74.

1925   **Luis Herrera Campins,** Venezuelan statesman; President, 1979– .

1928   **Hosni Mubarak,** Egyptian leader; President, 1981– .

1929   **Audrey Hepburn (Audrey Hepburn-Ruston),** Belgian-born U.S. actress.

1930   **Roberta Peters,** U.S. operatic soprano.

Historical Events

1041   The Lombards and Normans defeat the Greeks at **Montemaggiore.**

1256   **Pope Alexander IV** founds **Order of Augustine Hermits.**

1328   **Treaty of Northampton** is signed between England and Scotland; **Robert Bruce** is recognized as King of Scotland.

1471   **Edward, Prince of Wales,** son of **Henry VI of England,** is slain at the **Battle of Tewksbury (War of the Roses).**

1493   **Pope Alexander VI** divides the New World between Spain and Portugal.

1702   England, Holland, and the Holy Roman Empire declare war on France.

1776   **Rhode Island** is first American colony to renounce allegiance to **King George III.**

St. Helena in the recovery of the cross of Christ. [d. c. 133]

St. Florian, Roman army officer and martyr; patron of Poland, Linz, and Upper Austria. Invoked in danger from fire or water. [d. 304]

St. Pelagia of Tarsus, virgin and martyr. [d. c. 304]

St. Venerius, Bishop of Milan. [d. 409]

St. Godehard, Bishop of Hildesheim. Also called **Godard, Gothard.** [d. 1038]

The Martyrs of England and Wales. [d. 1535–1681]

The Beatified

Blessed Catherine of Parc-aux-Dames, virgin and visionary. [d. early 13th century]

Blessed Gregory of Verucchio. Invoked when rain is needed. [d. 1343]

Blessed Michael Giedroyé, Augustinian monk. [d. 1485]

Blessed John Martin Moye, missionary priest and founder of the Sisters of Divine Providence. [d. 1793]

1780	**American Academy of Arts and Sciences** is chartered at Boston.
1824	The **First Burma War** breaks out; the British take Rangoon.
1863	**Battle of Chancellorsville** ends with Union forces defeated by Confederates (**U.S. Civil War**).
1886	**Haymarket Riot** occurs in Chicago when an anarchist's bomb kills several policemen and injures many other policemen and civilians.
1919	Students in Peking protest the Versailles Peace Conference decision that Japan (rather than China) should retain Germany's possessions in Shantung Province. The **May Fourth Movement** marks the beginning of the **Chinese Communist Party.**
1938	**Douglas Hyde** is elected first president of Ireland under the new constitution.
1942	**Battle of the Coral Sea,** first carrier-vs.-carrier sea battle, begins (**World War II**).
1950	A 100-day strike of United Automobile Workers against the **Chrysler Corporation** ends.
1970	National Guardsmen fire on antiwar demonstrators at **Kent State University.** Four people are killed and at least nine are wounded.
1982	Argentina's computer-guided missile destroys British destroyer *Sheffield* in battle over **Falkland Islands.**

May 5

Holidays

Japan	**Children's Day** or **Kodomo-No-Hi**
	A day set aside to honor all children of the country and to wish them happiness.
Korea	**Children's Day**
Mexico	**Puebla Battle Day** or **Cinco de Mayo**
	Commemorates defeat of Napoleon III's forces, 1867.
The Netherlands	**Liberation Day**
	Commemorates the liberation from German occupation, 1945.

Birthdates

1282   **Juan Manuel,** Infante de Castile, Spanish soldier, statesman, writer; his writings provided models for the works of Chaucer, Boccaccio, and Lope de Vega. [d. c. 1349]

1809   **Frederick Augustus Porter Barnard,** U.S. educator; established **Barnard College for Women,** thus extending Columbia University's educational opportunities to women. [d. April 27, 1889]

1813   **Sören Kierkegaard,** Danish philosopher, theologian; called the *Father of Existentialism.* [d. November 11, 1855]

1818   **Karl Marx,** German social philosopher; chief theorist of modern **socialism** and **communism.** [d. March 14, 1883]

1832   **Hubert Howe Bancroft,** U.S. historian; directed the creation of *Western American Historical Series,* a 39-volume history of the American West. [d. March 2, 1918]

1846   **Henryk Sienkiewicz,** Polish novelist, short-story writer; Nobel Prize in literature, 1905. [d. November 15, 1916]

1852   **Pietro Gasparri,** Italian cardinal; Papal Secretary of State, 1914–34. [d. November 18, 1934]

1867   **Nellie Bly (Elizabeth Cochrane Seaman),** U.S. journalist; well known for her unorthodox and aggressive journalistic procedures. [d. January 27, 1922]

1882   **Sir Douglas Mawson,** Australian explorer of Antarctica; made some of most important discoveries regarding that region in the early twentieth century. [d. October 14, 1958]

1883   **Archibald Percival Wavell, 1st Earl Wavell,** British Army field marshal during World War II. [d. May 24, 1950]

1897   **Jacob Shapiro (Jake Gurrah),** U.S. mobster. [d. June 9, 1947]

1899   **Freeman Gosden,** U.S. radio comedian; played Amos in *Amos 'n' Andy* radio show. [d. December 10, 1982]

1903   **James Beard,** U.S. cooking authority, cookbook author.

1906   **Mary Astor (Lucille Langehanke),** U.S. actress.

1908   **Rex Harrison (Reginald Carey),** British stage and film actor.

1913   **Tyrone (Edmund) Power,** U.S. actor. [d. November 15, 1958]

1915   **Richard H(alworth) Rovere,** U.S. journalist, author; best known for the commentaries he contributed to the *New Yorker* called "Letter from Washington," 1948–79. [d. November 23, 1979]

1916   **Giani Zail Singh,** Indian statesman; President, 1982– .

Historical Events

1292   **Adolf, Count of Nassau,** is elected King of Germany.

1645   **Charles I** surrenders to Scottish army at Newark (**English Civil War**).

1705   Holy Roman Emperor **Leopold I** dies and is succeeded by **Josef I.**

1811   British defeat French at **Fuentes d'Oñoro,** Portugal (**Napoleonic Wars**).

Thailand	Coronation Day
	Celebrates the coronation of **King Bhumibol Adulyades,** the titular head of state, 1946.

St. Jutta, widow and recluse; patroness of Prussia. Also called **Judith.** [d. 1260]

St. Hydroc, hermit. Also called **Hydoc.** [death date unknown]

Religious Calendar

The Saints

St. Hilary, Bishop of Arles. [d. 449]

St. Mauruntius, abbot. Also called **Mauront.** [d. 701]

St. Avertinus. Invoked against dizziness and headache. Also called **Avertin.** [d. c. 1180]

St. Angelo, martyr and Carmelite. Also called **Angelus.** [d. 1220]

1821	**Napoleon I of France** dies at St. Helena, where he has been in exile since 1815.
1860	**Giuseppe Garibaldi** and his thousand Redshirts sail from Genoa to Sicily (**Italian Revolution**).
1867	Mexican army, led by Gen. **Ignacio Zaragoza,** defeats a large French force near **Puebla,** Mexico.
1893	Stocks on **New York Stock Exchange** drop sharply, setting off **Panic of 1893.**
1904	**Cy Young** of Boston Americans Baseball Team becomes first major league pitcher to pitch a perfect game.
1930	**Mahatma Gandhi** is arrested by the British for violating India's salt-tax law in his **civil disobedience** campaign.
1936	Italy captures **Addis Ababa,** ending Ethiopian resistance.
1945	Nazi occupation of **Denmark** ends (**World War II).**
1950	Phumiphon Adundet is crowned King of Thailand as **Rama IX** in ceremonies at Bangkok.
1955	Adler and Ross's ***Damn Yankees*** premieres in New York.
1961	**Alan B. Shepard** makes 15-minute flight in ***Freedom 7*** from Cape Canaveral, reaching altitude of 116 miles and becoming first American in space.
1964	Israel's pipeline from the Sea of Galilee to the southern Negev Desert begins operation.
1981	IRA hunger striker **Robert Burns** dies in Maze Prison, Belfast.

May 6

Holidays

Lebanon	Martyrs' Day
The Phillipines	Kagitingan Day
Syria	Martyrs' Day

Religious Calendar

St. Evodius, Bishop of Antioch; first to use the word *Christian*. [d. c. 64]

Birthdates

1501 **Pope Marcellus II,** pope 1555. [d. May 1, 1555]

1758 **Maximilien François Marie Isidore de Robespierre,** French revolutionary leader; a major figure in the Reign of Terror of the French Revolution. [d. July 28, 1794]

Duc André Massena, Prince d'Essling, French Army marshal during French Revolutionary and Napoleonic Wars. [d. April 4, 1817]

1806 **Chapin Aaron Harris,** U.S. dentist; leader in founding *American Journal of Dental Science* and **American Society of Dental Surgeons.**

1837 **John Mahlon Marlin,** U.S. firearms inventor, manufacturer. [d. July 1, 1901]

1843 **Grove Karl Gilbert,** U.S. geologist. [d. May 1, 1918]

1853 **Philander Chase Knox,** U.S. politician, lawyer; U.S. Secretary of State, 1909–13. [d. October 12, 1921]

1856 **Sigmund Freud,** Austrian neurologist; the founder of **psychoanalysis.** [d. September 23, 1939]

Robert Edwin Peary, U.S. Arctic explorer; leader of the first expedition to reach the **North Pole,** 1909. [d. February 20, 1920]

1859 **Luis María Drago,** Argentine statesman; famous mainly for his support of the principle of international law known as the **Drago Doctrine,** providing that a nation may not use armed force to collect debts from another nation. [d. 1921]

1867 **Władysław Stanisław Reymont,** Polish novelist; Nobel Prize in literature, 1924. [d. December 5, 1924]

1868 **Nicholas II (Nikolai Aleksandrovich), Czar of Russia,** 1894–1917; his efforts led to **International Peace Conference** at the Hague, 1899; the founding of the **Hague Tribunal;** his rule was terminated by **Russian Revolution** of 1917. Abdicated March 15, 1917. [Executed July 16/17, 1918]

1870 **Amadeo Peter Giannini,** U.S. banker; organized California's Bank of America. [d. June 3, 1949]

John McCutcheon, U.S. cartoonist; Pulitzer Prize in editorial cartooning, 1932.

1871 **Victor Grignard,** French chemist; Nobel Prize in chemistry for developing the **Grignard reaction** (with P. Sabatier), 1912. [d. December 13, 1935]

1875 **William Daniel Leahy,** U.S. admiral during World War II; Chief of Staff to Presidents Franklin Roosevelt and Harry Truman, 1942–49. [d. July 20, 1959]

1888 **Emmanuel Celler,** U.S. politician, lawyer; U.S. Congressman, 1923–72; wrote and guided passage of **U.S. Civil Rights Act.** [d. January 15, 1981]

1895 **Rudolph Valentino (Rodolpho d'Antonguolla),** U.S. actor born in Italy; one of the film idols of the 1920s. [d. August 23, 1926]

1898 **Daniel Gerber,** U.S. baby food manufacturer; President and Chairman of the Board of Gerber Products; responsible for introducing strained baby food into U.S. [d. March 16, 1974]

1902 **Harry (Lewis) Golden,** U.S. author; known for his humorous as well as historical studies of Jews in America. [d. October 2, 1981]

1904 **Harry Edmund Martinson,** Swedish novelist, poet; Nobel Prize in literature, 1974. [d. February 11, 1978]

1913 **Stewart Granger (James Stewart),** British actor.

St. John before the Latin Gate, patron of booksellers. [d. c. 94]

St. Edbert, Bishop of Lindisfarne. Also called **Eadbert.** [d. 698]

St. Petronax, Abbot of Monte Cassino. [d. c. 747]

The Beatified

Blessed Prudence, virgin and nun. [d. 1492]

Blessed Edward Jones and **Blessed Anthony Middleton,** martyrs. [d. 1590]

Blessed Francis de Montmorency-Laval. [beatified 1980]

1914 **Randall Jarrell,** U.S. poet, critic, novelist; recipient of two National Book Awards. [d. October 14, 1965]

1915 **Orson Welles,** U.S. actor, director, producer.

Theodore (Harold) White, U.S. journalist, author, chronicler of U.S. presidential campaigns; Pulitzer Prize in nonfiction, 1962.

1926 **Ross Hunter (Martin Fuss),** U.S. film producer.

1931 **Willie (Howard) Mays,** U.S. baseball player. Inducted into Baseball Hall of Fame, 1979.

1952 **Samuel K. Doe,** Liberian statesman; President, 1980– .

Historical Events

1432 **Jan van Eyck** finishes altarpiece for St. John's in Ghent, Belgium.

1527 Spanish and German mercenaries under **Charles V, Holy Roman Emperor,** sack Rome, bringing an end to the **Roman Renaissance.**

1757 **Frederick II of Prussia** captures Prague (**Seven Years' War**).

1840 First adhesive postage stamps, **Penny Blacks,** go on sale in England.

1861 **Arkansas** becomes the ninth state to secede from the Union (**U.S. Civil War**).

1882 The **Chinese Exclusion Act** bars Chinese laborers from entering the U.S.

Fenians murder Chief Secretary of Ireland, **Lord Frederick Cavendish,** and his under-secretary, **Thomas Burke,** in Dublin's Phoenix Park.

1889 **Eiffel Tower** in Paris is completed for the opening of the Universal Exhibition.

1910 **King Edward VII of Great Britain** dies and is succeeded by **George V.**

1919 **Togoland** in West Africa becomes a mandate of France and Great Britain.

1930 Riots and uprisings against British rule break out all over **India** following the arrest of **Mahatma Gandhi.**

1937 The dirigible *Hindenburg* bursts into flames while landing at Lakehurst, N.J., killing 36 persons.

1942 U.S. General **Jonathan Wainwright** surrenders **Corregidor** in the Philippines to the Japanese (**World War II**).

Bataan in the Philippines falls to Japan (**World War II**).

1954 **Dr. Roger Bannister** of Great Britain becomes the first person to run the mile in less than four minutes.

1960 U.S. President Dwight D. Eisenhower signs the **Civil Rights Act** of 1960.

Princess Margaret Rose, sister of Queen Elizabeth II of England, is married in Westminster Abbey to **Antony Armstrong-Jones.**

1962 U.S. *Polaris* missile, armed with a nuclear warhead, is launched from the nuclear submarine *Ethan Allen* and successfully explodes near Christmas Island. It is the first test of a nuclear warhead carried by a long-range missile and the first launched from a submarine.

1974 West German Chancellor **Willy Brandt** resigns in connection with an East German spy affair.

1976 An earthquake measuring 6.5 on the Richter scale kills an estimated 1,000 people in northeastern Italy.

1979 Austrian Chancellor **Bruno Kreisky** wins an unprecedented fourth term of office.

May 7

Holidays

U.S.S.R.   **Radio Day**

Religious Calendar

Feasts

C. F. W. Walter, Doctor. Minor Lutheran festival.

Birthdates

1426 **Giovanni Gioviano Pontano,** Italian poet, humanist; State Secretary to Ferdinand I of Naples, 1486–94. [d. September 1503]

1574 **Pope Innocent X,** pope, 1644–55. [d. January 7, 1655]

1812 **Robert Browning,** British poet; husband of Elizabeth Barrett; buried in Westminster Abbey. [d. December 12, 1889]

1833 **Johannes Brahms,** German composer; called one of the great musicians of all times. [d. April 3, 1897]

1836 **Joseph Gurney Cannon** (*Uncle Joe*), U.S. politician, lawyer; U.S. Congressman for 50 years, from 1873, except for 1891–93 and 1913–15. [d. November 12, 1926]

1840 **Peter Ilyich Tchaikovsky,** Russian composer; renowned for his symphonic works and ballet music. [d. November 6, 1893]

1851 **Adolf von Harnack,** German Protestant theologian; noted for his work on Martin Luther, *Luthers Theologie.* [d. June 10, 1930]

1861 **Rabindranath Tagore,** Bengali poet, playwright, essayist, novelist; Nobel Prize in literature, 1913; knighted, 1915. [d. August 7, 1941]

1870 **Harry Vardon,** British golfer; considered one of the greatest golfers who ever lived. Won six British Opens.

1885 **Gabby Hayes** (**George Hayes**), U.S. character actor. [d. February 9, 1969]

1892 **Archibald MacLeish,** U.S. poet, playwright; Pulitzer Prize, 1932, 1953, 1959; Librarian of Congress, 1939–44. [d. April 20, 1982]

Marshall (**Josip Broz**) **Tito,** Yugoslav communist leader; created the modern state of **Yugoslavia.** [d. May 4, 1980]

1901 **Gary Cooper** (**Frank James Cooper**), U.S. actor. [d. May 13, 1961]

1909 **Edwin Herbert Land,** U.S. inventor; invented the Polaroid lens, 1932 and the **Polaroid Land** instant camera, 1947.

1919 **Eva Duarte de Perón,** Argentine political leader; as wife of Argentine dictator **Juan Perón,** brought about numerous social reforms. [d. July 26, 1952]

Historical Events

1847 **American Medical Association** is founded in Philadelphia.

1902 **Mt. Soufrière volcano** in Guadeloupe erupts, killing two thousand people.

1915 The *Lusitania* is torpedoed by a German submarine off the coast of Ireland and sinks with a loss of 1198 lives, including 139 Americans, bringing the U.S. and Germany to the brink of war (**World War I**).

1918 **Treaty of Bucharest** is signed between Rumania, Germany, and Austro-Hungary with Rumanian indemnities and cession of territory (**World War I**).

1919 The Supreme Council of the Allies of World War I assigns **German East Africa (Tanganyika)** to the mandate of Great Britain.

1925 **Leon Trotsky** returns from exile in the Caucasus.

1936 First airborne piano recital is given aboard the dirigible *Hindenburg* by **Franz Wagner** on an aluminum grand piano.

1953 Cole Porter's musical comedy *Can Can* premieres in New York.

1954 **Dien Bien Phu** is captured from the French by Communist Vietnamese.

1960 U.S. government concedes that U.S. plane shot down by U.S.S.R. was equipped for intelligence purposes; Soviet Premier Khrushchev reports the captured pilot, **Francis Gary Powers,** has confessed to being on a photo-reconnaissance mission.

The Saints

St. Domitian, Bishop of Maestricht. Patron of Huy on the Meuse River, Belgium. [d. c. 560]

St. Liudhard, bishop. [d. c. 602]

SS. Serenicus and **Serenus,** brothers, recluses. Serenicus also called **Cerenicus** and **Seneridus.** [d. c. 669 and 680]

St. John of Beverly, Bishop of York. [d. 721]

The Beatified

Blessed Rose Venerini, virgin. Founder of many schools. [d. 1728]

Leonid I. Brezhnev is chosen by the Soviet Supreme Council as president of the U.S.S.R.

1975 Rally in Saigon celebrates emergence of new military authorities one week after the city's surrender, and marks the 21st anniversary of the communist victory over the French at **Dien Bien Phu.**

May 8

Red Cross Day
Celebrates the birth of Henri Dunant, founder of the International Red Cross, 1828.

V-E Day
Commemorates the end of World War II in Europe and the surrender of the Germans.

U.S. (Missouri) **Harry S. Truman's Birthday**

Religious Calendar

Feasts

The Appearing of St. Michael the Archangel.

Birthdates

1668 **Alain René Lesage,** French novelist, dramatist; author of *L'Historie de Gil Blas de Santellane.* [d. November 17, 1747]

1753 **Miguel Hidalgo y Costilla,** Mexican priest, revolutionary leader; known as the *Father of Mexican Independence.* [d. August 1, 1811]

1821 **William Henry Vanderbilt,** U.S. financier; son of Cornelius Vanderbilt (May 27), and successor to his empire. [d. December 8, 1885]

1828 **Jean Henri Dunant,** Swiss philanthropist; founded **International Red Cross.** Recipient of the first Nobel Peace Prize (with F. Passy), 1901. [d. October 30, 1910]

1829 **Louis Moreau Gottschalk,** U.S. pianist, composer; renowned in international music circles of the period for both his classical style and his own compositions. [d. December 18, 1869]

1847 **Oscar Hammerstein,** U.S. producer; pioneer opera impresario; grandfather of composer Oscar Hammerstein II (July 12). [d. August 1, 1919]

1864 **John Galen Howard,** U.S. architect. [d. July 18, 1931]

1877 **Oscar Bloch,** French linguist. [d. April 15, 1937]

1884 **Harry S. Truman,** U.S. politician, 33rd President of the United States (1945–1953), succeeding to presidency upon the death of Franklin D. Roosevelt; served as president during end of World War II; responsible for the decision to drop atomic bombs on Hiroshima and Nagasaki. His term also encompassed the Korean War and the era of McCarthyism. [d. December 26, 1972]

1885 **Thomas B(ertram) Costain,** U.S. historical novelist; author of *The Silver Chalice.* [d. October 8, 1965]

1895 **Fulton J(ohn) Sheen,** U.S. Roman Catholic bishop; well known for radio and television broadcasts during 1950s. [d. December 9, 1979]

Edmund Wilson, U.S. literary and social critic; noted for his criticisms of Ernest Hemingway's works. [d. June 12, 1972]

1897 **Philip F. La Follette,** U.S. politician, lawyer; Governor of Wisconsin, 1931–33; 1935–39. [d. August 18, 1965]

Roscoe H(enry) Hillenkoetter, U.S. naval officer, government official; first director of Central Intelligence Agency, 1947–50; helped establish CIA as vanguard anti-Communist espionage organization. [d. June 18, 1982]

1899 **Friedrich August von Hayek,** British economist born in Austria; Nobel Prize in economics (with G. Myrdal), 1974.

1902 **André Michael Lwoff,** French microbiologist; Nobel Prize in physiology or medicine for research in genetics and enzymes and virus synthesis (with J. Monod and F. Jacob), 1965.

1905 **Red Nichols (Ernest Loring Nichols),** U.S. musician, cornetist and bandleader; formed a group, *The Five Pennies,* very

The Saints

St. Victor Maurus, martyr. Patron of Milan, Italy. [d. c. 303]

St. Acacius, soldier and martyr. One of only two genuine ancient martyrs of Byzantium. Also called **Agathus.** [d. c. 303]

St. Gibrian, priest and hermit. Also called **Gobrian, Gybrian.** [d. c. 515]

St. Desideratus, Bishop of Bourges. Also called **Désiré.** [d. c. 550]

St. Boniface IV, pope. Elected 608. Converted the Pantheon in Rome into a Christian church. [d. 615]

St. Benedict II, pope. Elected 684. Streamlined the procedure of papal elections. [d. 685]

SS. Wiro and **Plechelm,** bishops, and **St. Otger,** missionary. [d. 8th century]

St. Peter, Archbishop of Tarentaise. [d. 1175]

---

popular during 1930s and 1940s. [d. June 28, 1965]

1910 **Mary Lou Williams,** U.S. pianist, composer, arranger; known as the *Queen of Jazz;* composed "What's Your Story, Morning Glory?" [d. May 28, 1981]

1920 **Sloan Wilson,** U.S. novelist; author of *The Man in the Gray Flannel Suit.*

1937 **Thomas Pynchon,** U.S. novelist; author of *Gravity's Rainbow.*

1940 **Peter (Bradford) Benchley,** U.S. novelist; author of *Jaws.*

Historical Events

1559 Elizabeth of England assents to new **Act of Supremacy** defining crown's authority in the church and establishing use of **Book of Common Prayer.**

1794 **U.S. Post Office** is established.

1846 **Zachary Taylor** and his American troops defeat Mexicans at the **Battle of Palo Alto (Mexican War).**

1852 **Treaty of London** is signed by Great Britain, France, Russia, Austria, Sweden, and Prussia, guaranteeing the integrity of **Denmark.**

1918 **Ferdinand Foch** of France is appointed Allied Commander-in-Chief at the **Conference of Doullens (World War I).**

1929 Norway annexes **Jan Mayen Island.**

1942 U.S. carrier-based planes inflict heavy damage on Japanese fleet in the **Coral Sea (World War II).**

1945 The German High Command surrenders unconditionally to the Allies (**World War II**).

1952 U.S. planes bomb **Suan, Korea (Korean War).**

1964 Former U.S. President **Harry S. Truman,** on his 80th birthday, becomes the first former president to address a regular session of the Senate.

1967 Heavyweight boxing champion **Muhammad Ali (Cassius Clay)** is indicted by a federal grand jury in Houston, Texas, after refusing induction into the U.S. armed forces.

1968 **Catfish Hunter** of the Kansas City A's pitches a perfect game against the Minnesota Twins.

1970 Construction workers disrupt student **antiwar demonstrations** in New York City's Wall Street.

1973 Siege of **Wounded Knee** ends after 70 days as occupying Indians surrender under terms of a new cease-fire1

1976 **Clarence M. Kelly,** Director of the **FBI,** apologizes to the public for some of the FBI's activities during J. Edgar Hoover's 48-year term as director.

May 9

Holidays

Czechoslova-kia	**Anniversary of Liberation** Celebrates the end of World War II in Europe.
Poland	**Victoria Day** Celebrates the end of World War II in Europe.
U.S.S.R.	**Victory Day** Celebrates the end of World War II in Europe.

Birthdates

1775   **Jacob Jennings Brown,** U.S. general; prominent in War of 1812. [d. February 24, 1828]

1785   **James Pollard Espy,** U.S. meteorologist; a pioneer in the scientific methods of predicting weather. [d. January 24, 1860]

1800   **John Brown,** U.S. abolitionist; legendary antislavery figure. [d. December 2, 1859]

1845   **Gustav de Laval,** Swedish scientist; developed first successful **steam turbines** for small engines. [d. February 2, 1913]

1860   **Sir J(ames) M(atthew) Barrie,** Scottish dramatist, novelist; author of *Peter Pan.* [d. June 19, 1937]

1873   **Howard Carter,** British Egyptologist; discovered tomb of **Tutankhamen,** 1922. [d. 1939]

1874   **Dame Lilian Baylis,** British theatrical manager; associated with **Old Vic Theatre** and **Sadler's Wells Theatre.** [d. 1937]

1882   **Henry John Kaiser,** U.S. industrialist; built **San Francisco Bay Bridge,** 1933; **Bonneville Dam,** 1934; **Grand Coulee Dam,** 1939. Built "Liberty Ships" in World War II: laying of keel to launching was only 30 days. [d. August 24, 1967]

1883   **José Ortega y Gasset,** Spanish philosopher; one of foremost Spanish thinkers of the 20th century. [d. October 18, 1955]

1918   **Mike Wallace,** U.S. television interviewer, commentator.

1927   **Manfred Eigen,** German physicist; Nobel Prize in chemistry for research on high-speed chemical reactions (with R. G. Norrish and G. Porter), 1967.

1928   **Richard Alonzo (*Pancho*) Gonzalez,** U.S. tennis player, coach; world professional tennis champion eight times.

1936   **Albert Finney,** British actor.

1949   **Billy Joel,** U.S. singer, songwriter, musician.

Historical Events

1846   Americans under Zachary Taylor defeat Mexicans in the **Battle of Resaca de la Palma (Mexican War).**

1901   **Australia** opens its first parliament at Melbourne.

1911   All Chinese railroads are nationalized.

1915   Portugal declares war on Germany (**World War I**).

The **Second Battle of Artois** starts on the Western Front with simultaneous French and British attacks on German positions (**World War I**).

1926   Rear Admiral **Richard Byrd** of the U.S. Navy and Floyd Bennett complete the first flight over the **North Pole.**

1936   **Ethiopia** is formally annexed to Italy (**World War II**).

1937   The coronation march by **William Walton,** *Crown Imperial,* is first performed by the BBC in London in anticipation of the coronation of **George VI.**

1940   British troops occupy **Iceland (World War II).**

1942   U.S. carrier *Wasp* launches British aircraft to reinforce troops in **Malta (World War II).**

1960   **Federation of Nigeria** is admitted to the British Commonwealth.

1965   U.S.S.R. launches an instrumented space station, *Lunik 5,* from a rocket previously placed in orbit around the Earth.

Religious Calendar

The Saints

St. Beatus, priest and hermit. [d. c. 112]

St. Pachomius, abbot. Founder of Christian monasticism. Also called **the Elder.** [d. 348]

St. Gerontius, Bishop of Cervia. [d. 501]

The Beatified

Blessed Nicholas Albergati, Bishop of Bologna and Cardinal. [d. 1443]

1969   Roman Catholic Church issues a revised calendar which eliminates more than 200 saints.

1974   U.S. House of Representatives begins committee hearings on possibility of impeachment of **Richard M. Nixon.**

1978   The body of former Italian prime minister **Aldo Moro,** kidnapped by **Red Brigade** terrorists, is found in Rome.

1979   U.S. and U.S.S.R. complete **SALT II** agreement to limit strategic arms.

1983   **Pope John Paul II** announces the reversal of the Catholic Church's condemnation of **Galileo Galilei,** the 17th-century scientist who espoused the heliocentric nature of the solar system.

May 10

Holidays

U.S. (North Carolina, South Carolina)   Confederate Memorial Day

Religious Calendar

The Saints

St. Calepodius, martyr. Also called **Galepodius.** [d. 222]

Birthdates

1755   **Robert Gray,** U.S. sailor, explorer; captained the first U.S. ship to circumnavigate the world, 1787-90; discovered the **Columbia River** in the American northwest. [d. 1806]

1770   **Louis Nicolas Davout,** Marshal of France during Napoleonic period, 1804; Minister of War during Hundred Days. [d. June 1, 1823]

1788   **Augustin Fresnel,** French physicist; established the transverse wave theory of light; designed **Fresnel lens.** [d. July 14, 1827]

1808   **Elisha Root,** U.S. mechanic, inventor; one of first to use principle of interchangeable parts in production. [d. August 31, 1865]

1813   **Montgomery Blair,** U.S. politician; Postmaster General, 1861–64. [d. July 27, 1883]

1823   **John Sherman,** U.S. politician, government official; leading financial expert. [d. October 22, 1900]

1826   **Henry Clifton Sorby,** British geologist; discovered the microstructure of steel, marking the beginning of modern metallurgical science. [d. March 9, 1908]

1838   **John Wilkes Booth,** U.S. actor; assassin of President Abraham Lincoln. [d. April 26, 1865]

1841   **James Gordon Bennett,** U.S. publisher; founder of Paris edition of the New York *Herald.* [d. May 14, 1918]

1843   **Kaufmann Kohler,** U.S. rabbi; leader of Reformed Judaism. [d. January 28, 1926]

1850   **Sir Thomas Johnstone Lipton,** British merchant; founder of a financial empire based on tea, coffee, and cocoa. [d. October 2, 1931]

1878   **Gustav Stresemann,** German statesman; Nobel Peace Prize (with A. Briand), 1926. [d. October 3, 1929]

1886   **Karl Barth,** Swiss theologian. [d. December 9, 1968]

1888   **Max Steiner,** U.S. composer, born in Austria. [d. December 28, 1971]

1890   **Alfred Jodl,** German army general; helped plan most of Germany's World War II military campaigns. [d. October 16, 1946]

1898   **Ariel Durant (Ada Kaufman Durant),** U.S. historian, writer; co-author with husband Will Durant of numerous works which provided detailed, comprehensive history of civilization in a popularized format. [d. October 25, 1981]

1899   **Fred Astaire (Frederick Austerlitz),** U.S. dancer and actor.

1902   **David O. Selznick,** U.S. film producer. [d. June 22, 1965]

1908   **Carl Albert,** U.S. lawyer, politician; Congressman, 1947–82.

1919   **Ella Tambussi Grasso,** U.S. politician; Governor of Connecticut, 1975–81. [d. February 5, 1981]

1946   **Donovan (Leitch),** Scottish folk-rock singer.

Historical Events

1307   **Robert Bruce,** Scottish king, defeats English at **Ayrshire.**

1774   **Louis XV of France** dies and is succeeded by his grandson, **Louis XVI.**

1775   **Second Continental Congress** convenes in Philadelphia.

SS. Alphius and his companions, martyrs; principal patrons of Vaste in the diocese of Otranto and of Lentini, in Sicily. [d. 251]

SS. Gordian and **Epimachus,** martyrs. [d. c. 362 and 250]

St. Catald, Bishop of Taranto, and **St. Conleth,** Bishop of Kildare. Also called **Cataldus** and **Conlaed.** [d. c. 685 and c. 520]

St. Solangia, virgin and martyr; patron of Berry Province, France. Also called **Genevieve of Berry, Solange.** [d. 880]

St. Antoninus, Archbishop of Florence. Also called **Antonino, Little Antony.** [d. 1459]

The Beatified

Blessed Beatrice of Este, virgin and nun. [d. 1226]

Blessed John of Avila, priest; one of the most influential and eloquent religious leaders of sixteenth-century Spain. [d. 1569]

Ethan Allen and his **Green Mountain Boys** capture **Fort Ticonderoga** from the British (**American Revolution**).

1796 Bonaparte of France defeats Austrians at **Lodi** (**Napoleonic Wars**).

1849 **Astor Place Riot** takes place in New York City, following a controversial performance of *Macbeth;* 22 people are killed and 36 hurt.

1869 **Golden Spike** is driven at Promontory, Utah, to complete the first transcontinental railroad in the U.S.

1871 Franco-German peace treaty is signed at Frankfurt; France cedes Alsace and Lorraine (**Franco-German War**).

1876 **U.S. Centennial Exposition** opens in Philadelphia.

1908 The first **Mothers' Day** is observed in Philadelphia, based on the suggestions of **Julia Ward Howe** and **Anne Jarvis.**

1917 Major General **John J. Pershing** is named to command the U.S. forces in France (**World War I**).

1921 **Greenland** is officially declared a Danish possession.

1940 Germany invades **Luxembourg, Netherlands,** and **Belgium** by land and air (**World War II**).

Winston Churchill becomes Prime Minister of Great Britain.

1951 Veterans of **Korean War** are officially acknowledged by U.S. Congress, thus entitling them to veteran's benefits.

1960 U.S. atomic submarine *Triton* completes an 84-day submerged voyage around the world.

Lunch counters at four national and two local stores in Nashville, Tennessee, are desegregated without incident after a month of negotiations.

1972 Irish voters overwhelmingly approve entry into the **European Economic Community** in a national referendum.

1981 **François Mitterand**, a Socialist, defeats incumbent Valéry Giscard in French presidential election.

May 11

Holidays

U.S.
(Minnesota)

Minnesota Day
Commemorating the state's admission into the Union in 1858.

Religious Calendar

Feasts

SS. Philip and **James**, (Formerly May 1, which see.)

The Saints

St. Mamertus, Bishop of Vienne. Author of the Rogation processions. Also called **Mammertus.** [d. c. 475]

St. Tudy, monk and abbot. Also called **Tudec.** [d. 6th century]

St. Comgall, Abbot of Bangor. One of the founders of Irish monasticism. [d. 603]

Birthdates

1720 **Karl Friedrich Hieronymous, Baron von Munchhausen,** German soldier, huntsman; reputedly a great storyteller whose name is now commonly associated with absurdly exaggerated stories. [d. February 22, 1797]

1722 **Pieter Camper,** Dutch naturalist, anthropologist; known for early experiments in **comparative anatomy**; discovered the comparatively large air content of bird bones. [d. April 7, 1789]

1752 **Johann Friedrich Blumenbach,** German naturalist, anthropologist; recognized as the *Father of Modern Anthropology.* [d. January 22, 1840]

1811 **George Whitfield Scranton,** U.S. manufacturer; developed process for smelting iron ore with anthracite coal; **Scranton, Pennsylvania** is named for him. [d. March 24, 1861]

1854 **Ottmar Mergenthaler,** U.S. inventor of **Linotype machine.** [d. October 28, 1899]

1880 **George Edmund Haynes,** U.S. sociologist, civil rights leader; one of founders of the **National Urban League,** 1910. [d. January 8, 1960]

1888 **Irving Berlin (Israel Baline),** U.S. composer, songwriter; writer of over 800 popular songs as well as dozens of Broadway musical scores.

1891 **Henry Morgenthau, Jr.,** U.S. government official, conservationist; as Secretary of the Treasury under Franklin D. Roosevelt, was responsible for engineering support and financing of the **New Deal** programs, as well as the unparalleled expansion of the U.S. budget during World War II. [d. February 6, 1967]

1892 **Dame Margaret Rutherford,** British character actress. [d. May 22, 1972]

1893 **Martha Graham,** U.S. dancer, teacher, and choreographer of modern dance.

1894 **Ellsworth Bunker,** U.S. diplomat; U.S. Ambassador-at-Large, 1966–67; 1973–78; Ambassador to Vietnam, 1967–73. [d. September 28, 1984]

1897 **Robert Ellsworth Gross,** U.S. industrialist. [d. September 3, 1961]

1904 **Salvador Dali,** Spanish surrealist painter.

1906 **Jay C. Higginbotham,** U.S. jazz trombonist, singer. [d. May 26, 1973]

1918 **Richard Philips Feynman,** U.S. physicist; Nobel Prize in physics for reserch in quantum electrodynamics (with J. S. Schwinger and S. I. Tomonaga), 1965.

1924 **Antony Hewish,** British radio astronomer; Nobel Prize in physics for developing revolutionary **radio telescope systems** (with Sir M. Ryle), 1974.

St. Asaph, bishop. Founded the church of Llanasa in Flintshire and at Llanelwy. [d. 7th century]

St. Gengulf, a Burgundian knight. Also called **Gengoul.** [d. 760]

St. Fremund, hermit and martyr. [d. 866]

St. Majolus, Abbot of Cluny. Also called **Maieul, Maiolus, Mayeul.** [d. 994]

St. Ansfrid, Bishop of Utrecht. [d. 1010]

St. Walter of L'Esterp, abbot. [d. 1070]

The English Carthusian Martyrs, with Blessed John Haile, monk. London community of monks martyred under the Tudor persecution. General feast kept in Archdiocese of Westminster and by the Carthusians. [d. 1540]

St. Francis di Girolamo, Jesuit priest. [d. 1716]

St. Ignatius of Laconi, Franciscan monk. [d. 1781]

The Beatified

Blessed Albert of Bergamo, Dominican tertiary. [d. 1279]

Blessed Vivaldo, a solitary. Also called **Ubaldo.** [d. 1300]

Blessed Benincasa, hermit. [d. 1426]

Blessed Aloysius Rabata, Carmelite prior. [d. 1490]

Blessed Ladislaus of Gielniow, Franciscan missioner; one of the principal patrons of Poland. [d. 1505]

Historical Events

330   **Constantinople** becomes new capital of the Roman Empire.

973   English **King Edgar** is crowned at Bath.

1258   **Treaty of Corbeil** between **Louis IX of France** and **James of Aragon** regulates the Pyrenees frontier.

1812   British Prime Minister **Spencer Percival** is assassinated in the lobby of the House of Commons by a bankrupt broker, **John Bellingham.**

1858   **Minnesota** enters the Union as the 32nd state.

1867   Grand Duchy of **Luxembourg** is declared independent by the Treaty of London.

1894   **Pullman strike** in U.S. ends in defeat for organized labor.

1910   **Glacier National Park** in Montana is established.

1931   The failure of the Austrian **Credit-Anstalt** (Austria's largest bank) marks the beginning of the financial collapse of central Europe.

1935   U.S. President Franklin D. Roosevelt creates the **Rural Electrification Administration** to extend electricity into rural areas of the U.S.

1938   Richard Rodgers' and Lorenz Hart's *I Married an Angel* premieres in New York.

1943   U.S. amphibious force lands on **Attu** in the Aleutians and annihilates 2,350 Japanese defenders (**World War II**).

1949   **Israel** is admitted to the United Nations.
       Siam is officially renamed **Thailand.**

1950   **Grand Coulee Dam** in the State of Washington is dedicated by U.S. President Harry S. Truman.

1973   Formal relations between **East** and **West Germany** are established by a treaty ratified by the West German Bundestag.

1978   Anti-government rioting spreads to Iranian capital where religious Muslim demonstrators demand the removal of **Shah Mohammad Reza Pahlavi.**

       Secessionist guerrillas of the **Congo National Liberation Front** invade Zaire's Shaba province with the active support of Angolan and Cuban forces.

May 12

Religious Calendar

The Saints

SS. Nereus, Achilleus and **Domitilla,** martyrs. [d. c. 1st century] Optional Memorial.

St. Pancras, martyr; in Middle Ages regarded as protector against false oaths and as the avenger of perjury. [d. c. 304] Optional Memorial.

St. Epiphanius, Bishop of Salamis. [d. 403]

Birthdates

1803 **Baron Justus von Liebig,** German organic chemist; established first practical teaching laboratory for study of chemistry. Discovered chloroform, aldehyde; considered the founder of agricultural chemistry. [d. April 10, 1873]

1804 **Robert Baldwin,** Canadian statesman; formed first Canadian administration after Act of Union. [d. December 9, 1858]

1812 **Edward Lear,** British author, artist; best known for limericks and nonsense verse. [d. January 29, 1888]

1816 **Sir Edmund Beckett, 1st Baron Grimthorpe,** British lawyer, author, inventor, architect; superintended construction of **Big Ben.** [d. April 29, 1905]

1820 **Florence Nightingale,** British nurse, hospital reformer, philanthropist. First woman to receive British Order of Merit. [d. August 13, 1910]

1828 **Dante Gabriel Rossetti (Gabriel Charles Dante),** British poet, painter; founder of **Pre-Raphaelite Brotherhood.** [d. April 9, 1882]

1842 **Jules Emile Frédéric Massenet,** French composer; winner of *Prix de Rome*, 1863. [d. August 13, 1912]

1850 **Henry Cabot Lodge,** U.S. politician, historian; grandfather of Henry Cabot Lodge, Jr. (July 5). [d. November 9, 1924]

1857 **William Archibald Dunning,** U.S. historian, educator; instructor in history, Columbia University, 1886–1922. [d. August 25, 1922]

1859 **Lillian Nordica,** U.S. operatic soprano, best known for Wagnerian roles. [d. May 10, 1914]

1880 **Lincoln Ellsworth,** U.S. polar explorer, scientist; first man to accomplish air crossings of both the Arctic, 1926, and Antarctic, 1933. [d. May 26, 1951]

1895 **William Francis Giauque,** U.S. chemist; Nobel Prize in chemistry for studies of properties of substances at extremely low temperatures, 1949. [d. March 29, 1982]

1901 **Sir Christopher Hinton, Lord Hinton of Bankshire, Baron of Dulwich,** British nuclear engineer; built first large scale nuclear power plant in England, 1956.

1902 **Philip Wylie,** U.S. novelist, critic; best known for *Generation of Vipers*, an attack on traditional American institutions. [d. October 25, 1971]

1903 **Wilfred Hyde-White,** British character actor.

1906 **William Maurice Ewing,** U.S. geologist, oceanographer; best known for studies of ocean floor and underwater exploration with seismic waves.

1910 **Dorothy C. Hodgkin,** British chemist; Nobel Prize in chemistry for work determining structure of **Vitamin B-12,** 1964.

1914 **Howard K. Smith,** U.S. news commentator.

1918 **Julius Rosenberg;** he and his wife, Ethel, were first U.S. civilians to be executed for espionage. [d. June 19, 1953]

1925 **(Lawrence Peter) Yogi Berra,** U.S. baseball player, manager, coach. Elected to Baseball Hall of Fame, 1972.

1929 **Burt Bacharach,** U.S. composer, pianist.

1938 **Andrei (Alekseyevich) Amalrik,** Soviet author, dissident, historian; outspoken in his criticism both of Russian and western policies. Died in an automobile accident. [d. November 11, 1980]

St. Modoaldus, Bishop of Trier and advisor to King Dagobert. Also called **Modowaldus.** [d. c. 640]

St. Rictrudis, widow and abbess. Founded the double Monastery at Marchiennes. Also called **Rictrudes.** [d. 688]

St. Germanus, Patriarch of Constantinople. [d. 732]

St. Dominic of the Causeway, hermit and hospice-builder. [d. c. 1109]

The Beatified

Blessed Francis Patrizzi, member of Servite Order. [d. 1328]

Blessed Gemma of Solmona, virgin and recluse. [d. 1429]

Blessed Jane of Portugal, virgin and Dominican lay-sister. Daughter of King Alphonso V of Portugal. [d. 1490]

Historical Events

1843   **Natal** in South Africa is proclaimed a British colony.

1846   U.S. declares war on Mexico (**Mexican War**).

1873   **King Oscar II** and his wife **Sophia** are crowned as rulers of **Sweden.**

1888   British establish protectorates over **North Borneo**, **Brunei,** and **Sarawak.**

1898   Louisiana adopts constitution disenfranchising blacks under property and literacy tests and the *grandfather clause.*

1917   **Thoroughbred Omar Khayyam** becomes first horse not born in America to win the **Kentucky Derby.**

1922   A twenty-ton **meteor** falls near Blackstone, Virginia, causing a 500-square-foot breach in the earth.

1926   **Joseph Pilsudski** leads successful military revolt against the Polish government.

Roald Amundsen, **Umberto Nobile,** and **Lincoln Ellsworth** fly over the **North Pole** in a 71-hour flight in the dirigible *Norge.*

1933   U.S. President Franklin D. Roosevelt signs the **Agricultural Adjustment Act** providing subsidies for farmers and establishing parity prices.

1936   Broadcast of the coronation of **George VI of England** is the first worldwide radio broadcast heard in the U.S. George VI succeeds his brother, **Edward VIII,** who has abdicated in order to marry U.S. divorcèe **Wallis Warfield Simpson.**

1943   German and Italian troops numbering 252,000 surrender to the Allies in **North Africa** (**World War II**).

Trident Conference in Washington, D.C., opens as **Franklin D. Roosevelt** and **Winston Churchill** plan global strategy and prepare for a second front in Europe (**World War II**).

1962   U.S. President **John F. Kennedy** orders troops into **Thailand** to defend the country against insurgents from Laos.

1975   Cambodia seizes U.S. merchant ship *Mayaguez.*

May 13

The Saints

St. Glyceria, virgin and martyr. [d. c. 177]

St. Mucius, martyr. Also called **Mocius.** [d. 304]

St. Servatius, Bishop of Tongres. Invoked against rodents and leg diseases, and for the success of enterprises. Also called **Servais, Servatus.** [d. 384]

Birthdates

1655 **Pope Innocent XIII,** pope 1721–24. [d. March 7, 1724]

1713 **Alexis Clairaut,** French mathematician; conducted mathematical investigations regarding the shape of the earth. [d. May 17, 1765]

1717 **Maria Theresa, Empress of Austria,** 1740–80; Archduchess of Austria, Queen of Hungary and Bohemia. [d. November 29, 1780]

1767 **John VI, King of Portugal** 1816–26. [March 10, 1826]

1792 **Pope Pius IX,** pope 1846–78; during his term the dogma of **infallibility** was promulgated. [d. February 7, 1878]

1842 **Sir Arthur S(eymour) Sullivan,** British composer, conductor; best known as collaborator with W. S. Gilbert (November 18) in popular satiric operettas. [d. November 22, 1900]

1845 **Gabriel Urbain Fauré,** French composer; credited with moving away from German influence in modern French music. [d. November 4, 1924]

1850 **Oliver Heaviside,** British physicist; **Heaviside layer** in the ionosphere (now called **E-layer**) was named after him. [d. February 3, 1925]

1857 **Sir Ronald Ross,** British bacteriologist; Nobel Prize in physiology or medicine for discovery of life cycle of **malaria** parasite, 1902. [d. September 16, 1932]

1882 **Georges Braque,** French painter, sculptor, stage designer; a principal figure in modern art. [d. August 31, 1963]

1883 **George Nicholas Papanicolaou,** U.S. physiologist; developer of **Pap smear** test for detection of cervical cancer. [d. February 19, 1962]

1907 **Daphne Du Maurier,** British novelist; author of *Rebecca.*

1913 **William R(ichard) Tolbert, Jr.,** Liberian statesman; President of Liberia, 1972–80; President of Baptist World Alliance, 1965–70. Killed in a coup. [d. April 12, 1980]

1914 **Joe Louis (Joseph Louis Barrow),** U.S. boxer; World Heavyweight Champion, 1937–49, longest reign in history; known as the *Brown Bomber.* [d. April 12, 1981]

1931 **Jim (James Warren) Jones,** U.S. fanatical leader of the **People's Temple,** an agrarian socialist cult that settled in Guyana, scene of mass suicide, 1978. [d. November 18, 1978]

1950 **Stevie Wonder (Steveland Morris),** U.S. singer, composer.

Historical Events

1532 **Scottish College of Justice** is established.

1568 **Mary, Queen of Scots,** is defeated by English at Langside.

1783 **Society of the Cincinnati** is founded at Newburgh, New York, by a group of Continental Army officers.

1888 **Serfdom** is abolished in Brazil.

1907 Legislation establishing **universal suffrage** is passed in Sweden.

1927 *Black Friday* signals the collapse of the German economic structure.

1965 **West Germany** and **Israel** open full diplomatic relations; Algeria, Iraq, Jordan, Saudi Arabia, Syria, the United Arab Republic, and Yemen sever relations with West Germany.

1967 About 70,000 persons march down Fifth Avenue in New York City in support of the U.S. soldiers fighting in Vietnam (**Vietnam War**).

1968 U.S. and North Vietnamese negotiators open talks aimed at ending **Vietnam War.**

St. John the Silent, hermit. Also called **the Sabaïte.** [d. 558]

St. Erconwald, Bishop of London and monastery founder. Also called **Earconwald**, **Erkenwald**, **Erkonwald.** [d. c. 693]

St. Euthymius the Enlightener, abbot. [d. 1028]

St. Peter Regalatus, Franciscan monk. Also called **Peter Regalati.** [d. 1456]

St. Andrew Hubert Fournet, co-founder of the Daughters of the Cross, also called the Sisters of St. Andrew. [d. 1834]

The Beatified

Blessed Imelda, virgin. [d. 1333]

Blessed Julian of Norwich, virgin and mystic. [d. c. 1423]

1981   **Pope John Paul II** is shot and wounded in an assassination attempt in Rome; a Turkish terrorist is arrested.

May 14

Guinea	**Anniversary of the Guinean Democratic Party**
Liberia	**National Unification Day** A day set aside to recognize the National Unification Party, which is dedicated to a unified Liberia.
Malawi (Nyasaland)	**Kamuzu Day** Commemorates the birthday of Dr. Kamuzu Banda, first president of the republic, 1906.
Paraguay	**National Flag Day** Beginning of a two-day celebration marking the achievement of independence from Spain, 1811.

Birthdates

1316 **Charles IV of Luxemburg,** Holy Roman Emperor 1355–78; known as a patron of the arts and sciences. [d. November 29, 1378]

1686 **Gabriel Daniel Fahrenheit,** German physicist; devised **Fahrenheit scale** which bears his name. [d. September 16, 1736]

1710 **Adolf Frederick, King of Sweden,** 1751–71. [d. February 12, 1771]

1727 **Thomas Gainsborough,** baptized on this day; English painter of landscapes and idyllic scenes. [d. August 2, 1788]

1752 **Timothy Dwight,** U.S. educator, theologian; one of **Hartford Wits**; President, Yale University, 1795–1817; grandson of Jonathan Edwards. [d. January 11, 1817]

1771 **Robert Owen,** Welsh sociologist; pioneer of cooperation in industry; founder of socialism in Great Britain; founder of **New Harmony, Indiana,** a utopian community. [d. November 17, 1858]

1827 **Jean Baptiste Carpeaux,** French sculptor; sculpted *The Dance,* now in the Louvre, Paris. [d. October 11, 1875]

1853 **Sir Thomas Henry Hall Caine,** British novelist, playwright. [d. August 31, 1931]

1872 **Mikhail Semenovich Tsvett,** Russian botanist; inventor of **chromatography,** 1906. [d. May 1920]

1885 **Otto Klemperer,** German conductor; known especially for interpretations of German Romantic works. [d. July 3, 1973]

1894 **Frank (Francis Marion) Folsom,** U.S. electronics executive; President of RCA, 1949–57.

1925 **Patrice Munsel,** U.S. soprano; the youngest singer ever to become a member of the Metropolitan Opera Company (at age 18).

1936 **Bobby Darin (Walden Robert Cassotto),** U.S. singer. [d. Dec. 20, 1973]

Historical Events

1509 **Venetians** are defeated at Agnadello by the **League of Cambrai,** consisting of Holy Roman Empire, France, Aragon, and the Papacy.

1607 **Jamestown, Virginia,** the first permanent English settlement in America, is founded.

1619 **Jan van Barneveldt,** Dutch statesman and champion of Dutch independence, is executed for treason.

1643 **Louis XIV of France** accedes to the throne (with **Anne of Austria** as Regent).

1796 **Dr. Edward Jenner** begins experiments which ultimately result in development of **vaccination.**

1801 **Yusef, Pasha of Tripoli,** declares war on the U.S. (**Tripolitan War**).

1930 **Carlsbad Caverns** in New Mexico becomes a national park.

Religious Calendar

Feasts

St. Matthias, apostle and martyr. Took the place among the twelve apostles left vacant by Judas Iscariot. Patron of carpenters, tailors, and reformed drunks. Invoked against smallpox. Feast formerly February 24. [d. 1st century]

St. Pontius, martyr. [d. c. 3rd century]

St. Boniface of Tarsus, martyr. [d. c. 306]

St. Carthage, bishop. Founded one of most famous of all Irish monastic schools, that of Lismore. Also called **Carthach, Carthagh, Mochuda, Mochudu.** [d. 637]

St. Erembert, Bishop of Toulouse. [d. c. 672]

St. Michael Garicoïts, founder of the Priests of the Sacred Heart of Bétharram. [d. 1863]

St. Mary Mazzarello, virgin and co-founder of the Daughters of Our Lady Help of Christians, founded for educating children. [d. 1881]

The Beatified

Blessed Giles of Portugal, Dominican friar. [d. 1265]

Blessed Petronilla of Moncel, virgin and abbess. [d. 1355]

Blessed Magdalen di Canossa, virgin and founder of the Canossian Daughters of Charity. [d. 1835]

1938 League of Nations recognizes unconditional neutrality of **Switzerland**.

1948 The U.S. becomes the first country to recognize the State of **Israel.**

1963 **Kuwait** becomes the 111th member of the United Nations.

1965 **Queen Elizabeth II** donates three acres of land at Runnymede to the U.S. for a memorial to assassinated U.S. President **John F. Kennedy.**

1973 *Skylab,* first orbiting U.S. space laboratory, is launched.

1974 **Archbishop Donald Coggan** is named 101st Archbishop of Canterbury by Queen Elizabeth II, succeeding Archbishop **Michael Ramsey.**

1978 **Franz Oppurg,** an Austrian climber, makes first successful solo ascent of **Mount Everest.**

May 15

Paraguay **Independence Day**
Celebrates the achievement of independence from Spain, 1811. The second day of a two-day celebration. (See Flag Day, May 14.)

U.S. **Peace Officers Memorial Day**
Commemorates all those law enforcement persons who have lost their lives in the line of duty.

Birthdates

1567 **Claudio Giovanni Antonio Monteverdi,** baptized on this day; Italian composer, music reformer; responsible for many innovations in musical compositions, including the elaboration on recitative forms; composed many madrigals. [d. November 29, 1643]

1633 **Sebastien le Prestre de Vauban,** French military engineer; Marshal of France, 1703. [d. March 30, 1707]

1773 **Klemens Wenzel Nepomuk Lothar von Metternich,** Austrian diplomat and statesman; played key role in making Austria a leading power of the 19th century. [d. June 11, 1859]

1788 **James Gadsden,** U.S. statesman; responsible for the **Gadsden Purchase** from Mexico by which the U.S. acquired southern **Arizona** and **New Mexico.** [d. December 25, 1858]

1808 **Michael William Balfe,** Irish operatic composer; composed *The Bohemian Girl,* which contains *I Dreamed I Dwelt in Marble Halls.* [d. October 20, 1870]

1814 **Stephen Heller,** Hungarian composer, pianist; intimate of Chopin, Liszt, and Berlioz. [d. January 14, 1888]

1845 **Elie Metchnikoff (Ilya Ilich Mechnikov),** French bacteriologist born in Russia; discovered **white corpuscles** in living cells; Nobel Prize in physiology or medicine for work on immunology (with P. Ehrlich), 1908. [d. July 15, 1916]

1855 **Louis Bamberger,** U.S. merchant. [d. March 11, 1944]

1856 **L(yman) Frank Baum,** U.S. writer of children's stories; known chiefly for the *Oz* books. [d. May 6, 1919]

1859 **Pierre Curie,** French chemist; Nobel Prize in physics for work on spontaneous radioactivity (with his wife Marie Curie and A. H. Becquerel), 1903. [d. April 19, 1906]

1862 **Arthur Schnitzler,** Austrian playwright, novelist. [d. October 21, 1931]

1870 **Henry Latham Doherty,** U.S. industrialist; founder of Cities Service Corporation, 1910. [d. December 26, 1939]

1889 **Bessie Hillman,** U.S. labor leader; founder of the **Amalgamated Clothing Workers of America.** [d. December 23, 1970]

1890 **Katherine Anne Porter,** U.S. short-story writer, novelist. [d. September 18, 1980]

1902 **Richard J. Daley,** U.S. political leader; Mayor of Chicago, 1955-76; called the last of the big-city bosses. [d. December 20, 1976]

1904 **Clifton Fadiman,** U.S. literary critic, author.

1905 **Joseph Cotten,** U.S. actor.

1909 **James Mason,** British actor. [d. July 27, 1984]

1910 **Constance Cummings (Constance Halverstadt),** U.S. stage and film actress.

1915 **Paul Anthony Samuelson,** U.S. economist; Nobel Prize in economics, 1970.

1918 **Eddy Arnold,** U.S. singer.

1921 **Erroll Garner,** U.S. jazz pianist, composer. [d. 1977]

1926 **(Levin) Peter Shaffer,** British playwright.

Religious Calendar

SS. Torquatus and his companions, martyrs. First Christian missionaries in Spain. [d. c. 1st century]

St. Isidore of Chios, martyr. [d. c. 251]

SS. Peter of Lampsacus and his companions, martyrs. [d. 251]

St. Hilary of Galeata, abbot and founder of the Monastery at Galeata. [d. 558]

SS. Dympna and **Gerebernus,** martyrs. Dympna is now regarded as patron saint of the insane. [d. c. 650]

St. Bertinus, abbot. Also called **Bercthun, Bertin, Brithun.** [d. c. 709]

SS. Bertha and **Rupert,** mother and son who established several hospices for the poor. [d. c. 840]

St. Hallvard, martyr; patron of Oslo, Norway. Invoked in defense of an innocent person. [d. 1043]

St. Isaias, Bishop of Rostov. [d. 1090]

St. Isidore the Husbandman, layman; patron of Madrid, Spain. [d. 1130]

The Beatified

Blessed Magdalen Albrizzi, virgin and superior of Convent at Brunate. [d. 1465]

1931 **Joseph Anthony Califano, Jr.,** U.S. government official; Secretary of Health, Education, and Welfare, 1977-79.

1936 **Anna Maria Alberghetti,** U.S. operatic soprano born in Italy.

Historical Events

1004 **Henry II of Germany** is crowned King of Lombardy.

1213 **King John of England** submits to **Pope Innocent III,** and England and Ireland become papal fiefs.

1455 Crusade against the Turks and for the capture of **Constantinople** is proclaimed by **Pope Calixtus III.**

1567 **Mary, Queen of Scots** marries **James Hepburn, Earl of Bothwell.**

1860 **Giuseppe Garibaldi** defeats Neapolitan army at Calatafimi (**War of Italian Unification**).

1867 Russia ratifies the treaty selling **Alaska** to the U.S. for $7 million.

1900 **Paderewski Fund** is established by Ignace Paderewski to award American orchestral composers.

1916 Austro-Hungarians successfuly launch offensive at Trentino, Italy (**World War I**).

1920 English army of occupation, known as the *Black and Tans,* arrives in Ireland.

1934 Coup d'état in **Latvia** is led by **Karlis Ulmanis,** the Prime Minister.

1940 Dutch army capitulates to Germany (**World War II**).

1951 **American Telephone & Telegraph Co.** becomes the world's first corporation to have one million stockholders.

1955 **Austria** and **Russia** conclude a state treaty restoring Austrian independence and ending Russian occupation.

1963 U.S. astronaut **Gordon Cooper** in *Faith 7* capsule is recovered near Midway after orbiting the earth 22 times.

1969 Students and others occupying **People's Park** on the campus of the University of California at Berkeley are attacked by police and national guardsmen during **Vietnam War protest.**

Justice Abe Fortas resigns from the U.S. Supreme Court because of criticism of his financial dealings.

1970 At **Jackson State College,** Mississippi, two students are killed when city and state police open fire on demonstrators.

1972 Alabama governor **George Wallace** is seriously wounded in an assassination attempt while campaigning in the Maryland Democratic presidential primary.

May 16

Religious Calendar

The Saints

St. Peregrine, Bishop of Auxerre, martyr. Evangelized much of his part of France. [d. c. 261]

St. Possidius, Bishop of Calama; a pupil and close associate of St. Augustine. [d. c. 440]

St. Germerius, Bishop of Toulouse. Also called **Germier.** [d. c. 560]

Birthdates

1782 **John Sell Cotman,** English painter; among his most famous pieces are *Silver Birches* and *Waterfall.* [d. July 24, 1842]

1801 **William Henry Seward,** U.S. politician, statesman; responsible for U.S. acquisition of **Alaska,** then known as *Seward's Folly.* [d. October 10, 1872]

1804 **Elizabeth Palmer Peabody,** U.S. educator; founded first **kindergarten** in U.S., 1860. [d. January 3, 1894]

1824 **Edmund Kirby-Smith,** Confederate Army officer during U.S. Civil War; the last Confederate commander to surrender. [d. March 28, 1893]

1831 **David Edward Hughes,** U.S. inventor of type-printing **telegraph** and **microphone.** [d. January 22, 1900]

1832 **Philip Danforth Armour,** U.S. meat-packing executive; President of Armour & Co., 1875–1901. [d. January 6, 1901]

1905 **Henry Fonda,** U.S. actor. [d. August 12, 1982]

1909 **Deighton Ward,** Governor-General of Barbados, 1976– .

1911 **Margaret (Brooke) Sullavan,** U.S. actress. [d. January 1, 1960]

1912 **Studs (Louis) Terkel,** U.S. writer; noted for books based on extensive personal interviews with average people.

1913 **Woody Herman (Woodrow Charles),** U.S. musician, orchestra leader.

1919 **Liberace (Wladziu Valentino),** U.S. entertainer.

1924 **Dawda Kairaba Jawara,** Gambian statesman; President, The Gambia, 1970– .

1955 **Olga Korbut,** Russian gymnast; Olympic gold medalist, 1972.

Historical Events

1568 **Mary, Queen of Scots,** flees to England for sanctuary after her defeat at **Langsides** (now Glasgow).

1763 **Samuel Johnson,** the great British lexicographer, meets his future biographer, **James Boswell,** for the first time.

1770 The French Dauphin, 15, (the future **Louis XVI**) marries **Marie Antoinette,** 14, at Versailles.

1868 U.S. Senate in impeachment trial of President **Andrew Johnson** votes for acquittal.

1915 The **Battle of the San** begins as Russians attempt to halt the advancing Austro-German army in Galicia (**World War I**).

1920 **Joan of Arc** is canonized.

1939 **Food stamps** are first introduced in the U.S.

1946 Irving Berlin's musical comedy, ***Annie Get Your Gun,*** premieres in New York.

1950 **Vladimir Houdek,** Czechoslovak delegate to the United Nations, resigns and seeks asylum in the U.S.

1974 **Helmut Schmidt** is sworn in as West German Chancellor.

1979 The problem of **boat people** and other peoples displaced by conflict in Southeast Asia is first addressed by the Association of Southeast Asian Nations.

St. Brendan, Abbot of Clonfert. [d. 577 or 583]

St. Domnolus, Bishop of Le Mans. Builder of several churches and a hospice. [d. 581]

St. Carantoc, abbot. Also called **Carannog.** [d. 6th century]

St. Honoratus, Bishop of Amiens. In France regarded as patron of bakers and all trades that deal with flour. Also called **Honorius.** [d. c. 600]

St. Ubald, Bishop of Gubbio. Also called **Ubaldo, Ubaldus.** [d. 1160]

St. Simon Stock, Carmelite friar; responsible for the tradition of wearing the scapular. [d. 1265]

St. John Nepomucen, martyr; principal patron of Bohemia and patron of bridges. His name is invoked against floods and slander, as well as for help in making a good confession. Also called **Nepomuc, Nepomucene, Nepomuk.** [d. 1393]

May 17

Holidays

World Telecommunications Day
Sponsored by United Nations.

Nauru   **Constitution Day**
Commemorates the adoption of the country's constitution and achievement of independence from Australia, 1968.

Norway   **Constitution Day**
Commemorates the adoption of Norway's constitution, 1814.

Birthdates

1749   **Edward Jenner,** English physician; developed vaccination for **smallpox.** [d. January 24, 1823]

1836   **Sir Joseph Norman Lockyer,** British astronomer; pioneered **solar spectroscopy.** [d. August 16, 1920]

1845   **Jacinto Verdaguer,** Catalan poet. [d. June 10, 1902]

1855   **Timothy Michael Healy,** Irish political leader; first Governor-General of the **Irish Free State.** [d. March 26, 1931]

1864   **Harry Chandler,** U.S. newspaper publisher. [d. September 23, 1944]

1866   **Erik Alfred-Leslie Satie,** French composer. [d. July 1, 1925]

1868   **Horace Elgin Dodge,** U.S. manufacturer; responsible for the initial success of the Dodge Company, automobile manufacturer. [d. December 10, 1920]

1875   **Joel Elias Spingarn,** U.S. educator, literary critic, civil rights leader; co-founder of **National Association for the Advancement of Colored People;** President, 1930–39; **Spingarn Medal,** established and endowed by Spingarn, is awarded annually to a black in recognition of service to his race. [d. July 26, 1939]

1886   **Alphonso XIII, King of Spain**; ruled during Spanish-American War when Spain lost Cuba, Puerto Rico, and the Philippines. Spanish Revolution forced his resignation, 1931. [d. February 28, 1941]

1897   **Odd Hassel,** Norwegian chemist; Nobel Prize in chemistry for helping establish conformational analysis (with D. Barton), 1969.

1900   **Ruholla Khomeini (Ruhollah Hendi),** Iranian ayatollah, Moslem religious and revolutionary leader; the chief political figure in Iran since 1979.

1904   **Jean Gabin (Alexis Moncourge),** French actor. [d. November 15, 1976]

1905   **John Patrick (Goggan),** U.S. playwright.

1911   **Maureen O'Sullivan,** U.S. actress.

1912   **Archibald Cox,** U.S. lawyer, professor; special prosecutor in **Watergate** investigation 1973.

1914   **Stewart Johonnot Oliver Alsop,** U.S. journalist, editor. [d. May 26, 1974]

1918   **Birgit Nilsson,** Swedish operatic soprano.

1956   **(Sugar) Ray Leonard,** U.S. boxer.

Historical Events

1198   **Frederick II, Holy Roman Emperor,** is crowned King of Sicily.

1540   **Humayun,** Sultan of Delhi, is defeated at Kanauj and is driven out of India by Sher Shah.

1579   Southern Netherlands recognizes **Philip II of Spain** in the **Peace of Arras (Dutch War of Liberation).**

1814   **Norway** declares independence from Sweden.

1875   First **Kentucky Derby** is held at Churchill Downs, Kentucky. *Aristides* is the winner of the $2850 purse.

1885   Apaches under **Geronimo** rise in revolt in Arizona and New Mexico.

1902   **Alfonso XIII** reaches his majority and is recognized as constitutional monarch in Spain, ending the long regency of his mother.

Religious Calendar

The Saints

St. Madron. Springs in the ruins of St. Madron's Church in Cornwall are noted for their curing powers, supposedly effective in helping skin diseases. Also called **Maden, Madern.** [d. c. 6th century]

St. Bruno, Bishop of Würzburg. Built cathedral of St. Kilian. [d. 1045]

St. Paschal Baylon, Friar Minor; patron of eucharistic congresses and organizations. Also called **Paschal Babylon.** [d. 1592]

The Beatified

Blessed Ratho of Andechs; a Bavarian monastery-builder, his name is invoked by invalids, especially those suffering from hernia and stone. [d. 953]

Blessed Andrew Abellon, Dominican prior. [d. 1450]

1904	*Shéhérazade* by Maurice Ravel premieres in Paris.
1925	**St. Thérèse of Lisieux** is canonized.
1930	The British administration restricts Jewish immigration to **Palestine.**
1944	British forces take **Cassino, Italy** from the Germans (**World War II**).
1954	U.S. Supreme Court issues ***Brown v. Board of Education*** decision, ruling that segregated schools are unconstitutional.

May 18

Holidays

Haiti   **Flag Day**

Uruguay   **La Piedras Battle Day**
Commemorates the end of conflict between Uruguay and Brazil and the achievement of Uruguayan Independence, 1828.

Religious Calendar

The Saints

St. Venantius, martyr. Also called **Verantius.** [d. c. 257]

Birthdates

1692 **Joseph Butler,** English clergyman, moralist, writer; Dean of St. Paul's, 1740; Bishop of Durham, 1750. [d. June 16, 1752]

1788 **Hugh Clapperton,** one of first European explorers of **Nigeria.** [d. April 13, 1827]

1814 **Mikhail Aleksandrovitch Bakunin,** Russian anarchist; leading revolutionary figure in Europe, 1861–76; his philosophy, *Bakuninism,* is based on atheism, destruction of the state, and extremes of individual rights. [d. July 13, 1876]

1830 **Karl Goldmark,** Hungarian composer. [d. January 2, 1915]

1872 **Bertrand (Arthur William) Russell, 3rd Earl Russell,** British philosopher, mathematician, writer. [d. February 2, 1970]

1883 **Walter (Adolph) Gropius,** German architect; founder of **Bauhaus** school of architecture. [d. July 5, 1969]

1889 **Thomas Midgley,** U.S. engineer, chemist; developer of **tetraethyl lead,** anti-knock additive for gasoline. [d. November 2, 1944]

1892 **Ezio Pinza,** Italian operatic bass. [d. May 9, 1957]

1897 **Frank Capra,** U.S. film director; a leading film director of 1930s and 1940s.

1901 **Vincent Du Vigneaud,** U.S. chemist; Nobel Prize in chemistry for work on **pituitary hormones** and first synthesis of **polypeptide hormone,** 1955. [d. December 11, 1978]

1902 **Meredith Willson,** U.S. composer; composed *The Music Man.*

1904 **Jacob (Koppel) Javits,** U.S. politician, lawyer; U.S. Congressman, 1946–54; U.S. Senator, 1956–80.

1907 **Clifford Curzon,** British pianist; knighted, 1977. [d. September 1, 1982]

1912 **Perry Como (Pierino Como),** U.S. singer.

Richard Brooks, U.S. film director; wrote and directed screenplays for *Cat on a Hot Tin Roof, Elmer Gantry, Sweet Bird of Youth,* and *In Cold Blood.*

1914 **Pierre Aléxandre Balmain,** French fashion designer. [d. June 29, 1982]

1919 **Margot Fonteyn (Margaret Hookham),** British prima ballerina.

1920 **Pope John Paul II (Karol Wojtyla),** pope, elected 1978; the first non-Italian pope in 455 years.

1946 **Reggie (Reginald) Jackson,** U.S. baseball player.

Historical Events

1291 **Mamelukes** conquer **Acre,** bringing end to Christian rule in the East.

1412 **Henry IV of England** abandons Duke of Burgundy and forms alliance with Duke of Orléans (**Hundred Years' War**).

1803 Great Britain declares war on France (**Napoleonic Wars**).

1804 **France** becomes an empire with **Napoleon Bonaparte** as Emperor.

1900 The **Tonga Islands** become a British protectorate.

1917 **U.S. Selective Service Act** is passed, providing for registration of men between ages of 21 and 31.

1918 The first British retaliatory air raid on German towns is carried out against **Cologne** (**World War I**).

SS. Theodotus, **Thecusa**, and their companions, martyrs. [d. c. 304]

St. Potamon, Bishop of Heraclea, martyr. Also called **Potamion.** [d. c. 340]

St. John I, pope and martyr. [d. 526] Feast formerly May 27. Optional Memorial.

St. Elgiva, founder of the Shaftesbury nunnery. Also called **Ælgifu, Ælgytha, Algyva.** [d. 944]

St. Eric of Sweden, King of Sweden and martyr. Did much to establish Christianity in Upper Sweden. Until Reformation was considered patron of Sweden. His banner is regarded as a portent of victory. [d. 1161]

St. Felix of Cantalice, Capuchin lay-brother and visionary. [d. 1587]

The Beatified

Blessed William of Toulouse, hermit and preacher. [d. 1369]

1920 **Iceland** adopts universal suffrage.

1933 **Tennessee Valley Authority** is created in U.S. to improve agriculture in that region.

1951 UN General Assembly, by unanimous vote, requests all nations to impose arms embargo against Communist China and North Korea.

1974 **India** explodes its first nuclear device, marking its entry into the nuclear age as the sixth nuclear power.

1978 Despite strong opposition from the Vatican, the Italian senate votes in favor of legalized **abortion.**

1980 **Mount St. Helens,** in Washington state, erupts, devastating a 122-square mile area, killing at least 60 people.

May 19

Holidays

Turkey — Youth and Sports Day
U.S.S.R. — Founding Day, V. I. Lenin Pioneer Organization

Religious Calendar

The Saints

SS. **Pudentiana** and **Pudens,** martyrs. Pudentiana also called **Pudenziana.** Pudentiana's feast suppressed 1969. [d. c. 1st century]

Birthdates

1593 **Jacob Jordaens,** Flemish painter; a follower of Rubens. [d. October 18, 1678]

1611 **Pope Innocent XI,** pope 1676–89. [d. August 12, 1689]

1762 **Johann Fichte,** German philosopher; developer of **ethical idealism.** [d. January 29, 1814]

1795 **Johns Hopkins,** U.S. merchant, philanthropist; left his fortune to found **Johns Hopkins University** and **Johns Hopkins Medical Hospital.** [d. December 24, 1873]

1861 **Nellie Melba (Helen Porter Mitchell),** Australian operatic soprano. [d. February 23, 1931]

1864 **Carl Akeley,** U.S. animal sculptor, naturalist; renowned for his African life exhibitions at Chicago's Field Museum and at New York City's American Museum of Natural History. [d. November 17, 1926]

1879 **Viscountess Nancy Witcher Langhorne Astor,** British politician; first woman member of the British House of Commons. [d. May 2, 1964]

1890 **Ho Chi Minh (Nguyen That Thanh),** Vietnamese leader; President of Democratic Republic of Vietnam (North Vietnam), 1954–69. [d. September 3, 1969]

1898 **Alan Frank Guttmacher,** U.S. physician, birth control advocate. [d. March 18, 1974]

1914 **Max Perutz,** British biochemist; Nobel Prize in chemistry for determination of the structure of **hemoproteins** (with J. C. Kendrew), 1962.

1925 **Malcolm X (Malcolm Little),** U.S. militant black leader. [assassinated February 21, 1965]

1930 **Lorraine Hansberry,** U.S. playwright. [d. January 12, 1965]

1935 **David (Downs) Hartman,** U.S. actor, talk show host.

Historical Events

1536 **Anne Boleyn,** second wife of **Henry VIII** of England, is beheaded.

1588 The **Spanish Armada** sets sail from Lisbon, bound for England.

1635 France declares war on Spain (**Thirty Years' War**).

1643 French defeat Spaniards at **Rocroi** (**Thirty Years' War**); considered end of supremacy of the Spanish forces.

New England Confederation is formed of representatives from Massachusetts, Plymouth, Connecticut, and New Haven colonies.

1802 **French Legion of Honor** is instituted.

1828 U.S. Congress passes **tariff of abominations,** raising duties on imports.

1849 Residents of **Colony of Cape of Good Hope,** Africa, successfully resist British attempt to make the Cape a penal colony.

1861 Spain annexes **Santo Domingo.**

1906 **Simplon Tunnel** through the Alps is opened in ceremonies by the King of Italy and the President of the Swiss Republic.

Federated Boys' Clubs of America is founded.

1918 *Codex Juris Canonici,* official collection of general Roman Catholic Church law, becomes effective.

1923 Cardinal **Robert Bellarmine** is beatified.

SS. Calocerus and **Parthenius,** martyrs. Brothers and eunuchs in the household of Emperor Decius' wife. [d. 304]

St. Dunstan, Archbishop of Canterbury; most famous of Anglo-Saxon saints. Regarded as father of English Benedictines. Patron of goldsmiths, jewelers, and locksmiths. [d. 988]

St. Celestine V, pope. Elected 1294; abdicated after five months; kept prisoner by the next pope, Boniface VIII. Also called **St. Peter Celestine.** Regarded as patron of book industry workers. [d. 1296]

St. Ivo of Kermartin, priest and lawyer; patron of lawyers, jurists, notaries, bailiffs, and orphans. Also called **Ives**, **Yves.** [d. 1303]

The Beatified

Blessed Alcuin, abbot. [d. 804]

Blessed Augustine Novello, Augustinian lay-brother; papal legate. [d. 1309]

Blessed Peter Wright, Jesuit priest and martyr. [d. 1651]

1934   Coup d'état of army officers under Gen. **Kimon Guerorguiev** takes place in Bulgaria.

1977   **Kenya** issues ban on big-game hunting.

May 20

Holidays

Cameroon	**National Day** Commemorates achievement of independence of the country, 1972.
U.S. (North Carolina)	**Anniversary of Mecklenburg Declaration of Independence,** 1775. The Declaration contained five resolutions of independence from England.
Zaire	**M.P.R. Day** Commemorates the founding of the *Movement Populaire de la Révolution,* 1976.

Birthdates

1470   **Pietro Bembo,** Italian humanist, man of letters, papal secretary. [d. January 18, 1547]

1537   **Hieronymous Fabricius,** Italian humanist, surgeon; known especially for work in comparative anatomy and embryology. [d. 1619]

1759   **William Thornton,** U.S. architect born in West Indies. Designed the **Capitol Building,** Washington, D.C. [d. March 28, 1828]

1772   **Dolley Madison,** U.S. First Lady; wife of President James Madison. [d. July 12, 1849]

1780   **Bernardino Rivadavia,** first President of the Argentine Republic, 1826–27. [d. September 2, 1845]

1799   **Honoré de Balzac,** French novelist; founder of school of realism in French literature; considered the greatest novelist in French literature; authored a comprehensive picture of French society, *La Comèdie Humaine.* [d. August 18, 1850]

1806   **John Stuart Mill,** British utilitarian economist, philosopher; first a champion of **utilitarianism;** later espoused more radical social philosophies. [d. May 8, 1873]

1818   **William George Fargo,** U.S. transportation executive; founder of American Express Co. and Wells Fargo & Co. [d. August 3, 1881]

1822   **Frederic Passy,** French economist; awarded first Nobel Peace Prize (with J. Dunant), 1901. [d. June 12, 1912]

1825   **Antoinette Louisa Blackwell,** U.S. clergywoman; first ordained woman minister in U.S. (Congregational), 1853. [d. November 5, 1921]

1826   **Potter Palmer,** U.S. merchant; a founder of Marshall Field & Co. [d. May 4, 1902]

1846   **Alexander von Kluck,** German Army general; headed First German Army in siege of Paris, 1914 (**World War I**). [d. October 19, 1934]

   Sir George Dashwood Taubman Goldie, British administrator; founder of **Nigeria.** [d. August 22, 1928]

1851   **Emile Berliner,** U.S. inventor of the flat (disk) **phonograph record.** [d. August 3, 1929]

1860   **Eduard Buchner,** German chemist; Nobel Prize in chemistry for discovery of **cell-free fermentation,** 1907. [d. August 24, 1917]

1882   **Sigrid Undset,** Norwegian novelist; Nobel Prize in literature, 1928. [d. June 10, 1949]

1890   **Allan Nevins,** U.S. historian; a prolific writer noted for his masterful political biographies; Pulitzer Prize in biography, 1933, 1937. [d. March 3, 1971]

1891   **Earl Russell Browder,** U.S. political leader; head of **U.S. Communist party.** [d. June 27, 1973]

1894   **Adela Rogers St. Johns,** U.S. journalist; noted for coverage of Lindbergh baby kidnapping and Bruno Hauptmann trial.

1908   **James (Maitland) Stewart,** U.S. actor.

1915   **Moshe Dayan,** Israeli public official and general; led invasion of Sinai Peninsula,

Religious Calendar

The Saints

St. Thalelaceus, martyr. Called *the Merciful* by the Greeks. [d. c. 284]

St. Basilla, virgin and martyr. Also called **Basilissa.** [d. 304]

St. Baudelius, martyr; principal patron of Nîmes, France. Also called **Baudille.** [d. c. 380]

St. Austregisilus, Bishop of Bourges. Also called **Outril.** [d. 624]

St. Ethelbert, King of the East Angles, martyr. Invoked against thieves. Also called **Aethelbert.** [d. 794]

St. Bernardino of Siena, Franciscan friar, apostle, reformer, and missionary throughout Italy. Called *the People's Preacher.* Also called **Bernardin of Siena, Bernardine.** [d. 1444]

The Beatified

Blessed Columba of Rieta, virgin; patron of Perugia, Italy. [d. 1501]

1956; Israeli Foreign Minister, 1977–79. [d. October 16, 1981]

Historical Events

1303   **Treaty of Paris** restores Gascony to England (**Hundred Years' War**).

1498   **Vasco da Gama** arrives at **Calicut,** completing his voyage around Africa to India.

1571   A great armada of the **Holy League** begins assembling at Messina under **Don John of Austria** to break Turkish sea power in the Mediterranean.

1774   English parliament passes **Quebec Act,** providing permanent and highly centralized civil government for Canada.

1862   U.S. President Abraham Lincoln signs into law the **Homestead Act,** which entitles every U.S. citizen who is over 21 and the head of a family to acquire 160 acres of land in the public domain by residing on it for five years and paying a nominal price per acre.

1882   **St. Gotthard Tunnel,** first great railroad tunnel through the Alps, opens, providing a link between Lucerne, Switzerland and Milan, Italy.

1902   **Cuba** gains independence from Spain.

1927   Treaty between Great Britain and **King Ibn Saud** recognizes the complete independence of the **Nejd-Hejaz (Saudi-Arabia).**

1929   Japanese evacuation of **Shantung Province** in China is completed.

1939   Italian and German forces are withdrawn from Spain (**Spanish Civil War**).

1958   **Japanese-American citizens** who renounced U.S. citizenship during World War II regain full citizenship.

1961   U.S. marshals are sent to **Alabama** to help settle racial unrest.

1966   U.S. makes its first sale of tactical military aircraft to **Israel.**

1969   U.S. and South Vietnamese troops capture **Hamburger Hill** after 10 days of bloody fighting (**Vietnam War**).

1972   **Cameroon** promulgates its constitution.

1973   Swiss voters, in a national referendum, repeal two anti-Catholic articles that had been in the constitution since 1874.

1978   **Chiang Ching-Kuo,** the 68-year old son of the late Chiang Kai-shek and Premier since June 1972, becomes President of the Nationalist Chinese government in Taiwan.

May 21

Holidays

Chile   Battle of Iquique
               Commemorates the naval battle
               at Iquique, 1879.

Religious Calendar

The Saints
St. Godric, hermit. Earliest known lyrical poet in

Birthdates

1471   **Albrecht Dürer,** German painter, graphic artist; one of the geniuses of the Renaissance in Germany. [d. April 6, 1528]

1527   **Philip II, King of Spain.** [d. September 13, 1598]

1688   **Alexander Pope,** English poet of the Augustan period; powerful figure in English literature. [d. May 30, 1744]

1759   **Joseph Fouché, Duke of Otranto,** French statesman, public official; known for his elaborate system of spies throughout the government; led provisional government after Napoleon's abdication. [d. December 25, 1820]

1796   **Reverdy Johnson,** U.S. public official; U.S. Senator, 1845–49; 1863–68; Attorney General, 1849–50; U.S. Minister to Great Britain, 1868–69. [d. February 10, 1876]

1817   **Rudolf Hermann Lotze,** German philosopher; influential in founding of science of **physiological psychology.** [d. July 1, 1881]

1843   **Charles A. Gobat,** Swiss lawyer, statesman; Nobel Peace Prize for work with **Bureau International Permanent de la Paix** (with E. Ducommun), 1902. [d. March 16, 1914]

1844   **Henri Rousseau,** French painter of the primitivist school of post-impressionism; known as *Le Douanier.* [d. September 2, 1910]

1851   **Léon V. A. Bourgeois,** French statesman; Nobel Peace Prize for promotion of the **League of Nations,** 1920. [d. September 29, 1925]

1856   **José Batlle Ordóñez,** Uruguayan statesman; President of Uruguay, 1902–1907. [d. October 20, 1929]

1860   **Willem Einthoven,** Dutch physiologist; Nobel Prize in physiology or medicine for development of the **electrocardiograph,** 1924. [d. September 29, 1927]

1878   **Glenn (Hammon) Curtiss,** U.S. inventor, aviator; made first public airplane flight in U.S., 1908; invented the **hydroplane.** [d. July 23, 1930]

1898   **Armand Hammer,** U.S. oil executive, art patron; Chairman of Occidental Petroleum Corporation, 1957– .

1902   **Marcel Lajos Breuer,** U.S. architect born in Hungary; recognized for his streamlined design and international style in architecture and the invention of the tubular metal chair that bears his name. [d. July 1, 1981]

1904   **Fats (Thomas) Waller,** U.S. musician; jazz pianist. [d. December 15, 1943]

         Robert Montgomery, U.S. actor, producer. [d. September 27, 1981]

1916   **Harold Robbins,** U.S. novelist.

1917   **Raymond Burr,** Canadian actor.

1921   **Andrei Sakharov,** Russian physicist; one of the leaders of the dissident movement in the U.S.S.R.; Nobel Peace Prize, 1975.

1923   **Ara (Raoul) Parseghian,** U.S. football coach; head coach, University of Notre Dame, 1964–75.

1930   **John Malcolm Fraser,** Australian politician; Prime Minister, 1975–83.

Historical Events

996   **Otto III** is crowned Holy Roman Emperor at Rome.

1369   **Charles V of France** declares war on England (**Hundred Years' War**).

1424   **James I** is crowned King of Scotland at Scone.

1471   **Henry VI, King of England,** dies in the Tower of London, supposedly murdered by order of his rival, **Edward IV.**

English; author of earliest known musical settings of English words. Also called **Godrick**. [d. 1170]

St. Andrew Bobola, Jesuit priest, missionary, and martyr. [d. 1657]

St. Theophilus of Corte, Franciscan priest noted for his oratory. [d. 1740]

St. Crispin of Viterbo, Capuchin brother. His life symbolized values of goodness. [d. 1750] Canonized May 21, 1982 by Pope John Paul II.

St. Collen, patron and founder of the Llangollen Church. Also called **Colan.** [death date unknown]

The Beatified

Blessed Benvenuto of Recanati, Franciscan lay-brother. [d. 1289]

1502 The island of **Saint Helena** is discovered by **Juan de Nova Castella,** on a return voyage from India.

1856 Proslavery border ruffians from Missouri ravage the free-soil town of **Lawrence, Kansas.**

1881 The **American Red Cross Society** is organized with **Clara Barton** as president.

1900 The British annex the **Orange Free State** to the British Empire as the **Orange River Colony** (**Boer War**).

1927 **Charles Lindbergh,** U.S. aviator, completes the first non-stop solo flight across the Atlantic (New York to Paris) in 33 hours, 29 minutes.

1932 **Amelia Earhart** completes first solo flight by a woman across the Atlantic.

U.S. Socialist Party convention nominates **Norman Thomas** for president.

1941 U.S. freighter *Robin Moor* is sunk by German submarine (**World War II**).

1961 Military rule is introduced in **South Korea** as 14-man military cabinet is sworn in.

1964 World's first **nuclear-powered lighthouse** goes into operation in Chesapeake Bay.

1968 Attempt by exiles to invade **Haiti** and overthrow the government of **President François Duvalier** is crushed by the Haitian government.

1978 Tokyo's new international airport at **Narita** is opened.

May 22

Haiti **National Sovereignty and Thanksgiving Day**
Day set aside to honor customs and rulers of Haiti.

Sri Lanka **National Heroes Day** (formerly **Republic Day**)
Commemorates ratification of Sri Lanka's constitution, 1972.

U.S. **National Maritime Day**
Commemorates the first transatlantic voyage by a steam-driven vessel, the *S.S. Savannah,* 1819.

Birthdates

1783 **William Sturgeon,** British inventor, electrician; developed first **electromagnet.** [d. 1850]

1813 **Richard Wagner,** German opera composer; best known for *Tannhäuser, Lohengrin,* and *The Ring of the Nibelung.* [d. February 13, 1883]

1844 **Mary Cassatt,** U.S. impressionist painter and printmaker in France; noted for her paintings of mothers and children. [d. June 14, 1926]

1851 **Emil Gustav Hirsch,** U.S. rabbi; a representative of the extreme wing of Reform Judaism. [d. January 7, 1923]

1859 **Sir Arthur Conan Doyle,** British novelist; creator of the fictional detective **Sherlock Holmes.** [d. July 7, 1930]

1871 **William McDougall,** U.S. psychologist born in England. [d. November 28, 1938]

1902 **Al Simmons (Aloys Szymanski),** U.S. baseball player; elected to Baseball Hall of Fame, 1953. [d. May 26, 1956]

1907 **Laurence (Kerr) Olivier,** British stage and film actor, especially well known for Shakespearean roles; knighted in 1947; in 1970 became the first actor in English history to be named a baron.

1912 **Herbert Brown,** U.S. physicist; Nobel Prize in chemistry for development of substances that facilitate very difficult chemical reactions (with G. Wittig), 1979.

1914 **Vance (Oakley) Packard,** U.S. author.

1934 **Peter Nero,** U.S. pianist.

1938 **Susan Strasberg,** U.S. actress.

1941 **Paul Edward Winfield,** U.S. actor.

1943 **Betty Williams,** Irish peace activist; Nobel Peace Prize for helping start **Northern Ireland Peace Movement** (with M. Corrigan), 1976.

Historical Events

1200 **Peace of Le Goulet** between **King John of England** and **Philip II of France** is signed.

1455 **War of the Roses** begins in England as Richard, Duke of York, defeats royal forces at **St. Albans.**

1526 **League of Cognac** between the pope, France, Venice, Florence, and Milan is established against **Charles V of Germany.**

1629 **Peace of Lübeck** between **Ferdinand II, Holy Roman Emperor,** and **Christian IV of Denmark** ends hostilities between the Empire and Denmark.

1900 **Associated Press** is founded in the U.S.

1911 The **gold escudo** becomes the official currency in Portugal.

1969 Canadian government decides to admit U.S. military deserters on the same basis as other immigrants.

Apollo 10 astronauts bring their lunar module, *Snoopy,* to within 9.4 miles of the moon and return it to the command ship, *Charlie Brown.*

1972 **Ceylon** officially becomes **Sri Lanka,** an independent republic.

Religious Calendar

The Saints

SS. Castus and **Æmilius,** martyrs. [d. 250]

St. Quiteria, virgin and martyr. Invoked against the bites of mad dogs. [d. c. 5th century]

St. Romanus, monk. Befriended St. Benedict; founded Monastery at Fontrouge, France. [d. c. 550]

St. Julia, martyr. [d. c. 6th century]

St. Aigulf, Bishop of Bourges. Also called **Ayoul.** [d. 836]

St. Margaret of Hulme, martyr. [d. 1170]

St. Humility, widow. Founder of Vallombrosan nuns. [d. 1310]

St. Rita of Cascia, widow and nun; patron of the impossible and advocate of desperate cases. [d. 1457]

St. Joachima des Mas y de Vedruna, widow and founder of the Carmelites of Charity. [d. 1854]

The Beatified

Blessed John Forest, martyr, priest, and confessor of Catherine of Aragon, first wife of Henry VIII. [d. 1538]

U.S. President **Richard Nixon** arrives in Moscow to begin the first official visit of a U.S. president to the U.S.S.R.

1977   After 94 years of service, the famed *Orient Express* makes its last regularly scheduled run across Europe.

1979   **Joe Clark,** the Progressive Conservative leader, replaces **Pierre Trudeau** as prime minister of Canada, thereby ending the 11-year rule of the Liberals.

May 23

Birthdates

1707 **Carolus Linnaeus,** (Carl von Linné) Swedish botanist; founder of modern **taxonomy.** [d. January 10, 1778]

1729 **Giuseppe Parini,** Italian didactic poet; best known for his epic satire *Il Giorno.* [d. August 15, 1799]

1734 **Franz Anton Mesmer,** Austrian physician; his discovery of cures by suggestion led to discovery of **hypnotism** and **mesmerism.** [d. March 5, 1815]

1795 **Sir Charles Barry,** English architect; designed the **Houses of Parliament** in London. [d. May 12, 1860]

1810 **Sarah Margaret Fuller, Marchioness Ossoli,** U.S. journalist, writer, foreign correspondent, critic; associated with Ralph Waldo Emerson and the Brook Farm experimental community. [d. July 19, 1850]

1824 **Ambrose Everett Burnside,** U.S. Civil War army general, political leader; was assigned to head Army of the Potomac during Civil War; Governor of Rhode Island, 1866-69; U.S. Senator, 1874–81. His style of facial whiskers led to the term *burnsides,* or *sideburns.* [d. September 13, 1881]

1848 **Otto Lilienthal,** German inventor, aeronautical engineer; contributed to improvement of wing designs of early planes. [d. August 9, 1896]

1883 **Douglas Fairbanks (Douglas Ullman),** U.S. actor, silent-screen star. [d. December 12, 1939]

1886 **James Gleason,** U.S. character actor, writer, director. [d. April 12, 1959]

1891 **Pär Fabian Lagerkvist,** Swedish novelist, poet, dramatist; Nobel Prize in literature, 1951. [d. July 11, 1974]

1908 **John Bardeen,** U.S. physicist; Nobel Prize in physics for development of **electronic transistors** (with W. B. Shockley and W. H. Brattain), 1956; Nobel Prize in physics for development of **theory of superconductivity** (with L. N. Cooper and J. R. Schrieffer), 1972.

1910 **Artie Shaw (Arthur Arshawsky),** U.S. bandleader, clarinetist.

1914 **Barbara Mary Ward, Baroness Jackson of Lodsworth,** British economist; author of *Spaceship Earth.* [d. May 31, 1981]

1920 **Helen O'Connell,** U.S. singer.

1923 **Alicia De Larrocha,** Spanish concert pianist; child prodigy who debuted at the age of four. Known for interpretations of Chopin.

1925 **Joshua Lederberg,** U.S. geneticist; Nobel Prize in physiology or medicine for studies on genetic function in **hereditary characteristic transfers** (with E. L. Tatum and G. W. Beadle), 1958.

Historical Events

1430 **Joan of Arc** is captured by Burgundians at Compiègne.

1474 **Pope Sixtus IV** confirms Order of the Hermits of St. Francis of Assisi, founded by **Francis of Padua.**

1493 **Treaty of Senlis** is signed between France and Holy Roman Empire; France renounces Netherlands and Burgundy.

1498 **Girolamo Savonarola,** Italian reformer and preacher of penitence, is burned to death at Florence.

1533 **Henry VIII** is divorced from **Catherine of Aragon.**

1611 **Matthias,** brother of Holy Roman Emperor **Rudolf II,** becomes King of Bohemia.

1618 **Defenestration of Prague** takes place as Protestants begin Bohemian revolt against Hapsburg **Emperor Ferdinand II,** starting the **Thirty Years' War.**

St. Guibert, monk and missionary. Founded celebrated Benedictine Monastery at Gembloux. Also called **Guilbert**, **Wibert**. [d. 962]

St. Leontius, Bishop of Rostov, martyr. [d. 1077]

St. Ivo, Bishop of Chartres. Also called **Yvo.** [d. 1116]

St. Euphrosyne of Polotsk, virgin and recluse. [d. 1173]

St. William of Rochester, martyr. [d. 1201]

St. John Baptist Rossi, priest. [d. 1764]

The Beatified

Blessed Gerard of Villamagna, hermit who joined the Third Crusade to the Holy Land. [d. 1245]

Blessed Bartholomew of Montepulciano, Franciscan monk. [d. 1330]

1706	Marlborough of England defeats French at **Ramillies** and conquers Spanish Netherlands (**War of the Spanish Succession**).
1788	**South Carolina** is admitted to the Union as the 8th state.
1895	**New York Public Library** is incorporated.
1903	**Wisconsin** becomes the first state in the U.S. to adopt the **direct primary system.**
1915	Italy, previously neutral, declares war on Austria-Hungary (**World War I**).
1950	**Harry Gold,** confederate of **Klaus Fuchs,** is arrested on espionage charges in U.S. for his dealings with Fuchs and passing of atomic secrets to the Russians.
1960	Israeli Prime Minister **David Ben-Gurion** reports the capture by Israeli agents of **Adolf Eichmann,** alleged leader in carrying out the Nazi program for extermination of the Jews.
1971	Body of **Ephraim Elrom,** Israeli Consul General in Istanbul, is found six days after being kidnapped by Turkish leftists who were demanding the release of political prisoners.
1973	U.S. agrees to grant commonwealth status to the **Mariana Islands.**
1977	South Moluccan extremists seize 100 children as hostages in the Netherlands.

May 24

Holidays

Bulgaria **Day of Slav Letters** or **Education Day**
A day of tribute to the nation's literature and culture.

Ecuador **Battle of Pichincha Day**
Commemorates the battle during the war for independence from Spain, 1822.

Birthdates

1494 **Jacopo da Pontormo (Jacopo Carrucci),** Italian painter of Florentine school; pupil of Leonardo da Vinci and Andrea del Sarto. [d. January 2, 1557]

1544 **William Gilbert,** English physician, physicist; known as *Father of Electricity.* First to use terms *electric force, magnetic pole.* [d. December 10, 1603]

1743 **Jean Paul Marat,** French Revolutionary politician born in Switzerland; advocate of extreme violence. [d. at the hand of **Charlotte Corday,** July 13, 1793]

1810 **Abraham Geiger,** German rabbi, scholar, author; leader of the second generation of Reform Judaism in Germany. [d. October 23, 1874]

1819 **(Alexandrina) Victoria, Queen of Great Britain and Ireland,** 1837–1901; Empress of India, 1876–1901. Ruled in dignified manner which created new concept of monarchy in the Empire. [d. January 22, 1901]

1854 **Richard Mansfield,** U.S. actor; known for his portrayal of the lead role in *Cyrano de Bergerac.* [d. August 30, 1907]

1855 **Alfred Cort Haddon,** British ethnologist, anthropologist; one of founders of modern **anthropology.** [d. April 20, 1940]

Arthur Wing Pinero, British playwright; his works marked the beginning of a new era in British drama, characterized by *problem plays.* [d. November 23, 1934]

1863 **George Grey Barnard,** U.S. sculptor; sculpted more than 30 pieces for state capitol at Harrisburg, Pennsylvania. [d. April 24, 1938]

1870 **Benjamin Nathan Cardozo,** U.S. jurist, lawyer; Justice of U.S. Supreme Court, 1932–38. Profound legal philosopher. [d. July 9, 1938]

Jan Christiaan Smuts, South African statesman, soldier; played a significant role in the creation of **Union of South Africa.** [d. September 11, 1950]

1878 **Harry Emerson Fosdick,** U.S. Protestant minister; stimulated heated controversy between liberals and fundamentalists. [d. October 5, 1969]

1891 **William F. Albright,** U.S. orientalist, archaeologist; authority on Dead Sea Scrolls. [d. September 19, 1971]

1899 **Suzanne Lenglen,** French tennis player; called the *Pavlova of Tennis.* [d. July 4, 1938]

1905 **Mikhail Aleksandrovich Sholokhov,** Russian novelist; Nobel Prize in literature, 1965.

1907 **Douglas Leigh,** U.S. advertising executive; best known for *Coca-Cola* and *Camel Cigarette* signs in Times Square, New York City.

1914 **Lilli Palmer,** U.S. actress, author, born in Germany.

1934 **Jane Byrne,** U.S. politician; Mayor of Chicago, 1979–82.

1941 **Bob Dylan (Robert Zimmerman),** U.S. singer, songwriter.

Historical Events

1153 **King David I of Scotland** dies and is succeeded by his grandson, **Malcolm IV.**

1370 **Peace of Stralsund** between Denmark-Norway and Hansa secures Hanseatic predominance in Northern Europe.

1822 **Ecuador** achieves independence.

1844 **Samuel F. B. Morse** transmits the first telegraphic message from the U.S. Supreme Court room in the Capitol, Washington, D.C., to Baltimore. The message: *What hath God wrought.*

Religious Calendar

The Saints

SS. Donatian and **Rogatian,** martyrs. Greatly venerated at Nantes and known there as *Les Enfants Nantais.* [d. 289 or 304]

St. Vincent of Lérins, hermit. [d. c. 445]

St. David I of Scotland, King of Scotland 1124–53. [d. 1153]

St. Nicetas of Pereaslau, martyr. Also called *the Wonder-Worker* for his miracles of healing. [d. 1186]

The Beatified

Blessed Lanfranc, Archbishop of Canterbury. [d. 1089]

Blessed John of Prado, Franciscan missionary and martyr. [d. 1613]

1846	U.S. General **Zachary Taylor** captures **Monterey** (**Mexican War**).
1856	**John Brown,** U.S. abolitionist, leads retaliatory massacre at **Pottawatomie Creek, Kansas,** in revenge for Quantril's raid on **Lawrence, Kansas** (see May 21).
1883	The **Brooklyn Bridge** opens, linking Manhattan to Brooklyn, New York.
1915	The U.S. proclaims its neutrality in the war between Italy and Austria-Hungary (**World War I**).
1917	Russians peasants rise against large land owners and Germans living in Russia (**Russian Revolution**).
1928	**Umberto Nobile,** in his last exploratory flight in the dirigible *Italia*, crashes on a return flight from the North Pole.
1930	**Amy Johnson** arrives in Australia, becoming first woman to complete solo flight from England to Australia.
1935	First major league **baseball night game** is played at Crosley Field, Cincinnati, Ohio, between Cincinnati Reds and the Philadelphia Phillies.
1941	German battleship *Bismarck* sinks the British battle cruiser *Hood.* British air and naval forces subsequently sink the *Bismarck* (**World War II**).
1960	U.S. Air Force launches *Midas II,* a 5,000 pound experimental satellite designed to give early warning of surprise missile attacks.
1962	**M(alcolm) Scott Carpenter** successfully completes second U.S. manned orbital space flight with three trips around the earth.
1976	Supersonic *Concorde* jets begin regular flights, less than four hours in duration, from London and Paris to Dulles International Airport near Washington, D.C., on a 16-month trial basis.
1978	**Princess Margaret of Great Britain** and her husband, the Earl of Snowden, are granted a divorce after 18 years of marriage.

May 25

Holidays

Argentina — **National Holiday (Revolución de Mayo)** Commemorates the revolution of 1810.

Chad, Liberia, Mali, Mauretania, Zambia, Zimbabwe — **Liberation of Africa Day** Commemorates the formation of the **Organization of African Unity,** 1963, and celebrates freedom and productivity.

Jordan — **Independence Day** Celebrates the coming to full independence of Jordan, 1949.

Libya — **National Day of Sudan** or **Revolution Day in the Sudan** Commemorates the overthrow of the government of King Idris I, 1969 (see below).

Sudan — **Revolution Day** Commemorates the military coup and takeover by Col. Jaafar al-Nimeiry, 1969.

Birthdates

1803 **Ralph Waldo Emerson,** U.S. philosopher, poet, essayist; leader of the **transcendental movement** in the U.S. [d. April 27, 1882]

1847 **John Alexander Dowie,** Scottish religious leader; established **Zion City** in Illinois; eventually deposed by his followers. [d. March 9, 1907]

1848 **Helmuth Johannes Ludwig, Graf von Moltke** (*Moltke the Younger*), German Army general; Chief of General Staff, 1906–16. [d. June 18, 1916]

1865 **Pieter Zeeman,** Dutch physicist; Nobel Prize in physics for research on influence of magnetism on radiation (with H. A. Lorentz), 1902. [d. October 9, 1943]

John Raleigh Mott, U.S. evangelist, Methodist layman; Nobel Peace Prize for his work in international church and missionary movements (with E. G. Balch), 1946. [d. January 31, 1955]

1878 **Bill** (*Bojangles*) **Robinson,** U.S. dancer. [d. November 25, 1949]

1879 **Lord Beaverbrook (William Maxwell Aitken),** British publisher, statesman; accumulated his fortune by investments in cement manufacturing plants. [d. June 9, 1964]

1886 **Philip Murray,** U.S. labor leader; President of CIO, 1940–52. [d. November 9, 1952]

1889 **Igor Ivanovich Sikorsky,** U.S. aviation engineer born in Russia; developed first successful **helicopter,** 1939. [d. October 26, 1972]

1898 **Gene Tunney,** U.S. boxer; World Heavyweight Champion, 1926–28. [d. November 7, 1978]

Bennett (Alfred) Cerf, U.S. publisher, editor, columnist; publisher of Modern Library; founder of Random House. [d. August 27, 1971]

1908 **Theodore Roethke,** U.S. poet; Pulitzer Prize in poetry, 1954. [d. August 1, 1963]

1910 **James N. Demaret,** U.S. golfer; first to win three Masters titles (1940, 1947, 1950).

1913 **Joseph Peter Grace,** U.S. business executive; President of W. R. Grace & Co., major manufacturer of chemicals, and owner of Grace Line, major shipping company.

1926 **Miles (Dewey) Davis, Jr.,** U.S. jazz musician, trumpeter.

1929 **Beverly Sills (Belle Silverman),** U.S. coloratura soprano.

| U.S. (New Mexico) | Memorial Day |
| U.S.S.R. | African Liberation Day |

Religious Calendar

The Saints

St. Urban I, pope and martyr. Elected 222 or 223. [d. c. 230]

St. Dionysius, Bishop of Milan. [d. c. 360]

St. Zenobius, Bishop of Florence; principal patron of the city of Florence, Italy. [d. c. 390]

St. Leo, Abbot of Monastery at Mantenay. Also called **Lyé.** [d. c. 550]

St. Aldhelm, first Bishop of Sherborne. Called the first English scholar of distinction. Also called **Adhelm.** [d. 709]

St. Bede the Venerable, Doctor of the Church. Known for his *Ecclesiastical History of the English People,* and for the first martyrology with historical notes. Also called **Beda.** [d. 735] Feast formerly May 27. Optional Memorial.

St. Gennadius, Bishop of Astorga; invoked by the Spaniards against fever. [d. 936]

St. Gregory VII, pope. Elected 1073. [d. 1085]

St. Mary Magdalen dei Pazzi, virgin, Carmelite nun, and mystic. [d. 1607] Feast formerly May 29. Optional Memorial.

St. Madeleine Sophie Barat, virgin, founder of the Society of the Sacred Heart, which provided for girls' education. [d. 1865]

The Beatified

Blessed Claritus, founder of convent of Augustinian nuns in Florence. Also called **Chiarito.** [d. 1348]

Historical Events

1085 **Alfonso VI of Castile** captures **Toledo,** thus bringing the Moorish center of science into Christian hands.

1659 **Richard Cromwell,** Lord Protector of England and son of **Oliver Cromwell,** resigns under pressure from Parliament.

1780 Mutiny by two Connecticut regiments at Washington's winter quarters, Morristown, N.J., is suppressed (**American Revolution**).

1787 The American **Constitutional Convention** meets in first session in Philadelphia to draw up a constitution for the new nation.

1810 Revolution occurs in **Argentina,** initiating the move toward independence, finally achieved July 9, 1816.

1909 The **India Councils Act** is enacted, providing some reform concerning powers of legislative councils in India.

1911 Mexican President **Porfirio Diaz** resigns after revolutionist **Francisco Madero's** forces defeat government troops (**Mexican Civil War**).

1915 **The Second Battle of Ypres,** begun April 22, ends with total casualties to all sides of about 105,000 (**World War I**).

German airplane raid on **Kent** and **Folkestone,** England, produces 290 casualties (**World War I**).

1921 The **League of Nations** assigns the **Aaland Islands** to Finland.

1933 Walt Disney's film, ***Three Little Pigs,*** with popular song *Who's Afraid of the Big Bad Wolf?* premieres in New York.

1946 **Abdallah** is proclaimed King of the Hashimite kingdom of **Transjordan,** thus establishing that country's independence from Great Britain.

1950 **Brooklyn-Battery Tunnel,** the longest roadway tunnel in the U.S., is formally opened to traffic.

1960 A team from the People's Republic of China completes the first ascent of **Mt. Everest** from the northern side.

1965 **Cassius Clay (Muhammad Ali)** knocks out **Sonny Liston** in the first round of a bout at Lewiston, Maine, to retain the world heavyweight boxing title.

1969 Sudanese coalition government led by Prime Minister **Muhammad Ahmed Mahgoub** is overthrown by leftist military coup; **Abubakr Awadallah** is named prime minister and foreign minister.

1971 Soviet supersonic jetliner, the ***Tu-144,*** makes its western debut, arriving in Paris for an air show.

1979 A *DC-10* jetliner crashes at Chicago's O'Hare International Airport, killing 274 persons.

May 26

Religious Calendar

Saints

St. Quadratus, Bishop of Athens; first of great line of Christian apologists. Also called **Codratus.** [d. c. 129]

SS. Priscus and his companions, martyrs. Also called **Prix.** [d. c. 272]

Birthdates

1478 **Pope Clement VII,** Pope 1523–34. [d. September 25, 1534]

1602 **Philippe de Champagne,** Belgian painter of the Flemish school. [d. August 12, 1674]

1650 **John Churchill, 1st Duke of Marlborough,** British general, politician; English leader during the **War of the Spanish Succession.** [d. June 16, 1722]

1784 **Joseph Stevens Buckminster,** U.S. clergyman; founder of the **Boston Atheneum.** [d. June 9, 1812]

1814 **Heinrich Geissler,** German glassblower, inventor; produced first **Geissler tubes** (most effective vacuum tubes created to that time), and the **Geissler pump.** [d. January 24, 1879]

1822 **Edmond Louis Antoine Huot de Goncourt,** French novelist, historian, art critic; brother of Jules Alfred Huot de Goncourt (December 17). Popularized naturalistic style of novel writing. By his will, established the **Académie des Goncourt,** which makes an annual award for imaginative fiction. [d. July 16, 1896]

1837 **Washington Augustus Roebling,** U.S. engineer and bridge builder born in Germany; with brother John, designed and constructed the **Brooklyn Bridge.** [d. July 21, 1926]

1859 **A(lfred) E(dward) Housman,** British classical scholar and poet. [d. April 30, 1936]

1863 **Shailer Mathews,** U.S. theologian, educator, writer; dean of Divinity School of University of Chicago. [d. October 23, 1941]

1876 **Robert Merans Yerkes,** U.S. psychologist; pioneer and leading authority on the great apes, particularly the chimpanzee. [d. February 3, 1956]

1884 **Charles Winninger,** U.S. character actor. [d. January 1969]

1886 **Al Jolson (Asa Yoelson),** U.S. singer, actor born in Russia; sang in blackface (his trademark), in vaudeville and minstrel companies, 1899–1926. Starred in first feature-length talking motion picture, *The Jazz Singer,* 1927. [d. October 23, 1950]

1891 **Paul Lukas,** U.S. actor born in Hungary. [d. August 15, 1971]

1897 **Norma Talmadge,** U.S. actress; silent-film star. [d. December 24, 1957]

1907 **John Wayne (Marion Michael Morrison),** known as *the Duke,* U.S. actor. [d. June 11, 1979]

1910 **Laurance Spelman Rockefeller,** U.S. executive; known for his numerous donations of land to U.S. government for parks, in particular the **Grand Teton Park,** Colorado. Chairman of Rockefeller Center, Inc., 1953–56, 1958–66.

1920 **Peggy Lee (Norma Egstrom),** U.S. singer.

1923 **James Arness (James Aurness),** U.S. actor.

1951 **Sally Ride,** astronaut, first U.S. woman in space.

Historical Events

1521 **Edict of Worms** outlaws **Martin Luther** and his followers.

1659 **Aurangzeb** formally ascends throne of Mogul dynasty, succeeding his deposed father, **Shah Jahan;** assumes title **Alamcir,** *conqueror of the world.*

1805 **Napoleon** crowns himself King of Italy in the Cathedral of Milan.

1834 **Dom Miguel of Portugal** capitulates to troops of **Dom Pedro,** ending the six-year **Portuguese Civil War.**

1879 The **Treaty of Gandamak** is signed by the British and Afghans giving the British occupation of the **Khyber Pass.**

St. Augustine, Archbishop of Canterbury; Apostle of the English. Also called **Austin.** [d. c. 605] Feast formerly May 28.

St. Lambert, Bishop of Vence, France. [d. 1154]

St. Philip Neri, priest; founder of the Congregation of the Oratory and of Trinity Hospital in Rome. Also called the **Apostle of the city of Rome.** [d. 1595] Obligatory Memorial.

St. Mariana of Quito, virgin. Also called the *Lily of Quito.* [d. 1645]

The Beatified

Blessed Eva of Liège, virgin and prioress of Mount Cornillon. [d. c. 1265]

Blessed Peter Sanz, bishop, and his companions, martyrs; missionaries in China. [d. 1747 and 1748]

1896   **Nicholas II,** destined to be the last Russian czar, is crowned in the Cathedral of the Assumption in Moscow.

1919   Women achieve full suffrage in **Sweden.**

1924   **Johnson-Reed Immigration Bill** is signed by U.S. President Calvin Coolidge, limiting number of immigrants from any one country to 2 percent of 1890 population of that nationality; Japanese are excluded entirely.

1932   Drainage of the **Zuider Zee** in the Netherlands is completed.

1961   U.S. *B-58* jet bomber flies from New York to Paris in record time of 3 hours 19 minutes 41 seconds.

1963   **Organization of African Unity** charter is adopted by heads of all 50 independent African states except those dominated by whites in the south.

1966   **Guyana** adopts a constitution and gains independence within the British Commonwealth. Constitution remains in effect until 1980, when the black majority **People's National Congress** takes power.

1968   **Sir Henry Tucker** of the United Bermuda Party is named Bermuda's first prime minister.

1978   Legalized **casino gambling** begins in **Atlantic City,** New Jersey, the first legal casino in the U.S. outside of Nevada.

       Dominican Republic President **Joaquin Balaguer** is unseated by Dominican Revolutionary Party candidate **Antonio Guzmán Fernandez.**

1979   Finnish president **Urho K. Kekkonen** names Social Democrat **Mauno Koivisto** prime minister of a new four-party coalition government; Koivisto assumes the presidency, 1982.

May 27

Religious Calendar

Feast of the Immaculate Heart of Mary. Formerly celebrated August 22. Optional Memorial.

The Saints

St. Restituta of Sora, virgin and martyr; principal patron of the Italian town of Sora. [d. c. 271]

Birthdates

1794   **Cornelius Vanderbilt,** U.S. financier, railroad builder; founder of the Vanderbilt empire. [d. January 4, 1877]

1799   **Jacques François Fromental Elie Levy (Halévy),** French opera composer; teacher of Gounod and Bizet. [d. March 17, 1862]

1818   **Amelia Bloomer,** U.S. social reformer, women's rights advocate; published the *Lily*, the first U.S. newspaper to be edited entirely by a woman, providing a forum for women's rights advocates as well as temperance reformers. Became involved in dress reform movement, and, by wearing trousers under a short skirt, gave rise to the term, and the fashion, called *bloomers*. [d. December 30, 1894]

1819   **Julia Ward Howe,** U.S. poet, writer, social reformer; author of the words for *The Battle Hymn of the Republic*. [d. October 17, 1910]

1836   **Jay Gould (Jason Gould),** U.S. financier, railroad executive; his gold speculations caused the *Black Friday* panic of 1869. [d. December 2, 1892]

1837   **James Butler (*Wild Bill*) Hickok,** U.S. frontier scout, marshal 1855–71; member of Buffalo Bill Cody's Wild West Show, 1872–73. [d. August 2, 1876]

1849   **Adolph Lewisohn,** U.S. financier, philanthropist; dedicated to reform of child labor laws and prisons. [d. August 17, 1938]

1867   **(Enoch) Arnold Bennett,** British novelist, dramatist; noted as a master of fiction; treated sordid aspects of English industrial life with infinite detail. [d. March 27, 1931]

1878   **Isadora Duncan,** U.S. dancer; her innovations in dance freed ballet from its previous restrictions and set the stage for the development of modern dance. [d. September 14, 1927]

1879   **Lucile Watson,** U.S. character actress. [d. June 24, 1962]

1894   **(Samuel) Dashiell Hammett,** U.S. writer of "tough-guy" detective stories; author of *The Maltese Falcon*. [d. January 10, 1961]

1897   **Sir John Douglas Cockcroft,** British physicist; first to cause **nuclear reaction** with artificially accelerated atomic particles. Knighted, 1948; Nobel Prize in physics (with E. T. S. Walton), 1951.

1902   **Peter Marshall,** U.S. Presbyterian clergyman; Chaplain to the U.S. Senate, 1947–48; subject of the book and film, *A Man Called Peter*. [d. January 25, 1949]

1903   **John Barth,** U.S. novelist; author of *The Sot-Weed Factor*.

1907   **Rachel Carson,** U.S. biologist, author. Her final book, *Silent Spring*, stimulated widespread national controversy about the use of chemical herbicides and pesticides and their potential danger to world ecological balance. [d. April 14, 1964]

1908   **Harold (Jacob) Rome,** U.S. composer of musicals; composed scores for *Pins and Needles, I Can Get It for You Wholesale*.

1911   **Hubert (Horatio) Humphrey,** U.S. politician; U.S. Senator; Vice-President, 1965–69; Democratic presidential candidate, 1968. [d. January 13, 1978]

       Vincent Price, U.S. stage and screen actor.

1912   **(Slammin') Sam Snead,** U.S. golfer.

       John Cheever, U.S. writer; Pulitzer Prize in fiction, 1979. [d. June 18, 1982]

1915   **Herman Wouk,** U.S. novelist; author of *The Caine Mutiny, Marjorie Morningstar, The Winds of War* trilogy.

1921   **Caryl (Whittier) Chessman,** U.S. criminal, author. Wrote four books which won him support by such figures as Albert Schweitzer, Aldous Huxley. [d. by electrocution, after eight stays of execution, May 2, 1960]

1923   **Henry Kissinger,** U.S. government official, diplomat, scholar, born in Germany; U.S.

SS. Julius and his companions, soldiers and martyrs. [d. c. 302]

St. Eutropius, Bishop of Orange. [d. c. 476]

St. John I, pope and martyr. Elected pope 523. [d. 526]

St. Melangell, virgin. Also called **Monacella.** [date unknown]

Secretary of State, 1973–77; Nobel Peace Prize, 1973.

1934 **Harlan Jay Ellison,** U.S. writer, known for his fantasy and speculative fiction; wrote numerous stories for *Star Trek* television series.

1935 **Ramsey Lewis,** U.S. musician, pianist, song-writer.

Historical Events

1471 **Ladislas,** son of **Casimir IV** of Poland, becomes King of Bohemia and Hungary.

1536 First **Helvetian Confession** is issued by Swiss Protestants.

1679 **Habeas Corpus Act** for protection against false arrest and imprisonment is passed in England.

1703 **St. Petersburg** (later **Leningrad**) is founded at the mouth of the Neva River by **Peter the Great.**

1860 **Giuseppe Garibaldi** takes Palermo and sets up a provisional government (**Unification of Italy**).

1883 **Czar Alexander III** and his consort, Marie, are crowned with great ceremony at Moscow.

1885 A new ship canal from St. Petersburg to Kronstadt in Russia is opened.

1905 Russian fleet is annihilated in the **Battle of Tsushima Strait** (**Russo-Japanese War**).

1918 **Third Battle of the Aisne** begins as Germans drive to Marne River, 13 miles from Paris (**World War I**).

1919 First west to east airplane crossing of the Atlantic is completed by **A. C. Read** and his U.S. Navy crew.

1933 U.S. Congress passes **Federal Securities Act** compelling full disclosure to investors.

1935 In *Schechter Poultry Corp. v. United States,* the U.S. Supreme Court unanimously rules that the **National Industrial Recovery Act** is unconstitutional.

1937 San Francisco's **Golden Gate Bridge** is opened.

1941 A state of *unlimited national emergency* is declared by U.S. President Franklin Roosevelt in response to sweeping German victories in Europe (**World War II**).

1944 U.S. troops land on **Biak,** off New Guinea (**World War II**).

1951 **Tibet** is incorporated into China by forced agreement of Dalai Lama, Panchen Lama, and the people's government.

1960 U.S. ends economic aid to **Cuba.**

1966 First French cabinet since 1948 to include Communists is sworn in.

May 28

Holidays

Puerto Rico   Memorial Day
U.S.S.R.   Frontier Corps Day

Religious Calendar

St. Senator, Bishop of Milan. Served as papal legate. [d. 475]

St. Justus, Bishop of Urgel. [d. c. 550]

St. Germanus, Bishop of Paris. Founded famous church of Saint-Germain-des-Prés, royal burial place for several generations. Also called **Germain.** [d. 576]

Birthdates

1660   **George I,** King of Great Britain; his reign saw the emergence of the prime minister as a powerful figure. [d. June 11, 1727]

1738   **Joseph Ignace Guillotin,** French politician, physician; defender of **capital punishment** as means of preventing crime. Proposed use of beheading machines (i.e., the **guillotine**) as most humane form of capital punishment [d. March 26, 1814]

1759   **William Pitt,** English statesman; Prime Minister of England, 1783–1801. [d. January 23, 1806]

1764   **Edward Livingston,** U.S. statesman, law reformer; U.S. Congressman, 1794–1801; 1823–29; Mayor of New York City, 1801–03; U.S. Senator, 1829–31; known throughout the world for his *System of Penal Law for the United States of America.* [d. May 23, 1836]

1779   **Thomas Moore,** Irish poet, patriot; known for his lyrical, patriotic songs. [d. February 25, 1852]

1789   **Bernhard Severin Ingemann,** Danish poet, playwright, novelist. [d. February 24, 1862]

1807   **Jean Louis Rodolphe Agassiz,** U.S. naturalist, educator, zoologist, geologist, born in Switzerland; founder of **Harvard's Museum of Comparative Zoology.** Innovator in teaching techniques for natural history. [d. December 14, 1873]

1818   **P(ierre) G(ustave) T(outant) Beauregard,** Confederate Army general during U.S. Civil War; ordered bombardment of **Fort Sumter,** which opened the war. [d. February 20, 1893]

1884   **Edvard Beneš,** Czechoslovak statesman; founder of modern Czechoslovakia. [d. September 3, 1948]

1888   **Jim (James Francis) Thorpe,** U.S. athlete; winner of pentathlon and decathlon at 1912 Olympics, he was later stripped of medals when he was declared a professional; the decision was reversed on January 18, 1983, when the medals Thorpe won were returned to his children. [d. March 28, 1953]

1908   **Ian (Lancaster) Fleming,** British writer of adventure novels; created **Secret Agent 007, James Bond.** [d. August 12, 1964]

1912   **Patrick White,** Australian novelist; Nobel Prize in literature, 1973.

1916   **Walker Percy,** U.S. essayist, novelist.

1917   **Barry Commoner,** U.S. biologist, environmentalist.

Gerald C. Cash, Bahamian statesman; Governor General, 1979– .

1925   **Dietrich Fischer-Dieskau,** German operatic baritone.

1934   **Dionne Quintuplets** (Marie, Emilie, Yvonne, Annette, and Cecile), world's first recorded surviving quintuplets. The quintuplets were delivered of **Oliva Dionne,** already the mother of six. [Marie d. February 27, 1970; Emilie d. August 5, 1954]

Historical Events

1037   Holy Roman Emperor **Conrad II** issues *Constitutis de Feudis,* which makes fiefs of small Italian land holders hereditary.

1156   **William of Sicily** destroys Byzantine fleet at **Brindisi.**

St. William of Gellone, founder of the Monastery at Gellone. [d. 812]

St. Bernard of Montjoux. Founded the two celebrated Alpine hospices of Great and Little Bernard which have saved the lives of many mountaineers. Known as patron of Alpinists and other mountaineers. [d. c. 1081]

St. Ignatius, Bishop of Rostov. [d. 1288]

The London martyrs of 1582, three priests, hanged, drawn, and quartered for denying that Elizabeth I was head of the Church. [d. 1582]

The Beatified

Blessed Margaret Pole, widow and cousin of **Henry VIII,** martyr; beheaded for denying Henry's supremacy over the Church in England. [d. 1541]

Blessed Mary Bartholomea of Florence, virgin. [d. 1577]

1167 **Frederick I (Frederick Barbarossa)** of Germany defeats Romans at Tusculum; enters Rome and enthrones the antipope, **Paschal III.**

1916 **Sir Julian Byng** becomes commander of the Canadian Corps (**World War I**).

1918 **Armenia** and **Azerbaijan** are declared republics independent of Russia.

U.S. forces in France score their first military success by the capture of **Cantigny** and hold it during three counterattacks (**World War I**).

1940 **Belgium** capitulates to Germany (**World War II**).

1963 **Jomo Kenyatta** is named first prime minister of **Kenya.**

1972 U.S. President **Richard Nixon** expresses his desire for peace in an unprecedented televised address to the Russian people during his visit in Moscow.

1979 **Greece** is formally admitted to membership in the European Economic Community (Common Market).

May 29

Holidays

U.S. (Rhode Island)   **Admission Day**
Celebrates Rhodes Island's ratification of the Constitution, 1790.

Religious Calendar

The Saints

St. Cyril of Caesarea, martyr. [d. c. 251]

Birthdates

1630   **Charles II,** King of Great Britain. [d. February 6, 1685]

1736   **Patrick Henry,** American patriot, lawyer, merchant; Governor of Virginia, 1776–79; 1784–86. Great orator of the American Revolution. [d. June 6, 1799]

1830   **Clémence Louise Michel,** French revolutionary, anarchist, agitator; took part in the **Paris Commune,** 1871; exiled; returned to France and continued to pursue anarchist activities. [d. January 10, 1905]

1859   **James Henry Rand,** U.S. business-equipment manufacturer; founder of Remington Rand, Inc., 1890. [d. September 15, 1944]

1874   **G(ilbert) K(eith) Chesterton,** British essayist, novelist, journalist, poet; created the priest-sleuth, **Father Brown.** [d. June 14, 1936]

1878   **Winford Lee Lewis,** U.S. chemist; discoverer of **Lewisite,** a poison gas. [d. January 1, 1943]

1880   **Oswald Spengler,** German writer on philosophy of history; proposed a theory that Western culture, like all other great cultures, follows a definite cycle, destined ultimately to decline. [d. May 8, 1936]

1898   **Beatrice Lillie (Constance Sylvia Munston),** English-Canadian comedienne, actress.

1903   **Bob Hope (Leslie Townes Hope),** U.S. comedian, actor.

1912   **Pamela Hansford Johnson,** British author; noted for her witty, often satirical fiction; wife of C.P. Snow (October 15). [d. June 18, 1981]

1917   **John Fitzgerald Kennedy,** U.S. politician, World War II naval hero, 35th President of the U.S. [assassinated November 22, 1963]

Historical Events

1453   Siege and fall of Constantinople takes place as **Mohammed II** and his Turkish forces capture the city and kill **Byzantine Emperor Constantine.**

1660   **Charles II** of England, an exile in France during the Cromwellian period, returns to England.

1765   **Patrick Henry** introduces resolutions in the Virginia House of Burgesses, challenging the British government.

1790   **Rhode Island** ratifies the U.S. Constitution, becoming the last of the 13 original states in the federal union.

1848   **Wisconsin** is admitted to the Union as the 30th state.

1889   Trial by jury is first introduced in Spain.

1921   **Salzburg** region votes for union with Germany.

1944   **_U.S.S. Block Island,_** torpedoed by a German submarine, becomes the only U.S. carrier lost in the Atlantic during **World War II.**

1953   **Sir Edmund Hillary** of New Zealand and Nepalese Sherpa tribesman **Tenzing Norgay** are the first men to reach the summit of **Mt. Everest.**

1961   U.S. Supreme Court upholds the constitutionality of state **blue laws** prohibiting commercial activity on Sunday.

St. Maximinus, Bishop of Trier. [d.c. 347]

SS. Sisinnius, Martyrius, and **Alexander,** missionaries and martyrs. [d. 397]

St. Theodosia, virgin, nun, and martyr. [d. 745]

SS. William, Stephen, Raymund, and their companions, martyrs. [d. 1242]

The Beatified

Blessed Peter Petroni of Siena; held in great veneration by the Carthusian order. [d. 1361]

Blessed Richard Thirkeld, priest and martyr. [d. 1583]

May 30

Holidays

U.S.   **Memorial Day**
Established as legal holiday to commemorate the U.S. war dead, 1868.

U.S. (Virginia)   **Confederate Memorial Day**

Religious Calendar

The Saints

St. Eleutherius, pope. Elected c. 174. [d. c. 189]

St. Felix I, pope. Elected 269. [d. 274]

St. Isaac of Constantinople, hermit and abbot. Founded Dalmatian Monastery, the oldest in Constantinople. [d. c. 410]

Birthdates

1845   **Amadeus I,** King of Spain, 1870–73; forced to abdicate. [d. January 18, 1890]

1846   **Peter Carl Fabergé (Karl Gustavovich Faberge),** Russian goldsmith, jeweler. [d. September 24, 1920]

1859   **Pierre Marie Félix Janet,** French psychopathologist, neurologist; known for research on hysteria. [d. February 24, 1947]

1887   **Alexander Archipenko,** U.S. sculptor born in Russia; one of first Cubists. [d. February 25, 1964]

1888   **James A(loysius) Farley,** U.S. politician; head of Democratic National Committee, 1932–40; U.S. Postmaster General, 1933–40. [d. June 9, 1976]

1896   **Howard Hawks,** U.S. film director; gained reputation for excellence in both comedy and drama in films during 1930s and 1940s. [d. December 26, 1977]

1901   **Cornelia Otis Skinner,** U.S. actress, author; known for her play, *The Pleasure of His Company* and her book *Our Hearts Were Young and Gay*; daughter of stage actor **Otis Skinner** (June 28). [d. July 9, 1979]

1904   **Roland Henry Wiley,** U.S. lawyer, farmer; responsible for numerous large developments near Las Vegas, Nevada, including Cathedral Canyon and Hidden Hills Ranch.

1908   **Hannes Alfvén,** Swedish physicist; Nobel Prize in physics for contributions in the study of plasmas, 1970.

1909   **Benny Goodman (Benjamin David Goodman),** U.S. orchestra leader, clarinetist.

1912   **Julian Gustave Symons,** British novelist, poet, biographer, critic; especially known for his crime novels.

       Julius Axelrod, U.S. biochemist; Nobel Prize in physiology or medicine for research on composition of nerve fibers (with B. Katz and U.S. Von Euler), 1970.

1920   **Godfrey Binaisa,** President of Uganda, 1979; successor to Idi Amin; ousted by a six-man military commission.

1934   **Aleksei Arkhipovich Leonov,** Russian cosmonaut; the first man to accomplish a **space walk,** 1965.

Historical Events

1431   **Joan of Arc** is burned at the stake at Rouen, France, by the English.

1536   **Henry VIII** of England marries **Jane Seymour,** his third wife.

1574   **Charles IX** of France dies and is succeeded by **Henry III.**

1814   **Malta** is annexed by Great Britain.

1848   U.S. acquires **New Mexico, Texas, California, Nevada, Utah, Arizona,** and parts of **Colorado** and **Wyoming** from Mexico; this constitutes more than 30 per cent of Mexico's territory.

1854   **Kansas-Nebraska Act** is passed in U.S., opening Nebraska territory to settlement with popular sovereignty on issue of slavery.

1868   **Memorial Day** is first celebrated in U.S.

St. Exuperantius, Bishop of Ravenna. Built the town of Argenta, so called because it paid a tribute in silver to the church of Ravenna. Also called **Superantius.** [d. 418]

St. Madelgisilus, recluse. Also called **Madelgisilus, Maguil, Maguille, Mauguille.** [d. c. 655]

St. Walstan, confessor. Invoked to cure fevers, palsies, lameness, and blindness. [d. 1016]

St. Ferdinand III of Castile, king. Reign of most importance in Spanish history because of great territorial gains. Founded the University of Salamanca. [d. 1252]

St. Joan of Arc, virgin, martyr, and patron of France. Also called *Jeanne la Pucelle*, *Joan the Maid*, and the *Maid of Orléans.* [d. 1431]

The Beatified

Blessed Andrew, Bishop of Pistola. [d. 1401]

Blessed James Bertoni, a Servite. [d. 1483]

Blessed William Scott and **Blessed Richard Newport,** priests and martyrs. [d. 1612]

1901	**Hall of Fame for Great Americans,** founded in 1900, is dedicated at New York University.
1911	First 500-mile automobile race at **Indianapolis Speedway** is held.
1913	**First Balkan War** between Bulgaria, Greece, Serbia, and Montenegro and the Turks, ends with signing of **Treaty of London.**
1915	Italian forces capture **Cortina** in the Venetian Alps (**World War I**).
1918	The first American troops arrive in **Italy** (**World War I**).
1922	**Lincoln Memorial** in Washington is dedicated.
1942	British send 1,000 bombers in raid on Cologne, Germany (**World War II**).
1961	Dominican strongman **Rafael Leonidas Trujillo Molina,** dictator of the Republic since 1930, is assassinated.
1967	**Biafra** secedes from Nigeria.
1981	**President Ziaur Rahmar** of Bangladesh is killed in an unsuccessful coup attempt by a group of military leaders.

May 31

Birthdates

1557   **Fyodor I, Emperor of Russia,** 1584–98; his brother-in-law, **Boris Godunov,** held real power. [d. January 7, 1598]

1750   **Prince Karl August von Hardenberg,** Prussian statesman; active in Prussian War against France, 1792–95; made a prince in recognition of service during War of Liberation, 1813–14. [d. November 26, 1822]

1819   **William Worrall Mayo,** U.S. physician, surgeon; father of William James and Charles Horace Mayo, who founded the **Mayo Clinic,** Rochester, Minnesota. [d. March 6, 1911]

       Walt(er) Whitman, U.S. poet; renowned for his free-form use of words, which gave rise to a new generation of poetry, and for his celebration of the individual and of democracy. [d. March 26, 1892]

1857   **Pope Pius XI,** a tireless worker for world peace. [d. February 10, 1939]

1861   **Emily Perkins Bissell,** U.S. welfare worker; responsible for concept and use of **Christmas seals** to aid tubercular children. [d. March 8, 1948]

1887   **Saint-John Perse,** French poet, diplomat; Nobel Prize in literature, 1960. [d. September 20, 1975]

1894   **Fred Allen (John Florence Sullivan),** U.S. comedian, radio personality of the 1930s and 1940s; introduced Jack Benny (February 14) to American radio audiences. [d. March 17, 1956]

1898   **Norman Vincent Peale,** U.S. clergyman, author; well known for his national radio program, *The Art of Living.*

1908   **Don Ameche (Dominic Felix Amici),** U.S. actor.

1912   **Henry (Martin) "Scoop" Jackson,** U.S. politician, lawyer; U.S. Congressman, 1941–52; U.S. Senator, 1953–1983. [d. September 1, 1983]

1919   **(Rupert) Vance Hartke,** U.S. politician; U.S. Senator, 1959–77.

1920   **Edward Bennett Williams,** U.S. criminal lawyer, sports franchise owner.

1923   **Prince Ranier III,** Head of State, Principality of Monaco, 1949– .

1924   **Patricia Roberts Harris,** U.S. government official, lawyer; Secretary of Housing and Urban Development, 1977–79; Secretary of Health, Education and Welfare; first black woman to reach both ambassadorial and cabinet rank.

1930   **Clint Eastwood,** U.S. actor.

1931   **John Robert Schrieffer,** U.S. physicist; Nobel Prize in physics for experiments in superconductivity (with J. Bardeen and L. Cooper), 1972.

1938   **Peter Yarrow,** U.S. singer, member of folk-singing group, *Peter, Paul, and Mary.*

1943   **Joe Namath,** U.S. football player, actor.

1957   **Jim Craig,** U.S. hockey player; goalie for 1980 U.S. hockey team which defeated the Soviets and won gold medal in Olympic competition.

Historical Events

1433   **Sigmund of Germany** is crowned Holy Roman Emperor by **Pope Eugene IV.**

1639   **Rev. Thomas Hooker** and his fellow settlers reach **Hartford, Connecticut.**

1653   **Pope Innocent X** declares propositions of **Cornelis Jansen** to be heretical; Jansen teaches that Augustinian interpretation of

The Saints

St. Petronilla, virgin and martyr. [d. c. 251]

SS. Cantius, Cantianus, and **Cantianella,** martyrs. [d. c. 304]

St. Mechtildis of Edelstetten, virgin and abbess. [d. 1160]

The Beatified

Blessed James the Venetian, friar and mystic. [d. 1314]

---

grace, free will, and predestination is against the teaching of Jesuit schools.

1740 **Frederick William I** of Prussia dies and is succeeded by **Frederick II.**

1775 **American Continental Army** is formed from the colonial troops assembled against the British at Boston.

1793 **Reign of Terror** begins in France.

1821 First Catholic cathedral in U.S., **Cathedral of the Assumption of the Blessed Virgin Mary,** is dedicated in Baltimore.

1868 First official **bicycle race** is held at **Parc de St. Cloud,** outside of Paris. It is won by **James Moore,** an Englishman.

1891 Construction of the **Trans-Siberian Railway,** linking Moscow with the Pacific Coast of Russia, begins.

1900 The British seize **Johannesburg (Boer War).**

1902 **Boer War** ends with the signing of the **Treaty of Vereeniging** in Pretoria, South Africa.

1910 **Union of South Africa** is inaugurated, uniting the **Cape of Good Hope, Natal,** the **Transvaal,** and the **Orange Free State.**

1913 **The 17th Amendment** to U.S. Constitution, providing for direct popular election of U.S. senators, goes into effect.

1915 German **Zeppelins** drop nearly a hundred incendiary bombs on London (**World War I**).

1916 **Battle of Jutland,** a naval battle between Germany and Britain, is fought, with both sides claiming victory. Britain retains command of the seas, but the German fleet escapes (**World War I**).

1918 The German advance in the **Third Battle of the Aisne** reaches the Marne, only 37 miles from Paris (**World War I**).

1935 An estimated 50,000 die in an **earthquake** in **Quetta, India.**

1961 **Union of South Africa** secedes from the British Commonwealth and becomes an independent republic.

1970 A devastating **earthquake** in the Andes destroys entire cities in Peru; death toll is estimated to exceed 50,000.

1979 **Bishop Abel Muzorewa** becomes Prime Minister of the new black-dominated government in **Rhodesia,** which later changed its name to **Zimbabwe.**

June

June is the sixth month of the Gregorian calendar and has 30 days. It was the fourth month of the early Roman 10-month calendar.

The Roman name for the month, *Junius*, probably derives from Juno, one of the most important goddesses in the Roman pantheon, consort of Jupiter and the patroness of women, invoked for propitious marriage and childbirth.

In the northern hemisphere the summer solstice, the day of the year with the longest daylight, occurs on June 21 or 22; this fact led to the celebration of Midsummer's Day,

June 24, one of the quarter days in Great Britain. June is also a popular month for marriages, and marks the end of the school year in many countries and the beginning of the vacation season.

In the astrological calendar, June spans the zodiac signs of Gemini, the Twins (May 21–June 21) and Cancer, the Crab (June 22–July 22).

The birthstone for June is the pearl, moonstone, or alexandrite, and the flower is the rose or the honeysuckle.

State, National, and International Holidays

Rose Harvest Festival
(Bulgaria)
First Sunday

Jefferson Davis's Birthday
(Alabama, Mississippi)
First Monday

(Florida, Georgia, South Carolina)
June 3

Labor Day
(Bahamas)
First Friday

Queen's Official Birthday
(Great Britain)
Second Saturday

(Australia, Bermuda, Cayman Islands, Fiji, and Papua New Guinea)
Second Monday

(New Zealand)
First Saturday

Flag Day
(United States)
June 14

Light Industry Workers' Day
(U.S.S.R.)
Second Sunday

Labor Day
(Trinidad and Tobago)
Third Saturday

Medical Workers' Day
(U.S.S.R.)
Third Sunday

Soviet Youth Day
(U.S.S.R.)
Final Sunday

Holland Festival
(The Netherlands)
First Three Weeks

Midsummer's Day
(Great Britain)
June 24

Midsummer Celebrations
(Sweden)
Weekend closest to summer solstice

Special Events and Their Sponsors

National Dairy Month
American Dairy Association
6300 North River Road
Rosemont, Illinois 60018

National Pest Control Month
National Pest Control Association
8150 Leesburg Pike
Suite 1100
Vienna, Virginia 22180

Philatelic Writers' Month
Franklin D. Roosevelt Philatelic Society
154 Laguna Court
St. Augustine Shores, Florida 32084

National Ragweed Month
Air Pollution Control League of Cincinnati
18 E. Fourth Street
Cincinnati, Ohio 45202

National Safe Boating Week
Second Week
National Safety Council
444 North Michigan Avenue
Chicago, Illinois 60611

Fan Fair Celebration
Second Full Week
International Fan Club Organization, Tri-Son, Inc.
Box 177
Wild Horse, Colorado 80862
(in conjunction with the Grand Ole Opry and the Country Music Association of Nashville, Tennessee)

National Little League Week
Second Week
Little League Baseball, Inc.
Williamsport, Pennsylvania 17701

Great Hudson River Revival
Third Weekend
Hudson River Sloop Clearwater, Inc.
112 Market Street
Poughkeepsie, New York 12601

Philatelic Journalists Day
June 6
Franklin D. Roosevelt Philatelic Society
154 Laguna Court
St. Augustine Shores, Florida 32084

Portuguese Day–Dia de Camões
Sunday nearest June 10
Luso-American Education Foundation
P.O. Box 1768
Oakland, California 94604

International Picnic Day
June 18
Makepeace Foundation
63 Adams Point
Barrington, Rhode Island 02806

Fathers' Day
Third Sunday
National Fathers' Day Committee
47 West 34th Street
New York, New York 10001

Special Days—Other Calendars

	Pentecost Sunday	Trinity Sunday	Shavuoth
1985		June 2	
1986			June 13
1987	June 7	June 14	June 3
1988			
1989			June 9
1990	June 3	June 10	

June 1

Holidays

Cape Verde Islands	Children's Day
Kenya	**Madaraka Day** A freedom celebration.
Western Samoa	**Independence Holiday** Celebrates the coming to independence, 1962. First day of a three-day celebration.
Tunisia	**Constitution Day** or **Victory Day** Commemorates promulgation of Tunisia's constitution, 1959. First day of a two-day celebration.
U.S.S.R.	**International Children's Protection Day**

Religious Calendar

The Saints

St. Justin, philosopher and martyr. First great Christian apologist. Feast formerly April 14. [d. 165] Obligatory Memorial.

Birthdates

1637 (Père) **Jacques Marquette,** French Jesuit missionary explorer in North America. [d. May 18, 1675]

1780 **Karl Maria von Clausewitz,** Prussian Army general, military strategist. [d. November 16, 1831]

1796 **Nicolas Leonard Sadi Carnot,** French physicist; his work formed foundation for study of thermodynamics. [d. August 24, 1832]

1801 **Brigham Young,** U.S. religious leader; one of the fathers of the **Mormon Church** in the U.S. Led migration to Utah and oversaw founding of **Salt Lake City.** [d. August 29, 1877]

1804 **Mikhail Ivanovich Glinka,** Russian composer; wrote first Russian national opera, *A Life for the Czar.* [d. February 15, 1857]

1813 **Evariste Régis Huc,** French Vincentian missionary to China, Mongolia, and Tibet. [d. April 26, 1860]

1814 **Philip Kearny,** U.S. soldier, cavalry expert; served as brigadier general of New Jersey militia during U.S. Civil War. [d. September 1, 1862]

1831 **John Bell Hood,** Confederate general in U.S. Civil War. [d. August 30, 1879]

1833 **John Marshall Harlan,** U.S. jurist, lawyer; Associate Justice of U.S. Supreme Court, 1877–1911. [d. October 14, 1911]

1849 **Francis Edgar Stanley,** U.S. inventor; with his twin brother, Freelan, developed first successful steam-powered automobile, the **Stanley Steamer.** [d. July 31, 1918]

1855 **Edward Hartley Angle,** U.S. orthodontist; founder of modern **orthodontics.** [d. August 11, 1930]

1862 **Simon Iturri Patino,** Bolivian mining executive; developer of world's richest tin reserves. [d. April 20, 1947]

1878 **John Masefield,** British poet; Poet Laureate, 1930–67. [d. May 12, 1967]

1882 **John Drinkwater,** British dramatist. [d. March 25, 1937]

1924 **William Sloane Coffin,** U.S. liberal clergyman; active in Vietnam War peace movement.

1926 **Marilyn Monroe (Norma Jean Baker),** U.S. actress, sex symbol of the 1950s. [d. August 5, 1962]

St. Proculus, *The Soldier,* and **St. Proculus,** Bishop of Bologna, martyrs. [d. c. 304 and 542]

St. Pamphilus and his companions, martyrs. St. Pamphilus, a priest, was the greatest Biblical scholar of his day. [d. 309]

St. Caprasius, Abbot of Lérins in France. Also called **Caprais.** [d. 430]

St. Wistan, prince and martyr. [d. 849]

St. Simeon of Syracuse, monk. [d. 1035]

St. Eneco, Abbot of Oña, in Castile. Also called **Iñigo.** [d. 1057]

St. Theobald of Alba, patron of cobblers and porters. [d. 1150]

St. Angela Merici, virgin; founder of the Company of St. Ursula, the first teaching order of women. [d. 1540]

The Martyrs of Japan. Numbering about 205, included many Dominican and Jesuit missionaries and many Japanese Christians, put to death in an effort to root out Christianity in Japan. [d. 1617–32]

St. Gwen Teirbron of Brittany. [death date unknown]

St. Ronan, bishop. [death date unknown]

St. Wite. One of two English saints to remain in their shrines undisturbed by the Protestant Reformation. Also called **Candida.** [death date unknown]

The Beatified

Blessed John Pelingotto, Franciscan monk. [d. 1304]

Blessed Herculanus of Piegaro, Franciscan preacher. [d. 1451]

Blessed John Storey, martyr. [d. 1571]

Blessed Felix of Nicosia, Capuchin monk. [d. 1787]

1930 **Frank Whittle,** British inventor; first developed **gas turbine** unit for jet propulsion in aircraft.

1934 **Pat Boone (Charles Eugene Boone),** U.S. pop singer.

1945 **Frederica von Stade,** U.S. operatic mezzo-soprano.

Historical Events

1783 **Bank of Ireland** is established.

1792 **Kentucky** is admitted to the Union as the 15th state.

1796 **Tennessee** is admitted to the Union as the 16th state.

1882 First scheduled train of **Gotthard Railway** makes trip from Lucerne, Switzerland, to Milan, Italy.

1918 American forces are rushed into battle at **Château-Thierry** to stem German advance on Paris in the **Third Battle of the Aisne (World War I).**

1932 **Franz von Papen** becomes German chancellor.

1959 Tunisian Constitution goes into effect, establishing Tunisia's independence from France.

1961 **Northern Cameroon,** a former British UN trust territory, merges with **Nigeria.**

1966 **Joaquín Balaguer** is elected President of the Dominican Republic and remains in power until 1978.

1973 Greek cabinet abolishes Greek monarchy, naming **George Papadopoulos** as Premier.

British Honduras officially changes its name to **Belize.**

1983 Swiss scientists announce confirmation of the existence of the **Z-zero** sub-nuclear particle. The announcement follows the January, 1983 announcement of the discovery of the sub-atomic **W particles.**

June 2

Holidays

Western Samoa	**Independence Holiday** Second day of a three-day celebration.
Tunisia	**Victory Day** Second day of a two-day celebration.

Religious Calendar

The Saints

St. Pothinus, Bishop of Lyons and his companions, the **Martyrs of Lyons and Vienne.** [d. 177]

Birthdates

1535   **Pope Leo XI,** pope, 1605. [d. April 27, 1605]

1624   **John III Sobieski,** King of Poland, 1674–96. [d. June 17, 1696]

1740   **Donatien Alphonse François de Sade, Marquis de Sade,** French man of letters; noted for his scandalous sex life, which inspired the term *sadism.* [d. December 2, 1814]

1743   **Count Alessandro Cagliostro,** Italian charlatan; with his wife, traveled widely through Europe posing as physician, alchemist, necromancer, and freemason. [d. August 26, 1795]

1773   **John Randolph,** U.S. politician, advocate of states' rights. [d. May 24, 1833]

1811   **Henry James,** U.S. theologian; father of William James (January 11), and Henry James (April 15). [d. December 18, 1882]

1835   **St. Pius X,** pope 1903–14; maintained a deep interest in social questions and in bettering the life of the poor. Beatified in 1951; canonized 1954. [d. August 20, 1914]

1840   **Thomas Hardy,** British novelist, poet; his works were major influence in poetry and novel writing of the late 19th and early 20th centuries. [d. January 11, 1928]

1845   **Arthur MacArthur,** U.S. Army officer; Congressional Medal of Honor for heroism at **Battle of Missionary Ridge** (Spanish-American War); father of Douglas MacArthur (January 26). [d. September 5, 1912]

1849   **Paul Albert Besnard,** French painter, etcher. [d. December 4, 1934]

1857   **Sir Edward William Elgar,** British composer; best known for his composition, *Pomp and Circumstance*, 1902. [d. February 23, 1934]

        Karl Adolf Gjellerup, Danish poet, novelist; Nobel Prize in literature (with H. Pontoppidan, 1917). [d. October 11, 1919]

1890   **Hedda Hopper,** U.S. actress, journalist, best known for her syndicated column about Hollywood, begun in 1938. [d. February 1, 1966]

1897   **R(euben) H(erbert) Mueller,** U.S. clergyman; leader in interfaith movement in the U.S.; President, National Council of Churches of Christ, 1963–66. [d. July 6, 1982]

1899   **Edwin Way Teale,** U.S. naturalist, writer, photographer; Pulitzer Prize for work entitled *Wandering Through Winter*, 1966. [d. June 2, 1899]

1903   **Johnny Weissmuller,** U.S. swimmer, actor; won 52 national championships, 3 Olympic gold medals (1924 and 1928 Olympic Games), and set 67 world records during 1920s. Played role of *Tarzan* in 19 films between 1930 and 1947. [d. January 22, 1984]

1909   **Michael Todd (Avron Hirsch Golbogen),** U.S. producer; husband of Elizabeth Taylor. [d. March 22, 1958]

1915   **Lester Del Rey (Ramon Alvarez del Rey),** U.S. science-fiction writer.

1930   **Charles (Pete) Conrad, Jr.,** U.S. astronaut on flight of *Gemini 5*, August 23, 1965; *Gemini 11*, September 12, 1966; and *Apollo 12*, November 14, 1969. Conrad, aboard Lunar Module, landed in Sea of Storms (with A.

St. Erasmus, bishop and martyr; patron of sailors who regard the corona discharge (St. Elmo's fire) seen before and after storms as manifestations of his protection. Invoked against cramp or colic, especially in children. Also called **Elmo, Ermo.** [d. c. 303]

SS. Marcellinus and **Peter,** martyrs. [d. 304] Optional Memorial.

St. Eugenius I, pope. Elected 654. [d. 657]

St. Stephen, Bishop in Sweden and martyr. Called **Apostle of the Helsings.** [d. c. 1075]

St. Nicholas the Pilgrim. Also called **Peregrinus.** [d. 1094]

The Beatified

Blessed Sadoc and his companions, martyrs. [d. 1260]

Bean). Also aboard first manned flight to *Skylab* space station, May 25, 1973.

1937 **Sally Kellerman,** U.S. actress.

1941 **Stacy Keach,** U.S. actor.

Historical Events

1420 **Henry V** of England marries **Catherine** of France.

1734 Russians take **Danzig** and expel **Stanislas Leszczinski** from Poland (**War of the Polish Succession**).

1774 **Quartering Act,** passed by British Parliament, legalizes quartering of troops in occupied dwellings; one of events precipitating **American Revolution.**

1793 The arrest of 31 Girondist deputies to national assembly leads to **Reign of Terror** during the French Revolution (see June 4).

1899 Spain cedes the **Carolinas, Pelews, Ladrones,** and **Mariannas Islands** to Germany.

1902 **Oregon** is first state to adopt **initiative** and **referendum** procedures on a general scale.

1916 Russians break through Austrian lines on eastern front and capture fortresses of **Lutzk** and **Dubno** (**World War I**).

1951 U.S. government prohibits all travel by U.S. citizens in **Czechoslovakia.**

1953 **Elizabeth II** of Great Britain is crowned by the Archbishop of Canterbury in Westminster Abbey, London.

1966 U.S. spacecraft *Surveyor I* makes successful soft landing on the moon and begins to relay first closeup pictures of the moon.

1967 U.S. Federal Communications Commission rules that radio and television stations must provide time for programming presenting the possible dangers of smoking as a balance to cigarette advertising.

1974 **Jigme Singye Wangchuk** is crowned King of **Bhutan.**

June 3

Holidays

Western Samoa	**Independence Day** Third day of a three-day celebration.
U.S. (Florida, Georgia, South Carolina)	**Jefferson Davis's Birthday**
U.S. (Kentucky, Louisiana)	**Confederate Memorial Day**

Religious Calendar

The Saints

St. Cecilius, priest. [d. c. 248]

SS. Pergentinus and **Laurentius,** martyrs. Patrons of Arezzo. [d. 251]

SS. Lucillian and his companions, martyrs. [d. 273]

Birthdates

1726 **James Hutton,** Scottish geologist; one of founders of modern geology; proposed principle of *uniformitarianism* which suggested that forces changing earth's crust are uniform and constant in nature, 1785. [d. March 26, 1797]

1793 **Antoni Malczewski,** Polish poet; intimate of Lord Byron; chief work was *Marja.* [d. May 2, 1826]

1804 **Richard Cobden,** British statesman, economist; known as the *Apostle of Free Trade.* [d. April 2, 1865]

1808 **Jefferson Davis,** U.S. political leader; President of the **Confederate States of America,** 1861–65 (U.S. Civil War). [d. December 6, 1889]

1819 **Thomas Ball,** U.S. sculptor; sculpted equestrian statue of George Washington now in Public Garden, Boston, Daniel Webster, now in Central Park, New York, plus numerous others. [d. December 11, 1911]

Johan Barthold Jongkind, Dutch luminist painter and etcher of Fontainebleau school. [d. February 9, 1891]

1843 **Frederick VIII,** King of Denmark, 1906–12. [d. May 14, 1912]

1844 **Garret Augustus Hobart,** U.S. lawyer, legislator; Vice-President of U.S., 1897–99. [d. November 21, 1899]

1864 **Ransom Eli Olds,** U.S. inventor, auto manufacturer; manufactured first Oldsmobile, 1895. Developed principles and methods for **assembly line** method of manufacturing. [d. August 26, 1950]

1865 **George V,** King of Great Britain. [d. January 20, 1936]

1873 **Otto Loewi,** U.S. physiologist born in Germany; Nobel Prize in physiology or medicine for discovery of chemical transmission of nerve impulses (with H. H. Dale), 1936. [d. December 25, 1961]

1877 **Raoul Dufy,** French painter, designer, associated with Fauvists. [d. March 23, 1953]

1887 **Roland Hayes,** U.S. tenor; one of first black American concert artists to achieve international fame. [d. December 31, 1976]

1899 **Georg von Békésy,** U.S. physiologist; Nobel Prize in physiology or medicine for findings concerning the cochlea of the ear, 1961. [d. June 13, 1972]

1901 **Maurice Evans,** British actor.

1904 **Jan Peerce,** U.S. operatic tenor; first American singer to appear at the Bolshoi Opera in Russia.

Charles Drew, U.S. physician, researcher in area of blood plasma; developed efficient way to store blood plasma in blood banks. [d. April 1, 1950]

St. Clotilda, Queen of France and widow. Converted her husband, Clovis, King of the Franks, to Christianity. Also called **Clotildis.** [d. 545]

SS. Liphardus and **Urbicius,** abbots and monks. Liphardus also called **Liéfard, Liphardus.** [d. 6th century]

St. Kevin, Abbot of Glendalough. Founder of Monastery at Glendalough, one of four principal pilgrimage-places of Ireland. One of the principal patrons of Ireland. Also called **Coemgen.** [d. c. 618]

St. Genesius, Bishop of Clermont. Also called **Genesis, Genêt.** [d. c. 660]

St. Isaac of Cordova, martyr. [d. 852]

St. Morand, missionary priest in Alsace. Patron of wine growers. [d. c. 1115]

SS. Charles Lwanga, Joseph Mkasa, and their companions, the Martyrs of Uganda, the first martyrs of Black Africa. [d. 1886] Optional Memorial.

The Beatified

Blessed Andrew of Spello, a disciple of St. Francis of Assisi. Called **Andrew of the Waters** because a providential rain resulted from a petition to him. [d. 1254]

Blessed John the Sinner, hospitaler. [d. 1600]

1906	**Josephine Baker,** U.S.-French dancer; star of the Folies-Bergère; owned her own club in Paris; traveled widely; well-known throughout Europe for her eccentric style, both on and off stage. [d. April 12, 1975 during 50th anniversary of her Paris debut]
1922	**Alain Resnais,** French film director.
1925	**Tony Curtis (Bernard Schwartz),** U.S. actor.
1926	**Allen Ginsburg,** U.S. poet of the beat generation.
1931	**(Thomas) Bert(ram) Lance,** U.S. banker, government official; forced to resign as Director of U.S. Office of Management and the Budget, 1977, after serious questions arose over his banking practices.
1933	**Celso Torrelio Villa,** Bolivian statesman; President, 1981–

Historical Events

1083	**Henry IV** of Germany storms Rome, making **Pope Gregory VII** a virtual prisoner.
1098	Crusaders take Antioch (**First Crusade**).
1539	**Fernando de Soto** claims **Florida** for Spain.
1621	**Dutch West Indies Company** is chartered.
1818	In India, the last **Marantha War** ends with British defeat of the resisting Maranthas.

1916	The Allies assume the administration of **Salonika, Greece** and proclaim martial law (**World War I**).
1942	Japanese launch carrier-borne air attack on U.S. Naval base in the **Aleutians** (**World War II**).
1963	**Pope John XXIII** dies at age 81; he is later succeeded by Cardinal Giovanni Battista Montini, **Pope Paul VI.**
1965	**Major Edward H. White II** spends 20 minutes outside the *Gemini 4* spacecraft launched earlier in the day from Cape Kennedy, Florida, completing the first American **space walk.**
	Silver is eliminated from coining of U.S. dimes and quarters, and percentage is reduced in half-dollars, in first major change in **U.S. coinage** since 1792.
1969	U.S. destroyer *Frank E. Evans* collides with Australian aircraft carrier *Melbourne* in the South China Sea; 73 U.S. seamen are killed.

June 4

Holidays

Finland   **Flag Day**
Finnish armed forces commemorate birthday of Carl Gustaf Mannerheim, Finnish military leader in fight for independence from Russia, 1867.

Tonga   **Emancipation Day**
Commemorates Tonga's achievement of independence, 1970.

Birthdates

1694   **François Quesnay,** French economist, physician; his theories formed the basis of the physiocratic approach to economics. [d. December 16, 1774]

1718   **Aleksandr Petrovich Sumarokov,** Russian playwright, poet; director of first permanent theater in St. Petersburg. [d. September 1, 1777]

1738   **George III,** King of Great Britain (1760–1820); ruled during the revolt of the American colonies. [d. January 29, 1820]

1744   **Jeremy Belknap,** U.S. clergyman, historian; founder of the **Massachusetts Historical Society.** [d. June 20, 1798]

1867   **Carl Gustav Emil, Baron von Mannerheim,** Finnish Field Marshal, public official; President of Finland, 1944–46. [d. January 27, 1951]

1877   **Heinrich Otto Wieland,** German chemist; Nobel Prize in chemistry for studies of bile acids, 1927. [d. 1957]

1879   **Alla Nazimova,** Russian actress; best known for interpretation of Ibsen roles. [d. July 13, 1945]

1911   **Rosalind Russell,** U.S. actress. [d. November 28, 1976]

1919   **Robert Merrill,** U.S. operatic baritone.

Historical Events

1133   **Lothair of Saxony** is crowned Holy Roman Emperor and is invested with Tuscany by **Pope Innocent II.**

1249   **Louis IX** of France, leader of the **Sixth Crusade,** lands in Egypt.

1316   **Louis X** of France dies and is succeeded by **Philip V.**

1793   **Robespierre** is declared President of France, marking the beginning of the **Reign of Terror** (see June 2).

1832   **Reform Act** passes Britain's House of Lords, redistributing parlimentary seats to favor growing industrial areas and, by lowering property qualifications, admitting the industrial middle class to the electorate.

1942   **Battle of Midway** begins, leading to a great American naval victory over Japan (**World War II**).

1944   U.S. troops liberate **Rome** (**World War II**).

1970   **Tonga** becomes an independent kingdom and member of the British Commonwealth.

1977   The **Soviet Union** releases for publication the draft of its most recent constitution, the fourth since the Russian Revolution of 1917, which states for the first time the dominant role of the Communist Party in ruling the U.S.S.R.

Religious Calendar

The Saints

St. Quirinus, Bishop of Siscia, martyr. [d. 308]

St. Metrophanes, Bishop of Byzantium. [d. c. 325]

St. Optatus, Bishop of Milevis or Milevum. One of most illustrious champions of the Church during the 4th century. [d. c. 387]

St. Petroc, abbot. Also called **Pedrog, Perreuse.** [d. 6th century]

St. Edfrith, Bishop of Lindisfarne. Wrote the Lindisfarne Gospels. Also called **Eadfrith.** [d. 721]

St. Francis Caracciolo, founder of the Minor Clerks Regular. [d. 1608]

St. Vincentia Gerosa, virgin; co-founder of the Sisters of Charity of Lovere. [d. 1847]

St. Ninnoc, nun. Also called **Ninnocha, Gwengusetle.** [death date unknown]

June 5

Holidays

World Environment Day
Commemorates anniversary of opening day of United Nations Conference on Human Environment, 1972.

Denmark   **Constitution Day**
Designated as day to remember signing of constitutions of 1849, 1953.

Birthdates

1718   **Thomas Chippendale,** English cabinet-maker, furniture designer, baptized on this day. [d. November, 1779]

1723   **Adam Smith,** Scottish economist, philosopher; author of *The Wealth of Nations.* [d. July 17, 1790]

1819   **John Couch Adams,** British astronomer, most noted for his discovery of **Neptune.** [d. January 21, 1892]

1826   **Ivar Christian Hallström,** Swedish composer of operas, ballets, and folk songs; composed *The Mountain King.* [d. April 11, 1901]

1854   **James Carroll,** U.S. bacteriologist, Army surgeon; noted for his work on **yellow fever.** [d. September 16, 1907]

1862   **Allvar Gullstrand,** Swedish ophthamologist, physicist; Nobel Prize for physiology or medicine for work on the dioptrics of the eye, 1911. [d. July 28, 1930]

1867   **Paul Jean Toulet,** French poet, novelist; his *Contrerimes* exerted significant influence on French poetry. [d. September 6, 1920]

1877   **John Henry Breck,** U.S. cosmetics manufacturer; best known for hair-care products. [d. February 16, 1965]

1878   **Francisco (*Pancho*) Villa** Mexican guerrilla leader and revolutionary. [d. June 20, 1923]

1883   **John Maynard Keynes,** British economist; proposed theory of economics whereby economic depression could be avoided by increased governmental investment in public works, encouragement of capital goods production, and stimulation of consumption. [d. April 21, 1946]

1887   **Ruth (Fulton) Benedict,** U.S. anthropologist; best known for her study of the influences of culture on personality development published as *Patterns of Culture.* Her study was translated into 14 languages and served to popularize anthropology. [d. September 17, 1948]

1895   **William Boyd,** U.S. actor; best known for his role as *Hopalong Cassidy.* [d. September 12, 1972]

1896   **Allyn Cox,** U.S. mural painter; known for the completion of the 300-foot mural depicting American historical scenes on great rotunda of U.S. capitol building. [d. September 26, 1982]

1899   **Federico García Lorca,** Spanish poet, playwright; known for the violence and passion of his works. Killed during Spanish Civil War. [d. August 1936]

1900   **Dennis Gabor,** British physicist born in Hungary; Nobel Prize in physics for invention of holography, 1971. [d. February 8, 1979]

1920   **Cornelius John Ryan,** U.S. novelist, journalist born in Ireland; author of *The Longest Day, A Bridge Too Far.* [d. November 23, 1974]

1934   **Bill Moyers,** U.S. journalist, editor, television news correspondent.

1936   **Bruce Dern,** U.S. actor.

1941   **Harry Nilsson (Harry Edward Nelson III),** U.S. singer, songwriter.

1942   **Teodoro Obiang Nguema Mbasogo,** Guinean statesman; President, Supreme Military Council, Republic of Equatorial Guinea, 1979– .

Historical Events

1806   **The Netherlands** is declared a kingdom; **Louis Bonaparte,** brother of Napoleon Bonaparte, is made king.

The Saints

St. Dorotheus of Tyre, priest and martyr. [d. c. 362]

St. Boniface, martyr and Archbishop of Mainz; patron of England and Apostle of Germany. Compiled first Latin grammar written in England. Also called **Winfrid.** [d. 754] Obligatory Memorial.

St. Eoban, bishop and martyr. [d. 754]

St. Sanctius. Aso called **Sancho.** [d. 851]

The Beatified

Blessed Meinwerk, Bishop of Paderborn. Made cathedral school of Paderborn famous throughout Germany. [d. 1036]

Blessed Ferdinand of Portugal, prince. Called the **Constant.** [d. 1443]

1864 **Greece** regains sovereignty over **Ionian Islands** after fifty years under British protection.

1873 **Sultan Barghash** of Zanzibar, under British pressure, signs treaty abolishing **slave trade.**

1900 The British under **Redvers Buller** capture **Pretoria,** Transvaal (**Boer War**).

1916 Field Marshal **Lord Kitchener,** on secret mission to Russia, is drowned when his ship is torpedoed off the Orkney Islands (**World War I**).

1945 **Germany** is placed under an Allied Control Council and divided into four occupation zones (**World War II**).

Marshall Plan is announced by U.S. Secretary of State **George C. Marshall** in address at Harvard University.

1950 U.S. Supreme Court rules that **segregation** of blacks in railroad dining cars violates the **Interstate Commerce Act.**

1953 **Danish Constitution** is adopted, making **Greenland** an integral part of Denmark.

1961 U.S. Supreme Court sustains constitutionality of 1950 **Internal Security Act** requiring registration of Communist organizations.

1963 British War Minister **John Dennis Profumo** resigns after admitting association with call girl **Christine Keeler,** who has also been involved with a known Soviet spy.

1965 U.S. State Department acknowledges combat activity in **South Vietnam** for the first time.

1967 Fighting breaks out between Israel and Egypt, Syria and Jordan (**Six-Day War**).

1968 **Robert F. Kennedy,** while campaigning for the presidential nomination, is shot by **Sirhan Bishara Sirhan,** a Jordanian-American, and dies the following day.

1975 **Suez Canal** reopens to shipping after eight years. The Canal has been closed since the **Arab-Israeli War of 1967.**

First national referendum in Great Britain is held; citizens vote to remain in **Common Market.**

1976 **Teton Dam** in Idaho collapses, resulting in a flood that kills 11 persons and leaves 30,000 homeless. The flood causes an estimated $1 billion damage and nearly wipes out the Idaho cattle industry.

1977 **Park Tong Sun** is identified as the agent who illegally spent millions of dollars to influence American policy toward **South Korea.**

1978 China releases 110,000 persons arrested during the 1957 antirightist campaign and the **Cultural Revolution** of the late 1960s.

June 6

South Korea   **Memorial Day**
Day set aside to commemorate Korean war dead.

Sweden   **Flag Day**
Commemorates ascension of Gustavus Eriksson Vasa to throne of Sweden as Gustavus I, 1523; marks signing of Swedish constitution, 1809.

U.S.   **Philatelic Journalists Day**
Sponsored by Franklin Delano Roosevelt Philatelic Society, St. Augustine Shores, Florida.

Birthdates

1436   **Regiomontanus (Johann Müller),** German astronomer, mathematician; recognized for his careful study of planetary motion. First to observe **Halley's Comet;** advanced study of algebra, trigonometry in Germany. [d. July 6, 1476]

1502   **John III** of Portugal (*the Pious*), instituted the **Inquisition,** 1531. [d. June 6, 1557]

1599   **(Diego Rodriguez de Silva y) Velázquez,** Spanish baroque painter; known for his portraits of Spanish noblemen, as well as dwarfs and jesters. [d. August 6, 1660]

1606   **Pierre Corneille,** French dramatist; called *Father of French Tragedy.* [d. September 30, 1684]

1755   **Nathan Hale,** American Revolutionary hero; hanged by British as a spy. Famous for his dying words: "I only regret that I have but one life to lose for my country." [d. September 22, 1776]

1756   **John Trumbull,** U.S. painter; best known for his scenes of the American Revolution. His most famous work, *The Declaration of Independence,* included more than 48 portraits, mostly painted from life. [d. November 10, 1843]

1799   **Alexander Sergeyevich Pushkin,** Russian poet, novelist, dramatist, short-story writer; the *Father of Modern Russian Literature.* [d. February 10, 1837]

1804   **Louis Antoine Godey,** U.S. publisher; best known as publisher of *Godey's Lady's Book,* most popular American periodical of mid-19th century. [d. November 29, 1878]

1850   **Karl F. Braun,** German physicist; Nobel Prize in physics for development of the wireless telegraph (with G. Marconi), 1909. [d. April 20, 1918]

1860   **William Ralph Inge,** British theologian; referred to as the *Gloomy Dean* because of his pessimism. [d. February 26, 1954]

1868   **Robert Falcon Scott,** British Antarctic explorer; reached South Pole January 18, 1912, shortly after Amundsen expedition; perished on return trip because of bad weather and lack of food. [d. c. March 19, 1912]

1875   **Thomas Mann,** German writer, exiled, 1933; became U.S. citizen in 1944; best-known novel: *The Magic Mountain;* Nobel Prize in literature, 1929. [d. August 12, 1955]

1886   **Paul Dudley White,** U.S. physician; leading heart specialist. [d. October 31, 1973]

1892   **Ted Lewis (Theodore Leopold Friedman),** U.S. bandleader, clarinetist. [d. August 25, 1971]

1896   **Italo Balbo,** Italian aviator, statesman; developer of Italy's Air Force under Benito Mussolini. [d. June 28, 1940]

1898   **Ninette de Valois (Edris Stannus),** British dancer, choreographer, ballet director.

1901   **Ahmed Sukarno,** Indonesian statesman; leader of the Indonesian independence movement and the nation's first president, 1949–65. [d. June 21, 1970]

1902   **Jimmie Lunceford,** U.S. bandleader, saxophonist. [d. July 13, 1947]

Religious Calendar

The Saints

St. Philip the Deacon. Surnamed *the Evangelist* because of his great zeal in spreading the faith, especially in Samaria. [d. 1st century]

St. Ceratius, Bishop of Grenoble. Also called **Cérase** [d. c. 455]

St. Eustorgius II, Bishop of Milan. [d. 518]

St. Jarlath, Bishop of Tuam, in Galway; opened a famous school in connection with the monastery. Principal patron of Tuam. Feast is kept throughout Ireland. [d. c. 550]

St. Gudwal. One of earliest missionaries to Brittany. Also called **Gudwall, Gurval.** [d. c. 6th century]

St. Claud, Bishop of Besançon. Also called **Claude.** [d. c. 699]

St. Norbert, Archbishop of Magdeburg, founder of the Canons Regular of Prémontré. [d. 1134] Optional Memorial.

The Beatified

Blessed Gerard of Monza. Principal patron of Monza, the ancient capital of Lombardy. [d. 1207]

Blessed Laurence of Villamagna, one of the greatest preachers of his age. [d. 1535]

Blessed Marcellinus Champagnat, founder of the teaching congregation of Little Brothers of Mary, or Marist Brothers. [d. 1840]

1903	**Aram Ilich Khachaturian,** Russian composer; *Saber Dance* is among his best-known works. [d. May 1, 1978]
1925	**Maxine Winokur Kumin,** U.S. poet, novelist, children's book writer; Pulitzer Prize in poetry, 1972.
1926	**Colleen Dewhurst,** Canadian actress.
1934	**Roy Innis,** U.S. civil rights leader, editor; National Director, Congress of Racial Equality, 1968– .
1956	**Bjorn Borg,** Swedish tennis player; Wimbledon Champion, 1976–80.

Historical Events

1513	Swiss papal forces defeat the French at **Novara** (**War of the Holy League**).
1654	**Christina of Sweden**, a convert to Catholicism, abdicates the Swedish throne to devote the remainder of her life to religion and art.
1660	**Treaty of Copenhagen** is signed, whereby Denmark surrenders southern half of Scandinavian peninsula to Sweden.
1801	War between Spain and Portugal ends with signing of **Treaty of Badajoz**; Portugal cedes part of **Guiana** to Spain.
1806	**Sweden** adopts a representative constitution.
1844	**YMCA** is organized in London by George Williams to combat unhealthy conditions arising from the Industrial Revolution.
1884	The **Treaty of Hué** establishes French control over **Annam** and places **Tonkin** under a French protectorate.
1913	First ascent of **Mount McKinley** in Alaska is made by **Hudson Stuck.**
1918	**Battle of Belleau Wood,** first sizable U.S. action of World War I, begins; battle results in American recapture of **Vaux, Bouresches,** and **Belleau Wood.**
1919	**Finland** declares war on Russia.
1934	**Securities & Exchange Commission** is created in U.S. to limit bank credit for speculators and to regulate the securities industry.
1942	**Battle of Midway** ends with first major defeat of Japanese naval forces (**World War II**).
1944	Allied forces invade **Normandy** on **D-Day,** the largest amphibious invasion in history. (**World War II**).
1966	*Gemini 9* splashes down after three-day, 44-orbit trip and a record space walk of 2 hours 9 minutes by **Eugene A. Cernan,** *Gemini* co-pilot.
1977	U.S. Supreme Court rules that **capital punishment** for rape is unconstitutional.
1978	California voters overwhelmingly endorse **Proposition 13,** a state constitutional amendment to reduce property taxes by 57 percent.

June 7

Religious Calendar

The Saints

St. Paul I, Bishop of Constantinople. [d. c. 350]

St. Colman, first Bishop of Dromore in County Down, Ireland. [d. 6th century]

St. Meriadoc, bishop. Subject of only complete miracle play written in English based on a saint. Also called **Meriadec, Meriasek.** [d. c. 6th century]

St. Vulflagius, hermit priest. Also called **Wulphy.** [d. c. 643]

Birthdates

1502 **Gregory XIII (Ugo Buoncompagni),** pope, 1572–85. Responsible for reformation of Julian calendar, promulgation of **Gregorian calendar.** [d. April 10, 1585]

1761 **John Rennie,** English engineer; builder of three bridges over the Thames in London. [d. October 4, 1821]

1778 **George Bryan (*Beau*) Brummell,** English dandy and wit; friend of Prince of Wales, later George IV of England. [d. March 30, 1840]

1811 **Sir James Young Simpson,** Scottish obstetrician; founder of modern **gynecology.** Discovered anesthetic properties of **chloroform**; first to use anesthesia (ether) in obstetric practice. [d. May 6, 1870]

1840 **Carlota (Marie-Charlotte Amélie Augustine Victoire Clémentine Léopoldine),** Empress of Mexico, 1864–67. Wife of Emperor Maximilian, Archduke of Austria, later imperial ruler of Mexico. [d. January 19, 1927]

1848 **(Eugène-Henri) Paul Gauguin,** French painter; one of the founders of the **Symbolist** school. From his studio in Tahiti, he sent many brilliant, primitive paintings to Paris. [d. May 8, 1903]

1862 **Philipp E. A. von Lenard,** German physicist; Nobel Prize in physics for research on cathode rays, 1905. [d. May 20, 1947]

1877 **Charles G. Barkla,** British physicist; Nobel Prize in physics for his work on x ray scattering, 1917. [d. October 23, 1944]

1896 **Robert S. Mulliken,** U.S. chemist; Nobel Prize in chemistry for fundamental investigations regarding molecules, 1966.

Imre Nagy, Hungarian communist leader; Premier, 1953–55; executed for anti-Soviet activities during Hungarian revolution, 1956. [d. June 16, 1958]

1899 **Elizabeth Bowen (Dorothea Cole),** British novelist, short-story writer. [d. February 22, 1973]

1909 **Jessica Tandy,** British actress.

1917 **Gwendolyn (Elizabeth) Brooks,** U.S. poet; the first black woman to win a Pulitzer Prize, 1950.

1922 **Rocky Graziano,** U.S. boxer, television personality; World Middleweight Boxing Champion, 1947–48.

1928 **Charles Strouse,** U.S. composer; best known for scores of *Bye Bye Birdie, Applause,* and *Annie.*

Historical Events

1329 **Robert Bruce,** King of Scotland, dies and is succeeded by **David II.**

1492 **Casimir IV** of Poland dies and is succeeded in Poland by **John Albert**; in Lithuania by **Alexander.**

1494 Spain and Portugal divide New World between themselves in the **Treaty of Tordesillas.**

1523 A victorious **Gustavus Vasa** is proclaimed **King Gustavus I** by the Swedish Riksrand after he frees the country of the Danes.

1840 **Frederick William III** of Prussia dies and is succeeded by **Frederick William IV.**

1905 **Union of Norway and Sweden** is dissolved.

1917 The **Battle of Messines,** a British offensive, opens in Flanders with the British capturing Messines Ridge, a German position overlooking British lines (**World War I).**

St. Willibald, first Bishop of Eichstätt. First known English pilgrim to the Holy Land. [d. 786]

St. Gottschalk, Prince of the Western Vandals. Also called **Godeschalc.** [d. 1066]

St. Robert, Abbot of Newminster. [d. 1159]

St. Antony Gianelli, Bishop of Bobbio; founder of the Missioners of St. Alphonsus and the Sisters of St. Mary dell'Orto. [d. 1846]

The Beatified

Blessed Baptista Varani, virgin and mystic. [d. 1527]

Blessed Anne of St. Bartholomew, virgin. [d. 1626]

1921 Parliament of **Northern Ireland** is seated for the first time.

1965 U.S. Supreme Court strikes down 1879 Connecticut law prohibiting sale of birth-control devices, establishing new constitutional precedent for **right to privacy.**

1971 *Soyuz II,* Soviet spacecraft, docks in earth orbit with the *Salyut* space station; its three cosmonauts begin laboratory experiments.

1979 The first direct elections for the **European Parliamentary Assembly** are held with an increase in seats from 198 to 410.

1981 Israeli fighter planes attack and destroy the **Osirak nuclear reactor** near Baghdad, Iraq.

June 8

Religious Calendar

The Saints

St. Maximinus of Aix. Legend calls him one of Christ's 72 disciples who accompanied the Three Marys to evangelize Provence. Principal patron of Aix, France. Also called **Maximus.** [d. c. 5th century]

Birthdates

1625   **Jean Dominique Cassini,** French astronomer; first director of Paris Observatory. Discovered four of Saturn's satellites, eccentricity of earth's orbit. [d. September 11, 1712]

1724   **John Smeaton,** English engineer, innovator in lighthouse building, canal construction, and pumping engines; noted for rediscovering **hydraulic cement,** unknown since Roman times. [d. October 28, 1792]

1772   **Robert Stevenson,** Scottish engineer; designed and built numerous **lighthouses**; invented the system of intermittent or flashing lights used in lighthouses. [d. 1850]

1810   **Robert Schumann,** German composer; regarded as one of greatest followers of Franz Schubert. [d. July 29, 1856]

1813   **David Dixon Porter,** Union admiral during U.S. Civil War. [d. February 13, 1891]

1814   **Charles Reade,** British novelist; known for his novels exposing social abuses. Best known for *The Cloister and the Hearth,* a novel about the father of Erasmus. [d. April 11, 1884]

1821   **Sir Samuel White Baker,** British traveler, explorer; discovered **Lake Albert**; explored tributaries of the **Nile.** [d. December 30, 1893]

1829   **Sir John Everett Millais,** British painter; originator, with Holman Hunt and D. G. Rossetti, of the **Pre-Raphaelite Movement.** [d. August 23, 1896]

1867   **Frank Lloyd Wright,** U.S. architect, writer; recognized for his highly unorthodox approach to building design, an approach which integrated color, form, and texture. [d. April 9, 1959]

1877   **Robert Ferdinand Wagner,** U.S. politician, public official born in Germany. Drafted numerous **New Deal** measures, including the **National Labor Relations Act,** which gave rise to the **National Labor Relations Board,** 1935. [d. May 4, 1953]

1916   **Francis Harry Compton Crick,** British biologist, biochemist, physicist; Nobel Prize in physiology or medicine for determining molecular structure of **DNA** (with J. D. Watson and M. H. F. Wilkins), 1962.

1917   **Byron Raymond White,** U.S. athlete, jurist; All-American and later professional football player (University of Colorado, Pittsburgh Pirates, Detroit Lions); Associate Justice of U.S. Supreme Court, 1962– .

1918   **Robert Preston,** U.S. actor.

1921   **Alexis Smith,** U.S. actress.

   Raden Suharto, Indonesian military officer, politician. Responsible for overthrow of President **Ahmed Sukarno.** President of Indonesia, 1968– .

1923   **Malcolm Boyd,** U.S. Episcopal priest, author.

1936   **Kenneth G. Wilson,** U.S. physicist; Nobel Prize in physics for theories about changes in matter, 1983.

Historical Events

632   **Muhammad** whose teachings converted all of Arabia to Islamic faith, dies. [born c. 570]

1042   **Hardecanute,** King of England, dies and is succeeded by **Edward the Confessor.**

1536   **Articles of Religion** are published by English clergy in support of Henry VIII's declarations.

1912   *Daphnis et Chloë,* a ballet by Maurice Joseph Ravel, premieres in Paris.

1915   **William Jennings Bryan,** U.S. Secretary of State and a pacifist, resigns in disagreement with President Wilson over U.S. policy on handling the *Lusitania* crisis (**World War I**).

St. Medard, Bishop of Vermandois; weather on his day is used to forecast weather for next 40 days. Invoked to cure toothache. [d. c. 560]

St. Clodulf, Bishop of Metz. Also called **Clodulphus, Clou, Cloud.** [d. c. 692]

St. William, Archbishop of York. Also called **William Fitzherbert** or **William of Thwayt.** [d. 1154]

The Beatified

Blessed John Rainuzzi. Also called **John Raynutius** or **John of Todi.** [d. c. 1330]

Blessed Pacifico of Cerano, Franciscan friar. [d. 1482]

1928 **Peking** is captured by Nationalist Chinese troops.

1937 *Carmina Burana* by **Carl Orff** premieres in Frankfurt.

1963 **American Heart Association** becomes the first U.S. voluntary public agency to open a drive against **cigarette smoking.**

1968 **James Earl Ray,** alleged assassin of the **Rev. Martin Luther King, Jr.,** is arrested by Scotland Yard detectives at Heathrow Airport in London.

Bermuda promulgates a new constitution placing most of the island's executive powers in the hands of the premier, while the British-appointed governor retains control over external affairs.

1973 Generalissimo **Francisco Franco (Bahamonde)** resigns as Premier of Spain, appointing Admiral **Luis Carrero Blanco** to succeed him, but retaining the title of Chief of State.

1981 Striking coal miners of the **United Mine Workers** end a 72-day strike, the second longest in the industry's history.

June 9

Holidays

U.S.   Senior Citizens Day
(Oklahoma)

Religious Calendar

SS. **Primus** and **Felician,** martyrs. Felician also called **Felicianus.** [d. c. 297]

St. **Vincent of Agen,** martyr. [d. c. 300]

St. **Pelagia of Antioch,** virgin and martyr. [d. c. 311]

Birthdates

1672   **Peter I,** Emperor of Russia, 1682–1725, known as **Peter the Great.** Introduced Western European civilization into Russia; founded **St. Petersburg** (now **Leningrad**). [d. February 8, 1725]

1768   **Samuel Slater,** U.S. textile manufacturer; one of the founders of the U.S. textile industry. [d. April 21, 1835]

1776   **Count Amedeo Avogadro,** Italian chemist; proposed theory (*Avogadro's Law*) which states that all gases at same pressure and temperature contain equal number of molecules. [d. July 9, 1856]

1781   **George Stephenson,** British inventor, credited with developing first successful **steam locomotive.** [d. August 12, 1848]

1785   **Sylvanus Thayer,** U.S. Army engineer, general, and educator. Controversial superintendent of U.S. military academy at West Point, 1817–33. Known as the *Father of the Military Academy.* [d. September 7, 1872]

1791   **John Howard Payne,** U.S. dramatist; composer of song *Home, Sweet Home;* known for the play *Clari: or, The Maid of Milan.* [d. April 9, 1852]

1812   **Johann Galle,** German astronomer; first to sight planet **Neptune,** 1846. [d. July 10, 1910]

1843   **Baroness Bertha von Suttner,** Austrian humanitarian; Nobel Peace Price, 1905; probably responsible for influencing Alfred Nobel to establish the Nobel Prize for Peace. [d. June 21, 1914]

1850   **Wilhelm Roux,** German zoologist, anatomist; founder of modern experimental embryology. [d. September 15, 1924]

1865   **Carl August Nielsen,** Danish composer; composed opera, *Saul and David.* [d. 1931]

1875   **Sir Henry H. Dale,** British physiologist; Nobel Prize in physiology or medicine for discoveries in the chemical transmission of nerve impulses (with O. Loewi), 1936. [d. July 23, 1968]

1892   **Cole Porter,** U.S. composer, lyricist; wrote some of the most popular, enduring music and lyrics of his time, including many musicals. [d. October 25, 1964]

1900   **Fred M. Waring,** U.S. orchestra conductor. [d. July 29, 1984]

1901   **Nelson Eddy,** U.S. singer, actor; mostly known for duet roles in operetta films with Jeanette MacDonald (June 18). [d. March 6, 1967]

1916   **Robert (Strange) McNamara,** U.S. banker, businessman, government official; U.S. Secretary of Defense, 1961–68; President of World Bank, 1968–81.

Historical Events

1549   English Parliament establishes uniformity of religious services and the first **prayer book.**

1732   Royal charter is granted to **James Oglethorpe** for formation of colony of **Georgia,** the last of the 13 original colonies to be settled.

1902   **Gustav Mahler** conducts the first complete performance of his **Third Symphony.**

1904   The **London Symphony Orchestra** presents its inaugural concert, **Hans Richter** conducting.

1918   The **Battle of the Metz** begins in German attempt to link the Soissons and Noyen salients, taken in the last two offensives **(World War I).**

1930   **King Carol II** assumes throne of Rumania.

St. Ephraem, Doctor of the Church. Writer and theologian. Also called **Ephrem.** [d. c. 373] Feast formerly June 18. Optional Memorial.

St. Columba, Abbot of Iona. The most famous of Scottish saints; actually an Irish missionary on Isle of Iona. Patron of Scotland. Also called **Colmcille, Columkille, Colum Cille.** [d. 597]

St. Richard, first Bishop of Andria in Apulia. [d. c. 12th cent.]

The Beatified

Blessed Diana, Cecilia, and **Amata,** virgins and Dominican nuns. [d. 1236 and 1290]

Blessed Silvester of Valdiseve, lay-brother. [d. 1348]

Blessed Henry the Shoemaker, founder of the Frères Cordonniers, a religious society for shoemakers. [d. 1666]

Blessed Anne Mary Taigi, matron. [d. 1837]

1973 **Secretariat** wins the Belmont Stakes, becoming the first horse since 1948 to win thoroughbred racing's **Triple Crown**.

1978 **Mormon Church** (The Church of Jesus Christ of the Latter-Day Saints) votes to allow blacks to become priests, thus ending a 148-year-old exclusionary policy.

June 10

Holidays

Macao	**Camoëns and Portuguese Communities Day** Commemorates death of Luiz Vaz de Camoëns, Portugal's national poet, 1580.
Portugal	**Portugal Day**

Religious Calendar

The Saints
SS. Getulius and his companions, martyrs. [d. c. 120]

Birthdates

1735   **John Morgan,** American physician; responsible for establishment of first medical school in the American colonies (College of Philadelphia, later **University of Pennsylvania**), 1765. Appointed Director-General of Hospitals and Physician-in-Chief to the American Army by the Continental Congress, 1775–77. [d. October 15, 1789]

1741   **Joseph Warren,** American Revolutionary general, physician. Active in American revolutionary politics; member of three provisional congresses held in Massachusetts. Dispatched **Paul Revere** and **William Dawes** to Lexington to warn of British approach. Killed at **Battle of Bunker Hill.** [d. June 17, 1775]

1819   **Gustave Courbet,** French realist painter, revolutionary; associated with the Commune, revolutionary regime in Paris, 1871. [d. December 31, 1877]

1819   **Gustave Cousbet,** French realist painter, revolutionary; associated with the Commune, revolutionary regime in Paris, 1871. [d. December 31, 1877]

1832   **Nikolaus August Otto,** German inventor; responsible for early form of **internal combustion engine** and first **four-cycle gasoline engine.** [d. January 26, 1891]

1841   **George Wallace Melville,** U.S. naval engineer, Arctic explorer. [d. March 17, 1912]

1850   **David Jayne Hill,** U.S. diplomat, author, historian, and educator. [d. March 2, 1932]

1854   **George Earle Buckle,** British editor of *The Times* of London, 1884–1912. [d. March 3, 1935]

1895   **Immanuel Velikovsky,** U.S. writer born in Russia; proposed controversial theory that Earth has been visited numerous times by beings from outer space. [d. November 17, 1979]

1901   **Frederick Loewe,** U.S. composer; most noted for works created in collaboration with A. J. Lerner (August 31); composed music for *Brigadoon*, *Paint Your Wagon*, and *My Fair Lady*.

1911   **Sir Terence (Mervyn) Rattigan,** British playwright; knighted 1971. [d. November 30, 1977]

1915   **Saul Bellow,** U.S. novelist; Nobel Prize in literature, 1976.

1921   **Prince Philip, Duke of Edinburgh,** husband and consort of **Queen Elizabeth II** of England.

1922   **Judy Garland (Frances Gumm),** U.S. singer, actress. [d. June 22, 1969]

1928   **Maurice (Bernard) Sendak,** U.S. author, illustrator of children's books.

1929   **James Alton McDivitt,** U.S. astronaut. Commanded *Gemini 4* space flight, 1965, and participated in *Apollo 9* flight, 1969.

1933   **F(rancis) Lee Bailey,** U.S. criminal lawyer.

Historical Events

1190   **Frederick I,** Holy Roman Emperor, drowns in the river Saleph in Cilicia.

1376   **Wenceslas,** son of **Charles IV,** Holy Roman Emperor, is elected King of the Romans.

St. Ithamar, Bishop of Rochester, the first Englishman to become a Bishop. [d. c. 656]

St. Landericus, Bishop of Paris. Founded the first real hospital in Paris. Also called **Landry.** [d. c. 660]

St. Bogumilus, Archbishop of Gniezno, Poland. Founder of the Cistercian Monastery of Coronowa. [d. 1182]

The Beatified

Blessed Olive of Palermo, virgin and martyr. Feast observed in dioceses of Carthage and Palermo. [d. 9th century]

Blessed Henry of Treviso. Also called **Henry of San Rigo.** [d. 1315]

Blessed Bonaventure of Peraga. The first Augustinian hermit to become a cardinal of the Roman Church. [d. 1386]

Blessed John Dominici, Archbishop of Ragusa and cardinal. [d. 1419]

1791	**Canada Constitution Act** is passed by British Parliament; Canada is divided into **Upper Canada** and **Lower Canada.**
1868	**Prince Michael III Obrenović** of Serbia is assassinated in Belgrade, after freeing Serbia from Ottoman rule.
1903	**King Alexander** and **Queen Draga** of Serbia are massacred along with aides and members of the palace guard in their palace at Belgrade in a radical coup d'état and revolution led by the military.
1924	**Giacomo Matteotti,** Italian Socialist Deputy, is kidnapped and murdered by Fascists.
1935	**Alcoholics Anonymous** is established in New York by ex-alcoholic **Bill Wilson** and **Dr. Robert H. Smith.**
1940	**Italy** declares war on France and Great Britain (**World War II**).
1942	**Lidice, Czechoslovakia** is destroyed and all the residents murdered or tortured by Nazis in reprisal for assassination of **Reinhard Heydrich**.
1943	Anglo-American forces begin invasion of **Sicily** by air and sea (**World War II**).
1962	Archdiocese of **Atlanta, Georgia,** announces nonracial admission policy for coming school year.
1963	U.S. President **John F. Kennedy** signs into law a bill guaranteeing equal pay for equal work, regardless of sex.
1967	Soviet Union breaks diplomatic relations with **Israel.**
1970	U.S. military attaché in Amman, Major **Robert Perry,** is shot to death by commandos.
1971	U.S. President **Richard Nixon** removes the 21-year old embargo on trade with **China.**
1977	**Rules of War Conference,** held to update 1949 Geneva conventions, approves a provision by which guerrillas have the same rights as soldiers engaged in international wars.

June 11

Holidays

| U.S. (Hawaii) | King Kamehameha Day |
| Libya | Evacuation Day |

Commemorates the closing of U.S. Air Force bases and the evacuation of U.S. military personnel, 1967.

Birthdates

1572?   **Ben(jamin) Jonson,** English playwright, poet; best known for his satires, comedies, and poetry. [d. August 6, 1637]

1776   **John Constable,** English landscape painter; known for his realistic landscapes and studies of rustic life. [d. March 31, 1837]

1815   **Otto von Böhtlingk,** German Sanskrit scholar; associated with Rudolf von Roth in effort to introduce Vedic studies into Germany. [d. April 1, 1904]

1842   **Carl von Linde,** German chemist, engineer; credited with developing first successful compression system using liquid ammonia as a refrigerant, 1873. [d. November 16, 1934]

1864   **Richard Strauss,** German composer, conductor; best known for his operas. Regarded as leader of the **New Romantic School.** [d. September 8, 1949]

1880   **Jeanette Rankin,** U.S. politician, social worker; first woman member of U.S. Congress, 1916–18; 1940–42. Maintained active role in social reform and women's liberation movements until her death at age 92. [d. May 18, 1973]

1895   **Nikolai Aleksandrovich Bulganin,** Russian political leader; Minister of Defense, 1947–49, 1953–55; Premier of Soviet Union, 1955–58. [d. February 24, 1975]

1899   **Kawabata Yasunari,** Japanese novelist; Nobel Prize in literature, 1968. [d. April 16, 1972]

1903   **Ernie Nevers,** U.S. football and baseball player. [d. May 3, 1976]

1904   **Clarence (Pinetop) Smith,** U.S. musician; originator of *boogie-woogie,* a musical form based on blues piano playing. [d. March 14, 1929]

1910   **Jacques-Yves Cousteau,** French marine explorer, writer, film producer; partly responsible for invention of **aqualung,** 1943. Creator of numerous award-winning documentary films.

1913   **Vince Lombardi,** U.S. football coach; elected to Pro Football Hall of Fame, 1971. [d. September 3, 1970]

Risé Stevens (Risé Steenberg), U.S. operatic mezzo-soprano.

1919   **Richard Todd,** British actor, producer.

1920   **Irving Howe,** U.S. literary and social critic.

Hazel (Dorothy) Scott, U.S. jazz pianist, singer; known for her numerous benefit performances on behalf of civil rights; wife of U.S. Congressman Adam Clayton Powell, Jr. (November 29). [d. October 2, 1981]

1935   **Gene Wilder (Jerry Silberman),** U.S. comedic actor, writer, and director.

1939   **Jackie Stewart,** Scottish auto racer, sportscaster.

Historical Events

1258   English barons, headed by **Simon de Montfort,** force **Henry III** to issue **Provisions of Oxford,** guaranteeing three Parliaments annually (**Mad Parliament**).

1488   **James III** of Scotland is murdered after **Battle of Bannockburn.** He is succeeded by **James IV.**

1917   **Constantine,** King of Greece, abdicates and is succeeded by his son, **Alexander.**

1926   General **Chiang Kai-shek** becomes Commander in Chief of the Nationalist Chinese army.

1963   **Quang Duc,** Buddhist monk, commits suicide by burning himself to death as protest against government of **South Vietnam.**

1975   The first oil flows from Britain's **North Sea oil fields.**

Religious Calendar

The Saints

St. Barnabas, Apostle. Not one of Christ's first 12 disciples but closely associated with St. Paul. Regarded as apostle because of his great dedication to apostolic works. [d. 1st century] Obligatory Memorial. [major holy day, Episcopal Church; minor festival, Lutheran Church.]

SS. Felix and **Fortunatus,** martyrs. [d. c. 296]

St. Parisio, priest, prophet, and miracle-worker. [d. 1267]

The Beatified

Blessed Paula Frassinetti, virgin, founder of the Sisters of St. Dorothy. [d. 1882]

June 12

Paraguay **Peace with Bolivia Day**
Commemorates end of Chaco
War between Paraguay and
Bolivia, 1935.

Philippines **Independence Day**
Commemorates Philippine
declaration of independence
from Spain, 1898.

Religious Calendar

The Saints

SS. Basilides and his companions, martyrs. [d. 3rd
century] Feast suppressed in 1969.

Birthdates

1519 **Cosimo I de Medici (*the Great*),** Florentine statesman; Duke of Florence, 1537–74.
[d. April 21, 1574]

1802 **Harriet Martineau,** British novelist, economist. [d. June 27, 1876]

1806 **John Augustus Roebling,** U.S. civil engineer, industrialist born in Germany; established first factory to manufacture **wire
rope** in America. Pioneered design of **suspension bridges,** including one over Niagara Falls. Conceived preliminary plans for
Brooklyn Bridge, built after his death. [d.
July 22, 1869]

1819 **Charles Kingsley,** British clergyman, novelist, chaplain to Queen Victoria; professor
of modern history, Cambridge, 1860–69;
author of *Westward Ho!* and *The Water Ba-
bies.* [d. January 23, 1875]

1851 **Sir Oliver Joseph Lodge,** British physicist, author. Conducted considerable investigation in field of electromagnetics,
wireless telegraphy. [d. August 22, 1940]

1864 **Frank Michler Chapman,** U.S. ornitholo-
gist, editor; Curator of Ornithology at
American Museum of Natural History, New
York, 1908–42. Founded magazine *Bird
Lore* which later became *Audubon Maga-
zine.* [d. November 15, 1945]

1897 **Sir Anthony Eden, First Earl of Avon,**
British statesman; Foreign Secretary, 1935–
38, 1940–45, 1951–55; Prime Minister, 1955–
57. [d. January 14, 1977]

1899 **Fritz Albert Lipmann,** U.S. biochemist
born in Russia; Nobel Prize in physiology
or medicine for studies on biochemical activity in cell metabolism, including discovery of **coenzyme A** (with H. A. Krebs), 1953.

1915 **David Rockefeller,** U.S. banker, philanthropist; head of Chase Manhattan Bank,
1955– ; one of most powerful financiers in
the world.

1919 **Uta Hagen,** German actress, teacher.

1924 **George Bush,** U.S. politician; Vice-President, 1980– .

1929 **Anne Frank,** Dutch writer; her diary, writ-
ten during two years of hiding with her
Jewish family from Nazis during World
War II, won acclaim after her death. [d. c.
March 1945]

Historical Events

1727 **George I** of England dies and is succeeded by **George II.**

1898 **Philippines** declares independence from
Spain.

1900 **Second German Naval Law** initiates program to double the number of German bat-
tleships, thus challenging England's supremacy at sea.

1917 Allied troops seize **Corinth** and **Larissa,
Greece (World War I).**

1930 **Max Schmeling** defeats **Jack Sharkey** for
world heavyweight boxing title.

1935 Armistice between **Bolivia** and **Paraguay**
ends **Chaco War.**

St. Antonina, martyr. [d. c. 304]

St. Onuphrius, hermit. [d. c. 400]

St. Ternan, Bishop of the Picts. [d. 5th or 6th century]

St. Peter of Mount Athos, hermit. [d. c. 8th century]

St. Leo III, pope. Elected 795. Famous for crowning Charlemagne Holy Roman Emperor at St. Peter's in 800. [d. 816]

St. Odulf, evangelizer of Friesland. [d. c. 855]

St. Eskil, bishop and martyr. Honored as one of the most illustrious martyrs of Scandinavia. [d. c. 1080]

St. John of Sahagun, priest and Augustinian hermit. [d. 1479]

The Beatified

Blessed Stephen Bandelli, Dominican preacher. [d. 1450]

1937	**Marshal Michael Tukhachevski** and seven other high-ranking generals are executed after a secret court martial in Russia.
1939	**Baseball Hall of Fame,** Cooperstown, New York, is dedicated.
1941	**U.S. Naval Reserves** are called to active duty (**World War II**).
1944	Aircraft from 15 U.S. carriers begin bombing the **Mariana Islands (World War II).** **V-1 rocket** is first used by Germans but is shot down by Allied gunners (**World War II**).
1948	U.S. Congress makes **Women's Army Corps** a permanent part of the army and creates the **Women's Air Force.**
1971	**Tricia Nixon,** elder daughter of U.S. President Nixon, is married to Edward Finch Cox in the White House rose garden.
1975	Indian Prime Minister **Indira Gandhi** is convicted of election violations in 1971 but refuses to resign.
1979	First man-powered flight across the English Channel is made by Bryan Allen in the ***Gossamer Albatross.***

June 13

Holidays

Portugal (Lisbon)	**St. Anthony's Day** Commemorates feast of St. Anthony of Padua, born in Lisbon, 1195.
Yemen Arab Republic	**Reform Movement's Anniversary** or **Corrective Movement Anniversary**

Birthdates

823   **Charles II (*the Bald*),** King of France, 843–877. [d. October 6, 877]

1752   **Frances (Fanny) Burney,** English novelist, also known as *Madame d'Arblay;* author of *Evelina, Camilla,* and *The Wanderer.* [d. January 6, 1840]

1773   **Thomas Young,** English physicist, physician, Egyptologist; first to describe and measure **astigmatism,** explain nature of color sensation in the human eye. Involved in translation of Egyptian hieroglyphics, especially the **Rosetta stone.** [d. May 10, 1829]

1786   **Winfield Scott** (*Old Fuss and Feathers*), U.S. army general, 1807–61; foremost military figure of the period. Saw action in War of 1812, Mexican War, pre-Civil War period. [d. May 29, 1866]

1795   **Thomas Arnold,** English educator; greatly influenced development of modern public school system in England, 1828–42. As headmaster of **Rugby,** introduced mathematics, modern history, and foreign languages into school's curriculum. [d. June 12, 1842]

1854   **Sir Charles Algernon Parsons,** British inventor, engineer; developed **compound steam turbine** used in ships, 1897. [d. February 11, 1931]

1865   **William Butler Yeats,** Irish poet, playwright, politician; considered leader of Irish literary revival; one of first senators of Irish Free State, 1922–28; Nobel Prize in literature, 1923. [d. January 28, 1939]

1870   **Jules Jean Baptiste Vincent Bordet,** Belgian bacteriologist, noted for his work in immunology, serology. Developed theories that laid basis for **Wasserman test** for syphilis; Nobel Prize in physiology or medicine, 1919. [d. April 6, 1961]

1879   **Robert Elkington Wood,** U.S. army officer, World War I; President, Sears, Roebuck and Company, 1928–54. Responsible for developing Sears from mail order house to largest merchandising company in the world. [d. November 6, 1969]

1884   **John McCormack,** U.S. operatic tenor. [d. September 16, 1945]

1892   **(Philip St. John) Basil Rathbone,** British actor. [d. July 21, 1967]

1893   **Dorothy L(eigh) Sayers,** British novelist; best known for sophisticated mystery stories. [d. December 17, 1957]

1894   **Mark Van Doren,** U.S. critic, poet, educator; film critic of *The Nation,* 1935–38; Pulitzer Prize in poetry, 1940. [d. December 10, 1972]

1897   **Paavo Nurmi,** Finnish long-distance runner; Olympic gold medalist, 1920 (10,000 meter run); 1924 (5,000 meter run); 1928 (10,000 meter run). [d. October 2, 1973]

1899   **Carlos Chávez,** Mexican composer, conductor; organized Mexican Symphony Orchestra, 1928. [d. August 2, 1978]

1903   **Harold Edward (*Red*) Grange,** U.S. football player, known as *The Galloping Ghost.*

1911   **Luis Walter Alvarez,** U.S. physicist; developed ground-controlled approach system for aircraft (with Lawrence Johnston), 1940–43. Renowned for his investigations into physics of subatomic particles. Albert Einstein Award, 1961; Nobel Prize in physics, 1968.

1915   **Don Budge,** U.S. tennis player. Elected to Tennis Hall of Fame, 1964.

1926   **Paul (Edward) Lynde,** U.S. comedian, actor; well-known for his quirky, sneering characterizations. [d. January 9, 1982]

Religious Calendar

The Saints

St. Felicula, martyr. [d. c. 90]

St. Aquilina, martyr. [d. c. end of 3rd century]

St. Triphyllius, Bishop of Nicosia. [d. c. 370]

St. Anthony of Padua, Doctor of the Church. A great preacher and biblical scholar; patron of Padua, Italy, of the poor and the illiterate; alms given to obtain his intercession are known as *St. Anthony's bread.* Also invoked for help in finding lost articles. Also called **Antonio, Antony.** [d. 1231] Obligatory Memorial.

The Beatified

Blessed Gerard of Clairvaux, brother and assistant of St. Bernard. [d. 1138]

1937   **Eleanor Holmes Norton,** U.S. government official, lawyer; Chairman, Equal Employment Opportunities Commission, 1977–81.

Historical Events

1515   **Martin Luther** marries **Catherine von Bora.**

1541   **John Calvin,** French religious reformer, begins organization of **Geneva** as theocratic state. Geneva becomes focal point for defense of Protestantism throughout Europe.

1898   **Yukon Territory** is formed from the **Northwest Territory** in Canada.

1911   Igor Stravinsky's ballet *Petrouchka* premieres in Paris.

1917   General **John J. Pershing,** leader of the American Expeditionary Force, arrives in France (**World War I).**

1935   **James J. Braddock** defeats **Max Baer** for world heavyweight boxing title.

1965   Military triumvirate led by Major General **Nguyen Van Thieu** takes control of the South Vietnam government.

1967   Attorney General **Thurgood Marshall** is appointed to **U.S. Supreme Court,** becoming the first black to be seated on the Supreme Court bench.

1971   *The New York Times* begins publishing the **Pentagon papers,** ending Daniel Ellsberg's long attempt to get those documents made public.

1983   *Pioneer 10*, an unmanned U.S. space probe, crosses the orbit of Neptune and becomes the first man-made object to leave the solar system.

June 14

Holidays

U.S.

Flag Day
Commemorates Continental Congress's adoption of flag for the 13 United States, consisting of 13 stripes, 7 red and 6 white, and 13 white stars arranged in a circle on a field of blue, 1777.

Birthdates

1736 **Charles Augustin de Coulomb,** French physicist; known for work on friction, electricity, and magnetism. The electrical unit, the *coulomb*, is named for him. [d. August 23, 1806]

1798 **Frantisek Palacký,** Czech historian, political leader; worked for creation of autonomous Czech nation. [d. April 26, 1876]

1811 **Harriet (Elizabeth) Beecher Stowe,** U.S. writer; best known for her novel, *Uncle Tom's Cabin*, 1852, which stimulated anti-slavery sentiment prior to U.S. Civil War. [d. July 1, 1896]

1820 **John Bartlett,** U.S. editor, bookseller; compiler of *Familiar Quotations*, a classic reference work. [d. December 3, 1905]

1838 **Yamagata Aritomo,** Japanese prince, army general; Premier of Japan, 1889–91, 1898–1900. [d. February 1, 1922]

1855 **Robert Marion La Follette,** U.S. public official, political leader; U.S. Senator, 1907–25. Introduced resolution calling for investigation of **Teapot Dome Scandal.** [d. June 18, 1925]

1862 **John Joseph Glennon,** U.S. Roman Catholic cardinal. [d. March 9, 1946]

1868 **Karl Landsteiner,** U.S. physician born in Austria; Nobel Prize in physiology or medicine for discovery of **human blood groups,** 1930. [d. June 26, 1943]

1895 **José Carlos Mariátegui,** Peruvian writer, reformer. [d. April 16, 1930]

1906 **Margaret Bourke-White,** U.S. photographer; noted for her photographs of numerous world events, including U.S. campaigns into North Africa, Italy, and Germany during World War II, and photo-essays on Russia, India, the American South. A founding editor of *Life* magazine. [d. August 27, 1971]

1909 **Burl Ives (Burl Icle Ivanhoe),** U.S. folk singer, character actor.

1925 **Pierre Salinger,** U.S. politician, journalist; Press Secretary to President John F. Kennedy, 1961–63.

1928 **Che Guevera (Ernesto Guevera de la Serna),** Latin American guerrilla, revolutionary theoretician and tactician; served as aide to Fidel Castro (August 13) during Cuban Revolution, 1959. [d. October 9, 1967]

1958 **Eric Heiden,** U.S. speed skater; winner of five gold medals in 1980 Winter Olympics.

Historical Events

1800 **Napoleon** defeats Austrians at **Marengo.**

1846 **Bear Flag Revolt** begins with proclamation of **Republic of California** by a group of settlers. California is annexed to U.S. on August 17, 1846.

1900 The **Hawaiian Islands** become the Territory of Hawaii, part of the United States.

1918 The **Battle of the Metz** ends in the failure of the German offensive (**World War I**).

1934 **Max Baer** knocks out **Primo Carnera** for world heavyweight boxing title.

1940 German troops enter **Paris (World War II).**

1942 Japanese garrisons arrive by sea and seize the Aleutian islands of **Kiska, Attu,** and **Agattu (World War II).**

1978 **Sierra Leone** ratifies a new constitution, making the All People's Congress the only recognized political party.

1982 Argentine troops surrender to British, ending fighting over **Falkland Islands.**

Religious Calendar

The Saints

SS. Valerius and **Rufinus,** martyrs. [d. c. 287]

St. Dogmael. In Britanny, mothers often invoke him to help their small children walk. Also called **Docmael, Dogfael, Dogwell**; and in Britanny, **Dogméel** and **Toël.** [d. c. 6th century]

St. Methodius I, Patriarch of Constantinople; greatly venerated in the East for his important role in the final overthrow of Iconoclasm. Also called **the Confessor** and **the Great.** [d. 847]

The Beatified

Blessed Castora Gabrielli, widow and Franciscan tertiary. [d. 1391]

June 15

Holidays

Fiji	Queen's Birthday
U.S. (Delaware)	Separation Day
U.S. (Idaho)	Pioneer Day

Commemorates first white settlement at Franklin, 1860.

Religious Calendar

The Saints

SS. Vitus, Modestus, and **Crescentia,** martyrs. Vitus is patron of Germany, Saxony, Bohemia, and Sicily. St. Vitus is especially venerated in Germany as the

Birthdates

1330 **Edward the Black Prince,** son of **King Edward III** of England. One of the outstanding commanders during the **Hundred Years' War;** accompanied Edward III on two successive campaigns to recover throne of France. Father of **King Richard II** of England. [d. June 8, 1376]

1843 **Edvard (Hagerup) Grieg,** Norwegian composer; based many of his compositions on Norwegian folk songs. [d. September 4, 1907]

1856 **Edward Channing,** U.S. historian, educator; began the *History of the United States,* a monumental single-handed work detailing the development of the U.S. beginning in A.D. 1000. Seven volumes were completed upon his death. Volume 6 awarded the Pulitzer Prize in history, 1926. [d. January 7, 1931]

1882 **Marshall Ion Antonescu,** Rumanian statesman, soldier; dictator of German-controlled government of Rumania, 1940–44; removed from office, 1944; executed as war criminal. [d. June 1, 1946]

1894 **Robert Russell Bennett,** U.S. composer, arranger, conductor; a leading orchestrator of Broadway musicals; scored more than 300 shows, including *Show Boat, Porgy and Bess, Annie Get Your Gun,* and *My Fair Lady.* [d. August 18, 1981]

1915 **Thomas Huckle Weller,** U.S. microbiologist; Nobel Prize in physiology or medicine for successful growth of **polio virus** in lab-oratory cultures and discovery of more effective methods of polio detection (with J. F. Enders and F. C. Robbins), 1954.

1916 **Herbert A. Simon,** U.S. economist; Nobel Prize in economics for research in the decision-making process within economic organizations, 1978.

1920 **Carol Fox,** U.S. opera producer; a founder of the Lyric Theatre of Chicago (frequently called *La Scala West*); introduced such famous European opera stars as Tito Gobbi and Maria Callas to American audiences. [d. July 21, 1981]

1922 **Morris (King) Udall,** U.S. lawyer; U.S. Congressman, 1961– .

Historical Events

1215 **Magna Carta** is signed at Runnymede as **King John** comes to terms with the English barons, laying foundation for English political and personal liberties.

1498 **Niccolò Machiavelli** is appointed Florentine secretary to the **Deici di Libertá e Pace.**

1520 **Pope Leo X** issues papal bull condemning **Martin Luther's** teaching on 41 counts.

1567 **Mary, Queen of Scots,** is imprisoned by her nobles and forced to abdicate in favor of her 13-month old son who is proclaimed **James VI** of Scotland.

special protector of epileptics; regarded as patron of dancers and actors; invoked against *St. Vitus's dance* or chorea, storms, over-sleeping, the bites of mad dogs and serpents, and other injuries of animals against man. Vitus also called **Guy.** [d. c. 300]

St. Hesychius, martyr. [d. 302]

St. Tatian Dulas, martyr. [d. c. 310]

St. Orsiesius, Abbot of Tabennisi in the Egyptian desert. [d. c. 380]

St. Landelinus, abbot. Founder of the great abbeys of Lobbes and Crespin. Also called **Landelin.** [d. c. 686]

St. Edburga of Winchester, virgin and abbess. Granddaughter of the Anglo-Saxon King Alfred. [d. 960]

St. Bordo, Archbishop of Mainz. [d. 1053]

St. Aleydis, virgin, Cistercian nun, and mystic. Also called **Aleydia** or **Alice.** [d. 1250]

St. Germaine of Pibrac, virgin. [d. 1601]

The Beatified
Blessed Jolenta of Hungary, widow. Founder of convent at Gnesen. Also called **Helena.** [d. 1299]

Blessed Aloysius Palazzolo, priest and founder of the Brothers of the Holy Family and the Sisters of the Poor. [d. 1886]

1775   **George Washington** is appointed commander-in-chief of the **Continental Army** by the **Continental Congress.**

1836   **Arkansas** is admitted to the Union as the 25th state.

1844   **Charles Goodyear** is granted a patent for **rubber vulcanization.**

1846   **Oregon Treaty** with Great Britain is signed by U.S., setting boundaries between U.S. and British Northwest Territory at 49th parallel.

1866   **Prussia** declares war against Hanover and Saxony (**European War**).

1888   Emperor **Frederick III** of Germany dies and is succeeded by **William II.**

1895   The territory of **Kenya** is made a British protectorate, the British government taking over for the British East Africa Company.

1898   U.S. ships destroy the fort and take possession of the outer bay at **Guantanamo, Cuba** (**Spanish-American War**).

1919   First nonstop aircraft crossing of the Atlantic is completed by Englishmen **J. W. Alcock** and **A. Whitten-Brown.**

1944   U.S. Marines land on **Saipan,** Mariana Islands (**World War II**).

1977   **Spain** holds first free elections in 41 years, with distinct turn toward democracy despite its status as a monarchy.

1978   U.S. Supreme Court rules that the **snail darter** is protected by the **Endangered Species Act** of 1973; as a consequence, the $100 million **Tellico Dam,** already 80 percent complete, cannot be finished.

June 16

International Day of Solidarity with the Struggling People of South Africa or **Soweto Day** Commemorates the start of uprising in Soweto and other areas, 1976, and expresses outrage at apartheid policies and other racist policies in South Africa. Sponsored by the United Nations.

Religious Calendar

The Saints

SS. Ferreolus and **Ferrutio,** missionaries and martyrs. Probably missionaries in area of Besançon,

Birthdates

1514 **Sir John Cheke,** English classical scholar, embroiled in political unrest; imprisoned by **Queen Mary** for serving as secretary of state to **Lady Jane Grey.** [d. September 13, 1557]

1858 **Gustavus V,** King of Sweden, 1907–50; responsible for maintaining Swedish neutrality during World War I. [d. October 29, 1950]

1874 **Arthur Meighen,** Canadian lawyer, statesman; Prime Minister, 1920–21; 1926. [d. August 5, 1960]

1889 **Nelson Doubleday,** U.S. publisher. [d. January 11, 1949]

1890 **Stan Laurel (Arthur Stanley Jefferson),** British comedian, best known for his film comedies with Oliver Hardy (January 18). Together they pioneered era of film comedy. [d. February 23, 1965]

1892 **Jennie Grossinger,** U.S. hotelier born in Austria. [d. November 20, 1972]

1897 **Georg Wittig,** German chemist; Nobel Prize in chemistry for his work with phosphorus compounds, 1979.

1899 **John L(awrence) Sullivan,** U.S. government official; U.S. Secretary of the Navy, 1947–59; resigned in protest over funding policies of the Truman administration. [d. August 8, 1982]

1910? **Jack Albertson,** U.S. actor. [d. November 25, 1982]

1917 **Katharine (Meyer) Graham,** U.S. publisher of the *Washington Post*, 1968–78; Chairman and Chief Executive Officer of Washington Post Co., 1973– .

1920 **José Lopez Portillo,** Mexican lawyer, statesman; President of Mexico, 1976–82.

John Howard Griffin, U.S. writer, musicologist; best known as author of *Black Like Me*, an account of discrimination in America written while traveling through the South disguised as a black man. [d. September 9, 1980]

1937 **Erich Segal,** U.S. novelist, classical scholar.

1938 **Joyce Carol Oates,** U.S. novelist, short-story writer, poet, critic, teacher.

1951 **Roberto Duran,** Panamanian boxer; world lightweight champion, 1972–79.

Historical Events

1654 **Queen Christina,** a convert to Catholicism, abdicates the Swedish throne to devote the remainder of her life to religion and art.

1919 Irving Berlin's *A Pretty Girl Is Like a Melody* premieres in New York at Ziegfeld Follies.

1933 U.S. Congress passes **Farm Credit Act,** an antidepression measure.

1941 U.S. State Department closes all German consulates in U.S. **(World War II).**

France. Also called **Fargeau** and **Ferrutius**. [d. c. 212]

SS. Cyricus and **Julitta**, martyrs. Cyricus also called **Circicus, Ciriacus, Cirycus, Quiricus**, and, in France, **Cirgues** or **Cyr.** [d. c. 304]

St. Aurelian, Bishop of Arles. Founded monastery and convent at Arles. [d. 551]

St. Ismael, bishop. Also called **Osmail, Ysfael.** [d. 6th cent.]

St. Tychon, very early Bishop of Amarthus on Cyprus; patron of vine growers. Also called **Tikhon.** [d. c. 5th century]

St. Benno, Bishop of Meissen. [d. 1106]

St. Lutgardis, virgin, Cistercian nun, and mystic. Also called **Lutgard.** [d. 1246]

St. John Francis Regis, Jesuit missionary. [d. 1640]

The Beatified

Blessed Guy of Cortona; an early disciple of St. Francis of Assisi. [d. c. 1245]

1963	First female in space, **Valentina V. Ter-eshkova,** is launched into orbit in Soviet ***Vostok VI***.
1977	Russian Communist Party general secretary, **Leonid I. Brezhnev,** is elected chief of state, becoming the first leader in the U.S.S.R. to occupy both posts concurrently.
1979	Executions of former leaders in **Ghana** begin in an anticorruption campaign by Flight Lieut. **Jerry Rawlings,** in control of the government since June 4.

June 17

Holidays

Federal Republic of Germany	National Day
Iceland	Independence Day Commemorates Iceland's separation from Denmark and independent status, 1944.
U.S. (Boston, Massachusetts)	Bunker Hill Day

Religious Calendar

The Saints

SS. Nicander and **Marcian,** martyrs. Nicander also called **Nicandeo, Nicanor.** [d. c. 303]

St. Bessarion, hermit. [d. 4th century]

St. Hypatius, abbot. Invoked as a protector against harmful beasts. [d. c. 446]

Birthdates

1239 **Edward I,** King of England; noted for strengthening the crown against the feudal nobility. [d. July 7, 1307]

1682 **Charles XII,** King of Sweden. Invaded Russia and Poland; was finally defeated at Poltava in 1709. [d. November 30, 1718]

1703 **John Wesley,** English evangelist, theologian; founder of the **Methodist movement.** [d. March 2, 1791]

1714 **César Cassini de Thury,** French surveyor; directed the first national geographical survey. [d. September 4, 1784]

1808 **Everhardus Johannes Potgieter,** Dutch poet, essayist, critic; founder and editor of *De Gids (The Guide)*, leading literary monthly of the Netherlands. [d. February 3, 1875]

Henrik Arnold Wergeland, Norwegian poet, playwright, and prose writer. [d. July 12, 1845]

1818 **Charles François Gounod,** French composer; especially well known for opera *Faust.* [d. October 18, 1893]

1832 **Sir William Crookes,** British physicist, chemist; discovered thallium, 1861; invented *Crookes' tube,* a high-exhaustion vacuum tube. [d. April 4, 1919]

1860 **Charles Frohman,** U.S. theatrical manager; developed Empire Theatre Stock Company, 1891, where such actors as Maude Adams, Ethel Barrymore, and William Gillette gained prominence. [d. May 7, 1915]

1871 **James Weldon Johnson,** poet, teacher, critic, civil rights leader; first black to serve as executive secretary of NAACP. [d. June 26, 1933]

1882 **Igor Fyodorovich Stravinsky,** U.S. composer born in Russia; controversial, avant-garde composer of symphonies, ballets, concertos; recognized as one of most influential composers of 20th century. [d. April 6, 1971]

1888 **Heinz Wilhelm Guderian,** German general; commander in chief of armored units, 1939–41. [d. May 15, 1954]

1907 **Charles Eames,** U.S. designer; best known for chair design developed with Eero Saarinen (August 20), which opened way for new approach to production of furniture and the coming of age of **industrial design.** [d. August 21, 1978]

1914 **John (Richard) Hersey,** U.S. educator, novelist, journalist; *A Bell for Adano* won Pulitzer Prize for fiction, 1945; also wrote *The Wall* and *Hiroshima,* an account based on survivors' documentation of atomic bombing of that city.

St. Avitus, abbot. Also called **Avy.** [d. c. 530]

St. Hervé, blind abbot. One of the most popular saints of Brittany. Invoked for eye troubles of all sorts. Also called **Harvey.** [d. 6th century]

St. Nectan, hermit. Also called the *Headless Saint*, **Nighton.** [d. c. 6th century]

St. Botulf, abbot, and **St. Adulf.** Botulf also called **Botolph** [d. c. 680]

St. Moling, Bishop of Leinster. One of the four prophets of Ireland. Also called **Daircheall, Dairchilla, Molingus, Mulling.** [d. 697]

St. Rainerius, patron saint of Pisa. Also called **Raniero** and nicknamed *de Aqua.* [d. 1160]

SS. Teresa and **Sanchia** of Portugal. [d. 1250 and 1229]

St. Gregory Barbarigo, Bishop of Padua and cardinal. [d. 1697]

St. Emily de Vialar, virgin; founder of the Sisters of Saint Joseph of the Apparition. [d. 1856]

St. Briavel, hermit; patron of St. Briavels. [death date unknown.]

The Beatified

Blessed Peter of Pisa, founder of the Poor Brothers of St. Jerome. [d. 1435]

1919   **Kingman Brewster,** U.S. educator, diplomat; President of Yale University, 1963–77; U.S. Ambassador to Great Britain, 1977–80.

1920   **François Jacob,** French biologist; Nobel Prize in physiology or medicine for discovery of body processes which contribute to genetic control of enzymes and virus synthesis (with J. L. Monod and A. M. Lwoff), 1965.

Historical Events

656   **Caliph Othman** of Arabia is murdered by Mohammed, son of **Abu-Bakr.**

1040   **Hardecanute (Harthacnut),** King of Denmark, becomes King of England, 1040–42.

1775   American forces meet British at **Breed's Hill** near Boston. The battle, known as the **Battle of Bunker Hill,** ends in an American defeat but only after heavy British losses.

1789   The French Third Estate declares itself the National Assembly and vows **Tennis Court Oath** not to disband until it has created a constitution for France (**French Revolution**).

1903   *Babes in Toyland* by Victor Herbert premieres in Chicago.

1925   The **Geneva Protocol** prohibiting use of poison gases in warfare is signed.

1944   Allied task force lands French troops on **Elba, Italy (World War II).**

      Iceland becomes a republic independent of Denmark.

1968   U.S. Supreme Court upholds 1866 law prohibiting racial discrimination in sales and rental of property.

1972   Five men are seized while apparently trying to install eavesdropping equipment in the Democratic National Committee headquarters at the Watergate building in Washington, D.C. (**Watergate Incident**).

June 18

Holidays

Egypt

Evacuation Day
Celebrates evacuation of French, British, and Israeli troops, who invaded after nationalization of Suez Canal in 1956.

International Peace Day
Sponsored by Makepeace Foundation, Barrington, Rhode Island

Birthdates

1754 **Anna Maria Lenngren,** Swedish satirical poet. [d. March 8, 1817]

1769 **Robert Stewart, Viscount Castlereagh,** British statesman; Chief Secretary for Ireland, 1799–1801; British Foreign Secretary and leader of House of Commons, 1812–22. [d. August 12, 1822]

1845 **Sir Sidney Colvin,** British art critic, biographer; intimate friend of Robert Louis Stevenson, and editor of Stevenson's works. [d. May 11, 1927]

Charles Louis Alphonse Laveran, French army surgeon; Nobel Prize in physiology or medicine for studies of protozoa-caused diseases, 1907. [d. May 18, 1922]

1850 **Cyrus Hermann Kotzschmar Curtis,** U.S. publisher, philanthropist; founder of Curtis Publishing Co., publishers of *Ladies Home Journal, Saturday Evening Post,* and the *Philadelphia Inquirer.* [d. June 7, 1933]

1854 **E(dward) W(yllis) Scripps,** U.S. newspaper publisher; with his brother, James Edmund Scripps, formed the Scripps-McRae League of Newspapers, which evolved into Scripps-Howard Newspapers. Also developed company to disseminate news by telegraph to subscriber newspapers, United Press International (UPI). [d. March 12, 1926]

1857 **Henry Clay Folger,** U.S. industrialist, philanthropist; Chairman, Standard Oil Co. of New York; avid collector of Shakespeare's works; built and endowed **Folger Shakespeare Library,** Washington, D.C. [d. June 11, 1930]

1869 **Miklos von Nagybanya Horthy,** Hungarian military officer; Commander in Chief of Austro-Hungarian fleet during World War I; commander in chief of national army in Hungary, 1919. Regent of Hungary, 1920–44. [d. February 9, 1957]

1883 **Baltasar Brum,** Uruguayan statesman, journalist, jurist; President of Uruguay, 1919–23. [d. March 31, 1933]

1884 **Edouard Daladier,** French politician; Premier of France 1933, 1934, 1938–40. [d. October 10, 1970]

1907 **Jeanette MacDonald,** U.S. singer, actress; best known for series of film operettas with Nelson Eddy (June 9). [d. January 14, 1965]

1910 **E(verett) G. Marshall,** U.S. actor.

1913 **Sylvia (Field) Porter,** U.S. journalist, financial adviser; author of *The Money Book.*

1937 **John D(avison) Rockefeller IV,** U.S. politician; Secretary of State for West Virginia, 1969–72; President of West Virginia Wesleyan College, 1973–75; Governor of West Virginia, 1977– .

1942 **Paul McCartney,** British musician; bass guitarist, vocalist and songwriter with John Lennon (October 9) for **The Beatles,** 1962–70.

Historical Events

1155 **Frederick I (*Barbarossa*)** is crowned Holy Roman Emperor, beginning a period of great advancements in intellectual areas and exploration.

1812 The U.S. declares war on Great Britain (**War of 1812**).

1815 Napoleon's troops are defeated at the **Battle of Waterloo** by the combined forces of the Duke of Wellington and General von Blücher.

The Saints

SS. Mark and **Marcellian,** martyred brothers. Also called **Marcus** and **Marcellianus.** [d. c. 287]

St. Amandus, Bishop of Bordeaux. Also called **Amand.** [d. c. 431]

St. Elizabeth of Schönau, virgin, visionary, and abbess. Also called **Elizabeth of Sconage.** [d. 1164]

1915	**Second Battle of Artois** ends with enormous numbers of British and French casualties **(World War I).**
1933	The **Nazi party** is dissolved in Austria.
1944	**Battle of the Philippine Sea** begins; Japan's defeat in this battle marks end of effective Japanese carrier power in the Pacific **(World War II).**
1948	First public demonstration of the 12-inch vinyl **long-playing phonograph record** is made in New York by CBS engineer Peter Goldmark.
1953	**Egypt** is declared a republic with **General Mohammed Naguib** as President.
1965	Air Vice-Marshal **Nguyen Cao Ky** is named Premier of South Vietnam under the new military regime of General **Nguyen Van Thieu.**
1975	**Prince Faisal ibn Musad** is beheaded in Riyadh, Saudi Arabia, for the assassination of his uncle **King Faisal.**
1979	U.S. President Jimmy Carter and Russian President Leonid Brezhnev sign the **Strategic Arms Limitation Treaty (SALT) II** in Vienna.

June 19

Birthdates

1566   **James I,** King of Great Britain, 1603–25 (King James VI of Scotland, 1567–1625); first king to rule both England and Scotland. [d. March 27, 1625]

1623   **Blaise Pascal,** French scientist, philosopher; contributed significantly to development of mathematical theories including **differential calculus.** Pascal's literary works, especially *Provinciales* and *Pensées*, are recognized as masterpieces of ironical style. [d. August 19, 1662]

1754   **Jean Baptiste Marie Meusnier,** French general, aeronautical theorist; his studies contributed to knowledge of aeronautical principles of balloons. [d. June 13, 1793]

1764   **Sir John Barrow,** English geographer; Secretary of the Admiralty, 1804–06; 1807–45. Founder of **Royal Geographical Society,** 1830. [d. November 23, 1848]

1783?   **Thomas Sully,** U.S. painter born in England; among his best-known works are portraits of the Marquis de Lafayette, Thomas Jefferson, James Madison, and Andrew Jackson. [d. November 5, 1872]

1861   **Douglas Haig, 1st Earl Haig,** British army officer; Commander in Chief of expeditionary forces in France, 1915–19 (World War I). [d. January 29, 1928]

     José Mercado Rizal, Philippine patriot, author; leader of a nationalist movement. [d. December 30, 1896]

1877   **Charles Coburn,** U.S. actor. [d. August 30, 1961]

1880   **Jóhann Sigurjónsson,** Icelandic dramatist, poet. [d. August 31, 1919]

1881   **James (John) Walker,** U.S. politician, lawyer; Mayor of New York City, 1925–32. [d. November 18, 1946]

1896   **(Bessie) Wallis Warfield, Duchess of Windsor,** U.S. socialite divorcee for whom King **Edward VIII** of England renounced his throne.

1897   **Sir Cyril Norman Hinshelwood,** British physical chemist; Nobel Prize in chemistry for research into the kinetics of chemical reactions (with N. N. Semenov), 1956. [d. October 9, 1967]

1902   **Guy Lombardo,** U.S. bandleader born in Canada; leader of *Royal Canadians* band whose New Year's Eve musical countdown became a U.S. radio and television tradition. [d. November 5, 1977]

1903   **(Henry) Lou(is) Gehrig,** U.S. baseball player; inducted into Baseball Hall of Fame, 1939. [d. June 2, 1941]

1906   **Ernst Boris Chain,** British biochemist born in Germany; Nobel Prize in physiology or medicine for discovery of **penicillin** (with A. Fleming and H. W. Florey), 1945.

1908   **Mildred Natwick,** U.S. character actress.

1910   **Abe Fortas,** U.S. jurist, lawyer; Associate Justice of U.S. Supreme Court, 1965–69. [d. April 5, 1982]

     Paul J. Flory, U.S. chemist; Nobel Prize in chemistry for his investigations of synthetic and natural macromolecules, 1974.

1921   **Louis Jourdan (Louis Gendre),** French actor.

1922   **(Aage) Niels Bohr,** Danish physicist; Nobel Prize in physics for discovery of connec-

Religious Calendar

The Saints

St. Deodatus, Bishop of Nevers. Also called **Dié** or **Didier.** [d. c. 679]

St. Bruno of Querfurt, bishop, missionary, and martyr; Apostle of Russia. Also called **Boniface.** [d. 1009]

St. Romualdo, abbot. Founder of the Camaldolese Benedictines. Also called **Romuald.** [d. 1027] Feast formerly February 7. Optional Memorial.

St. Juliana Falconieri, virgin, founder of the Servite order. [d. 1341]

St. Gervase and **St. Protase,** martyrs. Venerated as the first martyrs of Milan. Also called **Gervasius** and **Protasius.** [death date unknown]

The Beatified

Blessed Odo, Bishop of Cambrai. [d. 1113]

Blessed Thomas Woodhouse, martyr. [d. 1573]

---

tion between collective motion and particle motion in atomic nucleus (with J. Rainwater and B. Mottelson), 1975.

Historical Events

1464 **Louis XI,** King of France, establishes **Poste Royale,** pioneering concept of national **postal service.**

1669 **Michael Wisniowiecki** is elected King of Poland following abdication of **John Casimir.**

1842 The British seize **Shanghai** in the **First Opium War** with China.

1846 First real **baseball game** with set rules is played at the Elysian Fields in Hoboken, New Jersey, between the **Knickerbocker Baseball Club** and the **New York Nine.** Knickerbocker Club is defeated by a score of 23–1.

1867 Mexico's **Emperor Maximilian** is executed by a firing squad, thus ending France's hopes for establishing an empire in Central America.

1910 **Father's Day** is observed for the first time under the sponsorship of the Spokane, Washington, Ministerial Association and YMCA.

1934 **U.S. Federal Communications Commission** is created to regulate interstate and foreign communications by telegraph, radio, and cable.

1961 **Kuwait** gains independence from Great Britain.

1965 Algerian President **Ahmed ben Bella** is ousted from office in a coup d'état headed by Defense Minister **Houari Boumedienne.**

1967 **Gamal Abdel Nasser** names himself Prime Minister of the **United Arab Republic.**

1968 **Poor People's Campaign** comes to an end in Washington, D.C., as more than 50,000 persons take part in a **Solidarity Day** march on the capital.

1970 Russian spacecraft *Soyuz 9* returns to earth concluding a record-breaking 17-day flight.

June 20

Holidays

Argentina	Flag Day
U.S. (West Virginia)	West Virginia Day
	Commemorates admission of West Virginia to the Union, 1863.

Religious Calendar

The Saints

St. Silverius, pope and martyr. Elected 536. [d. c. 537]

Birthdates

1389 **John of Lancaster, Duke of Bedford,** third son of **Henry IV** of England; English military leader. [d. September 14, 1435]

1700 **Peter Faneuil,** American merchant; donated **Faneuil Hall** in Boston to the city. [d. March 3, 1743]

1793 **Count Alexander Fredro,** Polish playwright, poet; called the *Polish Molière*. [d. July 15, 1876]

1819 **Jacques Offenbach (Jakob Eberst),** French composer born in Germany; best known for operettas and *opéra bouffe* written for his own theater in Paris as well as others; wrote *Gaiété Parisienne*, which contains traditional music for the can-can. [d. October 5, 1880]

1832 **Benjamin Helm Bristow,** U.S. lawyer, public official; highly effective in his opposition to the Ku Klux Klan and as protector of blacks' rights. Served as second president of American Bar Association. [d. June 22, 1896]

1833 **Léon Joseph Florentin Bonnat,** French painter, art collector; noted for his religious paintings. [d. September 8, 1922]

1858 **Charles Waddell Chestnutt,** U.S. lawyer, novelist; first black to have work published in *Atlantic Monthly*. Noted for his various fictional works on the lives and attitudes of blacks in America, as well as his successes as a lawyer. [d. November 15, 1932]

1863 **John Miller Turpin Finney,** U.S. surgeon, author, educator. [d. May 30, 1942]

1873 **Alberto Santos-Dumont,** Brazilian aeronaut; known for his experiments with balloons and early airships; built first airship station in France, 1903. [d. July 25, 1932]

1883 **Royal Eason Ingersoll,** U.S. naval officer; commanded U.S. Atlantic fleet, 1942–44 (World War II). [d. May 20, 1976]

1899 **Helen Traubel,** U.S. operatic soprano; member of Metropolitan Opera Company, 1940–53. [d. July 28, 1972]

1900 **Julian (Edwin) Levi,** U.S. artist, educator; known for his seascapes; member of the faculty of the New School for Social Research, 1945-66. [d. February 28, 1982]

1905 **Lillian Hellman,** U.S. playwright; plays include *Children's Hour*, *The Little Foxes*, *Watch on the Rhine*, as well as other dramas and plays written for or adapted for the screen. [d. June 30, 1984]

1909 **Errol Flynn,** U.S. actor. [d. October 14, 1959]

1924 **Chet Atkins (Chester B. Atkins),** U.S. country-and-western guitarist.

Audie Murphy, U.S. soldier, actor; most highly decorated U.S. soldier of World War II. [d. May 28, 1971]

Historical Events

1624 **Treaty of Compiègne** is signed between France and the Netherlands (**Thirty Years' War**).

1756 The Nawab of Bengal, Surāj-ud-Dawlah, captures Calcutta and imprisons 146 English residents in what is later called **The Black Hole of Calcutta.** Allegedly, only 23 prisoners survive the overnight imprisonment.

1782 U.S. Congress adopts the **Great Seal of the United States.**

1792 French mob marches on the **Tuileries** (**French Revolution**).

St. Goban, priest and martyr. Also called Gobain, Gobian. [d. c. 670]

St. Bagnus, Bishop of Thérouanne; principal patron of Calais. Also called Bain. [d. c. 710]

Translation of St. Edward the Martyr, King of England, from Wareham to Shaftsbury, 980.

St. Adalbert, Archbishop of Magdeburg. [d. 981]

St. John of Matera, Abbot of Pulsano. [d. 1139]

The English Martyrs of the Oates Plot [1678–1680].

The Beatified

Blessed Michelina of Pesaro, widow. [d. 1356]

Blessed Osanna of Mantua, virgin. [d. 1505]

1837 **William IV** of England dies and is succeeded by **Queen Victoria.**

Hanover is separated from England upon the accession of **Queen Victoria** because Hanoverian law forbids the succession of a woman to the throne (**Salic Law**).

1840 A patent for the **telegraph** is granted to **Samuel F. B. Morse.**

1863 **West Virginia** is admitted to the Union as the 35th state.

1900 **Boxer Rebellion** begins in China as one Chinese faction attempts to rid the nation of foreign control and interference.

1944 **Battle of the Philippine Sea** ends with heavy losses inflicted by U.S. planes on the Japanese fleet (**World War II**).

1960 **Floyd Patterson** knocks out **Ingemar Johansson** in the 5th round to become the first man to regain the world heavyweight boxing championship.

Senegal and **Sudanese Republic,** former French territories in Africa, obtain independence as **Federation of Mali.**

1977 The first oil from Alaska's frozen north slope begins flowing into the **trans-Alaska pipeline.**

1979 Ugandan president **Jusufu Lule** is forced from office and **Godfrey Binasia** is appointed in his place.

June 21

Birthdates

1639   **Increase Mather,** American colonial religious leader; father of **Cotton Mather.** Pastor of Boston's Second Church, 1664–1723; President of Harvard College, 1685–1701. [d. August 23, 1723]

1676   **Anthony Collins,** English deist, theological controversialist; intimate of John Locke. [d. December 13, 1729]

1757   **Alexander James Dalls,** U.S. lawyer, public official; U.S. Secretary of the Treasury, 1814–16. [d. January 16, 1817]

1781   **Siméon-Denis Poisson,** French mathematician; known for innovative applications of mathematical laws to physics. [d. April 25, 1840]

1792   **Ferdinand Christian Baur,** German theologian; founder of Tübingen School of Theology. [d. December 2, 1860]

1805   **Charles Thomas Jackson,** U.S. chemist, geologist; first state geologist of Maine, Rhode Island, and New Hampshire. Controversial for his claims of precedence of discovery of **electric telegraph** over Samuel F. B. Morse, and **ether** as an anesthetic over William T. G. Morton. [d. August 28, 1880]

1832   **Joseph Hayne Rainey,** U.S. banker, politician; first black to serve in U.S. House of Representatives. [d. August 2, 1887]

1850   **Daniel Carter Beard,** U.S. artist, naturalist; inaugurated first class in animal drawing at Woman's School of Applied Design, New York. Founder of **Sons of Daniel Boone,** 1905, which later merged with **Boy Scouts of America.** [d. June 11, 1941]

1880   **Arnold Lucius Gesell,** U.S. psychologist; developed standards for child development which outlined progressive stages of child development from infancy through adolescence (**Gesell Development Schedules**). Founded Yale Psycho-Clinic (Yale Clinic of Child Development), 1908. [d. May 29, 1961]

1882   **Rockwell Kent,** U.S. painter, illustrator; one of most successful American artists of his period, with works in permanent collections of many museums, both in U.S. and Europe. [d. March 13, 1971]

1884   **Sir Claude (John Eyre) Auchinleck,** British field marshal; commander of British forces in Egypt and Mesopotamia, World War I; commander of British forces in the Middle East, World War II; dismissed by Winston Churchill for refusal to pursue Erwin Rommel after British recapture of Tobruk. [d. March 23, 1981]

1891   **Pier (Luigi) Nervi,** Italian architect, engineer; a pioneer in the use of **reinforced concrete.** [d. January 9, 1979]

1892   **Reinhold Niebuhr,** U.S. theologian. His teachings and writings marked the beginning of the **neo-orthodox movement** in U.S. [d. June 1, 1971]

1905   **Jean-Paul Sartre,** French existentialist philosopher, novelist, playwright. [d. April 15, 1980]

1912   **Mary (Therese) McCarthy,** U.S. novelist, critic.

1921   **Jane Russell,** U.S. actress.

       Judy Holliday (Judith Tuvim), U.S. actress. [d. June 7, 1965]

1925   **Maureen Stapleton,** U.S. character actress.

1935   **Françoise Sagan (Françoise Quoirez),** French novelist.

1982   **Prince William** of Great Britain, first child of Prince Charles and Princess Diana, and second generation heir to British throne, is born.

Historical Events

1377   **Edward III** of England dies and is succeeded by his grandson, **Richard II.**

St. Alban of Mainz, martyr. Also called **Albinus.** [d. 5th century]

St. Méen, abbot. Famous as a healer of skin diseases. Also called **Main, Melanus, Mevennus, Mewan.** [d. c. 6th century]

St. Engelmund, abbot and missionary. [d. c. 720]

St. Leutfridus, abbot. Also called **Leufredus, Leufroi, Leufroy.** [d. 738]

St. Ralph, Archishop of Bourges. Also called **Radolphus, Radulf, Raoul.** [d. 866]

St. Aloysius, patron of Catholic youth. Also called **Luigi Gonzaga.** [d. 1591] Obligatory Memorial.

1684	**Massachusetts Bay Colony** charter is annulled by British Court of Chancery.
1788	**New Hampshire** ratifies the U.S. Constitution.
1791	**Louis XVI** and the royal family are arrested at Varennes and brought back to Paris after attempting to escape (**French Revolution**).
1813	Duke of Wellington defeats French at **Vitoria,** ending France's presence in Spain (**Napoleonic Wars**).
1834	**Cyrus H. McCormick** is awarded a U.S. patent for his **reaper.**
1868	Richard Wagner's comic opera, *Die Meistersinger,* premieres at Munich.
1887	**Queen Victoria** celebrates her golden jubilee.
	Zululand is annexed to the British Empire.
1919	The German High Seas Fleet is scuttled by ships' crews at **Scapa Flow** after surrendering to the British (**World War I**).
1932	**Jack Sharkey** defeats **Max Schmeling** to gain world heavyweight championship.
1942	**Tobruk** in Libya is taken by German Field Marshal **Erwin Rommel (World War II).**
1960	**Patrice Lumumba** is named to form the first government of the **Belgian Congo.**
1963	**Giovanni Battista Cardinal Montini** is elected as 262nd pope of the Roman Catholic Church, taking the name **Paul VI.**
1964	Haitian National Assembly affirms presidency of **François (*Papa Doc*) Duvalier** and proclaims a new constitution. Duvalier governs Haiti until his death in 1971.
1977	**Menachem Begin** becomes Prime Minister of Israel; resigns September 15, 1983.

June 22

Holidays

People's Democratic Republic of Yemen — Corrective Move Day

Religious Calendar

The Saints

St. Nicetas, Bishop of Remesiana, missionary and writer. [d. c. 414]

St. Paulinus of Nola, bishop and poet. [d. 431] Optional Memorial.

Birthdates

1748   **Thomas Day,** English reformer, author; attempted to reconcile Rousseau's doctrines with conventional morality. [d. September 28, 1789]

1757   **George Vancouver,** British navigator; explored coasts of Australia, New Zealand, Hawaiian Islands, 1791–92; led expedition along Pacific Coast of North America, 1792–94. **Vancouver Island** and city of **Vancouver, British Columbia,** are named for him. [d. May 10, 1798]

1767   **Wilhelm von Humboldt,** German scholar, statesman, philologist; influential in developing science of comparative philology. [d. April 8, 1835]

1805   **Giuseppe Mazzini,** Italian patriot, political theorist, and critic; devoted most of his life to unification of Italy. Helped organize Garibaldi's expeditions. [d. March 10, 1872]

1837   **Paul Morphy,** U.S. chessmaster; defeated world's best players of his era, gaining unofficial world chess championship, 1857. [d. July 10, 1884]

1844   **Harriet Mulford Lothrop (Margaret Sidney),** U.S. children's book writer. [d. August 2, 1924]

1856   **Sir Henry Rider Haggard,** British novelist; author of *She, King Solomon's Mines, Alan Quatermain.* [d. May 14, 1925]

1861   **Count Maximilian von Spee,** German admiral; defeated British squadron at Coronel, off Chilean coast, 1914. Went down with his ship when German fleet was destroyed near Falkland Islands, 1914 (World War I). [d. December 8, 1914]

1869   **Hendrik Colijn,** Dutch anti-Fascist leader, statesman; Minister of War, 1911–13; Premier, 1925–26; 1933–39. [d. September 15, 1944]

1887   **Julian Huxley,** British biologist, author; first director of UNESCO, 1946–48; proponent of evolutionary humanism; knighted, 1958; brother of Aldous Huxley (July 26). [d. February 14, 1975]

1888   **Harold Hitz Burton,** U.S. lawyer, jurist; Associate Justice, U.S. Supreme Court, 1945–58. [d. October 28, 1964]

        Alan Seeger, U.S. poet; author of *I Have a Rendezvous with Death* and *Ode in Memory of the American Volunteers Fallen in France.* Killed in World War I. [d. July 4, 1916]

1898   **Erich Maria Remarque (Erich Paul Remark),** German-U.S. anti-militaristic novelist; author of *All Quiet on the Western Front.* [d. September 25, 1970]

1903   **John Dillinger,** U.S. outlaw; designated as public enemy number one in the early 1930s; betrayed by mysterious "woman in red," shot to death by FBI agents. [d. July 22, 1934]

        Carl Hubbell, U.S. baseball player. Baseball Hall of Fame, 1947.

1906   **Ann Morrow Lindbergh,** U.S. writer, poet; wife of Charles A. Lindbergh (February 4).

        Billy Wilder, U.S. film writer, producer, director born in Austria.

1910   **Katherine Dunham,** U.S. dancer, choreographer, anthropologist; leading dancer and dance authority deriving much of her inspiration from primitive rituals of the Car-

St. Ebbe the Younger, martyr. [d. 870]

St. Eberhard, Archbishop of Salzburg. [d. 1164]

St. John Fisher, Bishop of Rochester and cardinal, martyr. [d. 1535] Feast formerly July 9. Optional Memorial.

St. Thomas More, martyr. [d. 1535] Feast formerly July 9. Optional Memorial.

St. Acacius, martyr. [death date unknown]

St. Alban, martyr. Protomartyr of Britain. [death date unknown]

The Beatified

Blessed Innocent V, pope. Elected 1276. Commonly known as **Peter of Tarentaise.** [d. 1277]

ibbean. Founded **Katherine Dunham Dance Company,** 1945 (later the **Katherine Dunham School of Cultural Arts**).

1921 **Gower Champion,** U.S. dancer, choreographer, director. [d. August 25, 1980]

Joseph Papp (Papirofsky), U.S. theatrical producer; founder, head of New York Shakespeare Festival, 1953– .

1922 **Bill Blass,** U.S. fashion designer.

1936 **Kris Kristofferson,** U.S. actor, singer, songwriter.

1947 **Jerry Rawlings,** Ghanaian statesman; President, Republic of Ghana, 1981– .

1948 **Pete Maravich,** U.S. basketball player.

1949 **Meryl Streep,** U.S. actress.

1954 **Freddie Prinze,** U.S. comedian. [d. January 29, 1977]

Historical Events

1377 **Richard II,** King of England, is crowned after the death of his grandfather, **Edward III.**

1812 French troops of the **Grande Armée** begin invasion of **Russia** under leadership of **Napoleon.**

1815 **Napoleon Bonaparte** abdicates for the second time.

1870 **U.S. Department of Justice** is established by Congress.

1894 **Dahomey** becomes a French colony.

1910 **Count Zeppelin** inaugurates first airship passenger service, with the *Deutschland.*

1921 First session of **Northern Ireland** Parliament is opened by **King George V.**

1922 **Sir Henry Wilson,** opponent of the **Sinn Fein** (Irish separatist radical group) is murdered by members of that group.

1937 **Joe Louis** knocks out **Jim Braddock,** becoming the world heavyweight boxing champion.

1940 France signs armistice with Germany at Compiègne (**World War II**).

1941 German armies invade **Russia** on a 2000-mile front (**World War II**).

1965 **Japan** and **Korea** sign treaty and normalize relations after a lapse of 55 years.

1973 Three *Skylab 2* astronauts, Charles Conrad, Jr., Joseph P. Kerwin and Paul J. Weitz return safely to earth after spending a record 28 days in space during which they make two major repairs to the orbiting *Skylab.*

1981 **Abolhassan Bani-Sadr** is dismissed as President of Iran by **Ayatollah Ruhollah Khomeini.**

June 23

Holidays

Luxembourg **National Holiday**
Celebration of the Grand Duke's birthday.

Religious Calendar

The Saints

St. Agrippina, virgin and martyr. Invoked against evil spirits, thunderstorms, and leprosy. [d. c. 262]

Birthdates

1668 **Giovanni Battista Vico,** Italian philosopher, historian, critic, poet; pioneer in the study of esthetics. [d. January 23, 1744]

1763 **Josephine (Beauharnais),** Empress of France, wife of Napoleon Bonaparte; divorced by him because she did not provide him with an heir. [d. May 29, 1814]

1775 **Etienne Louis Malus,** French engineer, physicist; pioneer in field of **optics.** First to describe polarization of light by reflection. [d. February 23, 1812]

1876 **Irvin S(hrewsbury) Cobb,** U.S. journalist, humorist, short-story writer, playwright. [d. March 10, 1944]

1894 **Edward VIII,** King of England; the only British king to abdicate voluntarily (reigned January 20 to December 11, 1936), to marry American divorcee Wallace Warfield (Simpson); became Duke of Windsor. [d. May 27, 1972]

Alfred Charles Kinsey, U.S. zoologist and student of human sexual behavior. Most famous for his *Sexual Behavior in the Human Male,* 1948, a study based on interviews with 18,000 people; the study stirred up national controversy and brought great attention to the subject of human sexual activity, an area previously considered taboo. [d. August 25, 1956]

1904 **Carleton S(tevens) Coon,** U.S. anthropologist, archaeologist, educator; author of *The Story of Man,* in which he put forward a theory that the apes are descended from a species of "ground-living" mammals that almost became man. [d. June 3, 1981]

1907 **James E. Meade,** British economist; Nobel Prize in economics for contributions to theory of international trade (with B. Ohlin), 1977.

1910 **Jean Anouilh,** French playwright; plays include *Antigone, La Valse des toréadors,* (translated into English as *The Waltz of the Toreadors.*)

1927 **Bob Fosse,** U.S. director, choreographer.

1936 **Richard (Davis) Bach,** U.S. author, aviator.

1940 **Wilma Rudolph,** U.S. sprinter; winner of three gold medals in 1960 Olympics.

1943 **James Levine,** U.S. conductor, pianist; Music Director of the Metropolitan Opera, New York, 1975– .

Historical Events

1372 French and Castilians defeat English off **La Rochelle, France (Hundred Years' War).**

1501 **Pedro Cabral** completes voyage establishing Portuguese trade with East Indies; he accomplishes this by traveling west, reaching **Brazil,** which he claims for Portugal, 1500.

1930 **Iceland** celebrates the 1,000th anniversary of the **Alting,** the oldest parliament in the world.

1947 U.S. Congress adopts the **Taft-Hartley Law** over President Truman's veto, prohibiting closed shops and restricting union activity.

1966 **Secular Affairs Institute,** Buddhist antigovernment stronghold, is seized by South Vietnamese troops (**Vietnam War**).

1967 **Pope Paul VI** issues encyclical *Sacerdotalis Caelibatus,* reaffirming church ruling on priestly **celibacy.**

1969 **Warren Earl Burger** is sworn in as Chief Justice of the U.S. Supreme Court.

St. Etheldreda, Abbess of Ely and widow. Founded double monastery for monks and nuns at the **Isle of Ely.** Also called **Aethelthryth, Audrey, Audry.** [d. 679]

St. Lietbertus, Bishop of Cambrai. Also called **Libert, Liébert.** [d. 1076]

St. Joseph Cafasso, priest of Turin; patron saint of prisons. [d. 1860]

The Beatified

Blessed Peter of Jully. [d. 1136]

Blessed Lanfranc, Bishop of Pavia. [d. 1194]

Blessed Mary of Oignies, virgin. [d. 1213]

Blessed Thomas Corsini, monk. [d. 1345]

June 24

Holidays

Andorra	**Feast of St. John**
Peru	**Countryman's Day**
Puerto Rico	**San Juan Day**
Quebec	**St. Jean Day**
Venezuela	**Battle of Carabobo**
	Commemorates Bolivar's victory at Carabobo, the final battle in war for independence against Spain, 1821.

Birthdates

1485   **Johann Bugenhagen,** German Protestant reformer; assisted Martin Luther (November 10) in translating the Bible. [d. April 20, 1558]

1542   **Saint John of the Cross** (in Spain, **Juan de la Cruz**), Spanish monk, lyric poet, mystic; one of greatest mystical poets; wrote *The Dark Night of the Soul*. [d. December 24, 1591]

1616   **Ferdinand Bol,** Dutch painter; a student of Rembrandt. [d. July 24, 1680]

1753   **William Hull,** U.S. army general, lawyer; court-martialed for uncontested surrender of **Detroit** to British, 1812. Death sentence stayed by President James Madison. [d. November 29, 1825]

1771   **Eleuthère Irénée Du Pont de Nemours,** U.S. industrialist born in France; established gunpowder manufacturing plant near Wilmington, Delaware, that his descendants developed into E. I. Du Pont de Nemours and Co., one of the world's largest chemical and industrial firms. [d. October 31, 1834]

1795   **Ernst Heinrich Weber,** German physiologist, anatomist; known for his research on the human senses. Developed theory that least noticeable increase of a stimulus is a constant directly proportionate to original stimulus (**Weber's Law**). [d. January 26, 1878]

1813   **Henry Ward Beecher,** U.S. religious leader, social reformer; famous for his oratorical style. [d. March 8, 1887]

1839   **Gustavus Franklin Swift,** U.S. meat packer, founder of Swift & Co., 1885. [d. March 29, 1903]

1850   **Horatio Herbert Kitchener, 1st Earl Kitchener of Khartoum,** British soldier; Governor-General of Sudan, 1886, 1898; Commander in Chief of British forces in India, 1902–09; Secretary of War, 1914. Organized British forces for World War I, 1914–16. [d. June 5, 1916]

1864   **Walther Hermann Nernst,** German physicist, chemist; researcher in areas of thermodynamics, theories of ions, chemical equilibrium and solutions; Nobel Prize in chemistry for application of thermodynamics to chemistry, 1920. [d. November 18, 1941]

1883   **Victor F. Hess,** U.S. physicist born in Austria; Nobel Prize in physics for discovery of **cosmic rays** (with C. D. Anderson), 1936. [d. December 17, 1964]

1895   **Jack Dempsey (William Harrison Dempsey),** U.S. boxer; world heavyweight champion, 1919–26. [d. May 31, 1983]

1915   **Norman Cousins,** U.S. editor, author; editor of *Saturday Review*, 1940–77.

Historical Events

1314   The **Battle of Bannockburn** is won by the Scottish forces under **Robert Bruce,** completely defeating the English under **Edward II,** and establishing Bruce on the throne of Scotland.

1340   English defeat French off **Sluys,** giving England control of the English Channel until 1372 (**Hundred Years' War**).

1497   **John Cabot,** Italian-born explorer sailing from England, lands on North American soil (exact location is subject of debate, but it was probably Newfoundland, Labrador, or Cape Breton Island).

Religious Calendar

Solemnities

The Nativity of St. John the Baptist, forerunner and herald of Jesus Christ; sanctified in his mother's womb; invoked against hail, epilepsy, convulsions, and spasms, and for the protection of lambs. [d. c. 30] [major holy day, Episcopal Church; minor festival, Lutheran Church]

The Saints

The Martyrs under Nero. [d. 64 A.D.]

St. Simplicius, Bishop of Autun. [d. 4th or 5th century]

St. Bartholomew of Farne, hermit. [d. 1193]

1916   **Battle of the Somme** begins in France as British artillery bombards German lines **(World War I).**

1922   American Professional Football Association becomes **National Football League.**

1948   Soviet Union imposes total blockade on all land traffic between **Berlin** and West Germany.

U.S. President Harry Truman signs the **Selective Service Act**, requiring men between 18 and 25 to register for military service.

1963   Internal self-government is informally introduced in **Zanzibar,** with Sheikh Mohammed Shamte Hamadi as Prime Minister.

1967   **Zaire** ratifies a new constitution, providing for a federal system of government with a strong president and unicameral legislature.

1983   U.S. space shuttle *Challenger* lands at Edwards Air Force Base, completing its second flight. Crew member **Sally K. Ride** is the first U.S. woman astronaut to go into space.

June 25

Holidays

Mozambique   **Independence Day**
Commemorates Mozambique's
achievement of independence
from Portugal, 1975.

Religious Calendar

Presentation of the Augsburg Confession. [minor
festival, Lutheran Church]

The Saints

St. Febronia, virgin and martyr. [d. c. 304]

St. Gallicanus. [d. c. 352]

St. Prosper of Aquitaine, layman, poet, and author.
Secretary to Pope St. Leo the Great. [d. c. 465]

Birthdates

1768   **Lazare Hoche,** French Revolutionary general. [d. September 19, 1797]

1865   **Robert Henri,** U.S. painter, art teacher; influential artist of the period who, with Maurice Prendergast (October 10) and others, attempted to convey *new realism;* group became known as the **Ashcan School.** [d. July 12, 1929]

1886   **Henry Harley (*Hap*) Arnold,** U.S. Air Force five-star general; as commander of U.S. forces, 1941–46, was responsible for building the world's largest air force. Planned massive air strikes against Germany in World War II. [d. January 15, 1950]

1887   **George Abbot,** U.S. producer, director, and playwright.

1907   **J. Hans Daniels Jensen,** German physicist; Nobel Prize in physics for discoveries of atomic nucleus shell structure (with M. Goeppert-Mayer and E. P. Wigner), 1963. [d. February 11, 1973]

1911   **William Howard Stein,** U.S. biochemist; Nobel Prize in chemistry for research related to chemical structure of ribonuclease (with C. B. Anfisen and S. Moore), 1972.

1921   **Celia Franca,** British ballet dancer, director, choreographer; founder of **National Ballet of Canada.**

Historical Events

1080   **Synod of Brixen** elects imperial anti-pope **Clement III** after **Pope Gregory VII** is deposed.

1115   **Abbey of Clairvaux** is founded with St. Bernard as its first abbot.

1580   *Book of Concord,* official collection of Lutheran confessional treatises, is published.

1857   **Prince Albert,** husband of **Queen Victoria** of England, is named Prince Consort.

1861   The **Order of the Star of India** is instituted by the British.

1870   **Queen Isabella II** of Spain abdicates in favor of her son, **Alfonso XII.**

1876   Gen. **George Custer** and his men are massacred by **Sitting Bull** and his Sioux at **Little Big Horn,** South Dakota.

1910   **Igor Stravinsky's** first ballet, *The Firebird,* premieres in Paris, performed by Ballet Russe.

U.S. Congress passes **Mann Act** (*White Slave Traffic Act*), prohibiting interstate transportation of women for immoral purposes.

1918   U.S. Marine brigade captures **Belleau Wood** after weeks of fighting (**World War I).**

1950   People's Army of North Korea drives across the 38th parallel in invasion of **South Korea (Korean War).**

1975   After 470 years of colonial rule, **Portuguese East Africa** becomes the independent **People's Republic of Mozambique.**

St. Prosper, Bishop of Reggio; principal patron of Reggio. [d. c. 466]

St. Maximus, Bishop of Turin. [d. c. 467]

St. Molaug, abbot. Founded Scottish Monastery of Lismore. Invoked for cures from madness. Also called **Lugaid, Molloch.** [d. 592]

St. Adalbert of Egmond, missionary. Also called **Adelbert.** [d. 8th century]

St. Eurosia, virgin and martyr. Honored as protector of the fruits of the field and invoked against bad weather. Also called **Eurosis.** [d. 8th century]

St. Gohard, Bishop of Nantes, and his companions, martyrs. [d. 843]

St. William of Vercelli, Abbot of Monte Vergine. [d. 1142]

St. Cyneburga of Gloucester, princess. [death date unknown]

The Beatified

Blessed Henry Zdik, Bishop of Olomuc. [d. c. 1150]

Blessed John the Spaniard, prior. [d. 1160]

Blessed Guy Maramaldi, theologian and preacher. [d. 1391]

June 26

Holidays

United Nations Charter Day
Commemorates the signing of the Charter, 1945.

Madagascar   **Independence Day**

Religious Calendar

The Saints

St. John and **St. Paul,** martyrs. [d. c. 362] Feast suppressed in 1969.

Birthdates

1730   **Charles Messier,** French astronomer; credited with discovery of numerous comets. His catalog of nebulae gave rise to system of identification called *Messier numbers.* [d. April 11, 1817]

1819   **Abner Doubleday,** U.S. sportsman, soldier; legendary originator of game of **baseball** (a story now debunked). Manned the guns at Fort Sumter when first shots of Civil War were fired. [d. January 26, 1893]

1824   **William Thomson, 1st Baron Kelvin,** British engineer, mathematician, physicist; established the **absolute (Kelvin) scale** of temperature, 1848. [d. December 17, 1907]

1854   **Robert Laird Borden,** Canadian statesman; Prime Minister, 1917–20. [d. June 10, 1937]

1891   **Sidney (Coe) Howard,** U.S. playwright; best known for screenplay version of *Gone With the Wind.* [d. August 23, 1939]

1892   **Pearl (Sydenstricker) Buck,** U.S. author; educator; well-known expert on life in China, the basis for most of her writing; wrote *The Good Earth,* later a film; Nobel Prize in literature, 1938. [d. March 6, 1973]

1894   **Pyotr Kapitsa,** Russian scientist; Nobel Prize in physics for his work in low-temperature physics, 1978.

1898   **Willy (Wilhelm) Messerschmitt,** German aviation engineer. [d. September 15, 1978]

       Lewis Burwell Puller, U.S. Marine Corps general, World War II. [d. October 11, 1971]

1901   **Stuart Symington,** U.S. politician, businessman; President of Emerson Electric Manufacturing Co., 1938–45; U.S. Secretary of the Air Force, 1947–50; U.S. Senator, 1952–77.

1902   **Antonia Brico,** U.S. conductor, teacher; first woman to conduct Berlin Philharmonic, 1935; founder of **Brico Symphony,** 1935.

1914   **(Mildred Ella) Babe Didrikson Zaharias,** U.S. athlete; winner of two gold medals, 1932 Olympics. Leading woman golfer, 1932–55. Recognized as one of greatest woman athletes of all time. [d. September 27, 1956]

Historical Events

1306   The English are victorious over Robert Bruce, Scottish king, at **Methuen.**

1483   **Richard of Gloucester** assumes the English throne, succeeding **Edward V,** who was murdered in the Tower of London on June 23. Richard reigns as **Richard III.**

1794   Austrians are defeated by French at **Fleurus** and lose Belgium (**French Revolutionary period**).

1830   **George IV** of England dies and is succeeded by **William IV.**

1858   The **Treaty of Tientsin** is signed, ending hostilities between China and Great Britain and giving diplomatic and trade rights to Britain.

1900   Imperial edict declares war on all foreigners and orders their expulsion from China (**Boxer Rebellion**).

1917   First U.S. troops arrive in France (**World War I**).

1935   U.S. President Franklin D. Roosevelt establishes **National Youth Administration** to provide jobs for those aged 16–25.

St. Vigilius, Bishop of Trent, martyr. First martyr to be canonized by the Holy See. Principal patron of Trentino and the Italian Tirol. [d. 405]

St. Maxentius, abbot. [d. c. 515]

St. Salvius, bishop, and **St. Superius,** martyrs. Salvius also called **Sauve.** [d. c. 768]

St. John, Bishop of the Goths. [d. c. 800]

St. Pelagius, boy martyr. Also called **Pelayo.** [d. 925]

St. Anthelm, Bishop of Belley. First minister general of the Carthusian monks. [d. 1178]

1945   **United Nations** charter is signed in San Francisco, to become effective October 24, 1945.

1959   **St. Lawrence Seaway,** connecting the Great Lakes with the Atlantic, officially opens.

         Ingemar Johansson defeats **Floyd Patterson** for world heavyweight boxing title.

1960   **Malagasy Republic** (formerly **Madagascar,** a French possession) and **Somaliland** (formerly British protectorate) become independent.

1968   The **Bonin Islands,** including **Iwo Jima,** are returned to Japan by the U.S.

1975   State of emergency is declared in **India** in an attempt to control critics of Prime Minister **Indira Gandhi.**

June 27

Holidays

Djibouti
Independence Feast Day
Commemorates achievement of independence from France, 1977.

Religious Calendar

The Saints
St. Zoilus and his companions, martyrs. [d. c. 304]

Birthdates

1462 **Louis XII,** King of France, 1498–1515; called the *Father of his People.* [d. January 1, 1515]

1550 **Charles IX,** King of France; remembered for ordering the massacre of Protestants on **St. Bartholomew's Day,** August 24, 1572. [d. May 30, 1574]

1838 **Bankim Chandra Chatterjee,** Indian novelist; creator of an Indian school of fiction based on European model. [d. April 8, 1894]

Peter Paul Mauser, German arms inventor and manufacturer; invented the Mauser magazine rifle. [d. May 29, 1914]

1846 **Charles Stewart Parnell,** Irish nationalist leader; advocate of Irish Home Rule. [d. October 6, 1891]

1849 **Harriet Hubbard Ayer,** U.S. manufacturer of cosmetics; author. [d. November 23, 1903]

1850 **Lafcadio Hearn,** U.S. journalist born in Greece of British parents; wrote extensively on Japan in attempt to interpret Japan to English-speaking people. Became a Japanese citizen, writing under name of **Yakumo Koizumi.** [d. September 26, 1904]

1869 **Hans Spemann,** German zoologist; Nobel Prize in physiology or medicine for discovery of organizing effect in embryonic development, 1935. [d. September 12, 1941]

Emma Goldman, U.S. anarchist born in Lithuania; active in organizing laborers in New York, working against U.S. involvement in World War I and military conscription of U.S. citizens. Founded and edited *Mother Earth,* an anarchist journal suppressed in 1917. Died while working on behalf of antifascist cause in Spanish Civil War. [d. May 14, 1940]

1872 **Paul Lawrence Dunbar,** U.S. poet, short-story writer, novelist. The son of former slaves, he wrote of the lives of blacks in America. [d. February 9, 1906]

1876 **Percy Selden Straus,** U.S. merchant; co-owner of **Macy's** Department Store, New York, with his brother, Jesse Isidor Straus. [d. April 6, 1944]

1899 **Juan (Terry) Trippe,** U.S. commercial airline pioneer; founder of Pan American Airways. [d. April 3, 1981]

1913 **Philip Guston,** U.S. artist; leading representative of abstract expressionist school; best known for his depiction of the plight of blacks in America. [d. June 7, 1980]

1934 **Anna Moffo,** U.S. operatic soprano.

Historical Events

1375 Anglo-French **Truce of Bruges** confines English to Bordeaux, Bayonne, and Calais (**Hundred Years' War**).

1450 **Cade's Insurrection** begins when **Jack Cade** and 20,000 Kentsmen defeat and slay **Sir Humphry Stafford** at Sevenoaks, enter London and behead the Lord Treasurer, Lord Saye, in an attempt to stop oppressive taxation and corruption at the court of **Henry VI.**

1743 **George II** of England and his allies defeat French at **Dettingen** (**First Silesian War**).

1844 **Joseph Smith,** leader of the **Mormons,** is murdered by a mob in Carthage, Illinois.

1864 **Battle of Kennesaw Mountain,** Georgia, results in Confederate victory, temporarily checking Sherman's march to Atlanta (**U.S. Civil War**).

St. Cyril, Archbishop of Alexandria and Doctor of the Church; called *Doctor of the Incarnation.* [d. 444] Feast formerly February 9.

St. Samson of Constantinople, physician and priest. [d. 5th century]

St. John of Chinon, hermit. Also known in France as **Jean de Tours,** or **St. Jean du Moustier.** [d. 6th century]

St. George Mtasmindeli, Abbot of Iviron. [d. 1066]

St. Ladislaus of Hungary, King of Hungary. Helped organize First Crusade. [d. 1095]

The Beatified

Blessed Benvenuto of Gubbio, monk. [d. 1232]

Blessed Madeleine Fontaine and her companions, virgins and martyrs. [d. 1794]

1950   U.S. President **Harry S. Truman** orders U.S. forces into battle in aid of South Korea (**Korean War**).

1961   **Arthur Michael Ramsey** is enthroned as the 100th Archbishop of Canterbury.

1977   **Republic of Djibouti** is proclaimed.

June 28

The Saints

St. Irenaeus, bishop and martyr. [d. c. 202] Obligatory Memorial.

SS. Plutarch, Potamiaena and their companions, martyrs. [d. c. 202]

Birthdates

1476 **Pope Paul IV,** pope 1555–59. [d. August 18, 1559]

1491 **Henry VIII,** King of England, 1509–47. Notorious for his conflicts with Roman Catholic Church over issue of divorce. Married six times in an attempt to father a male heir to the throne. Separated Anglican Church from Roman Catholic Church. [d. January 28, 1547]

1577 **Peter Paul Rubens,** Flemish painter; renowned for excellence of his coloring and for painting plump female nudes as well as historical and sacred subjects. [d. May 30, 1640]

1712 **Jean-Jacques Rousseau,** French philosopher, educator, author whose theories greatly influenced the development of the French Revolution and Romanticism. [d. July 2, 1778]

1819 **Carlotta Gris,** Italian ballerina; cousin of **Girdetta** and **Guilio Grisi,** famous Italian operatic singers. [d. May 20, 1899]

1824 **Pierre Paul Broca,** 19th-century French anthropologist, surgeon; *convolution of Broca* (area of the brain) named for him. [d. July 9, 1880]

1831 **Joseph Joachim,** Hungarian violinist, composer; Director of musical **Hochschule** at Berlin, 1868–1907. [d. August 15, 1907]

1858 **Otis Skinner,** U.S. stage actor. [d. January 4, 1942]

1865 **Sir David Young Cameron,** British painter and etcher. [d. September 16, 1945]

1867 **Luigi Pirandello,** Italian playwright, novelist, short-story writer; Nobel Prize in literature, 1934. [d. December 10, 1936]

1873 **Alexis Carrel,** U.S. surgeon, born in France; Nobel Prize in physiology or medicine for development of vascular suture and surgical transplantation of blood vessels and organs. [d. November 5, 1944]

1875 **Henri Lebesque,** French mathematician; revolutionized integral calculus. [d. July 26, 1941]

1883 **Pierre Laval,** French lawyer, politician; Premier of France, 1931–32; 1935–36; 1942–45; executed for treason for collaborationist policy toward Germans. [d. October 15, 1945]

1889 **Harold W(illis) Dodd,** U.S. educator; president, Princeton University, 1933–57. [d. October 25, 1980]

1891 **Carl Spaatz,** U.S. air force general; led U.S. troops in World Wars I and II both in European and Pacific theaters. Orchestrated strategic bombings of Japan which ended with dropping of atomic bombs on Hiroshima and Nagasaki. [d. July 14, 1974]

1902 **Richard Rodgers,** U.S. composer; famous for his music for the theater, written in collaboration with Lorenz Hart (May 2), and Oscar Hammerstein II (July 12). [d. December 30, 1979]

1905 **Ashley Montagu (Montague Francis),** British-U.S. anthropologist, writer.

1906 **Marie Goeppert-Mayer,** German-U.S. physicist; Nobel Prize in physics for discoveries regarding atomic nucleus shell structure (with J. Hans D. Jensen), 1963. [d. February 20, 1972]

1909 **Eric Ambler,** British novelist; a specialist in novels of international intrigue.

1926 **Mel Brooks (Melvin Kaminsky),** U.S. filmmaker, comedian.

Historical Events

1098 Crusaders defeat Turks at **Antioch** (**First Crusade**).

1519 **Charles I** of Spain is elected Holy Roman Emperor assuming the name **Charles V.**

1629 **Peace of Alais** ends **Huguenot Wars.** Huguenots obtain religious freedom and dissolve their political organization.

St. Austell, monk. [d. 6th century]

Pope St. Paul I. Elected pope 757. [d. 767]

St. Heimrad. [d. 1019]

St. Sergius and **St. Germanus** of Valaam, abbots. Germanus also called **Herman.** [death date unknown]

1840 British fleet blockades **Canton (First Opium War).**

1841 Jean Coralli's ballet, *Giselle,* premieres in Paris at the Théâtre de l'Académie Royale de Musique. It is destined to become one of the classic tragedies of ballet.

1894 U.S. Congress establishes the first Monday in September as **Labor Day.**

1914 **Archduke Francis Ferdinand,** heir to the Austrian throne, and his wife are murdered at **Sarajevo, Bosnia** by a student, **Gavrilo Princip,** acting as an agent of the Serbian terrorist group *The Black Hand.* The incident touches off **World War I**.

1919 The **Treaty of Versailles,** ending World War I, is signed in the Hall of Mirrors at Versailles.

China refuses to sign the **Treaty of Versailles** because of a stipulation awarding Shantung Concessions to Japan.

1934 **Federal Housing Administration** is created to insure loans for new construction in an effort to stimulate activity in the U.S. housing industry.

1939 First commercial **trans-Atlantic passenger air service** begins with Pan American Airways *Yankee Clipper* flight from Port Washington, New York, to Marseilles, France.

1948 The **Cominform** (Communist Information Bureau) expels **Yugoslavia** from membership for doctrinal errors and hostility to the Soviet Union.

Independence National Historical Park in Philadelphia, Pennsylvania becomes part of the U.S. National Park System. The Park includes the **Liberty Bell Pavilion** and **Independence Hall.**

1950 **Seoul, South Korea** is captured by invading North Korean Communist troops. President **Syngman Rhee** escapes to Taejon (**Korean War**).

1951 First commercial **color television** broadcast is aired in New York City by Columbia Broadcasting System.

1967 All tariffs on industrial goods moving within the **European Economic Community** member countries are abolished.

June 29

Holidays

Colombia, Costa Rica, Peru, San Marino, Vatican City, Venezuela	Feast of SS. Peter and Paul
Seychelles	**Independence Day** Commemorates Seychelles' proclamation of independence from Great Britain, 1976.

Birthdates

1721 **Johann, Baron de Kalb,** French army officer born in Germany; accompanied Lafayette to America; he died in Battle of Camden (American Revolution). [d. August 16, 1780]

1798 **Count Giacomo Leopardi,** Italian poet, scholar; leading Italian poet of **pessimism.** [d. June 14, 1837]

1849 **Count Sergei Yulievich Witte,** Russian statesman; first constitutional Russian premier, 1905–06. [d. March 13, 1915]

1852 **John Bach McMaster,** U.S. historian, educator; noted for his eight-volume *Volumes of the History of the People of the United States from the Revolution to the Civil War,* as well as numerous historical textbooks which focus on social and economic forces influencing history. [d. May 24, 1932]

1858 **George Washington Goethals,** U.S. army officer; engineer in charge of construction of **Panama Canal,** 1907–14. Appointed first Governor of Canal Zone, 1914. [d. January 21, 1928]

Julia Clifford Lathrop, U.S. social worker; chief of U.S. Dept. of Labor, Children's Bureau, 1912–25. Member of Advisory Committee on Child Welfare for League of Nations, 1925–32. Friend and co-worker of Jane Addams (September 6). [d. April 15, 1932]

1861 **William James Mayo,** U.S. surgeon; with his brother, Charles Horace Mayo (July 19), founded the Mayo Foundation for Medical Education and Research (**Mayo Clinic**), 1915. [d. July 28, 1939]

1863 **James Harvey Robinson,** U.S. historian, educator; co-founder of the **New School for Social Research.** Author of *The Mind in the Making,* a study of the intellectual history of mankind. [d. February 16, 1936]

1865 **William Edgar Borah,** U.S. lawyer, politician; U.S. Senator, 1907–40; maintained an isolationist policy toward all proposed American involvement in foreign relations during his political career; strongly opposed U.S. joining League of Nations. [d. January 19, 1940]

1868 **George Ellery Hale,** U.S. astronomer; influential in establishment of **Yerkes Observatory,** Wisconsin; director of **Mt. Wilson Observatory,** California, where he pioneered solar research; responsible for securing funding for construction of **Mt. Palomar Observatory,** California. Invented **spectroheliograph** for photographing surface of the sun. [d. February 21, 1938]

1871 **Luisa Tetrazzini,** Italian operatic coloratura soprano. [d. April 28, 1940]

1875 **Edwin Walter Kemmerer,** U.S. economist; financial adviser to numerous foreign governments. [d. December 16, 1945]

1910 **Frank Loesser,** U.S. composer, lyricist; noted for his musical film and stage scores, including *Guys and Dolls, Most Happy Fella.* Also achieved fame for war songs, including *Praise the Lord and Pass the Ammunition,* 1942. [d. July 28, 1969]

1919 **Slim Pickens (Louis Bert Lindley),** U.S. character actor, principally in 1940s westerns. [d. December 8, 1983]

1930 **Oriana Fallaci,** Italian journalist, writer; frequent contributor to *New York Times Magazine, Life, Look;* well-known for her in-depth interviews of world famous persons.

Religious Calendar

The Saints

St. Peter, Apostle and martyr. One of the 12 original disciples of Jesus Christ, first Bishop of Rome, leader of Christian community after Christ's death. Patron of fishermen, locksmiths, cobblers. [d. c. 64] [major holy day, Episcopal Church; minor festival, Lutheran Church]

St. Paul, Apostle of the Gentiles. Through his letters he has had a profound and lasting influence on the development of Christianity. Patron of Rome and of ropemakers. Invoked against hail and snakebite. [d. c. 67] [major holy day, Episcopal Church; minor festival, Lutheran Church]

St. Cassius, Bishop of Narni. [d. 538]

St. Salome and **St. Judith.** [d. 9th century]

St. Emma, widow. Also called **Hemma.** [d. c. 1045]

St. Elwin, Bishop of Lindsey. Also called Æthelwine. [death date unknown]

1936   **Harmon (Clayton) Killebrew,** U.S. baseball player; elected to Baseball Hall of Fame, 1984.

1941   **Stokely Carmichael,** U.S. black militant leader; Chairman of **Student Nonviolent Coordinating Committee,** 1966; Prime Minister of **Black Panther Party,** 1967–69. Proponent of Black Power and militant tactics to achieve racial equality in U.S.

Historical Events

1236   **Ferdinand III** of Castile recaptures **Cordoba** from the Moors after 400 years of Moorish possession.

1312   **Henry VII** is crowned Holy Roman Emperor at Rome.

1408   **Council of Pisa** is called to end schism in Catholic Church, hearing charges against **Gregory XII** at Rome and **Benedict XII** at Avignon. Both are deposed and **Peter Philarges** is elected **Pope Alexander V.**

1767   **Townshend Revenue Acts** are passed by British parliament, establishing duties on tea, glass, paint, oil, lead, and paper imported into American colonies.

1880   France annexes **Tahiti** in South Pacific.

1906   **Mesa Verde National Park** in Colorado is established by an act of Congress. The park contains prehistoric cliff dwellings.

1916   **Sir Roger Casement,** the Irish leader, is convicted of high treason by a British court and sentenced to death for conspiracy with Germany (**World War I**).

1933   **Primo Carnera** knocks out **Jack Sharkey** at Madison Square Garden and becomes world heavyweight boxing champion.

1976   **Seychelles** gain independence.

1981   **Hu Yaobang** succeeds **Hua Guofeng** as Chinese Communist Party Chairman.

June 30

Holidays

Guatemala   **Army Day**
Commemorates revolution for agrarian reform, 1871.

Zaire   **Independence Day**
Commemorates Zaire's achievement of independence from Belgium, 1960.

Religious Calendar

The Saints

Martyrs of Rome. Feast of the protomartyrs of Roman Church who died in the persecution of Nero in the late 1st century. Optional Memorial.

Birthdates

1470   **Charles VIII,** King of France. [d. April 7, 1498]

1755   **Count Paul François Jean Nicolas Barras,** French revolutionary. [d. January 29, 1829]

1861   **Sir Frederick Gowland Hopkins,** British biochemist; Nobel Prize in physiology or medicine for discovery of **vitamins A and B** (with C. Eijkman), 1929. [d. May 16, 1947]

1893   **Harold Joseph Laski,** British political scientist, educator; Professor at London School of Economics, 1926–50. [d. March 24, 1950]

1896   **Wilfrid Pelletier,** Canadian conductor, pianist; founder of *Société des Concerts Symphoniques de Montréal*, 1935. [d. April 9, 1982]

1909   **Juan Bosch,** Dominican political leader; elected President of Dominican Republic, 1932.

1911   **Czeslaw Milosz,** U.S. writer born in Poland; Nobel Prize for literature, 1980.

1917   **Lena Horne,** U.S. singer.

       Buddy Rich (Bernard Rich), U.S. jazz drummer.

1919   **Susan Hayward (Edythe Marrener),** U.S. actress. [d. March 14, 1975]

1925   **Dorothy Malone,** U.S. actress.

Historical Events

1815   U.S. Captain **Stephen Decatur** concludes treaty for U.S. with Dey of Algiers, ending war declared on March 3, 1815. War was the result of Dey's harrassing U.S. ships and insisting upon tribute payments.

1854   Treaty is signed between Mexico and U.S. providing for the purchase of territory now comprising **Arizona** and **New Mexico** by the U.S. (**Gadsden Purchase**).

1892   **Homestead (Steel) Plant** strike in U.S. ends in violence and use of state troops to protect Carnegie property; the state troops remain in Homestead for 95 days protecting the plant.

1903   **Harry Lawrence Freeman,** U.S. black composer, conducts the premiere of his opera, *African Kraal,* with an all-black cast.

1906   **U.S. Pure Food and Drug Act** is passed, prohibiting the misbranding and adulteration of foods.

1908   **Meteorites** fall along the **Stony Tunguska River** in northern Siberia, creating the only meteorite craters known to have been formed in historic times.

1913   **Second Balkan War** begins as Bulgaria attacks Greece and Serbia.

1934   **Great Blood Purge** takes place in Germany as 77 Reichstag leaders are executed because of an alleged plot against Hitler.

1936   Ethiopian Emperor **Haile Selassie** addresses League of Nations, denouncing Mussolini's bombing of Ethiopia. He utters the often repeated threat *"God and history will remember your judgment."*

1943   U.S. Marines and Army land in New Georgia area, **Solomon Islands (World War II).**

St. Martial, Bishop of Limoges and missionary. [d. c. 250]

St. Bertrand, Bishop of Le Mans. Also called **Bertichramnus.** [d. 623]

St. Erentrude, virgin and abbess. [d. c. 718]

St. Theobald of Provins, hermit. Also called **Thibaud.** [d. 1066]

The Beatified

Blessed Arnulf of Villers, lay-brother. Also called **Arnoul Cornebout.** [d. 1228]

Blessed Philip Powell, martyr. [d. 1646]

1960   Independence of the **Republic of the Congo**, now **Zaire**, (formerly **Belgian Congo**) is proclaimed in Léopoldville by King Baudouin of Belgium.

1969   Spain returns southern Atlantic region of **Ifni** to Morocco after 35 years of occupation.

1971   Russian *Soyuz 11* cosmonauts Georgi T. Dobrovolsky, Victor I. Volkov, and Vladislav N. Patsayev complete a flight setting a new space endurance record of 570 hours, 22 minutes (although all 3 cosmonauts died 30 minutes before landing due to a sudden drop in air pressure when the ship's seals failed.)

     The **26th Amendment** to the U.S. Constitution, extending full voting rights to 18-year-olds, receives necessary ratification when Ohio legislature approves it.

1977   **The Southeast Asia Treaty Organization,** a regional defense league founded in 1954, is dissolved after 23 years.

July

July is the seventh month of the Gregorian Calendar and has 31 days. In the early Roman 10-month calendar it was named *Quintilis* 'fifth,' designating the position it occupied in that calendar. The name of the month was changed to *Iulius* (hence our *July*) in honor of Julius Caesar; ironically, the adoption of the change took effect in 44 B.C., the year of Caesar's assassination.

The "dog days" of summer, the hottest part of the year in the northern hemishpere, were recognized by the Romans as corresponding to the heliacal rising of the star they called *Canicula*, 'Little Dog,' which is now known as Sirius. This star, in the constellation Canis Major, rises above the horizon before sunrise during the period of July 3 to August 11. Its brightness apparently suggested that it added to the heat from the sun, hence, the "dog days," with allusion to the Roman name for Sirius.

In the astrological calendar, July spans the zodiac signs of Cancer, the Crab (June 22–July 22) and Leo, the Lion (July 23–August 22).

The birthstone for July is the ruby, and the flower is the larkspur or water lily.

State, National, and International Holidays

Independence or Decoration Day
(United States)
July 4

Kadooment Day
(Barbados)
First Monday

Constitution Day
(Cayman Islands)
First Monday

Caribbean Day
(Guyana)
First Monday

Family Day
(Lesotho)
First Monday

Heroes Day
(Zambia)
First Monday

International Cooperation Day
(U.S.S.R.)
First Saturday

Feria de San Fermin
(Spain)
Second Week

Fishermen's Day
(U.S.S.R.)
Second Sunday

Unity Day
(Zambia)
Second Tuesday

Girls' Fair
(Romania)
Third Sunday

Il Redentore
(Venice; gondola race and procession)
Third Sunday

Metallurgists' Day
(U.S.S.R.)
Third Sunday

President's Day
(Botswana)
Second or Third Monday

Trade Workers' Day
(U.S.S.R.)
Fourth Sunday

Special Events and Their Sponsors

July Belongs to Blueberries
North American Blueberry Council
P.O. Box 166
Marmora, New Jersey 08223

Eye Safety Month
American Society for the Prevention of Blindness
79 Madison Avenue
New York, New York 10016

Hitch Hiking Month
Richard R. Falk Associates
1472 Broadway
New York, New York 10036

National Hot Dog Month
National Hot Dog and Sausage Council
400 West Madison Avenue
Chicago, Illinois 60606

Man Watchers' Compliment Week
First Week
Man Watchers, Inc.
8033 Sunset Boulevard
Suite 363
Los Angeles, California 90046

National Ice Cream Week
Week containing July 15
Dairymen, Inc.
10140 Linn Station Road
Louisville, Kentucky 40233

National Cheer Up the Lonely Day
July 11
The Cheerer Upper Club
66 Maryland Drive
Battle Creek, Michigan 49017

Carnation Day
July 4
Puns Corp.
c/o Robert L. Birch
Box 2364
Falls Church, Virginia 22042

Special Days—Other Calendars

	10 Dhu'1 Hijjah	1 Muharram	Tish Ab B'Ab
1985			July 27
1986			
1987			
1988	July 26		July 23
1989	July 15		
1990	July 5	July 24	July 31

July 1

Birthdates

1481 **Christian II,** King of Denmark and Norway, 1513–23, and of Sweden, 1520–22. [d. January 25, 1559]

1506 **Louis II** of Hungary, 1516–26. [d. August 29, 1526]

1534 **Frederick II** of Denmark and Norway. [d. April 4, 1588]

1646 **Gottfried Wilhelm von Leibniz,** German philosopher, mathematician, diplomat. [d. November 14, 1716]

1725 **Jean Baptiste Donatien de Vimeur, Comte de Rochambeau,** French Army marshal; commanded French forces in America during the American Revolution. [d. May 10, 1807]

1804 **George Sand (Amandine Aurore Lucie Dupin),** French writer; known for her controversial writings and lifestyle. Liaisons, both romantic and artistic, were formed with Jules Sandeau, Alfred de Musset, and Frédéric Chopin. [d. June 8, 1876]

1846 **William Howard Brett,** U.S. librarian; responsible for many innovations in library science. [d. August 24, 1918]

1854 **Albert Bushnell Hart,** U.S. historian, professor, and editor; leading contributor to field of American history; Professor of History, Harvard College, 1883–1926. [d. June 16, 1943]

1872 **Louis Blériot,** French aviator; first to cross the **English Channel** in a heavier-than-air machine. [d. August 2, 1936]

1877 **Benjamin Oliver Davis,** U.S. army general; first black general in U.S. Army [d. November 26, 1970]

1879 **Léon Jouhaux,** French labor leader, politician; Secretary-General of Confèdèration Gènèrale du Travail, 1909–40, 1945–47; Nobel Peace Prize, 1951. [d. April 28, 1954]

1893 **Walter Francis White,** U.S. author, civil rights leader; Secretary of NAACP, 1930–35. [d. March 21, 1955]

1899 **Charles Laughton,** British actor. [d. December 15, 1962]

1902 **William Wyler,** U.S. film director, producer. [d. July 27, 1981]

José Luis Sert, U.S. architect born in Spain; Dean, Harvard University Graduate School of Design, 1953–69. [d. March 15, 1983]

1916 **Olivia de Havilland,** U.S. actress, born in England.

1921 **Sir Seretse M. Khama,** Botswanean statesman; Prime Minister of Bechuanaland, 1965–66; President of Botswana, 1966–80. [d. July 13, 1980]

1925 **Farley Granger,** U.S. actor.

1929 **Gerald Maurice Edelman,** U.S. biochemist; Nobel Prize in physiology or medicine for research into chemical structure of **antibodies,** 1972.

1942 **Genevieve Bujold,** French-Canadian actress.

Karen Black (Karen Ziegler), U.S. actress.

1961 **Carl Lewis,** U.S. athlete.

Somali Democratic Republic	**Union Day** Commemorates the reunification of the British and Italian sectors, 1960.
Surinam	**Day of Freedom**
Nationalist China	**Bank Holiday**

Religious Calendar

The Saints

St. Shenute, abbot. Also called **Shenoudi.** [d. c. 466]

St. Theodoric, abbot. Also called **Thieri, Thierry.** [d. 533]

St. Carilefus, abbot. Also called **Calais, Carilephus.** [d. c. 540]

St. Gall, Bishop of Clermont. [d. 551]

St. Eparchius. Also called **Cybar, Cybard, Separcus.** [d. 581]

St. Simeon Salus, monk and hermit. [d. c. 590]

St. Serf, bishop; patron of the **Orkney Islands** off the coast of Scotland. Also called **Servanus, Suranus.** [d. 6th century]

The Beatified

Blessed Thomas Maxfield, priest and martyr. Also called **Macclesfield.** [d. 1616]

Blessed Oliver Plunket, Archbishop of Armagh and martyr. [d. 1681] Feast Formerly July 11.

Historical Events

1097 Crusaders defeat Turks at **Dorylaeum (First Crusade).**

1190 **Richard I** of England and **Philip II** of France start on the **Third Crusade.**

1543 **Peace of Greenwich** between England and Scotland provides that **Prince Edward** will marry **Mary, Queen of Scotland.**

1569 **Union of Lublin** merges **Poland** and **Lithuania.**

1810 **Louis Bonaparte,** King of Holland, abdicates.

1863 **Battle of Gettysburg,** one of the decisive battles of the **U.S. Civil War,** begins.

1867 **Dominion of Canada** is created by the **British North America Act;** the Dominion consists of Nova Scotia, New Brunswick, Lower and Upper Canada.

1885 **King Leopold** of Belgium is proclaimed sovereign of the state of the **Congo.**

1898 The **Battle of San Juan Hill,** Cuba, is fought between the Americans and Spanish forces, with Col. **Theodore Roosevelt** commanding the **Rough Riders**. (**Spanish-American War**).

1916 **Battle of the Somme,** Allied offensive on the Western front, opens with bombardment of German positions (**World War I**).

1927 *First Piano Concerto* by **Béla Bartók** premieres in Frankfurt.

1931 First trip around the world by airplane is completed by **Wiley Post,** pilot, and Harold Gatty, navigator (New York to New York in 8 days, 15 hours).

Benguela-Katanga railway, the first trans-Africa line, is completed.

1942 **Sevastopol** falls to Germans after an 8-month siege (**World War II**).

1944 **Bretton Woods Conference,** a UN conference making financial plans for the postwar world, begins.

1960 **Italian Somaliland** and **British Somaliland** are united to form the independent **Somali Democratic Republic.**

1962 **Kingdom of Burundi, Republic of Rwanda** become independent.

1969 **Queen Elizabeth II** invests her son, Prince Charles, as **Prince of Wales** in ceremonies at Caernarvon Castle, Wales.

U.S. Truth-in-Lending Law goes into effect.

1974 **Isabel Perón** becomes the first woman chief of state in the Americas when she assumes presidency of Argentina upon the death of her husband, **Juan Perón.**

1980 *Ó Canada* is officially proclaimed Canada's national anthem.

July 2

Holidays

Italy (Siena)   **Il Palio**
A day of medieval sport, featuring horse racing and flag throwing in medieval garb.

Religious Calendar

The Saints

St. Monegundis, widow. Also called **Monegoude.** [d. 570]

St. Otto, Bishop of Bamberg. Also called **Otho.** [d. 1139]

St. Processus and Martinian, martyrs. [death date unknown]

Birthdates

1489   **Thomas Cranmer,** English churchman, reformer; Archbishop of Canterbury, 1533–55. Adviser to Henry VIII, especially in Henry's divorces and declaration of supremacy over the Church of England. One of the principal authors of *Book of Common Prayer.* Convicted of heresy during reign of Queen Mary I; burned at the stake. [d. March 21, 1556]

1714   **Christoph Willibald (Ritters von) Gluck,** German composer; innovator in operatic composition, his masterpieces such as *Orfeo ed Eurydice* (Italian libretto) revolutionized opera. [d. November 15, 1787]

1724   **Friedrich Gottlieb Klopstock,** German poet; first to use free verse in German; reformer of German literature. [d. March 14, 1803]

1821   **Sir Charles Topper,** Canadian statesman; Prime Minister, 1896; responsible for Nova Scotia's becoming a province of Canada. [d. October 30, 1915]

1861   **John Sanburn Phillips,** U.S. editor, publisher. [d. February 28, 1949]

1862   **Sir William Henry Bragg,** British physicist; with his son, W. L. Bragg, pioneered study of **molecular structures of crystals;** Nobel Prize in physics (with W. L. Bragg), 1915.

1877   **Hermann Hesse,** German author living in Switzerland, whose works include *Siddhartha,* and *Steppenwolf;* Nobel Prize in literature, 1946. [d. August 9, 1962]

1893   **Emanuel Neumann,** U.S. Zionist leader, lawyer, business executive; key figure in establishment of **Israel;** founder of **Tarbuth Foundation for the Advancement of Hebrew Culture.** [d. October 26, 1980]

1898   **Anthony Clement McAuliffe,** U.S. army general; distinguished himself during World War II, particularly during **Battle of the Bulge.** [d. August 11, 1975]

1903   **Olaf V,** King of Norway, 1957– .

1906   **Hans Albrecht Bethe,** U.S. physicist born in Germany; Nobel Prize in physics for contributions to theory of **nuclear reaction,** 1967.

1908   **Thurgood Marshall,** U.S. jurist, lawyer; Associate Justice, U.S. Supreme Court, 1967– . First black to serve on Supreme Court.

1918   **Robert William Sarnoff,** U.S. electronics and communications executive; President of RCA Corporation, 1966–71; Chairman of Board of RCA, 1970–75; Director of RCA Global Communications, 1973– .

1925   **Medgar Evers,** U.S. civil rights leader; field secretary, NAACP, 1954–63. Assassinated. [d. June 12, 1963]

Patrice Lumumba, African nationalist; leader and first premier of **Republic of the Congo,** 1960. [d. February 12, 1961]

1931   **Imelda Marcos,** Philippine political leader; wife of Philippine President Ferdinand Marcos.

1937   **Richard Petty,** U.S. auto racer.

The Beatified

Blessed Peter of Luxemburg, Bishop of Metz and Cardinal; patron of **Avignon.** [d. 1387]

Historical Events

1819 **Factory Act** is passed in Great Britain, prohibiting employment of children under 9 years of age in cotton mills.

1853 Russian army crosses Pruth River, invading Turkey and beginning **Crimean War.**

1862 **Morrill Act** is passed by U.S. Congress, providing for endowment of at least one agricultural (land-grant) college in each state.

1871 The government of newly unified **Italy** establishes its seat at Rome.

1881 **James A. Garfield,** U.S. president, is shot by **Charles J. Guiteau;** Garfield dies on September 19.

1890 **Sherman Anti-Trust Law** is enacted in U.S., curtailing the powers of U.S. business monopolies.

1900 *Finlandia* by **Jean Sibelius** premieres.

1917 The pro-Allied Greek government under King **Alexander** declares war on Germany and Austria-Hungary, Bulgaria, and Turkey **(World War I).**

1932 **Franklin Delano Roosevelt,** accepting Democratic presidential nomination, pledges a *New Deal* for the American people.

1937 U.S. aviator **Amelia Earhart** disappears over the Pacific during an attempt to circumnavigate the globe.

1940 **Lake Washington** floating bridge in Seattle, the greatest floating structure ever built, opens to traffic.

1947 The U.S.S.R. rejects U.S. **Marshall Plan** for European recovery.

1964 U.S. President **Lyndon B. Johnson** signs the **Civil Rights Act** of 1964, prohibiting discrimination on the basis of race, sex, or national origin in public accommodations and federally assisted programs.

1976 **North and South Vietnam** are reunited, with **Hanoi** as the capital. The country had been divided since the 1954 Geneva Agreement following the French defeat at Dien Bien Phu.

July 3

Religious Calendar

Feast

St. Thomas, Apostle of the Indies and martyr; patron of architects, builders, and divines; surnamed *Didymus* or *the Twin.* [d. 1st century] Feast formerly December 21.

Birthdates

1728 **Robert Adam,** English architect, furniture designer, decorator. [d. March 3, 1792]

1738 **John Singleton Copley,** American painter; known for his direct, realistic portraits of New Englanders, biblical scenes, and historical events; one of first great American painters. [d. September 9, 1815]

1746 **Henry Grattan,** Irish statesman; worked for Irish independence and Catholic emancipation. [d. June 6, 1820]

1854 **Leoš Janáček,** Czech composer; most of his works are based upon Czech folk music. [d. August 12, 1928]

1878 **George M(ichael) Cohan,** U.S. composer, playwright, actor, producer; known as much for his exuberant stage presence as for his talents; received Congressional Medal of Honor for spirited efforts in elevating morale in World War I, especially for song, *Over There!*. [d. November 5, 1942]

1883 **Franz Kafka,** Austrian novelist; his psychological and philosophical works display a desperation in man's awareness of his plight in modern society. Most of his works were published posthumously. [d. June 3, 1924]

1909 **Stavros Spyros Niarchos,** Greek shipping executive; pioneer of **supertanker shipping.**

1927 **Ken Russell,** British film director; achieved worldwide acclaim for his BBC film documentaries of famous people including Henri Rousseau, Isadora Duncan, Richard Strauss.

1935 **Harrison (*Jack*) Schmitt,** U.S. politician, geologist, astronaut; U.S. Senator, 1977– .

1937 **Tom Stoppard (Thomas Straussler),** British writer born in Czechoslovakia; noted for such award winning plays as *Rosencrantz and Guildenstern Are Dead.*

1947 **Michael Burton,** U.S. swimmer. Olympic gold medalist, 1968 and 1972.

1951 **Jean-Claude Duvalier,** Haitian leader; President, 1971– .

Historical Events

1608 **Samuel de Champlain** establishes European settlement on site of city of **Quebec.**

1775 **George Washington** takes command of **Continental Army** at Cambridge, Massachusetts (**American Revolution**).

1866 **Venetia** is ceded to Italy, marking a major step in the unification of **Italy.**

Battle of Königgrätz or **Sadowa,** decisive battle of the **Seven Weeks' War** between the Prussians and Austrians, ends in a tactical victory for the Prussians.

1880 **Madrid Convention** is signed by leading European powers and the U.S., recognizing independence and integrity of Morocco.

1890 **Idaho** joins the Union as the 43rd state.

1930 **U.S. Veterans Administration** is created by **Veterans Administration Act.**

1962 France formally proclaims the independence of **Algeria.**

1970 **Portugal** recalls its ambassador to the Vatican and delivers a formal protest over the meeting of **Pope Paul VI** with leaders of independence movements in Portugal's African territories.

1979 West German government votes to continue prosecution of **Nazi war criminals** by removing the statute of limitations on murder.

The Saints

St. Anatolius, Bishop of Laodicea. [d. c. 283]

St. Julius and **St. Aaron,** martyrs. [d. 304]

St. Heliodorus, Bishop of Altino. [d. c. 400]

St. Anatolius, Bishop and Patriarch of Constantinople. [d. 458]

St. Germanus of Man, bishop. Also called **Garmon, German.** [d. c. 475]

St. Leo II, pope; elected 682. [d. 683]

St. Rumold, martyr and bishop. Also called **Rombaut.** [d. c. 775]

St. Bernardino Realino, Jesuit. [d. 1616]

July 4

Holidays

Denmark	**Rebildfest** Largest celebration of America's independence held outside U.S.
Philippines	**Philippine-American Friendship Day**
Tonga	**Birthday of His Majesty, King Taufa'ahau Tupou IV**
U.S. (including Guam, Puerto Rico, Virgin Islands)	**Independence Day** Celebrates the signing of the Declaration of Independence, 1776.
U.S. (Wisconsin)	**Indian Rights Day**
Yugoslavia	**Fighter's Day**

Birthdates

1610 **Paul Scarron,** French comic poet, novelist, and dramatist. [d. October 6, 1660]

1736 **Robert Raikes,** British publisher, philanthropist; developer of concept of **Sunday School.** [d. April 5, 1811]

1793 **Friedrich Bleek,** German theologian, Bible scholar. [d. February 27, 1859]

1799 **Oscar I, King of Sweden,** 1844–59. [d. July 8, 1859]

1804 **Nathaniel Hawthorne,** U.S. author of *The Scarlet Letter*; member of the *Concord Circle* of great American writers. His work is marked by a preoccupation with evil and the dark side of man's nature. [d. May 19, 1864]

1807 **Giuseppe Garibaldi,** Italian military leader; key figure in the movement of **Italian unification;** with his Redshirts, defeated the Kingdom of the Two Sicilies, 1860, by expelling Francis II from Naples. Marched against Rome twice, 1862, 1867, but was defeated both times. [d. June 2, 1882]

1826 **Stephen (Collins) Foster,** U.S. composer; most famous for his ballads and minstrel songs inspired by a romantic view of life in the *Old South*. Some of his best known works are: *Oh, Susannah, My Old Kentucky Home,* and *Beautiful Dreamer.* [d. January 13, 1864]

1845 **Jan Hendrik Hofmeyr,** South African politician, editor; member of Cape Parliament, 1879–95; firm supporter of federation in South Africa. [d. October 16, 1909]

1858 **Emmeline Pankhurst,** British suffragist, barrister, radical; known for her unorthodox, often extreme methods of achieving attention for her cause, including arson, bombing, and hunger strikes. [d. June 14, 1928]

1872 **(John) Calvin Coolidge,** (*Silent Cal*) U.S. lawyer; 30th President of U.S., 1923–29; administration was marked by conservative economic policies and nonaggressive foreign policies. [d. January 5, 1933]

1885 **Louis B(urt) Mayer,** U.S. film producer born in Russia; his fortune was based on the establishment of the *motion picture* as the foundation of American entertainment; founded Louis B. Mayer Picture Corporation, which eventually evolved into Metro-Goldwyn-Mayer Studio. [d. October 29, 1957]

1898 **Gertrude Lawrence,** British actress. [d. September 6, 1952]

1900 **(Daniel) Louis (*Satchmo*) Armstrong,** U.S. jazz musician. [d. July 6, 1971]

1905 **Lionel Trilling,** U.S. critic, author. [d. November 5, 1975]

1918 **Ann Landers (Esther Pauline Friedman),** U.S. journalist; syndicated columnist of extremely popular advice-to-the-lovelorn column. Twin sister of Abigail Van Buren.

Abigail Van Buren (Pauline Esther Friedman), U.S. journalist; syndicated ad-

Religious Calender

St. Bertha, widow and abbess. [d. c. 725]

St. Andrew of Crete, Archbishop of Gortyn; preacher, and poet. Also called **St. Andrew of Jerusalem.** [d. c. 740]

St. Oda, Archbishop of Canterbury. Also called **Oda** or **Odo the Good.** [d. 959]

St. Ulric, Bishop of Augsburg. Also called **Udalric.** [d. 973]

St. Elizabeth, widow and queen of Portugal. Also called **Isabel, Isabella.** [d. 1336] Feast formerly July 8. Optional Memorial.

The Beatified

Blessed William of Hirschau, abbot. [d. 1091]

Blessed John Cornelius and his companions, the Dorchester martyrs. [d. 1594]

Blessed William Andleby and his companions, martyrs. William Andleby also called **Anlaby.** [d. 1597]

Birthdates

1610   **Paul Scarron,** French comic poet, novelist, and dramatist. [d. October 6, 1660]

1736   **Robert Raikes,** British publisher, philanthropist; developer of concept of **Sunday School.** [d. April 5, 1811]

1793   **Friedrich Bleek,** German theologian, Bible scholar. [d. February 27, 1859]

1799   **Oscar I, King of Sweden,** 1844–59. [d. July 8, 1859]

vice columnist, creator of *Dear Abby.* Twin sister of Ann Landers.

    King Taufa'ahau Tupou IV, King of Tonga, 1965– .

1924   **Eva Marie Saint,** U.S. actress.

1927   **Neil Simon,** U.S. playwright; author of highly successful comedies for stage and screen.

1928   **Gina Lollobrigida,** Italian actress.

1935   **Paul Scoon,** Governor-General, State of Grenada, 1978– .

Historical Events

1776   In Philadelphia, American **Declaration of Independence** is adopted by delegates to the Continental Congress.

1804   **U.S. Military Academy** at **West Point** formally opens.

1817   Construction of **Erie Canal** begins; the canal officially opens on October 26, 1825.

1828   **Baltimore and Ohio Railroad,** the first public railroad in the U.S., is begun.

1863   **Vicksburg** surrenders to Union forces, giving Union control of the Mississippi River **(U.S. Civil War).**

1884   The **Statue of Liberty** is formally presented to the U.S. by France.

1903   First Pacific **telegraph cable,** between San Francisco and Manila, is put into operation.

1919   **Jack Dempsey** knocks out **Jess Willard** to win the heavyweight boxing championship.

1946   **Republic of the Philippines** is proclaimed with **Manuel A. Roxas** as first president.

1960   New 50-star **U.S. flag** is officially flown for the first time.

1966   **Queen Elizabeth II** and **Prince Philip** of Great Britain escape injury in Belfast, Northern Ireland, when a 30-pound concrete block drops on the car in which they are riding.

1976   The U.S. celebrates its **Bicentennial** with pageantry, prayer, games, parades, picnics, and fireworks. In New York City millions watch an armada of tall-masted sailing ships from 31 countries pass in review on the Hudson River.

1979   Former Algerian President, **Ahmed Ben Bela,** is released after 14 years of house arrest; he is considered by many a national hero for his role in Algeria's struggle for independence.

July 5

Birthdates

1731 **Samuel Huntington,** American jurist; signer of the Declaration of Independence. [d. January 5, 1796]

1755 **Sarah Siddons (Sarah Kemble),** Welsh actress; renowned for her portrayal of various Shakespearean roles, especially Lady Macbeth. [d. June 8, 1831]

1801 **David Glasgow Farragut,** U.S. naval officer; Union admiral during U.S. Civil War; first person to hold rank of admiral in U.S. history. Renowned for his aggressive naval tactics. [d. August 14, 1870]

1803 **George Henry Borrow,** British linguist, writer, traveler; especially known for his Romany lexicon. [d. July 26, 1881]

1810 **P(hineas) T(aylor) Barnum,** U.S. showman. Formed **Barnum and Bailey Circus,** *the Greatest Show on Earth*, basing his success on the gullibility of audiences. Specialized in human and animal curiosities and extravagant exaggerations. [d. April 7, 1871]

1820 **William John McQuorn Rankine,** Scottish civil engineer, physicist; best known for research in **molecular physics.** [d. December 24, 1872]

1841 **William Collins Whitney,** U.S. businessman, government official; influential in breaking up the Tweed Ring; U.S. Secretary of the Navy, 1885–89. [d. February 2, 1904]

1853 **Cecil John Rhodes,** British administrator, financier; acquired fortune in Kimberley diamond fields; formed De Beers Consolidated Mines, 1888; Prime Minister of Cape Colony, 1890–96; endowed 70 scholarships for education at Oxford University (**Rhodes Scholarships**). [d. March 26, 1902]

1870 **Richard Bedford Bennett,** Canadian statesman; Prime Minister, 1930–35. [d. June 26, 1947]

1872 **Edouard Herriot,** French statesman; Prime Minister, 1924–25, 1932; served in nine different cabinets. [d. March 26, 1957]

1877 **Wanda Landowska,** Polish harpsichordist, musicologist, in France. [d. August 16, 1959]

1879 **Dwight Filley Davis,** U.S. sportsman; donor of the **Davis Cup,** trophy awarded to the winner of an international tennis tournament. [d. November 28, 1945]

1888 **Herbert Spencer Gasser,** U.S. physiologist; Nobel Prize in physiology or medicine for discovery of highly differentiated functions of nerve fibers (with E. J. Erlanger), 1944. [d. May 11, 1963]

1889 **Jean Cocteau,** French poet, novelist (*Les Enfants Terribles*), playwright, essayist, filmmaker (*Orpheus*), craftsman, artist. [d. October 11, 1963]

1891 **John Howard Northrop,** U.S. biochemist; Nobel Prize in chemistry for preparation of enzymes and virus proteins in pure form (with W. M. Stanley), 1946.

1902 **Henry Cabot Lodge, Jr.,** U.S. politician, diplomat; U.S. Senator, 1936–44, 1946–52; Chief of U.S. Mission to U.N., 1953–60; U.S. Ambassador to South Vietnam, 1963–64,

The Saints

St. Athanasius the Athonite, abbot. Built first monastery at Mount Athos. [d. c. 1000]

St. Antony Zaccaria, founder of Clerks Regular of St. Paul; founded the Congregation of St. Paul (*Barnabites*). [d. 1539]

1965–67. U.S. Ambassador to Federal Republic of Germany, 1968–69; Chief U.S. negotiator at Paris peace talks on Vietnam; special U.S. envoy to Vietnam, 1970–77.

1911 **Georges Pompidou,** French statesman; Premier of France, 1962–68; President of Fifth Republic, 1969–74. [d. April 2, 1974]

1926 **Salvador Jorge Blanco,** Dominican statesman; President, Dominican Republic, 1982– .

1977 Leaders of 48 nations, all members of the **Organization of African Unity,** conclude a four-day meeting in Gabon endorsing the efforts for black rule in **Rhodesia.**

Historical Events

1809 Napoleon defeats Austrians at **Wagram.**

1821 **Venezuela** gains independence under **Simón Bolívar.**

1830 A French expeditionary force captures **Algiers** and deposes the ruler.

1884 A treaty with the king of **Togo** puts that African area under German sovereignty.

1932 **António de Oliveira Salazar** becomes Premier of Portugal.

1935 The U.S. **Wagner-Connery Act** establishes a new **National Labor Relations Board,** protecting employees' right to collective bargaining.

1943 U.S. warships bombard **Vila, Kolombangara,** and **Bairoko Harbor, New Georgia, Solomon Islands (World War II).**

1962 **Algeria** gains its independence from France.

1975 **Cape Verde Islands** achieve independence from Portugal.

July 6

Holidays

Malawi — **Republic Day**
Commemorates Malawi's (Nyasaland) declaration of independence from Great Britain, 1967.

Zambia — **Unity Day**

Religious Calendar

St. Romulus, Bishop of Fiesole, martyr. [d. c. 90]

St. Dominica, virgin and martyr. [d. c. 303]

Birthdates

1747 **John Paul Jones,** American naval officer, born in Scotland; known for his highly successful campaign against the British; honored with the only gold medal awarded by Congress to a naval officer in the Revolution, 1787. [d. July 18, 1792]

1755 **John Flaxman,** English sculptor; as designer with Josiah Wedgewood's pottery company, was responsible for the cameo-like decorations which became the **Wedgewood** trademark. [d. December 7, 1826]

1759 **Joshua Barney,** U.S. naval officer, prominent in American Revolution and War of 1812. [d. December 1, 1818]

1766 **Alexander Wilson,** U.S. ornithologist born in Scotland; pioneered science of **ornithology** in America, collecting and recording specimens for entire East Coast; published multi-volume work considered a pioneering effort in the field. [d. August 23, 1813]

1796 **Nicholas I,** Emperor of Russia, 1825–55, a reactionary ruler whose reign was marked by militarism and bureaucracy. [d. March 2, 1855]

1831 **Daniel Coit Gilman,** U.S. educator; first president of **Johns Hopkins University**; first president of **Carnegie Institution**, Washington, D.C. [d. October 13, 1908]

1832 **Maximilian (Ferdinand Maximilian Joseph),** Archduke of Austria, 1864–67; Emperor of Mexico, 1864–67 under auspices of French Emperor Napoleon III. Condemned by court martial and shot to death. [d. June 19, 1867]

1858 **José Miguel Gómez,** Cuban soldier, patriot; president, 1909–13. [d. June 13, 1921]

1859 **Verner von Heidenstam,** Swedish author, poet; Nobel Prize in literature, 1916. [d. May 20, 1940]

1863 **Ronald McKenna,** British politician; first Lord of Admiralty, 1908–11; Chairman of Midland Bank, Ltd., 1919–43. [d. September 6, 1943]

1875 **Roger Ward Babson,** U.S. statistician, economist; pioneered in developing charts to forecast business trends (**Babson charts**); presidential candidate, 1940. Founded **Babson Institute,** 1919; **Webber College,** 1927; **Utopia College,** 1946. [d. March 5, 1967]

1877 **Robert Morris Ogden,** U.S. psychologist, educator. [d. March 2, 1959]

1896 **James Spencer Love,** U.S. textile manufacturer; founder of Burlington Industries, 1923. [d. January 20, 1962]

1903 **(Alex) Hugo (Teodor) Theorell,** Swedish biochemist; Nobel Prize in physiology or medicine for his work on enzymes, 1955. [d. August 15, 1982]

1909 **Andrei Gromyko,** Russian diplomat; long-time Soviet delegate to the United Nations.

1925 **Merv Griffin,** U.S. entertainer, talk-show host.

1927 **Janet Leigh (Jeanette Morrison),** U.S. actress.

1932 **Della Reese (Delloreese Patricia Early),** U.S. entertainer.

1937 **Vladimir Ashkenazy,** Russian pianist; international concert star.

1946 **Sylvester Stallone,** U.S. film actor, writer, director.

St. Sisoes, hermit. Also called Sisoy. [d. c. 429]

St. Monenna, abbess and founder of nunnery at Killeevy. Also called Bline, Darerca. [d. c. 518]

St. Goar, solitary. [d. c. 575]

St. Sexburga, Abbess of Ely, widow. Also called Sexburgh. [d. 699]

St. Modwenna, virgin. Also called Modwena, Modwina, or Monenna. [d. 7th century]

St. Godeleva, laywoman and martyr. Locally invoked against sore throats. Also called Godeleine, Godelive. [d. 1070]

St. Mary Goretti, virgin and martyr. Also called Maria. [d. c. 1902] Optional Memorial.

The Beatified

Blessed Thomas Alfield, martyr. [d. 1585]

Historical Events

1189	Henry II of England, dies and is succeeded by Richard I.
1415	John Hus, Bohemian religious reformer and nationalist, is burned at the stake for heresy.
1535	Sir Thomas More is beheaded for refusal to recognize Henry VIII of England as the supreme head of the church.
1540	The marriage of Henry VIII of England and Anne of Cleves is declared invalid.
1553	Edward VI of England dies and is succeeded by Queen Mary I.
1777	British troops capture Fort Ticonderoga (American Revolution).
1854	First state convention of the Republican Party is held in Jackson, Michigan.
1898	By a joint resolution of Congress, Hawaii is declared a U.S. territory.
1917	Col. T. E. Lawrence (Lawrence of Arabia) leads a force of Arabs in capturing Aqaba from the Turks (World War I).
1919	First Atlantic crossing by dirigible is completed by Major G. H. Scott in British dirigible R-34.
1943	U.S. naval forces are victorious over Japanese in Battle of Kula Gulf in the Solomon Islands (World War II).
1964	Nyasaland gains independence from Great Britain as the African state of Malawai. H. Kamazu Banda is named prime minister.
1967	Civil war breaks out in Nigeria after the eastern region declares its independence as the Republic of Biafra.
1975	The Comoros Islands in the Indian Ocean declare their independence from France.

July 7

Holidays

Belgium	**Ommegang Pageant** Medieval pageant presented in the Grand Place in Brussels recreating an entertainment given in honor of **Charles V** and his court.
Solomon Islands	**Independence Day** Commemorates the gaining of independence from British rule, 1978.
Tanzania	**Saba Saba Peasants Day**

Birthdates

1586 **Thomas Hooker,** American clergyman, colonist; founded **Hartford, Connecticut;** called the *Father of Connecticut.* [d. July 19, 1647]

1673 **George Graham,** English watchmaker; developed many specialized astronomical instruments for Edmund Halley, James Bradley, and the French Academy. [d. November 16, 1751]

1752 **Joseph Marie Jacquard,** French inventor of first **machine loom** to weave intricate patterns; the machine was controlled by cards containing patterned perforations, very much like the Hollerith cards later developed for computers. [d. August 7, 1834]

1843 **Camillo Golgi,** Italian physician; known for study of nervous system; Nobel Prize in physiology or medicine for study of **nervous system** and cell distribution (with R. C. Santiago), 1906. [d. January 21, 1926]

1860 **Gustav Mahler,** Bohemian composer, conductor. [d. May 18, 1911]

1887 **Marc Chagall,** French artist born in Russia; works include paintings and engravings, murals, costumes, ceramics, stained-glass windows; avante-garde style influenced by Fauvism and Cubism.

1899 **George Cukor,** U.S. film director; director for Metro Goldwyn Mayer, 1933–82. [d. January 24, 1983]

1901 **Vittorio De Sica,** Italian film director. [d. November 13, 1974]

1906 **(Leroy Robert) Satchel Paige,** U.S. baseball player; generally regarded as one of professional baseball's greatest pitchers; elected to Baseball Hall of Fame, 1971. [d. June 8, 1982]

1907 **Robert A(nson) Heinlein,** U.S. science fiction writer.

1911 **Gian Carlo Menotti,** Italian composer, librettist, producer; Pulitzer Prize in music, 1950 and 1954. Composer of *The Medium, The Telephone,* and *Amahl and the Night Visitors,* the first opera written for television, 1951.

1917 **Lawrence O'Brien,** U.S. government official, politician; active in presidential campaigns of John F. Kennedy and George McGovern; U.S. Postmaster General, 1965–68.

1919 **William Kunstler,** U.S. lawyer, noted for his flamboyant style and defense of U.S. political activists.

1922 **Pierre Cardin,** French fashion designer.

1938 **Edmund G. Brown, Jr.,** U.S. politician, lawyer; Governor of California, 1975–82.

1940 **Ringo Starr (Richard Starkey),** British musician; drummer for The Beatles.

Historical Events

1307 **Edward I** of England dies and is succeeded by **Edward II.**

1572 **Sigismund II** of Poland dies, ending the **Jagellon Dynasty;** Poland becomes an elective kingdom.

1807 **Treaty of Tilsit** is signed by Russia, Prussia, and France, ending the fighting among them and bringing Russia into secret alliance with Napoleon.

1839 The murder of Chinese villagers by drunken British seamen precipitates the **First Opium War.**

Religious Calendar

The Saints

St. Pantaenus, one of the Fathers of the Church. Nicknamed the *Sicilian Bee.* [d. c. 200]

St. Palladius, bishop and missionary. Apostle of the Scots. [d. 432]

St. Felix, Bishop of Nantes. [d. 582]

St. Ethelburga, St. Ercongota, and **St. Sethrida,** virgins. Ethelburga is also called **Aubierge** or **Edelburge** by the French. [d. c. 664 and 660]

St. Hedda, Bishop of Winchester. [d. 705]

St. Maelruain, abbot and founder of the **Monastery of Tallaght.** Most influential figure in the reform movement of the Culdees, a monastic community in Ireland between 8th and 10th century. [d. 792]

The Beatified

Blessed Benedict XI, pope. Elected 1303. [d. 1304]

Blessed Roger Dickenson and his companions, martyrs. [d. 1591]

St. Boisil, Abbot of Melrose. Also called **Boswell.** [d. 664] Feast formerly February 23.

1919	The German government ratifies the **Versailles Treaty** ending **World War I.**
1946	**Mother Frances Xavier Cabrini** is canonized in ceremonies conducted by Pope Pius XII; she is the first American to be canonized.
1948	First **WAVE** enlisted women (Women Appointed for Voluntary Emergency) are sworn into Regular **U.S. Navy.**
1969	French and English are designated as official languages of **Canada.**
1978	**Solomon Islands** gain independence from Great Britain.
1979	First civilian elections since 1966 take place in **Nigeria.**
1981	U.S. President Ronald Reagan nominates **Sandra Day O'Connor** to become a Supreme Court justice; she becomes the first woman member of the **U.S. Supreme Court.**

July 8

Birthdates

1478 **Giangiorgio Trissino,** Italian writer, scholar; protègè of Popes Leo X, Clement VII, and Paul III; urged the standardization of Italian language, made up of parts from various Italian dialects. [d. December 8, 1550]

1621 **Jean de La Fontaine,** French poet, fabulist; created 12 volumes of fables, 1668–94. [d. March 13, 1695]

1838 **Count Ferdinand von Zeppelin,** German soldier, aeronautical engineer; responsible for construction of first rigid-bodied airship, 1900. [d. March 8, 1917]

1857 **Alfred Binet,** French psychologist; with Thèodore Simon, developed standard for measuring degrees of intelligence (**Binet** or **Binet-Simon** test). [d. October 18, 1911]

1867 **Käthe Kollwitz,** German printmaker, sculptor, etcher, and painter. [d. April 22, 1945]

1887 **Hermann Rauschning,** German statesman; noted for his strong anti-Nazi stance during World War II; immigrated to the U.S., 1942; author of *The Revolution of Nihilism* and other anti-Nazi works. [d. 1982]

1892 **Richard Aldington,** British novelist, poet. [d. July 27, 1962]

1895 **Igor Yevgenyevich Tamm,** Russian physicist; Nobel Prize in physics for discovery of **Cherenkov effect** in which radiated electrons accelerate in water to speeds greater than that of light in the same medium (with P. A. Cherenkov and I. M. Frank), 1958. [d. April 12, 1971]

1898 **Alec (Alexander Raban) Waugh,** British novelist; brother of Evelyn Waugh. [d. September 3, 1981]

1899 **David E(li) Lilienthal,** U.S. government official, lawyer; director of the Tennessee Valley Authority, 1933–45, seeing it become the largest producer of electricity in America; Chairman, Atomic Energy Commission, 1947–50. [d. January 15, 1981]

1906 **Philip (Cortelyou) Johnson,** U.S. architect, theorist; developer and proponent of **International Style** of architecture.

1908 **Nelson Aldrich Rockefeller,** U.S. politician; Governor of New York, 1959–73; U.S. Vice-President, 1974–76. [d. January 26, 1979]

1913 **Walter Francis Kerr,** U.S. journalist, playwright, drama critic for *New York Herald Tribune*, 1951–56; *New York Times*, 1956– .

1917 **Faye Emerson,** U.S. actress; noted for her starring film roles during the 1940s; one of the pioneers of early television; hosted a late-night interview show which set precedent for later shows of the same type. [d. March 9, 1983]

1933 **Marty Feldman,** British comic actor. [d. December 2, 1982]

Historical Events

1497 **Vasco da Gama** leaves Lisbon on his voyage to India during which he discovers the **Cape of Good Hope.**

1709 **Battle of Poltava** is a resounding victory for **Peter the Great** over **Charles XII** of Sweden and marks Russia's emergence as the dominant power in northern Europe (**Great Northern War**).

1853 U.S. Commodore **Matthew Perry** and his fleet arrive at **Edo Bay** with first formal bid for trade and diplomatic relations with **Japan.**

1859 **Oscar I** of Sweden dies and is succeeded by **Charles XV.**

1889 Last bare-knuckles championship **boxing** match is staged between **John L. Sullivan** and **Jake Kilrain.** Kilrain is defeated after 75 rounds.

St. Withburga, virgin. Also called **Withburge.** [d. c. 743]

St. Adrian III, pope. Elected 884. [d. 885]

St. Grimbald, monk. Also called **Grimald.** [d. 903]

St. Sunniva and her companions. [d. c. 10th century]

St. Raymund of Toulouse, Canon Regular. [d. 1118]

St. Urith of Chittlehampton, virgin and founder of Church of Chittlehampton. Also called **Erth,** or **Hieritha.** [death date unknown]

The Beatified
Blessed Eugenius III, pope. Elected 1145. [d. 1153]

1895 The **Delagoa Bay Railway** is opened from Johannesburg and Pretoria to the sea, giving the Boers in the Transvaal an economic outlet free of British influence.

1937 **Peel Report** of Great Britain recommends dividing **Palestine** into Arab and Jewish states.

1944 U.S. naval bombardment of Japanese-held **Guam** begins (**World War II**).

1950 U.S. President **Harry S. Truman** appoints General **Douglas MacArthur** commander-in-chief of all U.N. forces in Korea.

1963 U.S. government bans all financial transactions with **Cuba.**

1975 Argentine cabinet of President **Isabel Perón** resigns.

1976 Former U.S. President **Richard M. Nixon** is ordered disbarred by a New York court for obstructing the due administration of justice during his presidency.

1976 **Indonesia** launches a communications satellite from Cape Canaveral in the U.S.; the spacecraft links 40 Indonesian cities with telephone and television signals. (The only other countries with domestic satellite systems are the U.S., Canada, and the Soviet Union.)

1979 New constitution is approved in the **Congo.**

July 9

Argentina **Independence Day**
Commemorates Argentina's declaration of independence from Spain, 1816.

Religious Calendar

St. Everild, virgin. Also called **Everildis.** [d. c. 700]

St. Nicholas Pieck and his companions, the martyrs of Gorkum. [d. 1572]

Birthdates

1578 **Ferdinand II, Holy Roman Emperor,** 1619; deposed by Bohemian Protestants, beginning **Thirty Years' War.** [d. February 15, 1637]

1764 **Ann Radcliffe,** English gothic novelist. [d. February 7, 1823]

1775 **Matthew Gregory (*Monk*) Lewis,** English gothic novelist, playwright, poet; inspired by Ann Radcliffe (see above). [d. May 14, 1818]

1777 **Henry Hallam,** English historian; his son Arthur is subject of Alfred Lord Tennyson's *In Memoriam.* [d. January 21, 1859]

1819 **Elias Howe,** U.S. inventor; developed the **sewing machine,** for which he was awarded patent rights after lengthy conflict with **Isaac M. Singer,** 1854. [d. October 3, 1867]

1835 **Tomàs Estrada Palma,** first president of Cuba, 1902–1906. [d. November 4, 1908]

1839 **John D(avison) Rockefeller,** U.S. industrialist, philanthropist; founder of Standard Oil Co., 1870; built a financial empire; devoted more than $500 million to philanthropic causes. [d. May 23, 1937]

1845 **Sir George Howard Darwin,** British astronomer, mathematician; authority on tidal friction as cause of decrease in earth's rotation and angular momentum; son of **Charles Darwin.** [d. December 7, 1912]

1856 **Nikola Tesla,** U.S. electrical engineer, inventor born in Yugoslavia; developed induction, synchronous, and split-phase motors; conceived and built new types of generators and transformers which constituted basis of **alternating-current** electric power system. [d. January 7, 1943]

Daniel Guggenheim, U.S. industrialist; son of **Meyer Guggenheim;** responsible for development and management of American Smelting and Refining Company, which became the largest and most modern mining enterprise in the world, 1905–19. Established **Daniel and Florence Guggenheim Foundation** and **Daniel Guggenheim Fund for the Promotion of Aeronautics.** [d. September 28, 1930]

1858 **Franz Boas,** U.S. anthropologist born in Germany; Columbia University's first professor of anthropology; greatly influenced many subsequently great anthropologists such as Margaret Mead and Ruth Benedict. His careful study and documentation destroyed the theory of innate racial differences. [d. December 22, 1942]

Richard Achilles Ballinger, U.S. lawyer, administrator; Secretary of the Interior, 1909–11. [d. June 6, 1922]

1878 **H.V. (Hans von) Kaltenborn,** U.S. journalist, radio commentator, news analyst; chief news commentator for Columbia Broadcasting System, 1929–40; chief commentator for National Broadcasting Company, 1940–55; noted for his coverage of world news events. [d. June 14, 1965]

1887 **Samuel Eliot Morison,** U.S. historian; Professor of History, Harvard University, 1925–55; historian of naval operations in World War II, 1942–45; prolific writer whose 25 works in various aspects of American history won him wide acclaim; Pulitzer Prizes in biography, 1941, 1959. [d. May 15, 1976]

1894 **Dorothy Thompson,** U.S. journalist; syndicated columnist with *New York Herald Tribune,* 1936–42; one of the most widely-read columnists of the 1930s and 1940s. [d. January 31, 1961]

St. Veronica Giuliani, virgin, abbess, and mystic. [d. 1727]

The Martyrs of Orange. [d. 1794]

The Martyrs of China, under the Boxers. [d. 1900]

The Beatified

Blessed Jane of Reggio, virgin. [d. 1491]

1908   **Paul Brown,** U.S. football coach, executive; elected to Pro Football Hall of Fame, 1967.

1916   **Edward (Richard George) Heath,** British statesman; Prime Minister, 1970–74.

1926   **Ben Ray Mottelson,** Danish physicist; Nobel Prize in physics for discovery of connection between collective and particle motion in **atomic nucleus** (with J. Rainwater and A. N. Bohr), 1975.

1929   **Hassan II,** King of Morocco, 1961– .

1947   **O(renthal) J(ames) Simpson,** U.S. football player, actor, sportscaster.

Historical Events

1386   **Leopold III** of Austria is defeated and killed by the Swiss at **Sempach** during Swiss struggle for independence.

1686   **League of Augsburg** is created, setting the Holy Roman Empire, Spain, Sweden, Saxony, and Palatinate against **Louis XIV** of France.

1755   English General **Edward Braddock** is defeated near **Ft. Duquesne** by French and Indians at **Battle of the Wilderness (French and Indian War).**

1810   **Holland** is annexed to France after the abdication of Holland's King **Louis Bonaparte,** brother of France's Napoleon Bonaparte.

1816   **Argentina** gains independence from Spain.

1850   U.S. President **Zachary Taylor** dies in office and is succeeded by **Millard Fillmore.**

1962   **Trans-Tasman submarine telephone cable** linking Sydney, Australia, and Auckland, New Zealand, is formally opened.

1963   **Federation of Malaysia** is created, including Malaya, Sarawak, Sabah, Brunei, and Singapore; Brunei withdraws at the last moment.

1973   **Clarence M. Kelley,** former Kansas City, Missouri, police chief, is sworn in as Director of the **FBI.**

July 10

Holidays

Bahamas	**Independence Day** Commemorates Bahamas' achievement of independence from Great Britain, 1973.
Japan	**Bon** or **O-Bon** or **Feast of Fortune**
Mauritania	**Armed Forces Day**

Religious Calendar

The Saints

The Seven Brothers and **St. Felicity,** their mother, martyrs. Invoked for the birth of male children. Felicity also called **Felicitas.** [d. 2nd century]

Birthdates

1509 **John Calvin (Jean Chauvin),** French theologian, ecclesiastical reformer; brought into focus the scattered reform theologies of Europe. Founder of **Calvinism.** [d. May 27, 1564]

1723 **Sir William Blackstone,** English jurist; author of *Commentaries on the Law of England,* a history of the fundamental doctrines of law, 1765–69. [d. February 14, 1780]

1752 **David Humphreys,** American Revolutionary war officer, diplomat, poet. [d. February 21, 1818]

1825 **Richard King,** U.S. rancher, steamboatman; developed and controlled the **King Ranch,** the largest cattle ranch in the U.S. [d. April 14, 1885]

1830 **Camille Pissarro,** French Impressionist painter. [d. November 13, 1903]

1834 **Jan Neruda,** Czech poet, story writer, journalist, and critic. [d. August 22, 1891]

James (Abott) McNeill Whistler, U.S. painter, etcher; his *Arrangement in Gray and Black, No. 1: The Artist's Mother* (later known as **Whistler's Mother**) is among his most famous works. [d. July 17, 1903]

1839 **Adolphus Busch,** U.S. brewery executive; founded Anheuser-Busch Brewery in St. Louis. [d. October 10, 1913]

1867 **Finley Peter Dunne,** U.S. humorist, creator of *Mr. Dooley,* a nationally syndicated column whose main character issued pithy, humorous observations on the people and events of his time. [d. April 24, 1936]

1871 **Marcel Proust,** French novelist, known for his autobiographical *Remembrance of Things Past.* [d. November 18, 1922]

1875 **Mary McLeod Bethune,** U.S. educator, government administrator; first black woman to hold administrative position in U.S. federal government (Office of Minority Affairs). [d. May 18, 1955]

1885 **Mary O'Hara,** U.S. novelist; most famous for her novel *My Friend Flicka,* (1941) which was later adapted for the screen. [d. October 15, 1980]

1895 **Carl Orff,** German composer; known for his neo-medieval style in such compositions as *Carmina Burana.* [d. March 29, 1982]

Nahum Goldmann, German Zionist leader born in Lithuania; noted for his efforts at establishing the state of Israel; President of World Jewish Congress, 1951–78; President of World Zionist Organization, 1956–68. [d. August 29, 1982]

1897 **John Gilbert (John Pringle),** U.S. silent-screen actor. [d. January 9, 1936]

1897 **Manlio (Giovanni) Brosio,** Italian statesman; leader of the Liberal party; Ambassador to Soviet Union, 1947–52; to Great Britain, 1952–54; to U.S. 1955–60; and to France, 1961–64; Secretary General of NATO, 1964–71. [d. March 14, 1980.]

1902 **Kurt Adler,** German organic chemist; Nobel Prize in chemistry for developing

St. Rufina and **St. Secunda,** virgins and martyrs. [d. c. 257]

St. Amalburga of Sustern, widow. Also called **Amelberga, Amelia.** [d. c. 690]

St. Anthony and **St. Theodosius Pechersky,** abbots of the caves of Kiev; founders of the first Russian monastery. [d. 1073, 1074]

The Beatified

Blessed Emmanuel Ruiz, Francis Masabki, and their companions, the **Martyrs of Damascus.** [d. 1860]

method for synthesizing organic compounds of the **diene group** (with O. P. H. Diels), 1950. [d. June 20, 1958]

1920 **David (McClure) Brinkley,** U.S. television news correspondent and commentator.

Owen Chamberlain, U.S. physicist; Nobel Prize in physics for discovery of **antiproton** (with E. G. Segræe), 1959.

1943 **Arthur Ashe,** U.S. professional tennis player.

1947 **Arlo Guthrie,** U.S. folk-rock singer, son of Woody Guthrie (July 14).

Historical Events

1460 **Richard of York** defeats **Henry VI** of England at Northampton and takes him prisoner (**War of the Roses**).

1584 **William of Orange,** stadtholder of Holland and Zealand, is assassinated; he is succeeded by his son **Maurice of Nassau.**

1898 U.S. troops begin bombardment of **Santiago Harbor,** Cuba (**Spanish-American War**).

1913 Rumania declares war on Bulgaria (**Second Balkan War**).

1934 **Franklin D. Roosevelt** becomes first U.S. president to visit South America.

1945 Aircraft from 14 U.S. carriers begin striking mainland Japan (**World War II**).

1962 *Telstar I,* experimental communications satellite developed by American Telephone and Telegraph Co., is launched from Cape Canaveral and later relays live television pictures from Andover, Maine, to France and Great Britain.

1973 **Bahamas** become independent of Great Britain.

July 11

Religious Calender

The Saints

St. Pius I, pope and martyr. Elected 142. [d. c. 155]

St. Benedict, abbot; patriarch of Western monks. Founded the Benedictine order. Invoked against the devil, fever, and inflammatory and kidney diseases. Also called **Bennett.** [d. c. 547] Feast formerly March 21. Obligatory Memorial.

St. Drostan, Abbot of Deer. [d. c. 610]

Birthdates

1274 **Robert I (the Bruce),** King and liberator of Scotland; defeated the forces of **Edward III** of England numerous times, finally forcing Edward to recognize Scotland's independence, 1328. Died of leprosy. [d. June 7, 1329]

1657 **Frederick I,** first King of Prussia, 1701–13. [d. February 25, 1713]

1767 **John Quincy Adams,** U.S. politician, diplomat, political writer; sixth President of U.S., 1825–29. [d. February 23, 1848]

1838 **John Wanamaker,** U.S. merchant, government official; founded one of first major department stores in U.S.; Postmaster General, 1889–93. [d. December 12, 1922]

1861 **George William Norris,** U.S. politician, lawyer; drafted the **20th Amendment** to U.S. Constitution, specifying the terms of the president and the Congress, as well as determining succession to presidency in case of death of the president. [d. August 29, 1944]

1888 **Bartolomeo Vanzetti,** Italian fish merchant, political radical; accused with **Nicola Sacco** (April 22) of murder of factory workers in South Braintree, Massachusetts, during a robbery attempt. Their cause won world-wide sympathy and roused protests against the system of justice that had condemned them. [executed August 23, 1927]

1890 **Arthur William Tedder, 1st Baron Tedder,** British air chief marshal; active in World War I in France and Egypt; instrumental in development of Royal Air Force training and development; Chief of Air Staff, 1946–50. [d. June 3, 1967]

1893 **Thomas B(ayard) McCabe,** U.S. business executive; president, Scott Paper Company, 1927–67; Chairman, Federal Reserve Board, 1948–51. [d. May 27, 1982]

1899 **E(lwyn) B(rooks) White,** U.S. author, editor; frequent contributor to *New Yorker* magazine, 1938–43; famous children's books include *Stuart Little* and *Charlotte's Web.*

1906 **Harry Von Zell,** U.S. entertainer; known for his mellow voice; provided support for such early entertainers as George Burns, Jack Benny, Fred Allen, and Eddie Cantor. [d. November 21, 1981]

1916 **Aleksander Prokhorov,** Russian scientist; Nobel Prize in physics for research in **quantum electronics,** leading to development of **maser principle** (with C. H. Towne and N. G. Basov), 1964.

1920 **Yul Brynner,** U.S. actor.

1925 **Nikolai Gedda (Nikolai Ustinov),** Swedish operatic tenor.

Historical Events

1302 **Philip IV** of France is defeated by the Flemish at **Courtrai.**

1533 **Pope Clement VII** excommunicates **Henry VIII** of England.

1804 **Alexander Hamilton** is fatally wounded in pistol duel with **Aaron Burr,** former U.S. Vice-President.

1890 **Wyoming** is admitted to Union as the 44th state.

St. John, Bishop of Bergamo. [d. c. 690]

St. Hildulf, bishop. Also called **Hidulphus.** [d. c. 707]

St. Olga, widow. [d. 969]

The Martyrs of Indo-China, I. [d. 1745–1840]

The Beatified

Blessed Adrian Fortescue, martyr. [d. 1539]

1921	**Mongolian People's Republic** is established.
1934	**Franklin D. Roosevelt** becomes the first U.S. President to sail through the **Panama Canal.**
1955	**U.S. Air Force Academy** is dedicated at its temporary location at Lowry Air Force Base, Colorado.
1960	Czechoslovakian constitution is adopted, signifying a liberalizing of Czechoslovakian society and government.
1966	Canada and the U.S.S.R. sign agreement providing for first direct air service between Soviet Union and North America.
1974	**Burundi** adopts its constitution, amid hostilities between Tutsis and Hutus.
1979	U.S. space station *Skylab,* in orbit since 1973, returns to earth and disintegrates over Indian Ocean.

July 12

Holidays

São Tome and Principe — **Anniversary of National Independence** Commemorates the coming of independence after 500 years of Portuguese rule, 1975.

Northern Ireland — **Orangeman's Day** Commemorates the Battle of the Boyne, 1690.

Birthdates

100 B.C. **Gaius Julius Caesar,** Roman general, statesman, writer, soldier. [Assassinated March 15, 44 B.C.]

1590 **Pope Clement X,** pope 1670–76. [d. July 22, 1676]

1730 **Josiah Wedgwood,** English potter, inventor; baptized on this day; his pottery techniques gained him renown; developed *queen's ware*, a cream colored domestic earthenware, and *jasperware.* Maternal grandfather of Charles Darwin (February 12). [d. January 3, 1795]

1811 **Vissarion Grigorievich Belinski,** Russian critic; first widely publicized literary critic; his works are the foundation of Russian literary criticism. (Born June 30, Old Style calandar.) [d. June 7, 1848 (May 26, Old Style calandar)]

1813 **Claude Bernard,** French physiologist; noted for discoveries related to the liver and pancreas. [d. February 10, 1878]

1817 **Henry David Thoreau,** U.S. essayist, poet, naturalist; associated with **transcendentalist school** of 19th-century American literature. [d. May 6, 1862]

1828 **Nikolay Gavrilovich Chernyshevsky,** Russian revolutionary, philsopher, economist, novelist, critic; spent 24 years in exile in Siberia. [d. October 17, 1889]

1852 **Hipòlito Irigoyen,** Argentine President, 1916–22, 1928–30. [d. July 3, 1933]

1854 **George Eastman,** U.S. inventor, industrialist, philanthropist; founder of Eastman Kodak Company, which for many years held a virtual monopoly in the film and camera industry. Contributed more than $75 million to various institutions, including Massachusetts Institute of Technology and Tuskegee Institute. [d. March 14, 1932]

1884 **Amedeo Modigliani,** Italian modernist painter, sculptor. [d. January 24, 1920]

1895 **R(ichard) Buckminster Fuller,** U.S. engineer, architect, author; developer of **geodesic dome.** [d. July 1, 1983]

Kirsten Flagstad, Norwegian operatic soprano; renowned for Wagnerian interpretations. [d. December 7, 1962]

Oscar Hammerstein II, U.S. lyricist; collaborator with Richard Rodgers in numerous Broadway musicals. [d. August 23, 1960]

1904 **Pablo Neruda,** Chilean poet; Nobel Prize in literature, 1971. [d. September 23, 1973]

1908 **Milton Berle (Milton Berlinger),** U.S. television comedian; became known as *Mr. Television.*

1912 **Peter Stambolic,** Yugoslav statesman; President, Socialist Federal Republic of Yugoslavia, 1982– .

1913 **Willis E. Lamb,** U.S. physicist; Nobel Prize in physics for experimental work in **electromagnetic phenomena,** 1955.

1917 **Andrew Wyeth,** U.S. painter; renowned for his disciplined and symbolic style and depth of feeling.

1922 **Mark Hatfield,** U.S. politician, political scientist; Governor of Oregon, 1959–67; U.S. Senator, 1967– .

Religious Calendar

The Saints

St. Hermagoras and **St. Fortunatus,** martyrs. [d. 1st century]

St. Jason. [d. 1st century]

St. Veronica, said to have wiped the brow of Jesus on his way to Calvary. [d. 1st century]

SS. Nabor and Felix, martyrs. [d. c. 303]

St. John the Iberian, abbot. [d. c. 1002]

St. John Gualbert, abbot. Founder of the Vallombrosan Benedictines; patron of foresters. [d. 1073]

The Beatified

Blessed Andrew of Rinn. [d. 1462]

1934 **Van Cliburn (Harvey Levan, Jr.),** U.S. concert pianist; won first prize at International Tchaikovsky Piano Competition, Moscow, 1958.

1937 **Bill Cosby,** U.S. comedian, actor.

Historical Events

1174 **Henry II** of England, does penance at Canterbury for the murder of **Thomas à Becket.**

1191 **Richard I, the Lion-Hearted** and his Crusaders capture **Acre** (**Third Crusade**).

1542 **Henry VIII** of England marries **Catherine Parr,** his sixth wife.

1690 **Battle of the Boyne** in Ireland is fought with **William III** of Orange victorious over **James II,** whom he had just driven from the throne of England.

1862 U.S. Congress authorizes **Congressional Medal of Honor** for gallantry in action by noncommissioned officers.

1906 In France, controversial **Dreyfus affair** (in which **Alfred Dreyfus,** a French Army officer, had been convicted of treason), ends with Dreyfus' conviction being overthrown fter it is proven that he has been condemned on the basis of forged documents. **Émile Zola** is primarily responsible for Dreyfus' re-trial and release, especially through his *J'accuse*.

1941 British forces occupy **Syria** (**World War II**).

1948 The Democratic Party convenes in Philadelphia and nominates **Harry S. Truman** and **Alben W. Barkley** for president and vice president.

1953 United Nations fleet launches heavy air and sea attack on **Wonsan** (**Korean War**).

1975 **São Tomè** and **Principe,** tiny islands off the west coast of Africa, are the fourth independent country to emerge from the decolonization of Portugal's African territories.

July 13

Holidays

Tahiti   National Day Eve

Religious Calendar

The Saints

St. Silas, companion and fellow worker of St. Paul. Also called **Silvanus.** [d. 1st century]

Birthdates

1608   **Ferdinand III** of Hungary, 1625–57; Holy Roman Emperor, 1637–57; signed Peace of Westphalia, 1648, ending **Thirty Years' War.** [d. April 2, 1657]

1793   **John Clare,** English poet; known as *Northamptonshire peasant poet.* [d. May 20, 1864]

1808   **Marie-Edmé-Patrice-Maurice Mac-Mahon,** Comte de Mac-Mahon, duc de Magenta French politician, soldier; second president of Third Republic, 1873–79. [d. October 17, 1893]

1816   **Gustav Freytag,** German novelist, playwright; champion of German liberalism and the middle class. [d. April 30, 1895]

1821   **Nathan Bedford Forrest,** Confederate general in U.S. Civil War; first Grand Wizard of original **Ku Klux Klan.** [d. October 29, 1877]

1826   **Stanislao Cannizzaro,** Italian chemist; first to clearly define distinction between atomic and molecular weights. [d. May 10, 1910]

1859   **Sidney James Webb,** British socialist, economist; cofounder of the **London School of Economics** with wife, Beatrice, 1895. [d. October 13, 1947]

1886   **Edward Joseph Flanagan,** U.S. Roman Catholic priest; founder of **Boys Town,** Nebraska, a school and hostel for rehabilitating delinquentboys. [d. May 15, 1948]

1898   **Sidney Blackmer,** U.S. actor. [d. October 5, 1973]

1905   **F. Bosley Crowther,** U.S. film critic; film critic for the *New York Times,* 1940–67; an influential authority on motion-picture art. [d. March 7, 1981]

1909   **Souphanouvrong,** Laotian statesman; President of Laos, 1975– .

1913   **Dave Garroway,** U.S. television personality. [d. July 21, 1982]

1922   **Anker Joergensen,** Danish statesman; Prime Minister of Denmark, 1975–82.

1927   **Simone Veil,** French lawyer, politician; President of **Parliament of the European Community,** 1979– .

Historical Events

1793   **Jean Paul Marat,** French revolutionary leader, is assassinated by **Charlotte Corday.**

1841   **Straits Convention** is signed by major European powers, guaranteeing independence of **Turkey.**

1878   **Berlin Congress** provides for the dissolution of the **Ottoman Empire** after almost 600 years. **Montenegro, Romania,** and **Serbia** become independent.

1931   All banks in Germany close following failure of Germany's **Danatbank.**

1960   Massachusetts Senator **John F. Kennedy** is named the Democratic party's presidential candidate.

1962   **Eugene McNeely,** President of American Telephone and Telegraph Co., and **Jacques Marette,** French Minister of Communications, hold the first official trans-Atlantic telephone conversation via *Telstar.*

1977   **Blackout** strikes **New York City** at 9:34 p.m. and lasts until the next day. The sweltering evening turns into a night of near-total chaos. Police arrest some 3,200 looters.

St. Maura and **St. Brigid.** Brigid also called **Britta.** [d. c. 5th century]

St. Eugenius, Bishop of Carthage. [d. 505]

St. Mildred, Abbess of Minister-in-Thanet and virgin. Also called **Mildthryth.** [d. c. 700]

St. Henry the Emperor, Holy Roman Emperor, 1014–1024; patron of Benedictine oblates. [d. 1024] Feast formerly July 15.

St. Francis Solano, Franciscan friar and missionary to Peru. [d. 1610]

The Beatified

Blessed James of Voragine, Archbishop of Genoa. [d. 1298]

Blessed Thomas Tunstal, martyr. [d. 1616]

July 14

Holidays

France, French Guiana, New Caledonia, St. Pierre, Miquelon	**Bastille Day** Commemorates the fall of the Bastille and overthrow of regime of King Louis XVI, 1789.
French West Indies, Monaco, Tahiti	**National Holiday**
Iraq	**14th of July Revolution** Commemorates overthrow of King Faisal and proclamation of the republic, 1958.

Birthdates

1602 **Jules Mazarin (Giulio Mazarini),** French cardinal, statesman born in Italy; succeeded **Richelieu** (September 9) as prime minister of France; greatly increased France's position as a European power. [d. March 9, 1661]

1743 **Gavrila Derzhavin,** Russian poet; considered one of the most influential and significant poets before Aleksander Pushkin. [d. July 21, 1816]

1794 **John Gibson Lockhart,** Scottish critic, editor, novelist, and biographer of Sir Walter Scott (August 15) and Robert Burns (January 25). Married to Scott's oldest daughter, Charlotte Sophia. [d. November 25, 1854]

1816 **Joseph Arthur Gobineau,** French writer, diplomat; first to propose the theory of **Aryan supremacy** (**Gobinism**). [d. October 13, 1882]

1829 **Edward White Benson,** British theologian; Archbishop of Canterbury, 1882–96. [d. October 11, 1896]

1857 **Frederick Louis Maytag,** U.S. manufacturer; founder of Maytag Co., manufacturers of washing machines, 1907. [d. March 26, 1937]

1868 **Gertrude Bell,** British traveler, archaeologist, government official; an authority on Arabian culture; influential in molding administration of post-World War I **Mesopotamia**. [d. July 11/12, 1926]

1869 **Owen Wister,** U.S. novelist; his writings on life in Wyoming did much to create the popular romantic image of the American cowboy. [d. July 21, 1938]

1898 **Alexander Brook,** U.S. artist; known for his portraits of famous people of his period; called the *Unstruggling Artist.* [d. February 26, 1980]

1903 **Irving Stone,** U.S. author.

1904 **Isaac Bashevis Singer,** U.S. author, born in Poland; novels are based on his life in the Jewish ghettos of eastern Europe; Nobel Prize in literature, 1978.

1911 **Terry Thomas (Thomas Terry Hoar-Stevens),** British actor.

1912 **Woody Guthrie (Woodrow Wilson Guthrie),** U.S. folksinger, composer; father of Arlo Guthrie (July 10). [d. October 3, 1967]

1913 **Gerald (Rudolph J.) Ford,** U.S. lawyer, politician; 38th president of U.S., 1974–77. Succeeded to the presidency upon resignation of Richard M. Nixon; defeated in his bid for presidency, 1976.

1918 **(Ernst) Ingmar Bergman,** Swedish film director, screenwriter.

1920 **Bella Abzug,** U.S. lawyer, politician; spokeswoman for peace, full employment, women's rights, environmental programs.

Religious Calendar

The Saints

St. Deusdedit, Archbishop of Canterbury. [d. 664]

St. Marchelm, missionary. Also called **Marceaumes, Marcellinus, Marculf.** [d. c. 762]

St. Ulric of Zell, abbot. [d. 1093]

St. Camillus de Lellis, priest and founder of the Ministers of the Sick; patron of nurses and the sick. [d. 1614] Optional Memorial.

The Beatified

Blessed Hroznata, martyr. [d. 1217]

Blessed Humbert of Romans, cardinal. [d. 1277]

Blessed Boniface of Savoy, Archbishop of Canterbury. [d. 1270]

Blessed Caspar de Bono, friar. [d. 1604]

1921 **Sir Geoffrey Wilkinson,** British chemist; Nobel Prize in chemistry for research in merger of organic and metallic atoms (with E. O. Fischer), 1973.

1927 **John (William) Chancellor,** U.S. journalist, television newscaster.

1930 **Polly Bergen (Nellie Bergen),** U.S. actress, executive of beauty products company.

Historical Events

1223 **King Philip II Augustus** of France dies and is succeeded by **Louis VIII.**

1789 After two days of fighting in Paris, the **Bastille,** symbol of the power of **Louis XVI,** falls to revolutionaries, marking the end of the monarchy and the feudal system in France (**French Revolution**).

1865 First ascent of the **Matterhorn** is completed by Englishman **Edward Whymper.**

1890 **Sherman Act** is passed by Congress, regulating silver coinage in U.S.

1933 In Germany the **National Socialist German Workers (Nazi) Party** is declared the only political party.

1940 General **Fulgencio Batista** becomes President of Cuba.

1951 **Kaesong** is selected as neutral site for conferences to end **Korean War.**

1958 **Iraq** overthrows its monarchy and becomes a revolutionary republic.

1961 **Pope John XXIII** issues papal encyclical *Mater et Magistra* calling for aid to underdeveloped nations.

1964 **Iraq** nationalizes all private and foreign banks and insurance companies and 30 industrial and commercial concerns; foreign oil companies are not affected.

1978 Russian dissident **Anatoly B. Shcharansky** is convicted of treason, espionage, and anti-Soviet agitation and sentenced to three years in prison, to be followed by ten years in a labor camp.

July 15

Religious Calendar

The Saints

St. James, first Bishop of Nisibis. One of the principal Doctors of the Armenian National Church. [d. 338]

St. Barhadbesaba, martyr. [d. 355]

St. Donald. [d. 8th century]

St. Swithin, Bishop of Winchester; patron of **Winchester.** Superstition says that if it rains on his feast day it will rain for 39 more. Also called **Swithuin.** [d. 862]

Birthdates

1606   **Rembrandt (Rembrandt Harmenszoon van Rijn or Ryn),** Dutch artist; one of the leaders of the Dutch school and regarded as one of the greatest artists of all time. [d. October 4, 1669]

1779   **Clement (Clarke) Moore,** U.S. writer, poet, lexicographer; most widely recognized work is *A Visit from St. Nicholas*; devoted his life to teaching Greek and Oriental literature. [d. July 10, 1863]

1808   **Henry Edward Manning,** British archdeacon in Church of England; converted to Catholicism, becoming supervisor of Oblates of St. Charles, 1857. Eventually became Roman Catholic cardinal, 1875. [d. January 14, 1892]

1809   **Pierre Joseph Proudhoun,** French journalist, politician, and social theorist; sometimes called the *Father of Anarchism.* [d. January 16, 1865]

1813   **George Peter Alexander Healy,** U.S. portrait painter; responsible for series of the presidents of the U.S. in Corcoran Art Gallery, Washington, D.C., as well as portraits of Daniel Webster and Henry Wadsworth Longfellow. [d. July 24, 1894]

1817   **Sir John Fowler,** British civil engineer; pioneer in underground railway construction. [d. November 20, 1898]

1848   **Vilfredo Pareto,** Italian economist, sociologist; developed methods of applying mathematics to economic and social phenomena; his theories formed the basis of **Italian fascism.** [d. August 20, 1923]

1850   **Saint Frances Cabrini** (*Mother Cabrini*), Italian missionary; became naturalized U.S. citizen, 1909. Her work with the poor Italians in America and her campaign to establish convents, schools, orphanages, and hospitals throughout the Americas led to her canonization in 1946; first U.S. citizen to be canonized. [d. December 22, 1917]

1865   **Alfred Charles William Harmsworth, Viscount Northcliffe,** British publisher, politician; established publishing empire that included *Answers,* 1888, *Evening News,* 1894, *Daily Mail,* 1896, *Daily Mirror,* 1903, and the *Times,* 1908. Outspoken enemy of Germany; led many special missions during and after World War I. [d. August 14, 1922]

1919   **(Jean) Iris Murdoch,** British novelist, university lecturer.

1933   **Julian Bream,** British guitarist, lutist; his research into Elizabethan lute music led to revival of interest in that instrument.

1946   **Linda Ronstadt,** U.S. singer.

Historical Events

455   **Rome** is pillaged by **Genseric the Vandal.**

1099   Crusaders take **Jerusalem (First Crusade).**

1662   **Royal Society for the Improvement of Science** (later the **Royal Society of London**)is chartered at London and becomes center of English scientific activity in the 17th and 18th centuries.

1815   **Napoleon** surrenders to British Captain **Frederick Lewis Maitland** of the *Bellerophon* at Rochefort; he is sent to St. Helena, where he lives out his life in exile.

St. Athanasius, Bishop of Naples. [d. 872]

St. Edith of Polesworth. [d. c. 10th century]

St. Vladimir of Kiev, Russian prince. He and his grandmother, St. Olga, are regarded as the first Russian-born Christians. [d. 1015]

St. David of Munktorp, bishop. [d. c. 1080]

St. Bonaventure, Cardinal-Bishop of Albano, Doctor of the Church, and head of the Franciscans. Also called **Bonaventura.** [d. 1274] Feast formerly July 14. Optional Memorial.

St. Pompilio Pirrotti, priest and teacher. [d. 1756]

The Beatified

Blessed Bernard of Baden. [d. 1458]

Blessed Ignatius Azevedo and his companions, martyrs. [d. 1570]

Blessed Anne Mary Javouhey, virgin. Founder of the Congregation of St. Joseph of Cluny. [d. 1851]

1918	The **Second Battle of the Marne** begins with a German offensive from both sides of Reims which meets strong resistance from French and American forces (**World War I**).
1945	U.S. warships bombard steel and iron works at **Muroran, Japan (World War II**).
1960	**Gabon Republic** is granted full independence from France.
1968	First direct air service between U.S.S.R. and U.S. is opened by Aeroflot and Pan American World Airways.
1974	President **Makarios** of Cyprus is overthrown, marking the beginning of long-term fighting between Greek and Turkish sectors.
1977	U.S. President **Jimmy Carter** approves admittance of Indochinese **boat people** into U.S.

July 16

Religious Calendar

The Saints

Feast of Our Lady of Mount Carmel, commemorates day on which Our Lady appeared to St. Simon Stock and gave him the scapular. Optional Memorial.

St. Athenogenes, bishop and martyr. [d. c. 305]

Birthdates

1486 **Andrea del Sarto (Andrea Domenico d'Agnolo di Francesco Vannucci),** Florentine painter; best known for his frescoes; called the *Faultless Painter.* [d. September 29, 1530]

1661 **Pierre Le Moyne, Sieur d'Iberville,** French-Canadian explorer, commander; founder of French colony in Louisiana. [d. July 9, 1706]

1723 **Sir Joshua Reynolds,** English painter; foremost portrait painter in England, 1752–90. Responsible for establishment of the **Literary Club,** of which Dr. Samuel Johnson, David Garrick, and others were members. [d. February 23, 1792]

1746 **Giuseppe Piazzi,** Italian astronomer; discovered and named the first asteroid, **Ceres,** 1801. [d. July 22, 1826]

1773 **Josef Jungmann,** Czech philologist, critic, poet; produced 5-volume Czech-German dictionary which formed foundation for modern Czech lexicography; considered by some the *Father of Modern Czech Literature.* [d. November 14, 1847]

1796 **Jean Baptiste Camille Corot,** French landscape painter. [d. February 22, 1875]

1821 **Mary (Morse) Baker Eddy,** U.S. religious leader; founder of **Christian Science** movement, 1866. [d. December 3, 1910]

1845 **Theodore Newton Vail,** U.S. communications executive; first president of American Telephone and Telegraph Co., 1885–87, 1907–19; responsible for instituting first employees' pension plan in U.S., 1912. [d. April 16, 1920]

1860 **(Jens) Otto (Harry) Jespersen,** Danish linguist; authority on English grammar; proposed an international language, *Nonial.* [d. April 30, 1943]

1872 **Roald Amundsen,** Norwegian polar explorer; navigated Northwest Passage and discovered **South Pole,** 1911; disappeared during flight to rescue Umberto Nobile on his return from North Pole. [d. June 1928]

1888 **Frits Zernike,** Dutch physicist; Nobel Prize in physics for his invention of **phase contrast microscope,** 1953. [d. March 10, 1966]

1896 **Trygve Lie,** Norwegian government official; first Secretary-General of the United Nations, 1946–53. [d. December 30, 1968]

1907 **Barbara Stanwyck (Ruby Stevens),** U.S. actress.

1911 **Ginger Rogers (Virginia Katherine Mc-Math),** U.S. actress; associated with Fred Astaire (May 10) as his frequent dance partner in several films.

1942 **Margaret Court,** Australian tennis player; Wimbledon champion, 1963, 1965, 1970.

Historical Events

1048 **Benedict IX** (*Boy Pope*) resigns from papacy; had been elected by simony; considered anti-pope to Clement II.

1917 The **Bolsheviks** attempt to seize power from the Russian provisional government but are defeated. **Trotsky** is arrested and **Lenin** goes into hiding in Finland.

1918 Russian **Czar Nicholas II** and his family are executed by order of Bolsheviks.

1945 First **atomic bomb** is exploded in a test at Alamogordo, New Mexico.

1947 U.S. President **Harry Truman** signs the **National Security Act,** creating a national military establishment and uniting the Army, Navy, and Air Force.

St. Eustathius, Bishop of Antioch. [d. c. 340]

St. Helier, martyr. Also called **Elier.** [d. 6th century]

St. Reineldis, virgin and martyr. Also called **Raineld.** [d. c. 680]

St. Tenenan, Bishop of Lèon. Also called **Tinihor.** [d. 7th century]

St. Fulrad, Abbot of Saint-Denis monastery. [d. 784]

St. Mary Magdalen Postel, virgin. Founder of the Sisters of the Christian Schools of Mercy. [d. 1846]

The Beatified

Blessed Ermengard, virgin. [d. 866]

Blessed Milo of Sèlincourt, Bishop of Thèrouanne. [d. 1158]

1965   **Mont Blanc Tunnel,** a seven-mile vehicular tunnel through the heart of Mont Blanc and connecting France and Italy, is opened.

1969   *Apollo 11,* U.S. manned spacecraft, is launched, carrying astronauts Armstrong, Aldrin, and Collins into moon orbit, from which Armstrong and Aldrin will launch **lunar module** for 21-hour **moon landing** (see July 20).

July 17

Holidays

Iraq	**17th of July Revolution** or **Baath Revolution Day** Commemorates the overthrow of the government by Revolutionary Command Council under General Ahmed Hassan al-Bakr, 1968.
Puerto Rico	**Muñoz Rivera's Birthday** Commemorates the birthday of Luis Muñoz Rivera, Puerto Rican patriot and leader in gaining Puerto Rico's independence from Spain.
South Korea	**Constitution Day** Commemorates the adoption of the constitution, 1963.
Venice	**Feast of the Redeemer** Procession of gondolas and other craft commemorating the end of the epidemic of 1575.

Birthdates

1698 **Pierre Louis Moreau Maupertius,** French mathematician, astronomer; led expedition sent by **Louis XV** to Lapland to make accurate measurements of longitude. [d. July 27, 1759]

1744 **Elbridge Gerry,** U.S. statesman; signer of Declaration of Independence; Vice-President of U.S., 1812–14. [d. November 23, 1814]

1763 **John Jacob Astor,** U.S. businessman, born in Germany; the founder and promoter of one of the greatest financial dynasties in the U.S. [d. March 29, 1848]

1797 **Hippolyte Paul Delaroche,** French historical and portrait painter. [d. November 4, 1856]

1827 **Sir Frederick Augustus Abel,** British chemist; developed **cordite** with James Dewar (September 20), the first **smokeless gun powder;** chemist to British War Department, 1854–88. [d. September 6, 1902]

1862 **Oscar Ivan Levertin,** Swedish poet, novelist, man of letters. [d. September 22, 1906]

1888 **Shmuel Yosef Halevi Agnon,** Israeli novelist, short-story writer. [d. February 17, 1970]

1889 **Erle Stanley Gardner,** U.S. lawyer, author of detective stories; developed the character *Perry Mason,* the hero of over 100 books and stories and a television series. [d. May 11, 1970]

1894 **Georges Lemaître,** Belgian astrophysicist, mathematician; first to introduce the concept of the **expanding universe,** 1927. [d. June 20, 1966]

1899 **James Cagney,** U.S. actor, dancer, active in American theater and films since 1925.

1902 **Christina Ellen Stead,** British novelist.

1905 **William Gargan,** U.S. actor; leading man in 1930s and 1940s films. [d. February 16, 1979]

1912 **Art Linkletter,** U.S. radio and television personality, born in Canada.

1934 **Donald Sutherland,** Canadian actor.

1935 **Diahann Carroll (Carol Diahann Johnson),** U.S. singer, actress.

Historical Events

1245 **Pope Innocent IV** declares German **King Frederick II** deposed and orders Germans to elect a new king; war breaks out throughout the German territories.

Religious Calendar

The Saints

St. Speratus and his companions, the Scillitan martyrs. [d. 180]

St. Marcellina, virgin. [d. c. 398]

St. Alexis, called the *Man of God*; patron saint of the Alexian Brothers. Also called **Alexius.** [d. 5th century]

St. Ennodius, Bishop of Pavia. [d. 521]

St. Kenelm, martyr. Also called **Cynehelm** or **Kenelm.** [d. c. 812]

St. Leo IV, pope. Elected 847. [d. 855]

St. Clement of Okhrida and his companions, the **Seven Apostles of Bulgaria.** [d. 9th–10th century]

St. Nerses Lampronatsi, Archbishop of Tarsus. Also called **Narsus of Lampron.** [d. 1198]

The Carmelite Martyrs of Compiegne, sixteen victims of the French Revolution. [d. 1794]

The Beatified

Blessed Ceslaus. [d. 1242]

1453 French defeat English under **John Talbot, Earl of Shrewsbury,** at **Castillon (Hundred Years' War).**

1841 *Punch,* the British humor magazine, begins publication.

1868 **Edo,** renamed **Tokyo,** becomes the capital of **Japan.**

1890 **Cecil Rhodes** becomes Prime Minister of the Cape Colony of South Africa.

1898 The Spanish formally surrender **Santiago, Cuba,** to American forces (**Spanish-American War**).

1948 **Dixiecrats** opposed to U.S. President Harry Truman's strong civil rights stand, form the **States Rights Party** and nominate **J. Strom Thurmond** for president.

1951 **Leopold III** of Belgium abdicates and is succeeded by his son, **Baudouin I.**

1969 *Luna 15,* Soviet unmanned space craft, is launched into orbit.

1973 **Afghanistan** monarchy is abolished when Lieut. Gen. **Mohammad Daud Khan** deposes his brother-in-law, **King Mohammad Zahir Shah** and proclaims himself president.

1975 U.S. *Apollo 18* and U.S.S.R. *Soyuz 19* linkup in space takes place as a dramatic goodwill gesture between Russia and the United States.

1979 **Anastasio Somoza** resigns and leaves **Nicaragua** as Sandinistas take control of Managua, ending civil war.

1981 **Wayne B. Williams** is indicted on charges of murdering two black youths in Atlanta, Georgia. He is suspected of murdering more than 20 other black youths over a two-year period.

July 18

Holidays

Mexico   **Benito Juárez Memorial Day**
Commemorates the death of Mexican statesman who led the revolt against Maximilian and the French, 1872.

Uruguay   **Constitution Day**

Birthdates

1504   **Heinrich Bullinger,** Swiss religious reformer; head of Reformation in German Switzerland after the death of Zwingli. [d. September 17, 1575]

1635   **Robert Hooke,** English experimental scientist; proposed numerous theories of physics which were later substantiated by more sophisticated scientific techniques: theories of combustion, center of gravity of earth and moon, elasticity. [d. March 3, 1703]

1811   **William Makepeace Thackeray,** British novelist; known for his pointed satires on upper class society of London, including *Vanity Fair*; contributed regularly to *Punch*, 1842–54. [d. December 24, 1863]

1853   **Hendrik A. Lorentz,** Dutch physicist; Nobel Prize in physics for his theory of electromagnetic radiation (with P. Zeeman), 1902. [d. February 4, 1928]

1864   **Philip Snowden, 1st Viscount Snowden of Ickornshaw,** British politician, socialist; Chairman of Independent Labor Party, 1903–06, 1917–20. [d. May 15, 1937]

1883   **Lev Borisovich Kamenev,** Russian revolutionary, politician; Vice-President of U.S.S.R., 1923. After Lenin's death became member of ruling triumvirate with Stalin (December 21) and Zinoviev (September 11). [d. August 25, 1936]

1887   **Vidkun Quisling,** Norwegian politician, public official; founded National Union Party in Norway; collaborated with Germany in conquest of Norway; executed as a traitor. [d. October 24, 1945]

1890   **Charles Erwin Wilson,** U.S. industrialist, public official; President of General Motors Corporation, 1941–46; U.S. Secretary of Defense, 1952–57. [d. September 26, 1961]

1902   **Chill Wills,** U.S. character actor. [d. December 15, 1978]

1903   **Victor (David) Gruen,** U.S. architect, urban planner, born in Austria; known for his large-scale planned commercial projects (mainly shopping centers) which integrated architecture, art, and landscape design. [d. February 14, 1980]

1906   **Clifford Odets,** U.S. playwright; a leading writer of the Depression era; helped found the Group Theatre in New York with Lee Strasberg. [d. August 14, 1963]

       S(amuel) I(chiye) Hayakawa, U.S. educator, semanticist, politician, born in Canada; President of San Francisco State College, 1968–73; U.S. Senator, 1976–82.

1911   **Hume Cronyn (Hume Blake),** Canadian actor.

1913   **(Richard) Red Skelton,** U.S. comedian, actor.

1915   **Philip Leslie Graham,** U.S. newspaper executive; publisher of *Washington Post*, 1946–63. [d. August 3, 1963]

1921   **John (Herschel) Glenn, Jr.,** U.S. astronaut, politician; first American to complete earth orbit, February 22, 1962; U.S. Senator, 1975– .

1929   **Dick Button,** U.S. figure skater, broadcaster; Olympic gold medalist in figure skating, 1948, 1952; world titlist, 1948–52.

1933   **Yevgeny Aleksandrovich Yevtushenko,** Russian poet.

Historical Events

1536   Authority of **Bishop of Rome** (the Pope) is declared void in England.

1870   Dogma of **papal infallibility** is declared by Vatican Council.

1915   The **Second Battle of Isonzo** begins with the Italians again attacking Austrian bridgeheads (**World War I**).

The Saints

St. Pambo, monk. [d. c. 390]

St. Philastrius, Bishop of Brescia. [d. c. 397]

St. Arnulf, Bishop of Metz. Also called **Arnoul.** [d. c. 643]

St. Edburga of Bicester, nun. Also called **Eadburh of Aylesbury.** [d. c. 650]

St. Frederick, Bishop of Utrecht, martyr. Also called **Frederic.** [d. 838]

St. Bruno, Bishop of Segni. [d. 1123]

St. Symphorosa and her seven sons, martyrs. [death date unknown]

1918	**Second Battle of the Marne**: a turning point of **World War I** as French and Allies halt German offensive.
1928	The **Somport Tunnel,** connecting Spain and France through the Pyrenees, opens.
1936	**Spanish Civil War** begins with a revolt of the army chiefs, led by **General Francisco Franco,** at Melilla in Spanish Morocco.
1947	President Harry S. Truman signs the **Presidential Succession Act,** designating the Speaker of the House of Representatives and the President Pro Tempore of the Senate as next in line of succession after the Vice-President.
1951	**Jersey Joe Walcott** defeats **Ezzard Charles** in seven rounds for the world heavyweight boxing championship.
1968	**U.S. B-52 bombers** are first used during air raids of missile sites in North Vietnam (**Vietnam War**).

July 19

Holidays

Burma   Martyrs' Day

Nicaragua   Anniversary of the Sandinista Revolution

Commemorates the coming to power of the Sandinist National Liberation Front over the forces of President Somoza, 1979.

Birthdates

1573   **Inigo Jones,** baptized on this day; influential early English designer; responsible for design of the restoration of St. Paul's Cathedral in London (1634–1642). [d. June 21, 1652]

1698   **Johann Jakob Bodmer,** Swiss scholar, critic, poet; contributed to the development of an original German literature in Switzerland. [d. January 2, 1783]

1800   **Juan José Flores,** Ecuadorian general; first president, 1830–35. [d. October 1, 1864]

1814   **Samuel Colt,** U.S. inventor, businessman; developed the repeating firearm (*six-shooter*), which he put into production in the U.S. in a sophisticated production line technique; his invention is said to be one of the most influential of the 19th century. [d. January 10, 1862]

1819   **Gottfried Keller,** Swiss novelist, short-story writer, poet. [d. July 15, 1890]

1834   **(Hilaire Germaine) Edgar Degas,** French Impressionist painter; known for his depiction of theater life, especially of ballet dancers. [d. September 27, 1917]

1840   **José Manuel Balmaceda,** Chilean statesman; president, 1851–61. [d. September 18, 1891]

1860   **Lizzie (Andrew) Borden,** U.S. accused murderer; alleged to have murdered her father and step-mother in a brutal ax-slaying. [d. June 1, 1927]

1865   **Charles Horace Mayo,** U.S. surgeon; co-founder of the **Mayo Foundation for Medical Education and Research (Mayo Clinic).** Brother of William James Mayo (June 29). [d. May 26, 1939]

1878   **Don(ald Robert Perry) Marquis,** U.S. author, journalist; leading humorist of his period; known for his characters *Archy* and *Mehitabel*. [d. December 29, 1937]

1885   **Malcolm King,** U.S. publisher; President of McGraw-Hill, Inc., 1928–37; President of Newsweek, Inc., 1937–61. [d. January 30, 1979]

1893   **Vladimir Vladimirovich Mayakovsky,** Russian poet; leading futurist writer of Russian Revolutionary period. [d. April 14, 1930]

1896   **A(rchibald) J(oseph) Cronin,** U.S. writer; formerly a physician in Scotland; turned to writing and gained enormous success with *The Keys of the Kingdom, The Citadel*. [d. January 6, 1981]

1898   **Herbert Marcuse,** U.S. philosopher, born in Germany; considered the prophet of the *New Left*, his writings became the foundation for political thought of radical students during the 1960s; lectured at Columbia University, 1940; Brandeis University, 1954–65. [d. July 29, 1979]

1917   **William Warren Scranton,** U.S. lawyer, politician, diplomat; U.S. Congressman, 1961–63; Governor of Pennsylvania, 1963–67; Special Envoy to Middle East, 1968.

1921   **Rosalyn Yalow,** U.S. medical physicist; Nobel Prize in physiology or medicine for development of method for using isotopes for diagnostic purposes, 1977.

1922   **George (Stanley) McGovern,** U.S. politician; U.S. Senator, 1963–81; Democratic presidential candidate, 1972.

Historical Events

1101   **Robert of Normandy** invades England in attempt to take English throne from his younger brother, **Henry I;** forestalled by **Treaty of Alton.**

1333   **Edward III** of England defeats Scots army at **Halidon Hill** in struggle to place **Edward Balliol** on the throne of Scotland.

The Saints

St. Justa and St. Rufina, virgins and martyrs. [d. c. 287]

St. Macrina the Younger, virgin. [d. 379]

St. Arsenius the Great, scholar and monk. [d. c. 450]

St. Symmachus, pope. Elected 498. [d. 514]

St. Ambrose Autpert, abbot. [d. c. 778]

The Beatified

Blessed Stilla, virgin. [d. c. 1140]

1821	**George IV** of England is crowned king; refuses to allow his estranged queen, Caroline, to attend coronation.
1848	First **women's rights convention** is held at **Seneca Falls, New York,** under the leadership of **Elizabeth Cady Stanton** and **Lucretia Coffin Mott.**
1862	**Garibaldi** calls for volunteers with watchword "Rome or death!" in his first attempt to capture the city.
1870	France declares war on Prussia (**Franco-Prussian War**).
1949	**Laos** becomes independent sovereign state within the French Union.
1969	U.S. Senator **Edward Kennedy** reports to police that his car has plunged off **Chappaquiddick Island** bridge in Edgartown, Massachusetts, drowning a woman passenger, **Mary Jo Kopechne.**

July 20

Holidays

| Colombia | Independence Day |
| U.S.S.R. | International Chess Day |

Religious Calendar

The Saints

St. Joseph Barsabas, one of the disciples of Christ. [d. 1st century]

St. Aurelius, Bishop of Carthage. [d. 429]

Birthdates

1304 **Petrarch (Francesco Petrarca),** Italian poet, humanist; known for his collection of sonnets and odes written to Laura, his beloved. [d. July 18, 1374]

1519 **Pope Innocent IX,** pope in 1591 for two months. [d. December 30, 1591]

1591 **Anne Hutchinson,** American colonial religious leader, baptized on this day. Proposed a theology based on a covenant of grace; excommunicated from Puritan community and banished from Massachusetts. [d. August, 1643]

1656 **Johann Bernard Fischer von Erlach,** Austrian architect; responsible for original plans for **Schönbrunn Castle,** 1695, and **Royal Library in Vienna,** 1722. [d. April 5, 1723]

1785 **Mahmud II,** Sultan of Turkey. [d. July 1, 1839]

1830 **Sir Clements Robert Markham,** British geographer, historical writer. [d. January 30, 1916]

1847 **Max Liebermann,** German Postimpressionist painter. [d. February 8, 1935]

1850 **John Graves Shedd,** U.S. merchant; partner with Marshall Field (September 3) in development of Marshall Field & Co. President of Marshall Field & Co., 1906–22; donated **Shedd Aquarium** in Chicago. [d. October 22, 1926]

1864 **Erik Axel Karlfeldt,** Swedish poet; Nobel Prize in literature (posthumously), 1931. [d. April 8, 1931]

1890 **George II,** King of Greece. [d. April 1, 1947]

Theda Bara (Theodosia Goodman), U.S. silent screen star; created the role of the vamp. [d. April 7, 1955]

1893 **Alexander,** King of Greece, 1917–20; became king when his father was forced to abdicate; died of blood poisoning after being bitten by a pet monkey. [d. October 25, 1920]

1894 **Edmond H(arrison) Leavey,** U.S. army officer, businessman; Assistant Chief of Staff, Supreme Headquarters, Allied Powers in Europe, 1952–56; President, ITT, 1956–59. [d. February 11, 1980]

1897 **Tadeusz Reichstein,** Swiss chemist; Nobel Prize in physiology or medicine for research in hormones and discovery of **cortisone** (with P. S. Hench and E. C. Kendall), 1950.

1919 **Sir Edmund (Percival) Hilary,** New Zealand mountain climber, Arctic explorer, author; with **Tenzing Norkay** was first to reach summit of **Mt. Everest,** 1953; reached South Pole, January 4, 1958.

1920 **Juan Antonio Samaranch,** Spanish diplomat; president of International Olympic Committee, 1980–.

Elliot (Lee) Richardson, U.S. lawyer, government official, diplomat; U.S. Secretary of Health, Education and Welfare, 1970–72; Attorney General of U.S., 1973; Ambassador to United Kingdom, 1975–76; U.S. Secretary of Commerce, 1976–77.

1924 **Elias Sarkis,** Lebanese statesman; President, 1976–82.

1933 **John (Champlin) Gardner,** U.S. author, educator; noted for his experimental style of novel writing; author of *Grendel,* and *October Light.* [d. September 14, 1982]

1938 **Natalie Wood (Natasha Gurdin),** U.S. actress. [d. November 29, 1981]

St. Flavian, Patriarch of Antioch, and **St. Elias,** Patriarch of Jerusalem. [d. 518]

St. Vulmar, abbot and hermit. Also called **Ulmar, Wulmar.** [d. c. 700]

St. Ansegisus, abbot and advisor to Charlemagne. [d. 833]

St. Arild, virgin. Also called **Alkelda.** [death date unknown]

St. Margaret, virgin and martyr; patron of women. Invoked in childbirth and for the cure of kidney diseases. Also called **Marina.** Feast suppressed in 1969. [death date unknown]

St. Wilgefortis, princess. Invoked against troublesome husbands. Also called **Kümmernis, Liberta, Livrade, Ontkommer, Regentledis,** or **Uncumber.** [death date unknown]

The Beatified

Blessed Gregory Lopez, hermit. [d. 1596]

Blessed Leo Ignatius Mangin, Ann Wang, and their companions, martyrs. Four French Jesuits and 52 Chinese lay people martyred by the Boxers in 1900. [d. 1900]

Historical Events

1402 The **Battle of Angora** (Ankara) is won by **Timur (Tamerlane)** who defeats and captures **Bazazid I,** Sultan of Turkey.

1810 **Colombia** defies Spanish authority and declares its independence.

1866 Austria and France destroy Italian fleet off **Lissa,** setting back Italy's unification efforts.

1917 The **Pact of Corfu** declares that Serbs, Croats, and Slovenes will form a single nation to be called **Yugoslavia.**

1927 **Ferdinand I** of Rumania dies and is succeeded by Michael.

1942 U.S. Congress authorizes **Legion of Merit** medal to recognize meritorious efforts by armed forces members.

1951 **King Abdullah ibn Hussein** of Jordan is assassinated; he is succeeded by his son Talal.

1960 **Polaris missile** is launched for the first time from a submerged submarine near Cape Canaveral, Florida.

1969 U.S. astronauts **Neil A. Armstrong** and **Edwin E. Aldrin,** during the mission of *Apollo 11*, land their lunar excursion module *Eagle* on the moon. Armstrong becomes the first man to set foot on the moon.

1976 *Viking 1*, U.S. robot spacecraft, lands on **Mars** in the **Plain of Chryse.**

The last U.S. military personnel are withdrawn from **Vietnam,** marking an end to American military involvement begun in 1965.

1977 **CIA** experiments in behavior control from 1949 through the mid-1960s are revealed; experiments were conducted through the use of chemical, biological, and radiological agents on human subjects, including prisoners and mental patients.

July 21

Holidays

Belgium	**National Day** Commemorates accession of first king of independent Belgium, Leopold I, 1831.
French West Indies	**Schoelcher Day** Commemorates the birthday of Victor Schoelcher, French politician devoted to elimination of slavery in French possessions.
Guam	**Liberation Day** Commemorates liberation of the island by U.S. forces, 1944.

Birthdates

810 **Mohammed Ibn Ismail Al-Bukhari,** Arabic scholar, author of one of the sacred books of Islam, the *Sahih*, which ranks next to the *Koran* in importance for Sunni Muslims. [d. August 31, 870]

1414 **Pope Sixtus IV,** pope 1471–84. [d. August 12, 1484]

1816 **Baron Paul Julius von Reuter,** German pioneer in gathering and disseminating news. His carrier pigeon and telegraph outpost in France, 1849, became the foundation of **Reuter's News Service.** [d. February 25, 1899]

1821 **Vasile Alexandri,** Rumanian poet, playwright, politician; Minister of Foreign Affairs for Rumania, 1859–85; Ambassador to France, 1885–90. [d. 1890]

1851 **Sam Bass,** U.S. outlaw; had a short but spectacular career as a train robber and cattle thief; killed in a gunfight with Texas Rangers. [d. July 21, 1878]

1863 **Sir C(harles) Aubrey Smith,** British character actor. [d. December 20, 1948]

1885 **Frances Parkinson Keyes,** U.S. novelist. [d. July 3, 1970]

1899 **Ernest (Miller) Hemingway,** U.S. novelist, short-story writer; Nobel Prize in literature, 1954. [d. July 2, 1961]

(Harold) Hart Crane, U.S. poet. [d. April 27, 1932]

1911 **(Herbert) Marshall McLuhan,** Canadian author, educator; contemporary expert on theories of **mass communication.** [d. December 31, 1980]

1920 **Isaac Stern,** U.S. violinist, born in Russia.

1934 **Jonathan Wolfe Miller,** British physician, stage and film director; co-author of and actor in *Beyond the Fringe,* 1961; directed numerous plays for National Theatre of London, 1970–78.

1947 **Cat Stevens (Steven Georgiou),** British singer, songwriter.

Historical Events

1773 **Pope Clement XIV** suppresses **Jesuit Order.**

1796 **Mungo Park,** British explorer, reaches the **Niger River**, in Africa, and starts his trip downstream to trace the course of the river.

1798 French defeat the Mamluk cavalry and take **Cairo** during the **Battle of the Pyramids** in Bonaparte's Egyptian expedition.

1861 Union General Irvin McDowell is defeated at **First Battle of Bull Run.**

1944 U.S. Marines and Army troops land on **Guam (World War II).**

1960 Ceylon's first woman prime minister, Mme. **Sirimavo Bandaranaike,** is sworn in at ceremonies in Colombo.

1966 *Gemini 10,* U.S. spacecraft carrying astronauts **John Young** and **Michael Collins,** achieves rendezvous with two space targets, and Collins accomplishes two walks in space.

Religious Calendar

The Saints

St. Praxedes, virgin. Also called **Praxedis.** [d. 1st–2nd century] Feast suppressed 1969.

St. Victor of Marseilles, martyr; patron of cabinet-makers. Invoked against lightning. [d. c. 290]

St. Arbogast, Bishop of Strasburg. Also called **Arbogastus.** [d. 6th century]

St. Lawrence of Brindisi, theologian, missionary, and doctor of the church. [d. 1619]

The Beatified

Blessed Oddino of Fossano, parish priest. [d. 1400]

Blessed Angelina of Marsciano, widow and abbess. [d. 1435]

1976   Christopher T.E. Ewart-Briggs, British ambassador to **Ireland**, and others are killed by a land mine set off under their car.

1978   **Juan Pereda Asbún** declares himself President of Bolivia after deposing President **Hugo Banzer Suárez** in a military coup.

July 22

Holidays

Poland	National Liberation Day
Swaziland	King's Birthday

Commemorates birthday of King Sobhuza II, 1899; Sobhuza came to power in 1967.

Religious Calendar

The Saints

St. Mary Magdalen, a follower of Christ and the first to see the Risen Christ; patron of perfumers, glovemakers, tanners, and repentant women. Also called

Birthdates

1621 **Anthony Ashley Cooper Shaftesbury, First Earl of Shaftesbury, 1st Baron Ashley,** English statesman; a leading politician under Oliver Cromwell (April 25). [d. January 21, 1683]

1784 **Friedrich Wilhelm Bessel,** Prussian astronomer; calculated path of Halley's Comet; invented mathematical functions (*Bessel functions*) used in mathematical physics. [d. March 17, 1846]

1803 **Eugene Louis Gabriel Isabey,** French painter; known for his marine paintings. [d. April 25, 1886]

1822 **Gregor Johann Mendel,** Austrian botanist, Augustinian monk; described laws of biological inheritance (*Mendel's laws*). [d. January 6, 1884]

1849 **Emma Lazarus,** U.S. poet, essayist; her sonnet, *The New Colossus,* is inscribed on the base of the **Statue of Liberty.** [d. November 19, 1887]

1878 **Ernest Ball,** U.S. vaudeville actor, composer of such early 20th-century songs as *Mother Machree.* [d. May 3, 1927]

1882 **Edward Hopper,** U.S. painter; known as *Painter of Loneliness* because of his portrayal of stark, realistic scenes of contemporary life. [d. May 15, 1967]

1887 **Gustav Ludwig Hertz,** German physicist; Nobel Prize in physics for discovery of laws governing the collision of electron with an atom (with J. Franck), 1925. [d. October 30, 1975]

1888 **Selman Abraham Waksman,** U.S. microbiologist, born in Russia; Nobel Prize in physiology or medicine for discovery of uses for **streptomycin** in treating tuberculosis, 1952. [d. August 16, 1973]

1890 **Rose Kennedy,** mother of U.S. President John F. Kennedy (May 29), Senators Robert F. (November 20) and Edward M. (February 22) Kennedy.

1891 **Ely Culbertson,** U.S. bridge expert born in Rumania; world champion **contract bridge** player; responsible for popularity of the game, especially during 1930s and 1940s. Became deeply involved in world peace activities during his later years, 1949–55. [d. December 17, 1955]

1892 **Arthur Seyss-Inquart,** German politician, Nazi leader; Chancellor of Austria, 1938–39; German High Commissioner of the Netherlands, 1940–45. Hanged for war crimes. [d. October 16, 1946]

1893 **Karl Augustus Menninger,** U.S. psychiatrist; with his father, Charles Frederich Menninger and his brother, William Claire, created the **Menninger Foundation,** 1941, a national center for training of psychiatrists and treatment and research in mental health.

1898 **Stephen Vincent Benét,** U.S. poet, short-story writer, novelist; Pulitzer Prize in poetry, 1928, 1943. [d. March 13, 1943]

Alexander Calder, U.S. sculptor; best known for his mobiles and stabiles. Also recognized for his watercolors, jewelry, tapestries, and carving. [d. November 11, 1976]

1899 **King Sobhuz II,** King of Swaziland, 1921–82. [d. August 21, 1982]

Mawdleyn. [d. 1st century] Obligatory Memorial [major holy day, Episcopal Church; minor festival, Lutheran Church].

St. Joseph of Palestine, scholar. Also called **Count Joseph.** [d. c. 356]

St. Wandregisilus, abbot. Also called **Vandrille, Wandrille.** [d. 668]

The Beatified

Blessed Benno, Bishop of Osnabrück. [d. 1088]

1908 **Amy Vanderbilt,** U.S. journalist, etiquette expert, author. [d. December 27, 1974]

1913 **Charles B(ates) Thornton,** U.S. industrialist; head of Ford Motor Company's "Whiz Kids," who set up modern management systems at the company, 1948–53; a founder of Litton Industries; Chairman and Chief Executive Officer of Litton, 1953–81. [d. November 24, 1981]

1922 **Jason (Nelson) Robards, Jr.,** U.S. actor.

1923 **Robert J. Dole,** U.S. politician, lawyer.

1924 **Margaret Whiting** (*Madcap Maggie*), U.S. singer, big band era star.

1928 **Bob Selmer Bergland,** U.S. government official, farmer; U.S. Secretary of Agriculture, 1977–80.

1932 **Oscar de la Renta,** U.S. fashion designer.

1940 **Terence Stamp,** British actor.

Historical Events

1194 **Richard I** of England defeats **Philip Augustus** of France at Frèteval.

1298 **Edward I** of England defeats Scottish leader **William Wallace** at **Falkirk.**

1812 The **Battle of Salamanca** ends in the defeat of the French by the British under **Wellesley** during British drive into Spain.

1847 First large **Mormon** company enters Salt Lake Valley.

1876 **Maria Spelterina** walks across **Niagara Falls** on a tightrope.

1913 Turkey recaptures Adrianople and forces Bulgaria to capitulate (**Second Balkan War**).

1917 The reorganized Rumanian army joins with the Russians in launching an attack on the Germans in the **Battle of Marasesti** (**World War I**).

Siam declares war on Germany and Austria-Hungary (**World War I**).

1932 U.S. Congress adopts the **Federal Home Loan Bank Act** to help financial institutions lend money to homeowners.

1943 U.S. forces liberate **Palermo, Sicily** (**World War II**).

1963 **Sonny Liston** defeats **Floyd Patterson** in the first round to retain the world heavyweight championship.

1969 Prince **Juan Carlos (Alfonso Victor María de Borbón y) Borbón** is named legal successor and heir to the Spanish throne by General **Francisco Franco.** Juan Carlos assumes the throne upon the death of Franco, November 20, 1975.

July 23

Holidays

Egypt	**Revolution Anniversary** Commemorates the overthrow of the monarchy, 1952.
Libya	**A.R.E. National Day** Commemorates the overthrow of the monarchy in Egypt, 1952.
Syria	**Egyptian Revolution Day**

Religious Calendar

The Saints

The Three Wise Men, patrons of **Cologne** and of travellers. [d. 1st century]

Birthdates

1649 **Pope Clement XI,** pope 1700–21. [d. March 19, 1721]

1816 **Charlotte Saunders Cushman,** U.S. actress; best known for her portrayals of Lady Macbeth. [d. February 12, 1876]

1823 **Coventry Kersey Dighton Patmore,** British poet, political reactionary; assistant librarian of British Museum, 1846–65. [d. November 26, 1896]

1834 **James Gibbons,** U.S. Roman Catholic cardinal; founder of **Catholic University of America.** [d. March 24, 1921]

1863 **Samuel Henry Kress,** U.S. merchant, philanthropist; founder of S. H. Kress & Co., 5, 10, and 25 cent store. Established the **Samuel H. Kress Foundation** to distribute his significant art collection to selected museums throughout the U.S. [d. September 22, 1955]

Kelly Miller, U.S. black academician, editor; dean of Howard University School of Arts & Letters. [d. December 29, 1939]

1883 **Sir Alan Francis Brooke, 1st Viscount Alanbrooke,** British soldier; Commander in Chief of British home forces, 1940–41; Chief of Imperial General Staff, 1941; Field Marshal, 1944. [d. June 17, 1963]

1884 **Albert Warner,** U.S. film executive born in Poland; brother of Harry (December 12) and Jack (August 2); with his brothers, founded Warner Brothers Studios. [d. November 26, 1967]

1886 **Arthur W. Brown,** British aviator; with **John Alcock** made the first flight across the Atlantic, 1919. [d. October 4, 1948]

1888 **Raymond (Thornton) Chandler,** U.S. short-story writer, novelist; author of numerous detective stories revolving around the escapades of detective *Philip Marlowe.* [d. March 26, 1959]

1892 **Haile Selassie (Tafari Makonnen),** called the *Lion of Judah,* Emperor of Ethiopia, 1930–74. [d. August 27, 1975]

1894 **Arthur Treacher,** British actor; famous for his roles as a haughty butler. [d. December 14, 1975]

1906 **Vladimir Prelog,** Yugoslav-Swiss chemist; Nobel Prize in chemistry for his work in **stereochemistry** (with J. W. Cornforth), 1975.

1911 **Penitala Fiatau Teo,** Tuvaluan statesman; Governor-General, 1978– .

1912 **Michael Wilding,** British actor. [d. July 8, 1979]

1913 **Michael Foot,** British political leader; head of the Labour Party, 1980–83.

1925 **Dr. Quett Ketumile Joni Masire,** Botswanan statesman; President, 1980– .

1930 **Moon Landrieu,** U.S. politician; Mayor of New Orleans, 1970–78, Secretary of Housing and Urban Development, 1979–81.

Historical Events

1840 **Union Act** is passed by British Parliament, uniting **Upper** and **Lower Canada** into one government with one governor, one council, and one popularly elected assembly.

St. Liborius, Bishop of Le Mans. Invoked against gravel and the stone and allied complaints. [d. 4th century]

St. John Cassian, abbot. Founded two monasteries at Marseilles. Commonly known as **Cassian.** [d. c. 433]

St. Romula and her companions, virgins. [d. 6th century]

St. Anne, virgin. Also called **Susanna.** [d. c. 918]

St. Bridget of Sweden, widow and founder of the Order of the Most Holy Savior, or the *Bridgettines.* Patron of Sweden. [d. 1373]

St. Apollinaris, Bishop of Ravenna and martyr. [death date unknown]

The Beatified

Blessed Joan of Orvieto, virgin. [d. 1306]

1920	**British East Africa** becomes crown colony of **Kenya.**
1950	**King Leopold III** of Belgium returns after six years in exile and is met by Socialist demonstrations which force his abdication on July 17, 1951.
1952	Egypt's Lt. Col. **Gamal Abdel Nasser** and a group of military officers stage a coup d'état and exile **King Farouk.**
1967	U.S. National Guard troops are called into **Detroit** to quell racial violence.
1970	**Sultan Saʻīd ibn Taimur** of Oman is deposed by his son, **Qabus ibn Saʻīd,** in a palace coup.
1971	**William R. Tolbert, Jr.,** is sworn in as President of **Liberia** upon the death of William Tubman.
1977	Muslim leader **Hamaas Abdul Khaalis** and two followers are found guilty of kidnapping, conspiracy, and second-degree murder during their seizure in March of three buildings in Washington, D.C.
1979	**Ayatollah Khomeini, Islamic** religious leader of Iran, issues a ban on music and reaffirms bans on most Western movies, alcoholic drink, singing by women, and swimming of men and women in the same pool or at the same beaches.

July 24

Holidays

Ecuador, Venezuela	**Bolívar's Birthday** Commemorates birth of Simón Bolívar, the *George Washington of South America*, 1783.

Religious Calendar

The Saints

St. Declan, first Bishop of Ardmore. [d. 6th century]

St. Boris and **St. Gleb,** martyrs; patrons of Muscovy. Sometimes referred to by their christening names,

Birthdates

1738 **Elisabeth Wolff-Bekker, (Silviana),** Dutch novelist, essayist, poet, translator. [d. November 5, 1804]

1783 **Simón Bolívar,** South American soldier, statesman, revolutionary leader; leader of struggle for independence from Spain in Venezuela, Peru, and Colombia. [d. December 17, 1830]

1798 **John Adams Dix,** U.S. politician, soldier; U.S. Secretary of the Treasury, 1861; Governor of New York, 1872–74. [d. April 21, 1879]

1802 **Aléxandre Dumas (Dumas père),** French novelist, playwright; author of: *Les Trois Mousquetaires, Le Comte de Monte Cristo,* as well as numerous other novels and plays. [d. December 5, 1870]

1817 **Adolphus William,** Grand Duke of Luxembourg; the first ruler of the autonomous duchy. [d. November 17, 1905]

1827 **Francisco Solano López,** president of Paraguay, 1862–70. [d. March 1, 1870]

1842 **Ambrose (Gwinett) Bierce,** U.S. journalist, short-story writer; known for his scathing wit and preoccupation with the supernatural. His tales of the Civil War and *Devil's Dictionary* gained him wide recognition, especially by American writers like O. Henry and Stephen Crane. [d. 1914?]

1855 **William (Hooker) Gillette,** U.S. dramatist, actor; best known for his stage portrayals of legendary detective *Sherlock Holmes.* [d. April 29, 1937]

1857 **Juan Vincente Gómez,** Venezuelan soldier, political leader; dictator of Venezuela and commander-in-chief of its army, 1908–35. [d. December 17, 1935]

Henrik Pontoppidan, Danish novelist, short-story writer; Nobel Prize in literature (with K. Gjellerup), 1917. [d. August 21, 1943]

1898 **Amelia Earhart,** U.S. aviator; pioneer in development of U.S. aviation industry; first woman to cross the Atlantic by plane; disappeared over the Pacific during a flight from New Guinea to Howland Island. [d. July 2, 1937?]

1916 **John D. MacDonald,** U.S. mystery novelist, short-story writer.

1920 **Alexander H. Cohen,** U.S. theater and television producer.

1921 **Billy Taylor (William Edward Taylor),** U.S. musician, jazz pianist.

Historical Events

1758 British take **Louisburg** in Canada from the French (**French and Indian War**).

1918 Cornerstone of the **Hebrew University** in Jerusalem is laid by **Dr. Chaim Weizmann.**

1923 **Treaty of Lausanne** is concluded, by which **Turkey** gives up all claims to non-Turkish territories lost in World War I, but retains control over areas still regarded as modern Turkey.

1943 British and U.S. air forces begin concentrated bombing of **Hamburg,** Germany (**World War II**).

Romanus and David. Gleb is also called **Cliba, Hliba.** [d. 1015]

St. Christina the Astonishing, virgin. [d. 1224]

St. Cunegund, virgin. Also called **Cunegundes** or **Kinga.** [d. 1292]

St. Christina, virgin and martyr. Also called **Christine.** [death date unknown]

St. Lewina, virgin and martyr. Also called **Lewine.** [death date unknown]

St. Wulfhad and **St. Ruffin,** brothers, princes, and martyrs. [death date unknown]

The Beatified

Blessed Nicholas, Bishop of Linköping. [d. 1391]

Blessed Felicia of Milan, virgin and abbess. [d. 1444]

Blessed John of Tossignano, Bishop of Ferrara. [d. 1446]

Blessed Augustine of Biella. [d. 1493]

The Durham Martyrs of 1594: Blessed John Speed (or **Spence**); **Blessed John Boste,** priest; **Blessed George Swallowell; Blessed John Ingram,** priest.

1963   Cuban government expropriates the U.S. embassy building and grounds in **Havana.**

1974   U.S. Supreme Court orders President **Richard Nixon** to surrender 64 tapes to Washington district court (**Watergate Incident**).

1975   The three *Apollo 18* astronauts return to earth, ending an age of U.S. space exploration that began in 1961. The next U.S. venture into space does not occur until the launch of U.S. space shuttle *Columbia*, April 12, 1981.

July 25

Birthdates

1750 **Henry Knox,** American Revolutionary general; considered an artillery genius. [d. October 25, 1806]

1839 **Francis Garnier,** French explorer of mainland China. [d. December 21, 1873]

1844 **Thomas (Cowperthwait) Eakins,** U.S. artist; recognized posthumously as one of the greatest American artists; noted for his realism and use of geometrical perspective. [d. June 25, 1916]

1848 **Arthur James Balfour, 1st Earl of Balfour,** British statesman; Prime Minister, 1902–05. [d. March 19, 1930]

1849 **Richard Lydekker,** British naturalist, geologist, author. [d. April 16, 1915]

1853 **David Belasco,** U.S. producer, playwright; known for his innovations in staging techniques and technical precision. Author of *Madame Butterfly*, later made into an opera by Giacomo Puccini. [d. May 14, 1931]

1870 **Maxfield (Frederick) Parrish,** U.S. painter, illustrator; known for his use of sentimental, romantic, and dreamlike qualities in paintings. [d. March 30, 1966]

1880 **Morris Raphael Cohen,** U.S. philosopher, author; known for his independent thought that drew upon pragmatism, logical positivism, and linguistic analysis; recognized for his work in the area of legal philosophy. [d. January 28, 1947]

1884 **Davidson Black,** Canadian anatomist; discoverer of **Peking Man,** whose fossils date back to between 300,000 and 400,000 B.C.

1894 **Walter Brennan,** U.S. character actor. [d. September 21, 1974]

1895 **Gavrilo Princip,** Serbian assassin of Archduke **Francis Ferdinand** (December 18) and his wife Sophie, 1914. This assassination triggered **World War I.** [d. April 28, 1918]

1902 **Eric Hoffer,** U.S. philosopher, author; representative of the working class in the area of social and political thought. [d. May 21, 1983]

1906 **Johnny Hodges (John Cornelius Hodges),** U.S. jazz alto saxophonist of the 1930s and 1940s. [d. May 11, 1970]

1915 **Mario Del Monaco,** Italian opera singer; appeared with the Metropolitan Opera more than 100 times between 1951 and 1959. [d. October 16, 1982]

1917 **Fritz Honegger,** Swiss statesman; President, 1981– .

1924 **Frank Church,** U.S. politician and lawyer; U.S. Senator, 1957–1981. [d. April 7, 1984]

Historical Events

1139 **Alfonso Henriques** defeats the Moors in the **Battle of Ourique** and becomes King of Portugal.

1261 **Michael VIII Palaeologus,** Byzantine emperor, recovers Constantinople and overthrows **Latin Empire,** which had been established by the successful Crusaders in 1204.

1415 **Prince Henry** of Portugal sails for Morocco, the first of a series of voyages of exploration and conquest in Africa by Europeans.

1564 **Ferdinand I, Holy Roman Emperor,** dies and is succeeded by **Maximilian II.**

Religious Calendar

Feasts

St. James the Greater, Apostle. First apostle to be martyred. Patron saint of Spain and Chile. Also called **James Major, Santiago.** [d. 44] [Major holy day, Episcopal Church; minor festival, Lutheran Church.]

The Saints

St. Thea, St. Valentina and **St. Paul,** martyrs. [d. 308]

St. Magnericus, Bishop of Trier. [d. 596]

St. Christopher, martyr; patron of archers, fruit dealers, travelers, mariners, and motorists. Invoked against water, tempest, plagues and sudden death. Also called **Christoper,** or **Christophorus.** [death date unknown]

1712 The Protestant cantons led by the city of Bern win a decisive victory over the Catholic cantons at the **Battle of Villmergen,** ending the religious wars in **Switzerland.**

1848 In **Battle of Custozza,** Austrians defeat forces of **Charles Albert,** King of Sardinia, suppressing first efforts toward Italian independence.

1914 Austria and Serbia mobilize against one another in the wake of the assassination at Sarajevo of the Austrian heir, Archduke **Francis Ferdinand.**

1929 **Pope Pius XI** makes an appearance outside the Vatican; this is the first public appearance of a pope since the fall of the Papal States, 1870.

1934 **Franklin D. Roosevelt** reaches Hilo, Hawaii, on board *U.S.S. Houston*, becoming the first U.S. president to visit Hawaii.

Austrian Chancellor **Engelbert Dollfuss** is assassinated by Nazi adherents.

1943 Premier **Benito Mussolini** of Italy and his cabinet resign.

1956 Italian ocean liner ***Andrea Doria*** sinks after collision with the Swedish ship ***Stockholm*** off Cape Cod, killing approximately 50 people.

1978 The first documented **test-tube baby** is born in Lancashire, England. The five pound, 12-ounce girl, **Louise Joy Brown,** is delivered by Caesarean section.

July 26

Holidays

Cuba　　**National Holiday**
Commemorates the beginning of Fidel Castro's 26th of July Movement.

Liberia　　**Independence Day**
Commemorates ratification of Liberian constitution, 1847.

Maldives　　**Independence Day**
Commemorates achievement of independence from Great Britain, 1965.

Birthdates

1739 **George Clinton,** U.S. Revolutionary soldier, public official; Governor of New York, 1777–95, 1800–04; U.S. Vice-President, 1805–12. [d. April 2, 1812]

1779 **Thomas Birch,** U.S. artist; noted for his marine paintings. [d. January 13, 1851]

1796 **George Catlin,** U.S. painter, author; created a knowledgeable, first-hand account, in words and pictures, of the life and details of the American Indian. He produced numerous illustrated texts, the greatest of which is *Letters and Notes on the Manners, Customs, and Conditions of the North American Indians*, 1841. [d. December 23, 1872]

1799 **Isaac Babbitt,** U.S. inventor, metallurgist; founded the company which was to become Reed & Barton silversmiths; developed a new alloy ("Babbitt metal") for use in bearings. [d. May 26, 1862]

1805 **Constantino Brumidi,** U.S. painter born in Italy; artist of the frescoes in the Capitol, Washington, D.C. [d. 1880]

1829 **Auguste Marie François Beernaert,** Belgian diplomat; Nobel Peace Prize for his work as member of international peace conferences of 1899 and 1907 (with P. H. B. Estournelles de Constant), 1909. [d. October 6, 1912]

1856 **William Rainey Harper,** U.S. educator, scholar; first President of **University of Chicago,** 1891–1906. [d. January 10, 1906]

George Bernard Shaw, British playwright, critic; Nobel Prize in literature, 1925. [d. November 4, 1950]

1858 **Edward Mandell House,** U.S. statesman; most trusted adviser of President **Woodrow Wilson.** [d. March 28, 1938]

1860 **Philippe Jean Bunau-Varilla,** French engineer, diplomat; involved in early French efforts to construct **Panama Canal,** 1884–89, 1894. Negotiated **Hay-Bunau-Varilla Treaty** by which U.S. gained control of Canal Zone, 1903. [d. May 18, 1940]

1870 **Ignacio Zuloaga y Zabaleta,** Spanish painter; noted for his use of Spanish folklore themes. [d. October 31, 1945]

1874 **Serge Alexandrovitch Koussevitzky,** U.S. conductor, born in Russia; Director, Russian State Symphony Orchestra, 1918–20; Conductor, Boston Symphony Orchestra, 1924–49. Established **Berkshire Symphonic Festival,** 1934. [d. June 4, 1951]

1875 **Carl Gustav Jung,** Swiss psychologist, psychiatrist; founded analytical psychology. [d. June 6, 1961]

1885 **André Maurois (Émile Salomon Wilhelm Herzog),** French writer; known for his biographies of Balzac, Disraeli, Byron, and others. [d. October 9, 1967]

1894 **Aldous (Leonard) Huxley,** British novelist, essayist; best known for his works *Brave New World, Point Counter Point,* and *Eyeless in Gaza.* [d. November 22, 1963]

1897 **Paul William Gallico,** U.S. novelist, journalist. [d. July 15, 1976]

1903 **(Carey) Estes Kefauver,** U.S. politician, lawyer; Congressman, 1939–63. [d. August 10, 1963]

Religious Calendar

The Saints

St. Joachim, father of the Virgin Mary, and **St. Anne,** matron, mother of the Virgin Mary. Anne is patron of women in labor, miners, dealers in used clothing, seamstresses, carpenters, stablemen, and broommakers. Invoked against poverty and to find lost objects. [d. 1st century B.C.]

St. Simeon the Armenian, pilgrim. [d. 1016]

St. Bartholomea Capitanio, virgin and co-founder of the Sisters of Charity of Lovene. [d. 1833]

The Beatified

Blessed William Ward, martyr. [d. 1641]

1906 **Gracie Allen (Grace Ethel Cecile Rosalie Allen),** U.S. comedienne; always performed with husband, **George Burns** (January 20). [d. August 27, 1964]

1908 **Salvador Allende Gossens,** Chilean politician, physician; first Marxist to be elected president of Chile, 1970–73. [d. September 11, 1973]

1922 **Blake Edwards (William Blake McEdwards),** U.S. film director; noted for the *Pink Panther* film series.

1928 **Stanley Kubrick,** U.S.-born filmmaker, writer, producer, director.

1943 **Mick Jagger (Michael Philip Jagger),** British rock singer; lead singer of *The Rolling Stones* since 1962.

Historical Events

1648 Swedes and French, allied against the Holy Roman Emperor, capture **Prague (Thirty Years' War).**

1757 French defeat English at **Hastenbeck (Seven Years' War).**

British generals Amherst and Wolfe capture Louisburg, taking more than 6,000 French prisoners (**French and Indian War**).

1788 **New York State** ratifies the new Constitution and becomes the 11th of the 13 original American states.

1803 In England the **Surrey Iron Railway,** first public freight-carrying railroad, opens from Wandsworth to Croydon with horses supplying motive power.

1847 **Liberia** is established as the first free and independent republic in Africa.

1858 **Sir Nathan Meyer, 1st Baron Rothschild,** becomes the first Jew admitted to the House of Lords.

1941 U.S. President **Franklin D. Roosevelt** names **Gen. Douglas MacArthur** Commander in Chief of U.S. forces in the Far East.

President Roosevelt freezes all Japanese credit in the U.S., virtually stopping Japanese-American trade.

1951 U.S. Army disbands its oldest and last remaining all-black unit, the **24th Infantry Regiment.**

1953 **Fidel Castro** leads an armed opposition in an unsuccessful attack on the Moncado army barracks.

1956 Egypt nationalizes the **Suez Canal.**

1965 **Maldives** becomes independent of Great Britain.

1971 *Apollo 15,* U.S. manned lunar spacecraft, is launched, carrying astronauts **Scott, Worden,** and **Irwin** to the moon's surface, where they will perform experiments and explore in the lunar rover.

1973 U.S. President **Richard Nixon** refuses to comply with subpoenas ordering him to release the Watergate tapes (**Watergate Incident**).

1976 Nitrogen is found in Martian atmosphere by *Viking 1,* unmanned explorer, but there are no signs of life present.

July 27

Holidays

Cuba	National Holiday
Maldives	**Independence Day**
	The second day of the two-day national celebration.
Puerto Rico	**Barbosa's Birthday**
	Commemorates the birth of José Barbosa, political leader, 1857.

Religious Calendar

The Saints

St. Pantaleon, martyr; patron of doctors and midwives. Invoked against tuberculosis. Also called **Panteleimon.** [d. c. 305]

Birthdates

1768 **Charlotte Corday (Marie Anne Charlotte Corday d'Armont),** French patriot; assassin of French revolutionary leader Jean Paul Marat (May 24). [d. July 17, 1793]

1777 **Thomas Campbell,** Scottish poet, biographer; his biography of S. T. Coleridge (October 21) is considered the standard. [d. June 25, 1844]

1801 **Sir George Biddell Airy,** British mathematician, astronomer, physicist; discoverer of basis for study of astigmatism. [d. January 2, 1892]

1824 **Aléxandre Dumas (*Dumas fils*),** French dramatist, novelist; son of Aléxandre Dumas *(père)* (July 24). Author of *La Dame aux Camèlias,* 1848. [d. November 27, 1895]

1835 **Giosuè Carducci,** Italian poet, critic; Nobel Prize in literature, 1906. [d. February 16, 1907]

1852 **George Foster Peabody,** U.S. merchant, banker, philanthropist; amassed fortune in international commercial trade; established and endowed many institutions and funds. Founded Peabody Museum of natural history and science at Yale University. [d. March 4, 1938]

1857 **Sir Ernest Alfred Wallis Budge,** British orientologist, archaeologist; keeper of Egyptian and Assyrian antiquities at British Museum, 1893–1924. [d. November 23, 1934]

1870 **(Joseph-Pierre) Hilaire Belloc,** British writer, born in France; journalist, member of Parliament, 1906–10. [d. July 16, 1953]

1881 **Hays Fischer,** German chemist; Nobel Prize in chemistry for research into constitution of **hemin** and **chlorophyll,** 1930. [d. March 31, 1945]

1901 **George D(avid) Woods,** U.S. banker; President and Chief Executive Officer, World Bank, 1963–68; Chairman of J. Kaiser Foundation, 1968–82. [d. August 20, 1982]

1906 **Leo Ernest Durocher,** U.S. baseball player, manager; known both for his outstanding performances with the St. Louis Cardinals and Brooklyn Dodgers and for his flamboyant management style.

1912 **Igor Markevitch,** Swiss conductor born in Russia; began as a composing prodigy; later best known as a master of conducting precision.

1916 **Keenan Wynn,** U.S. actor.

1922 **Norman Lear,** U.S. television producer, director.

1948 **Peggy Fleming,** U.S. figure skater; Olympic gold medalist, 1968; world champion, 1966–68.

Historical Events

1054 **Siward of Northumbria** and **Malcolm** defeat **Macbeth** at **Dunsinane** in Scotland.

1214 **Battle of Bouvines** establishes France as a major European power, as Philip II of

St. Aurelius, St. Natalia, and their companions, martyrs. [d. c. 852]

St. Theobald of Marly, abbot. [d. 1247]

The Seven Sisters of Ephesus. Legend says they were sealed into a cave while still alive. Invoked against sleeplessness. [death date unknown]

The Beatified

Blessed Berthold of Garsten, abbot. [d. 1142]

Blessed Lucy of Amelia, virgin and prioress. [d. 1350]

Blessed Rudolf Aquaviva and his companions, martyrs. [d. 1583]

Blessed Mary Magdalen Martinengo, virgin and abbess. [d. 1737]

France, allied with Frederick II of Germany, defeats anti-Capetian coalition of England, Flanders, Belgium, Lorraine, and Holy Roman Emperor.

1689   Scottish Jacobites are defeated at **Killiecrankie.**

1694   **Bank of England** is incorporated.

1866   **Atlantic cable** is completed, establishing communication by telegraph between England and U.S.

1944   U.S. regains control of **Guam** after bitter fighting (**World War II**).

1953   Armistice is signed by United Nations and Communist delegates, ending **Korean War.**

1965   Belgium's longest governmental crisis since World War II is ended by the formation of a coalition cabinet by **Pierre Harmel** of the Social Christian Party.

1980   **Mohammed Reza Pahlavi,** the deposed Shah of Iran, dies in Cairo.

July 28

Holidays

Peru   **Independence Day**
Commemorates Peru's
declaration of independence
from Spain, 1821. The first day
of a two-day celebration.

Religious Calendar

St. Victor I, pope and martyr; elected 189. [d. c. 199]
Rome 189.

Birthdates

1804 **Ludwig Andreas Feuerbach,** German philosopher; after abandoning Hegelian idealism, adopted a philosophy of *naturalistic materialism* which culminated in the teaching that God is merely the outward projection of man's own nature. [d. September 13, 1872]

1812 **Józef Ignacy Kraszewski,** Polish writer of novels, plays, verse, criticism, and history; one of the most influential and prolific Polish authors of the 19th century. [d. March 19, 1887]

1830 **Charles Franklin Dunbar,** U.S. editor, economist; first professor of political economy at Harvard, 1870–1900. [d. January 29, 1900]

1844 **Gerard Manley Hopkins,** British Jesuit priest, poet; developed poetic techniques of *sprung rhythm, counterpoint,* and *inscape.* [d. June 8, 1889]

1859 **Ballington Booth,** U.S. reformer, born in England; son of William Booth (April 10), founder of the Salvation Army. Ballington headed the **Salvation Army** in Australia, 1885–87 and in U.S., 1887–96. After disagreement with his father, left organization and founded **Volunteers of America.** [d. October 5, 1940]

1866 **Beatrix Potter,** British author of children's books, illustrator; the creator of *Peter Rabbit.* [d. December 22, 1943]

1887 **Marcel Duchamp,** U.S. painter born in France; a founder of **Dadaism.** [d. October 2, 1968]

1892 **Joe E. Brown,** U.S. comedian. [d. July 6, 1973]

1901 **Rudy Vallee (Hubert Prior Vallee),** U.S. entertainer; first to popularize the singing style known as *crooning;* introduced Edgar Bergen (February 16) and Charlie McCarthy, George Burns (January 20) and Grace Allen (July 26).

1902 **Kenneth Flexner Fearing,** U.S. novelist, poet; noted for his radical style in poetry, marked by unconventional structure and use of vernacular phrases. [d. June 26, 1961]

1915 **Charles Hard Townes,** U.S. physicist; Nobel Prize in physics for development of **maser-laser principle** (with N. G. Basov and Aleksander M. Prokhorov), 1964.

1925 **Baruch S. Blumberg,** U.S. physician; Nobel Prize in physiology or medicine for discoveries relating to origin and spread of infectious diseases (with D. C. Gajdusek), 1976.

1929 **Jacqueline Bouvier Kennedy Onassis,** former U.S. First Lady; widow of U.S. President John F. Kennedy (May 29); widow of Greek shipping magnate Aristotle Onassis; editor, Doubleday & Co., 1978– .

1937 **Peter (Oelrichs) Duchin,** U.S. musician; pianist and orchestra leader; son of Eddy Duchin (April 1).

1943 **(William Warren) Bill Bradley,** U.S. politician, basketball player for New York Knickerbockers, 1967–77; U.S. Senator, 1979– .

Historical Events

1402 **Timur Link (Tamerlane)** and his Mongols defeat and capture Ottoman ruler **Bajazet I** at the **Battle of Angora** (Ankara).

1461 **Charles VII** of France dies and is succeeded by **Louis XI.**

1540 **Thomas Cromwell, Earl of Essex,** is beheaded for heresy in the Tower of London

St. Innocent I, pope; elected 402. [d. 417]

St. Samson, Bishop of Dol. Important figure in the evangelization of Cornwall and the Channel Islands. Also called **Sampson.** [d. c. 565]

St. Botvid, martyr; venerated as one of the apostles of Sweden.

St. Nazarius and **St. Celsus,** martyrs. [death date unknown]

The Beatified

Blessed Antony Della Chiesa, friar and prior. [d. 1459]

---

after alienating **Henry VIII**; he had arranged Henry's brief and unsuccessful marriage to **Anne of Cleves.**

Henry VIII of England marries **Catherine Howard,** his fifth wife.

1588 **Spanish Armada,** anchored in Calais, is dispersed by English ships.

1637 A combined force from Plymouth, Massachusetts and Connecticut destroys remnants of **Pequot Indians** near New Haven (**Pequot War**).

1794 **Robespierre** and 71 others are guillotined, ending the **Reign of Terror (French Revolution**).

1821 **Peru,** under the leadership of **José de San Martín** declares itself independent of Spain.

1868 The **14th Amendment to U.S. Constitution** is ratified, granting citizenship to U.S. blacks.

1904 **Vyacheslav Plehwe,** Russian Minister of the Interior, is assassinated.

1914 **Austria-Hungary** declares war on **Serbia (World War I**).

1916 **Battle of Kovel** renews the successful Russian offensive against Austria in southern Galicia (**World War I**).

1926 Panama-U.S. Treaty is signed, protecting **Panama Canal** in time of war.

1932 **Bonus March** on Washington, D.C. is disbanded by federal troops; the march resulted from dissatisfaction on the part of soldiers over U.S. government's honoring of soldiers' bonus certificates.

1972 Mexican President **Luis Echeverría** decrees the expropriation of some 500,000 acres of private estates and distribution of the land to peasants.

1973 U.S. astronauts **Alan L. Bean, Owen K. Garriott,** and **Jack R. Lousma** are launched into space for a 59-day mission in *Skylab*, demonstrating man's ability to withstand long periods in space.

1976 Two major **earthquakes,** occurring 16 hours apart and measuring 8.2 and 7.9 on the Richter scale, strike northeast **China,** resulting in nearly 750,000 deaths.

1977 First oil through the **Alaskan Pipeline** reaches Valdez, Alaska.

1979 The leader of a breakaway faction of the **Janata Party,** 77-year old **Charan Sinph,** is sworn in as Prime Minister of India but resigns within one month as Gandhi government regains power.

July 29

Holidays

Peru   **Independence Day**
The second day of a two-day
celebration.

Religious Calendar

The Saints

St. Martha, virgin; sister of Mary and Lazarus; min-
istered to Jesus. Patron of hotelkeepers, laundresses,

Birthdates

1793   **Jan Kollár,** Slovak poet, philologist born in
Hungary. [d. January 4, 1852]

1794   **Thomas Corwin,** U.S. lawyer, legislator;
U.S. Secretary of the Treasury, 1850–53. [d.
December 18, 1865]

1796   **Christian Winther,** Danish romantic poet;
author of epic poem *Hjortens Flugt.* [d. December 30, 1876]

1805   **Alexis de Tocqueville,** French writer; noted for his writings on American democra-
cy; author of *La Dèmocratie en Amérique.*
[d. April 26, 1859]

1820   **Clement Laird Vallandigham,** U.S. public
official, lawyer; leader of the *Peace Democrats* or *Copperheads* during the U.S. Civil
War; vehemently opposed President Abraham Lincoln's policies during the Civil
War; opposition resulted in his banishment to the Confederacy. [d. June 17, 1871]

1869   **(Newton) Booth Tarkington,** U.S. author;
popular for his novels portraying boyhood
and life in the American Midwest; author
of *Penrod* and *Seventeen.* [d. May 19, 1946]

1877   **(Charles) William Beebe,** U.S. naturalist,
author; Director of Tropical Research, New
York Zoological Society; with Otis Barton
developed the **bathysphere,** which was
capable of record depth exploration of the
ocean. [d. June 4, 1962]

1883   **Benito Mussolini,** Italian dictator; founder
of Fascism with the creation of *Fascio di
Combattimento,* 1919; dictator of Italy,
1922–43. [d. April 28, 1945]

1887   **Sigmund Romberg,** U.S. composer; composed nearly 80 scores for stage plays and
more than 2,000 songs; considered one of
the most popular U.S. composers; wrote
The Student Prince. [d. November 9, 1951]

1892   **William Powell,** U.S. actor. [d. March 5,
1984]

1896   **Clark M(ell) Eichelberger,** U.S. international relations specialist; director of
League of Nations Association (later
**American Association for the United Na-
tions),** 1934–64. [d. January 26, 1980]

1898   **I(sidor) I(saac) Rabi,** U.S. physicist, born
in Poland; Nobel Prize in physics for discoveries in **spectroscopy,** 1944.

1900   **Eyvind Johnson,** Swedish novelist, short-
story writer; Nobel Prize in literature, 1974.

1905   **Dag Hammarskjöld,** Swedish political
economist; Secretary-General of United Nations, 1953–61; Nobel Peace Prize, 1961. [d.
September 18, 1961]

1907   **Melvin (Mouron) Belli,** U.S. lawyer; known
for his dramatic style and controversial
status of his clients.

1908   **Edgar F(osburgh) Kaiser,** U.S. industrialist; head of Kaiser Industries Corporation;
son of Henry J. Kaiser (May 9). [d. December 11, 1981]

1914   **Marcel Bich,** U.S.-French manufacturer,
born in Italy; founder of Bic Pen Corporation, 1950.

1918   **Edwin (Greene) O'Connor,** U.S. novelist.
[d. March 23, 1968]

1930   **Paul (Belville) Taylor,** U.S. modern dancer,
choreographer; director of the Paul Taylor
Dance Co., 1950– .

Historical Events

1030   **Olaf Haraldson,** Norwegian pretender, is
defeated at the **Battle of Stiklestad** by
King Canute II.

1565   **Mary, Queen of Scots** is married to her
cousin, **Henry Stuart, Lord Darnley.**

housewives, cooks, and those of service to the needy. [d. 1st century]

St. Simplicius, St. Faustinus and **St. Beatrice,** martyrs. Beatrice is also called **Viatrix.** [d. c. 304]

St. Felix II, antipope. [d. 365]

St. Lupus, Bishop of Troyes. Also called **Loup.** [d. 478]

St. Sulian, founder of Luxulyan Monastery. Also called **Silin.** [d. 6th century]

St. Olaf of Norway, King of Norway and martyr; patron and national hero of Norway. Also called **Olaus,** or **Olave.** [d. 1030]

St. William Pinchon, Bishop of Saint-Brieuc. [d. 1234]

The Beatified

Blessed Urban II, pope. Elected 1088. [d. 1099]

1830   **Charles X** abdicates during the **Revolution of 1830** in France. He is replaced by the Bourbon Duc d'Orléans who will reign as **Louis-Philippe.**

1848   **O'Brien's Rebellion,** the result of severe food shortages, is suppressed in Ireland, and rebellion leader **Smith O'Brien** is jailed.

1900   **Humbert I** of Italy is assassinated by anarchist **Gaetano Bresci.**

1967   The aircraft carrier **U.S.S. Forrestal** is severely damaged off Vietnam by a fire; 134 lives are lost and 60 planes and helicopters destroyed or damaged (**Vietnam War**).

1968   **Pope Paul VI,** in an encyclical, **Humanae Vitae,** upholds the Roman Catholic Church's prohibition against all artificial means of contraception.

     Virtually all the governing bodies of the Soviet and Czechoslovak Communist parties meet in **Cierna,** Czechoslovakia, to try to bridge the divisions between them.

1981   **Charles, Prince of Wales,** and **Lady Diana Spencer** are married in St. Paul's Cathedral, in London.

July 30

Holidays

Vanuatu   **Independence Day**
Commemorates the
achievement of independence
from Great Britain and France,
1980.

Religious Calendar

The Saints

St. Julitta, widow and martyr. [d. c. 303]

St. Abdon and **St. Sennen,** martyrs. Abdon also
called **Abden.** [d. c. 303]

Birthdates

1511   **Giorgio Vasari,** Italian painter, architect,
art historian; author of *Lives of the Paint-
ers,* 1551, which provides a detailed account of the lives of the great Italian masters; referred to in several of Robert Browning's poems on Renaissance artists. [d.
June 27, 1574]

1818   **Emily Jane (Ellis Bell) Brontë,** British
novelist, poet; author of *Wuthering Heights.*
Sister of Anne (January 17) and Charlotte
Brontë (April 21). [d. December 19, 1848]

1856   **Richard Burdon Haldane, Viscount
Haldane of Cloan,** British statesman, author; member of Parliament, 1885–1911;
Lord Chancellor, 1912–15, 1924. [d. August
19, 1928]

1857   **Thorstein (Bunde) Veblen,** U.S. social scientist, economist; author of *Theory of the
Leisure Class,* 1899. [d. August 3, 1919]

1863   **Henry Ford,** U.S. industrialist; founder
and President of the Ford Motor Co.; introduced standardization and mass-produc-
tion techniques in the automobile industry; established the **Ford Foundation,**
1936. [d. April 7, 1947]

1870   **Lavrenti Georgievich Kornilov,** Russian
general; commander of Russian Army after
Revolution of 1917. [d. April 13, 1918]

1880   **Robert Rutherford (*Colonel*) McCormick,** U.S. editor; publisher of *Chicago
Tribune,* 1910–55; President of Tribune Co.,
1911–55; founder, with his cousin Robert
W. Patterson, of the *New York Daily News,*
1919. [d. April 1, 1955]

1881   **Smedley Darlington Butler,** U.S. Marine
commander, prominent in World War I. [d.
June 21, 1940]

1889   **Vladimir Kosma Zworykin,** U.S. engineer,
inventor, born in Russia; developed the
iconoscope, which made possible the development of **television.** Called the *Father
of Television.* [d. July 29, 1982]

1891   **Casey (Charles Dillon) Stengel,** U.S. base-
ball player and manager; as manager of
New York Yankees, 1949–60, led his team to
10 American League pennants and 7 World
Series championships; elected to Baseball
Hall of Fame, 1966. [d. September 30, 1975]

1898   **Henry Moore,** British sculptor.

1939   **Peter Bogdanovich,** U.S. film director,
producer, writer.

1941   **Paul Anka,** Canadian singer, composer.

1958   **Daley Thompson,** British athlete; winner
of 1980 and 1984 Olympic decathlon
events.

Historical Events

1178   **Frederick I, Holy Roman Emperor,** is
crowned King of Burgundy.

1619   First legislative assembly in America, the
House of Burgesses, is convened at
Jamestown, Virginia.

1866   Armistice between Austria and Prussia
ends the **Seven Weeks' War.**

1907   Foundation stone of Carnegie **Palace of
Peace** at The Hague is laid.

1945   U.S. cruiser *Indianapolis* is sunk by Japanese submarine in the Philippine Sea with
a loss of 880 lives (**World War II**).

St. Peter Chrysologus, Archbishop of Ravenna and Doctor of the Church. [d. c. 450] Feast formerly December 4. Optional Memorial.

The Beatified

Blessed Mannes, Augustinian monk. [d. c. 1230]

Blessed Archangelo of Calatafimi, hermit. [d. 1460]

Blessed John Soreth, Carmelite prior and reformer. [d. 1471]

Blessed Simon of Lipnicza, Franciscan Friar Minor. [d. 1482]

Blessed Peter of Mogliano, Observant Franciscan Friar. [d. 1490]

Blessed Edward Powell and **Richard Fetherston,** martyrs. [d. 1540]

Blessed Thomas Abel, priest and martyr. [d. 1540]

Blessed Everard Hanse, priest and martyr. [d. 1581]

1974   The U.S. House Judiciary Committee votes three articles of **impeachment** against President **Richard Nixon (Watergate Incident).**

1980   The **Republic of Vanuatu** (formerly **New Hebrides**) attains independence from Great Britain and France.

July 31

Holidays

Congo   Revolution Day

Religious Calendar

The Saints

St. Germanus, Bishop of Auxerre. Also called **Germain.** [d. 448] Feast formerly August 3.

Birthdates

1763   **James Kent,** U.S. jurist, legal writer; first professor of law at Columbia College 1793; produced first systematic work on Anglo-American law, 1830. [d. December 12, 1847]

1803   **John Ericsson,** U.S. engineer, inventor, born in Sweden; invented **screw propeller;** developed first propeller-driven commercial ship; designed U.S. Union warship *Monitor,* which defeated the *Merrimack* in the **Battle of Hampton Roads;** responsible for revolutionizing naval warfare. [d. March 8, 1889]

1814   **Amos Adams Lawrence,** U.S. merchant, philanthropist; partner in firm of Mason and Lawrence, leading Boston textile merchants; benefactor of **Lawrence University,** Appleton, Wisconsin, and a college at Lawrence, Kansas, that later became the **University of Kansas;** adamant anti-slavery figure. [d. August 22, 1886]

1816   **George Henry Thomas,** Union Army general during U.S. Civil War; known as the *Rock of Chickamauga* after his success at the **Battle of Chickamauga** during the Chattanooga Campaign. Inflicted heaviest losses of entire war on Confederates at **Battle of Nashville,** 1864. [d. March 28, 1870]

1822   **Abram Stevens Hewitt,** U.S. businessman, political figure, philanthropist; built first open hearth smelting furnace; U.S. Congressman, 1874–79, 1881–87; Mayor of New York City, 1886–88. [d. January 18, 1903]

1839   **William Clarke Quantrill,** U.S. guerrilla leader, outlaw; loosely attached to Confederate Army, he and his band of guerrillas carried out many bloody attacks on towns and organizations sympathetic to the Union; most notoriety gained from his raid on **Lawrence, Kansas,** during which he killed more than 180 citizens and burned the town. [d. June 6, 1865]

1859   **Theobald Smith,** U.S. pathologist; first to demonstrate that parasites could act as vectors of disease; pioneer in field of immunology; established distinction between bacillus of human tuberculosis and that of bovine strain. [d. December 10, 1934]

1899   **Robert T(en Broeck) Stevens,** U.S. government official, industrialist; U.S. Secretary of the Army, 1953–55; President and Chairman of the Board, J.P. Stevens Company, 1929–74. [d. January 30, 1983]

1900   **Antoine (Marie-Roger) de Saint-Exupéry,** French aviator, author; noted for his fable *The Little Prince* and for his novels, *Wind, Sand, and Stars* and *Night Flight* ("Vol de Nuit"). [disappeared, presumed deceased July 31, 1944]

1912   **Milton Friedman,** U.S. economist, author; leading conservative economist; anti-Keynesian and advocate of *laissez-faire* economics; Nobel Prize in economics, 1976.

1921   **Whitney Moore Young, Jr.,** U.S. civil-rights leader; advocate of a total spectrum black coalition. [d. March 11, 1971]

1944   **Geraldine Chaplin,** U.S. actress; daughter of Charlie Chaplin (April 16); granddaughter of Eugene O'Neill (October 16).

1951   **Evonne Goolagong,** Australian tennis player.

Historical Events

1559   **University of Lille** in France is authorized by a papal bull.

1790   **U.S. Patent Office** opens and issues its first patent to **Samuel Hopkins** of Vermont for new method of making potash and pearlash.

1877   **Thomas A. Edison** receives a U.S. patent on his **phonograph.**

St. Helen of Skövde, widow and martyr. [d. c. 1160]

St. Ignatius of Loyola, founder of the Society of Jesus; patron of spiritual exercises and retreats. [d. 1556] Obligatory Memorial.

St. Neot, monk. Also called **Niet.** [death date unknown]

St. Sidwell, virgin. Also called **Sativola.** [death date unknown]

The Beatified

Blessed John Colombini, founder of the Apostolic Clerics of St. Jerome. [d. 1367]

Blessed Justin de Jacobis, titular Bishop of Nilopolis and missionary. [d. 1860]

1897 **Guglielmo Marconi** is awarded patent for his **wireless telegraph.**

1914 Germany declares war on Russia (**World War I**).

France mobilizes its army and navy (**World War I**).

General mobilization is ordered for the **Austro-Hungarian Empire** (**World War I**).

1917 The **Third Battle of Ypres** opens in Flanders as a British offensive (**World War I**).

1919 The **Weimar Constitution** is adopted in Germany, establishing a new republic.

1942 U.S. President Franklin Roosevelt creates the **U.S. Army Transportation Corps** (**World War II**).

1964 U.S. lunar probe *Ranger 7* crashes on moon's surface after transmitting some 4,000 photographs back to earth.

1971 *Apollo 15* astronauts make the first of three planned excursions on the moon in their lunar rover.

1975 Former Teamsters Union President **James R. Hoffa** is reported missing; Hoffa is declared legally dead December 8, 1982.

August

August is the eighth month of the Gregorian calendar and has 31 days. In the early Roman 10-month calendar, it was called *Sextilis*, a reference to its position as the sixth month in that calendar. In 8 B.C., Augustus Caesar, the adopted son and heir to Julius Caesar, consented to have a month named in his honor. Rather than the month of his birth, September, he chose Sextilis, acknowledging the many events favorable to his political career that occurred during that month, e.g., his first election to the consulship in 43 B.C. and the conquest of Egypt in 31 B.C., the latter marking the end of protracted civil war. Also at this time, in a move designed in part to make his month equal in length to Julius Casear's month of July, Augustus instituted changes in the number of days in certain months: the new *Augustus* was increased to 31 days (equaling July) from its traditional 30, while February was reduced to 28 days (except in leap years). The length of the months following August were also set, with an alternation of 30-day and 31-day months through December. Hence, the months of the year were assigned the number of days that they still retain today.

In the astrological calendar, August spans the zodiac signs of Leo, the Lion (July 23–August 22) and Virgo, the Virgin (August 23–September 22).

The birthstone for August is the carnelian, sardonyx, or peridot, and the flower is the poppy or gladiolus.

State, National, and International Holidays

American Family Day
(Arizona, Minnesota)
First Sunday

Fiesta de Andorra la Vieja
(Andorra)
First Saturday, Sunday, and Monday

Colorado Day
(Colorado)
First Monday

Discovery Day
(Trinidad and Tobago)
First Monday

Bank Holiday
(Fiji, Grenada, Guyana, Hong Kong, Ireland, Malawi)
First Monday

Independence Day
(Jamaica)
First Tuesday

All Union Physical Education Day
(U.S.S.R.)
Second Saturday

Builders' Day
(U.S.S.R.)
Second Sunday

Hora de la Prisiop
(Romania)
Second Sunday

Victory Day
(Rhode Island)
Second Monday

Admission Day
(Hawaii)
Third Friday

Air Force Day
(U.S.S.R.)
Third Sunday

Miners' Day
(U.S.S.R.)
Final Sunday

Liberation Day
(Hong Kong)
Final Monday

Special Events and Their Sponsors

Florida Appreciation Month
California Depopulation Commission
P.O. Box 964
Ross, California 94957

National Clown Week
First Week
Clowns of America, Inc.
200 Powetton Avenue
Woodlynne, New Jersey 08107

Beauty Queen Week
First Week
Richard R. Falk Associates
1472 Broadway
New York, New York 10036

All American Soap Box Derby
Second Week
International Soap Box Derby, Inc.
789 Derby Downs Drive
Akron, Ohio 44306

National Hosiery Week
Week containing August 15
National Association of Hosiery Manufacturers
P.O. Box 35098
516 Charlottetown Mall
Charlotte, North Carolina 28235

Bald Eagle Days
Third Week
Eagle Valley Environmentalists, Inc.
Box 155
Apple River, Illinois 61001

Family Day
August 7
Kiwanis International
3636 Woodview Trace
Indianapolis, Indiana 46268

Special Days—Other Calendars

	1 Muharram	10 Muharram	10 Dhu'1 Hijjah	Tish Ab B'Ab
1985			August 28	
1986			August 17	August 14
1987	August 26		August 6	August 4
1988	August 14	August 23		
1989	August 4	August 13		August 10
1990		August 2		

August 1

Holidays

England	**Lammas Day**
	From Middle English *Lammasse* or *loaf mass*, celebrating occasion of blessing of first bread made from new wheat or corn; associated with celebration of deliverance of St. Peter from imprisonment. See Religious Calendar below.
Switzerland	**National Day** or **Confederation Day**
	Commemorates the formation of the Swiss confederation, 1291.
Zaire	**Parents' Day**

Birthdates

10 B.C. **Claudius (Tiberius Claudius Drusus Nero Germanicus),** Roman emperor. [d. October 13, A.D. 54]

1749 **Jean Baptiste Pierre Antoine de Monet, chevalier de Lamarck,** French naturalist; forerunner of Darwin; first to categorize animals into **vertebrates** and **invertebrates.** [d. December 18, 1829]

1770 **William Clark,** U.S. soldier, explorer; shared command with Meriwether Lewis (August 18) of the expedition to **Northwest Territory;** upon return, gathered all records from exploration, providing documentation for the journals published in 1814. [d. September 1, 1838]

1779 **Francis Scott Key,** U.S. poet, lawyer; author of the poem which eventually became the verse for the *Star-Spangled Banner,* the **U.S. national anthem.** [d. January 11, 1843]

1815 **Richard Henry Dana, Jr.,** U.S. lawyer, author; his novel, *Two Years before the Mast,* recounts his life as a crew member aboard the ship *Pilgrim.* As a lawyer, specialized in maritime law and published *The Seaman's Friend,* a guide to the law for common seamen. [d. January 6, 1882]

1818 **Maria Mitchell,** U.S. astronomer; was recognized in scientific circles for her discovery of a comet; became first woman member of the American Academy of Arts and Sciences; Professor of Astronomy, Vassar College, 1865–69. [d. June 28, 1889]

1819 **Herman Melville,** U.S. novelist; author of *Moby Dick.* [d. September 28, 1891]

1843 **Robert Todd Lincoln,** U.S. lawyer, cabinet officer, diplomat; the oldest son of President Abraham Lincoln. [d. July 25, 1926]

1863 **Gaston Doumergue,** French statesman; 12th president of French Republic, 1924–31. [d. June 18, 1937]

1885 **Georg Hevesy,** Hungarian chemist; Nobel Prize in chemistry for discovery of use of isotopes as **tracer elements,** 1943. [d. July 5, 1966]

1892 **Hugh Macdiarmid (Christopher Murray Grieve),** Scottish poet, critic. [d. August 11, 1892]

1899 **William F(riske) Dean,** U.S. Army major general; highest ranking U.S. military person to be taken prisoner during **Korean War.** [d. August 25, 1981]

Joseph (Herman) Hirshhorn, U.S. financier, art patron; amassed multi-million dollar fortune through speculation in mining and stock market; owner of one of largest private art collections in the world, later donated, with a museum to house it, to U.S., 1966. [d. August 31, 1981]

1931 **Harold Connolly,** U.S. athlete; Olympic Gold Medal for hammer throw, 1956.

1936 **Yves (Mathieu) St. Laurent,** French fashion designer.

1942 **Giancarlo Giannini,** Italian actor, known for his role in *Love and Anarchy.*

Religious Calendar

The Saints

St. Peter ad Vincula; commemorates chains binding Peter when he was imprisoned in Rome. Also called **St. Peter's Chains.** Feast day now in recession.

The Holy Machabees, martyrs. Also called **Maccabees.** [d. 168 B.C.] Feast suppressed 1969.

St. Aled, virgin and martyr. Also called **Almedha,** or **Eiluned.** [d. 6th century]

St. Kyned, monk and hermit. Also called **Cenydd, Kened,** or **Keneth.** [d. c. 6th century]

St. Ethelwold, Bishop of Winchester. Also called **Etholwold.** [d. 984]

St. Alphonsus de' Liguori, Bishop of Sant' Agata Dei Goti, Doctor of the Church and founder of the Congregation of the Most Holy Redeemer. [d. 1787] Feast formerly August 2.

SS. Faith, Hope, and Charity and their mother, St. Wisdom, martyrs. [death date unknown]

The Beatified

Blessed Thomas Welbourn and Blessed William Brown, martyrs. [d. 1605]

Historical Events

1137   **Louis VI** of France dies and is succeeded by **Louis VII.**

1291   **Swiss Confederation** is formed by the Forest Cantons of Uri, Unterwalden, and Schwyz for defense against the Austrians.

1658   **Leopold I** is elected Holy Roman Emperor.

1714   **Queen Anne** of England dies and is succeeded by George Lewis, Elector of Hanover, who becomes **George I.**

1798   British Admiral **Horatio Nelson** destroys Napoleon's French fleet in harbor at Abukir, Egypt (**Battle of the Nile**).

1808   English expedition lands in Portugal to oppose French (**Napoleonic Wars**).

1834   **Slavery** is abolished throughout the British Empire.

1849   **Dr. David Livingstone,** British explorer and missionary, becomes the first European to reach **Lake Ngami** in Africa.

1876   **Colorado** is admitted to the Union as the 38th state.

1894   China and Japan declare war on each other (**Sino-Japanese War**).

1935   The **Federal Music Project** is organized in Washington to provide work for unemployed American musicians.

1943   U.S. aircraft based at Libya stage successful low-level attack on Romanian oil refineries at **Ploesti (World War II).**

1946   U.S. President Harry S. Truman signs the **McMahon Act** creating the U.S. **Atomic Energy Commission.** President Truman signs the **Fulbright Act,** funding an international educational exchange in the form of **Fulbright Scholarships.**

1960   **Benin** (formerly **Dahomey**) proclaims its independence as a republic within the French Community.

1966   Lieut. Col. **Yakubu Gowon,** Nigerian Army Chief of Staff, assumes power following the overthrow of the government in a bloody coup d'état that sees thousands of Ibo tribesmen massacred and more than a million driven from homes in the northern sector of the country.

1976   Nearly one million Roman Catholics participate in the **41st International Eucharistic Congress.** The first such congress was held in Lille, France, in 1881.

August 2

Holidays

Costa Rica **Our Lady of the Angels**
St. Lucia, St. **Emancipation Day**
Vincent, Joint celebration of
Turks and emancipation from Great
Caicos Britain.
Islands

Birthdates

1754 **Pierre Charles L'Enfant,** French engineer, architect, urban designer; responsible for the design and layout of **Washington, D.C.** [d. June 14, 1825]

1820 **John Tyndall,** British physicist; responsible for discoveries in transmission and absorption of heat; discovered that the sky appeared blue owing in part to dust particles in the atmosphere. [d. December 4, 1893]

1823 **Edward Augustus Freeman,** British historian; Professor of Modern History at Oxford, 1884–92. [d. March 16, 1892]

1835 **Elisha Gray,** U.S. inventor; founder of Gray & Barton Co., the basis of Western Electric Company, 1872. Filed for patent on a telephone device only hours after Alexander Graham Bell filed for his patent; was granted 70 patents during his lifetime. [d. January 21, 1901]

1854 **Francis Marion Crawford,** U.S. author born in Italy; son of expatriate sculptor Thomas Crawford; advocate of romanticism in fiction. [d. April 9, 1909]

1865 **Irving Babbitt,** U.S. author, educator; with Paul Elmer More (December 12) founded the **neo-humanist** movement in the U.S. [d. July 15, 1933]

1868 **Constantine I, King of Greece**; deposed in 1917 as a result of his neutral stance on World War I; recalled 1920, but once again forced to abdicate, 1922, after a disastrous campaign against Turkey. [d. January 11, 1923]

1871 **John French Sloan,** U.S. artist; one of the founders of the **Ashcan School** of art. [d. September 7, 1951]

1892 **John Kieran,** U.S. writer, analyst; first bylined columnist of the *New York Times*; wrote *Sports of the Times* column, 1927–43; member of the radio quiz panel of *Information Please*; editor of *Information Please Almanac*, 1947–80. [d. December 10, 1981]

Jack Warner, U.S. motion picture executive; with his brothers, Harry (December 12) and Albert (July 23), founded Warner Brothers Pictures, Inc. [d. September 9, 1978]

1900 **Helen Morgan,** U.S. singer, actress. [d. October 8, 1941]

1905 **Myrna Loy (Myrna Williams),** U.S. actress.

1920 **Lonnie (William) Coleman,** U.S. author; wrote novel *Beulah Land*, 1963. [d. August 13, 1982]

1922 **Paul Laxalt,** U.S. politician, lawyer; Governor of Nevada, 1967–71; U.S. Senator, 1974– .

1924 **James Baldwin,** U.S. novelist, essayist; leading spokesman for the black community in U.S. as well as an outstanding figure in contemporary American literature.

1932 **Peter (Seamus) O'Toole,** Irish-born stage and screen actor; Associate Director, Old Vic Theatre, London, 1980– .

Historical Events

1100 **William II,** King of England, is killed in New Forest in a hunting accident and is succeeded by **Henry I.**

1589 **Henry III** of France is murdered; the House of Valois becomes extinct and **Henry of Navarre** claims throne.

1858 **India Bill** is passed, ending the rule of the **British East India Company.**

1909 First **Lincoln penny** is issued in U.S.

1914 **Germany** begins its invasion of France near Sirez-sur-Vezouze and other frontier posts (**World War I**).

1923 **Warren G. Harding** dies; Vice-President Calvin Coolidge is sworn in as President of U.S. the following morning at 2:30 a.m.

1935 The **Government of India Act** is passed by British parliament, separating **Burma** and **Aden** from India.

Religious Calendar

The Saints

St. Stephen I, pope. Elected 254. Patron of Vienna. [d. 257]

St. Theodata, martyr. [d. c. 304]

St. Etheldritha, recluse. Also called **Ælfryth** or

Alfreda. [d. c. 835]

St. Plegmund, Archbishop of Canterbury. [d. 914]

St. Thomas of Dover, monk. [d. 1295]

August 3

Holidays

Equatorial Guinea	**Armed Forces Day**
Guinea-Bissau	**Martyrs of Colonialism Day**
Niger	**Independence Day** Celebrates the achievement of independence from France, 1960.
Tunisia	**President Bourguiba's Birthday** Celebrates the birth of Habib Bourguiba, 1903.

Birthdates

1746 **James Wyatt,** English romantic architect; responsible for revival of **Gothic architecture** in England. [d. September 4, 1813]

1770 **Frederick William III,** King of Prussia, 1797–1846. [d. June 7, 1840]

1801 **Sir Joseph Paxton,** British architect, horticulturist; designed **Crystal Palace,** site of London exhibition, 1851. [d. June 8, 1865]

1808 **Hamilton Fish,** U.S. politician, lawyer; U.S. Secretary of State, 1869–77. [d. September 6, 1893]

1811 **Elisha Graves Otis,** U.S. inventor; developed the first safe passenger **elevator.** [d. April 8, 1861]

1867 **Stanley Baldwin, 1st Earl Baldwin,** British statesman; Prime Minister, 1923–29, 1935–37. [d. December 14, 1947]

1872 **Haakon VII,** King of Norway, 1905–57; first king of Norway after the restoration of its independence from Denmark. [d. September 21, 1957]

1887 **Rupert Brooke,** British poet; died of blood poisoning at beginning of World War I. [d. April 23, 1915]

1900 **Ernest (*Ernie*) Pyle,** U.S. journalist; managing editor of *Washington Daily News*, 1932–35; noted for his reporting of events in World War II, which eventually won him the Pulitzer Prize, 1944. Killed by enemy machine gun fire on Ie Shima, in the Pacific. [d. April 18, 1945]

1901 **Stefan Cardinal Wyszynski,** Roman Catholic cardinal; Primate of Poland; renowned for his staunch anti-Communist position. [d. May 28, 1981]

John Cornelius Stennis, U.S. politician, lawyer; U.S. Senator, 1947– .

1903 **Habib Bourguiba,** first president of Tunisia, 1957– .

1905 **Dolores Del Rio,** U.S. actress, born in Mexico. [d. April 11, 1983]

1906 **George Sanders,** U.S. actor, born in Russia. Committed suicide. [d. April 25, 1972]

1919 **Walter Bigelow Wriston,** U.S. banker; President and Director of Citibank, N.A., 1967–70; Chairman and Director of Citicorp, 1970– .

1926 **Tony Bennett (Anthony Benedetto),** U.S. singer.

Historical Events

1347 **Calais** in France surrenders to **Edward III** of England (**Hundred Years' War**).

1460 **James II** of Scotland is killed at Roxburgh; he is succeeded by **James III.**

1492 **Christopher Columbus** embarks from Palos, Spain, on his first voyage of exploration aboard the *Santa Maria.*

1858 Captain **John Speke** discovers **Lake Victoria**, which he recognizes as the source of the **White Nile.**

1880 **American Canoe Association** is organized at Lake George, New York.

1914 **Germany** and **France** declare war on each other (**World War I**).

1916 Sir Roger Casement, Irish nationalist leader in the **Easter Rebellion,** is hanged in London for treason.

1917 Mutiny breaks out in the German fleet at **Wilhemshaven** (**World War I**).

1942 First U.S. woman naval officer, **Mildred McAfee,** is commissioned.

Religious Calendar

Feasts

The Finding of St. Stephen. Also called *The Invention of St. Stephen.* Relics discovered 415. This feast day is now in recession.

The Saints

St. Waltheof, Abbot of Melrose. Also called **Walthen,** or **Walthenus.** [d. c. 1160]

St. Peter Julian Eymard, founder of the Priests of the Blessed Sacrament. [d. 1868]

St. Manaccus, bishop. Also called **Mancus.** [death date unknown]

The Beatified

Blessed Augustine, Bishop of Lucera. [d. 1323]

1945   All Germans and Hungarians in **Czechoslovakia** are deprived of their citizenship and subsequently expelled.

1958   U.S. atomic submarine *Nautilus* reaches the **North Pole.**

1967   **West Germany** and **Czechoslovakia** resume diplomatic relations, which have been severed since World War II.

August 4

Holidays

Cook Island
(New Zealand Dependency)

Constitution Day
Commemorates the attainment of internal self-government, 1965.

El Salvador
San Salvador's Feast (1st day)

Birthdates

1521   **Urban VII,** pope in 1590 (one month). [d. September 27, 1590]

1792   **Percy Bysshe Shelley,** English Romantic poet; the most aberrant of the English Romantics, both in his social and philosophical activities and opinions. Died at the age of 29, at the height of his career, in a boating accident. [d. July 8, 1822]

1805   **Sir William Rowan Hamilton,** Irish mathematician; pioneer in the science of **quantum mechanics**; discovered the phenomenon of **conical refraction.** [d. September 2, 1865]

1816   **Russell Sage,** U.S. financier, public official; U.S. Congressman, 1850–57. Built his fortune through investments in the stockmarket and railroading; his fortune used by his widow, Margaret Slocum Sage, to endow many philanthropic institutions including **Russell Sage Foundation** for study of social conditions. [d. July 22, 1906]

1839   **Walter (Horatio) Pater,** British essayist; associated with pre-Raphaelite school; devoted his life to interpretation of the humanism of the Renaissance. [d. July 30, 1894]

1841   **William Henry Hudson,** British naturalist, writer; author of *The Purple Land* and *Green Mansions.* [d. August 18, 1922]

1859   **Knut Hamsun (Knut Pedersen),** Norwegian novelist; wrote *Hunger* and *Growth of the Soil*; Nobel Prize in literature, 1920. [d. February 19, 1952]

1870   **Sir Harry Lauder,** Scottish entertainer; popular balladeer of British music halls and U.S. vaudeville theaters. [d. February 26, 1950]

1899   **Ezra Taft Benson,** U.S. agriculturist, religious leader; U.S. Secretary of Agriculture, 1953–61; member, Council of Twelve, Church of Jesus Christ of Latter-day Saints, 1943– .

1900   **Arturo (Umberto) Illia,** Argentinian physician, statesman; President of Argentina, 1963–66. [d. January 18, 1983]

1913   **Jerome Weidman,** U.S. novelist, short-story writer; author of *I Can Get It for You Wholesale.*

Historical Events

1060   **Henry I,** King of France, dies and is succeeded by **Philip I.**

1213   The **Council of St. Albans,** a precursor of the British parliament, is convened.

1265   **Prince Edward** of England represses barons' rebellion by defeating and killing **Simon de Montfort** at Evesham. Simon is henceforth revered as a martyr and called *Simon the Righteous.*

1704   English capture **Gibraltar** from Spain (**War of the Spanish Succession**).

1789   The **Declaration of the Rights of Man** is adopted in France.

1846   **Santa Barbara, California,** is taken by U.S. Marines and sailors (**Mexican War**).

1914   **Great Britain** declares war on **Germany** (**World War I**).

Germany declares war on **Belgium** as Belgian forces resist German advancement through Belgium (**World War I**).

U.S. President **Woodrow Wilson** declares neutrality in the European war (**World War I**).

1916   Denmark cedes **Danish West Indies,** including the **Virgin Islands,** to U.S. for $25 million.

1936   **Ioannis Metaxas** seizes power in Greece; his dictatorship will last into World War II and invasion by Italy, until his death. [d. January 29, 1941]

1972   **Arthur Bremer** is found guilty of having shot Governor **George Wallace** of Alabama and three other persons on May 15; he is sentenced to 63 years in prison.

St. Ia and her companions, martyrs. Ia also called **Is.** [d. c. 360]

St. John Vianney; principal patron saint of parish clergy throughout the world. Also known as the *Holy Curé of Ars* and **John-Baptist Vianney.** [d. 1859] Formerly celebrated August 8. Obligatory Memorial.

St. Sithney; patron of Sithney and mad dogs. Also called **Sezni.** [death date unknown]

1977   **U.S. Department of Energy** is created by presidential proclamation.

August 5

Birthdates

1540 **Joseph Justus Scaliger,** French scholar; laid the basis for modern **textual criticism.** [d. January 21, 1609]

1802 **Niels Henrik Abel,** Norwegian mathematician; known for his research in the theory of **elliptic functions.** [d. April 6, 1829]

1829 **Manuel Deodoro da Fonseca,** first president of the Republic of Brazil, 1889–91. [d. August 23, 1892]

1850 **Guy de Maupassant,** French short-story writer, novelist; considered a master of the short story. [d. July 6, 1893]

1856 **Asher Ginzberg (Ahab Ha'am),** Russian essayist, editor; expounded **cultural Zionism.** [d. January 2, 1927]

1889 **Conrad (Potter) Aiken,** U.S. poet; Pulitzer Prize in poetry, 1930. [d. August 17, 1973]

1906 **John Huston,** U.S. film director, actor; known for his direction of many action-adventure films.

Wassily Leontief, U.S. economist, born in Russia; Nobel Prize in economics for development of **input-output system of economic planning,** 1973.

1911 **Robert Taylor (Spangler Arlington Brugh),** U.S. actor. [d. June 8, 1969]

1923 **Chengara Veetil Devan Nair,** President, Republic of Singapore, 1981– .

1924 **Ahmadou Ahidjo,** President, United Republic of Cameroon, 1960–82.

1930 **Neil Alden Armstrong,** U.S. astronaut; first man to set foot on the moon, July 20, 1969; Professor of Engineering, University of Cincinnati, 1971–79.

1937 **Manuel Pinto da Costa,** President, Democratic Republic of São Tomé and Principe, 1975– .

Historical Events

1529 **Peace of Cambrai** is signed between **Charles V,** Holy Roman Emperor, and **Francis I** of France; Francis renounces claims in Italy; Charles renounces claims in Burgundy.

1850 **Australian Constitution Act** is passed, providing for redistricting of country and representative government for South Australia and Tasmania.

1857 **Atlantic cable** is completed, establishing means of telegraphic communication between U.S. and Great Britain.

1864 Union forces under Admiral **David Farragut** defeat the Confederate troops at **Battle of Mobile Bay (U.S. Civil War);** Farragut's battle cry, "Damn the torpedoes!" has become famous.

1884 Cornerstone of the **Statue of Liberty** is laid on Bedloe's (now Liberty) Island in New York Harbor.

1914 Cuba, Uruguay, Mexico, and Argentina all proclaim their separate neutralities in the start of **World War I; Montenegro** declares war on Austria-Hungary.

1915 **Warsaw,** evacuated by the Russians, is occupied by the Germans (**World War I**).

1933 **National Labor Board** is established by U.S. President Franklin D. Roosevelt to enforce the right to collective bargaining.

1949 Severe earthquake in **Ecuador** razes 50 towns and kills about 6,000.

1960 **Upper Volta** gains independence from France; Maurice Yameozo is named president.

St. Aîra, martyr. Venerated in Germany. [d. 304]

St. Nonna, matron. [d. 374]

St. Cassyon, bishop. Also called **Cassian.** [d. 4th century]

The Dedication of the Basilica of St. Mary Major. Also called **St. Mary ad Nives** or **of the Snow,** and **St. Mary ad Praesepe.** [dedicated 5th century] Optional Memorial.

August 6

Holidays

Bolivia	**Independence Day** Commemorates Bolivia's achievement of independence from Spain, 1825.
El Salvador	**San Salvador's Feast** (3rd day)
Abu Dhabi, United Arab Emirates	**Anniversary of the Accession of Sheik Zaid Bin Sultan Al-Nahayan** Commemorates the accession of the sheik, 1971.

Birthdates

1638 **Nicolas de Malebranche,** French philosopher, metaphysicist; espoused the belief that man cannot know anything external to himself except through his relation to God. [d. October 13, 1715]

1651 **François de Salignac de la Mothe Fánelon,** French religious writer; tutor to the grandson of Louis XIV of France. His writings were condemned, in part, by the papacy. [d. January 7, 1715]

1697 **Charles VII,** Holy Roman Emperor. [d. January 20, 1745]

1766 **William Hyde Wollaston,** British chemist; first observed dark lines in solar spectrum; the **Wollaston Medal,** awarded for mineralogical research, is given in his honor. [d. December 22, 1828]

1775 **Daniel O'Connell,** Irish leader; originated **Catholic Association,** 1823. [d. May 15, 1847]

1809 **Alfred, 1st Baron Tennyson (Alfred, Lord Tennyson),** British poet; Poet Laureate of England, 1850–92; recognized as the greatest English poet of the Victorian age. [d. October 6, 1892]

1811 **Judah Philip Benjamin,** U.S. lawyer, politician, statesman; outstanding secessionist leader during American Civil War; Attorney General and Secretary of State of the Confederacy; escaped to England after the war, where he achieved great success as an appeals lawyer. [d. May 6, 1884]

1868 **Paul (Louis-Marie) Claudel,** French diplomat, dramatist, poet; member of French diplomatic corps, 1892–55; associated with Symbolist school of poetry. [d. February 23, 1955]

1881 **Sir Alexander Fleming,** British bacteriologist; discoverer of penicillin, 1928; Nobel Prize in physiology or medicine for discovery of penicillin (with H. W. Florey and E. B. Chain), 1945. [d. March 11, 1955]

Louella O. Parsons, U.S. journalist; known for her flamboyant Hollywood gossip column, which was syndicated and appeared regularly in more than 400 Hearst newspapers, 1934–65. [d. December 9, 1972]

1889 **George Churchill Kenney,** U.S. military officer, Army Air Force general; commander of Allied air forces in Southwest Pacific during World War II.

1892 **(Edward) Hoot Gibson,** U.S. silent-film actor. [d. August 23, 1962]

1893 **Wright Patman,** U.S. politician, lawyer; U.S. Congressman, 1928–76. [d. March 7, 1976]

1895 **F(rancis) W(ilton) Reichelderfer,** U.S. meteorologist; Chief, U.S. Weather Bureau, 1938–63; implemented air-mass theory in forecasting services; first president, **World Meteorological Organization.** [d. January 25, 1983]

1902 **Dutch Schultz (Arthur Flegenheimer),** U.S. gangster; ran bootlegging syndicate during prohibition era in U.S. [d. October 24, 1934]

1905 **Clara Bow,** U.S. actress; star of jazz age silent films; acquired the name the *It Girl* after her starring role in the Elinor Glyn movie *It*. [d. September 26, 1965]

1909 **Karl Ulrich Schnabel,** U.S. concert pianist, born in Germany.

1911 **Lucille Ball,** U.S. actress; renowned comedienne; President of Desilu Productions,

460

Religious Calendar

Feasts

The Transfiguration of Our Lord Jesus Christ.
Celebrates Christ's revelation of his holiness to Saints Peter, James, and John on Mount Tabor. [Major holy day, Episcopal Church]

The Saints

St. Justus and St. Pastor, martyrs. [d. 304]

St. Hormisdas, pope. Elected 514. [d. 523]

1962–67; President of Lucille Ball Productions, 1967– .

1917   **Robert Mitchum,** U.S. actor.

1928   **Andy Warhol,** U.S. artist; famous for **pop art;** produced numerous commercial silk screens on canvas, including pictures of Campbell's tomato soup cans and portraits of Marilyn Monroe and Elvis Presley; experimented in film medium and rock music.

Historical Events

1825   **Bolivia** declares its independence from Spain.

1896   **Madagascar** is proclaimed a French colony.

1914   **Austria** declares war on Russia (**World War I**).

      Serbia declares war on Germany (**World War I**).

1918   General **Ferdinand Foch** is appointed Marshal of France (**World War I**).

1923   Direct railroad connection between the east and west coasts of New Zealand is established with the opening of the **Otira Tunnel.**

1926   **Gertrude Ederle,** U.S. swimmer, becomes first woman to swim the **English Channel** (14 hours, 34 minutes).

      Harry Houdini performs his most famous magic act, remaining under water, in a sealed tank, for 91 minutes.

1927   **Metropolitan University** is created at Peking, China, by union of nine government universities.

1930   The body of Swedish balloonist and explorer **S. A. Andrée,** who died in an 1897 attempt to cross the North Pole by balloon, is found on White Island in the Barents Sea by a Norwegian scientific expedition.

1945   U.S. drops first-ever atomic bomb on **Hiroshima, Japan** (**World War II**).

1962   **Jamaica** becomes an independent member of the British Commonwealth.

1978   **Pope Paul VI** dies of a heart attack at age 80.

August 7

Birthdates

1533 **Alonso de Ercilla y Zúñiga,** Spanish soldier; author of *La Araucana*, an epic poem immortalizing the Araucanian heroes of the resistance to Spanish supremacy. This work is considered by some as one of first significant literary works in the Americas. [d. November 29, 1594]

1578 **Georg Stiernhielm (Georgius Olai),** Swedish poet, scholar; known as the *Father of Swedish Poetry*. [d. April 22, 1672]

1742 **Nathanael Greene,** American Revolutionary general; second in command of American army under General George Washington; largely responsible for the triumph of the American campaigns in the South. [d. June 19, 1786]

1876 **Mata Hari (Margartha Geertruida Macleod),** Dutch dancer; convicted and executed as a spy during World War I for passing Allied secrets to Germany. [d. October 15, 1917]

1887 **Carl Eric Wickman,** U.S. transportation executive; founder of Greyhound Bus Corporation; President of Greyhound, 1930–46. [d. February 5, 1954]

1890 **Elizabeth Gurley Flynn,** U.S. labor leader; first chairperson of **U.S. Communist Party National Committee,** 1961. [d. September 5, 1964]

1896 **John J(oseph) Bergen,** U.S. financier; responsible for relocation of New York's **Madison Square Garden,** 1968, from 50th Street and Eighth Avenue to the lower stories of a building over Pennsylvania Station. [d. December 11, 1980]

1903 **L(ouis) S(eymour) B(azett) Leakey,** British archaeologist, anthropologist; discovered evidence of early humanoid existence in Africa, weakening theory that earliest man came from Asia. [d. October 1, 1972]

1904 **Ralph Bunche,** U.S. diplomat, educator; Nobel Peace Prize for negotiating peace between Arabs and Israel, 1950. [d. December 9, 1971]

Historical Events

1803 **Second Maratha War** begins as British under Sir Arthur Wellesley attack Ahmadnagar, India.

1830 **Louis-Philippe** is elected king of France; known as the *Citizen King* during his six-year reign.

1914 City of **Liège, Belgium,** falls to invading Germans (**World War I**).

First troops of the **British Expeditionary Force** arrive in France (**World War I**).

1918 The **Second Battle of the Marne** ends with the Allies forcing a German retreat over the Marne (**World War I**).

1942 First U.S. land offensive in Pacific Theater of World War II begins in **Solomon Islands** as Marines land on Japanese-held **Guadalcanal.**

1958 Nuclear-powered U.S. submarine *Nautilus* completes history-making cruise under the Arctic ice pack and across the North Pole, traveling 1,830 miles in 4 days under the polar ice.

1960 **Ivory Coast** achieves full independence from France.

1964 U.S. Congress passes a joint resolution approving U.S. action in Southeast Asia (**Tonkin Gulf Resolution**).

1965 **Singapore** secedes from the Malaysian Federation and becomes independent.

St. Sixtus II, pope, **St. Felicissimus,** and **St. Agapitus,** with their companions, martyrs. Sixtus elected pope in 257. Sixtus also called **Xystus.** [d. 258] Optional Memorial.

St. Dometius the Persian, martyr. [d. c. 362]

St. Victricius, Bishop of Rouen. [d. c. 407]

St. Albert of Trapani. Also called **St. Albert of Sicily.** [d. c. 1307]

St. Cajetan, co-founder of the Theatine Clerks Regular. Also called **Gaetano.** [d. 1547]

The Beatified

Blessed Agathangelo and Cassian, martyrs. [d. 1638]

1972   A Protestant militiaman becomes the 500th victim in three years of sectarian violence in North Ireland when he is shot down outside his home in Armagh.

August 8

Religious Calendar

The Saints

The Fourteen Holy Helpers, a group of 14 German saints with special intercessory powers.

St. Hormisdas, martyr. Also called **Hormidz,** or **Hormizd.** [d. c. 420]

Birthdates

1646 **Sir Godfrey Kneller (Gottfried Kniller),** English portrait painter; court painter to **William III, Anne,** and **George I.** [d. October 8, 1723]

1694 **Francis Hutcheson,** Irish teacher, philosopher. [d. 1746]

1763 **Charles Bulfinch,** U.S. architect; designed the **Beacon Hill Monument, Connecticut State House**; served as architect of the Capitol, 1817–30. [d. April 4, 1844]

1799 **Nathaniel Brown Palmer,** U.S. explorer; discovered **Antarctica,** 1820. [d. June 21, 1877]

1807 **Emilie Flygare-Carlèn,** Swedish novelist, feminist. [d. February 5, 1892]

1839 **Nelson Appleton Miles,** U.S. army officer; fought in the Civil War, the Indian wars, and the Spanish-American War. [d. May 15, 1925]

1846 **Samuel Milton (*Golden Rule*) Jones,** U.S. inventor, businessman, philanthropist, reform politician. [d. July 12, 1904]

1876 **Patrick A. McCarran,** U.S. politician, lawyer; U.S. Senator, 1932–54. [d. September 28, 1954]

1879 **Robert Holbrook Smith,** U.S. reformer; founder of **Alcoholics Anonymous,** 1935. [d. November 6, 1950]

1882 **Edward John Noble,** U.S. business executive; one of founders of American Broadcasting Company. [d. December 28, 1958]

1883 **Emiliano Zapata,** Mexican revolutionary leader; championed agrarian movements, 1911–16. [d. April 10, 1919]

1884 **Sara Teasdale,** U.S. poet; Pulitzer Prize in poetry, 1918. [d. January 29, 1933]

1896 **Marjorie Kinnan Rawlings,** U.S. novelist; best known for her novel, *The Yearling,* 1939. [d. December 14, 1953]

1901 **Ernest Orlando Lawrence,** U.S. physicist; Nobel Prize in physics for development of **cyclotron,** 1939. [d. August 27, 1958]

1902 **Paul Adrien Maurice Dirac,** British physicist, mathematician; Nobel Prize in physics for development of new atomic theories (with E. Schrödinger), 1933.

1907 **Benny Carter (Bennett Lester Carter),** U.S. jazz musician, composer; composed music for *Stormy Weather* and *Guns of Navarone.*

Jesse Stuart, U.S. writer, educator; author of works dealing with mountain regions of Kentucky.

1908 **Arthur Joseph Goldberg,** U.S. lawyer, government official, diplomat; U.S. Secretary of Labor, 1961–62; Associate Justice, U.S. Supreme Court, 1962–65; U.S. Representative to United Nations, 1965–68.

1910 **Sylvia Sidney (Sophia Koskow),** U.S. actress, author.

1919 **Dino De Laurentiis,** Italian film producer.

1922 **Rudi Gernreich,** U.S. fashion designer.

1923 **Esther Williams,** U.S. swimmer/actress; starred in many movies with an aquatic theme; widow of Fernando Lamas.

1937 **Dustin Hoffman,** U.S. actor.

Historical Events

1502 **James IV** of Scotland marries **Margaret Tudor,** daughter of **Henry VII** of England.

1570 **Peace of St. Germain** grants **Huguenots** in France general amnesty.

1588 **Spanish Armada** is defeated by England; decline of Spanish power follows.

1786 First ascent of **Mont Blanc** is accomplished by **Dr. Michel Paccard** and **Jacques Balmat.**

1815 **Napoleon** is banished to **St. Helena** after his final defeat.

1881 **Pretoria Convention** restores South African Republic to British suzerainty.

St. Altman, Bishop of Passau. [d. 1091]

St. Dominic, founder of the Order of Preachers. This order also called Blackfriars, or Dominicans. [d. 1221] Feast formerly August 4. Obligatory Memorial.

St. Lide, Celtic hermit. Also called **Elid,** or **Elidius.** [death date unknown]

The Beatified

Blessed Joan of Aza, matron. Mother of **St. Dominic.** [d. c. 1190]

Blessed John Felton, martyr. [d. 1570]

1890 National Society of the **Daughters of the American Revolution** is organized in Washington, D.C.

1940 German bombers begin major offensive designed to destroy British air power (**World War II**).

1942 U.S. Marines win control of **Tulagi, Gavutu,** and **Tanambogo** in the Solomon Islands (**World War II**).

1963 Bandits rob the Glasgow-London mail train and escape with approximately $7 million in banknotes.

1967 **Association of Southeast Asian Nations** is established by Thailand, Indonesia, Singapore, the Philippines, and Malaysia, to promote regional growth, social progress, and cultural development.

1974 President **Richard Nixon** announces his resignation, marking the culmination of events known as the **Watergate Incident.** The resignation occurs six years to the day after he was nominated by the Republican party as its presidential candidate.

August 9

Holidays

Singapore   **National Day**
Celebrates Singapore's achievement of independence from Malaysia, 1965.

Religious Calendar

The Saints
St. Romanus, martyr. [d. 258]

Birthdates

1593 **Izaak Walton,** English biographer, author; author of *The Compleat Angler or the Contemplative Man's Recreation* and of biographies of John Donne and George Herbert. [d. December 15, 1683]

1613 **John Dryden,** English poet, dramatist, critic; Poet Laureate of England, 1670–1700. [d. May 1, 1700]

1757 **Thomas Telford,** Scottish civil engineer; designer of the **Menai suspension bridge,** and of numerous canals and bridges in northern Scotland. [d. September 2, 1834]

1809 **William Barret Travis,** Texas lawyer, soldier; leader in the revolt against Mexico. Commander of Texan forces at the **Battle of the Alamo,** 1836. [d. March 6, 1836]

1819 **William Thomas Green Morton,** U.S. dentist; pioneered in use of **anesthetics (ether)** for surgery. [d. July 15, 1868]

1896 **Jean Piaget,** Swiss psychologist; famous for his theories of child's cognitive development; Professor of Psychology, University of Lausanne, 1937–54; Director of International Bureau of Education, 1929–67. [d. September 17, 1980]

A(loysius) M(ichael) Sullivan, U.S. poet, businessman, editor; Editor, *Dun's Review,* 1954–61; moderator, *New Party Program,* 1932–40, a broadcast of readings by prominent poets of the period. [d. June 10, 1980]

1898 **(Lawrence) Brooks Hays,** U.S. politician; U.S. Congressman, 1943–59; noted for his efforts at compromise in civil rights issues. [d. October 11, 1981]

1905 **Robert C. Nix,** U.S. Congressman, 1958–72; Pennsylvania Supreme Court Justice, 1972–.

1913 **Herman Eugene Talmadge,** U.S. lawyer, politician; Governor of Georgia, 1948–55; U.S. Senator, 1957–80.

1922 **Philip (Arthur) Larkin,** British poet, novelist, editor, librarian; Librarian of Brynmor Janes Library, University of Hull, 1955– .

1928 **Bob Cousy (Robert Joseph Cousy),** U.S. basketball player, coach, sportscaster; inducted into Basketball Hall of Fame, 1970.

1938 **Rod(ney George) Laver,** Australian tennis player; 1962 and 1969 winner of tennis Grand Slam: U.S., Australian, French, and British championships.

1942 **David Steinberg,** Canadian comedian.

1945 **Ken Norton,** U.S. boxer, world heavyweight champion, 1978.

Historical Events

378 **Roman Emperor Valens** is killed at **Adrianople** as the mounted Visigoths easily defeat Roman footsoldiers.

870 **Treaty of Mersen** divides Lorraine between Germany and France.

1757 French army under **Montcalm** captures **Fort William Henry** from British; on August 10 many British are killed by Indians allied with the French (**French and Indian War**).

1807 Robert Fulton's steam boat, *Clermont,* begins regular service on Hudson River from New York to Albany.

1842 The **Webster-Ashburton Treaty** settles the boundary between the U.S. and British Canada from Maine to beyond the Great Lakes.

1851 The **Australian Gold Rush** is triggered by the discovery of large nuggets of gold at Bathhurst, New South Wales.

1903 **Pope Pius X** is anointed Bishop of Rome and Pope of the Roman Catholic Church.

1905 **Portsmouth Peace Conference** brings an end to the **Russo-Japanese War**; Ja-

St. Nathy and St. Felim, bishops. Felim also called **Fedhlimidh, Fedlemid,** or **Felimy.** [d. c. 6th century]

St. Oswald, King of Northumbria, martyr. Patron of Zug, Switzerland. [d. 642]

The Beatified

Blessed John of Salerno, Dominican monk. [d. 1242]

Blessed John of Rieti. [d. c. 1350]

---

pan secures recognition of its rights in **Korea** and consolidates its position in **Manchuria.**

1935   The **U.S. Motor Carrier Act** is adopted, giving the **Interstate Commerce Commission** regulatory power over trucks and buses.

August 10

Holidays

Ecuador   **Independence Day**
Celebrates Ecuador's achievement of independence, 1822.

Religious Calendar

The Saints
St. Laurence, martyr. Patron of cooks, vintners, and restaurateurs; invoked against lumbago and fire.

Birthdates

1729   **William Howe, 5th Viscount Howe,** British Army general; Commander in Chief of British army in North America, 1776–78. [d. July 12, 1814]

1753   **Edmund Jennings Randolph,** U.S. lawyer, politician; Attorney General, 1789–94; Secretary of State, 1794–95. [d. September 12, 1813]

1790   **George McDuffie,** U.S. politician; Congressman, 1821–34; Governor of South Carolina, 1834–36; greatly influenced John C. Calhoun on issue of nullification. [d. March 11, 1851]

1810   **Camillo Benso, Comte de Cavour,** Italian statesman; Premier of Sardinia, 1852–59, 1860–61; one of main figures in the campaign for Italian unity. [d. June 6, 1861]

1821   **Jay Cooke,** U.S. financier; founder of Jay Cooke & Co., a banking house; responsible for U.S. bond selling during Civil War; speculator in railroad construction. [d. February 18, 1905]

1848   **William Michael Harnett,** U.S. still-life painter; executed painfully detailed, realistic paintings of common objects. [d. October 29, 1892]

1856   **Edward Lawrence Doheny,** U.S. oilman; major figure in the **Teapot Dome Scandal** of 1921. [d. September 8, 1935]

1861   **Sir Almroth E. Wright,** British physician; introduced immunization against **typhoid fever** by means of inoculation. [d. April 30, 1947]

1865   **Aleksandr Konstantinovich Glazunov,** Russian composer. [d. March 21, 1936]

1869   **Laurence Binyon,** British poet, art critic; supervisor of Oriental prints and drawings at British Museum, 1913–32. [d. March 10, 1943]

1873   **William E. Hocking,** U.S. Idealist philosopher; Professor of Philosophy, Harvard University, 1914–43. [d. June 12, 1966]

1874   **Herbert (Clark) Hoover,** 31st President of the U.S., 1929–33. [d. October 20, 1964]

1894   **V(arahagiri) V(enkata) Giri,** Indian statesman; President of India, 1969–74; key figure in organization of India's government after independence from Great Britain. [d. June 25, 1980]

1895   **Harry Richman,** U.S. singer, vaudeville sensation. [d. November 3, 1972]

1902   **Arne W. K. Tiselius,** Swedish biochemist; Nobel Prize in chemistry for discoveries in biochemistry and the invention of important laboratory apparatus for separating and detecting **colloids** and **serum proteins,** 1948. [d. October 29, 1971]

1904   **Norma Shearer,** U.S. actress. [d. June 12, 1983]

Pavel Alekseyevich Cherenkov, Soviet physicist; Nobel Prize in physics for discovery of **Cherenkov effect** (radiated electrons accelerate in water to speeds greater than speed of light in that medium) (with I. M. Frank and I. Y. Tamm), 1958.

1913   **Noah Beery, Jr.,** U.S. actor.

1922   **Rhonda Fleming (Marilyn Louis),** U.S. actress.

1928   **Eddie Fisher (Edwin Jack Fisher),** U.S. singer.

Historical Events

955   **Otto I** of Germany defeats the Magyars at **Battle of Lechfeld,** ending the threat of Magyar invasion of the West.

Also called **Lawrence.** [d. 258] [Minor festival, Lutheran Church]

St. Bettelin, patron of Stafford. [death date unknown]

St. Philomena. Also called **Philumena.** [death date unknown] Feast suppressed, 1961.

1388	**Battle of Chevy Chase** is fought between English forces under Hotspur, Lord Percy, and the Scots under the Earl of Douglas.
1557	England and Spain defeat France at **Battle of St. Quentin,** thereby driving France from Italy.
1759	**Ferdinand V** of Spain dies and is succeeded by **Charles III.**
1792	A Parisian mob storms the **Tuileries** and massacres 5,000 Swiss Guards; the legislative assembly suspends the monarchy (**French Revolution**).
1821	**Missouri** is admitted to the Union as the 24th state.
1913	**Treaty of Bucharest** is signed between Bulgaria and the Balkan allies, Greece, Serbia, Montenegro, and Rumania, ending the **Second Balkan War.**
1920	**Treaty of Sevres,** stripping Turkey of a major portion of her possessions, is signed by Allied and Associated Powers.
1941	**Dean Dixon,** first black to lead a major U.S. orchestra, conducts a concert by the **New York Philharmonic Orchestra.**
1944	U.S. troops recapture **Guam** (**World War II**).
1949	U.S. President Harry S. Truman signs the **National Security Act**, which creates the **Department of Defense.**
1954	The union of the **Netherlands** and **Indonesia** is dissolved.
1964	**Pope Paul VI** issues the encyclical *Ecclesiam Suam,* which states his readiness to mediate in international disputes.
1966	U.S. air base at **Sattahid, Thailand** is dedicated, officially acknowledging cooperation between Thailand and the U.S. in the **Vietnam War.**
1981	U.S. announces its decision to produce **neutron weapons.**

August 11

Holidays

Jordan	**Accession of H. M. King Hussein**
	Celebrates the accession to the throne of Hussein, 1952.
Zimbabwe	**Heroes' Day**

Religious Calendar

The Saints

St. Alexander the Charcoal-Burner, bishop of Comana, martyr; patron of charcoal burners. [d. c. 275]

Birthdates

1778 **Friedrich Ludwig Jahn,** German educator; opened the first gymnasium in Berlin, 1811; called the *Father of Gymnastics.* [d. October 15, 1852]

1821 **Octave Feuillet,** French novelist, dramatist. [d. December 29, 1890]

1833 **Robert Green Ingersoll,** U.S. lawyer, orator, and lecturer; Attorney General of Illinois, 1867–69; major advocate of scientific and humanistic rationalism in the debates over Darwin's theory of evolution. Lectured widely, presenting a clear and logical summary of agnosticism. [d. July 21, 1899]

1837 **Marie François Sadi Carnot,** French statesman; fourth president of the French Republic, 1887–94; assassinated by Italian anarchist. [d. June 25, 1894]

1858 **Christiaan Eijkman,** Dutch physician; Nobel Prize in physiology or medicine for discovery of **Vitamin B,** 1929. [d. November 5, 1930]

1921 **Alex (Palmer) Haley,** U.S. author; Pulitzer Prize, 1977 (special citation for his fictional biography, *Roots*).

1925 **Carl T. Rowan,** U.S. journalist, columnist.

1926 **Aaron Klug,** British biochemist; Nobel Prize in chemistry for research on **genes and proteins,** 1982.

1928 **Arlene Dahl,** U.S. actress, beauty columnist, model.

Historical Events

1332 **Edward Balliol** deposes **King David II** and assumes the throne of Scotland by his victory at **Dupplin.**

1863 **Cambodia** becomes French protectorate.

1914 The invasion of **Serbia** by Austria-Hungary begins (**World War I**).

1949 U.S. General **Omar Bradley** is appointed the first chairman of the **Joint Chiefs of Staff.**

1965 Rioting by blacks begins in the **Watts** section of Los Angeles. The 6 days of looting and burning result in 34 deaths and more than $40 million worth of property damage.

1966 The three-year undeclared war between **Indonesia** and **Malaysia** ends with the signing of a peace treaty at Jakarta.

1979 **Morocco** formally annexes **Tiris el-Gharbia,** an area of the Western Sahara, formerly part of Spain.

SS. Tiburtius and Susanna, martyrs. Susanna also called **Susan.** [d. c. 3rd cent.]

St. Equitius, abbot. [d. c. 560]

St. Blaan, bishop. Aso called **Blane,** or **Blaun.** [d. c. 590]

St. Attracta, virgin; patron of diocese of Achonry, Ireland. Also called **Araght,** or **Tarahata.** [d. c. 6th cent.]

St. Lelia, virgin. [d. c. 6th cent.]

St. Clare, virgin and foundress of the Poor Clares or Minoresses. Patron of embroidery workers, guilders, washerwomen. Invoked against eye diseases. Feast formerly August 12. [d. 1253] Obligatory Memorial.

The Beatified

Blessed Peter Favre. Also called **Peter Faber.** [d. 1546]

Blessed Innocent XI, pope. Elected 1676. [d. 1689]

August 12

Birthdates

1503 **Christian III,** King of Denmark and Norway; called the *Father of the People*; introduced the Reformation to Denmark. [d. January 1, 1559]

1753 **Thomas Bewick,** English engineer, book illustrator; stimulated a rebirth of interest in wood engraving as an art form.

1762 **George IV,** King of Great Britain and Ireland, 1820–30. [d. June 26, 1830]

1781 **Robert Mills,** U.S. architect; Architect of Public Buildings 1830–51; designed the Washington Monument, although it was not built until 30 years after his death. [d. March 3, 1855]

1815 **Benjamin Pierce Cheney,** U.S. business executive; founder of New England stagecoach business that evolved into American Express Co., 1879. [d. July 23, 1895]

1856 **James Buchanan (*Diamond Jim*) Brady,** U.S. salesman of railroad carriages; bon vivant, flamboyant U.S. businessman known widely for his phenomenal selling ability, extravagant habits, and philanthropic leanings. Donated funds to **Johns Hopkins University** for establishment of its Urological Institute. [d. April 13, 1917]

1859 **Katherine Lee Bates,** U.S. author, educator; wrote the poem *America the Beautiful*, on which the song is based. [d. March 28, 1929]

1866 **Jacinto Benavante y Martínez,** Spanish dramatist; noted for his realistic and satirical plays of Spanish life; Nobel Prize in literature, 1922. [d. July 14, 1954]

1872 **Louis Loucheur,** French industrialist, statesman; French Minister of Labor, 1928–30; Minister of Commerce, 1930–31. [d. November 22, 1931]

1876 **Mary Roberts Rinehart,** U.S. novelist; noted for her popular mystery novels which appeared between 1908–53 and sold more than 10 million copies by the time of her death; a founder of Farrar & Rinehart, publishers. [d. September 22, 1958]

1880 **Christy Mathewson,** U.S. baseball player; inducted into Baseball Hall of Fame, 1936. [d. October 7, 1925]

1881 **Cecil B(lount) De Mille,** U.S. director, producer, Hollywood pioneer in production of films; first to establish the medium as a serious dramatic form. Noted for his extravagant large-scale productions on universally appealing themes such as Bible stories and American growth and expansion. [d. January 21, 1959]

1882 **George Wesley Bellows,** U.S. painter; exponent of realism; he brought modern art to America with his efforts at organizing the **Armory Show of 1913.** Renowned for his bold and vigorous paintings of city life, boxing events, and World War II. Among his most famous works are *Stag at Sharkey's* and *Forty-two Kids*. [d. January 8, 1925]

Vincent Bendix, U.S. inventor, industrialist; founder of Bendix Company, a pioneer in car manufacturing. Established Bendix Brake Company, the first mass producer of four-wheel brakes, and Bendix Aviation Corporation. [d. March 27, 1945]

1887 **Erwin Schrödinger,** Austrian physicist; Nobel Prize in physics for development of new forms of atomic theory (with P. Dirac), 1933. [d. January 4, 1961]

1904 **Alexis, Czarevitch of Russia,** son of Nicholas II and Alexandra. Executed with his parents and sisters by Bolsheviks. [d. July 16, 1918]

1924 **Mohammad Zia ul-Haq,** Pakistani statesman; President, Islamic Republic of Pakistan, 1977– .

1925 **Dale Bumpers,** U.S. politician, lawyer; Governor of Arkansas, 1971–75; U.S. Senator, 1975– .

Norris Dewar McWhirter and **(Alan) Ross McWhirter,** British editors and authors; twin brothers; creators and editors of *Guinness Book of World Records*, 1955–

Religious Calendar

The Saints

St. Euplus, martyr. Also called **Euplius.** [d. 304]

St. Murtagh, bishop. Also called **Muredach.** [d. c. sixth century]

SS. Porcarius and his Companions, martyrs. [d. c. 732]

St. Jambert, Archbishop of Canterbury. Also called **Jaenbeorht.** [d. 792]

75. Ross was killed in an Irish Republican Army terrorist attack on November 27, 1975.

1932 **John Richard Lane,** U.S. artist, author; Creative Director (1969–75), editorial cartoonist (1975–78), Art Director (1978–) for Newspaper Enterprise Association (now NEA-United Features Syndicate); illustrated such books as *Rockin' Steady* (1974) and *Secret Hidy Holes* (1979).

1936 **Andre Kolingba,** Head of State, Central African Republic, 1981– .

Historical Events

1099 Crusaders defeat Egyptians at **Ascalon (First Crusade).**

1450 French recover **Cherbourg** from English (**Hundred Years' War**).

1876 **Benjamin Disraeli** is created Earl of Beaconsfield by Queen Victoria.

1877 **Henry M. Stanley,** journalist, explorer, reaches the mouth of the Congo River in his search for explorer David Livingstone.

1898 The **Hawaiian Islands** are formally annexed by the United States.

Spanish-American War ends with the signing of a protocol by Spain and the United States. Spain relinquishes **Cuba** and cedes **Puerto Rico** to the U.S.

1914 Great Britain declares war on Austria-Hungary (**World War I**).

1922 German stock market collapses, with the **Deutschmark** declining in value from 162:1 U.S. dollar to 7,000:1 U.S. dollar.

1960 *Echo I,* U.S. balloon communications satellite (100 feet in diameter) is placed in orbit from Cape Canaveral.

1967 **Pope Paul VI** announces changes in the structure of the Roman Catholic Church's central administrative organ, the Curia, including the appointment of non-Italian bishops from all parts of the world to Curia posts.

1978 The first papal funeral ever held outdoors is conducted for **Pope Paul VI** in St. Peter's Square, Rome.

China and Japan sign an historic treaty of peace and friendship in Peking.

August 13

Holidays

| Central African Republic | **Proclamation of Independence** Commemorates the adoption of a parliamentary form of government, 1960. |
| Tunisia | **Women's Day** |

Religious Calendar

The Saints

St. Hippolytus, martyr; patron of horses and their riders. Also called **Hippolytas.** [d. c. 235] Optional Memorial.

Birthdates

1740 **Ivan VI,** Emperor of Russia, 1740–41; forced to abdicate; kept in prison after abdication; murdered, 1764. [d. July 15, 1764]

1814 **Anders Jonas Ångström,** Swedish physicist, astronomer; **Ångstrom unit,** used in measuring length of **light waves,** is named for him. [d. June 21, 1874]

1818 **Lucy Stone,** U.S. social reformer; leader in women's rights movement; founded American Woman Suffrage Association, 1869; founded *Woman's Journal*, a leading publication promoting woman's suffrage, 1870–1917. [d. October 18, 1893]

1820 **Sir George Grove,** British musicologist; editor of *Dictionary of Music and Musicians*, a standard work which bears his name even after numerous revisions by other editors. [d. May 28, 1900]

1860 **Annie Oakley (Phoebe Anne Oakley Mozee),** U.S. markswoman, entertainer; member of **Buffalo Bill Cody's Wild West Show** which toured America for over 17 years. [d. November 3, 1926]

1871 **Karl Liebknecht,** German Communist leader, lawyer; led opposition to Germany's involvement in World War I; murdered with Rosa Luxemburg (December 25) after **Spartacist Rebellion,** 1919. [d. January 15, 1919]

1872 **Richard M. Willstätter,** German chemist; Nobel Prize in chemistry for study of **chlorophyll** and other plant pigments, 1915. [d. August 3, 1942]

1888 **John Logie Baird,** Scottish engineer, an early contributor to science of visual transmission; developed first apparatus for transmitting visual record of moving objects, a forerunner of **television,** 1924. [d. June 14, 1946]

1895 **Bert Lahr (Irving Lahrheim),** U.S. comedian. [d. December 4, 1967]

1897 **Detlev Wulf Bronk,** U.S. biophysicist, educator; President of Johns Hopkins University, 1949–53; President of National Academy of Sciences, 1950–62; President of Rockefeller Institute for Medical Research, 1953–68. Received Presidential Medal of Freedom, 1964. [d. November 17, 1975]

1899 **Alfred (Joseph) Hitchcock,** British film director; master of the suspense film. [d. April 29, 1980]

1912 **(William) Ben(jamin) Hogan,** U.S. golfer; inducted into PGA Hall of Fame, 1953.

Salvador Edward Luria, U.S. biologist, educator, university professor, born in Italy; Nobel Prize in physiology or medicine for discoveries in genetic structure of viruses (with M. Delbrück and A. D. Hershey), 1969.

1913 **Makarios III (Mikhail Khristodolou Mouskos),** Cypriot leader; first president of Cyprus, 1960–74; Archbishop of the Orthodox Church of Cyprus, 1950–77. [d. August 13, 1977]

1916 **Daniel (Louis) Schorr,** U.S. news correspondent; commentator for CBS TV news, 1966–76; aroused national controversy by passing secret congressional report on the CIA to the *Village Voice*.

1917 **Philip Handler,** U.S. biochemist, educator; head of Department of Biochemistry, Duke University, 1950–69; Chairman, National

St. Pontian, pope and martyr. Elected to papacy 230. [d. c. 236] Optional Memorial. Feast formerly November 19.

St. Radegund, Queen of the Franks, matron. Founder of the nunnery at Poitiers. Also called Radegundes. [d. 587]

St. Maximus the Confessor, abbot. [d. 662]

St. Wigbert, abbot. [d. c. 738]

St. Nerses Klaiëtsi, Primate of the Armenians; foremost writer and poet of his time. Also called Narses, or Narses III. Also known as *Shnorhali*, or *the Gracious*. [d. 1173]

St. Benildus, teaching brother. [d. 1862]

St. Cassian of Imola, martyr. [death date unknown]

The Beatified

Blessed Novellone. [d. 1280]

Blessed Gertrude of Altenberg, virgin. [d. 1297]

Blessed John of Alvernia. Also called John of Fermo. [d. 1322]

Blessed William Freeman, martyr. Also called William Mason. [d. 1595]

Science Board, 1966–69. [d. December 29, 1981]

1918 Frederick Sanger, British biochemist; Nobel Prize in chemistry for determination of the structure of the **insulin** molecule, 1958.

1919 George Shearing, British musician; blind since birth; his jazz quintet has maintained great popularity for nearly 40 years.

1924 Leon (Marcus) Uris, U.S. novelist; best known for his novels *Exodus* and *Trinity*.

1926 Fidel Castro, Cuban political leader; Premier of Cuba, 1959– . Leader in establishing Cuba as the first Communist nation in the Western Hemisphere.

1914 France declares war on Austria-Hungary (World War I).

1918 Czechoslovakia declares war on Germany (World War I).

1961 Construction by the Soviets of the Berlin Wall, which blocks passage between East and West Berlin, is begun.

1960 Chad, the Congo, and the Central African Republic gain independence from France.

Historical Events

1624 Cardinal Richelieu becomes first Chief Minister of France.

1704 Battle of Blenheim is fought, in which French troops are routed by a combined English and Austrian force (War of the Spanish Succession).

1814 The Colony of the Cape of Good Hope in South Africa is formally ceded to the British by the Dutch.

1831 Nat Turner slave insurrection begins in Southampton County, Virginia. During the uprising 55 whites and about 100 blacks are killed.

1889 London Dock Strike, which lasts for more than one month, begins the spread of trade unionism in Great Britain.

1898 U.S. forces capture Manila (Spanish-American War).

August 14

Holidays

Pakistan	Independence Day
San Marino	Summer Holiday
Vatican City	Mid-August Holiday

Religious Calendar

The Saints

St. Marcellus, Bishop of Apamaea, martyr. [d. c. 389]

St. Eusebius (Vercelli) of Rome, priest. [d. 371]

Birthdates

1742   **Pius VII,** pope, 1800–23; imprisoned by Napoleon, 1809–14; restored Jesuit order. [d. August 20, 1823]

1840   Baron **Richard Krafft-Ebbing,** German neurologist; noted for studies of **forensic psychiatry** and **aberrant sexual practices.** [d. December 22, 1902]

1860   **Ernest Thompson Seton,** Canadian artist, author, lecturer; one of originators of **American Boy Scout** movement; Chief Scout of Boy Scouts of America, 1910–15. [d. October 23, 1946]

1867   **John Galsworthy (John Sinjohn),** British novelist, dramatist; Nobel Prize in literature, 1932. [d. January 31, 1933]

1883   **Ernest Everett Just,** U.S. biologist, educator; recipient of the first Spingarn Medal awarded by the National Association for the Advancement of Colored People for his dedication to improvement of medical education for black students, 1914. [d. October 27, 1941]

1920   **Nehemiah Persoff,** U.S. character actor, born in Israel.

1925   **Russell (Wayne) Baker,** U.S. journalist; Pulitzer Prize in commentary, 1979.

1952   **Debbie Meyer,** U.S. swimmer; Olympic gold medalist, 1968.

Historical Events

1040   **Duncan** is slain by **Macbeth,** who becomes king of Scots, reigning for 17 years.

1385   **John I** of Portugal defeats **John I** of Castile and secures independence of his country.

1765   American colonists challenge British governor in Boston by hanging effigies on what is later called the **Liberty Tree.**

1900   The **Imperial Court** flees Peking as international forces march on the city (**Boxer Rebellion**).

As consequence of **Boxer Rebellion,** Russian forces seize both banks of the Amur River and drive thousands of Chinese civilians to their death.

1912   U.S. Marines begin 21-year military presence in **Nicaragua** to protect American interests there.

1935   U.S. President **Franklin D. Roosevelt** signs **Social Security Act,** establishing Social Security Board to supervise payments of old-age benefits.

1941   The **Atlantic Charter** is signed by U.S. President **Franklin D. Roosevelt** and British Prime Minister **Winston Churchill;** the Charter forms the basis for the **United Nations Declaration.**

1945   Japanese acceptance of terms of surrender is announced to the American citizenry by President **Harry Truman,** touching off celebration known as **V-J Day.**

1947   **Indian Independence Act** is enacted by British parliament, dividing Indian subcontinent into **Pakistan** and **India.**

1960   First broadcast via satellite is made from Bell Laboratories in New Jersey to the Jet Propulsion Laboratory in California.

1962   A gang of thieves holds up a U.S. mail truck in Plymouth, Massachusetts, and escapes with more than $1.5 million.

1970   After nearly 18 years of separation, **Yugoslavia** and the **Vatican** resume full diplomatic relations.

St. Fachanan, Bishop; patron of diocese of Ross, Ireland. Also called **Eachanan,** or **Fachtna.** [d. 6th cent.]

St. Athanasia, matron. [d. c. 860]

St. Maximilian Kolbe. [canonized 1982]

The Beatified

Blessed Anthony Primaldi and his Companions, martyrs. [d. 1480]

August 15

Holidays

India	Independence Day
	Commemorates the independence of India from Great Britain, 1947.
Republic of Korea	Liberation Day
	Celebrates Korea's liberation from Japan, 1945, and the establishment of the Republic, 1948.

Birthdates

1688 **Frederick William,** King of Prussia, 1713–40; helped transform Prussia into a prosperous modern state; was himself illiterate and hostile to cultural development. [d. May 31, 1740]

1740 **Matthias Claudius,** German poet; known for his lyric poems. [d. January 21, 1815]

1769 **Napoleon I (Bonaparte),** called *le Petit Corporal* or *the Little Corporal* as well as *the Corsican;* French military and political leader; one of the foremost historical figures of Europe; established the basis of the current French legal system; controlled much of central Europe during his reign. Defeated by alliance of European powers; exiled to Elba, where he plotted his return to power (**Hundred Days**); utterly defeated at Waterloo and exiled to St. Helena, where he died. [d. May 5, 1821]

1771 **Sir Walter Scott,** Scottish novelist, historian; wrote many historical romances, including *Ivanhoe.* [d. September 21, 1832]

1785 **Thomas DeQuincy,** English essayist, critic; noted for his genius in exposition, particularly in his personal account, *Confessions of an English Opium Eater.* [d. December 8, 1859]

1807 **François Paul Jules Grévy,** French politician; President of the Third Republic, 1879–87. [d. September 9, 1891]

1858 **Emma Calvé (Emma de Roquer),** French operatic soprano. [d. January 6, 1942]

1875 **Robert Abram (*Captain Bob*) Bartlett,** Canadian Arctic explorer; commander of the *Roosevelt* on Robert Peary's expedition, 1905–09. Led numerous other expeditions to Greenland, Siberia, Labrador, and the Arctic. [d. April 28, 1946]

1879 **Ethel Barrymore,** U.S. actress; sister of Lionel and John Barrymore. [d. June 18, 1959]

1885 **Edna Ferber,** U.S. novelist, short-story writer, playwright; Pulitzer Prize in fiction, 1925. [d. April 16, 1968]

1888 **T(homas) E(dward) Lawrence (*Lawrence of Arabia*),** British archaeologist, soldier, author; led Arab revolt against Turks, 1917–18; noted for his controversial military strategies. Killed in a motorcycle accident. [d. May 19, 1935]

1892 **Prince Louis-Victor (Pierre-Raymond) de Broglie,** French physicist; Nobel Prize in physics for his revolutionary theory of the wave nature of electrons, 1929.

1896 **(Sol) Sheldon Glueck,** U.S. criminologist; noted for his research into prevention of **juvenile delinquency;** author of *The Problem of Delinquency,* 1958. [d. March 10, 1980]

1912 **Julia Child,** U.S. cooking expert, author, TV personality; known for her knowledge of and ability to teach the art of French cooking.

1919 **Robert Francis Goheen,** U.S. educator, diplomat; Ambassador to India, 1977–81.

1924 **Robert (Oxton) Bolt,** British playwright; noted for his stage play *A Man for All Seasons,* later adapted for film, and filmscript for *Lawrence of Arabia* and *Dr. Zhivago.*

Phyllis Schlafly, U.S. political activist, author; led opposition to Equal Rights Amendment.

1925 **Oscar (Emanuel) Peterson,** Canadian jazz pianist.

1930 **Tom Mboya,** Kenyan political leader; active in Kenyan struggle for independence.

San Marino	Summer Holiday
Vatican City	Mid-August Holiday
Roman Catholic Countries	Assumption Day

Celebrates the taking of the Blessed Virgin Mary, body and soul, into heaven, A.D. 40.

Religious Calendar

Solemnities

Feast of the Assumption of the Blessed Virgin Mary. [major holy day, Episcopal Church; minor festival, Lutheran Church]

The Saints

St. Tarsicius, martyr. [d. 3rd cent.]

St. Arnulf, Bishop of Soissons. Also called **Arnoul,** or **Arnulphus.** [d. 1087]

Assassinated by member of opposition political party (Kikuyu) while serving as Economics Minister. [d. July 5, 1969]

1935 **Vernon E. Jordan, Jr.,** U.S. civil rights spokesman, lawyer; president of National Urban League, 1972–81.

1950 **Princess Anne** of Great Britain.

Historical Events

1057 **Malcolm** kills **Macbeth of Scotland;** Macbeth's stepson **Lulach** succeeds him as king of Scotland.

1169 **Henry VI** is elected Holy Roman Emperor.

1307 **Henry of Carinthia** is elected king of Bohemia.

1534 **Jesuit Order** is founded at Paris as **Ignatius Loyola** and six companions take their vows.

1684 **Truce of Ratisbon** is signed between Holy Roman Empire and France, guaranteeing peace for 20 years.

1812 Indians massacre settlers and soldiers at **Fort Dearborn** (now **Chicago**).

1824 The colony on the West African coast for freed U.S. slaves is named **Liberia.**

1850 **Queen's University** in Ireland is established.

1867 **Second Reform Act** in Great Britain extends suffrage to householders and landowners, nearly doubling the electorate.

1914 The French repulse the Germans at the **Battle of Dinant** (**World War I**).

Panama Canal is opened to international commercial vessels.

1917 **Czar Nicholas II** and his family are moved from their residence at Tsarskoe Selo to further imprisonment in Tobolsk, Siberia (**Russian Revolution**).

1943 U.S. and Canadian troops reoccupy **Kiska** in the Aleutian Islands after Japanese withdrawal (**World War II**).

1947 **India** becomes independent, self-governing dominion within the Commonwealth of Nations.

1948 **Syngman Rhee** becomes first President of the new **Republic of Korea.**

1950 Severe earthquake affects 30,000 square miles in **Assam, India,** killing 20,000 to 30,000 persons.

1960 **Republic of the Congo** is proclaimed an independent nation within the French community in ceremonies at Brazzaville.

1967 **Rev. Martin Luther King, Jr.,** issues his call for massive campaigns of **civil disobedience.**

1969 **Woodstock Music and Art Fair,** held in Bethel, New York, begins.

1971 **Bahrain** gains independence from Great Britain.

1975 Bangladesh president, **Sheikh Mujibur Rahman,** is assassinated in an army coup. **Khandakar Mustaque Ahmed** is sworn in as president of the civilian regime.

1975 **Joanne Little,** a black 21-year-old, is acquitted in Raleigh, N.C., of second degree murder in the death of her jailer, a white man, contending she defended herself against rape.

1979 **Andrew Young** resigns as U.S. Ambassador to the U.N. as a result of disagreement with the U.S. policy in the Middle East.

August 16

Holidays

Dominican Republic — **Restoration of the Republic** Celebrates the 1963 restoration to independence and first free elections since 1924.

Gabon Republic — **Independence Anniversary** Celebrates Gabon's achievement of independence from France, 1960. A three-day holiday.

Liechtenstein — **Birthday of Prince Franz Josef II**

Birthdates

1397 **Albert II,** King of Germany, 1438–39; also king of Hungary and Bohemia. [d. October 27, 1439]

1557 **Agostino Carracci,** Italian painter; one of the pioneers of the **Italian baroque.** [d. February 23, 1602]

1645 **Jean de La Bruyère,** French moral satirist. [d. May 11, 1696]

1794 **Jean Henri Merle d'Aubigné,** Swiss theological historian. [d. October 21, 1872]

1798 **Mirabeau Buonaparte Lamar,** U.S. soldier; second president of the Republic of Texas; founded the capital at **Austin,** 1840. [d. December 19, 1859]

1813 **Sarah Porter,** U.S. educator; founder of **Miss Porter's School for Girls** in Connecticut; sister of **Noah Porter,** editor of first two editions of Noah Webster's unabridged dictionary. [d. February 17, 1900]

1821 **Arthur Cayley,** British mathematician; Professor of Pure Mathematics, Cambridge University, 1863–95; contributed significantly to development of mathematical theory; published more than 900 papers during his career. [d. January 26, 1895]

1830 **Diego Barros Arana,** Chilean historian, educator; renowned expert on Chilean history; wrote *Historia General de Chile*, 16 volumes, 1884–1902. [d. November 4, 1907]

1832 **Wilhelm Wundt,** German physiologist; founder of first laboratory of **experimental psychology,** 1879. [d. August 31, 1920]

1845 **Gabriel Lippmann,** French physicist; Nobel Prize in physics for producing the first **color photographic plate,** 1908. [d. July 13, 1921]

1862 **(Amos) Alonzo Stagg,** U.S. football coach; member of first all-American football team; coach of University of Chicago, 1892–1933; first college coach to achieve full faculty status; known as the *Grand Old Man of Football.* [d. March 17, 1965]

1894 **George Meany,** U.S. labor union leader; President of AFL-CIO, 1955–79; awarded Presidential Medal of Freedom, 1964. [d. January 10, 1980]

1904 **Wendell Meredith Stanley,** U.S. biochemist; Nobel Prize in chemistry for preparation of pure forms of **enzymes** and **virus proteins** (with J. H. Northrop), 1946. [d. June 15, 1971]

1906 **Franz Josef II,** Crown Prince of Liechtenstein, 1938– .

1913 **Menachem Begin,** Israeli political leader; Prime Minister of Israel, 1977–83.

1919 **Merce Cunningham,** U.S. dancer, choreographer; member of Martha Graham Dance Co., 1939–45; founder of **Merce Cunningham School of Dance,** 1959.

1923 **Lee Kuan Yew,** Prime Minister, Republic of Singapore, 1959– .

1925 **Fess Parker,** U.S. actor.

1928 **Ann Blyth,** U.S. actress.

1930 **Frank Gifford,** U.S. football player, broadcaster; elected to Football Hall of Fame, 1975.

1945 **Suzanne Farrell,** U.S. ballerina.

Historical Events

1513 **Battle of Spurs** is fought, in which Holy Roman Emperor **Maximilian I** and **Henry VIII** of England defeat French at **Guinegate.**

| Vermont | Bennington Battle Day |
| Vatican City | Mid-August Holiday |

Commemorates the defeat of the British at Bennington, 1777.

Religious Calendar

The Saints

St. Arsacius. Also called **Ursacius.** [d. 358]

St. Armel, abbot. Also called **Arkel, Arthmael, Arzel, Erme, Ermel,** or **Ermyn.** [d. c. 570]

St. Stephen of Hungary, first Christian king of Hungary. Also called **Stephens.** Feast formerly September 2. [d. 1038] Optional Memorial.

St. Rock, patron of surgeons and tile makers. Invoked against plague, knee afflictions, and cattle diseases. Also called **Roch,** or **Roche.** [d. c. 1378]

The Beatified

Blessed Laurence Loricatus. [d. 1243]

1773 **Jesuits** are expelled from Rome by **Pope Clement XIV.**

1777 American patriots defeat the British at the **Battle of Bennington** (**American Revolution**).

1780 Americans are defeated by British at Camden, New Jersey (**American Revolution**).

1807 **Gas street-lights** are first introduced in London at Golden Lane.

1812 U.S. forces at Detroit surrender to British (**War of 1812**).

1819 **Peterloo Massacre** in Manchester, England, results in several deaths and hundreds of injuries as British soldiers attempt to break up gathering listening to speakers on parliamentary reform and repeal of Corn Laws.

1896 **Klondike gold rush** is set off as gold is discovered on **Bonanza Creek,** near Dawson, Canada, 50 miles east of Alaska border.

1914 **Fort Flemalle,** the last of the fortresses at Liège, falls to the Germans; the Belgian government and royal family leave Brussels for Antwerp (**World War I**).

1921 **King Peter** of Yugoslavia dies and is succeeded by his son, **Alexander I.**

1943 **Messina, Sicily** is taken by U.S. Seventh Army (**World War II**).

1960 **Cyprus** proclaims its independence from Great Britain, which has held the island since 1878.

1966 **Declaration of Bogatá** is issued by presidents of Colombia, Chile, and Venezuela, calling for economic integration of Latin America.

August 17

Holidays

Argentina	**Anniversary of the Death of General San Martin** Commemorates the event which occurred in 1850.
Gabon Republic	**Independence Anniversary** Second day of a three-day celebration.
Indonesia	**Independence Day** Commemorates establishment of the republic, 1945.

Birthdates

1601 **Pierre de Fermat,** French mathematician, referred to as the *Founder of Modern Number Theory*; developer of differential calculus and probability theory.

1603 **Lennart Torstenson, Count of Ortala,** Swedish soldier; Commander in Chief of Swedish Army, 1641. [d. April 7, 1651]

1629 **John III Sobieski,** King of Poland, 1674–96; responsible for saving his country from Turks; Polish hero and patron of arts and sciences. [d. June 17, 1696]

1786 **Davy Crockett,** U.S. frontiersman, politician; U.S. Congressman, 1827–31, 1833–35; hero of Texas war for independence from Mexico; killed at **Battle of the Alamo.** [d. March 6, 1836]

1801 **Fredrika Bremer,** Swedish novelist, women's rights advocate. [d. December 31, 1865]

1819 **Jón Arnason,** Icelandic folklorist; author of *Popular Legends of Iceland*, 1862. [d. September 4, 1888]

1840 **Wilfrid Scawen Blunt,** British poet; severe critic of **white supremacy** policies and British exploitation of native races. Supported nationalist movements in Egypt, Ireland, and India. [d. September 11, 1922]

1847 **Alice Meynell,** British poet, essayist; wife of **Wilfred Meynell,** British journalist, biographer. [d. November 27, 1922]

1868 **Gene(ra) Grace Stratton Porter,** U.S. novelist; author of numerous books for children, nature books; at the time of her death, more than 10 million of her books had been sold. [d. December 6, 1924]

1887 **Charles I,** last Emperor of Austria and King of Hungary, abdicated November 11, 1918. [d. April 1, 1922]

Marcus (Moziah) Garvey, U.S. social reformer, black nationalist leader; advocate of black pride and **back to Africa** movement. [d. June 10, 1940]

1888 **Monty Woolley (Edgar Montillion Woolley),** U.S. actor, director. [d. May 6, 1963]

1890 **Harry (Lloyd) Hopkins,** U.S. public official; head of U.S. Emergency Relief Administration, 1933–38. Served as U.S. Secretary of Commerce, 1938–40; member of Roosevelt's **Little War Cabinet.** [d. January 29, 1946]

1892 **Mae West,** U.S. actress, burlesque queen; stage career extended from 1897–1969; considered the embodiment of the Gay Nineties femme fatale. [d. November 22, 1980]

1904 **John Hay Whitney,** U.S. financier, diplomat, publisher; chairman, Selznick-International Pictures, producers of *Gone with the Wind*, 1936–40; U.S. Ambassador to Great Britain, 1956–61; publisher, *New York Herald Tribune*, 1957–66. [d. February 8, 1982]

1906 **Marcello (Jose) Gaetano,** Portuguese statesman; Prime Minister, 1968–74; protégé of Dictator Antonio Salazar; ousted by revolution of the Army; exiled to Brazil. [d. October 26, 1980]

Hazel (Gladys) Bishop, U.S. chemist, cosmetics manufacturer; founder of Hazel Bishop, Inc.; director of marketing, Fashion Institute of Technology, 1978– .

1918 **George Scratchley Brown,** U.S. Air Force general; member of Chiefs of Staff, 1973–74; Chairman of Joint Chiefs of Staff, 1974–78. [d. December 5, 1978]

Religious Calendar

The Saints

St. Mamas, martyr. Also called **Manus.** [d. c. 275]

St. Eusebius, pope. Elected 310. [d. 310]

SS. Liberatus and his Companions, martyrs. Also called **Libertas.** [d. 484]

St. Hyacinth, Dominican missionary and apostle of Poland. Also called **Jacek.** [d. 1257]

St. Clare of Montefalco, virgin. Also called **Chiara,** or **Claire.** [d. 1308]

St. Joan Delanoue, virgin and founder of the Sisters of St. Anne of The Providence of Saumur. [d. 1736] [canonized 1982]

1921   **Maureen O'Hara (Maureen Fitzsimmons),** U.S. actress, born in Ireland.

1923   **Larry Rivers (Yitzroch Loiza Grossberg),** U.S. artist.

1929   **Francis Gary Powers,** U.S. pilot; shot down over Soviet territory in his U-2 reconnaissance plane, setting off an international diplomatic crisis, 1960; imprisoned by Russians; exchanged for Soviet agent, Rudolf Abel, 1962. [d. August 1, 1977]

1932   **V(idiadhar) S(urajpresad) Naipaul,** West Indian writer; BBC broadcaster; recorded cultural portraits of the Carribbean area.

1943   **Robert De Niro,** U.S. actor.

1952   **Guillermo Vilas,** Argentine tennis player.

Historical Events

1585   **Duke of Parma** takes Antwerp and regains Flanders and Brabant (**Dutch War of Liberation**).

1648   **Oliver Cromwell** defeats the Scots at the **Battle of Preston.**

1786   **Frederick the Great** of Prussia dies and is succeeded by **Frederick William II.**

1850   Denmark cedes all forts and property rights on the **Gold Coast of Africa** to Great Britain.

1900   International force of 19,000 British, French, Russian, American, German, and Japanese troops lift the seige of the imperial compound in Peking (**Boxer Rebellion**).

1942   First U.S. strategic bombing in Europe takes place as American B-17s attack German-controlled **Rouen, France (World War II).**

1945   **Indonesia** proclaims itself an independent republic.

1961   U.S. and all Latin American nations except Cuba formally proclaim **Alliance for Progress.**

1962   German citizen **Peter Fechter** is killed at the Berlin Wall, stimulating anti-East German demonstrations.

1967   **Stokely Carmichael,** militant U.S. black leader, calls for U.S. blacks to arm for **total revolution.**

1969   **Hurricane Camille,** the most violent storm to strike the U.S. since 1935, devastates the Gulf Coast of Mississippi, killing more than 300.

1975   Heir to the **Seagram** dynasty is released by kidnappers after payment of $2.3 million ransom.

1976   A severe **earthquake** shakes the island of **Mindanao** in the Philippines, producing tidal waves that kill more than 8,000 persons and leave 175,000 homeless.

1978   Three American balloonists cross the Atlantic in their helium-filled *Double Eagle II,* establishing an endurance record of 137 hours, 3 minutes and a distance record of 5,023 km (3,120 miles).

August 18

Holidays

| Gabon Republic | Independence Anniversary Third day of the celebration. |

Religious Calendar

The Saints

St. Helen, widow and empress. Mother of Constantine the Great. Also called **Helena.** [d. c. 330]

Birthdates

1564   **Federigo Borromeo,** Italian cardinal, archbishop; founder of the **Ambrosian Library** at Milan, 1609. [d. September 22, 1631]

1587   **Virginia Dare,** first English child to be born in colonial America. She and all other members of the **Roanoke settlement,** in Virginia, disappeared, the group being later referred to as the *lost colony of Roanoke.* [d. c. 1587]

1685   **Brook Taylor,** British mathematician; published the first treatise on **finite differences in calculus,** 1715. [d. December 29, 1731]

1774   **Meriwether Lewis,** U.S. explorer, soldier, public official; private secretary to President Thomas Jefferson, 1801–03; head of the great **Lewis and Clark Expedition** into the Northwest Territory of the U.S., 1803–06; Governor of Louisiana Territory, 1807–09. [d. October 11, 1809]

1807   **Charles Francis Adams,** U.S. statesman, economist; son of U.S. President John Quincy Adams; candidate for vice-presidency, 1848; U.S. Congressman, 1858–61; U.S. Ambassador to Great Britain, 1861–68. [d. November 21, 1886]

1830   **Francis Joseph I,** Emperor of Austria-Hungary; father of Archduke Francis Ferdinand, whose assassination in 1914 precipitated World War I. [d. November 21, 1916]

1834   **Marshall Field,** U.S. businessman, philanthropist; founder of Marshall Field & Co., 1881; donated large sums of money to the University of Chicago; established the **Field Museum of Natural History.** [d. January 16, 1906]

1854   **James Hervey Hyslop,** U.S. psychologist, philosopher, and educator; founder of American Society of Psychical Research. [d. June 17, 1920]

1900   **Vijaya Lakshmi Pandit,** Indian politician, diplomat; first woman Minister of Uttar Pradesh government, 1937–39; 1946–47; head of Indian delegation to UN, 1946–51, 1963; President of UN General Assembly, 1953–54.

1922   **Alain Robbe-Grillet,** French author, film-maker, agronomist; Chargé de Mission, Institute Nationale de la Statistique, 1945–48; author of numerous **nouveau roman** works.

       Shelley Winters, U.S. actress.

1925   **Brian (Wilson) Aldiss,** award-winning British science fiction writer; literary editor of *Oxford Mail,* 1957–69.

1927   **Rosalynn Carter,** wife of former U.S. President Jimmy Carter (October 1).

1933   **Roman Polanski,** film director; known for *Repulsion, Rosemary's Baby,* and *Tess.*

1934   **Roberto Clemente,** U.S. baseball player; inducted into Baseball Hall of Fame, 1973. Killed in plane crash. [d. December 31, 1972]

1935   **Rafer Johnson,** U.S. athlete; Olympic decathlon champion, 1960.

1937   **Robert Redford,** U.S. actor.

Historical Events

1765   Holy Roman Emperor **Francis I** dies and is succeeded by **Josef II.**

1825   **Alexander Gordon Laing** becomes the first European to reach **Timbuktu** in Africa.

1846   U.S. troops occupy **Santa Fé (Mexican War).**

1896   France annexes **Madagascar.**

St. Alipius, Bishop of Tagaste, companion of St. Augustine. [d. c. 430]

St. Agapitus, martyr. Also called **Agapitue,** or **Agapetus.** [death date unknown]

SS. Florus and Laurus, martyrs. [death dates unknown]

The Beatified

Blessed Angelo Augustine of Florence. [d. 1438]

Blessed Beatrice da Silva, virgin and foundress of the Conceptionist Nuns. Also called **Brites.** [d. 1490]

Blessed Haymo of Savigliano. [d. 1495]

1903   First U.S. transcontinental automobile trip is completed in 61 days, from San Francisco to New York, by **Tom Fitch** and **Marcus Kraarup.**

1917   First two-way **radiotelephone communication** between a plane and the ground is established.

1938   Benjamin Britten's *First Piano Concerto* premieres in London.

August 19

Holidays

Afghanistan   Independence Day
Commemorates the signing of
the **Treaty of Rawalpindi,**
1919.

Religious Calendar

The Saints
St. Andrew the Tribune, martyr. [d. c. 300]
SS. Timothy, Agapius, and Thecla, martyrs. [d. 304]

Birthdates

1398   **Iñigo López de Mendoza,** Marquis of Santillana, Spanish poet, humanist; noted for his contributions to Spanish poetry; composed sonnets imitating **Petrarch.** [d. March 25, 1458]

1560   **James Crichton,** Scottish prodigy; known as the *Admirable Crichton;* disputed scientific and philosophical questions in major centers of learning in France and Italy. [d. July 3, 1582]

1646   **John Flamsteed,** English astronomer; contributed to the discoveries of Sir Isaac Newton; established observatory at Greenwich, marking **prime meridian.** [d. December 31, 1719]

1689   **Samuel Richardson,** English novelist, baptized on this day; noted for his contributions to development of modern English novel; wrote *Pamela: or, Virtue Rewarded.* [d. July 4, 1761]

1743   **Comtesse Du Barry (Marie Jeanne Bécu),** French adventuress and mistress of **King Louis XV,** 1768–74; arrested by Robespierre, 1793, and executed. [d. December 7, 1793]

1793   **Samuel Griswold Goodrich (*Peter Parley*),** U.S. author, educator; famous for his series of *Peter Parley* books, of which over 7 million copies were sold between 1827–56. [d. May 9, 1860]

1808   **James Nasmyth,** British engineer; invented the **steam hammer,** 1839. [d. May 7, 1890]

1830   **Julius Lothar Meyer,** German chemist; known for his independent studies related to **periodic law.** [d. April 11, 1895]

1843   **Charles Montagu Doughty,** British poet, traveler; author of *Travels in Arabia Deserta,* 1888, a graphic narration describing his travels through Saudi Arabia disguised as an Arab. [d. January 20, 1926]

1853   **Aleksei Alekseevich Brusilov,** Russian general; highly successful military leader in World War I; appointed to Russian Supreme Command, 1917. [d. March 17, 1926]

1859   **Henry Ives Cobb,** U.S. architect; noted for his expertise in steel construction. [d. March 27, 1931]

1870   **Bernard M(annes) Baruch,** U.S. financier, public official; adviser to and confidant of every U.S. president from Woodrow Wilson to John F. Kennedy. [d. June 20, 1965]

1871   **Orville Wright,** U.S. inventor, aviator; with his brother Wilbur (April 16), succeeded in developing first machine capable of powered flight, December 17, 1903. [d. January 30, 1948]

1878   **Manuel Luis Quezon y Molina,** first president, Commonwealth of Philippines, 1935–44; head of Philippine government in exile after Japanese conquest, 1942–44. [d. August 1, 1944]

1883   **Gabrielle Bonheur Chanel (*Coco*),** French fashion designer; influenced women's fashion industry after World War I with introduction of clean, simple designs later classified as **Chanel look.** [d. January 10, 1971]

1902   **(Frederic) Ogden Nash,** U.S. poet; member, editorial staff of *New Yorker* magazine; noted for his humorous, often satirical verse and witty observations on light subjects. [d. May 19, 1971]

1903   **James Gould Cozzens,** U.S. novelist; most popular novel was *By Love Possessed.* [d. August 9, 1978]

St. Sixtus III, pope. Elected 432. [d. 440]

St. Mochta, abbot; last of St. Patrick's personal disciples. Also called **Mochteus.** [d. c. 535]

St. Bertulf, abbot. [d. 640]

St. Credan, Abbot of Evesham. [d. 8th cent.]

St. Sebald, patron of Nuremberg, Bavaria. [d. 8th cent.]

St. John Eudes, founder of the Congregations of Jesus and Mary and of Our Lady of Charity of the Refuge. Also called **John of Eudes.** [d. 1680]

St. Louis of Anjou, Bishop of Toulouse. Also called **Lewis.** [d. 1297]

The Beatified

Blessed Emily of Vercelli, virgin. [d. 1314]

1907   **Thurston Ballard Morton,** U.S. Congressman, 1946–52; U.S. Senator, 1957–69.

1931   **Willie Shoemaker,** U.S. jockey; rode Kentucky Derby winners, 1955, 1959, 1965.

1940   **Jill St. John,** U.S. actress.

Historical Events

1388   Scots, under the Earl of Douglas, defeat the English forces under Lord Percy Hotspur, at the **Battle of Chevy Chase** at **Otterburn.**

1477   **Maximilian,** son of Holy Roman Emperor Frederick III, marries Mary of Burgundy.

1493   Holy Roman Emperor **Frederick III** dies and is succeeded by **Maximilian I.**

1561   **Mary Queen of Scots** arrives in Scotland to assume the throne.

1587   **Sigismund III,** son of John of Sweden, is elected king of Poland.

1772   Revolution in Sweden, backed by France, re-establishes **Gustavus III** as monarch. He abolishes torture, improves code of laws, and establishes religious tolerance.

1812   The *U.S.S. Constitution,* captained by **Isaac Hull,** defeats *H.M.S. Guerrière* (**War of 1812**).

1839   Academy of Sciences in Paris makes public the details of Louis Daguerre's first practical **photographic process.**

1914   The Germans occupy **Louvain** after a battle with the Belgian army (**World War I**).

1918   *Yip, Yip, Yaphank,* revue with book, music, and lyrics by Irving Berlin, is first performed at Camp Upton, New York; contains songs *Oh, How I Hate to Get Up in the Morning* and *God Bless America.*

1919   **Korea** becomes a Japanese province under a new plan of civil government.

1934   German plebiscite approves Hitler's assumption of the presidency in addition to being chancellor.

1942   British and Canadian troops launch suicidal attack on **Dieppe** (**World War II**).

1969   British army assumes full responsibility for security in **Northern Ireland.**

1973   **Georgios Papadopoulos** is sworn in as the first president of Greece; vestiges of martial law in effect since 1967 are lifted and amnesty is granted to some political prisoners. He is unseated by military junta in Nov., 1973.

1976   U.S. President **Gerald Ford** is nominated as the Republican Party's presidential candidate.

1978   Theater fire set by Muslim extremists in **Abadan, Iran,** kills 430 people. The arrested suspects espouse belief that movie theaters are incompatible with Islamic teachings.

August 20

Holidays

Hungary   **Constitution Day**
Commemorates the establishment of the People's Republic, 1949.

Religious Calendar

The Saints

St. Oswin, king of Deria in Britain, and martyr. [d. 651]

Birthdates

1632 **Louis Bourdaloue,** French Jesuit theologian; known for his saintly character. [d. May 13, 1704]

1745 **Francis Asbury,** U.S. religious leader; only English missionary in U.S. at outbreak of Revolutionary War; first bishop of **Methodist Episcopal Church** ordained in America, 1784; established Methodism as one of principal U.S. denominations. [d. March 31, 1816]

1749 **Aleksandr Nikolayevich Radishchev,** Russian poet, reformer; noted for his *Voyage from Petersburg to Moscow*, 1790, in which he criticized serfdom, government absolutism and religion; exiled to Siberia as a result of his criticism. [d. September 12, 1802]

1779 **Baron Jons Jakob Berzelius,** Swedish chemist; determined molecular weights of many substances; introduced system of **chemical symbols** in use today; advocated using chemical composition as method of classifying minerals. [d. August 7, 1848]

1808 **Narcisse Virgile Diaz de la Peña,** French landscape painter; member of Barbizon school; noted for his nymphs, Venuses, and cupids. [d. November 18, 1876]

1832 **Thaddeus S. C. Lowe,** U.S. inventor; developed the **compression ice machine,** leading to the mechanical **refrigerator,** 1865. [d. January 16, 1913]

1833 **Benjamin Harrison,** 23rd president of the U.S., 1889–93; noted for his achievements in foreign affairs. [d. March 13, 1901]

1847 **Bolesław Prus (Alexander Głowacki),** Polish novelist and short-story writer. [d. May 19, 1912]

1860 **Raymond Poincaré,** French statesman, writer; 9th president of French Republic, 1913–20; member of French cabinet, 1893–1903; Prime Minister, 1912–13; 1922–24. [d. October 15, 1934]

1864 **Ion Bratianu,** Romanian statesman; Prime Minister, several terms, 1909–27. [d. November 24, 1927]

1873 **Eliel Saarinen,** Finnish architect; achieved his greatest recognition with his son Eero (below) for designs executed in the U.S.; exerted enormous influence on American architecture, particularly in the development of the **skyscraper.** [d. July 1, 1950]

1881 **Edgar A(lbert) Guest,** U.S. poet, journalist born in England; noted for his *Breakfast Table Chat,* daily verse column which was syndicated in more than 300 newspapers at its peak. Published numerous collections of folksy verse. [d. August 5, 1959]

1886 **Paul Tillich,** U.S. philosopher, theologian, born in Germany; outspoken critic of the Nazis; spokesman for Religious Socialism in the 1920s; developed a systematic theology that included psychology, philosophy, and art. [d. October 22, 1965]

1901 **Salvatore Quasimodo,** Italian poet, writer; Nobel Prize in literature for his lyrical poetry, 1959. [d. June 14, 1968]

1905 **Jack Weldon Lee Teagarden,** U.S. trombonist, orchestra leader. [d. January 15, 1964]

1910 **Eero Saarinen,** U.S. architect born in Finland; with his father Eliel (above), achieved wide recognition for his flamboyant steel and glass structures. [d. September 1, 1961]

1916 **Van Johnson,** U.S. actor.

St. Philibert, abbot. The filbert (fruit or nut of the cultivated hazel) derived its name from being ripe near St. Philibert's day. [d. c. 685]

St. Bernard, abbot of Clairvaux, Doctor of the Church, founder of the Cistercian Order. Called *Doctor mellifluus,* the *Honey-sweet Doctor.* [d. 1153]

St. Amadour, hermit. [death date unknown]

The Beatified

Blessed Mary de Mattias, virgin and founder of the Sisters Adorers of the Precious Blood. [d. 1866]

Blessed Teresa Jornet Ibars, founder of the Little Sisters of the Aged Poor. [d. 1897]

1921   **Jacqueline Susann,** U.S. novelist; author of *The Valley of the Dolls.* [d. September 21, 1974]

1936   **Wilt(on Norman) Chamberlain,** U.S. basketball player.

         Carla Fracci, Italian prima ballerina.

1942   **Isaac Hayes,** U.S. singer, composer, actor.

Historical Events

636   **Syria** is lost to the Arabs at the **Battle of Yarmuk.**

1846   U.S. General Winfield Scott defeats the Mexicans at the **Battle of Churubusco** (**Mexican War**).

1914   400,000 German soldiers under General Von Kluck enter Brussels, and the Belgian Army retreats to Antwerp (**World War I**).

1917   The French under General Pètain launch an offensive at **Verdun** (**World War I**).

1920   First **commercial radio broadcast** featuring musical numbers is made by WWJ in Detroit; this claim is disputed by some, who say that KDKA, Pittsburgh, on November 2, was the first to broadcast commercially.

1942   German army crosses **Don River** in Russia (**World War II**).

1944   U.S. and British forces destroy the German Seventh Army at **Falaise-Argentan Gap,** west of Paris, capturing some 50,000 Germans (**World War II**).

1960   **Mali Federation** of Senegal and Sudan is split by a Senegalese declaration of secession, resulting from irreconcilable political differences.

1968   Warsaw Pact troops invade and occupy **Czechoslovakia.**

1971   Chiefs of state of Egypt, Syria, and Libya sign a constitution forming the **Confederation of Arab Republics.**

1974   Former New York governor **Nelson Rockefeller** is nominated as Vice-President by President **Gerald Ford,** who has assumed the presidency of the U.S. upon the resignation of **Richard M. Nixon.**

1979   **Diana Nyad** becomes the first person to swim the 89 miles between the Bahamas and the U.S.

1980   First successful ascent of **Mt. Everest** by a solo climber is completed by **Reinhold Messner** of Italy.

August 21

Religious Calendar

The Saints

SS. Luxorius, Cisellus and Camerinus, martyrs. [d. c. 303]

SS. Bonosus and Maximian, martyrs. Maximian also called **Maxmilian.** [d. 363]

Birthdates

1165 **Philip II,** King of France; one of the chief consolidators of the French monarchy. [d. July 14, 1223]

1609 **Jean de Rotron,** French dramatist; one of Cardinal Richelieu's *Fine Poets.* [d. June 27, 1650]

1789 **Augustin-Louis Cauchy,** French mathematician; developed **calculus of residues;** conducted research in applied and pure mathematics. [d. May 23, 1857]

1796 **Asher Brown Durand,** U.S. painter, illustrator, engraver; one of founders of National Academy of Design, 1826; credited with being one of the founders of the **Hudson River School** of landscape painting. [d. September 17, 1886]

1798 **Jules Michelet,** French historian, essayist; head of Historical Division, National Archives of France, 1831; noted for his extensive treatment of French history, 1838–72. [d. February 10, 1874]

1823 **John Fritz,** U.S. metallurgist, industrialist; one of first to introduce **Bessemer process** of steel-making in U.S. [d. February 13, 1913]

1826 **Karl Gegenbauer,** German comparative anatomist; pioneer in using evolutionary approach to **anatomical development.** [d. June 14, 1903]

1872 **Aubrey (Vincent) Beardsley,** British illustrator, noted for his black-and-white drawings; illustrated Malory's *Morte d'Arthur,* Oscar Wilde's *Salome,* Pope's *Rape of the Lock,* and Jonson's *Volpone.* [d. March 16, 1898]

1896 **Roark Bradford,** U.S. writer, humorist; author of *Ol' Man Adam an' His Chillun.* [d. November 13, 1948]

1904 **(William) Count Basie,** U.S. jazz and blues musician, pianist, composer. [d. April 26, 1984]

1914 **Paul Hall,** U.S. labor union official; a founding member of **Seafarers' International Union,** 1938; renowned for his efforts to improve working conditions of merchant seamen. [d. June 22, 1980]

1930 **Princess Margaret Rose** of Great Britain, sister of Queen Elizabeth II.

1938 **Kenny Rogers,** U.S. country-rock singer and actor.

1954 **Archie (Mason) Griffin,** U.S. football player; only player to win Heisman Trophy twice: 1974, 1975.

Historical Events

1808 Arthur Wellesley and his British troops defeat the French at **Battle of Vimiera (Peninsular War).**

1810 Marshall **Bernadotte,** one of Napoleon's generals, is elected Crown Prince of Sweden under the name of **Charles John.**

1878 **American Bar Association** is created by a meeting of lawyers at Saratoga, New York.

1914 **Battle of Charleroi** opens with the Germans attacking the French and forcing their way over the Sambre River (**World War I**).

1915 **Gallipoli Campaign** ends in defeat for the British at the Battle of Scimitar Hill (**World War I**).

1918 The **Second Battles of the Somme** and of **Arras** open, extending the Allied offensive from Soissons to Arras (**World War I**).

1944 **Dumbarton Oaks Conference,** in Washington, D.C., begins outlining plans for the **United Nations.**

1959 **Hawaii** is admitted to the Union as the 50th state.

1961 **Jomo Kenyatta,** African nationalist leader imprisoned in Kenya since 1952, is released.

U.S. and El Salvador sign the first **Food for Peace** agreement.

St. Sidonius Apollinaris, Bishop of Clermont. [d. 479]

St. Abraham of Smolensk, abbot. [d. 1221]

St. Pius X, pope. Elected 1903. Feast formerly September 3. [d. 1914]

The Beatified

Blessed Humbeline, matron. Sister of St. Bernard, whose feast is celebrated on August 20. [d. 1135]

Blessed Bernard Tolomei, abbot and founder of the Benedictines of Monte Oliveto. Also called **Bernard Ptolemy.** [d. 1348]

1963 Martial law is declared in South Vietnam following raids on Buddhist pagodas and arrests of 100 Buddhist monks (**Vietnam War**).

1965 U.S. spacecraft *Gemini 5* is launched from Cape Kennedy, Florida, for a projected eight-day flight.

1983 Philippine opposition leader **Benigno S. Aquino Jr.** is assassinated in Manila moments after stepping off the plane that returned him to the island after a three-year exile in the U.S.

August 22

Religious Calendar

Queenship of Mary. Formerly celebrated May 31. Obligatory Memorial.

The Saints

SS. Timothy, Hippolytus, and Symphorian, martyrs. Feast suppressed in 1969. [d. 2nd to 4th cent.]

Birthdates

1647 **Denis Papin,** French physicist; invented the **pressure cooker** with safety valve; suggested the first cylinder and piston steam engine. [d. c. 1712]

1741 **Jean François de Galaup,** Comte de La Pérouse, French naval officer; led exploration of Asiatic waters; lost with his entire expedition by shipwreck. [d. 1788]

1760 **Leo XII,** pope 1823–29. [d. February 10, 1829]

1771 **Henry Maudslay,** British engineer; invented the **metal-cutting lathe;** considered *Father of the Machine-tool Industry.* [d. February 14, 1831]

1811 **William Kelly,** U.S. inventor; developed, simultaneously with Sir Henry Bessemer, what became known as the **Bessemer process** for steel-making. [d. February 11, 1888]

1834 **Samuel Pierpont Langley,** U.S. astronomer, aviation pioneer; pioneer in **solar research** and of flight of heavier-than-air craft. [d. February 27, 1906]

1847 **Sir John Forrest,** Australian explorer; first premier of Western Australia, 1890–1901; first Australian to be honored by a peerage. [d. September 3, 1918]

Sir Alexander Campbell Mackenzie, Scottish composer, conductor, teacher; conductor of London Philharmonic Society, 1892–99; knighted, 1895. [d. April 28, 1935]

1852 **Alfredo Oriani,** Italian writer; forerunner of Fascist theorists in Italy. [d. October 18, 1909]

1862 **Claude (Achille) Debussy,** French Romantic composer; leader of French **ultramodernist school of music.** [d. March 25, 1918]

1887 **Walter McLennan Citrine,** First Baron Citrine of Wembly, British labor union leader; General Secretary, British Trade Union Congress, 1925–46; knighted, 1935; raised to peerage, 1946. [d. January 22, 1983]

1893 **Dorothy (Rothschild) Parker,** U.S. author; associated with *The New Yorker,* 1927–33; member of the Algonquin Round Table, a group of renowned American wits who gathered at New York's Algonquin Hotel to lunch and discuss literary goings-on. [d. June 7, 1967]

1894 **Cecil Kellaway,** British character actor. [d. February 28, 1973]

1900 **Charles A. Halleck,** U.S. politician; U.S. Congressman, 1935–68; Conservative leader during 1950s and 1960s.

1908 **Henri Cartier-Bresson,** French photographer noted for his documentary photographs.

1920 **Ray (Douglas) Bradbury,** U.S. author, known for his science-fiction stories.

1928 **F. Ray Marshall,** U.S. government official and economist; U.S. Secretary of labor, 1977–81.

1939 **Carl Yastrzemski (*Yaz*),** U.S. baseball player.

1949 **Diana Nyad,** U.S. long-distance swimmer; the first person to swim the 89 miles between the Bahamas and the U.S.

Historical Events

1138 **Stephen,** King of England, defeats **David I** of Scotland near Northallerton at the **Battle of the Standard.**

1244 Egyptians and Khwarezmians capture **Jerusalem,** which never again falls in any subsequent Crusades.

1350 **Philip VI** of France dies and is succeeded by **John II.**

1485 **Richard III** of England is defeated and killed at **Bosworth.**

St. Sigfrid, Abbot of Wearmouth. [d. 690]

St. Andrew of Fiesole, deacon. [d. c. 9th cent.]

St. Arnulf, hermit. [death date unknown]

The Beatified

Blessed William Lacey and **Blessed Richard Kirkman,** martyrs. [d. 1582]

1642 **English Civil War** begins as Charles I sends Cavaliers against the Puritan parliament at York.

1791 Blacks in **San Domingo** revolt in effort to secure rights recently granted them by the French National Assembly.

1818 The *Savannah,* the first steamship to cross the Atlantic, is launched.

1864 Geneva Convention for Protection of the Wounded (**International Red Cross**) is founded.

1910 **Korea** is annexed by Japan after five years as a protectorate.

1914 **Austria-Hungary** declares war on Belgium (**World War I**).

The first air battle of the war occurs over Maubeuge, France, between British and German airplanes (**World War I**).

General **Paul von Hindenburg** is appointed commander of the German Eighth Army with **Erich von Ludendorff** as his chief of staff (**World War I**).

1922 **Michael Collins,** head of the Irish Free State Provisional Government, is killed by Republicans.

1945 U.S. destroyer escort *Levy* accepts surrender of first Japanese garrison to capitulate in World War II.

1962 U.S. nuclear ship *Savannah,* the world's first nuclear-powered cargo ship, completes her maiden voyage from Yorktown, Virginia, to Savannah, Georgia.

1972 **International Olympic Committee,** in a move to head off a boycott by African and other black athletes, bars Rhodesia from participating in the forthcoming games.

1973 **Henry Kissinger** is named U.S. Secretary of State, replacing William Rogers, who has resigned.

1978 Twenty-five **Sandinista National Liberation Front** members take control of the national palace in Managua, Nicaragua, killing six guards and holding 1,000 persons captive.

493

August 23

Holidays

Romania   **National Holiday**
Commemorates overthrow of the pro-Axis government of **Ion Antonescu**, 1944.

Religious Calendar

The Saints
SS. Claudius, Asterius, Neon, Domnina, and Theonilla, martyrs. [d. c. 303]

Birthdates

1754   **Louis XVI,** King of France, 1774–93, during the French Revolution; with his wife, **Marie Antoinette,** was imprisoned and later executed. [d. January 21, 1793]

1761   **Jedediah Morse,** American religious leader, geographer; author of the first American geography textbooks. [d. June 9, 1826]

1769   **Baron Georges Jean-Léopold-Nicolas-Frédéric Cuvier,** French anatomist; *Father of Comparative Anatomy*; considered by some as founder of modern **paleontology**; developed natural system of animal classification. [d. May 13, 1832]

1785   **Oliver Hazard Perry,** U.S. naval officer; responsible for securing Great Lakes region for U.S. during the War of 1812; issued the famous message, "We have met the enemy and they are ours." Recognized as American naval hero. [d. August 23, 1819]

1849   **William Ernest Henley,** British poet; collaborated with Robert Louis Stevenson on four plays; author of numerous volumes of verse. [d. June 11, 1903]

1864   **Eleutherios Venizelos,** Greek statesman, diplomat; Prime Minister of Greece, 1910–15, 1917–20, 1924, 1928–32, 1933; led Greece during World War I. [d. March 18, 1936]

1869   **Edgar Lee Masters,** U.S. poet, biographer; best known for his poetic monologues of persons speaking from the graveyard of Spoon River, Illinois, a fictitious town. The volume, *Spoon River Anthology*, was widely acclaimed and went through 70 editions between 1915 and 1940. [d. March 5, 1950]

1883   **Jonathan (Mayhew) Wainwright,** U.S. Army general; defender of Corregidor and Bataan; succeeded Douglas MacArthur as commander-in-chief of U.S. forces. [d. September 2, 1953]

1901   **John Sherman Cooper,** U.S. politician, lawyer; U.S. Senator, 1946–48, 1952–54, 1956–73; U.S. Ambassador to India and Nepal, 1955–56; U.S. Ambassador to East Germany, 1974–76.

1904   **William Primrose,** U.S. violist; considered one of the greatest violists of his time. [d. May 1, 1982]

1912   **Gene (Curran) Kelly,** U.S. dancer, movie star, choreographer.

1921   **Kenneth J. Arrow,** U.S. economist; Nobel Prize in economics for his contributions to the general equilibrium theory (with J. R. Hicks), 1972.

1930   **Vera Miles (Vera Helena Hruba Ralston),** U.S. actress.

1931   **Hamilton O. Smith,** U.S. biochemist; Nobel Prize in physiology or medicine for discoveries in restriction enzymes control of genes on chromosomes (with D. Nathans and W. Arber), 1978.

1934   **Barbara Eden (Barbara Huffman),** U.S. actress.

       Sonny Jurgenson (Christian Adolf Jurgenson III), U.S. football player.

Historical Events

1305   **William Wallace,** Scottish rival of **Edward I** of England, is executed at Smithfield after being convicted of treason by an English court.

1628   **Duke of Buckingham, George Villiers,** is assassinated as he prepares to lead a relief expedition to save **La Rochelle,** seat of power of the Huguenots.

St. Eugene, bishop. Also called **Eoghan, Eugenius,** or **Owen.** [d. 6th cent.]

St. Philip Benizi, Servite friar. Also called **Beniti,** or **Benize.** [d. 1285]

St. Rose of Lima, virgin; first South American saint, patron of Lima, Peru. Feast formerly August 30. [d. 1617]

The Beatified

Blessed James of Bevagna, Dominican friar. [d. 1301]

1645	Denmark loses her possessions in Sweden with the signing of the **Peace of Brömsebro.**
1833	Act for abolition of **slavery** throughout the British colonies is passed by Parliament.
1866	**Treaty of Prague** brings an end to **Germanic Confederation of 1815.**
1914	German troops execute 664 Belgian civilians at **Dinant,** then sack and burn the town (**World War I**).
	Japan declares war on Germany (**World War I**).
1942	**Battle of the Eastern Solomons** begins a three-day naval engagement against the Japanese, which is finally won by the Americans (**World War II**).
1944	Coup in Romania overthrows pro-Axis government of **Ion Antonescu.**
1961	*Ranger I,* first in a series of successful lunar probes is launched from Cape Canaveral, Florida.
1979	**Aleksandr Godunov,** a principal dancer with the Bolshoi Ballet, defects to the U.S.

August 24

Birthdates

1113   **Geoffrey, Count of Anjou,** called **Geoffrey Plantagenet.** [d. September 7, 1151]

1198   **Alexander II, King of Scotland,** 1214–49; maintained peace with England and strengthened Scottish monarchy. [d. July 8, 1249]

1724   **George Stubbs,** English animal painter; known especially for his accurate drawings of horses. [d. July 10, 1806]

1759   **William Wilberforce,** English statesman and reformer; instrumental in abolition of slavery in Great Britain, 1833. [d. July 29, 1833]

1772   **William I (William the Silent), King of Holland**, 1815–40. [d. December 12, 1843]

1787   **James Weddell,** British Antarctic explorer; discovered **Weddell Sea,** which was named for him. [d. September 9, 1834]

1817   **Count Alexey Tolstoy,** Russian poet, dramatist, and satirist. [d. September 28, 1875]

1846   **Henry Gannett,** U.S. geographer; called the *Father of American Mapmaking.* [d. November 5, 1914]

1847   **Charles Follen McKim,** U.S. architect; founder of McKim, Mead and White, one of foremost architectural firms in U.S.; designed **Boston Public Library;** leading exponent of Neo-classical style in U.S. [d. September 14, 1909]

1865   **Ferdinand I, King of Romania,** 1914–27. [d. July 20, 1927]

1872   **Sir Max Beerbohm,** British essayist, caricaturist, critic; noted for his satirical stories and parodies. [d. May 20, 1956]

1895   **Richard James Cushing,** U.S. Roman Catholic cardinal; archbishop of Boston, 1944–70. [d. November 2, 1970]

1898   **Malcolm Cowley,** U.S. writer, critic, and editor; literary editor of *The New Republic,* 1929–40; literary adviser to Viking Press, 1948– .

1899   **Albert Claude,** U.S. microbiologist born in Belgium; Nobel Prize in physiology or medicine for research in cell biology (with C. R. de Duve and G. E. Palade), 1974.

     Jorge Luis Borges, Argentine author, educator; Director, National Library of Buenos Aires, 1955–73; winner of numerous prizes for his original fictional narratives.

1901   **Preston Foster,** U.S. actor. [d. July 14, 1970]

1903   **Graham (Vivian) Sutherland,** British artist; best known for his controversial portrait of Winston Churchill, which was eventually destroyed by Lady Spencer Churchill. [d. February 17, 1980]

1905   **Siaka P. Stevens,** President, Republic of Sierra Leone, 1971– .

1925   **Shirley Hufstedler,** U.S. jurist; first U.S. Secretary of Education, 1979–81.

Historical Events

79   **Mount Vesuvius** on the Bay of Naples erupts, burying the cities of **Herculaneum** and **Pompeii** and killing 200,000 citizens.

410   **Rome** is sacked by **Alaric.**

1572   **St. Bartholemew's Day Massacre** of the Huguenots begins in Paris; up to 70,000 were eventually put to death throughout France.

1814   **Washington, D.C.** is captured and burned by the British (**War of 1812**).

1918   Bolshevik forces are defeated by the Allies at the **Battle of Dukhouskaya.**

1944   Romanian government surrenders as Soviet troops capture **Jassy** and **Kishinev** (**World War II**).

1958   Submarine *U.S.S. Nautilus* completes record setting six and one-half day underwater trans-Atlantic crossing.

1964   The Reverend Frederick McManus of Catholic University celebrates the first full **Roman Catholic Mass** in English at St. Louis, Missouri.

1968   France explodes its first **hydrogen bomb** in the South Pacific, becoming the world's fifth nuclear power.

Religious Calendar

The Saints

St. Bartholomew, apostle; patron of butchers, tanners, and bookbinders. [d. 1st cent.]

The Martyrs of Utica. [d. c. 258]

St. Audoenus, Bishop of Rouen. Also called **Audoen, Dado,** or **Ouen.** [d. 684]

St. Bregwine, Archbishop of Canterbury. [d. 764]

August 25

Holidays

Paraguay	**Constitution Day**
	Commemorates the adoption of the constitution of 1967.
Uruguay	**Independence Day**
	Commemorates Uruguay's achievement of independence from Brazil, 1825.

Religious Calendar

The Saints

St. Genesius of Arles, martyr. Also called **Genes.** [d. c. 303]

Birthdates

1530 **Ivan IV,** Emperor of Russia, 1547–84; known as *Ivan the Terrible,* he became czar at the age of 3. [d. March 18, 1584]

1744 **Johann Gottfried von Herder,** German critic, philosopher, author; influenced Goethe and development of German Romanticism. [d. December 18, 1803]

1745 **Henry Mackenzie,** Scottish novelist and essayist; known as the *Man of Feelings* and the *Addison of the North.* [d. January 14, 1831]

1819 **Allan Pinkerton,** U.S. detective, born in Scotland; founder of **Pinkerton National Detective Agency,** 1850; established first counterespionage unit in U.S. government, 1861. [d. July 1, 1884]

1836 **(Francis) Bret(t) Harte,** U.S. author; noted for his use of Western local color subjects, such as scenes from the exotic California gold-mining era, descriptions of pioneer characters, etc. His works include *The Luck of Roaring Camp* and *The Outcasts of Poker Flat.* [d. May 5, 1902]

1841 **Emil Theodar Kocher,** Swiss surgeon; Nobel Prize in physiology or medicine for his research on the **thyroid gland,** 1909. [d. July 27, 1917]

1850 **Charles R. Richet,** French physiologist; Nobel Prize in physiology or medicine for his work on **anaphylaxis,** 1913. [d. December 4, 1935]

1862 **William Cooper Procter,** U.S. manufacturer; founder and president of Procter & Gamble Co., 1907–34. [d. May 2, 1934]

1873 **John North Willys,** U.S. manufacturer, diplomat; founder of Willys-Overland Auto Co., 1907, developers of the "Jeep"; U.S. Ambassador to Poland, 1930–32. [d. August 26, 1935]

1880 **Joshua Lionel Cowen,** U.S. businessman; founder of Lionel Corporation, manufacturers of toy electric trains, 1945; invented the **flashlight** and the **dry cell battery.** [d. September 8, 1965]

1900 **Sir Hans Adolf Krebs,** British biochemist born in Germany; 1953 Nobel Prize in physiology or medicine for biochemical studies of cell metabolism (with F. A. Lipmann), 1953.

1909 **Ruby Keeler (Ethel Keeler),** U.S. dancer, actress.

1912 **Erich Honecker,** Chairman, East German Democratic Republic, 1976– .

1916 **Frederick Chapman Robbins,** U.S. microbiologist; Nobel Prize in physiology or medicine for successful growth of polio virus in tissue cultures and discoveries in polio detection (with J. F. Enders and T. Weller), 1954.

1917 **Mel Ferrer,** U.S. actor.

1918 **Leonard Bernstein,** U.S. composer, conductor; wrote music for *West Side Story;* Conductor of New York Philharmonic orchestra, 1957–58; Musical Director, 1958–69; Laureate Conductor for Life, 1969–; highly diversified in his approach to bringing music to the masses.

1919 **George (Corley) Wallace,** U.S. politician, lawyer; U.S. presidential candidate, Ameri-

498

St. Mennas, Patriarch of Constantinople. [d. 552]

St. Ebba, Abbess of Coldingham and virgin. Also called Aebba, Ebba the Elder, or Tabbs. [d. 683]

St. Gregory of Utrecht, abbot. [d. c. 775]

St. Louis of France, (King Louis IX); patron of builders, haberdashers, distillers, embroidery workers, hairdressers, and barbers. [d. 1270]

St. Joseph Calasanctius, founder of the Clerks Regular of the Religious Schools, commonly called Piarists or Scolopi. Also called Joseph Calasanz. Feast formerly August 27. [d. 1648]

St. Joan Antide-Thouret, virgin; founder of the Sisters of Charity under St. Vincent's Protection. [d. 1826]

St. Mary Michaela Desmaisières, virgin and founder of the Handmaids of the Blessed Sacrament. [d. 1865]

St. Genesius the Comedian, martyr. Also called Gelasinus, or Genesius the Actor. [death date unknown]

St. Patricia, virgin. [death date unknown]

can Independent Party, 1968; victim of assassination attempt which left him partially paralyzed, 1972.

1927 **Althea Gibson,** U.S. tennis player; first black player to win a major U.S. tennis championship.

1930 **Sean Connery (Thomas Connery),** Scottish actor; best known for his portrayal of Ian Fleming's James Bond, Agent 007.

1931 **Cecil D. Andrus,** U.S. politician; Governor of Idaho, 1971–77; U.S. Secretary of the Interior, 1977–81.

Historical Events

325 **Council of Nicaea** ends after establishing the method of calculating the day on which **Easter** would be celebrated (the first Sunday after the first full moon after the spring equinox), and making decrees regarding several other theologically significant issues.

1270 **Louis IX** of France dies and is succeeded by **Philip III.**

1786 **Punctation of Ems,** a congress of German bishops, meets with the aim of creating a National Catholic Church.

1825 **Uruguay** establishes its independence from Brazil.

1830 Revolt of French-speaking provinces of the Netherlands (now **Belgium**) begins.

1875 **Captain Matthew Webb** becomes the first person to swim across the **English Channel** (21 hours, 45 minutes).

1883 France assumes protectorate over **Annam** and **Tonkin** with the signing of the **Treaty of Huè.**

1914 Japan declares state of war with Austria-Hungary (**World War I**).

British first employ the **aircraft patrol** in their retreat from Mons (**World War I**).

1916 **U.S. National Park Service** is established as part of the Department of Interior.

1921 The U.S. and Germany sign a peace treaty ending the state of war between them (**World War I**).

1940 **Lithuania, Latvia,** and **Estonia** are incorporated into the U.S.S.R.

1943 **Lord Louis Mountbatten** is appointed Supreme Allied Commander in Southeast Asia (**World War II**).

1960 **XVII Summer Olympics** open in Rome.

1967 **American Nazi Party** leader, **George Lincoln Rockwell,** is shot to death in Arlington, Virginia.

Paraguay promulgates a new constitution.

1981 U.S. *Voyager 2* spacecraft speeds past Saturn, transmitting photos of the planet's rings and moons.

August 26

Holidays

U.N. Member Nations   Namibia Day

Religious Calendar

The Saints

St. Zephyrinus, pope and martyr. Elected bishop of Rome 198. Feast suppressed 1969. [d. c. 217]

Birthdates

1676 **Robert Walpole,** English statesman; Prime Minister, 1721–42; first to unify cabinet under leadership of a prime minister; established basis for Britain's colonial policy. [d. March 18, 1745]

1728 **Johann Heinrich Lambert,** German mathematician, physicist; devised methods of measuring light intensity and absorption; demonstrated **irrationality of pi.** [d. September 25, 1777]

1740 **Joseph Michel Montgolfier,** French inventor; with his brother, Jacques Etienne Montgolifer (January 7), invented the **hot air balloon,** 1783. [d. June 26, 1810]

1743 **Antoine Laurent Lavoisier,** French chemist, known as the *Founder of Modern Chemistry;* explained phenomenon of combustion; theorized on compounding of chemicals; executed by the Convention during the French Revolution. [d. May 8, 1794]

1819 **Prince Albert of Saxe-Coburg-Gotha,** Prince Consort of England, husband of Queen Victoria. [d. December 14, 1861]

1827 **Annie Turner Wittenmyer,** U.S. social reformer; first president of the National Woman's Christian Temperance Union, 1874–79. [d. February 2, 1906]

1873 **Lee De Forest,** U.S. inventor; developed the triode amplifier tube, thereby ushering in the electronics age; known as the *Father of Radio.* [d. June 30, 1961]

1875 **Sir John Buchan,** Scottish writer known for his adventure stories such as *The 39 Steps* and *Prester John.* [d. 1940]

1882 **James Franck,** U.S. physicist born in Germany; Nobel Prize in physics for discovery of laws related to impact of electrons in an atom (with G. Hertz), 1925. [d. May 21, 1964]

1884 **Earl Derr Biggers,** U.S. mystery-story writer and novelist; noted for his *Charlie Chan* stories. [d. April 5, 1933]

1898 **Peggy Guggenheim,** U.S. art patron and collector. [d. December 23, 1979]

1901 **Maxwell (Davenport) Taylor,** U.S. general, diplomat; chairman, Joint Chiefs of Staff, 1962–64; U.S. Ambassador to South Vietnam, 1964–65.

1903 **Jimmy Rushing,** U.S. jazz-blues singer; member of Count Basie's orchestra, 1935–50.

1904 **Christopher Isherwood,** British novelist, living in U.S.; noted for his novel *Goodbye to Berlin,* 1935, which was adapted to the stage as *I Am a Camera,* 1951, and to film as *Cabaret,* 1966; frequently collaborated with **W. H. Auden.**

1906 **Albert Bruce Sabin,** U.S. immunologist, born in Poland; developed the **Sabin vaccine** for polio, which resulted in significant reduction of the disease on an international scale.

Historical Events

1346 English longbowmen under **Edward III** rout the French crossbowmen at the **Battle of Crécy.** England is established as a dominant military power (**Hundred Years' War**).

1541 Conquest of **Hungary** by the Turks is completed.

1791 **John Fitch** is granted a U.S. patent for his invention of the **steamboat.**

1858 **Treaty of Edo** opens Japan to British trade.

1883 **Krakatoa volcano** in the South Pacific explodes, destroying its island, causing catastrophic tidal waves, killing more than

St. Pandonia, virgin. Also called **Pandwyna.** [d.c. 904]

St. Elizabeth Bichier des Ages, virgin and cofounder of the Daughters of the Cross or Sisters of St. Andrew. [d. 1838]

The Beatified
Blessed Herluin, abbot. [d. 1078]

Blessed Timothy of Montecchio. [d. 1504]

Blessed Thomas Percy, martyr. [d. 1572]

Blessed Bernard of Offida. [d. 1694]

30,000 people, and destroying hundreds of villages.

1896 Attack on the Ottoman Bank at **Constantinople** by Armenian revolutionaries results in a massacre of Armenians: 6,000 killed.

1914 **First Battle of Lemberg** between Russia and Austria opens in the Austrian province of **Galicia (World War I).**

World's largest power dam to date, **Keokuk Dam,** is opened, across Mississippi River from Keokuk, Iowa.

Germans crush the Russian army at the **Battle of Tannenberg (World War I).**

1920 **19th Amendment** to the U.S. Constitution is ratified, giving women the right to vote.

1924 The Kuomintang, Chinese national congress, creates a **Labor Corps** in Canton which becomes the **Red Army.**

1964 President **Lyndon B. Johnson** and Senator **Hubert H. Humphrey** are selected as the Democratic candidates for president and vice-president.

1972 **XX Summer Olympics** open at Munich, Germany.

1976 **Prince Bernhard** of the Netherlands, husband of Queen Juliana, resigns most of his military and business posts because of his disgrace in a scandal involving bribes by Lockheed Aircraft Company.

1977 **Quebec** assembly passes bill intended to extend and encourage the use of French in the province.

1978 Albino Cardinal Luciani, patriarch of Venice, is elected pope of the Roman Catholic Church and chooses the name **John Paul I.** He served in the position for only 34 days [d. Sept. 29, 1978]

1981 **Queen Juliana** of the Netherlands becomes the first ruling sovereign of the House of Orange to visit **Indonesia.**

August 27

Holidays

Texas   **Lyndon B. Johnson's Birthday**
Commemorates the birth of the
36th President of the U.S., 1908.

Religious Calendar

The Saints

St. Marcellus and his Companions, martyrs.
Marcellus also called **Marcellinus.** [d. 287]

Birthdates

1730   **Johann Georg Hamann,** German philosophical writer; known as the *Magus of the North.* [d. June 21, 1788]

1770   **Georg Wilhelm Friedrich Hegel,** German Idealist philosopher; established a system of metaphysics based on the concept of the *Absolute;* profoundly influenced the development of philosophy during the middle of the 19th century. [d. November 14, 1831]

1797   **Ramón Castilla,** Peruvian soldier, President of Peru, 1845–51. [d. August 29, 1867]

1809   **Hannibal Hamlin,** U.S. politician, lawyer, farmer; U.S. Congressman, 1842–47; U.S. Senator, 1848–57; U.S. Vice-President under Abraham Lincoln, 1860–64. [d. July 4, 1891]

1865   **Charles Gates Dawes,** U.S. politician, diplomat, financier; Nobel Peace Prize (with Sir Austen Chamberlain), 1925; U.S. Vice-President under Calvin Coolidge, 1925–29; U.S. Ambassador to Great Britain 1929–32. [d. April 23, 1951]

James Henry Breasted, U.S. Egyptologist, archaeologist, and historian; professor of Egyptology and Oriental History, University of Chicago, 1905–19; head of University's archaeological expedition to Egypt, 1905–07; published many volumes of history of Egypt and dictionaries of ancient languages. First archaeologist elected to National Academy of Sciences, 1920. [d. December 2, 1935]

1871   **Theodore (Herman Albert) Dreiser,** U.S. novelist; controversial proponent of naturalism in novel writing; his first work, *Sister Carrie,* aroused widespread controversy and was suppressed by its publisher; achieved recognition finally with *An American Tragedy.* [d. December 28, 1945]

1874   **Carl Bosch,** German industrial chemist; Nobel Prize for chemistry for development of chemical high-pressure methods (with F. Bergius), 1931. [d. April 26, 1940]

1877   **Lloyd C(assel) Douglas,** U.S. novelist, teacher of religion; known for his popular, religiously oriented novels, including *Magnificent Obsession, The Robe,* and *A Time to Remember.* [d. February 13, 1951]

1878   **Baron Petr Nikolayevich Wrangel,** Russian general; leader of counter-revolutionary forces in Russia, 1917–20. [d. April 25, 1928]

1884   **Samuel Goldwyn (Samuel Goldfish),** U.S. motion-picture industry pioneer, born in Poland; founded Goldwyn Pictures, 1917, which became Metro-Goldwyn-Mayer Studios, 1924. [d. January 31, 1974]

1890   **Man Ray (Emmanuel Radinski),** U.S. painter, photographer; with Marcel Duchamp founded Dadaism; one of first members of Surrealist movement; noted for his innovative, unpredictable style. [d. November 18, 1976]

1899   **C(ecil) S(cott) Forester,** British novelist; noted for *Horatio Hornblower* novels. [d. April 2, 1966]

1908   **Lyndon Baines Johnson,** U.S. teacher, politician; 36th President of U.S., 1963–68; became president upon assassination of John F. Kennedy; served during period of civil strife, racial unrest, and Vietnam War. [d. January 22, 1973]

1909   **Lester Young,** U.S. jazz musician. [d. March 15, 1959]

1910   **Mother Teresa** of Calcutta, the *Saint of the Gutters,* Italian-born humanitarian; Nobel Peace Prize for her work with the poor of India, 1979.

St. Monica, widow. Mother of St. Augustine; patroness of the Augustinian nuns. Feast formerly May 4. [d. 387] Obligatory Memorial.

St. Poemen, abbot. Also called **Pastor.** [d. 5th cent.]

St. Caesarius, Bishop of Arles. Founded first women's convent in Gaul. [d. 543]

St. Decuman, monk and hermit; patron of Watchet and St. Decumans. [d. 6th cent.]

St. Syagrius, Bishop of Autun. [d. 600]

Little St. Hugh of Lincoln. His martyrdom is subject of Chaucer's *Prioress's Tale.* [d. 1255]

St. Rufus of Capua, martyr. Also called **Rufinus.** [death date unknown]

The Beatified

Blessed Angelo of Foligno, Augustinian friar. [d. 1312]

Blessed Gabriel Mary, Franciscan friar. [d. 1532]

Blessed Dominic Barberi, priest. [d. 1849]

1913	**Martin David Kamen,** U.S. biochemist, born in Canada; discovered carbon-14 isotope, used in archaeological research. Also known as the world's foremost amateur viola player.
1916	**Martha Raye (Maggie Yvonne O'Reed),** U.S. actress.
1929	**Ira Levin,** U.S. novelist, playwright; author of *No Time for Sergeants, The Boys from Brazil,* and *Deathtrap.*
1932	**Lady Antonia Fraser,** British author; best known for her biographies of British royalty and statesmen.
1943	**Tuesday Weld (Susan Ker Weld),** U.S. actress.

Historical Events

1664	**New Amsterdam** surrenders to the English under Col. Richard Nicolls.
1828	**Uruguay** becomes a sovereign nation under the **Treaty of Rio de Janeiro,** which ends war between Brazil and Argentina.
1859	U.S. prospector **Edwin Drake** drills first successful oil well in U.S. at Titusville, Pennsylvania, striking oil at 69 feet.
1916	**Romania** declares war on Austria-Hungary (**World War I**).
	Italy declares war on Germany (**World War I**).
1928	**Kellogg-Briand Pact** is signed by 62 nations at Paris, outlawing war as an instrument of national policy.
1936	**Egypt** and **Great Britain** sign a treaty providing for withdrawal of British forces except in Suez Canal area.
1946	France concludes agreement with **Laos,** establishing a kingdom under French domination.

1962	Spacecraft *Mariner II* is launched from Cape Canaveral on a projected 15-week trajectory toward the planet **Venus.**
1976	Scientists at the **Massachusetts Institute of Technology** synthesize a gene and implant it in a living bacterial cell.
1977	Philippine military authorities release 500 prisoners imprisoned since the imposition of martial law on September 23, 1972.
1979	**Louis Mountbatten, 1st Earl Mountbatten of Burma,** is killed when a bomb planted by I.R.A. destroys his boat off the Irish coast.
1983	An estimated 250,000 people gather in Washington D.C. to commemorate the 20th anniversary of the march on Washington and Rev. Martin Luther King's "I have a dream" speech.

August 28

Religious Calendar

The Saints

St. Hermes, martyr. [d. c. 2nd cent.]

St. Julian of Brioude, martyr. Also called **Julian of Auvergne.** [d. 3rd cent.]

Birthdates

1481   **Francisco de Sá de Miranda,** Portuguese poet, playwright; author of first Portuguese prose comedy; first classical tragedy. [d. 1558]

1592   **George Villiers, 1st Duke of Buckingham,** English courtier, royal favorite; led British to relieve Rochelle. Assassinated. [August 23, 1628]

1728   **John Stark,** American Revolutionary War general; hero of the **Battle of Bennington,** 1777. [d. May 8, 1822]

1735   **Count Andreas Peter von Bernstorff,** Danish statesman, diplomat; leader in Danish reform movement, liberation of Danish peasants. [d. June 21, 1797]

1749   **Johann Wolfgang von Goethe,** German poet, dramatist, novelist; inaugurated German *Sturm and Drang* literary movement introduced Romanticism and Modernism in literary development of Germany. Author of *Faust.* [d. March 22, 1832]

1774   **Elizabeth Ann Seton,** U.S. educator, religious leader; founder of Sisters of St. Joseph; canonized, 1975; first U.S.-born saint. [d. January 4, 1821]

1814   **Joseph Sheridan Le Fanu,** Irish novelist; editor of *Dublin Evening Mail,* 1838–58; noted for his stories of the supernatural. [d. February 7, 1873]

1823   **James Oliver,** U.S. inventor, born in Scotland; invented the **chilled plow,** which used **annealed steel** for hardness, 1868. [d. March 2, 1908]

1833   **Sir Edward Coley Burne-Jones,** British painter; student of Rossetti; noted for his large oil paintings, frequently done in series: *The Golden Stairs,* 1880. [d. June 17, 1898]

1878   **George H. Whipple,** U.S. physiologist; Nobel Prize in physiology or medicine for discoveries concerning treatment of **pernicious anemia,** then a fatal disease (with G. R. Minot and W. P. Murphy), 1934. [d. February 1, 1976]

1894   **Karl Bühn,** Austrian musician, conductor; Director, Dresden State Opera, 1934–42; Director, Vienna State Opera, 1943–45; 1954–56; Conductor of Vienna Philharmonic Orchestra, 1933–81. [d. August 14, 1981]

1899   **Charles Boyer,** French actor. [d. August 26, 1978]

1903   **Bruno Bettleheim,** U.S. psychologist, born in Austria; director of Sonia Shankman Orthogenic School at University of Chicago, 1944–73; expert on emotionally disturbed children.

1905   **Sam Levene,** U.S. comic character actor; [d. December 29, 1980]

1910   **Tjalling Koopmans,** U.S. economist, born in the Netherlands; Nobel Prize in economics for contributions to the theory of optimum allocation of resources (with F. A. von Hayek), 1975.

1914   **Richard Tucker (Reuben Ticker),** U.S. operatic tenor; sang with Metropolitan Opera, 1945–75. [d. January 8, 1975]

1919   **Godfrey Newbold Hounsfield,** British scientist; Nobel Prize in physiology or medicine for development of computer-assisted tomography, **CAT scan** (with A. M. Cormack), 1979.

1925   **Donald O'Connor,** U.S. actor, singer, dancer.

1930   **Ben Gazzara,** U.S. actor.

1940   **William Cohen,** U.S. politician, lawyer; U.S. Congressman, 1973–77; U.S. Senator, 1979–.

1950   **Ron(ald Ames) Guidry,** U.S. baseball player.

Historical Events

1619   **Ferdinand II** is elected Holy Roman Emperor.

1850   Richard Wagner's *Lohengrin* premieres under the direction of **Franz Liszt** at Weimar, Germany.

SS. Alexander, John III, and Paul IV, Patriarchs of Constantinople. [d. 340, 577, 784]

St. Moses the Black, one of the Fathers of the Desert. [d. c. 405]

St. Augustine, Bishop of Hippo, and Doctor of the Church; patron of theologians and scholars. Also called **Austin** and the *Greatest of the Fathers.* [d. 430]

The London Martyrs of 1588. Fifteen or sixteen victims of anti-Catholic repression in England. [d. 1588]

1913 **Palace of Peace** at the Hague is dedicated.

1914 First major encounter between British and German naval forces occurs off **Heligoland (World War I).**

1916 Germany declares war on Rumania (**World War I**).

The Romanians begin an invasion of **Transylvania.**

1944 U.S. Third Army reaches **Marne River** in France (**World War II**).

1963 Approximately 200,000 demonstrators, supporting the demands for **civil rights** for U.S. blacks, march on Washington; Dr. **Martin Luther King, Jr.** delivers his "I have a dream" speech.

1968 U.S. Vice-president **Hubert H. Humphrey** is nominated as Democratic candidate for U.S. president.

Violence erupts between Chicago police and demonstrators at the headquarters for the Democratic National Convention.

John Gordon Mein, U.S. Ambassador to Guatemala, is assassinated by terrorists.

August 29

Religious Calendar

The Beheading of St. John the Baptist. [d. c. 30] Obligatory Memorial.

The Saints

St. Medericus, abbot. Also called **Merri,** or **Merry.** [d. c. 700]

Birthdates

1619 **Jean Baptiste Colbert,** French government official, businessman; minister to Louis XIV; a financial reformer and organizer; responsible for creation of French Navy. [d. September 6, 1683]

1632 **John Locke,** English philosopher; known as the *Father of English Empiricism.* [d. October 28, 1704]

1780 **Jean-Auguste-Dominique Ingres,** French painter; recognized as a leader among French classicists; best known as a historical painter. [d. January 14, 1867]

1805 **John Frederick Denison Maurice,** British writer and clergyman; founder of **Christian Socialism.** [d. April 1, 1872]

1809 **Oliver Wendell Holmes,** U.S. physician, educator, author; key figure in U.S. literary development; author of *Breakfast Table* series of essays. [d. October 7, 1894]

1826 **George Frisbie Hoar,** U.S. lawyer, public official; U.S. Congressman, 1877–1904; frequent crusader for civil service reform and honesty in government. [d. September 30, 1904]

1862 **Andrew Fisher,** Australian statesman, political leader; Prime Minister, 1908–09; 1910–13; 1913–15. [d. October 22, 1928]

Maurice (Polydore Marie Bernard) Maeterlinck, Belgian poet, dramatist, and essayist. [d. May 6, 1949]

1871 **Albert Lebrun,** 14th president of France, 1932–40; author of scientific works. [d. March 6, 1950]

1876 **Charles Franklin Kettering,** U.S. engineer, inventor; perfected the **electric self-starter** for automobiles. [d. November 25, 1958]

1899 **Lyman L. Lemnitzer,** U.S. Army general; U.S. Chief of Staff, 1959–60; Chairman, Joint Chiefs of Staff, 1960–62; Supreme Allied Commander, 1963.

1904 **Werner Forssmann,** German surgeon; Nobel Prize for physiology or medicine for research into **heart disease** (with D. W. Richards and A. F. Cournand), 1956. [d. June 1, 1979]

1912 **(Patrick) Barry Sullivan,** U.S. actor.

1915 **Ingrid Bergman,** Swedish actress; international star of stage and screen. [d. August 29, 1982]

1920 **Charlie (*Bird*) Parker,** U.S. jazz musician, composer; helped develop musical form called **bebop.** [d. March 12, 1955]

1923 **Sir Richard (Samuel) Attenborough,** British actor, producer, and film director.

1924 **Dinah Washington,** U.S. jazz singer. [d. December 14, 1963]

1938 **Elliott Gould (Elliot Goldstein)** U.S. actor.

1939 **Sir Julius Chan,** Papua-New Guinea statesman; Prime Minister 1980–82.

1945 **Wyomia Tyus,** U.S. sprinter; gold medalist in 1964 and 1968 Olympics.

1946 **Jean Baptiste Bagaza,** President, Republic of Burundi, 1976– .

1958 **Michael Jackson,** U.S. entertainer.

Historical Events

1268 **Conradin,** the 16-year-old ruler of Germany, is defeated by Charles of Anjou at Tagliacozzo. Conradin is beheaded, setting off waves of disapproval throughout Europe and creating long-lasting alienation between Germany and the Roman Church whose leader, **Pope Clement IV,** approved of the execution.

1475 **Peace of Picquigny** between **Edward IV** of England and **Louis XI** of France is signed, guaranteeing Edward an annual subsidy and stipulating the marriage of his daughter to the French dauphin.

1521 **Sultan Suleiman I,** the Magnificent, of Turkey conquers Belgrade as the Ottomans move across Hungary.

St. Edwold of Cerne, hermit. Also called **Eadwold.** [d. 9th cent.]

St. Sabina, martyr. [death date unknown]

The Beatified

Blessed Richard Herst, martyr. [d. 1628]

Blessed Joanna Jugan. [beatified 1982]

1664 English annex **New Netherlands**, which becomes **New York.**

1708 A party of French and Indians kill 16 inhabitants of **Haverhill, Massachusetts,** and capture 35 more (**Haverhill Massacre**).

1756 **Seven Years' War** breaks out as **Frederick II** of Prussia invades Saxony.

1820 Portuguese rebel against the regency and adopt a democratic constitution under King **John VI.**

1825 Portugal recognizes the independence of **Brazil.**

1833 **Shaftesbury Factory Act** is passed in Great Britain, authorizing factory inspection and forbidding employment of children under age 9.

1842 **Treaty of Nanking** ends the First Opium War; **Hong Kong** is ceded to Great Britain.

1916 **General von Hindenburg** becomes German Chief of the General Staff, with Gen. Ludendorff as first quartermaster general.

1960 **Hazza El-Majali**, Premier of Jordan, is assassinated.

1975 **General Juan Velasco Alvarado,** President of the leftist military government in Peru, is overthrown in a bloodless coup.

August 30

Holidays

Peru   **St. Rose of Lima**
Commemorates feast of St. Rose, a native of Peru and the first South American to be canonized.

Turkey   **Victory Day**
Commemorates Turkey victory at **Battle of Dumlupinar,** 1922.

Birthdates

1705   **David Hartley,** English philosopher, physician. [d. August 28, 1757]

1748   **Jacques-Louis David,** French artist; founder of French Classical school of painting; painter to Napoleon. [d. December 29, 1825]

1794   **Stephen Watts Kearny,** U.S. Army general; commanded American Army of the West during Mexican War. [d. October 31, 1948]

1797   **Mary Wollstonecraft Shelley,** English novelist; author of *Frankenstein*, 1818; wife of Percy Bysshe Shelley. [d. February 1, 1851]

1852   **Jacobus H. Van't Hoff,** Dutch physical chemist; Nobel Prize in chemistry for work on rates of reaction, chemical equilibrium, and osmotic pressure, 1901. [d. March 1, 1911]

1871   **Ernest Rutherford,** 1st Baron Rutherford of Nelson, British physicist; Nobel Prize in chemistry for discoveries in chemistry of **radioactive elements,** 1908. [d. October 19, 1937]

1884   **Theodor H. E. Svedberg,** Swedish chemist; Nobel Prize in chemistry for work on **colloids,** 1926. [d. February 26, 1971]

1893   **Huey P(ierce) Long (*The Kingfish*),** U.S. politician, lawyer; Governor of Louisiana, 1928–32; U.S. Senator, 1932–35. Assassinated [d. September 10, 1935]

1896   **Raymond Massey,** U.S. actor, born in Canada. [d. July 29, 1983]

1901   **John Gunther,** U.S. journalist, author, radio and television commentator; noted for his series of books providing analyses of various countries and regions: *Inside Europe*, 1936, *Inside Russia Today*, 1958, etc. [d. May 29, 1970]

Roy Wilkins, U.S. civil rights leader; Executive Director, NAACP, 1964–77. [d. September 8, 1981]

1904   **Charles E. (*Chip*) Bohlen,** U.S. diplomat; Soviet affairs specialist; U.S. Ambassador to U.S.S.R., 1953–57; U.S. Ambassador to the Philippines, 1957–59; U.S. Ambassador to France, 1962–68. [d. January 2, 1974]

1907   **Shirley Booth (Thelma Booth Ford),** U.S. actress.

1908   **Fred(erick Martin) Macmurray,** U.S. actor.

1909   **Joan Blondell,** U.S. comedic actress. [d. December 25, 1979]

1912   **Edward Mills Purcell,** U.S. physicist; Nobel Prize in physics for development of methods for precise measurement of atomic nucleic magnetic fields (with F. Bloch), 1952.

1943   **Jean-Claude Killy,** French skier. Olympic gold medalist, 1968; World Cup championship, 1967, 1968.

1944   **Frank Edwin (*Tug*) McGraw,** U.S. baseball player.

Historical Events

1125   **Lothair of Saxony** is elected king of Germany.

1483   **Louis XI** of France dies and is succeeded by Charles VIII.

1757   Russians win at Gross Jägersdorf and occupy East Prussia (**Seven Years' War**).

1914   The German 8th Army under von Hindenburg envelops and practically annihilates a Russian army in the **Battle of Tannenberg.** General Samsonov, the Russian commander, commits suicide (**World War I**).

Germans make first air raid on Paris (**World War I**).

Louisiana   **Huey P. Long Day.**

Religious Calendar

The Saints
SS. Felix and Adauctus, martyrs. [d. c. 304]
St. Pammachius, layman. [d. 410]
St. Rumon. Also called **Ruan.** [d. c. 6th century]
St. Fantinus, abbot. [d. 10th century]

The Beatified
Blessed Bronislava, virgin. [d. 1259]

1916 Turkey joins her allies, Germany and Austria, and declares war against Romania (**World War I**).

1918 Lenin survives an assassination attempt by social revolutionary **Dora Kaplan.**

1928 **Jawaharlal Nehru** founds **Independence of India League** to work toward freedom from British rule.

1942 U.S. Naval and Army forces occupy **Adak** in the Aleutian Islands.

1945 U.S. occupation forces land at Tokyo Bay and begin U.S. occupation of Japan (**World War II**).

1957 U.S. Senator **Strom Thurmond** of South Carolina sets a new filibuster record in the U.S. Congress when he speaks for 24 hours, 27 minutes against a civil rights bill.

August 31

Holidays

Afghanistan	Pushtoonistan Day
Malaysia	National Day
	Celebrates Malaysia's achievement of independent status in British Commonwealth, 1957.
Trinidad and Tobago	Independence Day
	Celebrates the achievement of independence and membership in the Commonwealth of Nations, 1962, and the promulgation of a new constitution, 1976.

Birthdates

12 **Caligula (Gaius Caesar Augustus Germanicus)**, Roman emperor, 37-41; great-grandson of Augustus Caesar. [d. January 24, 41]

1821 **Hermann Ludwig Ferdinand von Helmholtz,** German physiologist, physicist; known for numerous contributions to science; one of the formulators of the principle of the **conservation of energy.** [d. September 8, 1894]

1822 **Fitz-John Porter,** Union Army general during U.S. Civil War. [d. May 21, 1901]

1838 **Abel Bergaigne,** French linguist, philologist, and Sanskrit scholar. [d. August 6, 1888]

1870 **Maria Montessori,** Italian physician, educator; first woman in Italy to receive medical degree (1894); developed **Montessori method** of child education. [d. May 6, 1952]

1880 **Wilhelmina,** Queen of the Netherlands, 1890–1948; abdicated in favor of her daughter, Beatrix. [d. November 28, 1962]

1885 **Du Bose Heyward,** U.S. poet, novelist, and playwright; author of novel *Porgy* from which opera *Porgy and Bess* was developed. [d. June 16, 1940]

1897 **Fredric March (Frederic McIntyre Bickel),** U.S. actor; popular leading dramatic actor during 1930s and 1940s. [d. April 14, 1975]

1903 **William Saroyan,** U.S. short-story writer, playwright, known for his light-hearted, poignant stories; declined the 1940 Pulitzer Prize for *The Time of Your Life.* [d. May 18, 1981]

Arthur Godfrey, U.S. broadcaster and entertainer; his audience reached over 82 million in the 1950s. [d. March 16, 1983]

1907 **Ramón Magsaysay,** President of the Philippine Republic, 1953–57. [d. March 17, 1957]

1913 **Sir Alfred Charles Bernard Lovell,** British astronomer; front-runner in development of radio telescopic devices; responsible for development of the first major **radio telescope,** for Nuffield Radio Astronomy Labs, 1957.

1914 **Richard Basehart,** U.S. actor. [d. September 18, 1984]

1918 **Alan Jay Lerner,** U.S. playwright, lyricist; frequent collaborator with Frederick Loewe (June 10) for Broadway musical scores.

(Theodore Samuel) Ted Williams, U.S. baseball player; last major leaguer to hit over .400 (.406 in 1941); inducted into Baseball Hall of Fame, 1966.

1924 **Buddy Hackett (Leonard Hucker),** U.S. comedian.

1928 **James Coburn,** U.S. actor.

1935 **Eldridge Cleaver,** U.S. social critic, writer; former member of the Black Panther Party.

Frank Robinson, U.S. baseball player, manager; first black to manage a major league team (Cleveland Indians, 1974); elected to Baseball Hall of Fame, 1982.

Religious Calendar

The Saints

St. Paulinus, Bishop of Trier. [d. 358]

St. Aidan, Bishop of Lindisfarne. Also called **Ædan.** [d. 651]

St. Cuthburga, Abbess of Wimborne, and widow. Feast formerly September 3. [d. c. 725]

St. Quenburga, nun. Also called **Coenburga.** [d. c. 735]

St. Raymund Nonnatus, cardinal; patron saint of midwives, women in labor, and little children. [d. 1240]

The Beatified

Blessed Laurence Nerucci and his companions, martyrs. [d. 1420]

Blessed Juvenal Ancina, Bishop of Saluzzo. [d. 1604]

1945   **Van Morrison,** Irish-born singer, song-writer.

1955   **Edwin Moses,** U.S. hurdler; Olympic gold medalist, 1976, 1984.

Historical Events

1422   **Henry V** of England dies and is succeeded by **Henry VI,** 9 months old.

1823   **Battle of Trocadero** is lost by Spanish revolutionaries, bringing the revolution to an end and restoring the repressive **Ferdinand VII** to the throne.

1895   First U.S. **professional football game** is played at **Latrobe, Pennsylvania,** between the Latrobe team of profit-sharing players and the **Jeannette, Pennsylvania** team. In hiring a substitute quarterback for $10 in expenses, Latrobe employed the first professional player, **John Brallier.**

1907   Anglo-Russian agreement is signed aligning Russia, Britain, and France against the **Triple Alliance** of Germany, Austria-Hungary, and Italy.

1914   **Greece** declares her neutrality in **World War I.**

1919   **Communist Labor Party of America** is founded at Chicago, Illinois.

1928   *Die Dreigroschenoper (The Threepenny Opera)* premieres in Berlin, starring Lotte Lenya, with music by Kurt Weill, and lyrics by Bertolt Brecht.

1935   U.S. President Franklin D. Roosevelt signs the **Neutrality Act** of 1935.

1942   **Battle of Alam El Halfa** in Egypt begins, with Rommel's German forces attacking the superior British (**World War II**).

1944   U.S. naval ships and aircraft attack **Iwo Jima** and the Bonin Islands (**World War II**).

1957   **Malaya** becomes an independent member of the British Commonwealth.

1962   Colony of **Trinidad and Tobago** becomes an independent member of the Commonwealth of Nations.

1964   U.S. President Lyndon B. Johnson signs the **Food Stamp Act**, designed to aid needy families by establishing a cooperative federal-state food assistance program.

1976   **Trinidad and Tobago** adopts a new constitution under which it becomes a republic.

September

September is the ninth month of the Gregorian calendar and has 30 days. The name is derived from the Latin *septem*, 'seven,' designating its position as the seventh month in the early Roman calendar. As with the other numerically named months, October, November and December, September has retained this anachronistic designation; attempts by the Roman Senate to change the name after *Januarius* was adopted as the first month of the 12-month calendar met with failure, and the misleading etymology remains today.

In the northern hemisphere, September is the month of the autumnal equinox, occurring about September 22, after which nighttime is longer than daylight. September is also associated with harvest festivals, cider-making, the southerly migration of birds, the beginning of the school year, and the end of the summer vacation period.

In the astrological calendar, September spans the zodiac signs of Virgo, the Virgin (August 23–September 22) and Libra, the Balance (September 23–October 22).

The birthstone for September is the sapphire, and the flower is the aster or the morning glory.

State, National, and International Holidays

Labor Day
(United States)
First Monday

Primary Election Day
(Wisconsin)
First Tuesday

(Wyoming)
Second Tuesday

Rose of Tralee Festival
(Ireland)
Early in the Month

Sherry Wine Harvest
(Jerez de la Frontera, Spain)
Mid-Month

Tank Forces' Day
(U.S.S.R.)
Second Sunday

Forestry Workers' Day
(U.S.S.R.)
Third Sunday

Special Events and Their Sponsors

Cable TV Month
Richard R. Falk Associates
1472 Broadway
New York, New York 10036

Philatelic Publications Month
Franklin D. Roosevelt Philatelic Society
154 Laguna Court
St. Augustine Shores, Florida 32084

Sight Saving Month
American Society to Prevent Blindness
79 Madison Avenue
New York, New York 10016

Youth Activities Month
Rotary International
160 Ridge Avenue
Evanston, Illinois 60201

National Rub a Bald Head Week
Second Week
Bald Headed Men of America, Inc.
4006 West Arendell-Carteret Village
Morehead City, North Carolina 28557

Constitution Week
Third Week
National Society of the Daughters
of the American Revolution
Administration Building
1776 D Street, N.W.
Washington, D.C. 20006

National Farm Safety Week
Third Week
National Safety Council
444 North Michigan Avenue
Chicago, Illinois 60611

National Rehabilitation Week
Third Week
Allied Services for the Handicapped, Inc.
475 Morgan Highway
Scranton, Pennsylvania 18508

Tolkien Week
Week containing September 22
American Tolkien Society
Box 277
Union Lake, Michigan 48085

Snack a Pickle Time
Final Two Weeks
Pickle Packers International, Ltd.
One Pickle and Pepper Plaza
P.O. Box 31
St. Charles, Illinois 60174

Be Late for Something Day
September 5
Procrastinators' Club of America
111 Broad-Locust Building
Philadelphia, Pennsylvania 19102

Swap Ideas Day
September 10
Puns Corp.
c/o Robert L. Birch
Box 2364
Falls Church, Virginia 22042

National Play-Doh Day
September 16
Kenner Products
1014 Vine Street
Cincinnati, Ohio 45202

Constitution Day
September 17
Federal Union, Inc.
1875 Connecticut Avenue N.W.
Suite 128
Washington, D.C. 20009

Hobbit Day
September 22
American Tolkien Society
Box 277
Union Lake, Michigan 48085

Kids' Day
September 24
Kiwanis International
3636 Woodview Trace
Indianapolis, Indiana 46268

National Grandparents' Day
First Sunday after Labor Day
Marion McQuade, Founder
National Grandparents Day
140 Main Street
Oak Hill, West Virginia 25901

Defenders' Day
Sunday nearest Sunday 13-14
Star-Spangled Banner Flag House and 1812 Museum
844 East Pratt Street
Baltimore, Maryland 21202

National Hunting and Fishing Day
Fourth Saturday
National Shooting Sports Foundation
P.O. Box 1075
Riverside, Connecticut 06878

National Good Neighbor Day
Fourth Sunday
Good Neighbor Day Foundation
Dr. Richard C. Mattson
Drawer R
Lakeside, Montana 59922

Special Days—Other Calendars

	1 Muharram	10 Muharram	Rosh Hashanah	Yom Kippur	Sukkoth
1985	September 16	September 25	September 16	September 25	September 30
1986	September 6	September 15			
1987		September 4	September 24		
1988			September 12	September 21	September 26
1989			September 30		
1990			September 20	September 28	

September 1

Religious Calendar

The Saints

St. Lupus, Bishop of Sens. Also called **Leu.** [d. 623]

St. Fiacre, hermit; invoked against all kinds of physical ills, including hemorrhoids and venereal disease; patron saint of gardeners and of cab drivers in Paris. Also called **Fefre, Fiachra,** or **Fiaker.** [d. c. 670]

St. Sebbe, co-ruler of the East Saxons. Also called

Birthdates

1792 **Chester Harding,** U.S. portrait painter; noted for portraits of such famous Americans as Daniel Boone, Daniel Webster, and John C. Calhoun. [d. April 1, 1866]

1795 **James Gordon Bennett,** U.S. journalist, publisher, born in Scotland; founder of the *New York Herald*, 1834. [d. June 1, 1872]

1813 **Mark Hopkins,** U.S. railroad organizer, executive. [d. March 29, 1878]

1822 **Hiram Rhodes Revels,** U.S. clergyman, educator, politician; first black member of U.S. Congress, 1870–71. [d. January 16, 1901]

1854 **Engelbert Humperdinck,** German composer, best known for his fairy-tale operas, *Hansel und Gretel* and *Die Königskinder.* [d. September 27, 1921]

1864 **Sir Roger David Casement,** British civil servant, Irish rebel; knighted, 1910; later sought German assistance for Irish nationalist cause; hanged as a traitor by the British. [d. August 3, 1916]

1866 **James J. (*Gentleman Jim*) Corbett** , U.S. boxer; commonly regarded as the first scientific boxer, a reputation he earned by the techniques he developed to compensate for his small hands. [d. February 18, 1933]

1875 **Edgar Rice Burroughs,** U.S. novelist, known especially for his *Tarzan* novels, 1914–49, which had sold more than 35 million copies by the time of his death. [d. March 19, 1950]

1877 **Francis William Aston,** British chemist; Nobel Prize in chemistry for discovery of **isotopes** using the mass spectrograph, 1922. [d. November 20, 1945]

1878 **John Frederick Charles Fuller,** British military officer, theorist; wrote numerous books dealing with concept of mechanized warfare; greatly influenced military theories of post-World War I Europe. [d. February 10, 1966]

1900 **Don Wilson,** U.S. entertainer, radio and television announcer, producer; known for his role as Jack Benny's straight man. [d. April 25, 1982]

1907 **Walter (Philip) Reuther,** U.S. labor leader; President, United Auto Workers, 1946–70; President, Congress of Industrial Organization, 1952–70; played significant role in formation of AFL-CIO, 1955. [d. May 10, 1970]

1922 **Vittorio Gassman,** Italian actor.

Melvin (Robert) Laird, U.S. politician, government official; U.S. Congressman, 1953–69; U.S. Secretary of Defense, 1967–73; espoused reduction of size of U.S. armed forces; Counsellor for National and International Affairs, Reader's Digest Association, 1974– .

1923 **Rocky Marciano (Rocco Marchegiano),** U.S. boxer; undefeated world heavyweight champion, 1952–56. [d. August 31, 1969]

1924 **Yvonne De Carlo (Peggy Middleton),** Canadian actress.

1933 **Conway Twitty,** U.S. country-and-western singer.

1935 **Seiji Ozawa,** Japanese orchestra conductor; Musical Director, Boston Symphony Orchestra, 1973– .

1936 **Lily Tomlin,** U.S. actress, comedienne.

Sebba, Sebbi. [d. c. 694]

St. Drithelm, layman and visionary. [d. c. 700]

St. Giles, abbot; patron of Edinburgh, the indigent and crippled, and of spurmakers. Invoked against cancer, sterility in women, insanity, and night dangers. Also called **Aegidius.** [death date unknown]

St. Priscus of Capua, martyr. [death date unknown]

The Twelve Brothers, martyrs. [death date unknown]

St. Verena, virgin. [death date unknown]

The Beatified

Blessed John of Perugia and Blessed Peter of Sassoferrato, martyrs. [d. 1231]

Blessed Joan Soderini, virgin. [d. 1367]

Blessed Hugh More, martyr. [d. 1588]

Blessed Gabra Michael, martyr. Also called **Gabra Mika'el, Gilmichael, Michel Ghæebræe.** [d. 1855]

Historical Events

891 **Arnulf,** Holy Roman Emperor, defeats the Normans at **Louvain.**

1192 **Richard I** of England (**the Lion-Hearted**) and **Saladin** of Damascus sign a truce, allowing the Crusaders free access to the Holy Sepulchre (**Third Crusade**).

1494 **Charles VIII** of France invades Italy in support of **Lodovico the Moor.**

1715 **Louis XIV of France** dies and is succeeded by his great-grandson, **Louis XV.**

1836 The party of **Marcus Whitman** reaches **Fort Walla Walla** on the Columbia River, establishing the first U.S. settlement in (what was then) Territory of Northern Oregon.

1858 **East India Company's** government of India ends with the British Crown taking over its territories and duties.

1864 **Charlottetown Conference** is convened on Prince Edward Island, representing the beginning of steps toward Canadian confederation.

1900 **South African Republic** is annexed by Great Britain.

1905 Canadian Provinces of **Alberta** and **Saskatchewan** are established.

1916 U.S. Federal **Child Labor Act** (**Keating-Owen Act**) bars the products of **child labor** from interstate commerce.

Bulgaria declares war against Romania (**World War I**).

1923 Great **earthquake** in Japan completely destroys **Yokohama** and nearly destroys **Tokyo;** more than 100,000 lives are lost.

The **Royal Australian Air Force** is established.

1929 *Graf Zeppelin* completes first aerial circumnavigation of globe by a **dirigible.**

1937 **National Housing Act** (**Wagner-Steagall Act**) establishes **U.S. Housing Authority.**

1939 Germany, invades Poland without warning, precipitating **World War II.**

1969 Military officers overthrow government of **Libya;** Libyan Arab Republic is proclaimed under Colonel **Mu'ammar al-Qadhafi.**

1977 **Cuba** and the U.S. exchange low-level missions, a step toward restoration of full diplomatic relations.

1979 The U.S. unmanned spacecraft *Pioneer 11,* launched in 1973, transmits data to earth after coming within 20,200 km (12,560 miles) of Saturn's clouds; it surveyed Jupiter in 1974.

1980 **Sandy Hawley,** U.S. jockey, wins his 4,000th race, the 11th jockey in thoroughbred racing history to do so.

1981 A bloodless coup ousts President **David Dacko** of **Central African Republic;** General **Andrè Kolingba** is new government head.

1983 Korean Air Line **Flight 007,** an unarmed commercial airliner, crosses into Soviet airspace and is shot down over the Sea of Japan by a Soviet fighter; all 269 aboard perish.

September 2

Religious Calendar

The Saints

St. Antoninus, martyr. [d. 4th cent.]

St. Castor, Bishop of Apt. [d. c. 425]

St. Agricolus, Bishop of Avignon; invoked to bring both rain and fair weather. [d. 7th cent.]

Birthdates

1778 **Louis Bonaparte,** brother of Napoleon I and King of the Netherlands, 1806–10. [d. July 25, 1846]

1837 **James Harrison Wilson,** Union Army general during U.S. Civil War. [d. February 23, 1925]

1838 **Lydia Kamekeha Liliuokalani,** Queen of Hawaiian Islands; last sovereign to rule Hawaii before annexation by U.S.; deposed, 1893. [d. November 11, 1917]

1839 **Henry Georgne,** U.S. economist, social reformer, journalist; noted for his theories of economics based on land ownership. [d. October 29, 1897]

1840 **Giovanni Verga,** Italian novelist; leader of Sicilian realist school. [d. January 27, 1922]

1841 **Prince Hirobumi Ito,** Japanese statesman; Prime Minister, 1886–1901; assassinated by a Korean radical. [d. October 26, 1909]

1850 **Eugene Field,** U.S. poet, journalist; pioneer of personal feature column. [d. November 4, 1895]

1853 **Friedrich Wilhelm Ostwald,** German chemist; Nobel Prize in chemistry for work on **rates of chemical reaction,** 1909. [d. April 4, 1932]

1864 **Miguel de Unamuno y Jugo,** Spanish philosopher, writer, educator; subject of controversy because of his pro-republican leanings. [d. December 31, 1936]

1866 **Hiram Warren Johnson,** U.S. lawyer, politician; governor of California, 1911–17; U.S. Senator, 1917–45; favored U.S. neutrality in World War I. [d. August 6, 1945]

1877 **Frederick Soddy,** British chemist; Nobel Prize in chemistry for his work with **radioactive substances,** 1921. [d. Sept. 22, 1956]

1917 **Cleveland Amory,** U.S. journalist, author.

1918 **Allen Stuart Drury,** U.S. novelist, journalist; known for his penetrating novels about U.S. politics; Pulitzer Prize in fiction, 1960, for *Advise and Consent.*

1923 **Marge Champion (Marjorie Celeste Belcher),** U.S. dancer, actress; with her husband, Gower (June 22), appeared in numerous musical films during 1930s and 1940s.

1928 **Horace Ward Martin Tavares Silver,** U.S. jazz musician, pianist, composer (*Senor Blues, Sister Sadie*); leader of **Horace Silver Quintet.**

1933 **Ahmed Kerekou,** President, People's Republic of Benin, 1972– .

1952 **Jimmy Connors,** U.S. tennis player.

Historical Events

31 B.C. **Mark Antony** is defeated at **Actium** by Roman legions under Octavian (Augustus Caesar).

1644 In England, the army of the 3rd earl of Essex surrenders to **Charles I** at **Lostwithiel (English Civil War).**

1666 **Great Fire of London** begins, lasting four days and destroying almost all of the City of London.

1789 **U.S. Department of the Treasury** is established.

1864 Union forces under **General Sherman** occupy Atlanta, Georgia (**U.S. Civil War**).

1870 **Napoleon III** capitulates to Prussians at **Sedan (Franco-Prussian War).**

1898 **Lord Kitchener** decisively defeats the Dervishes at the **Battle of Omdurman** in the Sudan.

1914 The French government moves to **Bordeaux** as German troops move toward Paris (**World War I**).

1918 U.S. recognizes **Czechoslovakia** as a nation.

St. William, Bishop of Roskilde. Also called Bishop of Roschild. [d. c. 1070]

St. Brocard, cofounder of the Order of Carmelite Friars. Also called **Burchard.** [d. c. 1231]

The Beatified

Blessed Margaret of Louvain, virgin and martyr. [d. c. 1225]

Blessed John du Lau, Archbishop of Arles, and his Companions, the martyrs of September. Victims of the French Revolution. [d. 1792]

1930   Captain **Dieudonne Coste** and **Maurice Ballante** complete first nonstop flight from Paris to New York.

1945   Japanese premier and military leaders sign formal surrender on board the *U.S.S. Missouri* in Tokyo Bay, ending **World War II.**

The Viet-Minh coalition proclaims the **Democratic Republic of Vietnam,** with **Ho Chi Minh** as president.

1969   Rock music festival on the **Isle of Wight** attracts more than 250,000 spectators.

September 3

Holidays

Monaco	**Liberation of Monaco**
Qatar	**Independence Day** Commemorates Qatar's achievement of independence from Great Britain, 1971.
San Marino	**St. Marinus Day** Official Foundation Day. A celebration of the patron saint of the country.
Tunisia	**Commemoration of September 3, 1934** Commemorates the beginning of the Tunisian independence movement, 1934.

Birthdates

1803 **Prudence Crandall,** U.S. educator; arrested after she admitted black girls to her Connecticut school in 1833. [d. January 28, 1890]

1827 **Gísli Brynjúlfsson,** Icelandic poet; spread the influences of European romanticism in Icelandic literature. [d. May 29, 1888]

1849 **Sarah Orne Jewett,** U.S. novelist, short-story writer. [d. June 24, 1909]

1856 **Louis H. Sullivan,** U.S. architect; considered the *Father of Modern American Architecture*, especially noted for early **skyscraper** design. [d. April 14, 1924]

1859 **Jean Léon Jaures,** French Socialist leader; founder and editor of *L'Humanité*, 1904–14. [d. July 31, 1914]

1860 **Edward Albert Filene,** U.S. merchant, philanthropist; founder of Filene's, one of Boston's leading department stores; promoter of credit union movement in U.S. [d. September 26, 1937]

1869 **Fritz Pregl,** Austrian chemist; Nobel Prize in chemistry for development of methods of **microanalysis of organic substances,** 1923. [d. December 13, 1930]

1899 **Sir Frank Macfarlane Burnet,** Australian physician; Nobel Prize in physiology or medicine for discovery of **acquired immunity** (with P. B. Medawar), 1960.

1900 **Sally Benson,** U.S. novelist, short-story writer; author of *Meet Me in St. Louis*, an autobiographical novel that was made into a highly successful film, 1944. [d. July 19, 1972]

1905 **Carl David Anderson,** U.S. physicist; Nobel Prize in physics for discovery of the **positron,** 1936.

1907 **Loren C(orey) Eiseley,** U.S. anthropologist, naturalist; noted for his writings on early human habitations of North America and interpretations of Darwin's influence on scientific development in the 20th century. [d. July 9, 1977]

1913 **Alan Ladd,** U.S. actor. [d. January 29, 1964]

1914 **Dixy Lee Ray,** U.S. politician, marine biologist; chairperson of Atomic Energy Commission, 1973–75; U.S. Assistant Secretary of State, 1975–77; Governor of Washington, 1977–80.

1920 **Marguerite Higgins,** U.S. journalist; Pulitzer Prize for her coverage of front-line action during Korean War, 1951; reported on Vietnam War, 1960s. [d. January 3, 1966]

1926 **Irene Papas,** Greek actress.

1936 **Anne Jackson,** U.S. actress.

Historical Events

1650 **Oliver Cromwell** of England defeats Scots at **Dunbar.**

1651 **Oliver Cromwell** defeats royal army of **Charles I** at **Worcester.**

1654 **First Protectorate** Parliament under **Oliver Cromwell** meets in England.

1658 **Oliver Cromwell,** Protector of England, dies and is succeeded by his son, Richard.

Religious Calendar

The Saints

St. Phoebe. [d. 1st cent.]

St. Macanisius, bishop. Also called **Aengus Mac Nisse, Macrisius.** [d. 514]

St. Simeon Stylites the Younger, [d. 592]

St. Aigulf, martyr. [d. c. 676]

St. Hildelitha, Abbess of Barking and virgin. Also called **Hildilid.** [d. c. 717]

The Beatified

Blessed Guala, Bishop of Brescia. [d. 1244]

Blessed Andrew of Borgo San Sepolcro, Servite friar. [d. 1315]

1783	**Treaty of Paris,** signed between the U.S. and Great Britain, recognizes the independence of the **United States.**
1826	**Nicholas I** is crowned czar of all the Russias at Moscow.
1879	British residents of **Kabul** are massacred by native Afghans.
1914	**Pope Benedict XV** is elected.
1918	**Second Battles of the Somme and of Arras** end with the Germans being pushed back behind the Hindenburg Line from which they had first advanced in March (**World War I**).
1939	Great Britain and France declare war against Germany following Germany's invasion of Poland (**World War II**).
1943	British 8th Army invades Italy from Sicily (**World War II**).
1944	U.S. naval task group attacks **Wake Island** (**World War II**).
1967	Military ticket of **Nguyen Van Thieu** and **Nguyen Cao Ky** wins by an overwhelming majority in South Vietnamese presidential and vice-presidential elections.
1976	U.S. satellite, *Viking 2*, lands on **Mars** and begins sending back photographs of the Martian landscape.

September 4

Birthdates

1241 **Alexander III,** King of Scotland, 1249–86; responsible for consolidating royal power in Scotland. [d. March 18 or 19, 1286]

1768 **François-René Vicomte de Châteaubriand,** French writer, statesman; author of *René*, a seminal work in the French Romantic movement. [d. July 4, 1848]

1793 **Edward Bates,** U.S. politician; the first U.S. cabinet member (Attorney General, 1861–1864) from west of the Mississippi. [d. March 25, 1869]

1802 **Marcus Whitman,** U.S. Congregational missionary, pioneer, physician; responsible for the settlement of a large part of the **Northwest Territory;** massacred by Cayuse Indians. [d. November 29, 1847]

1824 **Anton Bruckner,** Austrian composer, organist; composed nine symphonies and three grand masses in the Romantic tradition. [d. October 11, 1896]

1846 **Daniel Hudson Burnham,** U.S. architect, city planner; member of the architectural firm, Burnham and Root, which designed the first building to be called a **skyscraper;** designed the site of the World's Columbian Exposition in Chicago, 1893; his *Report on Washington, D.C.,* which outlined a long-range plan of development for the city, marked the beginning of **city planning** in the U.S. [d. June 1, 1912]

1848 **Lewis Howard Latimer,** U.S. inventor, draftsman, engineer; associate of Alexander Graham Bell (March 3). [d. 1928]

1851 **John Dillon,** Irish nationalist politician; member of the British Parliament, 1880–83, 1885–1918. [d. August 4, 1927]

1899 **Ida Kaminska,** Polish actress, producer, director; head of government sponsored Jewish State Theatre of Poland, 1946–68; emigrated to U.S., 1968. [d. May 21, 1980]

1905 **Mary Renault (Mary Challens),** British novelist; noted for her historical novels of ancient Greece; author of *The King Must Die, The Nature of Alexander.* [d. December 13, 1983]

1906 **Max Delbrück,** U.S. biologist, physicist, born in Germany; Nobel Prize in physiology or medicine for discoveries in **genetic structure of viruses** (with A. D. Hershey and S. E. Luria), 1969. [d. March 9, 1981]

1908 **Richard Wright,** U.S. novelist, short-story writer; author of *Native Son,* 1940. [d. November 28, 1960]

1909 **Johannes Willebrands,** Dutch ecclesiastic; created cardinal, 1969; appointed Archbishop of Utrecht, 1975.

1913 **Stanford Moore,** U.S. biochemist; Nobel Prize in chemistry for research in life processes at the molecular level, and the biological activity of enzyme ribonuclease (with C. B. Anfinsen and W. H. Stein), 1972.

1917 **Henry Ford II,** U.S. auto executive; Chairman of the Board, Ford Motor Co., 1960– ; Chief Executive Officer, 1960–79.

1920 **Craig Claiborne,** U.S. cookery expert and author; food editor, *New York Times,* 1957–.

1931 **Mitzi Gaynor (Francesca Mitzi von Gerber),** U.S. dancer, actress.

1937 **Dawn Fraser,** Australian swimmer; Olympic gold medal winner, 1956, 1960, 1964.

1949 **Tom Watson,** U.S. professional golfer.

Historical Events

1439 **Pope Eugene IV** condemns reform decrees of **Basel Council** and excommunicates the members of the Council.

1882 **Thomas Edison** opens his first commercial electric station in New York City, thus beginning the **electric lighting industry** in the U.S.

1918 The would-be assassin of Lenin, **Dora Kaplan,** is executed at Moscow.

1939 **Argentina** proclaims her neutrality in **World War II.**

St. Boniface I, pope. Elected 418; patron of Germany. [d. 422]

St. Ultan, bishop. [d. 657]

St. Ida of Herzfeld, widow. [d. 825]

St. Rosalia, virgin; principal patron of Palermo. [d. c. 1160]

St. Rose of Viterbo, virgin. Also called Rosa. [d. c. 1252]

The Beatified

Blessed Catherine of Racconigi, virgin. [d. 1547]

1944   Brussels and Antwerp in Belgium are liberated by British and Canadian troops (World War II).

1948   Wilhelmina, Queen of the Netherlands, abdicates in favor of her daughter, Juliana.

1954   First transit of McClure Strait (Northwest Passage) is made by the U.S. Navy icebreaker, *Burton Island*, and U.S. Coast Guard icebreaker, *Northwind.*

1969   U.S. Food and Drug Administration issues final approval of oral contraceptives.

1972   Mark Spitz, U.S. swimmer becomes the first person to win seven gold medals in a single Olympics.

1974   Diplomatic ties are established between the U.S. and East Germany.

September 5

Holidays

U.S.	**Be Late for Something Day** Sponsored by the Procrastinators' Club of America, Philadelphia, Pennsylvania.
Macao	**Republic Day**

Birthdates

1568 **Tommaso Campanella,** Italian philosopher, poet; intimate of **Louis XIII** of France and **Cardinal Richelieu;** author of *Civitas Solis,* a utopian work similar to Plato's *Republic.* [d. May 21, 1639]

1638 **Louis XIV,** of France (*the Sun King,*) called *the Great;* reigned from 1643 to 1715, longest reign in European history; created an absolute monarchy in France; built the **Palace at Versailles;** in later years, as a result of great extravagances, brought France to financial ruin. [d. September 1, 1715]

1704 **Maurice Quentin de La Tour,** French painter; best known for pastel portraits. [d. February 17, 1788]

1733 **Christoph Martin Wieland,** German poet, novelist; called the *German Voltaire.* [d. January 20, 1813]

1735 **Johann Christian Bach,** German composer, organist, affiliated with the English royal family, 1759–82; called the *Milan* or *London Bach.* Composed many operas, sonatas, symphonies. Son of Johann Sebastian Bach (March 21). [d. January 1, 1782]

1847 **Jesse (Woodson) James,** U.S. outlaw; executed many daring robberies, 1866–82; murdered by a member of his own gang. [d. April 3, 1882]

1875 **Napoleon Lajoie,** U.S. baseball player; inducted into Baseball Hall of Fame, 1937. [d. February 7, 1959]

1897 **A(rthur) C(harles) Nielsen,** U.S. market researcher; initiated ratings for television programs, 1950. [d. June 1, 1980]

1901 **Florence Eldridge,** U.S. actress; wife of Fredric March (August 31).

1902 **Darryl F(rancis) Zanuck,** U.S. film producer; President and Chief Executive Officer of 20th-Century Fox Corp., 1962–79. [d. December 22, 1979]

1905 **Arthur Koestler,** British author, born in Hungary; noted for his anti-Communist writings and scientific and fictional novels. Author of *Darkness at Noon, The Art of Creation, Life After Death.* [d. March 3, 1983]

1912 **John Milton Cage, Jr.,** U.S. composer; subject of controversy because of his use of novel instruments and chance sounds in a style known as **aleatory music.**

1916 **Frank (Garvin) Yerby,** U.S. novelist.

1927 **Paul A. Volcker,** U.S. banker; Chairman, Federal Reserve Board, 1979– .

1934 **Ricardo de la Espriella,** President, Republic of Panama, 1982– .

1940 **Raquel Welch,** U.S. actress.

Historical Events

1338 **Louis IV,** Holy Roman Emperor, and **Edward III** of England conclude **Alliance of Coblenz,** which recognizes Edward's title to French throne.

Diet at Frankfurt declares that the Holy Roman Empire is divorced from the papacy.

1698 **English East India Company** (The General Society) is chartered.

1774 **First Continental Congress** opens at Philadelphia with all colonies except Georgia represented.

1905 A treaty of peace is signed at Portsmouth, New Hampshire, by Witte for the Russians and Baron Komura, the Japanese agent, ending the **Russo-Japanese War.**

1972 *Black September* Palestinian terrorists attack an Israeli dormitory in the Olympic Village in **Munich,** shooting two members of the Israeli team. Nine other Israelis, five terrorists, and a West German policeman die at a shoot-out at the Munich airport as the Palestinians attempt to escape.

The Saints

St. Laurence Giustiniani, patriarch of Venice. Also called **Laurence Justinian.** [d. 1455]

The Beatified

Blessed Gentilis, martyr. [d. 1340]

Blessed Raymund Lull, martyr. [d. 1316]

1975   **Lynette (*Squeaky*) Fromme**, 26, attempts to assassinate U.S. President **Gerald Ford** at Sacramento, California.

September 6

Holidays

Pakistan — Defense of Pakistan Day

São Tomé and Principe — National Heroes Day

Swaziland — Somhlolo Day

Birthdates

1711 **Heinrich Melchior Muhlenberg,** U.S. Lutheran clergyman, born in Germany; known as the founder of Lutheranism in America. [d. October 7, 1787]

1729 **Moses Mendelssohn,** German philosopher, Biblical scholar, translator, and critic; called the *German Socrates*. [d. January 4, 1786]

1757 **Marie Joseph Paul, Marquis de Lafayette,** French soldier, statesman; entered American Army during Revolutionary War, 1777; responsible for securing French aid to American cause. After his return to France, 1789, remained active in politics; served in Chamber of Deputies, 1815, 1818–24; leader of opposition, 1825–30. [d. May 20, 1834]

1766 **John Dalton,** English scientist; established the **quantitative atomic theory** in chemistry, 1808. [d. July 27, 1844]

1795 **Frances (Fanny) Wright,** U.S. social reformer, born in Scotland; author of *Views of Society and Manners in America*, 1821; established **Nashoba Community** in Indiana; espoused radical views on religion, politics, education, women's rights, and marriage. [d. December 13, 1852]

1800 **Catharine Esther Beecher,** U.S. educator; established the **Hartford Female Seminary;** devoted her life to attainment of equal education for women, although she opposed women's suffrage. [d. May 12, 1878]

1805 **Horatio Greenough,** U.S. sculptor, author; noted for his large-scale sculptures of famous Americans, especially the statue of George Washington at the Smithsonian Institution. [d. December 18, 1852]

1814 **Sir George Etienne Cartier,** Canadian statesman; Prime Minister of Canada, 1858–62. [d. May 20, 1873]

1817 **Alexander Tilloch Galt,** Canadian businessman and politician; first Minister of Finance, 1867–72; High Commissioner in England, 1880–83. [d. September 19, 1893]

1819 **William Starke Rosecrans,** Union Army general during U.S. Civil War; responsible for one of most disastrous Union defeats of the war, at **Chickamauga;** U.S. Minister to Mexico, 1868–69; U.S. Congressman, 1881–85. [d. March 11, 1898]

1828 **Aleksandr Mikhailovich Butlerov,** Russian chemist; one of chief developers of theory of structure of organic compounds; recognized as discoverer of **tertiary alcohols.** [d. August 17, 1886]

1869 **Jane Addams,** U.S. social reformer, social worker; founder of **Hull House,** one of first settlement houses in U.S.; Nobel Peace Prize (with N. M. Butler), 1931. [d. May 21, 1935]

1876 **John James Rickard Macleod,** Scottish physiologist; Nobel Prize in physiology or medicine for production of **insulin** and discovery of its effectiveness in combating diabetes (with F. G. Banting), 1923. [d. March 16, 1935]

1878 **Henry Seidel Canby,** U.S. editor, critic; a founder of *Saturday Review of Literature*. [d. April 5, 1961]

1885 **Otto Kruger,** U.S. actor. [d. September 6, 1974]

1888 **Joseph Patrick Kennedy,** U.S. financier, diplomat; patriarch of Kennedy political dynasty; first chairman of **Securities and Exchange Commission;** U.S. Ambassador to Great Britain, 1937–40; father of John F. Kennedy, Robert Kennedy, and Edward M. Kennedy. [d. November 18, 1969]

1890 **Claire Lee Chennault,** U.S. Army Air Force general, creator of the **Flying Tigers,** a World War II combat unit in Southeast Asia. [d. July 27, 1958]

Religious Calendar

The Saints

SS. Donatian, Laetus and Others, bishops and martyrs. Donatian also called **Donation.** [d. c. 484]

St. Eleutherius, abbot. [d. 6th cent.]

St. Chainoaldus, Bishop of Laon. Also called **Cagnoald, Cagnou.** [d. c. 633]

St. Bega, virgin and nun. Also called **Bee, Bees,** or **Begh.** [d. 7th cent.]

The Beatified

Blessed Bertrand of Garrigues, Dominican prior. [d. c. 1230]

Blessed Peregrine of Falerone, layman. [d. 1240]

Blessed Liberatus of Loro, hermit. [d. c. 1258]

1892 **Sir Edward Victor Appleton,** British physicist; knighted, 1941; Nobel Prize in physics for investigations of physics of upper atmosphere, 1947. [d. April 21, 1965]

1895 **Walter R(obert) Dornberger,** German missile expert; led Nazi guided missile program during World War II; later became adviser to U.S. Air Force; Vice-President, Bell Aerosystems, 1960–65. [d. June 1980]

1899 **Billy Rose (William Samuel Rosenberg),** U.S. entrepreneur, songwriter; produced numerous variety shows, 1931–44, and Aquacade at New York World's Fair, 1939. [d. February 10, 1966]

1906 **Luis F. Leloir,** Argentinian chemist, born in France; Nobel Prize in chemistry for investigations into the breakdown of complex sugars, 1970.

Historical Events

1512 The constitution of **Florence** is altered, restoring the Medici family to power.

1898 **Queen Wilhelmina** of the Netherlands is crowned.

1901 U.S. President **William McKinley** is shot by **Leon Czolgosz,** an anarchist; dies September 14.

1914 **First Battle of the Marne (World War I)** opens with a general offensive by French and British forces against the German advance.

1940 U.S. transfers the first destroyers to Great Britain under the destroyers-for-bases agreement (**Lend-Lease Act**).

1947 U.S. successfully fires first **V-2 rocket** launched from a ship.

1950 **Yongchong, Korea,** is recaptured by UN forces (**Korean War**).

U.S.S.R. vetoes a Security Council resolution condemning North Korea for continued defiance of the UN and asking all nations to withhold aid to North Korea.

1951 **Prince Talal,** elder son of King Abdullah, takes oath as King of Jordan.

An agreement is signed in Lisbon giving U.S. additional rights in the Azores and including the islands in the defense framework of **NATO.**

1961 **Afghanistan** breaks off diplomatic relations with **Pakistan,** closing its embassy, consulates, and trade agencies there.

1968 **Swaziland** becomes independent, ending Britain's colonial links with Africa.

1970 **Philibert Tsiranana** is elected President of the **Malagasy Republic.**

Arab commandos hijack three jetliners that eventually land in the Jordanian desert, where the planes are blown up.

1975 Violent earthquake in eastern **Turkey** kills more than 2,000 people.

1976 A **Soviet MiG-25 jet,** believed to be the Soviet Union's most advanced fighter, is flown to Japan by a pilot seeking U.S. asylum; President Ford grants him asylum; after a long delay, the plane is shipped back to the U.S.S.R.

1977 Korean businessman **Park Tong Sun,** in the U.S., is indicted on 36 felony charges and is also accused of making illegal campaign contributions and failing to register as a foreign agent.

1982 The Communist Party of **China** adopts a new party constitution which abolishes the post of Chairman and creates a new central Advisory Committee.

All private Mexican banks are nationalized and placed under the control of the **Bank of Mexico.**

Labor Day centennial is celebrated in the U.S.

September 7

Holidays

Brazil   Independence Day

Religious Calendar

The Saints

St. John of Nicomedia, martyr. Also called **Euetios, Euhtis.** [d. 303]

St. Clodoald, Frankish prince. Venerated in France as patron of nail makers. Also called **Cloud.** [d. c. 560]

Birthdates

1533 **Elizabeth I** of England, 1558–1603, ruled England during the literary Renaissance later identified as the **Elizabethan period;** as regent, defeated Mary, Queen of Scots; oppressed the Roman Catholics of England; defeated Philip of Spain and the Spanish Armada. [d. March 23, 1603]

1677 **Stephen Hales,** English scientist; conducted early studies on physiological phenomena; known as the *Founder of Science of Physiology.* [d. January 4, 1761]

1707 **Georges Louis Leclerc du Buffon,** French naturalist; Director of Jardin du Roi and Royal Museum, 1739; member, French Academy, 1753–88; published *Histoire Naturelle,* a 44-volume catalog of nature, 1749–1804 (portions published posthumously). [d. April 16, 1788]

1829 **Friedrich August Kekule von Stradonitz,** German organic chemist; known for his work on the constitution of organic compounds; first to propose theory of leaking carbon atoms; first to theorize on the ring formation of the benzene molecule. [d. July 13, 1896]

1860 **Anna Mary Robertson (*Grandma*) Moses,** U.S. painter; renowned as one of America's finest primitive painters; began painting in her seventies; produced over 2000 paintings by the time of her death. [d. December 13, 1961]

1867 **J. P. Morgan Jr.,** U.S. financier; son of John Pierpont Morgan (April 17); prime successor to the financial empire left by his father. [d. March 13, 1943]

1873 **Carl Lotus Becker,** U.S. historian, educator; noted for his popular analyses of American institutions and events; author of *The Declaration of Independence;* President, American Historical Society, 1931–41. [d. April 10, 1945]

1884 **Charles Tomlinson Griffes,** U.S. composer; impressionistic in his style and exotic in his themes; directly influenced by Debussy and Ravel. [d. April 8, 1920]

1887 **Dame Edith Sitwell,** British poet, author; known for her wit and eccentricity. [d. December 9, 1964]

1900 **(Janet Miriam) Taylor Caldwell,** U.S. novelist.

1908 **Michael Ellis Debakey,** U.S. heart surgeon; noted for his advanced techniques in heart surgery and heart transplants.

1909 **Elia Kazan,** U.S. director, producer, author, born in Turkey.

1911 **Todor Zhivkov,** President, People's Republic of Bulgaria, 1971– .

1913 **(John) Anthony Quayle,** British actor, director, known for his Shakespearean roles.

1914 **James Alfred Van Allen,** U.S. physicist; discovered the **Van Allen belt** of radiation around the earth; pioneer in high-altitude rocket research.

1917 **John Cornforth,** Australian-British chemist; Nobel Prize in chemistry for contributions to **stereochemistry** (with V. Prelog), 1975.

1923 **Louise Suggs,** U.S. golfer; winner of 50 tournaments on the Ladies' PGA Tour, two-time winner of U.S. Open.

 Peter Lawford, British actor.

1924 **Daniel Ken Inouye,** U.S. politician, lawyer; U.S. Congressman, 1959–62; U.S. Senator, 1963– .

St. Evurtius, Bishop of Orlèans. Also called **Enurchus, Evortius.** [d. 4th cent.]

SS. Alcmund and Tilbert, bishops of Hexham. Alcmund also called **Alchmund;** Tilbert also called **Tilberht.** [d. 781 and 789]

St. Grimonia, virgin and martyr. Also called **Germana.** [death date unknown]

St. Regina, virgin and martyr. Also called **Reine.** [death date unknown]

St. Sozon, martyr. [death date unknown]

The Beatified

Blessed Mark, Stephen, and Melchior, martyrs. [d. 1619]

Blessed John Duckett and Ralph Corby, martyrs. [d. 1644]

1930   **Baudouin I** of Belgium; acceded to throne in 1951 on his father's abdication; helped restore confidence in the Belgian monarchy.

1935   **Abdou Diouf,** President, Republic of Senegal, 1981– .

1936   **(Charles Harden) Buddy Holly,** U.S. singer, guitarist; had significant influence on rock 'n' roll music worldwide [d. February 2, 1959]

Historical Events

1714   **Peace of Baden** between France and Holy Roman Empire is achieved; France keeps Alsace.

1812   **Battle of Borodino,** fought 70 miles west of Moscow, is a costly victory over the Russians for Napoleon's Grand Army.

1822   **Brazil** declares its independence from **Portugal.**

1848   **Serfdom** in **Austria** is abolished.

1856   **Alexander II** is crowned Czar of Russia in Moscow.

1860   **Garibaldi** and his troops take **Naples;** the unification of Italy ensues.

1892   **John L. Sullivan** defeats **James J. Corbett** in the first modern **boxing** match to be held using **Marquis of Queensbury rules.**

1901   **Boxer Rebellion,** led by anti-foreign element in China, ends as 12 nations sign **Boxer Protocol.**

1941   U.S. merchant ship, the *Steel Seafarer,* is the first to be lost to air attack (**World War II**).

1944   Germans fire first **V-2 rocket** on London (**World War II**).

1945   **General Douglas MacArthur** enters Tokyo as Supreme Commander for the Allied Powers in Japan.

1978   **Sri Lanka** adopts a new constitution, establishing a strong presidency, and abandoning the former name of the country, **Ceylon** to **Sri Lanka.**

1979   **Robert Runcie,** Bishop of St. Albans, is named 102nd **Archbishop of Canterbury.**

September 8

Holidays

International Literacy Day
Sponsored by the United
Nations, New York, New York.

Andorra   **Our Lady of Meritxell**
Celebrates the finding of a
madonnalike figure under an
almond tree which was in
bloom out of season.

U.S.S.R.   **International Journalists'
Solidarity Day**

Birthdates

1157   **Richard I** (*the Lion-Hearted*), King of England, 1189–99; led the **Third Crusade,** 1189–92; kidnapped by Austrians, 1191; ransomed and returned to England, 1194; the subject of numerous legends. [d. April 6, 1199]

1474   **Ludovico Ariosto,** Italian poet, famous for his *Orlando Furioso.* [d. July 6, 1533]

1767   **August Wilhelm Schlegel,** German translator, critic, orientalist, and poet; founder of literary journal *Athenaeum,* the primary organ of the German Romantic school; best known for his poetical translation, with Ludwig Tieck, of Shakespeare. [d. May 12, 1845]

1778   **Clemens Maria Brentano,** German poet, novelist; described the visions of German nun and visionary **Anna Katharina Emmerick.** [d. July 28, 1842]

1828   **Margaret Olivia Sage,** U.S. philanthropist; wife of Russell Sage (August 4); established the **Russell Sage Foundation** for the improvement of social conditions, 1907. [d. November 4, 1918]

1830   **Frédéric Mistral,** Provençal poet and writer; Nobel Prize in literature, 1904. [d. March 25, 1914]

1837   **Joaquin Miller (Cincinnatus Hiner Miller),** U.S. poet, journalist; best known in Europe for his flamboyant and romantic poems of the Old West; his poetry was regarded as overly sentimental by American critics. [d. February 17, 1913]

1841   **Antonín Dvořák,** Czech composer; Director, National Conservatory of Music, New York, 1892–95; composed numerous symphonies, including *New World Symphony.* [d. May 1, 1904]

1848   **Viktor Meyer,** German chemist; noted for his research in organic compounds and physical chemistry. [d. August 8, 1897]

1863   **W(illiam) W(ymark) Jacobs,** British short-story writer; known for his sea stories. [d. September 1, 1943]

1886   **Siegfried (Lorraine) Sassoon,** British poet; known for his anti-war poetry and semi-autobiographical fiction, especially *Memoirs of a Fox-Hunting Man.* [d. September 1, 1967]

1889   **Robert A(lphonso) Taft,** U.S. politician; Senator, 1939–53; drafted the **Taft-Hartley Act,** aimed at preventing labor strikes that could endanger the public good; son of William Howard Taft (September 15). [d. July 31, 1953]

1892   **Theodore V. Houser,** U.S. business executive; Chairman of the Board of Sears, Roebuck & Co. [d. December 17, 1963]

1922   **Sid Caesar,** U.S. actor, comedian.

1924   **Grace Metalious,** U.S. novelist; wrote *Peyton Place.* [d. February 25, 1964]

1925   **Peter Sellers,** British comedian, actor; best known for his portrayal of **Inspector Clouseau** in the *Pink Panther* film series. [d. July 24, 1980]

Historical Events

1565   The first permanent settlement in what is now the U.S., **St. Augustine, Florida,** is established by Don Pedro Menéndez.

1755   William Johnson achieves British victory at **Battle of Lake George (French and Indian War).**

1760   English capture Montreal from French **(French and Indian War).**

Religious Calendar

Feasts

The Birthday of the Blessed Virgin Mary. Feast observed in the West since about A.D. 600.

The Saints

SS. Adrian and Natalia, martyrs. Adrian is patron of soldiers and butchers, invoked against plagues. [d. c. 304]

SS. Eusebius, Nestabus, Zeno, and Nestor, martyrs. [d. c. 362]

St. Kinemark. Also called **Cynfarch Oer.** [d. 5th cent.]

St. Ethelburga, princess of Kent and Abbess of Lyming. Also called **Aedilburh, Tata.** [d. 647]

St. Disibod, Irish monastery-founder. Also called **Disen, Disibode.** [d. c. 674]

St. Sergius I, pope. Elected 687. [d. 701]

St. Corbinian, bishop. [d. 725]

1847   **Battle of Molino del Rey** results in U.S. victory (**Mexican War**).

1883   **Northern Pacific Railroad** across the U.S. is completed as the final spike is driven in at Gold Creek, Montana, after 13 years of construction.

1900   Hurricane in **Galveston**, Texas, with winds up to 120 m.p.h. kills 6,000; the resulting crisis leads to the creation of the first **city commission government** in the U.S.

1919   An agreement between the British and French recognizes the French right to all territory west of the Nile basin, including most of the **Sahara.**

1935   **Huey P. Long,** Louisiana Senator, is fatally wounded by an assassin in Baton Rouge, Louisiana; he dies two days later.

1943   **Italy** accepts Allied terms of unconditional surrender (**World War II**).

1944   **Bulgaria** surrenders to the Allies (**World War II**).

1951   **San Francisco Treaty of Peace** with Japan is signed, establishing mutual assistance between the U.S. and Japan.

1974   U.S. President **Gerald Ford** grants former President **Richard M. Nixon** an unconditional pardon for all federal crimes committed while in office.

September 9

Holidays

Bulgaria	National Holiday
Japan	Choxo-no-Sekku or Chrysanthemum Day
California	Admission Day

Religious Calendar

The Saints

St. Isaac, Primate of the Armenian Church. Also called **Isaac the Great, Sahak I.** [d. 439]

St. Kieran, Abbot of Clonmacnois. Also called **Ciaran, Kiaran,** or **Kieran the Younger.** [d. c. 556]

Birthdates

1585   **Richelieu,** Armand Jean de Plessis, Duc de *Eminence Rouge*, French statesman, cardinal; chief minister of Louis XIII; directed domestic and foreign policies of France, 1624–42. [d. December 4, 1642]

1711   **Thomas Hutchinson,** American colonial official; Governor of Massachusetts Bay Colony, 1771–74; opposed revolutionary elements in America and returned to England as adviser to George III. [d. June 3, 1780]

1737   **Luigi Galvani,** Italian physician, physicist; known for his research into function of electrical current on muscle movements. [d. December 4, 1798]

1754   **William Bligh,** English naval officer; master of *H.M.S. Bounty*; cast adrift by mutinous sailors, sailed 4000 miles to East Indies with a crew of 18 men; Governor of New South Wales, 1805–08. [d. December 7, 1817]

1778   **Fabian Gottlieb von Bellingshausen,** Russian naval officer and Antarctic explorer; commanded **Antarctic expedition** which discovered Peter I Island and Alexander I Island. [d. January 13, 1852]

1789   **William Cranch Bond,** U.S. astronomer; the first director of the Harvard College Observatory; took the first photograph of a star, 1850. [d. January 29, 1859]

1828   **Leo Nikolayevich Tolstoi,** Russian novelist, philosopher, religious mystic; regarded as one of the great authors of all time; known not only for such works as *War and Peace*, but also for his system of **Christian anarchism;** founded sect of Tolstoyists who believed in nonresistance to evil. [d. November 20, 1910]

1890   **Harland Sanders,** U.S. businessman; founder of Kentucky Fried Chicken Corporation, 1956. [d. December 16, 1980]

1900   **James Hilton,** British novelist; author of *Lost Horizon, Goobye, Mr. Chips,* and *Random Harvest.* [d. December 20, 1954]

1901   **Granville Hicks,** U.S. writer, literary critic; known for his Marxist writings; author of *The Great Tradition.* [d. June 18,1982]

1923   **Daniel C. Gajdusek,** U.S. physician; Nobel prize in physiology or medicine for discoveries concerning mechanisms involved in the origin and spread of **infectious diseases** (with B. S. Blumberg), 1976.

     Cliff Robertson, U.S. actor, director.

Historical Events

1513   **James IV** of Scotland is defeated by the English and killed at the **Battle of Flodden Field**; he is succeeded by **James V.**

1850   **California** is admitted to the Union as the 31st state.

1884   **American Historical Association** is founded at Saratoga, New York.

1895   **American Bowling Congress** is organized at New York.

1914   **First Battle of the Marne** ends with the Germans beginning a retreat to the **Aisne River (World War I).**

1942   The only aerial bombing of the continental U.S. during **World War II** takes place from plane launched by Japanese submarine off

St. Audomarus, Bishop of Thèrouanne. Also called **Omer.** [d. c. 670]

St. Bettelin, hermit; patron of Stafford. Also called **Beccelin** or **Berthelm.** [d. 8th cent.]

St. Wulfhilda, Abbess of Barking. Also called **Wulfhildis.** [d. c. 1000]

St. Peter Claver, Jesuit priest. Missionary to Negro slaves in South America. [d. 1654]

St. Gorgonius, martyr. [death date unknown]

The Beatified

Blessed Seraphina Sforza, widow. [d. c. 1478]

Blessed Louisa of Savoy, widow. [d. 1503]

Blessed James D. Laval. [beatified 1979]

the Oregon coast. Only damage is a small forest fire.

1943   U.S. Fifth Army under General Mark Clark makes amphibious landings at **Salerno, Italy** (**World War II**).

1948   **Democratic People's Republic of Korea** (**North Korea**) is established.

1968   **Arthur Ashe** wins the U.S. Open tennis title at Forest Hills, New York, in the first tournament open to both professionals and amateurs.

September 10

Holidays

Belize   National Day
Bulgaria   National Holiday

Religious Calendar

The Saints

SS. Nemesian and companions, martyrs. [d. 257]
St. Pulcheria, virgin and Empress of Byzantium. [d. 453]
St. Finnian of Moville, bishop. Also called Finian. [d. c. 579]

Birthdates

1487 **Julius III,** Pope 1550-55; resumed session of **Council of Trent,** 1551. [d. March 23, 1555]

1753 **Sir John Soane,** English architect; redesigned **Bank of England** in Roman Corinthian style; donated his antiquarian paintings, sculptures, drawings to the English nation as the basis of the **Soane Museum in London.** [d. January 20, 1837]

1771 **Mungo Park,** Scottish-born African explorer, surgeon; discovered the source and course of the **Nile River,** 1796. [d. 1806]

1787 **John Jordan Crittenden,** U.S. politician, lawyer; U.S. Senator, 1817–19; 1835–41; 1842–48; 1855–61. U.S. Attorney General, 1841; 1850–53. Governor of Kentucky, 1848–50. [d. July 26, 1863]

1835 **William Torrey Harris,** U.S. Hegelian philosopher, educator; U.S. Commissioner of Education, 1889–1906; Editor-in-Chief of the first edition of *Webster's New International Dictionary,* 1909. [d. November 5, 1909]

1836 **Joseph (*Fighting Joe*) Wheeler,** U.S. Union and Confederate Army general (served in Union Army for two years, then resigned his commission to fight for the Confederacy); saw continuous action during the entire Civil War; U.S. Congressman, 1881–1900; returned to the army during the Spanish-American War. [d. January 25, 1906]

1839 **Isaac (Kauffman) Funk,** U.S. editor, publisher, lexicographer; founder, with Adam Willis Wagnalls, of the *Standard Series* publications, and editors and producers of the *Standard Dictionary of the English Language.* [d. April 4, 1912]

Charles Santiago Sanders Peirce, U.S. mathematician, logician, philosopher; *Father of Pragmatism;* from 1867 to 1914 was probably the world's leading logician. [d. April 19, 1914]

1847 **John R. Lynch,** U.S. Congressman, 1873–77; 1881–83; first black to preside over a national convention of the Republican Party, 1884. [d. November 2, 1939]

1856 **Elbridge Amos Stuart,** U.S. manufacturer; founder of Carnation Co.; President, 1899–1932; Chairman of the Board, 1932–44. [d. January 14, 1944]

1885 **Carl Van Doren,** U.S. author, editor; while at Columbia University, 1911–30, greatly influenced the revival of interest in American literature; author of Pulitzer Prize winning biography of Benjamin Franklin, 1939. [d. July 18, 1950]

1886 **Hilda Doolittle,** U.S. poet; major voice in the Imagist movement. [d. September 27, 1961]

1890 **Franz Werfel,** Austrian poet, playwright, and novelist; member of Expressionist movement. [d. August 26, 1945]

1892 **Arthur Holly Compton,** U.S. physicist; Nobel Prize in physics for discovery of **Compton effect,** the change in wave length of x rays colliding with electrons, 1927. [d. March 25, 1962]

1898 **Adele Astaire (Adele Austerlitz),** U.S. dancer; with her brother, Fred Astaire (May 10), formed a famous dance team of the 1920s. [d. January 25, 1981]

St. **Theodard,** Bishop of Tongres-Maastricht. [d. c. 670]

St. **Aubert,** Bishop of Avranches; founder of Church of Mont-Saint-Michel. [d. c. 725]

St. **Frithestan,** Bishop of Winchester. [d. c. 932]

St. **Nicholas of Tolentino,** Augustinian friar; patron of souls in purgatory. [d. 1305]

St. **Barloc,** hermit. [death date unknown]

The Beatified

Blessed Apollinaris Franco, Charles Spinola, and their companions, martyrs in the great martyrdom in Japan. [d. 1622]

1914 **Robert (Earl) Wise,** U.S. film director, producer; noted for his films, *Run Silent, Run Deep, West Side Story, The Sound of Music.*

1915 **Edmond O'Brien,** U.S. actor.

1929 **Arnold Palmer,** U.S. golfer; winner of 79 professional titles; first $1 million winner in golf.

1934 **Roger Maris,** U.S. baseball player; hit record 61 home runs in 1961.

1945 **José Feliciano,** U.S. composer, guitarist.

Historical Events

1721 **Treaty of Nystad** is signed, in which Russia obtains territories from Sweden: Livonia, Estonia, Ingria, and Eastern Karelia. (Old Style: August 30).

1813 **Battle of Lake Erie** results in important American victory as **Oliver Perry** defeats the British (**War of 1812**).

1846 **Elias Howe** patents his first **sewing machine.**

1893 Women are granted the right to vote in **New Zealand.**

1919 Austria signs the **Treaty of St. Germain,** ending **World War I** with the Allies and recognizing the independence of Czechoslovakia, Yugoslavia, Poland, and Hungary.

1944 German troops seize **Rome** (**World War II**).

1967 **Gibraltar** votes to remain under British sovereignty rather than return to Spanish rule.

1980 Coup d'état led by **General Kenan Evren** in Turkey gives power to the military.

September 11

Holidays

Ethiopia	**Ethiopian New Year and Reunion of Eritrea with Ethiopia** Commemorates the New Year of the Coptic Calendar, and the reunification of Eritrea, former Italian colony, with Ethiopia by U.N. mandate, 1952.
Pakistan	**Anniversary of the Death of Quaid-e-Azam** Commemorates the death of **Mohammed Ali Jinnah,** founder and first leader of Pakistan, 1948.

Birthdates

1524 **Pierre de Ronsard,** French poet; head of group of poets known as *Pléiade,* who were devoted to revitalizing the use of French language in great literature; called the *Father of Lyric Poetry in France.* [d. December 27, 1585]

1611 **Henri de La Tour d'Auvergne, Vicomte de Turenne,** French Army marshal; active during the Thirty Years' War, 1618–48; sided with the Fronde in rebellion against the French monarchy, 1648–53; led French troops in war in Holland, the Palatinate, and Alsace, 1672–75. Considered by Napoleon to be one of history's greatest military leaders. [d. July 27, 1675]

1723 **Johann Bernhard Basedow (Bernhard Nordalbingen),** German educator, educational reformer; established the **Philanthropinum,** a model school for children, 1774. [d. July 25, 1790]

1821 **Erastus Flavel Beadle,** U.S. publisher; his experiments in publication of *cheap* books led to the first *dime novel,* which was based on thrills, violence, suspense, and improbable narrative; this literary form became the most popular in 19th-century America. [d. December 21, 1894]

1862 **O. Henry (William Sidney Porter),** U.S. short-story writer; prolific master of the tightly plotted, superbly executed short story with a surprise ending. [d. June 5, 1910]

1877 **Sir James Hopwood Jeans,** British physicist, astronomer, author; noted for his work on **kinetic theory of gases and ra-** diations; knighted, 1928. [d. September 17, 1946]

1883 **D(avid) H(erbert) Lawrence,** British novelist, short-story writer, poet; noted for his passionate, primitive handling of controversial subjects. [d. March 2, 1930]

Grigori Evsevich Zinoviev, Russian political leader and associate of Lenin in forming Bolshevik party; member of ruling triumvirate with Kamenev and Stalin after Lenin's death; accused of plotting against Stalin; expelled from office; accused of complicity in the murder of Sergei Kirov. [executed August 25, 1936]

1895 **Vinoba Bhave,** Indian mystic, social reformer; heir to the spiritual empire of Mahatma Gandhi; after assassination of Gandhi, assumed leadership in movement for social reform and economic revolution begun by Gandhi. [d. November 15, 1982]

1896 **Robert Samuel Kerr,** U.S. politician, oilman; Governor of Oklahoma, 1943–47; U.S. Senator, 1949–63. [d. January 1, 1963]

1898 **Sir Gerald (Walter Robert) Templer,** British army officer; Chief of Imperial General Staff, 1935–54; knighted, 1949. [d. October 25, 1979]

1913 **Paul (*Bear*) Bryant,** U.S. football coach; coach for University of Alabama, 1958–82. [d. January 26, 1983]

1917 **Ferdinand Edralin Marcos,** Philippine leader; President of Philippines, 1965–73; prime minister, 1973– .

Religious Calendar

The Saints

St. Paphnutius, bishop. [d. c. 350]

St. Patiens, Bishop of Lyons. [d. c. 480]

St. Deiniol, bishop. Also called **Daniel of the Bangors, Deinoil.** [d. c. 584]

St. Peter of Chavanon, priest and monastery founder. [d. 1080]

SS. Protus and Hyacinth, martyrs. Hyacinth also called **Hyacinthus.** [death date unknown]

St. Theodora of Alexandria. [death date unknown]

The Beatified

Blessed Louis of Thuringia, king. Also called **Ludwig.** [d. 1227]

Blessed Bonaventure of Barcelona, Franciscan lay brother and hermitage-founder. [d. 1684]

Blessed John Gabriel Perboyre, martyr. [d. 1840]

1922   **James Charles Evers,** U.S. political, civil rights leader; Mayor of Fayette, Mississippi, 1969– .

1924   **Tom Landry,** U.S. football coach; head coach of Dallas Cowboys, 1960– .

Historical Events

1297   Scots under **William Wallace** defeat an English army of more than 50,000 at **Sterling Bridge.**

1649   **Oliver Cromwell** of England sacks **Drogheda** in Ireland, suppressing an Irish uprising led by the Marquis of Ormonde, James Butler.

1700   **Battle of Malplaquet** is fought as British, Dutch, and Austrian forces defeat the French in the last great battle of the **War of the Spanish Succession.**

1814   **Battle of Lake Champlain** (sometimes called **Battle of Plattsburg Bay**) results in American naval victory over the British (**War of 1812**).

1855   **Sebastopol** capitulates to England, France, and Turkey (**Crimean War**).

1941   U.S. President **Franklin D. Roosevelt** issues shoot-on-sight order to warships in U.S. defensive waters (**World War II**).

1943   Italian fleet surrenders to Allies (**World War II**).

1962   **The Beatles,** British rock group, make their first recordings, *Love Me, Do,* and *P.S., I Love You.*

1972   **Bay Area Rapid Transit,** first new **mass transit system** in the U.S. since 1907, begins limited service in the San Francisco Bay area.

1973   Leftist government of Chilean President **Salvador Allende** is overthrown by a military coup; Allende is reported to have committed suicide.

September 12

Holidays

Cape Verde Islands	Nationality Day
Ethiopia	Popular Revolution Commemoration Day Commemorates the coup which removed Emperor Haile Selassie from power, 1974.
Guinea-Bissau	National Day
Saudi Arabia	National Day
U.S. (Missouri)	Defenders' Day

Birthdates

1494 **Francis I** of France, 1515–47. [d. March 31, 1547]

1788 **Alexander Campbell,** U.S. editor, clergyman born in Ireland. Founder of Bethany College; son of Thomas Campbell, with whom he founded the **Churches of Christ** in the U.S. [d. March 4, 1866]

1806 **Andrew Hull Foote,** U.S. naval officer; prominent in the U.S. Civil War, distinguishing himself at the battles of Fort Henry and Fort Donelson. [d. June 26, 1863]

1812 **Richard March Hoe,** U.S. inventor; perfected a **rotary printing press,** which revolutionized the newspaper publishing business in the U.S. [d. June 7, 1886]

1818 **Richard Jordan Gatling,** U.S. inventor; developed the **Gatling gun,** the first **machine gun,** for use during the U.S. Civil War. [d. February 26, 1903]

1852 **Herbert Henry Asquith, 1st Earl of Oxford and Asquith,** British statesman; Prime Minister, 1908–16; achieved passage of Parliament Act, Home Rule Bill for Ireland, and Welsh Disestablishment Act. [d. February 15, 1928]

1855 **William Sharp,** Scottish poet; promoter of Celtic literary revival; wrote under the pseudonym **Fiona Macleod.** [d. December 14, 1905]

1880 **H(enry) L(ouis) Mencken,** U.S. journalist, critic, editor; noted social observer and expert on the American language. [d. January 29, 1956]

1888 **Maurice Chevalier,** French singer, actor. [d. January 1, 1972]

1891 **Arthur Hays Sulzberger,** U.S. newspaper publisher; publisher of *New York Times,* 1935–68; a director of Associated Press, 1943–52. [d. December 11, 1968]

1892 **Alfred A. Knopf,** U.S. publisher; founder of Alfred A. Knopf, Inc., 1915; recognized as one of the foremost publishers of all time. [d. August 11, 1984]

1893 **Lewis Blaine Hershey,** U.S. Army general; Director, U.S. Selective Service System, 1941–70.

1897 **Irène Joliot-Curie,** French physicist; Nobel Prize in chemistry for synthesizing new radioactive elements, including radioactive nitrogen and phosphorus (with F. Joliot-Curie), 1935. [d. March 17, 1956]

1898 **Ben(jamin) Shahn,** U.S. painter, graphic artist, born in Russia; devoted his art to social and political causes; responsible for murals at Rockefeller Center, New York (with Diego Rivera), Bronx Central Annex Post Office, and the Social Security Building, Washington, D.C., as well as numerous posters, oils, gouaches, and book illustrations. [d. March 14, 1969]

1901 **Ben Blue,** U.S. comedian. [d. March 7, 1975]

1904 **George K(ung) C(hao) Yeh,** Chinese National statesman, educator; Foreign Minister, 1949–58; Ambassador to U.S., 1958–62. [d. November 20, 1981]

1909 **Robert E(dmonds) Kintner,** U.S. broadcasting company executive; President, American Broadcasting Co., 1950–56; President, National Broadcasting Co., 1958–65. [d. December 20, 1980]

1913 **Jessie Owens,** U.S. athlete; winner of four gold medals at the 1936 Olympics in Berlin. [d. March 31, 1980]

Religious Calendar

The Holy Name of Mary. Feast originated in 14th century. Suppressed 1969.

The Saints

St. Ailbhe, bishop. Also called **Ailbe, Albeus.** [d. c. 526]

St. Eanswida, virgin. Also called **Eanswide, Eanswitho.** [d. c. 640]

St. Guy of Anderlecht. Also called **Guidon, Guy of Anderlent,** or **Wye.** [d. c. 1012]

The Beatified

Blessed Victoria Fornari-Strata, widow and foundress of the Blue Nuns of Genoa. [d. 1617]

Historical Events

490 B.C. Athenian force defeats the Persian army at the **Battle of Marathon.**

1683 The Turkish siege of **Vienna** is raised by a German-Polish army under the command of **John III Sobieski** of Poland.

1848 A new federal constitution, closely modeled on that of the United States, is adopted in **Switzerland.**

1908 *Lusitania,* world's largest steamship, arrives in New York on her maiden voyage.

1919 Gabriele d'Annunzio, with volunteer troops, seizes **Fiume,** under dispute between Yugoslavia and Italy, for Italy.

1966 U.S. spacecraft *Gemini 11* is launched from Cape Kennedy, Florida.

1973 Eleven black miners are killed by South African police at the Western Deep Levels gold mine in **Carletonville** during a riot over wages.

1974 **Haile Selassie,** Emperor of Ethiopia since 1930, is deposed in an army coup.

September 13

Religious Calendar

The Saints

St. John Chrysostom, archbishop of Constantinople and Doctor of the Church. Patron of preachers. Invoked against epilepsy. Surnamed Chrysostomus, 'golden-mouthed,' because of his eloquence. [d. 407] Obligatory Memorial.

Birthdates

1520 **William Cecil, Baron Burghley,** English statesman under Queen Elizabeth I; carried out execution of **Mary, Queen of Scots.** [d. August 4, 1598]

1722 **François Joseph Paul de Grasse, Marquis de Grasse-Tilly,** French admiral; aided America in its war for independence; supported General Washington at Yorktown, leading to the defeat of Cornwallis. [d. January 11, 1788]

1755 **Oliver Evans,** U.S. inventor; patented **high-pressure steam engine,** 1797; his work anticipated both the **steamboat** and the **automobile.** [d. April 15, 1819]

1851 **Walter Reed,** U.S. physician, bacteriologist; responsible for discovery of method to prevent **yellow fever.** [d. November 23, 1902]

1857 **Milton Snavely Hershey,** U.S. manufacturer; founded Hershey Chocolate Corp., the largest U.S. producer of chocolate products. [d. October 13, 1945]

1860 **John Joseph (*Black Jack*) Pershing,** U.S. Army general; led an unsuccessful pursuit of Mexican revolutionary Pancho Villa, 1915–17; headed American Expeditionary Force during World War I. Awarded the Pulitzer Prize for his memoirs, *My Experiences in the World War,* 1931. [d. July 15, 1948]

1863 **Baron Franz von Hipper,** German admiral prominent in World War I; Commander-in-Chief of German High Seas Fleet, 1918. [d. May 25, 1932]

Cyrus Adler, U.S. religious leader, educator; President, Dropsie College for Hebrew and Cognate Learning, 1908–40; President Jewish Theological Seminary, 1924–40; recognized as a major force in conservative Judaism in the U.S. [d. April 7, 1940]

Arthur Henderson, British diplomat; Nobel Peace Prize for work as head of World Disarmament Conference, 1934. [d. October 20, 1935]

1866 **Adolf Meyer,** U.S. psychiatrist, neurologist, born in Switzerland; *Father of the Mental Hygiene Movement* in the U.S.; developed the theory of objective psychobiology. [d. March 17, 1950]

1874 **Arnold Schönberg,** Austrian composer; revolutionized modern music through use of a 12-tone system. [d. July 13, 1951]

1883 **Lewis Edward Lawes,** U.S. penologist; warden of Sing Sing Prison, 1919–40; firm advocate of reform rather than punishment of prison inmates; opposed capital punishment. [d. April 23, 1947]

1886 **Sir Robert Robinson,** British chemist; Nobel Prize in chemistry for his work with **alkaloids** and other plant products, 1947. [d. February 8, 1975]

1887 **Leopold Ruzicka,** Swiss chemist; Nobel Prize in chemistry for work on **ringed molecules** and **terpenes,** 1939. [d. September 1976]

1894 **J(ohn) B(oynton) Priestley,** British novelist, dramatist, essayist; noted for his evocation of *déjà vu* in his writings. [d. August 14, 1984]

1916 **Roald Dahl,** British short-story and children's book writer; best known for his *Charlie and the Chocolate Factory.*

1925 **Mel Torme,** U.S. singer.

Historical Events

1515 **Battle of Marignano** results in a French victory over the Swiss in the **War of the Holy League.**

St. Maurilius, Bishop of Angers. [d. 453]

St. Eulogius, Patriarch of Alexandria. [d. c. 607]

St. Amatus, abbot. Also called **Ameè.** [d. c. 630]

1598   **Philip II** of Spain dies and is succeeded by **Philip III.**

1609   **Henry Hudson,** sailing for the Netherlands, enters harbor at New York and sails up Hudson River as far as Albany, thus establishing Dutch claims to this region.

1635   General Court of Massachusetts Bay Colony banishes **Roger Williams,** who leaves to establish the colony of **Rhode Island.**

1788   **New York** is declared the first federal capital and seat of U.S. Congress.

1846   U.S. General **Winfield Scott** defeats Mexicans at the **Battle of Chapultepec (Mexican War).**

1899   First successful climb of **Mt. Kenya,** over 17,058 feet, is accomplished by **H. J. Mackinder.**

1942   German army enters **Stalingrad,** Russia (**World War II**).

1968   **Albania** withdraws from the **Warsaw Pact.**

1971   Prisoners riot at the state prison in **Attica, New York;** 28 prisoners are killed.

1973   General **Augusto Pinochet Ugarte** becomes President of Chile.

September 14

Birthdates

1547   **Jan van Olden Barnveldt,** Dutch statesman; a champion of Dutch independence. [d. May 13, 1619]

1769   **Alexander von Humboldt,** German scientist and explorer; conducted numerous experiments dealing with the earth's magnetic field, climatic conditions, rock formations and volcanic activity; noted for his *Kosmos*, a description of the physical universe, 1845–62. [d. May 6, 1859]

1791   **Franz Bopp,** German philologist; founder of the science of **comparative philology.** [d. October 23, 1867]

1849   **Ivan Petrovich Pavlov,** Russian physiologist; best known for his studies of **conditioned reflexes** in dogs; Nobel Prize in physiology or medicine, 1904. [d. February 27, 1936]

1860   **(Hannibal) Hamlin Garland,** U.S. short-story writer, novelist, essayist; Pulitzer Prize in autobiography for *A Daughter of the Middle Border*, 1922. [d. March 4, 1940]

1864   **Edgar Algernon Robert, 1st Viscount Cecil of Chelwood,** British statesman; Nobel Peace Prize, 1919, for his work in drafting the 1919 League of Nations pact. [d. November 24, 1958]

1867   **Charles Dana Gibson,** U.S. artist, illustrator; best known for his creation of the *Gibson girl*, a model for women's fashion and hair style from 1890–1914. [d. December 23, 1944]

1883   **Margaret Higgins Sanger,** U.S. nurse, social reformer; founder of birth control movement in U.S.; responsible for establishment of the first birth control clinic in the U.S.; first president of **International Planned Parenthood Federation,** 1953–66; worked in India and Japan, as well as the U.S., to further the cause of intelligent contraceptive practices. [d. September 6, 1966]

1886   **Jan (Garrigue) Masaryk,** Czechoslovakian statesman; Minister to Great Britain, 1925–38; Foreign Minister, 1940–48; Vice-Premier of Czechoslovak provisional government in London, 1941–45. [d. March 10, 1948]

1887   **Karl Taylor Compton,** U.S. educator, physicist; President, M.I.T., 1930–46. [d. June 22, 1954]

1896   **John Robert Powers,** U.S. model agency pioneer; founder of **John Robert Powers Agency,** 1921. [d. July 19, 1977]

1898   **Hal (Brent) Wallis,** U.S. motion picture producer; in charge of production for Warner Brothers Studios, 1930–44; founded Hal Wallis Productions, 1944.

1920   **Lawrence R. Klein,** U.S. economist; Nobel Prize for economics for developing **forecasting models,** 1980.

1938   **Nicol Williamson,** Scottish actor, known for his Shakespearean roles.

Historical Events

1262   **Alfonso X** of Castile captures **Cadiz** from the Moors, thus ending a 500-year Moorish occupation of the city.

1752   England adopts the **Gregorian calendar;** September 14 of this year was preceded by September 3, thus effectively causing the loss of 11 days in the English calendar and sparking much unrest.

1770   **Censorship** is abolished in Denmark.

1814   **Francis Scott Key,** Maryland lawyer, is inspired to write the words to the song that is to become the American national anthem, *The Star-Spangled Banner*, as he witnesses the bombardment of **Fort McHenry (War of 1812).**

Day. [major holy day, Episcopal Church; minor festival, Lutheran Church]

1829   **Peace of Adrianople** is signed between Russia and the Turks with Russia securing the mouth of the Danube and the eastern coast of the Black Sea (**Russo-Turkish War**).

1846   U.S. General **Winfield Scott** captures **Mexico City,** effectively ending the **Mexican War.**

1854   Allied armies (Britain, France, Turkey) land in the Crimea to oppose Russia (**Crimean War**).

1901   U.S. President **William McKinley** dies from an assassin's bullet (see September 6); Vice-President **Theodore Roosevelt,** 42, becomes the youngest president ever to occupy the office.

1911   Russian premier **Peter Stolypin** is fatally wounded at a theater in Kiev by a reputed agent of the secret police.

1914   **General von Moltke** is succeeded as German Chief of Staff by **General von Falkenhayn** (**World War I**).

1930   General election in Germany gives **National Socialist Party** (**Nazis**) a majority in the Reichstag.

1939   First successful **helicopter** is flown by designer **Igor Sikorsky,** an American inventor born in Russia.

1975   **Mother Elizabeth Ann Bayley Seton,** first U.S.-born saint, is canonized in Rome by Pope Paul VI.

September 15

Holidays

Costa Rica, El Salvador, Guatemala, Honduras, Nicaragua	**Independence Day** Commemorates the achievement of independence from Spain, 1821.
Japan	**Respect for the Aged Day**

Birthdates

1584 **Georg Rodolf Weckherin,** German poet, translator, and parliamentary secretary to two English kings; responsible for introduction of Renaissance verse forms into German literature. [d. February 13, 1653]

1613 **François, duc de La Rochefoucauld,** French moralist and maxim writer; involved in plot against Richelieu; joined the Fronde; noted for his *Réflexions ou Sentences et Maximes Morales,* 1665. [d. March 16, 1680]

1765 **Manuel Maria Barbosa du Bocage,** Portuguese poet; leader of *Nova Arcádia group of poets. [d. December 21, 1805]*

1789 **James Fenimore Cooper,** U.S. author; the first truly American novelist; the Cooper hero, a woodsman characterized by an almost poetic solitude, courage, and stalwartness, can be seen in the characters of **Natty Bumppo, Leather-Stocking, Pathfinder,** and **Hawkeye.** [d. September 14, 1851]

1830 **Porfirio Diaz,** Mexican statesman; President of Mexico, 1877–80; 1884–1911; ruled as a dictator, advancing the material status of the country but not improving the lot of the masses; exiled, 1911. [d. July 2, 1915]

1834 **Heinrich Gotthard von Treitschke,** German historian and patriot; contributed to rise of anti-British sentiment in Germany. [d. April 28, 1896]

1852 **Jan Ernst Matzeliger,** U.S. inventor; developed the **shoe-lasting machine,** which totally revolutionized the shoe manufacturing industry. [d. August 24, 1889]

1857 **William Howard Taft,** U.S. jurist; 17th President of the U.S., 1909–13; represented the conservative wing of a divided Republican party; actively supported anti-trust legislation; Chief Justice of U.S. Supreme Court, 1921–30. [d. March 8, 1930]

1876 **Bruno Walter (Schlesinger),** German conductor; conductor of Vienna Imperial Opera, 1901–12; Vienna State Opera, 1935–38; guest conductor in New York, 1922–26, 1932–35, and London, 1924–32. [d. February 17, 1962]

1879 **Sir Joseph Aloysius Lyons,** Australian statesman; Premier of Tasmania, 1923–28; Prime Minister of Australia, 1932–39. [d. April 7, 1939]

1889 **Robert Charles Benchley,** U.S. humorist, critic; on the staff of *Life* magazine, 1920–30; drama critic, *New Yorker,* 1930–40; noted for his depiction of the struggles of an ordinary man; author of *My Ten Years in a Quandary.* [d. November 21, 1945]

1890 **Dame Agatha (Mary Clarissa) Christie,** British novelist, playwright; known for her popular mystery novels; created crime-solving characters of Belgian detective **Hercule Poirot** and eccentric spinster **Miss Jane Marple.** [d. January 12, 1976]

1894 **Jean Renoir,** French film director; son of Pierre Auguste Renoir (February 25). [d. February 12, 1979]

1904 **Umberto II** of Italy, assumed throne upon the abdication of his father, **Victor Emmanuel III,** 1946; third king of united Italy; exiled 1946 when Italy became a republic. [d. March 18, 1983]

1914 **Creighton Williams Abrams,** U.S. Army general; active in Vietnam War, 1968–72; U.S. Army Chief of Staff, 1972–74. [d. September 4, 1974]

1916 **Margaret Lockwood,** British actress.

1922 **Jackie Cooper,** U.S. actor, television director, producer.

The Seven Sorrows of the Blessed Virgin Mary. Also called the **Compassion of Our Lady,** or **Our Lady of Sorrows.** Obligatory Memorial.

The Saints

St. Nicetas the Goth, martyr. [d. 375]

St. Aichardus, abbot. Also called **Achard, Achart, Aicard.** [d. c. 687]

St. Mirin. Irish missionary to Scotland. Also called **Meadhran.** [d. c. 7th century]

St. Adam, Bishop of Caithness and martyr. [d. 1222]

St. Catherine of Genoa, widow and mystic. [d. 1510]

St. Nicomedes, monk, religious writer, and martyr. [death date unknown]

1923   **Hank Williams,** U.S. country-music singer, songwriter. [d. January 1, 1953]

1928   **Cannonball Adderley (Julian Edwin Adderley),** U.S. musician; jazz saxophonist. [d. August 8, 1975]

1929   **Murray Gell-Mann,** U.S. physicist; Nobel Prize in physics for development of *Eightfold Way*, a system of grouping nuclear particles, 1969; proposed the existence of the quark.

Historical Events

1776   British troops, under General Howe, seize **New York City,** which had been recently evacuated by Washington's troops (**American Revolution**).

1812   **Moscow** is burned by the Russians in an attempt to make the city untenable for Napoleon and the French army.

1821   **Costa Rica, El Salvador, Guatemala, Honduras, and Nicaragua** achieve independence from Spain.

1830   **Liverpool and Manchester Railway** in England opens, launching the railroad era.

1914   **Battle of the Aisne** marks the end of the Allied advance and the beginning of trench warfare in World War I.

1916   The first use of **tanks** in battle, by the British in an Allied attack at **Flers-Courcelette** during the **Battle of the Somme (World War I)**.

1935   **Nürnberg Laws** deprive Jews of citizenship in Germany.

1944   Allied forces begin **Rhineland Campaign** in Germany (**World War II**).

1950   Amphibious UN landing at **Inchon** proves decisive in defeat of North Korean troops (**Korean War**).

1972   U.S.S.R. and Spain sign a trade agreement, the first between the two countries since the 1936–39 Spanish Civil War.

1973   **King Gustaf VI Adolf** of Sweden dies at the age of 90 and is succeeded by his grandson, **Carl XVI Gustaf.**

       East and West Germany and the **Bahamas** are accepted as members of the UN at the opening session of the 28th General Assembly.

1977   1,200 South African students, who have gathered to commemorate the death of **Steven Biko,** the country's best known young black leader, are arrested for violating the **Riotous Assemblies Act.**

1978   **Muhammad Ali** defeats **Leon Spinks** in 15 rounds in New Orleans to win an unprecedented fourth world heavyweight boxing title.

September 16

Holidays

Mexico	Independence Day
Papua New Guinea	Independence Day
Oklahoma	Cherokee Strip Day

Commemorates the opening of the Cherokee Strip, 1893.

Religious Calendar

The Saints

St. Cornelius, pope and martyr. Elected 251. [d. 253] Obligatory Memorial.

Birthdates

1387 **Henry V** of England; began the **Hundred Years' War** against France. [d. August 31, 1422]

1678 **Henry St. John, 1st Viscount Bolingbroke,** English politician, historian, philosopher; supporter of James Stuart, the *Old Pretender;* associated with Pope and Swift, he contributed the philosophical basis for the former's *Essay on Man,* 1730. [d. December 12, 1751]

1685 **John Gay,** English playwright, poet; author of *The Beggar's Opera,* later adapted by Bertold Brecht and Kurt Weill for *The Threepenny Opera.* [d. December 4, 1732]

1745 **Prince Mikhail Illarionovich Golenishchev Kutuzov,** Russian Army field marshal; commander of army in Russian war against Poland, 1805–12; defeated at Austerlitz; military governor of Kiev, 1805–12; his defeat at **Battle of Borodino** allowed Napoleon to enter Moscow. [d. April 28, 1813]

1777 **Nathan Mayer, 1st Baron Rothschild,** British financier, born in Germany; son of Meyer Amschel Rothschild; head of financial institution's branch at London; made loans to European countries fighting Napoleon. [d. July 28, 1836]

1785 **Thomas Barnes,** Editor of *The* **(London)** *Times* 1817–41.

1822 **Charles Crocker,** U.S. railroad executive; founder of the Central Pacific Railroad Co., 1861, and of Southern Pacific Railroad, 1871. [d. August 14, 1888]

1823 **Francis Parkman,** U.S. historian, author; compiled the massive *France and England in North America.* [d. November 8, 1893]

1837 **Pedro V,** King of Portugal, 1853–61. [d. November 11, 1861]

1838 **James Jerome Hill,** U.S. railroad magnate, financier; organized the Great Northern Railway; developed the **Mesabi Range** iron ore mines in Minnesota, 1904–16. [d. May 29, 1916]

1853 **Albrecht Kossel,** German biochemist; Nobel Prize in physiology or medicine for contributions to the knowledge of **cellular chemistry,** 1910. [d. July 5, 1927]

1858 **Andrew Bonar Law,** British politician; Prime Minister of Great Britain, 1922–23. [d. October 30, 1923]

1875 **James Cash Penney,** U.S. merchant; founded the J.C. Penney Co., retail store; Chairman of the Board, 1917–58. [d. February 12, 1971]

1877 **Jacob Schick,** U.S. manufacturer; developed the **Schick razor.** [d. July 3, 1937]

1883 **T(homas) E(rnest) Hulme,** British critic, philosopher, poet; developed *Imagist theory* later popularized by T. S. Eliot and Ezra Pound. [d. September 28, 1917]

1885 **Karen Horney,** Norwegian-Dutch psychoanalyst, writer, teacher. [d. December 4, 1952]

1887 **Hans (or Jean) Arp,** French painter, sculptor, poet; founder of **Dadaism,** 1916; became member of Surrealist group, 1925. [d. June 7, 1966]

Nadia Juliette Boulanger, French music teacher, conductor; first woman conductor

St. Cyprian, bishop of Carthage, martyr. Primate of the African church. Also known as **Caecilius Cyprianus,** or **Thascius.** [d. 258] Obligatory Memorial.

St. Euphemia, virgin and martyr. [d. c. 303]

SS. Abundius, Abundantius, and their Companions, martyrs. [d. c. 304]

St. Ninian, bishop. Missionary in Scotland. Also called **Ninias, Ninnidh, Ninyas, Nynia,** or **Ringan.** [d. c. 432]

St. Ludmila, martyr. [d. 921]

St. Edith of Wilton, virgin and nun. Also called **Eadgyth, Editha.** [d. 984]

The Beatified

Blessed Victor III, pope. Elected 1086. [d. 1087]

Blessed Vitalis of Savigny, abbot. [d. 1122]

Blessed Louis Allemand, Archbishop of Arles and cardinal. Also called **Louis Aleman.** [d. 1450]

---

of Boston Symphony and New York Philharmonic. [d. October 22, 1979]

1888   **Frans Eemil Sillanpää,** Finnish novelist, short-story writer; Nobel Prize in literature, 1939. [d. June 3, 1964]

1891   **Karl Doenitz,** German admiral; commander-in-chief of German navy, 1943–45; Chancellor of Germany after Hitler's death, 1945; unconditionally surrendered to Allies. [d. December 24, 1980]

1893   **Albert Szent-Györgyi,** U.S. biochemist, born in Hungary; Nobel Prize in physiology or medicine for studies of effects of **Vitamins A and C,** 1937.

1896   **Lester B. Granger,** U.S. social worker; Director, National Urban League, 1941–61. [d. January 9, 1976]

1919   **Lawrence (Johnston) Peter,** U.S. educator, author, born in Canada; developed the **Peter Principle** of competence in organizations.

1924   **Lauren Bacall (Betty Joan Perske),** U.S. actress.

1925   **B. B. King (Riley B. King),** U.S. blues musician and guitarist.

1926   **John Knowles,** U.S. novelist; author of *A Separate Peace.*

1927   **Peter Falk,** U.S. actor.

Historical Events

1380   **Charles V** of France dies and is succeeded by **Charles VI.**

1620   *Mayflower* sails from Plymouth, England.

1810   **Mexico** claims independence from Spain. (The republic is established December 6, 1822.)

1824   **Louis XVIII** of France dies and is succeeded by **Charles X.**

1859   **David Livingstone,** British explorer, discovers **Lake Nyasa** in Africa.

1893   **Cherokee Strip,** land between Kansas and Oklahoma, is opened for *land rush* settlement.

1963   **Federation of Malaysia** is formed from Malaya, Singapore, and other former British colonies.

1966   New **Metropolitan Opera House** in New York City's Lincoln Center opens with the world premiere of Samuel Barber's ***Antony and Cleopatra.***

1974   Under a proclamation signed by U.S. President Gerald Ford, thousands of **Vietnam War deserters** and draft evaders become eligible for clemency if they swear allegiance to the U.S. and submit to alternate public service.

   Mary Louise Smith of Iowa becomes the first woman to head the U.S. Republican National Committee.

1975   **Papua New Guinea** gains full independence from Australia.

1976   The **Episcopal Church** approves the ordination of woman priests and bishops.

September 17

Holidays

Angola   **Day of the National Hero**

U.S.   **Citizenship Day**

Constitution Day
Sponsored by Federal Union, Inc., Washington, D.C.

Religious Calendar

The Impression of the Stigmata upon St. Francis (1224). Celebrates stigmata that appeared on hands and feet of **St. Francis of Assisi** at La Verna.

Birthdates

879   **Charles III** of France; called *Charles the Simple.* [d. October 7, 929]

1552   **Paul V,** pope 1605–21. [d. January 28, 1621]

1580   **Francisco Gómez de Quevedo y Villegas,** Spanish satirist, novelist; renowned author of Spain's Golden Age of Literature. [d. September 8, 1645]

1730   **Baron Friedrich Wilhelm Augustus von Steuben,** American Revolutionary general, born in Prussia; responsible for training Continental Army during American Revolution. [d. November 28, 1794]

1740   **John Cartwright,** English parliamentary reformer; called the *Father of Reform.* [d. September 23, 1824]

1743   **Marie-Jean-Antoine-Nicolas Caritat, Marquis de Condorcet,** French philosopher, educational theorist, mathematician, political economist; leading thinker of the Enlightenment. [d. March 25 or 29, 1794]

1800   **Franklin Buchanan,** U.S. naval officer; fought with the Confederate Navy; officer in charge of the *Merrimac* but not active in its historic battle with the *Monitor* because of a battle wound; captured at the Battle of Mobile Bay, 1864; released, 1865. [d. May 11, 1874]

1826   **Georg Friedrich Bernhard Riemann,** German mathematician; developed new, non-Euclidean geometry; conceptualized the Riemann's surface. [d. July 20, 1866]

1854   **David Dunbar Buick,** U.S. pioneer automobile builder; developed the Buick automobile; lost control of his company and died in obscurity as a clerk in a trade school. [d. March 5, 1929]

1857   **Konstantin Eduardovich Tsiolkovsky,** Soviet physicist; pioneer in development of Soviet rockets and space science. [d. September 19, 1935]

1869   **Christian Louis Lange,** Norwegian pacifist and historian; Nobel Peace Prize for his guidance of the Inter-Parliamentary Union, 1921. [d. December 11, 1938]

1883   **William Carlos Williams,** U.S. poet, physician; noted for his objective poetic form, utilizing idiomatic speech and informal structure; he viewed his style as an extension of the Imagism of Ezra Pound. [d. March 4, 1963]

1896   **Sam(uel James) Ervin, Jr.,** U.S. politician, lawyer; U.S. Senator, 1954–75; major opponent to Richard Nixon's claim of **executive privilege** during the **Senate Watergate Hearings.**

1900   **John Willard Marriott,** U.S. hotel and restaurant executive; founder of the Marriott Hotel chain.

1904   **Sir Frederick Ashton,** British choreographer, dancer; principal choreographer, Royal Ballet, 1935–70.

1906   **Junius Richard Jayawardene,** President, Democratic Socialist Republic of Sri Lanka, 1978– .

1907   **Warren Earl Burger,** U.S. jurist, lawyer; Justice of U.S. Court of Appeals for the District of Columbia, 1955–69; Chief Justice, U.S. Supreme Court, 1969– .

1916   **Mary Stewart,** British novelist; author of romantic suspense novels.

Yumzhagiyen Tsedenbal, Chairman, Mongolian People's Republic, 1974– .

1918   **Chaim Herzog,** Israeli statesman; Ambassador to UN, 1975–78; President, 1983– .

The Saints

St. Satyrus, brother of St. Ambrose. [d. c. 379]

St. Lambert, Bishop of Maestricht, martyr. Also called **Landebert.** [d. c. 705]

St. Columba, virgin and martyr. [d. 853]

St. Hildegard, virgin. First of the great German mystics. Also called **Hildegardis.** [d. 1179]

St. Peter Arbues, martyr. [d. 1485]

St. Robert Ballarmine, Archbishop of Capua, cardinal, and Doctor of the Church. Feast formerly May 13. [d. 1621] Optional Memorial.

SS. Socrates and Stephen, martyrs. [death date unknown]

1930 **Edgar D. Mitchell,** U.S. astronaut; participant in *Apollo 14* moon landing.

Thomas Patten Stafford, U.S. astronaut; participated in the following flights: *Gemini 6,* 1965; *Gemini 9,* 1966; *Apollo 10,* 1969.

1931 **Anne Bancroft (Anna Maria Italiano),** U.S. actress; noted for her dramatic roles on stage and in films; married to Mel Brooks (June 28).

1934 **Maureen Connolly,** U.S. tennis player; U.S. singles champion, 1951–53; Wimbledon champion, 1952–54; Associated Press Woman Athlete of the Year, 1952–54. [d. June 21, 1969]

1935 **Ken Kesey,** U.S. novelist, editor; author of *One Flew Over the Cuckoo's Nest.*

Historical Events

1631 **Battle of Breitenfeld,** fought near Leipzig, Germany, results in victory for Swedish and Protestant German forces under **Gustavus Adolphus** over Catholic troops led by the **Count of Tilly** (**Thirty Years' War**).

1665 **Philip IV** of Spain dies and is succeeded by **Charles II.**

1787 **U.S. Constitution** is signed by the delegates to the Constitutional Convention.

1796 U. S. President **George Washington** delivers his Farewell Address to the American people.

1806 Sweden cedes **Finland** to Russia by the **Peace of Frederikshamm.**

1838 **Great Western Railroad** from Liverpool to London is opened.

1862 **Battle of Antietam** halts Confederate advance into the North; known as the bloodiest battle of the Civil War (**U.S. Civil War**).

1920 **American Professional Football Association,** forerunner of **NFL,** is formed at Canton, Ohio.

1930 Construction of **Boulder Dam** (now **Hoover Dam**) begins near Las Vegas, Nevada. The dam is completed in 1936.

1935 **Manuel Quezon y Molina** is elected first president of the Philippines.

1939 **U.S.S.R.** invades **Poland.**

1947 **James V. Forrestal** is sworn in as first U.S. Secretary of Defense.

1948 UN mediator Count **Folke Bernadotte** is assassinated in Jerusalem.

1978 Egyptian President **Anwar al Sadat** and Israeli Prime Minister **Menachem Begin** sign documents providing machinery for peaceful relations, thus fulfilling purpose of Middle East summit at Camp David supported by U.S. President **Jimmy Carter.**

1980 **General Anastasio Somoza Debayle,** former president of Nicaragua, is assassinated in Paraguay.

September 18

Birthdates

1709   **Samuel Johnson,** English author, critic, essayist, lexicographer; one of the great figures of English literature; renowned for his learned works, among which were the *Dictionary of the English Language*, 1755, and the *Lives of the Poets*, 1779–81. [d. December 13, 1784]

1765   **Gregory XVI,** pope 1831–46. [d. June 1, 1846]

1779   **Joseph Story,** U.S. jurist, legal writer; Associate Justice, U.S. Supreme Court, 1811–45; noted for his opinions on **patent law.** [d. September 10, 1845]

1786   **Christian VIII,** King of Denmark, 1839–48. [d. January 20, 1848]

1819   **Jean Bernard Léon Foucault,** French physicist; developed the **Foucault pendulum,** which visually demonstrated the rotation of the earth; invented the **gyroscope.** [d. February 11, 1868]

1857   **John Hessin Clarke,** U.S. jurist; associate justice of U.S. Supreme Court, 1916–22; noted for his liberal interpretations of the Constitution. [d. March 22, 1945]

1883   **Elmer Henry Maytag,** U.S. manufacturer; developer of the modern **washing machine;** founder, president, and chairman of the board of the Maytag Co., 1926–40. [d. July 20, 1940]

1886   **Powel Crosley, Jr.,** U.S. industrialist; developed radio **vacuum tube socket;** established Crosley Corporation, 1921. [d. March 28, 1961]

1895   **John George Diefenbaker,** Canadian lawyer, political leader; Prime Minister of Canada, 1957–63. [d. August 16, 1979]

1901   **Harold Clurman,** U.S. director, critic; founded **Group Theater,** which introduced the **Stanislavsky Method** of acting; discovered Lee Strasberg, Elia Kazan, John Garfield, Lee J. Cobb; first to produce plays by Clifford Odets, William Saroyan, and Irwin Shaw. [d. September 9, 1980]

1905   **Greta Garbo (Greta Lovisa Gustafsson),** born in Sweden, one of the most glamorous and popular stars in motion-picture history; has lived in seclusion since 1941.

Eddie (*Rochester*) Anderson, U.S. character actor, best known for his role as Jack Benny's butler on radio and television, 1953–65. [d. February 28, 1977]

Claudette Colbert (Lily Claudette Chauchoin), U.S. actress, born in France.

1907   **Edwin Mattison McMillan,** U.S. physicist; Nobel Prize in chemistry for work in **synthetic transuranic elements** (with Glenn T. Seaborg), 1951.

1916   **John J. Rhodes,** U.S. politician, lawyer; U.S. Congressman, 1952–81.

1918   **Derek Harold Richard Barton,** British organic chemist; Nobel Prize in chemistry for studies on **conformation analysis** (with O. Hassel), 1969.

1919   **Pal Losonczi,** President, Hungarian People's Republic, 1967– .

Historical Events

1180   **Louis VII** of France, dies and is succeeded by his son **Philip II.**

1502   **Christopher Columbus** lands at **Costa Rica** on his fourth and last voyage to the New World.

1544   **Treaty of Crespy** between **Charles V** of Germany and **Francis I** of France is signed; France abandons claims to Naples.

1679   **New Hampshire** province is separated from Massachusetts.

1810   **Chile** gains independence from Spain.

Religious Calendar

The Saints

St. Ferreolus, martyr. Also called **Ferreol.** [d. c. 3rd cent.]

St. Methodius of Olympus, bishop and martyr. [d. c. 311]

St. Richardis, widow. [d. c. 895]

St. Joseph of Cupertino, Franciscan friar and ecstatic. [d. 1663]

The Beatified

Blessed John Massias, Dominican brother of Lima, Peru. Also called **Masias.** [d. 1645]

1873 **Panic of 1873,** financial depression caused partly by unbridled railroad speculation, causes widespread depression in U.S.

1900 Minneapolis holds first direct **primary election** in U.S.

1914 The Germans begin bombarding **Rheims,** France (**World War I**).

General von Hindenburg is named Commander in Chief of the German armies on the Eastern Front (**World War I**).

1917 **Ukulele** is patented by the Honolulu Ad Club.

1922 Hungary is admitted to the League of Nations.

1931 **Mukden Incident,** a bomb explosion damaging part of the South Manchurian railroad, provides a pretext for military action by the Japanese in **Manchuria**.

1934 The **U.S.S.R.** joins the League of Nations.

1950 General **Omar N. Bradley,** Chairman of the U.S. Joint Chiefs of Staff, is promoted to the rank of 5-Star General of the Army.

1961 U.N. Secretary-General **Dag Hammarskjöld** and 12 others are killed when their plane crashes in Northern Rhodesia.

1975 Fugitive **Patricia Hearst** is arrested in San Francisco after spending more than six months with the **Symbionese Liberation Army.**

September 19

Holidays

Chile   Armed Forces Day

Religious Calendar

The Saints

St. Januarius, Bishop of Benevento, and his Companions, martyrs. Januarius is patron of Naples. Januarius also called **Gennaro.** [d. c. 305] Optional Memorial.

Birthdates

1551   **Henry III,** King of France, 1574–89; last king of the **House of Valois.** [d. August 2, 1589]

1802   **Lajos Kossuth,** Hungarian statesman, patriot; President of Hungary, 1848–49; imprisoned in Turkey, 1849–51; lived in exile in U.S. and England, 1851–94. [d. March 20, 1894]

1851   **William Hesketh Lever, 1st Viscount Leverhulme,** British manufacturer; founded Lever Brothers, Inc., a soap manufacturer; established Port Sunlight, a model community for Lever Brothers employees. [d. May 7, 1925]

1867   **Arthur Rackham,** British artist; renowned for his book illustrations, especially for Grimm's *Fairy Tales.* [d. September 6, 1939]

1894   **Rachel (Lyman) Field,** U.S. author of New England novels and children's books: *Hitty, Her First Hundred Years, Time Out of Mind, All This and Heaven Too, And Now Tomorrow.* [d. March 15, 1942]

1895   **J(oseph) B(anks) Rhine,** U.S. psychologist; pioneer in research on **extrasensory perception** and **psychic phenomena;** author of *New Frontiers of the Mind,* 1937. [d. February 20, 1980]

1904   **Bergen Evans,** U.S. grammarian, educator, critic; author, with his sister, Cornelia, of *Dictionary of Contemporary American Usage,* 1957. [d. February 4, 1978]

1905   **Leon Jaworski,** U.S. lawyer; Watergate Special Prosecutor, 1973–74. [d. December 9, 1982]

1907   **Lewis F. Powell, Jr.,** U.S. jurist, lawyer; Associate Justice, U.S. Supreme Court, 1972– .

1911   **William (Gerald) Golding,** British novelist; author of *Lord of the Flies,* 1954; Nobel Prize in Literature, 1984.

1912   **(Elbert) Clifton Daniel, Jr.,** U.S. journalist, foreign correspondent; editor, *The New York Times,* 1964– ; married to Margaret Truman, daughter of former U.S. President Harry S. Truman.

1914   **Rogers C. B. Morton,** U.S. politician; U.S. Congressman, 1962–71; U.S. Secretary of the Interior, 1971–75; U.S. Secretary of Commerce, 1975–76. [d. April 19, 1979]

1915   **Oscar Handlin,** U.S. historian; Pulitzer Prize in history, 1952.

1927   **Harold Brown,** U.S. government official; President, California Institute of Technology, 1969–77; U.S. Secretary of Defense, 1977–81.

1932   **Mike Royko,** U.S. journalist; Pulitzer Prize in commentary, 1972.

1936   **Al Oerter,** U.S. discus thrower; gold medalist, four consecutive Olympics, 1956–68.

1940   **Paul Williams,** U.S. singer, composer.

1941   **Cass Elliott,** U.S. singer; member of *The Mamas and the Papas.* [d. July 29, 1974]

1945   **Jane Blalock,** U.S. professional golfer.

1949   **Twiggy (Leslie Hornby),** British model, actress, and singer.

Historical Events

1370   **Black Prince of England** sacks **Limoges, France (Hundred Years' War).**

1783   First balloon to carry a cargo (a sheep, a duck, and a rooster) makes its ascent in France.

1881   U.S. President **James Garfield** dies two months after being shot; Vice-President **Chester A. Arthur** becomes president.

St. Peleus and his Companions, martyrs. [d. 310]

St. Sequanus, abbot. Also called **Seine.** [d. c. 580]

St. Goericus, Bishop of Metz. Also called **Abbo.** [d. 647]

St. Theodore, Archbishop of Canterbury. First bishop of all England. [d. 690]

St. Mary of Cerevellon, virgin. [d. 1290]

SS. Theodore, David, and Constantine. Theodore also called *the Black.* [d. 1299, 1321]

St. Emily de Rodat, virgin and foundress of the Congregation of the Holy Family of Villefranche. Also called **Emilie.** [d. 1852]

The Beatified

Blessed Alphonsus de Orozco, Augustinian friar. Also called **Alonso.** [d. 1591]

1914   **Reims Cathedral** is badly damaged by German bombardment (**World War I**).

1928   The cartoon character later to be known as **Mickey Mouse** is introduced in a **Walt Disney** animated feature called *Steamboat Willie.*

1955   Argentine President **Juan Perón** resigns and goes into exile after his government is overthrown.

1957   First underground **atomic explosion** is set off near Las Vegas, Nevada.

       U.S. **bathyscaphe** *Trieste* reaches record depth of 3,200 meters in Mediterranean.

1961   **Jamaica** votes to secede from the West Indies Federation.

1973   **India** and **Pakistan** begin an exchange of the more than 250,000 persons isolated by the 1971 war.

September 20

Birthdates

1737   **Charles Carroll,** American Revolutionary leader; member of Continental Congress, 1776–78; signer of Declaration of Independence; U.S. Senator, 1789–92. [d. November 14, 1832]

1833   **David Ross Locke (*Petroleum V. Nasby*),** U.S. political satirist, journalist; creator of the **Nasby letters** which maintained a running attack on slavery, the Democratic Party, etc.; his work was favored by President Abraham Lincoln. [d. February 15, 1888]

       Ernesto T. Moneta, Italian journalist; Nobel Peace Prize for his activities fostering disarmament and international arbitration, 1907. [d. February 10, 1918]

1842   **Sir James Dewar,** Scottish physicist, chemist; first to produce liquid hydrogen, 1898; invented the **Dewar vessel,** a forerunner of the **vacuum bottle;** with Frederick A. Abel invented the explosive, **cordite.** [d. March 27, 1923]

1849   **George Bird Grinnel,** U.S. naturalist, author; editor of *Forest and Stream*, a leading journal of natural history and conservation, 1880–1911; a founder of the **Audubon Society;** responsible, in large part, for the establishment of **Glacier National Park,** 1910. [d. April 11 1938]

1878   **Upton (Beall) Sinclair,** U.S. novelist, politician; author of *The Jungle* and other novels aimed at social reform; instrumental in establishment of **American Civil Liberties Union** in California. [d. November 25, 1968]

1884   **Maxwell (Evarts) Perkins,** U.S. editor; as editor for Charles Scribner's Sons (1910–47), edited and promoted the work of F. Scott Fitzgerald, Ernest Hemingway, and Thomas Wolfe. [d. June 17, 1947]

1885   **Jellyroll Morton (Ferdinand Morton),** U.S. jazz musician, composer; noted as a pioneer in **ragtime music** and one of the great innovators in **jazz** in the U.S. [d. July 10, 1941]

1886   **Sister Elizabeth Kenny,** Australian nurse; developed method of treating **infantile paralysis.** [d. 1952]

1934   **Sophia Loren (Sophia Scicoloni),** Italian actress.

1936   **Sam Church, Jr.,** U.S. labor leader; head of United Mine Workers, 1979– .

Historical Events

622   **Muhammad** arrives at **Yathrib (Medina)** after completing his flight ("hegira") from Mecca. This year marks the beginning of the Muhammadan era.

1066   **Harald Haardraade, King of Norway** and **Tostig, Earl of Northumbria,** defeat troops loyal to **Harold II** of Engand at **Fulford.**

1697   **Treaty of Ryswyck** between France, Holland, England, and Spain is signed; Spain cedes some of West Indies possessions to France; this constitutes end of 11-year **War of the League of Augsburg.**

1819   **Carlsbad Decrees** to check revolutionary and liberal movements in Germany are enacted in reaction to the murder of **August von Kotzebue,** reactionary journalist, by university student **Karl Ludwig Sand.**

1850   **Compromise of 1850** becomes law as U.S. Congress passes resolution abolishing the **slave trade** in Washington, D.C.

1862   The Russian monarchy celebrates the 1,000th anniversary of its founding at **Novgorod.**

SS. Eustace and his companions, martyrs. St. Eustace patron of hunters. Invoked against fires and for protection from hell. St. Eustace also called **Eustachius, Eustasius, Eustathius,** or **Eustochius.** [death date unknown]

Blessed Francis de Posadas, Dominican priest. [d. 1713]

1927   Rightist **National Revolutionary Government** is formed by **Chiang Kai-shek** at Nanking, marking the end of the warlord era of Chinese history.

1949   Government of the **Federal Republic of Germany** is established.

1973   **Billie Jean King** defeats **Bobby Riggs,** 6–4, 6–3, 6–3, in a $100,000 tennis match in Houston, Texas, billed as the *Battle of the Sexes.*

1974   **Hurricane Fifi** strikes **Honduras,** killing thousands and leaving millions of dollars worth of devastation in its wake.

1976   Social Democratic Party of **Sweden** is narrowly defeated in parliamentary elections after more than 40 years in power.

1977   **Vietnam** and **Djibouti** are admitted to the UN.

1979   Central African **Emperor Bokassa I** is deposed by former president **David Dacko,** who returns the country to the status of a republic.

September 21

Belize   **Independence Day**
Commemorates the achievement of independence from England, 1981.

Religious Calendar

Feasts

St. Matthew, apostle and evangelist. Patron of bankers, tax collectors, and customs officers. Probably

Birthdates

1415   **Frederick III,** Holy Roman Emperor, 1452–93; laid the foundations for the greatness of the Habsburgs. [d. August 19, 1493]

1452   **Girolamo Savonarola,** Italian reformer, member of Dominican order; drove Pietro de' Medici from power; dictatorial leader of Florence, 1494–97; excommunicated, tried for sedition and heresy; tortured and burned. [d. May 23, 1498]

1645   **Louis Joliet,** French-Canadian explorer; with Father Jacques Marquette, explored the northern portions of the Mississippi River between the Fox River confluence and the Arkansas River, 1673; explored Hudson Bay and Labrador coast; appointed Royal Hydrographer of New France, 1697. [d. May 1700]

1708   **Prince Dimitrie Cantemir,** Russian author, diplomat; Prince of Moldavia, 1710–11; joined with Peter the Great in war against Turks. [d. April 11, 1744]

1722   **John Home,** Scottish dramatist, clergyman; Minister at Athelstaneford, 1747–57; secretary to Prime Minister John Stuart, 3rd Earl of Bute, 1762; tutor to the Prince of Wales. [d. September 5, 1808]

1737   **Francis Hopkinson,** U.S. public official, judge, author; member of the Continental Congress; signer of the Declaration of Independence; known for his political satire; one of the designers of first U.S. flag. [d. May 9, 1791]

1756   **John Loudon McAdam,** Scottish engineer; developed process for building roads of crushed stone, called **macadamized roads.** [d. November 26, 1836]

1792   **Johann Peter Eckermann,** German writer; friend and literary assistant to **Goethe;**

helped him prepare final editions of his work. [d. December 3, 1854]

1832   **Louis Paul Cailletet,** French physicist; credited with discovery of process for liquefying oxygen, nitrogen, etc., 1877–78. [d. January 5, 1913]

1849   **Sir Edmund William Gosse,** British poet, critic, and biographer; noted for his literary criticism and introduction of Scandinavian literature to the English reading public; on staff of British Museum, 1865–75; librarian to House of Lords, 1904–14. [d. May 16, 1928]

1853   **Heike Kamerlingh-Onnes,** Dutch physicist; Nobel Prize in physics for experiments in properties of matter at low temperatures, 1913. [d. February 21, 1926]

1866   **H(erbert) G(eorge) Wells,** British writer; renowned for his science fiction writings, which combined scientific kowledge, bold imagination, and high adventure. Among his works are *The Time Machine, The War of the Worlds,* and *Outline of History.* [d. August 13, 1946]

Charles J. H. Nicolle, French bacteriologist; Nobel Prize in physiology or medicine for discovery that typhus is transmitted by the body louse, 1928. [d. February 28, 1936]

1867   **Henry Lewis Stimson,** U.S. government official; U.S. Secretary of War, 1911–13, 1940–45; made final recommendation to President Harry Truman to drop the **atomic bomb** on Japan. [d. October 20, 1950]

1874   **Gustav Theodore Holst,** British composer, teacher; best known for his orchestral suite, *The Planets.* [d. May 25, 1934]

1895   **Juan de la Cierva,** Spanish aeronautical engineer; inventor of the **autogiro** aircraft;

originally called **Levi.** [d. 1st cent.] [major holy day, Episcopal Church; minor festival, Lutheran Church]

The Saints

St. Maura of Troyes, virgin. [d. c. 850]

St. Michael of Chernigov and **St. Theodore,** martyrs. [d. 1246]

The Beatified

Blessed Laurence Imbert and his companions, the **Martyrs of Korea.** [d. 1839]

---

killed in an airplane accident. [d. December 9, 1936]

1902 **Sir Allen Lane (Williams),** British publisher; founder of Penguin Books, Ltd., the first paperback book publisher in England. [d. July 7, 1970]

1909 **Kwame Nkrumah,** Ghanaian politician, President; the first man to lead an African nation to independence from colonial rule. [d. April 27, 1972]

1921 **Robert David Muldoon,** Prime Minister of New Zealand, 1975– .

1926 **Donald Arthur Glaser,** U.S. physicist; Nobel Prize in physics for invention of **bubble chamber** for studying subatomic particles, 1960.

1930 **Tore Lokoloko,** Governor-General, Papua New Guinea, 1977– .

1944 **(William) Hamilton Jordan,** U.S. government official; campaign director for U.S. President Jimmy Carter, 1975–76; assistant to the President, 1977–81; White House Chief of Staff, 1979–81.

1947 **Stephen King,** U.S. novelist; author of *Carrie*, *The Shining*, and other horror stories, many of which have become films achieving considerable box-office success.

Historical Events

1435 **Peace of Arras** is formalized between **Charles VII** of France and **Philip** of Burgundy who obtains Macon, Auxerre, and part of Picardy.

1870 Italian army invades Rome following withdrawal of French troops; the **unification of the Kingdom of Italy** under Victor Emmanuel II is completed.

1914 German troops in New Guinea surrender to the Australians (**World War I**).

1915 **Stonehenge,** prehistoric British landmark, is sold by auction to C. H. E. Chubb of Salisbury, England, for the equivalent of $6,600.

1930 Great Britain abandons the **gold standard.**

1938 Devastating hurricane hits **New England,** causing widespread destruction and loss of nearly 500 lives.

1944 Aircraft from 12 U.S. carriers attack Japanese shipping and airfield on **Luzon, Philippines** (**World War II**).

1957 **Haakon VII** of Norway dies and is succeeded by **Olaf V.**

1964 **Malta** becomes an independent nation within the British Commonwealth.

1965 **The Gambia,** the **Maldive Islands,** and **Singapore** are admitted to the UN.

1972 **Philippines** are placed under martial law by President Ferdinand Marcos.

1976 Former Chilean cabinet minister, **Orlando Letelier,** is killed in Washington, D.C., by a bomb placed in his car.

1978 **Nigeria** lifts a ban on political parties which had been in effect since 1966.

1981 **Belize** (formerly **British Honduras**) becomes fully independent from Great Britain.

September 22

Holidays

Haiti	**National Sovereignty Day**
Republic of Mali	**National Holiday** Celebrates Mali's independence from France, 1960.
U.S.	**Hobbit Day** Sponsored by American Tolkien Society, Union Lake, Michigan.

Birthdates

1606 **Richard Busby,** English scholar, grammarian; headmaster of Westminster School, 1638–95, numbering Dryden, South, Locke, and others among his students. [d. April 6, 1695]

1694 **Philip Dormer Stanhope, 4th Earl of Chesterfield (Lord Chesterfield),** English author; famous for his advice to his natural son, Philip, regarding the manners and standards of a man of the world. [d. March 24, 1773]

1791 **Michael Faraday,** English physicist, chemist; noted for his discovery of **benzene** and **carbon chloride;** did extensive research in field of **electricity** and **electromagnetism;** published numerous pioneering papers which led to the practical use of electricity. [d. August 25, 1867]

1882 **Wilhelm Keitel,** German Army Field Marshal; commanded German troops at Russian front during World War II; tried and executed as a war criminal, 1946. [d. October 16, 1946]

1885 **Erich von Stroheim,** U.S. film director, born in Austria. [d. May 2, 1957]

1895 **Paul Muni,** U.S. actor, born in Austria. [d. August 25, 1967]

1901 **Charles Brenton Huggins,** U.S. surgeon, born in Canada; Nobel Prize in physiology or medicine for discovering hormonal treatment of prostate cancer, 1966.

1902 **John Houseman (Jacques Haussman),** U.S. actor, producer, director, born in Romania.

1922 **Chen Ning Yang,** U.S. physicist, born in China; Nobel Prize in physics for discovery of **parity conservation** law in physics (with T. D. Lee), 1957.

Historical Events

1499 Swiss independence is acknowledged in fact by Holy Roman Emperor Maximilian I with the signing of the **Treaty of Basel.**

1586 **Sir Philip Sidney** is mortally wounded at the **Battle of Zutphen.**

1776 American patriot and spy **Nathan Hale** is executed by the British. Before he is hanged he issues his famous statement, "I only regret that I have but one life to lose for my country." (**American Revolution**)

1792 **French Republic** is proclaimed (**French Revolution**).

1862 U.S. President **Abraham Lincoln** declares all slaves in rebellious states to be free as of January 1, 1863.

1914 A German U-boat sinks the English cruisers *Hogue, Cressy,* and *Aboukir* in the North Sea (**World War I**).

 First Battle of Picardy opens in another Allied attempt to dislodge the Germans along the Western Front (**World War I**).

1915 **Second Battle of Champagne** opens with one of the heaviest artillery bombardments of World War I preceding the French attack.

1940 Japanese attack French forces in Vietnam and bomb **Haiphong** (**World War II**).

1960 **Sudanese Republic** renames itself the **Republic of Mali** as it gains independence from France.

1961 **Peace Corps** becomes permanent agency of U.S. government.

 Antonio Abertondo, of Argentina, makes first two-way, nonstop swim of the **English Channel** (43 hours, 5 minutes).

1969 San Francisco Giant outfielder **Willie Mays** becomes the second player (the other, **Babe Ruth**) to hit 600 career home runs.

Religious Calendar

The Saints

SS. Maurice and his companions, martyrs of the Theban Legion. Maurice is patron of infantrymen, weavers, and sword-makers. Invoked against gout. [d. c. 287]

St. Felix III (IV), pope. Elected 526. [d. 530]

St. Laudus, Bishop of Coutances. Also called **Lo.** [d. 6th century]

St. Salaberga, matron, and **St. Bodo,** bishop. [d. c. 665 and c. 670]

St. Emmeramus, bishop. Also called **Emmeram, Emmeran,** or **Haimhrammus.** [d. 7th cent.]

St. Thomas of Villanova, Archbishop of Valencia. Also called **Thomas of Villanueva.** [d. 1555]

St. Phocas, martyr; patron of sailors. [death date unknown]

1975 U.S. President **Gerald Ford** is the target of an attempted assassination by **Sara Jane Moore,** California radical. He is not hurt.

1980 War breaks out between **Iran** and **Iraq.**

September 23

Birthdates

63 B.C. **Julius Caesar Octavianus Augustus (Octavian),** first Roman Emperor, 27 B.C.–A.D. 14; adopted son and heir to Julius Caesar; his reign was known as the **Augustan Age** and was marked by the flowering of Roman literature, art, and imperial administration. [d. August 19, A.D. 14]

1713 **Ferdinand VI,** King of Spain, 1746–59; supported economic and military reforms. [d. August 10, 1759]

1728 **Mercy Otis Warren,** U.S. playwright, historian; noted for her chronicles of the American Revolution; wrote a three-volume history of the Revolution, *A History of the Rise, Progress, and Fermentation of the American Revolution.* [d. October 19, 1814]

1738 **Moses Brown,** U.S. manufacturer; perfected the first **water mill** in America. [d. September 7, 1836]

1745 **John Sevier,** U.S. frontiersman, soldier, public official; member of North Carolina legislature, 1789–90; first governor of Tennessee, serving from 1796–1801; U.S. Congressman, 1811–15. [d. September 24, 1815]

1800 **William Holmes McGuffey,** U.S. educator, author; noted for his development of the *Eclectic Reader* which was destined to become one of the most influential early textbooks in America. [d. May 4, 1873]

1819 **Armand Fizeau,** French physicist; first to successfully measure speed of light without using astronomical calculations. [d. September 18, 1896]

1829 **George Crook,** U.S. soldier, Indian fighter; fought in U.S. Civil War, distinguishing himself at **Battle of Chickamauga**; led American troops in conflicts with Indians in Idaho and Arizona; responsible for capturing **Geronimo** and placing him and his tribe on their Arizona reservation. [d. March 21, 1890]

1838 **Victoria Woodhull,** U.S. social reformer, radical; with the support of **Cornelius Vanderbilt,** established herself in the forefront of the women's liberation movement in the U.S.; responsible for the libelous accusations against **Henry Ward Beecher** which brought him to trial on charges of adultery; was first female candidate for U.S. presidency, running on Equal Rights Party ticket, 1872. [d. June 10, 1927]

1852 **William Stewart Halsted,** U.S. surgeon; discovered anesthetic properties of **cocaine;** performed the first **blood transfusion** in the U.S.; established the first school of surgery in the U.S. at **Johns Hopkins University,** 1890; contributed extensively to development of surgical procedures. [d. September 7, 1922]

1867 **John Avery Lomax,** U.S. folklorist; made significant contributions to the study of **folk music;** first curator of Archives of American Folk Song in Library of Congress. [d. January 26, 1948]

1880 **Lord John Boyd-Orr of Brechin Mearns,** British nutritionist; Nobel Peace Prize for his work on diet, nutrition, and world food supply, 1949. [d. June 25, 1971]

1884 **Adna Romanza Chaffee, Jr.,** U.S. Army officer; saw action in U.S. Civil War, Spanish American War; chief of staff of military government in Cuba, 1898–1900; led U.S. contingent of relief expedition to China to quell Boxer Rebellion; commander of U.S. forces in the Philippines, 1901–02; Chief of Staff of U.S. Army, 1904–06. [d. August 22, 1941]

1889 **Walter Lippmann,** U.S. journalist, editor; noted for his penetrating political criticism; through his syndicated news column, became a prime source of political and social analysis between 1931 and 1962,

St. Linus, pope and martyr. First successor of St. Peter. Feast suppressed in 1969. [d. c. 79]

St. Adamnan, Abbot of Iona. Also called **Adomnan, Eunan.** [d. 704]

The Beatified

Blessed Mark of Modena, Franciscan prior. [d. 1498]

Blessed Helen of Bologna, widow. [d. 1520]

---

being syndicated in more than 200 newspapers worldwide. [d. December 24, 1974]

1898   **Walter Pidgeon,** Canadian actor. [d. September 25, 1984]

1899   **Thomas Campbell Clark,** U.S. jurist; Associate Justice, U.S. Supreme Court, 1949–67; U.S. Attorney General, 1945–49; father of Ramsey Clark. [d. June 13, 1977]

1916   **Aldo Moro,** Italian statesman; Prime Minister of Italy, 1963–68, 1974–76; kidnapped and killed by Red Brigade leftist terrorists. [d. May 9, 1978]

1920   **Mickey Rooney (Joe Yule, Jr.),** U.S. actor.

1930   **Ray Charles (Ray Charles Robinson),** U.S. singer, composer; widely regarded for his jazz, pop, and country music.

1938   **Romy Schneider,** Austrian actress. [d. May 29, 1982]

1949   **Bruce Springsteen,** U.S. rock singer, songwriter, musician.

Historical Events

1122   Holy Roman Emperor **Henry V** renounces right of investiture in the **Concordat of Worms.**

1719   **Liechtenstein** becomes independent principality within the Holy Roman Empire.

1780   British agent **Major John André** is captured bearing incriminating papers near Tarrytown, N.Y. (**American Revolution**).

1862   **Otto von Bismarck** becomes Premier of Prussia.

1926   **Gene Tunney** wins world heavyweight boxing title from **Jack Dempsey.**

1932   The Kingdom of Hijaz and Nejd is renamed **Saudi Arabia.**

1952   **Rocky Marciano** gains world heavyweight boxing title by knocking out **Jersey Joe Walcott.**

1973   **Juan Perón** and his wife Isabel are elected President and Vice-President of Argentina.

September 24

Holidays

Dominican Republic and Peru   **Feast of Our Lady Mary**

Ghana   **Third Republic Day**
Recognizes the coming to power of Flight Lieutenant Jerry Rawlings, 1981.

Guinea-Bissau   **Establishment of the Republic**
Commemorates independence from Portugal and creation of the Republic, 1974.

Birthdates

1501   **Girolamo Cardano,** Italian mathematician, physician; noted for his development of **algebraic solutions.** [d. 1576]

1583   **Albrecht Eusebius Wenzel von Wollenstein,** Duke of Friedland and Mecklenburg, Prince of Sagan, Austrian general; led Austrian forces during Thirty Years' War 1625–30, 1632–34; subject of jealousy of the princes of the empire; assassinated. [d. February 25, 1634]

1625   **Jan De Witt,** Dutch statesman; led Dutch in war against England, 1665–67; concluded Triple Alliance with Sweden and England against France, 1668. Upon invasion of the United Provinces by France, was forced to resign position as Grand Pensionary; killed by a rioting mob. [d. August 20, 1672]

1717   **Horace Walpole, 4th Earl of Orford,** English novelist, letter-writer; wrote thousands of letters describing Georgian England, 1732–97; his fictional works were forerunners of the **supernatural romance.** [d. March 2, 1797]

1755   **John Marshall,** U.S. jurist; U.S. Secretary of State, 1800–01; Chief Justice, U.S. Supreme Court, 1801–35; established the Supreme Court's precedent for **judicial review** of statutes not in conformity with the Constitution; established practice of allowing only one opinion to be presented by the court, thus keeping dissension from the public view; primarily responsible for establishing unity of the federal court system in the U.S. [d. July 6, 1835]

1834   **Marcus Alonzo Hanna,** U.S. merchant, politician; backed William McKinley's successful bid for U.S. presidency; U.S. Senator, 1897–1904. [d. February 15, 1904]

1884   **Ismet Inönü,** Turkish general, statesman; President 1938–1950. [d. December 25, 1973]

1895   **André F. Cournand,** U.S. physician; Nobel Prize in physiology or medicine for development of catheter that can be inserted into heart to diagnose circulatory problems (with D. W. Richards and W. Forssmann), 1956.

1896   **F(rancis) Scott Fitzgerald,** U.S. novelist, short-story writer. [d. December 21, 1940]

1898   **Howard Walter Florey, Baron Florey of Adelaide,** British pathologist, born in Australia; Nobel Prize in physiology or medicine for discovery of **penicillin** (with A. Fleming and E. B. Chain), 1945. [d. February 22, 1968]

1899   **Georges Frederic Doriot,** U.S. educator, businessman; professor of Industrial Management, Harvard Business School, 1929–66; Professor Emeritus, 1966– ; Director, American Research & Development Corporation 1946–72; Chairman of the Board, 1972– .

1905   **Severo Ochoa,** U.S. biochemist, born in Spain; Nobel Prize in physiology or medicine for synthesis of **RNA** and **DNA** (with A. Kornberg), 1959.

1911   **Konstantin Chernenko,** Russian politician; Soviet premier 1983– .

1930   **John (Watts) Young,** U.S. astronaut; on *Gemini 3*, *Gemini 10*, and *Apollo 10* flights.

1931   **Anthony Newley,** British actor, singer.

John M. G. Adams, Prime Minister, Barbados, 1976– .

New Caledonia	Territorial Day
Trinidad and Tobago	Republic Day
U.S.	Kids' Day
	Sponsored by Kiwanis International.

Religious Calendar

Our Lady of Ransom. Celebrates founding of Order for the Redemption of Captives in Spain in 13th century.

The Saints

St. Geremarus, abbot. Also called **Geremar, Germer.** [d. c. 658]

St. Gerard, Bishop of Csanad, martyr. Protomartyr of Venice. Also called **Gerard Sagredo.** [d. 1046]

St. Pacifico of San Severino, Friar Minor. [d. 1721]

The Beatified

Blessed Robert of Knaresborough, hermit. [d. c. 1218]

Blessed Antonius Gonzdez, one of the Martyrs of Nagasaki. [beatified 1981]

1932   **Svetlana Beriosova,** British ballerina, born in Lithuania; performed with Metropolitan Ballet, 1946–49; Sadler's Wells Theatre Ballet, 1949–52; Sadler's Wells Ballet (Royal Ballet), 1952– .

1936   **James (Maury) Henson,** U.S. puppeteer, television producer; creator of the **Muppets.**

Historical Events

787   **Second Council of Nicaea** convenes to limit the veneration of icons.

1326   **Queen Isabella** of England and **Roger Mortimer** rebel against **King Edward II**.

1834   **Dom Pedro** of Portugal dies and is succeeded by **Queen Maria da Gloria.**

1869   **Jay Gould** and **James Fisk** create a financial panic in the U.S. (by attempting unsuccessfully to corner the gold market) in what is subsequently referred to as **Black Friday.**

1916   The French conduct an air raid on the **Krupp Works** at Essen, Germany (**World War I**).

1957   U.S. President **Dwight D. Eisenhower** orders the National Guard to enforce court-ordered **racial integration** of schools in **Little Rock, Arkansas.**

1960   *U.S.S. Enterprise,* first U.S. atomic-powered aircraft carrier, is launched at Newport News, Virginia.

1968   **Swaziland** is admitted to the United Nations.

1969   The trial of the **Chicago Seven,** radical leaders accused of inciting riots during the 1968 Democratic National Convention, begins.

September 25

Holidays

Mozambique	**Mozambican Popular Liberation Forces Day** Celebrates the coming to power of the Front for Liberation of Mozambique, 1974.
Rwanda	**Kamarampaka Day**

Religious Calendar

The Saints

St. Ferminus, bishop and martyr. Also called **Firmin.** [d. c. 4th cent.]

Birthdates

1599 **Francesco Borromini,** Italian architect, sculptor; master of the baroque style. [d. August 3, 1667]

1711 **Ch'ien Lung,** 4th Manchu emperor. [d. February 7, 1799]

1725 **Nicholas Cugnot,** French engineer; designed and built the world's first **automobile**, a steam-driven vehicle, 1769. [d. October 2, 1804]

1744 **Frederick William II** of Prussia; responsible for significant territorial expansion of Prussia. [d. November 16, 1797]

1832 **William Le Baron Jenney,** U.S. civil engineer, architect; pioneer in steel skeletal construction with curtain-wall exteriors, which made possible the **skyscraper** form of architecture. [d. June 15, 1907]

1866 **Thomas Hunt Morgan,** U.S. geneticist; Nobel Prize in physiology or medicine for discoveries related to bone-marrow's production of red blood cells, 1933. [d. December 4, 1945]

1877 **Plutarco Elias Calles,** Mexican statesman; President of Mexico, 1924–28. [d. October 19, 1945]

1896 **Alessandro Pertini,** Italian statesman; President of Italy, 1978– .

1897 **William (Harrison) Faulkner,** U.S. author; noted for his novels about the American South; Nobel Prize in literature, 1949. [d. July 6, 1962]

1898 **Robert Brackman,** U.S. artist; widely recognized for his portraits of the rich and famous, such as the Rockefellers and Lindberghs. [d. July 16, 1980]

1902 **Elliott V(allance) Bell,** U.S. publisher, editor; editor and publisher, *Business Week*, 1950–67. [d. January 11, 1983]

1903 **Olive Ann Beech,** U.S. aircraft industry executive; assisted her husband, Walter H. Beech, in founding Beech Aircraft Company; served as President and Chief Executive Officer, 1950–68.

Mark Rothko, U.S. painter, born in Russia; a leader in school of Abstract Expressionism; committed suicide. [d. February 25, 1970]

1905 **Walter Wellesley (*Red*) Smith,** U.S. sports columnist. [d. January 15, 1982]

1906 **Dimitri Shostakovich,** Russian composer; his style and pro-Soviet political leanings made him a source of controversy. [d. August 9, 1975]

1909 **Florizel A. Glasspole,** Jamaican statesman; Governor-General of Jamaica, 1973– .

1911 **Eric (Eustace) Williams,** Prime Minister, Trinidad and Tobago, 1962–80. [d. March 29, 1981]

1922 **Hammer DeRoburt,** President, Republic of Nauru, 1978– .

1931 **Barbara Walters,** U.S. newscaster, interviewer.

1932 **Adolfo Suarez Gonzalez,** Spanish lawyer, political leader; Prime Minister and President of Council of Ministers, 1976–1982.

Glenn Gould, Canadian composer, musician; first North American musician invited to play in the Soviet Union; retired from highly successful concert career to concentrate on recording, which he consid-

St. Cadoc, abbot. Also called **Cadog, Catwg.** [d. c. 575]

St. Aunacharius, Bishop of Auxerre. Also called **Aunaire.** [d. 605]

St. Finbar, first bishop of Cork. Also called **Bairre, Barr, Barrocus, Barrus.** [d. c. 633]

St. Ceolfrid, Abbot of Wearmouth. Also called **Ceufroy.** [d. 716]

St. Albert, Patriarch of Jerusalem. [d. 1214]

St. Sergius of Radonezh, most beloved of all Russian saints. [d. 1292]

St. Vincent Strambi, Bishop of Macerata and Tolentino. [d. 1824]

The Beatified

Blessed Herman the Cripple. [d. 1054]

---

ered to be a distinct and even superior art form. [d. October 4, 1982]

1936   **Moussa Traore,** President, Republic of Mali, 1969– .

1944   **Michael Douglas,** U.S. actor and producer; son of Kirk Douglas.

Historical Events

1066   **Harold II** of England, defeats invading forces of Harald Haardraade of Norway and Tostig, Earl of Northumbria at **Stamford Bridge.**

1493   **Christopher Columbus** embarks on his second voyage of discovery to the New World.

1513   **Vasco Núñez de Balboa** crosses Isthmus of Panama and sights the **Pacific Ocean.**

1555   **Religious Peace of Augsburg** is signed, resolving bitter disputes between Protestants and Catholics in the German states.

1629   **Truce of Altmark** is signed by Sweden and Poland; Sweden obtains Livonia and parts of Prussia.

1780   Treason of **Benedict Arnold** is exposed; Arnold flees New York in British warship (**American Revolution**).

1846   Zachary Taylor's troops defeat the Mexicans at the **Battle of Monterey (Mexican War).**

1915   **Third Battle of Artois** begins as a British diversion to the **Battle of Champagne (World War I).**

1932   **Catalonia,** in Spain, is granted autonomy.

1943   Russians liberate **Smolensk (World War II).**

1956   First **transatlantic telephone cable** is put into service.

1962   **Sonny Liston** knocks out **Floyd Patterson** in first round of world heavyweight championship fight in Chicago.

1973   *Skylab 2* astronauts return to earth after 59½ days in orbit.

1977   The funeral of **Steven Biko,** a 30-year-old black leader who died in police custody on September 12, attracts unprecedented support for South African blacks.

September 26

Holidays

Yemen Arab   Anniversary of the Revolution
Republic   of 1962

Religious Calendar

The Saints

St. Colman of Lann Elo, abbot. Also called **Coarb of MacNisse, Colman Elo.** [d. 611]

St. Nilus of Rossano, abbot. Also called **Nil** or **Nilus the Younger.** [d. 1004]

St. John of Meda, layman. [d. c. 1159]

Birthdates

1774 **John Chapman (***Johnny Appleseed***),** U.S. farmer; reputed planter of apple orchards from the Allegheny Mountains of Pennsylvania to Indiana; stories of him usually have a legendary quality and tell of his numerous brave and generous acts. [d. March 1845]

1791 **(Jean Louis André) Theodore Gèricault,** French Romantic painter. [d. January 26, 1824]

1842 **George Frederick Baer,** U.S. lawyer, businessman; President, Philadelphia and Reading Railway Co. and Central Railroad Company; represented business interests in the U.S. which were shaken by the upstart labor movement. [d. April 26, 1914]

1862 **Arthur B(owen) Davies,** U.S. painter, printmaker, tapestry designer; member of the **Ashcan School**; led young American artists in a revolt against the conservatism and traditionalism of the National Academy. [d. October 24, 1928]

1870 **Christian X** of Denmark, acceded to throne 1912; symbolized nation's resistance to German occupation during World War II. [d. April 20, 1947]

1886 **Archibald Vivian Hill,** British physiologist; Nobel Prize in physiology or medicine for discoveries concerning the production of heat in muscles, 1922. [d. June 3, 1977]

1888 **T(homas) S(tearns) Eliot,** U.S.-born poet; noted for his original use of metrics and diction; responsible for a revolution in poetry; Nobel Prize in literature, 1948. [d. January 4, 1965]

James Frank Dobie, U.S. folklorist, educator; known for his expertise in and writing about the folklore of the Southwest; editor of publications of the Texas Folklore Society, 1922–42. [d. September 18, 1964]

1889 **Martin Heidegger,** German philosopher; chief existential philosopher of the 1920s and 1930s. [d. May 26, 1976]

1891 **Charles Munch,** French conductor; cofounder and conductor, Paris Philharmonic Orchestra, 1935–38; conductor, Boston Symphony Orchestra, 1949–62; conductor, Tanglewood Berkshire Music Center, 1951–62. [d. November 6, 1968]

1895 **George Raft (George Ranft),** U.S. actor; best known for gangster roles. [d. November 24, 1980]

1897 **Pope Paul VI** (born Giovanni Battista Montini), pope 1963–78; noted for his efforts toward social justice and church reunion. [d. August 6, 1978]

1898 **Richard Lockridge,** U.S. novelist, short-story writer; creator of the husband and wife detective team, **The Norths.** [d. June 19, 1982]

George Gershwin, U.S. composer; Pulitzer Prize, 1931, for *Of Thee I Sing*, the first musical to win the Pulitzer; wrote numerous scores for motion pictures. [d. July 11, 1937]

Historical Events

1687 The Venetian army bombards **Athens** and destroys the Parthenon and Propylaea.

1901 **Ashanti** is formally annexed by Great Britain and placed under the administration of the **Gold Coast Colony.**

1907 **New Zealand** becomes a dominion rather than a colony of Great Britain.

The Martyrs of North America. Commemorates 8 French Jesuit missionaries slain by Indians in North America. [d. 1642–49]

St. Francis of Camporosso, Capuchin laybrother. Feast formerly September 17. [d. 1866]

SS. Cosmas and Damian, martyrs; patrons of physicians, druggists, and midwives. Invoked for good health. Feast formerly September 27. [death dates unknown]

SS. Cyprian and Justina, martyrs. Cyprian also called **Cyprian the Magician** and **Cyprian of Antioch.** [death dates unknown]

The Beatified

Blessed Lucy of Caltagirone, virgin. [d. 13th century]

Blessed Dalmatius Moner, Friar, preacher. [d. 1341]

Blessed Teresa Couderc, virgin and co-foundress of the Congregation of Our Lady of the Retreat in the Cenacle. [d. 1885]

1918   **Battle of the Argonne,** the final Allied offensive of **World War I,** begins.

1919   U.S. President **Woodrow Wilson** is paralyzed by a stroke.

1950   **Seoul, Korea** falls to U.S. troops (**Korean War**).

1957   *West Side Story* by Leonard Bernstein premieres in New York.

1962   Algerian national assembly designates **Ahmed Ben Bella** to form the first regular government of **Algeria.**

1977   **Laker Airways** begins cheap trans-Atantic flights with its 345-seat DC-10 **Skytrain.**

September 27

Holidays

Ethiopia   Feast of the Finding of the True Cross

Religious Calendar

The Saints

St. Barry, hermit. Also called Barnic, or Barruc. [d. 6th century]

Birthdates

1601   **Louis XIII** of France, *the Just*; reigned during the **Thirty Years' War.** [d. May 14, 1643]

1627   **Jacques Bénigne Bossuet,** French bishop, historian, and orator; tutor to the Dauphin; renowned for his oratorical skills. [d. April 12, 1704]

1722   **Samuel Adams,** American Revolutionary patriot, statesman; helped instigate Stamp Act riots; leader of the Boston Tea Party; signer of the Declaration of Independence; member of Congress, 1776–81; Governor of Massachusetts, 1794–97. [d. October 2, 1803]

1772   **Sándor Kisfaludy,** Hungarian poet, the *Father of Lyric Poetry in Hungary.* [d. October 28, 1844]

1783   **Peter Joseph von Cornelius,** German painter; known as the *Founder of the German School of Painting.* [d. March 6, 1867]

        Agustin de Iturbide, Mexican soldier; Emperor of Mexico, 1822–23. [d. July 19, 1824]

1809   **Raphael Semmes,** Confederate naval commander; responsible for the destruction or capture of 64 Union ships; after the Civil War, he lectured and wrote several books based on his war experiences. [d. August 30, 1877]

1818   **Adolph Wilhelm Hermann Kolbe,** German organic chemist; responsible for development of methods of synthesizing organic compounds, especially **acetylsalicylic acid (aspirin),** 1859. [d. November 25, 1884]

1839   **Henry Phipps,** U.S. manufacturer, philanthropist; Director, U.S. Steel Corporation, 1901–30. [d. September 22, 1930]

1840   **Alfred Thayer Mahan,** U.S. admiral, naval historian, and theorist; author of numerous classic studies of naval history and strategy; his works influenced the direction of naval development in most major countries of the world prior to World War II. [d. December 1, 1914]

        Thomas Nast, U.S. cartoonist, illustrator, born in Germany; his pointed political cartoons led to the fall of the **Tweed Ring** in New York City's **Tammany Hall,** 1869–72; conceived the Democratic Party's donkey symbol and the Republicans' elephant. [d. December 7, 1902]

1855   **Joy Morton,** U.S. manufacturer; founder and president of the Morton Salt Company. [d. May 9, 1934]

1862   **Louis Botha,** South African statesman, soldier; Premier of Transvaal, 1907–10; first Prime Minister of Union of South Africa, 1910–19. [d. August 27, 1919]

1875   **Grazia Deledda,** Italian novelist; Nobel Prize in literature for sympathetic portrayal of Sardinian life, 1926. [d. August 16, 1936]

1898   **Vincent (Millie) Youmans,** U.S. composer; wrote *Tea for Two, Great Day.* [d. April 5, 1946]

1914   **(Sarah) Catherine Marshall,** U.S. nonfiction writer, editor; known for her biography of her husband, Peter Marshall, entitled *A Man Called Peter.* [d. March 18, 1983]

1917   **Louis Stanton Auchincloss,** U.S. novelist, short-story writer.

1918   **Sir Martin Ryle,** British radio astronomer; Nobel Prize in physics for developing revolutionary **radio telescope systems** (with Anthony Hewish), 1974.

1919   **Charles Harting Percy,** U.S. politician, business executive; President, Bell & Howell Co., 1949–61; U.S. Senator, 1967–84.

1922   **Arthur Penn,** U.S. director of plays and films such as *The Miracle Worker, Two for*

St. Elzear and **Blessed Delphina,** his wife. Elzear also called **Eleazar.** [d. 1323 and 1360]

St. Vincent de Paul, founder of the Congregation of the Mission (Vincentians, or Lazarists) and the Sisters of Charity. Patron of all charitable societies. Feast formery July 19. [d. 1660] Obligatory Memorial.

the Seesaw, Alice's Restaurant, and *Bonnie and Clyde.*

1924 **Bud Powell,** U.S. pianist, composer, and modern jazz pioneer. [d. August 1, 1966]

Historical Events

1825 The world's first public **railroad** to use locomotive traction opens in England between Stockton and Darlington.

1831 **British Association for the Advancement of Science** is formed.

1914 **First Battle of Artois** opens another Allied attempt to dislodge the Germans along the Western Front (**World War I**).

1939 **Warsaw** falls to invading Germans (**World War II**).

1940 German-Italian-Japanese pact is concluded at Berlin, providing for 10-year military and economic alliance (**World War II**).

1961 Former U.S. Vice-President **Richard Nixon** announces his candidacy for governorship of California.

Sierra Leone is admitted to the United Nations.

1964 **Warren Report** on the assassination of U.S. President **John F. Kennedy** is issued.

1969 South Vietnamese President Thieu states that the withdrawal of U.S. troops would take "years and years" because his country had "no ambition" to take over the fighting (**Vietnam War**).

September 28

Holidays

Taiwan	Birthday of Confucius
Minnesota	Frances Willard Day

Religious Calendar

The Saints

St. Exsuperius, Bishop of Toulouse. Also called **Exuperius.** [d. c. 412]

St. Eustochium, virgin. [d. c. 419]

St. Faustus, Bishop of Riez. [d. c. 493]

St. Machan, bishop. Also called **Manchan.** [d. 6th century]

Birthdates

1573 **Caravaggio,** Italian painter; founder of naturalistic school of Italian painting. [d. July 18, 1610]

1803 **Prosper Mérimée,** French man of letters; Senator, 1853–70; noted for his translations of Russian classics, which brought literature of Russia to the French; author of *Carmen.* [d. September 23, 1870]

1839 **Frances Willard,** U.S. reformer; organizer and first president of **World Woman's Christian Temperance Union,** 1883–98. [d. February 18, 1898]

1841 **Georges Clemenceau,** known as the *Tiger,* French statesman; member of Chamber of Deputies, 1876–93; Senator, 1902–06; Premier of France, 1906–09, 1917. [d. November 24, 1929]

1852 **Henri Moissan,** French chemist; Nobel Prize in chemistry for isolation of the element **fluorine** and the development of the **Moissan furnace,** 1906. [d. February 20, 1907]

1856 **Kate (Douglas) Wiggin,** U.S. educator, author; organized first free **kindergarten** in the Far West, 1898; author of *Rebecca of Sunnybrook Farm,* one of the best-selling books of the 20th century. [d. August 24, 1923]

1887 **Avery Brundage,** U.S. sports figure; President, U.S. Olympic Association, 1929–53; President, International Olympic Committee, 1952–72. [d. May 8, 1975]

1888 **Herman Cyril McNeile (Sapper),** British novelist; author of a series of crime and adventure novels featuring *Bulldog Drummond.* [d. August 14, 1937]

1892 **Elmer (Leopold) Rice,** U.S. playwright; author of *The Adding Machine, Street Scene,* for which he won the 1929 Pulitzer Prize in drama. [d. May 8, 1967]

1893 **Marshall Field III,** U.S. publisher, philanthropist; established the Chicago *Sun* (later the *Sun-Times*). [d. November 8, 1956]

1895 **Wallace Kirkman Harrison,** U.S. architect; partner in architecture firm Harrison and Abramovitz, 1941–78; designer of Rockefeller Center, 1930, United Nations Headquarters, 1947, and Metropolitan Opera House, Lincoln Center, New York, 1955, New York State Capitol, South Mall, Albany, New York. [d. December 2, 1981]

1901 **William S. Paley,** U.S. communications executive; founder of CBS, president 1928–1946, chairman 1946–83; trustee of Museum of Modern Art, 1937– ; chairman of board, 1972– .

1902 **Ed(ward Vincent) Sullivan,** U.S. journalist, TV host; Broadway gossip columnist, 1929–39; radio columnist, 1929–48; television emcee of CBS's *Toast of the Town* (later known as the *Ed Sullivan Show*); on his television show, introduced nearly every major show-business personality of the period. His program was on CBS for 23 years. [d. October 13, 1974]

1905 **L(ucius) Mendel Rivers,** U.S. Congressman, 1941–70.

Max Schmeling, German boxer; World Heavyweight Champion, 1930–32.

1909 **Al Capp,** U.S. cartoonist; creator of *Li'l Abner,* satirical comic strip set in Dogpatch, U.S.A., and featuring various hillbilly citi-

St. Annemund, Bishop of Lyons. Also called **Dalfinus.** [d. 658]

St. Lioba, virgin. Also called **Leoba, Liobgetha.** [d. 780]

St. Wenceslaus of Bohemia, martyr; patron of **Czechoslovakia.** Also called **Vaclav, Wenceslas,** or **Wenzel.** [d. 929] Optional Memorial.

The Beatified

Blessed Laurence of Ripafratta, Dominican friar. [d. 1457]

Blessed John of Dukla, Franciscan friar. [d. 1484]

Blessed Bernardino of Feltre, Franciscan friar. Also called **Bernardino Tomitani.** [d. 1494]

Blessed Francis of Calderola, Friar Minor. [d. 1507]

Blessed Simon de Rojas. [d. 1624]

---

zens whose lives were occasionally interjected with visits from famous political figures of the day. [d. November 5, 1979]

1913 **Alice Marble,** U.S. tennis player; U.S. singles champion, 1936, 1938–40; Wimbledon singles champion, 1939.

1915 **Ethel Rosenberg,** U.S. traitor; arrested and convicted with her husband, Julius (May 12) of passing secrets to the Russians; executed for espionage. [d. June 19, 1953]

1917 **Michael Somes,** British ballet dancer; principal of Sadler's Wells Ballet Co., 1938–63; director of Royal Ballet Co., 1963–70.

1924 **Marcello Mastroianni,** Italian actor; starred in *La Dolce Vita; Yesterday, Today, and Tomorrow.*

1934 **Brigitte Bardot,** French actress; sex symbol.

Historical Events

1066 **Norman Conquest** of England begins when **William of Normandy** lands at Pevensey.

1914 Germans lay siege to **Antwerp (World War I).**

1916 The British take the fortress of **Kut-el-Amara** from the Turks (**World War I**).

1918 **Battle of Ypres** begins (**World War I**).

1935 **Protestant Church** in Germany is placed under state control.

1941 **Ted Williams** of the Boston Red Sox finishes baseball season with .406 batting average.

1950 **Indonesia** is admitted to the United Nations.

1958 **Fifth Republic** is established in **France.**

1960 **Mali and Senegal** are admitted to the United Nations.

1971 **Joszef Cardinal Mindszenty** arrives at the Vatican after spending 15 years as a virtual prisoner of the state in the U.S. Embassy in Hungary.

1977 Cambodian leader **Pol Pot** is received in Peking by top Chinese leaders as the secretary of the Central Committee of the **Cambodian Communist Party,** whose existence had never been acknowledged before. The 17th anniversary of its founding was announced simultaneously by a Phnom Penh radio station.

September 29

Holidays

Brunei **Constitution Day**
Commemorates the
promulgation of the
constitution, 1959.

Paraguay **Battle of Boqueron Day**

Religious Calendar

Feasts

St. Michael and All the Angels. Commonly called
Michaelmas Day. Feast originated in the sixth century. [major holy day, Episcopal Church; minor festival, Lutheran Church]

Birthdates

1547 **Miguel de Cervantes (Saavedra),** Spanish novelist, dramatist, poet; nicknamed *The Handless One* because of injury to his left hand. Author of **Don Quixote,** the burlesque novel of a country lord and his squire and their chivalric misadventures. [d. April 23, 1616]

1640 **Antoine Coysevox,** French sculptor; noted for his sculptural decorations at Versailles and his busts of such prominent figures as King Louis XIV, Richelieu, Mazarin, and Condé. [d. October 10, 1720]

1703 **François Boucher,** French painter, tapestry and porcelain designer and engraver; a favorite of Madame Pompadour; known for his historical and pastoral painting. [d. May 30, 1770]

1725 **Robert Clive, Baron Clive of Plassey,** English administrator, soldier; obtained sovereignty over Bengal for East India Company; his governorship of India, 1758–59, was marked by corruption. Committed suicide after dishonorable return to Engand. [d. November 22, 1774]

1758 **Viscount Horatio Nelson,** British naval hero; won great victories in wars with Revolutionary and Napoleonic France; recognized for conspicuous bravery at **Battle of Cape St. Vincent,** 1797; defeated Danish fleet at Copenhagen; most famous for defeat of French fleet at **Trafalgar,** 1805. [d. October 21, 1805]

1838 **Henry Hobson Richardson,** U.S. architect, noted for his neo-Romanesque style; examples of his work are Trinity Church, Boston, and Harvard University Law School. [d. April 27, 1886]

1865 **Elizabeth Cleghorn Gaskell,** British novelist; wrote about life in the manufacturing cities of the English Midlands; biographer of Charlotte Brontë. [d. November 12, 1865]

1871 **Gerardo Machado y Morales,** Cuban patriot, president 1924–33. [d. March 29, 1939]
Emma Wold, U.S. lawyer, reformer; women's rights activist. [d. July 21, 1950]

1897 **Herbert (Sebastian) Agar,** U.S. journalist, author; Pulitzer Prize in history, 1933; after World War II, lived in London. [d. November 24, 1980]

1901 **Enrico Fermi,** U.S. physicist born in Italy; pioneer in research on **man-made nuclear chain reaction;** Nobel Prize in physics for work on **radioactive elements,** including artificial ones produced by neutron bombardment, 1938. [d. November 28, 1954]

1907 **(Orvon) Gene Autry,** U.S. actor, business executive; known as *The Singing Cowboy,* starred in over 80 Westerns, 1934–54.

1910 **Virginia Bruce,** U.S. actress of the 1930s.

1912 **Michelangelo Antonioni,** Italian film director, scriptwriter, noted for his surrealistic films such as *The Red Desert, Zambriskie Point, Blow Up.*

1913 **Stanley Kramer,** U.S. producer, director; noted for his production of such classics as *Death of a Salesman, High Noon,* and *The Caine Mutiny.*

1916 **Trevor (Wallace) Howard,** British actor.

The Saints

SS. Rhipsime, Gaiana, and their Companions, virgins and martyrs. Protomartyrs of the Armenian Church. Rhipsime also called **Arepsima,** [d. c. 312]

St. Theodata, martyr. [d. c. 318]

The Beatified

Blessed Richard of Hampole, hermit. Also called **Richard Rolle.** [d. 1349]

Blessed Charles of Blois. [d. 1364]

Blessed Guillelmus Courtet, Michael de Aozaraza, Vincentius Schiwozuka, Laurentius Ruiz and Lazarus de Kyoto, the Martyrs of Nagasaki. [beatified 1981]

1920	**Peter Mitchell,** British chemist; Nobel Prize in chemistry for study of energy reception of human cells, 1978.
1925	**John Goodwin Tower,** U.S. politician, political scientist; U.S. Senator, 1961– .
1927	**Paul N. McCloskey, Jr.,** U.S. politician, lawyer; U.S. Congressman, 1967– .
1933	**Samora Machel,** President, People's Republic of Mozambique, 1975– .
1935	**Jerry Lee Lewis,** U.S. musician; one of the early rock stars.
1943	**Lech Wałęsa,** Polish labor leader; founder of **Solidarity** union.
1956	**Sebastian Coe,** British distance runner.

Historical Events

1829	**Robert Peel** remodels London police, henceforth known as **bobbies.**
1833	**King Ferdinand VII** of Spain dies and his wife becomes regent for their infant daughter, **Isabella II.**
1868	**Queen Isabella II** of Spain flees to France in the wake of a revolution and is declared deposed.
1879	A proclamation of the British government declares the **Transvaal** in South Africa a British Territory.
1911	**Italy** declares war on Turkey over Tripoli and Cyrenaica.
1918	The British pierce the **Hindenburg Line** of German defense between Cambrai and St. Quentin in the final offensive of **World War I.**
1950	General Douglas MacArthur, on behalf of the UN command, hands over the city of **Seoul** to President Syngman Rhee of the Republic of **Korea.**
1964	Roman Catholic Church's Ecumenical Council approves admission of married men to the deaconate.
1972	**China** and **Japan** agree to end the legal state of war existing between them since 1937 and to establish diplomatic relations.
1978	**Pope John Paul I** dies after a reign of only 34 days.
1979	China condemns the **Cultural Revolution of 1966-69.**
	Equatorial Guinea executes deposed President **Macias Nquema** after a trial attended by international observers.

September 30

Birthdates

1714 **Etienne Bonnot de Condillac,** French philosopher; exponent of doctrine of **sensationalism.** [d. April 2, 1780]

1732 **Jacques Necker,** French financier, statesman, born in Switzerland; appointed Director of Finances, 1776; dismissed, 1781; supervised establishment of the States-General, 1788; exiled, 1790; father of Madame de Staël (April 22) [d. April 9, 1804].

1788 **Fitzroy James Henry Somerset Raglan, 1st Baron Raglan,** British Army field marshal; commander of British troops during Crimean War, 1853–55; responsible for loss of the **Light Brigade** at **Battle of Balaklava,** 1854. His name survives in the *raglan* sleeve, styled after the slit potato sacks his men were forced to wear. [d. June 28, 1855]

1861 **William Wrigley, Jr.,** U.S. manufacturer; founder of the Wrigley Chewing Gum Company, 1891. [d. January 26, 1932]

1870 **Jean Baptiste Perrin,** French physicist; Nobel Prize in physics for confirming the **atomic nature of matter** through studies of **Brownian movement,** 1926. [d. April 17, 1942]

1882 **(Johannes) Hans Wilhelm Geiger,** German physicist; invented the **Geiger counter,** the first device to successfully detect **radioactivity.** [d. September 24, 1945]

1905 **Sir Nevill Francis Mott,** British physicist; Nobel Prize in physics for advancement of **solid state circuitry** and basic theories of magnetism and conduction (with P. W. Anderson and J. H. Van Vleck), 1977.

1915 **Lester Maddox,** U.S. politician; Governor of Georgia, 1967–71; Lieutenant-Governor, 1971–75; American Independent Party candidate, 1976 U.S. Presidential election; avowed segregationist.

1917 **Park Chung Hee,** South Korean leader, military officer; President of South Korea, 1963–79; assassinated. [d. October 26, 1979]

1924 **Truman Capote,** U.S. novelist, short-story writer; author of *In Cold Blood.* [d. August 24, 1984]

1935 **Johnny Mathis,** U.S. singer.

1943 **(Joseph Lester) Jody Powell, Jr.,** U.S. government official; Press Secretary for President Jimmy Carter, 1977–81.

Historical Events

1174 **Treaty of Montlouis** between **Henry II** of England and **Louis VII** of France ends family conspiracy against Henry.

1399 **Henry IV** of England, son of **John of Gaunt,** succeeds to English throne after **Richard II** is deposed.

1877 First **U.S. swimming championship** is held on Harlem River, New York.

1918 **Bulgaria** signs armistice with Allies (**World War I**).

1927 **Leon Trotsky** is expelled from the executive body of the Communist International.

1935 *Porgy and Bess,* George Gershwin's folk opera, premieres in Boston.

1949 **Berlin air lift** ends its successful operation after 277,264 flights.

1954 First atomic powered submarine, *U.S.S. Nautilus,* is commissioned at Groton, Connecticut.

1958 Governor **Orval E. Faubus** of Arkansas defies Supreme Court ruling against **segregation** by closing four high schools in Little Rock.

1962 Black student **James H. Meredith** is escorted onto the formerly white-only campus of the University of Mississippi by deputy U.S. marshals.

1966 **Bechuanaland** gains its independence from Great Britain as the nation of **Botswana.**

Religious Calendar

The Saints

St. Gregory the Enlightener, bishop of Ashtishat. Also surnamed the *Apostle of Armenia* and the *Illuminator.* [d. c. 330]

St. Jerome, Doctor of the Church. One of greatest Biblical scholars; patron of students. [d. 420]

St. Honorius, Archbishop of Canterbury. [d. 653]

SS. Tancred, Torthred, and Tova, hermits and martyrs; venerated at Thorney. [d. 870]

St. Simon of Crèpy, royal monk. [d. 1082]

1974   Establishment of year-round **Daylight Saving Time** is rescinded; it was instituted on January 1 as an energy-saving measure.

1976   **California** becomes the first U.S. state to recognize the **right to die.**

October

October is the tenth month of the Gregorian calendar and has 31 days. The name is derived from the Latin *octo*, 'eight,' designating the position October held in the early Roman 10-month calendar. Following the adoption of January as the first month in the 12-month calendar (see also **September**), various attempts to rename the month in honor of celebrated Romans all met with failure.

October was a month of notable Roman festivals honoring Mars, the god of war. On the Ides of October, October 15, one ritual involved the *Equus October* 'October Horse,' consisting of a horse race after which one horse was sacrificed to Mars. On October 19 the *Armilustrium* involved a ritual purification of arms prior to their being put away for the winter; winter campaigning was virtually unknown in the ancient world.

In the New England region, the frost and snow flurries of the beginning of October came to be called "Squaw Winter," and the warm days that generally followed were known as "Indian Summer," expressions which remain in use in colder climes throughout the United States.

In the astrological calendar, October spans the zodiac signs of Libra, the Balance (September 23–October 22) and Scorpio, the Scorpion (October 23–November 21).

The birthstone for October is the opal or tourmaline, and the flower is the calendula or cosmos.

State, National, and International Holidays

All-Union Petroleum & Gas Workers' Day
(U.S.S.R.)
First Sunday

Teachers' Day
(U.S.S.R.)
First Sunday

Child Health Day
(United States)
First Monday

United Nations' Day
(Barbados)
First Monday

National Sports' Day
(Lesotho)
during First Week

Foundation of Workers' Party
(North Korea)
during First Week

All-Union Farm Workers' Day
(U.S.S.R.)
Second Sunday

Columbus Day
(most of the United States)
Second Monday
except:
(Maryland, Puerto Rico)
October 12

Fraternal Day
(Alabama)
Second Monday

Discoverers' Day
(Hawaii)
Second Monday

Farmers' Day
(Florida)
Second Monday

Pioneer's Day
(South Dakota)
Second Monday

Thanksgiving Day
(Canada)
Second Monday

Kruger Day
(South Africa)
during Second Week

Food Industry Workers' Day
(U.S.S.R.)
Third Sunday

Heroes' Day
(Jamaica)
Third Monday

Taiwan Restoration Day
(Taiwan)
Fourth Monday

Chulalongkorn's Day
(Thailand)
Fourth Monday

Independence Day
(Zambia)
Fourth Monday

Angam Day
(Nauru)
Fourth Wednesday

Special Events and Their Sponsors

National Apple Month
National Apple Month
P.O. Box 657
6707 Old Dominion Drive
McLean, Virginia 22101

National B'nai B'rith Month
B'nai B'rith International
1640 Rhode Island Avenue, N.W.
Washington, D.C. 20036

Country Music Month
Country Music Association
Nashville, Tennessee 37202

Episcopal School Month
National Association of Episcopal Schools
815 Second Avenue
New York, New York 10017

Lazy Eye Alert Month
American Society to Prevent Blindness
79 Madison Avenue
New York, New York 10016

Pizza Festival Time
Richard R. Falk Associates
1472 Broadway
New York, New York 10036

National Popcorn Month
The Popcorn Institute
One Illinois Center
111 East Wacker Drive
Chicago, Illinois 60601

National Pretzel Month
National Pretzel Bakers Institute
P.O. Box 1433
800 New Holland Avenue
Lancaster, Pennsylvania 17603

National Spinal Health Month
American Chiropractic Association
1916 Wilson Boulevard
Arlington, Virginia 22201

Vocational Service Month
Rotary International
1600 Ridge Avenue
Evanston, Illinois 60201

National Spinning and Weaving Week
First week
The Weaving and Spinning Council
4860 Riverbend Road
Suite 1
Boulder, Colorado 80301

National 4-H Week
Week of the First Sunday
Extension Service
U.S. Department of Agriculture
Washington, D.C. 20250

National Fire Prevention Week
Second Week
National Fire Protection Association
Batterymarch Park
Quincy, Massachusetts 02269

The National Exchange Club
3050 Central Avenue
Toledo, Ohio 43606

National Safety Council
444 Michigan Avenue
Chicago, Illinois 60611

International Letter Writing Week
Second Week
Franklin D. Roosevelt Philatelic Society
154 Laguna Court
St. Augustine Shores, Florida 32084

National Newspaper Week
Second Week
Newspaper Association Managers
c/o Phil Berkebile
Nebraska Press Association
723 Sharp Building
Lincoln, Nebraska 68508

National YWCA Teen Week
Second Week
National Board of the YWCA of the United States
4th Floor
135 West 50th Street
New York, New York 10020

National Vocation Awareness Week
Mid-Month
National Catholic Vocation Council
1307 South Wabash
Suite 350
Chicago, Illinois 60605

National Sunshine Week
Week of the Third Sunday
National Society for Shut-ins
P.O. Box 1392
Reading, Pennsylvania 19603

National Handicapped Awareness Week
Third Week
National Easter Seal Society
2023 West Ogden Avenue
Chicago, Illinois 60612

National Lupus Week
Third Week
American Lupus Society
23751 Madison Street
Torrance, California 90505

National Safety on the Streets Week
Fourth Week
National Safety Council
444 North Michigan Avenue
Chicago, Illinois 60611

National Cleaner Air Week
Final Full Week
Air Pollution Control League of Greater Cincinnati
18 East Fourth Street
Cincinnati, Ohio 45202

National Storytelling Festival
First Full Weekend
National Association for the Preservation
    and Perpetuation of Storytelling
Box 112
Jonesboro, Tennessee 37659

Eleanor Roosevelt Birthday Anniversary
October 11
Franklin D. Roosevelt Philatelic Society
154 Laguna Court
St. Augustine Shores, Florida 32084

National Poetry Day
October 15
National Poetry Day Committee, Inc., and
    World Poetry Day Committee, Inc.
Dr. Frances Clark Handler, International Director
1110 North Venetian Drive
Miami Beach, Florida 33139

Good Bears of the World Day
October 27
Good Bears of the World
Box 1940
Washington, D.C. 20013

Sweetest Day
Third Saturday

Boss's Day
Third Sunday

National Shut-in Day
Third Sunday
National Society for Shut-ins
P.O. Box 1392
Reading, Pennsylvania 19603

Mother-in-Law's Day
Fourth Sunday

Special Days--Other Calendars

	12 Rabi Al-Awal	Rosh Hashanah	Yom Kippur	Sukkoth	Shemini Atzereth	Simhath Torah
1985					October 7	October 8
1986		October 4	October 13	October 18	October 25	October 26
1987			October 3	October 8	October 15	October 16
1988	October 24				October 3	October 4
1989	October 14		October 9	October 14	October 21	October 22
1990	October 3			October 4	October 11	October 12

October 1

Holidays

Botswana	**Botswana Day** (continued) Continuation of the celebration of Botswana Day, September 30.
People's Republic of China	**National Day**
Korea	**Armed Forces Day**
Nigeria	**National Holiday** Celebrates Nigeria's achievement of independent status within the British Commonwealth, 1960, and establishment of the Republic, 1963.

Birthdates

1207 **Henry III** of England, 1216–72. [d. November 16, 1272]

1685 **Charles VI,** Holy Roman Emperor. [d. October 20, 1740]

1746 **John Peter Gabriel Muhlenberg,** American Revolutionary clergyman, general, congressman; commanded first American light infantry brigade, 1777; member of first U.S. Congress, 1788–1801. [d. October 1, 1807]

1754 **Paul I,** Emperor of Russia, 1796–1801; successor to Catherine the Great; assassinated. [d. March 23, 1801]

1781 **James Lawrence,** U.S. naval captain; commander of the *Hornet*, which defeated the British *Peacock* in the War of 1812, and of the *Chesapeake*, which was defeated by the British outside of Boston Harbor, 1813; issued the rallying cry, "Don't give up the ship." [d. June 1, 1813]

1799 **Rufus Choate,** U.S. lawyer, statesman; leading trial lawyer of his time; Massachusetts state attorney general, 1853–54. [d. July 13, 1859]

1847 **Annie Besant,** British theosophist, reformer, Indian political leader; President, **Theosophical Society,** 1907–33; organized Indian Home Rule League; President, Indian National Congress, 1917. [d. September 20, 1933]

1885 **Louis Untermeyer,** U.S. poet, editor; compiled popular poetry anthologies. [d. December 18, 1977]

1893 **Faith (Cuthrell) Baldwin,** U.S. author; known for popular romantic novels. [d. March 19, 1978]

1904 **Vladimir Horowitz,** U.S. pianist, born in Russia; internationally recognized for his virtuosity.

Otto Robert Frisch, British physicist, born in Austria; responsible for significant work on uranium atom, which led to development of the **atomic bomb.**

1910 **Bonnie Parker,** U.S. outlaw; with Clyde Barrow (March 24) carried out a two-year crime spree in the U.S. Southwest that resulted in 12 murders and numerous robberies; died in an ambush by Texas Rangers. [d. May 23, 1934]

1914 **Daniel J. Boorstin,** U.S. historian, author, librarian; Director of National Museum of History and Technology, 1969–73; Pulitzer Prize for history, 1974; Librarian of Congress, 1975–.

1920 **Walter Matthau,** U.S. actor; starred in *The Odd Couple* and *The Sunshine Boys.*

1921 **James (Allen) Whitmore,** U.S. actor; noted for his impersonations of such famous figures as Will Rogers, Harry Truman.

1924 **Jimmy (James Earl) Carter,** 39th president of U.S.; first president from the deep South since the Civil War.

William Rehnquist, U.S. jurist, lawyer; Associate Justice, U.S. Supreme Court, 1972–.

San Marino	Captain Regents' Day
U.S.	Agricultural Fair Day

U.S. — Agricultural Fair Day
The basis for this celebration is in the first agricultural fair in the U.S., at Pittsfield, Massachusetts, and the formation of the first permanent agricultural association, 1810.

Religious Calendar

The Saints

St. Remigius, Bishop of Rheims. Apostle of France. Also called **Remi, Remigus.** [d. c. 530]

St. Romanus the Melodist, Byzantine hymn-writer. [d. 6th century]

St. Bavo, hermit and penitent; patron of Ghent and Haarlem. Also called **Allowin.** [d. c. 655]

St. Francis of Pesaro, hermit. Also called **Cecco.** [d. c. 1350]

The Canterbury Martyrs of 1588 and others.

St. Melorus, martyr. Also called **Melar, Mylor.** [death date unknown]

Theresa of the Child Jesus (St. Teresa of Lisieux), virgin; patron of all foreign missions. [d. 1897] Feast formerly October 3. Obligatory Memorial.

The Beatified

Blessed Nicholas of Forca Palena, hermit. [d. 1449]

1928 **Laurence Harvey, (Larushka Mischa Skikne)** British actor, born in Lithuania. [d. November 25, 1973]

1930 **Richard (St. John) Harris,** British actor.

1935 **Julie Andrews (Julia Elizabeth Wells),** British singer and actress.

1936 **Edward Villella,** U.S. ballet dancer; principal dancer with New York City Ballet and other major dance companies, from 1957.

Historical Events

1810 First **agricultural fair** in the U.S. is held at Pittsfield, Massachusetts.

1869 First **postcards** are introduced in Austria by the government.

1890 **McKinley Tariff Act** is passed by Congress, significantly raising import tariffs.

1896 First **Rural Free Delivery** of U.S. mail begins.

1908 Henry Ford's **Model T** automobile is introduced at a price of $850.

1914 Turkey closes the **Dardanelles** to the Allies (**World War I**).

1918 **Damascus** is seized by the British and Arabs (**World War I**).

1923 **Southern Rhodesia** becomes a self-governing colony within the British Commonwealth.

1928 U.S.S.R. inaugurates its first **Five-Year Plan.**

1936 General **Francisco Franco Bahamonde** is appointed Chief of the Spanish State by the insurgents (**Spanish Civil War**).

1943 U.S. troops enter **Naples,** burned by the departing Germans (**World War II**).

1946 International Military Tribunal in **Nuremberg** sentences 12 Nazi leaders to death.

1957 First meeting of the **International Atomic Energy Agency** in Vienna, Austria.

1960 **Nigeria** becomes an independent member of the British Commonwealth.

1961 **Roger Maris** of New York Yankees breaks **Babe Ruth's** record by hitting 61st home run in one season.

1966 **Albert Speer,** minister for armaments and war production in Nazi German government, and **Baldur von Schirach,** leader of Hitler Youth, are released from Spandau War Crimes Prison in Berlin after 20 years' imprisonment.

1974 **Watergate** coverup trial opens in Washington, D.C.

1979 **Pope John Paul II** arrives in U.S. on visit.

October 2

Holidays

People's Republic of China	National Day
Guinea	**Anniversary of Guinean Independence** Celebrates Guinea's achievement of independence from France, 1958.
India	**Mahatma Gandhi's Birthday**

Birthdates

1452 **Richard III** of England, 1483–85; upon death of his predecessor, **Edward IV,** assumed power as protector of the young **Edward V;** allegedly had Edward V slain, claiming the crown for himself; suppressed rebellion by Duke of Buckingham but was killed by Earl of Richmond who became **Henry VII,** first in the Tudor line. [d. August 22, 1485]

1791 **Alexis Petit,** French physicist; developed methods for determining **atomic weights;** studied phenomenon of **thermal expansion** and **specific heat.** [d. June 21, 1820]

1800 **Nat Turner,** U.S. slave; led insurrection at Southampton, Va. which resulted in murder of more than 50 whites; the rebellion failed. Turner, his followers, and many innocent blacks were killed in retaliation, and most Southern states passed even harsher slave laws. [d. November 11, 1831]

1830 **Charles Pratt,** U.S. oil magnate; founder of one of first oil operations in Pennsylvania; bought out by John D. Rockefeller; executive with Standard Oil Co.; founded **Pratt Institute,** New York City; established Pratt Institute Free Library, the first free public library in New York City. [d. May 4, 1891]

1847 **Paul von Hindenburg,** German statesman, soldier; during World War I, led Germans in East Prussian campaign; commanded successful campaign against Russians in Poland, 1915; Chief of Staff for German army, 1917–18; second president of Germany, 1925–32; re-elected, 1932–34; forced to appoint Adolf Hitler as chancellor. [d. August 2, 1934]

1851 **Ferdinand Foch,** French Army marshal; Supreme Commander of Allied Armies, 1918. [d. March 20, 1929]

1852 **Sir William Ramsay,** Scottish chemist; Nobel Prize in chemistry for discovery of **helium, xenon,** and **krypton,** 1904. [d. July 23, 1916]

1869 **Mahatma Gandhi (Mohandas Karamchand Gandhi**), leader of the Indian nationalist movement against British rule; known for advocacy of nonviolent civil disobedience to achieve political and social progress. Assassinated by a Hindu fanatic. [d. January 30, 1948]

1871 **Cordell Hull,** U.S. statesman, diplomat, lawyer; U.S. Secretary of State, 1933–44; developed **Good Neighbor Policy** between U.S. and Latin America; Nobel Peace Prize, 1945. [d. July 23, 1955]

1877 **Carl Trumbull Hayden,** U.S. politician; U.S. Congressman, 1912–69, the longest term in the nation's history. [d. January 25, 1972]

1879 **Wallace Stevens,** U.S. poet, businessman; Vice-President of Hartford Accident and Indemnity Co.; Pulitzer Prize in poetry, 1954. [d. August 2, 1955]

1885 **Ruth Bryan Rohde,** U.S. politician, diplomat; U.S. Congresswoman, 1929–33; U.S. Minister to Denmark, 1933–36; first woman diplomat appointed by U.S. government. [d. July 26, 1954]

1890 **Julius (***Groucho***) Marx,** U.S. comedian. With his brothers Chico (March 26), Harpo (November 21), Zeppo (February 25), formed one of the most outrageously funny comedy teams of the 1930s and 1940s. [d. August 20, 1977]

1895 **Bud Abbot (William Abbott),** U.S. comedian; with his partner, Lou Costello (March 6), formed popular comedy team of the 1940s and 1950s. [d. April 24, 1974]

Religious Calendar

Feasts

Feast of the Guardian Angels Obligatory Memorial.

The Saints

St. Leodegarius, Bishop of Autun and martyr. Also called **Leger, Leodegar.** [d. 679]

St. Eleutherius, martyr. [death date unknown]

1901   **(Ignatius) Roy (Dunnachie) Campbell,** South African poet. [d. April 22, 1957]

1904   **Graham Greene,** British novelist, short story writer, playwright; noted for his works set in exotic locations and dealing with major moral questions.

1906   **Willy Ley,** German-U.S. scientist, engineer; responsible for research leading to development of German **V-2 rocket** during World War II; defected to U.S., 1935; contributed significantly to U.S. entry into space age. [d. June 24, 1969]

1907   **Alexander Robertus Todd, Baron Todd of Trumpington,** Scottish biochemist; Nobel Prize in chemistry for studies of the compounds comprising **nucleic acid,** 1957.

1917   **Christian Renè de Duve,** Belgian physiologist; Nobel Prize in physiology or medicine for research in cell biology (with A. Claude and G. E. Palade), 1974.

1921   **Robert Runcie,** British clergyman; Archbishop of Canterbury, 1980– .

Historical Events

1187   **Saladin** of Damascus takes **Jerusalem.**

1889   First **Pan-American Conference** takes place in Washington, D.C.

1940   *S.S. Empress of Britain,* carrying children being evacuated from England to Canada, is sunk (**World War II**).

1944   U.S. First Army begins operations against the West Wall near **Aachen, Germany (World War II).**

October 3

Holidays

Honduras   **Francisco Morazán's Birthday**
Commemorates the birth of the Honduran responsible for the establishment of government after Honduras gained independence from Spain and who sought a unified Central America.

Korea   **National Foundation Day**
Celebrates the foundation of Korea in 2333 B.C.

Birthdates

1554   **Sir Fulke Greville, 1st Baron Brooke,** English statesman and poet in Queen Elizabeth I's court; Secretary of principality of Wales, 1583–1628; member of Parliament, 1592–1620; Chancellor of the Exchequer, 1614–21. [d. September 30, 1628]

1784   **Ithiel Town,** U.S. architect, engineer; known for his designs of custom house, Wall Street, New York; capitol buildings for states of Indiana and North Carolina; his collection of books on art and architecture was the best in the country. [d. June 13, 1844]

1800   **George Bancroft,** U.S. diplomat, historian; author of the *History of the United States,* 10 volumes, 1834–74; U.S. Secretary of the Navy, 1845–46; U.S. Minister to England, 1846–49. [d. January 17, 1891]

1802   **George Ripley,** U.S. journalist, social reformer; founder and editor of *The Dial,* the organ of the New England transcendentalists, 1840–44; instrumental in organizing **Brook Farm,** a utopian community which attempted to bring into effect the social ideals of transcendentalism; a founder of *Harper's New Monthly Magazine,* 1850. [d. July 4, 1880]

1804   **Townsend Harris,** U.S. merchant, diplomat; first U.S. consul general to Japan, 1855–60; responsible for securing first commercial trade agreement with Japan; achieved nearly legendary importance in Japan after his return to U.S. [d. February 25, 1878]

1809   **Alexey Vasilyevich Koltsov,** Russian poet. [d. October 19, 1842]

1844   **Sir Patrick Manson,** British physician, parasitologist; first to hypothesize on the mosquito's role in spread of malaria; called the *Father of Tropical Medicine.* [d. April 9, 1922]

1854   **William Crawford Gorgas,** U.S. army officer, physician; Surgeon General of U.S. Army, 1914–18; responsible for major breakthroughs in prevention of **yellow fever.** [d. July 3, 1920]

1858   **Percy Faraday Frankland,** British chemist; known for his work on fermentation and stereochemistry, purification of water, and bacterial treatment of sewage. [d. October 28, 1946]

1859   **Eleanora Duse,** Italian actress; international star, best known for playing Marguerite Gautier in *La Dame Aux Camélias.* [d. April 21, 1924]

1888   **Carl von Ossietzky,** German journalist; Nobel Peace Prize for his exposure of Nazi secret rearmament before World War II, 1935; incarcerated in a concentration camp, where he died. [d. May 4, 1938]

1889   **Gertrude Berg (Gertrude Edelstein),** U.S. comedic actress and writer; noted for her portrayal of Molly Goldberg of *The Goldbergs,* radio and television series. [d. September 14, 1966]

1895   **Sergei Aleksandrovich Esenin,** Soviet poet; founder of Imagist school of Russian poetry; poet laureate of Russian Revolution; married to Isadora Duncan (May 27). [committed suicide December 27, 1925]

1897   **Louis Aragon,** French poet, novelist, critic; member of Dadaist and Surrealist schools.

Religious Calendar

The Saints

St. Hesychius, monk. [d. 4th cent.]

The Two Ewalds, missionaries and martyrs. Patrons of Westphalia. Also called **Hewald.** [d. c. 695]

St. Gerard of Brogne, abbot. [d. 959]

St. Froilan, Bishop of Leon, and **St. Attilanus,** bishop of Zamora. Froilan also called **Foilan, Froylan.** [d. 10th cent.]

St. Thomas Cantelupe, Bishop of Hereford. [d. 1282]

The Beatified

Blessed Dominic Spadafora, priest and missionary. [d. 1521]

1898 **Leo McCarey,** U.S. producer, director; known for films *Duck Soup* and *Going My Way.* [d. July 5, 1969]

1900 **Thomas (Clayton) Wolfe,** U.S. novelist; known for his novels *Look Homeward, Angel, Of Time and the River,* and *You Can't Go Home Again.* [d. September 15, 1938]

1908 **Johnny Burke,** U.S. songwriter; known for *Pennies from Heaven* and *Moonlight Becomes You,* among others. [d. February 25, 1964]

1925 **Gore Vidal,** U.S. novelist, playwright, critic.

1928 **Erik Bruhn (Belton Evers),** Danish ballet dancer; artistic director of National Ballet of Canada, 1983– .

Kare Isaachsen Willock, Norwegian statesman; Prime Minister, 1981– .

1941 **Chubby Checker (Ernest Evans)** U.S. rock-'n'-roll singer; popularized the **Twist.**

Historical Events

1691 **Treaty of Limerick** is signed, ending the **Irish Rebellion.**

1777 Washington is defeated by English troops at **Germantown (American Revolution).**

1866 Treaty of peace between Italy and Austria is signed, ending the **Seven Weeks' War.**

1884 The **Palace at Christiansborg,** Denmark, the Danish National Gallery, Parliament, and royal reception rooms, are destroyed by fire.

1895 **Bechuanaland** is annexed to the British Cape Colony in South Africa.

1910 First **National Assembly** meets in Peking, China.

1929 **Yugoslavia** becomes the official name of the Kingdom of the Serbs, Croats and Slovenes.

1932 **Iraq** becomes one of the first Arab countries to free itself from Western Europe.

1935 Italian fascist forces begin invasion of **Ethiopia,** forcing exile of **Haile Selassie.**

1945 Great Britain explodes its first **atomic weapon** on Monte Bello Islands, near Australia.

1962 U.S. astronaut **Walter M. Schirra, Jr.,** makes third U.S. orbital flight, circling the earth six times in 10 hours, 46 minutes.

1965 U.S. **immigration quota system** is abolished.

October 4

Holidays

Lesotho (Basutoland)   **Independence Day**
Celebrates attainment of independence from Great Britain, 1966.

Birthdates

1289   **Louis X,** King of France; (the *Headstrong*), 1314–16. [d. June 5, 1316]

1550   **Charles IX,** King of Sweden, 1604–11. [d. October 30, 1611]

1787   **François Pierre Guillaume Guizot,** French historian, statesman; Premier of France, 1840–48. [d. September 13, 1874]

1797   **Albrecht Bitzius (Jeremias Gotthelf),** Swiss novelist, short-story writer; known for his novels depicting Swiss village life. [d. October 22, 1854]

1819   **Francesco Crispi,** Sicilian revolutionist; first representative of Palermo to Italian parliament; leader of radical leftists; Premier, 1887–91, 1893–96. [d. August 11, 1901]

1822   **Rutherford B(irchard) Hayes,** 19th President of U.S.; his presidency marked the end of Reconstruction in the South; fought to achieve reforms in government which lost him much support; became increasingly disillusioned with concentration of wealth and power in certain segments of the population. [d. January 17, 1893]

1861   **Frederic Remington,** U.S. painter, sculptor, illustrator; known for his depiction of life in the American West; prolific in his output, completed thousands of drawings. [d. December 26, 1909]

1881   **Heinrich Alfred Walther Brauchitsch,** German field marshal; Commander in Chief of German Army, 1938–41; planned and carried out occupation of Austria, Czechoslovakia, and Poland. [d. October 18, 1948]

1884   **(Alfred) Damon Runyon,** U.S. short-story writer, journalist; known for his colorful, humorous, sentimental portrayals of the low life of New York City, capturing the character and language of those who frequented Broadway: horseplayers, gamblers, grifters. [d. December 10, 1946]

1891   **Henri Gaudier-Brzeska,** French sculptor; associated with Ultramodernists. [d. June 5, 1915]

1892   **Engelbert Dollfuss,** Austrian statesman; Dictator of Austria, 1932–34; came into conflict with Nazi regime when he attempted to maintain Austria's independence; assassinated by Austrian Nazi rebels. [d. July 25, 1934]

1895   **Buster Keaton (Joseph Francis Keaton),** U.S. comedian, actor; one of the great clowns of the silent movie era; his career declined with advent of talkies but experienced a revival in the 1950s. [d. February 1, 1966]

1924   **Charlton Heston,** U.S. actor.

Historical Events

1190   **Richard I** of England (*the Lion-Hearted*) storms Messina (**Third Crusade**).

1209   **Otto IV** is crowned Holy Roman Emperor at Rome.

1511   **Holy League** is formed between Pope Julius II, Ferdinand of Aragon, Henry VIII of England, and Venice, against France.

1582   **Gregorian Calendar** is first introduced in Roman Catholic countries by Pope Gregory XIII, who abolishes the Julian Calendar and restores the vernal equinox to March 21.

1777   **Battle of Germantown** results in a British victory over Washington's disorganized troops (**American Revolution**).

1830   **Belgium** declares its independence from the Netherlands.

1877   **Chief Joseph** surrenders, ending U.S. warfare with the **Nez Percé Indians.**

1895   First **U.S. Golfers Association Open** is held at 9-hole course, Newport, Rhode Island.

1914   Hindenburg's army begins its advance on **Warsaw** (**World War I**).

St. Ammon, hermit. [d. c. 350]

St. Petronius, Bishop of Bologna. [d. c. 445]

St. Francis of Assisi, founder of the Friars Minor, or Franciscans, or Lesser Brothers. Also called St. Francis of Assisium and the Seraphic. [d. 1226] Obligatory Memorial.

1922   The **University of the Witwatersrand** is established in the Union of South Africa.

1931   *Dick Tracy,* Chester Gould's popular detective comic strip, makes its debut in U.S. newspapers.

1957   *Sputnik I,* the first artificial satellite, is launched from the Soviet Union.

1966   **Lesotho,** formerly the British colony of **Basutoland,** becomes an independent nation.

1970   U.S. Commission on Campus Unrest issues its report describing the **Kent State** shooting as unwarranted.

1976   U.S. Secretary of Agriculture **Earl Butz** is forced to resign after a furor over a "gross indiscretion" in remarks made about blacks.

October 5

Holidays

Portugal — **Republic Day** Commemorates the declaration of the Republic in Portugal, 1910.

Vanuatu — **Constitution Day** Commemorates the framing of a constitution for the former French possession, 1979.

Birthdates

1703 **Jonathan Edwards,** American colonial theologian, philosopher. [d. March 22, 1758]

1713 **Denis Diderot** (*Pantophile*), French philosopher and writer. Created the *Encyclopédie*, a 20-year, 28-volume attempt to incorporate all human knowledge into one organized whole; his work stimulated much thinking during the age of the Enlightenment. [d. July 30, 1784]

1813 **Antonio García Gutiérrez,** Spanish dramatist; noted as the foremost dramatist of the romantic era of Spanish literature. [d. August 26, 1884]

1819 **Jon Thoroddsen,** pioneer Icelandic novelist and poet; produced the first Icelandic novel, 1850; regarded as a master of Icelandic prose. [d. March 8, 1868]

1829 **Chester A(lan) Arthur,** U.S. lawyer; 21st president of the U.S. (assumed presidency upon the assassination of Garfield, 1881). [d. November 18, 1886]

1864 **Louis Lumière,** French inventor; with his brother, Auguste, invented a process for **color photography** and an early **motion-picture camera.** [d. June 6, 1948]

1879 **Francis Peyton Rous,** U.S. physician; Nobel Prize in physiology or medicine for discovery of a **cancer virus** (with C. B. Huggins), 1966. [d. February 16, 1970]

1882 **Robert Hutchings Goddard,** U.S. physicist; developed and built the first **liquid fuel rocket,** 1926; developed and patented more than 200 inventions in the field of **rocketry.** [d. August 10, 1945]

1887 **René Cassin,** French jurist; President, UN Human Rights Commission, 1946–68; Nobel Peace Prize, 1968. [d. February 20, 1976]

1902 **Ray A. Kroc,** U.S. businessman; founder of **McDonald's Corporation,** one of the first fast food chains in the U.S. [d. January 14, 1984]

1908 **Joshua Logan,** U.S. producer, director, author; producer of *Mr. Roberts, South Pacific,* and *Bus Stop.* Pulitzer Prize for *South Pacific,* 1950.

1929 **Richard F. Gordon,** U.S. astronaut; pilot of *Gemini II* mission, 1966.

Historical Events

1285 **Philip III** of France dies of the plague and is succeeded by **Philip IV** (*the Fair*).

1735 **Treaty of Vienna** ends **War of the Polish Succession** and assures Russian-Austrian dominance in Poland.

1853 Turks declare war on Russia, beginning the **Crimean War.**

1908 **Bulgaria** proclaims its independence from the Ottoman Empire.

1910 **Portugal** is declared a republic after successful revolt against **King Manuel II,** who flees to England.

1918 The French seize **Beirut** (**World War I**).

1947 U.S. President Harry S. Truman delivers the first televised address from the White House.

1965 **Pope Paul VI** makes unprecedented 14-hour visit to New York to plead for world peace before the UN.

Religious Calendar

The Saints

St. Apollinaris, Bishop of Valence; patron of Valence. Also called **Aplonay.** [d. c. 520]

St. Maurus, Abbot of Glanfeuil, afterwards called **Saint-Mausur-Loire.** [d. 584]

St. Placid, monk and martyr. Also called **Placidus.** [d. 6th cent.]

St. Magenulf. Also called **St. Méen, Meinulf.** [d. c. 857]

St. Flora of Beaulieu, virgin. [d. 1347]

The Beatified

Blessed Raymund of Capua, spiritual guide and biographer of St. Catherine of Siena. [d. 1399]

Blessed Aloisius Scrosoppi. [beatified 1981]

Blessed Joseph de Anchieta. [beatified 1981]

1970 French-Canadian separatists kidnap British diplomat **James R. Cross** in Montreal; he is freed December 3, unharmed, after his kidnappers fly to Cuba.

1978 **Norway** announces a strict austerity program to combat a large foreign debt and to improve the nation's economy.

1983 **Lech Walesa,** founder of Solidarity, the federation of Polish Trade Unions, is awarded the Nobel Peace Prize.

October 6

Birthdates

1744 **James McGill,** Canadian businessman, philanthropist, born in Scotland; his estate was left to found **McGill University.** [d. December 19, 1813]

1767 **Henri Christophe,** Haitian statesman; first president of the Republic of Haiti. [d. October 8, 1820]

1769 **Sir Isaac Brock,** British general; forced surrender of Hall's forces at Detroit, War of 1812; known as *Hero of Upper Canada.* [d. October 13, 1812]

1773 **Louis-Philippe,** King of France, 1830–48; known as the *Citizen King.* [d. August 26, 1850]

1795 **Joshua Reed Giddings,** U.S. public official; Congressman, 1838–59; outspoken abolitionist; Consul General to Canada, 1861–64. [d. May 27, 1864]

1808 **Frederick VII,** King of Denmark, 1848–63; adopted a representative government, thus forfeiting absolute power; last of the **Oldenburg** line. [d. November 15, 1863]

1820 **Jenny Lind (Johanna Maria Lind),** Swedish soprano; known as the *Swedish Nightingale* because of her exquisite voice. [d. November 2, 1887]

1824 **Henry Chadwick,** U.S. journalist; one of earliest sports writers in U.S.; member of first baseball rules committee; responsible for developing baseball's scoring system. [d. April 20, 1908]

1831 **Richard Dedekind,** German mathematician; produced first rigorous theory of irrationals. [d. February 12, 1916]

1836 **Heinrich Wilhelm Gottfried von Waldeyer,** German anatomist; noted for his theories of the composition of the nervous system. [d. January 23, 1921]

1846 **George Westinghouse,** U.S. engineer; inventor of the **air brake**; founder of Westinghouse Electric Corporation, 1886; responsible for standardization of electrical transmission in U.S. to alternating current. [d. March 12, 1914]

1862 **Albert Jeremiah Beveridge,** U.S. politician, historian; U.S. Senator, 1899–1911. [d. April 27, 1927]

1867 **George Horace Lorimer,** U.S. editor, writer; editor of the *Saturday Evening Post,* 1899–1936. [d. October 22, 1937]

1887 **Le Corbusier (Charles-Edouard Jenneret Gris),** French architect, designer, painter, and city planner born in Switzerland; the father of modern functional architecture. [d. August 27, 1965]

1903 **Ernest Thomas Sinton Walton,** Irish physicist; Nobel Prize in physics for transmutation of atomic nuclei with artificially accelerated atomic particles (with J. D. Cockroft), 1951.

Brien McMahon, U.S. politician, lawyer; U.S. Senator, 1944–52; sponsored the legislation that resulted in the establishment of the **Atomic Energy Commission.** [d. July 28, 1952]

1905 **Helen Wills,** U.S. tennis player; U.S. champion, 1923–25, 1927–29, 1931; Wimbledon champion, 1927–30, 1932–33, 1935, 1938.

1906 **Janet Gaynor (Laura Gainer),** U.S. actress. [d. September 14, 1984]

1908 **Carole Lombard (Jane Peters),** U.S. actress; wife of Clark Gable (February 1). [d. January 16, 1942]

1914 **Thor Heyerdahl,** Norwegian anthropologist, explorer; led **Kon Tiki** expedition from Peru to Polynesia, to prove that Peruvian Indians could have settled Polynesia, 1947; led **Ra** expedition from Morocco to Barbados, to prove that Mediterranean civilization could have reached the Americas, 1970; author of numerous books on early civilizations.

1942 **Britt Ekland,** Swedish actress.

Religious Calendar

The Saints

St. Faith, virgin and martyr. Also called **Fides, Foi,** or **Foy.** [d. c. 3rd cent.]

St. Nicetas of Constantinople, monk. [d. c. 838]

St. Bruno, founder of the **Carthusian Order.** [d. 1101] Optional Memorial

St. Mary Frances of Naples, virgin. [d. 1791]

The Beatified

Blessed Maria Rosa Durocher. [beatified 1982]

Historical Events

1404 In England, the **Unlearned Parliament** of Canterbury demands appropriation of all Church property.

1876 **American Library Association** is founded in Philadelphia by Melvil Dewey, F. W. Poole, and Charles Cutter.

1884 **U.S. Naval War College** is established at Newport, Rhode Island.

1892 **Alfred Austin** is named poet laureate of England upon the death of **Alfred, Lord Tennyson.**

1913 Japan and Russia recognize the **Republic of China.**

1915 The great Austro-German offensive and invasion of **Serbia** begins under the direction of General von Mackensen (**World War I**).

1927 *The Jazz Singer*, starring Al Jolson, opens in New York City. It is the first commercially successful motion picture with pre-recorded sound.

1973 Egyptian and Syrian forces attack Israeli-held territory on the east bank of the Suez Canal and in the Golan Heights.

1976 The government of **Thailand** falls to a military coup after three years of democratic regimes.

1978 The U.S. Senate votes to extend, to June 30, 1982, the deadline for individual states to ratify the proposed **Equal Rights Amendment**. Despite the extension, the Amendment does not receive the necessary support and is not adopted.

October 7

Holidays

German Democratic Republic (East Germany)	Day of Foundation of the German Democratic Republic
Libya	Evacuation Day
U.S.S.R.	Constitution Day Commemorates the adoption of the new Constitution, 1977.

Birthdates

1471 **Frederick I,** King of Denmark; encouraged spread of Lutheranism in Denmark. [d. April 10, 1533]

1573 **William Laud,** Archbishop of Canterbury; condemned and beheaded for high treason. [d. January 10, 1645]

1728 **Caesar Rodney,** American Revolutionary statesman; member of Continental Congress, 1774–76, 1777, 1778; signer of Declaration of Independence; President of Delaware, 1778–82. [d. June 26, 1784]

1734 **Sir Ralph Abercromby,** British Army general; led British forces that conquered Trinidad; defeated French at Alexandria, 1801; contributed to establishment of strict discipline among British troops. [d. March 28, 1801]

1746 **William Billings,** U.S. composer, hymnwriter; composed religious and patriotic songs during his lifetime; a founder of the **Stoughton Musical Society,** the oldest extant society of its type in the U.S. [d. September 29, 1800]

1748 **Charles XIII,** King of Sweden and Norway, 1809–18; first King of the Union of Sweden and Norway. [d. February 5, 1818]

1849 **James Whitcomb Riley** (*The Hoosier Poet*), U.S. poet, wrote poems representing rustic life in middle America. [d. July 22, 1916]

1854 **Christiaan Rudolph De Wet,** Boer general, politician; one of the Boer leaders in the war against the British. [d. February 3, 1922]

1885 **Niels Henrik David Bohr,** Danish physicist; Nobel Prize in physics for studies of atomic structure, 1922. [d. November 18, 1962]

1888 **Henry Agard Wallace,** U.S. politician, editor, agricultural expert; U.S. Secretary of Agriculture, 1935–40; U.S. Vice-President, 1940–44; U.S. Secretary of Commerce, 1945–46. [d. November 18, 1965]

1898 **Alfred Wallenstein,** U.S. conductor, cellist. [d. February 8, 1983]

1900 **Heinrich Himmler,** German Nazi official; Chief of Gestapo, 1936–45; captured by the British; committed suicide. [d. May 23, 1945]

1905 **Andy Devine,** U.S. character actor; known for his unusual voice; appeared in hundreds of movies between 1930 and 1975. [d. February 18, 1977]

1907 **Helen Clark MacInnes,** U.S. novelist, born in Scotland; author of numerous suspense and espionage novels.

1911 **Vaughn Monroe,** U.S. bandleader, popular singer of the 1940s. [d. May 21, 1973]

1912 **Fernando Belaúnde Terry,** Peruvian political leader; President, 1963–68, 1980– .

1914 **Alfred Drake (Alfred Capurro),** U.S. singer, actor; musical comedy star of the 1940s and 1950s.

1923 **June Allyson (Ella Geisman),** U.S. actress.

Historical Events

1290 **Margaret,** the Maid of Norway, and heiress to the Scottish throne, dies en route to England to marry **Prince Edward,** son of **Edward I** of England.

1571 **Don John** of Austria and his Christian forces overwhelmingly defeat the Turkish Navy at the **Battle of Lepanto.**

Religious Calendar

Feasts

Feast of Our Lady of the Rosary. Previously celebrated on the first Sunday of October. Obligatory Memorial.

The Saints

St. Mark, pope. Elected 336. [d. 336]

St. Osyth, virgin, queen of the East Saxons, and martyr. Also called **Osith, Sythe.** [d. c. 675]

St. Artaldus, Bishop of Belley. Also called **Arthaud.** [d. 1206]

St. Justina, virgin and martyr. Patroness of Padua and Venice. [death date unknown]

The Beatified

Blessed Matthew of Mantua. [d. 1470]

1763	**George III** of Great Britain issues the **Proclamation of 1763**, closing lands in North America north and west of the Alleghenies to white settlement.
1765	**Stamp Act Congress** meets in New York to protest British Stamp Act, which requires purchase of revenue stamps for certain export items.
1780	The British are defeated at the **Battle of King's Mountain** in North Carolina (**American Revolution**).
1883	**Pope Leo XIII** recognizes **Italian unity.**
1915	**Cape Cod Canal** in Massachusetts is opened for navigation.
1916	**Georgia Tech** defeats Cumberland University in football, 222–0, the biggest margin of victory on record.
1949	A constitution for the **German Democratic Republic (East Germany)** is proclaimed.
1960	**Nigeria** is admitted to the United Nations.
1977	**Soviet Union** adopts a new constitution, replacing the one adopted in 1936.

October 8

Holidays

Peru   Combat of Angamos

Religious Calendar

The Saints
St. Holy Simeon. [d. 1st century]
SS. Sergius and Bacchus, martyrs; patrons of desert wanderers. [d. c. 303] Feast suppressed in 1969.

Birthdates

1619   **Philipp von Zesen,** German novelist, lyric poet; founded a literary society to purify the language of barbarisms. [d. November 13, 1689]

1708   **Albrecht von Haller,** Swiss scientist, physician, and poet; known for enunciation of doctrine of irritability of living tissue. [d. December 12, 1777]

1810   **James Wilson Marshall,** U.S. pioneer; discoverer of gold on **Sutter's Creek** in California that started the Gold Rush, 1849. [d. August 10, 1885]

1838   **John Hay,** U.S. statesman, diplomat, author; close associate and private secretary to U.S. President Abraham Lincoln, 1861–65; U.S. Secretary of State, 1898–1905; promoted U.S. Open Door Policy with China. [d. July 1, 1905]

1846   **Elbert Henry Gary,** U.S. lawyer, businessman; led in organization of U.S. Steel Corporation, 1901; Chairman of Board of Directors U.S. Steel Corporation, 1901–27; **Gary, Indiana,** is named for him. [d. August 15, 1927]

1850   **Henri Louis Le Châtelier,** French physical chemist; known for his research on chemical equilibrium. [d. September 17, 1936]

1873   **Ejnar Hertzsprung,** Danish astronomer. [d. October 21, 1967]

1883   **Otto Heinrich Warburg,** German biochemist; Nobel Prize in physiology or medicine for discovery of character of respiratory enzyme, 1931. [d. August 1, 1970]

1890   **Edward (Vernon) Rickenbacker,** U.S. aviator, airline executive; noted for his aerial heroics during World War I; head of Eastern Airlines, 1938–63; special representative of War Department to South Pacific air bases, 1942. [d. July 23, 1973]

1895   **Juan (Domingo) Perón,** Argentine political leader; President, 1946–55; 1973–74. [d. July 1, 1974]

1899   **Bruce Catton,** U.S. historian, editor, journalist; Pulitzer Prize in history, 1954. [d. August 28, 1978]

1905   **Meyer Levin,** U.S. Zionist leader, novelist, scriptwriter; author of *Compulsion,* a novel about the Leopold and Loeb murder case.

1912   **John William Gardner,** U.S. psychologist, educator, public official; President, Carnegie Corporation of New York, 1955–65; U.S. Secretary of Health, Education and Welfare, 1965–68; Chairman of **Common Cause,** 1970–77.

1917   **Rodney Robert Porter,** British biochemist; Nobel Prize in physiology or medicine for research into chemical structure of antibodies, 1972.

            Billy Conn, U.S. boxer; light-heavyweight champion, 1939–41; defeated by Joe Louis in heavyweight title bout, 1941.

1925   **Alvaro Alfredo Magana,** President, Republic of El Salvador, 1982–84.

1941   **Jesse Jackson,** U.S. politician, civil rights leader.

1943   **Chevy Chase (Cornelius Crane Chase),** U.S. comedian.

Historical Events

1755   **Acadians,** refusing to swear loyalty to British crown, are expelled from **Nova Scotia.**

1856   **Arrow War** of Britain and France against China is instigated when Chinese police board the British vessel *Arrow,* arrest 12 Chinese crewmen, and lower the British flag.

St. Keyne, virgin. Also called **Cain, Keyna.** [d. c. 6th century]

St. Iwi, monk, deacon, and hermit. Also called **Ywi.** [d. 7th cent.]

St. Demetrius, martyr; local patron of Salonika. Also patron of soldiers and chivalry. [death date unknown]

SS. Marcellus and Apuleius, martyrs. [death date unknown] Feast suppressed 1969.

St. Pelagia the Penitent. Also called **Margaret, Pelagius.** [death date unknown]

St. Reparata, virgin and martyr. [death date unknown]

St. Thais, penitent. [death date unknown]

St. Triduana, virgin and abbess. Patron of Kintradwell, Caithness. Invoked for curing diseases of the eyes. Also called called **Tradwell, Trollhaena.** [death date unknown]

1871   **Great Chicago Fire,** which kills 250, leaves nearly 100,000 homeless, and destroys $200 million worth of property, begins in a stable on the west side of the Chicago River, when, according to legend, Mrs. O'Leary's cow kicks over an oil lamp.

Entire community of **Peshtigo, Wisconsin** is destroyed by fire, killing more than 600 people.

1912   **Montenegro** declares war on Turkey and hostilities begin (**First Balkan War**).

October 9

Holidays

	Universal Postal Union Day Sponsored by United Nations.
Ecuador	**Independence of Guayaquil** Celebrates the declaration of Guayaquil's independence from Spain, 1820.
Republic of Korea	**Korean Alphabet Day** or **Han'gu Day** Celebrates the promulgation of Hangul alphabet, 1443.
Uganda	**Independence Day** Commemorates attainment of independence from Great Britain, 1962.
U.S. (especially Wisconsin and Minnesota)	**Leif Ericsson Day** Celebrates the landing of Erikson in America, ca. 1000.

Birthdates

1751 **Pierre Louis Lacretelle,** French lawyer, journalist; active in French Revolution; member of Commune of Paris, States General, and Legislative Assembly; noted for his treatises on France of the Revolutionary period. [d. 1824]

1757 **Charles X,** King of France; deposed by the July Revolution of 1830 after attempting to restore absolute monarchy. [d. November 6, 1836]

1782 **Lewis Cass,** U.S. general, government official; senator, 1845–57; U.S. Secretary of State, 1857–60. [d. June 17, 1866]

1835 **(Charles) Camille Saint-Saëns,** French composer, pianist. [d. December 16, 1921]

1852 **Emil Hermann Fischer,** German chemist; Nobel Prize in chemistry for synthesizing sugars and purines, 1902. [d. July 15, 1919]

1854 **Myron Timothy Herrick,** U.S. banker, diplomat, and lawyer; Governor of Ohio, 1903–04; Ambassador to France, 1912–14; 1921–29; organized ambulance corps in France (World War I); active in U.S. post-war relief efforts. [d. March 31, 1929]

1860 **Leonard Wood,** U.S. soldier, physician; with Theodore Roosevelt, organized the Rough Riders; Military Governor of Cuba, 1899–1903; Chief of Staff of U.S. forces, 1910–14. [d. August 7, 1927]

1863 **Gamaliel Bradford,** U.S. biographer, historian; author of *Lee, the American.* [d. April 11, 1932]

Edward William Bok, U.S. editor, author, born in The Netherlands; editor of *Ladies Home Journal,* 1889–1919; Pulitzer Prize in biography for *The Americanization of Edward Bok.* [d. January 9, 1930]

1879 **Max von Laue,** German physicist; Nobel Prize for his discovery of x-ray diffraction, 1914. [d. April 24, 1960]

1884 **Helene Deutsch,** U.S. psychoanalyst, born in Austria.

1888 **Nikolai Ivanovich Bukharin,** Russian Communist leader; member of Politburo, 1918–29; head of Third International, 1926–29; expelled from Communist Party, 1937; executed with other Bolshevik leaders, 1938. [d. March 13, 1938]

1890 **Aimee Semple McPherson (A. Elizabeth Kennedy),** U.S. religious leader; founder of the **International Church of the Four-Square Gospel**; known for her extravagant, dramatic style of fundamentalist preaching. [d. September 27, 1944]

1906 **Leopold Sedar Senghor,** Senegalese poet, statesman; President of Senegalese Republic, 1960–70.

Religious Calendar

The Saints

St. Dionysius the Areopagite. [d. 1st century]

St. Demetrius, bishop of Alexandria. [d. 231]

SS. Denys, Bishop of Paris, **Rusticus,** and **Eleutherius,** martyrs. Denys patron saint of France. Also called **Dionysius, Denis.** [d. c. 258] Optional Memorial.

St. Publia, widow. [d. c. 370]

SS. Andronicus and Athanasia. [d. 5th century]

St. Savin, Apostle of Lavedan. [d. c. 5th century]

St. Gislenus, abbot. Also called **Ghislain, Guislain.** [d. c. 680]

St. Louis Bertrand, Dominican friar, missionary. Principal patron of Colombia. Also called **Lewis Bertrand, Luis Bertran.** [d. 1581]

St. John Leonardi, founder of the Clerks Regular of the Mother of God. [d. 1609] Optional Memorial.

The Beatified

Blessed Gunther, hermit. [d. 1045]

1908 **Jacques Tati,** French film director, writer, producer, actor; known for his characterization of **Monsieur Hulot,** a bumbling Frenchman, befuddled by modern life. [d. November 4, 1982]

1918 **Robert Schwarz Strauss,** U.S. government official, politician; special U.S. Envoy to the Middle East, 1979; chairman of President Carter's Campaign Committee, 1979.

1940 **John Lennon,** British singer, composer; member of **The Beatles.** [d. December 8, 1980]

1955 **Steve Ovett,** British middle-distance runner; Great Britain's outstanding athlete of 1980.

Historical Events

1651 **First Navigation Act** establishes English monopoly on shipping in foreign trade.

1831 **Ioannes Capodistrias,** President of Greece, is assassinated.

1870 **Rome** is incorporated with Italy by royal decree.

1899 The **Kruger Telegram,** considered the immediate cause of the **Boer War,** is sent to the British government, demanding immediate withdrawal of British troops from South Africa.

1914 **Antwerp** falls to the Germans (**World War I**).

Battle of Warsaw, first German offensive against that city, opens (**World War I**).

1915 **Belgrade,** capital of Serbia, falls to the Germans and Austrians (**World War I**).

1918 Canadian troops take **Cambrai** (**World War I**).

1921 *Taras Bulba* by Leoš Janáček premieres in Brno, Yugoslavia.

1943 Yugoslav partisans under Marshal Tito begin assault against Axis forces near Trieste (**World War II**).

1962 **Uganda** gains its independence from Great Britain.

1967 In Bolivia, **Che Guevara** is killed while leading a Cuban-sponsored guerrilla force.

1970 Cambodian leadership abolishes the monarchy.

1975 **Andrei Sakharov,** father of the Soviet hydrogen bomb, becomes the first Soviet citizen to win the Nobel Peace Prize.

October 10

Holidays

Taiwan	**National Day** Commemorates the proclamation of the Republic, 1912.
Cuba	**Beginning of Independence Wars**
Japan	**Physical Education Day**
Namibia (South Africa)	**Kruger Day** Celebrates the birthday of **Paulus Kruger (Oom Paul),** South African statesman, President of Transvaal, 1825.

Birthdates

1560   **Jacob Arminius,** Dutch theologian; originator of doctrine known as **Arminianism.** [d. October 19, 1609]

1684   **(Jean) Antoine Watteau,** French rococo painter. [d. July 18, 1721]

1731   **Henry Cavendish,** English chemist; determined specific gravity of hydrogen and carbon dioxide; first to isolate hydrogen as an element of water; first to isolate argon; his work led to later experiments on electricity by Faraday. [d. February 24, 1810]

1738   **Benjamin West,** U.S. painter; first American to study art in Italy; appointed charter member of Royal Academy in London; painter to King George III, 1771–92; although he never returned to U.S., he remained faithful to his Quaker religion and American heritage. [d. March 11, 1820]

1813   **Giuseppe Verdi,** Italian opera composer. [d. January 17, 1901]

1825   **Stephanus Johannes Paulus Kruger,** South African statesman; founder and President of **Transvaal,** 1883–1900. [d. July 14, 1904]

1830   **Isabella II,** Queen of Spain; came to throne at age 3 and ruled until deposed by Revolution of 1868. [d. April 9, 1904]

1861   **Fridtjof Nansen,** Norwegian Arctic explorer; Nobel Peace Prize for work in repatriating war prisoners, 1922. [d. May 13, 1930]

1870   **Ivan Alekseyevich Bunin,** Russian short-story writer, novelist, poet; Nobel Prize in literature, 1933. [d. November 8, 1953]

1892   **Ivo Andrić,** Yugoslavian novelist; Nobel Prize in literature, 1961. [d. March 13, 1975]

1900   **Helen Hayes (Helen Brown),** U.S. actress; known as the *First Lady of the American Stage.*

1901   **Alberto Giacometti,** Swiss sculptor. [d. January 11, 1966]

1914   **Dorothy Lamour (Dorothy Kaumeyer),** U.S. actress; leading lady of 1930–40's films.

1918   **Yigal Allan,** Israeli statesman; a leader in the fight for Israeli independence, 1948. [d. February 29, 1980]

        Theolonius (Sphere) Monk, U.S. musician; pianist, composer; noted for his jazz compositions and interpretations. [d. February 17, 1982]

1924   **James Dumaresq Clavell,** U.S. novelist, screenwriter, director, born in England; especially known for his novels of Japan.

1930   **Adlai E(wing) Stevenson III,** U.S. politician, lawyer; U.S. Senator, 1970–81.

1956   **Martina Navratilova,** U.S. tennis player, born in Czechoslovakia; Wimbledon Champion, 1978, 1979, 1982–84.

Historical Events

1845   **U.S. Naval School** (later **U.S. Naval Academy**) opens at **Annapolis,** Maryland.

1874   **Fiji** is ceded to Great Britain.

1911   **Chinese Revolution** begins with revolt of military officers in Hankow.

| Oklahoma | Oklahoma Historical Day |
| | Commemorates first settlement of whites in Oklahoma Territory, 1802. |

St. Francis Borgia, third Father General of the Jesuits, and 4th Duke of Gandia. [d. 1572]

St. Gereon and his companions, martyrs. [death date unknown]

Religious Calendar

The Saints

SS. Eulampius and Eulampia, martyrs. [d. c. 310]

St. Maharsapor, martyr. [d. 421]

St. Cerbonius, Bishop of Populonia; patron of the Diocese of Massa Marittima. [d. c. 575]

St. Paulinus, Bishop of York, and missionary. [d. 644]

SS. Daniel and his companions, martyrs. Second martyrs of the Franciscan Order. [d. 1227]

1918 The Irish mail boat *Leinster* is sunk by a German submarine with the loss of 480 lives (**World War I**).

Battle of Argonne Forest ends with very costly American and French victory (**World War I**).

1928 General **Chiang Kai-shek** is inaugurated in Nanking as President of China.

1944 U.S. aircraft bomb **Okinawa** and other islands in the Ryukyus (**World War II**).

1964 **XVIII Summer Olympic Games** open in Tokyo.

1965 Yale University discloses the existence of the **Vinland Map,** dating from about 1440, which contains indisputable cartographic representation of the Americas, including Greenland.

1970 **Fiji** gains independence from Great Britain.

Pierre Laporte, Quebec Labour Minister, is kidnapped from his Montreal home by French-Canadian separatists. Three suspects in his kidnap and murder are arrested on December 12.

1972 **Sir John Betjeman** is named Britain's Poet Laureate.

1973 U.S. Vice-President **Spiro Agnew** resigns, on the same day pleading *nolo contendere* to income-tax evasion; he is fined $10,000 and placed on probation for three years.

1977 Soviet cosmonauts abort space mission of their *Soyuz 25* spacecraft; no official explanation is given.

October 11

Holidays

Day of Solidarity with South African Political Prisoners. Sponsored by the United Nations.

Panama   **Revolution Anniversary** Commemorates the overthrow of the 11-day-old Arias government by the National Guard, 1968.

U.S. (Indiana)   **General Pulaski Memorial Day** Commemorates death of Polish General **Casimir Pulaski,** American Revolutionary War hero, 1779.

Birthdates

1671   **Frederick IV,** King of Denmark and Norway, 1699–1730. [d. October 12, 1730]

1675   **Samuel Clarke,** English theologian, metaphysician; disciple of Isaac Newton; noted for his demonstration of the existence of God. [d. May 17, 1729]

1814   **John Baptist Lamy,** U.S. Roman Catholic priest born in France; established Catholic missions and schools in New Mexico, Arizona, and parts of Colorado, Utah, and Nevada. Was the model for the main character in Willa Cather's *Death Comes for the Archbishop.* [d. February 13, 1888]

1821   **Sir George Williams,** British philanthropist; founder of the Young Men's Christian Association, 1844. [d. 1905]

1844   **Henry John Heinz,** U.S. food-products manufacturer; founder of H. J. Heinz Co. [d. May 14, 1919]

1872   **Harlan Fiske Stone,** U.S. jurist; Associate Justice, U.S. Supreme Court, 1925–41; Chief Justice, U.S. Supreme Court, 1941–46. [d. April 22, 1946]

1884   **Friedrich Karl Rudolf Bergius,** German chemist; Nobel Prize in chemistry for development of chemical high pressure methods (with C. Bosch), 1931. [d. March 30, 1949]

(Anna) Eleanor Roosevelt, U.S. First Lady, syndicated columnist, diplomat; wife of U.S. President Franklin D. Roosevelt. [d. November 7, 1962]

1885   **François Mauriac,** French novelist, essayist, dramatist; Nobel Prize in literature, 1952. [d. September 1, 1970]

1887   **Willie Hoppe,** U.S. billiards player; winner of more than 50 world billiards titles. [d. February 1, 1959]

1897   **Nathan Farragut Twining,** U.S. Air Force general; Chairman, Joint Chiefs of Staff, 1957–60. [d. March 29, 1982]

1902   **Frances Lillian Ilg,** U.S. pediatrician, educator; cofounder and director, Gesell Institute for Human Development, 1950–70. [d. July 26, 1981]

1906   **Charles (Haskell) Revson,** U.S. cosmetics manufacturer; founder of Revlon, Inc., world's largest cosmetics manufacturer. [d. August 24, 1975]

1910   **Joseph Wright Alsop, Jr.,** U.S. journalist, author; with his brother, Stewart (May 17), wrote *Matter of Fact,* a syndicated column for the New York *Herald Tribune,* 1946–58; sole author of the same for Los Angeles *Times* Syndicate, 1958–74.

1918   **Jerome Robbins,** U.S. ballet dancer, choreographer; associate artistic director, New York City Ballet, 1949–1959; ballet master, New York City Ballet, 1969– .

1939   **Maria Bueno,** Brazilian tennis player; Wimbledon Singles Champion, 1959, 1960, 1964.

Feasts

Feast of the Motherhood of Our Lady, promoted by Pope Pius XI in 1931.

The Saints

SS. Tarachus, Probus, and Andronicus, martyrs. [d. 304]

St. Nectarius, Archbishop of Constantinople. [d. 397]

St. Canice, abbot. Also called **Cainnech, Canicus, Kenneth, Kenny.** [d. 599]

St. Agilbert, Bishop of Paris. [d. c. 685]

St. Gummarus. Also called **Gomar, Gommaire, Gummar.** [d. c. 774]

St. Bruno the Great, Archbishop of Cologne. [d. 965]

St. Alexander Sauli, Bishop of Pavia and Barnabite Clerk Regular. [d. 1592]

The Beatified

Blessed James of Ulm, laybrother. [d. 1491]

Blessed Mary Soledad, virgin and foundress of the Handmaids of Mary Serving the Sick. [d. 1887]

Historical Events

1531 The Catholic cantons of Switzerland win the **Battle of Kappel** against the city of Zurich and her Protestant allies, and **Ulrich Zwingli,** the Protestant reformer, is killed.

1614 **New Netherlands Company** is chartered.

1698 **First Partition Treaty** divides Spanish possessions between Bavaria and other German states.

1865 **Governor Edward John Eyre** is recalled to Great Britain after exercising unnecessary harshness in quelling an insurrection of Jamaican natives. Eyre had ordered the execution of 450 natives and more than 1,000 native homes burned.

1899 **Boers** of the Transvaal and Orange Free State, hoping to destroy British supremacy in South Africa, declare war (**Boer War**).

1906 **San Francisco** school board orders **segregation** of all Japanese, Chinese, and Korean children into a separate Oriental school.

1912 **Leopold Stokowski** makes his first appearance as Director of the Philadelphia Orchestra.

1914 Cathedral of **Notre Dame** suffers some damage in a German air raid on Paris (**World War I**).

1939 **Albert Einstein** and other American scientists inform U.S. President Franklin Roosevelt of the possibilities of developing an **atomic bomb.**

1950 **Columbia Broadcasting System** receives authorization from the Federal Communications Commission to begin transmission of **color television** broadcasts.

1961 U.S. Air Force Major Robert M. White flies an **X-15 rocket plane** to a height of 217,000 feet, a record for winged, man-controlled aircraft.

1962 **Pope John XXIII** opens the **Second Vatican Council** in Rome.

1972 **Panama** promulgates a new constitution.

1977 **Col. Ibrahim al-Hamdi,** President of the Yemen Arab Republic, is killed by unidentified assassins.

1980 Two Soviet cosmonauts conclude longest **space mission** up to that time, 185 days.

October 12

Holidays

Bahamas, Honduras	**Discovery Day** Celebrates Columbus' discovery of the New World.
Chile, Colombia, Costa Rica, Paraguay, Spain, Uruguay	**Day of the Race** Celebrates Spanish influences and contributions to the New World.
Equatorial Guinea	**National Day** Celebrates end of Equatorial Guinea's status as a Spanish colony, 1968.

Birthdates

1710 **Jonathan Trumbull,** American colonial leader; Governor of Connecticut, 1769–84. [d. August 17, 1785]

1775 **Lyman Beecher,** U.S. religious leader, social reformer; vigorous critic of Roman Catholicism; adamant abolitionist; father of Harriet Beecher Stowe (June 14) and Henry Ward Beecher (June 24). [d. January 10, 1863]

1798 **Pedro IV,** King of Portugal, 1826; abdicated in favor of his daughter, Donna Maria da Gloria. [d. September 24, 1834]

1844 **George Washington Cable,** U.S. author, reformer; literary voice of old New Orleans; a leading figure in **Western local color movement** in American fiction. [d. January 31, 1925]

1860 **Elmer A(mbrose) Sperry,** U.S. inventor; developed the **gyrocompass,** gyroscopic stabilizer, and nearly 400 other inventions to which he held patents; a founder of the American Institute of Electrical Engineers and the American Electro-Chemical Society. [d. June 16, 1930]

1865 **Sir Arthur Harden,** English biochemist; Nobel Prize in chemistry for investigations into fermentation and fermentative enzymes (with Hans von Euler-Chelpin), 1929. [d. June 17, 1940]

1866 **James Ramsay MacDonald,** British statesman; Secretary of Labor Party, 1900–12; Treasurer of the Party, 1912–24; leader of Labor Party, 1911–14; Prime Minister of Great Britain, 1924, 1929–31; organized first Labor ministry in British history. [d. November 9, 1937]

1874 **Abraham Arden Brill,** U.S. psychiatrist; popularizer of Sigmund Freud. [d. March 2, 1948]

1884 **Sir Godrey Tearle,** British actor. [d. June 9, 1953]

1891 **Pearl Mesta,** U.S. diplomat, hostess; the unofficial hostess of Washington, D.C., during the 1940s; U.S. Envoy to Luxembourg, 1949–53. [d. January 11, 1975]

1896 **Eugenio Montale,** Italian poet; Nobel Prize in literature, 1975. [d. September 28, 1981]

1901 **F(elix) Edward Hebert,** U.S. politician; Congressman, 1947–76; wrote award winning exposé of Huey Long's political career in Louisiana. [d. December 29, 1979]

1927 **Charles Gordone,** U.S. playwright; Pulitzer Prize in drama, 1970.

1932 **Dick Gregory,** U.S. comedian, political activist.

1935 **Luciano Pavarotti,** Italian opera singer.
Joan Rivers, U.S. comedian, TV host.

Historical Events

1297 **Edward I** of England solemnly confirms **Magna Carta,** restricting sovereign's right to raise taxes.

1492 **Christopher Columbus** makes first landfall in the New World in what is today San Salvador.

1518 **Martin Luther** is interrogated at Augsburg and refuses to recant.

| Spain, Central America, South America, United States (some states) | Columbus Day
Commemorates Columbus' first landfall in the New World, 1492. | **St. Edwin,** first Christian king of Northumbria, martyr. [d. 633]

St. Ethelburga, Abbess of Barking, virgin. Also called **Ædilburh, Æthelburh.** [d. c. 678] |

Religious Calendar

The Saints

St. Maximilian, Bishop of Lorch and martyr. [d. c. 284]

St. Felix and Cyprian and many other martyrs. [d. c. 484]

1576	Holy Roman Emperor **Maximilian II** dies and is succeeded by his brother, **Rudolf II.**
1811	**Paraguay** declares its independence from Spain and Argentina.
1822	**Brazil** declares its independence from Portugal.
1908	The **Convention of the South African Union** opens at Durban, Natal, to prepare the way for the union of the Cape Colony, Natal, the Transvaal, and the Orange River Colony.
1914	The Germans enter **Lille, France** and begin an occupation that lasts until 1918 (**World War I**).
1915	**Edith Cavell,** a British nurse in Brussels, is shot by the Germans for aiding Allied soldiers (**World War I**).
1944	U.S. carrier-based planes bomb Formosa and northern Luzon in the Philippines (**World War II**).
1965	U.S. Navy formally concludes *Sealab II* program in which teams of aquanauts lived and worked in an underwater capsule submerged off the California coast.
1968	**Equatorial Guinea** achieves its independence from Spain.
1971	Celebration of the 2,500th anniversary of the **Persian Empire** begins in Persepolis, Iran.
1976	Mao Tse-tung's widow, **Chiang Ch'ing,** and three other radical leaders (the **Gang of Four**) are arrested for plotting a military takeover.

October 13

Religious Calendar

The Saints
SS. Faustus, Januarius, and Martial, martyrs. Martial also called Martialis. [d. c. 304]

Birthdates

1754   **Mary McCauley (*Molly Pitcher*)**, American Revolutionary heroine; earned her nickname when she carried water to the soldiers at the **Battle of Monmouth** during the American Revolution. [d. January 22, 1832]

1807   **Hans Conon von der Gabelentz**, German historian and linguist; known for his studies of languages of remote areas of Africa, Asia, and Pacific Islands. [d. September 3, 1874]

1821   **Rudolph Virchow**, German pathologist; father of cellular pathology; a leader of the German Liberal Party; member of the Reichstag, 1880–93. [d. September 5, 1902]

1850   **Pellegrino Matteucci**, Italian explorer; the first European to traverse the whole of Africa north of the Equator from Egypt to the Gulf of Guinea, 1880–81. [d. August 8, 1881]

1853   **Lillie Langtry (Emilie Charlotte Le Breton)**, British actress; toured the world as *the Jersey Lily*. [d. February 12, 1929]

1862   **John Rogers Commons**, U.S. labor economist; author of numerous multi-volume studies of American industrial society; professor of economics, University of Wisconsin, 1904–13; director of American Economic Association, 1920–28. [d. May 11, 1944]

1872   **Ralph Vaughan Williams**, British composer. [d. August 26, 1958]

1877   **Theodore Gilmore Bilbo**, U.S. politician; U.S. Senator, 1935–46; known for his bigotry and his filibustering, especially on Southern populist issues. [d. August 21, 1947]

1902   **Luther H(arris) Evans**, U.S. educator, librarian; Librarian of Congress, 1945–53; Director General, UNESCO, 1953–58. [d. December 23, 1981]

1909   **Herbert Lawrence Block (*Herblock*)**, U.S. cartoonist; Pulitzer Prize for cartoons, 1942, 1954, 1979.

1910   **Ernest K(ellogg) Gann**, U.S. novelist; author of *The High and the Mighty*, *Fate Is the Hunter*.

1918   **Cornel(ius Louis) Wilde**, U.S. actor.

1925   **Margaret (Hilda) Thatcher**, British barrister, politician; first woman Prime Minister of Great Britain, 1979– .

     Lenny Bruce (Leonard Alfred Schneider), U.S. comedian, satirist. [d. August 3, 1966]

1936   **Donald F. McHenry**, U.S. diplomat; U.S. Ambassador to the UN, 1979– .

1942   **Art(hur) Garfunkel**, U.S. singer, songwriter; known for his singing and songwriting efforts with partner Paul Simon (November 13).

1959   **Marie Osmond**, U.S. singer.

Historical Events

1501   **Peace of Trento** is signed between France and Holy Roman Emperor, Maximilian I, who recognizes French conquests in Upper Italy.

1851   Permanent telegraphic communications are first established between France and England.

1877   **Satsuma Rebellion** is crushed by a modern army of Japanese commoners, ending the power of the warrior class as a separate group.

1914   Continuing German advance in Flanders forces Belgian government to move to **Havre, France** from Ostend (**World War I**).

1919   France ratifies the **Treaty of Versailles,** ending **World War I.**

1922   The Colony of the **Niger** is formed by the French government.

1964   Three Soviet cosmonauts manning the world's first multi-seat spacecraft, ***Voskhod***, land safely after orbiting the earth 16 times.

1970   **Fiji** becomes the 127th member of the UN.

St. Comgan, abbot. [d. 8th century]

St. Gerald of Aurillac. Also called **Gerard.** [d. 909]

St. Coloman, martyr. Also called **Colman.** [d. 1012]

St. Edward the Confessor, King of England. Patron of England, especially of Westminster. [d. 1066]

St. Maurice of Carnoët, abbot. [d. 1191]

The Beatified

Blessed Magdalen Panattieri, virgin. [d. 1503]

1976   Scientists at the University of Michigan announce the identification of the mummy of King Tutankhamun's grandmother, who lived from 1397 to 1360 B.C.

October 14

Holidays

Yemen People's Democratic Republic

National Day
Celebrates the proclamation of the Republic, 1962.

Zaire

Founders' Day and **Youth Day**

Birthdates

1633 **James II,** King of England (James VII of Scotland). His abdication in 1688 established Parliament's strength in England. [d. September 16, 1701]

1644 **William Penn,** English Quaker leader in America; founder of **Pennsylvania.** [d. July 30, 1718]

1696 **Samuel Johnson,** American clergyman; first president of King's College (now **Columbia University**). [d. June 6, 1772]

1712 **George Grenville,** English politician; first Lord of the Admiralty, 1762–63; first Lord of the Treasury, Chancellor of the Exchequer, and Prime Minister, 1763–65; best known for enactment of the Stamp Act; nicknamed the *Gentle Shepherd.* [d. November 13, 1770]

1734 **Francis Lightfoot Lee,** American Revolutionary leader; member of Virginia House of Burgesses, 1758–68; 1769–76; delegate to Continental Congress; signer of Declaration of Independence. [d. January 11, 1797]

1784 **Ferdinand VII,** King of Spain, 1808, 1814–33; repressive reign was marked by periodic rebellion and reaction; Spain lost all her possessions in North and South America during his reign. [d. September 29, 1833]

1857 **Elwood Haynes,** U.S. inventor; creator of an early practical automobile, 1894. Patented **Stellite,** a cobalt alloy. [d. April 13, 1925]

1873 **Ray Ewry,** U.S. track and field star; winner of eight Olympic gold medals, 1900, 1904, 1908. [d. September 29, 1937]

1882 **Eamon De Valera,** Irish statesman; led the Easter Rising of 1916; President of Sinn Fein, 1917–26; Prime Minister, 1937–48; 1951–54; 1957–59. [d. August 29, 1975]

1888 **Katherine Mansfield (Kathleen Murry),** British writer; masterful short-story writer; most of her works were published after her death. [d. January 9, 1923]

1890 **Dwight David Eisenhower,** U.S. Army general, statesman, university president; 34th President of the U.S., 1953–61; Supreme Commander of Allied Expeditionary Force in Europe during World War II. [d. March 28, 1969]

1892 **(Benjamin) Sumner Welles,** U.S. diplomat; laid foundation of U.S. Good Neighbor Policy with Latin America; U.S. Under-Secretary of State, 1933–43. [d. September 24, 1961]

1894 **e(dward) e(stlin) cummings,** U.S. poet; noted for his unorthodox typography and experimental approach to style and diction. [d. September 3, 1962]

1896 **Lillian Gish,** U.S. silent-screen actress.

1906 **Hannah Arendt,** U.S. political scientist born in Germany; known for her studies of totalitarianism; first woman to hold full professorship at Princeton; author of *Origins of Totalitarianism*, 1951; *The Human Condition*, 1958. [d. December 4, 1975]

1930 **Joseph Mobutu (Mobotu Sese Seko),** Congolese general; President of the Congo, now Zaire, 1965– .

1950 **Sheila Young,** U.S. speed skater; winner of three medals in 1976 Winter Olympics.

Historical Events

1066 **King Harold** of England is defeated and killed by the Normans at the **Battle of Hastings.**

1322 **Robert Bruce,** King of Scotland, defeats **Edward II** of England at **Byland.**

1656 Massachusetts General Court passes the first punitive legislation against **Quakers** in the colony, imposing a 40 shilling fine on anyone harboring a Quaker.

1705 English navy captures **Barcelona (War of the Spanish Succession).**

Religious Calendar

The Saints

St. Callistus I, pope and martyr. Elected c. 217. Also called **Calixtus, Callixtus I.** [d. c. 222] Optional Memorial.

St. Justus, Bishop of Lyons. [d. c. 390]

St. Manacca, abbess. [d. c. 5th–6th cent.]

St. Manechildis, virgin. Also called **Ménéhould.** [d. c. 6th century]

St. Angadrisma, virgin. Also called **Angadrême.** [d. c. 695]

St. Burchard, Bishop of Würzburg. Also called **Burckard, Burkardi.** [d. 754]

St. Dominic Loricatus. [d. 1060]

1806	Napoleon defeats Prussians and Saxons at Jena and Auerstädt.
1809	**Peace of Vienna** is signed; Austria cedes Trieste and Illyria to France; Galicia to Poland and Russia; Salzburg and Inn District to Bavaria.
1915	Bulgaria declares war on Serbia (**World War I**).
1920	**Treaty of Dorpat** is signed by Finland and Russia, ending war between the two and defining boundaries.
1923	First mechanical **telephone switchboard** is installed in New York City.
1930	*Girl Crazy* by George Gershwin opens in New York.
1933	Germany withdraws from the Disarmament Conference and from the League of Nations.
1937	Socialist party is banned in Germany.
1947	American rocket-propelled *Bell X-1* becomes the first aircraft to exceed the speed of sound in level flight.
1966	U.S. extends its exclusive **coastal fishing zone** to 12 miles.
1974	**Palestine Liberation Organization** is recognized by the UN.

October 15

Holidays

Tunisia	**Evacuation Day**
U.S.	**White Cane Safety Day**
	Day dedicated to the visually handicapped citizens of the U.S. Sponsored by National Federation of the Blind.
	World Poetry Day
	Sponsored by National Poetry Day Committee, Inc., and World Poetry Day Committee.

Birthdates

70 B.C. **Vergil** (or **Virgil**) (**Publius Vergilius Maro**), Roman poet; the chief poet of the Golden Age of Rome; wrote *The Aeneid*, the epic poem relating the story of Aeneas and the founding of Rome. [d. September 21, 19 B.C.]

1542 **Akbar** (**Jala ud-Din Mohammad**), Emperor of Hindustan, 1556–1605; considered one of the greatest Indian emperors. [d. 1605]

1608 **Evangelista Torricelli,** Italian physicist, mathematician; developed early barometer; made improvements in telescope; constructed simple microscope. [d. October 25, 1647]

1758 **Johann Heinrich von Dannecker,** German sculptor; associate of Schiller, Goethe, Herder, Canova; best known for busts of Schiller, Gluck. [d. December 8, 1841]

1783 **François Magendie,** French physiologist; pioneered in research on functions of spinal nerves, blood flow; introduced morphine, codeine and bromide compounds into medical practice. [d. October 7, 1855]

1795 **Frederick William IV,** King of Prussia, 1840–61; forced to promulgate a new constitution by the Revolution of 1848; suffered from insanity; his reign carried out by his brother William (William I) as regent, 1858–61. [d. January 2, 1861]

1805 **Wilhelm von Kaulbach,** German painter; noted for his ceilings and wall murals, including the grand staircase of the Neves Museum in Berlin. [d. April 7, 1874]

1814 **Mikhail Yurievich Lermontov,** Russian poet, novelist; early Romantic poet; exiled to Caucasus, where he died. [d. July 27, 1841]

1829 **Asaph Hall,** U.S. mathematical astronomer; noted especially for his discovery of the **moons of Mars,** 1877. [d. December 7, 1914]

1830 **Helen Hunt Jackson,** U.S. novelist, poet, essayist; known for her sympathetic portrayal of the American Indian; appointed by U.S. government to investigate condition of Mission Indians of California; author of *Ramona.* [d. August 12, 1885]

1844 **Friedrich Nietzsche,** German philosopher; noted for his philosophy of the perfectability of man, which has been said to have influenced the development of the Nazi movement of the 1930s; proposed theory of the superman (*Übermensch*); suffered mental breakdown, 1889, which affected him for remainder of his life. [d. August 25, 1900]

1847 **Ralph Albert Blakelock,** U.S. romantic painter; unnoticed during his lifetime, many of his works are now in the collections of leading U.S. galleries. [d. August 9, 1919]

1858 **John L. Sullivan,** U.S. boxer; last bareknuckle heavyweight champion, 1882–92. [d. February 2, 1918]

William Sowden Sims, U.S. admiral; developed new theories of naval warfare that contributed to Allied victories in World War I; Pulitzer Prize in history, 1920. [d. September 28, 1936]

1878 **Paul Reynaud,** French statesman; Minister of Finance, 1930, 1938–40; Premier of France at time of defeat by Germans; imprisoned by Germans, 1943–45. [d. September 21, 1966]

Religious Calendar

The Saints

St. Leonard of Vandoeuvre, abbot. [d. c. 570]

St. Thecla, Abbess of Kitzingen, and virgin. Also called **Heilga, Tecla.** [d. c. 790]

St. Euthymius the Younger, abbot. [d. 898]

St. Teresa of Avila, virgin. Founder of the Discalced Carmelites, and Doctor of the Church. [d. 1582] Obligatory Memorial.

The Beatified

Blessed Magdalena de Nagasaki [one of the Martyrs of Nagasaki] [beatified 1981]

1881   **Sir P(elham) G(renville) Wodehouse,** British author; noted for his humorous stories of the life of English gentry; developed characters of *Jeeves*, *Bertie Wooster*; interned in Germany during World War II; became U.S. citizen, 1955. [d. February 14, 1975]

1905   **C(harles) P(ercy) Snow,** British novelist, scientist, government official; British Civil Service Commissioner, 1945–60; author of *Strangers and Brothers*, an 11-volume novel sequence, 1935–70. [d. July 1, 1980]

1908   **John Kenneth Galbraith,** U.S. economist, author, diplomat, born in Canada; noted for his work on the American economy, especially *The Affluent Society*; U.S. Ambassador to India, 1961–63; Chairman of Americans for Democratic Action, 1967–68.

1917   **Arthur M(eier) Schlesinger, Jr.,** U.S. historian, public official; author of Pulitzer Prize-winning *The Age of Jackson*, 1945; *A Thousand Days*, 1965; professor of history, Harvard University, 1946–61; a founder of Americans for Democratic Action; speechwriter for Adlai E. Stevenson and John F. Kennedy during their presidential campaigns.

1920   **Lee Iacocca,** U.S. businessman, auto manufacturing executive; President, Ford Motor Co., 1970–78; Chief Executive, Chrysler Corporation, 1978– .

     Mario Puzo, U.S. author; best known for his novel *The Godfather.*

1926   **Evan Hunter,** U.S. novelist; author of *The Blackboard Jungle*, 1954.

     Jean Peters, U.S. actress.

1938   **John Wesley Dean, 3rd,** U.S. lawyer; counsel to President Richard Nixon; achieved notoriety as chief prosecution witness during Watergate hearings.

Historic Events

1080   **Henry IV** of Germany is defeated and **Rudolf,** Duke of Swabia is killed at **Pegau.**

1581   *Ballet Comique de la Reine,* regarded as the first ballet, is performed in Paris.

1788   **Jean François Pilatre de Rozier,** French aeronautical designer, becomes the first human to ascend into the air by balloon; duration: 5 minutes; height: 60 feet.

1815   **Napoleon** arrives at **St. Helena,** where he remains for the rest of his life.

1900   Symphony Hall in Boston is inaugurated as the home of the **Boston Symphony Orchestra.**

1915   **Third Battle of Artois** ends with the British failing to reach the main objective of Lens and suffering some 60,000 casualties (**World War I**).

     Great Britain declares war on **Bulgaria (World War I).**

1918   **Poland** declares itself free and independent with **Josef Piłsudski** as Chief of State.

1919   The British and Italian governments ratify the **Treaty of Versailles.**

1943   U.S. establishes Naval Supply Depot at **Guantanamo Bay,** Cuba.

1964   **Nikita S. Khrushchev** is removed from all government and Communist Party posts; **Aleksei N. Kosygin** is named Premier, and **Leonid I. Brezhnev** becomes First Party Secretary.

1970   U.A.R. Acting President **Anwar al-Sadat** is elected president in a national plebiscite.

1978   General **João Baptista da Figueiredo** is elected president of Brazil.

October 16

Holidays

World Food Day
Sponsored by United Nations.

Religious Calendar

The Saints

SS. Martinian and other martyrs, and **Maxima.**
[d. 458]

Birthdates

1430   **James II,** King of Scotland, 1437–60. [d. August 3, 1460]

1708   **Albrecht von Haller,** Swiss physiologist, anatomist, botanist, poet; founder of experimental physiology and neurology. [d. December 12, 1777]

1758   **Noah Webster,** U.S. lexicographer, writer; creator of the first dictionary of American English, *An American Dictionary of the English Language,* 1828. [d. May 28, 1843]

1760   **Jonathan Dayton,** U.S. politician, lawyer, American Revolutionary soldier; U.S. Congressman, 1791–99; U.S. Senator, 1799-1805; city of **Dayton, Ohio,** is named for him. [d. October 9, 1824]

1806   **William Pitt Fessenden,** U.S. politician, lawyer; played major role in founding of Republican Party, 1856; U.S. Secretary of the Treasury, 1864–65; Chairman of Joint Congressional Committee on Reconstruction, 1866. [d. September 9, 1869]

1826   **Giovanni Battista Donati,** Italian astronomer; discovered six comets, one of which is named for him. [d. September 20, 1873]

1851   **Frederick Huntington Gillett,** U.S. Congressman, 1892–1925; responsible for legislation which established General Accounting Office of U.S.; U.S. Senator, 1924–30. [d. July 31, 1935]

1854   **Oscar (Fingall O'Flahertie Wills) Wilde,** Irish poet, dramatist; known for his light-hearted, sparkling comedies including *The Importance of Being Earnest*; produced French drama *Salome*; convicted of sodomy and jailed; while in jail wrote *De Profundis.* [d. November 30, 1900]

1863   **Sir Joseph Austen Chamberlain,** British statesman; Nobel Peace Prize, 1925. [d. March 16, 1937]

1886   **David Ben-Gurion,** Israeli statesman, born in Poland; first Prime Minister of Israel, 1949–53; 1957–63. [d. December 1, 1973]

1888   **Eugene (Gladstone) O'Neill,** U.S. playwright; first American to win Nobel Prize in literature, 1936; awarded Pulitzer Prize in drama, 1920, 1922, 1928, 1957. [d. November 27, 1953]

1890   **Michael Collins,** Irish revolutionary leader; Minister of Finance of Sinn Fein ministry, 1919–22; Commander in Chief of Military Forces. Killed in revolutionary action, 1922. [d. August 22, 1922]

1893   **Carl Carmer,** U.S. writer, folklorist. [d. September 11, 1976]

1898   **William O(rville) Douglas,** U.S. jurist; Associate Justice, U.S. Supreme Court, 1939–75. [d. January 19, 1980]

1906   **Edward (Jeffrey Irving) Ardizzone,** British artist; known for his illustrations of more than 200 books, including works by Thackeray, Trollope, Cervantes, and Mark Twain. [d. November 8, 1979]

1908   **Robert Ardrey,** U.S. author; known for his controversial anthropological books including *African Genesis,* and *The Territorial Imperative.* [d. January 14, 1980]

1921   **Linda Darnell (Manetta Eloisa Darnell),** U.S. actress. [d. April 10, 1965]

1925   **Angela Lansbury,** U.S. actress, born in England.

1927   **Günter Grass,** German novelist; spokesman for post-Nazi German literary movement.

1931   **Charles W. Colson,** U.S. government official; gained notoriety during Watergate scandal, 1973–74.

1941   **Baddeley Devesi,** Governor-General, Solomon Islands, 1978– .

St. Gall, monk and missionary; patron of Switzerland. [d. c. 635]

St. Mommolinus, Bishop of Noyon. Also called **Mommolin, Mummolin.** [d. c. 686]

St. Bercharius, abbot. [d. c. 696]

St. Lull, Bishop of Mainz. Also called **Lullon, Lullus.** [d. 786]

St. Anastasius of Cluny. [d. c. 1085]

St. Bertrand, Bishop of Comminges. [d. 1123]

St. Hedwig, widow and laywoman. Also called **Jadwiga.** [d. 1243] Optional Memorial

St. Margaret Mary Alacoque, virgin and visionary. [d. 1690] Optional Memorial.

St. Gerard Majella, Redemptorist lay brother. [d. 1755]

Historical Events

1076   Princes opposed to **Henry IV** of Germany meet at **Trebur.**

1171   **Henry II** of England invades Ireland at the request of deposed King Dermot Macmurrough.

1793   **Marie Antoinette** is beheaded.

1813   Allies defeat Napoleon at the **Battle of Leipzig,** causing French retreat from Germany.

1859   **John Brown,** U.S. abolitionist, leads unsuccessful raid on government arsenal at **Harper's Ferry.**

1904   French federal government is established in **Senegal.**

1915   France and Serbia declare war on **Bulgaria (World War I).**

1917   **Margaret Sanger** and others open the first **birth control clinic,** in Brooklyn, New York.

1938   Aaron Copland's ballet *Billy the Kid* opens in Chicago.

1946   **Joachim von Ribbentrop,** Nazi leader, convicted of war crimes by **Nuremberg Tribunal,** hanged; **Hermann Goering,** sentenced to hang with von Ribbentrop, commits suicide just prior to the scheduled execution.

1965   **Singapore** formally becomes a member of the Commonwealth of Nations.

1968   Two American black athletes at Olympic Games, **Tommie Smith** and **John Carlos,** demonstrate for **black power** during their victory celebration. The Olympic Committee suspends them two days later.

1975   Argentine President **Isabel Perón** returns to office in response to the nation's political and economic troubles.

1978   The Roman Catholic College of Cardinals elects first non-Italian pope in 456 years, Cardinal **Karol Wojtyla** of Poland, who takes the name **John Paul II.**

October 17

Holidays

Haiti   **Dessalines Memorial Day**
Commemorates the assassination of **Jean Jacques Dessalines,** early black leader of the country, 1806.

Malawi   **Mothers Day**
A day of tribute to the mothers of the country.

Birthdates

1803   **Ferencz Deák,** Hungarian statesman; generally acknowledged ruler of Hungary, 1861–67; effected restoration of Hungarian Constitution, 1867; responsible for establishment of dual monarchy of **Austria-Hungary.** [d. January 29, 1876]

1851   **Thomas Fortune Ryan,** U.S. financier; established first holding company in U.S. in order to gain control of New York City street railways; notorious for his shady financial operations and exploitation of U.S. companies and the Belgian Congo. [d. November 23, 1928]

1859   **Childe Hassam,** U.S. painter, printmaker; one of leading exponents of Impressionism; allowed substantial bequest to the American Academy of Arts and Letters, which provided its support for many years; known as the leader of the **Ten American Painters.** [d. August 27, 1935]

1864   **Robert Lansing,** U.S. lawyer, diplomat; leading American expert on international law; U.S. Secretary of State, 1915–20; responsible for U.S. purchase of **Virgin Islands.** [d. October 30, 1928]

1880   **Charles Herbert Kraft,** U.S. food-products manufacturer; founder of the J. L. Kraft Co., 1909, and Kraft Foods, Inc., 1945. [d. March 25, 1952]

1895   **Doris Humphrey,** U.S. dancer, choreographer, teacher; major influence in U.S. modern dance movement. [d. December 29, 1958]

1909   **(William Randolph) Cozy Cole,** U.S. jazz drummer.

1912   **Pope John Paul I (Albino Luciani),** pope for 34 days, 1978. [d. September 29, 1978]

1914   **Sarah Churchill,** British actress; daughter of Sir Winston Churchill (November 30). [d. September 24, 1982]

1915   **Arthur Miller,** U.S. dramatist; author of *Death of a Salesman, The Crucible, A View from The Bridge.* Awarded Pulitzer Prize in drama, 1949.

1918   **Rita Hayworth (Margarita Carmen Cansino),** U.S. actress.

1920   **Montgomery Clift,** U.S. actor. [d. July 23, 1966]

1930   **Jimmy Breslin,** U.S. journalist, novelist; noted for his Runyonesque syndicated column and novels. Wrote *The Gang that Couldn't Shoot Straight.*

1938   **(Robert Craig) Evel Knievel,** U.S. stunt motorcyclist.

Historical Events

1346   **Queen Philippa** of England, wife of **Edward III,** defeats and captures **David II** of Scotland at **Neville's Cross.**

1483   **Spanish Inquisition** is placed under joint direction of state and church.

1777   English **General John Burgoyne** capitulates to American troops at **Saratoga (American Revolution).**

1797   **Peace of Campo Formio** between France and Austria is signed; Austria cedes Belgium and Lombardy and obtains Istria, Dalmatia, and Venice.

1854   **Siege of Sebastopol** begins, pitting Allies (Turkey, Britain, France, Austria) against Russia (**Crimean War**).

1907   Wireless telegraph newspaper service between England and U.S. begins.

1918   **Hungary** declares independence from Austria.

1941   Prior to U.S. entry into World War II, U.S. destroyer *Kearny,* escorting British ships, is torpedoed off Iceland; 11 men are lost.

The Saints

St. Ignatius, Bishop of Antioch and martyr. Also called **Theophorous,** or *God Bearer.* [d. c. 107]. Feast formerly February 1. Obligatory Memorial.

St. John the Dwarf, hermit. [d. 5th century]

St. Anstrudis, virgin. Also called **Anstru, Austrude.** [d. c. 700]

St. Nothelm, Archbishop of Canterbury. [d. c. 740]

St. Seraphino, Capuchin laybrother. [d. 1604]

St. Margaret Mary, virgin and visionary. [d. 1690]

The Ursuline Martyrs of Valenciennes. [d. 1794]

The Beatified

Blessed John Baptist Turpin du Cormier, Blessed Mary L'Huilier, and their companions, martyrs. [d. 1794]

All U.S. merchant ships in Asiatic waters are ordered into friendly ports.

1944 Chicago's first **subway** formally opens.

1960 U.S. variety store chains, Woolworth's, W. T. Grant's, and McCrory-McLellan, begin racial **integration** of their lunch counters in more than 100 southern cities.

1966 **Botswana** and **Lesotho** are admitted to the UN.

1973 Organization of Arab Petroleum Exporting Countries imposes a cut in the flow of oil to force the U.S. to change its Middle East policy, marking the beginning of the **Arab oil embargo.**

1977 U.S. Supreme Court permits the supersonic *Concorde* to begin test flights to New York's Kennedy International Airport.

October 18

Holidays

U.S. (Alaska)   **Alaska Day**
Commemorates the transfer of Alaska from Russia to the U.S., 1867.

Birthdates

1405   **Pius II,** pope 1458–64. [d. August 14 or 15, 1464]

1631   **Michael Wigglesworth,** American colonial poet, clergyman; best known for his 224-stanza poem *The Day of Doom: Or a Poetical Description of the Great and Last Judgment,* 1662, a dramatic exposition of Calvinist theology. [d. June 10, 1705]

1697   **Canaletto (Giovanni Antonio Canal),** Italian painter, etcher, known for his urban scenes, especially of Venice. [d. April 19, 1768]

1824   **Juan Valera y Alcalá Galiano,** Spanish novelist, man of letters; Minister of Public Instruction, 1871–1905; Ambassador to Washington, 1883–86; Minister to Lisbon, 1886–88; Ambassador to Vienna, 1893–95. [d. April 18, 1905]

1831   **Thomas Hunter,** U.S. educator; founder of Normal College of City of New York (later **Hunter College**). [d. October 14, 1915]

       Frederick III, King of Prussia, 1888; ruled for only 88 days. [d. June 15, 1888]

1836   **Ellen Browning Scripps,** U.S. newspaper publisher, philanthropist; with her brother E. W. Scripps (March 19) was active in family-owned newspaper chain; founder of **Scripps College for Women** (later part of the **Claremont Colleges,** Claremont, California). [d. August 3, 1932]

1844   **Harvey W. Wiley,** U.S. chemist; responsible for enactment of U.S. **Pure Food & Drug Act of 1906.** [d. June 30, 1930]

1854   **(Salomon) August Andrée,** Swedish balloonist; lost during 1897 attempt to cross the North Pole in a balloon. [d. 1897]

1859   **Henri Bergson,** French philosopher, founder of **Bergsonism,** a philosophy based on concept of time as duration; Nobel Prize in literature, 1927. [d. January 4, 1941]

1878   **James Truslow Adams,** U.S. historian; Pulitzer Prize in history, 1922; noted for his popular books on American history, including the six-volume *Dictionary of American History.* [d. 1849]

1889   **Fannie Hurst,** U.S. novelist, short-story writer. [d. February 23, 1968]

1900   **Lotte Lenya (Karoline Blamauer),** Austrian actress, singer; known for her interpretation of first husband Kurt Weill's songs and characters, especially as Jenny in *The Threepenny Opera.* [d. November 27, 1981]

1903   **Evelyn (Arthur St. John) Waugh,** British novelist; noted for sophisticated, satirical portrayals of 20th-century society. [d. April 10, 1966]

1905   **Felix Houphouet-Boigny,** President, Republic of Ivory Coast, 1960– .

1919   **Pierre Elliott Trudeau,** Canadian political leader; Prime Minister of Canada, 1968–79; 1980–84; leader of federal Liberal Party, 1968–84.

1921   **Jesse A. Helms,** U.S. politician, newspaper editor; U.S. Senator from North Carolina, 1973– .

1922   **Richard (Peter) Stankiewicz,** U.S. sculptor; a pioneer in **junk art;** his works are on display in most major American museums of art.

1925   **Melina (Amalia) Mercouri,** Greek actress, political activist; Minister of Culture of Greece.

1927   **George C(ampbell) Scott,** U.S. actor, director.

1939   **Lee Harvey Oswald,** alleged assassin of U.S. President John F. Kennedy; was in turn killed by Jack Ruby two days after Kennedy's assassination. [d. November 24, 1963]

Religious Calendar

Feasts

St. Luke, evangelist. Patron of doctors, painters, glassmakers, lacemakers, and artists. [d. 1st century] [major holy day, Episcopal Church; minor festival, Lutheran Church.]

The Saints

St. Gwen of Cornwall. Also called **Wenn.** [death date unknown]

St. Justus of Beauvais, martyr. Also called **Justin.** [death date unknown]

Historical Events

1469   **Isabella of Castile** marries **Ferdinand II of Aragon,** thus uniting nearly all of the Christian areas of Spain in one monarchy.

1685   **Louis XIV** of France revokes **Edict of Nantes**, which had given religious freedom to French Huguenots.

1748   **Peace of Aix-la-Chapelle** ends the **War of the Austrian Succession.**

1854   **Ostend Manifesto** of the U.S. declares that if Spain refuses to sell Cuba to the U.S., the U.S. can take it by force.

1904   **Gustav Mahler** conducts the premiere performance of his Fifth Symphony.

1908   **Congo Free State** becomes **Belgian Congo** as Leopold II of Belgium transfers control of the territory to parliament.

1912   **First Balkan War** escalates as Bulgaria, Serbia, and Greece Montenegro join against Turkey.

       Italian-Turkey **Treaty of Lausanne** gives Italy control of Tripoli and Cyrenaica; Turkey gets Dodecanese.

1922   **British Broadcasting Co., Ltd.,** is established as a private corporation.

1933   **Commodity Credit Corporation** is established in U.S., primarily to extend loans to farmers.

October 19

Religious Calendar

The Saints

SS. Ptolemaeus, Lucius, and Another, martyrs. Ptolemaeus also called Ptolemy. [d. c. 161]

St. Varus, martyr, and St. Cleopatra, widow. [d. c. 4th century]

St. Ethbin, abbot. Also called Egbin. [d. 6th century]

Birthdates

1433 **Marsilio Ficino,** Italian philosopher, scholar; known as translator of Plato into Latin. [d. October 1, 1499]

1605 **Sir Thomas Browne,** English physician; best known for book of reflections, *Religio Medici.* [d. October 19, 1682]

1784 **(James Henry) Leigh Hunt,** English critic, essayist, poet, and playwright; associate of the major British Romantic poets, Keats, Shelley, and Byron; best known for his essays and *Autobiography,* 1850. [d. August 28, 1859]

James McLaughlin, Canadian fur trader; known as the father of Oregon because of the assistance he gave American settlers in that region. [d. September 13, 1857]

1859 **Alfred Dreyfus,** Jewish French Army officer; victim of anti-Semitism, convicted of treason on false evidence and sent to Devil's Island; was championed by Emile Zola, who wrote *J'accuse* in his defense; it eventually won him his pardon. [d. July 11, 1935]

1862 **Auguste Lumière,** French inventor, with his brother Louis, of the **motion picture.** [d. April 10, 1954]

1895 **Lewis Mumford,** U.S. social critic, author; noted for his writing and teaching, particularly in the areas of art, architecture, urban planning, and conservation.

1899 **Miguel Angel Asturias,** Guatemalan novelist, short-story writer; Nobel Prize in literature, 1967. [d. June 9, 1974]

1901 **Arleigh Burke,** U.S. naval commander; Chief of U.S. Naval Operations, 1955–61.

1922 **Jack Anderson,** U.S. journalist; successor to Drew Pearson (December 13).

1931 **John Le Carré (David John Moore Cornwell),** British novelist; author of *The Spy Who Came in from the Cold, The Little Drummer Girl,* and other spy novels.

Historical Events

1216 **King John** of England dies and is succeeded by **Henry III.**

1453 Bordeaux surrenders to the French; English retain only Calais and the Channel Islands (**Hundred Years' War**).

1781 British General Lord Cornwallis surrenders to Americans at **Yorktown (American Revolution).**

1914 The Germans open the **First Battle of Ypres (World War I).**

1915 Russia and Italy declare war on Bulgaria (**World War I**).

1941 German submarine sinks U.S. merchant ship *Lehigh* (**World War II**).

1943 **Moscow Conference of Foreign Ministers** opens; it is the first Allied meeting of World War II.

1983 U.S. Senate passes a bill making **Martin Luther King Jr.'s** birthday an annual federal holiday, beginning in 1986.

St. Aquilinus, Bishop of Eureux. [d. c. 695]

St. Frideswide, virgin and abbess. Also called **Frévisse.** Patron of Oxford, England and the University of Oxford. [d. c. 735]

St. Peter of Alcántara, hermit and mystic. Patron of night watchmen. [d. 1562]

St. Issac Jogues and his Companions. [d. 1647] Optional Memorial.

St. Jean de Brébeuf, Jesuit priest and martyr. Protomartyr of North America. [d. 1649]

St. Paul of the Cross, founder of the Barefooted Clerks of the Holy Cross and Passion, also called the Passionist Congregation. Feast formerly April 28. [d. 1775] Optional Memorial.

The Beatified

Blessed Thomas of Bioille, deacon. [d. 1257]

October 20

Holidays

Guatemala	**1944 Revolution Day** Commemorates the overthrow of military strongman, **General Federico Ponce,** 1944.
Kenya	**Kenyatta Day** Commemorates **Jomo Kenyatta,** the nation's first president.

Birthdates

1616   **Thomas Bartholin,** Danish physician; noted for discovery of **lymphatic vessels.** [d. December 4, 1680]

1632   **Sir Christopher Wren,** English architect, astronomer; proposed plan for rebuilding London after Great Fire, 1666; designed more than 50 churches in London, especially **St. Paul's Cathedral,** London. [d. February 25, 1723]

1741   **Angelica Kauffman,** Swiss-Italian painter and engraver. [d. November 5, 1807]

1762   **André-Marie Chénier,** French poet; one of greatest French classical poets after Racine; guillotined during Reign of Terror, 1794. [d. July 25, 1794]

1784   **(Henry John Temple), Viscount Palmerston,** English statesman; known as *Pam;* Home Secretary, 1853–55; Prime Minister, 1855–65; effected independence of Belgium, 1830; annexed Hong Kong, 1840–41. [d. October 18, 1865]

1822   **Thomas Hughes,** English reformer, author, jurist; founder of **Working Men's College** and its principal, 1872–83; established a model community in America which failed, 1879; best known as author of *Tom Brown's School Days* and *Tom Brown at Oxford.* [d. March 22, 1896]

1854   **Patrick Geddes,** British biologist, sociologist, educator, and city planner; noted for his avante-garde theories of the interrelationships between biology and sociology. [d. April 17, 1932]

       (Jean Nicolas) Arthur Rimbaud, French poet; known for his highly imaginative verse forms; associated with Symbolist School; wrote most of his poetry before the age of 20. [d. November 10, 1891]

1859   **John Dewey,** U.S. philosopher, educator, psychologist; head of Department of Philosophy, Psychology, and Pedagogy at the University of Chicago, 1894–1904; established Laboratory School to test his educational theories; a founder of the American Association of University Professors. [d. June 1, 1952]

1874   **Charles Edward Ives,** U.S. composer; Pulitzer Prize in music, 1947. [d. May 19, 1954]

1891   **Sir James Chadwick,** British physicist; Nobel Prize in physics for discovery of the **neutron,** 1935. [d. July 24, 1974]

1900   **Wayne Morse,** U.S. politician, lawyer; U.S. Senator, 1944–69. [d. July 22, 1974]

1904   **George Woodcock,** British labor leader, union official; General Secretary, Trades Union Congress, 1960–69. [d. October 30, 1979]

1905   **Frederic Dannay,** U.S. mystery writer; with his partner, Manfred B. Lee (January 11), created the **Ellery Queen** series. [d. September 3, 1982]

1925   **Art Buchwald,** U.S. journalist; his syndicated columns describe current controversies in a humorous tone.

1931   **Mickey Mantle,** U.S. baseball player; by the time of his retirement, 1969, he had 536 home runs and more than 1700 strikeouts. Elected to Baseball Hall of Fame, 1974.

1944   **William Albright,** U.S. composer; noted chiefly for experimental techniques.

Historical Events

1740   **Charles VI,** last male heir to **Hapsburg empire,** dies; he is succeeded by his daughter **Maria Theresa,** Queen of Bohemia and Hungary.

Religious Calendar

The Saints

St. Caprasius, martyr. [d. 3rd century]

St. Artemius, martyr. [d. 363]

St. Acca, Bishop of Hexham. [d. 740]

St. Andrew of Crete, martyr. Also called the *Calybite* [d. 766]

St. Bertilla Boscardin, virgin and nursing sister. [d. 1922]

The Beatified

Blessed Mary Teresa de Soubiran, virgin and founder of the Society of Mary Auxiliatrix. [d. 1889]

1818 Boundary between Canada and U.S. from Lake of the Woods to crest of Rocky Mountains is set at **49th parallel.**

1827 **Battle of Navarino** results in the destruction of the Egyptian-Turkish fleet by British, French, and Russian squadrons.

1883 **Peace of Ancón** ends **Saltpeter War** between Peru and Chile.

1899 Boers launch attack on British garrison at **Ladysmith, Natal (Boer War).**

1928 **French Academy** rules that **celibacy** is no longer a *conditio sine qua non* for applicants for the **Prix de Rome.**

1944 Russian and Yugoslav forces capture **Belgrade (World War II).**

1950 **Pyongyang,** capital of North Korea, is captured by UN forces (**Korean War**).

1973 **Sydney (Australia) Opera House** is officially opened by **Queen Elizabeth II.**

U.S. Attorney General **Elliott Richardson** resigns in dispute with U.S. President Richard Nixon over Watergate special prosecutor **Archibald Cox.**

October 21

Holidays

British Virgin Islands	**St. Ursula's Day**
Honduras	**Armed Forces Day**
Somali Democratic Republic	**Revolution Anniversary** Commemorates the rise to power of **Major General Mohammed Siad Barre** and establishment of a Supreme Revolutionary Council, 1969.

Birthdates

1660 **Georg Ernst Stahl,** German physician, chemist; proposed theory of phlogiston to explain combustion; enunciated a doctrine of animism, wherein the soul is the vital principle in organic development. [d. May 14, 1734]

1760 **Katsushika Hokusai,** Japanese painter, printmaker; noted for his technical excellence; his work has had great influence on artists of other countries; among his works are *Hundred Views of Mount Fuji*, 1835, and the 15-volume *Ten Thousand Sketches*, through 1836. [d. May 10, 1849]

1772 **Samuel Taylor Coleridge,** English poet, critic, essayist; one of spokesmen of the Romantic movement in English literature. [d. July 25, 1834]

1785 **Henry Miller Shreve,** U.S. riverboat captain; initiated commercial transportation on America's rivers; developed the snagboat, which was used to clear rivers of debris and make them navigable; superintendent of river improvements in the West, 1827–42; **Shreveport, Louisiana** is named for him. [d. March 6, 1851]

1790 **Alphonse Marie Louis Prat de Lamartine,** French man of letters; his *Méditations Poétiques* greatly influenced the Romantic movement in French literature. [d. February 28, 1869]

1833 **Alfred Bernhard Nobel,** Swedish industrialist, inventor, philanthropist; inventor of **dynamite;** his fortune was left to support the **Nobel Prizes** in peace, medicine, chemistry, physics, and literature, awarded annually since 1901. [d. December 10, 1896]

1861 **Prince Georgy Yevgenyevich Lvov,** first president of the Russian Provisional Government after Russian Revolution, 1917. [d. March 6, 1925]

1869 **William Edward Dodd,** U.S. educator, historian, and diplomat; U.S. Ambassador to Germany, 1933–37. [d. February 9, 1940]

1877 **Ostwald T. Avery,** Canadian bacteriologist; conducted early studies of DNA molecules. [d. February 20, 1955]

1912 **Sir Georg Solti,** British conductor, born in Hungary; Music Director, Royal Opera House, Covent Garden, 1961–71; Principal Conductor, Artistic Director, London Philharmonic Orchestra, 1979– .

1917 **(John Birks), Dizzy Gillespie** U.S. jazz musician.

Historical Events

1345 English, under **Earl of Derby,** defeat French at **Auberoche (Hundred Years' War).**

1422 **Charles VI** of France dies and is succeeded by **Charles VII.**

1805 **Lord Horatio Nelson** of Great Britain destroys Franco-Spanish fleet in the **Battle of Trafalgar (Napoleonic Wars).**

1879 **Thomas Edison** successfully demonstrates for the first time a carbon-filament **incandescent lamp.**

1914 British and Japanese forces take the German **Mariana and Marshall Islands** in the Pacific (**World War I**).

1915 First **transatlantic radio-telephone transmission** is made, from Arlington, Virginia, to Paris.

1918 **Czechoslovakia** declares its independence from Austria-Hungary.

The Saints

St. Hilarion, abbot and hermit. [d. c. 371]

St. Malchus. Also called **Malek.** [d. 4th cent.]

St. Fintan of Taghmon, abbot. Also called **Munnu.** [d. c. 635]

St. Tuda, Bishop of Northumbria. [d. 664]

St. Condedus, hermit. Also called **Condé, Condède.** [d. c. 685]

St. John of Bridlington, Canon Regular. [d. 1379]

St. Ursula and her Maidens, martyrs; patron of educators of young girls. Invoked for a good death. Ursuline Order named in her honor. [death date unknown]

The Beatified

Blessed James Strepar, Archbishop of Galich. [d. c. 1409]

Blessed Peter of Tiferno, confessor. [d. 1445]

Blessed Matthew, Bishop of Girgenti. [d. 1450]

1937 Franco's troops capture **Gijon,** completing the conquest of northwest Spain (**Spanish Civil War**).

1938 Japanese troops take Chinese city of **Canton,** which had been mercilessly bombed for months (**World War II**).

1944 U.S. First Army takes **Aachen,** after eight days of fierce fighting; it is the first large German city to fall to the Allies (**World War II**).

1960 Queen Elizabeth II launches Britain's first nuclear submarine, the *Dreadnought.*

1966 A colliery slag heap slips and crushes more than 140 persons and buries a school and several other buildings in **Aberfan, Wales.**

1973 Kuwait, Bahrain, Qatar, and Dubai announce a boycott of oil shipments to the U.S., completing the **Arab oil embargo** begun on October 17.

1976 Americans win all five Nobel prizes for 1976.

Cincinnati Reds win the World Series against the New York Yankees, becoming the first National League baseball team in 54 years to win two consecutive series.

1979 Israeli Foreign Minister **Moshe Dayan** resigns cabinet post in controversy over Palestinian autonomy.

October 22

Holidays

Somali Democratic Republic — **Revolution Anniversary** Second day of the celebration.

Birthdates

1740 **Sir Philip Francis,** British politician; reputed author of *Letters of Junius,* 69 letters attacking prominent British figures of the day. [d. December 23, 1818]

1811 **Franz Liszt,** Hungarian piano virtuoso, composer; known for his advanced musical techniques and methods of composition; in later years, became member of Franciscan order; known as *Abbé Liszt.* [d. July 31, 1886]

1818 **Charles Marie René Leconte de Lisle,** French poet; identified with Parnassian school; wrote poetry of disillusionment and skepticism inspired by the works of the ancients. [d. July 17, 1894]

1844 **Sarah Bernhardt (Henriette Rosine Bernard),** French actress; known as *The Divine Sarah*; renowned for her dramatic portrayals of tragic heroines as well as for her flamboyant lifestyle; continued her stage career in spite of an amputated leg, 1914; named to Legion of Honor, 1914. [d. March 23, 1923]

1881 **Clinton Joseph Davisson,** U.S. physicist; Nobel Prize in physics for discovery of diffraction of electrons by crystals (with G. P. Thomson), 1937. [d. February 1, 1958]

1887 **John Reed,** U.S. poet, radical journalist; as a reporter for *Metropolitan* magazine, was sent to cover several world-famous events, including Pancho Villa's revolutionary activities in Mexico, World War I action on the Eastern Front, and the October Revolution in Russia, 1917, about which he wrote *Ten Days That Shook the World.* Became a close friend of V. I. Lenin. Was named as seditious radical in U.S. and was arrested numerous times; escaped to Finland; died in Russia at age of 33; buried in Kremlin. [d. October 19, 1920]

1900 **Edward Reilly Stettinius, Jr.,** U.S. statesman, industrialist; executive, U.S. Steel Corp., 1935–39; Chairman, War Resources Board, 1939–40; administrator of Lend-Lease, 1941–43; U.S. Secretary of State, 1944–45; Chairman of U.S. delegation to UN, 1945–46. [d. October 31, 1949]

1903 **George Wells Beadle,** U.S. geneticist; Nobel Prize in physiology or medicine for discovery that genes transmit hereditary traits (with E. L. Tatum), 1958.

1904 **Constance Bennett,** U.S. actress; a leading lady of 1930s films.

1905 **Karl Guthe Janksy,** U.S. radio engineer; his experiments in determining sources of radio waves led to the development of radio astronomy. [d. February 14, 1950]

1917 **Joan Fontaine,** U.S. actress, born in Japan of British parents; sister of Olivia de Haviland (July 1).

1919 **Doris Lessing,** British novelist, short-story writer.

1920 **Timothy Francis Leary,** U.S. psychologist, educator; at the forefront of the drug controversy of the 1960s in the U.S.

1936 **Bobby Seale,** U.S. radical; a founder of **Black Panther Party,** 1966.

1942 **Annette Funicello,** U.S. actress; an original Disney Mousketeer in 1950s.

1943 **Catherine Deneuve,** French actress.

Historical Events

1721 **Peter I** is proclaimed Emperor of All the Russias.

1797 **André Jacques Garnerin,** French aeronaut and inventor of the **parachute,** makes first parachute jump from a balloon, at height of 2000 feet.

1836 **Sam Houston** takes the oath of office as President of the **Texas Republic.**

1873 New York's **Metropolitan Opera House** opens with a performance of Gounod's *Faust.*

1881 **Boston Symphony Orchestra** is founded with Georg Henschel as its first conductor.

Religious Calendar

The Saints

St. Abercius, Bishop of Hieropolis. [d. c. 200]

SS. Philip, Bishop of Heraclea, and his companions, martyrs. [d. 304]

St. Mallonus, Bishop of Rouen. Also called Melanius, Mello, Mellon. [d. c. 4th cent.]

SS. Nunilo and Alodia, virgins and martyrs. Nunilo also called Nunelo. [d. 851]

St. Donatus, Bishop of Fiesole. [d. c. 876]

1916 **Constanza,** a Romanian port on the Black Sea, is captured by a German-Bulgarian force under von Mackensen (**World War I**).

1935 Mikhail Sholokhov's opera, *Quiet Flows the Don,* opens in Leningrad.

1938 First true **xerographic** image is produced by New York Law School student **Chester Carlson.**

1962 U.S. establishes naval blockade of **Cuba** to prevent introduction of Soviet nuclear weapons there.

1964 **Jean-Paul Sartre,** French writer and philosopher, rejects the Nobel Prize for literature. [d. April 15, 1980]

1968 *Apollo 7* manned space flight comes to a successful conclusion as astronauts Schirra, Eisele, and Cunningham splash down in the Atlantic.

1979 Iran's deposed Shah, **Reza Pahlavi**, arrives secretly in U.S. for medical treatment.

October 23

Religious Calendar

Feasts

St. James of Jerusalem, Brother of Our Lord Jesus Christ, and martyr. [major holy day, Episcopal Church]

The Saints

St. Theodoret, martyr. [d. 362]

St. Severinus, Bishop of Bordeaux; patron of Bordeaux. Also called **Seurin, Surin.** [d. 420]

Birthdates

1715 **Peter II,** Emperor of Russia, 1727–30; died at age 14 of smallpox. [d. January 29, 1730]

1734 **Nicolas-Edme Restiff (de la Bretonne),** French novelist; known as the *Rousseau of the Gutter* and the *Voltaire of Chambermaids.* [d. February 3, 1806]

1773 **Francis Jeffrey,** Scottish critic and longtime editor of the *Edinburgh Review.* [d. January 26, 1850]

1817 **Pierre Athanase Larousse,** French lexicographer, encyclopedist; among his most notable accomplishments was the *Grand Dictionnaire Universal du XIX Siècle,* the great dictionary of France. [d. January 3, 1875]

1831 **Basil Lanneau Gildersleeve,** U.S. educator, philologist; recognized as one of the foremost classical scholars of the U.S. in the 19th century. [d. January 9, 1924]

1835 **Adlai E(wing) Stevenson,** U.S. Congressman, 1875–77; 1879–81; Vice-President of U.S., 1893–97; grandfather of Adlai E. Stevenson (February 5). [d. June 14, 1914]

1838 **Francis Hopkinson Smith,** U.S. author; wrote chiefly novels about the American South. [d. April 7, 1915]

1844 **Robert Seymour Bridges,** British poet; known for innovations in English verse, giving more freedom to accentuation and flexibility to rhythm; Poet Laureate, 1913–30. [d. April 21, 1930]

1873 **William David Coolidge,** U.S. physicist; invented ductile tungsten; developed **Coolidge tube** for production of x rays, 1913. [d. February 3, 1975]

1890 **Robert McGowan,** U.S. Army general, government official; Chief Quartermaster, U.S. forces, 1942–46; as such, was responsible for supplying food, clothing, and fuel for the two million U.S. combat troops during World War II. [d. May 6, 1982]

1899 **Bernt Balchen,** U.S. aviator, born in Norway; pilot of Richard Byrd's flight over the South Pole, November 28, 1929. [d. October 17, 1973]

1905 **Felix Bloch,** U.S. physicist, born in Switzerland; Nobel Prize in physics for development of nuclear precision measurements of magnetic fields of atomic nuclei (with E. M. Purcell), 1952.

1906 **Gertrude Ederle,** U.S. swimmer; first woman to swim the English Channel, 1926.

1908 **Ilya Mikhaylovich Frank,** Russian physicist; Nobel Prize in physics for discovery of Cherenkov effect (with I. Y. Tamm and P. A. Cherenkov), 1958.

1923 **Ned Rorem,** U.S. composer; Pulitzer Prize in music, 1977.

1925 **Johnny Carson,** U.S. comedian; longtime host of TV's *Tonight Show,* 1962– .

1931 **Diana Dors (Diana Fluck),** British actress. [d. May 4, 1984]

1940 **Pelé (Edson Arantes Do Nascimento),** Brazilian soccer player; led Brazilian national team to three World Cup championships, 1958, 1962, 1970.

1942 **(John) Michael Crichton,** U.S. novelist, filmmaker; well-known for his mystery stories, especially related to science and medicine; wrote *Andromeda Strain, Coma, Terminal Man.*

Historical Events

1385 **University of Heidelberg** is founded by **Pope Urban VI.**

St. Severinus Boethius, martyr and philosopher. Also called **Severin.** [d. 524]

St. Romanus, Bishop of Rouen. [d. c. 640]

St. Ignatius, Patriarch of Constantinople. [d. 877]

St. Ethelfleda, Abbess of Romsey. Also called **Elfleda.** [d. c. 960]

St. Allucio, shepherd; patron of Pescia in Tuscany. [d. 1134]

St. John of Capistrano, Franciscan missionary priest. Feast formerly March 28. [d. 1456] Optional Memorial.

St. Antony Claret, Archbishop of Santiago de Cuba. Founder of the Missionary Sons of the Immaculate Heart of Mary, and confessor to Queen Isabella II. [d. 1870]

The Beatified

Blessed John Buoni, penitent. [d. 1249]

Blessed Bartholomew, Bishop of Vicenza. [d. 1271]

1452	English recapture **Bordeaux** from France (**Hundred Years' War**).
1915	First national championship of **horseshoe pitching** is held at Kellerton, Kansas.
1917	In Russia, a Red Guard unit takes control of **Fortress of Peter and Paul** in Petrograd, beginning the Bolsheviks' **October Revolution.**
	The **Battle of Malmaison,** a French offensive on the Western Front, opens against the Germans (**World War I**).
1927	**Trotsky** and **Linoviev** are expelled from the Central Committee of the Russian Communist Party for their opposition to Stalin's policies.
1955	Premier **Ngo Dinh Diem** wins national referendum establishing him as Chief of State of **South Vietnam**.
1973	North Vietnamese negotiator Le Duc Tho refuses to accept the Nobel Peace Prize because "peace has not yet really been established in South Vietnam."
1980	**Alexei Kosygin** resigns as Chairman of the U.S.S.R. Council of Ministers and as a member of the Politburo for reasons of health.
1983	A terrorist driving a truck filled with explosives makes a suicide attack on **U.S. Marine Corps** headquarters in Beirut, Lebanon. The resulting explosion kills 239 Marines and destroys the building. A similar attack two miles away destroys a French barracks, killing 58.

October 24

Holidays

United Nations Day
Commemorates the effective date of the UN Charter, 1945.

Egypt — **Suez National Day**

Zambia — **Independence Day**
Commemorates gaining of independence of **Northern Rhodesia** as Zambia, 1964.

World Development Information Day
Sponsored by United Nations.

Birthdates

1618 **Aurangzeb (Aurungzeb, Aurungzebe),** 6th emperor of Hindustan; overthrew his father, 1658; last of the great Mughal emperors; conquered Muhammadan kingdoms; alienated both Muhammadans and Hindus with his bigotry. [d. March 3, 1707]

1632 **Anton van Leeuwenhoek,** Dutch biologist; pioneer in development of the **microscope,** with which he made discoveries about the blood, muscle fibers, lens of the human eye, and numerous characteristics of plants. [d. August 26, 1723]

1710 **Alban Butler,** English hagiographer, professor; compiler of *Lives of the Principal Saints,* which remains a classic source today. [d. May 15, 1773]

1788 **Sarah Josepha Buell Hale,** U.S. editor, writer, and feminist; editor of *Godey's Lady's Book,* most influential women's magazine in America of that time; advocate of women's education. [d. April 30, 1879]

1830 **Belva Anna Bennett Lockwood,** U.S. lawyer, suffragist, and reformer; the first woman to argue before the U.S. Supreme Court. [d. May 19, 1917]

1882 **Dame Sybil Thorndike,** English actress; manager of numerous London theaters; created a Dame of the British Empire, 1931. [d. June 9, 1976]

1889 **Arde Bulova,** U.S. manufacturer; founder of Bulova Watch Company. [d. March 19, 1958]

1891 **Rafael (Leonidas) Trujillo Molina,** Dominican political leader, army officer; led revolt against Horacio Vasquez, 1930; ruled as dictator, 1930–61; assassinated. [d. May 30, 1961]

1904 **Moss Hart,** U.S. playwright; collaborated with George S. Kaufman (November 16), Ira Gershwin (September 26), and Kurt Weill (March 2); Awarded the Pulitzer Prize in drama, 1937. [d. December 20, 1961]

1911 **Clarence M. Kelley,** U.S. government official; FBI Director, 1973–78.

Historical Events

1260 **Chartres Cathedral** in France is consecrated.

1360 Final **Peace of Calais** is signed, allowing **Edward III** of England to keep Calais, Angoulême, Channel Islands, and other formerly-French territories (**Hundred Years' War**).

1604 **James I** is declared King of Great Britain, France, and Ireland.

1648 **Peace of Westphalia** is signed, ending **Thirty Years' War** and guaranteeing independence of Switzerland, Netherlands, and all German states.

1795 **Poland** ceases to exist as an independent state when Russia, Prussia, and Austria divide remaining Polish territory in the **Third Partition of Poland.**

1820 **Spain** cedes **Florida** to U.S.

1910 *Naughty Marietta,* a light opera by Victor Herbert, premieres in Syracuse, New York.

1911 **Winston Churchill** is appointed First Lord of Admiralty.

1917 **Battle of Caporetto** in Italy ends in defeat of the Italians by the Austrian and German armies (**World War I**).

Religious Calendar

The Saints

St. Martin, hermit. Also called **Mark.** [d. c. 58]

St. Felix, Bishop of Thibiuca, martyr. [d. 303]

St. Proclus, Archbishop of Constantinople. [d. 446]

St. Aretas and the Martyrs of Najran, and **St. Elesbaan.** [d. 523]

St. Senoch, abbot. Also called **Senou.** [d. 576]

St. Maglorius, Bishop of Dol. Also called **Maelor, Magloire.** [d. 6th century]

St. Martin of Vertou, abbot. [d. 6th century]

St. Evergislus, Bishop of Cologne. Also called **Ebregiselus.** [d. c. 600]

The Beatified

Blessed John Angelo Porro. Patron of novice masters. [d. 1506]

1922 **Irish Free State** constitution is adopted; the Irish Free State is officially proclaimed on December 6, 1922.

1929 **Black Thursday** at the New York Stock Exchange, so named because of panic selling that resulted from downward trend in the market during previous several weeks, marks the beginning of the collapse of the stock market on October 29.

1933 Work begins on the **Ft. Peck Dam** on the Missouri River in Montana, the biggest earth-filled hydroelectric dam in the world at that time.

1944 During **Battle of Leyte Gulf,** U.S. planes sink Japanese battleship *Musashi,* one of the largest ships sunk during **World War II**.

1964 **Republic of Zambia** gains independence from Great Britain.

October 25

Holidays

Taiwan **Taiwan Restoration Day** Commemorates the return of Taiwan to the possession of China after 50 years of occupation by the Japanese, 1945.

Birthdates

1759 **William Wyndham Grenville, Baron Grenville,** English politician; Foreign Secretary, 1791–1801; frequently associated with coalition government called the *All-the-Talents Administration*, 1806–07, which abolished the **English slave trade.** [d. January 12, 1834]

1767 **Henri Benjamin Constant de Rebecque,** French novelist, statesman; protégé of Madame de Staël; member of French Chamber of Deputies, 1819–30. [d. December 8, 1830]

1789 **Heinrich Samuel Schwabe,** German astronomer; discovered 11-year cycle of **sunspots,** 1843. [d. April 11, 1875]

1800 **Thomas Babington Macaulay,** British historian, statesman; member of Parliament, 1830–34; 1839–47; 1852–56; author of *History of England*, five volumes covering period 1848–61; noted for his numerous essays on Milton and others, as well as biographical sketches, speeches, etc. [d. December 28, 1859]

1811 **Evariste Galois,** French mathematician; a founder of **theory of groups** and modern **theory of functions.** [d. May 31, 1832]

1825 **Johann Strauss, (the Younger),** Austrian composer, known as the *Waltz King*; succeeded his father, Johann Strauss, as leader of orchestra of Vienna; toured widely before 1863; thereafter, devoted himself to composition; wrote *Die Fledermaus, The Blue Danube*. [d. June 3, 1899]

1838 **Georges (Aléxandre César Léopold) Bizet,** French composer; composed *Carmen, Jeux d'enfants*. [d. June 3, 1875]

1848 **William Henry Moore,** U.S. financier; founder of National Biscuit Co., 1898; American Can Co., 1901; and Rock Island Railroad Co., 1901. [d. January 11, 1923]

1864 **John Francis Dodge,** U.S. manufacturer; with his brother, Horace (May 17), founded the Dodge Automobile Co., 1901. [d. January 14, 1920]

1877 **Henry Norris Russell,** U.S. astronomer; developer of the method of determining stellar types; with Ejnar Hertzsprung, after 1910, developed the **Hertzsprung-Russell Diagram** for illustrating relationship of spectral class and absolute magnitude of stars. [d. February 18, 1957]

1881 **Pablo Picasso,** Spanish painter, sculptor; one of foremost figures in modern art. [d. April 8, 1973]

1888 **Richard Evelyn Byrd,** U.S. admiral, aviator, explorer, author; made first flight over North Pole, 1926, and over South Pole, 1929; later conducted scientific expeditions to the South Pole. [d. March 11, 1957]

1890 **Floyd Bennett,** U.S. aviator; with Admiral Richard Byrd was the first to fly over the North Pole, 1926. [d. April 25, 1928]

1891 **Charles Edward Coughlin,** U.S. Roman Catholic priest, political activist; known for his opposition to the policies of the Roosevelt administration, expressing his reactionary and anti-Semitic views in the magazine *Social Justice* and on radio. [d. October 27, 1979]

1892 **Leo G. Carroll,** British character actor. [d. October 16, 1972]

Dolly Sisters (Rosie and Jenny), twins; a popular vaudeville dance act. [Rosie d.

Religious Calendar

The Saints

St. Gaudentius, Bishop of Brescia. [d. c. 410]

SS. Chrysanthus and Daria, martyrs. [death date unknown]

SS. Crispin and Crispinian, martyrs; patron saints of shoemakers, cobblers, and other workers in leather. [death date unknown]

SS. Fronto and George, bishops. [death date unknown]

The Beatified

Blessed Christopher of Romagnola, Friar Minor. [d. 1272]

Blessed Thomas of Florence, lay brother. [d. 1447]

Blessed Balthasar of Chiavari, Friar Minor. Patron of playing card makers. Invoked against epilepsy. [d. 1492]

Blessed Thaddeus, Bishop of Cork and Cloyne. [d. 1497]

The Martyrs of England and Wales, a festival of all 200 beatified English and Welsh martyrs, 1535–1681; includes **London Martyrs of 1588.**

February 1, 1970; Jenny committed suicide June 1, 1941]

1902 **Henry Steele Commager,** U.S. historian; major interpreter of American history and development; author of *The American Mind, Documents of American History.*

1912 **Minnie Pearl (Sarah Ophelia Colley Cannon),** U.S. country singer, comedienne.

1914 **John Berryman,** U.S. poet; Pulitzer Prize in poetry, 1965, for *Dream Songs.* [committed suicide January 7, 1972]

1930 **Hanna Holborn Gray,** U.S. educator, born in Germany; acting president, Yale University, 1977–78; President, University of Chicago, 1978– .

1941 **Helen Reddy,** Australian singer.

Historical Events

732 **Charles Martel** defeats the Arabs at Poitiers, marking the total overthrow of Muslims in France.

1154 **King Stephen** of England dies and is succeeded by **Henry II,** establishing the house of **Plantagenet,** who rule England until 1399.

1415 **Henry V** of England defeats French at **Agincourt (Hundred Years' War).**

1555 **Charles V,** Holy Roman Emperor, resigns Italy and the Netherlands to his son, **Philip II** of Spain, in ceremonies at the Hall of the Golden Fleece in the Netherlands.

1760 **George II** of Great Britain dies and is succeeded by **George III,** his grandson.

1812 **Stephen Decatur,** in the *U.S.S. United States,* captures the *H.M.S. Macedonian* **(War of 1812).**

1854 **Battle of Balaclava** (in which the **Charge of the Light Brigade** occurs) between the Russians and Great Britain and her Turkish allies, begins **(Crimean War.).**

1874 Great Britain annexes **Fiji Islands.**

1900 The British formally annex the **South African Boer Republic** during the course of the Boer War and rename it **Transvaal Colony.**

1918 **Battle of Vittorio Veneto,** the final Italian offensive against the Austrians, opens between the Brenta and Piave Rivers (**World War I**).

1920 **Terence MacSweney,** Lord Mayor of Cork, dies on 74th day of hunger strike in Brixton jail, Cork.

1938 **Mussolini** declares **Libya** a part of Italy.

Chinese city of **Hankow** falls to Japanese.

1944 **Battle of Leyte Gulf** (last and greatest naval engagement of World War II) ends in decisive defeat for Japanese.

1955 **Austria** becomes free and independent for the first time since 1938 as the **Austrian State Treaty** ends the Soviet-administered four power (Potsdam) occupation.

1961 **Outer Mongolia** and **Mauritania** are admitted to **United Nations.**

1962 **Uganda** becomes a member of the **United Nations.**

1971 UN General Assembly approves admission of **People's Republic of China** to the UN and expels **Nationalist China (Taiwan).**

1983 An assault force led by U.S. Marines and Army Rangers invades the Caribbean island of **Grenada.**

October 26

Holidays

Austria	National Holiday
Benin,	Armed Forces Day
Rwanda	

Religious Calendar

The Saints

St. Evaristus, pope and martyr. Elected 97 or 99. [d. c. 107]

SS. Lucian and Marcian, martyrs. [d. c. 250]

Birthdates

1466   **Desiderius Erasmus,** Dutch scholar; regarded as the leader of the Renaissance in northern Europe. [d. July 12, 1536]

1673   **Dimitrie Kantemir (Cantemir),** Hospodar of Moldavia, historian and writer; author of *History of the Growth and Decay of the Ottoman Empire.* [d. August 21, 1723]

1685   **(Giuseppe) Domenico Scarlatti,** Italian composer; especially noted for harpsichord music. [d. July 23, 1757]

1757   **Charles Pinckney,** U.S. politician, diplomat; one of most important contributors to U.S. constitution; creator of the **Pinckney Draught;** Governor of South Carolina, 1790–96; U.S. Senator, 1798–1801; U.S. Minister to Spain, 1801–04. [d. October 29, 1824]

1759   **Georges Jacques Dainton,** French revolutionary leader; a founder of the **Cordelier;** overthrown by **Robespierre** and leaders of **Reign of Terror**; condemned and guillotined. [d. April 5, 1794]

1786   **Henry Deringer,** U.S. firearms inventor, manufacturer; invented the short-barreled pocket pistol called the *derringer.* [d. 1868]

1787   **Vuk Stefanović Karadžić,** Serbian lexicographer, folklorist; credited with simplifying Cyrillic alphabet used in Serbia; expert on Serbian grammar; published anthology of Serbian folk songs. [d. January 26, 1864]

1800   **Count Helmuth von Moltke,** Prussian soldier, field marshal; Chief of Staff of Prussian Army, 1858–88. [d. April 24, 1891]

1802   **Dom Miguel,** King of Portugal, 1828–33. [d. November 14, 1866]

1854   **Charles William Post,** U.S. breakfast food manufacturer; founder of C. W. Post Co., 1894. [d. May 9, 1914]

1858   **Take Ionescu,** Romanian politician, writer, and orator; Prime Minister of Romania, 1921–22. [d. June 21, 1922]

1876   **H(erbert) B(ryan) Warner,** British actor. [d. December 24, 1958]

1879   **Leon Trotsky,** Russian Communist leader; People's Commissar for Foreign Affairs, 1917; Commissar of War, 1918; close associate of Lenin; exiled after defeat by Stalin in conflict for control of Party, 1929; murdered in Mexico. [d. August 21, 1940]

1889   **Millar Burrows,** U.S. clergyman; authority on Dead Sea Scrolls. [d. April 29, 1980]

1894   **John S(hively) Knight,** U.S. newspaper publisher; founder of Knight-Ridder Newspapers, Inc.; Pulitzer Prize in editorial writing, 1968. [d. June 16, 1981]

1909   **Igor Gorin,** U.S. operatic baritone, composer, born in Russia; well known for his showmanship as well as his musicianship. [d. March 24, 1982]

1914   **Jackie Coogan (John Leslie),** U.S. actor. [d. March 1, 1984]

1916   **François Mitterand,** French statesman; President, 1981– .

1919   **Shah Mohammed Reza Pahlavi,** Shah of Iran, 1941–79; forced into exile by fundamentalist Shi'ite Moslems led by Ayatollah Khomeini, 1979. [d. July 27, 1980]

      Edward W. Brooke, U.S. Senator, 1966–80; first black senator to be elected since 1876.

Historical Events

1825   **Erie Canal** is opened in New York State.

1856   First Portuguese railway is opened.

St. Rusticus, Bishop of Narbonne. Also called **Rotiri.** [d. c. 461]

St. Cedd, Bishop of the East Saxons. [d. 664]

St. Eata, Bishop of Hexham. [d. 686]

St. Bean, Bishop of Mortlach. [d. 11th century]

The Beatified

Blessed Damian of Finario, Dominican priest. [d. 1484]

Blessed Bonaventure of Potenza, Conventual Friar Minor. [d. 1711]

1863 **International Committee of the Red Cross** is established at a meeting of nations in Geneva, Switzerland.

1896 **Treaty of Addis Ababa** is signed, establishing peace between Italy and Abyssinia (Ethiopia), and recognizing the independence of **Abyssinia.**

1905 Russian workers in St. Petersburg establish first *soviet* (assembly).

A treaty of separation, nullifying the 91-year-old **Union of Sweden and Norway,** is signed.

1951 **Winston Churchill** is appointed Prime Minister of Great Britain, for the second time, by King George VI.

1955 **Republic of South Vietnam** is established. **Ngo Dinh Diem** proclaims himself President under a provisional constitutional act.

1967 First unmanned docking in space is accomplished between two Russian *Cosmos* satellites.

1973 Widespread violence in **Northern Ireland** includes at least 17 bomb explosions and more than 50 bomb scares.

1976 The first of South Africa's black homelands, the **Republic of Transkei,** is given its independence.

1979 South Korean President **Park Chung Hee** is assassinated by **Kim Jae Kyu,** head of Korean Central Intelligence.

October 27

Holidays

Nauru	**Angam Day**
St. Vincent	**Thanksgiving and Independence Day**
	Commemorates achievement of independence from Great Britain, 1979.
Zaire	**Anniversary of Country's Name Change**
	Celebrates the renaming of the Congo, 1971.

Birthdates

1728   **James Cook,** British navigator; known for his exploration of the South Pacific, especially **Australia, New Zealand,** and the **Hawaiian Islands.** [d. February 14, 1779]

1736   **James Macpherson,** Scottish poet, historian; claimed to have discovered Gaelic epic *Fingal*, which he translated and published; his discovery was disputed by Dr. Johnson and never rebutted by Macpherson; member of Parliament, 1780–96. [d. February 17, 1796]

1760   **August Wilhelm, Count Neithardt von Gneisenau,** Prussian field marshal; noted for his participation in campaigns against Napoleon. [d. August 24, 1831]

1782   **Niccolo Paganini,** Italian composer, violin virtuoso. [d. May 27, 1840]

1811   **Isaac M. Singer,** U.S. inventor; invented the first practical domestic **sewing machine,** 1851. [d. July 23, 1875]

1827   **Marcelin Berthelot,** French chemist; noted for contributions to the field of thermochemistry and his investigations into explosives, dyestuffs, and synthesis of organic compounds. [d. March 18, 1907]

1838   **John Davis Long,** U.S. lawyer, statesman, and author; Governor of Massachusetts, 1880–82; Congressman, 1883–89; U.S. Secretary of the Navy, 1897–1902. [d. August 28, 1915]

1842   **Giovanni Giolitti,** Italian politician; Prime Minister of Italy 1892–93; 1903–05; 1906–09; 1911–14; 1920–21. [d. July 17, 1928]

1844   **Klas P. Arnoldson,** Swedish writer, politician; Nobel Peace Prize for his work in solving problems of the Norwegian-Swedish Union, 1908. [d. February 20, 1916]

1856   **Kenyon Cox,** U.S. mural and figure painter, conservative art critic. [d. March 17, 1919]

1858   **Theodore Roosevelt,** U.S. politician, 26th president of the U.S., 1901–09; as commander of the First U.S. Volunteers Cavalry (the *Rough Riders*) in Cuba, became national hero; as President, pursued antitrust legislation; awarded Nobel Peace Prize for negotiating end of Russo-Japanese War, 1905. [d. January 6, 1919]

1872   **Emily Post,** U.S. journalist; wrote a definitive book of **etiquette** and a syndicated column on that subject. [d. September 25, 1960]

1889   **Enid Bagnold (Lady Roderick Jones),** British novelist, playwright; best known for her novel *National Velvet*. [d. March 31, 1981]

1914   **Dylan (Marlais) Thomas,** Welsh poet, author; known for his innovative poetic style based on rhythm and sound; author of *A Child's Christmas in Wales* and *Under Milk Wood*. [d. November 9, 1953]

1923   **Roy Lichtenstein,** U.S. painter, a leader in the **pop art** movement.

1926   **H(arry) R. Haldeman,** U.S. government official, advertising executive; Chief of Staff of U.S. President Nixon's presidential campaign; convicted of wrongdoing in **Watergate incident.**

1932   **Sylvia Plath,** U.S. poet; became famous posthumously for her volume of poetry, *Ariel*, which was written shortly before her suicide but not published until 1968; author of *The Bell Jar*. [d. February 11, 1963]

Religious Calendar

The Saints

St. Frumentius, Bishop of Aksum. Apostle of Ethiopia. [d. c. 380]

St. Otteran, abbot. Also called **Odhran, Odhuran.** [d. 563]

The Beatified

Blessed Contardo Ferrini, scholar. [d. 1902]

Historical Events

1553 **Michael Servetus,** Spanish physician, theologian, and anti-Trinitarian, is convicted of heresy and blasphemy and burned at the stake at Geneva.

1659 Massachusetts, having outlawed **Quakers,** hangs two who defiantly return to the colony.

1662 **Charles II** of England sells **Dunkirk** to France.

1795 **Treaty of San Lorenzo,** or **Pinckney's Treaty,** is signed between the U.S. and Spain, establishing southern boundary of U.S. at 31st parallel and giving Americans right to navigate the Mississippi.

1807 **Treaty of Fontainebleau,** whereby Napoleon would help Spain conquer Portugal, is signed between Spain and France.

1871 Great Britain annexes diamond fields of **Kimberley** in South Africa.

1904 New York City opens the first section of a **subway system.**

1905 **King Oscar II** of Sweden announces his renunciation of the Norwegian throne and his recognition of **Norway** as an independent and separate nation.

1914 The Belgians open the flood gates at **Nieuport,** allowing sea water to flood their front, thereby halting the German advance (**World War I**).

British superdreadnought *Audacious* is sunk by a German mine off the north coast of Ireland (**World War I**).

1916 Earliest mention of jazz bands in print occurs in *Variety* (spelled *jass*).

1918 **General Ludendorff,** mastermind of the German offensives on the Western Front during 1918, resigns his command.

1961 U.S. and Soviet tanks confront each other at the crossing point between East and West Berlin as U.S. insists on free entry to **East Berlin** by U.S. citizens.

1971 **Congo** government announces change of the name of the country to **Republic of Zaire.**

October 28

Holidays

Greece   Greek National Day

Religious Calendar

Feasts

SS. Simon and Jude, apostles. Simon, patron of curriers; Jude, patron of the impossible. Jude also

Birthdates

1017 **Henry III** (*the Black*), Holy Roman Emperor 1039–56; deposed three rival popes, appointing **Clement II;** a patron of learning. [d. October 5, 1056]

1585 **Cornelis Jansen,** Dutch theologian; Bishop of Ypres and founder of the theological system called **Jansenism.** [d. May 6, 1638]

1846 **Georges Auguste Escoffier,** French chef. [d. February 12, 1935]

1847 **J(ames) Walter Thompson,** U.S. advertising executive; responsible for raising the level of respectability of advertising in the eyes of the public. [d. October 16, 1928]

1885 **Per Albin Hansson,** Swedish statesman; Premier, 1932–46. [d. October 5, 1946]

1891 **Hans Driesch,** German embryologist; conducted early investigations of development of cells. [d. April 16, 1941]

1896 **Howard Harold Hanson,** U.S. composer, conductor; Pulitzer Prize in music, 1944. [d. February 26, 1981]

1902 **Elsa Lanchester (Elizabeth Sullivan),** British character actress.

1907 **Edith Head,** U.S. fashion designer; noted in the film industry since the 1930s. [d. October 24, 1981]

1909 **Francis Bacon,** British painter; noted for expressionistic style, especially in portraits marked by terror.

1914 **Jonas Edward Salk,** U.S. microbiologist; developed the first **polio vaccine,** 1953.

Richard Laurence Millington Synge, British biochemist; Nobel Prize in chemistry for development of method for separating and identifying chemical substances (with A. J. P. Martin), 1952.

1926 **Bowie Kuhn,** U.S. sports executive; U.S. Commissioner of Baseball, 1969–1984.

1929 **Joan (Anne) Plowright,** British actress; wife of Sir Laurence Olivier (May 22).

1932 **Spyros Kyprianou,** President, Republic of Cyprus, 1977– .

1949 **Bruce Jenner,** U.S. athlete, sportscaster; Olympic decathlon winner, 1976.

Historical Events

1492 **Christopher Columbus** discovers **Cuba** and claims it for Spain.

1497 **John II** of Denmark defeats Swedes at Brunkeberg and revives **Scandinavian Union.**

1628 **Siege of La Rochelle** ends with Huguenot capitulation after 14 months' resistance.

1636 **Harvard College** is founded with the **Rev. Henry Dunster** as its first president; the College receives its official name on March 13, 1639.

1871 Meeting of **David Livingstone** and **H. M. Stanley,** British explorers, takes place in Ujiji, Africa.

1886 **Statue of Liberty** is dedicated by U.S. President **Grover Cleveland.**

1891 An earthquake in Japan kills 10,000 and leaves 300,000 homeless.

1918 **Czechoslovakia** proclaims itself a republic; **Thomas G. Masaryk** is elected first president.

The Italian offensive at **Vittorio Veneto** drives Austrians back (**World War I**).

1922 **Benito Mussolini** and his Fascist followers make their march on Rome, taking control of Italy.

1924 France officially recognizes the government of the **U.S.S.R.**

1973 UN issues a report stating that a drought in **Ethiopia** has killed nearly 100,000 people.

1975 Violence in **Beirut, Lebanon,** intensifies, leaving the city in shambles; large foreign corporations relocate.

1981 West Germany and East Germany complete exchanges of convicted spies.

called **Judas, Lebbaeus, Lebbeaus, Libbius, Thaddeus.** Simon also called the *Cananaean*, the *Zealot*. [d. 1st century] [major holy day, Episcopal Church; minor festival, Lutheran Church]

The Saints

St. Fidelis of Como, martyr. [d. c. 303]

St. Salvius, hermit. Also called **Saire.** [d. c. 6th cent.]

St. Faro, Bishop of Meaux. [d. c. 672]

SS. Anastasia and Cyril, martyrs. [death date unknown]

October 29

Holidays

Turkey   **Turkish National Day**
Commemorates proclamation
of Turkish Republic, 1923.

U.S.S.R   **Komsomal Foundation Day,**
marks foundation of Russian
Communist Youth Organization

Birthdates

1507   **Fernando Alvarez de Toledo, Duke of Alba**; Spanish soldier and statesman, remembered for his conquest of Portugal and tyranny while governor general of the Netherlands. [d. December 11, 1582]

1740   **James Boswell,** Scottish biographer; best known for *The Life of Samuel Johnson,* 1791. [d. May 19, 1795]

1811   **(Jean Joseph Charles) Louis Blanc,** French utopian socialist; considered to be the father of state socialism. [d. December 6, 1882]

1815   **Daniel Decatur Emmett,** U.S. minstrel, songwriter; organized one of first blackface minstrel shows in U.S., known as *Virginia Minstrels,* 1843; composed *Dixie,* 1859. [d. June 28, 1904]

1831   **Othniel Charles Marsh,** U.S. paleontologist; first professor of vertebrate paleontology in U.S., Yale University, 1866; established the **Peabody Museum of Natural History** with funds contributed by his uncle, George Peabody, 1868. [d. March 18, 1899]

1837   **Abraham Kuyper,** Dutch theologian; formed alliance between Calvinist and Catholic clerics; formed Christian Conservative ministry, 1901; Minister of Interior, 1901–05; Minister of State, 1907. [d. November 8, 1920]

1865   **Charles Henry Ingersoll,** U.S. manufacturer; with his brother Robert Hawley Ingersoll (December 26) founded firm of Robert H. Ingersoll and Brother, which created and distributed the **one dollar watch,** frequently referred to as *the watch that made the dollar famous.* [d. September 21, 1948]

1882   **(Hippolyte) Jean Giraudoux,** French dramatist, diplomat; Chief of Propaganda, 1939–40; author of *Siegfried,* 1882. [d. January 31, 1944]

1884   **Bela Lugosi,** U.S. actor, born in Hungary; best known for parts in horror films. [d. August 16, 1956]

1891   **Fanny Brice (Fannie Borach),** U.S. entertainer; known primarily as a star of the Ziegfeld Follies, 1910–36; featured as *Baby Snooks* on radio, 1936–51. [d. May 29, 1951]

1897   **Joseph (Paul) Goebbels,** German Nazi official; Minister of Propaganda, 1929–45; member of Adolf Hitler's cabinet, 1938–45; committed suicide at the end of World War II. [d. May 1, 1945]

1911   **Mahalia Jackson,** U.S. gospel singer. [d. January 27, 1972]

1926   **Jon Vickers,** Canadian opera singer.

1947   **Richard (Stephen) Dreyfuss,** U.S. actor.

Historical Events

1814   U.S. launches its first steam warship, *U.S.S. Fulton.*

1888   **Suez Canal Convention,** signed at Constantinople, internationalizes and neutralizes the **Suez Canal.**

1889   **British South Africa Company,** headed by **Cecil Rhodes,** is granted a charter by the British government giving it almost unlimited powers and rights in the area that becomes Rhodesia.

1914   **Prince Louis of Battenberg (Mountbatten)** is replaced as First Lord of the British admiralty by Lord Fisher, primarily due to his German heritage (**World War I**).

1923   **Turkish Republic** is formally proclaimed, with **Mustapha Kemal** as president.

1940   First peacetime **draft** in U.S. history goes into effect.

1950   **Gustavus V** of Sweden dies and is succeeded by his son, **Gustavus VI Adolf.**

1966   **National Organization of Women** (**NOW**) is founded in U.S.

The Saints

St. Narcissus, Bishop of Jerusalem. [d. c. 215]

St. Theuderius, abbot. Also called **Chef.** [d. c. 575]

St. Colman of Kilmacduagh, Bishop and solitary. [d. c. 632]

St. Abraham of Rostov, abbot. [d. 12th century]

The Martyrs of Douax, English missionary priests. [d. 16th and 17th century]

October 30

Religious Calendar

The Saints
St. Serapion, Bishop of Antioch. [d. c. 212]
St. Marcellus the Centurion, martyr. [d. 298]
St. Asterius, Bishop of Amasea. [d. c. 410]
St. Germanus, Bishop of Capua. [d. c. 540]

Birthdates

1632   **Jan Vermeer,** Dutch painter of landscapes and portraits; noted especially for composition. [d. December 15, 1675]

1735   **John Adams,** U.S. politician, diplomat, second President of U.S., 1797–1801; father of John Quincy Adams (July 11). [d. July 4, 1826]

1839   **Alfred Sisley,** French impressionist painter. [d. January 29, 1899]

1840   **William Graham Sumner,** U.S. educator, sociologist, economist; professor of political and social science, Yale University, 1872–1910; champion of *laissez-faire* economics and government; author of *Folkways*, an in-depth study of customs and mores. [d. April 12, 1910]

1857   **Gertrude Franklin Atherton,** U.S. novelist; author of *The Californians.* [d. June 14, 1948]

1861   **Emile Antoine Bourdelle,** French sculptor, painter; collaborator with Auguste Rodin (November 12). [d. October 1, 1929]

1871   **Paul Ambroise Toussaint Jules Valery,** French man of letters; associated with symbolist school. [d. July 20, 1945]

1873   **Francisco Indalécio Madero,** Mexican patriot; president, 1911-13. [d. February 22, 1913]

1882   **William Frederick (*Bull*) Halsey, Jr.,** U.S. naval officer; commander of U.S. South Pacific fleet and South Pacific area, 1942–45; victor at **Battle of Leyte Gulf,** most overwhelming naval victory in history. [d. August 16, 1959]

1885   **Ezra (Loomis) Pound,** U.S. poet, critic; noted for his singularly profound influence on the development of modern poetry; responsible for recognition of Robert Frost, T. S. Eliot; diagnosed as mentally ill and committed to an institution, 1946–58; died an exile in Venice. [d. November 1, 1972]

1886   **Zoe Akins,** U.S. dramatist, screenwriter; Pulitzer Prize in drama, 1935. [d. October 29, 1958]

1895   **Gerhard Domagk,** German bacteriologist, pathologist; Nobel Prize in physiology or medicine for discoveries leading to introduction and use of first of **sulfa drugs,** 1939. [d. April 24, 1964]

Dickinson W. Richards, Jr., U.S. physiologist; Nobel Prize in physiology or medicine for research in heart disease and techniques for diagnosing circulatory ailments (with A. F. Cournand and W. Forssmann), 1956. [d. February 23, 1973]

1896   **Ruth Gordon,** U.S. stage and film actress, screenwriter.

1900   **Ragnar Granit,** Swedish neurophysiologist; Nobel Prize in physiology or medicine for work on the physiology of vision (with H. K. Hartline and G. Wald), 1967.

1915   **Fred W. Friendly,** U.S. communications executive, educator; collaborator with Edward R. Murrow in radio and television series, *See It Now*, 1951–59; President of CBS News, 1964–66; Professor of Journalism, Columbia University, 1966– .

1917   **Ruth Hussey (Ruth Carol O'Rourke),** U.S. actress.

1928   **Daniel Nathans,** U.S. biologist; Nobel Prize in physiology or medicine for research on restriction enzymes (with W. Arber and H. Smith), 1978.

1930   **Harold Pinter,** British playwright, actor; author of *The Birthday Party, The Homecoming.*

1932   **Louis Malle,** French film director.

1937   **Claude Lelouch,** French film director.

1945   **Henry Winkler,** U.S. actor.

St. Ethelnoth, Archbishop of Canterbury. Also called **Ednoth, Eadnodus, Adelnodus.** [d. 1038]

St. Alphonsus Rodriguez, Jesuit lay brother. [d. 1617]

The Beatified

Blessed Benvenuta of Cividale, virgin. [d. 1292]

Blessed Dorothy of Montau, widow. Popularly regarded as the patroness of Prussia. [d. 1394]

Blessed John Slade, martyr. [d. 1583]

Blessed Angelo of Acri, Franciscan priest. [d. 1739]

Historical Events

1340 Alfonso XI of Castile defeats Moors at **River Salado.**

1611 **Charles IX** of Sweden dies and is succeeded by **Gustavus II Adolphus.**

1769 **Captain Cook** makes landfall in **New Zealand** and claims it for Great Britain.

1864 **Peace of Vienna** is signed; Denmark cedes Schleswig, Holstein, and Lauenburg to Prussia.

1905 **October Manifesto** is issued at St. Petersburg by **Nicholas II** giving Russia a constitution, a legislative duma, civil liberties, and a prime minister.

1918 Turkey signs **Armistice of Mudros** with Allies, ending its participation in **World War I.**

1930 **Treaty of Ankara** between Turkey and Greece resolves property claims and agrees on naval equality.

1939 The broadcast in the U.S. of Orson Welles' radio drama, *War of the Worlds,* causes a national panic.

1967 **Shah Mohammad Reza Pahlavi** of Iran formally crowns himself and his wife, Empress Farah, at a lavish ceremony in Teheran.

1974 **Mohammad Ali** knocks out **George Foreman** in 8 rounds for world heavyweight boxing title.

1975 **Prince Juan Carlos** assumes the powers of Spain's chief of state, marking the end of the 36-year-old Franco regime.

1981 British Parliament enacts **British Nationality Bill,** creating three separate categories of citizenship.

October 31

Holidays

	National UNICEF Day Sponsored by United Nations.
Taiwan	**Birthday of President Chiang Kai-shek** Celebrates the event which occurred 1887.
U.S. (Nevada)	**Nevada Day** Commemorates Nevada's admission to the Union, 1864.
U.S.	**National Magic Day** A day for meetings of magicians occasioned by the death of **Harry Houdini,** 1926.

Birthdates

1705 **Clement XIV,** Pope 1769–74. [d. September 22, 1774]

1795 **John Keats,** British lyric poet. [d. February 23, 1821]

1802 **Benoit Fourneyron,** French inventor; developed the **water-turbine.** [d. July 31, 1867]

1815 **Karl Weierstrass,** German mathematician; developed many calculus innovations; founded theory of functions of a complex variable. [d. February 19, 1897]

1817 **Heinrich Graetz,** Jewish historian; author of *Geschichte der Juden von den Altesten Zeiten.* [d. September 7, 1891]

1821 **Karl Havlíček (Havel Borouský),** Czech critic, journalist, poet; imprisoned for his liberal opinions. [d. July 29, 1856]

1827 **Richard Morris Hunt,** U.S. architect; noted most for his advocacy of the Beaux-Arts design of the **Metropolitan Museum of Art,** New York, 1900; designed residences for Vanderbilts, Astors, Belmonts, and other wealthy Americans; designed The Breakers and Marble House, Newport, R.I., and the Biltmore estate, Asheville, N.C. [d. July 31, 1895]

1828 **Sir Joseph Wilson Swan,** British chemist; a pioneer in photographic chemistry; invented **dry plate photography,** 1871. [d. May 27, 1914]

1835 **Adolph von Baeyer,** German chemist; Nobel Prize in chemistry for his work with dye and uric acid derivatives, 1905. [d. August 20, 1917]

1838 **Luis I,** King of Portugal, ruled 1861–89; freed slaves in Portuguese colonies. [d. October 19, 1889]

1852 **Mary Eleanor Wilkins Freeman,** U.S. novelist and short-story writer; member of *local color* school. [d. March 13, 1930]

1860 **Juliette Gordon Low,** U.S. youth leader; established first American troop of **Girl Guides** (which later became the **Girl Scouts**). [d. January 17, 1927]

Andrew Joseph Volstead, U.S. politician; author of **Volstead Act,** enforcing **prohibition** in U.S. [d. January 20, 1947]

1863 **William Gibbs McAdoo,** U.S. government official, lawyer; U.S. Secretary of the Treasury, 1912–18; first chairman, Federal Reserve Board; U.S. Senator, 1932–38; son-in-law of U.S. President Woodrow Wilson (December 28). [d. February 1, 1941]

1887 **Chiang Kai-shek,** Chinese government leader; President, Republic of China, 1928–49; assumed presidency in exile in Taiwan, 1949–75. [d. April 5, 1975]

1888 **Sir George Hubert Wilkins,** Australian polar explorer; leader of a number of Arctic and Antarctic expeditions, 1913–39. Advanced use of airplane and submarine in polar research and exploration. [d. December 1, 1958]

1895 **B(asil) H(enry) Liddell Hart,** British military scientist; military editor of *Encyclopaedia Britannica*; wrote numerous books on defense that influenced British military strategy. [d. January 29, 1970]

Religious Calendar

All Hallow Even, Vigil of All Saints, All Hallow's Eve, or **Hallowe'en**; corresponds with the eve of **All Saints' Day,** November 1; based on ancient pagan festival of autumn and Roman festival of Pomona, goddess of gardens. **Halloween** is celebrated as a night of pranks and ghost stories.

Reformation Day Celebrated by many Protestant denominations as the day on which Martin Luther affixed his *95 Theses* to the church door at Wittenberg, 1517. [minor festival, Lutheran Church]

The Saints

St. Foillan, abbot. [d. c. 655]

St. Wolfgang, Bishop of Regensburg (Ratisbon). Invoked to heal the good and to keep sheep and oxen fat. [d. 994]

St. Bega, nun. Also called **Begu.** [death date unknown]

St. Quintinus, martyr. Invoked against coughs. Also called **Quentin, Quintin, Quintus.** [death date unknown]

1900	**Ethel Waters,** U.S. actress, singer. [d. September 1, 1977]
1912	**Oscar Dystel,** U.S. publisher; President and Chairman of the Board, Bantam Books, 1954–80.
	Dale Evans (Frances Smith), U.S. actress, singer; with husband, Roy Rogers (November 5), starred in numerous 1940s Western films and on television's *The Roy Rogers Show,* 1951–57.
1921	**Yves Montand (Ivo Levi),** French actor, born in Italy.
1922	**Barbara Bel Geddes,** U.S. actress.
	Prince Norodom Sihanouk, King of Cambodia, 1941–55; established government in exile; established Royal Government of National Union of Cambodia, 1970; restored as Head of State when CRUNC forces overthrew Khmer Republic, 1975; abdicated, 1976; special envoy of Khmer Rouge to UN, 1979.
1925	**Robin Moore (Robert Lowell Moore, Jr.),** U.S. novelist; author of *The French Connection.*
1930	**Michael Collins,** U.S. astronaut; co-pilot of U.S. *Gemini 10* space flight; pilot of command module, *Apollo 11,* lunar exploration flight.
1931	**Dan(iel) Rather,** U.S. television broadcast journalist.
1947	**Frank Shorter,** U.S. distance runner; winner of Olympic marathon gold medal, 1972.

Historical Events

1517	**Martin Luther** affixes **95 Theses** to door of Wittenberg Palace Church.
1754	**King's College** (now **Columbia University**) in New York City is granted a charter by **King George II.**
1864	**Nevada** is admitted to Union as the 36th state.
1879	**Irish National Land League** is founded, with **Charles Parnell** as president, for the purpose of destroying English landlordism in Ireland and establishing **home rule.**
1922	**Benito Mussolini** becomes Prime Minister of Italy.
1928	*Graf Zeppelin* completes first round-trip crossing of the Atlantic.
1941	U.S. destroyer *Reuben James* is torpedoed and sunk in the North Atlantic, becoming the first U.S. Navy warship to be sunk in the Atlantic during **World War II.**
1981	Caribbean islands of **Antigua** and **Barbuda** become a single independent nation, ending three centuries of British rule.

November

November is the eleventh month of the Gregorian calendar and has 30 days. The name is derived from the Latin *novem*, 'nine,' designating the position November held in the early Roman ten-month calendar (see also at **September**).

November generally marks, in the temperate zones of the northern hemisphere, the time when work on the land ceases and, in the United States, is the month for general elections, the Thanksgiving holiday, and preparation for December holidays, with the pre-Christmas shopping season beginning late in the month.

In the astrological calendar, November spans the zodiac signs of Scorpio, the Scorpion (October 23–November 21) and Sagittarius, the Archer (November 22–December 21).

The birthstone for November is the topaz, and the flower is the chrysanthemum.

State, National, and International Holidays

General Election Day
(United States)
First Tuesday after First Monday

Thanksgiving Day
(Liberia)
First Thursday

Sadie Hawkins Day
(United States)
First Saturday after November 11

Remembrance Day
(Cayman Islands)
Second Monday

Oklahoma Heritage Week
(Oklahoma)
Week containing November 16

Thanksgiving Day
(United States)
Fourth Thursday

Nellie Taylor Ross's Birthday
(Wyoming)
November 29

(Nebraska, Illinois, New Hampshire)
Day after Thanksgiving

Special Events and Their Sponsors

Alcohol Education Month
Parents Without Partners
7910 Woodmont Avenue
Bethesda, Maryland 20814

National Epilepsy Month
Epilepsy Foundation of America
4351 Garden City Drive
Landover, Maryland 20781

National Ice Skating Month
Ice Skating Institute of America
1000 Skokie Boulevard
Wilmette, Illinois 60091

National Jewish Book Month
JWB Jewish Book Council

One Nation Under God Month
The National Exchange Club
3050 Central Avenue
Toledo, Ohio 43606

Home and Family Month
from Thanksgiving to Christmas
Fraternal Order of Eagles
2401 West Wisconsin Avenue
Milwaukee, Wisconsin 53233

National Stamp Collecting Month
Franklin D. Roosevelt Philatelic Society
154 Laguna Court
St. Augustine Shores, Florida 32084

Rotary Foundation Month
Rotary International
1600 Ridge Avenue
Evanston, Illinois 60201

National Notary Public Week
Week containing November 7
American Society of Notaries
810 18th Street, N.W.
Washington, D.C. 20006

World Mutual Service Week
Second Full Week
National Board of the YWCA of the U.S.A.
4th Floor
135 West 50th Street
New York, New York 10022

Holidays are Pickle Days
Final Two Weeks and Month of December
Pickle Packers International, Inc.
One Pickle and Pepper Plaza
P.O. Box 31
St. Charles, Illinois 60174

Christmas Seal Campaign
November 15–December 31
American Lung Association
1740 Broadway
New York, New York 10019

National Children's Book Week
Third Week
Children's Book Council
67 Irving Place
New York, New York 10003

National Farm City Week
Third Week
Kiwanis International
3636 Broadview Trace
Indianapolis, Indiana 46268

National Adoption Week
Week of Thanksgiving
North American Council on Adoptable Children
1346 Connecticut Avenue, N.W.
Washington, D.C. 20036

National Bible Week
Week of Thanksgiving
Laymen's National Bible Committee, Inc.
815 Second Avenue
New York, New York 10017

Latin American Week
Last Full Week
Richard R. Falk Associates
1472 Broadway
New York, New York 10036

Death Anniversary of Eleanor Roosevelt
November 7
Franklin D. Roosevelt Philatelic Society
154 Laguna Court
St. Augustine Shores, Florida 32084

National Notary Public Day
November 7
American Society of Notaries
810 18th Street N.W.
Washington, D.C. 20006

National Thanksgiving Salute to Older Americans
Thanksgiving Day
No Greater Love
1750 New York Avenue, N.W.
Washington, D.C. 20006

Special Days—Other Calendars

	12 Rabi Al-Awal	Beginning of Advent
1985	November 26	
1986	November 15	November 30
1987	November 5	November 29
1988		November 27

November 1

Holidays

Algeria	**Anniversary of the Revolution** Commemorates the beginning of the struggle for independence from France by the National Liberation Front, 1954.
Congo	**Day of the Dead** or **All Saints' Day**
Louisiana	**All Saints' Day**
U.S. Virgin Islands	**Liberty Day**

Religious Calendar

Solemnities

All Saints' Day, a feast in Roman Catholic countries, and a holy day of obligation in the Roman Catholic

Birthdates

1530 **Étienne de La Boétie,** French poet, translator; intimate of Michel de Montaigne (February 28). [d. August 18, 1563]

1596 **Pietro Berretini da Cortona,** Italian painter, architect; noted for his individualistic style in architecture; designed numerous churches in Rome and Florence. [d. May 16, 1669]

1609 **Sir Matthew Hale,** English judge; active in bringing about the Restoration. [d. December 25, 1676]

1636 **Nicolas Boileau-Despréaux,** French poet, critic; regarded as the founder of principles upon which French classical literature is based. [d. March 11, 1711?]

1757 **Antonio Canova,** Italian sculptor; founder of modern classic school of sculpture. [d. October 13, 1822]

George Rapp, U.S. religious leader born in Germany; founded **Harmony, Pennsylvania, Harmony, Indiana,** and **Economy, Pennsylvania,** all communities founded on religious, communistic principles. [d. August 7, 1847]

1778 **Gustavus IV Adolphus,** King of Sweden, 1792–1809; exiled, 1809; died in poverty. [d. February 7, 1837]

1815 **Crawford Williamson Long,** U.S. surgeon; despite his failure to publish his results, he is generally recognized as first to use **ether** as an anesthetic in surgery, 1842. [d. June 16, 1878]

1818 **James Renwick,** U.S. architect; noted for Gothic Revival architecture; designed **St. Patrick's Cathedral,** New York City; **Smithsonian Institution** building, Washington, D.C.; facade of the New York Stock Exchange Building. [d. June 23, 1895]

1871 **Stephen (Townley) Crane,** U.S. novelist, short-story writer; best known for his novel, *The Red Badge of Courage.* [d. June 5, 1900]

1878 **Carlos de Saavedra Lamas,** Argentine statesman; Foreign Minister, 1932–38; Nobel Peace Prize, 1936. [d. May 5, 1959]

1880 **(Henry) Grantland Rice,** U.S. sportswriter; Chairman of Selection Committee for All-American Football Team, 1925–54; author of numerous books of verse; syndicated columnist, 1930–47. [d. July 13, 1954]

Sholem Asch, U.S. novelist, born in Poland; known for his novels with Biblical themes written in both English and Yiddish. [d. July 10, 1957]

Alfred Wegener, German geophysicist; one of first to clearly state the **continental drift theory,** 1915. [d. November 1930]

1889 **Philip J. Noel-Baker,** British politician; Nobel Peace Prize for his work in the League of Nations and disarmament conferences, 1959. [d. October 9, 1982]

1895 **George Joseph Hecht,** U.S. publisher; founder of *Parents' Magazine,* 1926–78. [d. April 23, 1980]

Church. Celebrates all the saints of the church. Also known as **All Hallows Day.** [major holy day, Episcopal Church; minor festival, Lutheran Church]

The Saints

St. Benignus of Dijon, martyr, apostle of Burgundy. [d. c. 3rd century]

St. Austremonius, first bishop of Clermont. Apostle of Auvergne. [d. c. 4th century]

St. Mary, virgin and martyr. [d. c. 4th century]

St. Maturinus, priest; patron of fools. Also called **Mathurin.** [d. 4th century]

St. Marcellus, Bishop of Paris. [d. c. 410]

St. Vigor, Bishop of Bayeux. [d. c. 537]

St. Cadfan, abbot; patron of warriors. [d. c. 6th century]

SS. Caesarius and Julian, martyrs. [death date unknown]

St. Dingad, Welsh church founder of the tribe of Brychan; patron of Llandingat, Wales. Also called **Digat.** [death date unknown]

St. Gwythian, patron of the parish of this name in North Cornwall. Also called **Gwithian,** or **Gothian.** [death date unknown]

1912   **Leo Kerz,** U.S. theatrical designer, director, born in Germany.

1935   **Gary Player,** South African golfer; first foreign player to win U.S. Open Championship, 1965.

Historical Events

1700   **Philip of Anjou,** grandson of Louis XIV of France, is proclaimed King **Philip V** on the death of **Charles II** of Spain; marks the beginning of **War of Spanish Succession.**

1755   Great earthquake at **Lisbon,** Portugal, accompanied by fire and flood, kills tens of thousands and destroys city.

1762   French troops capitulate at **Cassel** and evacuate right bank of the Rhine (**Seven Years' War**).

1894   **Alexander III** of Russia dies and is succeeded by **Nicholas II.**

1914   **Persia** declares neutrality in **World War I.**

1917   **Battle of Malmaison** ends in victory for France (**World War I**).

British troops capture **Beersheba** in Palestine and begin to break the Turkish line in the **Third Battle of Gaza** (**World War I**).

1918   The Serbs reclaim their capital of **Belgrade** while German-Austrian troops under von Mackensen begin a rapid retreat through Transylvania (**World War I**).

An independent Hungarian government is established under **Count Michael Karolyi** as **Austria-Hungary** breaks apart.

1922   **Mustapha Kemal (Ataturk)** of Turkey proclaims the abolition of the sultanate.

1925   First train passes through the **Khyber Pass.**

1941   **Rainbow Bridge,** an international bridge at Niagara Falls, opens to the public.

U.S. President **Franklin Roosevelt** places **United States Coast Guard** under Navy control.

1947   UN approves trusteeship arrangement for **Nauru,** to be administered jointly by Australia, New Zealand, and Great Britain.

1950   **Pope Pius XII,** in a papal bull, proclaims the **assumption of the Virgin Mary** as a dogma of the Roman Catholic Church.

1956   **Hungary** proclaims neutrality and withdraws from the Warsaw Pact during political uprisings within the Pact countries.

1960   Economic union between Belgium, Luxembourg, and the Netherlands comes into effect.

1964   **Antigua, Barbados, Dominica, Montserrat, St. Kitts, St. Lucia,** and **St. Vincent** reach agreement on forming a new independent **West Indies Federation.**

1976   Military coup overthrows the government of **Burundi;** Lt. Col. **Bagaza** gains control.

1981   **Antigua** and **Barbuda** gain independence from Great Britain. **Vere Bird** is named the first Prime Minister.

November 2

Birthdates

1734   **Daniel Boone,** American frontiersman, explorer; primarily responsible for expansion and development of lands west of the Alleghenies. [d. September 26, 1820]

1755   **Marie Antoinette,** Queen of France; wife of **King Louis XVI;** extremely unpopular with the French people because of insensitivity to miseries of the poor; imprisoned with the king and her children, 1792. Convicted of treason and beheaded. [d. October 16, 1793]

1766   **Joseph Wenzel Radetzky, Count Radetzky von Radetz,** Austrian field marshal, national hero; victorious over Sardinians at Custoza and Novara; responsible for Austria's capture of Venice. [d. January 5, 1858]

1795   **James Knox Polk,** U.S. lawyer, politician; 11th President of the U.S., 1845–49; the youngest man at that time ever to be elected to the presidency; led U.S. during Mexican War, 1846–48. [d. June 15, 1849]

1815   **George Boole,** British mathematician; helped establish modern symbolic logic; his algebra of logic, **Boolean algebra**, is basic to the design of digital computers. [d. December 8, 1864]

1849   **Friedrich von Bernhardi,** German soldier, military historian; gave distinguished service in Franco-Prussian War and World War I. [d. July 10, 1930]

1865   **Warren Gamaliel Harding,** U.S. teacher, journalist, politician; 29th President of the U.S., 1921–23. Died in office. [d. August 2, 1923]

1879   **Jacob Aall Bonnevie Bjerknes,** U.S. meteorologist, born in Norway. [d. July 7, 1975]

1885   **Harlow Shapley,** U.S. astronomer; known for his research into sizes of galaxies and composition of Milky Way. [d. October 20, 1972]

1897   **Richard B. Russell,** U.S. politician, lawyer; U.S. Senator, 1933–71; President *pro tempore* of Senate, 1969–71. [d. January 21, 1971]

1903   **Emile Zola Berman,** U.S. lawyer; noted for his defense of Sirhan Sirhan, assassin of Robert F. Kennedy. [d. July 3, 1981]

1905   **James Dunn,** U.S. actor. [d. September 3, 1967]

1906   **Luchino Visconti,** Italian film director. [d. March 17, 1976]

1913   **Burt Lancaster,** U.S. actor.

1917   **Ann Rutherford,** U.S. actress, born in Canada.

     Andrew Fielding Huxley, British physiologist; Nobel Prize in physiology or medicine for research on nerve cells (with A. L. Hodgkin and J. C. Eccles), 1963.

1934   **Ken Rosewall,** Australian tennis player.

1941   **David Hemmings,** British actor.

1942   **Shere D. Hite,** U.S. author: *The Hite Report: A Nationwide Study of Female Sexuality*, 1976.

Historical Events

1164   **Thomas Becket,** Archbishop of Canterbury, opponent of **King Henry II** of England, flees to France.

The Commemoration of All the Faithful Departed, commonly called **All Souls' Day.** Optional Memorial. [minor festival, Lutheran Church]

The Saints

St. Victorinus, Bishop of Pettau and martyr. [d. c. 303]

St. Marcian, hermit. [d. c. 387]

St. Ernin, hermit. Invoked to cure headaches. [d. 6th century]

St. Erc, patron of St. Erth, Cornwall. Also called **Ercius, Ercus,** or **Erth.** [death date unknown]

The Beatified

Blessed Thomas of Walden. Confessor to King Henry V. [d. 1430]

Blessed John Bodey, martyr. [d. 1583]

1439   **Charles VII** of France establishes the *taille,* a permanent tax.

1642   Swedes defeat army of Holy Roman Empire at **Breitenfeld** (**Thirty Years' War**).

1687   **Mohammed IV** of Turkey is deposed; he is succeeded by **Suleiman III.**

1795   **French Directory,** a moderate government, is installed.

1841   British envoys are murdered during Afghan uprisings in Kabul, during the **First Afghan War.**

1852   **Second Empire** is established in France under **Emperor Napoleon III.**

1889   **North Dakota** and **South Dakota** are admitted to Union as 39th and 40th states.

1899   Boer forces begin the siege of **Ladysmith,** held by the British (**Boer War**).

1914   **Russia** declares war on **Turkey** (**World War I**).

1917   **Balfour Declaration** states the British objective of establishing a Jewish state in Palestine.

   Lansing-Ishi Agreement between the U.S. and Japan recognizes Japanese interests in China but maintains China's sovereignty; the *Open Door Policy* is supported; and Japan joins the Allies in the war against Germany (**World War I**).

1920   Radio station **KDKA, Pittsburgh,** broadcasts the first commercial news, the returns of the Harding-Cox presidential election.

1923   **Union of Soviet Socialist Republics** is officially adopted as the name of the newly federated Russian republic.

1930   **Haile I Selassie** is crowned Emperor of Abyssinia (**Ethiopia**).

1938   Hungary acquires southern **Slovakia** following the dismemberment of **Czechoslovakia** after German invasion.

1942   British decisively defeat Rommel's German troops at **Tel-el Aqqaqir** (**World War II**).

1947   Howard Hughes's mammoth wooden flying boat, *The Spruce Goose,* makes its first and only flight.

1964   **King Saud** of Saudi Arabia is dethroned and replaced by his younger half-brother, **Prince Faisal**.

1965   **John V. Lindsay** becomes the first Republican mayor of New York City since Fiorello H. LaGuardia (1933).

   Norman R. Morrison, a Quaker, burns himself to death in front of the Pentagon as a protest against U.S. policy in **Vietnam.**

1978   Two Soviet cosmonauts descend to earth in the *Soyuz 31* spacecraft after setting a new endurance record of 139 days and 14 hours aboard the orbiting *Salyut 6* space station.

November 3

Holidays

Dominica   **Independence Day**
Celebrates Dominica's achievement of independence from Great Britain, 1978.

Ecuador   **Independence of Cuenca**
Commemorates declaration of the city, 1820.

Japan   **Culture Day**
A day for the people of Japan to reflect on liberty and peace and to emphasize the importance of promoting culture.

Panama   **Independence from Colombia**
Commemorates the event, 1903.

Religious Calendar

The Saints

St. Clydog, king and martyr. Also called **Clitaucus,** or **Clodock.** [d. 6th cent.]

Birthdates

1500   **Benvenuto Cellini,** Italian goldsmith, sculptor, writer; student of Michelangelo; protégé of Cosimo de' Medici; his *Autobiography* is a record of Renaissance life in Italy. [d. February 13, 1571]

1611   **Henry Ireton,** English general; a close ally of Oliver Cromwell. [d. November 26, 1651]

1793   **Stephen Fuller Austin,** U.S. colonizer, public official; leader in settlement of Texas by Americans. Austin, Texas is named for him. [d. December 27, 1836]

1794   **William Cullen Bryant,** U.S. poet, critic, editor, and part owner of the New York *Evening Post*; author of *Thanatopsis*, 1817. [d. June 12, 1878]

1801   **Vincenzo Bellini,** Italian composer; composed operas *La Sonnambula* and *Il Pirata*. [d. September 23, 1835]

1816   **Jubal Anderson Early,** U.S. Confederate Army general during U.S. Civil War; led a raid on Washington, D.C., during war but was turned back by General U. S. Grant. [d. March 2, 1894]

1834   **Paul Arrell Brown Widener,** U.S. financier, philanthropist; supported development of transit systems in New York, Philadelphia, and Chicago; noted for his art col-

lection, which was bequeathed to city of Philadelphia. [d. November 6, 1915]

1845   **Edward Douglass White,** U.S. jurist; Associate Justice, U.S. Supreme Court, 1894–1910; Chief Justice, U.S. Supreme Court, 1910–21; responsible for *White Doctrine* of incorporated and unincorporated territories; issued the *rule of reason* in interpretation of antitrust laws. [d. May 19, 1921]

1852   **Mutsuhito,** Emperor of Japan, 1867–1912. [d. July 30, 1912]

1879   **Vilhjalmur Stefansson,** U.S. explorer, ethnologist, born in Canada; noted for his extensive Arctic expeditions and adaptation to Eskimo life; spent five years living north of the Arctic Circle. [d. August 26, 1962]

1901   **Leopold III,** King of Belgium, 1934–51; abdicated in favor of son Baudouin in 1951. [d. September 25, 1983]

   André Malraux, French novelist, art historian, public official; leader of French resistance during World War II; Minister of Cultural Affairs, 1959–69. [d. November 23, 1977]

1903   **Julian (Parks) Boyd,** U.S. editor, historian; edited 19 volumes of the 60 volumes of Thomas Jefferson's works, one of the most

St. Winifred, virgin and martyr; patron of virgins. Also called **Gwenfrewi, Wenefride,** or **Winefride.** [d. c. 650]

St. Rumwald, patron of Brackley. Also called **Rumald.** [d. c. 7th century]

St. Hubert, Bishop of Liège; patron of Liège, and of hunters, foresters, furriers, smelters, and makers of precision instruments. He is invoked against rabies and for the protection of dogs. [d. 727]

St. Pirminus, bishop. [d. 753]

St. Amicus, solitary. [d. c. 1045]

St. Malachy, Archbishop of Armagh. Also called **Malachi.** [d. 1148]

St. Martin de Porres, Dominican lay brother; patron of workers for social justice. In U.S., patron of work for interracial justice and harmony. Feast formerly November 5. [d. 1639] Optional Memorial.

St. Wulganus, confessor; patron of Lens. Also called **Wulgan.** [death date unknown]

The Beatified

Blessed Alpais, virgin. [d. 1211]

Blessed Ida of Toggenburg, matron. [d. 1226]

Blessed Simon of Rimini, lay brother. [d. 1319]

---

ambitious projects in the history of U.S. publishing. [d. May 21, 1980]

1908 **Giovanni Leone,** Italian politician, professor; President of Chamber of Deputies, 1948–49; President, 1955–63; President of Italian Republic, 1971–78.

1909 **James Barrett (*Scotty*) Reston,** U.S. journalist, born in Scotland; *New York Times* columnist, 1953–64; editor, 1964–69; director, 1973– ; Pulitzer Prize in national correspondence, 1944, 1957.

1912 **Alfredo Stroessner,** President, Republic of Paraguay, 1954– .

1918 **Russell (Billiu) Long,** U.S. politician, lawyer; U.S. Senator, 1948– ; son of Huey P. Long (August 30).

1936 **Roy Emerson,** Australian tennis player.

1949 **Larry Holmes,** U.S. boxer; World Boxing Council heavyweight champion, 1978–84.

Historical Events

1492 **Peace of Etaples** is signed between England and France.

1760 **Frederick the Great** of Prussia scores brilliant victory over a superior Austrian force at **Torgau (Seven Years' War).**

1839 **First Opium War** between China and Great Britain begins; **Hong Kong** is taken by British.

1903 Under U.S. instigation and backing, **Panama** revolts and declares itself independent of Colombia.

1917 American forces are involved in trench fighting in **World War I** for the first time.

1918 Mutiny breaks out in the German fleet at **Kiel** and rapidly spreads through northwestern Germany (**World War I**).

Polish Republic is declared at Warsaw.

An **armistice** is signed at Belgrade between the Allies and Austria-Hungary (**World War I**).

The Italian army seizes **Trieste** and **Trent** at the end of the successful offensive of **Vittorio Veneto** against the Austrians (**World War I**).

1928 Roman alphabet is adopted by **Turkey.**

1957 The U.S.S.R. launches space satellite *Sputnik II*, carrying a dog.

1956 Soviet forces invade **Hungary** and crush a national uprising against the Communist coalition government; nearly 200,000 Hungarians flee the country.

1960 **Ivory Coast** adopts its constitution.

November 4

Holidays

Andorra	**Feast of St. Charles Borromeo**
Dominica	**Independence Day** Second day of the independence celebration.
Panama	**Flag Day**
Tonga	**Constitution Day** Commemorates the granting of the constitution by George I, 1875.
U.S. (Oklahoma)	**Will Rogers Day** Commemorates the birth of the world-famous actor and humorist, 1879.

Birthdates

1569 **Guillén de Castro y Bellvís,** Spanish dramatist; author of *Las Mocedades del Cid,* the basis for Pierre Corneille's *Le Cid.* [d. July 28, 1631]

1751 **Richard Brinsley (Butler) Sheridan,** Irish playwright, politician, baptized on this day; noted for his comedies of manners, *The Rivals, The School for Scandal,* and *The Critic.* [d. July 7, 1816]

1790 **Carlos Antonio López,** President and Dictator of Paraguay, 1844–62. [d. September 10, 1862]

1809 **Benjamin Robbins Curtis,** U.S. jurist, lawyer; Associate Justice, U.S. Supreme Court, 1851–57; issued dissenting opinion in the **Dred Scott Case,** 1857. [d. September 15, 1874]

1812 **Aleardo Aleardi,** Italian poet, patriot; participated in insurrection against Austrian control in Lombardy, 1848. [d. July 17, 1878]

1837 **James Douglas,** U.S. metallurgist, mine executive, and philanthropist; achieved reforms in U.S. mining industry; town of **Douglas, Arizona** is named for him. [d. June 25, 1918]

1841 **B(enjamin) F(ranklin) Goodrich,** U.S. manufacturer; founder of B. F. Goodrich Rubber Co. [d. August 3, 1888]

1876 **James (Earle) Fraser,** U.S. sculptor; known for his monumental sculptures of historical figures, as well as allegorical figures such as *Law* and *Justice* at U.S. Supreme Court Building; designed the buffalo nickel. [d. October 11, 1953]

1879 **Will(iam Penn Adair) Rogers,** U.S. humorist, actor; known throughout the world for his wry wit and satirical observations; killed in plane crash in Alaska with Wiley Post (November 22) at height of his career. [d. August 15, 1935]

1906 **Robert Bernard Considine,** U.S. journalist. [d. September 25, 1975]

1916 **Walter (Leland) Cronkite, Jr.,** U.S. broadcast journalist; anchored the popular *CBS Evening News* telecast, 1962–81.

1917 **Gig Young (Byron Barr),** U.S. actor.

1918 **Art(hur) Carney,** U.S. actor.

1936 **Didier Ratsiraka,** President, Democratic Republic of Madagascar, 1975– .

Historical Events

1307 **Swiss Confederation** declares its independence of Austria.

1520 **Christian II** of Denmark is crowned king of Sweden after defeating the Swedes in battle.

1854 **Florence Nightingale,** with a staff of 38 nurses, arrives at Scutari (**Crimean War**).

1890 The British protectorate over **Zanzibar** is formally announced.

1908 Belgium assumes sovereignty over the **Congo State** of Africa.

1909 **Sergei Rachmaninoff,** Russian pianist and composer, makes his American debut

Religious Calendar

The Saints

St. Pierius, priest. [d. c. 310]

St. John Zedazneli and his Companions, Fathers of the Iberian church. [d. c. 580]

St. Clether, hermit. Also called **Clanis,** or **Cleer.** [d. c. 6th century]

St. Clarus, martyr. [d. c. 8th century]

St. Joannicius, monk and hermit. [d. 846]

St. Charles Borromeo, archbishop of Milan and cardinal; patron of libraries, religious education. [d. 1584] Obligatory Memorial.

SS. Vitalis and Agricola, martyrs. [death date unkown] [Celebrated in particular calendars.]

The Beatified

Blessed Emeric, Hungarian prince. Also called **Imre;** generally referred to as **St. Emeric.** [d. 1031]

Blessed Frances D'Ambrose, widow. Established first Carmelite convent in France. [d. 1485]

---

in a recital at Smith College, Northampton, Massachusetts.

1918 Italy and Austria-Hungary sign armistice, ending conflict between the two countries (**World War I**).

The Allies formally agree to the U.S. demand for peace based on President Wilson's **Fourteen Points** (**World War I**).

1921 **Takashi Hara,** Premier of Japan, is assassinated.

1939 **U.S. Neutrality Act of 1939** repeals an arms embargo and authorizes *cash and carry* exports of arms and munitions.

1942 British defeat Germans at **El Alamein** in North Africa, forcing Rommel's troops to retreat (**World War II**).

1946 United Nations Educational, Scientific, and Cultural Organization (**UNESCO**) is established.

1966 Soviet-U.S. agreement for direct air service between New York City and Moscow is signed in Washington, D.C.

1979 **Iranian militants** seize U.S. Embassy in Teheran and take 90 hostages, who are not released until January 20, 1981.

November 5

Holidays

El Salvador | **Anniversary of First Cry of Independence**
Commemorates first battle for independence from Spain, 1811.

Great Britain | **Guy Fawkes Day**
Commemorates the thwarting of the attempt to blow up Parliament by Guy Fawkes and his fellow Roman Catholic conspirators, 1605.

Birthdates

1494   **Hans Sachs,** German poet, dramatist, meistersinger; composed more than 6000 musical works. [d. January 19, 1576]

1558   **Thomas Kyd,** English dramatist; author of *The Spanish Tragedy*, an early masterpiece of English drama. [d. December 1594]

1779   **Washington Allston,** U.S. painter, author; a leading U.S. Romantic painter, noted for his use of color; close friend of Samuel Taylor Coleridge (October 21) and teacher of Samuel F. B. Morse (April 27). [d. July 9, 1843]

1787   **Franz Xavier Gruber,** Austrian musician, composer of *Silent Night*, 1818. [d. June 7, 1863]

1818   **Benjamin Franklin Butler,** Union Army general during U.S. Civil War; Military Governor of New Orleans during Civil War; U.S. Congressman, 1867–75; 1877–79; Governor of Massachusetts, 1882–84. [d. January 11, 1893]

1854   **Paul Sabatier,** French chemist; Nobel Prize in chemistry for developing process for hydrogenating organic compounds, 1912. [d. August 14, 1941]

1855   **Eugene V(ictor) Debs,** U.S. socialist leader, labor organizer; Socialist party presidential candidate four times, 1900–1912; presidential candidate while in prison for sedition, 1920; released by presidential order, 1921. [d. October 20, 1926]

1857   **Ida Minerva Tarbell,** U.S. journalist; best known as a muckraker of the early 20th century; noted for her *History of the Standard Oil Company*, 1904. [d. January 6, 1944]

1863   **James Ward Packard,** U.S. manufacturer; creator of the Packard automobile, 1899; founder of Packard Motor Car Co. [d. March 20, 1928]

1869   **Nicholas Longworth,** U.S. lawyer, politician; husband of Alice Lee Roosevelt (February 12), daughter of U.S. President Theodore Roosevelt (October 27); prominent member of the Republican Party. [d. April 9, 1931]

1885   **Will(iam James) Durant,** U.S. historian, philosopher, author; Pulitzer Prize in general nonfiction, 1968. [d. November 7, 1981]

1892   **J(ohn) B(urdon) S(anderson) Haldane,** British geneticist; performed early studies on sex linkage in chromosomes. [d. December 1, 1964]

1895   **Charles G(ordon) MacArthur,** U.S. journalist, playwright; married to actress Helen Hayes. [d. April 21, 1956]

1901   **Martin Dies,** U.S. politician; U.S. Congressman, 1931–45; 1953–59; first chairman of **Dies Committee,** pinpointing infiltration of Communism into U.S. organizations; the committee later became the **Committee on Un-American Activities.** [d. November 14, 1972]

1905   **Joel McCrea,** U.S. actor.

1912   **Roy Rogers (Leonard Slye),** U.S. actor, singer; most famous for his role as cowboy hero in films from 1935–55; owner of Roy Rogers fast food restaurants. Husband of Dale Evans (October 31).

1913   **John McGiver,** U.S. actor. [d. September 9, 1975]

        Vivien Leigh (Vivien Hartley), British actress; best known for her portrayal of Scarlett O'Hara in *Gone with the Wind*. [d. July 8, 1967]

Religious Calendar

The Saints

SS. Zachary and Elizabeth, parents of St. John the Baptist. [d. 1st century]

St. Bertilla, virgin and Abbess of Chelles. Also called **Bertila,** or **Bertille.** [d. 705]

SS. Galation and Episteme, martyrs. [death date unknown]

St. Kea, monk and bishop; invoked for the cure of toothache. Also called **Ke,** or **Quay.** [death date unknown]

The Beatified

Blessed Gomidas Keumurgian, martyr. [d. 1707]

1934   **Jeb Stuart Magruder,** U.S. government official; gained notoriety during **Watergate Incident.**

1941   **Elke Sommer,** U.S. actress, born in Germany.

Historical Events

1414   Roman Catholic **Council of Constance** convenes in order to condemn heresy of **John Wyclif** and **John Hus.**

1556   **Akbar the Great,** Mogul leader, defeats Hindus at **Panipat.**

1605   **Gunpowder Plot** in England is discovered, a conspiracy of prominent Roman Catholics attempting to destroy the English government by blowing up Parliament; the affair ends with the arrest of conspirator **Guy Fawkes.**

1630   **Treaty of Madrid** ends war between England and Spain (**Thirty Years' War**).

1903   **Minneapolis Symphony Orchestra** makes its first appearance as a permanent organization under the direction of **Emil Oberhoffer.**

1911   **Tripoli** is annexed by Italy.

1912   First U.S. **cross-country flight** by Calbraith P. Rogers is successfully completed, taking 82 hours, 4 minutes.

1914   Great Britain and France declare war on Turkey (**World War I**).

1921   **Mongolia** declares its independence from China.

1974   **District of Columbia** residents vote for the first time for a mayor and 14-member city council; previously the posts were filled by presidential appointments.

1975   **São Tomé and Príncipe** promulgate a constitution.

November 6

Holidays

| Morocco | Al-Massira Celebration Day |
| Sweden | **Gustavus Adolphus Day** |

Commemorates the death of the famous military leader, 1632.

Religious Calendar

Feasts

Feast of All Saints of Ireland. [observed only in Ireland.]

Birthdates

1661 **Charles II,** King of Spain, 1665-1700; his death signalled beginning of **War of Spanish Succession.** [d. November 1, 1700]

1671 **Colley Cibber,** English actor, playwright; known for eccentric parts he portrayed in early English theater; named Poet Laureate, 1730; source of much debate, especially in his interpretation of Shakespeare. [d. December 11, 1757]

1771 **Aloys Senefelder,** Hungarian inventor; invented **lithography,** 1796; invented process of lithographing in color. [d. February 26, 1834]

1825 **Jean Louis Charles Garnier,** French architect; designed the Paris Opéra, the Nice Conservatory, Monte Carlo Casino, and tombs of Bizet and Offenbach. [d. August 3, 1898]

1833 **Jonas Lauritz Idemil Lie,** Norwegian novelist, playwright, and poet. [d. July 5, 1908]

1854 **John Philip Sousa,** U.S. conductor, composer; conductor of U.S. Marine Band, 1880–92; formed own band and became renowned for his marches; during World War I, directed all U.S. Navy bands; composed more than 100 marches. [d. March 6, 1932]

1861 **James Naismith,** Canadian educator, credited with inventing **basketball,** 1891. [d. November 28, 1939]

1890 **Henry Knox Sherrill,** U.S. clergyman; considered to be one of the most influential post-war church leaders in the U.S.; President, World Council of Churches, 1954–61. [d. May 11, 1980]

1892 **John W. Alcock,** British aviator; with Arthur Brown, made pioneer flight across the Atlantic, 1919 [d. December 18, 1919]

1893 **Edsel Bryant Ford,** U.S. auto executive; only son of Henry Ford (July 30); President of Ford Motor Co., 1919–43. [d. May 26, 1943]

1907 **Charles W(oodruff) Yost,** U.S. diplomat; played significant role in founding the **United Nations;** chief UN delegate, 1969–71. [d. May 21, 1981]

1912 **George Cakobau,** Governor-General, Dominion of Fiji, 1973– .

1921 **James Jones,** U.S. novelist. [d. May 9, 1977]

1923 **Robert P. Griffin,** U.S. politician, lawyer; U.S. Congressman, 1957–66; U.S. Senator, 1966–78.

1931 **Mike Nichols (Michael Igor Peschowsky),** U.S. stage and film director, producer, born in Germany.

Historical Events

1860 **Abraham Lincoln** is elected President of the U.S.

1869 First modern American **football game** is played between Rutgers and Princeton; the teams field 25 players on each side; Rutgers defeats Princeton, 6–4.

1911 **Francisco Madero,** having led successful revolution in Mexico, becomes president, an office he occupies for only two years.

1914 The U.S. declares its neutrality in hostilities between Great Britain and Turkey (**World War I**).

Egypt declares war on Turkey (**World War I**).

The Saints

St. Melaine, Bishop of Rennes. Also called **Malanius.** [d. c. 530]

St. Illtud, abbot. Also called **Eltut, Hildutus, Iltet, Iltut, Illtutus,** or **Illtyd.** [d. 6th century]

St. Leonard of Noblac; patron of prisoners, coppersmiths, blacksmiths, locksmiths, porters, coalminers, greengrocers, barrelmakers, and women in labor. [d. 6th century]

St. Winnoc, abbot. Also called **Winoc.** [d. c. 717]

St. Demetrian, Bishop of Khytri. [d. c. 912]

St. Barlaam of Khutyn, abbot. Also called **Varlaam.** [d. 1193]

The Martyrs of Indo-China. [d. 1862]

The Beatified

Blessed Christina of Stommeln, virgin. [d. 1312]

Blessed Joan Mary de Maillé, widow. [d. 1414]

Blessed Nonius, lay brother and a national hero of Portugal. Also called **Nuñes.** [d. 1431]

Blessed Margaret of Lorraine, widow. [d. 1521]

1915 **Second Battle of Champagne** ends with appalling casualties to the Allies and Germany and almost no gain for the French and British (**World War I**).

1917 Bolsheviks in Petrograd, Russia, take over telephone exchanges, railway stations, and electric power plants (**Revolution of 1917**).

1918 **Sedan,** in northeast France, is taken by French and American forces (**World War I**).

1923 First **electric shaver** patent is awarded to **Col. Jacob Schick.**

1935 **Edwin Armstrong** first demonstrates **FM radio transmission,** a method which he developed in 1933 but which did not come into popular use until 1940.

1943 Carl Orff's *Catulli Carmina* is first performed in Leipzig.

1978 An 88-day strike against the *New York Times* and the *Daily News* ends.

November 7

Holidays

Bangladesh	**National Revolution Day** Commemorates the overthrow of the government of **Abdus Sattar,** 1982.
Bulgaria, Hungary, Mongolia, U.S.S.R.	**October Revolution Day** Commemorates the socialist revolution of 1917.

Birthdates

1598   **Francisco de Zurbaran,** Spanish baroque painter, baptized on this day; noted for his religious paintings and monastic portraiture. [d. August 27, 1664]

1811   **Karel Jaromir Erben,** Czech poet and scholar; several composers have drawn inspiration from his ballads. [d. November 21, 1870]

1832   **Andrew Dickson White,** U.S. educator, diplomat; cofounder, with Ezra Cornell (January 11), of Cornell University, 1865; served as President of Cornell, 1868–85; U.S. Minister to Germany, 1879–81; Minister to Russia, 1892–94; U.S. Ambassador to Germany, 1897–1902; U.S. delegate to Hague Conference. [d. November 4, 1918]

1838   Jean Marie Mathias Philippe Auguste, Comte de Villiers de L'Isle-Adam (***Comte de L'Isle)***, French short-story writer, dramatist; founder of *Symbolist School* in French literature. [d. August 19, 1889]

1867   **Marie Curie,** French physical chemist, born in Poland; with her husband, Pierre Curie (May 15), pioneered in investigation of radioactivity; Nobel Prize in physics for study of radiation phenomenon (with P. Curie and A. H. Becquerel), 1903; Nobel Prize in chemistry for discovery of radium and polonium, 1911. [d. July 4, 1934]

1878   **Lise Meitner,** Swedish physicist, born in Austria; noted for work on disintegration products of radium, thorium, and protoactinium; with Otto Hahn and Fritz Strassman, accomplished fission of uranium, 1938. [d. October 17, 1968]

1888   **Sir Chandrasekhara Venkata Raman,** Indian physicist; Nobel Prize in physics for discoveries in light diffusion, called Raman effect, 1930. [d. November 21, 1970]

1895   **Clement D(ixon) Johnston,** U.S. business executive; President, U.S. Chamber of Commerce, 1954–55. [d. October 16, 1979]

1903   **Konrad Zacharias Lorenz,** Austrian ethologist; Nobel Prize in physiology or medicine (with K. von Frisch and N. Tinbergen), 1973.

1905   **Dean Jagger (Dean Jeffries),** U.S. character actor.

1913   **Albert Camus,** French philosopher, novelist, dramatist, journalist. [d. January 4, 1960]

1922   **Al Hirt,** U.S. jazz musician.

1926   **Dame Joan Sutherland,** Australian coloratura soprano.

Historical Events

680   **Sixth Council of Constantinople** is convened; it condemns **Monophysitism** and **Monotheletism.**

1153   **Treaty of Wallingford** is signed; **Stephen,** King of England, recognizes **Henry II** as his successor.

1811   **General William Henry Harrison** defeats Indians at the **Battle of Tippecanoe.**

1837   A pro-slavery mob in Alton, Illinois, destroys printing press and kills abolitionist printer **Elijah Lovejoy.**

1860   **Victor Emmanuel** enters Naples as King.

1900   Spain cedes the **Cagayan and Sibutu Islands** in the **Philippines** to the U.S. for $100,000.

Religious Calendar

The Saints

St. Herculanus, Bishop of Perugia, martyr. [d. c. 547]

St. Florentius, Bishop of Strasburg. [d. 7th century]

St. Willibrord, Bishop of Utrecht and missionary. Surnamed **Clement.** [d. 739]

St. Engelbert, Archbishop of Cologne, and martyr. [d. 1225]

St. Congar, patron of Hope, Wales. [death date unknown]

The Beatified

Blessed Helen of Arcella, virgin. [d. 1242]

Blessed Margaret Colonna, virgin. [d. 1280]

Blessed Matthia of Matelica, virgin and abbess. [d. 1300]

Blessed Peter of Ruffia, martyr. [d. 1365]

Blessed Antony Baldinucci, Jesuit priest. [d. 1717]

1914 **Tsingtao,** German leasehold in China, surrenders to Japanese and British forces (**World War I**).

1917 **Bolshevik** minority, led by **Lenin,** rises in revolution, capturing most of the government offices in Petrograd, seizing the Winter Palace, and arresting members of the provisional government except Premier Kerensky, who manages to escape (**Russian Revolution**).

The British capture Gaza from the Turks, ending the **Third Battle of Gaza (World War I)**.

1934 Rachmaninoff's ***Rhapsody on a Theme by Paganini*** premieres in Baltimore with Leopold Stokowski conducting the Philadelphia Orchestra and the composer as soloist.

1944 U.S. President **Franklin D. Roosevelt** is reelected for a historic fourth term.

November 8

Religious Calendar

The Saints

The Four Crowned Ones, martyrs. A feast in commemoration of four masons martyred when they refused to sculpt a pagan god for the Emperor Diocletian. [d. c. 306]

Birthdates

1086   **Henry V,** Holy Roman Emperor, reigned 1106–1125. [d. May 23, 1125]

1622   **Charles X Gustav,** King of Sweden. [d. February 13, 1660]

1656   **Edmund Halley,** English astronomer; best known for his study of comets; **Halley's comet** is named for him. [d. January 14, 1742]

1711   **Mikhail Vasilievich Lomonosov,** Russian scientist, poet, scholar; considered the founder of modern literary Russian, and the *Father of Modern Russian Poetry.* [d. April 4, 1765]

1732   **John Dickinson,** American patriot, lawyer; called the *Penman of the Revolution.* [d. February 14, 1808]

1818   **Marca Minghetti,** Italian premier, 1863–64; 1873–76. [d. December 10, 1886]

1821   **George Henry Bissell,** U.S. oil executive; responsible for establishing the Pennsylvania Oil Co., the first oil company in the U.S. [d. November 19, 1884]

1830   **Oliver Otis Howard,** U.S. Army general, educator; founder of **Howard University,** 1867. [d. October 26, 1909]

1848   **Gottlob Frege,** German mathematician, philosopher; founder of modern mathematical logic. [d. July 26, 1925]

1869   **Joseph Franklin Rutherford,** U.S. religious leader, author; a leader of the Russellites (Jehovah's Witnesses) in the U.S., 1916–42; outspoken proponent of conscientious objection. [d. January 8, 1942]

1884   **Hermann Rorschach,** Swiss psychiatrist; developed the ink blot test for psychiatric analysis (**Rorschach Test**), 1921. [d. April 2, 1922]

1885   **Tomoyuki Yamashita,** Japanese Army general; commander of Japanese forces in Malayan Campaign during World War II; executed as war criminal. [d. February 23, 1946]

1897   **Dorothy Day,** U.S. reformer; a founder of the **Catholic Worker Movement** in the U.S. [d. November 29, 1980]

1900   **Margaret Mitchell,** U.S. novelist; wrote *Gone with the Wind;* Pulitzer Prize, 1937. [d. August 16, 1949]

1909   **Katharine Hepburn,** U.S. actress; star in films and on stage; winner of four Academy Awards as Best Actress.

1916   **Peter Weiss,** Swedish writer, born in Germany; an important post-war European experimental playwright; author of *The Persecution and Assassination of Jean Paul Marat,* 1964. [d. May 10, 1982]

        June Havoc (June Hovick), Canadian actress; sister of Gypsy Rose Lee (January 9).

1918   **Florence Chadwick,** U.S. professional distance swimmer; the first woman to swim the English Channel both ways.

1921   **Jerome Hines (Jerome Heinz),** U.S. operatic bass.

        Gene Michael Saks, U.S. director; directed *Mame, The Odd Couple.*

1922   **Christiaan (Neethling) Barnard,** South African surgeon; performed first successful **heart transplant,** 1967.

1927   **Patti Page (Clara Anne Fowler),** U.S. singer.

1931   **Morley Safer,** U.S. broadcast journalist, born in Canada.

1935   **Alain Delon,** French actor.

St. Cybi, abbot. Also called **Cuby,** or **Kebie.** [d. 6th cent.]

St. Deusdedit, pope. Elected in 615 under the name **Adeodatus I.** [d. 618]

St. Tysilio, abbot. Also called **Suliau.** [d. c. 7th century]

St. Willehad, Bishop of Bremen and missionary. [d. 789]

St. Gerardin, monk and hermit. Also called **Garnard, Garnat, Gernardius,** or **Gervardius.** [d. c. 934]

St. Godfrey, Bishop of Amiens. Also called **Geoffrey.** [d. 1115]

Historical Events

1519 **Montezuma** receives **Hernando Cortés** in Aztec capital.

1520 Invasion of Sweden by **Christian II** of Denmark results in *Blood Bath of Stockholm,* in which nobility of Stockholm are massacred.

1576 **Pacification of Ghent** unites all Dutch provinces against Spain (**Dutch War of Liberation**).

1830 **Ferdinand II** accedes to the throne of Naples.

1889 **Montana** is admitted to the Union as the 41st state.

1917 **Second Congress of Soviets** convenes in Petrograd, Russia, and names Council of People's Commissars for the governing of the country with Lenin as chairman, Trotsky foreign commissar, and Stalin as commissar of nationalities.

   Lenin issues a decree of nationalization, abolishing private ownership of land in Russia.

1933 **Nadir Shah,** ruler of Afghanistan, is assassinated and succeeded by his son, **Mohammed Zahir Shah.**

1942 Allied forces begin landings in North Africa, beginning **Algeria-Morocco Campaign** (**World War II**).

1974 The eight National Guardsmen charged in the deaths of four people during an antiwar demonstration at **Kent State University** in 1970 are acquitted.

November 9

Holidays

Turks and Caicos Islands

Remembrance Day
Day set aside to commemorate all the Bahamian war dead.

Religious Calendar

Feasts

The Dedication of the Archbasilica of the Most Holy Savior, commonly called **St. John Lateran,** the acknowledged mother of churches and cathedral of the popes.

Birthdates

1731   **Benjamin Banneker,** U.S. inventor, mathematician, almanac maker. [d. 1806]

1801   **Robert Dale Owen,** U.S. social reformer, born in Scotland; U.S. Congressman, 1843–47; a founder of the **Smithsonian Institution,** 1845. [d. June 24, 1877]

  Gail Borden, U.S. inventor, manufacturer; opened the first factory for the production of **evaporated milk,** 1860. [d. January 11, 1874]

1802   **Elijah Parish Lovejoy,** U.S. abolitionist, newspaperman; killed during riot over slavery issue; known as the *martyr abolitionist.* [d. November 7, 1837]

1818   **Ivan Sergeyevich Turgenev,** Russian novelist, short-story writer; author of *Fathers and Sons.* [d. September 3, 1883]

1825   **Ambrose Powell Hill,** Confederate general during U.S. Civil War; commanded the best division of troops in Confederacy. [d. April 2, 1865]

1841   **King Edward VII** of Great Britain, ruled 1901–10. [d. May 6, 1910]

1853   **Stanford White,** U.S. architect; designed original **Madison Square Garden,** New York, 1889. [d. June 25, 1906]

1865   **Frederick Funston,** U.S. soldier, army general; primarily known for his guerrilla activities during Spanish American War. [d. February 19, 1917]

1869   **Marie Dressler (Leila von Koeber),** Canadian actress. [d. July 28, 1934]

1873   **Fritz Thyssen,** German industrialist; controller of *Vereingte Stahlwerke;* early supporter of Hitler; later lost all his property after a falling out with Hitler over policies in Germany. [d. February 8, 1951]

1886   **Ed Wynn (Isaiah Edwin Leopold),** U.S. comedic actor; father of Keenan Wynn. [d. June 19, 1966]

1888   **Jean Omer Marie Gabriel Monnet,** French economist, government official; founder of the **European Coal and Steel Community;** helped to rebuild European economy after World War II. [d. March 16, 1979]

1897   **Ronald George Wreyford,** British chemist; Nobel Prize in chemistry for studies of chemical reactions affected by short energy pulsations (with M. Eigen and G. Porter) 1967.

1915   **R. Sargent Shriver, Jr.,** U.S. government official, diplomat; Director of Peace Corps, 1961–66; U.S. Ambassador to France, 1968–70.

1918   **Spiro Agnew,** U.S. politician, lawyer; Governor of Maryland, 1967–68; U.S. Vice-President, 1969–73. Resigned as Vice-President when faced with charge of federal income tax evasion, 1973.

1922   **Dorothy Dandridge,** U.S. actress. [d. September 8, 1965]

1928   **Anne Sexton,** U.S. poet; Pulitzer Prize in poetry, 1966. [d. October 4, 1974]

1934   **Carl Sagan,** U.S. astronomer; popularized studies of astronomy through television series, *Cosmos.* Pulitzer Prize, 1978, for *The Dragons of Eden.*

Historical Events

1918   The German delegates are received by General Foch in the Compiègne Forest and given the Allies' armistice terms.

The Saints

St. Theodore Tiro, martyr. One of the patrons of warriors. Also called **Theodore Tyro, Theodore the Recruit,** or **Theodorus.** [d. c. 306]

St. Benignus, bishop. Also called **Benen,** or **Binen.** [d. 467]

St. Vitonus, Bishop of Verdun. Also called **Vanne.** [d. c. 525]

The Beatified

Blessed George Napper, martyr. Also called **Napier.** [d. 1610]

German **Kaiser Wilhelm II** is forced to abdicate (**World War I**).

Poland proclaims its independence as a free and reconstituted state with Marshal Jòzef Piłsudski as chief of state.

1935   **John L. Lewis** creates the **Congress of Industrial Organizations** within the **American Federation of Labor.**

1943   **United Nations Relief and Rehabilitation Administration** is established.

1944   U.S. General **George Patton** launches an all-out drive to capture **Metz, France** (**World War II**).

1949   **Costa Rica** promulgates its constitution.

1965   Largest **power failure** in history blacks out New York City, parts of eight northeastern states, and parts of Ontario and Quebec for several hours.

1967   First *Saturn V* rocket carrying the unmanned *Apollo 4* spacecraft is launched from Cape Kennedy.

November 10

Holidays

| U.S.S.R. | Soviet Militia Day |
| | World Youth Day |

Religious Calendar

The Saints

St. Leo the Great, pope (elected 440) and Doctor of the Church. Feast formerly April 11. [d. 461] Obligatory Memorial.

Birthdates

1433 Charles, Duke of Burgundy, known as *Charles the Bold*; the last Duke of Burgundy. [d. January 5, 1477]

1483 Martin Luther, German religious reformer; father of the Protestant Reformation in Germany; founder of the Lutheran church. [d. February 18, 1546]

1493 Paracelsus (Philippus Aureolus Theophrastus Bombastus von Hohenheim), Swiss alchemist, physician; noted for his early theories of disease and medicine. [d. September 24, 1541]

1577 Jacob Cats, Dutch poet, statesman; known as Holland's *Household Poet*. [d. September 12, 1660]

1668 François Couperin, French composer, harpsichordist; first great composer of harpsichord music. [d. September 12, 1773]

1683 George II, King of Great Britain, 1727– 60. [d. October 25, 1760]

1697 William Hogarth, English painter, engraver; noted for his pictorial satire; responsible for legislation (**Hogarth's Act,** 1735) protecting artists from piracy. [d. October 26, 1764]

1728 Oliver Goldsmith, English poet, playwright, novelist; author of *The Vicar of Wakefield* and *She Stoops to Conquer*. [d. April 4, 1774]

1759 Johann Christoph Friedrich Schiller, German dramatist, poet, historian, and philosopher. [d. May 9, 1805]

1801 Samuel Gridley Howe, U.S. humanitarian, physician, educator; Director, Perkins School for the Blind, 1831–65; a pioneer in education of the blind in the U.S.; husband of Julia Ward Howe (May 27), composer of *The Battle Hymn of the Republic*. [d. January 9, 1876]

1843 Miguel Antonio Caro, Colombian statesman; President, 1894–98. [d. August 5, 1909]

1874 Donald Baxter Macmillan, U.S. Arctic explorer; assisted Robert Peary during polar expedition, 1908–09; spent the rest of his life exploring Arctic region; author of *Four Years in the White North* and *How Peary Reached the Pole*. [d. September 7, 1970]

1879 (Nicholas) Vachel Lindsay, U.S. poet, noted for the rhythm and phonetics of his poetry. [d. December 5, 1931]

1887 Arnold Zweig, German novelist. [d. November 26, 1968]

1889 Claude Rains, U.S. actor, born in England [d. May 30, 1967]

1892 John Merrill Olin, U.S. manufacturer; head of Olin-Matheson Chemical Corporation, 1944–57.

1893 J(ohn) P(hillips) Marquand, U.S. novelist; Pulitzer Prize in fiction, 1938. [d. July 16, 1960]

1895 John Knudsen Northrup, U.S. aircraft manufacturer; a founder of Lockheed Aircraft Corporation, 1927.

1912 Bernard Haring, German theologian; active in reforms brought about by Vatican Council II.

1913 Karl Jay Shapiro, U.S. poet, critic; Pulitzer Prize in poetry, 1945.

1918 Ernst Otto Fischer, German chemist; Nobel Prize in chemistry for study of methods of merging organic and metallic atoms (with G. Wilkinson), 1973.

1919 Moise (Kapenda) Tshombe, Congolese political leader; President of Katanga State, 1960–63; exiled, 1965. [d. June 29, 1969]

1925 Richard Burton (Richard Jenkins), Welsh stage and screen actor. [d. Aug. 5, 1984]

St. Aedh Mac Bricc, bishop. Popularly invoked to cure headaches. Also called **Aed, Aid,** or **MacBrice.** [d. 589]

St. Justice, Archbishop of Canterbury, missionary, and the first bishop of Rochester. [d. c. 627]

St. Andrew Avellino, priest. [d. 1608]

St. Theoctista, virgin. [death date unknown]

SS. Trypho, Respicius, and Nympha, martyrs. [death dates unknown] Feast suppressed 1969.

1935   **Roy (Richard) Scheider,** U.S. actor.

Historical Events

1444   The Turks win a decisive victory at **Varna** over Christian crusaders led by **Ladislas of Hungary.**

1917   **Third Battle of Ypres** ends near Passchedaile with massive British losses (**World War I**).

1918   Professor **T. G. Masaryk,** President of National Council, is elected President of the **Republic of Czechoslovakia.**

1919   First **air mail service** is established between Paris and London.

1938   **Kemal Atatürk,** President of Turkey, dies and is succeeded by **Ismet Inönü.**

1941   First U.S.-escorted troop convoy of **World War II** sails from Halifax, Nova Scotia.

1942   U.S. warships and carrier aircraft engage French naval forces at **Casablanca, Morocco (World War II).**

1971   U.S. ratifies the treaty returning **Okinawa** and the southern Ryukyus to Japan.

1980   Polish Supreme Court rules that independent trade unions such as **Solidarity** are legal.

November 11

Holidays

Angola	**Independence Day** Commemorates the achievement of independence from Portugal, 1975.
Belgium, French Guiana, Tahiti	**Armistice Day** Commemorates the signing of the Armistice ending World War I, 1918.
Bhutan	**Birthday of His Majesty the King** Celebrates the birthday of King **Jigme Singye Wangchuk,** 1955.
Canada, Bermuda	**Remembrance Day** Commemorates all who participated in the two world wars.

Birthdates

1050 **Henry IV,** Holy Roman Emperor, 1056–1106. [d. August 7, 1106]

1491 **Martin Bucer** (or **Butzer,**) German Protestant clergyman; a leader of the Reformation in Germany. [d. February 28, 1551]

1729 **Louis Antoine de Bougainville,** French navigator; commanded first French expedition around the world; an island and two straits in the South Pacific are named for him; the flowering vine *bougainvillaea* is also named for him. [d. April 31, 1811]

1744 **Abigail Adams,** U.S. First Lady; wife of President John Adams, mother of President John Quincy Adams. [d. October 28, 1818]

1748 **Charles IV,** King of Spain, 1788–1808; abdicated, 1808. [d. January 20, 1819]

1771 **Marie François Xavier Bichat,** French physician, founder of the science of **histology.** [d. July 22, 1802]

Ephraim McDowell, U.S. surgeon; performed first successful removal of an ovarian tumor, previously considered impossible, 1809. [d. June 25, 1830]

1821 **Fyodor Mikhailovich Dostoyevsky,** Russian novelist; his best-known works are *Crime and Punishment* and *The Brothers Karamazov.* [d. February 9, 1881]

1836 **Thomas Bailey Aldrich,** U.S. poet, editor; editor of *Atlantic Monthly,* 1881–90. [d. March 19, 1907]

1852 **Franz Conrad von Hötzendorf,** Austrian general during World War I; Chief of Staff of Austro-Hungarian army, 1914–17. [d. August 26, 1925]

1868 **(Jean) Edouard Vuillard,** French painter, graphic artist; developer of **intimist style;** known for his interiors, still lifes, and flowers. [d. June 21, 1940]

1869 **Victor Emmanuel III,** last king of Italy; reigned 1900–46; forced into exile, 1946. [d. December 28, 1947]

1872 **Maude Adams (Maude Kiskadden),** U.S. actress. [d. July 17, 1953]

1882 **Gustav VI Adolf,** King of Sweden, 1950–73; the last Swedish king to have any real political power. [d. September 15, 1973]

1883 **Ernest Alexandre Ansermet,** Swiss conductor, composer. [d. February 20, 1969]

1885 **George S(mith) Patton, Jr.,** U.S. army officer, armored-warfare tactician; prominent commander in World War II. [d. December 21, 1945]

1889 **Sir Alexander Fleck,** Scottish industrialist; helped develop polyethylene and Dacron. [d. August 6, 1968]

1891 **René Clair,** French filmmaker; first member of the French Academy elected solely for his contributions to the art of filmmaking. [d. March 15, 1981]

1896 **Charles (Lucky) Luciano (Salvatore Lucania),** U.S. gangster, born in Italy; an infa-

France	**Veterans Day**	
	Commemorates the signing of the Armistice ending World War I, 1918, and pays tribute to all members of French armed forces.	
French West Indies, Monaco, New Caledonia	**Victory Day**	
Maldives	**Republic Day**	
	Celebrates the establishment of the Republic, 1953.	
U.S., Guam, Puerto Rico, Virgin Islands	**Veterans Day**	
	A national holiday commemorating the signing of the armistice ending World War	

I, 1918, and honoring all men and women who have served in U.S. armed forces; prior to 1954, called **Armistice Day.**

Religious Calendar

The Saints

St. Martin, Bishop of Tours; apostle of the Gauls, and patron of reformed drunkards. This day also called **Martinmas Day**; a Quarter Day in Scotland. [d. 397] Obligatory Memorial.

St. Theodore the Studite, abbot. [d. 826]

St. Bartholomew of Grottaferrata, abbot. [d. c. 1050]

St. Mennas, martyr. Also called **Menas.** [death date unknown]

---

mous figure of 1930s in U.S.; deported to Italy in 1946. [d. January 26, 1962]

1899 **Pat O'Brien,** U.S. actor. [d. October 15, 1983]

1904 **Alger Hiss,** U.S. public official; central figure in widely publicized spy case in U.S. in early 1950s; U.S. State Department official, 1936–46.

1913 **Sun Yun-suan,** Chinese leader; Prime Minister, Republic of China (Taiwan), 1978– .

1915 **William Proxmire,** U.S. Senator, 1957– ; gained national attention with his *Golden Fleece Awards* to government-sponsored groups or persons whose subsidization he deems unwarranted.

1922 **Kurt Vonnegut, Jr.,** U.S. novelist.

1925 **Jonathan Winters,** U.S. comedian.

1928 **Carlos Fuentes,** Mexican author, critic; head of Mexico's Department of Culture, 1956–59; Ambassador to France, 1975.

1935 **Bibi Andersson,** Swedish actress.

Historical Events

1500 **Treaty of Granada** is signed by France and Spain, determining partition of Italy.

1630 **Cardinal Richelieu** overthrows conspiracy of **Maria de' Medici,** the Queen Mother; referred to as the *Day of Dupes.*

1861 **Peter V** of Portugal dies and is succeeded by **Louis I.**

1889 **Washington** is admitted to the Union as the 42nd state.

1918 **Armistice** ending **World War I** goes into effect.

1921 **Tomb of the Unknown Soldier** is dedicated at **Arlington, Virginia.**

1922 **British Broadcasting Company** begins wireless transmissions of musical programs.

1941 British navy attacks and badly damages Italian fleet in **Malta** (**World War II**).

1944 Naval assault on **Iwo Jima** begins (**World War II**).

1945 **Marshal Tito's** Communist-dominated National Front wins elections in **Yugoslavia.**

1961 **Stalingrad,** Soviet city on the Volga River, is renamed **Volgograd.**

1966 U.S. spacecraft *Gemini 12* with James A. Lovell, Jr., and Edwin E. Aldrin, Jr., aboard, is launched from Cape Kennedy and later makes a successful rendezvous and linkup with an Agena target vehicle.

Methodist and **Evangelical United Brethren** churches of the U.S. vote to merge into the **United Methodist Church.**

1975 **Angola** gains independence from Portugal.

November 12

Holidays

Maldives   **Republic Day**
Second day of the celebration.

Republic of China (Taiwan)   **Birthday of Dr. Sun Yat-sen**
Celebrates the birth of the famous Chinese statesman and revolutionary leader, 1866; he is called the *Father of the Revolution.*

Religious Calendar

The Saints

St. Nilus the Elder, solitary. [d. c. 430]

St. Emilian Cucullatus, abbot. A patron of Spain. [d. 574]

Birthdates

1493 **Baccio Bandinelli,** Italian Renaissance sculptor; sculpture of *Adam and Eve* and bas-relief in choir of the Florence cathedral. [d. February 7, 1560]

1651 **Sor Juana Inés de la Cruz,** Mexican poet, nun; one of the great women of Mexican history. [d. 1695]

1746 **Jacques Alexandre César Charles,** French physicist, chemist, inventor; first to use hydrogen for balloon inflation; anticipated Gay-Lussac's (December 6) discovery of law governing expansion of gases. [d. April 7, 1823]

1815 **Elizabeth Cady Stanton,** U.S. reformer; a leader in the movement for women's suffrage; with Lucretia Mott (January 3) organized the **Seneca Falls Convention** on Women's Rights, 1848. [d. October 26, 1902]

1833 **Aleksandr Profiryevich Borodin,** Russian composer; one of the *Mighty Five* figures in Russian nationalist school. [d. February 27, 1887]

1840 **Auguste Rodin,** French sculptor; creator of *The Burghers of Calais, The Kiss,* and *The Thinker.* [d. November 17, 1917]

1842 **John William Strutt, 3rd Baron Rayleigh,** English physicist; Nobel Prize in physics for discovery of **argon,** 1904. [d. June 30, 1919]

1866 **Sun Yat-sen,** Chinese revolutionary leader and national hero; led fight to overthrow Manchu dynasty; head of South Chinese Republic, 1921. [d. March 12, 1925]

1889 **Dewitt Wallace,** U.S. publisher; with his wife, Lila Bell Acheson, founded and edited *Reader's Digest,* 1921–65. [d. March 30, 1981]

1908 **Harry Andrew Blackmun,** U.S. jurist, lawyer; Associate Justice, U.S. Supreme Court, 1970– .

1915 **Roland Barthes,** French critic, writer; noted especially for his theories of **semiology,** or the study of signs and symbols. [d. March 25, 1980]

1918 **Jo Stafford,** U.S. singer; popular during Big Band era of 1930s and 1940s.

1929 **Princess Grace** of Monaco **(Grace Kelly),** U.S. film star prior to her marriage to Prince Rainier III of Monaco, 1956. [d. September 14, 1982]

1934 **Charles (Milles) Manson,** U.S. criminal; convicted murderer of actress Sharon Tate and six others; leader of a radical cult of drifters.

1945 **Neil Young,** Canadian-born rock musician.

1949 **André Laplante,** Canadian pianist; first Canadian to win a medal in the International Tchaikovsky Competition in Moscow, 1978.

1961 **Nadia Comaneci,** Romanian gymnast; winner of three Olympic gold medals, 1976.

Historical Events

1893 **Durand Agreement** is signed between Great Britain and Afghanistan fixing the

St. Machar, bishop. Also called **Mochumma.** [d. 6th cent.]

St. Cunibert, Bishop of Cologne. [d. c. 663]

St. Cadwaladr, Welsh king. Also called *battle-shunner.* [d. 664]

St. Cumian, abbot. Also called **Cuimine Fota.** [d. c. 665]

St. Lebuin, monk and missionary. Also called **Lebwin,** or **Liafwine.** Patron of Daventer (Daventry), England [d. c. 773]

St. Benedict and his Companions, martyrs. Venerated in Poland as the *Five Polish Brothers.* [d. 1003]

St. Astrik, Archbishop of the Hungarians. Also called **Anastasius, Radla.** [d. 1040]

St. Josaphat, Archbishop of Polotsk and martyr. Feast formerly November 14. [d. 1623] Obligatory Memorial.

St. Livinus, bishop and martyr. Also called **Livin.** [death date unknown]

The Beatified

Blessed Rainerius of Arezzo, Franciscan Friar Minor. [d. 1304]

Blessed John Della Pace, hermit. [d. c. 1332]

Blessed Gabriel of Ancona, Franciscan friar and missionary. [d. 1456]

frontier with India from Chitral to Baluchistan.

1912   Spain's Liberal Prime Minister **Josè Canalejas** is assassinated by anarchist **Pardinas.**

1918   **Charles I** of Austria, last Hapsburg emperor of **Austria-Hungary,** abdicates; **Austria** and **Hungary** are proclaimed republics.

1921   **Washington Armament Conference,** set to discuss reduction of naval armaments after World War I, begins in Washington, D.C.

1942   Naval battle of **Guadalcanal** begins (**World War II**).

1958   **Guinea** promulgates its constitution.

1969   U.S. Army Lieutenant **William L. Calley, Jr.,** is charged with the murder of an undetermined number of Vietnamese civilians in the village of **My Lai.**

1975   Ailing U.S. Supreme Court Justice **William O. Douglas** resigns from the court after 36 years of service.

1981   Second launching of U.S. space shuttle *Columbia* marks the first reuse of a space vehicle.

November 13

Religious Calendar

The Saints

St. Arcadius and his Companions, martyrs. [d. 437]

St. Brice, Bishop of Tours; invoked against stomach diseases. Also called **Brictio,** or **Britius.** [d. 444]

St. Eugenius, Archbishop of Toledo. [d. 657]

St. Maxellendis, virgin and martyr. [d. c. 670]

Birthdates

354 **Saint Augustine,** early Christian philosopher, theologian, and Father of the Church. Feast day is August 28. [d. August 28, 430]

1312 **Edward III,** King of England; 1327–77; a brilliant military leader who commanded the finest army in medieval Europe. [d. June 21, 1377]

1567 **Maurice of Nassau,** stadtholder of Dutch Republic; the Dutch Republic's greatest military leader of 16th and 17th centuries. [d. April 23, 1625]

1729 **Aleksandr Vasilievich Suvorov,** Count Suvorov Rimniksy, Prince Itolsky, Russian field marshal and tactician. [d. May 6, 1800]

1782 **Esaias Tegner,** Swedish poet, scholar, bishop, and orator; representative of Gothic school of literature; one of great poets of Sweden. [d. November 2, 1846]

1814 **Joseph Hooker,** Union Army general during U.S. Civil War; Commander of Army of the Potomac, 1863. [d. October 31, 1879]

1831 **James Clerk Maxwell,** Scottish mathematician, physicist; proposed electromagnetic nature of light, 1873; experimented in color perception, color blindness, and kinetic theory of gases. [d. November 5, 1879]

1833 **Edwin Booth,** U.S. actor; outstanding U.S. stage actor of 19th century; noted for his portrayal of Shakespeare's *Hamlet.* Brother of John Wilkes Booth (May 10). [d. June 7 1893]

1854 **George Whitefield Chadwick,** U.S. composer; Director, New England Conservatory of Music, 1897–1931. [d. April 4, 1931]

1856 **Louis (Dembitz) Brandeis,** U.S. jurist, lawyer; Associate Justice, U.S. Supreme Court, 1916–39; Brandeis University is named for him. [d. October 5, 1941]

1859 **Robert Louis (Balfour) Stevenson,** Scottish novelist, essayist, critic, poet; author of *Treasure Island* and *A Child's Garden of Verses.* [d. December 3, 1894]

1893 **Edward A. Doisy,** U.S. biochemist; Nobel Prize in physiology or medicine for research into antihemorrhagic substances and the discovery of **vitamin K** (with C. P. H. Dam), 1943.

1915 **Nathaniel (Goddard) Benchley,** U.S. novelist, editor, journalist; son of Robert Benchley (September 15); father of Peter Benchley (May 8).

1922 **Charles Bronson (Charles Buchinsky),** U.S. actor.

Oskar Werner, U.S. actor, born in Austria.

Historical Events

1002 Danish settlers in England are massacred at **St. Brice** on order of **Ethelred II.**

1092 **Malcolm III** of Scotland is defeated and killed near Alnwick.

1851 First submarine telegraph cable is completed from Dover to Calais.

1940 Walt Disney's ***Fantasia*** premieres at the Broadway Theater in New York; first film to attempt to use stereophonic sound.

1966 U.S. astronaut **Edwin E. Aldrin, Jr.** completes **space walk** during *Gemini 12* mission.

1971 *Mariner 9,* unmanned U.S. spacecraft, goes into orbit around Mars, the first man-made object to orbit another planet.

St. Kilian, preacher. Also called **Chilianus, Chillen, Kilien,** or **Killian.** [d. 7th century]

St. Nicholas I, pope. Elected 858; patron of Russia, Aberdeen, mariners, thieves, and parish clerks. Called *the Great.* [d. 867]

St. Abbo of Fleury, abbot and martyr. [d. 1004]

St. Homobonus, merchant; patron of tailors, clothmakers, and Cremona, Italy. Also called **Gutman.** [d. 1197]

St. Didacus, Franciscan lay brother. Also called **Diego.** [d. 1463]

St. Stanislaus Kostka, Jesuit. A lesser patron of Poland. Also called **Stanislas.** [d. 1568]

November 14

Holidays

Jordan	**H. M. King Hussein's Birthday** Commemorates the event, 1935.
St. Kitts	**Prince of Wales' Birthday** Celebrates the occasion of the prince's birth, 1948.

Birthdates

1650 **William III,** King of Great Britain, 1688–1702. [d. March 19, 1702]

1668 **Johnann Lucus von Hildebrandt,** Austrian baroque architect, military engineer. [d. November 16, 1745]

1765 **Robert Fulton,** U.S. inventor; developed first practical **steamship,** 1807. [d. February 24, 1815]

1779 **Adam Gottlob Oehlenschläger,** Danish poet, dramatist; named Danish national poet, 1849; leader of Romantic movement in Danish poetry. [d. January 20, 1850]

1797 **Sir Charles Lyell,** Scottish geologist; the father of modern geology. [d. February 22, 1875]

1820 **Anson Burlingame,** U.S. legislator, diplomat; noted for his great achievements as U.S. Minister to China, 1860–67; appointed by Chinese government to head a three-man mission to U.S. and Europe in 1868, charged with establishing diplomatic relations with the U.S., Great Britain, and Russia; (resulted in the **Burlingame Treaty,** July 28, 1868.) [d. February 23, 1870]

1828 **Charles Louis de Saulces de Freycinet,** French statesman; Premier of France, 1879–80; 1882; 1886; 1890–92. [d. May 14, 1923]

1840 **Claude Monet,** French artist; Impressionist painter. [d. December 5, 1926]

1861 **Frederick Jackson Turner,** U.S. historian; noted for his revolutionary interpretation of American history; author of *The Significance of Sections in American History*, for which he received the Pulitzer Prize, 1933. [d. March 14, 1932]

1862 **Count Johann-Heinrich von Bernstorff,** German diplomat; German Ambassador to U.S., 1908–17; Chairman, German League of Nations Union; Vice-Chairman, League of Nations. [d. October 6, 1939]

1863 **Leo Hendrik Baekeland,** U.S. chemist, born in Belgium; developed **bakelite,** one of first widely used **plastics.** [d. February 23, 1944]

1885 **Sonia Delaunay,** French-Russian artist; influenced creative and applied arts, 1920–70; experimented with *infinite rhythm* in her paintings.

1889 **Jawaharlah Nehru,** Indian statesman; first Prime Minister of India, 1947–64; became known throughout the world for his exercise of civil disobedience while striving for independence of India. [d. May 27, 1964]

1891 **Sir Frederick Grant Banting,** Canadian physiologist; Nobel Prize in physiology or medicine for production of **insulin** (with J. J. R. Macleod), 1923. [d. February 21, 1941]

1895 **Frank J. Lausche,** U.S. statesman; U.S. Senator, 1956–68.

Wilmarth Sheldon Lewis, U.S. author, editor; his extensive works related to Horace Walpole; senior editor of projected 50-volume edition of Walpole's correspondence. [d. October 7, 1979]

1896 **Mamie Doud Eisenhower,** U.S. First Lady; wife of Dwight David Eisenhower, 34th U.S. President. [d. November 1, 1979]

1900 **Aaron Copland,** U.S. composer; Pulitzer Prize in music, 1945.

1904 **Dick Powell,** U.S. actor, producer, director. [d. January 3, 1963]

1908 **Joseph (Raymond) McCarthy,** U.S. politician, lawyer, farmer; U.S. Senator, 1947–57; responsible for controversial hearings into Communism in U.S., which became known as a witch-hunt because of the terrorizing tactics of him and his staff; slandered many people using unsubstantiated evidence. [d. May 2, 1957]

Religious Calendar

The Saints

St. Dubricius, bishop. Also called **Dyfrig.** [d. 6th century]

St. Laurence O'Toole, Archbishop of Dublin. Also called **Lawrence,** or (in Gaelic) **Lorcan Ua Tuathail.** [d. 1180]

The Beatified

Blessed Serapion, martyr. [d. 1240]

Blessed John Liccio, Dominican preacher, prior. [d. 1511]

Harrison (Evans) Salisbury, U.S. journalist; editor and writer for *The New York Times*, 1954– ; Pulitzer Prize in international correspondence, 1955.

1912   **Barbara Hutton,** U.S. heiress. [d. May 11, 1979]

1919   **Veronica Lake (Constance Ockleman),** U.S. actress. [d. July 7, 1973]

1930   **Edward White,** U.S. astronaut; first man to walk in space (during *Gemini 4* mission, 1965). Killed in fire aboard *Apollo I.* [d. January 27, 1967]

1935   **Hussein ibn Talal,** King of Jordan, 1953–.

1948   **Charles, Prince of Wales,** oldest son of Queen Elizabeth II and Prince Philip; heir apparent to British throne.

Historical Events

1532   **King Henry VIII** of England marries **Anne Boleyn.**

1847   **Chloroform** is first used as an anesthetic by Scottish physician **James Y. Simpson.**

Civil war breaks out in **Switzerland** between the federal government and the Sonderbund of the seven Catholic cantons.

1863   Great Britain cedes **Ionian Islands** to Greece.

1888   **St. Andrew's Golf Club,** Yonkers, New York, is organized, the first American golf club.

1914   First issue of ***Popolo d'Italia,*** edited by **Benito Mussolini,** is published.

1969   ***Apollo 12*** spacecraft is successfully launched from Cape Kennedy, Florida.

1973   **Princess Anne** of Britain and Captain Mark Phillips are married in Westminster Abbey.

November 15

Holidays

Brazil   **Proclamation of the Republic**
                  Commemorates the event, 1889.

Religious Calendar

The Saints

SS. Gurius, Samonas, and Abibus, martyrs. Venerated as avengers of unfulfilled contracts. [d. 4th century]

Birthdates

1397   **Nicholas V,** pope from 1447–55. [d. 1455]

1708   **William Pitt, the Elder,** English statesman; Secretary of State, 1756–61; 1766–68; led England during the Seven Years' War, 1756–63; responsible for England's rise to power and acquisition of Canada and other territories. Called *The Great Commoner.* [d. May 11, 1778]

1738   **Sir William Herschel (Friedrich Wilhelm Herschel),** English astronomer, born in Germany; refined telescope quality; discovered **Uranus.** [d. August 25, 1822]

1741   **Johann Kaspar Lavater,** Swiss philosopher, mystic, writer; founder of science of **physiognomy.** [d. January 2, 1801]

1816   **Isidore Kalish,** U.S. rabbi, author, leader; pioneer of Reform Judaism in the U.S. [d. May 11, 1886]

1849   **James O'Neill,** U.S. actor, born in Ireland; father of Eugene O'Neill (October 16). [d. August 10, 1920]

1862   **Gerhart Hauptmann,** German dramatic poet; one of most noted German writers of the early twentieth century; Nobel Prize in literature, 1912. [d. June 8, 1946]

1874   **Schack August Steenberg Krogh,** Danish physiologist; Nobel Prize in physiology or medicine for discovery of regulating mechanism in blood capillary action. [d. September 13, 1949]

1882   **Felix Frankfurter,** U.S. jurist; Associate Justice, U.S. Supreme Court, 1939–62. [d. February 22, 1965]

1887   **Marianne (Craig) Moore,** U.S. poet; noted for her highly personal subject matter, strict adherence to set metrical form, wit, and concern for abiding moral issues. Pulitzer Prize in poetry, 1952.

         Georgia O'Keeffe, U.S. painter; known for her abstract style and intensity of her images and colors. Married to Alfred Stieglitz (January 1).

1891   **Erwin (Johannes Eugin) Rommel,** German field marshall; head of Nazi forces in Africa, 1941–43. [d. October 14, 1944]

         W(illiam) Averell Harriman, U.S. statesman, diplomat, banker; special representative of the U.S. government to Great Britain and Russia, 1941–43; U.S. Ambassador to Russia, 1943–46; U.S. Ambassador to Great Britain, 1946; U.S. Secretary of Commerce, 1946–48; Chief Representative of U.S. to Paris Peace Talks (Vietnam War), 1968–69.

1897   **Aneurin Bevan,** British political leader, Labour Party leader; Minister of Health, 1945–51; responsible for establishment of National Health Service in Great Britain. [d. July 6, 1960]

1906   **Curtis (Emerson) Lemay,** U.S. Air Force general; U.S. Commander of Strategic Air Command (SAC), 1957–61; U.S. Air Force Chief of Staff, 1961–65; ran for Vice President on Wallace ticket, 1968.

1925   **Howard Henry Baker, Jr.,** U.S. politician, lawyer; U.S. Senator, 1967–85.

1929   **Edward Asner,** U.S. actor.

1931   **John Kerr,** U.S. actor, lawyer.

Historical Events

1315   **Battle of Morgarten** is won by the Swiss, throroughly defeating **Leopold of Austria** and beginning the brilliant career of the **Swiss infantry.**

1635   **University of Budapest** opens.

1715   Austria obtains **Spanish Netherlands** in the **Barrier Treaty** with Holland.

St. Disiderius, Bishop of Cahors. Also called **Didier,** or **Géry.** [d. 655]

St. Malo, Bishop of Aleth. Also called **Machutus, Maclou, Maclovius,** or **Mallou.** [d. 7th century]

St. Fintan of Rheinau, solitary. Also called **Findan** [d. 879]

St. Leopold of Austria, prince; patron of Austria. Also called *the Good.* [d. 1136]

St. Albert the Great, Bishop of Regensburg and Doctor of the Church. Patron of Prussia and of students of the natural sciences. Called *the Universal Teacher.* [d. 1280] Optional Memorial.

1777 **Continental Congress** adopts the **Articles of Confederation** for the American colonies.

1806 **Pike's Peak** is first sighted by Zebulon M. Pike.

1853 **Maria II** of Portugal dies and is succeeded by **Pedro V.**

1863 **Frederick VII** of Denmark dies and is succeeded by **Christian IX.**

1864 **General William Sherman** and 60,000 Union troops leave Atlanta, beginning their famous *March to the Sea* (**U.S. Civil War**).

1889 **Pedro II** of Brazil abdicates and a republic is proclaimed.

1908 **Congo Free State** becomes the **Belgian Congo.**

1914 **Battle of Cracow** begins in the second Russian offensive in Galicia (**World War I**).

1920 First meeting of the Assembly of the **League of Nations,** with 42 member nations, takes place in London.

1921 **Russian State Bank** opens in Moscow and is granted a monopoly on purchase and sale of foreign currency and precious metals.

1942 **Battle of Guadalcanal** ends with decisive U.S. victory over the Japanese (**World War II**).

1950 U.S. Marines occupy **Hagaru, Korea** (**Korean War**).

1960 *U.S.S. George Washington,* the first U.S. submarine armed with **thermonuclear missiles,** sails from Charleston, S.C., on its first patrol.

1971 **People's Republic of China** delegation, headed by Deputy Foreign Minister Chiao Kuan-hua, assumes its seats in the UN General Assembly.

1979 **Sir Anthony Blunt,** knight of the British Empire, advisor on art to Queen Elizabeth II, is discovered to be a spy for the Soviet Union and is stripped of his knighthood.

November 16

Religious Calendar

The Saints

St. Eucherius, Bishop of Lyons. [d. c. 449]

St. Afan, bishop. Also called **Avan, Avanus,** or **Llanafan.** [d. c. 6th century]

St. Margaret of Scotland, queen and matron. Wife of Malcolm of Scotland. Patroness of Scotland. [d. 1093] Optional Memorial.

Birthdates

42 B.C. **Tiberius (Tiberius Claudius Nero Caesar),** second Emperor of Rome, A.D. 14–37. [d. March 16, A.D. 37]

1758 **Peter Andreas Heiberg,** Danish poet, playwright; author of many satirical pieces aimed at Danish government; exiled, 1799; accompanied Talleyrand (February 2) on numerous diplomatic missions. [d. April 30, 1841]

1807 **Jónas Hallgrímsson,** Icelandic poet, patriot, scientist; exerted great influence in purifying the Icelandic language. [d. May 26, 1845]

1810 **Karel Hynek Mácha,** Czech poet, novelist; a leader in the Czech romantic movement. [d. November 6, 1836]

1811 **John Bright,** British politician, orator; leading proponent of Irish independence. [d. March 27, 1889]

1836 **David Kalakaua,** 7th King of the Hawaiians, 1874–91, elected by the Hawaiian assembly. [d. January 30, 1891]

1839 **Louis-Honoré Fréchette,** Canadian poet, journalist; preeminent French-Canadian poet of 19th century. [d. May 31, 1908]

1873 **W(illiam) C(hristopher) Handy,** U.S. composer; regarded by many as the father of the blues; wrote *Memphis Blues*, *St. Louis Woman*. [d. March 28, 1958]

1881 **Joel Hildebrand,** U.S. chemist, educator; member of the faculty, University of California at Berkeley for nearly 70 years. It is estimated that he taught over 40,000 students during his career. [d. May 2, 1983]

1889 **George S(imon) Kaufman,** U.S. dramatist, drama critic, director; Pulitzer Prize in drama, 1932, 1937. [d. June 2, 1961]

1895 **Paul Hindemith,** U.S. composer born in Germany; noted for his ultramodern style of composition. [d. December 23, 1963]

1896 **Sir Oswald Ernald Mosely,** British politician; founder of British Union of Fascists; member of House of Commons, 1918–31. [d. December, 2 1980]

1898 **Ben Pearson,** U.S. archery promoter. [d. March 2, 1971]

1899 **Mary Margaret McBride,** U.S. radio commentator. [d. April 7, 1976]

1909 **Burgess Meredith,** U.S. actor.

1919 **Anatoliy F. Dobrynin,** Russian diplomat; Russian Ambassador to U.S., 1962– .

1935 **France-Albert Rene,** President, Republic of Seychelles, 1977– .

1942 **Donna Ruth McKechnie,** U.S. dancer; Tony award, 1975, for role of Cassie in *A Chorus Line*.

Historical Events

1272 **Henry III** of England dies and is succeeded by **Edward I.**

1621 Papal Chancery first adopts **January 1** as beginning of the year.

1632 **Battle of Lützen** is fought, in which Protestant forces under Swedish **King Gustavus Adolphus** are victorious over Imperialist Catholic troops; Gustavus Adolphus is killed (**Thirty Years' War**).

1797 **Frederick William II** of Prussia dies and is succeeded by **Frederick William III.**

1900 **Philadelphia Orchestra** presents its inaugural concert.

1907 **Oklahoma** is admitted to Union as the 46th state.

1914 **Battle of Łódź** begins in the second German offensive against the Russians at **Warsaw** (**World War I**).

SS. Gertrude the Great and Mechtildis, virgins and mystics. [d. 1302 and 1298] Optional Memorial.

St. Edmund of Abingdon, Archbishop of Canterbury. Also called **St. Edme.** [d. 1240]

St. Agnes of Assisi, virgin and abbess. [d. 1253]

The Beatified

Blessed Louis Morbioli, Carmelite tertiary. [d. 1485]

Blessed Gratia of Cattaro, Augustinian lay brother. [d. 1508]

Blessed Lucy of Narni, virgin and mystic. [d. 1544]

1918 **Hungarian Republic** is proclaimed in the break-up of the Austro-Hungarian Empire (**World War I**). (See November 13)

The Allied armies begin their march into Germany (**World War I**).

1944 The U.S. First and Ninth Armies begin co-ordinated drive to the **Roer River** in western Germany (**World War II**).

1959 Rodgers & Hammerstein's musical comedy, *The Sound of Music,* premieres in New York.

1973 U.S. President Richard Nixon signs a bill authorizing construction of a **trans-Alaska oil pipeline.**

Skylab 3, with a crew of 3, is launched from Kennedy Space Center for a 60-day mission.

November 17

Holidays

Federal Republic of Germany	Day of Penance
U.S.S.R.	International Students' Day
Zaire	Armed Forces Day

Religious Calendar

The Saints

St. Dionysius, Bishop of Alexandria. Also called *the Great.* [d. 265]

St. Gregory the Wonderworker, Bishop of Neocaesarea. Invoked in time of earthquake and flood. Also called **Thaumaturgus.** [d. 268]

Birthdates

1612 **Pierre Mignard,** French painter; preeminent court portrait painter of the mid-seventeenth century. [d. May 30, 1695]

1685 **Pierre Gaultier de Varennes, Sieur de La Verendrye,** French-Canadian fur trader, explorer; discoverer of **Manitoba,** the **Dakotas,** and **western Minnesota.** [d. December 5, 1749]

1717 **Jean Le Rond d'Alembert,** French mathematician and scientist; one of the leading figures of the French Enlightenment. [d. October 29, 1783]

1755 **Louis XVIII,** King of France; first king to rule France after the restoration of the monarchy, 1814. [d. September 16, 1824]

1790 **August Ferdinand Möbius,** German mathematician, astronomer; **Möbius strip,** a three-dimensional, one-sided band with a continuous surface, is named for him. [d. September 26, 1868]

João Carlos Saldanha, Portuguese general and statesman; Premier, 1846–49; 1851–56; 1870. [d. November 21, 1876]

1794 **George Grote,** English historian of Greece; primarily known for his 8-volume *History of Greece.* [d. June 18, 1871]

1867 **Henri Joseph Eugène Gourand,** French soldier. [d. September 14, 1946]

1878 **Grace Abbott,** U.S. social worker, public administrator; chief of U.S. Children's Bureau, 1921–34; leader in movement to legislate child labor and immigrant exploitation; author of *The Child and the State,* 1938. [d. June 19, 1939]

1887 **Bernard Law Montgomery, 1st Viscount of Alamein,** British Army field marshal; responsible for defeat of **Erwin Rommel** (November 15) at **El Alamein** in World War II. [d. March 24, 1976]

1901 **Lee Strasberg,** U.S. theatrical director, prominent acting teacher, born in Austria; cofounder of the Group Theatre. [d. February 17, 1982]

Walter Hallstein, German diplomat, lawyer; Secretary of Foreign Affairs, West Germany, 1951–58; a founder and first president of the **European Economic Community,** 1958–67. [d. March 29, 1982]

1902 **Eugene Paul Wigner,** U.S. physicist, born in Hungary; Nobel Prize in physics for research on structure of atom and its nucleus (with M. G. Mayer and J. H. D. Jensen), 1963.

1904 **Isamu Noguchi,** U.S. sculptor, designer.

1918 **(William Franklin) Billy Graham,** U.S. Baptist clergyman, evangelist.

1919 **Hershy Kay,** U.S. composer, arranger; arranged scores for *Candide, Once Upon a Mattress, A Chorus Line,* and *Evita.* [d. December 2, 1981]

1923 **Aristide Pereira,** President, Republic of Cape Verde, 1975– .

1925 **Rock Hudson (Roy Fitzgerald),** U.S. actor.

1930 **Bob Mathias,** U.S. athlete; U.S. Olympic decathlon winner, 1948, 1952; U.S. Congressman, 1967–73.

1938 **Gordon Lightfoot,** Canadian singer.

SS. Alphaeus and Zachaeus, martyrs. Also called **Alphoeus** and **Zachoeus.** [d. 303]

SS. Acisclus and Victoria, martyrs. [d. c. 4th century]

St. Anianus, Bishop of Orleans. Also called **Agnan, Aignan,** or **Anian.** [d. c. 453]

St. Gregory, Bishop of Tours and historian. [d. 594]

St. Hilda, Abbess of Whitby and virgin. Also called **Hild;** patron saint of business and professional women. [d. 680]

St. Hugh, Bishop of Lincoln. [d. 1200]

St. Elizabeth of Hungary, widow and Landgravine (countess) of Thuringia. Feast formerly November 19. [d. 1231] Obligatory Memorial.

The Beatified

Blessed Salome, widow. [d. 1268]

Blessed Joan of Signa, virgin. [d. 1307]

Blessed Elizabeth the Good, virgin and mystic. [d. 1420]

Blessed Roque Gonzalez and His Companions, the martyrs of Paraguay. [d. 1628]

Blessed Philippine Duchesne, virgin. [d. 1852]

Blessed Hyacinthus Ansalone, one of the Martyrs of Nagasaki. [beatified 1981]

Blessed Thomas Hioji Rokuzayemon Nishi, one of the Martyrs of Nagasaki. [beatified 1981]

1943   **Lauren Hutton,** U.S. model.

Historical Events

1292   **Edward I** of England awards vacant Scottish throne to **John Baliol.**

1558   **Queen Mary I** of England dies and is succeeded by **Elizabeth I.**

1637   **Anne Hutchinson,** American religious leader, is banished from Massachusetts by the General Court.

1796   **Catherine the Great,** Empress of Russia, dies and is succeeded by her son, **Paul.**

1855   **Dr. David Livingstone** discovers **Victoria Falls** in Africa and names it for the British Queen.

1869   **Suez Canal** opens for navigation.

1870   **Amadeus,** Duke of Aosta, is proclaimed king of Spain as **Amadeo I** upon election by the Cortes.

1933   U.S. recognizes **Soviet government** in Russia.

1941   U.S. Congress amends the **Neutrality Act** to allow arming of U.S. merchant ships.

1958   Civilian government of **Sudan** is overthrown in a military coup.

1968   Unmanned Soviet spacecraft **Zond 6** completes its circumlunar flight.

1970   **Luna 17,** Soviet unmanned spacecraft, lands a **lunokhod,** a self-propelled, 8-wheel vehicle, on the moon.

1972   **Juan Perón** arrives in Buenos Aires from Rome, ending 17 years of exile.

November 18

Holidays

Haiti   **Vertieres Day**
Commemorates the **Battle of Vertieres,** 1803.

Morocco   **Independence Celebration Day**
Celebrates achievement of independence from France, 1956.

Birthdates

1647   **Pierre Bayle,** French philosopher, critic; founder of 18th-century rationalism. [d. December 28, 1706]

1743   **Johannes Ewald,** Danish poet, playwright; author of the first original Danish tragedy, *Rolf Krage,* 1770. [d. March 17, 1781]

1768   **Zacharias Werner,** German dramatist, preacher; author of one of the first **fate tragedies,** 1810. [d. January 17, 1823]

     Carl Maria von Weber, German composer; the founder of German Romantic opera. [d. June 5, 1826]

1786   **Sir Henry Rowley Bishop,** English conductor and composer of operas; composed music incidental to Shakespearean plays; known especially for refrain of *Home Sweet Home.* [d. April 30, 1855]

1789   **Louis Jacques Mandé Daguerre,** French artist, inventor; invented the **daguerreotype process,** an early photographic technique. [d. July 10, 1851]

1810   **Asa Gray,** U.S. botanist; author of *Manual of the Botany of the Northern United States,* the fundamental resource in the area; chief advocate of Darwin's theory of evolution in the U.S. [d. January 30, 1888]

1832   **(Nils) Adolf Nordenskiöld,** Swedish Arctic explorer, scientist; first to successfully navigate the **Northeast Passage,** 1878–80. [d. August 12, 1901]

1836   **Sir William Schwenck Gilbert,** British poet and librettist; with his partner, Sir Arthur Sullivan (May 13), composed numerous comic operas. [d. May 29, 1911]

1860   **Ignace Jan Paderewski,** Polish statesman, pianist, composer; leader in Polish cause during World War I; Prime Minister of Polish coalition government, January–November, 1919; preeminent pianist, known for his interpretations of Schumann, Chopin, Liszt, and Rubinstein. [d. June 29, 1941]

1870   **Elizabeth Meriwhether Gilmer,** U.S. journalist; known for her syndicated advice to the lovelorn column written under byline **Dorothy Dix.** [d. December 16, 1951]

1874   **Clarence (Shepard) Day, Jr.,** U.S. essayist; author of series of essays upon which stage play *Life with Father* was based. [d. December 28, 1935]

1875   **Walter Seymour Allward,** Canadian sculptor; creator of massive Canadian war memorial on Vimy Ridge in France. [d. April 24, 1955]

1882   **Jacques Maritain,** French philosopher; representative of liberal apologist school of Catholic thought; author of numerous influential works, including *Art and Scholasticism* and *True Humanism.* [d. April 28, 1973]

1883   **Carl Vinson,** U.S. politician; U.S. Congressman, 1914–64, and Chairman House Armed Services Committee. [d. June 1, 1981]

1884   **(Percy) Wyndham Lewis,** British novelist, artist; representative of Post-Impressionist Vorticist school; author of *The Art of Being Ruled, Time and Western Man,* and *The Apes of God.* [d. March 7, 1957]

1886   **James S(cott) Kemper,** U.S. insurance executive; Chairman and Chief Executive Officer, Kemper Group, one of the world's largest underwriting organizations, 1945–66; U.S. Ambassador to Brazil, 1953–54. [d. September 17, 1981]

1894   **(Justin) Brooks Atkinson,** U.S. drama critic; preeminent U.S. critic, 1920–40; Pulitzer Prize in correspondence, 1947. [d. January 13, 1984]

The Dedication of the Basilicas of St. Peter and of St. Paul, 1626 and 1854.

The Saints

St. Romanus of Antioch, martyr. [d. 304]

St. Mabyn, nun. [d. c. 6th century]

St. Mawes, abbot. Also called **Maudez.** [d. c. 6th century]

St. Odo of Cluny, abbot. Invoked for rain. Also called **Odo of Cluni.** [d. 942]

1897 **Lord Patrick Maynard Stuart Blackett,** British physicist; Nobel Prize in physics for discoveries in **cosmic radiation,** 1948. [d. July 13, 1974]

1899 **Eugene Ormandy,** U.S. conductor, born in Hungary; toured Europe as child prodigy violinist; conductor of Minneapolis Symphony, 1931–36; conductor of Philadelphia Symphony Orchestra, 1936–80; exercised great influence on development of U.S. symphony orchestras during 1930s and 1940s.

1901 **George Horace Gallup,** U.S. public-opinion statistician; creator of the **Gallup Poll;** innovator in area of scientific analysis of public opinion. [d. July 27, 1984]

1906 **George Wald,** U.S. chemist; Nobel Prize in physiology or medicine for experimentation and discovery of processes in human eye, including color reception process (with H. K. Hartline and R. A. Granit), 1967.

1907 **Pierre Dreyfus,** French industrialist; President, Renault, 1948– .

1909 **Johnny Mercer,** U.S. lyricist; composer of numerous popular songs, 1940s–1960s. [d. June 25, 1976]

1923 **Alan (Bartlett) Shepard, Jr.,** U.S. astronaut; first American in space, May 1961; Chief, Astronaut Office, 1965–74; commander *Apollo XIV* mission, 1971.

Theodore Fulton Stevens, U.S. politician, lawyer; U.S. Senator from Alaska, 1968– .

1939 **Brenda Vaccaro,** U.S. actress.

1942 **Qabus ibn Said,** Sultan, Sultanate of Oman, 1970– .

Historical Events

1188 Richard (later **Richard I** of England), the rebellious son of **King Henry II** of England, allies with **Philip II** of France against his father.

1189 **William II** of Sicily dies and is succeeded by **Tancred the Bastard.**

1210 **Pope Innocent III** excommunicates Holy Roman Emperor **Otto IV.**

1905 **Prince Charles** of Denmark is elected King of Norway; assumes the title **King Haakon VII.**

1914 The Russians are defeated at **Soldau,** East Prussia, in their second invasion of that German province (**World War I**).

1918 Belgian army reoccupies **Brussels** for the first time in more than four years (**World War I**).

Sovereign free state of **Latvia** is proclaimed.

1928 The first animated talking cartoon movie, *Steamboat Willie,* is shown in New York featuring the character of **Mickey Mouse,** the creation of **Walt Disney.**

1936 Germany and Italy recognize the government of Gen. Francisco Franco (**Spanish Civil War**).

1943 Planes from 11 U.S. carriers attack **Gilbert Islands** in the Pacific (**World War II**).

1966 U.S. spacecraft *Lunar Orbiter 2* begins transmission of photographs of moon's surface, allowing analysis of possible landing sites for future lunar craft.

1978 Murder of U.S. congressman Leo J. Ryan and four other Americans in **Jamestown, Guyana** triggers mass suicides and murders of more than 900 members of the **People's Temple** and their leader, **Jim Jones.**

November 19

Holidays

Belize	**Garifuna Settlement Day**
Monaco	**Prince of Monaco Holiday**
	Celebrates the official birthday of Prince Rainier III.
Oman	**National Days**
	The second day of a three-day celebration.

Birthdates

1600 **Charles I,** King of England, 1625–49; his authoritarian rule provoked a civil war that led to his execution. [d. January 30, 1649]

1752 **George Rogers Clark,** U.S. frontiersman, army general; known for his capture of Vincennes during American Revolution. [d. February 13, 1818]

1805 **Ferdinand De Lesseps,** French diplomat, engineer; the builder of the **Suez Canal.** [d. December 7, 1894]

1812 **Franz Felix Adalbert Kuhn,** German linguist, mythologist; a pioneer of **comparative mythology.** [d. May 5, 1881]

1831 **James Abram Garfield,** college president, lay preacher; U.S. Congressman, 1863–80; 20th President of U.S.; shot July 2, 1881, after six months in office. [d. September 9, 1887]

1839 **Emil von Skoda,** Czech industrialist; founder of **Skoda Works,** famous for its manufacture of munitions, especially heavy artillery and cannons. [d. August 8, 1900]

1853 **Albert Auguste Gabriel Hanotaux,** French historian and statesman; Minister of Foreign Affairs, 1894–95; 1896–98; author of several excellent histories of France. [d. April 11, 1944]

1859 **Mihail Mihailovich Ippolitov-Ivanov,** Russian composer; noted especially for his *Sketches from the Caucasus.* [d. January 28, 1935]

1862 **(William Ashley) Billy Sunday,** U.S. revivalist, professional baseball player. [d. November 6, 1935]

1875 **Mikhail Ivanovich Kalinin,** Russian revolutionary and Soviet official; President, U.S.S.R., 1923–46. [d. June 3, 1946]

1887 **James Batcheller Sumner,** U.S. biochemist; Nobel Prize in chemistry for crystallizing enzymes (with J. H. Northrop and W. M. Stanley), 1946. [d. August 12, 1955]

1896 **Clifton Webb,** U.S. character actor. [d. October 13, 1966]

1899 **(John Orley) Allen Tate,** U.S. critic, poet, novelist; a major figure in New Criticism.

1905 **Tommy Dorsey,** U.S. musician; major figure in U.S. Big Band era; performed with brother Jimmy (February 29) and in own band. [d. November 26, 1956]

1912 **George Emil Palade,** U.S. physiologist born in Rumania; Nobel Prize in physiology or medicine for research in science of **cell biology** (with A. Claude and C. R. de Duve), 1974.

1915 **Earl Wilbur Sutherland,** U.S. biochemist; Nobel Prize in physiology or medicine for discoveries in **chromosome research,** 1971.

1917 **Indira Gandhi,** Indian stateswoman; Prime Minister of India, 1966–77; 1980–84; assassinated. [d. October 31, 1984]

1918 **Hendrik van de Hulst,** Dutch astronomer; his discoveries contributed to mapping structure of **Milky Way.**

1922 **Emil Zatopek,** Czech distance runner; winner of 3 Olympic gold medals, 1952.

1936 **Dick Cavett,** U.S. entertainer, talk-show host.

1942 **Calvin Klein,** U.S. fashion designer.

Historical Events

1794 **Jay's Treaty** between the U.S. and Great Britain is concluded, settling remaining disputes between the two countries.

1863 Abraham Lincoln delivers the **Gettysburg Address.**

1918 **Metz, Alsace** is occupied by the French (**World War I**).

Puerto Rico	Discovery of Puerto Rico
	Commemorates discovery of the island by Christopher Columbus on his second voyage of discovery, 1493.
U.S.S.R.	Rocket and Artillery Forces Day

Religious Calendar

The Saints

St. Nerses I, Primate of the Armenians and martyr. Also called **Narses I** and *the Great.* [d. c. 373]

St. Barlaam, martyr of Antioch. [d. c. 4th century]

St. Ermenburga, abbess. Also called **Domneva,** or **Eormenburh.** [d. c. 700]

Antwerp, Belgium is reoccupied by Belgian troops (**World War I**).

1942 Russian counteroffensive against Germans begins on the **Stalingrad front** (**World War II**).

1965 **Ecumenical Council** of Roman Catholic Church declares **freedom of conscience** is official Church doctrine.

1969 U.S. astronauts **Charles Conrad, Jr.,** and **Alan L. Bean** land on the moon in the *Apollo 12* lunar module and begin the first of two scheduled moon walks.

Pelé (**Edson Arantes do Nascimento**), Brazilian soccer star, scores his 1000th goal, at the Maracaña Stadium, Rio de Janeiro.

1976 **Algeria** promulgates a new constitution.

November 20

Holidays

Mexico   **Mexican Revolution Anniversary**
              Anniversary of the overthrow of the dictatorship of Porfirio Diaz, 1910.

Religious Calendar

The Saints
St. Dasius, martyr. [d. c. 303]

SS. Nerses, Bishop of Sahgerd, and other martyrs. [d. 343]

Birthdates

1602 **Otto von Guericke,** German scientist; invented the **Magdeburg hemispheres** for demonstration of pressure of the atmosphere; credited with development of first **electrical generating machine.** [d. May 11, 1686]

1725 **Oliver Wolcott,** American Revolutionary leader; Governor of Connecticut, 1796–97; signer of the Declaration of Independence. [d. December 1, 1797]

1752 **Thomas Chatterton,** English poet; creator of **Thomas Rowley,** an imaginary 15th-century monk, whose works were the subject of debate for nearly 100 years; committed suicide in desperation over failure of his own literary works. [d. August 24, 1770]

1761 **Pope Pius VIII,** pope 1829–30. [d. November 30, 1830]

1841 **Sir Wilfrid Laurier,** Canadian statesman; Prime Minister of Canada, 1896–1911. [d. February 17, 1919]

1855 **Josiah Royce,** U.S. idealist philosopher; professor of philosophy, Harvard University, 1882–1916. Noted for his contributions to logic, religion, metaphysics, and the philosophy of mathematics; developed system of philosophy based on concepts of the Absolute. [d. September 14, 1916]

1858 **Selma Lagerlöf,** Swedish novelist, short-story writer; the first woman to win the Nobel Prize in literature, 1909. [d. March 16, 1940]

1866 **Judge Kenesaw Mountain Landis,** U.S. jurist, sports executive; first commissioner of professional baseball. [d. November 25, 1944]

1873 **William Weber Coblentz,** U.S. physicist, pioneer in **infrared spectrophotometry.** [d. September 15, 1962]

1884 **Norman (Mattoon) Thomas,** U.S. socialist leader, reformer, editor, clergyman; a founder of **American Civil Liberties Union,** 1920; leader of **American Socialist Party,** 1926–48; conscience candidate for American liberals in numerous elections. [d. December 19, 1968]

1885 **Albert Kesselring,** German Air Force field marshal; commanded German invasions of Poland, 1939, and France, 1940; condemned as German war criminal; committed to life imprisonment. [d. July 16, 1960]

1886 **Karl von Frisch,** German zoologist, born in Austria; Nobel Prize in physiology or medicine for research in **ethology** (with K. Lorenz and N. Tinbergen), 1973.

1889 **Edwin Powell Hubble,** U.S. astronomer; developed **Hubble's constant,** a numerical value applied to the speed of recession of distant galaxies; contributed greatly to development of cosmology and concept of **expanding universe.** [d. September 28, 1953]

1908 **(Alfred) Alistair Cooke,** U.S. journalist, broadcaster, born in England; chief correspondent of Manchester *Guardian*, 1948–72; master of ceremonies of *Masterpiece Theatre*, a dramatic series, produced by the BBC, on National Public Television, 1971– .

1914 **Emilio Pucci,** Italian fashion designer.

St. Edmund the Martyr, King of the East Angles. [d. 870]

St. Bernward, bishop of Hildesheim. [d. 1022]

St. Felix of Valois, co-founder of the Order of the Most Holy Trinity. [d. 1212]

St. Maxentia, virgin and martyr. Also called **Masentia.** [death date unknown]

The Beatified

Blessed Ambrose of Camaldoli, abbot. [d. 1439]

1917 **Robert Carlyle Byrd,** U.S. politician, lawyer; U.S. Senator, 1958–; Senate Majority Leader, 1977–81.

1920 **Gene Tierney,** U.S. actress.

1925 **Maya Michailovna Plisetskaya,** Soviet prima ballerina.

Robert Francis Kennedy, U.S. politician, lawyer; Attorney General, 1961–64; brother of U.S. President John F. Kennedy (May 29). Assassinated. [d. June 6, 1968]

1938 **Dick Smothers,** U.S. folksinger, comedian; with brother Tom (February 2) became center of controversy during 1960s when their program was edited by television censors.

Historical Events

1541 **John Calvin** establishes a theocratic government at Geneva, creating a base for Protestantism in Europe.

1759 Engish defeat French off **Quiberon, France (Seven Years' War).**

1910 **Francisco I. Madero** leads a rebellion that overthrows the government of Mexican dictator of **Porfirio Díaz.**

1917 First demonstration of effectiveness of **tanks** in warfare is made as British attack German lines during **Battle of Cambrai (World War I).**

1921 Madame **Marie Spaak-Janson,** Belgian socialist, becomes first woman elected to Belgian parliament.

1922 **Lausanne Conference,** to conclude peace between Turkey and the Allies of World War I, opens in Switzerland.

1943 U.S. infantry invades **Makin Island,** one of the Gilbert Islands in the Central Pacific **(World War II).**

1945 **Nuremburg Trials** begin in Germany, an international military tribunal, trying Nazi offenders for crimes against peace, humanity, and the laws of war.

1962 U.S. President John Kennedy signs executive order prohibiting **racial discrimination** in housing built or purchased with federal funds.

1969 U.S. Department of Agriculture orders a halt in the use of the pesticide **DDT** in residential areas.

1978 **Ethiopia** signs a 20-year treaty of friendship and cooperation with the U.S.S.R. which insures a foothold for the Soviet Union in the Horn of Africa.

November 21

The Presentation of the Blessed Virgin Mary. Commemorates Mary's being brought by her parents to the Temple at Jerusalem. Of 6th-century origin; formally recognized in 1585. Obligatory Memorial.

Birthdates

1495 **John Bale,** English bishop, reformer, antiquary, and dramatist; author of several controversial works on Protestantism. [d. November 1563]

1694 **François Marie Arouet de Voltaire,** French philosopher, writer; master of satire; champion of victims of religious intolerance; author of *La Siècle de Louis XIV,* 1751. [d. May 30, 1778]

1729 **Josiah Bartlett,** American physician, Revolutionary War patriot; representative to Continental Congress; signer of Declaration of Independence; Chief Justice of Superior Court of New Hampshire, 1788–90; President of New Hampshire, 1790–92; first governor of New Hampshire, 1793–94. [d. May 19, 1795]

1785 **William Beaumont,** U.S. surgeon; pioneer in experimental medicine; wrote treatise on digestion, *Experiments and Observations on the Gastric Juice and the Physiology of Digestion,* 1833. [d. Apri 25, 1853]

1787 **Sir Samuel Cunard,** Canadian shipowner; founder of Cunard Shipping Co., 1839; with others, established Royal Mail Steam Packet Co., the first regularly scheduled trans-Atlantic mail service, 1839. [d. April 28, 1865]

1789 **Cesare Balbo,** Italian author, statesman; first premier of Piedmont, 1848. [d. June 3, 1853]

1834 **(Henrietta Howland) Hettie Green,** U.S. financier; reputedly the richest woman of her time in the U.S.; shrewd, eccentric, financial genius; investments in real estate, railroad securities, and government bonds estimated at $100 million at her death. [d. July 3, 1916]

1851 **Désiré Joseph Mercier,** Belgian cardinal; the spokesman for Belgians during German occupation (World War I). [d. January 23, 1926]

1854 **Pope Benedict XV,** pope 1914–22; a strict neutral during World War I, he refrained from condemning any actions of the belligerents. [d. January 22, 1922]

1867 **Vladimir Nikolaevich Ipatieff,** U.S. chemist, born in Russia; developed numerous high-pressure catalytic reactions; important in synthesis of hydrocarbons; head of Russian chemical works during World War I. [d. November 29, 1952]

1869 **William Henry Murray,** U.S. politician; U.S. Congressman, 1913–17; Governor of Oklahoma, 1931–35. [d. October 15, 1956]

1886 **Sir Harold George Nicolson,** British diplomat, biographer, historian; husband of **Victoria Mary Sackville West.** [d. May 1, 1968]

1893 **(Arthur)** *Harpo* **Marx,** U.S. comedian, screen actor; silent member of **Marx Brothers** comedy team. [d. September 28, 1964]

1898 **René François-Ghislain Magritte,** Belgian surrealist painter. [d. August 15, 1967]

1907 **Jim Bishop,** U.S. journalist, author; known for his detailed portrayals of deaths of Jesus, Abraham Lincoln, John F. Kennedy.

1912 **Eleanor Powell,** U.S. dancer. [d. February 11, 1982]

1920 **Stan(ley Frank) "the Man" Musial,** U.S. baseball player; Baseball Hall of Fame, 1960.

1940 **Natalia Romanovna Makarova,** U.S. ballerina; defected from Russia, 1970.

1945 **Goldie Hawn,** U.S. actress, comedienne, singer, dancer, producer; 1969 Academy Award for best supporting actress in *Cactus Flower.*

Historical Events

1620 **Mayflower Compact,** a preliminary plan of government for the Pilgrims, is signed in the cabin of *The Mayflower,* near Provincetown, Massachusetts.

The Saints

St. Gelasius I, pope. Elected 492. [d. 496]

St. Albert of Louvain, Bishop of Liège and martyr. [d. 1192]

1783 Two Frenchmen, **Jean François Pilâtre de Rozier** and the **Marquis d'Arlandes,** make first successful **balloon ascent,** lasting 25 minutes and covering more than five miles.

1789 **North Carolina** becomes the twelfth state to ratify the U.S. Constitution.

1916 **Emperor Franz Josef** of Austria-Hungary dies and is succeeded by his nephew, Karl.

1918 The German High Seas Fleet is surrendered to the British near Rosyth, Scotland, for internment at **Scapa Flow** (**World War I**).

1920 Fourteen secret British agents in Dublin are slain by the I.R.A. in what is henceforth called *Bloody Sunday.*

1934 Cole Porter's musical comedy, *Anything Goes,* opens in New York, including title song and *I Get a Kick Out of You.*

1945 Sergei Prokofiev's opera ballet, *Cinderella,* opens in Moscow.

1946 **Harry S. Truman** becomes first U.S. president to travel underwater in a submarine.

1963 Ecumenical Council of Roman Catholic Church (Vatican II) authorizes use of **vernacular languages** in all churches.

1964 **Verrazano-Narrows Bridge** between Brooklyn and Staten Island, then the world's longest suspension bridge, is formally opened.

November 22

Birthdates

1643   **René Robert Cavelier, Sieur de La Salle,** French explorer in North America; expeditions of wilderness south of Lakes Ontario and Erie helped him to eventually take possession of the waterway region of the Mississippi River, dubbed Louisiana, and to claim it for France; killed by mutinous companions while exploring for the mouth of the Mississippi River. [d. March 19, 1687]

1767   **Andreas Hofer,** Tirolean patriot; led rebellion against Bavarian army; defeated and killed. [d. February 20, 1810]

1808   **Lionel Nathan Rothschild,** British banker; first Jewish member of Parliament. [d. June 3, 1879]

1819   **George Eliot (Mary Ann Evans),** British novelist; known for her irregular lifestyle and humorous descriptions of rural life in England. [d. December 22, 1880]

1842   **José María de Heredia,** French poet, bibliophile, born in Cuba; leading representative of French Parnassians; author of *Les Trophées*, a collection of 50 sonnets, 1893. [d. October 2, 1905]

1852   **Paul H. B. B. d'Estournells de Constant de Rebecque,** French diplomat, politician; Nobel Peace Prize for his work for international conciliation and disarmament, 1909. [d. May 15, 1924]

1857   **George (Robert) Gissing,** British novelist and man of letters; noted for portrayal of middle-class life in England. [d. December 28, 1903]

1868   **John Nance (*Cactus Jack*) Garner,** U.S. Congressman, 1903–33; U.S. Vice President, 1933–41; two-time running mate of U.S. President Franklin D. Roosevelt; upon retirement became known as a minor political sage. [d. November 7, 1967]

1869   **André (Paul Guillaume) Gide,** French novelist, esssayist; a founder of *Nouvelle Revue Française*. [d. February 19, 1951]

1890   **Charles (André Joseph Marie) De Gaulle,** French statesman, soldier, writer; head of French government in exile during World War II; President of Fifth Republic, 1958–69. [d. November 9, 1970]

1899   **Wiley Post,** U.S. aviator; first solo pilot to successfully circumnavigate the globe; with Will Rogers (November 4), killed on flight across Alaska. [d. August 15, 1935]

     Hoagy Carmichael (Hoagland Howard Carmichael), U.S. composer, singer, pianist; wrote *Stardust*, *Georgia on My Mind*, and *Nearness of You*. [d. December 27, 1981]

1904   **Louis Eugene Felix Neel,** French physicist; Nobel Prize in physics for discoveries in area of magneto-hydrodynamics (with H. O. G. Alfven), 1970.

1913   **(Edward) Benjamin Britten,** British composer; leading figure in development of 20th-century music. [d. December 4, 1976]

1921   **Rodney Dangerfield,** U.S. comedian.

1924   **Geraldine Page,** U. S. actress.

1943   **Billie Jean King,** U.S. tennis player.

Historical Events

1497   **Vasco da Gama** rounds the **Cape of Good Hope** in Africa, discovering for Portugal an ocean passage to India.

1878   **Second Afghan War** begins when Ali Mujid is shelled and occupied by the British.

1914   **Battle of Ypres** ends with the failure of a second massive German offensive (**World War I**).

1917   **National Hockey League** is established at Montreal.

1928   Ravel's ***Bolero*** opens at Paris Opera with **Ida Rubenstein** dancing.

1931   Ferde Grofé's ***Grand Canyon Suite*** premieres in Chicago.

The Saints

SS. Philemon and Apphia, martyrs. Apphia also called **Apphis,** or **Appia.** [d. 1st cent.]

St. Cecilia, virgin and martyr. Patron of church music, musicians, makers of musical instruments, and of music generally. Also called **Cecily.** [death date unknown] Obligatory Memorial.

1941 **Lebanon** achieves independence from France, which has maintained control under a mandate from the League of Nations.

1943 **First Cairo Conference** begins as U.S. President Franklin Roosevelt, British Prime Minister Churchill, and Chinese Premier Chiang Kai-shek confer.

1944 **Metz** in France falls to U.S. Third Army under Patton (**World War II**).

1963 **John F. Kennedy,** 35th President of the U.S., is assassinated in Dallas, Texas. Vice-President **Lyndon Baines Johnson** is sworn in as president.

1965 **Cassius Clay** retains his world heavyweight championship by defeating Floyd Patterson in the 12th round in Las Vegas, Nevada.

1975 **Juan Carlos I** takes oath as the king of Spain, two days after the death of Geralissimo **Francisco Franco.**

November 23

Holidays

Japan

Labor Thanksgiving Day or **Kinro-Kansha-No-Hi**
A day of rest for workers in Japan on which they reflect on the dignity of labor and express gratitude for success and abundance.

Birthdates

912   **Otto I, (the Great)**, King of Germany and Holy Roman Emperor, 936–973; consolidated the German state and decisively defeated the Magyars in 955. [d. May 7, 973]

1221   **Alfonso X (the Wise)**, King of Castile and Leon. [d. April 4, 1284]

1608   **Francisco Manuel de Melo**, Portuguese moralist, historian, playwright, and poet; accused of attempted assassination of **King John IV** of Portugal; exiled to Brazil, 1653–59. [d. August 24, 1666]

1712   **Andrew Foulis**, Scottish publisher, printer; with his brother, Robert, noted for editions of Thomas Gray's poetry and Milton's *Paradise Lost*. [d. September 18, 1775]

1803   **Theodore Dwight Weld**, U.S. social reformer; called the *Great Abolitionist*. [d. February 3, 1895]

1804   **Franklin Pierce**, U.S. lawyer; 14th President of the U.S., 1853–57. [d. October 8, 1869]

1837   **Johannes D. van der Waals**, Dutch physicist; discovered *van der Waals forces*; Nobel Prize in physics for research on mathematical equations describing the continuity of gaseous and liquid states of matter, electrolytic dissociation, and the thermodynamic theory of capillarity, 1910. [d. March 9, 1923]

1859   *Billy the Kid* **(William H. Bonney)**, U.S. outlaw; one of most highly publicized outlaws in U.S. history; killed 21 men before being shot to death at age of 21. [d. July 15, 1881]

1860   **Karl Hjalmar Branting**, Swedish statesman, diplomat; awarded Nobel Peace Prize for his conciliatory international diplomacy from 1900–1920, 1921. [d. February 24, 1925]

1869   **Valdemar Poulsen**, Danish scientist; developed methods of recording of sound with magnetization, 1898; invented **arc generator** for high-frequency oscillations used in **wireless telegraphy.** [d. July 1942]

1876   **Manuel de Falla**, Spanish composer; known for his nationalistic and impressionistic themes; wrote *The Three-Cornered Hat*. [d. November 14, 1946]

1878   **Ernest Joseph King**, U.S. admiral; first man to act as commander of the Combined Fleet (COMINCH), simultaneously acting as chief of naval operations; as such he commanded the largest fleet of ships, planes, and men in the history of the Navy; also acted as adviser to U.S. President Franklin Roosevelt on naval issues. [d. June 25, 1956]

1883   **José Clemente Orozco**, Mexican painter; master of fresco painting. [d. September 7, 1949]

1887   **Henry Gwyn-Jeffreys Moseley**, British physicist; noted for research on x-ray elements; killed during World War I. [d. August 10, 1915]

       Boris Karloff (William Henry Pratt), British actor. [d. February 3, 1969]

1927   **Otis Chandler**, U.S. newspaper publisher; publisher of *Los Angeles Times*, 1960–78; Vice-Chairman of the Board, Times Mirror Co., 1968– .

Historical Events

1890   **Grand Duchy of Luxembourg** is separated from the Netherlands.

1914   **Turkey** issues a formal declaration of war against the Allies (**World War I**).

1938   *The Boys from Syracuse*, Richard Rodgers' musical comedy based on Shakespeare's *A Comedy of Errors*, premieres in New York.

The Saints

St. Clement I, pope and martyr. Elected 88. First of the Apostolic Fathers. Patron of the Gild, Fraternity, and Brotherhood House of the Most Glorious and Undivided Trinity of London, or Trinity House; patron of boatmen, hatters, tanners, and stonecutters. Invoked to aid sick children. [d. c. 99]

St. Amphilochius, Bishop of Iconium. [d. c. 400]

St. Gregory, Bishop of Girgenti. [d. c. 603]

St. Columban, Abbot of Luxeuil and Bobbio, and missionary-monk. [d. 615] Optional Memorial.

St. Trudo, missionary. Also called **Tron,** or **Trond.** [d. c. 690]

1961 The name of the capital of the Dominican Republic is changed from **Ciudád Trujillo** to **Santo Domingo.**

1970 **Pope Paul VI** issues a decree barring cardinals over age 80 from voting for a new pope.

1979 The assassin of Earl Mountbatten of Burma, **Thomas McMahon,** is convicted by a special criminal court in Dublin and sentenced to life imprisonment.

1980 A violent **earthquake** devastates southern **Italy,** killing 3,000 and leaving 200,000 homeless.

1983 Two Soviet cosmonauts return to earth safely after spending 150 days in the *Salyut 7 space station.*

November 24

Holidays

Zaire   **Anniversary of the New Regime**
               Marks the beginning of the new
               government, 1964.

Religious Calendar

The Saints
St. Chrysogonus, martyr. [d. c. 304]
St. Colman of Cloyne, bishop. [d. 6th century]

Birthdates

1394 **Charles, duc de Orléans,** French poet. [d. January 5, 1465]

1632 **Baruch Spinoza,** Dutch philosopher; pre-eminent pantheistic philosopher of 17th century. [d. February 21, 1677]

1655 **Charles XI,** King of Sweden, 1660–97; responsible for establishment of an absolute monarchy. [d. April 5, 1697]

1713 **Laurence Sterne,** English novelist; author of *Tristram Shandy.* [d. March 18, 1768]

Junipero Serra (Miguel José Serra), Spanish Franciscan missionary in Mexico; ascetic, founder of **Mission San Diego,** the first European settlement in Upper California; also responsible for missions at **San Francisco, Santa Barbara, San Luis Obispo, Santa Clara,** and **San Juan Capistrano.** [d. August 28, 1784]

1784 **Zachary Taylor,** U.S. soldier; 12th President of the U.S., 1849–50; hero of the War with Mexico; favored annexation of California. [d. July 9, 1850]

1826 **Carlo Collodi (Carlo Lorenzini),** Italian author, journalist; creator of *Pinocchio.* [d. October 26, 1890]

1848 **Lilli Lehmann,** German operatic soprano, lieder singer; known for her interpretations of Wagner and Mozart. [d. May 17, 1929]

1849 **Frances Eliza Hodgson Burnett,** U.S. novelist, born in England; author of *Little Lord Fauntleroy* and *The Secret Garden.* [d. October 29, 1924]

1859 **Cass Gilbert,** U.S. architect; designed the Woolworth Building, New York, 1913; the Supreme Court Building, Washington, D.C., 1935. [d. May 17, 1934]

1864 **Henri de Toulouse-Lautrec,** French artist; known primarily for his paintings of Parisian life and his poster drawings. [d. September 9, 1901]

1868 **Scott Joplin,** U.S. pianist; gained significant place in history of American music as pioneer of **ragtime**; the *Maple Leaf Rag* is his most famous composition. [d. April 1, 1917]

1877 **Alben William Barkley,** U.S. lawyer; Vice-President of U.S., 1949–53; U.S. Senator, 1927–49, 1954–56. [d. April 30, 1956]

1888 **Dale Carnegie,** U.S. writer, teacher of public speaking, author of *How to Win Friends and Influence People.* [d. November 1, 1955]

Cathleen (Mary) Nesbitt, British actress; known as a grande dame of the stage, having portrayed numerous characters in more than 300 roles on the London and Broadway stages and in films. [d. August 2, 1982]

1892 **Konstantin Aleksandrovich Fedin,** Soviet novelist.

1912 **Garson Kanin,** U.S. playwright, director, author, screenwriter; husband of Ruth Gordon (October 30).

1914 **Geraldine Fitzgerald,** Irish actress.

1921 **John V(liet) Lindsay,** U.S. politician, lawyer, author; U.S. Congressman, 1959–65; Mayor of New York City, 1966–74.

1926 **Tsung-Dao Lee,** U.S. physicist, born in China; Nobel Prize in physics for disproving law of parity conservation in nuclear physics (with C. N. Yang), 1957.

Historical Events

1642 **Abel Tasman,** Dutch explorer, discovers **Tasmania,** which he names Van Diemen's Land.

St. Minver, virgin and nun. Also called **Menefreda.** [d. c. 6th century]

St. Enfleda, Abbess of Whitby. Also called **Eanflaed.** [d. c. 704]

SS. Flora and Mary, virgins and martyrs. [d. 851]

The Beatified

Blessed Maria Anna Sala. [beatified 1982]

Blessed Salvator Lilli and his Seven Companions. [beatified 1982]

1865 **Mississippi** is first of Southern state legislatures to enact a **Black Code,** a body of apprenticeship laws binding freedmen to the land.

1918 **United Kingdom of the Serbs, Croats, and Slovenes** is proclaimed at Zagreb with **King Peter** of Serbia as king (World War I).

1935 **George II** of Greece returns from exile in England.

1950 Frank Loesser's musical *Guys and Dolls,* based on characters from Damon Runyon's stories, premieres in New York.

1963 **Lee Harvey Oswald,** accused by Dallas police of assassinating President John F. Kennedy, is shot and killed by **Jack Ruby** in the basement of the Dallas municipal building while in police custody.

1965 **Sheikh Abdullah of Kuwait** dies and is succeeded by his younger brother, **Sabah as-Salim as-Sabah.**

1972 **Finland** becomes the first Western state to formally recognize **East Germany,** and the first to establish ties with both Germanys.

UN grants permanent observer status to **East Germany** based on UNESCO's approval of East German membership in that body on November 21; this effectively gives East Germany the same status as West Germany.

1976 **Earthquake** in eastern **Turkey** takes an estimated 4,000 lives; relief efforts in the mountain villages are hampered by blizzards.

November 25

Holidays

Suriname   **Independence Day**
Celebrates achievement of independence from The Netherlands, 1975.

Birthdates

1562   **Lope (Felix) de Vega** *El Fenix de España,* Spanish dramatist, poet; developed the comic character *gracioso* or clown; author, reputedly, of more than 1,800 plays and several hundred other works. [d. August 27, 1635]

1778   **Joseph Lancaster,** English educator; founder of a free school based on man's conventional principles that competed with the system supported by the Church of England; emigrated to U.S., 1818. [d. October 24, 1838]

1814   **Julius von Mayer,** German physicist; pioneer in thermodynamic investigations, 1842. [d. March 20, 1878]

1835   **Andrew Carnegie,** U.S. industrialist, philanthropist, born in Scotland; founder of Carnegie Steel Company. [d. August 11, 1919]

1844   **Karl Friedrich Benz,** German engineer; pioneer in design and development of the automobile; founder of automobile manufacturing company that makes **Mercedes Benz,** named for his daughter. [d. April 4, 1929]

1846   **Carrie (Amelia) Nation,** U.S. temperance advocate; famed for her hatchet-wielding rampages through the saloons of Kansas; always appeared dressed in deaconess garb. [d. June 9, 1911]

1869   **Benjamin Barr Lindsey,** U.S. jurist, publicist; pioneer in handling of juvenile delinquents; established a conciliation court to deal with divorce cases; espoused principle of *compassionate marriage,* or trial marriage. [d. March 26, 1943]

1877   **Harley Granville-Barker,** British playwright, actor, director, and critic; a major figure in the London theater of the early 1900s. [d. August 31, 1946]

1878   **Georg Kaiser,** German playwright; leader in Expressionist movement in Germany. [d. June 4, 1945]

1881   **John XXIII,** pope 1958–63; convened the **Second Vatican Council,** 1959–65. [d. June 3, 1963]

1894   **Laurence Stallings,** U.S. playwright.

       Lawrence Mario Giannini, U.S. banker; President, Transamerica Corporation, 1930–32; President, Bank of America, 1936–52. [d. August 19, 1952]

1896   **Virgil Thomson,** U.S. composer, music critic.

1897   **Willie (*The Lion*) Smith, (William Henry Bertholoff),** U.S. musician; a major contributor to development of ragtime music in U.S.

1900   **Helen Gahagan Douglas,** U.S. politician, actress; U.S. Congresswoman, 1945–51; candidate for U.S. Senate in opposition to Richard Nixon, 1951 (defeated); wife of Melvyn Douglas (April 5). [d. June 28, 1980]

1914   **Joe DiMaggio,** U.S. baseball player.

1915   **Augusto Pinochet Ugarte,** President, Republic of Chile, 1973– .

1920   **Ricardo Montalban,** U.S. actor, born in Mexico.

1923   **Mauno Koivisto,** President, Republic of Finland, 1982– .

1925   **William F(rank) Buckley, Jr.,** U.S. publisher, editor, writer, television interviewer; political conservative; unsuccessful candidate for mayor of New York City, 1965.

Historical Events

1034   **Malcolm II,** King of Scots dies and is succeeded by **Duncan,** his grandson.

1542   **Henry VIII** of England is victorious over the forces of **James V** of Scotand at the **Battle of Solvay Moss.**

1758   British forces led by Washington take **Fort Duquesne** (Pittsburgh) from French (**French and Indian War**).

1783   Last British troops leave New York City (**American Revolution**).

Religious Calendar

The Saints

St. Moses, priest and martyr. [d. 251]

St. Catherine of Alexandria, virgin and martyr; patron of Christian philosophers and students of philosophy. Also called **Catharine,** or **Katherine.** [death date unknown]

St. Mercurius, martyr. Also called **Abu Saifain,** *the Father of Swords,* or **Mercury.** [death date unkown]

1863 Confederates are driven from Tennessee and roads are opened into Georgia by the **Battle of Chattanooga (U.S. Civil War).**

1882 Gilbert and Sullivan's comic opera *Iolanthe* opens simultaneously in London and New York.

1885 **King Alfonso XII** of Spain dies and is succeeded by his mother, Maria Christina, who reigns as regent for Alfonso's son, born posthumously, who ascends to the throne in 1902.

1901 **Gustav Mahler** conducts the world premiere, in Munich, of his *Fourth Symphony in G Major.*

1904 Russian sailors of the Black Sea Fleet mutiny at **Sevastopol.**

1918 **Strasbourg, Alsace,** is occupied by the French (**World War I**).

1943 Five U.S. destroyers sink three Japanese destroyers and severely damage two others at the **Battle of Cape St. George (World War II).**

1950 Hurricane winds cause severe damage on the eastern seaboard, while a record blizzard, killing more than 100 persons, paralyzes western Pennsylvania, Ohio, and West Virginia.

1961 *U.S.S. Enterprise,* nuclear-powered aircraft carrier, the largest, fastest, and most powerful warship built to date, is commissioned at Newport News, Virginia.

1962 Supporters of French President **Charles De Gaulle** win control of national assembly in run-off elections; it is the first time in modern French history that one group has gained a clear majority.

1970 Japanese poet and writer **Yukio Mishima** commits ritual suicide in Tokyo in protest against Japan's westernization and the weakness of the post-World War II Japanese Constitution.

1971 Denmark and Norway become the first NATO members to establish full diplomatic relations with **North Vietnam.**

1975 Aluminum-producing South American territory of **Suriname** becomes independent after 308 years of Dutch colonial rule and promulgates a constitution.

November 26

Holidays

São Tomé and Príncipe — Anniversary of Signing of Argel Agreement

Religious Calendar

The Saints

St. Peter, Bishop of Alexandria, and martyr. [d. 311]
St. Siricius, pope. Elected 384. [d. 399]

Birthdates

1731 **William Cowper,** English poet; despite periods of great mental instability, produced numerous significant poems, including *Olney Hymns,* with John Newton, 1779; *The Task;* early proponent of break with strict guidelines of classicism; foreshadowed Romantic movement in English poetry. [d. April 25, 1800]

1792 **Sarah Moore Grimké,** U.S. reformer, abolitionist, and women's rights advocate; sister of Angelina Grimké (February 20). [d. December 23, 1873]

1832 **Mary Walker,** U.S. physician, women's rights advocate, assistant surgeon of Union Army (U.S. Civil War), 1864–65; only woman to receive Medal of Honor, 1865. [d. February 21, 1919]

1842 **Prince Peter Alexeyevich Kropotkin,** Russian geographer, social philosopher; after escape from prison, lived in England, 1886–1914, and Russia, 1917–21; author of numerous books on social subjects. [d. February 8, 1921]

1861 **Albert Bacon Fall,** U.S. politician, lawyer, rancher; U.S. Senator, 1912–21; U.S. Secretary of the Interior, 1921–23; convicted in **Teapot Dome** scandal; imprisoned, 1931–32. [d. November 30, 1944]

1894 **Norbert Wiener,** U.S. mathematician; creator of the field of **cybernetics.** [d. March 18, 1964]

1895 **William Griffith Wilson,** U.S. reformer; founder of **Alcoholics Anonymous,** 1935. [d. January 24, 1971]

1898 **Karl Ziegler,** German chemist; Nobel Prize in chemistry for research in plastics (with G. Natta), 1963. [d. August 12, 1973]

1901 **Melville Bell Grosvenor,** U.S. editor; member of the founding family of the **National Geographic Society;** editor in chief, *National Geographic Magazine,* 1967–77; led the society to be the largest private educational and scientific association in the world. [d. April 22, 1982]

1912 **(Arnold) Eric Sevareid,** U.S. broadcast journalist; correspondent with CBS News, 1939–77.

Eugene Ionesco, French playwright, born in Romania; author of absurdist dramas, incuding *Rhinoceros,* 1959, *The Bald Soprano,* 1950, and *Exit the King,* 1963.

1922 **Charles M(onroe) Schulz,** U.S. cartoonist; creator of *Peanuts,* a cartoon strip.

1925 **Gregorio Conrodo Alvarez Armelino,** President, Oriental Republic of Uruguay, 1981– .

Historical Events

1917 **Bolshevik** government abolishes all class privileges in the Russian Republic.

1965 France places its first space satellite in orbit from its test center in the Algerian Sahara.

1966 U.S. military authorities in Vietnam announce the end of **Operation Attleboro,** the biggest U.S. offensive of the war (**Vietnam War**).

1969 U.S. President Richard Nixon authorizes legislation establishing a **draft lottery.**

1974 Japan's Prime Minister **Kakuei Tanaka** resigns under pressure.

1979 More than 300,000 Afghan refugees flee into Pakistan as a result of civil war between Muslim rebels and government troops; Soviet military personnel are used against rebel positions.

St. Basolus, monk and hermit. Also called **Basle.** [d. c. 620]

St. Conrad, Bishop of Constance. [d. 975]

St. Nikon (Metanoeite) missionary. Also called **Nicon.** [d. 998]

St. Silvester Gozzolini, abbot and founder of the Silvestrine Benedictines. Also called **Sylvester.** [d. 1267]

St. John Berchmans, patron of altar boys. [d. 1621]

St. Leonard of Port Maurice, Franciscan friar and missionary. [d. 1751]

The Beatified

Blessed Pontius of Faucigny, abbot. [d. 1178]

Blessed James, Bishop of Mantua. [d. 1338]

November 27

Religious Calendar

The Saints

St. James Intercisus, martyr. Also called **James Intercisius.** [d. c. 421]

St. Secundinus, bishop. Also called **Seachnal, Sechnall,** or **Secundin.** [d. 447]

St. Maximus, Bishop of Riez; patron of the Diocese of Boulogne in Picardy. Also called **Masse.** [d. c. 460]

Birthdates

1701   **Anders Celsius,** Swedish astronomer; the originator of the Celsius scale, also called centigrade, in which the freezing point of water is 0 (degrees) and the boiling point is 100 (degrees). [d. April 25, 1744]

1746   **Robert R. Livingston,** U.S. diplomat, lawyer; a drafter of the Declaration of Independence, 1776; administered the oath of office to President George Washington; with Robert Fulton, built first steamboat; U.S. Minister to France, 1801–04. [d. February 26, 1813]

1754   **Johann George Adam Forster,** German traveler, scientist, author, and revolutionary; accompanied Captain James Cook (October 27) on his voyage around the world, 1772. [d. January 10, 1794]

1809   **Fanny Kemble,** British author, actress; her 1829 debut as Juliet in Shakespeare's Romeo and Juliet brought prosperity to the Covent Garden theatre; her *Journals*, 1835 and 1863, contain valuable information of 19th-century stage and social history. [d. January 15, 1893]

1857   **Sir Charles Scott Sherrington,** British neurologist; Nobel Prize in physiology or medicine for studies on physiology of the nervous system (with E. D. Adrian), 1932. [d. March 4, 1952]

1870   **Joseph Sanford Mack,** U.S. silk manufacturer, trucking executive; with his brothers, founded Mack Brothers Wagon Co., 1889, builders of gasoline-powered buses and trucks. [d. July 25, 1953]

1874   **Charles A(ustin) Beard,** U.S. historian; a founder of the **New School for Social Research,** 1919; author of *The Rise of American Civilization*, 1927–39; severe critic of policies of Franklin D. Roosevelt. [d. September 1, 1948]

Chaim Weizmann, Zionist leader, biochemist, born in Russia; first president of Israel, 1949–52. [d. November 9, 1952]

1903   **Lars Onsager,** U.S. chemist; Nobel Prize in chemistry for developing theory of irreversible chemical processes, 1968. [d. October 5, 1976]

1909   **James Agee,** U.S. writer, film critic; Pulitzer Prize, 1958. [d. May 16, 1955]

1912   **David Merrick (David Margulois),** U.S. theatrical producer.

1917   **Bob Smith (*Buffalo Bob*),** U.S. entertainer; best known for his role in the *Howdy Doody Show,* a television program popular in the early 1950s.

1927   **William (Edward) Simon,** U.S. government official, financier; U.S. Secretary of the Treasury, 1974-77.

1937   **Gail (Henion) Sheehy,** U.S. journalist, writer; author of *Passages* and *Predictable Crises of Adult Life.*

Historical Events

1295   **Model Parliament** meets in England, granting money for French and Scottish wars.

1308   **Henry VII,** Count of Luxembourg is elected German king.

1919   **Treaty of Neuilly** is signed by Bulgaria, ending World War I with the Allies and recognizing the independence of **Yugoslavia.**

1942   French fleet is scuttled at **Toulon** to prevent its being taken by the Germans (**World War II**).

1965   Between 15,000 and 35,000 persons take part in a march on Washington for peace in Vietnam, initiated by the Committee for a Sane Nuclear Policy.

St. Cungar, abbot. Also called **Congar,** or **Cyngar.** [d. 6th century]

St. Virgil, Bishop of Salzburg; apostle of the Slovenes. Also called **Feargal, Fergal,** or **Ferghil.** [d. 784]

St. Fergus, bishop and missionary. Also called *the Pict.* [d. c. 8th century]

SS. Barlaam and Josaphat. Josaphat also called **Joasaph.** [death date unknown]

The Beatified

Blessed Bernardino of Fossa, Friar Minor of the Observance. [d. 1503]

Blessed Humilis of Bisignano, lay brother. [d. 1637]

1977 **Upper Volta** promulgates a new constitution.

1978 **Masayoshi Ohira** becomes the President of the ruling Liberal-Democratic Party and Prime Minister of Japan.

November 28

Holidays

Albania	**Independence Proclamation Day** Commemorates Albania's declaration of independence from Turkey, 1912.
Chad	**Proclamation of the Republic** Commemorates the proclamation which established Chad as a member state in the French community, 1958.
Mauritania	**Independence Day** Celebrates achievement of independence from France, 1960.

Birthdates

1632 **Jean-Baptiste Lully,** French composer, born in Italy; primarily known for his operas and ballets; called the *Founder of the French National Opera*. [d. March 22, 1687]

1757 **William Blake,** English poet, artist; noted for mystical nature of his poetry; author of *Songs of Innocence* and *Songs of Experience*; his engravings illustrated a famous edition of Milton's *Paradise Lost*. [d. August 12, 1827]

1792 **Victor Cousin,** French philosopher, educational administrator; leader of Eclectic School. [d. January 13, 1867]

1820 **Friedrich Engels,** German philosopher, businessman; with Karl Marx, regarded as the founder of modern Communism; with Marx, co-authored *The Communist Manifesto*. [d. August 5, 1895]

1829 **Anton Grigorievich Rubinstein,** Russian composer, pianist. [d. November 20, 1894]

1832 **Sir Leslie Stephen,** British author, critic, editor; first editor of *Dictionary of National Biography*; father of Virginia Woolf (January 25). [d. February 22, 1904]

1847 **Prince Taro Katsura,** Japanese military leader and statesman; Premier of Japan, 1901–06; 1908–11; 1912–13. [d. October 10, 1913]

1851 **Albert Henry George Grey, 4th Earl Grey,** British official; Governor-General of Canada, 1904–11. [d. August 29, 1917]

1857 **Alfonso XII,** King of Spain, 1875–85; his short reign led to hopes for a constitutional Spanish monarchy. [d. November 25, 1885]

1858 **Sir Robert Abbott Hadfield,** British metallurgist; developer of **manganese steel.** [d. September 30, 1940]

1866 **Henry Bacon,** U.S. architect; designer of **Lincoln Memorial.** [d. 1924]

1873 **Frank Phillips,** U.S. oilman; a founder of Phillips Petroleum Co. [d. August 23, 1950]

1880 **Aleksandr Aleksandrovich Blok,** Russian poet; leader of Symbolist School in Russian poetry. [d. August 9, 1921]

1887 **Ernst Röhm,** German soldier; National Socialist Workers leader; commander of Hitler's *Brown Shirts*; acted as Reich's Secretary of State for Bavaria; executed by Hitler's troops, 1934. [d. June 30, 1934]

1895 **José Iturbi,** U.S. pianist, born in Spain; began his professional career at the age of seven; noted for his flamboyant lifestyle and enormous energy during his long history of concerts. [d. June 28, 1980]

1904 **Nancy Mitford,** British novelist, biographer, editor; noted for her biographies of Voltaire and Louis XIV of France. [d. June 30, 1973]

James O. Eastland, U.S. politician, lawyer, farmer; U.S. Senator, 1941–78; President pro-tempore of the U.S. Senate, 1972–78.

1908 **Claude Levi-Strauss,** French anthropologist, university professor, writer; developed concept of **structural anthropology.**

Panama	**Independence from Spain**

Celebrates Panama's achievement of independence from Spain, 1821.

Religious Calendar

The Saints

St. Stephen the Younger, martyr. [d. 764]

St. Simeon Metaphrastes, principal compiler of the legends of the saints found in the menologies of the Byzantine church. [d. c. 1000]

St. James of the March, priest. [d. 1476]

St. Joseph Pignatelli, Jesuit. [d. 1811]

St. Catherine Labouré, virgin, nun and visionary. Also called **Katherine.** [d. 1876]

St. Juthwara, virgin and martyr. Also called **Aude.** [death date unknown]

The Beatified

Blessed James Thompson, priest and martyr. [d. 1582]

Historical Events

1821 **Panama** declares its independence from Spain and joins **Republic of Colombia.**

1855 Russians capture Turkish fortress of **Kars** in the Caucasus (**Crimean War**).

1885 British forces occupy **Mandalay** in the **Third Burmese War.**

1888 **Gambia** becomes a separate British Crown Colony.

1895 First recorded automobile race in America is held, sponsored by *Chicago Times Herald*, over a 54-mile course.

1902 **Lord Horatio Herbert Kitchener,** distinguished British soldier, becomes the new commander in chief of the Indian army.

1919 **Lady Nancy Witcher Astor** becomes first woman to be elected to the British Parliament.

1922 Polish President **Józef Piłsudski** convokes new national assembly.

1925 *Grand Ole Opry,* a medley of cowboy tunes and ballads, is first broadcast as *Barn Dance.*

1941 **Benjamin Britten's** *Scottish Ballad* is first performed by the Cincinnati Symphony Orchestra.

1943 **Teheran Conference** begins; Roosevelt, Churchill, and Stalin meet to plan Allied invasion of Europe (**World War II**).

1960 **Mauritania** gains independence from France.

1966 **Dominican Republic** promulgates a new constitution.

November 29

Holidays

Albania	**Liberation Day** Continuation of the celebration of November 28, commemorating the withdrawal of occupation troops, 1944.
Liberia	**President Tubman's Birthday** Celebrates the birthday of William Tubman, the nation's president, 1944–71.
U.N. Member Nations	**International Day of Solidarity with the Palestinian People** Sponsored by the United Nations.

Birthdates

1607 **John Harvard,** American colonial clergyman, baptized on this date; his library and estate, left to a Massachusetts college, became the foundation of **Harvard University.** [d. September 14, 1638]

1781 **Andrés Bello,** Chilean poet, statesman, scholar; one of Chile's greatest poets; edited the Civil Code of Chile. [d. October 15, 1865]

1797 **Gaetano Donizetti,** Italian opera composer; composer of *Lucrezia Borgia* and *Lucia di Lammermoor.* [d. April 8, 1848]

1799 **Amos Bronson Alcott,** U.S. philosopher, teacher, reformer; a leader of the Transcendentalist movement in New England; father of Louisa May Alcott (November 29). [d. March 4, 1888]

1803 **Christian Johann Doppler,** Austrian physicist, mathematician; first to explain the change in sound frequencies when a source approaches and departs from a listener (later called the *Doppler effect*). [d. March 17, 1853]

1811 **Wendell Phillips,** U.S. orator, reformer; eloquent advocate of abolition of slavery. [d. February 2, 1884]

1825 **Jean-Martin Charcot,** French neurologist, known for his research in areas of **hysteria** and **hypnosis.** [d. August 16, 1893]

1832 **Louisa May Alcott,** U.S. novelist; author of *Little Women*; daughter of Amos Bronson Alcott (November 29). [d. March 6, 1888]

1834 **George Holmes Howison,** U.S. mathematician and philosopher; one of chief exponents of **personalism.** [d. December 31, 1916]

1849 **John Ambrose Fleming,** British electrical engineer; inventor of the **diode thermionic valve (radio tube),** 1904. [d. April 18, 1945]

1856 **Theobald von Bethmann-Hollweg,** German politician; Chancellor of Germany, 1909–17. [d. January 1, 1921]

1866 **Ernest William Brown,** U.S. astronomer, mathematician; professor of mathematics, Yale University, 1907–32; noted for his investigations of celestial mechanics. [d. July 22, 1938]

1874 **Antonio Caetano de Abreu Freire Egas Moniz,** Portuguese surgeon, statesman; Nobel Prize in physiology or medicine for development of technique of **prefrontal lobotomy** in treatment of psychoses (with W. R. Hess), 1949. [d. December 13, 1955]

1898 **C(live Hamilton) S(taples) Lewis,** British novelist, critic, scholar; known for his science fiction works and allegories. [d. November 22, 1963]

1908 **Adam Clayton Powell, Jr.,** U.S. politician, clergyman; prominent black leader; U.S. Congressman, 1945–67; removed from U.S. Congress for improper activities. [d. April 4, 1972]

1916 **Sir Sydney Douglas Gun-Munro,** Governor-General, Saint Vincent and the Grenadines, 1977– .

1920 **Elmo Russell Zumwalt, Jr.,** U.S. naval officer; Commander of U.S. naval forces in

U.S. (Wyoming)	Nellie Taylor Ross' Birthday
Vanuatu	Unity Day
Yugoslavia	Day of the Republic
	Commemorates the proclamation of the Republic, 1945.

Religious Calendar

St. Saturninus, first bishop of Toulouse, and martyr. Also called **Sernin.** [d. c. 3rd century]

St. Saturninus, priest and martyr. [d. c. 309]

St. Brendan of Birr, abbot and chief of the prophets of Ireland. [d. 573]

St. Ethelwin, monk and hermit. Also called **Ailwin,** or **Egelwin.** [d. 7th century]

St. Radbod, Bishop of Utrecht. [d. 918]

The Beatified

Blessed Frederick of Regensburg, lay brother. [d. 1329]

Blessed Dionysius, Carmelite priest, and **Redemptus,** lay brother; martyrs. [d. 1638]

Blessed Francis Antony of Lucera, priest. Also called *Padre Maestro,* **Father Master.** [d. 1742]

Vietnam Conflict, 1968–70; Chief of Naval Operations, 1970–74.

1933 **David Robert Reuben,** U.S. psychiatrist, author; became known for series of *Everything You Wanted to Know* books.

1934 **Willie Morris,** U.S. editor, novelist, nonfiction writer; executive editor and editor-in-chief of *Harper's Magazine.* 1965–71.

Historical Events

1314 **Philip IV,** King of France, dies and is succeeded by **Louis X.**

1890 First **Japanese Diet** opens, seating first freely elected public officials in Japan's history.

1900 **Lord Horatio Herbert Kitchener** becomes supreme commander of British forces during the **Boer War.**

1914 The Serbs evacuate their capital of **Belgrade** in the face of the Austrian advance (**World War I**).

1916 **Sir David Beatty** succeeds Admiral Jellicoe as commander-in-chief of the British fleet (**World War I**).

1922 **Tomb of Tutankhamun** is discovered in Egypt by British archaeologists **Howard Carter** and **Lord Carnarvon.**

1929 **Richard E. Byrd** and **Bernt Balchen** pilot *The Floyd Bennett* in the first flight over the **South Pole.**

1945 Federal People's Republic of **Yugoslavia** is proclaimed.

1947 UN approves the partition of **Palestine.**

1950 **National Council of the Churches of Christ** [in the U.S.] is formally established by delegates of 25 Protestant denominations and 4 Eastern Orthodox churches.

1963 President Lyndon B. Johnson creates a special commission headed by Chief Justice Earl Warren to investigate the assassination of President Kennedy and the murder of his presumed assassin, **Lee Harvey Oswald (Warren Commission).**

1964 Revolutionary changes in the Roman Catholic liturgy, including the use of English in many prayers and responses, become effective in the U.S.

1974 Great Britain outlaws **Irish Republican Army** in the wake of bombings and terrorist attacks.

France's National Assembly votes to legalize **abortion,** overturning a 1920 law.

November 30

Holidays

Barbados   **Independence Day**
Commemorates the achievement of independence from Great Britain, 1966.

Benin   **National Day**
Commemorates the establishment of the country, formerly **Dahomey**, 1975.

Philippines   **Bonifacio Day** or **National Heroes' Day**
Celebrates the birthday of revolutionary leader **Andres Bonifacio,** 1863.

Birthdates

1508   **Andrea Palladio (Andrea di Pietro della Gondola),** Italian architect; his designs exerted great influence on later European domestic architecture. [d. August 19, 1580]

1554   **Sir Philip Sidney,** English poet, courtier, scholar, soldier; author of *Arcadia* and *Astrophel and Stella,* an early sonnet sequence. [d. October 17, 1586]

1667   **Jonathan Swift,** English satirist, clergyman; author of *Gulliver's Travels.* [d. October 19, 1745]

1699   **Christian VI,** King of Denmark and Norway. [d. August 6, 1746]

1756   **Ernst Florens Friedrich Chladni,** German physicist; authority in **acoustics;** did extensive experimentation in measuring **velocity of sound.** [d. April 3, 1827]

1817   **Theodor Mommsen,** German historian, writer; Nobel Prize in literature for his history of Rome, 1902. [d. November 1, 1903]

1819   **Cyrus West Field,** U.S. businessman, science promoter; used his fortune to promote laying of first transatlantic cable. [d. July 12, 1892]

1835   **Samuel Langhorne Clemens (Mark Twain),** U.S. humorist and novelist; among his books are: *Huckleberry Finn* and *The Adventures of Tom Sawyer.* [d. April 21, 1910]

1858   **Charles Allerton Coolidge,** U.S. architect; designed **Chicago Public Library** and **Rockefeller Institute** in New York. [d. April 1, 1936]

1869   **Nils G. Dalén,** Swedish physicist; Nobel Prize in physics for his invention of the **automatic sun valve** in lighting, 1912. [d. December 9, 1937]

1872   **John McCrae,** Canadian physicist, poet; surgeon to first brigade of Canadian artillery, World War I; author of poem *In Flanders Field.* [d. January 28, 1918]

1874   **Sir Winston Churchill,** British statesman, author; guided British policy during the World War II years; Prime Minister, 1939–45; 1951–55; Nobel Prize in literature, 1953. [d. January 24, 1965]

1889   **Edgar Douglas Adrian, Baron of Cambridge,** British physiologist; Nobel Prize in physiology or medicine for studies in physiology of the nervous system (with C. S. Sherrington), 1932. [d. August 4, 1977]

1894   **Donald Ogden Stewart,** U.S. actor and author; member of the famous **Algonquin Round Table** of the 1920s; one of the most successful scriptwriters in Hollywood during the 1930s and 1940s; blacklisted during the McCarthy anti-Communist era; moved to England where he continued to write movie scripts and books of humor. [d. August 2, 1980]

1904   **Clyfford Still,** U.S. artist; although a recluse, exerted a profound influence on contemporary American artists; the subject of the largest one-man exhibition the Metropolitan Museum of Art ever devoted to a living artist. [d. June 23, 1980]

Upper Volta	Youth Day
People's Democratic Republic of Yemen (Southern Yemen)	Independence Day Commemorates the establishment of the new government and achievement of independence from Great Britain, 1967.
Yugoslavia	Day of the Republic Continuation of the celebration of November 29.

Religious Calendar

Feasts

St. Andrew, apostle and first-called of the followers of Christ. Patron of Scotland, Russia, the Order of the Golden Fleece of Burzmund, the Order of the Cross of St. Andrew, fishermen, and fish dealers. Invoked for motherhood. [d. 1st century] [major holy day, Episcopal Church; minor festival, Lutheran Church]

The Saints

SS. Sapor and Isaac, bishops and martyrs. [d. 339]

The Beatified

Blessed Andrew of Antioch, Augustinian canon regular. [d. c. 1348]

1907	**Jacques Barzun,** U.S. educator, historian, born in France; author of several books on music, art, and education.
1923	**Efrem Zimbalist, Jr.,** U.S. actor.
1926	**Andrew Schally,** U.S. biochemist, born in Poland; Nobel Prize in physiology or medicine for research in pituitary hormones (with R. C. L. Guillemin and R. S. Yalow), 1977.
1930	**G(eorge) Gordon Liddy,** U.S. lawyer, government official; one of original conspirators in **Watergate Incident.**

Historical Events

1016	**Edmund Ironside,** King of England, dies; **Cnut of Denmark** is recognized as King of England.
1554	**Roman Catholicism** is restored in England as **Queen Mary I** achieves reconciliation with Rome.
1700	**Peter the Great** of Russia is decisively defeated at **Narva** by **Charles XII** of Sweden (**Great Northern War**).
1718	**Charles XII** of Sweden is killed near **Frederikshall** and is succeeded by his sister, **Ulrica Eleanor.**
1853	Russia destroys Turkish fleet at **Sinope,** precipitating **Crimean War.**
1864	**Battle of Franklin, Tennessee** results in costly Confederate defeat (**U.S. Civil War**).
1914	**Battle of Lowicz** between Russia and Germany begins in Poland (**World War I**).
1918	**Iceland** is granted autonomy by Denmark.
1939	Russian armies attack Finland on three fronts (**Russo-Finnish War**).
1959	**Floyd Patterson** knocks out **Archie Moore** for World Boxing Association heavyweight title.
1965	**Declaration of Rio** is signed at Second Special Inter-American Conference.
1966	**Barbados** achieves complete independence from Great Britain.
1967	**South Yemen People's Republic,** formerly the **South Arabian Federation,** is declared independent of Great Britain.
1970	South Yemen changes its name to the **People's Democratic Republic of Yemen.**
1975	**Dahomey** changes its name to the People's Republic of **Benin.**

December

December is the twelfth month of the Gregorian calendar and has 31 days. The Latin *decem* 'ten,' in the name of this month, refers to December's original position as the final month in the early Roman 10-month calendar. The name remained as December even after the Roman adoption of a 12-month calendar, with December still the final month. (See also at **September.**)

The Romans celebrated the Saturnalia in late December, a festival of great merriment dedicated to the god Saturn, marked by exchange of gifts, temporary liberty for slaves, and the playful honoring of a mock king, the Lord of Misrule, known by the Romans as *Saturnalicius princeps.* The Anglo-Saxons celebrated the great Yule feast, associated with Christmas but probably originating in an ancient, pre-Christian festival.

The occurrence of the winter solstice—the shortest day of the year—approximately on December 22 in the northern hemisphere is very likely the reason that many ancient religions celebrated important festivals at this time. The lengthening of daylight after the solstice was a reassurance that the solar cycle was continuing and that warmer weather would return.

In the astrological calendar, December spans the zodiac signs of Sagittarius, the Archer (November 22–December 21) and Capricorn, the Goat (December 22–January 19).

The birthstone for December is the turquoise or zircon, and the flower is the holly or narcissus.

State, National, and International Holidays

The King's Birthday
(Thailand)
First Monday
Nine Days of Posada
(Mexico)
Third Week

Russian Winter Festival
(U.S.S.R.)
December 25 through First Week in January
Christmas Day
December 25

Boxing Day
(Great Britain)
December 26

Special Events and Their Sponsors

Tinsel Day
December 5
Tandem Day
December 13

Puns Corp.
c/o Robert L. Birch
Box 2364
Falls Church, Virginia 22042

Special Days—Other Calendars

	Hanukkah	Beginning of Advent
1985	December 8	December 1
1986	December 27	
1987	December 16	
1988	December 4	
1989	December 23	December 3
1990	December 12	December 2

December 1

Holidays

Central African Republic	**Anniversary of the Proclamation of the Republic** Celebrates the achievement of independence from France, 1958.
Portugal	**Restoration of Independence**

Religious Calendar

The Saints

St. Ansanus, martyr and first apostle of Siena. Also called the *Baptizer.* [d. 304]

St. Agericus, Bishop of Verdun. Also called **Airy.** [d. 588]

Birthdates

1751 **Johan Henrik Kellgren,** Swedish poet, critic; private secretary and literary advisor to **King Gustavus III** of Sweden. [d. April 20, 1795]

1766 **Nikolai Mikhaylovich Karamzin,** Russian writer; author of a 12-volume *History of Russia*; brought about reforms in the literary language of Russia; exerted significant influence on development of the language and literature. [d. May 22, 1826]

1792 **Nikolai Ivanovich Lobachevsky,** Russian mathematician; an early developer of non-Euclidean geometries. [d. February 24, 1856]

1830 **Luigi Cremona,** Italian mathematician; known for his work in geometry and graphical statistics; reorganized technical schools in major cities in Italy. [d. June 10, 1903]

1846 **William Henry Holmes,** U.S. anthropologist; Chief, Bureau of American Ethnology, 1902–09; Head Curator of Anthropology, U.S. National Museum, 1910–20; Director, National Gallery of Art, 1920–33. [d. April 20, 1933]

1854 **William Temple Hornaday,** U.S. zoologist, wild life conservator; early promoter of game preserves and protection of wildlife through conservation laws. [d. March 6, 1937]

1879 **Lane Bryant (Lena Himmelstein),** U.S. merchant, born in Lithuania; founder of Lane Bryant chain of stores that cater to larger-size women's clothes and maternity clothes. [d. September 26, 1951]

1886 **Rex (Todhunter) Stout,** U.S. novelist; known for his creation of **Nero Wolfe** detective stories. [d. October 27, 1975]

1897 **Cyril Ritchard,** Australian actor, director. [d. December 18, 1977]

1904 **W(illiam) A(nthony) (Tony) Boyle,** U.S. labor leader; President of United Mine Workers, 1963–72; convicted of murder of union leader **Joseph Yablonski** and his family, 1970.

1910 **Dame Alicia Markova (Lilian Alicia Marks),** British ballerina; first prima ballerina of Vic-Wells Ballet (now Royal Ballet Company), 1933–35; Vice-President, Royal Academy of Dancing, 1958– ; Governor, Royal Ballet, 1973– .

1913 **Mary Martin,** U.S. actress, singer.

1935 **Lou Rawls,** U.S. rhythm and blues singer.

Woody Allen (Allen Stewart Konigsberg), U.S. comedian, film maker.

1939 **Lee Trevino,** U.S. golfer.

1940 **Richard Pryor,** U.S. comedian, actor.

1945 **Bette Midler,** U.S. singer, musical comedy actress.

Historical Events

1135 **Henry I** of England dies and is succeeded by his nephew, **Stephen of Blois.**

1145 **Pope Eugene III** proclaims the **Second Crusade.**

St. Tudwal, bishop. Also called **Pabu, Tugdual,** or **Tutwal.** [d. 6th cent.]

St. Eligius, Bishop of Noyon; patron of all kinds of smiths and metalworkers. Invoked on behalf of horses. Also called **Eloi,** or **Eloy.** [d. 660]

The Beatified

Blessed Bentivoglia, Franciscan friar minor. [d. 1232]

Blessed John of Vercelli, 6th master general of the Dominican Order of Preachers. [d. 1283]

Blessed Gerard Gagnoli, Franciscan lay brother. [d. 1345]

Blessed Antony Bonfadini, Franciscan friar minor. [d. 1482]

Blessed Hugh Faringdon, abbot of Reading, and his Companions, martyrs. [d. 1539]

Blessed John Beche, Abbot of Colchester and martyr. Also called **Thomas Marshall.** [d. 1539]

Blessed Richard Whiting, Abbot of Glastonbury, and his Companions, martyrs. [d. 1539]

1640   **Portugal** gains independence from Spain.

1887   The infant **King Alfonso XIII** is crowned king of Spain.

China cedes **Macao** to Portugal.

1918   British and American troops begin the occupation of Germany following **World War I.**

1924   George Gershwin's musical revue, ***Lady Be Good,*** containing *Fascinating Rhythm,* opens in New York.

1925   **Locarno Treaties** are signed with Germany; Belgium, France, Britain, and Italy mutually guarantee peace in Western Europe, and Germany promises arbitration in any disputes with Poland, France, Belgium, and Czechoslovakia.

1934   **Serge Kirov,** a close collaborator of Stalin, is assassinated in Russia, followed by an outbreak of terror and purges within the Communist Party.

1943   **Declaration of Cairo** by U.S., Great Britain, and China, clarifies goals of war against Japan (**World War II**).

Nationwide **gasoline rationing** goes into effect in the U.S.

1950   U.S. Marines rescue 1,200 American soldiers at **Chosin, Korea** (**Korean War**).

1951   Benjamin Britten's opera ***Billy Budd*** premieres in London.

1956   Leonard Bernstein's musical comedy ***Candide*** premieres in New York.

1959   **Antarctic Treaty** is signed in Washington, D.C., guaranteeing international use of continent for peaceful purposes only.

1963   **Queen Elizabeth II** officially opens the Commonwealth Pacific submarine telephone cable extending from Vancouver Island to Australia.

1970   **Divorce** is legalized in Italy.

December 2

Holidays

| Laos | National Day |
| United Arab Emirates | National Day |

United Arab Emirates National Day Commemorates the achievement of independence from Great Britain, 1971.

Birthdates

1738 **Richard Montgomery,** American Revolutionary general; killed leading assault on Quebec. [d. December 31, 1775]

1813 **Matthias Alexander Castrén,** Finnish linguist and ethnologist; pioneer in **Ural-Altaic philology.** [d. May 7, 1852]

1825 **Pedro II,** second and last Emperor of Brazil; forced to abdicate in 1889 when federal republic was established. [d. December 5, 1891]

1842 **Enos Melancthon Barton,** U.S. manufacturer; founder of Western Electric Co. [d. May 3, 1916]

1859 **Georges Seurat,** French painter; a pioneer of **Neo-impressionism;** creator of **pointillism.** [d. March 29, 1891]

1866 **Harry Thacker Burleigh,** U.S. singer, composer; noted for his exquisite voice, as well as his renditions of the Negro spiritual which he popularized during numerous European concert tours. [d. September 12, 1949]

1885 **George R. Minot,** U.S. physician; Nobel Prize in physiology or medicine for new discoveries in the treatment of **pernicious anemia,** at that time a uniformly fatal disease (with W. P. Murphy and G. H. Whipple), 1934. [d. February 25, 1950]

1906 **Peter Carl Goldmark,** U.S. inventor, born in Hungary; credited with invention of **color television.** [d. December 7, 1977]

1914 **Alexander (Meigs) Haig, Jr.,** U.S. Army general; NATO Supreme Allied Commander in Europe, 1974–79; White House chief of staff, 1973–74; U.S. Secretary of State, 1980–82.

1915 **Marais Viljoen,** President, Republic of South Africa, 1979– .

1925 **Julie Harris,** U.S. actress.

1962 **Tracy Austin,** U.S. tennis player.

Historical Events

1254 **Manfred,** King of Sicily retains his kingdom against claims of **Charles of Anjou** at the **Battle of Foggia.**

1804 **Napoleon Bonaparte** is crowned French Emperor **Napoleon I** of France.

1805 **Napoleon** scores one of his greatest victories in the **Battle of Austerlitz,** defeating the combined Russian and Austrian armies.

1823 **Monroe Doctrine** is expressed by U.S. President James Monroe in his annual message to Congress.

1848 **Emperor Ferdinand** of Holy Roman Empire abdicates in favor of his nephew, **Franz Joseph.**

1851 **Napoleon III** is proclaimed emperor of France following a coup d'etat.

1859 **John Brown** is hanged at Charlestown for treason against the state of Virginia.

1903 **First Panama Canal Treaty** is ratified.

1911 **King George V** and **Queen Mary** arrive at Bombay, the first British sovereigns to visit India.

1942 Scientists at the University of Chicago achieve the first self-sustaining **nuclear reaction.**

1943 *Carmen Jones,* Oscar Hammerstein II's Americanization of Bizet's **Carmen,** premieres in New York.

1962 Record **thorium** deposits in the White Mountains of New Hampshire are found by geologists; they constitute a reserve for nuclear fuel equal to the nation's uranium deposits.

1966 **U.S. Catholic Bishops Conference** abolishes rule of **abstinence from meat** except on Ash Wednesday and Fridays during Lent.

1971 Six Persian Gulf sheikdoms proclaim their independence as the **United Arab Emirates.**

Religious Calendar

The Saints

St. Chromatius, Bishop of Aquileia. [d. c. 407]

St. Bibiana, virgin and martyr. Also called **Bibiania,** or **Viviana.** [death date unknown]

The Beatified

Blessed John Ruysbroeck, priest and contemplative. Also called **Jan Van Ruysbroeck,** or **Joannes Rusbrochius.** [d. 1381]

1982   **Dr. William DeVries** and a team of surgeons at Utah Medical Center successfully implant an **artificial heart** in **Barney Clark,** a Washington State dentist (who lives for 112 days after the surgery).

December 3

Religious Calendar

The Saints

St. Cassian, martyr. Also called Cassian of Tangier; patron of stenographers. [d. c. 298]

St. Birinus, first bishop of Dorchester, and Apostle of Wessex. Also called Berin, or Birin. Feast formerly December 5. [d. c. 650]

Birthdates

1368 Charles VI of France, the *Well-Beloved;* also known as Charles the Mad because of his periods of insanity beginning in 1392. [d. October 21, 1422]

1684 Baron Ludvig Holberg, Danish writer, historian, philosopher; known as the father of Danish literature; claimed also by Norway as the founder of its literature. [d. January 28, 1754]

1753 Samuel Crompton, English inventor; in 1779 developed the *mule,* a spinning machine which revolutionized the cotton industry. [d. June 26, 1827]

1755 Gilbert Charles Stuart, U.S. painter; created the *Athenaeum Head,* the most popular, romantic portrait ever done of George Washington. [d. July 9, 1828]

1764 Mary Ann Lamb, English author; sister of Charles Lamb (February 10); with her brother wrote various poems, especially children's verses. [d. May 20, 1847]

1795 Sir Rowland Hill, British postal authority; creator of the first postage stamp, the *Penny Black;* responsible for the reform of the British postal system; Secretary to the Post office, 1854–64. [d. August 27, 1879]

1805 Ernest Adolphe Hyacinthe Constantin Guys, French artist; noted for his detailed sketches of life during the Second Empire. [d. March 13, 1892]

1812 Hendrik Conscience, Flemish novelist; regarded as the *Founder of Modern Flemish Literature.* [d. September 10, 1883]

1826 George Brinton McClellan, Union Army general, public official; Commander of the Army of the Potomac during U.S. Civil War, 1861–62. [d. October 29, 1885]

1830 Frederick Leighton, Baron Leighton, British artist; noted for his detailed draftsmanship, especially in *Venus Disrobing for the Bath.* [d. January 25, 1896]

1838 Cleveland Abbe, U.S. astronomer; the first meteorologist to issue daily weather forecasts; advocate of standard time system. [d. October 28, 1916]

1842 Charles Alfred Pillsbury, U.S. milling executive; founder of Charles A. Pillsbury & Co., 1872. [d. September 17, 1899]

1845 Henry Bradley, British philologist, lexicographer; became editor and eventually senior editor of *Oxford English Dictionary,* 1889–1923. [d. May 23, 1923]

1857 Joseph Conrad (Jozef Teodor Konrad Korzeniowski), British novelist, short-story writer, born in Poland; one of the master stylists of English literature. [d. August 3, 1924]

1864 Herman Heijermans (Koos Habbema, Samuel Falkland), Dutch dramatist, short-story writer; author of numerous works of fiction, especially of Dutch small-town life. [d. November 22, 1924]

1880 (Moritz Albert Franz Friedrich) Fedor von Bock, German field marshal, World War II; chief of northern armies during invasion of Poland; commanded armies on Russian front, 1941. [d. c. May 1, 1945]

1886 Karl Manne Georg Siegbahn, Swedish physicist; Nobel Prize in physics for discovery of M series in the x-ray spectrum, 1925. [d. September 30, 1978]

1895 Anna Freud, Austro-English psychoanalyst; considered the definitive interpreter of the theories of her father, Sigmund Freud. [d. October 9, 1982]

1896 Carlo Schmid, West German statesman; leader of the Social Democrat Party; helped reshape West Germany after World War II. [d. December 11, 1979]

1899 Hayoto Ikeda, Japanese statesman; signed the treaty of peace with U.S. ending World War II. [d. August 13, 1965]

St. Sola, priest and solitary. Also called **Sualo.** [d. 794]

St. Francis Xavier, apostle of India and one of the first Jesuits. Patron saint of the East Indies and of Roman Catholic missionaries in foreign parts as well as all works for the spreading of the faith. Invoked against plague. [d. 1552] Obligatory Memorial.

SS. Claudius, Hilaria, and their Companions, martyrs. [death date unknown]

St. Lucius, king. [death date unknown]

1900	**Richard Kuhn,** German chemist; Nobel Prize in chemistry for work on **carotenoids** and **vitamins,** 1938. [d. August 1, 1967]
1923	**Maria Callas (Cecilia Sophia Anna Maria Kalogeropoulos),** U.S. prima donna operatic soprano. [d. September 16, 1977]
1930	**Jean-Luc Godard,** French film director; leader of the nouvelle vague cinéma.
	Andy Williams, U.S. singer.
1951	**Alberto Juantorena,** Cuban middle-distance runner; Olympic gold medalist, 1976.

Historical Events

1170	**Thomas Becket,** Archbishop of Canterbury, returns to Canterbury after exile in France.
1800	**Battle of Hohenlinden,** in Upper Bavaria, results in great French victory over the Austrians (**War of the Second Coalition**).
1818	**Illinois** is admitted to Union as the 21st state.
1849	**Mt. Kenya** in Africa is discovered by **Dr. Lewis Krapf.**
1909	**Housing and Town Planning Act** goes into effect in Great Britain.
1912	**First Balkan War** ends with armistice between Turkey, Bulgaria, Serbia, and Montenegro.
1914	**Battle of the Kolubara River** opens between the Austrians and the Serbs (**World War I**).
1915	**General Joseph Joffre** is named commander in chief of all French armies (**World War I**).
1917	Negotiations are opened at **Brest-Litovsk** between Russia and Germany in an attempt at peace (**World War I**).
1944	Civil war breaks out in **Greece** between the government in power, backed by British troops, and its Communist-dominated opposition group.
1953	Robert Wright's and George Forrest's musical, ***Kismet,*** opens in New York.
1960	Frederick Loewe's ***Camelot*** premieres in New York.
1967	**Christiaan Barnard** of South Africa performs first successful human **heart transplant** operation at a Cape Town hospital.
1973	***Pioneer 10,*** U.S. unmanned spacecraft, reaches its closest approach to **Jupiter,** 21 months after its launch.
1974	U.S. space vehicle ***Pioneer 11*** begins a five-year journey to **Saturn.**
1979	**Iran** adopts an Islamic constitution.

December 4

Holidays

Mexico   **Day of the Artisans**
Set aside to honor the workers
of the nation.

Religious Calendar

The Saints

St. Clement of Alexandria. Feast suppressed 1969.
[d. c. 215]

Birthdates

1585   **John Cotton,** American colonial leader;
Puritan leader of Massachusetts Bay Colony; responsible for expulsion of Anne
Hutchinson (July 20) and Roger Williams
from the colony. [d. December 23, 1652]

1595   **Jean Chapelain,** French poet, critic; one
of founders of **Académie Française.** [d.
February 22, 1674]

1730   **William Moultrie,** American Revolutionary general; his defense of Charleston, 1776,
delayed British infiltration of the South for
years. [d. September 27, 1805]

1795   **Thomas Carlyle,** British essayist, philosopher, historian. [d. February 5, 1881]

1835   **Samuel Butler,** British novelist, satirist;
known for his novels, *The Way of All Flesh*
and *Erewhon.* [d. June 18, 1902]

1860   **George Albert Hormel,** U.S. businessman;
founder of George A. Hormel & Co., first
company to produced canned hams in
U.S. [d. June 5, 1946]

1861   **Lillian Russell (Helen Louise Leonard),**
U.S. entertainer, actress. [d. June 6, 1922]

1865   **Luther Halsey Gulick,** U.S. educator; cofounder of **Camp Fire Girls of America.**
[d. August 13, 1918]

        Edith Cavell, British nurse; executed by
German soldiers in Brussels for harboring
Allied soldiers. [d. October 12, 1915]

1875   **Rainer Maria Rilke,** German lyric poet,
author; known for his somewhat mystical
works, often dealing with death. [d. December 29, 1926]

1892   **Francisco Franco,** Spanish government
leader; dictator of Spain, 1936–75. [d. November 20, 1975]

1904   **Harry N(athan) Abrams,** U.S. publisher;
founder and Chairman of the Board, Harry
N. Abrams Inc., the largest American publisher of art books. [d. November 25, 1979]

1908   **Alfred Day Hershey,** U.S. biologist; Nobel
Prize in physiology or medicine for research into **genetic structure of viruses**
(with M. Delbruck and S. E. Luria), 1969.

1911   **Robert Payne,** British-American author,
linguist; produced over 100 books, including biographies of Karl Marx and Charlie
Chaplin; founding director, Columbia University translation center. [d. February 18,
1983]

1918   **John Bell Williams,** U.S. politician; U.S.
Congressman, 1947–67; Governor of Mississippi, 1968–72; staunch segregationist. [d.
March 26, 1983]

1922   **Deanna Durbin (Edna Mae Durbin),** U.S.
singer, actress.

Historical Events

963   Roman synod deposes **Pope John XII.**

1214   **William the Lion,** King of Scotland, dies
and is succeeded by **Alexander II.**

1867   **The Grange** (The Order of Patrons of Husbandry), is founded at Washington, D.C.

1920   The French colony of Upper Senegal-Niger
is renamed the **French Sudan.**

1961   **Floyd Patterson** knocks out **Tom McNeeley** to retain the world heavyweight boxing
title.

1965   U.S. spacecraft *Gemini 7*, with Frank Borman and James A. Lovell, Jr., aboard, is
successfully launched into orbit from Cape
Kennedy, Florida.

1974   Church of England **Worship and Doctrine Measure** is passed, giving power to
change Anglican liturgy.

St. Maruthas, bishop of Maiferkat. Considered one of the chief Syrian doctors. [d. c. 415]

St. John Damascene, Doctor of the Church. Last of the Greek fathers and one of the two greatest poets of the Eastern church. Also called **Mansur.** Feast formerly March 27. [d. c. 749] Optional Memorial.

St. Anno, Archbishop of Cologne. [d. 1075]

St. Osmund, Bishop of Salisbury. [d. 1099]

St. Bernard, Bishop of Parma, and cardinal. [d. 1133]

St. Barbara, virgin and martyr; patron of gunners, miners, mathematicians, architects, smelters, brewers, oilers, masons, and captives. Invoked against lightning, fire, and sudden death. [death date unknown] Feast suppressed 1969.

1976   **Jean-Bédel Bokassa** declares himself emperor of the Central African Republic in a $20 million extravaganza. Though the country is one of the world's poorest, it is believed to have great undeveloped mineral deposits.

December 5

Holidays

Haiti	**Discovery Day** Celebrates the discovery of the island by Christopher Columbus, 1492.
U.S.S.R.	**Constitution Day** Commemorates the promulgation of the Russian constitution, 1936.

Birthdates

1443 **Julius II, pope,** 1503–13; greatest art patron of all the popes; commissioned Michelangelo's Sistine chapel frescoes. [d. February 21, 1513]

1782 **Martin Van Buren,** U.S. Senator, 1821–28; U.S. Secretary of State, 1829–31; U.S. Vice-President, 1833–37; 8th President of U.S., 1837–41. [d. July 24, 1862]

1803 **Fyodor Tyutchev,** Russian lyric poet, essayist. [d. August 8, 1873]

1830 **Christina (Georgina) Rossetti,** British poet; noted chiefly for her sacred poetry. [d. December 29, 1894]

1839 **George Armstrong Custer,** U.S. cavalry officer; known primarily for his defeat by Sitting Bull and Crazy Horse at the **Battle of Little Bighorn,** which is often called **Custer's Last Stand.** [d. June 25, 1876]

1841 **Marcus Daly,** U.S. miner, businessman; founder of the Anaconda Mining Co.; exerted great influence on Democratic politics in Montana. [d. November 12, 1900]

1859 **Sir Sidney Lee,** British scholar, editor; editor-in-chief of *Dictionary of National Biography,* 1891–1917. [d. March 3, 1926]

John Rushworth Jellicoe, Earl Jellicoe, British naval officer in World War I; commander of the grand fleet in **Battle of Jutland,** 1916. [d. November 20, 1935]

1867 **Joseph Piłsudski,** Polish military officer, statesman; Chief of State, 1920; Dictator of Poland, 1921; 1926–28; 1930; Minister of War and Commander in Chief of Army, 1930–35. [d. May 12, 1935]

1879 **Clyde Vernon Cessna,** U.S. aircraft manufacturer; founder of Cessna Airplane Co., 1927. [d. November 20, 1954]

1894 **P(hilip) K(night) Wrigley,** U.S. manufacturer; President and Chairman of the Board of William Wrigley & Co., the world's largest **chewing gum** manufacturer; son of W. Wrigley, Jr. (September 30). [d. April 12, 1977]

1896 **Carl Ferdinand Cori,** U.S. biochemist, born in Czechoslovakia; Nobel Prize in physiology or medicine for research in **carbohydrate metabolism** (with G. T. Cori), 1947. [d. October 26, 1957]

1901 **Werner Karl Heisenberg,** German physicist; known for the **uncertainty principle,** which maintains that observations are affected by the observer; Nobel Prize in physics for discoveries in study of **hydrogen,** 1932. [d. February 1, 1976]

Walt(er Elias) Disney, U.S. film producer; pioneer in **movie animation;** creator of **Mickey Mouse,** 1928; produced first feature length cartoon, *Snow White,* 1938. [d. December 15, 1966]

1902 **(James) Strom Thurmond,** U.S. politician, farmer, lawyer; Governor of South Carolina, 1947–51; U.S. Senator, 1954– .

1903 **Cecil Frank Powell,** British physicist; Nobel Prize in physics for development of photographic method of tracking nuclear particles, 1950. [d. August 9, 1969]

1905 **Mohammad Abdullah,** Kashmiri statesman; known as the *Lion of Kashmir;* Chief Minister, Kashmir, 1947–53; 1975–82. [d. September 8, 1982]

1906 **Otto Preminger,** U.S. film director, born in Austria.

1908 **Lin Piao (Lin Biao),** Chinese communist military leader; reported to have died in

The Saints

St. Crispina, martyr. [d. 304]

St. Sabas, abbot and one of the most renowned patriarchs of the monks of Palestine. Founded the monastery called **Mar Saba** near Jerusalem, one of the oldest occupied monasteries in the world. Also called **Sebas.** [d. 532]

St. Nicetius, Bishop of Trier. [d. c. 566]

St. Justinian, priest, hermit, and martyr. Also called **Jestin.** [d. 6th cent.]

St. Sigiramnus, abbot. Also called **Cyran,** or **Siran.** [d. c. 655]

St. Christina of Markyate, virgin. Also called **Theodora.** [d. c. 1161]

The Beatified

Blessed Nicholas of Sibenik, Franciscan friar minor and martyr. [d. 1391]

Blessed Bartholomew of Mantua, Dominican preacher. [d. 1495]

---

airplane crash, 1971. [d. September 12, 1971]

1925   **Anastasio Somoza-Debayle,** Nicaraguan political leader; President of Nicaragua, 1967–72; 1974–79. [d. September 17, 1980]

1927   **Bhumibol Adulyadej,** King of Thailand, 1946– .

1932   **Sheldon L. Glashow,** U.S. physicist; Nobel Prize in physics for formulating theory concerning interaction of elementary particles (with S. Weinberg), 1979.

1934   **Joan Didion,** U.S. novelist, journalist.

1947   **Jim Messina,** U.S. rock musician.

Historical Events

1189   **King Richard I** of England acknowledges independence of **Scotland** and sells Roxburgh and Berwick to **William the Lion,** of Scotland.

1301   **Pope Boniface VIII** issues papal bull against **Philip IV** of France over issue of king's right to tax the clergy.

1484   **Pope Innocent VIII** issues papal bull against witchcraft and sorcery.

1560   **Francis II** of France dies and is succeeded by **Charles IX,** his brother, under regency of Catherine de' Medici, their mother.

1776   **Phi Beta Kappa** fraternity is founded at William and Mary College as a social fraternity; in 1831, it becomes an honorary fraternity for students achieving academic distinction.

1870   **Rome** is declared the capital of Italy.

1892   Tchaikovsky's ballet *The Nutcracker* premieres at St. Petersburg, Russia.

1897   The authority of the British South Africa Company under **Cecil Rhodes** is extended over Northern Rhodesia.

1919   **Yugoslavia** signs treaties of peace with Austria and Bulgaria ending **World War I.**

1930   **The Swedish National Socialist Party** (Fascist) holds its first meeting.

1933   21st Amendment, revoking the **18th (Prohibition) Amendment,** is ratified in the U.S.

1936   U.S.S.R. adopts a new constitution recasting the Soviet federation.

1967   More than 1,000 persons, including numerous nationally known personalities, are arrested during a **Stop the Draft Week** demonstration in New York City.

1977   **Tripoli Declaration** is issued by Arab critics of President **Anwar Sadat** of Egypt; Sadat, in retaliation, breaks off diplomatic relations with Algeria, Iraq, Libya, Yemen, and Syria.

December 6

Holidays

Ecuador	**Day of Quito** Commemorates the founding of the city, 1534.
Finland	**Independence Day** Commemorates Finland's declaration of independence from Russia, 1917.
Ivory Coast Republic	**Independence Day** Commemorates Ivory Coast's achievement of independence from France, 1960.

Birthdates

1478 **Count Baldassare Castiglione,** Italian diplomat, soldier, and author; known for his writings on courtly life; author of *The Courtier*. [d. February 7, 1529]

1637 **Sir Edmund Andros,** English governor of New England, 1674–86. [d. February 24, 1714]

1719 **John Phillips,** U.S. merchant, educational benefactor; founded **Phillips Exeter Academy,** New Hampshire, 1781. [d. April 21, 1795]

1732 **Warren Hastings,** English administrator; first governor-general of British India. [d. August 22, 1818]

1778 **Joseph Louis Gay-Lussac,** French chemist; developer of **Gay-Lussac's Law** of volumes of gases, 1808. [d. May 9, 1850]

1792 **William II,** King of the Netherlands, 1840–49; his reign saw the Netherlands transformed into a constitutional monarchy. [d. March 17, 1849]

1810 **Robert Cornelis Napier, 1st Baron Napier of Magdala,** British Army field marshal, administrator; Commander in Chief in India, 1770–76; Governor of Gibraltar, 1876–82. [d. January 14, 1890]

1824 **Emmanuel Frémiet,** French sculptor; a leading sculptor of animals. [d. September 10, 1910]

1863 **Charles Martin Hall,** U.S. chemist; discovered an inexpensive method for the isolation of pure **aluminum** from its compounds. [d. December 27, 1914]

1886 **(Alfred) Joyce Kilmer,** U.S. poet; best known for his poem *Trees*. [d. July 30, 1918]

1887 **Lynn Fontanne,** U.S. actress, born in England. [d. July 30, 1983]

1892 **Sir (Francis) Osbert Sacheverell Sitwell, 5th Baronet Sitwell,** British poet, author, critic; brother of Edith Sitwell (September 7). [d. May 4, 1969]

1896 **Ira Gershwin,** U.S. lyricist; frequent collaborator with brother George (September 26) on Broadway musicals; wrote *Porgy and Bess* and *Of Thee I Sing*, first musical to win Pulitzer Prize, 1932. [d. August 17, 1983]

1897 **Milton R. Young,** U.S. politician, farmer; U.S. Senator, 1945–81; served the longest continuous Senate term of any Republican. [d. May 31, 1983]

1898 **Gunnar Myrdal,** Swedish economist, sociologist, public official; Nobel Prize in economics (with F. von Hajek), 1974.

1906 **Agnes Moorehead,** U.S. actress. [d. April 30, 1974]

1908 **George (***Baby Face***) Nelson,** U.S. bank robber; member of the Dillinger gang. [d. November 28, 1934]

1920 **George Porter,** British chemist; Nobel Prize in chemistry for studies of chemical reactions affected by energy pulsations (with M. Eigen and R. G. W. Norrish), 1967.

Dave (David Warren) Brubeck, U.S. musician; a prime mover in the development of modern jazz.

1924 **Wally Cox,** U.S. comedian. [d. February 15, 1973]

Historical Events

1506 **Macchiavelli** creates **Florentine Militia,** first national Italian troops.

Religious Calendar

The Saints

St. Nicholas, called *St. Nicholas of Bari*, Bishop of Myra; patron of Russia, Greece, Sicily, Lorraine, mariners, children, virgins, merchants, pawnbrokers, coopers, brewers, those who lose in lawsuits unjustly, scholars, dock workers, and the worshipful company of parish clerks of the city of London. Invoked by and on behalf of prisoners. Also called **Santa Claus, Sint Klaes,** or **Sinta Klaas.** [d. 4th century] Optional Memorial.

SS. Dionysia, Majoricus, and other martyrs. [d. 484]

St. Abraham, Bishop of Kratia. [d. c. 558]

The Beatified

Blessed Peter Pascual, Bishop of Jaén, martyr; commonly called *saint.* [d. 1300]

1822 **Republic of Mexico** is established following achievement of independence from Spain.

Britain extends suffrage to agricultural workers.

1907 Mononagh, West Virginia, **coal mine disaster**, one of worst in U.S. history, kills 361 men.

1914 **Łódź, Poland** falls to Germans (**World War I**).

Battle of the Kolubara River ends in an Austrian defeat and flight from Serbia (**World War I**).

1916 German army enters **Bucharest** (**World War I**).

1917 **Finland** declares its independence from Russia.

1921 **Irish Peace Treaty** is signed, giving Ireland dominion status and establishing **Irish Free State.**

1971 **India** recognizes the Bangladesh rebel government as the government of **East Pakistan;** Pakistan breaks diplomatic relations with India.

1977 South African government officially grants independence to the black homeland of **Bophuthatswana.**

1978 A new constitution is approved in **Spain,** providing for a constitutional monarchy, a parliamentary system of government, and general individual liberties.

December 7

Holidays

Ivory Coast	**Independence Day**
	Commemorates achievement of independence from France, 1960
U.S. (Delaware)	**Delaware Day**

Birthdates

1598   **Giovanni Lorenzo Bernini,** Italian sculptor, architect, painter, designer; the *Father of Italian Baroque Style.* [d. November 28, 1680]

1784   **Allan Cunningham,** Scottish poet; close associate of Sir Walter Scott; edited Robert Burns's work, 1834. [d. October 30, 1842]

1801   **Johann Nepomuk Edward Ambrosius Nestroy,** Austrian dramatist, actor; leading actor of his time. [d. May 25, 1862]

1810   **Theodor Schwann,** German physiologist; developed the **cell theory of life.** [d. January 11, 1882]

1823   **Leopold Kronecker,** German mathematician; known for his work in algebra and theory of numbers. [d. December 29, 1891]

1830   **Judah Loeb Gordon,** Hebrew poet; the leading Hebrew poet of the 19th century. [d. September 16, 1892]

1841   **Michael Cudahy,** U.S. meat packer; founder of Cudahy Packing Co., 1890. [d. November 27, 1910]

1876   **Willa Cather,** U.S. novelist, short-story writer; Pulitzer Prize in fiction, 1923. [d. April 24, 1947]

1879   **(Charles) Rudolf Friml,** U.S. composer, born in Czechoslovakia; composer of several popular operettas. [d. November 12, 1972]

1888   **(Arthur) Joyce Lunel Cary,** British novelist; author of *The Horse's Mouth.* [d. March 29, 1957]

     Heywood Campbell Broun, U.S. journalist, founder of the Newspaper Guild; the **Heywood Campbell Broun Award** is named for him. [d. December 18, 1939]

1893   **Virginia Kirkus,** U.S. literary critic, author; founder of **Kirkus Service,** which was later sold to the *New York Review of Books.* [d. September 10, 1980]

1894   **Stuart Davis,** U.S. artist; leading exponent of abstract art in the U.S. [d. June 24, 1964]

1910   **Vere Cornwall Bird,** Prime Minister, Antigua and Barbuda, 1981– .

1915   **Eli Wallach,** U.S. actor.

1924   **Mario Soares,** Portuguese political leader; Prime Minister, 1976–78.

1928   **Noam Chomsky,** U.S. linguist, writer, political activist; father of **transformational grammar.**

1932   **Ellen Burstyn,** U.S. actress.

Historical Events

1767   **John Street Theatre,** America's leading theater until 1797, opens in New York City.

1787   **Delaware** votes to adopt the newly created federal constitution, thus becoming the first state of the United States.

1829   The custom of **suttee,** or self-immolation of widows on their husbands' funeral pyres, is outlawed in parts of India under the control of the British East India Company.

1835   **Steam locomotive** is first used in Germany when a railroad opens from Nürnberg to Fürth.

1842   **New York Philharmonic Society** is formed in the U.S.

1889   *The Gondoliers,* a comic opera by Sir Arthur Sullivan and W. S. Gilbert, premieres in London.

1916   **Lloyd George** of Great Britain forms a war cabinet after the resignation of the Asquith coalition cabinet (**World War I**).

1917   **Battle of Cambrai** ends with the British losing much of what they had gained in the initial offensive (**World War I**).

     U.S. declares war on Austria-Hungary (**World War I**).

1937   **Romansch** is recognized as a fourth national language in Switzerland.

Religious Calendar

The Saints

St. Eutychian, pope. Elected 275. [d. 283]

St. Ambrose, Bishop of Milan and Doctor of the Church; patron of Milan, bees, and domestic animals. Introduced Ambrosian chant. Obligatory Memorial [d. 397]

St. Diuma, Bishop of Middle Angles and Mercians. Also called **Dionia.** [d. 658]

St. Josepha Rossello, virgin and founder of the Daughters of Our Lady of Mercy. [d. 1880]

1941 Japanese carrier-based planes make a surprise attack on U.S. fleet at **Pearl Harbor,** Hawaii, destroying 188 U.S. aircraft and many ships and precipitating U.S. declaration of war on Japan. (**World War II**)

1945 American military commission sentences Japanese general **Tomoyuki Yamashita** to be hanged.

1965 **Pope Paul VI** and the Ecumenical Patriarch, **Athenagoras I** of the Greek Church, issue a joint declaration constituting an act of reconciliation between their two churches.

1971 A capsule launched from the Soviet Union's *Mars 3* space probe on December 2 makes soft landing on Mars.

December 8

Holidays

Panama   **Mothers' Day**
Consistent with the celebration of the Immaculate Conception, the people of Panama honor mothers on this day.

Birthdates

65 B.C.   **Horace (Quintus Horatius Flaccus),** the great lyric poet of Rome; under the patronage of Maecenas, wrote numerous works describing the Age of Augustus; known for his *Odes, Satires, Epistles,* and *Ars Poetica.* [d. November 27, 8 B.C.]

1542   **Mary, Queen of Scots (Mary Stuart),** Queen of Scotland; unpopular with her subjects owing to her **Roman Catholicism** and possible involvement in death of her husband, Lord Darnley; forced to abdicate, 1567; imprisoned in England by **Elizabeth I;** executed. [d. February 8, 1587]

1626   **Christina,** Queen of Sweden, 1632–44; her reign was disturbed by the **Thirty Years' War** and great civil unrest; abdicated in favor of her cousin, **Charles X Gustavus.** [d. April 19, 1689]

1708   **Francis I,** Holy Roman Emperor, 1745–65; overshadowed by his wife, **Maria Theresa of Austria.** [d. August 18, 1765]

1730   **Jan Ingenhousz,** Dutch physician, plant physiologist; early developer of theory of **photosynthesis.** [d. September 7, 1799]

1765   **Eli Whitney,** U.S. inventor; invented the **cotton gin,** which revolutionized the cotton growing industry; used early form of **assembly line** method of manufacturing in his musket factory. [d. January 8, 1825]

1826   **Friedrich Siemens,** German inventor; industralist; together with his brother, Sir William Siemens (April 4) developed the **regenerative furnace** used in steel manufacturing. [d. April 24, 1904]

1856   **Henry Thomas Mayo,** U.S. naval commander in World War I; Commander in Chief, Atlantic Fleet, 1916–18. [d. February 23, 1937]

1861   **William Crapo Durant,** U.S. auto manufacturer; founder of the Buick Motor Co., General Motors Company, Chevrolet Motor Co.; President of General Motors Co., 1916–20; founder of Durant Motors, 1921. [d. March 17, 1947]

      Aristide Maillol, French sculptor, designer, and illustrator; best known for monument to Cézanne. [d. October 5, 1944]

1862   **Georges Leon Jules Marie Feydeau,** French dramatist; known for his bedroom farces; wrote *Le Tailleur pour Dames,* 1887. [d. June 5, 1921]

1865   **Jean Sibelius,** Finnish composer; pioneer of Finnish national music; composed *Finlandia,* 1900. [d. September 20, 1957]

1881   **Padraic Colum,** Irish-American poet, dramatist, a founder of the Irish theater. [d. January 11, 1972]

1885   **Kenneth Lewis Roberts,** U.S. novelist; Pulitzer Prize (Special Citation) for historical novels that increased interest in early American history, 1957. [d. July 21, 1957]

1886   **Diego Rivera,** Mexican painter, muralist; his work was controversial because of his communist sympathies, resulting in his murals at Rockefeller Center, New York, being removed. [d. November 25, 1957]

1894   **James (Grover) Thurber,** U.S. humorist, cartoonist; known for his numerous contributions to *The New Yorker,* 1927–52. [d. November 2, 1961]

1898   **Emmett Kelly,** U.S. clown. [d. March 28, 1979]

1901   **Manuel Urrutia Lleo,** Cuban statesman; President of Cuba, 1959. Defected to U.S., 1963, where he headed Anti-Castro Democratic Revolutionary Alliance. [d. July 5, 1981]

1908   **Adele Simpson,** U.S. fashion designer.

Religious Calendar

Solemnities

Feast of the Immaculate Conception of the Blessed Virgin Mary; celebrates the conception of Mary, the Mother of Christ, in the womb of St. Anne; prior to 1854, the feast was known as the **Conception of St. Anne.** A public holiday in many Catholic countries.

The Saints

St. Budoc, abbot. Also caled **Beuzec, Budeaux,** or **Buoc.** Feast formerly December 7. [d. c. 6th century]

St. Romaric, abbot. Also called **Romaricus.** [d. 653]

1911   **Lee J. Cobb,** U.S. actor. [d. February 11, 1976]

1925   **Sammy Davis, Jr.,** U.S. entertainer.

1930   **Maximilian Schell,** Austrian actor.

1932   **Bjørnstjerne Bjørnson,** Norwegian poet, novelist, playwright; political and social leader; the national poet of Norway; Nobel Prize in literature, 1903. [d. April 26, 1910]

1939   **James Galway,** Irish virtuoso flautist.

1943   **Jim Morrison,** U.S. musician; a leading rock vocalist of the 1960s. [d. July 3, 1971]

Historical Events

1795   **Gagging Act** is passed to protect king and government of Great Britain from seditious meetings.

1854   Dogma of the **Immaculate Conception** is made an article of faith in Roman Catholic Church.

1886   **American Federation of Labor** is organized at Columbus, Ohio, with **Samuel Gompers** as first president.

1907   **King Oscar II** of Sweden dies and is succeeded by his son, **Gustavus V.**

1911   **San Francisco Symphony Orchestra** is established.

1914   **Battle of the Falkland Islands** between Great Britain and Germany results in victory for the British. German Admiral Maximilian von Spee dies when his ship is sunk (**World War I**).

1940   U.S. professional championship football game is first broadcast on radio, with Chicago defeating Washington, 73–0.

1941   U.S. declares war on Japan (**World War II**).

   U.S.S. Wake becomes the only American warship to surrender during World War II as it surrenders to the Japanese near Shanghai.

   Japanese troops land on **Bataan**, the east coast of Malaya, and invade **Thailand** (**World War II**).

1949   **Chinese Nationalists** flee the Chinese mainland, moving their capital to **Formosa (Taiwan).**

   Jule Styne's musical comedy *Gentlemen Prefer Blondes* premieres in New York.

1966   Canada adopts a **medicare** program providing for payment by federal government of one half of medical costs.

   28 world nations, including the U.S. and U.S.S.R., reach agreement on a treaty to prohibit use of **outer space** for placement of weapons of mass destruction.

1980   Rock star **John Lennon,** originally the leader of the Beatles, is shot and killed in New York City.

December 9

Holidays

Tanzania   Independence/Republic Day
Commemorates the achievement of complete independence from Great Britain, 1961, and the establishment of the Republic, 1962.

Birthdates

1594   **Gustavus II Adolphus,** King of Sweden, 1611–32; called the *Lion of the North;* responsible for making Sweden a major European power. [d. November 6, 1632]

1608   **John Milton,** English poet, essayist; one of the masters of English literature; wrote *Paradise Lost,* 1665–74, considered the greatest epic in English language; blind from 1652. [d. November 8, 1674]

1717   **Johann Joachim Winckelmann,** German archeologist; founder of the history of ancient art and scientific archaeology. [d. June 8, 1768]

1742   **Karl Wilhelm Scheele,** Swedish pharmacist-chemist; among many of his discoveries were: **chlorine, ammonia, prussic acid,** and **oxygen;** his work on oxygen done independently of Joseph Priestley (March 13). [d. May 21, 1786]

1748   **Claude Louis Berthollet,** French chemist; with Lavoisier, established system of **chemical nomenclature** still in use today. [d. November 6, 1822]

1848   **Joel Chandler Harris,** U.S. journalist, short-story writer, novelist; creator of **Uncle Remus,** the cartoon character whose stories became extremely popular in the late 19th and early 20th centuries. [d. July 3, 1908]

1868   **Fritz Haber,** German physical chemist; Nobel Prize in chemistry for development of process for synthesizing **ammonia** from nitrogen and hydrogen. [d. January 29, 1934]

1886   **Clarence Birdseye,** U.S. businessman, inventor; developed the quick freeze process of food preservation; founder of General Foods Corporation. [d. October 7, 1956]

1895   **Dolores Ibarruri,** Spanish politician, journalist; Secretary General of Spanish Communist Party (Partido Communista Español), 1942–60; President in exile 1960–77; returned to Spain, 1977.

1909   **Douglas Fairbanks, Jr.,** U.S. actor, television producer; son of silent-film star Douglas Fairbanks (May 23).

1912   **Thomas P. (*Tip*) O'Neill,** U.S. politician; U.S. Congressman, 1952– ; Speaker of the House of Representatives, 1976– .

1915   **Elisabeth Schwarzkopf,** German operatic soprano.

1917   **L. James Rainwater,** U.S. physicist; Nobel Prize in physics for development of theory of **structure of the atomic nucleus** (with B. R. Mottelson and A. N. Bohr), 1975.

1918   **Kirk Douglas,** U.S. actor.

1919   **William N. Lipscomb,** U.S. chemist; Nobel Prize in chemistry for investigation of the **structure of boranes,** 1976.

1925   **Dina Merrill (Nedenia Hutton),** U.S. actress; heiress to the Post cereal fortune.

1929   **John Cassavetes,** U.S. actor, director, screenwriter.

1932   **Bill Hartack,** U.S. jockey; rode five Kentucky Derby winners, in 1957, 1960, 1962, 1964, 1969.

Historical Events

1165   **Malcolm IV,** King of Scotland dies and is succeeded by his brother, **William the Lion.**

1625   **Treaty of the Hague** is signed, in which England and the Netherlands agree to subsidize Denmark against the Holy Roman Emperor, **Ferdinand.**

1865   **Leopold I** of Belgium dies and is succeeded by **Leopold II.**

1905   Richard Strauss's one-act opera, *Salome,* opens at the Dresden Opera.

Religious Calendar

The Saints

SS. Hipparchus and his Companions, the **Seven Martyrs of Samosata.** [d. c. 297]

St. Leocadia, virgin and martyr. [d. c. 304]

St. Gorgonia, matron. [d. c. 372]

St. Peter Fourier, co-founder of the Augustinian Canonesses Regular of Our Lady. [d. 1640]

The Beatified

Blessed Francis Antony Fasani, priest. [d. 1742]

1913	Richard Strauss's ***Der Rosenkavalier*** premieres in New York.
1917	**Cossacks** revolt against the Bolshevik government in the Ural and Don regions of Russia.
1918	**Romania** signs treaties of peace with Austria and Bulgaria, ending **World War I.**
1958	**John Birch Society** is founded in Boston for the purpose of combatting Communism.
1961	**Tanganyika** gains its independence from Great Britain with **Julius Nyerere** as Prime Minister.
1962	**Tanganyika** changes to a republic, with **Julius Nyerere** as first president.
1966	**Barbados** becomes the 122nd member of the UN.
1974	Greek Parliament is re-established after seven years; **King Constantine** is stripped of his title.

December 10

Holidays

Angola	**M.P.L.A. Foundation Day** Commemorates the founding of the **Popular Movement for the Liberation of Angola.**
Equatorial Guinea	**Human Rights Day**
Thailand	**Thai Constitution Day** Commemorates the promulgation of the first Thai constitution, 1932.
UN Member Nations	**Human Rights Day** Commemorates the adoption of the **Universal Declaration of Human Rights** by the UN, 1948.

Birthdates

1787 **Thomas Hopkins Gallaudet,** U.S. educator; founder of first free school for the deaf, **American Asylum,** 1817; **Gallaudet College** in Washington, D.C., is named in his honor. [d. September 10, 1851]

1804 **Karl Gustav Jacobi,** German mathematician; known for his work in theoretical mathematics, differential equations, and calculus. [d. February 18, 1851]

1805 **William Lloyd Garrison,** U.S. journalist, abolitionist leader; editor of *The Liberator,* the chief abolitionist publication of the pre-Civil War period in America, 1831–65. [d. May 24, 1879]

1813 **Zachariah Chandler,** U.S. government official; U.S. Senator, 1857–63; 1863–69; 1877–79. [d. November 1, 1879]

1822 **César Auguste Franck,** French composer, organist, born in Belgium; regarded as the founder of the modern French instrumental school. [d. November 8, 1890]

1830 **Emily Dickinson,** U.S. poet; known only posthumously for her highly unorthodox, whimsical yet profound poetry; lived a reclusive life. [d. May 15, 1886]

1843 **Queen Elizabeth** of Rumania (Carmen Sylvia), 1881–1914; writer and folk tale collector. [d. March 2, 1916]

1851 **Melvil Dewey,** U.S. librarian; developer of the **Dewey Decimal System,** 1876. [d. December 26, 1931]

1891 **Nelly Leonie Sachs,** German poet, dramatist; Nobel Prize in literature (with S. Y. Agnon), 1966. [d. May 12, 1970]

1891 **Harold Rupert Leofric George Alexander,** 1st Earl Alexander of Tunis, British Army general; in charge of evacuation of British forces from Dunkirk, 1940; Commander in Chief of Allied Forces, Italy, 1944–45. [d. June 16, 1969]

1906 **Walter Henry Zinn,** U.S. physicist, born in Canada; developer of the **breeder reactor,** 1951.

1911 **Chester (*Chet*) Huntley,** U.S. television newscaster, best known for his news program with David Brinkley (July 10), 1956–70. [d. March 20, 1974]

1912 **Philip A. Hart,** U.S. politician, lawyer; U.S. Senator, 1959–76. [d. December 26, 1976]

1934 **Howard Martin Temin,** U.S. molecular biologist; Nobel Prize in physiology or medicine for discoveries in area of tumor viruses (with D. Baltimore and R. Dulbecco), 1975.

Historical Events

1508 **League of Cambrai** is formed between Holy Roman Emperor **Maximilian I, Louis XII** of France, and **Ferdinand of Aragon,** against Venice.

1520 **Martin Luther** burns the papal bull excommunicating him.

U.S.
(Wyoming)

Wyoming Day
Commemorates Wyoming's admission to the Union, 1890.

The Beatified

Blessed Thomas Somers, Benedictine priest and martyr. [d. 1610]

Religious Calendar

The Saints

St. Eulalia of Mérida, virgin and martyr. Most celebrated virgin martyr of Spain. [d. c. 304]

St. Miltiades, pope and martyr. Elected 311. Also called **Melchiades.** [d. 314]

St. Gregory III, pope. Elected 731. [d. 741]

The London Martyrs of 1591 SS. Mennas, Hermogenes, and Eugraphus, martyrs. Mennas also called **Menas.** [death date unknown]

1710 French defeat Austrians at **Villa Viciosa,** leaving **Philip V** as master of Spain (**War of the Spanish Succession**).

1817 **Mississippi** is admitted to the Union as the 20th state.

1848 **Louis Napoleon** is elected President of the French Republic.

Second Sikh War between Great Britain and rebel Indian leaders begins.

1869 **Territory of Wyoming** grants **women's suffrage,** becoming first U.S. possession to do so.

1896 First **intercollegiate basketball game** is played, at New Haven, Connecticut, between Wesleyan University and Yale; Yale wins, 39 to 4.

1898 **Treaty of Paris** between U.S. and Spain settles **Spanish-American War,** with U.S. gaining Cuba, Puerto Rico, Guam, and the Philippines.

1916 Sergei Prokofiev's *The Ugly Duckling* premieres.

1936 **Edward VIII** of Great Britain abdicates in order to marry **Wallis Warfield Simpson,** becoming the first monarch to abdicate voluntarily in British history. He becomes known as the **Duke of Windsor,** and is succeeded on the throne by his brother, **George VI.**

1941 Japanese troops capture **Guam** (**World War II**).

1963 **Zanzibar** becomes an independent member of the Commonwealth of Nations.

December 11

Holidays

UN Member Nations	UNICEF Anniversary Day
Upper Volta	**National Holiday** Commemorates the attainment of independent standing within the French community, 1958.

Birthdates

1475 **Pope Leo X,** pope 1513–21. [d. December 1, 1521]

1803 **(Louis) Hector Berlioz,** French composer; leader in the Romantic movement in French music; known as a pioneer in **modern orchestration.** [d. March 8, 1869]

1810 **(Louis Charles) Alfred de Musset,** French dramatist and poet; intimate of George Sand (July 1); some of his best poetry was composed at end of their liaison. [d. May 2, 1857]

1838 **Emil Rathenau,** German industrialist; founder of Deutsche Edison Gesellschaft, which eventually became Telefunken, a leading German electronics firm. [d. June 20, 1915]

1843 **Robert Koch,** German physician, bacteriologist; Nobel Prize in physiology or medicine for developments in **bacteriology** and discoveries related to **tuberculosis,** 1905. [d. May 27, 1910]

1847 **Michel Joseph Maunoury,** French army commander; commanded the French 6th Army that checked the German offensive on Paris during World War I. [d. March 28, 1923]

1849 **Ellen Karoline Sofia Key,** Swedish sociologist, author, feminist. [d. April 24, 1926]

1856 **Georgi Plekhanov,** Russian political philosopher; proponent of Marxism and chief advocate of development of socialist thought. [d. May 30, 1918]

1863 **Annie Jump Cannon,** U.S. astronomer; developed a spectral classification system by which she eventually cataloged hundreds of thousands of stars; her work published as the *Henry Draper Catalogue,* 1918–24, consisted of 9 volumes, and effected a great evolution in the science of **astronomy.** [d. April 13, 1941]

1882 **Max Born,** British physicist; Nobel Prize in physics for his statistical studies of **wave functions,** 1954. [d. January 5, 1970]

Fiorello H(enry) LaGuardia, U.S. politician; Congressman, 1916–17; 1918–20; 1922–32; Mayor of New York City, 1933–45; noted for his honesty; well-loved by his constituents and the people of the city. [d. September 20, 1947]

1913 **Carlo Ponti,** Italian film producer.

1918 **Alexander Isayevich Solzhenitsyn,** Soviet novelist; Nobel Prize in literature (declined), 1970; deported to the West, 1974. Awarded the Nobel Prize when he arrived in Switzerland, 1974.

Historical Events

1205 **John de Grey** is elected Archbishop of Canterbury but is rejected by **Pope Innocent III.**

1776 U.S. General **George Washington** retreats across the Delaware, escaping capture by the British (**American Revolution**).

1816 **Indiana** is admitted to the Union as the 19th state.

1845 **Sonderbund** is formed in Switzerland by the seven Catholic cantons to support education by the Jesuits and to protect their interests against the Liberal cantons.

1901 First **transatlantic radio signal** is transmitted by **Guglielmo Marconi** from Cornwall to St. John's, Newfoundland.

1917 **Lithuania** proclaims its independence from Russia.

1930 **Bank of the United States** in New York, with more than 400,000 depositors, fails, another indication of the **Great Depression** in the U.S.

1941 Germany and Italy declare war on U.S. (**World War II**).

Religious Calendar

The Saints

St. Damasus, pope. Elected 366. Also called **Damascus I.** [d. 384] Optional Memorial.

St. Daniel the Stylite, priest. Best known of the disciples of St. Simeon the Stylite. [d. 493]

St. Barsabas, abbot and martyr. Also called **Barsabias.** [death date unknown]

SS. Fuscian, Victoricus, and Gentian, martyrs. [death date unknown]

Blessed Peter of Siena, Franciscan tertiary. [d. 1289]

Blessed Franco of Grotti, Carmelite lay brother. [d. 1291]

Blessed Hugolino Magalotti, Franciscan tertiary. [d. 1373]

Blessed Jerome Ranuzzi, Servite priest. [d. 1455]

1946 United Nations International Children's Emergency Fund (**UNICEF**) is established by the United Nations General Assembly.

1973 **Czechoslovakia** and **West Germany** sign a treaty establishing diplomatic relations and voiding the 1938 Munich pact.

December 12

Holidays

Kenya	**Independence Day** Commemorates the achievement of independence from Great Britain, 1963.
Mexico	**Our Lady of Guadalupe** Commemorates the appearance of the Blessed Virgin to a young Indian, 1531.

Birthdates

1520   **Pope Sixtus V,** pope 1585–90. [d. August 27, 1590]

1731   **Erasmus Darwin,** English physician, poet, and speculative thinker; grandfather of Charles Darwin (February 12). [d. April 18, 1802]

1745   **John Jay,** American public official, jurist; President of Continental Congress, 1778; first Chief Justice of the U.S. Supreme Court, 1789–94. [d. May 17, 1829]

1786   **William Learned Marcy,** U.S. politician; first to articulate the concept of the spoils system; Governor of New York, 1833–39; U.S. Secretary of War, 1844–50; U.S. Secretary of State, 1853–57. [d. July 4, 1857]

1803   **James Challis,** British astronomer; one of first to observe the planet **Neptune.** [d. December 3, 1882]

1805   **Henry William Dwight Wells,** U.S. transportation executive; with his partner, William George Fargo (May 20), formed the Wells, Fargo & Co., 1852, express and commercial transportation company. [d. December 10, 1878]

1821   **Gustave Flaubert,** French novelist; author of *Madame Bovary*, a classic of French literature. [d. May 8, 1880]

1838   **Sherburne Wesley Burnham,** U.S. astronomer; noted for his discovery and cataloging of double stars. [d. March 11, 1921]

1849   **William Kissam Vanderbilt,** U.S. financier; with his brother Cornelius, managed the assets and investments of the Vanderbilt empire, 1878–1903. [d. July 12, 1920]

1864   **Arthur Brisbane,** U.S. journalist; noted for his exploitation of the media and use of **yellow journalism** to build his fortune. [d. December 25, 1936]

Paul Elmer More, U.S. philosopher, editor, critic; founder, with Irving Babbitt (August 2), of the **neo-humanist** movement in the U.S. [d. March 4, 1937]

1866   **George Swinnerton Parker,** U.S. games manufacturer; founder of Parker Brothers, manufacturers of **Monopoly.** [d. September 26, 1952]

Alfred Werner, Swiss chemist; Nobel Prize in chemistry for studies of molecular structure, 1913. [d. November 15, 1919]

1872   **Albert Payson Terhune,** U.S. novelist; known for his novels about collies, including *Lad, a Dog*. [d. February 18, 1942]

1875   **Karl Rudolf von Rundstedt,** German Army field marshal; Chief of General Staff, World War I; Commander in Chief on Western Front, 1942–45. [d. February 24, 1953]

1881   **Harry Warner,** U.S. motion picture executive; co-founder of Warner Brothers movie empire with his brothers Jack (August 2) and Albert (July 23). [d. July 25, 1958]

1893   **Edward G. Robinson (Emanuel Goldenburg),** U.S. actor, born in Hungary; noted for gangster roles during 1930s. [d. January 26, 1973]

1915   **Frank (Francis Albert) Sinatra,** U.S. singer, actor.

1917   **Dan Dailey,** U.S. actor. [d. October 17, 1978]

1918   **Eugene Burdick,** U.S. novelist, political theorist. [d. July 26, 1965]

1924   **Edward Irving Koch,** U.S. politician, lawyer; U.S. Congressman, 1969–76; Mayor of New York City, 1977– .

1928   **Helen Frankenthaler,** U.S. painter.

1929   **John James Osborne,** British playwright, screenwriter.

Religious Calendar

The Saints

SS. Epimachus and Alexander and other Martyrs. [d. 250]

St. Finnian of Clonard, bishop. Also called **Finan,** or **Finian.** [d. c. 549]

St. Edburga, Abbess of Minster and virgin. Also called **Eadburge,** or **Eadburh.** [d. 751]

St. Vicelin, Bishop of Staargard, evangelizer of the Wends. [d. 1154]

St. Jane Frances de Chantal, widow and co-founder of the Order of the Visitation. Feast formerly August 21. [d. 1641] Optional Memorial.

The Beatified

Blessed Thomas Holland, Jesuit priest and martyr. [d. 1642]

Historical Events

1417　**Sir John Oldcastle, Lord Cobham,** leader of the Lollards, is burned and hanged. He is later portrayed as **Falstaff** by Shakespeare.

1787　**Pennsylvania** ratifies the Constitution and becomes the second state in the Union.

1911　The capital of British India is changed from Calcutta to **Delhi.**

1936　**Chiang Kai-shek,** Chinese leader, declares war on Japan.

1963　**Kenya** gains independence from Great Britain.

1966　**Francis Chichester,** British yachtsman, completes a solo voyage from England to Sydney, Australia, a distance of more than 14,000 miles, in 107 days.

1972　**Orange soil** is discovered by *Apollo 17* astronauts Eugene A. Cernan and Harrison H. Schmitt during their second day of exploration on the lunar surface.

December 13

Holidays

Japan	**Sosuharai** or **Soot Sweeping Day** A time of traditional year-end house cleaning.
Malta	**Repubic Day** Commemorates the establishment of the Republic, 1974.
Sweden	**St. Lucia Day**

Birthdates

1553   **Henry IV,** King of France, 1589–1610; first of the **Bourbon line;** made enemies by giving tolerance to Protestants in the **Edict of Nantes;** assassinated. [d. May 14, 1610]

1720   **Count Carlo Gozzi,** Italian dramatist; author of many fairy plays. [d. April 4, 1806]

1797   **Heinrich Heine (Chaim Harry Heine),** German lyric poet; his lyrics are among the best loved in German music. [d. February 17, 1856]

1804   **Joseph Howe,** Nova Scotian official, editor; Governor of Nova Scotia, 1873. [d. June 1, 1873]

1810   **Clark Mills,** U.S. sculptor; best known for his equestrian statues of George Washington and Andrew Jackson. [d. January 12, 1883]

1816   **(Ernst) Werner von Siemens,** brother of Friedrich Siemens (December 8), German inventor, industrialist; a pioneer in producing telegraphic equipment and the **open-hearth process** used in steel manufacturing. [d. December 6, 1892]

1818   **Mary Todd Lincoln,** U.S. First Lady; wife of Abraham Lincoln, 16th President. [d. July 26, 1882]

1835   **Phillips Brooks,** U.S. Episcopal clergyman, hymn writer; author of *O Little Town of Bethlehem,* 1868. [d. January 23, 1893]

1844   **John Henry Patterson,** U.S. manufacturer; founder of the National Cash Register Co. [d. May 7, 1922]

1856   **Abbott Lawrence Lowell,** U.S. political scientist, educational administrator; President, Harvard University, 1909–33; responsible for establishment of schools of architecture, business administration, education, and public health. [d. January 6, 1943]

1879   **Eleanor Robson Belmont,** U.S. socialite, actress; legendary *grande dame* of New York society; wife of August Belmont (February 18); subject of George Bernard Shaw's play, *Major Barbara.* [d. October 24, 1979]

1887   **Alvin Cullum York,** U.S. soldier; one of most popular and decorated heroes of World War I; the subject of the movie *Sergeant York.* [d. December 2, 1964]

1890   **Marc(us Cook) Connelly,** U.S. dramatist; Pulitzer Prize in drama, 1930. [d. December 21, 1980]

1897   **Drew Pearson,** U.S. columnist; known for his muckraking column, (*Washington Merry-Go-Round*) which exposed and caused the retirement of numerous corrupt public figures. [d. September 1, 1969]

1902   **Talcott Parsons,** U.S. sociologist; Professor of Sociology, Harvard University, 1927–73; first chairman of Department of Social Relations. [d. May 8, 1979]

1905   **Carey McWilliams,** U.S. author, editor; social critic; editor, *The Nation,* 1955–75; author of more than 20 books on U.S. social problems. [d. June 27, 1980]

1910   **Lillian Roth (Lillian Rutstein),** U.S. singer of 1920s and 1930s. [d. May 12, 1980]

1913   **Archie Moore (Archibald Lee Wright),** U.S. boxer; World light-heavyweight champion, 1952–61.

1915   **Ross MacDonald (Kenneth Millar),** U.S. novelist, mystery writer; creator of fictional detective *Lew Archer.* [d. July 11, 1983]

Balthazar Johannes Vorster, South African political leader; noted for his extremist policies; Prime Minister, 1966–78.

Religious Calendar

The Saints

St. Lucy, virgin and martyr. Patron of Syracuse, Sicily. Invoked against eye diseases, dysentery, and hemorrhages. Also called **Lucia.** [d. 304] Obligatory Memorial.

St. Judoc, priest and hermit. Also called **Jodoc,** or **Josse.** [d. 668]

St. Aubert, Bishop of Cambrai and Arras. Also called **Autbertus.** [d. c. 669]

St. Odilia, virgin and abbess; patron of Alsace. Invoked for sore eyes and other ophthalmic troubles. Also called **Odile, Othilia, Othilla,** or **Ottilia.** [d. c. 720]

St. Eustratius and his Companions, martyrs. [death date unknown]

The Beatified

Blessed John Marinoni, priest. [d. 1562]

Blessed Antony Grassi, priest. [d. 1671]

1923 **Philip Warren Anderson,** U.S. physicist; Nobel Prize in physics for developments in **solid state circuitry** and **theories of magnetism and conduction** (with J. H. Van Vleck and N. F. Mott), 1977.

Historical Events

1250 **Frederick II** of Germany dies and is succeeded by **Conrad IV.**

1545 **Council of Trent** is opened, during which Roman Catholics deal with doctrinal issues raised by Protestants.

1577 **Sir Francis Drake** embarks on voyage to circumnavigate the globe.

1642 **New Zealand** is discovered by the Dutch navigator **Abel Jansen Tasman.**

1664 **New Haven General Court** holds last meeting as the **Colony of New Haven** becomes part of **Connecticut.**

1843 **Basutoland,** a native state under British protection, is established.

1862 **Battle of Fredericksburg** ends in defeat of Union troops by Confederate General **Robert E. Lee** (**U.S. Civil War**).

1928 George Gershwin's *American in Paris* premieres in New York.

1937 Chinese city of **Nanking** falls to Japanese after heavy fighting (**World War II**).

1951 **Bogotá Charter** creating **Organization of American States** goes into effect.

1981 Martial law is declared in **Poland** in response to increasing demands for independence by **Solidarity Union.**

December 14

The Saints

St. Spiridion, Bishop of Tremithus. Also called **Spyridon.** [d. 4th century]

St. Nicasius, Bishop of Rheims, and his Companions, martyrs. [d. c. 451]

St. Venantius Fortunatus, Bishop of Poitiers. [d. c. 605]

Birthdates

1546 **Tycho Brahe,** Danish astronomer; with Johannes Kepler (December 27), made numerous significant discoveries which aided in the development of modern scientific **astronomy.** [d. October 24, 1601]

1739 **Pierre Samuel Du Pont de Nemours,** French economist; exponent of Physiocratic school of thought; member of States-General, 1789–92; emigrated to U.S.; developed a national scheme for education, which was never adopted in U.S., but parts of which were incorporated in French national plan. [d. August 6, 1817]

1775 **Thomas Cochrane, 10th Earl of Dundonald,** British admiral noted for his capture of foreign sailing vessels, 1800–06; member of Parliament, 1806–09; expelled from Navy because of political jealousies; led Chilean navy in fight for freedom from Spain; led Brazilian navy in war for independence, 1819–22; one of first to utilize **screw propeller** on warships; pioneered in use of **steamship** in combat; reinstated in English navy, 1832. [d. October 31, 1860]

1829 **John Mercer Langston,** U.S. public official; the first black elected to public office in the U.S., 1855; Minister to Haiti, 1877–85; President, Virginia Normal and Collegiate Institute, 1885–88; U.S. Congressman, 1888–90. [d. November 15, 1897]

1856 **Louis Marshall,** U.S. lawyer, political leader; known for his pioneer work in securing better conditions for blacks and Jews in the U.S.; led fight for international tolerance; founder and president of **American Jewish Committee;** founder and head of **American Jewish Relief Committee.** [d. September 11, 1929]

1870 **Dirk Jan de Geer,** Dutch statesman; Prime Minister, 1926–29, 1939–40. [d. November 28, 1960]

1893 **John Cowles,** U.S. newspaper publisher; founded a newspaper empire based on education of readers, promotion of tolerance, and provision of unbiased information; adviser to U.S. Presidents Eisenhower, Kennedy, and Johnson. [d. February 25, 1983]

1895 **George VI,** King of Great Britain, 1936– 52; acceded upon abdication of his brother, Edward VIII, 1936. [d. February 6, 1952]

Paul Eluard, French poet; a pioneer of **surrealism.** [d. November 18, 1952]

1896 **James Harold Doolittle,** U.S. Army aviator; one of most popular U.S. heroes of World War II; led first bombing raid on Japan, 1942.

1897 **Margaret Chase Smith,** U.S. politician, columnist; U.S. Congresswoman, 1940–49; U.S. Senator, 1948–72; first woman to be elected to both houses of Congress.

1909 **Edward Lawrie Tatum,** U.S. biochemist; Nobel Prize in physiology or medicine for discovery of role of genes in **heredity** (with G. W. Beadle and J. Lederberg), 1958. [d. November 5, 1975]

1914 **Karl Carstens,** West German statesman; President, West Germany (Federal Republic of Germany), 1979–84.

Solomon Spiegelman, U.S. microbiologist; recognized for his extensive research on DNA and RNA. [d. January 21, 1983]

1919 **Shirley Jackson,** U.S. short-story writer, novelist. [d. August 8, 1965]

1922 **Nikolai Gennadievich Basov,** Russian physicist; Nobel Prize in physics for research in **quantum electronics** and contributions to development of **maser-laser principle** (with A. Prokhorov and C. H. Townes), 1964.

1946 **Patty Duke Aston (Anna Marie Duke),** U.S. actress.

St. Hybald, abbot. Also called **Hibald,** or **Higbald.** [d. 7th century]

St. John of the Cross, Doctor of the Church, and co-founder of the Barefooted Carmelite Friars. Feast formerly November 24. [d. 1591] Obligatory Memorial.

The Beatified

Blessed Bartholomew of San Gimignano, priest. Also called **Bartolo.** [d. 1300]

Blessed Conrad of Offida, priest. [d. 1306]

Blessed Bonaventure Buonaccorsi, priest. [d. 1315]

Blessed Nicholas Factor, Friar Minor of the Observance. [d. 1583]

Historical Events

1542   **James V** of Scotland dies and is succeeded by **Arran** who is appointed Regent for 6-day-old **Mary, Queen of Scots.**

1788   **Charles III** of Spain dies and is succeeded by **Charles IV.**

1819   **Alabama** is admitted to Union as the 22nd state.

1911   **Roald Amundsen,** Norwegian explorer becomes first to reach the **South Pole.**

1914   Allies launch a general attack along the entire **Western Front** from Nieuport to Verdun (**World War I**).

1918   **President Sidonia da Silva Paes of Portugal** is assassinated.

Women vote for the first time in Great Britain.

1927   New Iraqi-British treaty is signed, recognizing independence of **Iraq** and promising British support for Iraq's admission to the League of Nations in 1932.

1946   UN General Assembly votes to accept a gift of $8.5 million from **John D. Rockefeller, Jr.,** to acquire a site on the East River in New York for the **UN Headquarters.**

1951   **San Salvador Charter** creating **Organization of Central American States** becomes effective.

1960   Western European nations and the U.S. and Canada sign agreement for the creation of an **Organization for Economic Cooperation and Development.**

1961   **Tanganyika** is admitted to the UN as the 104th member.

1962   U.S. space probe *Mariner II,* on its 109th day of flight, transmits information about **Venus.**

1967   **King Constantine II** of Greece flees to Italy after an abortive attempt to overthrow the military junta in power since earlier that year.

Stanford University biochemists report they have produced a synthetic version of **DNA,** the master chemical of all life.

December 15

Holidays

Netherlands Antilles	**Statute Day** Commemorates the achievement of autonomy, 1954.
U.S.	**Bill of Rights Day** Commemorates the passage of the Bill of Rights, 1791.

Birthdates

1787   **Charles Cowden Clarke,** English critic, bookseller, and lecturer; intimate of Keats, Shelley, Leigh Hunt, and Charles and Mary Lamb; lectured on Shakespeare, 1834–56. [d. March 13, 1877]

1793   **Henry Charles Carey,** U.S. economist; renowned for progressive economic theories that won him recognition in the U.S. and Europe. [d. October 13, 1879]

1802   **János Bolyai,** Romanian mathematician; pioneer in development of **non-Euclidean geometries.** [d. January 27, 1860]

1832   **Alexandre Gustave Eiffel,** French engineer; known chiefly for construction of the **Eiffel Tower,** Paris; also constructed framework of Bartholdi's **Statue of Liberty.** [d. December 27, 1923]

1848   **Edwin Howland Blashfield,** U.S. painter; decorated the central dome of the Library of Congress, Washington, D.C. [d. October 12, 1936]

1852   **Antoine Henri Becquerel,** French physicist; Nobel Prize in physics for discovery of **spontaneous radioactivity** (with M. and P. Curie), 1903. [d. August 25, 1908]

1859   **Ludwik Lazanz Zamenhof,** Polish linguist; developer of **Esperanto,** an artificial language, 1887. [d. April 14, 1917]

1860   **Niels R. Finsen,** Danish physician; Nobel Prize in physiology or medicine for his development of **phototherapy,** the treatment of diseases by light, 1903. [d. September 24, 1904]

1863   **Arthur D(ehon) Little,** U.S. industrial chemist; patented **rayon,** the first successful cellulose fiber. [d. August 1, 1935]

1877   **John Timothy McNichols,** U.S. Roman Catholic archbishop; founder of **National Legion of Decency,** a group established to boycott immoral or obscene films; Archbishop of Cincinnati, 1925–50. [d. April 22, 1950]

1888   **Maxwell Anderson,** U.S. dramatist; famous for verse plays and his drama, *What Price Glory?*, Pulitzer Prize in drama, 1933. [d. February 28, 1959]

1892   **J(ean) Paul Getty,** U.S. oilman; one of the richest men in the world; left a fortune estimated at over $1 billion. [d. June 6, 1976]

1906   **Betty Smith,** U.S. novelist, playwright; author of *A Tree Grows in Brooklyn*, 1948. [d. January 17, 1972]

1913   **Muriel Rukeyser,** U.S. poet; known for her poetry protesting social injustice and reflecting on political and economic issues. [d. February 12, 1980]

1916   **Maurice Hugh Frederick Wilkins,** British physicist; Nobel Prize in physiology or medicine for research into **molecular structure of DNA** (with J. D. Watson and F. H. C. Crick), 1962.

1922   **Alan Freed,** disk jockey; first to introduce the term **rock-'n'-roll** to the American public. [d. January 20, 1965]

Historical Events

1791   **Bill of Rights,** the first ten amendments to U.S. Constitution, are passed.

1794   **Revolutionary Tribunal** is abolished in France (**French Revolution**).

1821   U.S. government representatives negotiate the purchase of a strip of land on the West African coast for the establishment of a colony of freed slaves, naming it **Monrovia.**

1914   **Battle of Łódź** ends with Russians falling back toward Warsaw (**World War I**).

1917   **Moldavian Republic** declares its independence from Russia.

1941   *U.S.S. Swordfish* becomes first U.S. submarine to sink a Japanese ship in **World War II.**

Religious Calendar

St. Niō, virgin. [d. 4th century]

St. Valerian and other Martyrs in Africa. [d. 457 and 482]

St. Offa of Essex, king. [d. c. 709]

St. Stephen, Bishop of Surosh. [d. c. 760]

St. Paul of Latros, hermit. [d. 956]

St. Mary di Rosa, virgin, and founder of the Handmaids of Charity of Brescia. Also called **Paula,** or **Pauline.** [d. 1855]

The Beatified

Blessed Mary Margaret d'Youville, founder of the Grey Nuns of Canada. [d. 1771]

1951   **British Foreign Exchange Market** opens for first time since the end of World War II.

1961   **Adolf Eichmann** is convicted by an Israeli court in Jerusalem of war crimes committed during World War II.

1964   **Canada** adopts a national flag with a red maple leaf on a white background with vertical red bars at each end.

1965   U.S. spacecraft **Gemini 6** is launched and effects a rendezvous with **Gemini 7.**

1970   **Venera 7,** Soviet unmanned spacecraft, lands on **Venus.**

1973   **J. Paul Getty III,** grandson of U.S. oil magnate J. Paul Getty, is found in southern Italy more than five months after his disappearance, following payment of a reported $2.8 million ransom.

December 16

Holidays

Bahrain	**National Day of Bahrain**
Bangladesh	**Victory Day**
	Commemorates the end of conflict with Pakistan, 1971.
Namibia	**Day of the Covenant**
Nepal	**Constitution Day**
	Commemorates the adoption of Nepal's Constitution, 1962.
South Africa	**Day of the Vow**

Birthdates

1485   **Catherine of Aragon,** 1st wife of **King Henry VIII** of England and mother of **Queen Mary** of England. [d. January 7, 1536]

1742   **Gebhard Liberecht Blücher von Wahlstatt,** Prussian field marshal; known for his role in aiding Wellington in defeat of Napoleon at **Waterloo.** [d. September 12, 1819]

1770   **Ludwig van Beethoven,** German composer; known as one of the foremost musical geniuses of all time. [d. March 26, 1827]

1775   **Jane Austen,** English novelist; noted for her novels of the manners of provincial English men and women, such as *Pride and Prejudice.* [d. July 18, 1817]

1776   **Johann Wilhelm Ritter,** German physicist; discoverer of ultraviolet rays; conducted numerous experiments in electricity that led to various discoveries, as electroplating. [d. 1810]

1790   **Leopold I,** first King of the Belgians; elected king by a national congress in 1831. [d. December 10, 1865]

1792   **Abbott Lawrence,** U.S. manufacturer, government official; U.S. Congressman, 1835–40; U.S. Minister to Great Britain, 1849–52; town of Lawrence, Massachusetts is named for him. [d. August 18, 1855]

1857   **Edward Emerson Barnard,** U.S. astronomer; famed for his photographic surveys of the **Milky Way.** [d. February 6, 1923]

1859   **Francis Thompson,** British poet; known for his poetry on religious themes, especially *The Hound of Heaven.* [d. November 13, 1907]

1863   **George Santayana,** U.S. philosopher, poet, novelist, born in Spain; significant contributions to aesthetics, speculative philosophy, and literary criticism. Wrote *The Life of Reason, Scepticism and Animal Faith,* and other philosophical works. [d. September 26, 1952]

  Ralph Adams Cram, U.S. architect; noted for his design of Gothic structures, including the **Cathedral of St. John the Divine,** New York City; Professor of Architecture, Massachusetts Institute of Technology, 1914–21; Chairman of Boston City Planning Board, 1915–22. [d. September 22, 1942]

1882   **Zoltán Kodály,** Hungarian composer, teacher; noted for his collections of classic Hungarian folk tales. [d. March 6, 1967]

1888   **Alexander I,** King of the Serbs, Croats, and Slovenes, 1921–29, and of Yugoslavia, 1929–34; struggled to unite his ethnically divided country. [d. October 9, 1934]

1899   **Sir Noel (Pierce) Coward,** British playwright, actor, composer, and director. [d. March 26, 1963]

1901   **Margaret Mead,** U.S. anthropologist; especially well known for studies of cultural, sexual, and adolescent development in primitive areas and in the U.S. [d. November 15, 1978]

1912   **Robert M(artin) Fouss,** U.S. editor, advertising executive; Editor, *Saturday Evening Post,* 1942–62. [d. January 27, 1980]

1913   **Buddy Parker,** U.S. football coach. [d. March 22, 1982]

1917   **Arthur Charles Clarke,** British author; best known for his science fiction works, including *2001: A Space Odyssey.*

1939   **Liv Ullmann,** Norwegian actress.

1950   **Ieremia Tabai,** President, Republic of Kiribati, 1979– .

Religious Calendar

The Saints

St. Adelaide, widow. Also called **Alice.** [d. 999]

The Beatified

Blessed Ado, first archbishop of Vienne. [d. 875]
Blessed Sebastian of Brescia, preacher. [d. 1496]
Blessed Mary of Turin, virgin, prioress, and mystic. [d. 1717]

Historical Events

1653   In England, the **Protectorate** is established with **Oliver Cromwell** as Lord Protector.

1773   A group of American patriots dressed as Indians dumps British tea overboard in Boston Harbor, protesting taxes levied by the British government; the event is referred to as the **Boston Tea Party.**

1815   **Brazil** becomes seat of the empire under **John, Prince Regent of Portugal.**

1835   Great fire in **New York City** destroys $20 million worth of property and levels 674 buildings.

1838   Boers under **Andries Pretorius** defeat the Zulus under Dingaan at **Blood River, Natal.**

1856   **South African Republic (Transvaal)** is established with Pretoria as its capital.

1864   **Battle of Nashville** ends as Confederate army commanded by General John B. Hood is almost destroyed by Union troops under General George Thomas (**U.S. Civil War**).

1944   **Battle of the Bulge**, the major German offensive in the Ardennes, begins (**World War II**).

1962   **Nepal** promulgates its constitution.

1963   **Zanzibar** and **Kenya** are admitted as the 112th and 113th members of the UN.

1968   Spanish government declares void a 1492 decree expelling Jews from Spain.

1971   **Bangladesh** comes into existence, being formed from the old state of **Bengal.**

December 17

Holidays

Bhutan	**National Day**
U.S.	**Wright Brothers Day** Commemorates the first flight of the Wright Brothers at Kitty Hawk, North Carolina, 1903.
Venezuela	**Bolívar Day** Commemorates the death of Simon Bolívar, 1830.

Birthdates

1758   **Nathaniel Macon,** U.S. legislator; U.S. Congressman, 1791–1815; U.S. Senator, 1815–19. [d. June 29, 1837]

1778   **Sir Humphrey Davy,** English chemist; first to isolate **potassium, sodium, calcium;** discovered that chlorine is an element; discovered that a diamond is carbon; identified role of hydrogen in acids; developed miners' safety lamp known as the **Davy lamp.** [d. May 29, 1829]

1787   **Jan Evangelista Purkinje,** Czech physiologist; renowned for basic discoveries in physiology and microscopic anatomy; named for him are the **Purkinje cells** in the brain and **Purkinje tissue** in the heart. [d. July 18, 1869]

1797   **Joseph Henry,** U.S. physicist; pioneer in development of **electromagnetism;** did extensive research in coil behavior; developed early versions of the telegraph and the electric motor; first secretary and director of the Smithsonian Institution, 1846; developed method of tracking and recording weather which led to establishment of **U.S. Weather Bureau.** [d. May 13, 1878]

1807   **John Greenleaf Whittier,** U.S. poet, social reformer. [d. September 7, 1892]

1853   **Sir Herbert (Draper) Beerbohm Tree,** British actor, producer, playwright; noted for his Shakespearean roles; half-brother of Sir Max Beerbohm (August 24). [d. July 2, 1917]

1860   **James Herbert McGraw,** U.S. publisher; a founder of McGraw-Hill Publishing Co., 1916. [d. February 21, 1948]

1861   **Arthur Edwin Kennelly,** U.S. electrical engineer, born in India; assistant to Thomas A. Edison, 1887–94; discovered, in conjunction with Oliver Heaviside, the **Kennelly-Heaviside Layer** in the upper atmosphere. [d. June 18, 1939]

1873   **Ford Madox Ford (Ford Madox Heuffer),** British novelist, editor, critic. [d. July 26, 1939]

1874   **William Lyon Mackenzie King,** Canadian statesman; Prime Minister, 1921–26; 1926–30; 1935–48. [d. July 22, 1950]

1894   **Arthur Fiedler,** U.S. conductor; conducted the **Boston Pops Orchestra,** 1930–79. [d. July 10, 1979]

1903   **Erskine (Breston) Caldwell,** U.S. novelist; known especially for his novels of the rural South, including *God's Little Acre,* 1933.

1906   **William McChesney Martin, Jr.,** U.S. financier; President of New York Stock Exchange, 1938–41; Chairman of Federal Reserve Board, 1951–70.

1908   **Willard Frank Libby,** U.S. chemist; Nobel Prize in chemistry for development of a technique of radioactive carbon dating that determines geological age by measuring **carbon 14** in organic objects, 1960. [d. September 8, 1980]

1938   **Peter Snell,** New Zealand distance runner; Olympic gold medalist, 1960, 1964.

Historical Events

1819   **Republic of Colombia** is established with **Simon Bolívar** as president.

1903   **Wright Brothers** at **Kitty Hawk, North Carolina** make first successful flight of self-powered heavier-than-air craft, lasting 12 seconds.

1917   The confiscation of the property of the Russian church and abolition of religious instruction in schools is announced by the Bolshevik government.

Religious Calendar

The Saints

St. Lazarus, Bishop at Kition. Raised from the dead by Jesus. [d. 1st century]

St. Olympias, widow. [d. c. 408]

St. Begga, widow and abbess; patroness of the Béguines of Belgium. [d. 693]

St. Sturmi, abbot and apostle of the Saxons. First German known to have become a Benedictine monk. Also called **Sturm.** [d. 779]

St. Wivina, virgin and abbess. [d. c. 1170]

1933 First **National Football League** championship game is played at Wrigley Field, Chicago, between the New York Giants and the Chicago Bears; the Bears win 23–21.

1962 **Monaco** promulgates restoration of the National Council and a new constitution.

1973 Arab guerrillas kill 31 persons at Rome airport and hijack a West German airliner to Athens where they demand the release of Palestinian terrorists being held there.

1978 **Rwanda** promulgates a new constitution.

1983 A car bomb explodes outside **Harrods** department store in London, killing 5 and injuring 91. The **Irish Republican Army (IRA)** later acknowledged responsibility.

December 18

Holidays

Niger

National Day
Celebrates the establishment of the constitutional government and achievement of independence from France, 1960.

Birthdates

1709   **Elizabeth,** Empress of Russia, 1741–61; daughter of **Peter the Great.** [d. January 5, 1762]

1819   **Isaac Thomas Hecker,** U.S. Roman Catholic priest; founder of Congregation of the Missionary Priests of St. Paul the Apostle (**Paulist Fathers**). [d. December 22, 1888]

1856   **Sir Joseph John Thomson,** British physicist; Nobel Prize in physics for investigations into **conductivity of gases,** 1906. [d. August 30, 1940]

1861   **Edward Alexander MacDowell,** U.S. composer, pianist, teacher; the **Edward MacDowell Medal** is presented annually to recognize individual contributions in the arts. [d. January 3, 1908]

1863   **Francis Ferdinand,** Archduke of Austria; heir to the Austrian throne whose assassination was the immediate cause of **World War I.** [d. July 28, 1914]

1870   **H(ector) H(ugh) Munro (Saki),** British short-story writer, journalist, born in Burma. [d. November 14, 1916]

1879   **Paul Klee,** Swiss painter, etcher; Surrealist artist known for his works showing strong African influence. [d. June 29, 1940]

1886   **Ty(rus Raymond) Cobb,** U.S. baseball player; inducted into Baseball Hall of Fame, 1936. [d. July 17, 1961]

       Chu Teh, Chinese military leader; commander in chief of Chinese Communist Army; led his army to victory over Nationalist Chinese forces, 1949. [d. July 6, 1976]

1888   **Robert Moses,** U.S. public official; known as the master builder of New York City. [d. July 29, 1981]

1890   **Edwin Howard Armstrong,** U.S. engineer, inventor; invented the **regenerative circuit,** which revolutionized the field of radio; developed system of frequency modulation (FM) radio transmission; also responsible for development of **multiplex-**ing system that allowed more than one FM transmission on the same frequency. [d. February 1, 1954]

1904   **George Stevens,** U.S. film director. [d. March 8, 1975]

1907   **Christopher Fry,** British dramatist.

1912   **Benjamin Oliver Davis, Jr.,** U.S. Air Force general; first black graduate of West Point, 1936; first black general in the Air Force.

1913   **Betty Grable,** U.S. actress. [d. July 2, 1973]

       Willy Brandt (Karl Herbert Frahn), German politician; Chancellor of Federal Republic of Germany, 1969–74; Nobel Peace Prize, 1971.

1927   **(William) Ramsey Clark,** U.S. lawyer, government official; U.S. Attorney General, 1967–69.

Historical Events

1398   **Timur Lenk (Tamerlane),** ruler of Mongols, conquers **Delhi.**

1437   **Albert V** of Austria becomes King of Hungary.

1787   **New Jersey** becomes the third state to ratify the U.S. Constitution.

1865   **13th Amendment** to U.S. Constitution, prohibiting slavery, is ratified.

1914   British declare a protectorate over **Egypt** and begin to provide for its defense (**World War I**).

1916   **Battle of Verdun,** a German offensive and the longest battle of **World War I,** ends with little gain for the Germans and combined casualties of about 750,000.

1933   The government of **Newfoundland** collapses; Great Britain establishes a commission to govern.

1940   **Hitler** orders full military preparations for German invasion of Russia (**World War II**).

1964   Organization of American States Council approves the **Act of Washington,** estab-

The Saints

SS. Rufus and Zosimus, martyrs. Zosimus also called **Zozimus.** [d. c. 107]

St. Gatian, Bishop of Tours. [d. c. 301]

St. Flannan, first bishop of Killaloe. [d. c. 7th century]

St. Samthann, nun. [d. 739]

St. Winebald, abbot. Also called **Wynbald.** [d. 761]

St. Mawnan. Also called **Maunanus.** [death date unknown]

lishing procedures for admission of new members.

1965   **Japan** and **South Korea** establish formal diplomatic relations.

1968   *Intelsat 3A,* first in a series of communications satellites, is launched from Cape Kennedy, Florida.

1969   **Capital punishment** is abolished in the **United Kingdom.**

     Kuwait and **Saudi Arabia** sign an agreement formally establishing new international boundaries.

December 19

Religious Calendar

The Saints

SS. Nemesius and other Martyrs. [d. 250]

St. Anastasius I, pope. Elected 399. [d. 401]

Birthdates

1683 **Philip V,** King of Spain, 1700–1746; first of the **Spanish Bourbon dynasty.** [d. July 9, 1746]

1790 **Sir William Edward Parry,** British naval officer; famous for his discovery of an entrance to the **Northwest Passage** in the Arctic as well as for development of **polar survival techniques.** [d. July 8, 1855]

1814 **Edwin McMasters Stanton,** U.S. statesman; U.S. Secretary of War, 1862–68. [d. December 24, 1869]

1820 **Mary Ashton Livermore,** U.S. social reformer; noted for her ardent advocacy of suffrage for women and temperance; editor of *The Agitator*, a suffragist paper, 1869–72; editor of *Woman's Journal*, 1872–82. [d. May 23, 1905]

1849 **Henry Clay Frick,** U.S. industrialist; Chairman, Carnegie Steel Co., 1889–1900; leader in negotiations that resulted in formation of United States Steel Corporation; his art collection and home donated to New York City as the **Frick Museum.** [d. December 2, 1919]

1852 **Albert Abraham Michelson,** U.S. physicist; received first U.S. Nobel Prize in physics for development of **spectroscopic and meteorological measuring equpment,** 1907. [d. May 9, 1931]

1865 **Minnie Madern Fiske,** U.S. actress; noted for her brilliant performances on the New York stage; managed the Manhattan Theater, 1901–07. [d. February 15, 1932]

1875 **Carter Godwin Woodson,** U.S. educator, historian, publisher; known as the *Father of Negro History in the U.S.* [d. April 3, 1950]

1888 **Fritz Reiner,** U.S. conductor, born in Hungary; conductor of Metropolitan Opera, 1948–53; noted for his interpretations of Wagner and Strauss. [d. November 15, 1963]

1894 **Ford Frick,** U.S. baseball executive; professional baseball commissioner, 1951–65. [d. April 8, 1978]

1901 **Oliver Lafarge,** U.S. novelist, anthropologist; Pulitzer Prize in fiction, 1930. [d. August 2, 1963]

1902 **Sir Ralph David Richardson,** British actor; noted for his Shakespearean roles; his career spanned over 50 years in the theater, as well as in films. [d. October 10, 1983]

1906 **Leonid I. Brezhnev,** Soviet leader; Chairman of Presidium of Supreme Soviet of U.S.S.R., 1960–64, 1977–82. [d. November 12, 1982]

1910 **Jean Genet,** French dramatist, essayist, existentialist; a founder of the **theater of the absurd.**

1915 **Edith Piaf (Edith Giovanna Gassion),** French singer; renowned as a song stylist. [d. October 11, 1963]

1920 **David (Howard) Susskind,** U.S. producer, television host.

1929 **Howard Sackler,** U.S. playwright; Pulitzer Prize in drama, 1969.

1939 **Cicely Tyson,** U.S. actress; co-founder of the **Dance Theatre of Harlem.**

1944 **Richard E(rskine) F. Leakey,** British paleontologist, born in Nairobi, Kenya; with his parents, Louis S. B. Leakey (August 7) and Mary Leakey (February 6), made significant discoveries regarding the origins of man; Director of National Museum of Kenya.

Historical Events

1777 American Continental Army establishes camp at **Valley Forge,** Pennsylvania.

1915 **Sir Douglas Haig** replaces **Sir John French** as supreme commander of the British Army in France (**World War I**).

1946 Vietnamese independence forces in **Hanoi** attack the French garrison, beginning an eight-year war for independence from France which ends with defeat of the French in 1954.

The Beatified

Blessed William of Fenoli, Carthusian lay brother. [d. 1205]

Blessed Urban V, pope. Elected c. 1361. [d. 1370]

1961 New transatlantic submarine cable between Britain and Canada (first link in a proposed around-the-world Commonwealth system) is inaugurated by a telephone conversation between Queen Elizabeth II and Prime Minister Diefenbaker of Canada.

1962 **Nyasaland** secedes from the **Central African Federation.**

1975 **John Paul Stevens** is named to the U.S. Supreme Court, taking the seat of retired justice **William O. Douglas.**

December 20

Birthdates

1743 **James Rumsey,** U.S. inventor; ran first steamboat on the Potomac. [d. December 20, 1792]

1805 **Thomas Graham,** Scottish chemist; discovered **dialysis process;** known for his research in **colloids.** [d. September 16, 1869]

1813 **Samuel Jordan Kirkwood,** U.S. politician; U.S. Senator, 1866–67; 1877–81; U.S. Secretary of the Interior, 1881–82. [d. September 1, 1894]

1841 **Ferdinand Edouard Buisson,** French educator; Nobel Peace Prize for his work with the **League of Human Rights** and efforts for Franco-German friendship after World War I (with Ludwig Quidde), 1927. [d. February 16, 1932]

1849 **Harry Pratt Judson,** U.S. educator; President of Chicago University, 1907–23. [d. March 4, 1927]

1851 **Theodore Elijah Burton,** U.S. lawyer, legislator; U.S. Senator, 1909–15. [d. October 28, 1929]

1853 **Husayn Kamil,** Sultan of Egypt, 1914–17. [d. October 9, 1917]

1856 **Baron Shibasaburo Kitazato,** Japanese bacteriologist; responsible for isolation of bacilli for **tetanus, anthrax, dysentery,** and **bubonic plague.** [d. June 13, 1931]

1865 **Maude Gonne,** Irish patriot; impassioned advocate of Irish freedom; subject of various literary works by William Butler Yeats (June 13). [d. April 27, 1953]

1868 **Harvey Samuel Firestone,** U.S. tire manufacturer; founder of Firestone Tire & Rubber Co., 1900. [d. February 7, 1938]

1871 **Henry Kimball Hadley,** U.S. orchestral composer, conductor; Conductor, San Francisco Orchestra, 1911–15; Conductor, Manhattan Symphony, 1929–37. [d. September 6, 1937]

1876 **Walter Sidney Adams,** U.S. astronomer, born in Turkey; ascertained velocities and distances of thousands of stars by spectroscopic analysis; contributed to planning of **Mt. Palomar Observatory** in California. [d. May 11, 1956]

1881 **Branch (Wesley) Rickey,** U.S. baseball executive. [d. December 9, 1965]

1890 **Jaroslav Heyrovsky,** Czech chemist; Nobel Prize in chemistry for discovery and development of **polarography,** 1959. [d. March 27, 1967]

1893 **Richard Paul Carlton,** U.S. manufacturer; President, Minnesota Mining and Manufacturing Co. 1949–53. [d. June 17, 1953]

1894 **Robert Gordon Menzies,** Prime Minister of Australia, 1939–41; responsible for industrial growth of Australia after World War II.

1899 **John J. Sparkman,** U.S. politician, lawyer; U.S. Congressman, 1937–46; U.S. Senator, 1946–79.

Finn Ronne, U.S. arctic explorer, engineer; member of nine expeditions to Antarctica; member of Admiral Richard Byrd's expedition, 1933. Author of several books dealing with his explorations. [d. January 2, 1980]

1902 **Max Lerner,** U.S. journalist.

1904 **Irene Dunne,** U.S. actress.

1914 **Harry (Flood) Byrd,** U.S. politician; U.S. Senator, 1965–81.

Historical Events

1046 Holy Roman Emperor **Henry III** deposes both antipope **Silvester II** and **Pope Gregory VI.**

1803 U.S. takes formal possession of the **Louisiana Territory.**

1848 **Prince Louis Napoleon (Napoleon III)** takes oath as President of the French Republic.

1852 **Pegu (Lower Burma)** is annexed to the Indian Empire.

1860 **South Carolina** secedes from the Union (**U.S. Civil War**).

1914 **First Battle of Champagne** opens with a French attack on the Western Front between Verdun and Reims (**World War I**).

St. Philogonius, Bishop of Antioch. [d. 324]

St. Ursicinus, abbot. Also called **Ursinus.** [d. c. 625]

St. Dominic of Silos, abbot. [d. 1073]

1917   **Lenin** creates the **Revolutionary Tribunal (Cheka)** for suppression of counter-revolutionary activity, marking the beginning of the **red terror.**

1928   **Nanking** government of China is recognized by the British.

1968   U.S. government lifts its ban on cultural exchanges with the U.S.S.R.

1973   **Spanish Premier Carrero** is assassinated in Madrid.

1979   **Kim Jae Kyu,** former head of the Korean Central Intelligence Agency, and five of his aides are sentenced to death for the assassination of President **Park Chung Hee** and five of his bodyguards.

1981   **Romauld Spasowski,** the Polish Ambassador to the U.S., is granted political asylum in the U.S.

December 21

Holidays

São Tomé and Príncipe	Anniversary of the Coming into Power of the Transition Government
U.S.	Forefathers' Day

Religious Calendar

The Saints

St. Thomas, apostles of the Indies and martyr patron of architects, builders, and divines. Sur-

Birthdates

1401   **Masaccio (Tommaso Guidi),** Italian painter; his works mark the beginning of Renaissance painting in Italy. [d. 1428]

1795   **Leopold von Ranke,** German historian; founder of the modern school of history, utilizing writings based on fact and source material rather than tradition and legend. [d. May 23, 1886]

1804   **Benjamin Disraeli,** Earl of Beaconsfield, British statesman; Prime Minister of England, 1868; 1874–80; responsible for British involvement in **Suez Canal;** one of founders of modern **conservatism** in Great Britain. [d. April 19, 1881]

1823   **Jean Henri Fabre,** French entomologist; noted for his direct observation and study of insects; author of 10-volume *Souvenirs Entomologiques,* 1879–1907. [d. October 11, 1915]

1842   **Prince Pëtr Kropotkin,** Russian geographer, social philosopher, revolutionist; active in extreme branch of International Workingmen's Association, 1872; escaped to England after arrest by Russian authorities, 1876; lived in England, 1886–1914; again in Russia, 1917–21. [d. February 8, 1921]

1860   **Henrietta Szold,** U.S. Zionist leader; founder of **Hadassah,** U.S. Women's Zionist organization. [d. February 13, 1945]

1879   **Joseph Stalin (Josif Vissarionovich Dzhugashvili),** Russian political leader; after death of Lenin, established himself as virtual dictator, 1929–53; responsible for establishment of Russia as a world power. [d. March 5, 1953]

1890   **Herman Joseph Muller,** U.S. biologist; Nobel Prize in physiology or medicine for discovering use of **x-rays in genetics,** 1946. [d. April 5, 1967]

1891   **John W. McCormack,** U.S. politician, lawyer; U.S. Congressman, 1928–71.

1892   **Walter Hagen,** U.S. golfer; P.G.A. champion, 1921; 1924–27; British Open Champion, 1922, 1924, 1928–29. [d. October 5, 1969]

1909   **George Ball,** U.S. lawyer, diplomat; UN Ambassador, 1968–69.

1917   **Heinrich Böll,** U.S. German novelist, short-story writer; Nobel Prize in literature, 1972.

1921   **Alicia Alonso,** Cuban prima ballerina.

1935   **Edward Richard Schreyer,** Canadian politician; Governor-general of Canada, 1979– ; youngest person to hold that position.

1937   **Jane Fonda,** U.S. actress, social activist; daughter of Henry Fonda (May 16).

1954   **Chris Evert Lloyd,** U.S. tennis player.

Historical Events

1192   **Richard I** of England, having returned from Palestine on the **Third Crusade,** is captured by **Leopold,** Duke of Austria.

1864   **General William Sherman** and his Union Army take Savannah, Georgia, concluding Sherman's famous **March to the Sea (U.S. Civil War).**

1902   First **wireless telegraph** message is exchanged between Canada and England.

1913   The first **crossword puzzle** is printed in a New York newspaper.

1914   First air raid on **England** by German planes occurs near **Dover (World War I).**

1923   **Nepal** gains independence from Great Britain.

named **Didymus,** or **the Twin.** [d. 1st century] Celebrated by Episcopal and Lutheran churches on this date. Roman Catholic Church celebrates this Memorial on July 3.

St. Anastasius II, Patriarch of Antioch and martyr. [d. 609]

St. Peter Canisius, Jesuit priest, writer, educator, and Doctor of the Church; second Apostle of Germany. Feast formerly April 27. [d. 1597] Optional Memorial.

Dirigible **Dixmude,** largest airship in the world, disappears over Tunis.

1943 U.S. General **Joe Stilwell** begins campaign against the Japanese in northern Burma (**World War II**).

1951 119 miners are killed in a **coal mine explosion** near West Frankfort, Illinois.

1958 **Charles De Gaulle** is named President of the Fifth French Republic.

1968 **Apollo 8,** first manned flight around the moon, with astronauts Frank Borman, William A. Anders, and James A. Lovell Jr. aboard, is launched from Cape Kennedy.

1973 First peace conference between Israel and Arab countries is opened in Geneva.

1975 **Madagascar** promulgates a constitution.

1976 Liberian-registered tanker **Argo Merchant** spills 7.5 million gallons of crude oil into the North Atlantic.

December 22

Holidays

Japan	Toji or Winter Solstice
	Marks the beginning of the solar new year.
U.S.S.R.	Electric Power Workers' Day

Birthdates

1400 **Luca della Robbia,** Italian sculptor; creator of **della Robbia** reliefs. [d. September 22, 1482]

1639 **Jean Racine,** French dramatist; known for his classical drama; intimate of La Fontaine (July 8) and Molière (January 15). [d. April 21, 1699]

1696 **James Edward Oglethorpe,** English colonist of America; founder of colony of **Georgia.** [d. July 1, 1785]

1755 **Georges Couthon,** French revolutionist; associate of Robespierre (May 6); guillotined with him. [d. July 28, 1794]

1768 **John Crome (*Old Crome*),** English landscape painter; founder of **Norwich school of painting.** [d. April 22, 1821]

1807 **Johan Sebastian Welhaven,** Norwegian poet, critic; champion of conservatism in literature. [d. October 21, 1873]

1823 **Thomas Wentworth Storrow Higginson,** U.S. writer; advocate of woman's suffrage; a confidant of Emily Dickinson. [d. May 9, 1911]

1842 **Joseph Bernard Bloomingdale,** U.S. merchant; a founder of Bloomingdale's department store, 1872. [d. November 21, 1904]

1857 **Frank Billings Kellogg,** U.S. politician, diplomat, lawyer; author of the **Kellogg-Briand Pact**; U.S. Senator, 1917–23; U.S. Ambassador to Great Britain; U.S. Secretary of State, 1925–29; Nobel Peace Prize, 1929. [d. December 21, 1937]

1858 **Giacomo Puccini,** Italian opera composer. [d. November 19, 1924]

1869 **Edward Arlington Robinson,** U.S. poet; Pulitzer Prize in poetry, 1925, 1928. [d. April 6, 1935]

1883 **Arthur W. Mitchell,** U.S. politician; U.S. Congressman, 1934–42; first black Democrat elected to Congress. [d. May 1968]

1901 **André Kostelanetz,** U.S. conductor, born in Russia. [d. January 14, 1980]

1903 **Haldan Keffer Hartline,** U.S. physiologist; Nobel Prize in physiology or medicine for discoveries in physiology of the eye (with G. Wald and R. A. Granit), 1967.

1905 **Kenneth Rexroth,** U.S. poet, historian, critic; elder statesman of the American **beat generation.** [d. June 6, 1982]

1912 **Claudia Alta (*Ladybird*) Johnson,** U.S. First Lady; wife of Lyndon B. Johnson, 36th President of the U.S.

1921 **Clifton Canter Garvin, Jr.,** U.S. oil executive; Chairman of the Board and Chief Executive Officer, Exxon Corporation, 1975– .

Historical Events

640 **Saracens** conquer **Alexandria, Egypt.**

1807 **Thomas Jefferson,** U.S. President, gets Congress to pass **Embargo Act,** to force France and Britain to withdraw restrictions on American trade.

1894 **U.S. Golf Association** is founded.

1917 Peace negotiations begin at **Brest-Litovsk** between Germany and Russia (**World War I**).

1928 **Mahatma Gandhi** regains leadership at the **All-Parties Conference** in Calcutta and calls for mass **civil disobedience** if dominion status is not given India in one year.

1929 **Russia** and **China** reach agreement, ending prolonged dispute over conflicting claims to the **Chinese Eastern Railway.**

1930 **Oslo Agreement,** concerning tariffs between Scandinavian countries, the Netherlands, Belgium, and Luxembourg is signed.

1941 Japanese capture **Wake Island** (**World War II**).

1950 *U.S.S. Meredith Victory* evacuates 14,000 refugees from Hungnam, Korea, establishing world's passenger carrying record.

1968 83-man crew of the *U.S.S. Pueblo*, captured in the Sea of Japan on January 23, are released by North Korea.

Religious Calendar

The Saints

SS. Chaeremon, Ischyrion and other Martyrs.
[d. 250]

The Beatified

Blessed Jutta of Diessenberg, virgin and recluse.
[d. 1136]

Blessed Adam of Loccum, priest. [d. c. 1210]

1969   Bernadette Devlin, Irish activist, is found
        guilty of inciting to riot and riotous behav-
        ior during Catholic-Protestant clashes in
        Londonderry in August.

December 23

Religious Calendar

The Ten Martyrs of Crete. [d. 250]
St. Servulus, paralytic beggar. [d. c. 590]
St. Dagobert II of Austrasia, king. [d. 679]
St. Frithebert, Bishop of Hexham. [d. 766]

Birthdates

1597   **Martin Opitz von Boberfeld,** German poet, literary theorist; founder of the first **Silesian school of poets.** [d. August 20, 1639]

1732   **Sir Richard Arkwright,** English textile manufacturer; inventor of a spinning machine called the **water frame.** [d. August 3, 1792]

1777   **Alexander I,** Emperor of Russia, 1801–25; founded the coalition that defeated Napoleon I. [d. December 1, 1825]

1783   **Giovanni Berchet,** Italian romantic poet; author of *Lettera Semiseria,* the manifesto of the Italian Romantic movement. [d. December 23, 1851]

1790   **Jean François Champollion,** French archaeologist; founded the Egyptian museum at the Louvre; from study of trilingual **Rosetta Stone,** established principles for deciphering Egyptian hieroglyphics. [d. March 4, 1832]

1805   **Joseph Smith,** U.S. religious leader; founder of the **Church of Jesus Christ of Latter-Day Saints** or **Mormon Church.** [d. June 27, 1844]

1815   **Henry Highland Garnet,** U.S. clergyman, orator, and political activist; leader in abolition movement among blacks; called upon slaves to rise up and kill their masters; U.S. Minister to Liberia, 1881–82. [d. 1882]

1854   **Victoriano Huerta,** Mexican revolutionary politician; responsible for the rise to power of **Porfirio Diaz** and for the overthrow of Francisco Madero's government, 1913; provisional president of Mexico, 1913–14. [d. January 13, 1916]

1856   **James Buchanan Duke,** U.S. industrialist, philanthropist; founder of American Tobacco Company; major benefactor of **Duke University.** [d. October 10, 1925]

1918   **Helmut Schmidt,** German political leader; Chancellor of West Germany, 1974–82.

1926   **Robert Bly,** U.S. poet; gained political prominence by helping found the **American Writers Against the Vietnam War.**

1935   **Paul Hornung,** U.S. football player, broadcaster.

1947   **Bill Rodgers,** U.S. distance runner; winner of Boston Marathon, 1975; 1978–79.

Historical Events

1861   **Moldavia** and **Wallachia** are united as the principality of **Romania** under **Alexander Cuza.**

1893   *Hansel und Gretel,* by Humperdinck premieres in Weimar, Germany.

1910   **Padlock Bill** is passed in Spain, prohibiting the establishment of any new religious houses without the consent of the government in an attempt to curb the power of the Roman Catholic Church.

1914   The Russians are forced to end their siege of **Cracow** (**World War I**).

1919   **Government of India Act** introduces the **Montagu-Chelmsford reforms** and establishes a system of government called "dyarchy."

1938   Spanish insurgents begin great drive in **Catalonia** (**Spanish Civil War**).

        Boogie-woogie music is first performed in a public demonstration at Carnegie Hall, in a historical review, *From Spiritual to Swing.*

1941   **Wake Island** is captured by the Japanese (**World War II**).

1950   **Pope Pius XII** confirms that the **tomb of St. Peter** has been discovered beneath St. Peter's Basilica in Rome.

1961   All foreign-owned land in **Egypt** is nationalized.

1972   Massive **earthquake** devastates the city of **Managua, Nicaragua.**

1975   **Richard S. Welch,** station chief of the U.S. Central Intelligence Agency, is shot and killed outside his suburban Athens residence.

St. Thorlac, Bishop of Skalholt. [d. 1193]

St. John of Kanti, priest and scholar. Also called **John Cantius.** Feast formerly October 20. [d. 1473] Optional Memorial.

SS. Victoria and Anatolia, virgins and martyrs. [death date unknown]

The Beatified

Blessed Hartman, Bishop of Brixen. [d. 1164]

Blessed Margaret of Savoy, widow. [d. 1464]

December 24

Religious Calendar

The Vigil of the Nativity of Jesus Christ.

The Saints

St. Gregory of Spoleto, priest and martyr. [d. c. 304]

St. Delphinus, Bishop of Bordeaux. [d. 403]

Birthdates

1167 **John (Lackland),** King of England, 1199–1216; forced by the English barons to sign the **Magna Carta**; brother of **Richard I.** [d. October 19, 1216]

1737 **Silas Deane,** American diplomat, lawyer, merchant. [d. September 23, 1789]

1745 **Benjamin Rush,** American physician, educator; first surgeon general of American Army, 1777; established first **free dispensary** in America, 1786; Treasurer of the U.S., 1797–1813; author of *Medical Inquiries and Observations upon the Diseases of the Mind*, the first systematic study of the subject in America. [d. April 19, 1813]

1754 **George Crabbe,** English poet. [d. February 3, 1832]

1798 **Adam (Bernard) Mickiewicz,** Polish poet, playwright, and scholar; author of epic *Pan Tadeusz*; first professor of Slavic literature, Collège de France, 1840–44. [d. November 26, 1855]

1809 **Kit Carson,** U.S. frontiersman, soldier, Indian agent; best known as Indian scout in Mexican War. [d. May 23, 1868]

1818 **James Prescott Joule,** English physicist; discoverer (with William Thomson, Baron Kelvin) of the **Joule-Thomson effect** of expanding gases. [d. October 11, 1889]

1822 **Matthew Arnold,** British poet, critic. [d. April 15, 1888]

Charles Hermite, French mathematician; first to solve equations to fifth degree. [d. January 14, 1901]

1845 **George I,** King of Greece. [d. March 18, 1913]

1881 **Juan Ramón Jiménez,** Spanish lyric poet; Nobel Prize in literature, 1956. [d. May 29, 1958]

Charles Wakefield Cadman, U.S. composer; best known for his studies of **North American Indian songs.** [d. December 30, 1946]

1893 **Harry Warren,** U.S. composer; composed the popular songs: *Lullaby of Broadway* and *You'll Never Know.* [d. September 22, 1981]

1894 **Georges M. Guynemer,** French aviator; the outstanding air ace of France in World War I. [d. September 11, 1917]

1895 **Maurice (Richard) Robinson,** U.S. publisher, editor; founder of Scholastic Magazine, Inc. publishers of magazines for young people. [d. February 7, 1982]

1905 **Howard (Robard) Hughes, Jr.,** U.S. industrialist; was one of the world's richest men and became an eccentric recluse. [d. April 5, 1976]

1907 **I(sidor) F(einstein) Stone,** U.S. journalist.

John Patrick, Cardinal Cody, U.S. Roman Catholic Archbishop of Chicago. [d. April 25, 1982]

1922 **Ava Gardner (Lucy Johnson),** U.S. actress.

1930 **Robert Joffrey,** U.S. dancer, choreographer, ballet director; founder of the **Joffrey Ballet,** 1956.

Historical Events

1046 **Clement II** is elected pope at the **Synod of Rome.**

1800 **Bank of France** is founded by Napoleon, aided by **Count Mollien.**

1814 **Treaty of Ghent** is signed between the U.S. and Great Britain, ending the **War of 1812.**

1851 Two-thirds of the collection of the **Library of Congress** and a portion of the Capitol are destroyed by fire.

1859 First **iron-clad ship** is launched at Toulon, France.

1865 **Ku Klux Klan** is first formed in Pulaski, Tennessee.

1941 British Prime Minister Winston Churchill and U.S. President Franklin Roosevelt meet

SS. Tharsilla and Emiliana, virgins. [d. c. 550]

St. Mochua of Timahoe, monk. [d. c. 657]

SS. Irmina, virgin, and **Adela,** widow. [d. c. 710 and c. 734]

The Beatified

Blessed Paula Cerioli, widow and founder of the Institute of the Holy Family of Bergamo. [d. 1865]

in Washington to discuss fundamental war strategy (**World War II**).

1943 U.S. Air Force makes first major raid on German secret weapon targets near the **Pas de Calais (World War II).**

1951 Gian Carlo Menotti's opera *Amahl and the Night Visitors* premieres on NBC television; it is the first opera written for television.

Libya declares its independence and proclaims a constitutional and hereditary monarchy under **King Idris I.**

1974 **Pope Paul VI** inaugurates Holy Year 1975.

Holidays

December 25

Christmas Day
Celebrated in all the Christian countries of the world; commemorates the birth of Jesus Christ; the feast was instituted in the mid 4th century.

Angola, São Tomé and Príncipe	Family Day
Congo	Children's Day

Birthdates

1564 **Johannes Buxtorf (the Elder),** German Protestant scholar; an authority on Hebrew and rabbinical literature. [d. September 13, 1629]

1642 **Sir Isaac Newton,** English scientist, mathematician; discovered the law of universal **gravitation;** one of the fathers of modern science. [d. March 20, 1727]

1709 **Julien Offroy de La Mettrie,** French philosopher, physician; espoused materialistic philosophy; believed that the only pleasures are sensual and that the soul ceases to exist after the death of the body. [d. November 11, 1751]

1717 **Pope Pius VI,** pope 1775–99. [d. August 29, 1799]

1721 **William Collins,** English poet; best known for his ode on the death of his friend, James Thomson, *Elegy on Thomson,* 1749. [d. June 12, 1759]

1763 **Claude Chappe,** French engineer; developed the first **semaphore,** 1793. [d. January 23, 1805]

1821 **(Clarissa Harlowe) Clara Barton,** U.S. humanitarian; founder of the **American Red Cross.** [d. April 12, 1912]

1829 **Patrick Sarsfield Gilmore,** U.S. bandmaster, born in Ireland; author, under pseudonym **Louis Lambert;** wrote *When Johnny Comes Marching Home Again.* [d. September 24, 1892]

1851 **Herman Frasch,** U.S. chemical engineer, born in Germany; developed process for mining deep-lying sulfur deposits. [d. May 1, 1914]

1865 **Evangeline Cory Booth,** British social reformer; seventh child of William Booth (April 10), founder of Salvation Army; national commander of Salvation Army in U.S., 1904–34; international leader of Salvation Army, 1934. [d. July 17, 1950]

1870 **Rosa Luxemburg (*Red Rosa*),** German socialist revolutionary; associated with Karl Liebknecht (August 3); a founder of the **Spartacus Union.** [d. 1919]

1876 **Giuseppe de Luca,** Italian operatic baritone. [d. August 26, 1950]

Mohammed Ali Jinnah, Muslim leader; first governor-general of Pakistan, 1947–48. [d. September 11, 1948]

Adolf Windaus, German chemist; Nobel Prize in chemistry for research on **steroids** and **vitamins,** 1928. [d. June 9, 1959]

1886 **(Edward) Kid Ory,** U.S. musician; chief exponent of New Orleans jazz. [d. January 23, 1973]

1887 **Conrad (Nicholson) Hilton,** U.S. hotelier; founder of Hilton Hotels Corporation, 1946. [d. January 3, 1979]

1888 **David Lawrence,** U.S. journalist; editor of *U.S. News & World Report,* 1948–73. [d. February 11, 1973]

1889 **Lila Acheson Wallace,** U.S. publisher; with her husband, Dewitt Wallace (November 12), founded *Readers' Digest,* 1921. [d. May 8, 1984]

1892 **Dame Rebecca West (Cicily Isabel Fairfield),** British novelist, critic; noted for her writing on Yugoslavia, as well as her reports on the Nuremberg trials. [d. March 16, 1983]

1893 **Robert Leroy Ripley,** U.S. cartoonist; best known for his syndicated feature *Believe It*

| Pakistan | Birthday of Quaid-es-Azam |
| Taiwan (Republic of China) | **Constitution Day** Commemorates the adoption of the constitution, 1946. |

Religious Calendar

Solemnities

The Birthday of Our Lord Jesus Christ, commonly called **Christmas Day.**

Many Martyrs of Nicomedia. [d. 303]

St. Anastasia, martyr. [d. c. 304]

St. Alburga, founder of Wilton nunnery. [d. c. 810]

St. Eugenia, virgin and martyr. [death date unknown]

The Beatified

Blessed Jacopone of Todi, Franciscan lay brother. [d. 1306]

---

or Not, which described curiosities. [d. May 27, 1949]

1899 **Humphrey Bogart,** U.S. actor, known for his romantic tough guy image; won 1951 Academy Award for role in *The African Queen.* [d. January 14, 1957]

1904 **Gladys Swarthout,** U.S. mezzo-soprano; primarily known for her interpretation of **Carmen.** [d. July 7, 1969]

Gerhard Herzberg, Canadian chemist; Nobel Prize in chemistry for work in determining the electronic structure and geometry of molecules, 1971.

1907 **Cab(ell) Calloway,** U.S. musician.

1914 **Oscar Lewis,** U.S. anthropologist; author of *The Children of Sanchez,* 1961. [d. December 16, 1971]

1918 **Anwar Sadat,** Egyptian leader; known for his peace efforts with Israel; assassinated. [d. October 6, 1981]

1931 **Carlos Castaneda,** U.S. anthropologist, born in Brazil; best known for his writings about his apprenticeship to a Yaqui Indian sorcerer.

Historical Events

503 **Clovis,** King of the Franks, is baptized a Christian.

800 **Charlemagne** is crowned Holy Roman Emperor by **Pope Leo III** at Rome.

1066 **William I (the Conqueror)** is crowned King of England.

1100 **Baldwin I** is crowned King of Jerusalem at Bethlehem.

1130 **Roger II** is crowned King of Sicily.

1194 **Henry VI,** Holy Roman Emperor, is crowned King of Sicily.

1196 **Frederick II** is elected King of Germany.

1492 Columbus's flagship, the **Santa Maria,** is wrecked on northern coast of Hispaniola.

1497 **Vasco da Gama** sights the entrance to Durban harbor in South Africa and names the country **Terra Natalis (Natal).**

1776 **George Washington,** American general, crosses the Delaware River, staging a surprise attack on the British and Hessian troops in Trenton, New Jersey (**American Revolution**).

1926 **Hirohito** becomes emperor of Japan on the death of his father, **Yoshihito.**

1950 **Stone of Scone,** symbol of the union of the English and Scottish thrones, is stolen from Westminster Abbey in London.

1961 **Pope John XXIII** issues a papal bull convening the Roman Catholic Church's 21st ecumenical council, to be held in 1962.

1974 **Darwin, Australia,** is devastated by a **cyclone.**

December 26

Holidays

Great Britain and the United Kingdom	**Boxing Day** Traditionally the first weekday after Christmas, but generally on this day. A day when gifts (boxes) are given to servants or others who perform services.
Andorra, Austria, Ireland, Italy, Liechtenstein, San Marino, Switzerland	**St. Stephen's Day** Commemorates the feast of St. Stephen, first martyr of the Christian Church.

Birthdates

1194 **Frederick II,** Holy Roman Emperor, 1220–50; pursued many policies opposing papal authority. [d. December 13, 1250]

1542 **Iyeyasu Tokugawa,** Japanese feudal lord, general; founder of the **Tokugawa** shogunate, which lasted 1603–1867; made numerous attempts to open Japan to commercial trade with the West. [d. 1616]

1716 **Thomas Gray,** English poet; best known for his melancholy lyrics; wrote *Elegy Written in a Country Churchyard*, 1751. [d. July 30, 1771]

1738 **Thomas Nelson,** American merchant; member of Continental Congress, 1775–77; signer of the Declaration of Independence; Governor of Virginia, 1781. [d. January 4, 1789]

1769 **Ernest Moritz Arndt,** German poet, historian; his writings led to abolition of **serfdom** in Sweden; led opposition to Napoleonic movements in Germany. [d. January 29, 1860]

1792 **Charles Babbage,** English mathematician, inventor; a pioneer in development of calculating machines which ultimately resulted in the creation of the computer; also developed the **ophthalmoscope,** the **speedometer,** and the **skeleton key.** [d. October 18, 1871]

1820 **Dion Boucicault (Dionysius Lardner Boursiquot),** U.S. actor, playwright, born in Ireland; a leading figure in New York and London theater, 1853–69. [d. September 18, 1890]

1825 **Ernst Felix Hoppe-Seyler,** German biochemist, physiologist; noted for his articulation of **biochemistry** as a separate science. [d. August 10, 1895]

1837 **George Dewey,** U.S. naval officer; hero of the **Spanish-American War**; responsible for the destruction of the Spanish fleet in **Manila Bay,** Philippines. [d. January 16, 1917]

1859 **Robert Hawley Ingersoll,** U.S. manufacturer; with his brother, C. H. Ingersoll, founded the Ingersoll Watch Co., manufacturers of the **one dollar Ingersoll watch.** [d. September 4, 1928]

1872 **Sir Norman Thomas Angell (Ralph Norman Angell Lane),** British economist, author; Nobel Peace Prize, 1933. [d. October 7, 1967]

1878 **Isaiah Bowman,** U.S. geographer; President, Johns Hopkins University, 1935–49. [d. January 6, 1950]

1891 **Henry (Valentine) Miller,** U.S. author; because of the explicit sexual nature of his novels (*Tropic of Cancer, Tropic of Capricorn,*) his work was banned in the U.S. until the 1960s; a 1964 Supreme Court ruling allowed publication of his novels in the U.S. [d. June 6, 1980]

1893 **Mao Tse-tung,** Chinese communist leader; Chairman of the Chinese Communist Party, 1949–76; Chairman of the People's

Namibia	Family Day
South Africa	Day of Good Will
Vatican City	Christmas Holiday

Religious Calendar

Feasts

St. Stephen, the first martyr and one of the first seven deacons; patron of smelters and stonecutters. Also called Proto-Martyr of the Church. [d. c. 34]

The Saints

St. Dionysius, pope. Elected 259. [d. 269]

St. Zosimus, pope. Elected 417. [d. 418]

St. Tathai, founder of the Monastery of Llantathan. Also called **Atheus, Tathan,** or **Tathar.** [d. 5th–6th century]

St. Archelaus, Bishop of Kashkar. [death date unknown]

The Beatified

Blessed Vincentia Lopez y Vicuña, virgin and founder of the Daughters of Mary Immaculate. [d. 1890]

Republic of China, 1949–59. [d. September 9, 1976]

1901 **Georgy Rimsky-Korsakov,** Russian musician; an exponent of quarter-tone music; grandson of Nikolai Rimsky-Korsakov (March 18).

1905 **William Loeb,** U.S. publisher; known for his conservative position and brutal attacks on liberal Democrats; editor of *The Manchester Union Leader.* [d. September 13, 1981]

1907 **Albert Arnold Gore,** U.S. coal industry executive, politician; U.S. Congressman, 1939–53; U.S. Senator, 1953–70.

1914 **Richard Widmark,** U.S. actor.

1920 **Emmet John Hughes,** U.S. journalist, author; chief foreign correspondent, Time-Life Corporation, 1957–60. [d. September 20, 1982]

1921 **Steve Allen,** U.S. humorist, composer; the originator of the *Tonight Show,* 1950.

1937 **Gnassingbe Eyadema,** President, Republic of Togo, 1967– .

Historical Events

1776 **Washington** and his Continental troops defeat Hessian mercenaries at the **Battle of Trenton (American Revolution).**

1836 First settlers arrive at British colony of **South Australia.**

1900 *Ollanta,* by José Maria Valle-Riestra, the first truly national Peruvian opera, premieres in Lima.

1917 American pilots of the **Lafayette Escadrille** transfer from the French to the American service (**World War I**).

1941 **Manila** is declared an open city (**World War II**).

1950 UN forces in Korea are unified under the command of Lieutenant General **Matthew B. Ridgway.**

1973 *Soyuz 13,* Soviet-manned spacecraft, ends an eight-day flight orbiting the earth.

December 27

Birthdates

1571   **Johannes Kepler,** German astronomer; discovered the three laws of planetary action called **Kepler's Laws**; pioneered in research in optics; contributed to the invention of **calculus.** [d. November 15, 1630]

1654   **Jakob Bernoulli,** Swiss mathematician; developed calculus of variations; the **Bernoulli numbers** are named for him. [d. August 16, 1705]

1741   **Jean Etienne Boré,** U.S. sugar planter; the father of the sugar industry in Louisiana; Mayor of New Orleans, 1803. [d. February 2, 1820]

1769   **Alexander John Forsyth,** Scottish clergyman, inventor; invented the **percussion lock,** an improvement in the explosive mechanism of firearms. [d. June 11, 1843]

1798   **William Wilson Corcoran,** U.S. banker, philanthropist; founded the **Corcoran Art Gallery,** Washington, D.C. [d. February 24, 1888]

1822   **Louis Pasteur,** French chemist; proponent of the **germ theory of disease;** through research discovered the basic principle of **inoculation** as a method of preventing disease. [d. September 28, 1845]

1879   **Sydney Greenstreet,** British actor; known for his performances on stage and in the films; his film career began at age 62. [d. January 18, 1954]

1883   **Cyrus Stephen Eaton,** U.S. industrialist, financier; founder of Republic Steel Corporation, 1930; sponsored the annual **Pugwash Conference** for the international exchange of scholarly, scientific, and business information; supported improved relations with Russia; awarded Lenin Peace Prize, 1960. [d. May 9, 1979]

1896   **Louis Bromfield,** U.S. writer; Pulitzer prize in fiction, 1927. [d. March 18, 1956]

1901   **Marlene Dietrich (Maria Magdalena von Losch),** U.S. actress, born in Germany.

1906   **Oscar Levant,** U.S. concert pianist, comedic actor. [d. August 14, 1972]

1909   **Henryk Jablonski,** Chairman, Council of State, Poland, 1972– .

1915   **William Howell Masters,** U.S. physician, educator; with his wife, Virginia E. Johnson, contributed significant research to the understanding of **human sexual characteristics.**

Historical Events

1882   600th anniversary of the establishment of the **House of Hapsburg** is celebrated throughout Austrian Empire.

1917   Independent **Ukrainian Soviet Socialist Republic** is proclaimed.

Bolshevik government of Russia nationalizes all banks and confiscates all private accounts.

1927   **Jerome Kern's** musical comedy, ***Show Boat,*** with book and lyrics by Oscar Hammerstein II, based on Edna Ferber's novel, opens in New York.

Soviet Communist Congress expels **Leon Trotsky** and his followers from the Communist Party, marking final victory of **Joseph Stalin** in Soviet power struggle.

1932   **Radio City Music Hall** opens in New York City as the world's largest indoor theater with seating for 6,200 people.

1939   Severe **earthquakes** destroy city of **Erzincan, Turkey,** with about 100,000 casualties.

1941   **Rubber rationing** begins in the U.S. with restrictions placed on rubber tires.

1945   **Indonesia** becomes a new and independent state as The Netherlands relinquishes its sovereignty.

1948   **Jozef Cardinal Mindszenty,** Primate of Hungary, is arrested for anti-Communist statements. Later sentenced to death, the

Religious Calendar

Feasts

St. John the Evangelist, apostle; patron of Sweden and theologians. Invoked against poisons and burns and for forming friendships. Also called *the Divine, the Theologian.* [d. c. 100] [major holy day, Episcopal Church; minor festival, Lutheran church]

The Saints

St. Fabiola, matron. [d. 399]

St. Nicarete, virgin. [d. c. 410]

SS. Theodore and Theophanes, monks. Surnamed *Graptoi,* that is, *the written-on.* [d. c. 841 and 845]

sentence is commuted to life imprisonment.

1972 Belgium becomes the first NATO nation to extend full diplomatic recognition to **East Germany.**

1979 **Soviet Union** invades **Afghanistan.** President Hafizullah Amin is denounced and executed; **Babrak Karmal** is installed as president.

December 28

Birthdates

1619   **Abbé Antoine Furetière,** French poet, editor; compiled the *Dictionnaire Universel* over a 40-year period; was forbidden permission by the French government to publish it. [d. May 14, 1688]

1798   **Thomas Henderson,** Scottish astronomer; one of first to measure **stellar parallax** [d. November 23, 1844]

1818   **Carl Remigius Fresenius,** German chemist; known for research and writing in field of **analytical chemistry.** [d. June 11, 1897]

1856   **(Thomas) Woodrow Wilson,** U.S. political scientist, educator; 28th President of the U.S.; responsible for the **Fourteen Points** plan for peace after World War I; Nobel Peace Prize, 1919. [d. February 23, 1924]

1862   **Morris Rosenfeld (Moshe Jacob Alter),** foremost early Yiddish poet. [d. June 22, 1923]

1873   **William Draper Harkins,** U.S. chemist, known for his work on **atomic structure** and **isotopes.** [d. March 7, 1951]

1882   **Sir Arthur Stanley Eddington,** British scientist; with others, verified Einstein's prediction concerning bending of light rays, 1919; known for research on motion of stars and their evolution. [d. November 22, 1944]

1896   **Roger (Huntington) Sessions,** U.S. composer, teacher.

1903   **John von Neumann,** U.S. mathematician, born in Hungary; invented the **von Neumann algebras;** leader in movement to integrate all mathematics; contributed to the development of **atomic bomb** through his work in computer science; the *Father of Game Theory.* [d. February 8, 1957]

1905   **Earl (*Fatha*) Hines,** U.S. jazz musician; a profound influence on American jazz music particularly such jazz stars as Dizzy Gillespie and Sarah Vaughan. [d. April 22, 1983]

1908   **Lew Ayres,** U.S. actor; leading film star of the 1930s.

1911   **Sam(uel) Levenson,** U.S. comedian, author. [d. August 27, 1980]

1917   **Ellis E. I. Clarke,** President, Republic of Trinidad and Tobago, 1976– .

1925   **Hildegarde Neff,** German actress.

        Milton Obote, President, Republic of Uganda, 1980– .

1934   **Maggie Smith,** British actress.

1945   **Birendra Bir Bikram Shah Dev,** King of Nepal, 1972– .

Historical Events

1846   **Iowa** is admitted to the Union as the 29th state.

1885   The first **Indian National Congress** opens at Bombay.

1908   **Earthquake** in **Calabria** and **Sicily** destroys towns on both sides of Straits of Messina.

1937   First radio transmission of a musical score is made between Leipzig and Boston, transmitting last portions of Jean Sibelius' *Origin of Fire.*

1949   **Hungary** nationalizes all major industries.

1950   Chinese troops cross over the 38th parallel in Korea, posing the threat of war between China and the U.S. (**Korean War**)

1973   Comet **Kohoutek** makes its closest approach to the sun.

1974   Severe **earthquake** in northern **Pakistan** kills more than 5,000 persons.

Feasts

The Holy Innocents. Commemorates the suffering of the children of Bethlehem two years old and younger. Also called **Childermas.** [major holy day, Episcopal Church; minor festival, Lutheran Church]

The Saints

St. Theodore the Sanctified, abbot. [d. 368]

St. Antony of Lérins, monk and hermit. [d. c. 520]

December 29

Holidays

Costa Rica   Civic Holiday

Religious Calendar

The Saints
St. Trophimus, first bishop of Arles. [d. c. 3rd cent.]
St. Marcellus Akimetes, abbot. Also called

Birthdates

1721   **Madame de Pompadour (Jeanne Antoinette Poisson),** mistress of **Louis XV** of France; exerted enormous influence over the king and the political affairs of the country; responsible for France's involvement in the Seven Years' War. [d. April 15, 1764]

1766   **Charles Macintosh,** Scottish chemist; inventor of process of bonding rubber to cloth to produce raincoats (**macintoshes**), 1823. [d. July 25, 1843]

1796   **Ferdinand Petrovich, Baron von Wrangel,** Russian explorer; commander of Russian Polar expedition, 1820–24; Governor-General of Russian America (Alaska), 1829–34. **Wrangel Island** in the East Siberian Sea is named for him although he did not discover it. [d. June 6, 1870]

1800   **Charles Goodyear,** U.S. inventor; developed the **vulcanization process** which revolutionized the rubber industry; in spite of his discovery, he died deeply in debt because of infringement of his patent. [d. July 1, 1860]

1808   **Andrew Johnson,** U.S. tailor, politician; military governor of Tennessee, 1862–64; 17th President of the U.S., 1865–69, succeeding Abraham Lincoln after his assassination. [d. July 31, 1875]

1809   **William Ewart Gladstone,** British statesman; Prime Minister, 1868–74; 1880–85; 1886; 1892–94; advocate of Irish Home Rule. [d. May 19, 1898]

1816   **Carl Ludwig,** German physiologist; perfected the **kymograph,** an instrument for measuring blood pressure and circulation. [d. April 23, 1895]

1833   **John James Ingalls,** U.S. politician, lawyer, farmer; U.S. Senator, 1873–91. [d. August 16, 1900]

1859   **Venustiano Carranza,** Mexican revolutionist, political leader; opposed Victoriano Huerta (December 23); proclaimed First Chief of Mexico, 1914; President of Mexico, 1917–20; assassinated. [d. May 21, 1920]

1876   **Pablo Casals,** Spanish cellist, conductor; considered the greatest cellist of the 20th century. [d. October 22, 1973]

1879   **William (Billy) Mitchell,** U.S. Army Air Corps general, aviation pioneer; hero of World War I; court-martialed for criticism of U.S. Navy and War Departments regarding their neglect of air power; later vindicated by events during World War II. [d. February 19, 1936]

1891   **Joyce Clyde Hall,** U.S. manufacturer; founder, President and Chairman of the Board, Hallmark Cards, Inc., 1913–66, largest manufacturer of greeting cards in the world. [d. October 29, 1982]

1900   **Thomas Gardiner Corcoran,** U.S. lawyer; assisted in the drafting of the **Securities Act of 1933,** the **Securities Exchange Act of 1934** and other New Deal legislation. [d. December 6, 1981]

1907   **Robert C. Weaver,** U.S. economist, government official; first black cabinet member in U.S. history as Secretary of Housing and Urban Development, 1966–68; Professor of Urban Affairs, Hunter College, 1970– .

1915   **Robert (Chester) Ruark,** U.S. novelist, journalist. [d. June 30, 1965]

1917   **Thomas Bradley,** U.S. politician, lawyer; mayor of Los Angeles, 1973– .

1925   **Luis Alberto Monge Alvarez,** President, Republic of Costa Rica, 1982– .

1938   **Jon Voight,** U.S. actor.

1939   **Maumoon Abdul Gayoom,** President, Republic of Maldives, 1978– .

Marcellus the Righteous. [d. c. 485]

St. Ebrulf, abbot. Also called **Evroul,** or **Evroult.** [d. 596]

St. Thomas Becket, archbishop of Canterbury, and martyr. Patron of secular clergy, blind men, eunuchs, and sinners. Also called **Thomas à Becket.** [d. 1170] Optional Memorial.

The Beatified

Blessed Peter the Venerable, abbot. [d. 1156]

Historical Events

1170   **Thomas Becket,** Archbishop of Canterbury, is murdered by four Norman knights.

1778   General Clinton and British forces crush Americans and take **Savannah, Georgia (American Revolution).**

1845   **Texas** is admitted to the Union as the 28th state.

1874   The Spanish army proclaims **Alfonso,** son of the deposed Queen Isabella, king.

1890   U.S. authorities, seeking to curb religious rites of the Teton Sioux, massacre Indians at the **Battle of Wounded Knee.**

1911   **Sun Yat-sen** is elected President of the **United Provinces of China** by the revolutionary provisional assembly at Nanking.

1914   **Battle of Sarikamish** opens in the Caucasus between Russia and Turkey (**World War I**).

1937   **Irish Free State** is renamed **Eire.**

1941   Japanese bomb **Corregidor** for the first time (**World War II**).

1944   Russians enter **Budapest, Hungary** (**World War II**).

1954   **Paris Pacts** abolish all economic ties between **Laos** and France.

1975   Bomb explosion at New York's **La Guardia Airport** kills 11 people and injures 75.

1982   U.S. scientists unearth the oldest human bones yet found in North America at Anzick, Montana. The discovery of the skeleton, that of a woman estimated to be more than 12,000 years old, concludes 80 years of searching for ancient human remains.

1983   U.S. announces that it intends to end its membership in the **United Nations Educational Scientific and Cultural Organization (UNESCO)** by the end of 1984.

December 30

Holidays

Costa Rica	Civic Holiday
Madagascar	Anniversary of the Democratic Republic of Madagascar
Philippines	Rizal Day

Commemorates the death of José Mercado Rizal, Philippine nationalist, 1896.

Birthdates

1844 **Charles Albert Coffin,** U.S. manufacturer; founder of General Electric Corporation, 1892. [d. July 14, 1926]

1847 **John Peter Altgeld,** U.S. politician; governor of Illinois, 1892–96; defended industrial strikers against federal intervention. [d. March 12, 1902]

1850 **John Milne,** British geologist; developed the first accurate **seismograph.** [d. July 30, 1913]

1851 **Asa Griggs Candler,** U.S. businessman; founder of Coca-Cola Corporation, 1873; mayor of Atlanta, Georgia, 1917–18. [d. March 12, 1929]

1865 **(Joseph) Rudyard Kipling,** British poet, novelist, born in India; primarily known for his writings about India; Nobel Prize in literature, 1907. [d. January 18, 1936]

1867 **John Simon Guggenheim,** U.S. industrialist, philanthropist; son of Meyer Guggenheim (February 1); established the **Guggenheim Foundation,** 1925. [d. November 2, 1941]

1869 **Stephen Butler Leacock,** Canadian humorist, economist, and political scientist. [d. March 28, 1944]

1872 **William Augustus Larned,** U.S. champion lawn-tennis player; seven-time national singles champion. [d. December 16, 1926]

1873 **Alfred E(mmanuel) Smith,** U.S. politician; governor of New York, 1918–20; 1922–28; first man to serve four terms as governor of New York; twice a candidate for U.S. President. [d. October 4, 1944]

1884 **Hideki (*Eiki*) Tojo,** Japanese leader, military officer; Prime Minister of Japan, 1941–44; responsible for ordering Japanese attack on **Pearl Harbor.** [d. December 23, 1948]

1906 **Sir Carol Reed,** British film director. [d. April 25, 1976]

1928 **Bo Diddley (Elias McDaniel),** U.S. musician; one of early leaders in **rock-'n'-roll** music.

1935 **Albert-Bemard (Omar) Bongo,** President of Gabon, 1967– .

Historical Events

1460 **Queen Margaret** of England defeats and kills **Richard** of York at Wakefield (**War of the Roses**).

1880 Revolt of the **Transvaal Boers** breaks out against the British with the proclamation of a republic by Boer leaders Kruger, Pretorius, and Joubert.

1895 **Dr. Starr Jameson** of the Cape Colony begins his famous **Jameson Raid,** an effort to bring support to rebellious Uitlanders.

1903 Disastrous **Iroquois Theatre fire** in Chicago kills 588 but leads to new and better fire codes in most cities.

1916 **Rasputin** is assassinated in the house of Prince Felix Yussopov in St. Petersburg, Russia.

1917 Foreign intervention in Russia's **Bolshevik revolution** begins with the arrival of Japanese warships at Vladivostok.

1922 **Union of Soviet Socialist Republics** is established by confederation of Russia, Ukraine, White Russia, and Transcaucasia.

1947 **King Michael** of Romania abdicates under Communist pressure.

1971 Anglican-Roman Catholic International Commission announces agreement on essential teachings about the Eucharist.

The Saints

SS. Sabinus and his Companions, martyrs. [d. c. 303]

St. Anysius, Bishop of Thessalonica. [d. c. 410]

St. Peter of Canterbury, first abbot of St. Augustine's. [d. 607]

St. Egwin, Bishop of Worcester. [d. 717]

December 31

New Year's Eve
Traditionally, the vigil celebration ushering out the old year and in the new.

Benin	**Feed Yourself Day**
Japan	**Omisoka** or **Grand Last Day**
Lebanon	**Foreign Troops Evacuation Day**
Scotland	**Hogmanay Day**

Hogmanay Day
Traditional name given to New Year's Eve, celebrated by children who visit from house to house gathering sweets.

Birthdates

1378 **Pope Calixtus III,** pope 1455–58; his heroic crusade to recover Constantinople from the Turks failed. [d. August 6, 1458]

1514 **Andreas Vesalius,** Flemish anatomist. [d. October 15, 1564]

1668 **Hermann Boerhaave,** Dutch physician, philosopher; author of several encyclopedic medical books; responsible for systemizing **physiology.** [d. September 23, 1738]

1712 **Peter Bochler,** U.S. Moravian theologian, born in Prussia; leader of Moravians of Georgia in migration to **Bethlehem, Pennsylvania.** [d. April 27, 1775]

1738 **Charles, 1st Marquis Cornwallis,** British Army general; a primary force in the British presence in the American Revolution; Governor-General of India, 1786; 1805; Viceroy of Ireland, 1798–1801. [d. October 5, 1805]

1803 **José Maria Heredia,** French poet, born in Cuba; leader in French Parnassian movement. [d. May 2, 1939]

1815 **George Gordon Meade,** U.S. soldier; commander of the **Army of the Potomac,** 1863–65; victorious over Confederate forces at the **Battle of Gettysburg.** [d. November 6, 1872]

1830 **Ismail Pasha,** Viceroy of Egypt, 1866–79; his rule led directly to British occupation of Egypt, 1882. [d. March 2, 1895]

1853 **Tasker Howard Bliss,** U.S. soldier, diplomat; first commandant of U.S. Army War College; U.S. Army Chief of Staff, 1915–20. [d. November 9, 1930]

1869 **Henri-Emile Benoit Matisse,** French painter; leader of the Fauvist school. [d. November 3, 1954]

1880 **George Catlett Marshall,** U.S. Army general, statesman; U.S. Army Chief of Staff, 1939–45; U.S. Envoy to China, 1945–47; U.S. Secretary of State, 1947–49; U.S. Secretary of Defense, 1950–51; formulated plan for economic relief of war-ravaged Europe (**Marshall Plan**); Nobel Peace Prize, 1953. [d. October 16, 1959]

1884 **Stanley F(orman) Reed,** U.S. jurist; Associate Justice, U.S. Supreme Court, 1938–57. [d. April 3, 1980]

1894 **Pola Negri (Appolonia Chalupek),** U.S. actress, born in Poland.

1905 **Jule Styne (Julius Kerwin Stein),** U.S. composer, producer.

1930 **Odetta (Felious Gordon),** U.S. folk singer, known for the African motifs in her songs.

1937 **Anthony Hopkins,** Welsh actor.

1946 **Diane (Simone Michelle) von Furstenberg,** U.S. fashion designer, born in Belgium.

Historical Events

1584 In France the Guises and **Philip II** form **League of Joinville** against the Huguenots.

1600 **East India Company (London Company)** is chartered.

1908 **Sergei Prokofiev** makes first professional appearance at age 17 in St. Petersburg, Russia.

Religious Calendar

New Year's Eve [minor festival, Lutheran Church]

The Saints

St. Silvester I, pope. Elected 314. Also called **Sylvester.** [d. 335]

St. Melania the Younger, widow. [d. 439]

St. Columba of Sens, virgin and martyr. [death date unknown]

The Beatified

Blessed Israel, Augustinian precentor. [d. 1014]

1941   **Chester W. Nimitz** assumes command of U.S. Pacific Fleet (World War II).

1946   French troops evacuate **Lebanon.**

1963   Federation of **Rhodesia** and **Nyasaland** is dissolved; the two territories gain independence from Great Britain as the **Republic of Zambia** and **Malawi.**

1968   U.S.S.R. conducts the world's first test of a commercial supersonic jetliner.

1974   **Gold** sales become legal in the U.S. after 40 years of restriction.

Index

of

Names, Terms, and Events

Index

of

Names, Terms, and Events

Adrian, Edgar Douglas, Nov. 30, 1889.
Adrianople, Jul. 22, 1913.
Adrianople, Peace of, Sep. 14, 1829.
Adults' Day (Japan), Jan. 15.
Adundet, Phumiphon, May 5, 1950.
Aduwa, Battle of, Mar. 1, 1896.
Advent, Beginning of, Dec. intro.
Advent, beginning of, p. xii; Nov. intro.
Adzhubei, Aleksei I., Jan. 30, 1962.
aerial bombing of U.S.: only, Sep. 9, 1942.
Aeronautical Society of Great Britain, Jan. 12, 1866.
Afghanistan, Jan. 17, 1929; Sep. 6, 1961; monarchy abolished, Jul. 17, 1973; Apr. 27, 1978; Feb. 14, 1979; invaded by Soviet Union, Dec. 27, 1979; Feb. 22, 1980.
Afghan New Year (Afghanistan), Mar. intro.
Afghan War, First, Nov. 2, 1841.
Afghan War, Second: begins, Nov. 22, 1878.
AFL, Nov. 9, 1935.
Africa, German East (Tanganyika), Jan. 10, 1920.
Africa, North: German and Italian surrender, May 12, 1943.
African Kraal: premieres, Jun. 30, 1903.
African Liberation Day (U.S.S.R.), May 25.
African Unity, Organization of, May 26, 1963; concludes meeting, Jul. 5, 1977.
Afridi uprising, Mar. 11, 1898.
Afro-American (Black) History Month, National, Feb. intro.
Afro-American Unity Organization, Feb. 21, 1965.
Afro-Asian People's Solidarity Conference, Third, Feb. 10, 1963.
Agar, Herbert (Sebastian), Sep. 29, 1897.
Agassiz, Jean Louis Rodolphe, May 28, 1807.
Agattu (Aleutian Islands): seized by Japan, Jun. 14, 1942.
Agee, James, Nov. 27, 1909.
Agincourt, Battle of, Oct. 25, 1415.
Agnadello, Battle of, May 14, 1509.
Agnew, Spiro, Nov. 9, 1918; Jan. 20, 1969; resigns, Oct. 10, 1973; May 2, 1974.
Agnon, Shmuel Yosef Halevi, Jul. 17, 1888.
Agricola, Georgius, Mar. 24, 1494.
Agricultural Adjustment Act, May 12, 1933.
agricultural fair: first in U.S., Oct. 1, 1810.
Agricultural Fair Day (U.S), Oct. 1.
Agriculture Day, Mar. intro.
Agt, Andreas van, Feb. 2, 1931.
Aherne, Brian, May 2, 1902.
Ahidjo, Ahmadou, Aug. 5, 1924.
Aiaru, p. x.
Aiken, Conrad (Potter), Aug. 5, 1889.
Aiken, Howard Hathaway, Mar. 8, 1900.
Ailey, Alvin, Jan. 5, 1931.
Aimee, Anouk, Apr. 27, 1932.
air attack: first U.S. on Germany, Jan. 27, 1943.
aircraft crossing of Atlantic: first, Jun. 15, 1919.
Air Force Academy (U.S.): established, Apr. 1, 1954; dedicated, Jul. 11, 1955.
Air Force Day (Nicaragua), Feb. 1.
Air Force Day (U.S.S.R.), Aug. intro.
air mail service: first established, Nov. 10, 1919.

airplane trip around the world: first, Jul. 1, 1931.
airship passenger service: first, Jun. 22, 1910.
Airy, Sir George Biddell, Jul. 27, 1801.
Aisne, First Battle of, Sep. 15, 1914.
Aisne, Second Battle of, Apr. 16, 1917.
Aisne, Third Battle of, May 27, 1918; May 31, 1918; Jun. 1, 1918.
Aix, France, patron of, Jun. 8.
Aix-la-Chapelle, Peace of, Oct. 18, 1748.
Akbar (Emperor of Hindustan), Oct. 15, 1542.
Akbar the Great (Mogul), Nov. 5, 1556.
Akeley, Carl, May 19, 1864.
Akins, Zoe, Oct. 30, 1886.
Alabama: admitted to Union, Dec. 14, 1819; secedes from Union, Jan. 11, 1861; May 20, 1961.
Alabama, University of, Feb. 6, 1956.
Alais, Peace of, Jun. 28, 1629.
Alam El Halfa, Battle of: begins, Aug. 31, 1942.
Alamo, Mar. 6, 1836.
Alamogordo (New Mexico), Jul. 16, 1945.
Alarcòn, Pedro Antonio de, Mar. 10, 1833.
Alaska: purchased by U.S., Mar. 30, 1867; purchase, May 15, 1867; admitted to Union, Jan. 3, 1959.
Alaska Day (Alaska), Oct. 18.
Alaskan oil pipeline: Jan. 13, 1971; work begins, Mar. 9, 1975; first oil, Jul. 28, 1977.
al-Assad, Hafez (Syria), Mar. 12, 1971.
Albania, Jan. 23, 1916; Jan. 21, 1925; Apr. 7, 1939; Apr. 8, 1939; Sep. 13, 1968.
Albany (New York State), Jan. 6, 1797.
Albee, Edward Franklin, Mar. 12, 1928.
Alberghetti, Anna Maria, May 15, 1936.
Albert: named Prince Consort, Jun. 25, 1857.
Albert, Carl, May 10, 1908.
Albert, Eddie, Feb. 22, 1908.
Albert, Prince (England), Feb. 10, 1840.
Albert I (Belgium), Apr. 8, 1875; dies, Feb. 17, 1934.
Albert II (Germany), Aug. 16, 1397.
Albert V (Austria), Dec. 18, 1437; King of Germany, Mar. 18, 1438.
Alberta (Canada), Sep. 1, 1905.
Alberti, Leon Battista, Feb. 14, 1401.
Albert of Saxe-Coburg-Gotha, Prince, Aug. 26, 1819.
Albert (Sweden), Feb. 24, 1389.
Albertson, Jack, Jun. 16, 1910.
al-Bitar, Salah, Feb. 23, 1966.
Albright, William, Oct. 20, 1944.
Albright, William F., May 24, 1891.
Al-Bukhari, Mohammed Ibn Ismail, Jul. 21.
Albuquerque, Afonso de, Mar. 4, 1510.
Alcala Zamora y Torres, Niceto, Apr. 7, 1936.
Alcock, John W., Nov. 6, 1892; Jun. 15, 1919.
Alcohol Education Month, Nov. intro.
Alcoholics Anonymous: established, Jun. 10, 1935.
Alcott, Amos Bronson, Nov. 29, 1799.
Alcott, Louisa May, Nov. 29, 1832.
Alda, Alan, Jan. 28, 1936.

Aldershot, Feb. 22, 1972.
Aldington, Richard, Jul. 8, 1892.
Aldiss, Brian (Wilson), Aug. 18, 1925.
Aldrich, Thomas Bailey, Nov. 11, 1836.
Aldrin, Edwin Eugene (*Buzz*) Jr., Jan. 20, 1930; Nov. 13, 1966; Jul. 20, 1969.
Aleardi, Aleardo, Nov. 4, 1812.
Alegre, S., Apr. 13, 1913.
Aleichem, Sholem, Feb. 18, 1859.
Aleixandre, Vicente, Apr. 26, 1898.
Aleppo, Jan. 1, 1925.
Aleutians: Japanese carrier attack, Jun. 3, 1942.
Alexander, Harold Rupert Leofric George, Dec. 10, 1891.
Alexander, Sir William, Feb. 4, 1629.
Alexander (King of Greece), Jul. 20, 1893; Jun. 11, 1917; Jul. 2, 1917.
Alexander (Lithuania), Jun. 7, 1492.
Alexander (Russia), Apr. 30, 1815.
Alexander (Serbia), Mar. 6, 1889; massacred, Jun. 10, 1903.
Alexander I (Russia), Dec. 23, 1777; Mar. 23, 1801.
Alexander I (Scotland), Jan. 8, 1107; dies, Apr. 22, 1124.
Alexander I (Yugoslavia), Dec. 16, 1888; Aug. 16, 1921; Jan. 5, 1929; Mar. 22, 1929.
Alexander II (Russia), Apr. 29, 1818; Mar. 2, 1855; Sep. 7, 1856; Jan. 15, 1858; Apr. 3, 1861; Apr. 14, 1879; Feb. 17, 1880; assassinated, Mar. 13, 1881.
Alexander II (Scotland), Aug. 24, 1198; Dec. 4, 1214.
Alexander III (Russia), Mar. 10, 1845; May 27, 1883; dies, Nov. 1, 1894.
Alexander III (Scotland), Sep. 4, 1241; dies, Mar. 19, 1286.
Alexander IV (pope), May 4, 1256.
Alexander V (pope), Jun. 29, 1408.
Alexander VI (pope), May 4, 1493.
Alexander VII (pope), Feb. 13, 1599.
Alexander Cuza, King (Rumania), Feb. 23, 1866.
Alexanderson, Ernst Frederick Werner, Jan. 25, 1878.
Alexandra (Denmark), Mar. 10, 1863.
Alexandri, Vasile, Jul. 21, 1821.
Alexandria (Egypt), Dec. 22, 640.
alexandrite, Jun. intro.
Alexandr Pushkin: Soviet liner, Apr. 26, 1966.
Alexian Brothers, patron saint of the, Jul. 17.
Alexis, (Czarevitch of Russia), Aug. 12, 1904.
Alexius I Comnenus (Byzantine Emperor), Apr. 29, 1091.
Alfieri, Count Vittorio, Jan. 16, 1749.
Alfonso (Aragon), Feb. 26, 14·13.
Alfonso (King of Spain), Dec. 29, 1874.
Alfonso VI (Castile), May 25, 1085.
Alfonso X (Castile), Sep. 14, 1262.
Alfonso X (Germany, Holy Roman Emperor), Nov. 23, 1221.
Alfonso XI of Castile, Oct. 30, 1340.
Alfonso XII (Spain), Nov. 28, 1857; Jun. 25, 1870; Jan. 9, 1875; Jan. 14, 1875; dies, Nov. 25, 1885.
Alfonso XIII (Spain): crowned, Dec. 1, 1887; May 17, 1902; Apr. 13, 1913.

Angola, National Union for the Total Independence of, Apr. 4, 1978.

Angola, Popular Movement for Liberation of, Feb. 11, 1976.

Angora, Mar. 28, 1930.

Angora, Battle of (Ankara), Jul. 20, 1402; Jul. 28, 1402.

Angostura Bridge, Jan. 6, 1967.

Ångström, Anders Jonas, Aug. 13, 1814.

Anguilla, Feb. 16, 1967.

Anka, Paul, Jul. 30, 1941.

Ankara, Mar. 28, 1930.

Ankara, Treaty of, Oct. 30, 1930.

Ankerström, Count, Mar. 16, 1792.

Anna (Empress of Russia), Feb. 7, 1693; Feb. 11, 1730.

Annam: French control established, Jun. 6, 1884.

Anne, Princess (England), Aug. 15, 1950; Nov. 14, 1973.

Anne of Austria, May 14, 1643.

Anne of Cleves, Jan. 6, 1540; Jul. 6, 1540; Jul. 29, 1540.

Anne (Queen of England), Feb. 6, 1665; Mar. 8, 1702; dies, Aug. 1, 1714.

Annie Get Your Gun: premiere, May 16, 1946.

Ann-Margret (Ann Margret Olsson), Apr. 28, 1941.

Annunciation, Mar. intro.

Annunciation of our Lord to the Blessed Virgin Mary, Mar. 25.

Annunzio, Gabriele d', Sep. 12, 1919.

Anouilh, Jean, Jun. 23, 1910.

Ansermet, Ernest Alexandre, Nov. 11, 1883.

Anson, (Adrian) Cap, Apr. 17, 1851.

Anson, George, Apr. 23, 1697.

Antarctica, Mar. 2, 1958; Mar. 4, 1962.

Antarctic Treaty, Dec. 1, 1959.

Anthony, Susan Brownell, Feb. 15, 1820.

Antietam, Battle of, Sep. 17, 1862.

Antigua, Nov. 1, 1964; Feb. 16, 1967; Feb. 27, 1967; independence, Nov. 1, 1981.

Antigua and Barbuda: become a single independent nation, Oct. 31, 1981.

Antioch, Jun. 3, 1098; Jun. 28, 1098.

Anti-Semitic Day (Germany), Apr. 1, 1933.

anti-war demonstration: Wall Street (New York City), May 8, 1970.

Antonescu, Ion (Romania): Jun. 15, 1882; overthrown Aug. 23, 1944.

Antonio, Reynaldo Benito, Jan. 21, 1928.

Antonioni, Michelangelo, Sep. 29, 1912.

Antony and Cleopatra: premiere, Sep. 16, 1966.

Antwerp, Truce of, Apr. 9, 1609.

Antwerp (Belgium): German siege of, Sep. 28, 1914; falls to Germany, Oct. 9, 1914; reoccupied by Belgium, Nov. 19, 1918; Sep. 4, 1944.

Anything Goes: premiere, Nov. 21, 1934.

ANZAC Day (Australia, New Zealand, Samoa, Tonga), Apr. 25.

Anzick (Montana): oldest human bones found at, Dec. 29, 1982.

Apaches, May 17, 1885.

apartheid, Feb. 3, 1960.

apartheid, Feb. 10, 1963.

aperire, Apr. intro.

Apollo, May intro.

Apollo 4, Nov. 9, 1967.

Apollo 7, Oct. 22, 1968.

Apollo 8, Dec. 21, 1968.

Apollo 9, Mar. 3, 1969; Mar. 13, 1969.

Apollo 10, Mar. 18, 1969; May 22, 1969.

Apollo 11, Jul. 16, 1969; Jul. 20, 1969.

Apollo 12, Nov. 14, 1969; Nov. 19, 1969.

Apollo 13: launched, Apr. 11, 1970.

Apollo 14: launched, Jan. 31, 1971.

Apollo 15, Jul. 26, 1971; Jul. 31, 1971; Aug. 2, 1971.

Apollo 16: moon walk, Apr. 21, 1972; Apr. 27, 1972.

Apollo 17, Dec. 12, 1972.

Apollo 18, Jul. 17, 1975; Jul. 24, 1975.

Apollo spacecraft, Jan. 27, 1967.

Appearing of Our Lady at Lourdes, Feast of, Feb. 11.

Appearing of St. Michael the Archangel, Feast of the, May 8.

Apple Month, National, Oct. intro.

Appleton, Sir Edward Victor, Sep. 6, 1892.

Appomattox Court House, Apr. 9, 1865.

April Fools' Day, Apr. 1.

Aprilis, Apr. intro.

Aqaba (Jordan): captured by Arabia, Jul. 6, 1917.

aquamarine, Mar. intro.

Aquarius, Jan. intro.; Feb. intro.

Aquino, Benigno S., Jr.: assassinated, Aug. 21, 1983.

Aquitaine, Jan. 11, 1360.

Arab commandos, Sep. 6, 1970.

Arab countries: first peace conference with Israel, Dec. 21, 1973.

Arab Emirates, United: independence of, Dec. 2, 1971.

Arab Federation of Iraq and Jordan, Feb. 14, 1958.

Arab guerrillas: attack at Rome airport, Dec. 17, 1973.

Arabi Pasha, Jan. 10, 1883.

Arab-Israeli War of 1967, Jun. 5, 1975.

Arab League Day (Arab League Countries), Mar. 22.

Arab nations: policy regarding Israel, Jan. 12, 1965.

Arab oil embargo: begins, Oct. 17, 1973; Oct. 21, 1973.

Arago, François, Feb. 26, 1786.

Aragon, Jan. 19, 1497.

Aragon, Louis, Oct. 3, 1897.

Aragon, patron of, Mar. 26.

Arahsamnu, p. x.

Arana, Diego Barros, Aug. 16, 1830.

Arany, János, Mar. 2, 1817.

Aras, Second Battle of, Sep. 3, 1918.

Arbor Day, Apr. intro.

Arbor Day (Arizona, U.S.), Feb. 6.

Arbor Day (Delaware, Nebraska), Apr. 22.

Arbor Day (Jordan), Jan. 15.

Arbor Day (Korea), Apr. 5.

Arbor Day (Neb., Del., Wyo., Utah), Apr. intro..

Arbor Day (Spain), Mar. 26.

Arbor Day (Taiwan), Mar. 12.

Arbuckle, Fatty, Mar. 24, 1887.

Arcaro, Eddie, Feb. 19, 1916.

Archbasilica of the Most Holy Savior Dedication of the, Feast of, Nov. 9.

archers, patron of, Jan. 20; Jul. 25.

Archipenko, Alexander, May 30, 1887.

architects, patron of, Jul. 2; Dec. 4; Dec. 21.

Ardennes, Jan. 6, 1945.

Ardizzone, Edward (Jeffrey Irving), Oct. 16, 1906.

Ardrey, Robert, Oct. 16, 1908.

A.R.E. National Day (Libya), Jul. 23.

Arendt, Hannah, Oct. 14, 1906.

Aretino, Pietro, Apr. 20, 1492.

Arezzo, patrons of, Jun. 3.

Argentina, May 25, 1810; independence, Jul. 9, 1816; Sep. 4, 1939; Mar. 24, 1976; Jan. 7, 1977; May 4, 1982.

Argo Merchant: oil spill, Dec. 21, 1976.

Argonne, Feb. 20, 1915.

Argonne Forest, Battle of: Sep. 26, 1918; ends, Oct. 10, 1918.

Arianism, Feb. 27, 380.

Arias Navarro, Carlos, Jan. 3, 1974.

Aires, Mar. intro.; Apr. intro.

Ariosto, Ludovico, Sep. 8, 1474.

Aristides: first Kentucky Derby winner, May 17, 1875.

Arizona: purchased from Mexico, Jun. 30, 1854; admitted to Union, Feb. 14, 1912.

Arkansas: admitted to Union, Jun. 15, 1836; secedes, May 6, 1861.

Arkwright, Sir Richard, Dec. 23, 1732.

Arlandes, Marquis d', Nov. 21, 1783.

Arliss, George, Apr. 10, 1868.

Armada, Spanish, May 19, 1588; dispersed, Jul. 28, 1588.

Armed Forces Day (Benin, Rwanda), Oct. 26.

Armed Forces Day (Chile), Sep. 19.

Armed Forces Day (Egypt), Oct. 6.

Armed Forces Day (Equatorial Guinea), Aug. 3.

Armed Forces Day (Honduras), Oct. 21.

Armed Forces Day (Korea), Oct. 1.

Armed Forces Day (Liberia), Feb. 11.

Armed Forces Day (Mauritania), Jul. 10.

Armed Forces Day (United States), May intro.

Armed Forces Day (Zaire), Nov. 17.

Armenia, May 28, 1918.

Armenian Republic, Jan. 26, 1920.

Armenian revolt, Apr. 20, 1915.

Armenians: Turkish persecution, Apr. 8, 1915.

Armenian Soviet Socialist Republic, Apr. 2, 1921.

Armida: premiere, Mar. 25, 1904.

Armilustrium, Oct. intro.

Arminius, Jacob, Oct. 10, 1560.

armistice: signed, ends World War I, Nov. 3, 1918; goes into effect, Nov. 11, 1918.

Armistice Day, Nov. 11.

Armour, Philip Danforth, May 16, 1832.

Armstrong, (Daniel) Louis (*Satchmo*), Jul. 4, 1900.

Armstrong, Edwin H., Dec. 18, 1890; Nov. 6, 1935; Jan. 5, 1940.

Armstrong, Neil A.: first man to set foot on the moon, Aug. 5, 1930; Jul. 20, 1969.

Armstrong-Jones, Anthony, May 6, 1960.

Austrian Succession, War of the, Mar. 15, 1744; ends Oct. 18, 1748.

Austro-Hungarians, May 15, 1916.

autogyro: first, Jan. 10, 1923.

automobile race: first in U.S., Nov. 28, 1895.

Autry, (Orvon) Gene, Sep. 29, 1907.

autumnal equinox, Sep. intro.

Avery, Ostwald T., Oct. 21, 1877.

Avignon, patron of, Apr. 14.

Avignon, patron of, Jul. 2.

Avignonese papacy, Jan. 17, 1377.

Avogadro, Count Amedeo, Jun. 9, 1776.

Awadallah, Abubakr, May 25, 1969.

Awardene, Junius Richard Jay (Sri Lanka), Feb. 4, 1978.

Awolowo, Obafemi, Mar. 6, 1909.

Axelrod, Julius, May 30, 1912.

Ayala, Eligio (Paraguay): overthrown, Feb. 17, 1936.

Ayckbourn, Alan, Apr. 12, 1939.

Ayer, Francis Wayland, Feb. 4, 1848.

Ayer, Harriet Hubbard, Jun. 27, 1849.

Ayres, Lew, Dec. 28, 1908.

Ayrshire, May 10, 1307.

Azerbaijan, May 28, 1918.

Azores, Sep. 6, 1951.

B

B-50, Mar. 2, 1949.

B-52 bombers: first used, Jul. 18, 1968; crashes Jan. 22, 1968.

B-58: jet bomber, May 26, 1961.

Baath Party (Syria), Feb. 23, 1966.

Babbage, Charles, Dec. 26, 1792.

Babbitt, Irving, Aug. 2, 1865.

Babbitt, Isaac, Jul. 26, 1799.

Babes in Arms: premiere, Apr. 14, 1937.

Babes in Toyland: premiere, Jun. 17, 1903.

Babson, Roger Ward, Jul. 6, 1875.

Babylonian Exile, p. ix.

Babylonians, p. ix.

Bacall, Lauren, Sep. 16, 1924.

Bach, Johann Christian, Sep. 5, 1735.

Bach, Johann Sebastian, Mar. 21, 1685.

Bach, Karl Philipp Emanuel, Mar. 8, 1714.

Bach, Richard (Davis), Jun. 23, 1936.

Bacha-i-Saquao, Jan. 17, 1929.

Bacharach, Burt, May 12, 1929.

Bachelors' Day, Feb. 29.

Backhaus, Wilhelm, Mar. 26, 1884.

Bacon, Francis, Oct. 28, 1909.

Bacon, Henry, Nov. 28, 1866.

Bacon, Nathaniel, Jan. 2, 1647.

Bacon, Sir Francis, Jan. 22, 1561.

Badajoz, Treaty of, Jun. 6, 1801.

Baden, Peace of, Sep. 7, 1714.

Baden-Powell, Robert, Feb. 22, 1857.

Baekeland, Leo Hendrik, Nov. 14, 1863.

Baer, George Frederick, Sep. 26, 1842.

Baer, Karl Ernst von, Feb. 29, 1792.

Baer, Max, Jun. 14, 1934; Jun. 13, 1935.

Baeyer, Adolph von, Oct. 31, 1835.

Baez, Joan, Jan. 9, 1941.

Bagaza, Jean Baptiste, Aug. 29, 1946; Nov. 1, 1976.

Baghdad, Mar. 11, 1917.

Bagnold, Enid, Oct. 27, 1889.

Bahadur Shah II (India), Mar. 9, 1858.

Bahamas: independence, Jan. 7, 1964; Jan. 16, 1967; Jul. 10, 1973; U.N. membership, Sep. 15, 1973.

Bahrain: independence, Aug. 15, 1971.

Bailey, F(rancis) Lee, Jun. 10, 1933.

Bailey, Liberty Hyde, Mar. 15, 1858.

Bailey, Pearl, Mar. 29, 1918.

Baird, John Logie, Aug. 13, 1888.

Bajazet I (Ottoman ruler), Jul. 28, 1402.

Bajer, Fredrik, Apr. 21, 1837.

Baker, George Pierce, Apr. 4, 1866.

Baker, Howard Henry, Nov. 15, 1925.

Baker, Josephine, Jun. 3, 1906.

Baker, Russell (Wayne), Aug. 14, 1925.

Baker, Sir Samuel White, Mar. 14, 1864.

Bakunin, Mikhail Aleksandrovitch, May 18, 1814.

Balaclava, Battle of: begins, Oct. 25, 1854.

Balaguer, Joaquín, Jun. 1, 1966; May 26, 1978.

Balanchine, George, Jan. 9, 1904.

Balbo, Cesare, Nov. 21, 1789.

Balbo, Italo, Jun. 6, 1896.

Balch, Emily Green, Jan. 8, 1867.

Balchen, Bernt, Oct. 23, 1899; Nov. 29, 1929.

Bald Eagle Days, Aug. intro.

Baldwin, Faith (Cuthrell), Oct. 1, 1893.

Baldwin, James, Aug. 2, 1924.

Baldwin, Robert, May 12, 1804.

Baldwin, Roger Nash, Jan. 21, 1884.

Baldwin, Stanley, Aug. 3, 1867.

Baldwin I (Jerusalem), Dec. 25, 1100.

Bale, John, Nov. 21, 1495.

Balenciaga, Cristobal, Jan. 21, 1895.

Balfe, Michael William, May 15, 1808.

Balfour, Arthur James, Jul. 25, 1848.

Balfour, Lord, Apr. 1, 1925.

Balfour Declaration, Nov. 2, 1917.

Balikiapen (Borneo), Apr. 23, 1945.

Baliol, John, Nov. 17, 1292.

Balkan Pact, Feb. 9, 1934.

Balkan War, First: Mar. 6, 1912; begins, Oct. 7, 1912; Oct. 18, 1912; ends, Dec. 3, 1912; May 30, 1913.

Balkan War, Second: Mar. 26, 1913; begins, Jun. 30, 1913; Jul. 10, 1913; Jul. 22, 1913.

Ball, Ernest, Jul. 22, 1878.

Ball, George, Dec. 21, 1909.

Ball, Hugo, Feb. 22, 1886.

Ball, Lucille, Aug. 6, 1911.

Ball, Thomas, Jun. 3, 1819.

Ballante, Maurice, Sep. 2, 1930.

Ballantine, Ian Keith, Feb. 15, 1916.

Ballesteros, Severiano, Apr. 9, 1957.

Ballet Comique de la Reine: first ballet, Oct. 15, 1581.

Ballinger, Richard Achilles, Jul. 9, 1858.

Balliol, Edward (Scotland): assumes throne, Aug. 11, 1332; Jul. 19, 1333.

balloon: first to carry cargo, Sep. 19, 1783.

balloon ascent: first, Nov. 21, 1783.

balloon flight: first U.S., Jan. 9, 1793.

Ballou, Hosea, Apr. 30, 1771.

Balmaceda, José Manuel, Jul. 19, 1840.

Balmain, Pierre Aléxandre, May 18, 1914.

Balmat, Jacques, Aug. 8, 1786.

Baltimore: fire, Feb. 7, 1904.

Baltimore, David, Mar. 7, 1938.

Baltimore and Ohio Railroad, Mar. 4, 1828; Jul. 4, 1828.

Balzac, Honoré de, May 20, 1799.

Bamberger, Louis, May 15, 1855.

Banana, Cannan, Mar. 5, 1936.

Bancroft, Anne, Sep. 17, 1931.

Bancroft, George, Oct. 3, 1800.

Bancroft, Hubert Howe, May 5, 1832.

Banda, H. Kamazu, Apr. 14, 1906; Feb. 1, 1963; Jul. 6, 1964.

Bandaranaike, Sirimavo: first woman prime minister of Ceylon, Apr. 17, 1916; Jul. 21, 1960.

Bandinelli, Baccio, Nov. 12, 1493.

Bangalore, Mar. 21, 1791.

Bangao Islands, Apr. 2, 1945.

Bangladesh, Mar. 26, 1971; Apr. 12, 1971; Dec. 6, 1971; formed, Dec. 16, 1971; Jan. 24, 1972; Feb. 4, 1972; treaty with India, Mar. 19, 1972; Feb. 24, 1974; Apr. 9, 1974; Jan. 25, 1975; May 30, 1981; Mar. 24, 1982.

Bani-Sadr, Abolhassan, Jan. 25, 1980; dismissed, Jun. 22, 1981.

Bank Employees Day (Guatemala), Jul. 1.

bankers, patron of, Sep. 21.

Bankhead, Tallulah, Jan. 31, 1903.

bank holiday, U.S., Mar. 6, 1933.

Bank Holiday (Bangladesh), Jul. 1.

Bank Holiday (Fiji, Grenada, Guyana, Hong Kong, Ireland, Malawi), Aug. intro.

Bank Holiday (Somalia), Jan. 1.

Bank Holiday (Taiwan), Jul. 1.

Bank of England: incorporated, Jul. 27, 1694; nationalized, Feb. 14, 1946.

Bank of North America: first U.S. commercial bank, Jan. 7, 1782.

Bank of the United States: fails, Dec. 11, 1930.

Banks, Ernie, Jan. 31, 1931.

Banks, Nathaniel Prentiss, Jan. 30, 1816.

Banneker, Benjamin, Nov. 9, 1731.

Bannister, Roger, Mar. 23, 1929; May 6, 1954.

Bannockburn, Battle of, Jun. 24, 1314; Jun. 11, 1488.

Banque de France: founded, Apr. 14, 1800.

Bante, Teferi (Ethiopia): assassinated, Feb. 3, 1977.

Ban the Bomb rally (London), Apr. 15, 1963.

Banting, Sir Frederick Grant, Nov. 14, 1891.

Banzer Suárez, Hugo, Jul. 21, 1978.

Bao Dai, Feb. 7, 1950.

Baptista da Figueiredo, Gen. João (Brazil), Mar. 15, 1979; Oct. 15, 1978.

Bara, Theda, Jul. 20, 1890.

Bárány, Robert, Apr. 22, 1876.

Barbados, Nov. 1, 1964; independence, Nov. 30, 1966; admitted to U.N., Dec. 9, 1966.

Barbarossa, Frederick (Germany), May 28, 1167.

Barbecue Month, National, May intro.

barbed wire, Feb. 15, 1876.

Barber, Samuel, Mar. 9, 1910; Sep. 16, 1966.

barbers, patron of, Aug. 25 .

Barbosa's Birthday (Puerto Rico), Jul. 27.

Belgium: independence, Oct. 4, 1830; Apr. 19, 1839; Jan. 1, 1922; May 10, 1940; May 28, 1940; Apr. 3, 1979.

Belgrade, Nov. 29, 1914; falls to Germany and Austria, Oct. 9, 1915; recapture by Serbs, Nov. 1, 1918; Apr. 20, 1941; captured, Oct. 20, 1944.

Belinski, Vissarion Grigorievich, Jul. 12, 1811.

Belize, Jun. 1, 1973; independence, Sep. 21, 1981.

Belknap, Jeremy, Jun. 4, 1744.

Bell, Alexander Graham, Mar. 3, 1847; telephone patent, Mar. 7, 1876; Mar. 10, 1876; Feb. 12, 1877; Jan. 14, 1878; Jan. 25, 1915.

Bell, Andrew, Mar. 27, 1753.

Bell, Elliott V(allance, Sep. 25, 1902.

Bell, Gertrude, Jul. 14, 1868.

Bell, John, Feb. 1, 1797.

Bellamy, Edward, Mar. 26, 1850.

Bellarmine, Robert (Cardinal), May 19, 1923.

Belleau Wood: captured, Jun. 25, 1918.

Belleau Wood, Battle of: begins, Jun. 6, 1918.

Bellerophon, Jul. 15, 1815.

Belli, Melvin (Mouron), Jul. 29, 1907.

Bellingham, John, May 11, 1812.

Bellingshausen, Fabian Gottlieb von, Sep. 9, 1778.

Bellini, Vincenzo, Nov. 3, 1801.

bell-makers, patron of, Feb. 5.

Bello, Andrés, Nov. 29, 1781.

Belloc, (Joseph-Pierre) Hilaire, Jul. 27, 1870.

Bellow, Saul, Jun. 10, 1915.

Bellows, George Wesley, Aug. 12, 1882.

Bell X-1: breaks sound barrier, Oct. 14, 1947.

Belmondo, Jean-Paul, Apr. 9, 1933.

Belmont, August, Feb. 18, 1853.

Belmont, Eleanor Robson, Dec. 13, 1879.

Belsen, Apr. 15, 1945.

Belushi, John, Jan. 24, 1950.

Bembo, Pietro, May 20, 1470.

Bemelmans, Ludwig, Apr. 27, 1898.

Benavante y Martínez, Jacinto, Aug. 12, 1866.

Ben Bella, Ahmed, Sep. 26, 1962; Jun. 19, 1965; Jul. 4, 1979.

Benchley, Nathaniel (Goddard), Nov. 13, 1915.

Benchley, Peter, May 8, 1940.

Benchley, Robert Charles, Sep. 15, 1889.

Bendix, Vincent, Aug. 12, 1882.

Bendix, William, Jan. 14, 1906.

Bendjedid, Chadli, Apr. 14, 1929.

Benedict, Ruth (Fulton), Jun. 5, 1887.

Benedictine nuns and nunneries, patron of, Feb. 10.

Benedictine oblates, patron of, Jul. 13.

Benedict IX (Boy Pope): resigns, Jul. 16, 1048.

Benedict XII (pope), Jun. 29, 1408.

Benedict XIII (pope), Feb. 2, 1649.

Benedict XIV (pope), Mar. 31, 1675.

Benedict XV (pope), Nov. 21, 1854.

Benedict XV (pope), Sep. 3, 1914.

Benedict the Black, Apr. 4.

Benelux Economic Union: established, Feb. 3, 1958.

Benér, Stephen Vincent, Jul. 22, 1898.

Benér, William Rose, Feb. 2, 1886.

Benevente (Portugal), Apr. 23, 1909.

Beneš, Edvard, May 28, 1884.

Bengal, Apr. 23, 1795.

Bengal: becomes Bangladesh, Dec. 16, 1971.

Bengali New Year (Bangladesh), Apr. 15.

Benghazi (Libya), Feb. 7, 1941; Apr. 3, 1941.

Benguela-Katanga railway, Jul. 1, 1931.

Ben-Gurion, David, Oct. 16, 1886; May 23, 1960.

Benin: independence, Aug. 1, 1960; Nov. 30, 1975.

Benito Juárez Memorial Day (Mexico), Jul. 18.

Benjamin, Judah Philip, Aug. 6, 1811.

Benn, Tony, Apr. 3, 1925.

Bennett, Arnold, May 27, 1867.

Bennett, Constance, Oct. 22, 1904.

Bennett, Floyd, Oct. 25, 1890; May 9, 1926.

Bennett, James Gordon, Sep. 1, 1795; May 10, 1841.

Bennett, Richard Bedford, Jul. 5, 1870.

Bennett, Robert Russell, Jun. 15, 1894.

Bennett, Tony, Aug. 3, 1926.

Bennington, Battle of, Aug. 16, 1777.

Bennington Battle Day (Vermont), Aug. 16.

Benny, Jack, Feb. 14, 1894.

Benso, Camillo, Aug. 10, 1810.

Benson, Edward White, Jul. 14, 1829.

Benson, Ezra Taft, Aug. 4, 1899.

Benson, Sally, Sep. 3, 1900.

Bentham, Jeremy, Feb. 15, 1748.

Benton, Thomas Hart, Mar. 1, 1782.

Benton, Thomas Hart, Apr. 15, 1889.

Bentsen, Lloyd Millard Jr., Feb. 11, 1921.

Benz, Karl Friedrich, Nov. 25, 1844.

Berchet, Giovanni, Dec. 23, 1783.

Berchtoldstag (Switzerland), Jan. 2.

Berg, Gertrude, Oct. 3, 1889.

Bergamo, Apr. 19, 1428.

Bergen, Edgar, Feb. 16, 1903.

Bergen, John J(oseph), Aug. 7, 1896.

Bergen, Polly, Jul. 14, 1930.

Bergerac, Cyrano de, Mar. 6, 1619.

Bergius, Friedrich Karl Rudolf, Oct. 11, 1884.

Bergland, Bob Selmer, Jul. 22, 1928.

Bergman, (Ernst) Ingmar, Jul. 14, 1918.

Bergman, Ingrid, Aug. 29, 1915.

Bergson, Henri, Oct. 18, 1859.

Bering Expedition, Feb. 5, 1725.

Beriosova, Svetlana, Sep. 24, 1932.

Beriya, Lavrenti Pavlovich, Mar. 18, 1899.

Berkeley, George, Mar. 12, 1685.

Berkeley, University of California at, May 15, 1969.

Berle, Adolf Augustus, Jan. 29, 1895.

Berle, Milton, Jul. 12, 1908.

Berlin, Mar. 6, 1944; Russian troops enter, Apr. 24, 1945; May 2, 1945; Soviet blockade, Jun. 24, 1948.

Berlin, East, Jan. 31, 1971.

Berlin, Irving, May 11, 1888; Jun. 16, 1919; May 16, 1946.

Berlin, West, Jan. 31, 1971.

Berlin air lift: ends, Sep. 30, 1949.

Berlin Congress, Jul. 13, 1878.

Berliner, Emile, May 20, 1851.

Berlin Wall: construction begins, Aug. 13, 1961.

Berlioz, (Louis) Hector, Dec. 11, 1803.

Berman, Emile Zola, Nov. 2, 1903.

Bermuda, May 26, 1968.

Bernadette, Jan. 7, 1844.

Bernadotte, Folke (Count):, Jan. 2, 1895; assassinated Sep. 17, 1948.

Bernadotte, Marshall, Feb. 5, 1818.

Bernard, Claude, Jul. 12, 1813.

Bernhard, Prince (Netherlands): bribery scandal, Aug. 26, 1976.

Bernhardi, Friedrich von, Nov. 2, 1849.

Bernhardt, Sarah, Oct. 22, 1844.

Bernini, Giovanni Lorenzo, Dec. 7, 1598.

Bernoulli, Jakob, Dec. 27, 1654.

Bernstein, Carl, Feb. 14, 1944.

Bernstein, Elmer, Apr. 4, 1922.

Bernstein, Leonard, Aug. 25, 1918; Jan. 28, 1944; Dec. 1, 1956; Sep. 26, 1957.

Bernstorff, Count Andreas Peter von, Aug. 28, 1735.

Bernstorff, Count Johann-Heinrich von, Nov. 14, 1862.

Bern (Switzerland): Protestant victory, Jul. 25, 1712.

Berra, Yogi, May 12, 1925.

Berry, Chuck, Jan. 15, 1926.

Berryman, John, Oct. 25, 1914.

Berthelot, (Pierre Eugene) Marcelin, Mar. 18, 1827; Oct. 27, 1827.

Berthollet, Claude Louis, Dec. 9, 1748.

Berthoud, Ferdinand, Mar. 19, 1727.

Bertillon, Alphonse, Apr. 23, 1853.

Bertolucci, Bernardo, Mar. 16, 1940.

Bertrand, Louis Jacques Napoleon, Apr. 20, 1807.

Berzelius, Baron Jons Jakob, Aug. 20, 1779.

Besant, Annie, Oct. 1, 1847.

Besant Pancami (India), Jan. 26.

Besnard, Paul Albert, Jun. 2, 1849.

Bessarabia, Apr. 9, 1918.

Bessel, Friedrich Wilhelm, Jul. 22, 1784.

Betancourt, Romulo, Feb. 22, 1908.

Bethe, Hans Albrecht, Jul. 2, 1906.

Bethmann-Hollweg, Theobald von, Nov. 29, 1856.

Bethune, Mary McLeod, Jul. 10, 1875.

Betjeman, Sir John, Apr. 6, 1906.

Betjeman, Sir John, Oct. 10, 1972.

Better Hearing and Speech Month, May intro.

Bettleheim, Bruno, Aug. 28, 1903.

Bevan, Aneurin, Nov. 15, 1897.

Beveridge, Albert Jeremiah, Oct. 6, 1862.

Beveridge, William Henry, Mar. 5, 1879.

Bevin, Ernest, Mar. 9, 1881.

Bewick, Thomas, Aug. 12, 1753.

Bhave, Vinoba, Sep. 11, 1895.

Bhumibol Adulyadej (King of Thailand), Dec. 5, 1927.

Bhutan, Apr. 5, 1964.

(Bhutan) His Majesty the King, Birthday of, Nov. 11.

Biafra, Republic of: May 30, 1967; declares independence, Jul. 6, 1967; Apr. 13, 1968; Jan. 11, 1970; Jan. 12, 1970.

Biak: U.S. troops land on, May 27, 1944.

Bialik, Hayyim Nahman, Jan. 9, 1873.

bibbu, p. ix.

Bible, Revised Version, Feb. 10, 1899.

Bible Week, National, Nov. intro.

Bicentennial, American Revolution, Apr. 18, 1975.

Bicentennial, U.S., Jul. 4, 1976.

Bich, Marcel, Jul. 29, 1914.

Bichat, Marie François Xavier, Nov. 11, 1771.

bicycle race: first official, May 31, 1868.

Biddle, Nicholas, Jan. 8, 1786.

Bienville, Jean-Baptiste Le Moyne, sieur de, Feb. 23, 1680.

Bierce, Ambrose (Gwinett), Jul. 24, 1842.

Bierstadt, Albert, Jan. 7, 1830.

Bigelow, Erastus Brigham, Apr. 2, 1814.

Biggers, Earl Derr, Aug. 26, 1884.

Biggs, E. Power, Mar. 29, 1906.

Bike Safety Month, May intro.

Bike Safety Week, National, Apr. intro.

Biko, Steven, Sep. 15, 1977.

Biko, Steven: funeral, Sep. 25, 1977.

Bilbo, Theodore Gilmore, Oct. 13, 1877.

billiards championship: first U.S., Apr. 12, 1859.

Billings, John Shaw, Apr. 12, 1838.

Billings, William, Oct. 7, 1746.

Bill of Rights: passed, Dec. 15, 1791.

Bill of Rights Day (U.S.), Dec. 15.

Billy Budd: opera premieres, Dec. 1, 1951.

Billy the Kid (ballet): opens, Oct. 16, 1938.

Biloxi (Mississippi): riots, Apr. 24, 1960.

Binaisa, Godfrey, May 30, 1920; Jun. 20, 1979.

Binet, Alfred, Jul. 8, 1857.

Bing, Sir Rudolph, Jan. 9, 1902.

Bingham, George Caleb, Mar. 20, 1811.

Binyon, Laurence, Aug. 10, 1869.

biological weapons: treaty, Apr. 10, 1972.

Birch, Thomas, Jul. 26, 1779.

Bird, Vere: first Prime Minister of Antigua and Barbuda, Dec. 7, 1910; Nov. 1, 1981.

Bird Day (Oklahoma), May intro.; May 1.

Birdseye, Clarence, Dec. 9, 1886.

Birendra Bir Bikram Shah Dev (King of Nepal), Dec. 28, 1945.

Birkenhead (England), Jan. 20, 1885.

Birkoff, George David, Mar. 21, 1884.

Birney, James Gillespie, Feb. 4, 1792.

birth control clinic: first, Oct. 16, 1917.

birth control devices: sale of, Jun. 7, 1965.

Birth of a Nation, Feb. 8, 1915.

Bishop, Hazel (Gladys), Aug. 17, 1906.

Bishop, Jim, Nov. 21, 1907.

Bishop, Maurice (Grenada), Mar. 13, 1979.

Bishop, Sir Henry Rowley, Nov. 18, 1786.

Bismarck, Feb. 14, 1939; May 24, 1941.

Bismarck, Otto von, Apr. 1, 1815; Sep. 23, 1862; Mar. 18, 1890.

Bismarck Sea, Battle of, Mar. 2, 1943.

Bissell, Emily Perkins, May 31, 1861.

Bissell, George Henry, Nov. 8, 1821.

Bitzius, Albrecht (Jeremias Gotthelf), Oct. 4, 1797.

Bizet, Georges, Oct. 25, 1838; Mar. 3, 1875; Feb. 26, 1935; *First Symphony*: premiere, Feb. 26, 1935.

Bjerknes, Jacob Aall Bonnevie, Nov. 2, 1879.

Bjorling, Jussi, Feb. 2, 1911

Bjørnson, Bjørnstjerne, Dec. 8, 1932.

Björnsson, Sveinn, Feb. 27, 1881.

Black, Davidson, Jul. 25, 1884.

Black, Hugo Lafayette, Feb. 27, 1886.

Black, Joseph, Apr. 16, 1728.

Black, Karen, Jul. 1, 1942.

Black, Shirley Temple, Apr. 23, 1928.

Black and Tans, May 15, 1920.

Black Christ Festival (Guatemala), Jan. intro.

Black Code: enacted, Nov. 24, 1865.

Blackett, Lord Patrick, Maynard Stuart, Nov. 18, 1897.

Black Friday: financial panic, Sep. 24, 1869.

Black Friday: Germany, May 13, 1927.

Black Hand, The, Jun. 28, 1914.

Black Hole of Calcutta, The, Jun. 20, 1756.

black majority rule, Mar. 14, 1978.

Blackmer, Sidney, Jul. 13, 1898.

Blackmun, Harry Andrew, Nov. 12, 1908.

Blackout: New York City, Jul. 13, 1977.

Black Prince (England), Sep. 19, 1370.

black rule in Rhodesia, Jul. 5, 1977.

Blacks, North American, patron of, Apr. 4.

blacks disenfranchised: Louisiana, May 12, 1898.

Black Sea, Jan. 9, 1792.

Black September: terrorists, Sep. 5, 1972.

blacksmiths, patron of, Nov. 6.

Blackstone, Sir William, Jul. 10, 1723.

Blackstone (Virginia): meteor, May 12, 1922.

Black Thursday, Oct. 24, 1929.

Blackwell, Antoinette Louisa, May 20, 1825.

Blackwell, Elizabeth, Feb. 3, 1821.

Blackwell, Henry Browne, May 4, 1825.

Blaiberg, Philip, Jan. 2, 1968.

Blaine, James Gillespie, Jan. 31, 1830.

Blair, Francis Preston, Apr. 12, 1791.

Blair, Montgomery, May 10, 1813.

Blake, Eubie, Feb. 7, 1883.

Blake, Robert (Admiral), Apr. 20, 1657.

Blake, William, Nov. 28, 1757.

Blakelock, Ralph Albert, Oct. 15, 1847.

Blalock, Jane, Sep. 19, 1945.

Blanc, (Jean Joseph Charles) Louis, Oct. 29, 1811.

Blanchard, François, Jan. 7, 1785; Jan. 9, 1793.

Blanco, Salvador Jorge, Jul. 5, 1926.

Blanqui, Louis Auguste, Feb. 1, 1805.

Blasco Ibáñez, Vincente, Jan. 29, 1867.

Blashfield, Edwin Howland, Dec. 15, 1848.

Blass, Bill, Jun. 22, 1922.

Bleek, Friedrich, Jul. 4, 1793.

Blenheim, Battle of, Aug. 13, 1704.

Blèriot, Louis, Jul. 1, 1872.

Blessed Adam of Loccum, Dec. 22.

Blessed Ado, Dec. 16.

Blessed Adrian Fortescue, Jul. 11.

Blessed Agathangelo, Aug. 7.

Blessed Agnello of Pisa, Mar. 13.

Blessed Agnes of Bohemia, Mar. 2.

Blessed Alanus de Solminihac, Jan. 3.

Blessed Albert of Bergamo, May 11.

Blessed Alcuin, May 19.

Blessed Alda, Apr. 26.

Blessed Alexander Rawlins, Apr. 7.

Blessed Alix le Clercq, Jan. 9.

Blessed Aloisius Scrosoppi, Oct. 5.

Blessed Aloysius Palazzolo, Jun. 15.

Blessed Aloysius Rabata, May 11.

Blessed Alpais, Nov. 3.

Blessed Alphonsus de Orozco, Sep. 19.

Blessed Alvarez of Cordova, Feb. 19.

Blessed Amadeus IX of Savoy, Mar. 30.

Blessed Amata, Jun. 9.

Blessed Ambrose of Camaldoli, Nov. 20.

Blessed Ambrose of Siena, Mar. 20.

Blessed Andrew, May 30.

Blessed Andrew Abellon, May 17.

Blessed Andrew Bessette, Jan. 6.

Blessed Andrew Hilbernon, Apr. 18.

Blessed Andrew of Anagni, Feb. 17.

Blessed Andrew of Antioch, Nov. 30.

Blessed Andrew of Borgo San Sepolcro, Sep. 3.

Blessed Andrew of Montereale, Apr. 12.

Blessed Andrew of Peschiera, Jan. 19.

Blessed Andrew of Rinn, Jul. 12.

Blessed Andrew of Siena, Mar. 19.

Blessed Andrew of Spello, Jun. 3.

Blessed Andrew of Strumi, Mar. 10.

Blessed Angela de la Cruz Guerrero Gonzalez, Mar. 2.

Blessed Angela of Foligno, Feb. 28.

Blessed Angelina of Marsciano, Jul. 21.

Blessed Angelo Augustine of Florence, Aug. 18.

Blessed Angelo of Acri, Oct. 30.

Blessed Angelo of Borgo San Sepolcro, Feb. 15.

Blessed Angelo of Chivasso, Apr. 12.

Blessed Angelo of Foligno, Aug. 27.

Blessed Angelo of Furcio, Feb. 6.

Blessed Anne Mary Javouhey, Jul. 15.

Blessed Anne Mary Taigi, Jun. 9.

Blessed Anne of St. Bartholomew, Jun. 7.

Blessed Anthony Middleton, May 6.

Blessed Anthony Pavoni, Apr. 9.

Blessed Anthony Primaldi, Aug. 14.

Blessed Anthony Pucci, Jan. 12.

Blessed Antonia of Florence, Feb. 28.

Blessed Antonius Gonzdez, Sep. 24.

Blessed Antony Baldinucci, Nov. 7.

Blessed Antony Bonfadini, Dec. 1.

Blessed Antony Della Chiesa, Jul. 28.

Blessed Antony Grassi, Dec. 13.

Blessed Antony Neyrot, Apr. 10.

Blessed Antony of Siena, Apr. 27.

Blessed Antony of Stroncone, Feb. 7.

Blessed Antony the Pilgrim, Feb. 1.

Blessed Apollinaris Franco, Charles Spinola, Sep. 10.

Blessed Archangeklo of Bologna, Apr. 16.

Blessed Archangela Girlani, Feb. 13.

Blessed Archangelo of Calatafimi, Jul. 30.

Blessed Arnold Janssen, Jan. 15.

Blessed Arnulf of Villers, Jun. 30.

Blessed Augustine, Aug. 3.

Blessed Augustine Novello, May 19.

Blessed Augustine of Biella, Jul. 24.

Blessed Avertanus, Feb. 25.

Blessed Ayrald, Jan. 2.

Blessed Balthasar of Chiavari, Oct. 25.
Blessed Baptista Varani, Jun. 7.
Blessed Baptist of Mantua, Mar. 20.
Blessed Bartholomew, Oct. 23.
Blessed Bartholomew of Cervere, Apr. 22.
Blessed Bartholomew of Mantua, Dec. 5.
Blessed Bartholomew of Montepulciano, May 23.
Blessed Bartholomew of San Gimignano, Dec. 14.
Blessed Beatrice da Silva, Aug. 18.
Blessed Beatrice D'Este of Ferrara, Jan. 18.
Blessed Beatrice of Este, May 10.
Blessed Beatrice of Ornacieu, Feb. 13.
Blessed Benedict XI, Jul. 7.
Blessed Benedict of Coltiboni, Jan. 20.
Blessed Benedict of Urbino, Apr. 30.
Blessed Benincasa, May 11.
Blessed Benno, Jul. 22.
Blessed Bentivoglia, Dec. 1.
Blessed Benvenuta of Cividale, Oct. 30.
Blessed Benvenuto of Gubbio, Jun. 27.
Blessed Benvenuto of Recanati, May 21.
Blessed Bernardino of Feltre, Sep. 28.
Blessed Bernard of Baden, Jul. 15.
Blessed Bernard of Corleone, Jan. 19.
Blessed Bernard of Offida, Aug. 26.
Blessed Bernard Scammacca, Feb. 16.
Blessed Bernard the Penitent, Apr. 19.
Blessed Bernard Tolomei, Aug. 21.
Blessed Bernardino of Fossa, Nov. 27.
Blessed Berthold of Garsten, Jul. 27.
Blessed Bertrand of Garrigues, Sep. 6.
Blessed Bonaventure Buonaccorsi, Dec. 14.
Blessed Bonaventure of Barcelona, Sep. 11.
Blessed Bonaventure of Forli, Mar. 31.
Blessed Bonaventure of Peraga, Jun. 10.
Blessed Bonaventure of Potenza, Oct. 26.
Blessed Bonavita, Mar. 1.
Blessed Boniface of Savoy, Jul. 14.
Blessed Bronislava, Aug. 30.
Blessed Caspar de Bono, Jul. 14.
Blessed Cassian, Aug. 7.
Blessed Castora Gabrielli, Jun. 14.
Blessed Catherine of Pallanza, Apr. 6.
Blessed Catherine of Parc-aux-Dames, May 4.
Blessed Catherine of Racconigi, Sep. 4.
Blessed Cecilia, Jun. 9.
Blessed Ceslaus, Jul. 17.
Blessed Charlemagne, Jan. 28.
Blessed Charles of Blois, Sep. 29.
Blessed Charles the Good, Mar. 2.
Blessed Christian, Mar. 18.
Blessed Christina of Aquila, Jan. 18.
Blessed Christina of Spoleto, Feb. 13.
Blessed Christina of Stommeln, Nov. 6.
Blessed Christopher Bales, Mar. 4.
Blessed Christopher Macassoli, Mar. 11.
Blessed Christopher of Romagnola, Oct. 25.
Blessed Clare of Pisa, Apr. 17.
Blessed Clare of Rimini, Feb. 10.
Blessed Claud la Colombière, Feb. 15.
Blessed Clement of Osimo, Apr. 8.
Blessed Columba of Rieta, May 20.
Blessed Conrad of Ascoli, Apr. 19.
Blessed Conrad of Offida, Dec. 14.
Blessed Conrad of Seldenbüren, May 2.
Blessed Constantius of Fabrino, Feb. 25.

Blessed Contardo Ferrini, Oct. 27.
Blessed Crescentia of Kaufbeuren, Apr. 5.
Blessed Dalmatius Moner, Sep. 26.
Blessed Damian of Finario, Oct. 26.
Blessed Desiderius, Jan. 20.
Blessed Diana, Jun. 9.
Blessed Didacus of Cadiz, Mar. 24.
Blessed Diemoda, Mar. 29.
Blessed Dionysius, Nov. 29.
Blessed Dodo, Mar. 30.
Blessed Dominic, Apr. 26.
Blessed Dominic Barberi, Aug. 27.
Blessed Dominic Spadafora, Oct. 3.
Blessed Dorothy of Montau, Oct. 30.
Blessed Eberhard of Marchthal, Apr. 17.
Blessed Edmund Catherick, Apr. 13.
Blessed Edward Jones, May 6.
Blessed Edward Oldcorne, Apr. 7.
Blessed Edward Powell, Jul. 30.
Blessed Edward Stransham, Jan. 21.
Blessed Edward Waterson, Jan. 7.
Blessed Elizabeth of Mantua, Feb. 20.
Blessed Elizabeth the Good, Nov. 17.
Blessed Emeric, Nov. 4.
Blessed Emily of Vercelli, Aug. 19.
Blessed Emmanuel Ruiz, Jul. 10.
Blessed Ermengard, Jul. 16.
Blessed Eugenia Smet, Feb. 7.
Blessed Eugenius III, Jul. 8.
Blessed Eustochium of Messina, Feb. 16.
Blessed Eustochium of Padua, Feb. 13.
Blessed Evangelist, Mar. 20.
Blessed Eva of Liège, May 26.
Blessed Everard Hanse, Jul. 30.
Blessed Felicia of Milan, Jul. 24.
Blessed Felix of Nicosia, Jun. 1.
Blessed Ferdinand of Portugal, Jun. 5.
Blessed Ferreolus, Jan. 16.
Blessed Frances D'Ambrose, Nov. 4.
Blessed Francis Antony Fasani, Dec. 9.
Blessed Francis Antony of Lucera, Nov. 29.
Blessed Francis Coll, Apr. 2.
Blessed Francis de Capillas, Jan. 15.
Blessed Francis de Montmorency-Laval, May 6.
Blessed Francis de Posadas, Sep. 20.
Blessed Francis Dickenson, Apr. 30.
Blessed Francis Masabki, Jul. 10.
Blessed Francis of Calderola, Sep. 28.
Blessed Francis of Fabriano, Apr. 22.
Blessed Francis Page, Apr. 20.
Blessed Francis Patrizzi, May 12.
Blessed Franco of Grotti, Dec. 11.
Blessed Frederick of Regensburg, Nov. 29.
Blessed Fulco of Neuily, Mar. 2.
Blessed Gabra Michael, Sep. 1.
Blessed Gabriel Mary, Aug. 27.
Blessed Gabriel of Ancona, Nov. 12.
Blessed Gandulf of Binasco, Apr. 2.
Blessed Gemma of Solmona, May 12.
Blessed Gentilis, Sep. 5.
Blessed George Gervase, Apr. 11.
Blessed George Napper, Nov. 9.
Blessed George Swallowell, Jul. 24.
Blessed Gerard Gagnoli, Dec. 1.
Blessed Gerard of Clairvaux, Jun. 13.
Blessed Gerard of Monza, Jun. 6.
Blessed Gerard of Villamagna, May 23.
Blessed Gertrude of Altenberg, Aug. 13.

Blessed Gertrude of Delft, Jan. 6.
Blessed Giles Mary, Feb. 7.
Blessed Giles of Assisi, Apr. 23.
Blessed Giles of Lorenzana, Jan. 14.
Blessed Giles of Portugal, May 14.
Blessed Godfrey of Kappenberg, Jan. 13.
Blessed Gomidas Keumurgian, Nov. 5.
Blessed Gonsalo of Amarante, Jan. 16.
Blessed Gratia of Cattaro, Nov. 16.
Blessed Gregory, Apr. 26.
Blessed Gregory X, Jan. 10.
Blessed Gregory Lopez, Jul. 20.
Blessed Gregory of Verucchio, May 4.
Blessed Guala, Sep. 3.
Blessed Guillelmus Courtet, Sep. 29.
Blessed Gunther, Oct. 9.
Blessed Guy Maramaldi, Jun. 25.
Blessed Guy of Cortona, Jun. 16.
Blessed Hartman, Dec. 23.
Blessed Haymo of Savigliano, Aug. 18.
Blessed Hedwig of Poland, Feb. 28.
Blessed Helen Guerra, Apr. 11.
Blessed Helen of Arcella, Nov. 7.
Blessed Helen of Bologna, Sep. 23.
Blessed Helen of Udine, Apr. 23.
Blessed Henry de Osso y Cervello, Jan. 27.
Blessed Henry of Treviso, Jun. 10.
Blessed Henry Suso, Mar. 2.
Blessed Henry the Shoemaker, Jun. 9.
Blessed Henry Walpole, Apr. 7.
Blessed Henry Zdik, Jun. 25.
Blessed Herculanus of Piegaro, Jun. 1.
Blessed Herluin, Aug. 26.
Blessed Herman Joseph, Apr. 7.
Blessed Herman the Cripple, Sep. 25.
Blessed Hildegard, Apr. 30.
Blessed Hippolytus Galantini, Mar. 20.
Blessed Hroznata, Jul. 14.
Blessed Hugh Faringdon, Dec. 1.
Blessed Hugh More, Sep. 1.
Blessed Hugh of Anzy, Apr. 20.
Blessed Hugh of Fosses, Feb. 10.
Blessed Hugolino Magalotti, Dec. 11.
Blessed Hugolino of Cortona, Mar. 22.
Blessed Hugolino of Gualdo, Jan. 1.
Blessed Humbeline, Aug. 21.
Blessed Humbert III of Savoy, Mar. 4.
Blessed Humbert of Romans, Jul. 14.
Blessed Humilis of Bisignano, Nov. 27.
Blessed Hyacinthus Ansalone, Nov. 17.
Blessed Ida of Boulogne, Apr. 13.
Blessed Ida of Toggenburg, Nov. 3.
Blessed Ignatius Azevedo, Jul. 15.
Blessed Imelda, May 13.
Blessed Innocent V, Jun. 22.
Blessed Innocent XI, Aug. 11.
Blessed Innocent of Berzo, Mar. 3.
Blessed Isabel of France, Feb. 26.
Blessed Isaiah of Cracow, Feb. 8.
Blessed Isnardo of Chiampo, Mar. 22.
Blessed Jacopino of Canepaci, Mar. 3.
Blessed Jacopone of Todi, Dec. 25.
Blessed James, Jan. 28.
Blessed James, Mar. 14.
Blessed James, Nov. 26.
Blessed James Bell, Apr. 20.
Blessed James Bertoni, May 30.
Blessed James Bird, Mar. 25.
Blessed James D. Laval, Sep. 9.

Blessed Peter Favre, Aug. 11.
Blessed Peter Geremia, Mar. 10.
Blessed Peter Gonzalez, Apr. 14.
Blessed Peter Igneus, Feb. 8.
Blessed Peter of Castelnau, Jan. 15.
Blessed Peter of Gubbio, Mar. 23.
Blessed Peter of Jully, Jun. 23.
Blessed Peter of Luxemburg, Jul. 2.
Blessed Peter of Mogliano, Jul. 30.
Blessed Peter of Pisa, Jun. 17.
Blessed Peter of Ruffia, Nov. 7.
Blessed Peter of Sassoferrato, Sep. 1.
Blessed Peter of Siena, Dec. 11.
Blessed Peter of Tiferno, Oct. 21.
Blessed Peter of Treia, Feb. 17.
Blessed Peter Pascual, Dec. 6.
Blessed Peter Petroni of Siena, May 29.
Blessed Peter René Roque, Mar. 1.
Blessed Peter Sanz, May 26.
Blessed Peter the Venerable, Dec. 29.
Blessed Peter Wright, May 19.
Blessed Petronilla of Moncel, May 14.
Blessed Philippa Mareri, Feb. 16.
Blessed Philip Powell, Jun. 30.
Blessed Philippine Duchesne, Nov. 17.
Blessed Placida Viel, Mar. 4.
Blessed Placid Riccardi, Mar. 15.
Blessed Pontius of Faucigny, Nov. 26.
Blessed Prudence, May 6.
Blessed Rabanus Maurus, Feb. 4.
Blessed Rainerius Inclusis of Osnabruck, Apr. 11.
Blessed Rainerius of Arezzo, Nov. 12.
Blessed Ralph Ashley, Apr. 7.
Blessed Ralph Corby, Sep. 7.
Blessed Ratho of Andechs, May 17.
Blessed Raymund Lull, Sep. 5.
Blessed Raymund of Capua, Oct. 5.
Blessed Raymund of Fitero, Feb. 6.
Blessed Reginald of Orleans, Feb. 17.
Blessed Richard Fetherston, Jul. 30.
Blessed Richard Herst, Aug. 29.
Blessed Richard Kirkman, Aug. 22.
Blessed Richard Newport, May 30.
Blessed Richard of Hampole, Sep. 29.
Blessed Richard Pampuri, Feb. 3.
Blessed Richard Thirkeld, May 29.
Blessed Richard Whiting, Dec. 1.
Blessed Rizzerio, Feb. 7.
Blessed Robert Anderton, Apr. 25.
Blessed Robert Dalby, Mar. 16.
Blessed Robert of Arbrissel, Feb. 25.
Blessed Robert of Knaresborough, Sep. 24.
Blessed Roger Dickenson, Jul. 7.
Blessed Roger Le Fort, Mar. 1.
Blessed Roger of Ellant, Jan. 4.
Blessed Roger of Todi, Jan. 14.
Blessed Romaeus, Feb. 25.
Blessed Roque Gonzalez, Nov. 17.
Blessed Roseline, Jan. 17.
Blessed Rose Venerini, May 7.
Blessed Rudolf Aquaviva, Jul. 27.
Blessed Sadoc, Jun. 2.
Blessed Salome, Nov. 17.
Blessed Salvator Lilli, Nov. 24.
Blessed Santuccia, Mar. 21.
Blessed Sebastian Aparicio, Feb. 25.
Blessed Sebastian of Brescia, Dec. 16.
Blessed Sebastian Valfré, Jan. 30.

Blessed Seraphina Sforza, Sep. 9.
Blessed Serapion, Nov. 14.
Blessed Serlo, Mar. 3.
Blessed Sibyllina of Pavia, Mar. 23.
Blessed Simon de Rojas, Sep. 28.
Blessed Simon of Cascia, Feb. 3.
Blessed Simon of Lipnicza, Jul. 30.
Blessed Simon of Rimini, Nov. 3.
Blessed Simon of Todi, Apr. 20.
Blessed Stephana Quinzani, Jan. 2.
Blessed Stephen, Sep. 7.
Blessed Stephen Bandelli, Jun. 12.
Blessed Stephen Bellesini, Feb. 3.
Blessed Stilla, Jul. 19.
Blessed Teresa Couderc, Sep. 26.
Blessed Teresa Jornet Ibars, Aug. 20.
Blessed Teresa Verzani, Mar. 3.
Blessed Thaddeus, Oct. 25.
Blessed Thomas Abel, Jul. 30.
Blessed Thomas Alfield, Jul. 6.
Blessed Thomas Corsini, Jun. 23.
Blessed Thomas Hemerford, Feb. 12.
Blessed Thomas Hioji Rokuzayemon Nishi, Nov. 17.
Blessed Thomas Holland, Dec. 12.
Blessed Thomasius, Mar. 25.
Blessed Thomas Maxfield, Jul. 1.
Blessed Thomas of Bioille, Oct. 19.
Blessed Thomas of Cori, Jan. 19.
Blessed Thomas of Florence, Oct. 25.
Blessed Thomas of Walden, Nov. 2.
Blessed Thomas Percy, Aug. 26.
Blessed Thomas Plumtree, Feb. 4.
Blessed Thomas Reynolds, Jan. 21.
Blessed Thomas Sherwood, Feb. 7.
Blessed Thomas Somers, Dec. 10.
Blessed Thomas Tunstal, Jul. 13.
Blessed Thomas Welbourn, Aug. 1.
Blessed Thomas Woodhouse, Jun. 19.
Blessed Timothy of Montecchio, Aug. 26.
Blessed Torello, Mar. 16.
Blessed Ubald of Florence, Apr. 9.
Blessed Urban II, Jul. 29.
Blessed Urban V, Dec. 19.
Blessed Ursalina, Apr. 7.
Blessed Verdiana, Feb. 16.
Blessed Veronica of Binasco, Jan. 13.
Blessed Victoria Fornari-Strata, Sep. 12.
Blessed Victor III, Sep. 16.
Blessed Villana of Florence, Feb. 28.
Blessed Vincent, Mar. 8.
Blessed Vincentia Lopez y Vicuña, Dec. 26.
Blessed Vincentius Schiwozuka, Sep. 29.
Blessed Vitalis of Savigny, Sep. 16.
Blessed Vivaldo, May 11.
Blessed Waltman, Apr. 11.
Blessed William Andleby, Jul. 4.
Blessed William Brown, Aug. 1.
Blessed William Freeman, Aug. 13.
Blessed William Harringron, Feb. 18.
Blessed William Hart, Mar. 15.
Blessed William Lacey, Aug. 22.
Blessed William Marsden, Apr. 25.
Blessed William of Fenoli, Dec. 19.
Blessed William of Hirschau, Jul. 4.
Blessed William of Polizzi, Apr. 16.
Blessed William of Scicli, Apr. 7.
Blessed William of Toulouse, May 18.

Blessed William Patenson, Jan. 22.
Blessed William Richardson, Feb. 17.
Blessed William Scott, May 30.
Blessed William Tempier, Mar. 27.
Blessed William Ward, Jul. 26.
Blessed Wolfhelm, Apr. 22.
Blessed Zdislava, Jan. 1.
Bligh, William (Captain), Sep. 9, 1754; Apr. 28, 1789.
blindmen, patron of, Dec. 29.
Bliss, Tasker Howard, Dec. 31, 1853.
Blizzard of '88, Mar. 12, 1888.
Bloch, Felix, Oct. 23, 1905.
Bloch, Konrad Emil, Jan. 21, 1912.
Bloch, Oscar, May 8, 1877.
Block, Herbert Lawrence, Oct. 13, 1909.
Block Island, U.S.S.: torpedoed, May 29, 1944.
Blodgett, Katharine Burr, Jan. 10, 1898.
Bloemfontein, Mar. 13, 1900.
Bloemfontein, Convention of, Feb. 17, 1854.
Blok, Aleksandr Aleksandrovich, Nov. 28, 1880.
Blondell, Joan, Aug. 30, 1909.
Blondin, Charles, Feb. 28, 1824.
Blood River (Natal), Dec. 16, 1838.
bloodstone, Mar. intro.
Bloody Sunday (Dublin, Ireland), Nov. 21, 1920.
Bloody Sunday (Russia), Jan. 22, 1905.
Bloom, Claire, Feb. 15, 1931.
Bloomer, Amelia, May 27, 1818.
Bloomfield, Leonard, Apr. 1, 1887.
Bloomingdale, Joseph Bernard, Dec. 22, 1842.
Blount, William, Mar. 26, 1749.
Blücher: sunk, Jan. 24, 1915.
Blue, Ben, Sep. 12, 1901.
blue laws: upheld, May 29, 1961.
Blum, Léon (France), Apr. 9, 1872; Mar. 13, 1938.
Blumberg, Baruch S., Jul. 28, 1925.
Blumenbach, Johann Friedrich, May 11, 1752.
Blumenthal, Werner Michael, Jan. 3, 1926.
Blunt, Sir Anthony: discovered to be a spy, Nov. 15, 1979.
Blunt, Wilfrid Scawen, Aug. 17, 1840.
Bly, Nellie, May 5, 1867.
Bly, Robert, Dec. 23, 1926.
Blyth, Ann, Aug. 16, 1928.
B'nai B'rith Month, National, Oct. intro.
Boas, Franz, Jul. 9, 1858.
boatmen, patron of, Feb. 12.
boatmen, patron of, Nov. 23.
boat people: Indochinese people admitted into U.S., Jul. 15, 1977; problem addressed, May 16, 1979.
Bobbies (London Police), Sep. 29, 1829.
Bocage, Manuel Maria Barbosa du, Sep. 15, 1765.
Boccherini, Luigi, Feb. 19, 1743.
Bochler, Peter, Dec. 31, 1712.
Bock, (Moritz Albert Franz Friedrich) Fedor von, Dec. 3, 1880.
Bode, Johann Elert, Jan. 19, 1747.
Bodmer, Johann Jakob, Jul. 19, 1698.
Bodoni, Giambattista, Feb. 16, 1740.

Bouvines, Battle of: establishes France as European power, Jul. 27, 1214.

Bovet, Daniel, Mar. 23, 1907.

Bow, Clara, Aug. 6, 1905.

Bowditch, Nathaniel, Mar. 26, 1773.

Bowen, Elizabeth, Jun. 7, 1899.

Bowie, James, Mar. 6, 1836.

Bowles, Chester, Apr. 5, 1901.

bowling: first ten-pin match, Jan. 1, 1840.

Bowling Congress, American, Sep. 9, 1895.

Bowman, Isaiah, Dec. 26, 1878.

Boxer Protocol, Sep. 7, 1901.

Boxer Rebellion, Jan. 7, 1895; Jun. 20, 1900; war declared, Jun. 26, 1900; Aug. 14, 1900; Aug. 17, 1900; ends, Sep. 7, 1901; Jan. 3, 1903.

boxing: last bare-knuckles championship, Jul. 8, 1889.

Boxing Day, Dec. 26.

boxing match: first modern, Sep. 7, 1892.

Boycott, Charles Cunningham, Mar. 12, 1832.

Boyd, Julian (Parks), Nov. 3, 1903.

Boyd, William, Jun. 5, 1895.

Boyd-Orr of Brechin Mearns, Lord John, Sep. 23, 1880.

Boyer, Charles, Aug. 28, 1899.

Boyes, Sir Brian Barratt, Jan. 13, 1924.

Boyle, Robert, Jan. 25, 1627.

Boyle, W(illiam) A(nthony) (Tony), Dec. 1, 1904.

Boyne, Battle of the, Jul. 12, 1690.

Boys' Clubs of America, Federated, May 19, 1906.

Boy Scouts, patron of, Apr. 23.

Boy Scouts of America: incorporated, Feb. 8, 1910.

Boys from Syracuse, The: premiere, Nov. 23, 1938.

Brabham, Sir John Arthur, Apr. 2, 1926.

Brackley, patron of, Nov. 3.

Brackman, Robert, Sep. 25, 1898.

Bradbury, Ray, Aug. 22, 1920.

Braddock, Edward, Jul. 9, 1755.

Braddock, James J., Jun. 13, 1935.

Braddock, Jim, Jun. 22, 1937.

Bradford, Gamaliel, Oct. 9, 1863.

Bradford, Roark, Aug. 21, 1896.

Bradford, William, Mar. 19, 1589.

Bradley, Bill, Jul. 28, 1943.

Bradley, Henry, Dec. 3, 1845.

Bradley, Omar N., Feb. 12, 1893; appointed chairman, Joint Chiefs of Staff Aug. 11, 1949; promoted Sep. 18, 1950.

Bradley, Thomas, Dec. 29, 1917.

Brady, James Buchanan (Diamond Jim), Aug. 12, 1856.

Braga (Portugal), patron of, Apr. 26.

Bragg, Braxton, Mar. 22, 1817.

Bragg, Sir William Henry, Jul. 2, 1862.

Bragg, Sir William Lawrence, Mar. 31, 1890.

Brahe, Tycho, Dec. 14, 1546.

Brahms, Johannes, May 7, 1833.

Braille, Louis, Jan. 4, 1809.

Brailler, John: first professional football player, Aug. 31, 1895.

Bramah, Joseph, Apr. 13, 1748.

Brancusi, Constantin, Feb. 21, 1876.

Brand, Max, Mar. 20, 1892.

Brandeis, Louis (Dembitz), Nov. 13, 1856.

Brando, Marlon, Apr. 3, 1924.

Brandt, Willy, Dec. 18, 1913; Mar. 19, 1970; resigns, May 6, 1974.

Branting, Karl Hjalmar, Nov. 23, 1860.

Braque, Georges, May 13, 1882.

Brasilia (Brazil), Apr. 21, 1960.

Bratianu, Ion, Aug. 20, 1864.

Brattain, Walter Houser, Feb. 10, 1902.

Brauchitsch, Heinrich Alfred Walther, Oct. 4, 1881.

Braun, Eva, Feb. 6, 1912.

Braun, Karl F., Jun. 6, 1850.

Braun, Werner von, Mar. 23, 1912.

Brazil: discovered, Apr. 22, 1500; claimed for Portugal, Jun. 23, 1501; becomes empire, Dec. 16, 1815; independence from Portugal, Sep. 7, 1822; declares independence, Oct. 12, 1822; independence, Aug. 29, 1825; serfdom abolished, May 13, 1888; extradition treaty with U.S., Jan. 13, 1961; Jan. 18, 1963; Jan. 22, 1967; Feb. 24, 1976.

Brazzaville, Mar. 18, 1977.

Bream, Julian, Jul. 15, 1933.

breast cancer: X-ray treatment of, Jan. 29, 1896.

Breasted, James Henry, Aug. 27, 1865.

Brecht, Bertolt, Feb. 10, 1898.

Breck, John Henry, Jun. 5, 1877.

Breckinridge, John Cabell, Jan. 21, 1821; Mar. 4, 1857.

Breckinridge, Sophonisba, Apr. 1, 1866.

Breed's Hill, Jun. 17, 1775.

Breidfjord, Sigurdur Eirikson, Mar. 4, 1798.

Breitenfeld, Battle of, Sep. 17, 1631; Nov. 2, 1642.

Breitinger, Johann Jakob, Mar. 1, 1701.

Brel, Jacques, Apr. 8, 1929.

Bremer, Arthur: found guilty of attempted assassination of George Wallace, Aug. 4, 1972.

Bremer, Fredrika, Aug. 17, 1801.

Brennan, Walter, Jul. 25, 1894.

Brennan, William Joseph, Jr., Apr. 25, 1906.

Brenner Pass, Jan. 4, 1945.

Brentano, Clemens Maria, Sep. 8, 1778.

Bresci, Gaetano, Jul. 29, 1900.

Brescia, Apr. 19, 1428.

Brescia, patrons of, Feb. 15.

Breslau, Jan. 20, 1918.

Breslin, Jimmy, Oct. 17, 1930.

Bresse, Jan. 17, 1601.

Brest-Litovsk: negotiations between Russia and Germany, Dec. 3, 1917; peace negotiations begin, Dec. 22, 1917; Treaty of, Mar. 3, 1918; Mar. 16, 1918.

Breton, André, Feb. 18, 1896.

Breton, Jules Adolphe, May 1, 1827.

Brett, William Howard, Jul. 1, 1846.

Bretton Woods Conference: begins, Jul. 1, 1944.

Breuer, Josef, Jan. 15, 1842.

Breuer, Marcel Lajos, May 21, 1902.

Breuil, Henri Edouard-Prosper, Feb. 28, 1877.

brewers, patron of, Dec. 4.

brewers, patron of, Dec. 6.

Brewster, Kingman, Jun. 17, 1919.

Brezhnev, Leonid I., Dec. 19, 1906; May 7, 1960; Oct. 15, 1964; Jun. 16, 1977; Jun. 18, 1979.

Brezhnev Doctrine, Feb. 24, 1972.

Briand, Aristide, Mar. 28, 1862.

Brice, Fanny, Oct. 29, 1891.

Brico, Antonia, Jun. 26, 1902.

Bridger, James, Mar. 17, 1804.

Bridges, Calvin Blackman, Jan. 11, 1889.

Bridges, Robert Seymour, Oct. 23, 1844.

Bridgman, Percy Williams, Apr. 21, 1882.

Brigadoon: premiere, Mar. 13, 1947.

Bright, John, Nov. 16, 1811.

Brill, Abraham Arden, Oct. 12, 1874.

Brillat-Savarin, Anthelme, Apr. 1, 1755.

Brindisi (Italy): destruction of Byzantine fleet, May 28, 1156.

Brinkley, David (McClure), Jul. 10, 1920.

Brisbane, Arthur, Dec. 12, 1864.

Bristol (England), Jan. 9, 1969.

Bristow, Benjamin Helm, Jun. 20, 1832.

Britain, Jan. 22, 1760; suffrage to agricultural workers, Dec. 6, 1822; Jan. 20, 1841; Jan. 20, 1874.

British, May 5, 1811; Jan. 4, 1916; Jan. 26, 1931.

British Air Training Corps, Feb. 1, 1941.

British Association for the Advancement of Science: formed, Sep. 27, 1831.

British Broadcasting Company: begins transmission, Nov. 11, 1922; established Oct. 18, 1922.

British East India Company, Mar. 9, 1846, Aug. 2, 1858.

British Expeditionary Force: arrives in France, Aug. 7, 1914.

British Gazette and Sunday Monitor, The, Mar. 26, 1780.

British Honduras (Belize), Mar. 3, 1964; Jun. 1, 1973; Sep. 21, 1981.

British Museum: opens, Jan. 15, 1759.

British Nationality Bill, Oct. 30, 1981.

British North America Act, Jul. 1, 1867; Apr. 17, 1982.

British Road Traffic Act, Mar. 26, 1934.

British South Africa Company: granted charter, Oct. 29, 1889; May 3, 1895; Dec. 5, 1897.

Britten, (Edward) Benjamin, Nov. 22, 1913; Aug. 18, 1938; First Piano Concerto: premiere, Aug. 18, 1938; Nov. 28, 1941; Dec. 1, 1951.

Britton, Nathaniel Lord, Jan. 15, 1859.

Broca, Philippe Claude Alex de, Mar. 15, 1933.

Broca, Pierre Paul, Jun. 28, 1824.

Brock, Sir Isaac, Oct. 6, 1769.

Broglie, Prince Louis-Victor de, Aug. 15, 1892.

Bromfield, Louis, Dec. 27, 1896.

Brömsebro, Peace of: signed, Aug. 23, 1645.

Brongniart, Alexandre, Feb. 5, 1770.

Bronk, Detlev Wulf, Aug. 13, 1897.

Bronson, Charles, Nov. 13, 1922.

Brontë, Anne, Jan. 17, 1820.

Brontë, Charlotte, Apr. 21, 1816.

Brontë, Emily Jane (Ellis Bell), Jul. 30, 1818.

Brook, Alexander, Jul. 14, 1898.

Brook, Peter, Mar. 21, 1925.

Brooke, Edward W., Oct. 26, 1919.

Burnham, Daniel Hudson, Sep. 4, 1846.
Burnham, Linden Forbes, Feb. 20, 1923.
Burnham, Sherburne Wesley, Dec. 12, 1838.
Burns, Arthur, Apr. 27, 1904.
Burns, George, Jan. 20, 1896.
Burns, Robert, Jan. 25, 1759.
Burns, Robert: IRA hunger striker dies, May 5, 1981.
Burnside, Ambrose Everett, May 23, 1824.
Burpee, David, Apr. 5, 1893.
Burpee, W. Atlee, Apr. 5, 1858.
Burr, Aaron, Feb. 6, 1756; Mar. 4, 1801; Jul. 11, 1804.
Burr, Raymond, May 21, 1917.
Burroughs, Edgar Rice, Sep. 1, 1875.
Burroughs, John, Apr. 3, 1837.
Burroughs, William, Feb. 5, 1914.
Burroughs, William Seward, Jan. 28, 1855.
Burrows, Millar, Oct. 26, 1889.
Burstyn, Ellen, Dec. 7, 1932.
Burton, Charles, Apr. 11, 1982.
Burton, Harold Hitz, Jun. 22, 1888.
Burton Island, U.S.S., Sep. 4, 1954.
Burton, Michael, Jul. 3, 1947.
Burton, Richard, Feb. 23, 1854; Nov. 10, 1925; Feb. 8, 1577.
Burton, Sir Richard, Mar. 19, 1821; Feb. 13, 1858.
Burton, Theodore Elijah, Dec. 20, 1851.
Burundi, independence, Jul. 1, 1962; Jan. 30, 1965; Nov. 1, 1976.
Busby, Richard, Sep. 22, 1606.
Busch, Adolphus, Jul. 10, 1839.
Busch, Wilhelm, Apr. 15, 1832.
Bush, George, Jun. 12, 1924; Jan. 20, 1981.
Bush, Vannevar, Mar. 11, 1890.
Bushell, John, Mar. 23, 1752.
Bushman, Francis X., Jan. 10, 1883.
business and professional women, patron of, Nov. 17.
Busoni, Ferruccio Benvenuto, Apr. 1, 1866.
butchers, patron of, Jan. 17.
butchers, patron of, Aug. 24.
butchers, patron of, Sep. 8.
Butenandt, Adolf Friedrich Johann, Mar. 24, 1903.
Butler, Alban, Oct. 24, 1710.
Butler, Benjamin Franklin, Nov. 5, 1818.
Butler, James (Marquis of Ormonde), Sep. 11, 1649.
Butler, Joseph, May 18, 1692.
Butler, Nicholas Murray, Apr. 2, 1862.
Butler, Pierce, Mar. 17, 1866.
Butler, Samuel, Dec. 4, 1835.
Butler, Smedley Darlington, Jul. 30, 1881.
Butlerov, Aleksandr Mikhailovich, Sep. 6, 1828.
Buttigieg, Anton, Feb. 19, 1912.
Button, Dick, Jul. 18, 1929.
Butz, Earl: resigns, Oct. 4, 1976.
Buxtorf, Johannes (the Elder), Dec. 25, 1564.
Byland, Oct. 14, 1322.
Byng, Julian (Sir), May 28, 1916.
Byrd, Harry (Flood), Dec. 20, 1914.
Byrd, Richard E., Oct. 25, 1888; May 9, 1926; Nov. 29, 1929.
Byrd, Robert Carlyle, Nov. 20, 1917.
Byrne, Jane, May 24, 1934.

Byrnes, James Francis, May 2, 1879.
Byron, Lord, Jan. 22, 1788. *See also* Gordon, George.

C

Caballe, Montserrat, Apr. 12, 1933.
Caballo Island, Mar. 27, 1945.
cab drivers in Paris, patron of, Sep. 1.
Cabell, James Branch, Apr. 14, 1879.
cabinetmakers, patron of, Jul. 21.
Cable, George Washington, Oct. 12, 1844.
cable, transatlantic submarine: inaugurated, Dec. 19, 1961.
Cable TV Month, Sep. intro.
Cabot, John, Mar. 5, 1496.
Cabot, John, Jun. 24, 1497.
Cabral, Pedro, Apr. 22, 1500; Jun. 23, 1501.
Cabrini, Frances Xavier: first American canonized, Jul. 7, 1946.
Cade, Jack, Jun. 27, 1450.
Cade's Insurrection, Jun. 27, 1450.
Cadillac, Antoine de la Mothe, Mar. 5, 1658.
Cadiz (Spain), captured from Moors, Sep. 14, 1262; Apr. 19, 1587.
Cadman, Charles Wakefield, Dec. 24, 1881.
Caernarvon Castle (Wales), Apr. 25, 1284.
Caesar, Julius, p. x, xi; Jul. intro.; Aug. intro.; Jul. 12, 100 B.C.; Feb. 6, 46 B.C.; Feb. 15, 44 B.C.; assassinated Mar. 15, 44 B.C.; Mar. 17, 45 B.C.
Caesar, Sid, Sep. 8, 1922.
Caetano, Marcelo, Apr. 25, 1974.
Cagayan and Sibutu Islands (Philippines): ceded to U.S., Nov. 7, 1900.
Cage, John Milton, Jr., Sep. 5, 1912.
Cagliostro, Count Alessandro, Jun. 2, 1743.
Cagney, James, Jul. 17, 1899.
Cailletet, Louis Paul, Sep. 21, 1832.
Cain, Richard Harvey, Apr. 12, 1825.
Caine, Sir Thomas Henry Hall, May 14, 1853.
Cairo, Declaration of, Dec. 1, 1943.
Cairo Conference, First: begins, Nov. 22, 1943.
Caithness, patron of, Oct. 8.
Cakobau, George, Nov. 6, 1912.
Calabria (Italy): earthquake, Dec. 28, 1908.
Calais: regained by France, surrenders to Edward III (England), Aug. 3, 1347; Jan. 7, 1558; Jan. 20, 1558; Jan. 7, 1785.
Calais, patron of, Jun. 20.
Calais, Peace of, Oct. 24, 1360.
Calatafimi, Battle of, May 15, 1860.
Calcutta, University of (India), Jan. 24, 1857.
Calcutta (India): captured, Jun. 20, 1756; Dec. 12, 1911.
Caldecott, Randolph, Mar. 22, 1846.
Calder, Alexander, Jul. 22, 1898.
Calderon de la Barca, Pedro, Jan. 17, 1600.
Caldwell, Erskine, Dec. 17, 1903.
Caldwell, Taylor, Sep. 7, 1900.
calendar, Gregorian, Feb. 24, 1582.
calendar, Julian, Feb. 24, 1582.
calendula, Oct. intro.

Calhoun, John C., Mar. 18, 1782; Mar. 4, 1825; Mar. 4, 1829.
Calicut (India), May 20, 1498.
Califano, Joseph A., May 15, 1931; Apr. 28, 1977.
California, May 30, 1848; admitted to Union, Sep. 9, 1850; earthquake, Feb. 9, 1971; right to die recognized, Sep. 30, 1976.
California, Republic of: proclaimed, Jun. 14, 1846.
California, University of, Jan. 6, 1971.
californium: identified, Mar. 17, 1950.
Caligula (Roman emperor), Aug. 31, A.D. 12
Calixtus III (pope), Dec. 31, 1378; May 15, 1455.
Callaghan, James (England), Mar. 27, 1912; Apr. 5, 1976; Mar. 1, 1979.
Callas, Maria, Dec. 3, 1923.
Calles, Plutarco Elias, Sep. 25, 1877.
Calley, Lt. William L.: charged, Nov. 12, 1969; found guilty Mar. 29, 1971; sentenced Mar. 31, 1971.
Calloway, Cab(ell), Dec. 25, 1907.
Calvé, Emma, Aug. 15, 1858.
Calvin, John, Jul. 10, 1509; Apr. 21, 1538; Jun. 13, 1541; Nov. 20, 1541.
Cambodia, Jan. 29, 1950; Feb. 7, 1950; Jan. 31, 1964; May 3, 1965; Mar. 1, 1975; Apr. 17, 1975; seizure of *Mayaguez*, May 12, 1975; Jan. 5, 1976.
Cambodia, National Union of, Apr. 25, 1975.
Cambrai, Oct. 9, 1918.
Cambrai, Battle of, Nov. 20, 1917; ends, Dec. 7, 1917.
Cambrai, League of: formed, Dec. 10, 1508; May 14, 1509.
Cambrai, Peace of: signed, Aug. 5, 1529.
Camden, William, May 2, 1551.
Camelot: premiere, Dec. 3, 1960.
Cameron, Sir David Young, Jun. 28, 1865.
Cameroon, Feb. 18, 1916; independence, Jan. 1, 1960; admitted to U.N., Jan. 26, 1960; May 20, 1972.
Cameroon, Northern, Jun. 1, 1961.
Cammaerts, Emile, Mar. 16, 1878.
Camoëns and Portuguese Communities Day (Macao), Jun. 10.
Camões, Dia de, Jun. intro.
Camp, Walter Chauncey, Apr. 17, 1859.
Campanella, Tommaso, Sep. 5, 1568.
Campanile (Venice), Apr. 25, 1903.
Campbell, Alexander, Sep. 12, 1788.
Campbell, Glen, Apr. 22, 1938.
Campbell, (Ignatius) Roy (Dunnachie), Oct. 2, 1901.
Campbell, James B., Apr. 18, 1963.
Campbell, Mrs. Patrick, Feb. 9, 1865.
Campbell, Sir Malcolm, Mar. 11, 1885.
Campbell, Thomas, Jul. 27, 1777.
Campbell, William Wallace, Apr. 11, 1862.
Camp David, Middle East Summit at, Sep. 17, 1978.
Camp David Agreement, Apr. 25, 1982.
Camper, Pieter, May 11, 1722.
Camp Fire Birthday Week, Mar. intro.
Camp Fire Founder's Day, Mar. intro.
Camp Fire Founders Day (U.S.), Mar. 17.
Camp Fire Girls: established, Mar. 17, 1910.

Campion, Thomas, Feb. 12, 1567.

Campobello Island, Jan. 22, 1964.

Campo Formio, Peace of, Oct. 17, 1797.

Campora, Héctor José, Mar. 26, 1909; Mar. 11, 1973.

Camus, Albert, Nov. 7, 1913.

Canada, Jan. 22, 1964; flag adopted, Dec. 15, 1964; new flag, Feb. 15, 1965; Feb. 7, 1968; official languages, Jul. 7, 1969; Progressive Conservatives, May 22, 1979.

Canada, Dominion of: created, Jul. 1, 1867.

Canada, Lower, Jun. 10, 1791; Jul. 23, 1840; Jul. 1, 1867.

Canada, Upper, Jun. 10, 1791; Jul. 23, 1840; Jul. 1, 1867.

Canada-U.S. Goodwill Week, Apr. intro.

Canada and U.S.S.R.: first direct air service between, Jul. 11, 1966.

Canada Constitution Act: passed, Jun. 10, 1791.

Canadian Corps, May 28, 1916.

Canadian government: admission of U.S. deserters, May 22, 1969.

Canalejas, José (Spain): assassinated, Nov. 12, 1912.

Canaletto (Giovanni Antonio Canal), Oct. 18, 1697.

Canaris, Wilhelm Franz, Jan. 1, 1887.

Canary Islands, Mar. 6, 1480.

Canby, Henry Seidel, Sep. 6, 1878.

Can-Can: premiere, May 7, 1953.

Cancer, Jun. intro; Jul. intro.

Candide: premiere, Dec. 1, 1956.

Candlemas, Feb. 2.

Candlemas (Liechtenstein), Feb. 2.

Candler, Asa Griggs, Dec. 30, 1851.

Candolle, Augustine Pyrame, Feb. 4, 1778.

Canfield, Cass, Apr. 26, 1897.

Canicula, Jul. intro.

Canis Major, Jul. intro.

Canning, George, Apr. 11, 1770.

Cannizzaro, Stanislao, Jul. 13, 1826.

Cannon, Annie Jump, Dec. 11, 1863.

Cannon, Clarence, Apr. 11, 1879.

Cannon, Joseph Gurney, May 7, 1836.

Cannonball, Apr. 30, 1900.

Cano, Alonso, Mar. 19, 1601.

Canossa, Jan. 28, 1077.

Canova, Antonio, Nov. 1, 1757.

Cantemir, Prince Dimitrie, Sep. 21, 1708.

Canterbury, Archbishop of, Mar. 23, 1966.

Canterbury, 100th Archbishop of (Arthur Michael Ramsey), Jun. 27, 1961.

Canterbury Martyrs, Oct. 1, 1588.

Cantigny (France), May 28, 1918.

Canton (China): British blockade, Jun. 28, 1840; Jan. 20, 1924; Oct. 21, 1938.

Canton (Ohio), Sep. 17, 1920.

Cantor, Eddy, Jan. 31, 1892.

Cantor, Georg, Mar. 3, 1845.

cantus tradionalis, Jan. 8, 1904.

Canute II (Denmark), Feb. 3, 1014.

Canute II (Norway), Jul. 29, 1030.

Canutes Day (Sweden), Jan. 13.

Cape Canaveral (Florida), Jan. 31, 1961; May 5, 1961; Apr. 26, 1962. *See also* Cape Kennedy.

Cape Cod Canal: opens, Oct. 7, 1915.

Cape Colony, Apr. 6, 1652; Jan. 17, 1837; Jan. 12, 1879; Jul. 17, 1890; Jan. 6, 1896.

Cape Kennedy (Florida), Jan. 27, 1967. *See also* Cape Canaveral.

Cape of Good Hope: Feb. 3, 1488; British occupation of, Jan. 8, 1806; Colony of: ceded to British, Aug. 13, 1814; May 31, 1910.

Cape St. George, Battle of, Nov. 25, 1943.

Cape Town, Jan. 10, 1900.

Capetown, University of, Apr. 27, 1916.

Cape Verde Islands: independence, Jul. 5, 1975.

capital punishment: abolished in United Kingdom, Dec. 18, 1969; reinstated in U.S., Jan. 17, 1977; Jun. 6, 1977.

Capodistrias, Ioannes (Greece): assassinated, Oct. 9, 1831.

Capone, Al, Jan. 17, 1899.

Caporetto, Battle of: ends, Oct. 24, 1917.

Capote, Truman, Sep. 30, 1924.

Capp, Al, Sep. 28, 1909.

Capra, Frank, May 18, 1897.

Capricorn, Jan. intro; Dec. intro.

Captain Regents Day (San Marino), Apr. 1; Oct. 1.

captives, patron of, Dec. 4.

Carabobo Battle of (Venezuela), Jun. 24.

Caravaggio, Sep. 28, 1573.

Caraway, Hattie Wyatt, Feb. 1, 1878.

Cardano, Girolamo, Sep. 24, 1501.

Cardin, Pierre, Jul. 7, 1922.

Cardozo, Benjamin Nathan, May 24, 1870.

Carducci, Giosuè, Jul. 27, 1835.

Carey, Henry Charles, Dec. 15, 1793.

Carey, Hugh, Apr. 11, 1919.

Caribbean Day (Guyana), Jul. intro.

Carl XVI Gustaf (Sweden), Apr. 30, 1946; Sep. 15, 1973.

Carletonville (South Africa): wage riot, Sep. 12, 1973.

Carlos, Don, Apr. 22, 1834; Mar. 4, 1876.

Carlos, John, Oct. 16, 1968.

Carlos I (Portugal): assassinated, Feb. 1, 1908.

Carlota (Mexico), Jun. 7, 1840.

Carlsbad Caverns, May 14, 1930.

Carlsbad Decrees (Germany), Sep. 20, 1819.

Carlson, Chester, Feb. 8, 1906; Oct. 22, 1938.

Carlton, Richard Paul, Dec. 20, 1893.

Carlyle, Thomas, Dec. 4, 1795.

Carmelite Martyrs of Compiegne, Jul. 17.

Carmen: premiere, Mar. 3, 1875.

Carmen Jones: premiere, Dec. 2, 1943.

Carmer, Carl, Oct. 16, 1893.

Carmichael, Hoagy, Nov. 22, 1899.

Carmichael, Stokely, Jun. 29, 1941; calls for black revolution, Aug. 17, 1967.

Carmina Burana: premiere, Jun. 8, 1937.

Carnarvon, Lord, Nov. 29, 1922.

carnation, Jan. intro.

Carnation Day, Jul. intro.

Carnaval des Animaux: premiere, Feb. 25, 1922.

Carnegie, Andrew, Nov. 25, 1835.

Carnegie, Dale, Nov. 24, 1888.

carnelian, Aug. intro.

Carnera, Primo, Jun. 29, 1933; Jun. 14, 1934.

Carney, Art, Nov. 4, 1918.

Carnot, Marie François Sadi, Aug. 11, 1837.

Carnot, Nicolas Leonard Sadi, Jun. 1, 1796.

Caro, Miguel Antonio, Nov. 10, 1843.

Carol I (Romania), Apr. 20, 1839.

Carol II (Rumania), Jun. 9, 1930.

Carolina, South: secedes, Dec. 20, 1860.

Carothers, Wallace Hume, Apr. 27, 1896.

Carousel: premiere, Apr. 19, 1945.

Carpathian Passes. Battles of, Jan. 26, 1915.

Carpatho-Ukraine, Mar. 15, 1939.

Carpeaux, Jean Baptiste, May 14, 1827.

Carpenter, M(alcolm) Scott, May 1, 1925; May 24, 1962.

carpenters, patron of, Mar. 11.

carpenters, patron of, Mar. 19.

carpenters, patron of, Jul. 26.

Carracci, Agostino, Aug. 16, 1557.

Carracci, Ludovico, Apr. 21, 1555.

Carranza, Venustiano, Dec. 29, 1859.

Carrel, Alexis, Jun. 28, 1873.

Carrero Blanco, Luis (Spain):, Jun. 8, 1973; assassinated Dec. 20, 1973; Jan. 3, 1974.

Carroll, Charles, Sep. 20, 1737.

Carroll, Diahann, Jul. 17, 1935.

Carroll, James, Jun. 5, 1854.

Carroll, John, Jan. 8, 1735.

Carroll, Leo G., Oct. 25, 1892.

Carroll, Lewis, Jan. 27, 1832.

Carson, Johnny, Oct. 23, 1925.

Carson, Kit, Dec. 24, 1809.

Carson, Rachel, May 27, 1907.

Carstens, Karl, Dec. 14, 1914.

Carter, Benny, Aug. 8, 1907.

Carter, Howard, May 9, 1873; Nov. 29, 1922; Feb. 16, 1923.

Carter, Jimmy, Oct. 1, 1924; inaugurated, Jan. 20, 1977; Jan. 21, 1977; Mar. 5, 1977; Apr. 6, 1977; Jul. 15, 1977; Apr. 6, 1978; Sep. 17, 1978; Jun. 18, 1979.

Carter, Rosalynn, Aug. 18, 1927.

Cartier, Jacques, Apr. 20, 1534.

Cartier, Sir George Etienne, Sep. 6, 1814.

Cartier-Bresson, Henri, Aug. 22, 1908.

Cartwright, Edmund, Apr. 24, 1743.

Cartwright, John, Sep. 17, 1740.

Caruso, Enrico, Feb. 25, 1873; Feb. 1, 1904; Apr. 9, 1909.

Carver Day, George Washington (U.S.), Jan. intro.

Cary, (Arthur) Joyce Lunel, Dec. 7, 1888.

Casablanca Conference, Jan. 14, 1943.

Casablanca (Morocco): U.S. attacks French naval forces, Nov. 10, 1942.

Casadesus, Robert, Apr. 7, 1899.

Casals, Pablo, Dec. 29, 1876.

Casanova de Seingalt, Giovanni, Apr. 2, 1725.

Casement, Sir Roger, Sep. 1, 1864; Apr. 20, 1916; Jun. 29, 1916; hanged for treason, Aug. 3, 1916; Mar. 1, 1965.

Cash, Gerald C., May 28, 1917.

Cash, Johnny, Feb. 26, 1932.

Casimir III (Poland), Apr. 30, 1309.

Casimir IV (Poland), May 27, 1471; Apr. 6, 1490; dies, Jun. 7, 1492.

Cass, Lewis, Oct. 9, 1782.

Cassatt, Mary, May 22, 1844.

Cassavetes, John, Dec. 9, 1929.

Cassel, Battle of, Apr. 11, 1677.

Cassel, Battle of, Nov. 1, 1762.

Cassin, René, Oct. 5, 1887.

Cassini de Thury, César, Jun. 17, 1714.

Cassino (Italy), May 17, 1944.

Cassius, Mar. 15, 44.

Castaneda, Carlos, Dec. 25, 1931.

Castelbuono, patron of, Apr. 16.

Castello Branco, Camillo, Mar. 16, 1825.

Castiglione, Baldassare, Dec. 6, 1478.

Castile, Jan. 19, 1497.

Castilla, Ramón, Aug. 27, 1797.

Castillon, Jul. 17, 1453.

Castle, Irene, Apr. 7, 1893.

Castle, Vernon, May 2, 1887.

Castrén, Matthias Alexander, Dec. 2, 1813.

Castro, Fidel, Aug. 13, 1926; Jul. 26, 1953; Jan. 2, 1959; Feb. 16, 1959; Feb. 20, 1960; Apr. 20, 1961; Apr. 30, 1961; May 1, 1961.

Castro y Bellvís, Guillén de, Nov. 4, 1569.

Catalonian Union, Jan. 24, 1919.

Catalonia (Spain): autonomy, Sep. 25, 1932; Dec. 23, 1938.

Catania (Sicily), patron of, Feb. 5.

Cateau-Cambrésis, Treaty of, Apr. 3, 1559.

Cather, Willa, Dec. 7, 1876.

Catherine Cornaro (Cyprus), Mar. 14, 1489.

Catherine I (Russia), Apr. 5, 1684; Feb. 8, 1725.

Catherine of Aragon, Dec. 16, 1485; May 23, 1533.

Catherine of France, Jun. 2, 1420.

Catherine the Great (Russia):, Apr. 21, 1729; May 2, 1729; dies Nov. 17, 1796.

Catholic Bishops Conference, U.S.: rule of abstinence from meat abolished, Dec. 2, 1966.

Catholic Church, Jan. 3, 1521; first meeting of Pope with Orthodox Patriarch., Jan. 5, 1964; revised calendar, May 9, 1969; May 9, 1983.

Catholic college: first in U.S., Mar. 1, 1815.

Catholic youth, patron of, Jun. 21.

Catlin, George, Jul. 26, 1796.

Cato Street Conspiracy, Feb. 23, 1820.

Cats, Jacob, Nov. 10, 1577.

Catt, Carrie Chapman, Jan. 9, 1859.

Catton, Bruce, Oct. 8, 1899.

Catulli Carmina: premiere, Nov. 6, 1943.

Caucasus, Jan. 2, 1915; May 7, 1925.

Cauchy, Augustin-Louis, Aug. 21, 1789.

Cavadee (Mauritius), Jan. 30.

Cave, George, Feb. 23, 1856.

Cavell, Edith, Dec. 4, 1865; Oct. 12, 1915.

Cavendish, Henry, Oct. 10, 1731.

Cavendish, Lord Frederick, May 6, 1882.

Cavett, Dick, Nov. 19, 1936.

Cayley, Arthur, Aug. 16, 1821.

Ceauşescu, Nicolae (Romania), Jan. 26, 1918; Mar. 28, 1974.

Cecil, Lord Robert (1st Viscount Cecil of Chelwood), Feb. 3, 1830; Sep. 14, 1864.

celibacy, Oct. 20, 1928.

celibacy, priestly, Jun. 23, 1967.

Celler, Emmanuel, May 6, 1888.

Cellini, Benvenuto, Nov. 3, 1500.

Celsius, Anders, Nov. 27, 1701.

cemetary workers, patron of, Jan. 17.

Centennial Exposition, U.S., May 10, 1876.

Central African Federation, Dec. 19, 1962.

Central African Republic:, independence, Aug. 13, 1960; Jan. 2, 1975; Sep. 1, 1981.

Central American States, Organization of: created, Dec. 14, 1951.

Central Intelligence Agency, Feb. 13, 1967.

Central Planning Board (Cuba), Feb. 20, 1960.

Central provinces (Poland), Apr. 30, 1815.

Cerdagne, Jan. 19, 1493.

Cerf, Bennett, May 25, 1898.

Cermak, Anton, Feb. 15, 1933.

Cernan, Eugene A., Jun. 6, 1966; Dec. 12, 1972.

Cerro Gordo, Battle of, Apr. 18, 1847.

Cervantes (Saavedra), Miguel, Sep. 29, 1547.

Cessna, Clyde Vernon, Dec. 5, 1879.

Ceylon, Mar. 27, 1802; Jan. 10, 1883; Apr. 4, 1942; Feb. 4, 1948; Jul. 21, 1960; May 22, 1972; name changed to Sri Lanka, Sep. 7, 1978. *See also* Sri Lanka

Cezanne, Paul, Jan. 19, 1839

Chaco War: ends, Jun. 12, 1935.

Chad, Apr. 22, 1900; independence, Aug. 13, 1960; Apr. 14, 1962; Apr. 13, 1975; civil war ends, Mar. 15, 1979.

Chadwick, Florence, Nov. 8, 1918.

Chadwick, George Whitefield, Nov. 13, 1854.

Chadwick, Henry, Oct. 6, 1824.

Chadwick, Sir Edwin, Jan. 24, 1800.

Chadwick, Sir James, Oct. 20, 1891.

Chaffee, Adna Romanza, Jr., Apr. 14, 1842; Sep. 23, 1884.

Chaffee, Roger, Feb. 15, 1935.

Chagall, Marc, Jul. 7, 1887.

Chain, Ernst Boris, Jun. 19, 1906.

Chaing Kai-shek, Jun. 11, 1926.

Chair of Peter, Feb. 22.

Chakri Memorial Day (Thailand), Apr. 6.

Chaliapin, Fyodor Ivanovich, Feb. 13, 1873.

Challe, Maurice (General), Jan. 24, 1960.

Challenger (U.S. space shuttle): launched, Apr. 4, 1983; Jun. 24, 1983.

Challis, James, Dec. 12, 1803.

Chalmers, Thomas, Mar. 17, 1780.

Chama Cha Mapenduzi (CCM Day) (Tanzania), Feb. 5.

Chamberlain, Neville, Mar. 18, 1869.

Chamberlain, Owen, Jul. 10, 1920.

Chamberlain, Sir Joseph Austen, Oct. 16, 1863.

Chamberlain, Wilt, Aug. 20, 1936.

Chambers, Whittaker, Apr. 1, 1901; Jan. 21, 1950.

Chambord, Treaty of, Jan. 15, 1552.

Champagne, Battle of, Feb. 1, 1915; Feb. 16, 1915; Sep. 25, 1915.

Champagne, First Battle of: opens, Dec. 20, 1914; Mar. 17, 1915.

Champagne, Philippe de, May 26, 1602.

Champagne, Second Battle of, Sep. 22, 1915; ends, Nov. 6, 1915.

Champion, Gower, Jun. 22, 1921.

Champion, Marge, Sep. 2, 1923.

Champlain, Samuel de, Jul. 3, 1608.

Champollion, Jean François, Dec. 23, 1790.

Chan, Sir Julius, Aug. 29, 1939.

Chancellor, John (William), Jul. 14, 1927.

Chancellorsville, Battle of, May 4, 1863.

Chandler, Harry, May 17, 1864.

Chandler, Otis, Nov. 23, 1927.

Chandler, Raymond (Thornton), Jul. 23, 1888.

Chandler, Zachariah, Dec. 10, 1813.

Chanel, Gabrielle Bonheur, Aug. 19, 1883.

Chaney, Lon, Apr. 1, 1883.

Channing, Carol, Jan. 31, 1923.

Channing, Edward, Jun. 15, 1856.

Channing, William Ellery, Apr. 7, 1780.

Chapelain, Jean, Dec. 4, 1595.

Chaplin, Charlie, Apr. 16, 1889.

Chaplin, Geraldine, Jul. 31, 1944.

Chapman, Frank Michler, Jun. 12, 1864.

Chapman, John (*Johnny Appleseed*), Sep. 26, 1774.

Chappaquiddick Island, Jul. 19, 1969.

Chappe, Claude, Dec. 25, 1763.

Chapultepec, Battle of, Sep. 13, 1846.

charcoal burners, patron of, Aug. 11.

Charcot, Jean-Martin, Nov. 29, 1825.

Chardonnet, Louis Marie, May 1, 1839.

Charge of the Light Brigade, Oct. 25, 1854.

Charing Cross Railway Station, Jan. 11, 1864.

Charisse, Cyd, Mar. 8, 1923.

Charlemagne, Apr. intro.

Charlemagne (Holy Roman Emperor), Apr. 2, 742; Dec. 25, 800.

Charleroi, Battle of: opens, Aug. 21, 1914.

Charles, duc d'Orléans, Nov. 24, 1394.

Charles, Duke of Burgundy, Nov. 10, 1433.

Charles, Ezzard, Jul. 18, 1951.

Charles, Jacques Alexandre César, Nov. 12, 1746.

Charles, Prince of Hohenzollern, Feb. 23, 1866.

Charles, Prince of Wales, Nov. 14, 1948; Jul. 1, 1969; Jul. 29, 1981.

Charles, Ray, Sep. 23, 1930.

Charles I (Austria): Aug. 17, 1887; abdicates, Nov. 12, 1918.

Charles I (England), Nov. 19, 1600; Mar. 27, 1625; Apr. 13, 1640; Sep. 2, 1644; Jan. 21, 1645; May 5, 1645; Sep. 3, 1651; beheaded, Jan. 30, 1649.

Charles I (Spain), Jun. 28, 1519.

Charles II (England), May 29, 1630; May 29, 1660; crowned, Apr. 23, 1661; Oct. 27, 1662; Mar. 4, 1681; Feb. 6, 1685.

Charles II (Scotland), Jan. 1, 1651.

Charles II (Spain), Nov. 6, 1661; Sep. 17, 1665; dies, Nov. 1, 1700.

Charles II (*the Bald*), Jun. 13, 823.

Charles III (France), Sep. 17, 879.

Charles III (Holy Roman Emperor), Feb. 12, 881.

Charles III (Naples), Feb. 27, 1386.

Charles III (Spain), Jan. 20, 1716; Aug. 10, 1759; dies, Dec. 14, 1788; Mar. 1, 1797.

Charles IV (France), Jan. 3, 1322; dies, Feb. 1, 1328.

Charles IV (Holy Roman Emperor), May 14, 1316; Apr. 7, 1348; Apr. 5, 1355; Jan. 10, 1356.

Charles IV (Spain), Nov. 11, 1748; Dec. 14, 1788; Mar. 19, 1808; May 1, 1808.

Christian VI (Denmark and Norway), Nov. 30, 1699.

Christian VII (Denmark and Norway), Jan. 29, 1749.

Christian VIII (Denmark): Sep. 18, 1786; dies, Jan. 20, 1848.

Christian IX (Denmark), Apr. 8, 1818; Nov. 15, 1863.

Christian X (Denmark): Sep. 26, 1870; dies, Apr. 20, 1947.

Christian philosophers, patron of, Nov. 25.

Christiana, Jan. 1, 1925.

Christianborg Palace (Denmark): burned, Oct. 3, 1884.

Christie, Agatha, Sep. 15, 1890.

Christina (Queen of Sweden), Dec. 8, 1626; abdicates Jun. 6, 1654.

Christmas Day, Dec. 25.

Christmas (Ethiopia), Jan. 6.

Christmas Holiday (Vatican City State), Dec. 26.

Christmas Holiday (Vatican City State), Dec. 27.

Christmas Island, May 6, 1962.

Christmas Seal Campaign, Nov. intro.

Christofer, Michael, Jan. 22, 1945.

Christ of the Andes: dedicated, Mar. 13, 1904.

Christophe, Henri, Oct. 6, 1767.

chrysanthemum, Nov. intro.

Chryse, Plain of (Mars), Jul. 20, 1976.

Chrysler, Walter Percy, Apr. 2, 1875.

Chrysler Corporation, May 4, 1950.

Chulalongkorn's Day (Thailand), Oct. intro.

Chun Doo Hwan, Jan. 18, 1931.

Church, Frank, Jul. 25, 1924.

Church, Frederick Edwin, May 4, 1826.

Church, Sam, Jr., Sep. 20, 1936.

church music, patron of, Nov. 22.

Church of England, Jan. 14, 1604; Worship and Doctrine Measure passed, Dec. 4, 1974.

Church of Ireland: established, Jan. 1, 1871.

Church of Jesus Christ of the Latter-Day Saints, The (Mormon Church), Jun. 9, 1978.

Churchill, John, May 26, 1650.

Churchill, Lord Randolph, Feb. 13, 1849.

Churchill, Sarah, Oct. 17, 1914.

Churchill, Winston, Nov. 30, 1874; appointed First Lord of Admiralty, Oct. 24, 1911; May 10, 1940; Dec. 24, 1941; May 12, 1943; appointed Prime Minister, Oct. 26, 1951; Apr. 9, 1963; dies, Jan. 24, 1965.

Churubusco, Battle of, Aug. 20, 1846.

Chu Teh, Dec. 18, 1886.

CIA: experiments revealed, Jul. 20, 1977.

Cibber, Colley, Nov. 6, 1671.

Cierva, Juan de la, Sep. 21, 1895; Jan. 10, 1923.

cigarette advertising, Jun. 2, 1967.

cigarette smoking: first drive against, Jun. 8, 1963.

Cincinnati, Society of the, May 13, 1783.

Cincinnati (Ohio), May 24, 1935.

Cincinnati Reds, May 24, 1935; Oct. 21, 1976.

Cinderella: premiere, Nov. 21, 1945.

CIO, Nov. 9, 1935. *See also* Congress of Industrial Organizations.

Citeaux Monastery: founded, Mar. 21, 1098.

Citizenship Day (U.S.), Sep. 17.

Citrine, Walter McLennan, Baron, Aug. 22, 1887.

city commission government: first in U.S., Sep. 8, 1900.

City of Glasgow, Apr. 6, 1929.

Ciudád Trujillo, Nov. 23, 1961.

Civic Holiday (Costa Rica), Dec. 29; Dec. 30.

civil disobedience: India, Mar. 30, 1919; Mar. 18, 1922; Dec. 22, 1928; Mar. 12, 1930; May 5, 1930; Mar. 4, 1931; Mar. 5, 1931.

civil rights: march on White House, Aug. 28, 1963.

Civil Rights Act, May 6, 1960; signed, Jul. 2, 1964.

civil rights bill: housing, Apr. 11, 1968.

Civil Service Commission (U.S.): established, Mar. 4, 1871.

Civil Service (U.S.), Jan. 6, 1883.

Civil War, (U.S.), begins, Apr. 12, 1861; Dec. 13, 1862; ends, Apr. 9, 1865; centennial, Jan. 8, 1961.

Civilian Conservation Corps: established, Mar. 31, 1933.

civilians, patron of, Apr. 24.

Civita Vecchia, Apr. 26, 1849.

Claiborne, Craig, Sep. 4, 1920.

Clair, René, Nov. 11, 1891.

Clairaut, Alexis, May 13, 1713.

Clairvaux, Abbey of: founded, Jun. 25, 1115.

Clantarf, Battle of, Apr. 23, 1014.

Clapperton, Hugh, May 18, 1788.

Clare, John, Jul. 13, 1793.

Clark, Barney, Jan. 21, 1922; artificial heart implanted, Dec. 2, 1982; Mar. 21, 1983.

Clark, Champ (James Beauchamp), Mar. 7, 1850.

Clark, George Rogers, Nov. 19, 1752.

Clark, Joe, May 22, 1979.

Clark, Mark Wayne, May 1, 1896; Sep. 9, 1943.

Clark, Robert, Jan. 2, 1968.

Clark, Thomas Campbell, Sep. 23, 1899.

Clark, William, Aug. 1, 1770.

Clark, (William) Ramsey, Dec. 18, 1927.

Clarke, Arthur Charles, Dec. 16, 1917.

Clarke, Charles Cowden, Dec. 15, 1787.

Clarke, Ellis E.I., Dec. 28, 1917.

Clarke, John Hessin, Sep. 18, 1857.

Clarke, Samuel, Oct. 11, 1675.

Classified Advertising Week, International, May intro.

Claude, Albert, Aug. 24, 1899.

Claudel, Paul (Louis-Marie), Aug. 6, 1868.

Claudius, Matthias, Aug. 15, 1740.

Clausewitz, Karl Maria von, Jun. 1, 1780.

Clavell, James Dumaresq, Oct. 10, 1924.

Clay, Cassius, May 25, 1965; Nov. 22, 1965; May 8, 1967. *See also* Ali, Muhammad.

Clay, Henry, Apr. 12, 1777.

Clay, Lucius, Apr. 23, 1897.

Clayton-Bulwer Treaty, Apr. 19, 1850.

Cleaner Air Week, National, Oct. intro.

Cleaver, Eldridge, Aug. 31, 1935.

Clemenceau, Georges, Sep. 28, 1841; Jan. 18, 1919.

Clemens, Samuel Langhorne, Nov. 30, 1835. *See also* Twain, Mark.

Clemente, Roberto, Aug. 18, 1934.

Clement II (pope), Dec. 24, 1046.

Clement III (anti pope), Jun. 25, 1080; Mar. 31, 1084.

Clement III (pope), Apr. 3, 1189.

Clement IV (pope), Feb. 5, 1265.

Clement V (pope), Mar. 22, 1312.

Clement VI (pope), Apr. 13, 1346.

Clement VII (pope), May 26, 1478; Jul. 11, 1533.

Clement VIII (pope), Feb. 24, 1536.

Clement IX (pope), Jan. 28, 1600.

Clement X (pope), Jul. 12, 1590.

Clement XI (pope), Jul. 23, 1649.

Clement XII (pope), Apr. 7, 1652.

Clement XIII (pope), Mar. 7, 1693.

Clement XIV (pope), Oct. 31, 1705; Jul. 21, 1773; expells Jesuits from Rome, Aug. 16, 1773.

Clemson College, Jan. 28, 1963.

Clermont: begins regular service, Aug. 9, 1807.

Cleveland, Grover, Mar. 18, 1837; inaugurated, Mar. 4, 1885; dedicates Statue of Liberty, Oct. 28, 1886; second term, Mar. 4, 1893.

Cleveland (Ohio), Jan. 10, 1870.

Cliburn, Van, Jul. 12, 1934; Apr. 11, 1958.

Clift, Montgomery, Oct. 17, 1920.

Clinton, Dewitt, Mar. 2, 1769.

Clinton, George, Jul. 26, 1739.

Clive, Robert, Sep. 29, 1725.

clothing industry workers, patron of, Jan. 15.

clothmakers, patron of, Nov. 13.

Clovis (King of the Franks), Dec. 25, 503.

Clown Week, National, Aug. intro.

clowns, patron of, Feb. 12.

Clurman, Harold, Sep. 18, 1901.

Clymer, George, Mar. 16, 1739.

Cnut of Denmark, Nov. 30, 1016.

coal mine disaster: Mononagh (West Virginia), Dec. 6, 1907.

coal mine explosion: West Frankfort (Illinois), Dec. 21, 1951.

coalminers, patron of, Nov. 6.

coastal fishing zone, U.S.: extended, Oct. 14, 1966.

Coast Guard, United States, Jan. 28, 1915; Nov. 1, 1941.

Cobb, Henry Ives, Aug. 19, 1859.

Cobb, Irvin S(hrewsbury), Jun. 23, 1876.

Cobb, Lee J., Dec. 8, 1911.

Cobb, Ty(rus Raymond), Dec. 18, 1886.

cobblers, patron of, Jun. 29.

Cobden, Richard, Jun. 3, 1804.

Coblentz, William Weber, Nov. 20, 1873.

Coblenz, Alliance of, Sep. 5, 1338.

Coburn, Charles, Jun. 19, 1877.

Coburn, James, Aug. 31, 1928.

Cochin-China, Apr. 13, 1862.

Cochrane, Thomas, Dec. 14, 1775.

Cockcroft, Sir John Douglas, May 27, 1897.

Cocteau, Jean, Jul. 5, 1889.

code of ethics, Mar. 2, 1977.

Connolly, Maureen, Sep. 17, 1934.

Connors, Jimmy, Sep. 2, 1952.

Conrad, Charles (Pete) Jr., Jun. 2, 1930; Nov. 19, 1969; Jun. 22, 1973.

Conrad, Joseph, Dec. 3, 1857.

Conrad II (Holy Roman Emperor), Mar. 26, 1027; May 28, 1037.

Conrad III (Germany), Mar. 7, 1138.

Conrad IV (Holy Roman Emperor), Apr. 25, 1228; Dec. 13, 1250.

Conradin (Holy Roman Emperor), Mar. 25, 1252; beheaded, Aug. 29, 1268.

Conscience, Hendrik, Dec. 3, 1812.

conscription: British, Apr. 27, 1939.

Conservative Party, Great Britain, May 3, 1979.

Considine, Robert Bernard, Nov. 4, 1906.

Constable, John, Jun. 11, 1776.

Constance, Council of: convenes, Nov. 5, 1414.

Constance (Sicily), Jan. 27, 1186.

Constant de Rebecque, Henri Benjamin, Oct. 25, 1767.

Constantine (the Great), p. ix.

Constantine (Byzantine Emperor): killed, May 29, 1453.

Constantine I (Greece), Aug. 2, 1868; Mar. 18, 1913; abdicates, Jun. 11, 1917; Mar. 6, 1964.

Constantine II (Greece): flees, Dec. 14, 1967; stripped of title Dec. 9, 1974.

Constantinople, May 11, 330; Apr. 12, 1204; May 29, 1453; May 15, 1455; Mar. 28, 1930.

Constantinople, Peace of, Apr. 16, 1712.

Constantinople, Sixth Council of:convenes, Nov. 7, 680.

Constanza (Romania), Oct. 22, 1916.

Constitution, U.S.: signed, Sep. 17, 1787.

Constitution, U.S.S, Aug. 19, 1812; Feb. 20, 1815.

Constitution Act (Canada), Apr. 17, 1982.

Constitutional Convention, May 25, 1787.

Constitution Day, Sep. intro.

Constitution Day (Cayman Islands), Jul. intro.

Constitution Day (Brunei), Sep. 29.

Constitution Day (Cook Island), Aug. 4.

Constitution Day (Denmark), Jun. 5.

Constitution Day (Hungary), Aug. 20.

Constitution Day (Japan), May intro.

Constitution Day (Mexico), Feb. 5.

Constitution Day (Nauru), May 17.

Constitution Day (Nepal), Dec. 16.

Constitution Day (North Korea), Dec. 27.

Constitution Day (Norway), May 17.

Constitution Day or Victory Day (Tunisia), Jun. 1.

Constitution Day (Paraguay), Aug. 25.

Constitution Day (Poland), May 3.

Constitution Day (Puerto Rico), Jul. 25.

Constitution Day (South Korea), Jul. 17.

Constitution Day (Taiwan), Dec. 25.

Constitution Day (Tonga), Nov. 4.

Constitution Day (Uruguay), Jul. 18.

Constitution Day (U.S.), Mar. 4.

Constitution Day (U.S.), Sep. 17.

Constitution Day (U.S.S.R.), Oct. 7.

Constitution Day (U.S.S.R.), Dec. 5.

Constitution Day (Vanuatu), Oct. 5.

Constitution Memorial Day (Japan), May 3.

Constitution (U.S.), Jan. 2, 1788.

Constitution Week, Sep. intro.

Constitutis de Feudis, May 28, 1037.

Continental Army, formed, May 31, 1775; Jun. 15, 1775; Jul. 3, 1775; Valley Forge camp, Dec. 19, 1777.

Continental Congress, First, Sep. 5, 1774; Second, May 10, 1775; Jul. 4, 1776; Nov. 15, 1777; Jan. 14, 1784.

contraception, Jul. 29, 1968.

Conversion of St. Paul, Feast of, Jan. 25.

Coogan, Jackie, Oct. 26, 1914.

Cook, Frederick Albert, Apr. 21, 1865.

Cook, James (Captain), Apr. 19, 1770; Apr. 28, 1770; Oct. 27, 1728; landfall in New Zealand Oct. 30, 1769; murdered Feb. 13, 1779.

Cooke, (Alfred) Alistair, Nov. 20, 1908.

Cooke, Jay, Aug. 10, 1821.

Cooke, Terence James, Mar. 21, 1921.

Cooke, William F., May 4, 1806.

cooks, patron of, Jul. 29.

cooks, patron of, Aug. 10.

Cooley, Denton A., Apr. 4, 1969.

Coolidge, Charles Allerton, Nov. 30, 1858.

Coolidge, (John) Calvin, Jul. 4, 1872; Mar. 4, 1921; May 26, 1924; inaugurated, Mar. 4, 1925.

Coolidge, William David, Oct. 23, 1873.

Coon, Carleton S(tevens), Jun. 23, 1904.

Cooper, Gary, May 7, 1901.

Cooper, Jackie, Sep. 15, 1922.

Cooper, James Fenimore, Sep. 15, 1789.

Cooper, John Sherman, Aug. 23, 1901.

Cooper, Leon N., Feb. 28, 1930.

Cooper, Leroy Gordon, Mar. 6, 1927; May 15, 1963.

Cooper, Peter, Feb. 12, 1791.

coopers, patron of, Dec. 6.

Cooperstown (New York), Jan. 29, 1936.

Copenhagen, patron of, Mar. 4.

Copenhagen, Treaty of: signed, Jun. 6, 1660.

Copernicus, Nicolas, Feb. 19, 1473.

Copland, Aaron, Nov. 14, 1900; *Symphony:* premiere, Jan. 11, 1925; Oct. 16, 1938; Jan. 28, 1941.

Copley, John Singleton, Jul. 3, 1738.

coppersmiths, patron of, Nov. 6.

Coppola, Francis Ford, Apr. 7, 1939.

Coralli, Jean, Jun. 28, 1841.

Coral Sea, Battle of, May 4, 1942; May 8, 1942.

Corbeil, Treaty of, May 11, 1258.

Corbett, James J., Sep. 7, 1892.

Corbett, James J. (*Gentleman Jim*), Sep. 1, 1866.

Corbusier, Le, Oct. 6, 1887.

Corcoran, Thomas Gardiner, Dec. 29, 1900.

Corcoran, William Wilson, Dec. 27, 1798.

Corday, Charlotte, Jul. 27, 1768; Jul. 13, 1793.

Cordoba, Jun. 29, 1236.

Corelli, Franco, Apr. 8, 1921.

Corey, William Ellis, May 4, 1866.

Corfu, Jan. 11, 1916; Jan. 13, 1916.

Corfu, Pact of, Jul. 20, 1917.

Cori, Carl Ferdinand, Dec. 5, 1896.

Cori, Gerty Theresa, Aug. 15, 1896.

Corinth (Greece), Jun. 12, 1917.

Cormack, Allan MacLeod, Feb. 23, 1924.

Corneille, Pierre, Jun. 6, 1606.

Cornelius, Peter Joseph von, Sep. 27, 1783.

Cornell, Ezra, Jan. 11, 1807.

Cornell, Katherine, Feb. 16, 1893.

Cornforth, John, Sep. 7, 1917.

Cornwallis, Charles 1st Marquis, Dec. 31, 1738; Jan. 3, 1777.

Coronation Day (Thailand), May 5.

Corot, Jean Baptiste Camille, Jul. 16, 1796.

Correct Posture Month, Apr. intro.

Corrective Move Day (People's Democratic Republic of Yemen), Jun. 22.

Corregidor: first Japanese bombing, Dec. 29, 1941; (Philippines), May 6, 1942; Feb. 16, 1945.

Correll, Charles, Feb. 2, 1890.

Corrigan, Mairead, Jan. 27, 1944.

Cortés, Hernando, Nov. 8, 1519.

Cortina, May 30, 1915.

Cortona, Pietro Berretini da, Nov. 1, 1596.

Corwin, Thomas, Jul. 29, 1794.

Cosby, Bill, Jul. 12, 1937.

Cosell, Howard, Mar. 25, 1920.

Cosmonautics Day (U.S.S.R.), Apr. 12.

cosmos, Oct. intro.

Cosmos, Oct. 26, 1967.

Cosmos 954, Jan. 24, 1978.

Cossacks: revolt, Dec. 9, 1917; Jan. 10, 1918; Jan. 7, 1920.

Costain, Thomas B., May 8, 1885.

Costanzi Theater (Rome), Jan. 14, 1900.

Costa Rica: discovered, Sep. 18, 1502; independence, Sep. 15, 1821; Jan. 19, 1921; Nov. 9, 1949.

Coste, Dieudonne (Captain), Sep. 2, 1930.

Costello, Lou, Mar. 6, 1906.

Cotman, John Sell, May 16, 1782.

Cotten, Joseph, May 15, 1905.

Cotton, Charles, Apr. 28, 1630.

Cotton, John, Dec. 4, 1585.

cotton gin: patented, Mar. 14, 1794.

Coty, François, May 3, 1874.

Coubertin, Pierre, Jan. 1, 1863.

Coughlin, Charles Edward, Oct. 25, 1891.

Coulanges, Numa Denis Fustel de, Mar. 18, 1830.

Coulomb, Charles Augustin de, Jun. 14, 1736.

Council of Europe, May 2, 1951; Apr. 29, 1965.

Council of Four, Mar. 25, 1919.

Country Music Month, Oct. intro.

Countryman's Day (Peru), Jun. 24.

Couperin, François, Nov. 10, 1668.

Courbet, Gustave, Jun. 10, 1819.

Cournand, André F., Sep. 24, 1895.

Court, Margaret, Jul. 16, 1942.

Cousin, Victor, Nov. 28, 1792.

Cousins, Norman, Jun. 24, 1915.

Cousteau, Jacques Ives, Jun. 11, 1910.

Cousy, Bob, Aug. 9, 1928.

Couthon, Georges, Dec. 22, 1755.

Covenant, Day of the, Dec. 16.

Coward, Sir Noel (Pierce), Dec. 16, 1899.

Cowell, Henry Dixon, Mar. 11, 1897.

Cowen, Joshua Lionel, Aug. 25, 1880.

Cowles, John, Dec. 14, 1893.

Cowley, Malcolm, Aug. 24, 1898.

Cowpens (South Carolina), Jan. 17, 1781.

Cowper, William, Nov. 26, 1731.

Cox, Allyn, Jun. 5, 1896.

Cox, Archibald, May 17, 1912; Oct. 20, 1973.

Cox, Edward Finch, Jun. 12, 1971.

Cox, Kenyon, Oct. 27, 1856.

Cox, Wally, Dec. 6, 1924.

Coxey, Jacob Sechler, Apr. 16, 1854.

Coysevox, Antoine, Sep. 29, 1640.

Cozzens, James Gould, Aug. 19, 1903.

Crabbe, Buster, Feb. 7, 1909.

Crabbe, George, Dec. 24, 1754.

Cracow, Battle of: begins, Nov. 15, 1914; siege ends, Dec. 23, 1914.

Cracow, Jan. 9, 1493.

Crèvecoeur, Michael-Guillaume-Jean de, Jan. 31, 1735.

Craig, Jim, May 31, 1957.

Cram, Ralph Adams, Dec. 16, 1863.

Crandall, Prudence, Sep. 3, 1803.

Crane, (Harold) Hart, Jul. 21, 1899.

Crane, Stephen (Townley), Nov. 1, 1871.

Cranmer, Thomas, Jul. 2, 1489; burned at stake, Mar. 21, 1556.

Crawford, Francis Marion, Aug. 2, 1854.

Crawford, Joan, Mar. 23, 1908.

Creation, date of, p. x.

Crécy, Battle of, Aug. 26, 1346.

Credit-Anstalt: bank failure, May 11, 1931.

crematorium: first municipal, Jan. 2, 1901.

Cremer, Sir William Randal, Mar. 18, 1838.

Cremona, Italy, patron of, Nov. 13.

Cremona, Luigi, Dec. 1, 1830.

Crespy, Treaty of, Sep. 18, 1544.

Cressy, H.M.S.: sunk, Sep. 22, 1914.

Crete: union with Greece, Feb. 6, 1897.

Crete Greece, Mar. 18, 1897.

Crichton, James, Aug. 19, 1560.

Crichton, (John) Michael, Oct. 23, 1942.

Crick, Francis H.C., Apr. 25, 1953.

Crime Prevention Week, National, Feb. intro.

Crimea, Jan. 9, 1792.

Crimean War, Apr. 19, 1853; begins, Jul. 2, 1853; begins, Oct. 5, 1853; Nov. 30, 1853; Mar. 12, 1854; Mar. 27, 1854; Mar. 28, 1854; Sep. 14, 1854; Oct. 17, 1854; Oct. 25, 1854; Nov. 4, 1854; Sep. 11, 1855; Nov. 28, 1855; treaty ending, Mar. 30, 1856.

Crisler, Herbert Orin (Fritz), Jan. 12, 1899.

Crispi, Francesco, Oct. 4, 1819.

Cristofori, Bartolommeo, May 4, 1655.

Crittenden, John Jordan, Sep. 10, 1787.

Croatia (Yugoslavia), Jan. 26, 1699; Jan. 14, 1972.

Croce, Benedetto, Feb. 25, 1866.

Crocker, Charles, Sep. 16, 1822.

Crockett, Davy, Aug. 17, 1786; Mar. 6, 1836.

Crome, John, Dec. 22, 1768.

Crompton, Samuel, Dec. 3, 1753.

Cromwell, Oliver, Apr. 25, 1599; defeats Scots, Aug. 17, 1648; Jan. 30, 1649; Sep. 11, 1649; Sep. 3, 1650; Sep. 3, 1651; Apr. 20, 1653; Dec. 16, 1653; Sep. 3, 1654; Mar. 31, 1657; dies, Sep. 3, 1658; May 25, 1659.

Cromwell, Richard, Sep. 3, 1658; May 25, 1659.

Cromwell, Thomas (Earl of Essex): Apr. 12, 1533; beheaded, Jul. 28, 1540.

Cronin, A(rchibald) J(oseph), Jul. 19, 1896.

Cronkite, Walter (Leland), Jr., Nov. 4, 1916.

Cronyn, Hume, Jul. 18, 1911.

Crook, George, Sep. 23, 1829.

Crookes, Sir William, Jun. 17, 1832.

crops, patron of, Mar. 13.

Crosby, Bing, May 2, 1903.

Crosley, Powel, Jr., Sep. 18, 1886.

Crosley Field (Cincinnati), May 24, 1935.

Cross, James R., Oct. 5, 1970.

Cross, Wilbur Lucius, Apr. 10, 1862.

cross-country flight: first U.S., Nov. 5, 1912.

crossword puzzle: first printed, Dec. 21, 1913.

Crowdy, Oliver, Apr. 6, 1830.

Crown Imperial: first performed, May 9, 1937.

Crown of St. Stephen, Jan. 6, 1978.

Crown Prince Harald's Birthday (Norway), Feb. 21.

Crowther, F. Bosley, Jul. 13, 1905.

Crump, Diana, Feb. 7, 1969.

Crusade, First, Jul. 1, 1097; Jun. 3, 1098; Jun. 28, 1098; Jul. 15, 1099.

Crusade, Second: proclaimed, Dec. 1, 1145; Mar. 31, 1146; (Louis VII), Mar. 24, 1267.

Crusade, Third, Jul. 1, 1190; Jul. 12, 1191; Sep. 1, 1192; Dec. 21, 1192.

Crusade, Fourth, Apr. 12, 1204.

Crusade, Sixth, Mar. 18, 1229; Jun. 4, 1249.

Cuba, Oct. 18, 1854; independence, May 20, 1902; Mar. 10, 1952; May 27, 1960; Jan. 3, 1961; Apr. 17, 1961; May 1, 1961; expulsion from O.A.S., Jan. 31, 1962; Feb. 3, 1962; U.S. naval blockade, Oct. 22, 1962; U.S. bans financial transactions, Jul. 8, 1963; Jan. 9, 1970; Sep. 1, 1977.

Cudahy, Edward Aloysius, Feb. 1, 1859.

Cudahy, Michael, Dec. 7, 1841.

Cugnot, Nicholas, Sep. 25, 1725.

Cukor, George, Jul. 7, 1899.

Culbertson, Ely, Jul. 22, 1891.

Culloden, Battle of, Apr. 16, 1746.

Cultural Revolution, Chinese, Feb. 2, 1974; Jun. 5, 1978.

Cultural Revolution of 1966-69: condemned, Sep. 29, 1979.

Culture Day (Japan), Nov. 3.

Cumana (Venezuela), patron of, Jan. 21.

Cumberland, Mar. 8, 1862.

Cummings, Constance, May 15, 1910.

Cummings, E. E., Oct. 14, 1894.

Cunard, Sir Samuel, Nov. 21, 1787.

Cunningham, Allan, Dec. 7, 1784.

Cunningham, Imogen, Apr. 12, 1883.

Cunningham, Merce, Aug. 16, 1919.

Curie, Marie, Nov. 7, 1867.

Curie, Pierre, May 15, 1859.

Curran, Joseph Edwin, Mar. 1, 1906.

Currier, Nathaniel, Mar. 27, 1813.

curriers, patron of, Oct. 28.

Curtin, John, Jan. 8, 1885.

Curtis, Benjamin Robbins, Nov. 4, 1809.

Curtis, Charles, Jan. 25, 1860; Mar. 4, 1929.

Curtis, Cyrus Hermann Kotzschmar, Jun. 18, 1850.

Curtis, Tony, Jun. 3, 1925.

Curtiss, Glenn, May 21, 1878.

Curzon, Clifford, May 18, 1907.

Curzon, George Nathaniel, Jan. 11, 1859.

Cushing, Harvey Williams, Apr. 8, 1869.

Cushing, Richard James, Aug. 24, 1895.

Cushing, U.S.S.: bombed, Apr. 28, 1915.

Cushman, Charlotte Saunders, Jul. 23, 1816.

Custer, George A(rmstrong), Dec. 5, 1839; massacred, Jun. 25, 1876.

customs officers, patron of, Sep. 21.

Custozza, Battle of, Jul. 25, 1848.

Cuvier, Baron Georges (Jean-Léopold-Nicolas Frédéric), Aug. 23, 1769.

Cuza, Alexander, Dec. 23, 1861.

Cyane, Feb. 20, 1815.

cyclone: Darwin (Australia), Dec. 25, 1974.

Cyprus: independence, Aug. 16, 1960; Jul. 15, 1974; Feb. 13, 1975.

Czech language, Apr. 5, 1897.

Czechoslovakia, patron of, Sep. 28; proclaimed a republic, Oct. 28, 1891; declares war on Germany, Aug. 13, 1918; Sep. 2, 1918; declares independence, Oct. 21, 1918; Nov. 10, 1918; Nov. 2, 1938; deprives Germans and Hungarians of citizenship, Aug. 3, 1945; Mar. 17, 1951; Jun. 2, 1951; communist Party of, Jan. 5, 1968; Apr. 5, 1968; invaded by Warsaw Pact troops, Aug. 20, 1968; federal government Jan. 1, 1969; Jan. 16, 1969; treaty with West Germany Dec. 11, 1973; Jan. 6, 1977.

Czerny, Karl, Feb. 20, 1791.

Czolgosz, Leon, Sep. 6, 1901.

D

Dachau: liberated, Apr. 24, 1945.

Dacko, David, Sep. 20, 1979; Sep. 1, 1981.

daffodil, Mar. intro.

Daguerre, Louis Jacques Mandè, Nov. 18, 1789.

Dahl, Arlene, Aug. 11, 1928.

Dahl, Roald, Sep. 13, 1916.

Dahomey, Jun. 22, 1894; Nov. 30, 1975.

Dailey, Dan, Dec. 12, 1917.

Daimler, Gottlieb Wilhelm, Mar. 17, 1834.

Dainton, Georges Jacques, Oct. 26, 1759.

Dairy Month, National, Jun. intro.

dairy workers, patron of, Feb. 1.

daisy, Apr. intro.

Daladier, Edouard, Jun. 18, 1884.

Dalai Lama, May 27, 1951; Mar. 31, 1959.

Dalberg-Acton, John Emerich Edward, 1st Baron Acton, Jan. 10, 1834.

d'Albert, Eugen Francis Charles, Apr. 10, 1864.

Dale, Sir Henry H., Jun. 9, 1875.

d'Alembert, Jean Le Rond, Nov. 17, 1717.

Dalén, Nils G., Nov. 30, 1869.

Daley, Richard J., May 15, 1902.

Dali, Salvador, May 11, 1904.

Dallas, George M., Mar. 4, 1845.

Dalls, Alexander James, Jun. 21, 1757.

Dalton, John, Sep. 6, 1766.

Daly, Marcus, Dec. 5, 1841.

Dam, Henrik C. P., Feb. 21, 1895.

Damansky (Chanpao) Island, Mar. 2, 1969.

Damascus, Mar. 24, 1401; seized by British and Arabs Oct. 1, 1918; Jan. 1, 1925.

Damn Yankees: premiere, May 5, 1955.

Damrosch, Walter Johannes, Jan. 30, 1862.

Dana, Richard Henry, Jr., Aug. 1, 1815.

Da Nang, Mar. 30, 1975.

Danatbank: failure, Jul. 13, 1931.

Dandridge, Dorothy, Nov. 9, 1922.

Danes, Jan. 6, 871.

Dangerfield, Rodney, Nov. 22, 1921.

Daniel, Clifton, Jr., Sep. 19, 1912.

Daniels, Jonathan Worth, Apr. 26, 1902.

Däniken, Erich von, Apr. 14, 1935.

Danish Constitution: adopted, Jun. 5, 1953.

Danish West Indies, Aug. 4, 1916; Mar. 31, 1917.

Danish West Indies Emancipation Day (Virgin Islands), Jul. 3.

Dannay, Frederic, Oct. 20, 1905 .

Dannecker, Johann Heinrich von, Oct. 15, 1758.

d'Annunzio, Gabriele, Mar. 12, 1863.

Danzig, Jun. 2, 1734.

Daphnis et Chloë: premiere, Jun. 8, 1912.

D'Aquino, Iva Toguri, Jan. 19, 1977.

Dardanelles, Feb. 23, 1905; Oct. 1, 1914; Feb. 19, 1915.

Dare, Virginia, Aug. 18, 1587.

Darin, Bobby, May 14, 1936.

Dario, Rubén , Jan. 18, 1867.

Darnell, Linda, Oct. 16, 1921.

Darnley, Lord (Henry Stuart), Jul. 29, 1565; Feb. 10, 1567.

Darrow, Clarence, Apr. 18, 1857.

Dartmoor Prison, Mar. 20, 1806.

Darwin, Charles Robert, Feb. 12, 1809.

Darwin, Erasmus, Dec. 12, 1731.

Darwin, Sir George Howard, Jul. 9, 1845.

Darwin (Australia), Dec. 25, 1974.

Dato, Eduardo, Mar. 8, 1921.

d'Aubigné, Jean Henri Merle, Aug. 16, 1794.

Daubigny, Charles François, Feb. 15, 1817.

Daud Khan, Sardar Mohammad, Apr. 27, 1978.

Daughters of the American Revolution, Aug. 8, 1890.

Daumier, Honoré, Feb. 26, 1808.

Davenport, James, Feb. 14, 1764.

David, Jacques-Louis, Aug. 30, 1748.

David I (Scotland), Apr. 22, 1124; Apr. 27, 1124; Aug. 22, 1138; dies, May 24, 1153.

David II (Scotland), Jun. 7, 1329; deposed, Aug. 11, 1332; Oct. 17, 1346.

Davidson, Jo, Mar. 30, 1883.

Davies, Arthur B(owen), Sep. 26, 1862.

Davis, Adelle, Feb. 25, 1904.

Davis, Angela Yvonne, Jan. 26, 1944.

Davis, Benjamin Oliver, Jul. 1, 1877.

Davis, Benjamin Oliver, Jr., Dec. 18, 1912.

Davis, Bette, Apr. 5, 1904.

Davis, Dwight Filley, Jul. 5, 1879.

Davis, Jefferson, Birthday (U.S. southern states), Jun. intro; Jun. 3, 1808; Feb. 8, 1861.

Davis, Miles, Jr., May 25, 1926.

Davis, Richard Harding, Apr. 18, 1864.

Davis, Sammy, Jr., Dec. 8, 1925.

Davis, Stuart, Dec. 7, 1894.

Davis, William Morris, Feb. 12, 1850.

Davisson, Clinton Joseph, Oct. 22, 1881.

Davout, Louis Nicolas, May 10, 1770.

Davy, Sir Humphrey, Dec. 17, 1778.

Dawes, Charles Gates, Aug. 27, 1865; Mar. 4, 1925.

Dawson, William L., Apr. 26, 1886.

Day, Clarence (Shepard), Nov. 18, 1874.

Day, Doris, Apr. 3, 1924.

Day, Dorothy, Nov. 8, 1897.

Day, Thomas, Jun. 22, 1748.

Dayan, Moshe, May 20, 1915; Oct. 21, 1979.

Daylight Saving Time, Mar. 31, 1918; Sep. 30, 1974.

Dayton, Jonathan, Oct. 16, 1760.

DC-10 jetliner: crashes, May 25, 1979.

DDT: banned in residential areas, Nov. 20, 1969.

deaconate: married men admitted to Roman Catholic, Sep. 29, 1964.

Dead or All Saints' Day, Day of the (Congo), Nov. 1.

Deák, Ferencz, Oct. 17, 1803.

dealers in used clothing, patron of, Jul. 26.

Dean, Dizzy, Jan. 16, 1911.

Dean, James, Feb. 8, 1931.

Dean, John W. 3rd, Oct. 15, 1938; Apr. 30, 1973; Aug. 2, 1974.

Dean, William F(riske), Aug. 1, 1899.

Deane, Silas, Dec. 24, 1737.

Death of General San Martin Anniversary of the (Argentina), Aug. 17.

Death of Quaid-e-Azam Anniversary of the (Pakistan), Sep. 11.

death penalty: restoration in U.S.S.R., Jan. 12, 1950.

Debakey, Michael Ellis, Sep. 7, 1908.

Debs, Eugene V(ictor), Nov. 5, 1855.

Debussy, Claude, Aug. 22, 1862; Apr. 30, 1902; Mar. 1, 1907.

Debye, Peter J. W., Mar. 24, 1884.

De Carlo, Yvonne, Sep. 1, 1924.

Decatur, Stephen, Feb. 16, 1804; Oct. 25, 1812; Jun. 30, 1815.

decem, Dec. intro.

decimal currency: Britain, Feb. 15, 1971.

Declaration of Independence: adopted, Jul. 4, 1776.

Declaration of the Rights of Man (France): adopted, Aug. 4, 1789.

Decoration Day (Liberia), Mar. 13.

Decoration Day (Liberia), Mar. intro.

Decoration Day (U.S.), Jul. intro.

Dedekind, Richard, Oct. 6, 1831.

de Diego's Birthday (Puerto Rico), Apr. 16 .

de Duve, Christian René, Oct. 2, 1917.

Deere, John, Feb. 7, 1804.

Deerfield, Massachusetts, Feb. 28, 1704.

Defender of the Faith, Feb. 2, 1522.

Defenders' Day, Sep. intro.

Defenders' Day (Missouri), Sep. 12.

Defense of Pakistan Day (Pakistan), Sep. 6.

Defense Production Administration, Jan. 3, 1951.

De Forest, Lee, Aug. 26, 1873; Mar. 5, 1907; Apr. 9, 1909.

Degas, (Hilaire Germaine) Edgar, Jul. 19, 1834.

De Gaulle, Charles, Nov. 22, 1890; named president of Fifth Republic, Dec. 21, 1958; Jan. 8, 1959; Jan. 29, 1960; Apr. 14, 1962; Nov. 25, 1962; Jan. 31, 1964; Apr. 28, 1969.

de Havilland, Olivia, Jul. 1, 1916.

De Hostos' Birthday (Puerto Rico), Jan. intro.; Jan. 11.

Dekker, Eduard Douwes (*Multatuli*), Mar. 2, 1820.

Delacroix, Eugene, Apr. 26, 1798.

Delagoa Bay Railway, Jul. 8, 1875.

Delano, Jane, Mar. 12, 1862.

de la Renta, Oscar, Jul. 22, 1932.

Delarge, Robert C., Mar. 15, 1842.

Delaroche, Hippolyte Paul, Jul. 17, 1797.

De Larrocha, Alicia, May 23, 1923.

Delaunay, Sonia, Nov. 14, 1885.

De Laurentiis, Dino, Aug. 8, 1919.

Delavigne, Jean François Casimir, Apr. 4, 1793.

Delaware Day (Delaware), Dec. 7.

Delaware (U.S.): first state, Dec. 7, 1787.

Delbrück, Max, Sep. 4, 1906.

Deledda, Grazia, Sep. 27, 1875.

Delhi, Dec. 18, 1398; Jan. 3, 1399; Dec. 12, 1911.

Delhi Pact, Mar. 5, 1931.

Del Monaco, Mario, Jul. 25, 1915.

Delmonico, Lorenzo, Mar. 13, 1813.

Delon, Alain, Nov. 8, 1935.

Del Rey, Lester, Jun. 2, 1915.

Del Rio, Dolores, Aug. 3, 1905.

del Sarto, Andrea, Jul. 16, 1486.

de Luca, Giuseppe, Dec. 25, 1876.

Demaret, James N., May 25, 1910.

Demille, Cecil B(lount), Aug. 12, 1881.

Democracy Day (Nepal), Feb. 18.

Democracy Day (Rwanda), Jan. 28 .

Democratic convention: rioting, Aug. 28, 1968.

Democratic Republic of Madagascar Anniversary of the (Madagascar), Dec. 30.

Dempsey, Jack, Jun. 24, 1895; Jul. 4, 1919; Sep. 23, 1926.

Deneuve, Catherine, Oct. 22, 1943.

de Neve, Felipe, Feb. 3, 1777.

De Niro, Robert, Aug. 17, 1943.

Denmark, Apr. 4, 1611; Sep. 14, 1770; Jan. 14, 1814; May 8, 1852; Jan. 17, 1917; Apr. 22, 1918; Mar. 8, 1920; Apr. 9, 1940; Jan. 15, 1969.

Denmark, patron of, Feb. 3.

Denmark, patron saint of, Jan. 19 .

Dennison, Aaron Lufkin, Mar. 6, 1812.

Dennison, Robert Lee, Apr. 13, 1901.

dentists, patron of, Feb. 9.

Department of Defense (U.S.): created, Aug. 10, 1949.

Department of Energy (U.S.): created, Aug. 4, 1977.

Department of Labor and Commerce (U.S.), Feb. 14, 1903.

DeQuincy, Thomas, Aug. 15, 1785.

Derby Earl of, Oct. 21, 1345.
Deringer, Henry, Oct. 26, 1786.
Dern, Bruce, Jun. 5, 1936.
Derne (Tripoli), Apr. 27, 1805.
DeRoburt, Hammer, Sep. 25, 1922.
Derzhavin, Gavrila, Jul. 14, 1743.
Desai, Morarji R. (India), Mar. 24, 1977.
Descartes, René, Mar. 31, 1596.
desegregation: Nashville (Tennessee), May 10, 1960.
desert wanderers, patrons of, Oct. 8.
De Sanctis, Francesco, Mar. 28, 1817.
De Sica, Vittorio, Jul. 7, 1901.
Dessalines, Jean Jacques, Mar. 29, 1804.
Dessalines Memorial Day (Haiti), Oct. 17 .
d'Estournells de Constant de Rebecque, Paul H. B. B., Nov. 22, 1852.
Detroit (Michigan), Jan. 21, 1915; racial violence, Jul. 23, 1967.
Dettingen, Jun. 27, 1743.
Deutsch, Helene, Oct. 9, 1884.
Deutschland, Jun. 22, 1910.
Deux Images: premiere, Feb. 26, 1913.
De Valera, Eamon, Oct. 14, 1882; Apr. 5, 1919.
Devesi, Baddeley, Oct. 16, 1941.
Devine, Andy, Oct. 7, 1905.
Devlin, Bernadette, Apr. 23, 1947; Dec. 22, 1969.
De Voto, Bernard A., Jan. 11, 1897.
DeVries, William (Dr.), Dec. 2, 1982.
Dewar, Sir James, Sep. 20, 1842.
De Wet, Christiaan Rudolph, Oct. 7, 1854.
Dewey, George, Dec. 26, 1837; May 1, 1898.
Dewey, John, Oct. 20, 1859.
Dewey, Melvil, Dec. 10, 1851.
Dewey, Thomas E., Mar. 24, 1902.
Dewhurst, Colleen, Jun. 6, 1926.
De Witt, Jan, Sep. 24, 1625.
Dhu'l Hijjah, 10, p. xii; Aug. intro.
Día de la Candelaria (Mexico), Feb. 2.
Diaghilev, Sergei Pavlovich, Mar. 19, 1872.
diamond, Apr. intro.
Diamond, Neil, Jan. 24, 1941.
Dias, Bartholomeu, Feb. 3, 1488.
Díaz, Porfirio, Sep. 15, 1830; Nov. 20, 1910; May 25, 1911.
Diaz de la Peña, Narcisse Virgile, Aug. 20, 1808.
Dick, Albert Blake, Apr. 16, 1856.
Dickens, Charles, Feb. 7, 1812.
Dickinson, Emily, Dec. 10, 1830.
Dickinson, John, Nov. 8, 1732.
Dick Tracy: debut, Oct. 4, 1931.
Diddley, Bo, Dec. 30, 1928.
Diderot, Denis, Oct. 5, 1713.
Didion, Joan, Dec. 5, 1934.
Diefenbaker, John George, Sep. 18, 1895.
Diego Gestido, Oscar (Uruguay), Mar. 1, 1967.
Diels, Otto Paul Hermann, Jan. 23, 1876.
Diem, Ngo Dinh, Jan. 3, 1901.
Dien Bien Phu, Feb. 3, 1954; Mar. 13, 1954; May 7, 1954; May 7, 1975; Jul. 2, 1976.
Dieppe, Aug. 19, 1942.
Dierx, Léon, Mar. 31, 1838.
Dies, Martin, Nov. 5, 1901.
Diesel, Rudolf, Mar. 18, 1858.
Dietrich, Marlene, Dec. 27, 1901.

Diez, Friedrich Christian, Mar. 15, 1794.
Dillinger, John, Jun. 22, 1903.
Dillon, John, Sep. 4, 1851.
DiMaggio, Joe, Nov. 25, 1914.
Dinant, Battle of, Aug. 15, 1914.
d'Indy, Vincent, Mar. 27, 1851.
Dionne Quintuplets, May 28, 1934.
Dior, Christian, Jan. 21, 1905.
Diori, Hamani, Apr. 15, 1974; Apr. 17, 1974.
Diouf, Abdou, Sep. 7, 1935; Jan. 1, 1981.
dioxin, Feb. 22, 1983.
Dirac, Paul Adrien Maurice, Aug. 8, 1902.
direct primary system: adoption of, May 23, 1903.
dirigible: first use in warfare, Mar. 6, 1912; first Atlantic crossing, Jul. 6, 1919.
Dirksen, Everett McKinley, Jan. 4, 1896.
Discoverers' Day (Hawaii), Oct. intro.
Discovery Day (Bahamas), Oct. 12.
Discovery Day (Cayman Islands), May intro.
Discovery Day (Guam), Mar. 6.
Discovery Day (Haiti), Dec. 5.
Discovery Day (Honduras), Oct. 12.
Discovery Day (St. Vincent), Jan. 22 .
Discovery Day (Trinidad and Tobago), Aug. intro.
Discovery of Puerto Rico (Puerto Rico), Nov. 19.
Disney, Walt, Dec. 5, 1901; Nov. 18, 1928; May 25, 1933; Nov. 13, 1940.
Disraeli, Benjamin, Dec. 21, 1804; Feb. 29, 1868; Aug. 12, 1876.
distillers, patron of, Aug. 25.
Diu, Battle of, Feb. 2, 1509.
divines, patron of, Jul. 2; Dec. 2.
Dix, Dorothea, Apr. 4, 1802.
Dix, John Adams, Jul. 24, 1798.
Dixiecrats, Jul. 17, 1948.
Dixmude, Dec. 21, 1923.
Dixon, Dean, Jan. 10, 1915; Aug. 10, 1941.
Dixon, Jul. 1, 1977; Sep. 20, 1977.
Djibouti, Jun. 27, 1977; Sep. 20, 1977.
DNA: structure, Apr. 25, 1953; synthesized, Dec. 14, 1967.
Dobie, James Frank, Sep. 26, 1888.
Dobrolyubov, Nikolai, Jan. 24, 1836.
Dobrovolsky, Georgi T., Jun. 30, 1971.
Dobrynin, Anatoliy F., Nov. 16, 1919.
dock workers, patron of, Dec. 6.
Doctorow, E. L., Jan. 6, 1931.
doctors, patron of, Jul. 27; Oct. 18 .
Doctor's Day, Mar. intro.
Doctor's Day (Georgia), Mar. 30 .
Dodd, Harold W(illis), Jun. 28, 1889.
Dodd, William Edward, Oct. 21, 1869.
Dodecanese Islands, Mar. 31, 1947.
Dodge, Cleveland, Feb. 5, 1888.
Dodge, Horace Elgin, May 17, 1868.
Dodge, John Francis, Oct. 25, 1864.
Dodge, Mary Elizabeth, Jan. 26, 1831.
Dodgson, Charles. *See* Carroll, Lewis.
Doe, Samuel K., May 6, 1952; Apr. 12, 1980.
Doenitz, Karl, Sep. 16, 1891.
"dog days", Jul. intro.
Dogger Bank, Battle of (World War I), Jan. 24, 1915.
"Dog Star", p. viii.
Doheny, Edward Lawrence, Aug. 10, 1856.
Doherty, Henry Latham, May 15, 1870.

Dohrn, Bernadine Rae, Jan. 12, 1942.
Doisy, Edward A., Nov. 13, 1893.
Dole, Robert J., Jul. 22, 1923.
Dole, Sanford Ballard, Apr. 23, 1844.
Dollfuss, Engelbert, Oct. 4, 1892; Apr. 30, 1934; Jul. 25, 1934.
Dolls' Day (Japan), Mar. 3 .
Dolly Sisters (Rosie and Jenny), Oct. 25, 1892.
Domagk, Gerhard, Oct. 30, 1895.
domestic animals, patron saint of, Jan. 17 .
domestic workers, patron of, Apr. 27.
Domingo, Plácido, Jan. 21, 1941.
Dominica, Nov. 1, 1964; Feb. 16, 1967.
Dominican Republic, Feb. 27, 1844; May 30, 1961; Jan. 4, 1962; Feb. 27, 1963; Jun. 1, 1966; Nov. 28, 1966; May 26, 1978.
Dominion Day (Canada), Jul. 1.
Domitien, Elizabeth, Jan. 2, 1975.
Don, Republic of, Jan. 10, 1918.
Donat, Robert, Mar. 18, 1905.
Donati, Giovanni Battista, Oct. 16, 1826.
Donelson, Fort, Feb. 16, 1862.
Donizetti, Gaetano, Nov. 29, 1797.
Donleavy, J. P., Apr. 23, 1926.
Donovan, May 10, 1946.
Donovan, William Joseph (*Wild Bill*), Jan. 1, 1883.
Don River (Russia), Aug. 20, 1942.
Doolittle, Hilda, Sep. 10, 1886.
Doolittle, James (Col.), Dec. 14, 1896; Apr. 18, 1942.
Doornkop (South African Republic), Jan. 2, 1896.
Doppler, Christian Johann, Nov. 29, 1803.
Dorati, Antal, Apr. 9, 1906.
Dorchester Heights, Mar. 17, 1776.
Doriot, Georges Frederic, Sep. 24, 1899.
Dorji, Jigme, Apr. 5, 1964.
Dornberger, Walter R(obert), Sep. 6, 1895.
Dorpat, Treaty of, Feb. 2, 1920; signed, Oct. 14, 1920.
Dors, Diana, Oct. 23, 1931.
Dorsey, Jimmy, Feb. 29, 1904.
Dorsey, Tommy, Nov. 19, 1905.
Dorylaeum, Jul. 1, 1097.
Dos Passos, John, Jan. 14, 1896.
Dostoyevsky, Fyodor Mikhailovich, Nov. 11, 1821.
Doubleday, Abner, Jun. 26, 1819.
Doubleday, Frank Nelson, Jan. 8, 1862.
Doubleday, Nelson, Jun. 16, 1889.
Double Eagle II, Aug. 17, 1978.
Doughty, Charles Montagu, Aug. 19, 1843.
Douglas, Donald Willis, Apr. 6, 1892.
Douglas, Helen Gahagan, Nov. 25, 1900.
Douglas, James, Nov. 4, 1837.
Douglas, Kirk, Dec. 9, 1918.
Douglas, Lloyd C(assel), Aug. 27, 1877.
Douglas, Melvyn, Apr. 5, 1901.
Douglas, Michael, Sep. 25, 1944.
Douglas, Paul, Apr. 11, 1907.
Douglas, Paul Howard, Mar. 26, 1892.
Douglas, Stephen A., Apr. 23, 1813.
Douglas, William O., Oct. 16, 1898; Nov. 12, 1975; Dec. 19, 1975.
Douglas MacArthur Day (Arkansas), Jan. 26.
Doullens, Conference of, May 8, 1918.

Doumer, Paul, Mar. 22, 1857.

Doumergue, Gaston, Aug. 1, 1863.

Dover (England), Jan. 7, 1785; first German air raid, Dec. 21, 1914.

Dow, Herbert Henry, Feb. 26, 1866.

Dowding, Hugh Caswall Tremenheere, Apr. 24, 1882.

Dowie, John Alexander, May 25, 1847.

Dow Jones average: passes 1000, Mar. 11, 1976.

Downhearted Blues, Feb. 16, 1923.

Doyle, Sir Arthur Conan, May 22, 1859.

D'Oyly Carte, Richard, May 3, 1844.

draft: first peacetime in U.S., Oct. 29, 1940.

draft evaders: pardoned, Jan. 21, 1977.

draft lottery (U.S.): established, Nov. 26, 1969.

draft regulations (U.S.), Jan. 19, 1970.

Drafting Week, National, Apr. intro.

Draga (Serbia): massacred, Jun. 10, 1903.

Drago, Luis María, May 6, 1859.

Drake, Alfred, Oct. 7, 1914.

Drake, Edwin Laurentine, Mar. 29, 1819; Aug. 27, 1859.

Drake, Francis, Feb. 11, 1573; Dec. 13, 1577; Apr. 4, 1581; Apr. 19, 1587.

Draper, Henry, Mar. 7, 1837.

Dreadnought: first British nuclear submarine, Oct. 21, 1960.

Dred Scott decision, Mar. 7, 1857.

Dreiser, Theodore, Aug. 27, 1871.

Dresden: sunk, Mar. 14, 1915.

Dresden Opera, Jan. 25, 1909; Jan. 26, 1911.

Dressler, Marie, Nov. 9, 1869.

Drew, Charles, Jun. 3, 1904.

Dreyfus, Alfred, Oct. 19, 1859; Jul. 12, 1906.

Dreyfus, Pierre, Nov. 18, 1907.

Dreyfus case: Jan. 13, 1898; ends, Jul. 12, 1906.

Dreyfuss, Richard (Stephen), Oct. 29, 1947.

Driegroschenoper, Die (The Three Penny Opera): premiere, Aug. 31, 1928.

Driesch, Hans, Oct. 28, 1891.

Drinkwater, John, Jun. 1, 1882.

driving tests, Mar. 26, 1934.

Drogheda (Ireland): sack of, Sep. 11, 1649.

Dru, Joanne, Jan. 31, 1923.

druggists, patrons of, Sep. 26.

Druids, May intro.

Drury, Allen Stuart, Sep. 2, 1918.

Dryden, John, Aug. 9, 1613.

Duarte Nuna, Dom (Portugal), Apr. 17, 1922.

Duarte's Birthday (Dominican Republic), Jan. 26.

Du Barry, Comtesse (Marie Jeanne Bécu), Aug. 19, 1743.

Dubček, Alexander, Jan. 5, 1968; Apr. 5, 1968.

Dubinsky, David, Feb. 22, 1892.

Dublin (Ireland), Jan. 21, 1950.

Dubno, Jun. 2, 1916.

Dubois, W. E. B., Feb. 23, 1868.

Dubos, René, Feb. 20, 1901.

Dubs, Adolph: assassinated, Feb. 14, 1979.

Duchamp, Marcel, Jul. 28, 1887.

Duchin, Eddy, Apr. 1, 1909.

Duchin, Peter (Oelrichs), Jul. 28, 1937.

Ducommun, Elie, Feb. 19, 1833.

Dufy, Raoul, Jun. 3, 1877.

duGran, Claurène, Mar. 21, 1927.

Dukas, Paul Abraham, Oct. 1, 1865.

Duke, Benjamin Newton, Apr. 27, 1855.

Duke, Charles, Apr. 21, 1972; Apr. 27, 1972.

Duke, James Buchanan, Dec. 23, 1856.

Dukhouskaya, Battle of, Aug. 24, 1918.

Dulbecco, Renata, Feb. 2, 1914.

Dulles, Allen, Apr. 7, 1893.

Dulles, John Foster, Feb. 25, 1888.

Dulong, Pierre-Louis, Feb. 12, 1785.

Duma, Apr. 1, 1906.

Dumas, Aléxandre (père), Jul. 24, 1802.

Dumas, Aléxandre (fils), Jul. 27, 1824.

Du Maurier, Daphne, May 13, 1907.

du Maurier, Sir Gerald, Mar. 26, 1873.

Dumbarton Oaks Conference, Aug. 21, 1944.

Dunant, Jean Henri, Birthday Anniversary of, May intro.; May 8, 1828.

Dunbar, Battle of, Apr. 27, 1296; Sep. 3, 1650.

Dunbar, Charles Franklin, Jul. 28, 1830.

Dunbar, Paul Lawrence, Jun. 27, 1872.

Duncan, Isadora, May 27, 1878.

Duncan (King of Scotland), Nov. 25, 1034.

Dunham, Katherine, Jun. 22, 1910.

Dunkirk: sold to France, Oct. 27, 1662; bombed, Jan. 10, 1915.

Dunlop, John Boyd, Feb. 5, 1840.

Dunn, James, Nov. 2, 1905.

Dunne, Finley Peter, Jul. 10, 1867.

Dunne, Irene, Dec. 20, 1904.

Dunning, William Archibald, May 12, 1857.

Dunsinane (Scotland), Jul. 27, 1054.

Dunster, Rev. Henry, Oct. 28, 1636.

Dupes, Day of, Nov. 11, 1630.

Dupleix, Joseph, Jan. 1, 1697.

Du Pont, Pierre Samuel, Jan. 15, 1870.

Du Pont de Nemours, Eleuthère Irènèe, Jun. 24, 1771.

Du Pont de Nemours, Pierre Samuel, Dec. 14, 1739.

Dupré, Jules, Apr. 5, 1811.

Duran, Roberto, Jun. 16, 1951.

Durand, Asher Brown, Aug. 21, 1796.

Durand Agreement: signed, Nov. 12, 1893.

Durant, Ariel, May 10, 1898.

Durant, Thomas Clark, Feb. 6, 1820.

Durant, William Crapo, Dec. 8, 1861.

Durant, Will(iam James), Nov. 5, 1885.

Durante, Jimmy, Feb. 10, 1893.

Duras, Marguerite Donnadieu, Apr. 4, 1914.

Durban (South Africa), Jan. 21, 1898.

Durbin, Deanna, Dec. 4, 1922.

Dürer, Albrecht, May 21, 1471.

Durham, Martyrs of 1594, Jul. 24.

Durkheim, Emile, Apr. 15, 1858.

Durocher, Leo Ernest, Jul. 27, 1906.

Durrell, Gerald, Jan. 7, 1925.

Durrell, Lawrence, Feb. 27, 1912.

Durrenmatt, Friedrich, Jan. 5, 1921.

Duse, Eleanora, Oct. 3, 1859.

Dutch army, May 15, 1940.

Dutch East India Company: established, Mar. 20, 1602; Apr. 6, 1652.

Dutch War of Liberation, Nov. 8, 1576; Aug. 17, 1585; May 17, 1597.

Dutch West Indies Company: chartered, Jun. 3, 1621.

Du'uzu, p. x.

Duvalier, François, Apr. 14, 1907; Jun. 21, 1964; May 21, 1968; dies, Apr. 22, 1971.

Duvalier, Jean-Claude, Jul. 3, 1951; Apr. 22, 1971.

Dvinsk, Jan. 4, 1920.

Dvořák, Antonín, Sep. 8, 1841; Sep. 18, 1841; Mar. 25, 1904.

Dwight, Timothy, May 14, 1752.

dyarchy: established in India, Dec. 23, 1919.

Dylan, Bob, May 24, 1941.

Dystel, Oscar, Oct. 31, 1912.

E

Eagle, Jul. 20, 1969.

Eakins, Thomas (Cowperthwait), Jul. 25, 1844.

Eames, Charles, Jun. 17, 1907.

Earhart, Amelia, Jul. 24, 1898; May 21, 1932; disappears, Jul. 2, 1937.

Earl Beatty, David, Jan. 17, 1871.

Early, Jubal Anderson, Nov. 3, 1816.

Early Bird: launched, Apr. 6, 1965; begins transmission, May 2, 1965.

Earp, Wyatt, Mar. 19, 1848.

Earth Day, Apr. intro.; (U.S.), Apr. 22; Apr. 22, 1970.

earthquake: Andes (Peru), May 31, 1970.

earthquake: Calabria (Italy), Dec. 28, 1908.

earthquake: China, Jul. 28, 1976.

earthquake: Erzincan (Turkey), Dec. 27, 1939.

earthquake: Italy, May 6, 1976.

earthquake: Italy, Nov. 23, 1980.

earthquake: Japan, Oct. 28, 1891.

earthquake: Japan, Sep. 1, 1923.

earthquake: Managua (Nicaragua), Dec. 23, 1972.

earthquake: northern India, Apr. 4, 1905.

earthquake: Pakistan, Dec. 28, 1974.

earthquake: Quetta (India), May 31, 1935.

earthquake: Sicily (Italy), Dec. 28, 1908.

earthquake: Turkey, Mar. 28, 1969.

earthquake: Turkey, Sep. 6, 1975.

earthquake: Turkey, Nov. 24, 1976.

East Africa, British, Jul. 23, 1920.

East Berlin, Oct. 27, 1961.

Easter Sunday, p. xii; Mar. intro.; Apr. intro.; holiday established, Aug. 25, 325.

Eastern Solomons, Battle of the: begins, Aug. 23, 1942.

East Germany, Mar. 5, 1960; Nov. 24, 1972.

East India Company, Sep. 1, 1858; chartered, Dec. 31, 1600; Sep. 5, 1698.

East India Railway, Apr. 2, 1895; Mar. 5, 1928.

East Indies, patron saint of, Dec. 3.

Eastland, James O., Nov. 28, 1904.

Eastman, George, Jul. 12, 1854.

Eastwood, Clint, May 31, 1930.

Eaton, Cyrus Stephen, Dec. 27, 1883; May 3, 1960.

Enders, John Franklin, Feb. 10, 1897.

engaged couples, patron of, Feb. 14.

Engels, Friedrich, Nov. 28, 1820.

Engineer's Week, Feb. intro.

England, Jan. 20, 1301; Jan. 21, 1528; Jan. 21, 1645; Apr. 12, 1654; Jan. 23, 1668; May 4, 1702; union with Scotland, May 1, 1707; Jan. 4, 1717; Jan. 16, 1756; Jan. 4, 1762; first German air raid, Dec. 21, 1914.

England, Kingdom of, Protector of, Apr. 23.

English Carthusian Martyrs, May 11.

English Channel: first air crossing, Jan. 7, 1785; first swimmer, Aug. 25, 1875; Apr. 16, 1912; first two-way, non-stop swim, Sep. 22, 1961.

English Civil War: begins, Aug. 22, 1642; Sep. 2, 1644; Jan. 21, 1645; May 5, 1645.

English language in India, Feb. 17, 1965.

English Martyrs of the Oates Plot, Jun. 20.

Entente Cordiale, Apr. 8, 1904.

Enterprise, U.S.S.: launched, Sep. 24, 1960; Nov. 25, 1961; Jan. 14, 1969.

Environmental Protection Agency (EPA), Mar. 9, 1983.

Epilepsy Month, National, Nov. intro.

Epiphany, Jan. 6.

Epiphany Day (Cyprus), Jan. 6.

Episcopal Church: woman priests and bishops, Sep. 16, 1976; first woman priest, Jan. 1, 1977.

Episcopal School Month, Oct. intro.

equal pay for equal work: law signed, Jun. 10, 1963.

Equal Rights Amendment: passed by U.S. Senate, Mar. 22, 1972; ratification vote extended, Oct. 6, 1978.

Equatorial Guinea: independence, Oct. 12, 1968; Sep. 29, 1979.

Equus October, Oct. intro.

Erasmus, Desiderius, Oct. 26, 1466.

Erben, Karel Jaromir, Nov. 7, 1811.

Ercilla y Zúñiga, Alonso de, Aug. 7, 1533.

Erhard, Ludwig, Feb. 4, 1897.

Ericsson, John, Jul. 31, 1803.

Erie Canal: construction begins, Jul. 4, 1817; opens, Oct. 26, 1825.

Eritrea, Jan. 1, 1890; Feb. 15, 1975.

Eritrean Liberation Front, Feb. 10, 1975.

Erlanger, Joseph, Jan. 5, 1874.

Ernst, Max, Apr. 2, 1891.

Ervin, Sam, Sep. 17, 1896.

Erzerum, Feb. 16, 1916.

Erzincan (Turkey): earthquake, Dec. 27, 1939.

Esaki, Leo, Mar. 12, 1925.

Escoffier, Georges Auguste, Oct. 28, 1846.

escudo, gold, May 22, 1911.

Esenin, Sergei Aleksandrovich, Oct. 3, 1895.

Espriella, Ricardo de la, Sep. 5, 1934.

Espy, James Pollard, May 9, 1785.

Establishment of the Republic (Guinea-Bissau), Sep. 24.

Estonia, Feb. 2, 1920; Mar. 12, 1934; incorporated into U.S.S.R., Aug. 25, 1940.

Estrada Palma, Tomàs, Jul. 9, 1835.

Etaples, Peace of: signed, Nov. 3, 1492.

Ethan Allen: U.S. nuclear submarine, May 6, 1962.

Ethelred II (England), Mar. 18, 979; Apr. 14, 979; Nov. 13, 1002; Apr. 19, 1012.

Ethiopia, Apr. 3, 1930; invaded by Italy, Oct. 3, 1935; May 9, 1936; drought, Oct. 28, 1973; Feb. 15, 1975; treaty with U.S.S.R., Nov. 20, 1978.

Ethiopian New Year and Reunion of Eritrea with Ethiopia (Ethiopia), Sep. 11.

Ethiopian resistance: to Italy, May 5, 1936.

Eucken, Rudolph Christoph, Jan. 5, 1846.

Eugene III (pope), Dec. 1, 1145.

Eugene IV (pope), May 31, 1433; Sep. 4, 1439; Jan. 24, 1446.

Euler, Leonhard, Apr. 15, 1707.

Euler, Ulf Svante von, Feb. 7, 1905.

Euler-Chelpin, Hans Karl August Simon, Feb. 15, 1873.

eunuchs, patron of, Dec. 29.

European Economic Community, established, Mar. 25, 1957; Jan. 1, 1958; tariffs abolished, Jun. 28, 1967; Feb. 6, 1970; May 10, 1972; Jan. 1, 1973; Feb. 3, 1978; May 28, 1979; Jan. 1, 1981.

European economic union, Apr. 18, 1951.

European Free Trade Association, Jan. 4, 1960.

European Monetary System, Mar. 13, 1979.

European Parliamentary Assembly, Jun. 7, 1979.

European Social Charter, Feb. 26, 1965.

European War, Jun. 15, 1866.

Evacuation Day (Egypt), Jun. 18.

Evacuation Day (Libya), Mar. 28 .

Evacuation Day (Syria), Apr. 17 .

Evacuation Day (Tunisia), Oct. 15 .

Evangelical United Brethren, Nov. 11, 1966.

Evans, Bergen, Sep. 19, 1904.

Evans, Dale, Oct. 31, 1912.

Evans, Dame Edith, Feb. 8, 1888.

Evans, Luther H(arris), Oct. 13, 1902.

Evans, Maurice, Jun. 3, 1901.

Evans, Oliver, Sep. 13, 1755.

Eve of Epiphany (England), Jan. 5.

Everest, Mt., May 29, 1953; May 25, 1960; May 14, 1978.

Everett, Edward, Apr. 11, 1794.

Evers, James Charles, Sep. 11, 1922.

Evers, Medgar, Jul. 2, 1925.

Evren, Kenan (General), Sep. 10, 1980.

Ewald, Johannes, Nov. 18, 1743.

Ewart-Briggs, Christopher T.E., Jul. 21, 1976.

Ewing, William Maurice, May 12, 1906.

Ewry, Ray, Oct. 14, 1873.

Exaltation of the Holy Cross, Sep. 14.

Exclusion Act, Chinese, May 6, 1882.

Exodus, p. ix.

Expeditionary Force, American: arrives in France, Jun. 13, 1917.

Expeditionary Force, First U.S. (World War II), Jan. 26, 1942.

Explorer I: launched, Jan. 31, 1958.

Expo 70, Mar. 14, 1970.

Extension Homemaker Council Week, National, May intro.

Eyadéma, Etienne, Jan. 13, 1967.

Eyadema, Gnassingbe, Dec. 26, 1937.

Eyck, Jan van, May 6, 1432.

Eye Safety Month, Jul. intro.

Eylan, Battle of, Feb. 7, 1807.

Eyre, Governor Edward John: recalled, Oct. 11, 1865.

F

Fabergé, Peter Carl, May 30, 1846.

Fabre, Jean Henri, Dec. 21, 1823.

Fabricius, Hieronymous, May 20, 1537.

Factory Act (Great Britain): passed, Jul. 2, 1819.

Fadiman, Clifton, May 15, 1904.

Faenza, patron of, Feb. 23.

Fahrenheit, Gabriel Daniel, May 14, 1686.

Fairbanks, Charles Warren, Mar. 4, 1905.

Fairbanks, Douglas, May 23, 1883.

Fairbanks, Douglas, Jr., Dec. 9, 1909.

Fairclough, Ellen, Jan. 19, 1962.

Fairfax, Thomas, Third Baron Fairfax, Jan. 17, 1612; Jan. 21, 1645.

Faisal ibn Musad, Prince, Mar. 25, 1975.

Faisal I (Syria), Mar. 11, 1920.

Faisal II (Iraq), Apr. 4, 1939.

Faisal (Saudi Arabia), Nov. 2, 1964; assassinated, Mar. 25, 1975.

Faith 7, May 15, 1963.

Falaise-Argentan Gap, Aug. 20, 1944.

Falk, Peter, Sep. 16, 1927.

Falkenhayn, General von, Sep. 14, 1914.

Falkirk, Jul. 22, 1298.

Falkland Islands, Jan. 22, 1771; British sovereignity, Jan. 1, 1833; Battle of the, Dec. 8, 1914; seized by Argentina, Apr. 2, 1982; Apr. 25, 1982; May 4, 1982; Argentine troops surrender, Jun. 14, 1982.

Falköpping, Feb. 24, 1389.

Fall, Albert Bacon, Nov. 26, 1861.

Falla, Manuel de, Nov. 23, 1876.

Fallaci, Oriana, Jun. 29, 1930.

Fallersleben, August Heinrich Hoffmann von, Apr. 2, 1798.

Falstaff: portrayal of Sir John Oldcastle, Dec. 12, 1417.

Family Day, Aug. intro.

Family Day (Angola, São Tomé and Príncipe), Dec. 25.

Family Day (Lesotho), Jul. intro.

Family Day (Namibia), Dec. 26.

Family Day (U.S.), Aug. 7.

Fan Fair Celebration, Jun. intro.

Faneuil, Peter, Jun. 20, 1700.

Fantasia: premiere, Nov. 13, 1940.

Faraday, Michael, Sep. 22, 1791.

Fargo, William George, May 20, 1818.

Farley, James A., May 30, 1888.

Farm City Week, National, Nov. intro.

Farm Credit Act, Jun. 16, 1933.

Farm Safety Week, National, Sep. intro.

Farmer, Fannie, Mar. 23, 1857.

Farmer, James Leonard, Jan. 12, 1920.

Farmers' Day (Florida), Oct. intro.

Farouk I (Egypt), Feb. 11, 1920; Jul. 23, 1952; Apr. 28, 1936.

Farragut, Adm. David, Jul. 5, 1801; May 1, 1862; Aug. 5, 1864.

Farrell, Eileen, Feb. 13, 1920.

Flag Day (Finland), Jun. 4.
Flag Day (Haiti), May 18.
Flag Day (Mexico), Feb. 24 .
Flag Day (Panama), Nov. 4.
Flag Day (Sweden), Jun. 6 .
Flag Day (U.S.), Jun. intro.; Jun. 14.
Flagstad, Kirsten, Jul. 12, 1895.
Flamborough Head, Mar. 30, 1406.
flamethrower: first, Feb. 20, 1915.
Flamsteed, John, Aug. 19, 1646.
Flanagan, Edward Joseph, Jul. 13, 1886.
Flanders: British offensive, Jul. 31, 1917;
    Apr. 9, 1918.
Flanner, Janet, Mar. 13, 1892.
Flaubert, Gustave, Dec. 12, 1821.
Flaxman, John, Jul. 6, 1755.
Fleck, Sir Alexander, Nov. 11, 1889.
Fleming, Ian, May 28, 1908.
Fleming, John Ambrose, Nov. 29, 1849.
Fleming, Peggy, Jul. 27, 1948.
Fleming, Rhonda, Aug. 10, 1922.
Fleming, Sir Alexander, Aug. 6, 1881.
Flemming, Walther, Apr. 21, 1843.
Flers-Courcelette, Sep. 15, 1916.
Fletcher, Alice Cunningham, Mar. 15, 1838.
Fletcher, Frank Jack, Apr. 29, 1885.
Fleurus, Jun. 26, 1794.
Flexner, Simon, Mar. 25, 1863.
Flodden Field, Battle of, Sep. 9, 1513.
Flora, May intro.
Floralia, May intro.
Florence, patron of, May 25 .
Florence (Italy), Sep. 6, 1512.
Florentine Militia: created, Dec. 6, 1506.
Flores, Juan José, Jul. 19, 1800.
Florey, Howard Walter, Sep. 24, 1898.
Florida, Apr. 2, 1513; Jun. 3, 1539; Feb. 22,
    1819; Mar. 3, 1845; Jan. 10, 1861.
Florida Appreciation Month, Aug. intro.
Florida (confederate cruiser), Jan. 15, 1863.
florists, patron of, Feb. 6.
Flory, Paul J., Jun. 19, 1910.
Flower Festival (Japan), Apr. 8.
Flygare-Carlèn, Emilie, Aug. 8, 1807.
Flynn, Elizabeth Gurley, Aug. 7, 1890.
Flynn, Errol, Jun. 20, 1909.
Flynt, Larry C., Feb. 8, 1977.
FM radio, Jan. 5, 1940.
FM radio transmission: first
    demonstration, Nov. 6, 1935.
Foch, Ferdinand, Oct. 2, 1851; May 8, 1918;
    Aug. 6, 1918.
Foch, Nina, Apr. 20, 1924.
Fogarty, Anne, Feb. 2, 1919.
Foggia, Battle of, Dec. 2, 1254.
Fokine, Michel, Apr. 26, 1880.
Fokker, Anthony Herman Gerard, Apr. 6,
    1890.
Folger, Henry Clay, Jun. 18, 1857.
Foligno (Italy), patron of, Jan. 24.
Folkestone (England): German raid on,
    May 25, 1915.
Folsom, Frank, May 14, 1894.
Fonda, Henry, May 16, 1905.
Fonda, Jane, Dec. 21, 1937.
Fonseca, Manuel Deodoro da, Aug. 5, 1829.
Fontaine, Joan, Oct. 22, 1917.
Fontainebleau, Treaty of, Oct. 27, 1807.
Fontanne, Lynn, Dec. 6, 1887.

Fonteyn, Margot, May 18, 1919.
Food and Drug Administration, U.S., Sep.
    4, 1969.
Food for Peace agreement: signed, Aug. 21,
    1961.
Food Industry Workers' Day (U.S.S.R.), Oct.
    intro.
Food Stamp Act: signed, Aug. 31, 1964.
Food stamps: first introduced, May 16,
    1939.
fools, patron of, Nov. 1.
Foot, Michael, Jul. 23, 1913.
Football Association, American
    Professional: formed, Sep. 17, 1920.
football game: first American, Nov. 6, 1869;
    first professional game, Aug. 31, 1895;
    first broadcast of pro championship,
    Dec. 8, 1940.
Foote, Andrew Hull, Sep. 12, 1806.
Forbes, Kathryn, Mar. 20, 1909.
Forcheim, Diet of, Mar. 15, 1077.
Ford, Edsel Bryant, Nov. 6, 1893.
Ford, Ford Madox, Dec. 17, 1873.
Ford, Gerald, Jul. 14, 1913; Aug. 9, 1974;
    Sep. 8, 1974; Sep. 16, 1974; Mar. 1, 1975;
    Apr. 18, 1975; Sep. 5, 1975; Sep. 22, 1975;
    Feb. 17, 1976; Aug. 19, 1976; Jan. 19, 1977.
Ford, Glenn, May 1, 1916.
Ford, Harold, May 20, 1945.
Ford, Henry, Jul. 30, 1863.
Ford, Henry II, Sep. 4, 1917.
Ford, John, Apr. 17, 1586.
Ford, John, Feb. 1, 1895.
Ford, Tennessee Ernie, Feb. 13, 1919.
Ford Foundation, Jan. 15, 1936.
Ford's Theater, Apr. 14, 1865.
Forefathers' Day (U.S.), Dec. 21.
foreign aid bill: first U.S., Mar. 3, 1812.
Foreign Exchange Market, British: opens,
    Dec. 15, 1951.
Foreign Language Week, National, Mar.
    intro.
Foreign Troops Evacuation Day (Lebanon),
    Dec. 31.
Foreman, George, Jan. 10, 1949; Jan. 22,
    1973; Oct. 30, 1974.
Forest Hills (New York), Sep. 9, 1968.
Forester, C(ecil) S(cott), Aug. 27, 1899.
foresters, patron of, Jul. 12.
Forestry Workers' Day (U.S.S.R.), Sep. intro.
Formidable: sunk, Jan. 1, 1915.
Formigny, Battle of, Apr. 15, 1450.
Formosa, Dec. 8, 1949.
Forrest, Edwin, Mar. 9, 1806.
Forrest, George, Dec. 3, 1953.
Forrest, Nathan Bedford, Jul. 13, 1821.
Forrest, Sir John, Aug. 22, 1847.
Forrestal, James V., Feb. 15, 1892; first
    Secretary of Defense, Sep. 17, 1947.
Forrestal, U.S.S., Jul. 29, 1967.
Forssmann, Werner, Aug. 29, 1904.
Forster, E. M., Jan. 1, 1879.
Forster, Johann George Adam, Nov. 27,
    1754.
Forsyth, Alexander John, Dec. 27, 1769.
Fortas, Abe, Jun. 19, 1910; May 15, 1969.
Fort Christiana, Delaware, Mar. 29, 1638.
Fort Dearborn: Indian massacre, Aug. 15,
    1812.

Fort Duquesne (Pittsburgh), Jul. 9, 1755;
    Nov. 25, 1758.
Fort Flemalle (Belgium): falls to Germans,
    Aug. 16, 1914.
Fort Henry, Battle of, Feb. 6, 1862.
Fort Monmouth (New Jersey), Jan. 10,
    1946.
Fort Peck Dam, Oct. 24, 1933.
Fortress of Peter and Paul, Oct. 23, 1917.
Forty Martyrs of Sebastea, Mar. 10.
Fosbury, Dick, Mar. 6, 1947.
Fosdick, Harry Emerson, May 24, 1878.
Fosse, Bob, Jun. 23, 1927.
Foster, Preston, Aug. 24, 1901.
Foster, Stephen (Collins), Jul. 4, 1826.
Foucault, Jean Bernard Lèon, Sep. 18, 1819.
Fouché, Joseph, May 21, 1759.
Fougéres (France), Mar. 24, 1449.
Foulis, Andrew, Nov. 23, 1712.
Foundation of the German Democratic
    Republic Day of, Oct. 7.
Foundation of Workers's Party (North
    Korea), Oct. intro.
Founders' Day and Youth Day (Zaire), Oct.
    14.
Founders Day (Republic of South Africa),
    Apr. 6.
Founding Day, V.I. Lenin Pioneer
    Organization (U.S.S.R.), May 19.
Founding of the Republic of China
    (Taiwan), Jan. 1.
Four Chaplains Memorial Day (U.S.), Feb.
    3.
Four Crowned Ones, Nov. 8.
4-H Week, National, Oct. intro.
Fourier, François Marie, Apr. 7, 1772.
Fourier, Joseph Jean Baptiste, Mar. 21,
    1768.
Fourneyron, Benoit, Oct. 31, 1802.
Fourteen Holy Helpers, Aug. 8 .
Fourteen Points: U.S. peace demands, Nov.
    4, 1918.
Fourteenth Amendment (U.S.
    Constitution): ratified, Jul. 28, 1868.
Fourteenth of July Revolution (Iraq), Jul.
    14.
41st International Eucharistic Congress,
    Aug. 1, 1976.
Fouss, Robert M(artin), Dec. 16, 1912.
Fowler, Sir John, Jul. 15, 1817.
Fowles, John, Mar. 31, 1926.
Fox, Carol, Jun. 15, 1920.
Fox, Charles James, Jan. 24, 1749.
Fox, Sir William, Jan. 20, 1812.
Fox, Virgil, May 3, 1912.
Fox, William, Jan. 1, 1879.
Foy, Eddie, Mar. 9, 1857.
Foyt, A. J., Jan. 16, 1935.
Fracci, Carla, Aug. 20, 1936.
Fragonard, Jean-Honoré, Apr. 5, 1732.
Fragrance Day (U.S.), Mar. 21 .
Franca, Celia, Jun. 25, 1921.
France, Jan. 20, 1558; Jan. 17, 1601; allied
    with Swedes, Jul. 26, 1648; Jan. 23, 1668;
    May 4, 1702; Jan. 4, 1717; Jan. 22, 1760;
    annexes Geneva, Apr. 26, 1798; becomes
    Empire, May 18, 1804; May 5, 1811; war
    with Spain, Apr. 7, 1823; declares war on
    Austria, May 3, 1859; Apr. 23, 1860;
    mobilizes army, Jul. 31, 1914; declares

Frisch, Ragnar, Mar. 3, 1895.

Fritz, John, Aug. 21, 1823.

Froebel, Friedrich Wilhelm, Apr. 21, 1872.

Frohman, Charles, Jun. 17, 1860.

Fromm, Erich, Mar. 23, 1900.

Fromme, Lynette (*Squeaky*), Sep. 5, 1975.

From Spiritual to Swing, Dec. 23, 1938.

Frontier Corps Day (U.S.S.R.), May 28.

Frost, David, Apr. 7, 1939.

Frost, Robert, Mar. 26, 1874.

fruit dealers, patron of, Jul. 25.

Fry, Christopher, Dec. 18, 1907.

Fuad I (Egypt), Feb. 28, 1922; Mar. 15, 1922; Mar. 15, 1924; dies, Apr. 28, 1936.

Fuad Pasha, Ahmed (Egypt), Mar. 26, 1868.

Fuchs, Klaus, Feb. 10, 1950; May 23, 1950.

Fuchs, Leonhard, Jan. 17, 1501.

Fuchs, Sir Vivian, Mar. 2, 1958.

Fuentes, Carlos, Nov. 11, 1928.

Fuentes d'Oñoro (Portugal), May 5, 1811.

Fukuda, Takeo, Jan. 14, 1905.

Fulbright, William, Apr. 9, 1905.

Fulbright Act, Aug. 1, 1946.

Fulbright Scholarships: created, Aug. 1, 1946.

Fulford, Battle of, Sep. 20, 1966.

Fuller, Carl Alfred, Jan. 13, 1885.

Fuller, John Frederick Charles, Sep. 1, 1878.

Fuller, Melville Weston, Feb. 11, 1833.

Fuller, R(ichard) Buckminster, Jul. 12, 1895.

Fuller, Sarah Margaret, May 23, 1810.

Fulton, Robert, Nov. 14, 1765; Feb. 11, 1809.

Fulton, U.S.S.: first U.S. steam warship, Oct. 29, 1814.

Fundamental Orders of Connecticut: first constitution in America, Jan. 14, 1639.

Funeral Music: first performance, Jan. 22, 1936.

Funicello, Annette, Oct. 22, 1942.

Funk, Isaac, Sep. 10, 1839.

Funston, Frederick, Nov. 9, 1865.

Furetière, Abbé Antoine, Dec. 28, 1619.

furriers, patron of, Nov. 3.

Furstenberg, Diane (Simone Michelle) von, Dec. 31, 1946.

G

Gabelentz, Hans Conon von der, Oct. 13, 1807.

Gabin, Jean, May 17, 1904.

Gable, Clark, Feb. 1, 1901.

Gabon, Feb. 21, 1961.

Gabon Republic: independence, Jul. 15, 1960.

Gabor, Dennis, Jun. 5, 1900.

Gabor, Zsa Zsa, Feb. 6, 1919.

Gabrovo's Biannual Comedic Extravaganza (Bulgaria), May intro.

Gadsden, James, May 15, 1788.

Gadsden Purchase, Jun. 30, 1854.

Gaetano, Marcello (Jose), Aug. 17, 1906.

Gagarin, Yuri, Mar. 9, 1934; first man in space, Apr. 12, 1961.

Gagging Act (Great Britain), Dec. 8, 1795.

Gainsborough, Thomas, May 14, 1727.

Gairy, Sir Eric (Grenada), Mar. 13, 1979.

Gajdusek, Daniel C., Sep. 9, 1923.

Galapagos Islands, Feb. 12, 1832.

Galaup, Jean François de, Aug. 22, 1741.

Galbraith, John Kenneth, Oct. 15, 1908.

Galicia: Austro-German offensive, May 3, 1915.

Galilee, Sea of, May 5, 1964.

Galileo, Feb. 15, 1564; Jan. 7, 1610; May 9, 1983.

Gallagher, Capt. James, Mar. 2, 1949.

Gallatin, Albert, Jan. 29, 1761.

Gallaudet, Thomas Hopkins, Dec. 10, 1787.

Galle, Johann, Jun. 9, 1812.

Gallico, Paul William, Jul. 26, 1897.

Gallipoli Campaign, Apr. 25, 1915; ends, Aug. 21, 1915.

Gallup, George Horace, Nov. 18, 1901.

Galois, Evariste, Oct. 25, 1811.

Galsworthy, John, Aug. 14, 1867.

Galt, Alexander Tilloch, Sep. 6, 1817.

Galton, Sir Francis, Feb. 16, 1822.

Galvani, Luigi, Sep. 9, 1737.

Galveston (Texas): hurricane, Sep. 8, 1900.

Galway, James, Dec. 8, 1939.

Gama, Vasco da, Jul. 8, 1497; Nov. 22, 1497; Dec. 25, 1497; Mar. 1, 1498; May 20, 1498.

Gambetta, Léon, Apr. 2, 1838.

Gambia, Nov. 28, 1888; Feb. 18, 1965; admitted to U.N., Sep. 21, 1965; Apr. 23, 1970; Apr. 24, 1970; Feb. 1, 1982.

gambling, casino: legalized in Atlantic City, May 26, 1978.

Gamow, George, Mar. 4, 1904.

Gandamak, Treaty of, May 26, 1879.

Gandhi, Indira, Nov. 19, 1917; Jan. 19, 1966; Jan. 24, 1966; Jan. 19, 1970; Feb. 14, 1970; convicted, Jun. 12, 1975; Jun. 26, 1975; Jan. 18, 1977; Mar. 24, 1977.

Gandhi, Mahatma, Oct. 2, 1869; Mar. 30, 1919; Feb. 12, 1922; Mar. 10, 1922; Mar. 18, 1922; Feb. 4, 1924; Dec. 22, 1928; Mar. 12, 1930; Apr. 6, 1930; May 5, 1930; May 6, 1930; Jan. 26, 1931; Mar. 4, 1931; Mar. 5, 1931; Jan. 4, 1932; assassinated, Jan. 30, 1948.

Gandhi's Birthday (India), Oct. 2.

Gang of Four: arrested, Oct. 12, 1976.

Gann, Ernest K(ellogg), Oct. 13, 1910.

Gannett, Henry, Aug. 24, 1846.

Gantt, Harvey, Jan. 28, 1963.

Garand, John Cantius, Jan. 1, 1888.

Garbo, Greta, Sep. 18, 1905.

Garborg, Arne Evenson, Jan. 25, 1851.

García Gutiérrez, Antonio, Oct. 5, 1813.

García Lorca, Federico, Jun. 5, 1899.

Garcilaso de la Vega (El Inca), Apr. 12, 1539.

Gard, Roger Martin du, Mar. 23, 1881.

gardeners, patron of, Feb. 6.

Gardner, Ava, Dec. 24, 1922.

Gardner, Erle Stanley, Jul. 17, 1889.

Gardner, John (Champlin), Jul. 20, 1933.

Gardner, John William, Oct. 8, 1912.

Garfield, James, Nov. 19, 1831; inaugurated, Mar. 4, 1881; Jul. 2, 1881; dies, Sep. 19, 1881.

Garfield, John, Mar. 4, 1913.

Garfunkel, Art(hur), Oct. 13, 1942.

Gargan, William, Jul. 17, 1905.

Garibaldi, Giuseppe, Jul. 4, 1807; May 5, 1860; May 15, 1860; May 27, 1860; Sep. 7, 1860; Jul. 19, 1862.

Garifuna Settlement Day (Belize), Nov. 19.

Garland, Hamlin, Sep. 14, 1860.

Garland, Judy, Jun. 10, 1922.

Garner, Erroll, May 15, 1921.

Garner, James, Apr. 7, 1928.

Garner, John Nance (*Cactus Jack*), Nov. 22, 1868; Mar. 4, 1933.

Garnerin, André Jacques: first parachute jump, Oct. 22, 1797.

garnet, Jan. intro.

Garnet, Henry Highland, Dec. 23, 1815.

Garnier, Francis, Jul. 25, 1839.

Garnier, Jean Louis Charles, Nov. 6, 1825.

Garrick, David, Feb. 19, 1717.

Garriott, Owen K., Jul. 28, 1973.

Garrison, William Lloyd, Dec. 10, 1805.

Garroway, Dave, Jul. 13, 1913.

Garter, Order of the: established, Apr. 23, 1348.

Garvey, Marcus (Moziah), Aug. 17, 1887.

Garvin, Clifton Canter, Jr., Dec. 22, 1921.

Gary, Elbert Henry, Oct. 8, 1846.

gas, chlorine: first use as weapon, Apr. 22, 1915.

Gaskell, Elizabeth Cleghorn, Sep. 29, 1865.

gasoline rationing: begins in U.S., Dec. 1, 1943.

Gasparri, Pietro, May 5, 1852.

Gasperi, Alcide de, Apr. 3, 1881.

Gassendi, Pierre, Jan. 22, 1592.

Gasser, Herbert Spencer, Jul. 5, 1888.

Gassman, Vittorio, Sep. 1, 1922.

Gas street-lights: introduced in London, Aug. 16, 1807.

Gates, Thomas S., Jr., Apr. 10, 1906.

Gatling, Richard Jordan, Sep. 12, 1818.

Gatty, Harold, Jul. 1, 1931.

Gaudier-Brzeska, Henri, Oct. 4, 1891.

Gaudy, Frederic William, Mar. 8, 1865.

Gauguin, (Eugène-Henri-) Paul, Jun. 7, 1848.

Gauss, Karl Friedrich, Apr. 30, 1777.

Gavin, James Maurice, Mar. 22, 1907.

Gavutu, Solomon Islands: captured by U.S., Aug. 8, 1942.

Gay, John, Sep. 16, 1685.

Gay-Lussac, Joseph Louis, Dec. 6, 1778.

Gaynor, Janet, Oct. 6, 1906.

Gaynor, Mitzi, Sep. 4, 1931.

Gayoom, Maumoon Abdul, Dec. 29, 1939.

Gaza, Battle of, Mar. 26, 1917.

Gaza, Second Battle of, Apr. 19, 1917.

Gaza, Third Battle of, Nov. 1, 1917; Nov. 7, 1917.

Gazzara, Ben, Aug. 28, 1930.

Gedda, Nikolai, Jul. 11, 1925.

Geddes, Patrick, Oct. 20, 1854.

Geer, Dirk Jan de, Dec. 14, 1870.

Geer, Will, Mar. 9, 1902.

Gegenbauer, Karl, Aug. 21, 1826.

Gehrig, (Henry) Lou(is), Jun. 19, 1903.

Geiger, Abraham, May 24, 1810.

Geiger, (Johannes) Hans Wilhelm, Sep. 30, 1882.

Giscard D'Estaing, Valèry, Feb. 2, 1926.

Giselle: premiere, Jun. 28, 1841.

Gish, Dorothy, Mar. 11, 1898.

Gish, Lillian, Oct. 14, 1896.

Gissing, George (Robert), Nov. 22, 1857.

Givenchy, Hubert de, Feb. 21, 1927.

Gjellerup, Karl Adolf, Jun. 2, 1857.

Glacier National Park: established, May 11, 1910.

gladiolus, Aug. intro.

Gladstone, William Ewart, Dec. 29, 1809.

Glaser, Donald Arthur, Sep. 21, 1926.

Glasgow, Ellen, Apr. 22, 1874.

Glasgow, University of, Jan. 7, 1450.

Glashow, Sheldon L., Dec. 5, 1932.

Glass, Carter, Jan. 4, 1858.

glassmakers, patron of, Oct. 18.

Glasspole, Florizel A., Sep. 25, 1909.

Glaucoma Alert Month, Apr. intro.

glaziers, patron of, Apr. 25.

Glazunov, Aleksandr Konstantinovich, Aug. 10, 1865.

Gleason, Jackie, Feb. 26, 1916.

Gleason, James, May 23, 1886.

Glencoe Massacre (Scotland), Feb. 13, 1692.

Glenn, John, Jul. 18, 1921; Feb. 20, 1962.

Glennon, John Joseph, Jun. 14, 1862.

Glidden, Joseph Farwell, Jan. 18, 1813.

Glinka, Mikhail Ivanovich, Jun. 1, 1804.

Glorification of the Heroes of Independence, Day of the (Haiti), Jan. 1.

glovemakers, patron of, Jul. 21.

Gluck, Christoph Willibald (Ritters von), Jul. 2, 1714.

Glueck, (Sol) Sheldon, Aug. 15, 1896.

Gneisenau, Wilhelm August Count Neithardt von, Oct. 27, 1760.

Goa, Mar. 4, 1510.

Gobat, Charles A., May 21, 1843.

Gobineau, Joseph Arthur, Jul. 14, 1816.

Godard, Jean-Luc, Dec. 3, 1930.

Goddard, John, Jan. 20, 1724.

Goddard, Robert Hutchings, Oct. 5, 1882; Mar. 16, 1926.

Godey, Louis Antoine, Jun. 6, 1804.

Godfrey, Arthur, Aug. 31, 1903.

Godse, Nathuram, Jan. 30, 1948.

Godunov, Aleksandr, Aug. 23, 1979.

Godwin, Mary Wollstonecraft, Apr. 27, 1759.

Godwin, William, Mar. 3, 1756.

Goebbels, Joseph (Paul), Oct. 29, 1897.

Goeben, Jan. 20, 1918.

Goeppert-Mayer, Marie, Jun. 28, 1906.

Goering, Hermann, Oct. 16, 1946.

Goethals, George Washington, Jun. 29, 1858.

Goethe, Johann Wolfgang von, Aug. 28, 1749.

Gogol, Nikolai Vasilyevich, Mar. 31, 1809.

Goheen, Robert Francis, Aug. 15, 1919.

Gold, Harry, May 23, 1950.

gold-backed currency, U.S.: eliminated, Mar. 19, 1968.

Goldberg, Arthur Joseph, Aug. 8, 1908.

Goldberg, Sol Harry, Apr. 20, 1880.

Gold Coast (Africa), Feb. 1, 1642; Denmark cedes to Great Britain, Aug. 17, 1850;

Feb. 25, 1871; Feb. 2, 1872; Jan. 13, 1886; Apr. 5, 1873.

Gold Coast Colony, Sep. 26, 1901.

Gold Creek (Montana), Sep. 8, 1883.

Golden, Harry Lewis, May 6, 1902.

Golden Bull, Jan. 10, 1356.

Golden Fleece, Order of, Jan. 10, 1429.

Golden Gate Bridge: opened, May 27, 1937.

Golden Spike: first transcontinental railroad, May 10, 1869.

Goldhaber, Maurice, Apr. 18, 1911.

Goldie, Sir George Dashwood Taubman, May 20, 1846.

Golding, William, Sep. 19, 1911.

Goldman, Emma, Jun. 27, 1869.

Goldmann, Nahum, Jul. 10, 1895.

Goldmark, Karl, May 18, 1830.

Goldmark, Peter Carl, Dec. 2, 1906; Jun. 18, 1948.

Goldoni, Carlo, Feb. 25, 1707.

Gold Rush (California), Jan. 24, 1848.

Goldsmith, Oliver, Nov. 10, 1728.

gold standard: adopted by U.S., Mar. 14, 1900; Great Britain abandons, Sep. 21, 1930; Apr. 19, 1932.

Goldwater, Barry (Morris), Jan. 1, 1909.

Goldwyn, Samuel, Aug. 27, 1884.

Golf Association, U.S.: founded, Dec. 22, 1894.

golf club: first American, Nov. 14, 1888.

Golf Hall of Fame, Apr. 9, 1941.

Golgi, Camillo, Jul. 7, 1843.

Gómez, José Miguel, Jul. 6, 1858.

Gómez, Juan Vincente, Jul. 24, 1857.

Gomide, Aloysio Dias (Brazil), Feb. 21, 1971.

Gompers, Samuel, Dec. 8, 1886.

Gomulka, Wladyslaw, Feb. 6, 1905.

Goncourt, Edmond Louis Antoine Huot de, May 26, 1822.

Gondoliers: premiere, Dec. 7, 1889.

Gonne, Maude, Dec. 20, 1865.

González, Richard Alonzo (Pancho), May 9, 1928.

Good Bears of the World Day, Oct. intro.

Good Hope, Cape of: discovered, Jul. 8, 1497; Nov. 22, 1497.

Good Neighbor Day, National, Sep. intro.

Goodall, Jane (Baroness Jane Van Lawick-Goodall), Apr. 3, 1934.

Goodhue, Bertram Grosvenor, Apr. 28, 1869.

Goodman, Benny, May 30, 1909.

Goodrich, B(enjamin) F(ranklin), Nov. 4, 1841.

Goodrich, Samuel Griswold, Aug. 19, 1793.

Good Thief, Mar. 25.

Good Will Day of (South Africa), Dec. 26.

Goodyear, Charles, Dec. 29, 1800; Jun. 15, 1844.

Goolagong, Evonne, Jul. 31, 1951.

Gorboduc: first English tragedy, Jan. 18, 1562.

Gordon, Charles George, Jan. 28, 1833; Feb. 18, 1884; Jan. 26, 1885.

Gordon, Judah Loeb, Dec. 7, 1830.

Gordon, Richard F., Oct. 5, 1929.

Gordon, Ruth, Oct. 30, 1896.

Gordone, Charles, Oct. 12, 1927.

Gore, Albert Arnold, Dec. 26, 1907.

Goren, Charles Henry, Mar. 4, 1901.

Gorgas, William Crawford, Oct. 3, 1854.

Gorin, Igor, Oct. 26, 1909.

Göring, Hermann Wilhelm, Jan. 12, 1893.

Gorki, Maksim, Mar. 16, 1868.

Gorlice-Tarnow, Battle of, May 2, 1915.

Gorran (Cornwall), patron of, Apr. 7.

Gosden, Freeman, May 5, 1899.

Gossamer Albatross: first flight across English Channel, Jun. 12, 1979.

Gosse, Sir Edmund William, Sep. 21, 1849.

Gotthard Railway: first scheduled trip, Jun. 1, 1882.

Gotthard Railway Tunnel, Feb. 29, 1880.

Gottschalk, Louis Moreau, May 8, 1829.

Gould, Chester, Oct. 4, 1931.

Gould, Elliott, Aug. 29, 1938.

Gould, Glenn, Sep. 25, 1932.

Gould, Jay, May 27, 1836; Sep. 24, 1869.

Goulding, Ray Walter, Mar. 20, 1922.

Gounod, Charles François, Jun. 17, 1818.

Gourand, Henri Joseph Eugène, Nov. 17, 1867.

Government of India Act, Dec. 23, 1919; Aug. 2, 1935.

Government Printing Office (U.S): established, Mar. 4, 1861.

Gowan, Yakubu, Aug. 1, 1966; Jan. 15, 1969.

Goya, Mar. 30, 1746.

Gozzi, Count Carlo, Dec. 13, 1720.

Grable, Betty, Dec. 18, 1913.

Grace, Joseph Peter, May 25, 1913.

Grace of Monaco (Grace Kelly), Nov. 12, 1929.

Graetz, Heinrich, Oct. 31, 1817.

Graf Zeppelin, Oct. 31, 1928; Sep. 1, 1929.

Graham, Billy, Nov. 17, 1918.

Graham, George, Jul. 7, 1673.

Graham, Katharine (Meyer), Jun. 16, 1917.

Graham, Martha, May 11, 1893.

Graham, Philip Leslie, Jul. 18, 1915.

Graham, Sir Robert, Feb. 20, 1437.

Graham, Thomas, Dec. 20, 1805.

Grahame, Kenneth, Mar. 8, 1859.

Gramme, Zénobe Théophile, Apr. 4, 1826.

gramophone: patent, Feb. 19, 1878.

Granada, Jan. 2, 1492.

Granada, Treaty of: signed, Nov. 11, 1500.

Grand Alliance, Mar. 13, 1813.

Grand Armée, Jun. 22, 1812.

Grand Army (France), Sep. 7, 1812.

Grand Canyon National Park, Feb. 26, 1919.

Grand Canyon Suite: premiere, Nov. 22, 1931.

Grand Coulee Dam, May 11, 1950.

Grand Ole Opry, Nov. 28, 1925.

Grand Teton National Park, Feb. 26, 1929.

grandfather clause, May 12, 1898.

Grandparents' Day, National, Sep. intro.

Grange, Harold Edward (*Red*), Jun. 13, 1903.

Grange (*Order of Patrons of Husbandry*): founded, Dec. 4, 1867.

Grange Week, Apr. intro.

Granger, Farley, Jul. 1, 1925.

Granger, Lester B., Sep. 16, 1896.

Granger, Stewart, May 6, 1913.

Granit, Ragnar, Oct. 30, 1900.

Granson, Mar. 3, 1476.

Guggenheim, Meyer, Feb. 1, 1828.
Guggenheim, Peggy, Aug. 26, 1898.
Guiana: part ceded to Spain, Jun. 6, 1801.
Guicciardini, Francesco, Mar. 6, 1483.
guided missile: first submarine launching, Feb. 12, 1947.
Guidry, Ron(ald Ames), Aug. 28, 1950.
guilders, patron of, Aug. 11.
Guilford Courthouse, Battle at, Mar. 15, 1781.
Guillaume, Charles Edouard, Feb. 15, 1861.
Guillemin, Roger, Jan. 11, 1924.
Guillon, Treaty of, Jan. 11, 1360.
Guillotin, Joseph Ignace, May 28, 1738.
guillotine, Mar. 7, 1792; first use, Apr. 25, 1792.
Guinea, Nov. 12, 1958; Mar. 5, 1960.
Guinean Democratic Party, Anniversary of the (Guinea), May 14.
Guinean Independence, Anniversary of (Guinea), Oct. 2.
Guinness, Sir Alec, Apr. 2, 1914.
Guise, Duke of (France), Jan. 20, 1558.
Guiteau, Charles J., Jul. 2, 1881.
Guizot, François Pierre Guillaume, Oct. 4, 1787.
Gujarat, Battle of, Feb. 21, 1849.
Gulflight: sunk, May 1, 1915.
Gulick, Luther Halsey, Dec. 4, 1865.
Gullstrand, Allvar, Jun. 5, 1862.
Gun-Munro, Sir Sydney Douglas, Nov. 29, 1916.
gunners, patron of, Dec. 4.
Gunpowder Plot, Nov. 5, 1605.
Gunther, John, Aug. 30, 1901.
Gustaf VI Adolf (Sweden): dies, Sep. 15, 1973.
Gustavus I (Sweden), Jun. 7, 1523.
Gustavus II Adolphus (Sweden), Dec. 9, 1594; Oct. 30, 1611; Sep. 17, 1631; Nov. 16, 1632.
Gustavus Adolphus Day (Sweden), Nov. 6.
Gustavus III (Sweden), Jan. 24, 1746; Aug. 19, 1772; assassinated, Mar. 16, 1792; dies, Mar. 29, 1792.
Gustavus IV Adolphus (Sweden), Nov. 1, 1778; Mar. 29, 1792; Mar. 13, 1806; abdicates, Mar. 29, 1809.
Gustavus V (Sweden), Jun. 16, 1858; Dec. 8, 1907; dies, Oct. 29, 1950.
Gustav VI Adolf (Sweden), Nov. 11, 1882; Oct. 29, 1950.
Guston, Philip, Jun. 27, 1913.
Guthrie, Arlo, Jul. 10, 1947.
Guthrie, Janet, Mar. 7, 1938.
Guthrie, Woody, Jul. 14, 1912.
Guttmacher, Alan Frank, May 19, 1898.
Guyana, May 26, 1966; Feb. 23, 1970.
Guy Fawkes Day (Great Britain), Nov. 5.
Guynemer, Georges M., Dec. 24, 1894.
Guys, Ernest Adolphe Hyacinthe Constantin, Dec. 3, 1805.
Guys and Dolls: premiere, Nov. 24, 1950.
Guzmán Fernández, Antonio, May 26, 1978.
Gwinear (Cornwall), patron of, Mar. 23.
Gwyn, Nell, Feb. 2, 1650.
Gwythian, patron of, Nov. 1.

H

Haakon VII (Norway), Aug. 3, 1872; Nov. 18, 1905; dies, Sep. 21, 1957.
Habeas Corpus Act (England), May 27, 1679.
Habeas Corpus Constitution (Poland), Jan. 9, 1493.
Haber, Fritz, Dec. 9, 1868.
haberdashers, patron of, Aug. 25.
Habyarimana, Juvenal, Mar. 8, 1937.
Hackett, Bobby, Jan. 31, 1915.
Hackett, Buddy, Aug. 31, 1924.
Hackman, Gene, Jan. 30, 1931.
Haddon, Alfred Cort, May 24, 1855.
Hadfield, Sir Robert Abbott, Nov. 28, 1858.
Hadley, Arthur Twining, Apr. 23, 1856.
Hadley, Henry Kimball, Dec. 20, 1871.
Haeckel, Ernst Heinrich, Feb. 16, 1834.
Hagaru (Korea): U.S. occupies, Nov. 15, 1950.
Hagen, Uta, Jun. 12, 1919.
Hagen, Walter, Dec. 21, 1892.
Haggard, Sir Henry Rider, Jun. 22, 1856.
Hague, Alliance of the, Jan. 23, 1668.
Hague, Treaty of, Dec. 9, 1625.
Hague (Holland), Jan. 29, 1914.
Hahn, Otto, Mar. 8, 1879.
Hahnemann, Samuel Christian Friedrich, Apr. 10, 1755.
Haig, Alexander (Meigs), Jr., Dec. 2, 1914.
Haig, Douglas, Jun. 19, 1861; Dec. 19, 1915.
Haile I Selassie (Emperor of Ethiopia), Jul. 23; Apr. 3, 1930; Nov. 2, 1930; exiled Oct. 3, 1935; address to League of Nations Jun. 30, 1936; deposed Sep. 12, 1974.
Hainan Island, Apr. 23, 1950.
Haiphong: bombed, Sep. 22, 1940.
hairdressers, patron of, Aug. 25.
Haise, Fred W. Jr., Apr. 11, 1970.
Haiti, independence, Jan. 1, 1804; Mar. 29, 1804; May 21, 1968.
Haka Road, Apr. 20, 1890.
Halas, George, Feb. 2, 1895.
Haldane, J(ohn) B(urdon) S(anderson), Nov. 5, 1892.
Haldane, Richard Burdon, Jul. 30, 1856.
Haldeman, H. R., Oct. 27, 1926; Apr. 30, 1973; Jan. 1, 1975; Feb. 21, 1975.
Hale, Edward Everett, Apr. 3, 1822.
Hale, George Ellery, Jun. 29, 1868.
Hale, Nathan, Jun. 6, 1755; executed, Sep. 22, 1776.
Hale, Sarah Josepha Buell, Oct. 24, 1788.
Hale, Sir Matthew, Nov. 1, 1609.
Hálek, Vítezslav, Apr. 5, 1835.
Hales, Stephen, Sep. 7, 1677.
Halévy, Ludovic, Jan. 1, 1834.
Haley, Alex (Palmer), Aug. 11, 1921.
Half-year Holiday (Hong Kong), Jul. 1.
Halidon Hill, Jul. 19, 1333.
Halifax Gazette, Mar. 23, 1752.
Halifax Resolves, Anniversary of the Signing of(North Carolina), Apr. 12.
Hall, Asaph, Oct. 15, 1829.
Hall, Charles Martin, Dec. 6, 1863.
Hall, Granville Stanley, Feb. 1, 1844.
Hall, James, Apr. 22, 1887.

Hall, Joyce Clyde, Dec. 29, 1891.
Hall, Marshall, Feb. 18, 1790.
Hall, Paul, Aug. 21, 1914.
Hall, Sir James, Jan. 17, 1761.
Hallam, Henry, Jul. 9, 1777.
Halleck, Charles A., Aug. 22, 1900.
Halleck, Henry Wager, Jan. 16, 1815.
Haller, Albrecht von, Oct. 8, 1708; Oct. 16, 1708.
Halley, Edmund, Nov. 8, 1656.
Hallgrimsson, Jónas, Nov. 16, 1807.
Halliburton, Richard, Jan. 9, 1900.
Hall of Fame for Great Americans, May 30, 1901.
Hall of the Golden Fleece, Oct. 25, 1555.
Hallowe'en, Oct. 31.
Hallstein, Walter, Nov. 17, 1901.
Hallström, Ivar Christian, Jun. 5, 1826.
Halsey, William Frederick (Bull), Oct. 30, 1882.
Halsted, William Stewart, Sep. 23, 1852.
Halston, Apr. 23, 1932.
Ham: chimpanzee, Jan. 31, 1961.
Hamadan, Mar. 2, 1917.
Hamadi, Mohammed Shamte (Zanzibar), Jun. 24, 1963.
Hamann, Johann Georg, Aug. 27, 1730.
Hamburger Hill: Vietnam War, May 20, 1969.
Hamburg (Germany), Jul. 24, 1943.
Hamilton, Alexander, Jan. 11, 1755; dies, Jul. 11, 1804.
Hamilton, Sir William Rowan, Aug. 4, 1805.
Hamlin, Hannibal, Aug. 27, 1809; Mar. 4, 1861.
Hammarskjöld, Dag, Jul. 29, 1905; killed, Sep. 18, 1961.
Hammer, Armand, May 21, 1898.
Hammerstein, Oscar, May 8, 1847.
Hammerstein, Oscar II, Jul. 12, 1895; Dec. 27, 1927; Dec. 2, 1943; Apr. 19, 1945; Apr. 7, 1949.
Hammett, Dashiell, May 27, 1894.
Hammond, James Bartlett, Apr. 23, 1839.
Hampton, Lionel, Apr. 12, 1913; Apr. 20, 1914.
Hampton, Wade, Mar. 28, 1818.
Hampton Court Conference, Jan. 14, 1604.
Hampton Roads, Mar. 8, 1862.
Hampton Roads Conference, Feb. 7, 1865.
Hamstrom (Switzerland), Feb. intro.
Hamsun, Knut, Aug. 4, 1859.
Hana, Mar. 13, 1915.
Hana Matsuri (Japan), Apr. 8.
Hancock, John, Jan. 12, 1737.
Hancock, Winfield Scott, Feb. 14, 1824.
Handel, George Frederick, Feb. 23, 1685.
Handicapped Awareness Week, National, Oct. intro.
handicapped, discrimination, Apr. 28, 1977.
Handler, Philip, Aug. 13, 1917.
Handlin, Oscar, Sep. 19, 1915.
Handsel Monday (Scotland), Jan. intro.
Handwriting Day, Jan. intro.
Handy, Thomas Troy, Mar. 11, 1892.
Handy, W(illiam) C(hristopher), Nov. 16, 1873.
Hankow, Mar. 15, 1927.

Helvetius, Claude Adrien, Jan. 26, 1715.

Hemingway, Ernest, Jul. 21, 1899.

Hemmings, David, Nov. 2, 1941.

Henderson, Arthur, Sep. 13, 1863.

Henderson, Thomas, Dec. 28, 1798.

Hendricks, Thomas A., Mar. 4, 1885.

Henie, Sonja, Apr. 8, 1912.

Henley, William Ernest, Aug. 23, 1849.

Henri, Robert, Jun. 25, 1865.

Henriques, Alfonso (Portugal), Jul. 25, 1139.

Henry, Benjamin, May 1, 1764.

Henry, Joseph, Dec. 17, 1797.

Henry, O., Sep. 11, 1862.

Henry, Patrick, May 29, 1736; May 29, 1765; Mar. 23, 1775.

Henry, Prince de Condé, May 3, 1616.

Henry I (England), Aug. 2, 1100; Jul. 19, 1101; dies, Dec. 1, 1135.

Henry I (France): dies, Aug. 4, 1060.

Henry II (England), Nov. 7, 1153; Oct. 25, 1154; Jan. 6, 1169; Oct. 16, 1171; Jul. 12, 1174; Sep. 30, 1174; Nov. 18, 1188; dies, Jul. 6, 1189.

Henry II (France), Mar. 31, 1547; Jan. 15, 1552; Feb. 5, 1556; Mar. 19, 1519.

Henry II (Holy Roman Emperor), May 15, 1004; Feb. 14, 1014.

Henry III (England), Oct. 1, 1207; Oct. 19, 1216; Jun. 11, 1258; dies, Nov. 16, 1272.

Henry III (France), Sep. 19, 1551; May 30, 1574; murdered, Aug. 2, 1589; Mar. 14, 1590.

Henry III (Holy Roman Emperor), Oct. 28, 1017; Apr. 14, 1028; Dec. 20, 1046.

Henry IV (England), Apr. 3, 1367; Sep. 30, 1399; Mar. 30, 1406; May 18, 1412; dies, Mar. 21, 1413.

Henry IV (France), Dec. 13, 1553; Apr. 13, 1598.

Henry IV (King of Germany, Holy Roman Emperor), Nov. 11, 1050; Feb. 2, 1074; Jan. 24, 1076; Oct. 16, 1076; Jan. 28, 1077; Mar. 15, 1077; Mar. 7, 1080; Oct. 15, 1080; Jun. 3, 1083; Mar. 31, 1084.

Henry V (England), Sep. 16, 1387; Mar. 21, 1413; May 23, 1414; Oct. 25, 1415; Jan. 19, 1419; Jun. 2, 1420; dies, Aug. 31, 1422.

Henry V (Holy Roman Emperor), Jan. 8, 1081; Nov. 8, 1086; Jan. 6, 1099; Feb. 4, 1111; Feb. 12, 1111; Apr. 13, 1111; Apr. 7, 1118; Sep. 23, 1122.

Henry VI (England), Aug. 31, 1422; Jun. 27, 1450; Jul. 10, 1460; Mar. 4, 1461; Mar. 29, 1461; May 4, 1471; dies, May 21, 1471.

Henry VI (Holy Roman Emperor), Jan. 27, 1186; Apr. 14, 1191; Feb. 3, 1194; Dec. 25, 1194; Mar. 8, 1198.

Henry VI (Rome), Aug. 15, 1169.

Henry VII (England), Jan. 28, 1457; Mar. 5, 1496; Jan. 25, 1502; dies, Apr. 21, 1509; Aug. 16, 1513.

Henry VII (Holy Roman Emperor), Jun. 29, 1312.

Henry VII (Count of Luxembourg), Nov. 27, 1308.

Henry VIII (England), Jun. 28, 1491; Apr. 21, 1509; Apr. 5, 1513; Feb. 2, 1522; Nov. 14, 1532; Jan. 25, 1533; May 23, 1533; Jul. 11, 1533; Jul. 6, 1535; May 19, 1536; May 30, 1536; Jan. 6, 1540; Jul. 6, 1540; Jul. 28,

1540; Jul. 29, 1540; Jul. 12, 1542; Nov. 25, 1542; dies, Jan. 28, 1547.

Henry of Carinthia, Aug. 15, 1307.

Henry the Navigator, (Prince), Mar. 4, 1394; Jul. 25, 1415.

Henryk II (Duke of Silesia), Apr. 9, 1241.

Henschel, George, Oct. 22, 1881.

Henson, James (Maury), Sep. 24, 1936.

Hepburn, Audrey, May 4, 1929.

Hepburn, James (Earl of Bothwell), May 15, 1567.

Hepburn, Katharine, Nov. 8, 1909.

Herbert, George, Apr. 3, 1593.

Herbert, Victor, Feb. 1, 1859; Jun. 17, 1903; Oct. 24, 1910.

Herder, Johann Gottfried von, Aug. 25, 1744.

Heredia, José María de, Dec. 31, 1803; Nov. 22, 1842.

Hereros, Jan. 11, 1904.

Herman, Woody, May 16, 1913.

Hermite, Charles, Dec. 24, 1822.

Hermits of St. Francis of Assisi, Order of, May 23, 1474.

Heroes Day (Haiti), Jan. 1.

Heroes Day (Paraguay), Mar. 1.

Heroes Day (Zambia), Jul. intro.; Jul. 5.

Heroes' Day (Jamaica), Oct. intro.

Heroes' Day (Mozambique), Feb. 3.

Heroes' Day (Zimbabwe), Aug. 11.

Herrera, Felipe, Feb. 5, 1960.

Herrera Campins, Luis, May 4, 1925; Mar. 12, 1979.

Herrick, Myron Timothy, Oct. 9, 1854.

Herriot, Edouard, Jul. 5, 1872.

Herschel, Sir John Frederick, Mar. 7, 1792.

Herschel, Sir William, Nov. 15, 1738; Mar. 13, 1781.

Hersey, John (Richard), Jun. 17, 1914.

Hershey, Alfred Day, Dec. 4, 1908.

Hershey, Lewis Blaine, Sep. 12, 1893.

Hershey, Milton Snavely, Sep. 13, 1857.

Herter, Christian Archibald, Mar. 28, 1895.

Hertz, Gustav Ludwig, Jul. 22, 1887.

Hertz, Heinrich Rudolf, Feb. 22, 1857.

Hertzog, James Barry Munnik, Apr. 3, 1866.

Hertzsprung, Ejnar, Oct. 8, 1873.

Herzberg, Gerhard, Dec. 25, 1904.

Herzl, Theodor, May 2, 1860.

Herzog, Chaim, Sep. 17, 1918.

Heshvan, p. x.

Hess, Rudolf, Apr. 26, 1894.

Hess, Victor F., Jun. 24, 1883.

Hess, Walter, Mar. 17, 1881.

Hesse, Hermann, Jul. 2, 1877.

Heston, Charlton, Oct. 4, 1924.

Hevesy, Georg, Aug. 1, 1885.

Hewes, Joseph, Jan. 23, 1730.

Hewish, Antony, May 11, 1924.

Hewitt, Abram Stevens, Jul. 31, 1822.

Heydrich, Reinhard, Mar. 7, 1904; Jun. 10, 1942.

Heyerdahl, Thor, Oct. 6, 1914.

Heymans, Corneille J. F., Mar. 28, 1892.

Heyrovsky, Jaroslav, Dec. 20, 1890.

Heyse, Paul Johann Ludwig von, Mar. 15, 1830.

Heyward, Du Bose, Aug. 31, 1885.

Hickok, James Butler, May 27, 1837.

Hicks, Edward, Apr. 4, 1780.

Hicks, Granville, Sep. 9, 1901.

Hicks, Sir John R., Apr. 8, 1904.

Hidalgo y Costilla, Miguel, May 8, 1753.

Higginbotham, Jay C., May 11, 1906.

Higgins, Marguerite, Sep. 3, 1920.

Higginson, Thomas Wentworth Storrow, Dec. 22, 1823.

High Council of the Revolution (Portugal), Mar. 15, 1975.

Hijaz and Nejd, Kingdom of (Saudi Arabia), Sep. 23, 1932.

Hijaz (Saudi Arabia), Jan. 8, 1926.

Hilary, Sir Edmund (Percival), Jul. 20, 1919.

Hildebrand, Joel, Nov. 16, 1881.

Hildebrandt, Johnann Lucus von, Nov. 14, 1668.

Hildegarde, Feb. 1, 1906.

Hill, Ambrose Powell, Nov. 9, 1825.

Hill, Archibald Vivian, Sep. 26, 1886.

Hill, David Jayne, Jun. 10, 1850.

Hill, James Jerome, Sep. 16, 1838.

Hill, Sir Rowland, Dec. 3, 1795.

Hillary, Sir Edmund, May 29, 1953.

Hillenkoetter, Roscoe H., May 8, 1897.

Hillery, Patrick J., May 2, 1923.

Hillman, Bessie, May 15, 1889.

Hillman, Sidney, Mar. 23, 1887.

Hilo (Hawaii), Jul. 25, 1934.

Hilton, Conrad (Nicholson), Dec. 25, 1887.

Hilton, James, Sep. 9, 1900.

Himmler, Heinrich, Oct. 7, 1900.

Hina Matsuri (Japan), Mar. 3.

Hinckley, John W. Jr., Mar. 30, 1981.

Hindemith, Paul, Nov. 16, 1895; Jan. 22, 1936.

Hindenburg: first air-born piano recital, May 7, 1936; burns, May 6, 1937.

Hindenburg, Paul von, Oct. 2, 1847; Sep. 18, 1914; Aug. 29, 1916; Apr. 10, 1932.

Hindenburg Line, Feb. 24, 1917; Mar. 14, 1917; Apr. 5, 1917; Sep. 3, 1918; Sep. 29, 1918.

Hindi language, Jan. 26, 1965.

Hines, Duncan, Mar. 26, 1880.

Hines, Earl (*Fatha*), Dec. 28, 1905.

Hines, Jerome, Nov. 8, 1921.

Hinshelwood, Sir Cyril Norman, Jun. 19, 1897.

Hinton, Sir Christopher, May 12, 1901.

Hipper, Baron Franz von, Sep. 13, 1863.

Hirobumi Ito, Prince, Sep. 2, 1841.

Hirohito (Emperor of Japan), Apr. 29, 1901; world tour, Mar. 3, 1921; Dec. 25, 1926.

Hiroshima, Japan, Aug. 6, 1945.

Hirsch, Emil Gustav, May 22, 1851.

Hirshhorn, Joseph (Herman), Aug. 1, 1899.

Hirt, Al, Nov. 7, 1922.

Hiss, Alger, Nov. 11, 1904; Jan. 21, 1950.

Histoires Naturelles: premiere, Jan. 12, 1907.

Historic Preservation Week, National, May intro.

Historical Association; American: founded, Sep. 9, 1884.

Hitch Hiking Month, Jul. intro.

Hitchcock, Alfred (Joseph), Aug. 13, 1899.

Hite, Shere D., Nov. 2, 1942.

Howe, Richard, Mar. 8, 1726.

Howe, Samuel Gridley, Nov. 10, 1801.

Howe, William, Aug. 10, 1729.

Howells, William Dean, Mar. 1, 1837.

Howison, George Holmes, Nov. 29, 1834.

Hrdlihčka, Aleš, Mar. 29, 1869.

Hua Guofeng, Jun. 29, 1981.

Hubbard, L. Ron, Mar. 13, 1911.

Hubbell, Carl, Jun. 22, 1903.

Hubble, Edwin Powell, Nov. 20, 1889.

Hubertusburg, Treaty of, Feb. 15, 1763.

Hubmaier (Austrian Anabaptist), Mar. 10, 1528.

Huc, Evariste Régis, Jun. 1, 1813.

Hudson, Henry, Sep. 13, 1609.

Hudson, Rock, Nov. 17, 1925.

Hudson, William Henry, Aug. 4, 1841.

Hudson Bay Company, May 2, 1670; Mar. 9, 1869.

Hudson River: claimed for Netherlands, Sep. 13, 1609.

Hudson River Revival, Great, Jun. intro.

Hué, Mar. 26, 1975.

Hué, Treaty of: signed, Aug. 25, 1883; Jun. 6, 1884.

Huerta, Victoriano, Dec. 23, 1854.

Huey P. Long Day (Louisiana), Aug. 30.

Hufstedler, Shirley, Aug. 24, 1925.

Huggins, Charles Brenton, Sep. 22, 1901.

Huggins, Miller, Mar. 27, 1879.

Huggins, Sir William, Feb. 7, 1824.

Hughes, Charles Evans, Apr. 11, 1862.

Hughes, David Edward, May 16, 1831.

Hughes, Emmet John, Dec. 26, 1920.

Hughes, Howard, Dec. 24, 1905, autobiography hoax, Mar. 13, 1972.

Hughes, Langston, Feb. 1, 1902.

Hughes, Richard, Apr. 19, 1900.

Hughes, Thomas, Oct. 20, 1822.

Hugo, Victor, Feb. 26, 1802.

Huguenots, Apr. 13, 1598.

Huguenots, Massacre of the: begins, Aug. 24, 1572.

Huguenot War, First: ends, Mar. 19, 1563.

Huguenot Wars, Mar. 1, 1562; end, Jun. 28, 1629.

Huidobro, Vicente, Jan. 10, 1893.

Hull, Cordell, Oct. 2, 1871.

Hull, Isaac, Mar. 9, 1773; Aug. 19, 1812.

Hull, William, Jun. 24, 1753.

Hull (England), Jan. 2, 1901.

Hulme, T(homas) E(rnest), Sep. 16, 1883.

Hulst, Hendrik van de, Nov. 19, 1918.

Humanae Vitae: encyclical, Jul. 29, 1968.

human bones, oldest in North America, Dec. 29, 1982.

Human Rights Day, Dec. 10.

Human Rights Day (Equatorial Guinea), Dec. 10.

Humayun (Sultan of Delhi), May 17, 1540.

Humbert I (Italy): Jan. 9, 1878; assassinated, Jul. 29, 1900.

Humble Petition and Advice, Mar. 31, 1657.

Humboldt, Alexander von, Sep. 14, 1769.

Humboldt, Wilhelm von, Jun. 22, 1767.

Hume, David, Apr. 26, 1711.

Humperdinck, Engelbert, Sep. 1, 1854; Dec. 23, 1893.

Humphrey, Doris, Oct. 17, 1895.

Humphrey, George Magoffin, Mar. 8, 1890.

Humphrey, Hubert H., May 27, 1911; Democratic candidate for Vice-President, Aug. 26, 1964; Jan. 20, 1965; Democratic nomination for President, Aug. 28, 1968.

Humphreys, David, Jul. 10, 1752.

Hundred Days, The: begins, Mar. 20, 1815.

Hundred Years' War, May 20, 1303; Jan. 5, 1340; Jun. 24, 1340; Mar. 15, 1341; Oct. 21, 1345; Aug. 26, 1346; Aug. 3, 1347; Jan. 11, 1360; Oct. 24, 1360; Mar. 14, 1369; May 21, 1369; Sep. 19, 1370; Jun. 23, 1372; Jun. 27, 1375; May 18, 1412; Oct. 25, 1415; Jan. 19, 1419; Mar. 24, 1449; Apr. 15, 1450; Aug. 12, 1450; Oct. 23, 1452; Jul. 17, 1453; Oct. 19, 1453.

Hungarian Republic: proclaimed, Nov. 16, 1918.

Hungary, Aug. 26, 1541; Jan. 26, 1699; Apr. 14, 1849; Oct. 17, 1918; Nov. 1, 1918; Nov. 12, 1918; Mar. 22, 1919; Sep. 18, 1922; Apr. 11, 1939; Anti-Jewish laws, May 3, 1939; Dec. 28, 1949; Nov. 1, 1956; Nov. 3, 1956; Feb. 24, 1972.

Hung Hsiu-Ch'uan, Jan. 11, 1851.

Hungnam (Korea): evacuated, Dec. 22, 1950.

Hunley, Feb. 17, 1864.

Hunt, H. L., Feb. 7, 1889.

Hunt, (James Henry) Leigh, Oct. 19, 1784.

Hunt, Richard Morris, Oct. 31, 1827.

Hunt, (William) Holman, Apr. 2, 1827.

Hunter, Catfish, May 8, 1968.

Hunter, Evan, Oct. 15, 1926.

Hunter, Ross, May 6, 1926.

Hunter, Thomas, Oct. 18, 1831.

hunters, patron of, Sep. 20; Nov. 3.

Hunting and Fishing Day, National, Sep. intro.

Huntington, Henry Edwards, Feb. 27, 1850.

Huntington, Samuel, Jul. 5, 1731.

Huntley, Chester (*Chet*), Dec. 10, 1911.

Huong, Tran Van, Jan. 26, 1965.

Hurok, Sol, Apr. 9, 1888.

Hurricane Camille, Aug. 17, 1969.

Hurricane Fifi, Sep. 20, 1974.

Hurst, Fannie, Oct. 18, 1889.

Hus, John, Nov. 5, 1414; Jul. 6, 1415; Feb. 22, 1418.

Husák, Gustáv, Jan. 10, 1913.

Husayn Kamil (Egypt), Dec. 20, 1853.

Hussein, Abdullah ibn (Jordan): assassinated, Jul. 20, 1951.

Hussein, Saddam, Apr. 28, 1937.

Hussein ibn Talal (King of Jordan), Nov. 14, 1935.

Hussein (King of the Hejaz), Jan. 13, 1919.

Husserl, Edmund, Apr. 8, 1859.

Hussey, Ruth, Oct. 30, 1917.

Hustler, Feb. 8, 1977.

Huston, John, Aug. 5, 1906.

Huston, Walter, Apr. 6, 1884.

Hutcheson, Francis, Aug. 8, 1694.

Hutchinson, Anne, Jul. 20, 1591; Nov. 17, 1637.

Hutchinson, Thomas, Sep. 9, 1711.

Hutson, Don, Jan. 31, 1913.

Hutten, Ulrich von, Apr. 21, 1488.

Hutton, Barbara, Nov. 14, 1912.

Hutton, James, Jun. 3, 1726.

Hutton, Lauren, Nov. 17, 1943.

Huxley, Aldous (Leonard), Jul. 26, 1894.

Huxley, Andrew Fielding, Nov. 2, 1917.

Huxley, Julian, Jun. 22, 1887.

Huxley, Thomas Henry, May 4, 1825.

Hu Yaobang, Jun. 29, 1981.

Huygens, Christian, Apr. 14, 1629.

Huysmans, Joris Karl, Feb. 5, 1848.

Hyde, Douglas, Jan. 17, 1860; May 4, 1938.

Hyde, Edward, Feb. 18, 1609.

Hyde Park (London), May 1, 1851.

Hyde-White, Wilfred, May 12, 1903.

hydrogen bomb: first for France, Aug. 24, 1968.

Hyslop, James Hervey, Aug. 18, 1854.

I

Iacocca, Lee, Oct. 15, 1920.

Ibarruri, Dolores, Dec. 9, 1895.

Ibn Saud (Saudi Arabia), Jan. 8, 1926; May 20, 1927.

Ibsen, Henrik, Mar. 20, 1828.

Ice Cream Week, National, Jul. intro.

Ice Skating Month, National, Nov. intro.

Iceland, May 18, 1920; Jun. 23, 1930; May 9, 1940; independence, Jun. 17, 1944; Jan. 23, 1973; Feb. 19, 1976.

Icelandic Supreme Court: established, Oct. 6, 1919.

Idaho: admitted to the Union, Jul. 3, 1890; Teton Dam collapses, Jun. 5, 1976.

Ideal Husband, An: premieres, Jan. 3, 1895.

Ides, p. x.

Ides of March, Mar. 15, 44 B.C.

Idris I (Libya), Dec. 24, 1951.

Ie Shima, Apr. 16, 1945.

Ifni: returned to Morocco, Jun. 30, 1969.

Ignatius Loyola, Apr. 4, 1541.

Ikeda, Hayoto, Dec. 3, 1899.

Illia, Arturo (Umberto), Aug. 4, 1900.

Illinois: admitted to Union, Dec. 3, 1818.

illiterate, patron of, Jun. 13.

Il Palio (Italy), Jul. 2.

Ilq, Frances Lillian, Oct. 11, 1902.

I Married an Angel: premiere, May 11, 1938.

Immaculate Conception, Dogma of, Dec. 8, 1854.

Immaculate Conception of the Blessed Virgin Mary, Feast of, Dec. 8.

Immaculate Heart of Mary, Feast of the, May 27.

immigration quota system: abolished in U.S., Oct. 3, 1965.

immigration regulations (Canadian), Jan. 19, 1962.

impeachment: Richard M. Nixon, May 9, 1974; three articles against, Jul. 30, 1974.

impossible, patron of the, Oct. 28.

Impression of the Stigmata upon St. Francis, Sep. 17.

Inauguration Day (U.S.), Jan. 20.

Inayatullah (King of Afganistan), Jan. 14, 1929.

incandescent lamp, Oct. 21, 1879.

J

Johnson, Hiram Warren, Sep. 2, 1866.

Johnson, Jack, Mar. 31, 1878; Apr. 5, 1915.

Johnson, James Weldon, Jun. 17, 1871.

Johnson, John, Jan. 19, 1918.

Johnson, Lyndon B., Aug. 27, 1908; Jan. 20, 1961; Nov. 22, 1963; Jul. 2, 1964; Democratic candidate for President, Aug. 26, 1964; Jan. 4, 1965; inaugurated Jan. 20, 1965; Feb. 8, 1966; Jan. 5, 1967; Mar. 31, 1968; Apr. 11, 1968; dies Jan. 22, 1973.

Johnson, Pamela Hansford, May 29, 1912.

Johnson, Philip (Cortelyou), Jul. 8, 1906.

Johnson, Rafer, Aug. 18, 1935.

Johnson, Reverdy, May 21, 1796.

Johnson, Richard M., Mar. 4, 1837.

Johnson, Samuel, Oct. 14, 1696.

Johnson, Samuel, Sep. 18, 1709; May 16, 1763.

Johnson, Van, Aug. 20, 1916.

Johnson, William, Sep. 8, 1755.

Johnson, William Eugene, Mar. 25, 1862.

Johnson-Reed Immigration Bill, May 26, 1924.

Johnston, Albert (General), Apr. 6, 1862.

Johnston, Clement D(ixon), Nov. 7, 1895.

John Street Theater: opens, Dec. 7, 1767.

Joinville, League of, Dec. 31, 1584.

Joliet, Louis, Sep. 21, 1645.

Joliot-Curie, Iréne, Sep. 12, 1897.

Joliot-Curie, Jean Frédéric, Mar. 19, 1900; Apr. 28, 1950.

Jolson, Al, May 26, 1886.

Jonathan, Leabua (Lesotho), Jan. 30, 1970; Mar. 31, 1970.

Jones, Casey, Apr. 30, 1900.

Jones, Ernest, Jan. 1, 1879.

Jones, Inigo, Jul. 19, 1573.

Jones, James, Nov. 6, 1921.

Jones, James Earl, Jan. 17, 1931.

Jones, Jim, May 13, 1931; Nov. 18, 1978.

Jones, John Paul, Jul. 6, 1747.

Jones, Mary (*Mother Jones*), May 1, 1830.

Jones, Samuel Milton (*Golden Rule*), Aug. 8, 1846.

Jong, Erica, Mar. 26, 1942.

Jongkind, Johan Barthold, Jun. 3, 1819.

jonquil, Mar. intro.

Jonson, Ben(jamin), Jun. 11, 1572.

Joplin, Janis, Jan. 19, 1943.

Joplin, Scott, Nov. 24, 1868.

Jordaens, Jacob, May 19, 1593.

Jordan, Feb. 20, 1928; formed, Apr. 24, 1950; Apr. 6, 1972.

Jordan, Barbara, Feb. 21, 1936.

Jordan, David Starr, Jan. 19, 1851.

Jordan, Hamilton, Sep. 21, 1944.

Jordan, Vernon E., Jr., Aug. 15, 1935.

Jordon, Jan. 8, 1952.

Josef Ferdinand (Archduke of Austria), May 3, 1915.

Josef I (Holy Roman Emperor), May 5, 1705; dies, Apr. 17, 1711.

Josef II (Holy Roman Emperor), Mar. 13, 1741; Aug. 18, 1765; dies, Feb. 20, 1790.

Joseph, Chief: surrenders, Oct. 4, 1877.

Joseph I (Portugal): dies, Feb. 24, 1777.

Josephine (Beauharnais), Jun. 23, 1766.

Josephson, Brian David, Jan. 4, 1940.

Jouhaux, Léon, Jul. 1, 1879.

Joule, James Prescott, Dec. 24, 1818.

Jourdan, Louis, Jun. 19, 1921.

Jovellanos, Gaspar Melchor de, Jan. 5, 1744.

Jowett, Benjamin, Apr. 15, 1817.

Joyce, James, Feb. 2, 1882; Feb. 2, 1922.

Joyce, William (*Lord Haw-Haw*), Jan. 3, 1946.

Józef Pilsudski, Nov. 28, 1922.

Juana Inés de la Cruz, Sor, Nov. 12, 1651.

Juan Carlos (Alfonso Victor María de Borboón y Borbón), Jul. 22, 1969.

Juan Carlos I (Spain), Jan. 5, 1938; assumes power, Oct. 3b, 1975; Nov. 22, 1975.

Juan Manuel (Infante de Castile), May 5, 1282.

Juantorena, Alberto, Dec. 3, 1951.

Juárez, Benito, Mar. 21, 1806.

Judson, Harry Pratt, Dec. 20, 1849.

jugglers, patron of, Feb. 12.

Julesburg (Colorado), Jan. 7, 1865.

Julian calendar, p. x.

Julian, Percy Lavon, Apr. 11, 1899.

Juliana (Queen of the Netherlands), Apr. 30, 1909; Sep. 4, 1948; abdicates, Apr. 30, 1980; visits Indonesia Aug. 26, 1981.

Julius I (pope), Feb. 6, 337.

Julius II (pope), Dec. 5, 1443.

Julius III (pope), Sep. 10, 1487.

July Belongs to Blueberries, Jul. intro.

Jung, Carl Gustav, Jul. 26, 1875.

Jungmann, Josef *Jakub*, Jul. 16, 1773.

Junior Achievement Week, Jan. intro.

Junius, Jun. intro.

Juno, Jun. intro.

Jupiter, Jan. 7, 1610; approached by *Pioneer 10*, Dec. 3, 1973; Mar. 1, 1979; Mar. 5, 1979.

Jurgenson, Sonny, Aug. 23, 1934.

Just, Ernest Everett, Aug. 14, 1883.

Justice, U.S. Department of: established, Jun. 22, 1870.

Jutland, Battle of, May 31, 1916.

K

Kabul (Afghanistan): massacre of British, Sep. 3, 1879; Jan. 17, 1929.

Kadooment Day (Barbados), Jul. intro.

Kaesong (North Korea), Jul. 14, 1951.

Kafka, Franz, Jul. 3, 1883.

Kaganovich, Jan. 27, 1962.

Kagitingan Day (The Phillipines), May 6.

Kahn, Albert, Mar. 21, 1869.

Kahn, Otto Hermann, Feb. 21, 1867.

Kaiser, Edgar F(osburgh), Jul. 29, 1908.

Kaiser, Georg, Nov. 25, 1878.

Kaiser, Henry John, May 9, 1882.

Kalakaua, David, Nov. 16, 1836.

Kalanianaole Day, Prince Johan Kuhio (Hawaii), Mar. intro.

Kalb, Baron Johann de, Jun. 29, 1721.

Kaledin, Aleksei, Jan. 10, 1918; Feb. 13, 1918.

Kalends, p. x.

Kalevala Day (Finland), Feb. 28.

Kalinin, Mikhail Ivanovich, Nov. 19, 1875.

Kalish, Isidore, Nov. 15, 1816.

Kaltenborn, H. V. (Hans von), Jul. 9.

Kamahameha III (Hawaii), Mar. 7, 1814.

Kamarampaka Day (Rwanda), Sep. 25.

Kamen, Martin David, Aug. 27, 1913.

Kamenev, Lev Borisovich, Jul. 18, 1883.

Kamerlingh-Onnes, Heike, Sep. 21, 1853.

kamikaze attack, Apr. 6, 1945.

Kaminska, Ida, Sep. 4, 1899.

Kampala (Uganda), Apr. 11, 1979.

Kamuzu Day (Malawi), May 14.

Kanagawa, Treaty of, Mar. 31, 1854.

Kanauj (India), May 17, 1540.

K'ang-hsi (Manchu Dynasty), May 4, 1654.

K'ang Yu-wei, Mar. 19, 1858.

Kania, Stanislaw, Mar. 8, 1927.

Kanin, Garson, Nov. 24, 1912.

Kansas-Nebraska Act, May 30, 1854.

Kansas (U.S.): admitted to Union, Jan. 29, 1861.

Kant, Immanuel, Apr. 22, 1724.

Kantemir (Cantemir), Dimitrie, Oct. 26, 1673.

Kantor, McKinlay, Feb. 4, 1904.

Kantorovich, Leonid, Jan. 15, 1912.

Kapitsa, Pyotr, Jun. 26, 1894.

Kaplan, Dora: executed, Sep. 4, 1918.

Kappel, Battle of: ends, Oct. 11, 1531.

Karachi (India), Apr. 6, 1929.

Karadžić, Vuk Stefanović, Oct. 26, 1787.

Karajan, Herbert von, Apr. 5, 1904.

Karakatoa volcano: explodes, Aug. 26, 1883.

Karamanlis, Constantine, Feb. 23, 1907.

Karameh, Mar. 21, 1968.

Karamzin, Nikolai Mikhaylovich, Dec. 1, 1766.

Karjalainen, Ahti, Apr. 13, 1962.

Karlfeldt, Erik Axel, Jul. 20, 1864.

Karloff, Boris, Nov. 23, 1887.

Karlowitz, Treaty of, Jan. 26, 1699.

Karmal, Babrak, Dec. 27, 1979.

Karolyi, Count Michael, Nov. 1, 1918.

Karp, Haskell, Apr. 4, 1969.

Karrer, Paul, Apr. 21, 1889.

Kartini Day (Indonesia), Apr. 21.

Kasala, Mar. 19, 1896.

Kashmir, Mar. 9, 1846.

Kastler, Alfred, May 3, 1902.

Katanga Company, Apr. 15, 1891.

Katsura, Prince Taro, Nov. 28, 1847.

Katz, Sir Bernard, Mar. 26, 1911.

Kauffman, Angelica, Oct. 20, 1741.

Kaufman, George S(imon), Nov. 16, 1889.

Kaulbach, Wilhelm von, Oct. 15, 1805.

Kaunda, Kenneth D., Apr. 28, 1924; Jan. 22, 1964.

Kawabata Yasunari, Jun. 11, 1899.

Kay, Hershy, Nov. 17, 1919.

Kaye, Danny, Jan. 18, 1913.

Kaye, Sammy, Mar. 13, 1913.

Kazan, Elia, Sep. 7, 1909.

KDKA, Pittsburgh: first commercial news radio broadcast, Nov. 2, 1920.

Keach, Stacy, Jun. 2, 1941.

Kean, Edmund, Mar. 17, 1787.

Kearny, Philip, Jun. 1, 1814.

Kearny, Stephen Watts, Aug. 30, 1794.

Kearny, U.S.S.: sunk, Oct. 17, 1941.

Keating-Owen Act (Child Labor Act), Sep. 1, 1916.

Keaton, Buster, Oct. 4, 1895.

Keats, John, Oct. 31, 1795.

Keeler, Christine, Jun. 5, 1963.

Keeler, Ruby, Aug. 25, 1909.

Keen, William Williams, Jan. 19, 1837.

Keep America Beautiful Week, Apr. intro.

Kefauver, (Carey) Estes, Jul. 26, 1903.

Keitel, Wilhelm, Sep. 22, 1882.

Kekkonen, Urho K., May 26, 1979.

Kellaway, Cecil, Aug. 22, 1894.

Keller, Gottfried, Jul. 19, 1819.

Kellerman, Sally, Jun. 2, 1937.

Kelley, Clarence M., Oct. 24, 1911; Jul. 9, 1973.

Kellgren, Johan Henrik, Dec. 1, 1751.

Kellogg, Frank Billings, Dec. 22, 1857.

Kellogg, John Harvey, Feb. 26, 1852.

Kellogg, Will Keith, Apr. 7, 1860.

Kellogg-Briand Pact: signed, Aug. 27, 1928.

Kelly, Clarence M., May 8, 1976.

Kelly, Emmett, Dec. 8, 1898.

Kelly, Gene, Aug. 23, 1912.

Kelly, Grace. *See* Grace of Monaco.

Kelly, William, Aug. 22, 1811.

Kemble, Fanny, Nov. 27, 1809.

Kemble, John Philip, Feb. 1, 1757.

Kemmerer, Edwin Walter, Jun. 29, 1875.

Kemper, James S(cott), Nov. 18, 1886.

Kendall, Edward Calvin, Mar. 8, 1886.

Kendrew, John C., Mar. 24, 1917.

Kennan, George Frost, Feb. 16, 1904.

Kennedy, Edward M., Feb. 22, 1932; Jul. 19, 1969.

Kennedy, John F., May 29, 1917; Jul. 13, 1960; Mar. 1, 1961; inaugurated Jan. 20, 1961; Jan. 30, 1962; Feb. 3, 1962; May 12, 1962; Jun. 10, 1963; assassinated, Nov. 22, 1963; Sep. 27, 1964; memorial May 14, 1965; Jan. 3, 1967.

Kennedy, Joseph Patrick, Sep. 6, 1888.

Kennedy, Robert F., Nov. 20, 1925; shot, Jun. 5, 1968; Apr. 17, 1969; Apr. 23, 1969.

Kennedy, Rose, Jul. 22, 1890.

Kennedy Space Center (Florida), Apr. 12, 1981.

Kennelly, Arthur Edwin, Dec. 17, 1861.

Kennesaw Mountain, Battle of, Jun. 27, 1864.

Kenney, George Churchill, Aug. 6, 1889.

Kenny, Sister Elizabeth, Sep. 20, 1886.

Kent, James, Jul. 31, 1763.

Kent, Rockwell, Jun. 21, 1882.

Kent (England): German raid on, May 25, 1915.

Kenton, Stan, Feb. 19, 1912.

Kent State shootings: U.S. Commission report, Oct. 4, 1970.

Kent State University, May 4, 1970.

Kentucky: admitted to Union, Jun. 1, 1792.

Kentucky Derby: first, May 17, 1875; May 12, 1917.

Kenya: made British protectorate, Jun. 15, 1895; May 28, 1963; independence, Dec. 12, 1963; admitted to UN, Dec. 16, 1963; Jan. 31, 1968; May 19, 1977.

Kenya (British East Africa): becomes colony, Jul. 23, 1920.

Kenya, Mt.: discovered, Dec. 3, 1849; first climbed, Sep. 13, 1899.

Kenyatta, Jomo: released from prison, Aug. 21, 1961; May 28, 1963.

Kenyatta Day (Kenya), Oct. 20.

Keokuk Dam: opened, Aug. 26, 1914.

Kepler, Johannes, Dec. 27, 1571.

Kerekou, Ahmed, Sep. 2, 1933.

Kerenski, Aleksandr Feodorovich, Apr. 22, 1881.

Kern, Jerome, Jan. 27, 1885; Dec. 27, 1927.

Kerouac, Jack, Mar. 12, 1922.

Kerr, John, Nov. 15, 1931.

Kerr, Robert Samuel, Sep. 11, 1896.

Kerr, Walter Francis, Jul. 8, 1913.

Kerwin, Joseph P., Jun. 22, 1973.

Kerz, Leo, Nov. 1, 1912.

Kesey, Ken, Sep. 17, 1935.

Kesselring, Albert, Nov. 20, 1885.

Kettering, Charles Franklin, Aug. 29, 1876.

Key, Ellen Karoline Sofia, Dec. 11, 1849.

Key, Francis Scott, Aug. 1, 1779; Apr. 13, 1814; Sep. 14, 1814.

Keyes, Frances Parkinson, Jul. 21, 1885.

Keynes, John Maynard, Jun. 5, 1883.

Khaalis, Hamaas Abdul, Jul. 23, 1977.

Khachaturian, Aram Ilich, Jun. 6, 1903.

Khalid (Saudi Arabia), Mar. 25, 1975.

Khama, Sir Seretse M., Jul. 1, 1921; Mar. 8, 1950.

Khan, Mohammad Daud, Jul. 17, 1973; Jul. 28, 1973.

Khanh, Hguyen (General), Jan. 26, 1965.

Khartoum, Feb. 18, 1884; Jan. 26, 1885.

Khmer Rouge, Apr. 17, 1975; Apr. 25, 1975.

Khomeini, Ayatollah Ruhollah, May 17, 1900; Feb. 1, 1979; Mar. 16, 1979; issues bans Jul. 23, 1979; Jun. 22, 1981.

Khorana, Har Gobind, Jan. 9, 1922.

Khruschshev, Nikita S., Apr. 17, 1894; Mar. 20, 1953; Oct. 15, 1964.

Khyber Pass: massacre, Jan. 13, 1842; May 26, 1879; Mar. 11, 1898; first train through, Nov. 1, 1925.

Kiaochow Bay, Mar. 6, 1898.

Kids' Day, Sep. intro; Sep. 24.

Kiel: German naval mutiny, Nov. 3, 1918.

Kiel, Treaty of, Jan. 14, 1814.

Kieran, John, Aug. 2, 1892.

Kierkegaard, Sören, May 5, 1813.

Kiev, Feb. 18, 1918.

Kilimanjaro, Mar. 5, 1916.

Killebrew, Harmon (Clayton), Jun. 29, 1936.

Killiecrankie: Scottish Jacobites defeated, Jul. 27, 1689.

Killy, Jean-Claude, Aug. 30; 1943.

Kilmer, (Alfred) Joyce, Dec. 6, 1886.

Kilrain, Jake, Jul. 8, 1889.

Kimberley (South Africa): diamond fields annexed, Oct. 27, 1871.

Kim Il-Sung, Apr. 15, 1912.

Kim Jae Kyu, Oct. 26, 1979; sentenced, Dec. 20, 1979.

Kimmel, Husband Edward, Feb. 26, 1882.

King, B. B., Sep. 16, 1925.

King, Billie Jean, Nov. 22, 1943; Sep. 20, 1973.

King, Clarence, Jan. 6, 1842.

King, Coretta Scott, Apr. 27, 1927.

King, Ernest Joseph, Nov. 23, 1878.

King, Malcolm, Jul. 19, 1885.

King, Martin Luther Jr., Birthday (U.S.), Jan. intro; Jan. 15, 1929; Aug. 28, 1963; calls for civil disobedience Aug. 15, 1967; assassinated, Apr. 4, 1968; Jun. 8, 1968; birthday made federal holiday, Oct. 19, 1983.

King, Richard, Jul. 10, 1825.

King, Rufus, Mar. 24, 1755.

King, Stephen, Sep. 21, 1947.

King, William Lyon Mackenzie, Dec. 17, 1874.

King, William R., Mar. 4, 1853.

King Kamehameha Day (Hawaii), Jun. 11.

Kingdom of the Serbs, Croats, and Slovenes, Oct. 3, 1929.

King's Birthday (Lesotho), May intro.

King's Birthday (Swaziland), Jul. 22 .

King's Birthday (Thailand), Dec. intro.

King's College (Columbia University): chartered, Oct. 31, 1754.

Kingsley, Charles, Jun. 12, 1819.

Kings Lynn, Jan. 19, 1915.

King's Mountain, Battle of, Oct. 7, 1780.

Kinsey, Alfred Charles, Jun. 23, 1894.

Kintner, Robert E(dmonds), Sep. 12, 1909.

Kintradwell, patron of, Oct. 8.

Kipling, (Joseph) Rudyard, Dec. 30, 1865.

Kiplinger, William, Jan. 8, 1891.

Kirby-Smith, Edmund, May 16, 1824.

Kirchner, Leon, Jan. 24, 1919.

Kirchschlaeger, Rudolf, Mar. 20, 1915.

Kirkland, Lane, Mar. 12, 1922.

Kirkus, Virginia, Dec. 7, 1893.

Kirkwood, Samuel Jordan, Dec. 20, 1813.

Kirov, Serge: assassinated, Dec. 1, 1934.

Kisfaludy, Sàndor, Sep. 27, 1772.

Kishinev (Romania): captured by Soviets, Aug. 24, 1944.

Kiska (Aleutian Islands): seized by Japan, Jun. 14, 1942; reoccupied by U.S. and Canada, Aug. 15, 1943.

Kislev, p. x.

Kislimu, p. x.

Kismet: opens, Dec. 3, 1953.

Kissinger, Henry, May 27, 1923; named Secretary of State, Aug. 22, 1973; Feb. 24, 1976; Mar. 10, 1976.

Kitazato, Baron Shibasaburo, Dec. 20, 1856.

Kitchener, Lord Horatio Herbert, Jun. 24, 1850; Mar. 19, 1896; Sep. 2, 1898; Jan. 21, 1899; Jan. 10, 1900; Nov. 29, 1900; drowned Jun. 5, 1916.

Kitchener, Lord Horatio Herbert, Nov. 28, 1902.

Kitt, Eartha, Jan. 26, 1928.

Kitt Peak, Mar. 15, 1960.

Kitty Hawk (North Carolina), Dec. 17, 1903.

Kiukiang, Mar. 15, 1927.

Kiwanis International, Jan. 21, 1915.

Kiwanis Week, World-wide, Jan. intro.

Kiwanuka, Benedicto (Uganda): first prime minister, Mar. 1, 1962.

K-k-k-Ka-ty, Beautiful Katy: copyrighted, Oct. 10, 1916.

Klee, Paul, Dec. 18, 1879.

Klein, Calvin, Nov. 19, 1942.

Klein, Lawrence R., Sep. 14, 1920.

Kleindienst, Richard, Apr. 30, 1973.

Klemperer, Otto, May 14, 1885.

Klondike gold rush, Aug. 16, 1896.

Klopstock, Friedrich Gottlieb, Jul. 2, 1724.

Kluck, Alexander von, May 20, 1846.

Klug, Aaron, Aug. 11, 1926.

Kluge, Die: opens, Feb. 18, 1943.

Kneller, Sir Godfrey (Gottfried Kniller), Aug. 8.

Knickerbocker Baseball Club: first baseball game, Jun. 19, 1846.

Knievel, Evel, Oct. 17, 1938.

Knight, Eric Mowbray, Apr. 10, 1897.

Knight, John S(hively), Oct. 26, 1894.

Knights of Columbus: organized, Feb. 2, 1882; chartered, Mar. 29, 1882.

Knights of Pythias: founded, Feb. 19, 1864.

Knopf, Alfred A., Sep. 12, 1892.

Knowles, John, Sep. 16, 1926.

Knox, Henry, Jul. 25, 1750.

Knox, Philander Chase, May 6, 1853.

Koch, Edward Irving, Dec. 12, 1924.

Koch, Robert, Dec. 11, 1843.

Kocher, Emil Theodar, Aug. 25, 1841.

Kodály, Zoltán, Dec. 16, 1882.

Koestler, Arthur, Sep. 5, 1905.

Kohler, Kaufmann, May 10, 1843.

Köhler, Wolfgang, Jan. 21, 1887.

Koivisto, Mauno, Nov. 25, 1923; May 26, 1979.

Kokoschka, Oskar, Mar. 1, 1886.

Kolbe, Adolph Wilhelm Hermann, Sep. 27, 1818.

Kolbe, Georg, Apr. 4, 1877.

Kolingba, Andrè (General), Aug. 12, 1936; Sep. 1, 1981.

Kollŕ, Ján, Jul. 29, 1793.

Kollwitz, Käthe, Jul. 8, 1867.

Kölreuter, Josef Gottlieb, Apr. 27, 1733.

Koltsov, Alexey Vasilyevich, Oct. 3, 1809.

Kolubara River, Battle of, Dec. 3, 1914; ends, Dec. 6, 1914.

Komandorskie Islands, Battle of, Mar. 26, 1943.

Komenský, Jan Amos, Mar. 28, 1592.

Komsomal Foundation Day (U.S.S.R.), Oct. 29.

Königgrätz, Battle of: ends, Jul. 3, 1866.

Koopmans, Tjalling, Aug. 28, 1910.

Kopechne, Mary Jo, Jul. 19, 1969.

Koraës, Adamantios, Apr. 27, 1748.

Korbut, Olga, May 16, 1955.

Korea, Feb. 26, 1876; independence, Jan. 7, 1895; Jan. 30, 1902; annexed by Japan, Aug. 22, 1910; becomes Japanese province, Aug. 19, 1919; Chinese troops enter, Dec. 28, 1950; treaty with Japan, Jun. 22, 1965.

Korea, Democratic People's Republic of: established, Sep. 9, 1948.

Korea, North, May 18, 1951; Jan. 23, 1968.

Korea, South: invaded, Jun. 25, 1950; May 21, 1961; relations with Japan, Dec. 18, 1965.

Korean Air Lines Flight 007, Sep. 1, 1983.

Korean Alphabet Day or Han'gu Day (Republic of Korea), Oct. 9.

Korean nationalists, Apr. 27, 1919.

Korean War, Jun. 25, 1950; Jun. 27, 1950; Jun. 28, 1950; U.S. Marines land in Korea, Aug. 2, 1950; Sep. 6, 1950; Sep. 15, 1950; Sep. 26, 1950; Nov. 15, 1950; Dec. 1, 1950; Dec. 28, 1950; Jan. 4, 1951; Mar. 14, 1951; Mar. 15, 1951; Jul. 14, 1951; May 8, 1952; Oct. 25, 1952; Jul. 12, 1953; armistice signed, Jul. 27, 1953.

Korean War veterans, May 10, 1951.

Korietz, Feb. 9, 1904.

Kornberg, Arthur, Mar. 3, 1918.

Kornilov, Lavrenti Georgievich, Jul. 30, 1870.

Kosciusko, Thaddeus, Feb. 4, 1746.

Kosciuszko, Army of, Apr. 4, 1917.

Kossel, Albrecht, Sep. 16, 1853.

Kossuth: first performance, Jan. 13, 1904.

Kossuth, Lajos, Sep. 19, 1802.

Kostelanetz, André, Dec. 22, 1901.

Kosygin, Aleksei N., Feb. 20, 1904; Oct. 15, 1964; resigns Oct. 23, 1980.

Kotzebue, August von, Sep. 20, 1819.

Kountché, Seyni (Lt. Col.), Apr. 17, 1974.

Koussevitzky, Serge Alexandrovitch, Jul. 26, 1874.

Kovel, Battle of, Jul. 28, 1916.

Krafft-Ebbing, Baron Richard, Aug. 14, 1840.

Kraft, Charles Herbert, Oct. 17, 1880.

Kraft, Christopher Columbus, Feb. 28, 1924.

Kramer, Stanley, Sep. 29, 1913.

Krapf, Lewis (Dr.), Dec. 3, 1849.

Krasicki, Count Ignacy, Feb. 3, 1735.

Kraszewski, Józef Ignacy, Jul. 28, 1812.

Kraut & Frankfurter Week, National, Feb. intro.

Krebs, Sir Hans Adolf, Aug. 25, 1900.

Kreisky, Bruno, Jan. 22, 1911; Apr. 21, 1970; May 6, 1979.

Kreisler, Fritz, Feb. 2, 1875.

Kress, Samuel Henry, Jul. 23, 1863.

Kreuger, Ivar, Mar. 2, 1880.

Kristofferson, Kris, Jun. 22, 1936.

Kroc, Ray A., Oct. 5, 1902.

Kroger, Bernard Henry, Jan. 24, 1860.

Krogh, Schack August Steenberg, Nov. 15, 1874.

Kronecker, Leopold, Dec. 7, 1823.

Kronstadt (Russia): ship canal, May 27, 1885; Feb. 23, 1921.

Kropotkin, Prince Peter Alexeyevich, Nov. 26, 1842; Dec. 21, 1842.

Kruger Day (South Africa), Oct. intro.

Kruger, Otto, Sep. 6, 1885.

Kruger, Paul, Oct. 10, 1825; Apr. 16, 1883.

Kruger Day (Namibia), Oct. 10.

Kruger Telegram, Oct. 9, 1899.

Krupa, Gene, Jan. 15, 1909.

Krupp, Alfred, Apr. 26, 1812.

Krupp Works: French air raid on, Sep. 24, 1916.

Kubrick, Stanley, Jul. 26, 1928.

Kuhn, Bowie, Oct. 28, 1926.

Kuhn, Franz Felix Adalbert, Nov. 19, 1812.

Kuhn, Richard, Dec. 3, 1900.

Ku Klux Klan: formed, Dec. 24, 1865.

Kula Gulf, Battle of, Jul. 6, 1943.

Kumasi, Battle of, Feb. 4, 1874.

Kumin, Maxine Winokur, Jun. 6, 1925.

Kumpuchea, see Cambodia.

Kun, Béla (Hungary), Mar. 22, 1919.

Küng, Hans, Mar. 19, 1928.

Kunstler, William, Jul. 7, 1919.

Kuomintang, Apr. 15, 1927.

Kuo Min Tang National Congress, Jan. 20, 1924.

Kurdish people, Mar. 11, 1970.

Kurdish rebels, Mar. 14, 1974.

Kurosawa, Akira, Mar. 23, 1910.

Kusch, Polykarp, Jan. 26, 1911.

Kut-el-Amara, Jan. 4, 1916; Apr. 29, 1916; taken by British, Sep. 28, 1916.

Kutuzov, Prince Mikhail Illarionovich Golenishchev, Sep. 16, 1745.

Kuwait: independence, Jun. 19, 1961; May 14, 1963; boundaries established, Dec. 18, 1969.

Kuyper, Abraham, Oct. 29, 1837.

Kuznets, Simon, Apr. 30, 1901.

Kwang-su (Emperor of China), Jan. 12, 1875.

Ky, Nguyen Cao, Jun. 18, 1965; Feb. 8, 1966; Sep. 3, 1967.

Kyd, Thomas, Nov. 5, 1558.

Kyrpianou, Spyros, Oct. 28, 1932.

Kyushu, Japan, Mar. 18, 1945.

L

La Boheme: premiere, Feb. 1, 1896.

Labor Congress of China, National, May 1, 1922.

Labor Day, May 1.

Labor Day (Bahamas), Jun. intro.

Labor Day (Korea), Mar. 10.

Labor Day (Trinidad and Tobago), Jun. intro.

Labor Day (United States), established, Jun. 28, 1894; Sep. 6, 1982, Sep. intro.

Labor Thanksgiving Day or Kinro-Kansha-No-Hi (Japan), Nov. 23.

Labour Day (Jamaica), May 23.

Labour Day (Trinidad and Tobago), Jun. 19.

Labour Government, British: fall, Mar. 28, 1979.

Labrador, Apr. 20, 1534.

La Bruyère, Jean de, Aug. 16, 1645.

lacemakers, patron of, Oct. 18.

Lackland, John (King of England), Apr. 6, 1199.

Laclède, Pierre, Feb. 15, 1764.

Lacretelle, Pierre Louis, Oct. 9, 1751.

Ladd, Alan, Sep. 3, 1913.

Ladislas (Hungary), Nov. 10, 1444.

Ladislas II (King of Bohemia and Hungary), Mar. 1, 1456; May 27, 1471; Apr. 6, 1490;.

Ladislas V (Hungary), Feb. 22, 1440.

Ladislaus (King of Naples), Feb. 27, 1386; Apr. 21, 1408.

Lady Be Good: opens, Dec. 1, 1924.

Lady Day (Great Britain), Mar. 25.

Ladysmith, Seige of, Nov. 2, 1899; Feb. 28, 1900.

Le Châtelier, Henri Louis, Oct. 8, 1850.

Le Duc Tho: refuses Nobel Peace Prize, Oct. 23, 1973.

Lechfeld, Battle of, Aug. 10, 955.

Ledbetter, Huddie (*Leadbelly*), Jan. 20, 1889.

Lederberg, Joshua, May 23, 1925.

Lederer, William, Mar. 31, 1912.

Lee, Ann, Feb. 29, 1736.

Lee, Francis Lightfoot, Oct. 14, 1734.

Lee, Gypsy Rose, Jan. 9, 1914.

Lee, Henry (*Light-Horse Harry*), Jan. 29, 1759.

Lee-Jackson Day (Virginia), Jan. intro.

Lee, John D.: executed, Mar. 23, 1877.

Lee, Manfred Bennington, Oct. 20, 1905.

Lee, (Nelle) Harper, Apr. 28, 1926.

Lee, Peggy, May 26, 1920.

Lee, Richard Henry, Jan. 20, 1732.

Lee, Robert E., Jan. 19, 1807; appointed commander, Feb. 6, 1862; Dec. 13, 1862; Apr. 1, 1865; surrender, Apr. 9, 1865.

Lee, Robert E., Birthday (U.S. southern states), Jan. intro.

Lee, Sir Sidney, Dec. 5, 1859.

Lee, Tsung-Dao, Nov. 24, 1926.

Lee Kuan Yew, Aug. 16, 1923.

Leeuwenhoek, Anton van, Oct. 24, 1632.

Le Fanu, Joseph Sheridan, Aug. 28, 1814.

Leger, Fernand, Feb. 4, 1881.

Léger, Jules, Apr. 4, 1913.

Legionnaires' Disease, Jan. 18, 1977.

Legion of Honor, French, May 19, 1802.

Le Goulet, Peace of, May 22, 1200.

Leguía y Salcedo, Augusto Bernardino, Feb. 19, 1863.

Lehár, Franz, Apr. 30, 1870.

Lehigh: sunk, Oct. 19, 1941.

Lehmann, Lilli, Nov. 24, 1848.

Leibniz, Gottfried Wilhelm von, Jul. 1, 1646.

Leif Ericsson Day (U.S.), Oct. 9.

Leigh, Douglas, May 24, 1907.

Leigh, Janet, Jul. 6, 1927.

Leigh, Vivien, Nov. 5, 1913.

Leighton, Frederick, Dec. 3, 1830.

Leinsdorf, Erich, Feb. 4, 1912.

Leinster: sunk, Oct. 10, 1918.

Leipzig, Battle of, Oct. 16, 1813.

Leipzig (Germany), Jan. 10, 1921.

Leland, Henry Martyn, Feb. 16, 1843.

Leloir, Luis F., Sep. 6, 1906.

Lelouch, Claude, Oct. 30, 1937.

Lemaître, Georges, Jul. 17, 1894.

Lemay, Curtis (Emerson), Nov. 15, 1906.

Lemberg, First Battle of: begins, Aug. 26, 1914.

Lemmon, Jack, Feb. 8, 1925.

Lemnitzer, Lyman L., Aug. 29, 1899; Jan. 2, 1963.

Lemnos, Feb. 23, 1905.

Le Moyne, Pierre, Jul. 16, 1661.

Lenard, Philipp E. A. von, Jun. 7, 1862.

Lend-Lease Act, Sep. 6, 1940; passed, Mar. 11, 1941.

L'Enfant, Pierre Charles, Aug. 2, 1754.

Lenglen, Suzanne, May 24, 1899.

Lenin, Apr. 9, 1870; May 4, 1870; Jul. 16, 1917; Nov. 7, 1917; Dec. 20, 1917; Mar. 17, 1921.

Leningrad, May 27, 1703; Mar. 9, 1917; Apr. 22, 1920.

Lenin Peace Prize, May 3, 1960; Apr. 30, 1961.

Lenngren, Anna Maria, Jun. 18, 1754.

Lennon, John, Oct. 9, 1940; killed, Dec. 8, 1980.

Lennox (Scotland), patron of, Mar. 10.

LeNôtre, André, Mar. 12, 1613.

Lens, patron of, Nov. 3.

Lenya, Lotte, Oct. 18, 1900.

Lenz, Jakob Michael Reinhold, Jan. 12, 1751.

Leo, Jul. intro.; Aug. intro.

Leo III (pope), Dec. 25, 800.

Leo III (pope), Oct. 7, 1883.

Leo X (pope), Dec. 11, 1475; Apr. 5, 1513; Feb. 3, 1518; Jun. 15, 1520; Jan. 3, 1521; Feb. 2, 1522.

Leo XI (pope), Jun. 2, 1535.

Leo XII (pope), Aug. 22, 1760.

Leo XIII (pope), Mar. 2, 1810; Mar. 4, 1878.

Leonard, Ray, May 17, 1956.

Leonardo da Vinci, Apr. 15, 1452.

Leone, Giovanni, Nov. 3, 1908.

Leoni, Raul, Jan. 6, 1967.

Leonov, Aleksei Arkhipovich, May 30, 1934; Mar. 18, 1965.

Leontief, Wassily, Aug. 5, 1906.

Leontovich, Eugenie, Mar. 21, 1900.

Leopardi, Count Giacomo, Jun. 29, 1798.

Leopold, Duke of Austria, Dec. 21, 1192.

Leopold (Austria), Nov. 15, 1315.

Leopold I (Belgium), Dec. 16, 1790; dies, Dec. 9, 1865.

Leopold I (Holy Roman Emperor), Aug. 1, 1658; dies, May 5, 1705.

Leopold II (Belgium), Apr. 9, 1835; Dec. 9, 1865; May 2, 1885; Jul. 1, 1885; Oct. 18, 1908.

Leopold II (Holy Roman Emperor), Feb. 20, 1790; dies, Mar. 1, 1792.

Leopold III (Austria), Jul. 9, 1386.

Leopold III (Belgium), Nov. 3, 1901; Feb. 17, 1934; Jul. 23, 1950; abdicates, Jul. 17, 1951.

Lepanto: Battle of, Oct. 7, 1571.

Lerdo de Tejada, Sebastián, Apr. 25, 1825.

Le Redoutable: French nuclear submarine, Mar. 29, 1967.

Lermontov, Mikhail Yurievich, Oct. 15, 1814.

Lerner, Alan Jay, Aug. 31, 1918.

Lerner, Max, Dec. 20, 1902.

Lerner and Loewe, Mar. 15, 1955.

Lesage, Alain René, May 8, 1668.

Leskov, Nikolai Semyanovich, Feb. 16, 1831.

Lesotho (Basutoland), Feb. 2, 1884; Apr. 30, 1965; becomes independent, Oct. 4, 1966; admitted to UN, Oct. 17, 1966; Jan. 30, 1970; Mar. 31, 1970.

Lesseps, Ferdinand de, Nov. 19, 1805; Feb. 1, 1864.

Lessing, Doris, Oct. 22, 1919.

Lessing, Gotthold Ephraim, Jan. 22, 1729.

Leszczinski, Stanislas, Jun. 2, 1734.

Letelier, Orlando: killed, Sep. 21, 1976.

Letter Writing Week, International, Oct. intro.

Levant, Feb. 20, 1815.

Levant, Oscar, Dec. 27, 1906.

Levene, Sam, Aug. 28, 1905.

Levenson, Sam(uel), Dec. 28, 1911.

Lever, William Hesketh (1st Viscount Leverhulme), Sep. 19, 1851.

Le Verrier, Urbain, Mar. 11, 1811.

Levertin, Oscar Ivan, Jul. 17, 1862.

Levi, Julian (Edwin), Jun. 20, 1900.

Levin, Ira, Aug. 27, 1929.

Levin, Meyer, Oct. 8, 1905.

Levine, James, Jun. 23, 1943.

Levingston, Roberto Marcelo (Argentina), Mar. 22, 1971.

Levi-Strauss, Claude, Nov. 28, 1908.

Levitt, William Jaird, Feb. 11, 1907.

Levy, Jacques François Fromental Elie, May 27, 1799.

Levy, U.S.S., Aug. 22, 1945.

Lévy-Bruhl, Lucien, Apr. 10, 1857.

Lewes, George Henry, Apr. 18, 1817.

Lewis, Anthony, Mar. 27, 1927.

Lewis, Carl, Jul. 1, 1961.

Lewis, C(ecil) Day, Apr. 27, 1904; Jan. 1, 1968.

Lewis, C(live Hamilton) S(taples), Nov. 29, 1898.

Lewis, Francis, Mar. 21, 1713.

Lewis, Jerry, Mar. 16, 1926.

Lewis, Jerry Lee, Sep. 29, 1935.

Lewis, Joe E., Jan. 12, 1902.

Lewis, John L., Feb. 12, 1880; Nov. 9, 1935; Mar. 6, 1947.

Lewis, John Robert, Feb. 21, 1940.

Lewis, Matthew Gregory (*Monk*), Jul. 9, 1775.

Lewis, Meriwether, Aug. 18, 1774.

Lewis, Oscar, Dec. 25, 1914.

Lewis, (Percy) Wyndham, Nov. 18, 1884.

Lewis, Ramsey, May 27, 1935.

Lewis, Shari, Jan. 17, 1934.

Lewis, Sinclair, Feb. 7, 1885.

Lewis, Sir W. Arthur, Jan. 23, 1915.

Lewis, Ted, Jun. 6, 1892.

Lewis, Wilmarth Sheldon, Nov. 14, 1895.

Lewis, Winford Lee, May 29, 1878.

Lewisohn, Adolph, May 27, 1849.

Lexington, battle of, Apr. 19, 1775.

Lexington (Virginia), Jan. 8, 1961.

Ley, Willy, Oct. 2, 1906.

Leyte Gulf, Battle of, Oct. 24, 1944; ends, Oct. 25, 1944.

Libby, Willard Frank, Dec. 17, 1908.

Liberace (Wladziu Valentino), May 16, 1919.

Liberal Party (Canada), Apr. 6, 1968.

Liberation Anniversary of (Czechoslovakia), May 9.

Liberation Day (Albania), Nov. 29.

Liberation Day (Bulgaria), Mar. 3.

Liberation Day (Guam), Jul. 21.

Liberation Day (Hong Kong), Aug. intro.

Liberation Day (Hungary), Apr. 4.

Liberation Day (Italy), Apr. 25.

Liberation Day (Netherlands), May 5.

Liberation Day (Republic of Korea), Aug. 15.

Liberation Day (Togo), Jan. 13.

Liberation of Africa Day (African nations), May 25.

Liberation of Monaco (Monaco), Sep. 3.

London Naval Conference Treaty, Apr. 10, 1930.

London police, Sep. 29, 1829.

London Symphony Orchestra: inaugural concert, Jun. 9, 1904.

London *Times*: first color Sunday supplement, Feb. 4, 1964.

London University: chartered, Feb. 11, 1826.

Lone Ranger: radio debut, Jan. 30, 1933.

Long, Crawford Williamson, Nov. 1, 1815.

Long, Huey P., Aug. 30, 1893; assassinated, Sep. 8, 1935.

Long, John Davis, Oct. 27, 1838.

Long, Russell (Billiu), Nov. 3, 1918.

Longfellow, Henry Wadsworth, Feb. 27, 1807.

Longo, Luigi, Mar. 15, 1900.

Longstreet, James, Jan. 8, 1821.

Longworth, Alice Lee Roosevelt, Feb. 12, 1884.

Longworth, Nicholas, Nov. 5, 1869.

Lönnrot, Elias, Apr. 9, 1802.

Loos, Anita, Apr. 26, 1893.

López, Carlos Antonio, Nov. 4, 1790.

López, Francisco Solano, Jul. 24, 1827.

Lopez, Nancy, Jan. 1, 1957.

Lopez Arellano, Oswaldo, Apr. 22, 1975.

López de Ayala y Herrera, Adelardo, May 1, 1828.

Lopez de Santa Anna, Antonio, Feb. 21, 1794.

Lopez Portillo, Josè, Jun. 16, 1920.

Lopez Rega, Jan. 3, 1975.

Loren, Sophia, Sep. 20, 1934.

Lorentz, Hendrik A., Jul. 18, 1853.

Lorenz, Konrad Zacharias, Nov. 7, 1903.

Lorimer, George Horace, Oct. 6, 1867.

Lorraine, patron of, Dec. 6.

Los Angeles (California), Jan. 15, 1939.

Losonczi, Pal, Sep. 18, 1919.

Lostwithiel, Sep. 2, 1644.

Lothair of Saxony, Aug. 30, 1125; Jun. 4, 1133.

Lothrop, Harriet Mulford, Jun. 22, 1844.

Lotze, Rudolf Hermann, May 21, 1817.

Loucheur, Louis, Aug. 12, 1872.

Loudon, John Claudius, Apr. 8, 1783.

Loudun, Treaty of, May 3, 1616.

Louis, Joe, May 13, 1914; Jun. 22, 1937; Mar. 1, 1949.

Louis, Saint (France), Mar. 24, 1267.

Louis, the Child (Germany), Feb. 4, 900.

Louisburg (Canada), Jul. 24, 1758.

Louis Charles (Belgium), Feb. 3, 1831.

Louisiana, Apr. 9, 1682; admitted to Union, Apr. 30, 1812; May 12, 1898.

Louisiana Purchase, Feb. 22, 1819.

Louisiana Territory, Apr. 30, 1803; U.S. takes possession, Dec. 20, 1803.

Louis I (Hungary), Mar. 5, 1326.

Louis I (Portugal), Nov. 11, 1861.

Louis II (Anjou), Feb. 27, 1386.

Louis II (Hungary), Jul. 1, 1506.

Louis III (Bavaria), Jan. 7, 1845.

Louis IV (Holy Roman Emperor), Mar. 23, 1324; Jan. 17, 1328; Apr. 18, 1328; Sep. 5, 1338; Mar. 15, 1341; Apr. 13, 1346.

Louis VI (France): dies, Aug. 1, 1137.

Louis VII (France), Aug. 1, 1137; Jan. 6, 1169; Sep. 30, 1174; dies, Sep. 18, 1180.

Louis VIII (France), Jul. 14, 1223.

Louis IX (France), Apr. 25, 1214; Jun. 4, 1249; May 11, 1258; dies, Aug. 25, 1270.

Louis X (France), Oct. 4, 1289; Nov. 29, 1314; dies, Jun. 4, 1316.

Louis XI (France), Jul. 28, 1461; Jun. 19, 1464; dies, Aug. 30, 1483.

Louis XII (France), Jun. 27, 1462; Dec. 10, 1508; dies, Jan. 1, 1515.

Louis XIII (France), Sep. 27, 1601.

Louis XIV (France), Sep. 5, 1638; May 14, 1643; Oct. 18, 1685; Jul. 9, 1686; dies, Sep. 1, 1715.

Louis XV (France), Feb. 15, 1710; Sep. 1, 1715; dies, May 10, 1774.

Louis XVI (France), Aug. 23, 1754; May 16, 1770; May 10, 1774; Jul. 14, 1789; arrested, Jun. 21, 1791; beheaded, Jan. 21, 1793.

Louis XVII (France), Mar. 27, 1785.

Louis XVIII (France), Nov. 17, 1755; dies, Sep. 16, 1824.

Louis Napoleon, Dec. 20, 1848.

Louis of Battenberg (Mountbatten), Oct. 29, 1914.

Louis-Philippe (France), Oct. 6, 1773; Jul. 29, 1830; Aug. 7, 1830; abdication, Feb. 24, 1848.

Lousma, Jack R., Jul. 28, 1973.

Louvain, Battle of, Sep. 1, 891.

Louvain, Belgium: occupied by Germans, Aug. 19, 1914.

Love, James Spencer, Jul. 6, 1896.

Lovejoy, Elijah Parish, Nov. 9, 1802; killed, Nov. 7, 1837.

Lovell, James A. Jr., Mar. 25, 1928; Dec. 4, 1965; Dec. 21, 1968; Apr. 11, 1970.

Lovell, Sir Alfred Charles Bernard, Aug. 31, 1913.

Love Me, Do: Beatles first recording, Sep. 11, 1962.

lovers, Welsh patron of, Jan. 25.

Low, Juliet, Mar. 12, 1912.

Low, Juliette Gordon, Oct. 31, 1860.

Low, Sir David Alexander Cecil, Apr. 7, 1891.

Lowe, Thaddeus S. C., Aug. 20, 1832.

Lowell, Abbott Lawrence, Dec. 13, 1856.

Lowell, Amy, Feb. 9, 1874.

Lowell, James Russell, Feb. 22, 1819.

Lowell, Percival, Mar. 13, 1855.

Lowell, Robert Traill Spence, Mar. 1, 1917.

Lowicz, Battle of: begins, Nov. 30, 1914.

Lowry Air Force Base, Jul. 11, 1955.

Loy, Myrna, Aug. 2, 1905.

Loyalty Day (United States), May intro.

Loyola, Ignatius, Aug. 15, 1534.

Lübeck, Peace of, May 22, 1629.

Lublin, Union of, Jul. 1, 1569.

Lucca (Italy), patron of, Mar. 18.

Luce, Claire Boothe, Apr. 10, 1903.

Luce, Henry Robinson, Apr. 3, 1898.

Luciano, Charles (Lucky), Nov. 11, 1896.

Lucky Lady II, Mar. 2, 1949.

Ludendorff, Erich Friedrich Wilhelm, Apr. 9, 1865; resigns Oct. 27, 1916.

Ludwig, Carl, Dec. 29, 1816.

Ludwig, Christa, Mar. 16, 1928.

Ludwig I (Bavaria), Mar. 20, 1848.

Lugosi, Bela, Oct. 29, 1884.

Luis I (Portugal), Oct. 31, 1838.

Lukas, Paul, May 26, 1891.

Lule, Jusufu (Uganda), Jun. 20, 1979.

Lully, Jean-Baptiste, Nov. 28, 1632.

Lumière, Auguste, Oct. 19, 1862; Feb. 13, 1895.

Lumière, Louis Jean, Oct. 5, 1864; Feb. 13, 1895.

Lumumba, Patrice (Republic of the Congo): Jul. 2, 1925; Jun. 21, 1960; killed, Feb. 12, 1961.

Luna 9: moon landing, Feb. 3, 1966.

Luna 10: first lunar orbiter, Apr. 3, 1966.

Luna 15, Jul. 17, 1969.

Luna 17, Nov. 17, 1970.

Luna 20, Feb. 25, 1972.

Luna 1, Jan. 2, 1959.

lunar eclipse: first recorded, Mar. 19, 72.

lunar module, Mar. 13, 1969.

lunar month, p. viii.

Lunar Orbiter 2, Nov. 18, 1966.

Lunar Orbiter I: transmits photos of moon's surface, Aug. 18, 1966.

Lunar Orbiter III, Feb. 4, 1967.

lunar year, p. viii.

lunation, p. viii.

Lunceford, Jimmie, Jun. 6, 1902.

lundi, p. ix.

Lunéville, Peace of, Feb. 9, 1801.

Lunik 5, May 9, 1965.

Lunokhod 2, Jan. 16, 1973.

Lupercalia, Feb. intro.

Lupino, Ida, Feb. 4, 1918.

Lupus Week, National, Oct. intro.

Luria, Salvador Edward, Aug. 13, 1912.

Lusitania: maiden voyage, Sep. 12, 1908; Feb. 6, 1915; sunk, May 7, 1915; Jun. 8, 1915.

Luther, Martin, Feb. 18; Nov. 10, 1483; Jun. 13, 1515; Oct. 31, 1517; interrogated, Oct. 12, 1518; teachings condemned by Leo X, Jun. 15, 1520; Dec. 10, 1520; exccommunicated by Pope Leo X, Jan. 3, 1521; excommunicated by Diet of Worms, Apr. 17, 1521; May 26, 1521.

Lutheran Church, American: formed, Apr. 22, 1960.

Lutheran Church, Evangelical, Apr. 22, 1960.

Lutheran Church, United Evangelical, Apr. 22, 1960.

Lutyens, Sir Edwin Landseer, Mar. 29, 1869.

Lützen, Battle of, Nov. 16, 1632.

Lutzk: captured by Russians, Jun. 2, 1916.

Luxembourg, May 11, 1867; Nov. 23, 1890; 05 10, 1940.

Luxemburg, Rosa (*Red Rosa*), Dec. 25, 1870.

Luxemburgs, Feb. 10, 1364.

Luzán, Ignacio de, Mar. 28, 1702.

Luzon (Philippines): attack by U.S. carriers, Sep. 21, 1944; Jan. 9, 1945.

Lvov, Prince Georgy Yevgenyevich, Oct. 21, 1861.

Lwoff, André Michael, May 8, 1902.

Lydekker, Richard, Jul. 25, 1849.

Lydwina of Schiedam, Apr. 14.

Lyell, Sir Charles, Nov. 14, 1797.

Lynch, John R., Sep. 10, 1847.

Lynde, Paul (Edward), Jun. 13, 1926.

Lyndon B. Johnson's Birthday (Texas), Aug. 27.

Lynen, Feodor, Apr. 6, 1911.

Lynn, Loretta, Jan. 14, 1932.

Lyon, Mary, Feb. 28, 1797.

Lyons, Sir Joseph Aloysius, Sep. 15, 1879.

Lyons, Treaty of, Jan. 17, 1601.

M

Maazel, Lorin, Mar. 6, 1930.

Macao, Dec. 1, 1887.

MacArthur, Arthur, Jun. 2, 1845.

MacArthur, Charles G(ordon), Nov. 5, 1895.

MacArthur, Douglas, Jan. 26, 1880; Jul. 26, 1941; Feb. 5, 1945, Feb. 7, 1945; Sep. 7, 1945; Jul. 8, 1950; Sep. 29, 1950; Apr. 11, 1951.

Macaulay, Thomas Babington, Oct. 25, 1800.

Macbeth, May 10, 1849.

Macbeth, Jul. 27, 1054; killed Aug. 15, 1057.

MacBride, Sean, Jan. 26, 1904.

Macchiavelli, Dec. 6, 1506.

Macdiarmid, Hugh, Aug. 1, 1892.

MacDonald, Dwight, Mar. 24, 1906.

MacDonald, James Ramsay, Oct. 12, 1866; Jan. 22, 1924.

MacDonald, Jeanette, Jun. 18, 1907.

MacDonald, John D., Jul. 24, 1916.

MacDonald, Ross, Dec. 13, 1915.

Macdonald, Sir John, Jan. 11, 1815.

MacDowell, Edward Alexander, Dec. 18, 1861.

Macedonian, H.M.S., Oct. 25, 1812.

Mach, Ernst, Feb. 18, 1838.

Mácha, Karel Hynek, Nov. 16, 1810.

Machado y Morales, Gerardo, Sep. 29, 1871.

Machel, Samora, Sep. 29, 1933.

Machensen, General von, Apr. 28, 1915.

Machiavelli, Niccolò, May 3, 1469; Jun. 15, 1498.

Macias Nquema: executed, Sep. 29, 1979.

MacInnes, Helen Clark, Oct. 7, 1907.

Macintosh, Charles, Dec. 29, 1766.

Mack, Joseph Sanford, Nov. 27, 1870.

Mackay, Charles Hungerford, Apr. 17, 1874.

Mackensen, August von (General), Sep. 6, 1914; Oct. 6, 1915.

Mackenzie, Alexander, Jan. 28, 1822.

Mackenzie, Henry, Aug. 25, 1745.

Mackenzie, Sir Alexander Campbell, Aug. 22, 1847.

Mackenzie, William Lyon, Mar. 6, 1834.

Mackinder, H.J., Sep. 13, 1899.

Maclaine, Shirley, Apr. 24, 1934.

MacLeish, Archibald, May 7, 1892.

Macleod, John James Rickard, Sep. 6, 1876.

Mac-Mahon, Marie-Edmé-Patrice-Maurice, Jul. 13, 1808.

Macmillan, Donald Baxter, Nov. 10, 1874.

Macmillan, Harold, Feb. 10, 1894; Jan. 10, 1957; *Winds of Change*, Feb. 3, 1960.

Macmurray, Fred(erick Martin), Aug. 30, 1908.

Macon, Nathaniel, Dec. 17, 1758.

Macpherson, James, Oct. 27, 1736.

Macready, William Charles, Mar. 3, 1793.

MacSweney, Terence: dies, Oct. 25, 1920.

Madách, Imré, Jan. 21, 1823.

Madagascar: French colony, Aug. 6, 1896; annexed by France, Aug. 18, 1896; Mar. 26, 1960. *See also* Malagasy Republic.

Madame Butterfly: premiere, Feb. 17, 1904.

Madaraka Day (Kenya), Jun. 1.

mad dogs, patron of, Aug. 3.

Maddox, Lester, Sep. 30, 1915.

Madero, Francisco Indalécio, Oct. 30, 1873; Nov. 20, 1910; May 25, 1911; Nov. 6, 1911; assassinated Feb. 22, 1913.

Madison, Dolley, May 20, 1772.

Madison, James, Mar. 16, 1751; inaugurated, Mar. 4, 1809.

Mad Parliament, Jun. 11, 1258.

Madrid, Treaty of, Nov. 5, 1630.

Madrid, University of: closed, Mar. 17, 1929.

Madrid Convention: signed, Jul. 3, 1880.

Maeterlinck, Maurice, Aug. 29, 1862.

Magana, Alvaro Alfredo, Oct. 8, 1925.

Magellan, Ferdinand, Feb. 3, 1521; killed, Apr. 27, 1521.

Magellan Day (Guam), Mar. 6.

Magendie, François, Oct. 15, 1783.

Magna Carta: signed, Jun. 15, 1215; final form, Feb. 25, 1225; confirmed, Oct. 12, 1297.

Magnani, Anna, Mar. 7, 1908.

Magnuson, Warren G., Apr. 12, 1905.

Magritte, René François-Ghislain, Nov. 21, 1898.

Magruder, Jeb Stuart, Nov. 5, 1934.

Magsaysay, Ramón, Aug. 31, 1907.

Mahan, Alfred Thayer, Sep. 27, 1840.

Mahdi, Jan. 26, 1885.

Mahendra (King of Nepal): dies, Jan. 31, 1972.

Mahgoub, Muhammad Ahmed, May 25, 1969.

Mahler, Gustav, Jul. 7, 1860; Nov. 25, 1901; Jun. 9, 1902; Oct. 18, 1904; first American appearance, Jan. 1, 1908.

Mahler's *Fourth Symphony in G Major*: premiere, Nov. 25, 1901.

Mahler's *Third Symphony*: first complete performance of, Jun. 9, 1902.

Mahmud (Emperor of India), Jan. 3, 1399.

Mahmud II (Turkey), Jul. 20, 1785.

Maia, May intro.

Maia Majesta, May intro.

Mailer, Norman, Jan. 31, 1923.

Maillol, Aristide, Dec. 8, 1861.

Maimonides, Moses, Mar. 30, 1135.

Maine, Mar. 3, 1820; admitted to Union, Mar. 15, 1820.

Maine, Henry James Sumner, Aug. 15, 1822.

Maine, U.S.S., Feb. 15, 1898.

Maine Memorial Day (U.S.), Feb. 15.

Maistre, (Joseph Marie) de, Apr. 1, 1753.

Maitland, Frederick Lewis, Jul. 15, 1815.

Maitlisụnntig (Switzerland), Jan. intro.

Makarios (Cyprus): overthrown, Jul. 15, 1974.

Makarios III (Archbishop, Cyprus), Aug. 13, 1913.

Makarova, Natalia Romanovna, Nov. 21, 1940.

Makeba, Miriam, Mar. 4, 1932.

makers of precision instruments, patron of, Nov. 3.

Makin Island, Nov. 20, 1943.

Makino, Count Nobuaki, Apr. 22, 1861.

Malaga, Feb. 8, 1937.

Malagasy Republic (Madagascar): Mar. 26, 1960; independence, Jun. 26, 1960; Sep. 6, 1970; Feb. 11, 1975.

Malamud, Bernard, Apr. 26, 1914.

Malawi, Feb. 1, 1963; independence, Jul. 6, 1964.

Malaya: independent member of British Commonwealth, Aug. 31, 1957.

Malaya: Japanese landing, Dec. 8, 1941.

Malay Peninsula, Jan. 20, 1874.

Malaysia, Mar. 7, 1970.

Malaysia, Federation of: created, Jul. 9, 1963.

Malaysia, Federation of, Sep. 16, 1963.

Malcolm, Jul. 27, 1054.

Malcolm II (Scotland): dies, Nov. 25, 1034.

Malcolm III (Scotland): killed, Nov. 13, 1092.

Malcolm IV (Scotland), May 24, 1153; dies, Dec. 9, 1165.

Malcolm X: assassinated, Feb. 21, 1965.

Malczewski, Antoni, Jun. 3, 1793.

Malden, Karl, Mar. 22, 1913.

Maldive Islands: independence, Jul. 26, 1965; admitted to U.N., Sep. 21, 1965.

Malebranche, Nicolas de, Aug. 6, 1638.

Malenkov, Georgi Maximilianovich, Jan. 8, 1902; Jan. 27, 1962.

Mali, Federation of: Apr. 4, 1960; independence, Jun. 20, 1960; Aug. 20, 1960.

Mali, Republic of: independence, Sep. 22, 1960; admitted to U.N., Sep. 28, 1960.

Malinowski, Bronislaw Kasper, Apr. 7, 1884.

Mallarmé, Stéphane, Mar. 18, 1842.

Malle, Louis, Oct. 30, 1932.

Malmaison, Battle of, Oct. 23, 1917.

Malone, Dorothy, Jun. 30, 1925.

Malpighi, Marcello, Mar. 10, 1628.

Malplaquet, Battle of, Sep. 11, 1700.

Malraux, André, Nov. 3, 1901.

Malta, May 30, 1814; Apr. 15, 1942; May 9, 1942; Mar. 3, 1962; independence, Sep. 21, 1964; Apr. 29, 1965.

Malta, Knights of, patron of, Jan. 23.

Malthus, Thomas Robert, Feb. 14, 1766.

Malus, Etienne Louis, Jun. 23, 1775.

Mameluke, Mar. 1, 1811.

Mamelukes, May 18, 1291.

Man Watchers' Compliment Week, Jul. intro.

Man Watchers' Week, Jan. intro.

Managua (Nicaragua): earthquake, Dec. 23, 1972.

Manchester, William, Apr. 1, 1922.

Manchu Dynasty, Jan. 11, 1851; Feb. 12, 1912.

Manchukuo, Feb. 18, 1932.

Manchuria, Apr. 7, 1907; Apr. 14, 1929; Japanese military action in, Sep. 18, 1931.

Manchuria, War Lord of, Apr. 21, 1922.

Mancini, Henry, Apr. 16, 1924.

Mancini, Pasquale Stanislao, Mar. 17, 1817.

Mandalay, Nov. 28, 1885.

Manes, Apr. 24, 216.

Manet, Edouard, Jan. 23, 1832.

Manfred (King of Sicily), Dec. 2, 1254.

Manila (Philippines), captured by U.S., Aug. 13, 1898; Dec. 26, 1941; Japanese occupation, Jan. 2, 1942; Feb. 5, 1945; Feb. 7, 1945.

Manila Bay, Battle of, May 1, 1898.

Mankiewicz, Joseph Leo, Feb. 11, 1909.

Mann, Herbie, Apr. 16, 1930.

Mann, Horace, May 4, 1796.

Mann, Thomas, Jun. 6, 1875.

Mann Act (White Slave Traffic Act): passed, Jun. 25, 1910.

Mannerheim, Carl Gustav Emil, Jun. 4, 1867.

Manners, John, Jan. 2, 1721.

Manning, Henry Edward, Jul. 15, 1808.

Mansfield, Katherine, Oct. 14, 1888.

Mansfield, Michael Joseph, Mar. 16, 1903.

Mansfield, Richard, May 24, 1854.

Manson, Charles (Milles), Nov. 12, 1934.

Manson, Sir Patrick, Oct. 3, 1844.

Mantle, Mickey, Oct. 20, 1931.

Mantua, patron of, Mar. 18.

Manuel II (Portugal), Oct. 5, 1910.

Many Martyrs of Nicomedia, Dec. 25.

Manzoni, Alessandro Francesco Tommaso Antonio de, Mar. 7, 1785.

Maori insurrection: ends, Mar. 19, 1861.

Maori War: begins, Mar. 17, 1860.

Mao Tse-tung, Dec. 26, 1893; Jan. 19, 1975.

Marantha War: last, ends, Jun. 3, 1818.

Marasesti, Battle of, Jul. 22, 1917.

Marat, Jean Paul, May 24, 1743; assassinated, Jul. 13, 1793.

Maravich, Pete, Jun. 22, 1948.

Marble, Alice, Sep. 28, 1913.

Marceau, Marcel, Mar. 22, 1923.

Marcellus II (pope), May 6, 1501.

March, Fredric, Aug. 31, 1897.

March of Dimes, Jan. 3, 1938.

Marciano, Rocky, Sep. 1, 1923; Sep. 23, 1952.

Marconi, Guglielmo, Apr. 25, 1874; Jul. 31, 1897; Dec. 11, 1901.

Marcos, Ferdinand, Sep. 11, 1917; Sep. 21, 1972; Feb. 2, 1973; Apr. 7, 1978.

Marcos, Imelda, Jul. 2, 1931.

Marcus, Harold Stanley, Apr. 20, 1905.

Marcus Aurelius (Roman Emperor), Apr. 20, 121.

Marcuse, Herbert, Jul. 19, 1898.

Marcus Island, Mar. 4, 1942.

Marcy, William Learned, Dec. 12, 1786.

mardi, p. ix.

Mare, Walter de la, Apr. 25, 1873.

Marengo, Jun. 14, 1800.

Marette, Jacques, Jul. 13, 1962.

Margaret (Queen of England), Mar. 23, 1430; Dec. 30, 1460; Feb. 17, 1461.

Margaret, Maid of Norway (Queen of Scotland), Mar. 19, 1286; dies Oct. 7, 1290.

Margarethe II (Denmark), Apr. 16, 1940; Jan. 15, 1972.

Margaret of Navarre, Apr. 11, 1492.

Margaret Rose, Princess (England), Aug. 21, 1930; May 6, 1960; May 24, 1978.

Margaret Tudor: Jan. 25, 1502; marries James IV (Scotland), Aug. 8, 1502.

Mariage de Figaro, Le: premiere, Apr. 27, 1784.

Maria I (Portugal), Feb. 24, 1777.

Maria II (Portugal):, Apr. 4, 1819; Sep. 24, 1834; dies Nov. 15, 1853.

Maria-Luisa (Austria), Feb. 11, 1810.

Mariana Islands: bombed, Jun. 12, 1944; May 23, 1973.

Mariana and Marshall Islands, Oct. 21, 1914.

Mariátegui, José Carlos, Jun. 14, 1895.

Maria Theresa (Austria), May 13, 1717; Oct. 20, 1740.

Marie Antoinette (France), Nov. 2, 1755; May 16, 1770; beheaded, Oct. 16, 1793.

Marie Louise (Austria), Apr. 1, 1810.

Marignano, Battle of, Sep. 13, 1515.

Mariner 9, Nov. 13, 1971.

Mariner II: launched, Aug. 27, 1962; Dec. 14, 1962; Feb. 26, 1963.

mariners, patron of, Apr. 14; Jul. 25; Nov. 13; Dec. 6.

Marines, U.S., Apr. 21, 1914.

Maris, Roger, Sep. 10, 1934; breaks Babe Ruth's record, Oct. 1, 1961.

Maritain, Jacques, Nov. 18, 1882.

Maritime Day, National (U.S.), May intro.

Maritime Day, World, Mar. intro.

Mark Antony, Sep. 2, 31 B.C.; Feb. 15, 44 B.C..

Markevitch, Igor, Jul. 27, 1912.

Markham, Edwin Charles, Apr. 23, 1852.

Markham, Sir Clements Robert, Jul. 20, 1830.

Markova, Dame Alicia, Dec. 1, 1910.

Marlborough (England), May 23, 1706.

Marlin, John Mahlon, May 6, 1837.

Marlowe, Christopher, Feb. 26, 1564.

Marne, First Battle of the, Sep. 6, 1914; ends, Sep. 9, 1914.

Marne, Second Battle of the: begins, Jul. 15, 1918; Jul. 18, 1918; ends, Aug. 7, 1918.

Marne River: reached by U.S. Third Army, Aug. 28, 1944.

Marquand, J(ohn) P(hillips), Nov. 10, 1893.

Marquette, Jacques, Jun. 1, 1637.

Marquis, Don(ald Robert Perry), Jul. 19, 1878.

married priests: excommunicated, Mar. 9, 1074.

Marriner, Neville, Apr. 15, 1924.

Marriott, John Willard, Sep. 17, 1900.

Mars 3: space probe, Dec. 7, 1971.

Mars, Jul. 20, 1976; Sep. 3, 1976.

Mars, Mar. intro; Oct. intro.

Marsh, Dame Ngaio, Apr. 23, 1899.

Marsh, Othniel Charles, Oct. 29, 1831.

Marshall, E(verett) G., Jun. 18, 1910.

Marshall, F. Ray, Aug. 22, 1928.

Marshall, George C., Dec. 31, 1880; Jun. 5, 1945.

Marshall, James Wilson, Oct. 8, 1810.

Marshall, John, Sep. 24, 1755.

Marshall, Louis, Dec. 14, 1856.

Marshall, Peter, May 27, 1902.

Marshall, (Sarah) Catherine, Sep. 27, 1914.

Marshall, Sir John Hubert, Mar. 19, 1876.

Marshall, Thomas R., Mar. 4, 1913; Mar. 4, 1917.

Marshall, Thurgood, Jul. 2, 1908; first black on U.S. Supreme Court, Jun. 13, 1967.

Marshall, Tully, Apr. 13, 1869.

Marshall Plan: launched, Jun. 5, 1945; U.S.S.R. rejects, Jul. 2, 1947; passed, Apr. 3, 1948.

Martel, Charles, Oct. 25, 732.

Martello, Pier Iacopo, Apr. 28, 1665.

Martens, Wilfried, Apr. 3, 1979.

Marti, José, Jan. 28, 1853.

Martian atmosphere: nitrogen found, Jul. 26, 1976.

Martin, Archer John Porter, Mar. 1, 1910.

Martin, Glenn Luther, Jan. 17, 1886.

Martin, Mary, Dec. 1, 1913.

Martin V (pope), Feb. 22, 1418.

Martin, William McChesney, Jr., Dec. 17, 1906.

Martineau, Harriet, Jun. 12, 1802.

Martinez de la Rosa, Francisco, Mar. 10, 1787.

Martin Luther King's Birthday (U.S. and Virgin Islands), Jan. 15.

Martinson, Harry Edmund, May 6, 1904.

Martius, Mar. intro.

Martyrs and Liberation Days of (São Tomé and Príncipe, Feb. 3.

Martyrs' Day (Bangladexh), Feb. 20.

Martyrs' Day (Benin), Jan. 16.

Martyrs' Day (Burma), Jul. 19.

Martyrs' Day (Lebanon), May 6.

Martyrs' Day (Malawi), Mar. 3.

Martyrs' Day (Nepal), Jan. 29.

Martyrs' Day (Syria), May 6.

Martyrs' Day (Tunesia), Apr. 9.

Martyrs in the Plague of Alexandria, Feast of, Feb. 28.

Martyrs of China, Feb. 17; Jul. 9.

Martyrs of Colonialism Day (Guinea-Bissau), Aug. 3.

Martyrs of Damascus, Jul. 10.

Martyrs of Douax, Oct. 29.

Martyrs of Ebsdorf, Feb. 2.

Martyrs of England and Wales, Oct. 25.

Martyrs of Independence (Zaire), Jan. 4.

Martyrs of Indo-China, Jul. 11; Nov. 6.

Martyrs of Japan, Feb. 5; Jun. 1.

Martyrs of Lyons and Vienne, Jun. 2.

Martyrs of Mar Saba, Mar. 20.

Martyrs of Mount Sinai, Jan. 14.

Martyrs of Nagasaki, Sep. 29.

Martyrs of North America, Sep. 26.

Martyrs of Orange, Jul. 9.

Martyrs of Rome, Jun. 30.

Martyrs of the Serapeum, Mar. 17.

Martyrs of Uganda, Jun. 3.

Martyrs of Utica, Aug. 24.

Martyrs under Nero, Jun. 24.

Martyrs under the Danes, Apr. 10.

McKuen, Rod, Apr. 29, 1938.
McLaughlin, James, Oct. 19, 1784.
McLuhan, (Herbert) Marshall, Jul. 21.
McMahon, Brien, Oct. 6, 1903.
McMahon, Thomas, Nov. 23, 1979.
McMahon Act, Aug. 1, 1946.
McMaster, John Bach, Jun. 29, 1852.
McMillan, Edwin Mattison, Sep. 18, 1907.
McMurdo Sound, Mar. 4, 1962.
McNamara, Robert (Strange), Jun. 9, 1916.
McNeeley, Tom, Dec. 4, 1961.
McNeely, Eugene, Jul. 13, 1962.
McNeile, Herman Cyril, Sep. 28, 1888.
McNichols, John Timothy, Dec. 15, 1877.
McPartland, Jimmy, Mar. 15, 1907.
McPartland, Marian Margaret, Mar. 20, 1920.
McPherson, Aimee Semple, Oct. 9, 1890.
McQueen, Steve, Mar. 24, 1930.
M'Culloch v. Maryland: Supreme Court decision, Mar. 6, 1819.
McWhirter, Alan Ross, Aug. 12, 1925.
McWhirter, Norris Dewar, Aug. 12, 1925.
McWilliams, Carey, Dec. 13, 1905.
Mead, Larkin Goldsmith, Jan. 3, 1835.
Mead, Margaret, Dec. 16, 1901.
Meade, George Gordon, Dec. 31, 1815.
Meade, James E., Jun. 23, 1907.
Meany, George, Aug. 16, 1894.
Mecca, Sep. 20, 622.
Mechlin, Treaty of, Apr. 5, 1513.
Mecklenburg Declaration of Independence Anniversary of (North Carolina), May 20.
Mecklenburg Independence Day (No. Car.), May intro.
Medawar, Peter Brian, Feb. 28, 1915.
Mediation, Act of, Feb. 28, 1803.
Medical Association, American, May 7, 1847.
Medical Workers' Day (U.S.S.R.), Jun. intro.
medicare program: Canada, Dec. 8, 1966.
Medici, Alessandro de', Jan. 5, 1537.
Medici, Catherine de, Dec. 5, 1560.
Medici, Cosimo de, Jun. 12, 1519; Apr. 17, 1555.
Medici, Lorenzo de, Jan. 1, 1449.
Medici, Maria de, Nov. 11, 1630.
Medici family, Sep. 6, 1512.
medicinal springs, patron of, Mar. 2.
Medici, Catherine de, Apr. 13, 1519.
Medina, Sep. 20, 622; Jan. 13, 1919.
Medina, Ernest L., Mar. 8, 1971.
Mehta, Zubin, Apr. 29, 1936.
Meighen, Arthur, Jun. 16, 1874.
Meiji (Emperor of Japan), Apr. 6, 1868.
Mein, John Gordon: assassinated, Aug. 28, 1968.
Meir, Golda, May 3, 1898; Mar. 17, 1969; Jan. 15, 1973; Apr. 10, 1974.
Meistersinger, Die: premiere, Jun. 21, 1868.
Meitner, Lise, Nov. 7, 1878.
Mekong River delta, Jan. 6, 1967.
Melanchthon, Philipp, Feb. 15, 1497.
Melba, Nellie, May 19, 1861.
Melbourne: Australian aircraft carrier, Jun. 3, 1969.
Melbourne (Australia), May 9, 1901.
Melcher, Frederick G., Apr. 12, 1879.
Melchior, Lauritz, Mar. 20, 1890.

Melgarejo, Mariano, Apr. 15, 1820.
Mellon, Andrew William, Mar. 24, 1855.
Melo, Francisco Manuel de, Nov. 23, 1608.
Melville, George Wallace, Jun. 10, 1841.
Melville, Herman, Aug. 1, 1819.
Memorial Day: first celebrated, May 30, 1868.
Memorial Day (Brazil), Nov. 2.
Memorial Day (Malagasy Republic), Mar. 29.
Memorial Day (New Mexico), May 25.
Memorial Day (Puerto Rico), May 28.
Memorial Day (South Korea), Jun. 6.
Memorial Day (U.S.), May 30.
Memorial Day (U.S., P.R.), May intro.
Memory Day (U.S.), Mar. 21.
Memory Day, Mar. intro.
Memphis (Tennessee), Apr. 4, 1968.
Mencken, H(enry) L(ouis), Sep. 12, 1880.
Mendel, Gregor Johann, Jul. 22, 1822.
Mendeleev, Dmitri Ivanovich, Feb. 7, 1834.
Mendelssohn, Felix, Feb. 3, 1809.
Mendelssohn, Moses, Sep. 6, 1729.
Mendes, Sergio, Feb. 11, 1941.
Mendes-France, Pierre, Jan. 11, 1907.
Menéndez de Avilés, Pedro, Feb. 15, 1519; Sep. 8, 1565.
Menéndez Pidal, Ramón, Mar. 13, 1869.
Mengelberg, Willem, Mar. 28, 1871.
Mengistu Haile-Mariam (Ethiopia), Feb. 3, 1977.
Menjou, Adolphe, Feb. 18, 1890.
Menninger, Karl Augustus, Jul. 22, 1893.
Menotti, Gian Carlo, Jul. 7, 1911; Dec. 24, 1951.
Mental Health Month, National, May intro.
Menuhin, Yehudi, Apr. 22, 1916.
Menzies, Robert Gordon, Dec. 20, 1894.
Mercator, Gerardus, Mar. 5, 1512.
Mercer, Johnny, Nov. 18, 1909.
merchants, patron of, Dec. 6.
Mercier, Désiré Joseph, Nov. 21, 1851.
Merciless Parliament, Feb. 3, 1388.
Mercouri, Melina, Oct. 18, 1925.
mercredi, p. ix.
Mercury (Project), Nov. 29, 1961.
Meredith, Burgess, Nov. 16, 1909.
Meredith, George, Feb. 12, 1828.
Meredith, James H., Sep. 30, 1962; first black to graduate from University of Mississippi, Aug. 18, 1963.
Meredith Victory, U.S.S., Dec. 22, 1950.
Mergenthaler, Ottmar, May 11, 1854.
Mérimée, Prosper, Sep. 28, 1803.
Merit, Legion of: authorized, Jul. 20, 1942.
Merman, Ethel, Jan. 16, 1909.
Merrick, David, Nov. 27, 1912.
Merrill, Dina, Dec. 9, 1925.
Merrill, Robert, Jun. 4, 1919.
Merrimac, Mar. 8, 1862.
Mersen, Treaty of, Aug. 9, 870.
Mersey Tunnel, Jan. 20, 1885.
Mesa Verde National Park: established, Jun. 29, 1906.
Mesmer, Franz Anton, May 23, 1734.
Messerschmitt, Willy (Wilhelm), Jun. 26, 1898.
Messiah (Handel): premiere, Apr. 13, 1742.
Messier, Charles, Jun. 26, 1730.

Messina, Jim, Dec. 5, 1947.
Messina, Sicily: captured by U.S., Aug. 16, 1943.
Messines, Battle of, Jun. 7, 1917.
Messner, Reinhold: solo ascent of Mt. Everest, Aug. 20, 1980.
Mesta, Pearl, Oct. 12, 1891.
Metalious, Grace, Sep. 8, 1924.
Metallurgists' Day (U.S.S.R.), Jul. intro.
metalworkers, patron of, Dec. 1.
Metastasio, Pietro Antonio Domenico Buonaventura, Jan. 3, 1698.
Metaxas, Ioannis (Greece), Aug. 4, 1936.
Metaxas, Johannes, Apr. 12, 1871.
Metchnikoff, Elie, May 15, 1845.
meteor: Blackstone (Virginia), May 12, 1922.
meteorites: craters found in northern Siberia, Jun. 30, 1908; China, Mar. 8, 1976.
Meteorological Day, World, Mar. intro.
Methodist Church, Nov. 11, 1966.
Methuen: English victory over Scots, Jun. 26, 1306.
Metropolitan Museum of Art (N.Y.), Apr. 13, 1870.
Metropolitan Opera House (New York City), Oct. 22, 1873; Apr. 9, 1909; Jan. 7, 1933; Sep. 16, 1966.
Metropolitan University (Peking): opens, Aug. 6, 1927.
Metternich, Klemens Wenzel Nepomuk Lothar von, May 15, 1773.
Metternich, Prince Clemens, Mar. 13, 1848.
Metz (France), Jan. 15, 1552; occupied by French Nov. 19, 1918; Nov. 9, 1944; Nov. 22, 1944.
Metz, Battle of, begins, Jun. 9, 1918; Jun. 12, 1918; ends, Jun. 14, 1918.
Meunier, Constantin Emile, Apr. 12, 1831.
Meusnier, Jean Baptiste Marie, Jun. 19, 1754.
Mexican army, May 5, 1867.
Mexican Civil War, May 25, 1911.
Mexican Revolution Anniversary (Mexico), Nov. 20.
Mexican War, Jan. 13, 1846; May 8, 1846; May 9, 1846; U.S. declares, May 12, 1846; May 24, 1846; Aug. 4, 1846; U.S. occupies Santa Fé, Aug. 18, 1846; Sep. 13, 1846; Sep. 25, 1846; Feb. 22, 1847; Mar. 29, 1847; Apr. 18, 1847; Sep. 8, 1847; treaty ending, Feb. 2, 1848.
Mexico: claims independence, Sep. 16, 1810; May 30, 1848; constitution, Feb. 5, 1917; expropriates oil companies, Mar. 18, 1938.
Mexico, Bank of, Sep. 6, 1982.
Mexico, Republic of: established, Dec. 6, 1822; proclaimed, Mar. 26, 1825.
Mexico City: capture of, Sep. 14, 1846.
Meyer, Adolf, Sep. 13, 1866.
Meyer, Debbie, Aug. 14, 1952.
Meyer, Julius Lothar, Aug. 19, 1830.
Meyer, Nathan, Jul. 26, 1858.
Meyer, Viktor, Sep. 8, 1848.
Meyerhof, Otto F., Apr. 12, 1884.
Meynell, Alice, Aug. 17, 1847.
Michael, Grand Duke (Russia), Mar. 15, 1917.

Monroe, Vaughn, Oct. 7, 1911.

Monroe Doctrine, Dec. 2, 1823.

Monroney, A. S., Mar. 2, 1902.

Monrovia: land purchased, Dec. 15, 1821.

Mons (Belgium), patron of, Apr. 9.

Montagu, Ashley, Jun. 28, 1905.

Montagu, Charles, Apr. 16, 1661.

Montagu-Clemsford reforms, Dec. 23, 1919.

Montaigne, Michel Eyquem de, Feb. 28, 1533.

Montalban, Ricardo, Nov. 25, 1920.

Montale, Eugenio, Oct. 12, 1896.

Montana: admitted to Union, Nov. 8, 1889; first old-age pension, Mar. 5, 1923.

Montand, Yves, Oct. 31, 1921.

Mont Blanc: first ascent, Aug. 8, 1786.

Mont Blanc Tunnel: opens, Jul. 16, 1965.

Montcalm, Louis Joseph, Feb. 28, 1712.

Montebello, Treaty of, Apr. 16, 1175.

Monte Cassino, Feb. 15, 1944.

Monteil, Mar. 14, 1369.

Montemaggiore, May 4, 1041.

Montenegro: independence, Jul. 13, 1878; declares war on Turkey, Oct. 8, 1912; declares war on Austria-Hungary, Aug. 5, 1914; Jan. 23, 1916; Apr. 20, 1920.

Monterey, May 24, 1846.

Monterey, Battle of, Sep. 25, 1846.

Montessori, Maria, Aug. 31, 1870.

Monteux, Pierre, Apr. 4, 1875.

Monteverdi, Claudio Giovanni Antonio, May 15, 1567.

Montezuma, Nov. 8, 1519.

Montfort, Simon de, Jun. 11, 1258; killed, Aug. 4, 1265.

Montgolfier, Jacques Etienne, Jan. 7, 1745.

Montgolfier, Joseph Michel, Aug. 26, 1740.

Montgomery, Bernard Law, Nov. 17, 1887.

Montgomery, Richard, Dec. 2, 1738.

Montgomery, Robert, May 21, 1904.

months, number of days, Aug. intro.

Montini, Giovanni Battista: elected Pope Paul VI, Jun. 21, 1963.

Montreal: captured from French, Sep. 8, 1700.

Montserrat, Nov. 1, 1964.

Moody, Dwight Lyman, Feb. 5, 1837.

moonstone, Jun. intro.

Moore, Archie, Dec. 13, 1913; Nov. 30, 1959.

Moore, Clement (Clarke), Jul. 15, 1779.

Moore, Garry, Jan. 31, 1915.

Moore, George, Feb. 24, 1852.

Moore, Henry, Jul. 30, 1898.

Moore, James, May 31, 1868.

Moore, Marianne (Craig), Nov. 15, 1887.

Moore, Robin, Oct. 31, 1925.

Moore, Sara Jane, Sep. 22, 1975.

Moore, Stanford, Sep. 4, 1913.

Moore, Thomas, May 28, 1779.

Moore, William Henry, Oct. 25, 1848.

Moorehead, Agnes, Dec. 6, 1906.

Moravia, Mar. 15, 1939.

More, Paul Elmer, Dec. 12, 1864.

More, Sir Thomas, Feb. 7, 1478.

More, Thomas: executed, Jul. 6, 1535.

Moréas, Jean, Apr. 15, 1856.

Moreau, Gustave, Apr. 6, 1826.

Moreau, Jean Victor Marie, Feb. 14, 1763.

Morgagni, Giovanni Battista, Feb. 25, 1682.

Morgan, Daniel, Jan. 17, 1781.

Morgan, Helen, Aug. 2, 1900.

Morgan, John, Jun. 10, 1735.

Morgan, J. P., Jr., Apr. 17, 1837; Sep. 7, 1867.

Morgan, Junius Spencer, Apr. 14, 1813.

Morgan, Thomas Hunt, Sep. 25, 1866.

Morgarten, Battle of, Nov. 15, 1315.

Morgenthau, Henry, Jr., May 11, 1891.

Morison, Samuel Eliot, Jul. 9, 1887.

Morisot, Berthe, Jan. 14, 1841.

Morley, Edward Williams, Jan. 29, 1838.

Mormon Church, Apr. 6, 1830.

Mormon Church (The Church of Jesus Christ of the Latter-Day Saints), Jun. 9, 1978.

Mormon exodus, Feb. 10, 1846.

Mormons, Jun. 27, 1844; enter Salt Lake Valley, Jul. 22, 1847.

morning glory, Sep. intro.

Moro, Aldo, Sep. 23, 1916; kidnapped, Mar. 16, 1978; May 9, 1978.

Morocco, Mar. 6, 1480; independence, Jul. 3, 1880; Franco-German agreement, Feb. 9, 1909; Mar. 2, 1956; Apr. 18, 1960.

Morocco National Day (Morocco), Mar. 3.

Morphy, Paul, Jun. 22, 1837.

Morrill Act: passed, Jul. 2, 1862.

Morris, Gouverneur, Jan. 31, 1752.

Morris, Lewis, Apr. 8, 1726.

Morris, Robert, Jan. 20, 1734; Jan. 31, 1734.

Morris, William, Mar. 24, 1834.

Morris, Willie, Nov. 29, 1934.

Morrison, Jim, Dec. 8, 1943.

Morrison, Norman R., Nov. 2, 1965.

Morrison, Van, Aug. 31, 1945.

Morristown (New Jersey), May 25, 1780.

Morse, Jedediah, Aug. 23, 1761.

Morse, Samuel F.B., Apr. 27, 1791; Jun. 20, 1840; May 24, 1844.

Morse, Wayne, Jan. 6, 1838; Oct. 20, 1900.

Mortimer, Roger, Sep. 24, 1326.

Morton, Joy, Sep. 27, 1855.

Morton, Julius Sterling, Apr. 22, 1832.

Morton, Levi P., Mar. 4, 1889.

Morton, Rogers C. B., Sep. 19, 1914.

Morton, Thurston Ballard, Aug. 19, 1907.

Morton, William Thomas Green, Aug. 9, 1819.

Moscow: burned, Sep. 15, 1812; Mar. 9, 1917; first official visit of U.S. president, May 22, 1972.

Moscow Conference of Foreign Ministers: opens, Oct. 19, 1943.

Moscow State Symphony: first U.S. performance, Jan. 3, 1960.

Moseley, Henry Gwyn-Jeffreys, Nov. 23, 1887.

Mosely, Sir Oswald Ernald, Nov. 16, 1896.

Moses, Anna Mary (Grandma) Robertson, Sep. 7, 1860.

Moses, Edwin, Aug. 31, 1955.

Moses, Robert, Dec. 18, 1888.

Moshoeshoe II (Lesotho), May 2, 1938; Mar. 31, 1970.

Moshoeshoe's Day (Lesotho), Mar. 12.

Mosilikatze (Chief of Zulus), Jan. 17, 1837.

Mossbauer, Rudolf Ludwig, Jan. 31, 1919.

Mother Cabrini, Saint Frances Xavier, Jul. 15.

Motherhood of Our Lady, Feast of the, Oct. 11.

Mother-in-Law's Day, Oct. intro.

Mothers' Day (Central African Republic), May intro.

Mothers' Day: first, May 10, 1908.

Mothers' Day (India), Feb. 22.

Mothers' Day (Malawi), Oct. 17.

Mothers' Day (Panama), Dec. 8.

Mother's Day (United States), May intro.

motion picture: first commercial, Apr. 23, 1896.

motion picture projector, Feb. 13, 1895.

Motor Carrier Act, U.S.: adopted, Aug. 9, 1935.

motorists, patron of, Jul. 25.

Mott, John Raleigh, May 25, 1865.

Mott, Lucretia Coffin, Jan. 3, 1793; Jul. 19, 1848.

Mott, Sir Nevill Francis, Sep. 30, 1905.

Mottelson, Ben Ray, Jul. 9, 1926.

Moultrie, William, Dec. 4, 1730.

mountaineers, patron of, May 28.

Mountain Meadow Massacre, Mar. 23, 1877.

Mountbatten, Lord Louis: appointed Supreme Allied Commander, Aug. 25, 1943; killed Aug. 27, 1979.

Mount Etna: erupts, Apr. 23, 1910.

Mountlouis, Treaty of, Sep. 30, 1174.

Mount St. Helens: erupts, Mar. 27, 1980.

Mount Vesusius: erupts, Aug. 24, 79.

Mourning Day of (Mexico), Feb. 14.

movable holidays, p. xii.

Moyers, Bill, Jun. 5, 1934.

Moynihan, Daniel Patrick, Mar. 16, 1927.

Mozambican Popular Liberation Forces Day (Mozambique), Sep. 25.

Mozambique, Mar. 1, 1498.

Mozambique, People's Republic of:independence, Jun. 25, 1975.

Mozart, Wolfgang Amadeus, Jan. 27, 1756.

Mozorewa, Abel, Apr. 14, 1925.

M.P.L.A. Foundation Day (Angola), Dec. 10.

M.P.R. Day (Zaire), May 20.

Mt. Everest: first solo ascent, Aug. 20, 1980.

Mt. Soufriére volcano, May 7, 1902.

Mt. Suribachi, Feb. 23, 1945.

Mubarak, Hosni, May 4, 1928.

Mudd, Roger, Feb. 9, 1928.

Mudros, Armistice of: signed, Oct. 30, 1918.

Mueller, Elizabeth: West German diplomat, Jan. 25, 1970.

Mueller, R(euben) H(erbert), Jun. 2, 1897.

Mugabe, Robert, Feb. 21, 1924.

Muhammad: arrives at Yathrib (Medina), Sep. 20, 622; dies, Jun. 8, 632.

Muharram, 1, p. xii; Jul. intro.; Aug. intro.; Sep. intro.

Muharram, 10, p. xii; Aug. intro.; Sep. intro.

Muhlenberg, Frederick Augustus Conrad, Jan. 1, 1750.

Muhlenberg, Heinrich Melchior, Sep. 6, 1711.

Muhlenberg, John Peter Gabriel, Oct. 1, 1746.

N

National Day (Nationalist China), Oct. 10.
National Day (Nepal), Dec. 28.
National Day (Niger), Dec. 18.
National Day (People's Republic of China), Oct. 1; Oct. 2.
National Day (San Marino), Apr. 1.
National Day (Saudi Arabia), Sep. 12.
National Day (Senegal), Apr. 4.
National Day (Singapore), Aug. 9.
National Day (United Arab Emirates), Dec. 2.
National Day (Yemen People's Democratic Republic), Oct. 14.
National Day Eve (Tahiti), Jul. 13.
National Day of Bahrain (Bahrain), Dec. 16.
National Day of Sudan or Revolution Day in the Sudan (Libya), May 25.
National Day or Confederation Day (Switzerland), Aug. 1.
National Days (Oman), Nov. 19.
National Defense Day (Paraguay), Mar. 1.
National Flag Day (Liberia), Aug. 24.
National Flag Day (Paraguay), May 14.
National Flag Day (Swaziland), Apr. 25.
National Football League: established, Jun. 24, 1922; first championship, Dec. 17, 1933; Jan. 15, 1939.
National Foundation Day (Japan), Feb. 11.
National Foundation Day (Korea), Oct. 3.
National Freedom Day (U.S.), Feb. 1.
National Gallery of Art (Washington): opens, Mar. 17, 1941.
National Guardsmen, May 4, 1970; acquitted, Nov. 8, 1974.
National Hero, Day of the (Angola), Sep. 17.
National Heroes Day (Cape Verde Islands), Jan. 20.
National Heroes Day (Costa Rica), Apr. 11.
National Heroes Day (Guinea-Bissau), Jan. 20.
National Heroes Day (São Tomé and Príncipe), Sep. 6.
National Heroes Day (Sri Lanka), May 22.
National Hockey League: established, Nov. 22, 1917.
National Holiday (Austria), Oct. 26.
National Holiday (Bulgaria), Sep. 9; Sep. 10.
National Holiday (Colombia), Aug. 7.
National Holiday (Cuba), Jul. 25; Jul. 26; Jul. 27.
National Holiday (French West Indies, Monaco, Tahiti), Jul. 14.
National Holiday (Liechtenstein), Jan. 23.
National Holiday (Luxembourg), Jun. 23.
National Holiday (Nigeria), Oct. 1.
National Holiday (Republic of Mali), Sep. 22.
National Holiday (Revolución de Mayo) (Argentina), May 25.
National Holiday (Romania), Aug. 23; Aug. 24.
National Holiday (Upper Volta), Dec. 11.
National Holiday (Zimbabwe), Aug. 12.
National Independence, Anniversary of (São Tomé and Príncipe), Jul. 12.
National Industrial Recovery Act, May 27, 1935.
National Institute of Arts & Letters, Feb. 4, 1913.
National Inventors Day (U.S.), Feb. 11.

Nationalist China (Taiwan): expelled from UN, Oct. 25, 1971.
Nationalist Chinese, Mar. 24, 1927; May 20, 1978.
Nationality Day (Cape Verde Islands), Sep. 12.
Nationalization Day (São Tomé and Príncipe), Sep. 30.
National Labor Board: established, Aug. 5, 1933.
National Labor Relations Board, Jul. 5, 1935.
National Liberation Day (Poland), Jul. 22.
National Magic Day (U.S.), Oct. 31.
National Maritime Day (U.S.), May 22.
National Mourning Day (Bangladesh), Feb. 20.
National-Mourning Day (Panama), Jan. 9.
National Mourning Day of (Mexico), Feb. 14.
National Organization of Cypriot Struggle, Feb. 10, 1978.
National Organization of Women (NOW): founded, Oct. 29, 1966.
National Park Service, U.S.: established, Aug. 25, 1916.
National Portrait Gallery (London), Jan. 15, 1859.
National Progressive Republican League, Jan. 21, 1911.
National Railroad Passenger Corporation, May 1, 1971.
National Revolutionary Government (China), Sep. 20, 1927.
National Revolutionary Movement (Bolivia), Apr. 9, 1952.
National Revolution Day (Bangladesh), Nov. 7.
National Revolution Day (Tunisia), Jan. 18.
National Security Act: signed, Aug. 10, 1949.
National Socialist (German Workers) Party (Nazi), Jan. 5, 1919; Sep. 14, 1930; Jul. 14, 1933.
National Sovereignty and Thanksgiving Day (Haiti), May 22.
National Sovereignty Day (Haiti), Sep. 22.
National Sovereignty Day (Turkey), Apr. 23.
National Student Association, Feb. 13, 1967.
National Traffic Safety Agency (U.S.), Jan. 31, 1967.
National Tree Planting Day (Lesotho), Mar. 22.
National UNICEF Day, Oct. 31.
National Unification Day (Liberia), May 14.
National Unity Day (Nepal), Jan. 11.
National Youth Administration, Jun. 26, 1935.
National Zoo (Washington, D.C.), Apr. 16, 1972.
NATO (North Atlantic Treaty Organization), Sep. 6, 1951; Jan. 2, 1963; Mar. 18, 1966; Supreme Military Headquarters opens Mar. 31, 1967.
Natta, Giulio, Feb. 26, 1903.
Natwick, Mildred, Jun. 19, 1908.
Naughty Marietta: premiere, Oct. 24, 1910.
Nauru, Nov. 1, 1947; independence, Jan. 29, 1968; independence, Jan. 31, 1968.

Nautilus, U.S.S.: launched, Jan. 21, 1954; commissioned Sep. 30, 1954; Mar. 4, 1958; Aug. 3, 1958; Aug. 7, 1958; underwater trans-Atlantic crossing Aug. 24, 1958.
Naval Reserves, U.S.: active duty, Jun. 12, 1941.
Navarino, Battle of, Oct. 20, 1827.
Navon, Yitzhak, Apr. 19, 1921.
Navratilova, Martina, Oct. 10, 1956.
Navy, U.S., Apr. 11, 1900; first enlisted women, Jul. 7, 1948.
Nazi leaders: sentenced, Oct. 1, 1946.
Nazi occupation: Denmark, May 5, 1945.
Nazi party: dissolved in Austria, Jun. 18, 1933; wins elections, Mar. 29, 1936.
Nazi war criminals: West Germany continues to prosecute, Jul. 3, 1979.
Nazimova, Alla, Jun. 4, 1879.
Neal, Patricia, Jan. 20, 1926.
Nebraska: admitted to Union, Mar. 1, 1867.
Necker, Jacques, Sep. 30, 1732.
Neel, Louis Eugene Felix, Nov. 22, 1904.
Neff, Hildegarde, Dec. 28, 1925.
Negev Desert, May 5, 1964.
Negri, Pola, Dec. 31, 1894.
Nehru, Jawaharlal:, Nov. 14, 1889; founds Independence of India League Aug. 30, 1928; Apr. 14, 1930; Jan. 19, 1966; Jan. 24, 1966.
Neilson, William Allen, Mar. 28, 1869.
Nejd-Hejaz (Saudi Arabia), May 20, 1927.
Nejd (Saudi Arabia), Jan. 8, 1926.
Nellie Taylor Ross' Birthday (Wyoming), Nov. 29.
Nelson, Adm. Horatio, Aug. 1, 1798.
Nelson, George (*Baby Face*), Dec. 6, 1908.
Nelson, Lord, Sep. 29, 1758; Apr. 2, 1801; Oct. 21, 1805.
Nelson, Thomas, Dec. 26, 1738.
Nemerov, Howard, Mar. 1, 1920.
Nenni, Pietro, Feb. 9, 1891.
Nepal: independence, Dec. 21, 1923.
Nernst, Walther Hermann, Jun. 24, 1864.
Nero, Apr. intro.
Nero, Peter, May 22, 1934.
Neronius, Apr. intro.
Neruda, Jan, Jul. 10, 1834.
Neruda, Pablo, Jul. 12, 1904.
nerves: first transplants, human, Apr. 18, 1963.
Nervi, Pier (Luigi), Jun. 21, 1891.
Nesbitt, Cathleen (Mary), Nov. 24, 1888.
Ness, Eliot, Apr. 19, 1903.
Nesselrode, Count Karl Robert, Mar. 23, 1780.
Nestroy, Johann Nepomuk Edward Ambrosius, Dec. 7, 1801.
Netherlands, Jan. 30, 1648; declared kingdom, Jun. 5, 1806; Jan. 1, 1917; Mar. 9, 1920; May 26, 1932; May 10, 1940.
Netherlands, Southern, May 17, 1597.
Netherlands, Spanish, May 23, 1706.
Netherlands East Indies, Mar. 19, 1942.
Neuilly, Treaty of: signed, Nov. 27, 1919.
Neumann, Emanuel, Jul. 2, 1893.
Neumann, John von, Dec. 28, 1903.
Neumann, St. John Nepomucene, Mar. 28, 1811.
Neutrality Act: amended, Nov. 17, 1941.

Neutrality Act of 1935: signed, Aug. 31, 1935.

Neutrality Act of 1939, U.S., Nov. 4, 1939.

neutron weapons: U.S. announces decision to produce, Aug. 10, 1981.

Neuve Chapelle, Battle of, Mar. 10, 1915; ends, Mar. 13, 1915.

Nevada, May 30, 1848; admitted to Union, Oct. 31, 1864; first old-age pension, Mar. 5, 1923.

Nevada Day (Nevada), Oct. 31.

Neva River, May 27, 1703.

Nevers, Ernie, Jun. 11, 1903.

Neville's Cross, Battle of, Oct. 17, 1346.

Nevins, Allan, May 20, 1890.

New Amsterdam: surrenders to English, Aug. 27, 1664.

New Brunswick, Jul. 1, 1867.

New Connecticut (Vermont), Jan. 15, 1777.

Newcomb, Simon, Mar. 12, 1835.

New Deal, Jul. 2, 1932.

New England Confederation, May 19, 1643.

New England: hurricane, Sep. 21, 1938.

Newfoundland: government collapses, Dec. 18, 1933; Mar. 31, 1949.

New Guinea, Mar. 13, 1884; German troops surrender, Sep. 21, 1914.

New Hampshire: separated from Massachusetts, Sep. 18, 1679; Jun. 21, 1788.

New Haven Colony: becomes part of Connecticut, Dec. 13, 1664.

New Haven General Court, Dec. 13, 1664.

New Hebrides, Jul. 30, 1980.

New Jersey: third state, Dec. 18, 1787.

New Jewel Movement (Grenada), Mar. 13, 1979.

Newley, Anthony, Sep. 24, 1931.

Newman, Barnett, Jan. 29, 1905.

Newman, Edwin, Jan. 25, 1919.

Newman, Paul, Jan. 26, 1925.

Newman, St. John Henry, Feb. 21, 1801.

New Mexico: May 30, 1848; purchased from Mexico, Jun. 30, 1854; admitted to Union, Jan. 6, 1912.

New Netherlands: annexed by England, Aug. 29, 1664.

New Netherlands Company: chartered, Oct. 11, 1614.

New Orleans, May 1, 1862; segregation, Mar. 27, 1962.

New Orleans Day, Battle of, Jan. intro.

New Orleans, Battle of, Jan. 8, 1815.

New Regime, Anniversary of the (Zaire), Nov. 24.

newspaper strike (New York City): ends, Nov. 6, 1978.

Newspaper Week, National, Oct. intro.

Newsweek, Feb. 17, 1933.

Newton, Sir Isaac, Dec. 25, 1642; Jan. 4, 1643.

New World: divided between Spain and Portugal, Jun. 7, 1494.

new year, beginning of the, Mar. intro.

New Year's Day, Jan. intro.; Jan. 1.

New Year's Eve, Dec. 31.

New York: annexed by England, Aug. 29, 1664; seized by British, Sep. 15, 1776; declared federal capital, Sep. 13, 1788; great fire Dec. 16, 1835; Jan. 25, 1915;

Jan. 17, 1917; five boroughs joined, Jan. 1, 1898; Jan. 7, 1927; May 1, 1931; Jan. 8, 1961; blackout Jul. 13, 1977.

New York, state of: Becomes 11th American state, Jul. 26, 1788.

New York Herald, Jan. 6, 1871.

New York Nine: first baseball game, Jun. 19, 1846.

New York Public Library, May 23, 1895.

New York Stock Exchange: panic selling, Oct. 24, 1929.

New York stock market, Mar. 13, 1907.

New York University, May 30, 1901.

New York University Medical Center, Apr. 18, 1963.

New Zealand, discovered, Dec. 13, 1642; Captain Cook arrives, Oct. 30, 1769; first British colonists, Jan. 22, 1840; Feb. 6, 1840; May 3, 1841; first settlers, Mar. 23, 1848; women vote, Sep. 10, 1893; Sep. 26, 1907; parliament opened, Jan. 12, 1954.

New Zealand, patron of, Feb. 1.

New Zealand Day, Feb. 6.

Ney, Michel, Jan. 10, 1769.

Nez Percé Indians, Oct. 4, 1877.

NFL, Sep. 17, 1920.

Ngo Dinh Diem, Oct. 23, 1955; Oct. 26, 1955.

Ngouabi, Marien (Congo/Brazzaville): assassinated, Mar. 18, 1977.

Niagara Falls, Jul. 22, 1876; Feb. 27, 1950.

Niagara River, Feb. 27, 1950.

Niarchos, Stavros Spyros, Jul. 3, 1909.

Nicaea, Council of: ends, Aug. 25, 325.

Nicaea, Second Council of, Sep. 24, 787.

Nicaragua, Feb. 12, 1978; Feb. 8, 1979; Jul. 17, 1979.

Nicholas I (Russia), Jul. 6, 1796; Sep. 3, 1826; dies, Mar. 2, 1855.

Nicholas II (pope), Apr. 13, 1059.

Nicholas II (Russia), May 6, 1868; Nov. 1, 1894; crowned, May 26, 1896; Oct. 30, 1905; Mar. 14, 1917; Mar. 15, 1917; abdicates, Mar. 17, 1917; Mar. 21, 1917; imprisoned in Siberia, Aug. 15, 1917; executed, Jul. 16, 1918.

Nicholas V (pope), Nov. 15, 1397; Feb. 25, 1455.

Nichols, Mike, Nov. 6, 1931.

Nichols, Red, May 8, 1905.

Nicholson, Ben, Apr. 10, 1894.

Nicholson, Jack, Apr. 28, 1937.

Nicklaus, Jack, Jan. 21, 1940.

Nicolai, Christoph Friedrich, Mar. 18, 1733.

Nicolle, Charles J. H., Sep. 21, 1866.

Nicolson, Sir Harold George, Nov. 21, 1886.

Niebuhr, Reinhold, Jun. 21, 1892.

Niehaus, Charles Henry, Jan. 24, 1855.

Nielsen, A(rthur) C(harles), Sep. 5, 1897.

Nielsen, Carl August, Jun. 9, 1865.

Nielsen, Leslie, Feb. 11, 1926.

Niemöller, Martin, Jan. 1, 1892.

Niepce, Joseph Nicéphore, Mar. 7, 1765.

Nietzsche, Friedrich, Oct. 15, 1844.

Nieuport (Belgium), Oct. 27, 1914.

Niger, Oct. 13, 1922; Apr. 15, 1974; Apr. 17, 1974.

Nigeria, Mar. 13, 1884; Jan. 1, 1914; elections, May 9, 1960; Oct. 1, 1960; admitted to U.N., Oct. 7, 1960; Jun. 1,

1961; civil war begins, Jul. 6, 1967; Jan. 12, 1970; Sep. 21, 1978; Jul. 7, 1979.

Nigeria, Southern, Jan. 19, 1904.

Nigeria (Lower), Jan. 1, 1900.

Nigeria (Upper), Jan. 1, 1900.

Niger River, Jul. 21, 1796; Mar. 22, 1830.

Nightingale, Florence, May 12, 1820; Nov. 4, 1854.

night watchmen, patron of, Oct. 19.

Nijinsky, Vaslav, Mar. 12, 1890.

Nile, Battle of the, Aug. 1, 1798.

Nile, flooding of the, p. viii.

Nile basin: French right to territory west of, Sep. 8, 1919.

Nile River, Feb. 23, 1854.

Niles, John Jacob, Apr. 28, 1892.

Nilsson, Birgit, May 17, 1918.

Nilsson, Harry, Jun. 5, 1941.

Nimeiri, Goafar Mohammed, Jan. 1, 1930.

Nimitz, Chester W., Feb. 24, 1885; Dec. 31, 1941.

Nin, Anaïs, Feb. 21, 1903.

Nineteenth Amendment: ratified, Aug. 26, 1920.

Ninety-five Theses, Oct. 31, 1517.

Nippur, p. ix.

Nirenberg, Marshall Warren, Apr. 10, 1923.

Nisan, p. x.

Nisanu, p. x.

Niven, David, Mar. 1, 1910.

Nix, Robert C., Aug. 9, 1905.

Nixon, Richard: Jan. 9, 1913; Jan. 20, 1953; Sep. 27, 1961; inaugurated Jan. 20, 1969; Apr. 3, 1970; Jun. 10, 1971; resigns presidency Jan. 5, 1972; China trip Feb. 17, 1972; China visit Feb. 21, 1972; May 22, 1972; address to Russian people, May 28, 1972; Jan. 15, 1973; Jul. 26, 1973; Feb. 6, 1974; May 9, 1974; Jul. 24, 1974; Jul. 30, 1974; Aug. 8, 1974; pardoned Sep. 8, 1974; second China visit Feb. 21, 1976; Mar. 10, 1976; disbarred Jul. 8, 1976.

Nixon, Tricia Jun. 12, 1971.

Nizer, Louis, Feb. 6, 1902.

Nkrumah, Kwame, Sep. 21, 1909.

Noah, Mar. 17.

Nobel, Alfred Bernhard, Oct. 21, 1833.

Nobile, Umberto, Jan. 24, 1885; May 12, 1926; May 24, 1928.

Noble, Edward John, Aug. 8, 1882.

Noel-Baker, Philip J., Nov. 1, 1889.

Noguchi, Isamu, Nov. 17, 1904.

Nones, p. xi.

Non-Intercourse Act, Jan. 9, 1809.

No No Nanette: opens, Mar. 11, 1925.

Nordenskiöld, (Nils) Adolf, Nov. 18, 1832.

Nordhoff, Charles Bernard, Feb. 1, 1887.

Nordica, Lillian, May 12, 1859.

Nordic Economic Union, Jan. 15, 1969.

Norell, Norman, Apr. 20, 1900.

Norfolk County (England), Jan. 19, 1915.

Norgay, Tenzing, May 29, 1953.

Norge: dirigible, May 12, 1926.

Norman Conquest of England: begins, Sep. 28, 1066.

Normandie, Feb. 9, 1942.

Normandy: invasion, Jun. 6, 1944.

Normans, May 4, 1041.

Norodom Sihanouk, Oct. 31, 1922; Apr. 25, 1975.

Norris, Benjamin Franklin, Mar. 5, 1870.

Norris, George William, Jul. 11, 1861.

Norstad, Lauris, Mar. 24, 1907.

North, Frederick, Apr. 13, 1732.

North, Lord, Mar. 19, 1782.

North America, Mar. 5, 1496.

North Atlantic Council, Dec. 19, 1950.

North Atlantic Treaty: signed, Apr. 4, 1949.

North Carolina: ratifies Constitution, Nov. 21, 1789.

North Carolina, University of: opens, Feb. 13, 1795.

North Dakota: admitted to Union, Nov. 2, 1889.

Northern Ireland, Feb. 7, 1970; Mar. 30, 1972; Mar. 8, 1973; Oct. 26, 1973.

Northern Pacific Railroad: completed, Sep. 8, 1883.

Northern Rhodesia, Mar. 29, 1963.

Northern War, May 3, 1660.

Northhampton, Treaty of, May 4, 1328.

North Korea, Jan. 4, 1951.

North Pole, Apr. 6, 1909; May 9, 1926; dirigible flight over, May 12, 1926.

Northrop, John Howard, Jul. 5, 1891.

Northrup, John Knudsen, Nov. 10, 1895.

North Sea oil fields: first oil, Jun. 11, 1975.

Northumbria, Earl of (Tostig), Sep. 20, 1966; Sep. 25, 1966.

North Vietnam, Feb. 8, 1965; Mar. 5, 1967.

Northwest Territory (Canada), Jun. 13, 1898; Jan. 24, 1978.

Northwind, U.S.S., Sep. 4, 1954.

Norton, Eleanor Holmes, Jun. 13, 1937.

Norton, Ken, Aug. 9, 1945.

Norton, Thomas, Jan. 18, 1562.

Norvo, Red, Mar. 31, 1908.

Norway: ceded to Sweden, Jan. 14, 1814; independence of, May 17, 1814; independence recognized, Oct. 27, 1905; Mar. 5, 1920; Jan. 18, 1928; May 8, 1929; Apr. 9, 1940; Feb. 1, 1942; Jan. 15, 1969; Oct. 5, 1978.

Norway, patron of, Feb. 3.

Norway, patron of, Jul. 29.

Norway and Sweden, Union of: dissolved, Jun. 7, 1905.

Notary Public Day, National, Nov. intro.

Notary Public Week, Natioinal, Nov. intro.

Notre Dame, University of, Jan. 15, 1844.

Notre Dame Cathedral (France): damaged, Oct. 11, 1914.

Nova Castella, Juan de, May 21, 1502.

Novara, Jun. 6, 1513.

Nova Scotia, Oct. 7, 1755; Jul. 1, 1867.

novem, Nov. intro.

Novgorod (Russia), Jan. 9, 1570; Sep. 20, 1862.

novice masters, patron of, Oct. 23.

Novikov, Nikolay Ivanovich, Apr. 27, 1744.

Novo 'Tcherksk, Jan. 7, 1895.

Novotny, Antonin, Jan. 5, 1968.

NOW: **see** National Organization of Women, Oct. 29, 1966.

Nu, Thakin, Jan. 4, 1948.

Nu, U, Apr. 5, 1960.

nuclear power plant: India's first, Jan. 19, 1970.

nuclear reaction: first self-sustaining, Dec. 2, 1942.

nuclear warhead: first launched from submarine, May 6, 1962; first carried by long-range missile, May 6, 1962.

Numa Pompilius, p. x; Feb. intro.; Jan. intro.

nundinae, p. xi.

Núñez de Balboa, Vasco, Sep. 25, 1513.

Nuremberg, Jan. 10, 1356; Trials begin, Nov. 20, 1945; International Military Tribunal, Oct. 1, 1946; Oct. 16, 1946.

Nuremberg, Bavaria, patron of, Aug. 19.

Nureyev, Rudolph, Mar. 17, 1938.

Nurmi, Paavo, Jun. 13, 1897.

Nürnberg Laws, Sep. 15, 1935.

nurses, patron of, Feb. 5.

nurses, patron of, Mar. 8.

nurses, patron of, Jul. 14.

Nursing Home Week, National, May intro.

Nutcracker: premiere, Dec. 5, 1892.

Nutrition Time, National, Mar. intro.

Nyad, Diana, Aug. 22, 1949; first swim Bahamas to U.S., Aug. 20, 1979.

Nyasa, Lake (Africa): discovered, Sep. 16, 1859.

Nyasaland, Dec. 19, 1962; Feb. 1, 1963; Dec. 31, 1963; Jul. 6, 1964.

Nyerere, Julius, May 1, 1961; Dec. 9, 1961.

Nystad, Treaty of, Sep. 10, 1721.

O

Oakley, Annie, Aug. 13, 1860.

Oates, Joyce Carol, Jun. 16, 1938.

Oberhoffer, Emil, Nov. 5, 1903.

Oberon, Merle, Feb. 19, 1911.

O-Bon or Feast of Fortune (Japan), Jul. 10.

Obote, Milton, Dec. 28, 1925; Feb. 22, 1966.

Obregón, Alvaro, Feb. 19, 1880.

O'Brian, Smith, Jul. 29, 1848.

O'Brian's Rebellion, Jul. 29, 1848.

O'Brien, Edmond, Sep. 10, 1915.

O'Brien, Lawrence, Jul. 7, 1917.

O'Brien, Margaret, Jan. 15, 1937.

O'Brien, Pat, Nov. 11, 1899.

O' Canada: Canada's national anthem, Jul. 1, 1980.

O'Casey, Sean, Mar. 30, 1880.

Ocean Pond, Battle of, Feb. 20, 1864.

Ochoa, Severo, Sep. 24, 1905.

Ochs, Adolph Simon, Mar. 12, 1858.

Ochsner, Alton, May 4, 1896.

O'Connell, Daniel, Aug. 6, 1775.

O'Connell, Helen, May 23, 1920.

O'Connor, Donald, Aug. 28, 1925.

O'Connor, Edwin (Greene), Jul. 29, 1918.

O'Connor, Flannery, Mar. 25, 1925.

O'Connor, Sandra Day, Mar. 26, 1930; Jul. 7, 1981.

Octave of Christmas, Jan. 1.

Octavian (Augustus Caesar), Sep. 2, 31 B.C..

octo, Oct. intro.

'October Horse', Oct. intro.

October Manifesto, Oct. 30, 1905.

October Revolution Day (Bulgaria, Hungary, Mongolia, U.S.S.R.), Nov. 7.

October Revolution (Russia), Oct. 23, 1917.

October Socialist Revolution Anniversary of the (U.S.S.R.), Nov. 8.

Odessa, Feb. 8, 1920.

Odets, Clifford, Jul. 18, 1906.

Odetta, Dec. 31, 1930.

Odoacer, Mar. 5, 493.

Oehlenschläger, Adam Gottlob, Nov. 14, 1779.

Oerter, Al, Sep. 19, 1936.

O'Faolain, Sean, Feb. 22, 1900.

Offenbach, Jacques, Jun. 20, 1819.

Official Languages Act (India), Jan. 26, 1965.

Ogden, Robert Morris, Jul. 6, 1877.

Oglala Sioux reservation, Feb. 27, 1973.

Oglethorpe, James, Dec. 22, 1696; Jun. 9, 1732; Feb. 12, 1733.

Oglethorpe Day (Georgia), Feb. 12.

O'Hair, Madalyn Murray, Apr. 13, 1919; Jan. 26, 1970.

O'Hara, Geoffrey, Oct. 10, 1916.

O'Hara, John Henry, Jan. 31, 1905.

O'Hara, Mary, Jul. 10, 1885.

O'Hara, Maureen, Aug. 17, 1921.

O'Hare, Edward Henry, Mar. 13, 1914.

O'Hare International Airport, May 25, 1979.

Ohio: admitted to Union, Mar. 1, 1803.

Ohira, Masayoshi, Mar. 12, 1910; Nov. 27, 1978.

Ohm, George Simon, Mar. 16, 1787.

oil embargo against U.S.: ended, Mar. 18, 1974.

oilers, patron of, Dec. 4.

oil spill (Cornwall, England), Mar. 18, 1967.

oil spill (Brittany Coast), Mar. 17, 1978.

O'Keeffe, Georgia, Nov. 15, 1887.

Okinawa: bombed, Oct. 10, 1944; U.S. invasion, Apr. 1, 1945; Apr. 6, 1945.

Oklahoma: Apr. 22, 1889; admitted to Union, Nov. 16, 1907.

Oklahoma!: premiere, Mar. 31, 1943.

Oklahoma Day (Oklahoma), Apr. intro.; Apr. 22.

Oklahoma Heritage Week (Oklahoma), Nov. intro.

Oklahoma Historical Day (Oklahoma), Oct. 10.

Okuchi, Nobuo, Mar. 11, 1970.

Olaf V (Norway), Jul. 2, 1903; Sep. 21, 1957.

Oldcastle, John: burned and hanged, Dec. 12, 1417.

Older Americans Month, May intro.

Olds, Ransom Eli, Jun. 3, 1864.

Olin, John Merrill, Nov. 10, 1892.

Oliva, Treaty of, May 3, 1660.

Oliver, James, Aug. 28, 1823.

Olivier, George Borg, Mar. 3, 1962.

Olivier, Laurence, May 22, 1907.

Ollanta: premiere, Dec. 26, 1900.

Olmsted, Frederick Law, Apr. 26, 1822.

Olustee, Battle of, Feb. 20, 1864.

Olympic Games: first modern, Apr. 6, 1896; XVIII Summer, Oct. 10, 1964; black power demonstration, Oct. 16, 1968.

Olympio, Sylvanus, Jan. 13, 1963.

Oman, Sir Charles, Jan. 12, 1860.

P

Palestine Liberation Organization: recognized by U.N., Oct. 14, 1974.

Palestinian terrorists: Munich, Sep. 5, 1972.

Paley, William S., Sep. 28, 1901.

Palladio, Andrea, Nov. 30, 1508.

Palmer, Alice Elvira Freeman, Feb. 21, 1855.

Palmer, Arnold, Sep. 10, 1929.

Palmer, Lilli, May 24, 1914.

Palmer, Nathaniel Brown, Aug. 8, 1799.

Palmer, Potter, May 20, 1826.

Palmerston, (Henry John Temple) Viscount, Oct. 20, 1784.

Palo Alto, Battle of, May 8, 1846.

Panama: independence from Spain, Nov. 28, 1821; independence, Nov. 3, 1903; Feb. 13, 1904; Oct. 11, 1972.

Panama, Isthmus of, Sep. 25, 1513.

Panama Canal, Feb. 1, 1864; opened to international commercial vessels, Aug. 15, 1914; Jul. 28, 1926; Jul. 11, 1934.

Panama Canal Treaty: ratified, Dec. 2, 1903; Apr. 18, 1978.

Panama-U.S. Treaty: signed, Jul. 28, 1926.

Pan American Airways, Jan. 6, 1942.

Pan-American Conference: first, Oct. 2, 1889.

Pan American Day, Apr. 14.

Panchen Lama, May 27, 1951.

pandas, giant, Apr. 16, 1972.

Pandit, Vijaya Lakshmi, Aug. 18, 1900.

Pan-German League, Apr. 9, 1891.

Pangkor, Treaty of, Jan. 20, 1874.

Panic of 1873, Sep. 18, 1873.

Panic of 1893, May 5, 1893.

Panic of 1907, Mar. 13, 1907.

Panipat (India), Nov. 5, 1556.

Panizzi, Antonio, Sep. 16, 1797.

Pankhurst, Emmeline, Jul. 4, 1858.

Papadopoulos, Georgios (Greece): Apr. 21, 1967; Jun. 1, 1973; first President, Aug. 19, 1973.

Papal Chancery: adopts January 1 as beginning of year, Nov. 16, 1621.

papal infallibility: declared, Jul. 18, 1870.

Papal States, May 1, 1809.

Papanicolaou, George Nicholas, May 13, 1883.

Papas, Irene, Sep. 3, 1926.

Papen, Franz von, Jun. 1, 1932.

Papin, Denis, Aug. 22, 1647.

Papp, Joseph, Jun. 22, 1921.

Papua New Guinea, Jan. 19, 1975; independence, Sep. 16, 1975.

Papua Republic, Jan. 19, 1975.

Paracelsus, Nov. 10, 1493.

parachute, Oct. 22, 1797.

Paraguay: declares independence, Oct. 12, 1811; Chaco War ends, Jun. 12, 1935; Mar. 11, 1936.

Parc de St. Cloud (Paris), May 31, 1868.

Parcel Post (U.S.), Jan. 1, 1913.

Parents' Day (Zaire), Aug. 1.

Parents Without Partners Founder's Month, Mar. intro.

Pareto, Vilfredo, Jul. 15, 1848.

Parini, Giuseppe, May 23, 1729.

Paris, Mar. 31, 1814; capitulates to Prussia, Jan. 28, 1871; Jan. 23, 1911; German bombardment, Mar. 23, 1918; Jan. 27, 1973.

Paris, Treaty of, May 20, 1303; Feb. 10, 1763; independence of U.S., Sep. 3, 1783; Jan. 14, 1784; Mar. 30, 1856; Spanish-American War, Dec. 10, 1898.

Paris Commune: uprising, Mar. 18, 1871; established, Mar. 26, 1871.

Paris (France): German troops enter, Jun. 14, 1940.

Paris (France), patroness of, Jan. 3.

parish clergy throughout the world, principal patron saint of, Aug. 3.

parish clerks, patron of, Nov. 13.

Paris Pacts, Dec. 29, 1954.

Paris Peace Conference, Jan. 18, 1919; Apr. 28, 1919.

Paris Peace Conference, Supreme Council of, Apr. 25, 1920.

Paris Peace Pact, Mar. 1, 1929.

Park, Mungo, Sep. 10, 1771; Jul. 21, 1796.

Park Chung Hee, Sep. 30, 1917; Mar. 10, 1976; assassinated, Oct. 26, 1979.

Parker, Bonnie, Oct. 1, 1910.

Parker, Buddy, Dec. 16, 1913.

Parker, Charlie (*Bird*), Aug. 29, 1920.

Parker, Dorothy, Aug. 22, 1893.

Parker, Fess, Aug. 16, 1925.

Parker, George Swinnerton, Dec. 12, 1866.

Parkhurst, Charles Henry, Apr. 17, 1842.

Parkman, Francis, Sep. 16, 1823.

Park Tong Sun, Jun. 5, 1977; Sep. 6, 1977; Mar. 9, 1978.

Parkyns, William (Sir), Apr. 3, 1696.

Parliament, British: opening first telecast, Apr. 21, 1966.

Parliament, English, May 20, 1774.

Parliament, Long, Apr. 20, 1653.

Parliament, Short, Apr. 13, 1640.

Parliamentary army (English Civil War), Jan. 21, 1645.

Parliament (British), Jan. 6, 1916.

Parliament of Lincoln (England), Jan. 20, 1301.

Parnell, Charles Stewart, Jun. 27, 1846; Oct. 31, 1879.

Parnis, Mollie, Mar. 18, 1905.

Parr, Kathrine, Jul. 12, 1542.

Parrish, Maxfield , Jul. 25, 1870.

Parry, Sir William Edward, Dec. 19, 1790.

Parseghian, Ara, May 21, 1923.

Parsons, Louella O., Aug. 6, 1881.

Parsons, Sir Charles Algernon, Jun. 13, 1854.

Parsons, Talcott, Dec. 13, 1902.

Parthenon: destroyed, Sep. 26, 1687.

Partition of Poland, Third, Oct. 24, 1795.

Partition Treaty, First, Oct. 11, 1698.

Parton, Dolly, Jan. 19, 1946.

Partridge, Eric Honeywood, Feb. 6, 1894.

Pascal, Blaise, Jun. 19, 1623.

Paschal II (pope), Feb. 4, 1111; Feb. 12, 1111.

Paschal III (antipope), May 28, 1167.

Pascua Florida Day (Florida), Apr. 2.

Pas de Calais: U.S. raids, Dec. 24, 1943.

Pass Law (South Africa), Mar. 21, 1960.

Passover, p. xii; Apr. intro.

Passy, Frederic, May 20, 1822.

Pasta, Giuditta, Apr. 9, 1798.

Pasternak, Boris, Feb. 10, 1890.

Pasteur, Louis, Dec. 27, 1822.

pastry cooks and confectioners, patron of, Jan. 2.

Patent Office, U.S.: opens, Jul. 31, 1790.

Pater, Walter Horatio, Aug. 4, 1839.

Patino, Simon Iturri, Jun. 1, 1862.

Patman, Wright, Aug. 6, 1893.

Patmore, Coventry Kersey Dighton, Jul. 23, 1823.

Paton, Alan Stewart, Jan. 11, 1903.

Patrick, John, May 17, 1905.

Patriot's Day (Maine, Mass.), Apr. intro.

Patsayev, Vladislav N., Jun. 30, 1971.

Patterson, Floyd, Jan. 4, 1935; Jun. 26, 1959; Nov. 30, 1959; Jun. 20, 1960; Mar. 13, 1961; Dec. 4, 1961; Sep. 25, 1962; Jul. 22, 1963.

Patterson, John Henry, Dec. 13, 1844.

Patton, George S(mith), Nov. 11, 1885; Nov. 9, 1944.

Paul, Alice, Jan. 11, 1885.

Paul I (Greece), Mar. 6, 1964.

Paul I (Russia), Oct. 1, 1754; Nov. 17, 1796; assassinated Mar. 23, 1801.

Paul II (pope), Feb. 23, 1417.

Paul III (pope), Feb. 29, 1468; Jan. 1, 1547.

Paul IV (pope), Jun. 28, 1476.

Paul V (pope), Sep. 17, 1552.

Paul VI (pope), Sep. 26, 1897; Jun. 3, 1963; Jun. 21, 1963; Jan. 5, 1964; *Ecclesiam Suam*, Aug. 10, 1964; Mar. 7, 1965; addresses UN, Oct. 5, 1965; Dec. 7, 1965; Feb. 17, 1966; Mar. 23, 1966; Jan. 29, 1967; Jun. 23, 1967; restructures Curia, Aug. 12, 1967; Jul. 29, 1968; priestly celibacy, Feb. 1, 1970; Jul. 3, 1970; Nov. 23, 1970; Jan. 15, 1973; Dec. 2, 1973; Dec. 24, 1974; Sep. 14, 1975; dies, Aug. 6, 1978.

Pauli, Wolfgang, Apr. 25, 1900.

Pauling, Linus Carl, Feb. 28, 1901.

Pavarotti, Luciano, Oct. 12, 1935.

Pavlov, Ivan Petrovich, Sep. 14, 1849.

pawnbrokers, patron of, Dec. 6.

Paxton, Sir Joseph, Aug. 3, 1801.

Payne system of income tax, Feb. 10, 1944.

Payne, John Howard, Jun. 9, 1791.

Payne, Robert, Dec. 4, 1911.

Payson, Joan Whitney, Feb. 5, 1903.

Pay Your Bills Week, National, Feb. intro.

Paz, Octavio, Mar. 31, 1914.

Paz Estenssoro, Victor, Apr. 9, 1952.

Peabody, Elizabeth Palmer, May 16, 1804.

Peabody, George, Feb. 18, 1795; Jul. 27, 1852.

Peace, Palace of, Jul. 30, 1907.

Peace Conference (World War I), Jan. 25, 1919.

Peace Corps: established, Mar. 1, 1961; Sep. 22, 1961.

Peace Day (Rwanda), Jul. 5.

Peace Officers Memorial Day (U.S.), May 15.

Peace of Trento, Oct. 13, 1501.

Peace with Bolivia Day (Paraguay), Jun. 12.

peace without victory: Wilson's speech, Jan. 22, 1917.

Peach Festival (Japan), Mar. 3.

Peale, Charles Wilson, Apr. 15, 1741.

Peale, Norman Vincent, May 31, 1898.

Peanut Month, National, Mar. intro.

pearl, Jun. intro.

Pearl, Minnie, Oct. 25, 1912.

Pearl Harbor, Jan. 20, 1887; Japanese attack on, Dec. 7, 1941.

Pearson, Ben, Nov. 16, 1898.

Pearson, Drew, Dec. 13, 1897.

Pearson, Karl, Mar. 27, 1857.

Pearson, Lester Bowles, Apr. 23, 1897.

Peary, Robert (Admiral), May 6, 1856; Apr. 6, 1909.

peasants, poor, patroness of, Sep. 14.

Peasants Day (Burma), Mar. 2.

Peck, Gregory, Apr. 5, 1916.

Peckinpah, Sam, Feb. 21, 1925.

Pedro, Dom (Portugal) abdicates, Apr. 7, 1831; Apr. 2, 1832; May 26, 1834; Sep. 24, 1834.

Pedro II (Brazil), Dec. 2, 1825; Apr. 7, 1831; abdicates, Nov. 15, 1889.

Pedro IV (Portugal), Oct. 12, 1798.

Pedro V (Portugal), Sep. 16, 1837; Nov. 15, 1853.

Peel, Sir Robert, Feb. 5, 1788; Sep. 29, 1829.

Peel Report, Jul. 8, 1937.

Peerce, Jan, Jun. 3, 1904.

Pegasus, Feb. 16, 1965.

Pegau, Battle of, Oct. 15, 1080.

Pegu (Lower Burma), Dec. 20, 1852.

Peguy, Charles, Jan. 7, 1873.

Pei, I. M., Apr. 26, 1917.

Peirce, Benjamin, Apr. 4, 1809.

Peirce, Charles Santiago Sanders, Sep. 10, 1839.

Peking (China): occupied, Oct. 12, 1860; Jan. 7, 1895; Apr. 8, 1913; captured, Jun. 8, 1928.

Pelé (Edson Arantes do Nascimento): Oct. 23, 1940; scores 1000th goal, Nov. 19, 1969.

Pella, Giuseppe, Apr. 18, 1902.

Pelléas et Mélisande: premiere, Apr. 30, 1902.

Pelletier, Wilfrid, Jun. 30, 1896.

Pelshe, Arvid Y., Feb. 7, 1899.

Peltz, Mary Ellis, May 4, 1896.

Penance, Day of (Federal Republic of Germany), Nov. 17.

Pendleton Act, Jan. 6, 1883.

Peninsular War, Feb. 16, 1808; Aug. 21, 1808; Mar. 12, 1814.

penitent women, patron of, Apr. 2.

Penjdeh, Feb. 13, 1886.

Penn, Arthur, Sep. 27, 1922.

Penn, William, Oct. 14, 1644; Mar. 4, 1681.

Penney, James Cash, Sep. 16, 1875.

Pennsylvania: second state, Dec. 12, 1787.

Penny Blacks: first adhesive postage stamps, May 6, 1840.

Pentagon Building, Jan. 15, 1943.

Pentagon Papers: published, Jun. 13, 1971.

Pentecost Sunday, p. xii; Jun. intro.; May intro.

Penzias, Arno Allan, Apr. 26, 1933.

People's National Congress (Guyana), May 26, 1966.

People's Park: Vietnam War protest, May 15, 1969.

People's Party (Populist Party): formation, Feb. 22, 1892.

People's Redemption Party (Liberia), Apr. 12, 1980.

People's Redemptive Council (Liberia), Apr. 25, 1980.

People's Republic of China: admitted to UN, Oct. 25, 1971; Mar. 13, 1972; Feb. 2, 1974.

People's Temple, Nov. 18, 1978.

Peppercorn Day (Bermuda), Apr. 23.

Pepys, Samuel, Feb. 23, 1633.

Pequot Indians, Jul. 28, 1637.

Pequot War, Jul. 28, 1637.

Perak (Malay Peninsula), Jan. 20, 1874.

Percival, Spencer, May 11, 1812.

Percy, Charles Harting, Sep. 27, 1919.

Percy, Walker, May 28, 1916.

Pereda Asbún, Juan, Jul. 21, 1978.

Pereira, Aristide, Nov. 17, 1923.

Perelman, S. J., Feb. 1, 1904.

Peres, Shimon, Apr. 8, 1977.

Pergaud, Louis, Jan. 22, 1882.

Pergolesi, Giovanni, Jan. 4, 1710.

peridot, Aug. intro.

Perkin, Sir William Henry, Mar. 12, 1838.

Perkins, Anthony, Apr. 4, 1932.

Perkins, Frances, Apr. 10, 1882.

Perkins, Maxwell, Sep. 20, 1884.

Permanent Court of International Justice: opens, Feb. 15, 1922.

Perón, Eva Duarte de, May 7, 1919.

Perón, Isabel, Feb. 6, 1931; Sep. 23, 1973; becomes President, Jul. 1, 1974; Jan. 3, 1975; Jul. 8, 1975; returns to office, Oct. 16, 1975; Mar. 24, 1976; Mar. 29, 1976.

Perón, Juan: Oct. 8, 1895; resigns, Sep. 19, 1955; ends 17-year exile, Nov. 17, 1972; Sep. 23, 1973; Jul. 1, 1974.

Perpetuation Bill, Apr. 20, 1653.

Perrault, Charles, Jan. 12, 1628.

Perrin, Jean Baptiste, Sep. 30, 1870.

Perry, Commodore Matthew, Apr. 10, 1794; Jul. 8, 1853; Mar. 31, 1854.

Perry, Oliver Hazard, Aug. 23, 1785; Sep. 10, 1813.

Perry, Robert: shot to death, Jun. 10, 1970.

Perse, Saint-John, Mar. 31, 1887; May 31, 1887.

Pershing, John J., Sep. 13, 1860; May 10, 1917; Jun. 13, 1917.

Persia: declares neutrality, Nov. 1, 1914; Jan. 30, 1915; Mar. 21, 1935.

Persia, Shah of, Apr. 25, 1926.

Persian Empire: 2,500th anniversary begins, Oct. 12, 1971.

Persian martyrs, Apr. 6.

Persigny, Jean Gilbert Fialin, Jan. 11, 1808.

Persoff, Nehemiah, Aug. 14, 1920.

Perth, Feb. 20, 1437.

Pertini, Alessandro, Sep. 25, 1896.

Peru: independence, Jul. 28, 1821; Jan. 26, 1827; declares war on Spain, Jan. 14, 1866; Apr. 5, 1879.

Perutz, Max, May 19, 1914.

Peruvian opera, first: *Ollanta*, Dec. 26, 1900.

Pescia in Tuscany, patron of, Oct. 23.

Peshtigo (Wisconsin), Oct. 7, 1871.

Pest Control Month, National, Jun. intro.

Pestalozzi, Johann H., Jan. 12, 1746.

Pétain, Henri Philippe Omer, Apr. 24, 1856.

Peter (Serbia), Nov. 24, 1918.

Peter (Yugoslavia): dies, Aug. 16, 1921.

Peter and the Wolf: premiere, May 2, 1936.

Peter II (Russia), Oct. 23, 1715; dies, Feb. 11, 1730.

Peter III (Russia), Feb. 21, 1728; Jan. 5, 1762.

Peter V (Portugal): dies, Nov. 11, 1861.

Peter of Castile, Mar. 14, 1369.

Peter the Great (Russia), Jun. 9, 1672; Nov. 30, 1700; May 1, 1703; May 27, 1703; Jul. 8, 1709; Oct. 22, 1721; dies, Feb. 8, 1725.

Peter, Lawrence (Johnston), Sep. 16, 1919.

Peterloo Massacre, Aug. 16, 1819.

Peters, Jean, Oct. 15, 1926.

Peters, Roberta, May 4, 1930.

Peterson, Oscar (Emanuel), Aug. 15, 1925.

Petit, Alexis, Oct. 2, 1791.

Petofi (Petrovics), Sandor, Jan. 1, 1823.

Petrarch, Jul. 20, 1304; Apr. 8, 1341.

Petrograd, Mar. 8, 1917; Apr. 22, 1920.

Petrograd Soviet of Workers and Soldiers Deputies: organized, Mar. 12, 1917.

Petrouchka: premiere, Jun. 13, 1911.

Petty, Richard, Jul. 2, 1937.

Pet Week, National, May intro.

Pevensey (England), Sep. 28, 1066.

Phelan, Michael, Apr. 12, 1859.

Phi Beta Kappa: founded, Dec. 5, 1776.

Philadelphia, Feb. 16, 1804.

Philadelphia (Pennsylvania), Sep. 5, 1774; May 25, 1787; May 7, 1847.

Philadelphia Contributionship, Apr. 13, 1752.

Philadelphia Orchestra: inaugural concert, Nov. 16, 1900; Jan. 3, 1941.

Philadelphia Phillies, May 24, 1935.

Philarges, Peter: elected Pope Alexander V, Jun. 29, 1408.

Philatelic Exhibitions Month, May intro.

Philatelic Journalists Day (U.S), Jun. 6; Jun. intro.

Philatelic Literature Month, Mar. intro.

Philatelic Publications Month, Sep. intro.

Philatelic Societies' Month, Apr. intro.

Philatelic Writers' Month, Jun. intro.

Philately Day, Jan. intro.

Philby, Harold *Kim*, Jan. 1, 1912.

Philharmonic Society, New York: formed, Dec. 7, 1842.

Philip, Duke of Swabia (Germany), Mar. 8, 1198.

Philip, Prince (England), Jun. 10, 1921; Jul. 4, 1966.

Philip I (France), Aug. 4, 1060.

Philip II Augustus (France):, Aug. 21, 1165; Sep. 18, 1180; Nov. 18, 1188; Jul. 1, 1190; Jul. 22, 1194; May 22, 1200; dies Jul. 14, 1223.

Philip II (Spain), May 21, 1527; Mar. 9, 1551; Oct. 25, 1555; Jan. 16, 1556; Feb. 5, 1556; Dec. 31, 1584; May 17, 1597; dies, Sep. 13, 1598.

Philip III (France), Aug. 25, 1270; Apr. 3, 1245; dies, Oct. 05, 1285.

Philip III (Spain), Apr. 14, 1578; Sep. 13, 1598; dies, Mar. 31, 1621.

Philip IV (France), Oct. 5, 1285; Dec. 5, 1301; Jul. 11, 1302; dies, Nov. 29, 1314.

Philip IV (Spain), Apr. 8, 1605; Mar. 31, 1621; dies, Sep. 17, 1665.

Philip V (France), Jun. 4, 1316; dies, Jan. 3, 1322.

Philip V (Spain), Dec. 19, 1683; Nov. 1, 1700; Dec. 10, 1710.

Philip VI (France), Feb. 1, 1328; Mar. 15, 1341; dies, Aug. 22, 1350.

Philip of Anjou, Nov. 1, 1700.

Philip of Burgundy, Jan. 11, 1360.

Philip the Good (Duke of Burgundy), Jan. 10, 1429; Sep. 21, 1435.

Philippa (Queen of England), Oct. 17, 1346.

Philippine-American Friendship Day (Philippines), Jul. 4.

Philippine Sea, Jul. 30, 1945.

Philippine Sea, Battle of: begins, Jun. 18, 1944; ends, Jun. 20, 1944.

Philippines, Apr. 27, 1521; independence, Jun. 12, 1898; Feb. 4, 1899; Mar. 24, 1934; first president of, Sep. 17, 1935; Jan. 2, 1942; Apr. 9, 1942; bombed, Oct. 12, 1944; martial law, Sep. 21, 1972; Apr. 7, 1978.

Philippines, National Bank of, Feb. 4, 1916.

Philippines, Republic of the: proclaimed, Jul. 4, 1946.

Phillips, Captain Mark, Nov. 14, 1973.

Phillips, Frank, Nov. 28, 1873.

Phillips, John, Dec. 6, 1719.

Phillips, John Sanburn, Jul. 2, 1861.

Phillips, Wendell, Nov. 29, 1811.

Phipps, Henry, Sep. 27, 1839.

Phnom Penh (Cambodia), Apr. 17, 1975; Jan. 7, 1979.

Phoenix Park (Dublin), May 6, 1882.

phonograph: patented, Jul. 31, 1877.

phonograph record, long-playing: first public demonstration, Jun. 18, 1948.

Phouma, Souvana (Laos), Apr. 5, 1974.

Physical Education Day (Japan), Oct. 10.

physicians, patrons of, Sep. 26.

Piaf, Edith, Dec. 19, 1915.

Piaget, Jean, Aug. 9, 1896.

Piatigorsky, Gregor, Apr. 20, 1903.

Piazzi, Giuseppe, Jul. 16, 1746.

Picardy, First Battle of, Sep. 22, 1914.

Picasso, Pablo, Oct. 25, 1881.

Piccard, Auguste, Jan. 28, 1884.

Pichincha Day Battle of (Ecuador), May 24.

Pickens, Slim, Jun. 29, 1919.

Pickett, George Edward, Jan. 25, 1825.

Pickford, Mary, Apr. 8, 1893.

Pickle Weeks, May intro.

Picnic Day, International, Jun. intro.

Picquigny, Peace of, Aug. 29, 1475.

Pidgeon, Walter, Sep. 23, 1898.

Pieck, Wilhelm, Jan. 3, 1876.

Pierce, Franklin, Nov. 23, 1804; inaugurated, Mar. 4, 1853.

Pike, James Albert, Feb. 14, 1913.

Pike, Zebulon M., Jan. 5, 1779; Nov. 15, 1806.

Pike's Peak, Nov. 15, 1806.

pilgrims, patron of, Feb. 12.

Pilgrim's Progress, Feb. 18, 1678.

Pillsbury, Charles Alfred, Dec. 3, 1842.

pilots: captured U.S. in Vietnam, Jan. 21, 1970.

Pilsudski, Josef (Poland), Dec. 5, 1867; Oct. 15, 1918; Apr. 19, 1919; May 12, 1926.

Pinckney, Charles, Oct. 26, 1757.

Pinckney, Charles Cotesworth, Feb. 25, 1746.

Pinckney's Treaty (Treaty of San Lorenzo), Oct. 27, 1795.

Pincus, Gregory, Apr. 9, 1903.

Pindling, Lynden O., Jan. 16, 1967.

Pinel, Philippe, Apr. 20, 1745.

Pinero, Arthur Wing, May 24, 1855.

Pinkerton, Allan, Aug. 25, 1819.

Pinkham, Lydia Estes, Feb. 9, 1819.

Pinkowski, Josef (Poland), Feb. 9, 1981.

pinmakers, patron saint of, Jan. 20.

Pinochet Ugarte, Augusto, Sep. 13, 1973; Mar. 11, 1981.

Pinter, Harold, Oct. 30, 1930.

Pinto da Costa, Manuel, Aug. 5.

Pinza, Ezio, May 18, 1892.

Pioneer 10, Mar. 2, 1972; Apr. 25, 1983; Jun. 13, 1983; Dec. 3, 1973.

Pioneer 11, Dec. 3, 1974; Sep. 1, 1979.

Pioneer Day (Idaho), Jun. 15.

Pioneers' Day (Liberia), Jan. 7.

Pioneer's Day (South Dakota), Oct. intro.

Pioneer V, Mar. 11, 1960.

Piper, William Thomas, Jan. 8, 1881.

Pirandello, Luigi, Jun. 28, 1867.

Pisa, Council of, Jun. 29, 1408.

Pisa, patron saint of, Mar. 17.

Pisces, Feb. intro.; Mar. intro.

Pissarro, Camille, Jul. 10, 1830.

Piston, Walter, Jan. 20, 1894.

Pitcher, Molly (Mary McCauley), Oct. 13, 1754.

Pitkin, Walter Boughton, Feb. 6, 1878.

Pitman, Sir Isaac, Jan. 4, 1813.

Pitt, William, Nov. 15, 1708; May 28, 1759; Feb. 16, 1801.

Pittsburgh (Pennsylvania), Jan. 28, 1944.

Pittsburgh Steelers football team, Jan. 21, 1979.

Pittsburg Landing (Tennessee), Apr. 6, 1862.

Pius II (pope), Oct. 18, 1405.

Pius IV (pope), Mar. 31, 1499.

Pius V (pope), Jan. 17, 1504; Feb. 25, 1570.

Pius VI (pope), Dec. 25, 1717.

Pius VII (pope), Aug. 14, 1742; May 1, 1809.

Pius VIII (pope), Nov. 20, 1761.

Pius IX (pope), May 13, 1792.

Pius X (pope), Jun. 2, 1835; Aug. 9, 1903; Jan. 8, 1904.

Pius XI (pope), May 31, 1857; Jul. 25, 1929.

Pius XII (pope), Mar. 2, 1876; Mar. 2, 1939; Jul. 7, 1946; Nov. 1, 1950; Dec. 23, 1950.

Pizza Festival Time, Oct. intro.

Planck, Max, Apr. 23, 1858.

Plantagenet, Edward: first Prince of Wales, Apr. 25, 1284.

Plantagenet, House of: established, Oct. 25, 1154.

Plath, Sylvia, Oct. 27, 1932.

Plattsburg Bay, Battle of, Sep. 11, 1814.

Play-Doh Day, National, Sep. intro.

Playa Giron, Apr. 20, 1961.

Player, Gary, Nov. 1, 1935.

Players, The (Club), Jan. 7, 1888.

Playfair, John, Mar. 10, 1748.

playing card makers, patron of, Oct. 25.

Plehwe, Vyacheslav: assassinated, Jul. 28, 1904.

Plekhanov, Georgi, Dec. 11, 1856.

Pleshette, Suzanne, Jan. 31, 1937.

Plimsall, Samuel, Feb. 10, 1824.

Plisetskaya, Maya Michailovna, Nov. 20, 1925.

Plowright, Joan (Anne), Oct. 28, 1929.

Plumer, Herbert Charles Onslow, Mar. 13, 1857.

Plunkett, Oliver, Mar. 17, 1918.

Pluto: discovered, Feb. 18, 1930; Apr. 25, 1983.

Plymouth (England), Sep. 16, 1620.

Pocahontas, Apr. 5, 1614.

Podgorica (Montenegro), Jan. 23, 1916.

Podgorny, Nikolai Viktorovich, Feb. 18, 1903; Jan. 29, 1967.

Poe, Edgar Allan, Jan. 19, 1809.

Poetry Day, National, Oct., intro.

poets, patron of, Mar. 1.

Poher, Alain, Apr. 28, 1969.

Poincaré, Jules Henri, Apr. 29, 1854.

Poincaré, Raymond, Aug. 20, 1860.

poison gas, Feb. 6, 1922.

poison gas prohibited: Geneva Protocol, Jun. 17, 1925.

Poison Prevention Week, National, Mar. intro.

Poisson, Siméon-Denis, Jun. 21, 1781.

Poitier, Sidney, Feb. 20, 1927.

Poland, Jan. 18, 1401; Jul. 1, 1569; Jan. 15, 1582; Jan. 26, 1699; Jun. 2, 1734; Seven Years' War, Jan. 10, 1757; Apr. 11, 1764; partition, Jan. 23, 1793; Third Partition of Poland, Oct. 24, 1795; Apr. 30, 1815; Mar. 30, 1917; declares independence, Oct. 15, 1918; independence, Nov. 9, 1918; Jan. 17, 1919; attacked by Germany, Sep. 1, 1939; invaded by U.S.S.R., Sep. 17, 1939; Jan. 6, 1946; thousandth anniversary of Christianity in, Jan. 8, 1966; Mar. 11, 1968; martial law declared, Dec. 13, 1981.

Poland, Bank of: established, Apr. 1, 1924.

Poland, patron of, Mar. 4; Apr. 11; Nov. 13.

Polanski, Roman, Aug. 18, 1933.

Polaris missile: launched for first time from submerged submarine, Jul. 20, 1960; May 6, 1962.

Polisario Republic (Saharan Arab Democratic Republic), Feb. 27, 1976.

Polish Falcons Societies, Union Of, Apr. 4, 1917.

Polish Republic, Nov. 3, 1918.

Polish Succession, War of the, Jun. 2, 1734; ends, Oct. 5, 1735.

Polk, James Knox, Nov. 2, 1795; inaugurated, Mar. 4, 1845.

Pollock, Jackson, Jan. 28, 1912.

Pol Pot: received in Peking (China), Sep. 28, 1977.

Poltava, Battle of, Jul. 8, 1709.

Pompadour, Madame de, Dec. 29, 1721.

Pompidou, Georges, Jul. 5, 1911; Apr. 14, 1962.

Ponce de León, Juan, Apr. 2, 1513.

Pons, Lily, Apr. 16, 1904.

Ponselle, Rosa Melba, Jan. 22, 1897.

Pontano, Giovanni Gioviano, May 7, 1426.

Pontecorvo, Bruno M., Apr. 21, 1963.

Provine, Dorothy, Jan. 20, 1937.
Proxmire, William, Nov. 11, 1915.
Prudhomme, Sully, Mar. 16, 1839.
Prus, Boleslaw, Aug. 20, 1847.
Prussia, proclaimed kingdom, Jan. 15, 1701; Jan. 16, 1756; Seven Years' War, Jan. 10, 1757; Jan. 23, 1793; new constitution, Jan. 31, 1850; Jan. 24, 1867; Jan. 28, 1871.
Prussia, patroness of, Oct. 30.
Prussia, patron of, Nov. 15.
Pryor, Richard, Dec. 1, 1940.
Przasnyz, Battle of, Feb. 27, 1915; Mar. 11, 1915.
Przemysl (Galicia), Mar. 22, 1915.
P.S., I Love You: Beatles first recording, Sep. 11, 1962.
Public Holiday (Botswana), Jan. 2.
Public Holiday (St. Lucia), Jan. 2.
Public Holiday (Zimbabwe), Dec. 27.
Public Order Act, Feb. 7, 1970.
Public Relations Week, May intro.
Public Safety Act (India), Apr. 12, 1929.
public school, first in America, Feb. 13, 1635.
public school segregation laws: Georgia, Jan. 27, 1961.
Publicity Stunt Week, Apr. intro.
Pucci, Emilio, Nov. 20, 1914.
Puccini, Giacomo, Dec. 22, 1858; Feb. 1, 1896; Jan. 14, 1900; Feb. 17, 1904.
Puebla Battle Day or Cinco de Mayo (Mexico), May 5.
Puebla (Mexico), May 5, 1867.
Pueblo, U.S.S., Jan. 23, 1968; Dec. 22, 1968.
Puerto Rico: U.S. territory, Mar. 2, 1917; Feb. 14, 1929.
Pugin, Augustus Welby, Mar. 1, 1812.
Pulaski, Count Casimir, Mar. 4, 1747.
Pulitzer, Joseph, Apr. 10, 1847.
Puller, Lewis Burwell, Jun. 26, 1898.
Pullman, George Mortimer, Mar. 3, 1831.
Pullman strike, May 11, 1894.
pulsar: discovery, Feb. 29, 1968.
Pultusk, May 1, 1703.
Punch: begins publication, Jul. 17, 1841.
Punjab, Feb. 21, 1849; Mar. 29, 1849; Apr. 2, 1849; Mar. 10, 1966.
Punta del Este, Jan. 31, 1962.
Purcell, Edward Mills, Aug. 30, 1912.
Pure Food and Drug Act, U.S., Jun. 30, 1906.
Purification of the Blessed Virgin Mary, Feb. 2.
Purim, p. xii; Mar. intro.
Puritans, Jan. 14, 1604.
purity, patron of, Jan. 21.
Purkinje, Jan Evangelista, Dec. 17, 1787.
Pushkin, Alexander Sergeyevich, Jun. 6, 1799.
Pushtoonistan Day (Afghanistan), Aug. 31.
Putnam, George Palmer, Feb. 7, 1814.
Putnam, Israel, Jan. 7, 1718.
Pu-Yi, Emperor (China), Feb. 12, 1912.
Puzo, Mario, Oct. 15, 1920.
Pya Martyrs Day (Togo), Jun. 21.
Pyle, Ernest (*Ernie*), Aug. 3, 1900.
Pyle, Howard, Mar. 5, 1853.
Pynchon, Thomas, May 8, 1937.

Pyongyang (North Korea): captured, Oct. 20, 1950.
Pyramids, Battle of, Jul. 21, 1798.

Q

Qabus ibn Said (Oman), Nov. 18, 1942; Jul. 23, 1970.
Qadhafi, Mu'ammar al-, Sep. 1, 1969.
Quadruple Alliance, Apr. 22, 1834.
Quaid-es-Azan Birthday of (Pakistan), Dec. 25.
Quakers, Oct. 14, 1656; hanged in Massachusetts, Oct. 27, 1659.
Quang Duc: suicide, Jun. 11, 1963.
Quant, Mary, Feb. 11, 1934.
Quantrill, William Clarke, Jul. 31, 1839.
Quarter Day (Great Britain), Mar. 25.
Quartering Act: passed, Jun. 2, 1774.
Quasimodo, Salvatore, Aug. 20, 1901.
Quayle, Anthony, Sep. 7, 1913.
Quebec, Jul. 3, 1608.
Quebec Act, May 20, 1774.
Queen Elizabeth, S.S., Jan. 9, 1972.
Queen Isabella Day (Spain), Apr. 22.
Queen Margrethe's Birthday (Denmark), Apr. 16.
Queen's Birthday (Fiji), Jun. 15.
Queen's Birthday (Netherlands and Netherlands Antilles), Apr. 30.
Queen's Official Birthday (U.K.), Jun. intro.
Queen's University (Ireland): founded, Aug. 15, 1850.
Queensbury, Marquis of: boxing rules, Sep. 7, 1892.
Queenship of Mary, Aug. 22.
Queiroz, Francisco Teixeira de, May 3, 1848.
Quental, Antero de, Apr. 18, 1842.
Quesnay, François, Jun. 4, 1694.
Quetelet, Adolphe, Feb. 22, 1796.
Quetta (India): earthquake, May 31, 1935.
Quevedo y Villegas, Francisco Gomez de, Sep. 17, 1580.
Quezon y Molina, Manuel Luis, Aug. 19, 1878; Sep. 17, 1935.
Quiberon (France), Nov. 20, 1759.
Quidde, Ludwig, Mar. 23, 1858.
Quiet City: premiere, Jan. 28, 1941.
Quiet Flows the Don: opens, Oct. 22, 1935.
Quimby, Harriet, Apr. 16, 1912.
Quinn, Anthony, Apr. 21, 1915.
Quintilis, Jul. intro.
Quisling, Vidkun, Jul. 18, 1887; Feb. 1, 1942.
Quito, Day of (Ecuador), Dec. 6.

R

Rabi Al-Awal, 12, p. xii; Oct. intro.; Nov. intro.
Rabi, I(sidor) I(saac), Jul. 29, 1898.
Rabin, Yitzak, Apr. 8, 1977.
Race, Day of the, Oct. 12.

Race Relations Sunday (U.S.), Feb. intro.
Rachmaninoff, Sergei, Apr. 1, 1873; Feb. 8, 1908; American debut, Nov. 4, 1909; Nov. 7, 1934; Jan. 3, 1941.
Rachmaninoff's *Second Symphony in E Minor*: premiere, Feb. 8, 1908.
racial discrimination: prohibited, Jun. 17, 1968.
racial integration: Little Rock, Arkansas, Sep. 24, 1957; begins in U.S. stores, Oct. 17, 1960; National Guard (U.S.), Apr. 3, 1962.
racial violence: Detroit (Michigan), Jul. 23, 1967.
Racine, Jean, Dec. 22, 1639.
Rackham, Arthur, Sep. 19, 1867.
Radcliffe, Ann, Jul. 9, 1764.
Radcliffe Library (Oxford University), Apr. 13, 1749.
Radetzky, Joseph Wenzel, Nov. 2, 1766.
Radford, Arthur William, Feb. 27, 1896.
radio: first commercial broadcast, Aug. 20, 1920.
radio broadcast: first composition, Mar. 5, 1907.
Radio City Music Hall: opens, Dec. 27, 1932.
Radio Day (U.S.S.R.), May 7.
radio signal: first transatlantic, Dec. 11, 1901.
radiotelephone: first between plane and ground, Aug. 18, 1917.
radio transmission of a musical score, first, Dec. 28, 1937.
Radishchev, Aleksandr Nikolayevich, Aug. 20, 1749.
Raeder, Erich, Apr. 24, 1876.
Raemaekers, Louis, Apr. 6, 1869.
Raft, George, Sep. 26, 1895.
Raglan, Fitzroy James Henry Somerset, Sep. 30, 1788.
Ragweed Month, National, Jun. intro.
Rahman, Mujibur (Sheikh), Mar. 26, 1971; Jan. 25, 1975; assassinated Aug. 15, 1975.
Rahmar, Ziaur: killed, May 30, 1981.
Raikes, Robert, Jul. 4, 1736.
railroad: first locomotive traction, Sep. 27, 1825.
Rainbow Bridge: opens, Nov. 1, 1941.
Rainey, Joseph Hayne, Jun. 21, 1832.
Rainey, Ma, Apr. 26, 1886.
Rains, Claude, Nov. 10, 1889.
Rainwater, L. James, Dec. 9, 1917.
Rákóczi II, Ferenc (Transylvania), Mar. 27, 1676.
Rama IX (Thailand), May 5, 1950.
Ramadan, 1, p. xii; Apr. intro.; Jun. intro.; Mar. intro.; May intro.
Ramakrishna, Feb. 18, 1836.
Raman, Sir Chandrasekhara Venkata, Nov. 7, 1888.
Ramillies, Battle of, May 23, 1706.
Ramón y Cajal, Santiago, May 1, 1852.
Ramos, João de Deus, Mar. 8, 1830.
Rampal, Jean-Pierre Louis, Jan. 7, 1922.
Ramsay, Sir William, Oct. 2, 1852.
Ramsey, Michael (Archbishop of Canterbury), Jun. 27, 1961; Mar. 23, 1966; May 14, 1974.
Rand, Ayn, Feb. 2, 1905.

Rand, James Henry, May 29, 1859.

Rand, Sally, Jan. 2, 1904.

Randolf, Asa Philip, Apr. 15, 1889.

Randolph, Edmund Jennings, Aug. 10, 1753.

Randolph, John, Jun. 2, 1773.

Ranger, U.S.S.: first aircraft carrier, Feb. 25, 1933.

Ranger I, Aug. 23, 1961.

Ranger 6, lunar probe, Feb. 2, 1964.

Ranger 7, Jul. 31, 1964.

Ranger 8, Feb. 20, 1965.

Ranger 9, Mar. 24, 1965.

Rangoon, May 4, 1824.

Ranier III, (Prince of Monaco), May 31, 1923.

Ranke, Leopold von, Dec. 21, 1795.

Rankin, Jeanette, Jun. 11, 1880.

Rankine, William John McQuorn, Jul. 5, 1820.

Ransom, John Crowe, Apr. 30, 1888.

Rapallo, Treaty of, Apr. 16, 1922.

Raphael, Mar. 28, 1483.

Rapp, George, Nov. 1, 1757.

Rasputin, Grigori Yefimovich: assassinated, Dec. 30, 1916; Jan. 1, 1917.

Rastatt, Peace of, Mar. 6, 1714.

Rathbone, Basil, Jun. 13, 1892.

Rathenau, Emil, Dec. 11, 1838.

Rather, Dan(iel), Oct. 31, 1931.

Ratisbon, Diet of, Feb. 25, 1803.

Ratisbon, Treaty of, Aug. 15, 1684.

Ratsimandrava, Richard: assassinated, Feb. 11, 1975.

Ratsiraka, Didier, Nov. 4, 1936.

Rattigan, Sir Terence (Mervyn), Jun. 10, 1911.

Rau, Sir Bengal Narsing, Feb. 26, 1887.

Rauschning, Hermann, Jul. 8, 1887.

Ravel, Maurice, Mar. 7, 1875; Mar. 5, 1904; May 17, 1904; Jan. 12, 1907; Jun. 8, 1912; Nov. 22, 1928.

Ravel's String Quartet in F: premiere, Mar. 5, 1904.

Ravenna, Mar. 5, 493.

Ravenna, Battle of, Apr. 11, 1512.

Rawalpindi, Mar. 12, 1849.

Rawlings, Jerry, Jun. 22, 1947; Jun. 16, 1979.

Rawlings, Marjorie Kinnan, Aug. 8, 1896.

Rawls, Lou, Dec. 1, 1935.

Ray, Dixy Lee, Sep. 3, 1914.

Ray, James Earl, Jun. 8, 1968; Mar. 10, 1969.

Ray, Man, Aug. 27, 1890.

Rayburn, Sam Taliaferro, Jan. 6, 1882.

Raye, Martha, Aug. 27, 1916.

Read, A.C., May 27, 1919.

Reagan, Ronald, Feb. 6, 1911; inaugurated Jan. 20, 1981; shot Mar. 30, 1981.

reaper: patented, Jun. 21, 1834.

Reasoner, Harry, Apr. 17, 1923.

Réaumur, René A. F. de, Feb. 28, 1683.

Rebildfest (Denmark), Jul. 4.

Reconstruction Act: passed, Mar. 2, 1867.

Reconstruction Finance Corporation: established, Feb. 2, 1932.

Red Army, Aug. 26, 1924.

Red Baron: dies, Apr. 21, 1918.

Red Brigade, Mar. 16, 1978; May 9, 1978; May 3, 1979.

Red Cross Day, May 8.

Red Cross Month, Apr. intro.

Red Cross Society, American, May 21, 1881.

Reddy, Helen, Oct. 25, 1941.

Redemption Day (Ghana), Jan. 13.

Redentore, II (Venice), Jul. intro.

Redford, Robert, Aug. 18, 1937.

Redgrave, Sir Michael, Mar. 20, 1908.

Redgrave, Vanessa, Jan. 30, 1937.

Redshirts, May 5, 1860.

red terror: begins, Dec. 20, 1917.

Reed, Donna, Jan. 27, 1921.

Reed, John, Oct. 22, 1887.

Reed, Oliver, Feb. 13, 1938.

Reed, Sir Carol, Dec. 30, 1906.

Reed, Stanley F(orman), Dec. 31, 1884.

Reed, Walter, Sep. 13, 1851.

Reese, Della, Jul. 6, 1932.

referendum and initiative devices: adopted by Oregon, Jun. 2, 1902.

Reform Act: passed in Great Britain, Jun. 4, 1832.

Reformation Day, Oct. 31.

reformed drunkards, patron of, Nov. 11.

Reform Movement's Anniversary (Yemen Arab Republic), Jun. 13.

refugees: South Vietnam, May 1, 1975.

Regatta Day (Hawaii), Mar. 26.

Regency Act, Feb. 5, 1811.

Rehabilitation Week, National, Sep. intro.

Rehnquist, William, Oct. 1, 1924.

Reichelderfer, F(rancis) W(ilton), Aug. 6, 1895.

Reichstag, first: opens, Mar. 21, 1871.

Reichstein, Tadeusz, Jul. 20, 1897.

Reid, Wallace, Apr. 15, 1890.

Reign of Terror, May 31, 1793; Jun. 2, 1793; Jun. 4, 1793; Jul. 28, 1794.

Reilly, Charles Nelson, Jan. 13, 1931.

Reims Cathedral: bombardment of, Sep. 19, 1914.

Reiner, Fritz, Dec. 19, 1888.

Reisenweber's Restaurant, Jan. 17, 1917.

religious education, patron of, Nov. 4.

Remagen Bridge, Mar. 7, 1945.

Remano, Umberto, Feb. 26, 1905.

Remarque, Erich Maria, Jun. 22, 1898.

Rembrandt, Jul. 15, 1606.

Remembrance Day (Canada, Bermuda), Nov. 11.

Remembrance Day (Cayman Islands), Nov. intro.

Remembrance Day (Papua New Guinea), Apr. 25.

Remembrance Day (Turks and Caicos Islands), Nov. 9.

Remington, Frederic, Oct. 4, 1861.

Remón, José Antonio: assassinated, Jan. 2, 1955.

Remsen, Ira, Feb. 10, 1846.

Renaissance, Roman, May 6, 1527.

Renan, Ernest, Feb. 28, 1823.

Renault, Mary, Sep. 4, 1905.

Rene, France-Albert, Nov. 16, 1935.

Renewal Anniversary of (Gabon Republic), Mar. 12.

Rennie, John, Jun. 7, 1761.

Renoir, Jean, Sep. 15, 1894.

Renoir, Pierre Auguste, Feb. 25, 1841.

Renovation Day (Gabon Republic), Mar. 12.

Renwick, James, Nov. 1, 1818.

repentant women, patron of, Jul. 22.

Representatives, U.S. House of, May 9, 1974.

Republic, Day of the (Yugoslavia), Nov. 29; Nov. 30.

Republican National Committee: first woman head of, Sep. 16, 1974.

Republic Anniversary Day (Sierra Leone), Apr. 19.

Republican Party: first state convention, Jul. 6, 1854.

Republic Day (Gambia), Feb. 18.

Republic Day (Guyana), Feb. 23.

Republic Day (Macao), Sep. 5.

Republic Day (Malawi), Jul. 6.

Republic Day (Maldives), Nov. 11; Nov. 12.

Republic Day (Malta), Dec. 13.

Republic Day (Portugal), Oct. 5.

Republic Day (Republic of South Africa, Namibia), May 31.

Republic Day (Trinidad, Tobago), Sep. 24.

Republic Day (Tunisia), Jul. 25.

Republic of China, Mar. 10, 1912.

Republic of Togo, Apr. 27, 1960.

Resaca de la Palma, Battle of, May 9, 1846.

Resistance Day (Burma), Mar. 27.

Resnais, Alain, Jun. 3, 1922.

Respect for the Aged Day (Japan), Sep. 15.

restaurateurs, patron of, Aug. 10.

Restif Nicolas-Edme, Oct. 23, 1734.

Restitution, Edict of, Mar. 6, 1629.

Reston, James Barrett, Nov. 3, 1909.

Restoration of Independence (Portugal), Dec. 1.

Restoration of the Republic (Dominican Republic), Aug. 16.

retirement age, mandatory, Apr. 6, 1978.

retreats, patron of, Jul. 31.

Reuben, David Robert, Nov. 29, 1933.

Reuben James, U.S.S.: sunk, Oct. 31, 1941.

Reuss, Henry S., Feb. 22, 1912.

Reuter, Baron Paul Julius von, Jul. 21, 1816.

Reuther, Walter (Philip), Sep. 1, 1907.

Revels, Hiram Rhodes, Sep. 1, 1822.

Revenue Cutter Service, Jan. 28, 1915.

Revere, Paul, Jan. 1, 1735; Apr. 18, 1775.

Revolution, American: begins, Apr. 19, 1775; Sep. 15, 1776.

Revolution, Anniversary of the (Algeria), Nov. 1.

Revolution Anniversary (Egypt), Jul. 23.

Revolution Anniversary (Panama), Oct. 11.

Revolution Anniversary (Somali Democratic Republic), Oct. 21.

Revolution Anniversary (Somali Democratic Republic), Oct. 22.

Revolutionary Council of Iran, Mar. 16, 1979.

Revolutionary Tribunal (Cheka): established, Dec. 20, 1917.

Revolutionary Tribunal (France): abolished, Dec. 15, 1794.

Revolution Day (Congo), Jul. 31.

Revolution Day (Guatemala), Oct. 20.

Revolution Day (Iran), Feb. 11.

Revolution Day (Sudan), May 25.

Revolution Day (Syria), Mar. 8.

Revolution Day (Upper Volta), Jan. 3.

Revolution Day (U.S.S.R.), Mar. 8.

Revolution of 1830 (France), Jul. 29, 1830.

Revolution of 1905 (Russia), Jan. 22, 1905.

Revolution of 1917 (Russia), Nov. 6, 1917.

Revolution of 1962, Anniversary of the (Yemen Arab Republic), Sep. 26.

Revson, Charles (Haskell), Oct. 11, 1906.

Rexroth, Kenneth, Dec. 22, 1905.

Reymont, Wladislaw Stanislaw, May 6, 1867.

Reynaud, Paul, Oct. 15, 1878.

Reynolds, Burt, Feb. 11, 1936.

Reynolds, Sir Joshua, Jul. 16, 1723.

Reza Khan, Feb. 21, 1921.

Rhapsody in Blue: premiere, Feb. 12, 1924.

Rhapsody on a Theme by Paganini: premiere, Nov. 7, 1934.

Rhee, Syngman (Republic of Korea): first President, Apr. 26, 1875; Aug. 15, 1948; Jun. 28, 1950; Sep. 29, 1950; Mar. 15, 1960.

Rheims (France): bombarded, Sep. 18, 1914.

Rhine, Mar. 7, 1945.

Rhine, J(oseph) B(anks), Sep. 19, 1895.

Rhineland Campaign, Sep. 15, 1944.

Rhode Island, Sep. 13, 1635; Mar. 24, 1644; May 4, 1776; May 29, 1790.

Rhodes, Cecil, Jul. 5, 1853; Oct. 29, 1889; Jul. 17, 1890; Jan. 06, 1896; Dec. 5, 1897.

Rhodes, John J., Sep. 18, 1916.

Rhodesia, name given, May 3, 1895; Dec. 31, 1963; Jan. 5, 1967; Apr. 10, 1968; Mar. 2, 1970; Apr. 4, 1975; Jul. 5, 1977; Mar. 14, 1978; Apr. 12, 1978; Feb. 28, 1979; Apr. 21, 1979; May 31, 1979; Apr. 17, 1980.

Rhodesia, Northern (Zambia), Jan. 22, 1964.

Rhodesia, Southern, Apr. 11, 1963.

Rhodesia, Southern, Apr. 13, 1964.

Ribbentrop, Joachim von, Apr. 30, 1893; executed, Oct. 16, 1946.

Ribicoff, Abraham A., Apr. 9, 1910.

Ricardo, David, Apr. 19, 1772.

Rice, Elmer (Leopold), Sep. 28, 1892.

Rice, (Henry) Grantland, Nov. 1, 1880.

Rich, Buddy, Jun. 30, 1917.

Richard (Duke of York), May 22, 1455.

Richard I (England), Sep. 8, 1157; Nov. 18, 1188; Jul. 6, 1189; Dec. 5, 1189; Jul. 1, 1190; Oct. 4, 1190; Jul. 12, 1191; Aug. 1, 1192; Dec. 21, 1192; Feb. 3, 1194; Apr. 17, 1194; Jul. 22, 1194; dies, Apr. 6, 1199.

Richard II (England), Jan. 6, 1367; Jun. 21, 1377; Jun. 22, 1377; Feb. 3, 1388; Sep. 30, 1399; murdered, Feb. 14, 1400.

Richard III (England), Oct. 2, 1452; Jun. 26, 1483; killed, Aug. 22, 1485.

Richard of Gloucester (England), Jun. 26, 1483.

Richard of York, Jul. 10, 1460; killed, Dec. 30, 1460.

Richards, Dickinson W., Jr., Oct. 30, 1895.

Richards, Laura Elizabeth, Feb. 27, 1850.

Richards, Theodore William, Jan. 31, 1868.

Richardson, Elliott: , Jul. 20, 1920; resigns Oct. 20, 1973.

Richardson, Henry Hobson, Sep. 29, 1838.

Richardson, Samuel, Aug. 19, 1689.

Richardson, Sir Owen Willans, Apr. 26, 1879.

Richardson, Sir Ralph David, Dec. 19, 1902.

Richelieu, Cardinal de: becomes first Chief Minister of France, Aug. 13, 1624; Nov. 11, 1630; Jan. 29, 1635.

Richelieu, Duc de (Armand Jean de Plessis), Sep. 9, 1585.

Richet, Charles R., Aug. 25, 1850.

Richman, Harry, Aug. 10, 1895.

Richmond (Virginia): surrender, Apr. 3, 1865.

Richter, Burton, Mar. 22, 1931.

Richter, Charles Francis, Apr. 26, 1900.

Richter, Hans, Apr. 4, 1843; Jun. 9, 1902.

Richter, Jean Paul Friedrich, Mar. 21, 1763.

Richthofen, Manfred von, May 2, 1892; dies Apr. 21, 1918.

Rickenbacker, Edward (Vernon), Oct. 8, 1890.

Rickey, Branch (Wesley), Dec. 20, 1881.

Rickover, Hyman George, Jan. 27, 1900.

Ride, Sally, May 26, 1951; Jun. 24, 1983.

Ridgway, Matthew B., Mar. 3, 1895; Dec. 26, 1950.

Riebeeck, Jan van, Apr. 21, 1634; Apr. 6, 1652.

Riemann, Georg Friedrich Bernhard, Sep. 17, 1826.

Riga, Treaty of, Mar. 18, 1921.

Riga (Latvia), Jan. 4, 1919.

Riggs, Bobby, Sep. 20, 1973.

Righting Day (Algeria), Jun. 19.

right to privacy, Jun. 7, 1965.

Riis, Jacob August, May 3, 1849.

Riley, James Whitcomb, Oct. 7, 1849.

Rilke, Rainer Maria, Dec. 4, 1875.

Rimbaud, (Jean Nicolas) Arthur, Oct. 20, 1854.

Rimski-Korsakov, Nicolai, Mar. 6, 1844.

Rimsky-Korsakov, Georgy, Dec. 26, 1901.

Rinehart, Mary Roberts, Aug. 12, 1876.

Rio, Declaration of: signed, Nov. 30, 1965.

Rio de Janeiro, Jan. 1, 1531.

Rio de Janeiro, Treaty of, Aug. 27, 1828.

Riotous Assemblies Act (South Africa), Sep. 15, 1977.

Ripley, George, Oct. 3, 1802.

Ripley, Robert Leroy, Dec. 25, 1893.

Ritchard, Cyril, Dec. 1, 1897.

Ritter, Johann Wilhelm, Dec. 16, 1776.

Ritter, Tex, Jan. 12, 1907.

Ritter, Thelma, Feb. 14, 1905.

Rivadavia, Bernardino, May 20, 1780.

Rivas Day Battle of (Costa Rica), Apr. 11.

Rivera, Diego, Dec. 8, 1886.

Rivers, Joan, Oct. 12, 1935.

Rivers, Larry, Aug. 17, 1923.

Rivers, L(ucius) Mendel, Sep. 28, 1905.

Rivers, William Halse, Mar. 12, 1864.

River Salado, Battle of, Oct. 30, 1340.

Rivières du Sud, Mar. 10, 1893.

Rivoli, Battle of, Jan. 14, 1797.

Rizal, José Mercado, Jun. 19, 1861.

Rizal Day (Philippines), Dec. 30.

Roa y Garcí, Raùl, Apr. 18, 1907.

Roach, Hal, Jan. 14, 1892.

Roanoke Island, N.C., Feb. 8, 1862.

Robards, Jason (Nelson), Jul. 22, 1922.

Robbe-Grillet, Alain, Aug. 18, 1922.

Robbia, Luca della, Dec. 22, 1400.

Robbins, Frederick Chapman, Aug. 25, 1916.

Robbins, Harold, May 21, 1916.

Robbins, Jerome, Oct. 11, 1918.

Robert, Henry Martyn, May 2, 1837.

Robert Bruce (Scotland), Oct. 14, 1322.

Robert E. Lee Day (Kentucky), Feb. 19.

Robert Green, Aug. 11, 1833.

Robert II (Scotland), Feb. 22, 1370; Mar. 2, 1316.

Robert III (Scotland): dies, Apr. 1, 1406.

Robert of Normandy, Jul. 19, 1101.

Robert's, J.J., Birthday (Liberia), Mar. 15.

Roberts, Field Marshal Lord, Jan. 10, 1900.

Roberts, Kenneth Lewis, Dec. 8, 1885.

Roberts, Lord Frederick, Mar. 13, 1900.

Roberts, Oral, Jan. 24, 1918.

Robertson, Cliff, Sep. 9, 1923.

Robeson, Paul, Apr. 9, 1898.

Robespierre, Maximilien François Marie Isidore de, May 6, 1758; Jun. 4, 1793; guillotined, Jul. 28, 1794.

Robin Moore: U.S. freighter sunk, May 21, 1941.

Robinson, Bill (Bojangles), May 25, 1878.

Robinson, Edward Arlington, Dec. 22, 1869.

Robinson, Edward G., Dec. 12, 1893.

Robinson, Frank, Aug. 31, 1935.

Robinson, Jackie Roosevelt, Jan. 31, 1919.

Robinson, James Harvey, Jun. 29, 1863.

Robinson, Maurice (Richard), Dec. 24, 1895.

Robinson, Sir Robert, Sep. 13, 1886.

Robinson, (*Sugar*) Ray, May 3, 1920.

Robson, May, Apr. 19, 1865.

Rochambeau, Comte de, Jul. 1, 1725.

Rochas, Alphonse Beau de, Apr. 9, 1815.

Rochefort, Victor-Henri, Jan. 31, 1830.

Rochelle, La (France), Jun. 23, 1372.

Rochester (Eddie Anderson), Sep. 18, 1905.

Rockefeller, David, Jun. 12, 1915.

Rockefeller, John D(avison), Jul. 9, 1839.

Rockefeller, John D(avison) IV, Jun. 18, 1937.

Rockefeller, John D. Jr., Jan. 29, 1874; Dec. 14, 1946.

Rockefeller, Laurance Spelman, May 26, 1910.

Rockefeller, Nelson, Jul. 8, 1908; nominated as Vice-President Aug. 20, 1974.

rocket: first liquid-fuel, Mar. 16, 1926; first to leave atmosphere, Mar. 22, 1946.

Rocket and Artillery Forces Day (U.S.S.R.), Nov. 19.

Rockne, Knute, Mar. 4, 1888.

Rockwell, George Lincoln: killed, Aug. 25, 1967.

Rockwell, Norman, Feb. 3, 1894.

Rocroi, Battle of, May 19, 1643.

Rod, Edouard, Mar. 31, 1857.

Rodgers, Bill, Dec. 23, 1947.

Rodgers, Richard, Jun. 28, 1902; Apr. 14, 1937; May 11, 1938; Nov. 23, 1938; Apr. 19, 1945; Apr. 7, 1949.

Rodgers and Hammerstein, Mar. 31, 1943; Mar. 30, 1951.

Rodin, Auguste, Nov. 12, 1840.

Rodney, Caesar, Oct. 7, 1728.

Roebling, John Augustus, Jun. 12, 1806.

Runeberg's Day (Finland), Feb. 5.
Runnymede (England), May 14, 1965.
Runyon, (Alfred) Damon, Oct. 4, 1884.
Rural Electrification Administration, May 11, 1935.
Rural Free Delivery: begins, Oct. 1, 1896.
Rush, Benjamin, Dec. 24, 1745.
Rushing, Jimmy, Aug. 26, 1903.
Rusk, Dean, Feb. 9, 1909.
Ruskin, John, Feb. 8, 1819.
Russell, Bertrand, May 18, 1872.
Russell, Henry Norris, Oct. 25, 1877.
Russell, Jane, Jun. 21, 1921.
Russell, Ken, Jul. 3, 1927.
Russell, Lillian, Dec. 4, 1861.
Russell, Pee Wee, Mar. 27, 1906.
Russell, Richard B., Nov. 2, 1897.
Russell, Rosalind, Jun. 4, 1911.
Russell, William Hepburn, Jan. 31, 1812.
Russia, Jan. 15, 1582; Seven Years' War, Jan. 10, 1757; Jan. 9, 1792; Jan. 23, 1793; French invasion, Jun. 22, 1812; emancipation of serfs, Mar. 3, 1861; May 15, 1867; first parliamentary elections, Apr. 1, 1906; declares war on Turkey, Nov. 2, 1914; Mar. 20, 1915; provisional government recognized, Mar. 22, 1917; Jan. 12, 1918; Jan. 28, 1918; German invasion, Jun. 22, 1941; May 15, 1955; Jan. 19, 1968. See also U.S.S.R.
Russia, patron of, Nov. 13; Nov. 30; Dec. 6.
Russian Church: confiscation by Bolsheviks, Dec. 17, 1917.
Russian monarchy: 1,000th anniversary, Sep. 20, 1862.
Russian Revolution, Jan. 7, 1895; Mar. 8, 1917; Mar. 10, 1917; Mar. 17, 1917; Mar. 27, 1917; May 24, 1917; Czar imprisoned in Siberia, Aug. 15, 1917; Nov. 7, 1917; Jan. 10, 1918; Jan. 4, 1919; Jan. 5, 1919; Jan. 30, 1920.
Russian serfs: liberation of, Apr. 3, 1861.
Russian State Bank: opens, Nov. 15, 1921.
Russian workers: establish first soviet, Oct. 26, 1905.
Russians, Jan. 26, 1915.
Russo-Finnish War, Nov. 30, 1939; ends, Mar. 12, 1940.
Russo-Japanese War, Feb. 4, 1904; Feb. 9, 1904; Jan. 2, 1905; May 27, 1905; ends, Aug. 9, 1905; ends, Sep. 5, 1905.
Russo-Turkish War, Sep. 14, 1829; treaty ending, Mar. 3, 1878.
Rustin, Bayard, Mar. 17, 1910.
Ruth, Babe, Feb. 6, 1895; Sep. 22, 1969.
Rutherford, Ann, Nov. 2, 1917.
Rutherford, Dame Margaret, May 11, 1892.
Rutherford, Ernest (1st Baron Rutherford of Nelson), Aug. 30, 1871.
Rutherford, Joseph Franklin, Nov. 8, 1869.
Ruyter, Michiel Adriaanszoon de, Mar. 24, 1607.
Ruzicka, Leopold, Sep. 13, 1887.
Rwanda, Republic of: independence, Jul. 1, 1962.
Ryan, Cornelius John, Jun. 5, 1920.
Ryan, Nolan, Jan. 31, 1947.
Ryan, Paddy, Feb. 7, 1883.
Ryan, Thomas Fortune, Oct. 17, 1851.
Ryan, Tubal Claude, Jan. 3, 1898.

Ryder, Albert Pinkham, Mar. 19, 1847.
Ryle, Sir Martin, Sep. 27, 1918.
Ryswyck, Treaty of, Sep. 20, 1697.
Ryuku Islands, Apr. 16, 1945.
Rzewuski, Count Henryk, May 3, 1791.

S

Saarinen, Eero, Aug. 20, 1910.
Saarinen, Eliel, Aug. 20, 1873.
Saavedra Lamas, Carlos de, Nov. 1, 1878.
Saavedra (Ramírez de Baquendano) Angel de, Mar. 10, 1791.
Sabah as-Salim as-Sabah (Kuwait), Nov. 24, 1965.
Saba Saba Peasants Day, Jul. 7.
Sabatier, Paul, Nov. 5, 1854.
Sabin, Albert Bruce, Aug. 26, 1906.
Sabbath, p. ix.
Sacco, Nicola, Apr. 22, 1891.
Sacerdotalis Caelibatus: encyclical, Jun. 23, 1967.
Sacher-Masoch, Leopold von, Jan. 27, 1836.
Sachs, Hans, Nov. 5, 1494.
Sachs, Nelly Leonie, Dec. 10, 1891.
Sackler, Howard, Dec. 19, 1929.
Sackville, Thomas, Jan. 18, 1562.
Sackville-West, Victoria Mary, Mar. 9, 1892.
Sacramento (California), Sep. 5, 1916.
Sadat, Anwar, Dec. 25, 1918; Mar. 28, 1973; Dec. 5, 1977; Sep. 17, 1978; Mar. 26, 1979.
Sade, Donatien Alphonse François de, Jun. 2, 1740.
Sadie Hawkins Day (United States), Nov. intro.
Sadler's Wells Theater, Jan. 6, 1931.
Sadowa, Battle of: ends, Jul. 3, 1866.
Safe Boating Week, National, Jun. intro.
Safer, Morley, Nov. 8, 1931.
Safety on the Streets Week, National, Oct. intro.
Safety Sabbath, National, Feb. intro.
Sagan, Carl, Nov. 9, 1934.
Sagan, Françoise, Jun. 21, 1935.
Sage, Margaret Olivia, Sep. 8, 1828.
Sage, Russell, Aug. 4, 1816.
Sagittarius, Dec. intro.; Nov. intro.
Sahara: French right to, Sep. 8, 1919.
Sa'id ibn Taimur (Oman), Jul. 23, 1970.
Saigon, Apr. 30, 1975; May 7, 1975.
Saigon, Treaty of, Apr. 13, 1862.
sailors, patron of, Apr. 2; Jun. 2; Sep. 22.
sailors in Ireland, patron of, Mar. 24.
Saint, Eva Marie, Jul. 4, 1924.
St. Abachum, Jan. 19.
St. Abbo of Fleury, Nov. 13.
St. Abdon, Jul. 30.
St. Abercius, Oct. 22.
St. Abibus, Nov. 14.
St. Abraham, Feb. 14; Dec. 6.
St. Abraham Kidunaia, Mar. 16.
St. Abraham of Rostov, Oct. 29.
St. Abraham of Smolensk, Aug. 21.
St. Acacius, Mar. 31; May 8; Jun. 22.
St. Acca, Oct. 20.
St. Achilleus, Apr. 23; May 12.

St. Acisclus, Nov. 17.
St. Adalbald of Ostrevant, Feb. 2.
St. Adalbert, Apr. 23; Jun. 20.
St. Adalbert of Egmond, Jun. 25.
St. Adalhard, Jan. 2.
St. Adam, Sep. 15.
St. Adamnan, Sep. 23.
St. Adamnan of Coldingham, Jan. 31.
St. Adauctus, Aug. 30.
St. Adaucus, Feb. 7.
St. Addai, Aug. 5.
St. Adela, Dec. 23.
St. Adelaide, Feb. 5; Dec. 16.
St. Adelemus, Jan. 30.
St. Adolf, Feb. 14.
St. Adrian, Jan. 9; Mar. 4; Mar. 5; Sep. 8.
St. Adrian III, Jul. 8.
St. Aedh Mac Bricc, Nov. 10.
St. Aelred, Mar. 3.
St. Aemilius, May 22.
St. Afan, Nov. 16.
St. Afra, Aug. 5.
St. Agape, Feb. 15; Apr. 2.
St. Agapitus, Aug. 18.
St. Agapitus I, Apr. 22.
St. Agapius, Aug. 19.
St. Agatha, Feb. 5.
St. Agathangelus, Jan. 23.
St. Agatho, Jan. 10.
St. Agathonice, Apr. 13.
St. Agathopus, Apr. 4.
St. Agericus, Dec. 1.
St. Agilbert, Apr. 1; Oct. 11.
St. Agnes, Jan. 21.
St. Agnes Eve (Great Britain), Jan. 20.
St. Agnes of Assisi, Nov. 16.
St. Agnes of Montepulciano, Apr. 20.
St. Agrecius, Jan. 13.
St. Agricola, Mar. 17; Nov. 4.
St. Agricolus, Sep. 2.
St. Agrippina, Jun. 23.
St. Aichardus, Sep. 15.
St. Aidan, Aug. 31.
St. Aidan of Ferns, Jan. 31.
St. Aigulf, May 22; Sep. 3.
St. Ailbhe, Sep. 12.
St. Alban, Jun. 22.
St. Alban of Mainz, Jun. 21.
St. Alban Roe, Jan. 21.
St. Albans, May 22, 1455; Feb. 17, 1461.
St. Albans, Council of, Aug. 4, 1213.
St. Alberic, Jan. 26.
St. Albert, Apr. 5; Sep. 25.
St. Albert of Cashel, Jan. 19.
St. Albert of Louvain, Nov. 21.
St. Albert of Trapani, Aug. 7.
St. Albert the Great, Nov. 15.
St. Albinus, Mar. 1.
St. Alburga, Dec. 25.
St. Alcmund, Mar. 19.
St. Aldate, Feb. 4.
St. Aldegundis, Jan. 30.
St. Aldemar, Mar. 24.
St. Aldhelm, May 25.
St. Aldric, Jan. 7.
St. Aled, Aug. 1.
St. Alexander, Feb. 26; Mar. 18; Apr. 22; May 3; May 29; Aug. 28.
St. Alexander Akimetes, Feb. 23.

St. Fachanan, Aug. 14.
St. Faith, Oct. 6.
St. Fantinus, Aug. 30.
St. Faro, Oct. 28.
St. Faustinus, Feb. 15; Jul. 29.
St. Faustus, Sep. 28; Oct. 13.
St. Febronia, Jun. 25.
St. Fechin, Jan. 20.
St. Felician, Jan. 24; Jun. 9.
St. Felicity, Mar. 7; Jul. 10.
St. Felicula, Jun. 13.
St. Felim, Aug. 9.
St. Felix, Mar. 26; Apr. 23; Jun. 11; Jul. 7; Jul. 12; Aug. 30; Oct. 23.
St. Felix I, May 30.
St. Felix II, Jul. 29.
St. Felix II (III), Mar. 1.
St. Felix III (IV), Sep. 22.
St. Felix of Bourges, Jan. 1.
St. Felix of Cantalice, May 18.
St. Felix of Dunwich, Mar. 8.
St. Felix of Nola, Jan. 14.
St. Felix of Valois, Nov. 20.
St. Ferdinand III of Castile, May 30.
St. Fergus, Nov. 27.
St. Ferminus, Sep. 25.
St. Ferreolus, Jun. 16; Sep. 18.
St. Ferrutio, Jun. 16.
St. Fiacre, Sep. 1.
St. Fidelis of Como, Oct. 28.
St. Fidelis of Signaringen, Apr. 24.
St. Fillan, Jan. 19.
St. Fina, Mar. 12.
St. Finan, Feb. 17.
St. Finan of Aberdeen, Mar. 18.
St. Finbar, Sep. 25.
St. Finnian Lobhar, Mar. 16.
St. Finnian of Clonard, Dec. 12.
St. Finnian of Moville, Sep. 10.
St. Fintan, Feb. 17.
St. Fintan of Rheinau, Nov. 15.
St. Fintan of Taghmon, Oct. 21.
St. Flannan, Dec. 18.
St. Flavian, Feb. 18; Jul. 20.
St. Flora, Nov. 24.
St. Flora of Beaulieu, Oct. 5.
St. Florentius, Nov. 7.
St. Florian, May 4.
St. Floribert, Apr. 27.
St. Foillan, Oct. 31.
St. Forannan, Apr. 30.
St. Fortunatus, Apr. 23; Jun. 11.
St. Franca of Piacenza, Apr. 26.
St. Frances of Rome, Mar. 9.
St. Franchea, Mar. 21.
St. Francis Borgia, Oct. 10.
St. Francis Caracciolo, Jun. 4.
St. Francis de Sales, Jan. 24.
St. Francis di Girolamo, May 11.
St. Francis of Assisi, Oct. 4.
St. Francis of Camporosso, Sep. 26.
St. Francis of Paola, Apr. 2.
St. Francis of Pesaro, Oct. 1.
St. Francis Solano, Jul. 13.
St. Francis Xavier, Dec. 3.
St. Francis Xavier Bianchi, Jan. 31.
St. Frederick, Jul. 18.
St. Fremund, May 11.
St. Frideswide, Oct. 19.

St. Fridolin, Mar. 6.
St. Frigidian, Mar. 18.
St. Frithebert, Dec. 23.
St. Frithestan, Sep. 10.
St. Froilan, Oct. 3.
St. Fronto, Oct. 25.
St. Fructuosus, Jan. 21; Apr. 16.
St. Frumentius, Oct. 27.
St. Fulbert, Apr. 10.
St. Fulgentius, Jan. 1.
St. Fulrad, Jul. 16.
St. Fursey, Jan. 16.
St. Gabriel Possenti, Feb. 27.
St. Gabriel the Archangel, Mar. 24.
St. Gaius, Apr. 22.
St. Galation, Nov. 5.
St. Galdinus, Apr. 18.
St. Gall, Jul. 1; Oct. 16.
St. Gallicanus, Jun. 25.
St. Gatian, Dec. 18.
St. Gaucherius, Apr. 9.
St. Gaudentius, Oct. 25.
St. Gaurinus, Feb. 6.
St. Gelasius I, Nov. 21.
St. Gemma Galgani, Apr. 11.
St. Genesius, Jun. 3.
St. Genesius of Arles, Aug. 25.
St. Genesius the Comedian, Aug. 25.
St. Geneviève, Jan. 3.
St. Gengulf, May 11.
St. Genulf, Jan. 17.
St. George, Feb. 21; Apr. 23; Oct. 25.
St. George Mtasmindeli, Jun. 27.
St. George's Day (England), Apr. 23.
St. George the Younger, Apr. 7.
St. Gerald of Aurillac, Oct. 13.
St. Gerald of Mayo, Mar. 13.
St. Gerard, Apr. 23; Sep. 24.
St. Gerardin, Nov. 8.
St. Gerard Majella, Oct. 16.
St. Gerard of Brogne, Oct. 3.
St. Gerasimus, Mar. 5.
St. Gerebernus, May 15.
St. Geremarus, Sep. 24.
St. Gereon and his Companions, Oct. 10.
St. Gerlac, Jan. 5.
St. Gerland, Feb. 25.
St. Germain, Edict of, Jan. 17, 1562.
St. Germain, Peace of, Aug. 8, 1570.
St. Germain, Treaty of, Sep. 10, 1919.
St. Germain-en-Laye, Treaty of, Mar. 29, 1632.
St. Germaine of Pibrac, Jun. 15.
St. Germanicus, Jan. 19.
St. Germanus, May 12; May 28; Jun. 28; Jul. 31; Oct. 30.
St. Germanus of Granfel, Feb. 21.
St. Germanus of Man, Jul. 3.
St. Germerius, May 16.
St. Geroldus, Apr. 19.
St. Gerontius, May 9.
St. Gertrude of Nivelles, Mar. 17.
St. Gertrude the Great, Nov. 16.
St. Gervase, Jun. 19.
St. Gervinus, Mar. 3.
St. Getulius, Jun. 10.
St. Gibrian, May 8.
St. Gilbert of Caithness, Apr. 1.
St. Gilbert of Sempringham, Feb. 4.

St. Gildas the Wise, Jan. 29.
St. Giles, Sep. 1.
St. Gislenus, Oct. 9.
St. Gleb, Jul. 24.
St. Glyceria, May 13.
St. Glywys, May 3.
St. Goar, Jul. 6.
St. Goban, Jun. 20.
St. Gobnet, Feb. 11.
St. Godeberta, Apr. 11.
St. Godehard, May 4.
St. Godeleva, Jul. 6.
St. Godfrey, Nov. 8.
St. Godric, May 21.
St. Goericus, Sep. 19.
St. Gohard, Jun. 25.
St. Goran, Apr. 7.
St. Gordian, May 10.
St. Gorgonia, Dec. 9.
St. Gorgonius, Mar. 12; Sep. 9.
St. Gotthard Tunnel, May 20, 1882.
St. Gottschalk, Jun. 7.
St. Govan, Mar. 26.
St. Gregory, Jan. 4; Mar. 9; Nov. 17; Nov. 23.
St. Gregory Barbarigo, Jun. 17.
St. Gregory III, Dec. 10.
St. Gregory Makar, Mar. 16.
St. Gregory Nazianzen, Jan. 2.
St. Gregory of Spoleto, Dec. 23.
St. Gregory of Utrecht, Aug. 25.
St. Gregory the Enlightener, Sep. 30.
St. Gregory the Wonderworker, Nov. 17.
St. Gregory VII, May 25.
St. Grimbald, Jul. 8.
St. Grimonia, Sep. 7.
St. Gualfardus, Apr. 30.
St. Guarinus, Bishop of Sion, Jan. 6.
St. Gudula, Jan. 8.
St. Gudwal, Jun. 6.
St. Guibert, May 23.
St. Guinoch, Apr. 13.
St. Gummarus, Oct. 11.
St. Gundleus, Mar. 29.
St. Guntramnus, Mar. 28.
St. Gurius, Nov. 15.
St. Guthlac, Apr. 11.
St. Guy of Anderlecht, Sep. 12.
St. Guy of Pomposa, Mar. 31.
St. Gwen of Cornwall, Oct. 18.
St. Gwen Teirbron of Brittany, Jun. 1.
St. Gwinear, Mar. 23.
St. Gwladys, Mar. 29.
St. Gwythian, Nov. 1.
St. Hallvard, May 15.
St. Hedda, Jul. 7.
St. Hedwig, Oct. 16.
St. Hegesippus, Apr. 7.
St. Heimrad, Jun. 28.
St. Heldrad, Mar. 13.
St. Helen, Aug. 18.
St. Helen of Skövde, Jul. 31.
St. Helena, May 21, 1502; Jan. 1, 1673; Napoleon arrives, Oct. 15, 1815; May 5, 1821; Apr. 22, 1834.
St. Helens, Mount: erupts, May 18, 1980.
St. Helier, Jul. 16.
St. Heliodorus, Jul. 3.
St. Helladius, Feb. 18.
St. Henry, Jan. 19.

St. Jutta, May 5.
St. Juvenal, May 3.
St. Juventinus, Jan. 25.
St. Kea, Nov. 5.
St. Kenelm, Jul. 17.
St. Kentigern, Jan. 14.
St. Kentigerna, Jan. 7.
St. Kessog, Mar. 10.
St. Kevin, Jun. 3.
St. Kew (Cornwall), patron of, Feb. 8.
St. Keyne, Oct. 8.
St. Kieran, Sep. 9.
St. Kieran of Saighir, Mar. 5.
St. Kilian, Jul. 8; Nov. 13.
St. Kinemark, Sep. 8.
St. Kitts, Nov. 1, 1964.
St. Kitts-Nevis, Feb. 16, 1967.
St. Kyned, Aug. 1.
St. Ladislaus of Hungary, Jun. 27.
St. Lambert, Apr. 14; May 26; Sep. 17.
St. Landelinus, Jun. 15.
St. Landericus, Jun. 10.
St. Landoald, Mar. 19.
St. Laserian, Apr. 18.
St. Laudus, Sep. 22.
St. Laurence, Aug. 10.
St. Laurence, Archbishop of Canterbury, Feb. 3.
St. Laurence, Bishop of Spoleto, Feb. 3.
St. Laurence Giustiniani, Sep. 5.
St. Laurence O'Toole, Nov. 14.
St. Laurent, Louis Stephen, Feb. 1, 1882.
St. Laurent, Yves (Mathieu), Aug. 1, 1936.
St. Laurentius, Jun. 3.
St. Lawrence of Brindisi, Jul. 21.
St. Lawrence River, Feb. 4, 1629; Mar. 29, 1632.
St. Lawrence Seaway: opens, Jun. 26, 1959.
St. Lazarus, Feb. 11; Dec. 17.
St. Leander, Feb. 27.
St. Lebuin, Nov. 12.
St. Lelia, Aug. 11.
St. Leo, Feb. 18; May 25.
St. Leo II, Jul. 3.
St. Leo III, Jun. 12.
St. Leo IV, Jul. 17.
St. Leo IX, Apr. 19.
St. Leobinus, Mar. 14.
St. Leocadia, Dec. 9.
St. Leocritia, Mar. 15.
St. Leodegarius, Oct. 2.
St. Leonard of Noblac, Nov. 6.
St. Leonard of Port Maurice, Nov. 26.
St. Leonard of Vandoeuvre, Oct. 15.
St. Leonides, Apr. 22.
St. Leontius, May 23.
St. Leopold of Austria, Nov. 15.
St. Leopold of Gaiche, Apr. 2.
St. Leo the Great, Nov. 10.
St. Leutfridus, Jun. 21.
St. Lewina, Jul. 24.
St. Liberatus, Aug. 17.
St. Liborius, Jul. 23.
St. Licinius, Feb. 13.
St. Lide, Aug. 8.
St. Lietbertus, Jun. 23.
St. Limnaeus, Feb. 22.
St. Linus, Sep. 23.
St. Lioba, Sep. 28.

St. Liphardus, Jun. 3.
St. Liudhard, May 7.
St. Livinus, Nov. 12.
St. Loman, Feb. 17.
St. Longinus, Mar. 15.
St. Louis, Missouri, Feb. 15, 1764.
St. Louis, Sons of, Apr. 7, 1823.
St. Louisa de Marillac, Mar. 15.
St. Louis Bertrand, Oct. 9.
St. Louis Mary of Montfort, Apr. 28.
St. Louis of Anjou, Aug. 19.
St. Louis of France, Aug. 25.
St. Lucia, Nov. 1, 1964; Feb. 16, 1967; Feb. 21, 1979.
St. Lucia Day (Sweden), Dec. 13.
St. Lucian, Oct. 26.
St. Lucian of Antioch, Jan. 7.
St. Lucian of Beauvais, Jan. 8.
St. Lucillian, Jun. 3.
St. Lucius, Feb. 11; Feb. 24; Mar. 4; Oct. 19; Dec. 3.
St. Lucy, Dec. 13.
St. Lucy Filippini, Mar. 25.
St. Ludan, Feb. 12.
St. Ludger, Mar. 26.
St. Ludmila, Sep. 16.
St. Ludolf, Mar. 29.
St. Lufthildis, Jan. 23.
St. Luke, Feast of, Oct. 18.
St. Luke the Younger, Feb. 7.
St. Lull, Oct. 16.
St. Lupicinus, Feb. 28.
St. Lupus, Jul. 29; Sep. 1.
St. Lutgardis, Jun. 16.
St. Luxorius, Aug. 21.
St. Mabyn, Nov. 18.
St. Macanisius, Sep. 3.
St. Macarius, Mar. 10.
St. Macarius of Alexandria, Jan. 2.
St. Macarius of Ghent, Apr. 10.
St. Macarius the Elder, Jan. 15.
St. Macarius the Wonder-worker, Apr. 1.
St. Macartan, Mar. 26.
St. Macedonius, Jan. 24.
St. Machan, Sep. 28.
St. Machar, Nov. 12.
St. Macrina the Elder, Jan. 14.
St. Macrina the Younger, Jul. 19.
St. Madelgisilus, May 30.
St. Madron, May 17.
St. Maelruain, Jul. 7.
St. Mafalda, May 2.
St. Magenulf, Oct. 5.
St. Maglorius, Oct. 23.
St. Magnericus, Jul. 25.
St. Magnus of Orkney, Apr. 16.
St. Maharsapor, Oct. 10.
St. Maimbod, Jan. 23.
St. Majolus, May 11.
St. Malachy, Nov. 3.
St. Malchus, Oct. 21.
St. Mallonus, Oct. 22.
St. Malo, Nov. 15.
St. Mamas, Aug. 17.
St. Mamertus, May 11.
St. Manacca, Oct. 14.
St. Manaccus, Aug. 3.
St. Manechildis, Oct. 14.
St. Mappalicus, Apr. 17.

St. Marcella, Jan. 31.
St. Marcellian, Jun. 18.
St. Marcellina, Jul. 17.
St. Marcellinus, Apr. 6; Apr. 20; Jun. 2.
St. Marcellus, Aug. 14; Aug. 27; Sep. 4; Nov. 1.
St. Marcellus I, Jan. 16.
St. Marcellus Akimetes, Dec. 29.
St. Marcellus the Centurion, Oct. 30.
St. Marchelm, Jul. 14.
St. Marcian, Jan. 10; Apr. 20; Jun. 17; Oct. 26; Nov. 2.
St. Marciana, Jan. 9.
St. Marculf, May 1.
St. Mardellinus, Apr. 26.
St. Margaret, Jul. 20.
St. Margaret Mary, Oct. 17.
St. Margaret Mary Alacoque, Oct. 16.
St. Margaret of Cortona, Feb. 22.
St. Margaret of England, Feb. 3.
St. Margaret of Hulme, May 22.
St. Margaret of Hungary, Jan. 26.
St. Margaret of Scotland, Nov. 16.
St. Mari, Aug. 5.
St. Marian, Apr. 30.
St. Mariana of Quito, May 26.
St. Marina, Feb. 12.
St. Marinus, Mar. 3; Sep. 4.
St. Marinus Day (San Marino), Sep. 3.
St. Marius, Jan. 19; Jan. 27.
St. Mark, Mar. 29; Apr. 25; Jun. 18; Oct. 7.
St. Maro, Feb. 14.
St. Maron's Day (Lebanon), Feb. 9.
St. Martha, Jan. 19; Jul. 29.
St. Martial, Jun. 30; Oct. 13.
St. Martin, Mar. 20; Oct. 23; Nov. 11.
St. Martin I, Apr. 13.
St. Martin de Porres, Nov. 3.
St. Martin of Vertou, Oct. 23.
St. Martina, Jan. 30.
St. Martinian, Oct. 16.
St. Martinian the Hermit, Feb. 13.
St. Martius, Apr. 13.
St. Martyrius, May 29.
St. Maruthas, Dec. 4.
St. Mary, Nov. 1; Nov. 24.
St. Mary di Rosa, Dec. 15.
St. Mary Euphrasia Pelletier, Apr. 24.
St. Mary Frances of Naples, Oct. 6.
St. Mary Goretti, Jul. 6.
St. Mary Magdalen, Jul. 22.
St. Mary Magdalen Postel, Jul. 16.
St. Mary Mazzarello, May 14.
St. Mary Michaela Desmaisières, Aug. 25.
St. Mary of Cerevellon, Sep. 19.
St. Mary of Cleophas, Apr. 9.
St. Mary of Egypt, Apr. 2.
St. Maternus, Sep. 14.
St. Matilda, Mar. 14.
St. Matrona, Mar. 15.
St. Matthew, Feast of, Sep. 21.
St. Matthias, Feast of, May 14.
St. Matthias the Apostle, Feb. 24.
St. Maturinus, Nov. 1.
St. Maughold, Apr. 27.
St. Maura, May 3.
St. Maura, Jul. 13.
St. Maura of Troyes, Sep. 21.
St. Maurice, Sep. 22.

St. Maurice of Carnoét, Oct. 13.
St. Maurilius, Sep. 13.
St. Mauruntius, May 5.
St. Maurus, Oct. 5.
St. Mawes, Nov. 18.
St. Mawnan, Dec. 18.
St. Maxellendis, Nov. 13.
St. Maxentia, Nov. 20.
St. Maxentius, Jun. 26.
St. Maximian, Aug. 21.
St. Maximilian, Mar. 12; Oct. 12.
St. Maximilian Kolbe, Aug. 14.
St. Maximinus, Jan. 25; May 29.
St. Maximinus of Aix, Jun. 8.
St. Maximus, Apr. 14; Apr. 30; Jun. 25; Nov. 27.
St. Maximus the Confessor, Aug. 13.
St. Mechtildis, Nov. 16.
St. Mechtildis of Edelstetten, May 31.
St. Medard, Jun. 8.
St. Medericus, Aug. 29.
St. Méen, Jun. 21.
St. Meingold, Feb. 8.
St. Meinrad, Jan. 21.
St. Mel, Feb. 6.
St. Melaine, Nov. 6.
St. Melangell, May 27.
St. Melania the Younger, Dec. 31.
St. Melchu, Feb. 6.
St. Meletius, Feb. 12.
St. Meleusippus, Jan. 17.
St. Melito, Apr. 1.
St. Mellitus, Apr. 24.
St. Melorus, Oct. 1.
St. Mennas, Aug. 25; Nov. 11.
St. Mercurius, Nov. 25.
St. Merewenna, Feb. 10.
St. Meriadoc, Jun. 7.
St. Mesrop, Feb. 19.
St. Methodius, Feb. 14.
St. Methodius I, Jun. 14.
St. Methodius of Olympus, Sep. 18.
St. Metrophanes, Jun. 4.
St. Michael and All the Angels, Feast of, Sep. 29.
St. Michael de Sanctis, Apr. 10.
St. Michael Garicoîts, May 14.
St. Michael of Chernigov, Sep. 21.
St. Milburga, Feb. 23.
St. Mildgyth, Jan. 17.
St. Mildred, Jul. 13.
St. Miltiades, Dec. 10.
St. Minver, Nov. 24.
St. Mirin, Sep. 15.
St. Mochoemoc, Mar. 13.
St. Mochta, Aug. 19.
St. Mochua of Timahoe, Dec. 23.
St. Modan, Feb. 4.
St. Modestus, Jun. 15.
St. Modoaldus, May 12.
St. Modomnoc, Feb. 13.
St. Modwenna, Jul. 6.
St. Molaug, Jun. 25.
St. Moling, Jun. 17.
St. Mommolinus, Oct. 16.
St. Monegundis, Jul. 2.
St. Monenna, Jul. 6.
St. Monica, Aug. 27.
St. Montanus, Feb. 24.

St. Morand, Jun. 3.
St. Moses, Feb. 7; Nov. 25.
St. Moses the Black, Aug. 28.
St. Mucius, May 13.
St. Mura, Mar. 12.
St. Murtagh, Aug. 12.
St. Nabor, Jul. 12.
St. Narcissus, Oct. 29.
St. Natalia, Sep. 8.
St. Nathalan, Jan. 19.
St. Nathy, Aug. 9.
St. Nazaire, Mar. 28, 1942.
St. Nazarius, Jul. 28.
St. Nectan, Jun. 17.
St. Nectarius, Oct. 11.
St. Neon, Aug. 23.
St. Neot, Jul. 31.
St. Nemesius, Dec. 19.
St. Nereus, May 12.
St. Nerses, Nov. 20.
St. Nerses I, Nov. 19.
St. Nerses Klaiëtsi, Aug. 13.
St. Nerses Lampronatsi, Jul. 17.
St. Nestabus, Sep. 8.
St. Nestor, Feb. 26; Sep. 8.
St. Nicander, Jun. 17.
St. Nicarete, Dec. 27.
St. Nicasius, Dec. 14.
St. Nicephorus, Feb. 9; Mar. 13.
St. Nicetas, Jan. 31; Apr. 2; Jun. 22.
St. Nicetas of Constantinople, Oct. 6.
St. Nicetas of Pereaslau, May 24.
St. Nicetas the Goth, Sep. 15.
St. Nicetius, Feb. 8; Apr. 2; Dec. 5.
St. Nicholas, Dec. 6.
St. Nicholas I, Nov. 13.
St. Nicholas of Tolentino, Sep. 10.
St. Nicholas Pieck and his companions, Jul. 9.
St. Nicholas Studites, Feb. 4.
St. Nicholas the Pilgrim, Jun. 2.
St. Nicholas von Flüe, Mar. 22.
St. Nicomedes, Sep. 15.
St. Nikon (Metanoeite), Nov. 26.
St. Nilus of Rossano, Sep. 26.
St. Nilus the Elder, Nov. 12.
St. Ninian, Sep. 16.
St. Ninnoc, Jun. 4.
St. Niõ, Dec. 15.
St. Non, Mar. 3.
St. Nonna, Aug. 5.
St. Norbert, Jun. 6.
St. Notburga, Sep. 14.
St. Nothelm, Oct. 17.
St. Nunilo, Oct. 22.
St. Nympha, Nov. 10.
St. Oda, Jul. 4.
St. Odilia, Dec. 13.
St. Odilio, Jan. 1.
St. Odo of Cluny, Nov. 18.
St. Odulf, Jun. 12.
St. Oengus, Mar. 11.
St. Offa of Essex, Dec. 15.
St. Olaf, Jul. 29.
St. Olga, Jul. 11.
St. Ollegarius, Mar. 6.
St. Olympias, Dec. 17.
St. Onesimus, Feb. 16.
St. Onuphrius, Jun. 12.

St. Opatatus, Apr. 16.
St. Opportuna, Apr. 22.
St. Optatus, Jun. 4.
St. Orsiesius, Jun. 15.
St. Osburga, Mar. 30.
St. Osmund, Dec. 4.
St. Oswald, Aug. 9.
St. Oswald of Worcester, Feb. 28.
St. Oswin, Aug. 20.
St. Osyth, Oct. 7.
St. Otger, May 8.
St. Otteran, Oct. 27.
St. Otto, Jul. 2.
St. Pachomius, May 9.
St. Pacian, Mar. 9.
St. Pacifico of San Severino, Sep. 24.
St. Palladius, Jul. 7.
St. Pambo, Jul. 18.
St. Pammachius, Aug. 30.
St. Pamphilus, Apr. 28; Jun. 1.
St. Pancras, Apr. 2; May 12.
St. Pandonia, Aug. 26.
St. Pantaenus, Jul. 7.
St. Pantaleon, Jul. 27.
St. Paphnutius, Sep. 11.
St. Papylus, Apr. 13.
St. Paregorius, Feb. 18.
St. Parisio, Jun. 11.
St. Parthenius, May 19.
St. Paschal I, Feb. 11.
St. Paschal Baylon, May 17.
St. Paschasius Radbertus, Apr. 26.
St. Pastor, Aug. 6.
St. Paternus, Apr. 16.
St. Paternus of Abdinghof, Apr. 10.
St. Patiens, Sep. 11.
St. Patricia, Aug. 25.
St. Patrick, Mar. 17.
St. Patrick's Day, Mar. intro.
St. Patrick's Day (Ireland), Mar. 17.
St. Patrick's Day: Irish bank holiday, Mar. 23, 1903.
St. Patroclus, Jan. 21.
St. Paul, Jan. 15; Jun. 26; Jun. 29; Jul. 25.
St. Paul I, Jun. 7; Jun. 28.
St. Paul IV, Aug. 28.
St. Paul Aurelian, Mar. 12.
St. Paul Miki, Feb. 6.
St. Paul of Cyprus, Mar. 17.
St. Paul of Latros, Dec. 15.
St. Paul of Narbonne, Mar. 22.
St. Paul of the Cross, Oct. 19.
St. Paul the Simple, Mar. 7.
St. Paula, Jan. 26.
St. Paulinus, Jan. 28; Aug. 31; Oct. 10.
St. Paulinus of Nola, Jun. 22.
St. Paul's Shipwreck (Malta), Feb. 10.
St. Pega, Jan. 8.
St. Pelagia of Antioch, Jun. 9.
St. Pelagia of Tarsus, May 4.
St. Pelagia the Penitent, Oct. 8.
St. Pelagius, Jun. 26.
St. Peleus, Sep. 19.
St. Peregrine, May 16.
St. Peregrine Laziosi, May 1.
St. Pergentinus, Jun. 3.
St. Perpetua, Mar. 7.
St. Perpetuus, Apr. 8.

St. Peter, Jan. 9; Mar. 12; Apr. 26; May 8; Jun. 2; Jun. 29; Nov. 26.
St. Peter ad Vincula, Aug. 1.
St. Peter Arbues, Sep. 17.
St. Peter Balsam, Jan. 3.
St. Peter Canisius, Dec. 21.
St. Peter Chrysologus, Jul. 30.
St. Peter Claver, Sep. 9.
St. Peter Damian, Feb. 21; Feb. 23.
St. Peter Fourier, Dec. 9.
St. Peter Julian Eymard, Aug. 3.
St. Peter Mary Chanel, Apr. 28.
St. Peter Nolasco, Jan. 28.
St. Peter of Alcántara, Oct. 19.
St. Peter of Atroa, Jan. 1.
St. Peter of Canterbury, Dec. 30.
St. Peter of Cava, Mar. 4.
St. Peter of Chavanon, Sep. 11.
St. Peter of Lampsacus, May 15.
St. Peter of Mount Athos, Jun. 12.
St. Peter of Verona, Apr. 29.
St. Peter Orseolo, Jan. 10.
St. Peter Regalatus, May 13.
St. Petersburg (Russia), May 27, 1703; ship canal, May 27, 1885; Jan. 22, 1905; Apr. 22, 1920.
St. Peter's Kaiserwerth, patron of, Mar. 1.
St. Peter Thomas, Jan. 28.
St. Petroc, Jun. 4.
St. Petronax, May 6.
St. Petronilla, May 31.
St. Petronius, Oct. 4.
St. Pharaídis, Jan. 4.
St. Philastrius, Jul. 18.
St. Phileas, Feb. 4.
St. Philemon, Mar. 8.
St. Philibert, Aug. 20.
St. Philip, Bishop of Heraclea, Oct. 22.
St. Philip Benizi, Aug. 23.
St. Philip Neri, May 26.
St. Philip of Zell, May 3.
St. Philip the Deacon, Jun. 6.
St. Philogonius, Dec. 20.
St. Philomena, Aug. 10.
St. Phocas, Sep. 22.
St. Phocas of Antioch, Mar. 5.
St. Phoebe, Sep. 3.
St. Photina, Mar. 20.
St. Pierius, Nov. 4.
St. Pionius, Feb. 1.
St. Piran, Mar. 5.
St. Pirminus, Nov. 3.
St. Pius I, Jul. 11.
St. Pius V, Apr. 30.
St. Pius X, Aug. 21.
St. Placid, Oct. 5.
St. Plato, Apr. 4.
St. Plechelm, May 8.
St. Plegmund, Aug. 2.
St. Poemen, Aug. 27.
St. Pollio, Apr. 28.
St. Polycarp, Feb. 23.
St. Polyeuctus, Feb. 13.
St. Pompilio Pirrotti, Jul. 15.
St. Pontian, Aug. 13.
St. Pontius, May 14.
St. Poppo, Jan. 25.
St. Porcarius, Aug. 12.
St. Porphyry, Feb. 26.

St. Possidius, May 16.
St. Potamon, May 18.
St. Pothinus, Jun. 2.
St. Praejectus, Jan. 25.
St. Praetextatus, Feb. 24.
St. Praxedes, Jul. 21.
St. Primus, Jun. 9.
St. Prisca, Jan. 18; Jul. 8.
St. Priscilla, Jan. 16.
St. Priscus, May 26.
St. Priscus of Capua, Sep. 1.
St. Probus, Oct. 11.
St. Processus and Martinian, Jul. 2.
St. Proclus, Oct. 23.
St. Procopius, Jul. 8.
St. Proculus, Jun. 1.
St. Prosper, Jun. 25.
St. Prosper of Aquitaine, Jun. 25.
St. Proterius, Feb. 28.
St. Prudentius, Apr. 6.
St. Ptolemaeus, Oct. 19.
St. Publia, Oct. 9.
St. Publius, Jan. 25.
St. Pudens, May 19.
St. Pudentiana, May 19.
St. Pulcheria, Sep. 10.
St. Quadratus, May 26.
St. Quenburga, Aug. 31.
St. Quentin, Battle of, Aug. 10, 1557.
St. Quintinus, Oct. 31.
St. Quirinus, Jun. 4.
St. Quiteria, May 22.
St. Radbod, Nov. 29.
St. Radegund, Aug. 13.
St. Rainerius, Jun. 17.
St. Ralph, Jun. 21.
St. Raphaela Mary, Jan. 6.
St. Raymond of Peñafort, Jan. 7.
St. Raymund Nonnatus, Aug. 31.
St. Raymund of Toulouse, Jul. 8.
St. Regina, Sep. 7.
St. Regulus, Mar. 30.
St. Reineldis, Jul. 16.
St. Reinold, Jan. 7.
St. Rembert, Feb. 4.
St. Remigius, Oct. 1.
St. Reparata, Oct. 8.
St. Respicius, Nov. 10.
St. Restituta of Sora, May 27.
St. Revocatus, Mar. 7.
St. Richard, Feb. 7; Jun. 9.
St. Richardis, Sep. 18.
St. Richard of Wyche, Apr. 2.
St. Richarius, Apr. 26.
St. Richimir, Jan. 17.
St. Rictrudis, May 12.
St. Rigobert, Jan. 4.
St. Rita of Cascia, May 22.
St. Robert, Jun. 7.
St. Robert Ballarmine, Sep. 17.
St. Robert of Chaise-Dieu, Apr. 17.
St. Robert of Molesmes, Apr. 29.
St. Rock, Aug. 16.
St. Roderic, Mar. 13.
St. Rogatian, May 24.
St. Romanus, Feb. 28; May 22; Aug. 9; Oct. 23.
St. Romanus of Antioch, Nov. 18.
St. Romanus the Melodist, Oct. 1.

St. Romaric, Dec. 8.
St. Romualdo, Jun. 19.
St. Romula and her companions, Jul. 23.
St. Romulus, Jul. 6.
St. Ronan, Feb. 7; Jun. 1.
St. Rosalia, Sep. 4.
St. Rose of Lima (Peru), Aug. 23.
St. Rose of Lima (Peru), Aug. 30.
St. Rose of Viterbo, Sep. 4.
St. Ruadan of Lothra, Apr. 15.
St. Rudesind, Mar. 1.
St. Ruffin, Jul. 24.
St. Rufina, Jul. 10; Jul. 19.
St. Rufinus, Jun. 14.
St. Rufus of Capua, Aug. 27.
St. Rumold, Jul. 3.
St. Rumon, Aug. 30.
St. Rumwald, Nov. 3.
St. Rupert, Mar. 29; May 15.
St. Rusticus, Oct. 9; Oct. 26.
St. Sabas, Dec. 5.
St. Sabas the Goth, Apr. 12.
St. Sabian, Jan. 29.
St. Sabina, Aug. 29.
St. Sabinus, Jan. 17; Feb. 9; Dec. 30.
St. Sadoth, Feb. 20.
St. Saethrith, Jan. 10.
St. Salaberga, Sep. 22.
St. Salome, Jun. 29.
St. Salvator of Horta, Mar. 18.
St. Salvius, Jan. 11; Jun. 26; Oct. 28.
St. Samonas, Nov. 14.
St. Samson, Jul. 28.
St. Samson of Constantinople, Jun. 27.
St. Samthann, Dec. 18.
St. Samuel, Feb. 16.
St. Sanchia, Jun. 17.
St. Sanctius, Jun. 5.
St. Sapor, Nov. 30.
St. Saturninus, Feb. 11; Mar. 7; Nov. 29.
St. Saturus, Mar. 7; Mar. 29.
St. Satyrus, Sep. 17.
St. Sava, Jan. 14.
St. Savin, Oct. 9.
St. Scholastica, Feb. 10.
St. Sebald, Aug. 19.
St. Sebastian, Jan. 20.
St. Sebastian Day (Rio de Janeiro, Brazil), Jan. 20.
St. Sebbe, Sep. 1.
St. Secunda, Jul. 10.
St. Secundinus, Nov. 27.
St. Secundulus, Mar. 7.
St. Seirol, Feb. 1.
St. Senan of Scattery Island, Mar. 8.
St. Senator, May 28.
St. Sennen, Jul. 30.
St. Senoch, Oct. 23.
St. Sequanus, Sep. 19.
St. Seraphino, Oct. 17.
St. Serapion, Mar. 21; Oct. 30.
St. Serenicus, May 7.
St. Serenus, May 7.
St. Serenus the Gardener, Feb. 23.
St. Serf, Jul. 1.
St. Sergius, Jun. 28.
St. Sergius I, Sep. 8.
St. Sergius of Radonezh, Sep. 25.
St. Servatius, May 13.

St. Victor the Hermit, Feb. 26.
St. Victricius, Aug. 7.
St. Vigilius, Jun. 26.
St. Vigor, Nov. 1.
St. Vincent, Nov. 1, 1964.
St. Vincent de Paul, Sep. 27.
St. Vincent Ferrer, Apr. 5.
St. Vincentia Gerosa, Jun. 4.
St. Vincentian, Jan. 2.
St. Vincent Madelgarius, Sep. 20.
St. Vincent of Agen, Jun. 9.
St. Vincent of Lérins, May 24.
St. Vincent of Saragossa, Jan. 22.
St. Vincent Pallotti, Jan. 22.
St. Vincent Strambi, Sep. 25.
St. Vindician, Mar. 11.
St. Virgil, Mar. 5; Nov. 27.
St. Vitalian, Jan. 27.
St. Vitalis, Apr. 28; Nov. 4.
St. Vitonus, Nov. 9.
St. Vitus, Jun. 15.
St. Vladimir of Kiev, Jul. 15.
St. Vodalus, Feb. 5.
St. Volusian, Jan. 18.
St. Vulflagius, Jun. 7.
St. Vulmar, Jul. 20.
St. Walaricus, Apr. 1.
St. Walburga, Feb. 25.
St. Waldebert, May 2.
St. Waldetrudis, Apr. 9.
St. Walfrid, Feb. 15.
St. Walstan, May 30.
St. Walter of L'Esterp, May 11.
St. Walter of Pontoise, Apr. 8.
St. Waltheof, Aug. 3.
St. Wandregisilus, Jul. 22.
St. Waningus, Jan. 9.
St. Wenceslaus of Bohemia, Sep. 28.
St. Werburga, Feb. 3.
St. Wiborada, May 2.
St. Wigbert, Aug. 13.
St. Wilfrid the Younger, Apr. 29.
St. Wilgefortis, Jul. 20.
St. Willehad, Nov. 8.
St. William, Jan. 10; Jun. 8; Sep. 2.
St. William Firmatus of Tours, Apr. 24.
St. William of Eskill, Apr. 6.
St. William of Gellone, May 28.
St. William of Maleval, Feb. 10.
St. William of Norwich, Mar. 24.
St. William of Rochester, May 23.
St. William of Saint Benignus, Jan. 1.
St. William of Vercelli, Jun. 25.
St. William Pinchon, Jul. 29.
St. Willibald, Jun. 7.
St. Willibrord, Nov. 7.
St. Willigis, Feb. 23.
St. Wiltrudis, Jan. 6.
St. Winebald, Dec. 18.
St. Winifred, Nov. 3.
St. Winnoc, Nov. 6.
St. Winwaloe, Mar. 3.
St. Wiro, May 8.
St. Wistan, Jun. 1.
St. Wite, Jun. 1.
St. Withburga, Jul. 8.
St. Wivina, Dec. 17.
St. Wolfgang, Oct. 31.
St. Wulfhad, Jul. 24.

St. Wulfhilda, Sep. 9.
St. Wulfram, Mar. 20.
St. Wulfric, Feb. 20.
St. Wulfstan, Jan. 19.
St. Wulganus, Nov. 3.
St. Wulsin, Jan. 8.
St. Zachaeus, Nov. 17.
St. Zachary, Mar. 15; Nov. 5.
St. Zeno, Apr. 12; Sep. 8.
St. Zenobius, Feb. 20; May 25.
St. Zephyrinus, Aug. 26.
St. Zita, Apr. 27.
St. Zoë, May 2.
St. Zoilus and his companions, Jun. 27.
St. Zosimus, Mar. 30; Dec. 26.
Saint Aubin, Stéphanie Félicité du Crest de, Jan. 25, 1746.
Saint-Denis, Charles de Marguetel de, Apr. 1, 1616.
Saint-Exupéry, Antoine (Marie-Roger) de, Jul. 31, 1900.
Saint-Gaudens, Augustus, Mar. 1, 1848.
Saint-Hilaire, Etienne Geoffroy, Apr. 15, 1672.
Saint-Pierre, Jacques Henri Bernardin de, Jan. 19, 1737.
Saint-Saëns, (Charles) Camille, Oct. 9, 1835; Feb. 25, 1922.
SS. Abundius, Abundantius, Sep. 16.
SS. Alcmund and Tilbert, Sep. 7.
SS. Alphius, May 10.
SS. Ammon, Dec. 20.
SS. Apphia and Philemon, Nov. 22.
SS. Chaeremon and Ischyrion, Dec. 22.
SS. Charles Lwanga and Joseph Mkasa, Jun. 3.
SS. Claudius and Hilaria, Dec. 3.
SS. Cosmas and Damian, Sep. 26.
SS. Cyprian and Justina, Sep. 26.
SS. Dionysia and Majoricus, Dec. 6.
SS. Donatian and Laetus, Sep. 6.
SS. Epimachus and Alexander, Dec. 12.
SS. Faith, Hope, Charity, and Wisdom, Aug. 1.
SS. Felix and Cyprian, Oct. 12.
SS. Florus and Laurus, Aug. 18.
SS. Fuscian and Victoricus, and Gentian, Dec. 11.
SS. James and Philip, Feast of, May 1.
SS. Marcellus and Apuleius, Oct. 8.
SS. Mennas, Hermogenes, and Eugraphus, Dec. 10.
SS. Nemesius and many Companions, Sep. 10.
SS. Peter and Paul, Feast of, Jun. 29.
SS. Philemon and Apphia, Nov. 22.
SS. Philip and James, Feast of, May 1.
SS. Plutarch and Potamiaena, Jun. 28.
SS. Protus and Hyacinth, Sep. 11.
SS. Rhipsime and Gaiana, Sep. 29.
SS. Rugus and Zosimus, Dec. 18.
SS. Sergius and Bacchus, Oct. 8.
SS. Tharsilla and Emiliana, Dec. 23.
SS. Thecusa and Theodotus, May 18.
SS. Theodore, David, and Constantine, Sep. 19.
SS. Theodotus and Thecusa, May 18.
SS. Tiburtius and Susanna, Aug. 11.
SS. Victoria and Anatolia, Dec. 23.

SS. William, Stephen and Raymund, May 29.
Saipan (Mariana Islands): U.S. Marines land, Jun. 15, 1944.
Sakharov, Andrei, May 21, 1921; Oct. 9, 1975.
Saks, Gene Michael, Nov. 8, 1921.
Saladin (Damascus): takes Jerusalem, Oct. 2, 1187; Sep. 1, 1192; dies Mar. 4, 1193.
Salam, Abdus, Jan. 29, 1926.
Salamanca, Battle of: ends, Jul. 22, 1812.
Salant, Richard, Apr. 14, 1914.
Salazar, António de Oliveira, Apr. 28, 1889; Jul. 5, 1932.
Saldanha, João Carlos, Nov. 17, 1790.
Salem Witch Trials: begin, Mar. 1, 1692.
Salerno (Italy): U.S. landing, Sep. 9, 1943.
Salic Law, Jun. 20, 1837.
Salinger, J. D., Jan. 1, 1919.
Salinger, Pierre, Jun. 14, 1925.
Salisbury, Harrison (Evans), Nov. 14, 1908.
Salk, Jonas Edward, Oct. 28, 1914.
Salome (opera): premiere, Dec. 9, 1905.
Salome: premiere, Jan. 22, 1907.
Salonika, patron of, Oct. 8.
Salonika (Greece), Jun. 3, 1916.
SALT II: agreements, May 9, 1979; Jun. 18, 1979.
Salt Lake Valley, Jul. 22, 1847.
Saltpetre War, Apr. 5, 1879; ends, Oct. 20, 1883.
Saluzzo, Apr. 3, 1559.
Salvation Army Week, National, May intro.
Salyut, Apr. 24, 1971; Jun. 7, 1971.
Salyut 6, Nov. 2, 1978.
Salyut 7, Nov. 23, 1983.
Salzburg: union with Germany, May 29, 1921.
Samaranch, Juan Antonio, Jul. 20, 1920.
Samoa (Western): independence, Jan. 1, 1962.
Samora (Portugal), Apr. 23, 1909.
Samuelson, Paul Anthony, May 15, 1915.
San, Battle of the, May 16, 1915.
Sandburg, Carl, Jan. 6, 1878.
Sanders, George, Aug. 3, 1906.
Sanders, Harland, Sep. 9, 1890.
Sand, George, Jul. 1, 1804.
Sandinista National Liberation Front, Feb. 12, 1978; seizes national palace in Managua, Nicaragua, Aug. 22, 1978.
Sandinista Revolution, Anniversary of the (Nicaragua), Jul. 19.
Sandinists, Jul. 17, 1979.
Sand, Karl Ludwig, Sep. 20, 1819.
San Domingo: blacks revolt, Aug. 22, 1791.
Sand River Convention, Jan. 17, 1852.
San Fermin, Feria de (Spain), Jul. intro.
San Francisco, Jan. 3, 1847; earthquake, Apr. 18, 1906; Oct. 11, 1906; Jan. 25, 1915.
San Francisco Symphony Orchestra: established, Dec. 8, 1911.
San Francisco Treaty of Peace, Sep. 8, 1951.
Sanga Sanga, Apr. 2, 1945.
Sanger, Frederick, Aug. 13, 1918.
Sanger, Margaret, Sep. 14, 1883; Oct. 16, 1917.
Sangster, Donald B. (Jamaica), Feb. 22, 1967.

San Jacinto, Apr. 21, 1836.

San Jacinto, Battle of (Nicaragua), Sep. 14.

San Jacinto Day (Texas), Apr. 21.

San Joaquin Valley, Jan. 24, 1848.

San Juan Day (Puerto Rico), Jun. 24.

San Juan Hill, Battle of, Jul. 1, 1898.

San Lorenzo, Treaty of (Pinckney's Treaty), Oct. 27, 1795.

San Martín, José de, Feb. 25, 1778; Jul. 28, 1821.

San Salvador Charter, Dec. 14, 1951.

San Salvador's Feast (El Salvador), Aug. 4; Aug. 5; Aug. 6.

San Stefano, Mar. 3, 1878.

Santa Anna, Mar. 6, 1836; Apr. 21, 1836; Feb. 22, 1847.

Santa Barbara (California): captured by U.S., Aug. 4, 1846.

Santa Clara de Asis, Mission: established, Jan. 12, 1777.

Santa Cruz de Tenerife, Apr. 20, 1657.

Santa Cruz (Philippines), May 3, 1945.

Santa Fé: occupied by U.S., Aug. 18, 1846.

Santa Maria: wrecked, Dec. 25, 1492.

Santana, Pedro (Santo Domingo), Mar. 18, 1861.

Santander (Spain), patrons of, Mar. 3.

Santayana, George, Dec. 16, 1863.

Santiago (Cuba): surrenders, Jul. 17, 1898; Jan. 2, 1959.

Santiago Harbor (Cuba), Jul. 10, 1898.

Santillana, Marquis of (Iñigo López de Mendoza), Aug. 19, 1398.

Santo Domingo, Mar. 18, 1861; Nov. 23, 1961.

Santos-Dumont, Alberto, Jun. 20, 1873.

São Tomé: independence, Jul. 12, 1975.

São Tomé and Príncipe, Nov. 5, 1975.

sapphire, Sep. intro.

Saracens, Dec. 22, 640.

Saragossa, Treaty of, Apr. 22, 1529.

Sarajevo (Bosnia), Jun. 28, 1914.

Saratoga, Oct. 17, 1777.

Sarawak, May 12, 1888.

sardonyx, Aug. intro.

Sargent, Francis W., Apr. 2, 1970.

Sargent, John Singer, Jan. 12, 1856.

Sarikamish, Battle of, Dec. 29, 1914; Jan. 2, 1915.

Sarkis, Elias, Jul. 20, 1924.

Sarnoff, David, Feb. 27, 1891.

Sarnoff, Robert William, Jul. 2, 1918.

Saroyan, William, Aug. 31, 1903.

Sartre, Jean-Paul, Jun. 21, 1905; rejects Nobel Prize for literature, Oct. 22, 1964.

Saskatchewan (Canada), Sep. 1, 1905.

Sassoon, Siegfried (Lorraine), Sep. 8, 1886.

satellite, international: first, Apr. 26, 1962.

satellite broadcast: first, Aug. 14, 1960.

satellite communications, Jan. 19, 1961.

satellite systems: Indonesian domestic, Jul. 8, 1976.

Satie, Erik Alfred-Leslie, May 17, 1866.

Sato, Eisako, Mar. 27, 1901.

Satsuma Rebellion, Oct. 13, 1877.

Sattahid, Thailand: U.S. air base dedicated, Aug. 10, 1966.

Saturday, p. ix.

Saturday Evening Post: suspends publication, Jan. 10, 1969; Feb. 8, 1969.

Saturn, Feb. 2, 1982.

Saturn V, Nov. 9, 1967.

Saturnalia, Dec. intro.

Saturnalicius princeps, Dec. intro.

Saud (Saudi Arabia):, Jan. 15, 1902; deposed Nov. 2, 1964.

Saudi Arabia: named, Sep. 23, 1932; Jan. 18, 1963; boundaries established, Dec. 18, 1969.

Saur Revolution Day (Afghanistan), Apr. 27.

Savage, Michael Joseph, Mar. 23, 1872.

Savage, Richard, Jan. 16, 1697.

Savalas, Telly, Jan. 21, 1927.

Savannah: first steamship to cross Atlantic, Aug. 22, 1818.

Savannah, Mar. 23, 1962; U.S. nuclear ship: completes maiden voyage, Aug. 22, 1962.

Savannah (Georgia): taken by British, Dec. 29, 1778; captured by General Sherman, Dec. 21, 1864.

Save Your Vision Week, National, Mar. intro.

Savonarola, Girolamo, Sep. 21, 1452; executed, May 23, 1498.

Savoy, Jan. 17, 1601; Apr. 23, 1860.

Saxons, Jan. 6, 871.

Saxony, patron of, Jun. 15.

Sayers, Dorothy L(eigh), Jun. 13, 1893.

Scaliger, Joseph Justus, Aug. 5, 1540.

Scaliger, Julius Caesar, Apr. 23, 1484.

Scandinavian Union, Oct. 28, 1497.

Scapa Flow, Nov. 21, 1918; German fleet scuttled, Jun. 21, 1919.

Scarlatti, Alessandro, May 2, 1660.

Scarlatti, (Giuseppe) Domenico, Oct. 26, 1685.

Scarron, Paul, Jul. 4, 1610.

Schacht, Hjalmar, Jan. 22, 1877.

Schaefer, Rudolph Jay, Feb. 21, 1863.

Schally, Andrew, Nov. 30, 1926.

Schechter Poultry Corp. vs. United States, May 27, 1935.

Scheele, Karl Wilhelm, Dec. 9, 1742.

Scheider, Roy (Richard), Nov. 10, 1935.

Schell, Maximilian, Dec. 8, 1930.

Schelling, Friedrich Wilhelm Joseph von, Jan. 27, 1775.

Schenectady, Feb. 8, 1690.

Scherman, Harry, Feb. 1, 1887.

Schick, Col. Jacob, Sep. 16, 1877; Nov. 6, 1923.

Schiller, Johann Christoph Friedrich, Nov. 10, 1759.

Schippers, Thomas, Mar. 9, 1930.

Schirach, Baldur von: released from prison, Oct. 1, 1966.

Schirra, Walter M., Jr., Mar. 12, 1923; Oct. 3, 1962.

Schlafly, Phyllis, Aug. 15, 1924.

Schlegel, August Wilhelm, Sep. 8, 1767.

Schlegel, Friedrich von, Mar. 10, 1772.

Schleiden, Matthias, Apr. 5, 1804.

Schlesinger, Arthur M(eier), Jr., Oct. 15, 1917.

Schlesinger, James Rodney, Feb. 15, 1929.

Schleswig and Holstein, Mar. 5, 1460; Jan. 24, 1867.

Schlieffen, Alfred Graf von, Feb. 28, 1833.

Schliemann, Heinrich, Jan. 6, 1822.

Schmeling, Max, Sep. 28, 1905; Jun. 12, 1930; Jun. 21, 1932.

Schmid, Carlo, Dec. 3, 1896.

Schmidt, Helmut, Dec. 23, 1918; May 16, 1974.

Schmitt, Harrison H. (*Jack*), Jul. 3, 1935; Dec. 12, 1972.

Schnabel, Karl Ulrich, Aug. 6, 1909.

Schneider, Romy, Sep. 23, 1938.

Schnitzler, Arthur, May 15, 1862.

Schoelcher Day (French West Indies), Jul. 21.

Schoenbrun, David Franz, Mar. 15, 1915.

scholars, patron of, Aug. 28; Dec. 6.

Schönberg, Arnold, Sep. 13, 1874.

Schoonover, Lawrence Lovell, Mar. 6, 1906.

Schopenhauer, Arthur, Feb. 22, 1788.

Schorr, Daniel, Aug. 13, 1916; Feb. 23, 1976.

Schreyer, Edward Richard, Dec. 21, 1935.

Schrieffer, John Robert, May 31, 1931.

Schrödinger, Erwin, Aug. 12, 1887.

Schubart, Christian Friedrich Daniel, Apr. 13, 1739.

Schubert, Franz Peter, Jan. 31, 1797.

Schulberg, Budd, Mar. 27, 1914.

Schultz, Dutch, Aug. 6, 1902.

Schultz, Theodore W., Apr. 30, 1902.

Schulz, Charles M., Nov. 26, 1922.

Schurz, Carl, Mar. 2, 1829.

Schwab, Charles Michael, Feb. 18, 1862.

Schwabe, Heinrich Samuel, Oct. 25, 1789.

Schwann, Theodor, Dec. 7, 1810.

Schwarzkopf, Elisabeth, Dec. 9, 1915.

Schweitzer, Albert, Jan. 14, 1875.

Schwinger, Julian Seymour, Feb. 12, 1918.

Scofield, Paul, Jan. 21, 1922.

Scone, May 21, 1424.

Scoon, Paul, Jul. 4, 1935.

Scorpio, Nov. intro.; Oct. intro.

Scotland: independence acknowledged, Dec. 5, 1189; Jan. 20, 1301; Jul. 19, 1333; Apr. 12, 1654; Union with England, May 1, 1707; Mar. 1, 1979.

Scotland, patron of, Nov. 16; Nov. 30.

Scott, David R., Jul. 26, 1971.

Scott, George C., Oct. 18, 1927.

Scott, G.H., Jul. 6, 1919.

Scott, Hazel (Dorothy), Jun. 11, 1920.

Scott, Hugh Doggett, Jr., Nov. 11, 1900.

Scott, Randolph, Jan. 23, 1903.

Scott, Robert, Jan. 17, 1912.

Scott, Robert Falcon, Jun. 6, 1868.

Scott, Sir Walter, Aug. 15, 1771.

Scott, Winfield, Jun. 13, 1786; Sep. 13, 1846; Sep. 14, 1846; Apr. 18, 1847.

Scott, Zachary, Feb. 21, 1914.

Scottish Ballad: first performance, Nov. 28, 1941.

Scottish College of Justice: established, May 13, 1532.

Scottish Jacobites, Jul. 27, 1689.

Scottish National Gallery: opens, Mar. 21, 1859.

Scottish Quarter Day (Scotland), Feb. 2.

Scouting Anniversary, Feb. intro.

Scranton, George Whitfield, May 11, 1811.

Scranton, William Warren, Jul. 19, 1917.

Scribner, Charles, Feb. 21, 1821.

Scripps, E(dward) W(yllis), Jun. 18, 1854.
Scripps, Ellen Browning, Oct. 18, 1836.
Scutaria (Albania), Jan. 23, 1916.
Seaborg, Glenn T., Apr. 19, 1912.
Sealab II, Oct. 12, 1965.
Seale, Bobby, Oct. 22, 1936.
Sealsfield, Charles, Mar. 3, 1793.
seamstresses, patron of, Jul. 26.
Sebastopol: capitulates to Allies, Sep. 11,
    1855.
Sebastopol, Siege of: begins, Oct. 17, 1854.
Sebour (Archbishop of Paris), Jan. 3, 1857.
Secondat, Charles-Louis de, Jan. 18, 1689.
Second Balkan War: ends, Aug. 10, 1913.
Second Coalition, War of, Mar. 12, 1799;
    Mar. 25, 1799; Dec. 3, 1800.
Second Empire (France), Nov. 2, 1852.
Second Maratha War, Aug. 7, 1803.
Second Reform Act (Great Britain), Aug. 15,
    1867.
Secretariat: Triple Crown winner, Jun. 9,
    1973.
secretaries, patron of, Jan. 3.
Secular Affairs Institute: seized, Jun. 23,
    1966.
secular clergy, patron of, Dec. 29.
Securities & Exchange Commission:
    created, Jun. 6, 1934.
Sedaka, Neil, Mar. 13, 1939.
Sedan (France), Nov. 6, 1918.
Sedgwick, Adam, Mar. 22, 1785.
Seeger, Alan, Jun. 22, 1888.
Seeger, Pete, May 3, 1919.
Seereiter, John, Apr. 12, 1859.
Seferis, Giorgos, Mar. 13, 1900.
Segal, Erich, Jun. 16, 1937.
Segovia, Andrés, Feb. 18, 1894.
Segrè, Emilio, Feb. 1, 1905.
segregation, Oct. 11, 1906; ruled illegal in
    railroad cars, Jun. 5, 1950.
Séguin, Marc, Apr. 20, 1786.
Selective Service Act, May 18, 1917; signed,
    Jun. 24, 1948.
Selective Service System, Jan. 19, 1970.
Selfridge, Harry Gordon, Jan. 11, 1864.
Sellers, Peter, Sep. 8, 1925.
Selznick, David O., May 10, 1902.
Semenov, Nikolay Nikolaevich, Apr. 15,
    1896.
Semmes, Raphael, Sep. 27, 1809.
Sempach, Jul. 9, 1386.
Senate, U.S., Apr. 18, 1978.
Sendak, Maurice, Jun. 10, 1928.
Senefelder, Aloys, Nov. 6, 1771.
Senegal: French government established,
    Oct. 16, 1904; Apr. 4, 1960; admitted to
    U.N., Sep. 28, 1960; Mar. 3, 1963; Feb. 1,
    1982.
Senegal and Sudanese Republic:
    independence, Jun. 20, 1960.
Senegal-Niger, Upper (French Sudan), Dec.
    4, 1920.
Senegambia: confederation, Feb. 1, 1982.
Senghor, Leopold Sedar, Oct. 9, 1906.
Senior Citizens Day (Oklahoma), Jun. 9.
Senlis, City and Diocese of, patron of, Mar.
    30.
Senlis, Treaty of, May 23, 1493.
Sennett, Mack, Jan. 17, 1880.

Seoul (Korea): captured, Jun. 28, 1950; falls
    to U.S., Sep. 26, 1950; handed over to
    Republic of Korea, Sep. 29, 1950; Jan. 4,
    1951; Mar. 14, 1951.
Separation Day (Delaware), Jun. 15.
Sepoy Mutiny, Mar. 9, 1858.
septem, Sep. intro.
Serbia, Mar. 3, 1878; independence, Jul. 13,
    1878; Jul. 28, 1914; declares war on
    Germany, Aug. 6, 1914; invaded by
    Austria-Hungary, Aug. 11, 1914; invasion
    begins, Oct. 6, 1915.
Serbia, patron, Jan. 14.
serfdom (Austria): abolished, Sep. 7, 1848.
Serge, Grand Duke (Russia): killed, Feb. 17,
    1905.
Serkin, Rudolf, Mar. 28, 1903.
Serra, Junipero, Nov. 24, 1713.
Sert, José Luis, Jul. 1, 1902.
servants, hired, partron of, Sep. 14.
Servetus, Michael: convicted and executed,
    Oct. 27, 1553.
Service, Robert W., Jan. 16, 1874.
service to the needy, patron of those of,
    Jul. 29.
Sessions, Roger (Huntington), Dec. 28,
    1896.
Seton, Elizabeth Ann, Aug. 28, 1774;
    beatified Mar. 17, 1963; Sep. 14, 1975.
Seton, Ernest Thompson, Aug. 14, 1860.
Setsubun (Japan), Feb. intro.
Seurat, Georges, Dec. 2, 1859.
Seuss, Dr. *See* Geisel, Theodore Seuss.
Sevareid, Eric, Nov. 26, 1912.
Sevastopol: Russian sailors mutiny, Nov.
    25, 1904; falls to Germany, Jul. 1, 1942.
Seven Apostles of Bulgaria, Jul. 17.
Seven Brothers, Jul. 10.
seven-day week, p. ix.
Seven Founders of the Servite Order, Feb.
    12; Feb. 17.
Seven oaks, Jun. 27, 1450.
Seven Sisters of Ephesus, Jul. 27.
Seven Sorrows of the Blessed Virgin Mary,
    Sep. 15.
Seven Weeks' War, Jul. 3, 1866; Jul. 30,
    1866; ends, Oct. 3, 1866.
Seven Years' War, Jan. 16, 1756; begins,
    Aug. 29, 1756; Jan. 10, 1757; May 6, 1757;
    Jul. 26, 1757; Aug. 30, 1757; Nov. 20, 1759;
    Nov. 3, 1760; Jan. 4, 1762; Nov. 1, 1762;
    ends, Feb. 10, 1763.
Seventeenth Amendment: U.S.
    Constitution, May 31, 1913.
Seventeenth of July Revolution or Baath
    Revolution Day (Iraq), Jul. 17.
Seventeenth Summer Olympics: open in
    Rome, Aug. 25, 1960.
Severndroog, Feb. 11, 1755.
Sevier, John, Sep. 23, 1745.
Sèvres, Treaty of, Aug. 10, 1920.
Sewall, Samuel, Mar. 28, 1652.
Seward, William Henry, May 16, 1801.
Seward's Day (Alaska), Mar. intro.
Seward's Folly, Mar. 30, 1867.
sewing machine: first patented, Sep. 10,
    1846.
Sextilis, Aug. intro.
Sexton, Anne, Nov. 9, 1928.
Seychelles: independence, Jun. 29, 1976.

Seymour, Jane, May 30, 1536.
Seyss-Inquart, Arthur, Jul. 22, 1892.
Shaba (Zaire), May 11, 1978.
Shabatu, p. x.
Shaffer, Peter, May 15, 1926.
Shaftesbury, Anthony Ashley Cooper, Jul.
    22, 1621.
Shaftesbury Factory Act: passed, Aug. 29,
    1833.
Shagari, Alhaji Shehu, Apr. 25, 1925.
Shah Jahan, Jan. 5, 1592; May 26, 1659.
Shah, Mohammad Zahir, Jul. 17, 1973.
Shaheed Day (Bangladesh), Feb. 20.
Shahn, Ben(jamin), Sep. 12, 1898.
Shah Rokh, Feb. 18, 1405.
Shaiba, Battle of, Apr. 12, 1915; ends, Apr.
    14, 1915.
Shakespeare, Frank Joseph Jr., Apr. 9, 1925.
Shakespeare, William, Apr. 26, 1564; dies,
    Apr. 23, 1616; anniversary, Apr. 23, 1964.
Shanghai: seized by British, Jun. 19, 1842;
    Jan. 3, 1903; Mar. 21, 1927; Jan. 28, 1932.
Shankar, Ravi, Apr. 7, 1920.
Shannon, Claude Elwood, Apr. 30, 1916.
Shantung, Mar. 6, 1898.
Shantung Concessions, Jun. 28, 1919.
Shantung Province (China), May 20, 1929.
Shapiro, Jacob, May 5, 1897.
Shapiro, Karl Jay, Nov. 10, 1913.
Shapley, Harlow, Nov. 2, 1885.
Sharif, Omar, Apr. 10, 1932.
Sharkey, Jack, Jun. 12, 1930; Jun. 21, 1932;
    Jun. 29, 1933.
Shark Island, Feb. 3, 1521.
Sharp, William, Sep. 12, 1855.
Sharpeville Massacre, Mar. 21, 1960.
Shastri, Lal Bahadun, Jan. 24, 1966.
Shavuoth, p. xii; May intro.; Jun. intro.
Shaw, Anna Howard, Feb. 14, 1847.
Shaw, Artie, May 23, 1910.
Shaw, George Bernard, Jul. 26, 1856.
Shaw, Irwin, Feb. 27, 1913.
Shays, Daniel, Feb. 4, 1787.
Shays' Rebellion, Feb. 4, 1787.
Shcharansky, Anatoly B.: sentenced, Jul.
    14, 1978.
Shearer, Moira, Jan. 17, 1926.
Shearer, Norma, Aug. 10, 1904.
Shearing, George, Aug. 13, 1919.
Shebat, p. x.
Shedd, John Graves, Jul. 20, 1850.
Sheed, Frank, Mar. 20, 1897.
Sheehy, Gail (Henion), Nov. 27, 1937.
Sheen, Fulton J., May 8, 1895.
Sheffield: British destroyer, May 4, 1982.
Shéhérazade: premiere, May 17, 1904.
Shehu, Mehmet, Jan. 10, 1913.
Shelley, Mary Wollstonecraft, Aug. 30, 1797.
Shelley, Percy Bysshe, Aug. 4, 1792.
Shemini Atzereth, p. xii; Oct. intro.
Shepard, Alan B., Nov. 18, 1923; first
    American in space, May 5, 1961.
shepherds, patron of, Feb. 12; Apr. 16.
Sheridan, Philip Henry, Mar. 6, 1831.
Sheridan, Richard Brinsley (Butler), Nov. 4,
    1751.
Sherman, James S., Mar. 4, 1909.
Sherman, John, May 10, 1823.
Sherman, Roger, Apr. 19, 1721.

Smith, Howard K., May 12, 1914.

Smith, Ian, Apr. 8, 1919; Apr. 13, 1964; Apr. 4, 1975; Apr. 12, 1978.

Smith, Jedediah Strong, Jan. 6, 1799.

Smith, Joseph, Dec. 23, 1805; Apr. 6, 1830; murdered, Jun. 27, 1844.

Smith, Kate, May 1, 1909.

Smith, Maggie, Dec. 28, 1934.

Smith, Margaret Chase, Dec. 14, 1897.

Smith, Mary Louise: first woman head of Republican National Committee, Sep. 16, 1974.

Smith, Robert H., Aug. 8, 1879; Jun. 10, 1935.

Smith, Sir C(harles) Aubrey, Jul. 21, 1863.

Smith, Theobald, Jul. 31, 1859.

Smith, Tommie, Oct. 16, 1968.

Smith, Walter Wellesley (Red), Sep. 25, 1905.

Smith, William, Mar. 23, 1760.

Smith, Willie (*The Lion*), Nov. 25, 1897.

smiths, patron of, Dec. 1.

Smithsonian Institution, Apr. 23, 1909; Apr. 7, 1983.

Smolensk: liberated, Sep. 25, 1943.

Smollett, Tobias George, Mar. 19, 1721.

Smothers, Dick, Nov. 20, 1938.

Smuts, Jan Christiaan, May 24, 1870; Mar. 5, 1916.

Snack a Pickle Time, Sep. intro.

snail darter, Jun. 15, 1978.

Snead, Sam, May 27, 1912.

Snell, Peter, Dec. 17, 1938.

Snodgrass, William Dewitt, Jan. 5, 1926.

Snoopy: lunar module, May 22, 1969.

Snow, C(harles) P(ercy), Oct. 15, 1905.

Snowden, Earl of, May 24, 1978.

Snowden, Philip, Jul. 18, 1864.

snowdrop, Jan. intro.

Soane, Sir John, Sep. 10, 1753.

Soap Box Derby, All American, Aug. intro.

Soares, Mario, Dec. 7, 1924; Apr. 25, 1983.

Sobell, Morton, Apr. 11, 1917.

Sobhuz II (Swaziland), Jul. 22.

Sobieski, John III (Poland), Jun. 2, 1624; Sep. 12, 1683. .

Social Christian Party (Belgium), Jul. 27, 1965; Apr. 3, 1979.

Social Democratic Party (Portugal), Apr. 25, 1983.

Social Democratic Party (Sweden), Sep. 20, 1976.

Socialist Party, U.S., May 21, 1932.

social justice, patron of, Nov. 3.

Social Security Act: signed, Aug. 14, 1935.

Société Nationale de Musique, Jan. 12, 1907.

Soddy, Frederick, Sep. 2, 1877.

Soderbert, Carl Richard, Feb. 3, 1895.

Söderblom, Nathan, Jan. 15, 1866.

Soil Conservation Service, U.S., Apr. 27, 1935.

Soissons, Battle of, Jan. 8, 1915; Jan. 14, 1915.

solar telescope: largest, Mar. 15, 1960.

solar year, length of, p. xi.

Soldau (East Prussia), Nov. 18, 1914.

soldiers, patron of, Sep. 8.

soldiers, patron of, Oct. 8.

soldiers, patron of, Jan. 20.

Solemnity of Mary, Jan. 1.

Solidarity Day: march, Jun. 19, 1968.

Solidarity (Poland): ruled legal, Nov. 10, 1980; Dec. 13, 1981.

Solidarity with South African Political Prisoners, Oct. 11.

Solomon, Elijah Ben, Apr. 23, 1720.

Solomon Islands, U.S. troops land, Jun. 30, 1934; U.S. offensive begins, Aug. 7, 1942; Mar. 6, 1943; independence, Jul. 7, 1978.

Solomos, Dionysius, Apr. 8, 1798.

Solovieff, Alexander, Apr. 14, 1879.

Solti, Sir Georg, Oct. 21, 1912.

Solvay, Ernest, Apr. 16, 1838.

Solvay Mass, Battle of, Nov. 25, 1542.

Solzhenitsyn, Alexander, Dec. 11, 1918; Feb. 13, 1974.

Somalia, Jan. 31, 1968.

Somali Coast, Mar. 13, 1884.

Somali Democratic Republic: formed, Jul. 1, 1960.

Somaliland, Jan. 27, 1950; independence, Jun. 26, 1960.

Somaliland, British, Jul. 1, 1960.

Somaliland, Italian, Jul. 1, 1960.

Somes, Michael, Sep. 28, 1917.

Somhlolo Day (Swaziland), Sep. 6.

Somme, Battle of the, Jun. 24, 1916; Jul. 1, 1916; Sep. 15, 1916; ends, Apr. 6, 1918.

Somme, Second Battle of the: opens, Aug. 21, 1918; Sep. 3, 1918.

Somme offensive: begins, Mar. 21, 1918.

Sommer, Elke, Nov. 5, 1941.

Somoza, Anastasio, Feb. 1, 1896; Dec. 5, 1925; resigns, Feb. 02, 1967; Jul. 17, 1979; assassinated, Sep. 17, 1980.

Somport Tunnel: opens, Jul. 18, 1928.

Sonderbund: formed in Switzerland, Dec. 11, 1845.

Sondheim, Stephen, Mar. 22, 1930.

Sontag, Susan, Jan. 28, 1933.

Sophia (Sweden), May 12, 1873.

Sopwith, Sir Thomas, Jan. 18, 1888.

Sora, Italy, patron of, May 27.

Sorby, Henry Clifton, May 10, 1826.

Sorge, Reinhard Johannes, Jan. 29, 1892.

Sorolla y Bastida, Joaquin, Feb. 27, 1863.

Sosigenes, p. xi.

Sosuharai or Soot Sweeping Day (Japan), Dec. 13.

Sothern, Ann, Jan. 22, 1912.

Sothis, p. ix.

Soto, Fernando de, Jun. 3, 1539.

souls in purgatory, patron of, Sep. 10.

souls on journey from this world to the next, patron of, Mar. 17.

Soult, Nicolas Jean de Dieu, Mar. 29, 1769.

Sound of Music, The: premiere, Nov. 16, 1959.

Souphanouvrong, Jul. 13, 1909.

soup kitchen: first, Jan. 8, 1800.

Sousa, John Philip, Nov. 6, 1854.

South Africa, Jan. 21, 1898; first European settlement, Apr. 06, 1652; Mar. 11, 1964; Catholic Schools in, Jan. 17, 1977; Sep. 15, 1977.

South Africa, Union of, May 31, 1910; Mar. 5, 1916; Apr. 27, 1916; May 31, 1961.

South Africa, University of, Apr. 27, 1916.

South African Boer Republic, Oct. 25, 1900.

South African Republic (Transvaal), established, Dec. 16, 1856; Jan. 6, 1857; Apr. 16, 1883; Jan. 2, 1896; Sep. 1, 1900.

South African Union, Convention of the: opens, Oct. 12, 1908.

South America, Jul. 10, 1934.

South Arabian Federation, Nov. 30, 1967.

South Bend (Indiana), Jan. 15, 1844.

South Carolina, admitted to Union, May 23, 1788; Apr. 12, 1861; Jan. 28, 1963.

South Dakota: admitted to Union, Nov. 2, 1889.

Southeast Asian Nations, Association of, May 16, 1979.

Southeast Asia Treaty Organization: dissolved, Jun. 30, 1977.

Southern Rhodesia: becomes self-governing colony, Oct. 1, 1923.

South Georgia Island (Falkland Islands), Apr. 25, 1982.

South Pacific: premiere, Apr. 7, 1949.

South Pole, Dec. 14, 1911; Jan. 17, 1912; first flight over, Nov. 29, 1929.

South Vietnam, Oct. 23, 1955; Republic of, established, Oct. 26, 1955; Mar. 9, 1962; Feb. 8, 1966; U.S. troops withdrawn, Mar. 29, 1973; Mar. 1, 1975; Communist victory, May 1, 1975.

South Yemen People's Republic: independence, Nov. 30, 1967.

Soviet Army and Navy Day U.S.S.R., Feb. 23.

Soviet Militia Day (U.S.S.R.), Nov. 10.

Soviets, Second Congress of: convenes, Nov. 8, 1917.

Soviet Socialist Republics, Union of: established, Dec. 30, 1922.

Soviet Union, Jan. 3, 1928; satellite station agreement with Cuba, Jan. 9, 1970; constitution, Jun. 4, 1977; adopts new constitution, Oct. 7, 1977.

Soviet Youth Day (U.S.S.R.), Jun. intro.

Soweto Day, Jun. 16.

Soyuz 9, Jun. 19, 1970.

Soyuz 10, Apr. 24, 1971.

Soyuz 11, Jun. 7, 1971.

Soyuz 11, Jun. 30, 1971.

Soyuz 13, Dec. 26, 1973.

Soyuz 19, Jul. 17, 1975.

Soyuz 25, Oct. 10, 1977.

Soyuz 27, Mar. 16, 1978.

Soyuz 31, Nov. 2, 1978.

Soyuz spacecraft, Jan. 16, 1969.

"Squaw Winter", Oct. intro.

Spaak, Paul Henri, Jan. 25, 1899.

Spaak-Janson, Marie: first woman elected to Belgian parliament, Nov. 20, 1921.

Spaatz, Carl, Jun. 28, 1891.

space endurance record, Jun. 30, 1971.

space: peaceful use of, Jan. 27, 1967.

space shuttle, manned, Jan. 5, 1972.

space walk, first, Mar. 18, 1965.

space walk: *Gemini 4*, Jun. 3, 1965.

Spahn, Warren, Apr. 23, 1921.

Spain, Jan. 2, 1492; Jan. 30, 1648; Jan. 4, 1762; Jan. 22, 1771; Jan. 20, 1801; Jan. 4, 1805; war with France, Apr. 7, 1823; concordat with papacy, Mar. 16, 1851; jury trial introduced, May 29, 1889; universal suffrage, Mar. 27, 1890; Apr. 4,

Stevens, Thaddeus, Apr. 4, 1792.

Stevens, Theodore Fulton, Nov. 18, 1923.

Stevens, Wallace, Oct. 2, 1879.

Stevenson, Adlai E., Oct. 23, 1835; Mar. 4, 1893; Feb. 5, 1900.

Stevenson, Robert Louis (Balfour), Nov. 13, 1859.

Stevenson III, Adlai E(wing), Oct. 10, 1930.

Stewart, Donald Ogden, Nov. 30, 1894.

Stewart, Jackie, Jun. 11, 1939.

Stewart, James, May 20, 1908.

Stewart, Mary, Sep. 17, 1916.

Stewart, Potter, Jan. 23, 1915.

Stewart, Robert, Jun. 18, 1769.

Stewart, Robert (King of Scotland), Apr. 1, 1406.

Stieglitz, Alfred, Jan. 1, 1864.

Stiernhielm, Georg, Aug. 7.

Stiklestad, Battle of, Jul. 29, 1030.

Still, Clyfford, Nov. 30, 1904.

Stilwell, Joseph Warren, Mar. 19, 1883; Dec. 21, 1943.

Stimson, Henry Lewis, Sep. 21, 1867.

Stock Exchange, New York, May 5, 1893; May 25, 1970.

Stockholm, Jul. 25, 1956.

Stockholm, Blood Bath of, Nov. 8, 1520.

Stokach, Mar. 25, 1799.

Stokowski, Leopold, Apr. 18, 1882; Oct. 11, 1912.

Stolypin, Peter, Sep. 14, 1911.

stomach patients, patron of, Jan. 26.

Stone, Amasa, Apr. 27, 1818.

Stone, Edward Durell, Mar. 9, 1902.

Stone, Harlan Fiske, Oct. 11, 1872.

Stone, Irving, Jul. 14, 1903.

Stone, I(sidor F(einstein), Dec. 24, 1907.

Stone, Lucy, Aug. 13, 1818.

stonecutters, patron of, Nov. 23.

stonecutters, patron of, Dec. 26.

Stonehenge: sold, Sep. 21, 1915.

stone masons, patron of, Jan. 7.

Stone of Scone: stolen, Dec. 25, 1950.

Stony Tunguska River (Siberia): meteorite craters found, Jun. 30, 1908.

Stoph, Willi, Mar. 19, 1970.

Stop the Draft Week, Dec. 5, 1967.

Stoppard, Tom, Jul. 3, 1937.

Story, Joseph, Sep. 18, 1779.

Storytelling Festival, National, Oct. intro.

Stout, Rex (Todhunter), Dec. 1, 1886.

Stowe, Harriet (Elizabeth) Beecher, Jun. 14, 1811.

Strachey, Lytton, Mar. 1, 1880.

Stradonitz, Friedrich August Kekule von, Sep. 7, 1829.

Straits Convention: signed, Jul. 13, 1841.

Stralsund, Peace of, May 24, 1370.

Strasberg, Lee, Nov. 17, 1901.

Strasberg, Susan, May 22, 1938.

Strasbourg, Peace of, Apr. 3, 1189.

Strasbourg (Alsace): occupied by France, Nov. 25, 1918.

Strategic Air Command: established, Mar. 21, 1946.

Stratford-on-Avon, Apr. 23, 1964.

Stratigic Arms Limitation Treaty (SALT) II, Jun. 18, 1979.

Straus, Isidor, Feb. 6, 1845.

Straus, Nathan, Jan. 31, 1848.

Straus, Oscar, Apr. 6, 1870.

Straus, Percy Selden, Jun. 27, 1876.

Strauss, Johann, Oct. 25, 1825.

Strauss, Richard, Jun. 11, 1864; Dec. 9, 1905; Jan. 22, 1907; Jan. 25, 1909; Jan. 26, 1911.

Strauss, Robert Schwarz, Oct. 9, 1918.

Stravinsky, Igor, Jun. 17, 1882; Jun. 25, 1910; Jun. 13, 1911.

Streep, Meryl, Jun. 22, 1949.

Streisand, Barbara, Apr. 24, 1942.

Stresemann, Gustav, May 10, 1878.

Strindberg, August, Jan. 22, 1849.

Stroessner, Alfredo, Nov. 3, 1912.

Stroheim, Erich von, Sep. 22, 1885.

Strouse, Charles, Jun. 7, 1928.

Strutt, John William, Nov. 12, 1842.

Struve, Friedrich Georg Wilson von, Apr. 15, 1793.

Stuart, Charles, Apr. 28, 1795.

Stuart, Elbridge Amos, Sep. 10, 1856.

Stuart, Gilbert Charles, Dec. 3, 1755.

Stuart, Henry (Lord Darnley), Jul. 29, 1565.

Stuart, Jeb, Feb. 6, 1833.

Stuart, Jesse, Aug. 8, 1907.

Stuart, John (Earl of Bute), Apr. 7, 1763.

Stubbs, George, Aug. 24, 1724.

Stuber, William George, Apr. 9, 1864.

Stuck, Hudson: first ascent of Mount McKinley, Jun. 6, 1913.

Studebaker, Clement, Mar. 12, 1831.

students, patron of, Sep. 30.

Students for a Democratic Society, Apr. 2, 1970.

students of philosophy, patron of, Nov. 25.

students of the natural sciences, patron of, Nov. 15.

Sturgeon, William, May 22, 1783.

Styne, Jule, Dec. 31, 1905; Dec. 8, 1949.

Suan (Korea), May 8, 1952.

Suarez Gonzales, Adolfo (Spain), Sep. 25, 1932; Mar. 1, 1979.

Suazo Córdova, Roberto, Jan. 5, 1982.

submarine attack, first, Feb. 17, 1864.

submarine blockade, German, Feb. 18, 1915.

submarine telephone cable, Trans-Tasman: opens, Jul. 9, 1962.

submarine warfare, Jan. 16, 1915; Feb. 1, 1917; Feb. 6, 1922; regulation of, Apr. 10, 1930.

subway: Chicago's first, Oct. 17, 1944.

subway system: first section opens in New York, Oct. 27, 1904.

Sucre, Josè Antonio de, Feb. 3, 1793.

Sudan, Jan. 26, 1885; Sep. 2, 1898; independence, Jan. 1, 1956; civilian government overthrown, Nov. 17, 1958; Apr. 4, 1960; Feb. 26, 1972.

Sudan, French (Upper Senegal-Niger), Dec. 4, 1920.

Sudanese Republic, Sep. 22, 1960.

Sudanese Republic and Senegal: independence as Federation of Mali, Jun. 20, 1960.

Suez Canal, Apr. 25, 1859; opens, Nov. 17, 1869; Oct. 29, 1888; nationalized, Jul. 26, 1956; Jan. 18, 1974; reopens, Jun. 5, 1975.

Suez National Day (Egypt), Oct. 23.

Suggs, Louise, Sep. 7, 1923.

Sukarno, Ahmed, Jun. 6, 1901; Jan. 13, 1959; Mar. 5, 1960.

Sukarno government, Apr. 24, 1965.

Sukkoth, p. xii; Sep. intro.; Oct. intro.

Suleiman I (Turkey): conquers Belgrade, Aug. 29, 1521.

Suleiman III (Turkey), Nov. 2, 1687.

Sullavan, Margaret, May 16, 1911.

Sullivan, A(loysius) M(ichael), Aug. 9, 1896.

Sullivan, Anne, Apr. 14, 1866.

Sullivan, Arthur (Sir), Dec. 7, 1889.

Sullivan, Barry, Aug. 29, 1912.

Sullivan, Ed(ward Vincent), Sep. 28, 1902.

Sullivan, John L., Oct. 15, 1858; Feb. 7, 1883; Jul. 8, 1889; Sep. 7, 1892.

Sullivan, John L(awrence), Jun. 16, 1899.

Sullivan, Louis H., Sep. 3, 1856.

Sullivan, Sir Arthur S., May 13, 1842; Nov. 25, 1882.

Sullivan Ordinance, Jan. 21, 1908.

Sully, Thomas, Jun. 19, 783?.

Sulzberger, Arthur Hays, Sep. 12, 1891.

Sumarokov, Aleksandr Petrovich, Jun. 4, 1718.

Sumatra, Jan. 1, 1596.

Sumerian calendar, p. ix.

Summer Holiday (San Marino), Aug. 14; Aug. 15.

summer solstice, Jun. intro.

Summerskill, Edith Clara, Apr. 19, 1901.

Sumner, Charles, Jan. 6, 1811.

Sumner, James Batcheller, Nov. 19, 1887.

Sumner, William Graham, Oct. 30, 1840.

Sumter, Fort, Apr. 10, 1861.

Sumter, Fort, Apr. 12, 1861.

Sunay, Cevdet, Feb. 10, 1900.

Sunday, p. ix.

Sunday, (William Ashley) Billy, Nov. 19, 1862.

Sunshine Week, National, Oct. intro.

Sun Yat-sen, Nov. 12, 1866; Dec. 29, 1911; Jan. 1, 1912; Feb. 15, 1912; Apr. 7, 1921; Jan. 20, 1924.

Sun Yat-sen, Dr. Birthday of (Taiwan), Nov. 12.

Sun Yun-suan, Nov. 11, 1913.

Super Bowl, Jan. 21, 1979.

supersonic jetliner: first test, Dec. 31, 1968.

Supremacy, Act of, Jan. 15, 1535.

Supreme Council of National Economy (U.S.S.R.), Mar. 13, 1963.

Supreme Court, U.S.: Jan. 8, 1798; Mar. 3, 1879; May 1, 1911; May 27, 1935; rules on segregation, Jun. 5, 1950; Jan. 15, 1951; May 17, 1954; ruling against segregation, Sep. 30, 1958; May 29, 1961; Feb. 18, 1963; rules on sale of birth control devices, Jun. 7, 1965; first black seated, Jun. 13, 1967; rules on racial discrimination, Jun. 17, 1968; Jan. 19, 1970; Jan. 22, 1973; rules on capital punishment, Jun. 6, 1977; Jun. 15, 1978; first woman member Jul. 7, 1981.

surgeons, patron of, Aug. 16.

Suriname: independent, Nov. 25, 1975.

Surrey Iron Railway: first public freight-carrying railway, Jul. 26, 1803.

Surveyor I, Jun. 2, 1966.

Teague, Olin E., Apr. 6, 1910.

Teale, Edwin Way, Jun. 2, 1899.

Tearle, Sir Godrey, Oct. 12, 1884.

Teasdale, Sara, Aug. 8, 1884.

Tebaldi, Renata, Jan. 2, 1922.

Tebet, p. x.

Tebetu, p. x.

Tedder, Arthur William, Jul. 11, 1890.

Tegner, Esaias, Nov. 13, 1782.

Teheran Conference: begins, Nov. 28, 1943.

Teilhard de Chardin, Pierre, May 1, 1881.

telecast address: first from White House, Oct. 5, 1947.

telegraph, Jan. 6, 1838; patented, Jun. 20, 1840; first message, May 24, 1844.

telegraph cable: first submarine, Nov. 13, 1851; first Pacific, Jul. 4, 1903.

telegraph communications: established between U.S. and England, Jul. 27, 1866.

telegraph service, wireless: opened, Jan. 26, 1930.

telegraph workers, patron of, Mar. 24.

telegraphic line: London to New Zealand, Feb. 18, 1876.

Tel-el Aqqaqir, Nov. 2, 1942.

telephone: patented, Mar. 7, 1876; first demonstration, Feb. 12, 1877; first demonstration to Queen Victoria, Jan. 14, 1878; inter-city link, Mar. 27, 1884; communication between London and Paris, Mar. 18, 1891; first transcontinental call, Jan. 25, 1915; first mechanical switchboard, Oct. 14, 1923; transatlantic service, Jan. 7, 1927.

telephone cable: first trans-Atlantic, Sep. 25, 1956; Commonwealth Pacific submarine, opened, Dec. 1, 1963.

telephone line: first submarine, Mar. 14, 1891.

telephone workers, patron of, Mar. 24.

television broadcast, first network, Feb. 1, 1940.

television broadcasts, color, Oct. 11, 1950; first broadcast, Jun. 28, 1951.

Telford, Thomas, Aug. 9, 1757.

Teller, Edward, Jan. 15, 1908.

Tellico Dam, Jun. 15, 1978.

Telstar I, Jul. 10, 1962; Jul. 13, 1962.

Temin, Howard Martin, Dec. 10, 1934.

Temple, Shirley. *See* Black, Shirley Temple.

Templer, Sir Gerald Walter Robert, Sep. 11, 1898.

Tenerife: air disaster, Mar. 27, 1977.

Ten Martyrs of Crete, Dec. 23.

Tennessee: admitted to Union, Jun. 1, 1796.

Tennessee Valley Authority, May 18, 1933.

Tenniel, Sir John, Feb. 28, 1820.

Tennis Court Oath, Jun. 17, 1789.

Tennyson, Alfred Lord, Aug. 6, 1809; Apr. 23, 1850; Oct. 6, 1892.

Teo, Penitala Fiatau, Jul. 23, 1911.

Teresa of Avila, Mar. 28, 1515.

Teresa of Calcutta, Mother, Aug. 27, 1910.

Tereshkova, Valentina Vladimirovna, Mar. 6, 1937; first female in space, Jun. 16, 1963.

Terhune, Albert Payson, Dec. 12, 1872.

Terkel, Studs, May 16, 1912.

Terman, Lewis Madison, Jan. 15, 1877.

Terni (Umbria), patron of, Feb. 15.

Terra Natalis (Natal), Dec. 25, 1497.

Territorial Day (New Caledonia), Sep. 24.

Territory Day (British Virgin Islands), Jul. 1.

Terry, Dame Ellen Alice, Feb. 27, 1847.

Terry, Fernando Belaúnde, Feb. 1, 1969.

Teruel (Spanish Civil War), Feb. 15, 1938.

Tesla, Nikola, Jul. 9, 1856.

Test Act (England), Mar. 22, 1673.

test-tube baby: first is born, Jul. 25, 1978.

Teton Dam: collapses, Jun. 5, 1976.

Tetrazzini, Luisa, Jun. 29, 1871.

Tewksbury, Battle of, May 4, 1471.

Texas: independence, Mar. 1, 1836; annexed to U.S., Mar. 1, 1845; admitted to Union, Dec. 29, 1845; May 30, 1848.

Texas Republic, Oct. 22, 1836.

Thackeray, William Makepeace, Jul. 18, 1811.

Thai Constitution Day (Thailand), Dec. 10.

Thailand, Japanese invasion of, Dec. 8, 1941; May 11, 1949; Mar. 6, 1962; May 12, 1962; Feb. 5, 1965; Mar. 7, 1970; Jan. 26, 1975; government falls, Oct. 6, 1976.

Thanksgiving and Independence Day (St. Vincent), Oct. 27.

Thanksgiving Day (Canada), Oct. intro.

Thanksgiving Day (Liberia), Nov. intro.

Thanksgiving Day (United States), Nov. intro.

Thanksgiving Salute to Older Americans, National, Nov. intro.

Thant, U, Jan. 22, 1909.

Thapsus, Feb. 6, 46.

Thatcher, Margaret, Oct. 13, 1925; Feb. 11, 1975; May 3, 1979.

Thayer, Sylvanus, Jun. 9, 1785.

Theiler, Max, Jan. 30, 1899.

Theodoric, Mar. 5, 493.

Theodosius, Emperor, Feb. 27, 380.

theologians, patron of, Aug. 28; Dec. 27.

Theorell, (Alex) Hugo (Teodor), Jul. 6, 1903.

thermonuclear missiles: first on U.S. submarine, Nov. 15, 1960.

Theroux, Paul, Apr. 10, 1941.

Thiers, Louis Adolphe, Apr. 15, 1797.

Thieu, Nguyen Van, Jun. 13, 1965; Jun. 18, 1965; Sep. 3, 1967; Sep. 27, 1969; Apr. 21, 1975.

thieves, patron of, Nov. 13.

Third Coalition, Apr. 11, 1805.

Third Coalition, War of, Feb. 7, 1807.

Third Crusade, Oct. 4, 1190.

Third Republic Day (Ghana), Sep. 24.

Third Togolese Republic, Jan. 13, 1967.

33 Immortals (Uruguay), Apr. 19.

Thirty Years' War, May 23, 1618; Mar. 10, 1624; Jun. 20, 1624; Nov. 5, 1630; Sep. 17, 1631; Mar. 29, 1632; Nov. 16, 1632; May 19, 1635; Nov. 2, 1642; May 19, 1643; Mar. 7, 1645; Mar. 14, 1647; Jan. 30, 1648; Jul. 26, 1648; ends, Oct. 24, 1648.

Thomas, Dylan (Marlais), Oct. 27, 1914.

Thomas, George, Jul. 31, 1816; Dec. 16, 1864.

Thomas, Kurt, Mar. 29, 1956.

Thomas, Lowell, Apr. 6, 1892.

Thomas, Martha Carey, Jan. 2, 1857.

Thomas, Norman, Nov. 20, 1884; May 21, 1932.

Thomas, Terry, Jul. 14, 1911.

Thomas, William Miles Webster, Mar. 2, 1897.

Thomas Jefferson's Birthday (Alabama, Oklahoma, Virginia), Apr. 13.

Thomas of Lancaster, Mar. 16, 1322.

Thompson, Daley, Jul. 30, 1958.

Thompson, David, Apr. 30, 1770.

Thompson, Dorothy, Jul. 9, 1894.

Thompson, Francis, Dec. 16, 1859.

Thompson, J(ames) Walter, Oct. 28, 1847.

Thompson, Sir Benjamin, Mar. 26, 1753.

Thomson, Charles Wyville, Mar. 5, 1830.

Thomson, Elihu, Mar. 29, 1853.

Thomson, Joseph, Feb. 14, 1858.

Thomson, Sir George Paget, May 3, 1892.

Thomson, Sir Joseph John, Dec. 18, 1856.

Thomson, Virgil, Nov. 25, 1896.

Thomson, William, Jun. 26, 1824.

Thorbecke, Jan Rudolf de, Jan. 14, 1798.

Thoreau, Henry David, Jul. 12, 1817.

Thorild, Thomas, Apr. 18, 1759.

thorium: deposits found, Dec. 2, 1962.

Thorndike, Dame Sybil, Oct. 24, 1882.

Thornton, Charles B(ates), Jul. 22, 1913.

Thornton, William, May 20, 1759.

Thoroddsen, Jon, Oct. 5, 1819.

Thorpe, Jim, May 28, 1888.

Three Kings' Day (Puerto Rico), Jan. intro.

Three Little Pigs: premiere, May 25, 1933.

Three Mile Island, Mar. 28, 1979.

Three Wise Men, Jul. 23.

Thresher, U.S.S.: lost, Apr. 10, 1963.

throat, suffers of afflictions of, patron of, Feb. 3.

Thule (Greenland), Jan. 22, 1968.

Thulin, Ingrid, Jan. 27, 1929.

Thunderbirds (U.S. Air Force flying team), Jan. 18, 1982.

Thurber, James (Grover), Dec. 8, 1894.

Thurmond, (James) Strom, Dec. 5, 1902; Jul. 17, 1948; sets filibuster record Aug. 30, 1957.

Thursday, p. ix.

Thyssen, Fritz, Nov. 9, 1873.

Tiberius (Roman emperor), Nov. 16, B.C..

Tibet, Apr. 21, 1912; incorporated into China, May 27, 1951.

Ticonderoga, Fort, May 10, 1775; captured by British, Jul. 6, 1777.

Tientsin, Treaty of: signed, Jun. 26, 1858.

Tierney, Gene, Nov. 20, 1920.

Tiffany, Charles Lewis, Feb. 15, 1812.

Tiffany, Louis Comfort, Feb. 18, 1848.

Tilden, Samuel Jones, Feb. 9, 1814.

tile makers, patron of, Aug. 16.

Tillich, Paul, Aug. 20, 1886.

Tilly, Count of, Sep. 17, 1631.

Tilsit, Treaty of: signed, Jul. 7, 1807.

Times Beach, Mo., Feb. 22, 1983.

Timket (Ethiopia), Jan. 19.

Timur (Tamerlane): conquers Delhi, Dec. 18, 1398; Jan. 3, 1399; Mar. 24, 1401; Jul. 20, 1402; Jul. 28, 1402; Feb. 18, 1405.

Tinbergen, Jan, Apr. 12, 1903.

Tinbergen, Nikolaas, Apr. 15, 1907.

Ting, Samuel Chao Chung, Jan. 26, 1936.

Tinsel Day (U.S.), Dec. 5.

Tinsel Day, Dec. intro.

Tippecanoe, Battle of, Nov. 7, 1811.

tipsy people, patron of, May 25.

Tiris el-Gharbia: annexed by Morocco, Aug. 11, 1979.

Tiros I: launched, Apr. 1, 1960.

Tirpitz, Admiral Alfred von, Mar. 19, 1849; Mar. 16, 1916.

Tiselius, Arne W. K., Aug. 10, 1902.

Tish Ab B'Ab, p. xii; Jul. intro.; Aug. intro.

Tishri, p. x.

Titanic: sinks, Apr. 15, 1912.

Tito, Marshal, May 7, 1892; Nov. 11, 1945; Apr. 7, 1963.

Tituba, Mar. 1, 1692.

Tobruk (Libya), Jun. 21, 1942.

Tocqueville, Alexis de, Jul. 29, 1805.

Todd, Alexander Robertus, Oct. 2, 1907.

Todd, Michael, Jun. 2, 1909.

Todd, Richard, Jun. 11, 1919.

Togliatti, Palmiro, Mar. 26, 1893.

Togo, Jan. 13, 1963; Jan. 13, 1967.

Togoland, May 6, 1919; Apr. 27, 1960.

Toji or Winter Solstice (Japan), Dec. 22.

Tojo, Hideki (*Eiki*), Dec. 30, 1884.

Tokugawa, Iyeyasu, Dec. 26, 1542.

Tokyo, Apr. 25, 1867; becomes capital of Japan, Jul. 17, 1868; Sep. 1, 1923; Apr. 18, 1942; Allied bombing, Apr. 13, 1945; Sep. 7, 1945; XVIII Summer Olympics, Oct. 10, 1964; May 21, 1978.

Tokyo Rose, Jan. 19, 1977.

Tolbert, William R. Jr., May 13, 1913; Jul. 23, 1971; Jan. 3, 1972; Apr. 14, 1979; Apr. 12, 1980.

Toledo, Treaty of, Mar. 6, 1480; Feb. 1, 1539.

Toledo (Spain), May 25, 1085.

Toler, Sidney, Apr. 28, 1874.

Tolkien, J. R. R., Jan. 3, 1892.

Tolkien Week, Sep. intro.

Tolman, Edward Chace, Apr. 14, 1886.

Tolstoi, Aleksei Nikolaevich, Jan. 10, 1882.

Tolstoi, Leo Nikolayevich, Count, Sep. 9, 1828.

Tolstoy, Count Alexey, Aug. 24, 1817.

Tombalbaye, François (Chad): assassinated, Apr. 13, 1975.

Tombaugh, Clyde, Feb. 18, 1930.

tomb of St. Peter: discovered, Dec. 23, 1950.

Tomb of the Unknown Soldier: dedicated, Nov. 11, 1921.

Tomlin, Lily, Sep. 1, 1936.

Tomonaga, Sin-Itiro, Mar. 31, 1906.

Tompkins, Daniel D., Mar. 4, 1817.

Tone, Wolfe, Jan. 20, 1763.

Tonga: independence, Jun. 4, 1970.

Tonga Islands, May 18, 1900.

Tongoland, Apr. 23, 1895.

Tonkin: made French protectorate, Jun. 6, 1884.

Tonkin Gulf Resolution, Aug. 7, 1964.

topaz, Nov. intro.

Topper, Sir Charles, Jul. 2, 1821.

Tordesillas, Treaty of: divides New World, Jun. 7, 1494.

Torgau, Battle of, Nov. 3, 1760.

Torme, Mel, Sep. 13, 1925.

Toronto: incorporated, Mar. 6, 1834.

Torrey Canyon, Mar. 18, 1967.

Torricelli, Evangelista, Oct. 15, 1608.

Torrijos-Herrera, Omar, Feb. 13, 1929.

Torstenson, Lennart, Count of Ortala, Aug. 17, 1603.

Tosca: premiere, Jan. 14, 1900.

Toscanini, Arturo, Mar. 25, 1867.

Tostig (Earl of Northumbria), Sep. 20, 1066; Sep. 25, 1066.

Toul, Jan. 15, 1552.

Toulet, Paul Jean, Jun. 5, 1867.

Toulon (France), Nov. 27, 1942.

Toulouse-Lautrec, Henri de, Nov. 24, 1864.

Touring Theater Month, May intro.

tourmaline, Oct. intro.

Tower, John Goodwin, Sep. 29, 1925.

Tower of London, May 21, 1471.

Town, Ithiel, Oct. 3, 1784.

Town Meeting Day (Vermont), Mar. intro.

Townes, Charles Hard, Jul. 28, 1915.

Townsend, Francis Everett, Jan. 13, 1867.

Townshend Acts passed, Jun. 29, 1767; Feb. 11, 1768.

Toynbee, Arnold, Apr. 14, 1889.

Tracy, Spencer, Apr. 5, 1900.

Trade Workers' Day (U.S.S.R.), Jul. intro.

Trades Disputes Act (India), Apr. 12, 1929.

Trafalgar, Battle of, Oct. 21, 1805.

tram cars: first in London, Mar. 23, 1861.

Tranquillity, Sea of, Feb. 20, 1965.

trans-Alaska oil pipeline: construction authorized, Nov. 16, 1973; first oil, Jun. 20, 1977.

transatlantic passenger service: first commercial, Jun. 28, 1939.

transatlantic radio broadcast: first, Mar. 12, 1922.

transatlantic radio-telephone transmission: first, Oct. 21, 1915.

Trans-Caucasian Soviet Socialist Republic: organized, Mar. 12, 1922.

transcontinental automobile trip: first U.S., Aug. 18, 1903.

Transfer Day (Virgin Islands), Mar. intro.

Transfiguration of Our Lord Jesus Christ, Feast of, Aug. 6.

Transit I-B: space lighthouse, Apr. 13, 1960.

Transjordan, Feb. 20, 1928; Mar. 22, 1946; Apr. 3, 1949.

Transjordan, Kingdom of, Apr. 24, 1950.

Transkei, Republic of: given independence, Oct. 26, 1976.

Transportation Corps, U.S.: created, Jul. 31, 1942.

Trans-Siberian Railway, May 31, 1891.

Trans-Tasman submarine telephone cable: opens, Jul. 9, 1962.

Transvaal Boers: revolt breaks out, Dec. 30, 1880.

Transvaal Colony, Oct. 25, 1900.

Transvaal (South African Republic), Jan. 17, 1852; established, Dec. 16, 1856; Jan. 6, 1857; Apr. 12, 1877; declared British territory, Sep. 29, 1879; Jan. 6, 1896; Jan. 21, 1898.

Transylvania, Jan. 26, 1699; Romanian invasion begins, Aug. 28, 1916; Jan. 10, 1919.

Traore, Moussa, Sep. 25, 1936.

Trapp, Maria Augusta von, Jan. 26, 1905.

Traubel, Helen, Jun. 20, 1899.

travelers, patron of, Feb. 12; Mar. 17; Jul. 25.

Travis, William Barret, Aug. 9, 1809.

Treacher, Arthur, Jul. 23, 1894.

Treasury, U.S. Department of, Sep. 2, 1789.

Trebizond, Apr. 18, 1916.

Trebur (Germany), Oct. 16, 1076.

Tree Planting Day (Lesotho), Mar. intro.

Tree, Sir Herbert (Draper) Beerbohm, Dec. 17, 1853.

Treitschke, Heinrich Gotthard von, Sep. 15, 1834.

Trenchard, Hugh Montague, Feb. 3, 1873.

Trent, Nov. 3, 1918.

Trent, Council of: opens, Dec. 13, 1545.

Trentino, patron of, Jun. 26.

Trentino (Italy), May 15, 1916.

Trenton, Battle of, Dec. 26, 1776.

Trevino, Lee, Dec. 1, 1939.

Trevithick, Richard, Apr. 13, 1771.

Trevor, Claire, Mar. 8, 1909.

Triangle Shirtwaist Co.: fire, Mar. 25, 1911.

Trident Conference, May 12, 1943.

Trier: Archbishop of, Jan. 24, 1446.

Trieste, Nov. 3, 1918.

Trieste: U.S. bathyscaphe, Sep. 19, 1957; Jan. 23, 1960.

Trifon Zarenzan (Bulgaria), Feb. 14.

Trilling, Lionel, Jul. 4, 1905.

Trinidad, Mar. 27, 1802.

Trinidad and Tobago, Feb. 23, 1967; independent member of Commonwealth of Nations, Aug. 31, 1962; becomes republic, Aug. 31, 1976.

Trinity House, patron of, Nov. 23.

Trinity Sunday, p. xii; May intro.; Jun. intro.

Triple Alliance, Jan. 4, 1717.

Triple Crown: Secretariat wins, Jun. 9, 1973.

Tripoli: annexed by Italy, Nov. 5, 1911; Mar. 6, 1912; Apr. 8, 1926; Jan. 24, 1943.

Tripoli Declaration, Dec. 5, 1977.

Tripolitan War, May 14, 1801.

Trippe, Juan (Terry), Jun. 27, 1899.

Trissino, Giangiorgio, Jul. 8, 1478.

Triton: U.S. atomic submarine, May 10, 1960.

Triumph of the Revolution Anniversary of the (Cuba), Jan. 1.

Trivia day, Jan. intro.

Trocadero, Battle of, Aug. 31, 1823.

Trollope, Anthony, Apr. 24, 1815.

Trotsky, Leon, Oct. 26, 1879; Jul. 16, 1917; Jan. 15, 1925; May 7, 1925; Sep. 30, 1927; Oct. 23, 1927; expelled from Communist Party, Dec. 27, 1927; Jan. 3, 1928; Jan. 19, 1929; Jan. 21, 1929.

Trudeau, Pierre Elliott, Oct. 18, 1919; Apr. 6, 1968; May 22, 1979.

Truffaut, François, Feb. 6, 1932.

Trujillo Molina, Rafael Leonidas: assassinated, May 30, 1961.

Truk, Feb. 16, 1944.

Truk (Caroline Islands), Apr. 29, 1944.

Truman, Bess, Feb. 13, 1885.

Truman, Harry S., May 8, 1884; Apr. 12, 1945; Nov. 21, 1946; Jul. 12, 1948; Jul. 17, 1948; inaugurated, Jan. 20, 1949; Feb. 6, 1950; Jan. 31, 1950; May 11, 1950; Jun. 27, 1950; Jan. 3, 1951; Apr. 6, 1951; Apr. 11, 1951; May 8, 1964.

Truman Day (Missouri), May intro.

Trumbull, John, Jun. 6, 1756.

Trumbull, Jonathan, Oct. 12, 1710.

Truth-in-Lending Law, U.S., Jul. 1, 1969.

Tryon, Thomas, Jan. 14, 1926.

Tsedenbal, Yumzhagiyen, Sep. 17, 1916.

Tshombe, Moise (Kapenda), Nov. 10, 1919.

Tsingtao (China), Nov. 7, 1914.

Tsiolkovsky, Konstantin Eduardovich, Sep. 17, 1857.

Tsiranana, Philibert, Sep. 6, 1970.

Tsushima Strait, Battle of, May 27, 1905.

Tsvett, Mikhail Semenovich, May 14, 1872.

TU-144: Soviet supersonic jetliner, May 25, 1971.

Tubman, William V.S., Jan. 20, 1960; Jul. 23, 1971.

Tuchman, Barbara, Jan. 30, 1912.

Tucker, Henry (Sir), May 26, 1968.

Tucker, Richard, Aug. 28, 1914.

Tucker, Sophie, Jan. 13, 1884.

Tuesday, p. ix.

Tuileries: mob marches, Jun. 20, 1792; stormed by Parisian mob, Aug. 10, 1792.

Tukhachevski, Michael: executed, Jun. 12, 1937.

Tulagi, Solomon Islands: captured by U.S., Aug. 8, 1942.

Tunisia, Apr. 9, 1938; Mar. 20, 1956; Jan. 10, 1957; independence, Jun. 1, 1959.

Tunisian workers rising, Jan. 26, 1978.

Tunney, Gene, May 25, 1898; Sep. 23, 1926.

Tupouto'a Crown Prince Birthday of (Tonga), May 4.

turbo-prop: first airliner, Feb. 1, 1957.

Turenne, Vicomte de (Henri de La Tour d'Auvergne), Sep. 11, 1611.

Turgenev, Ivan Sergeyevich, Nov. 9, 1818.

Turkey, Jan. 9, 1792; invasion of, Apr. 25, 1915; Jan. 27, 1822; independence, Jul. 13, 1841; invaded by Russia, Jul. 2, 1853; Apr. 18, 1897; Oct. 7, 1912; coup d'état, Jan. 23, 1913; recaptures Adrianople, Jul. 22, 1913; declares war against Allies, Nov. 23, 1914; declares war on Romania, Aug. 30, 1916; Greece declares war on, Jul. 2, 1917; Jan. 20, 1921; Jan. 2, 1922; Jul. 24, 1923; Apr. 9, 1928; U.S. aid cut, Feb. 5, 1975; coup d'état, Sep. 10, 1980.

Turkish Caliphate: abolished, Mar. 3, 1924.

Turkish Cypriots, Feb. 13, 1975.

Turkish forces (World War I), Jan. 26, 1915.

Turkish National Day (Turkey, Cyprus), Oct. 29.

Turkish Republic: proclaimed, Oct. 29, 1923.

Turkish troops (World War I), Jan. 9, 1917.

Turks, Jan. 26, 1699; Jan. 30, 1915; Jan. 4, 1916.

Turner, Frederick Jackson, Nov. 14, 1861.

Turner, Henry McNear, Feb. 1, 1831.

Turner, J. M. W., Apr. 23, 1775.

Turner, Lana, Feb. 8, 1920.

Turner, Nat, Oct. 2, 1800; slave insurrection begins, Aug. 13, 1831.

Turner, Stansfield, Feb. 1, 1923.

turquoise, Dec. intro.

Tutankhamen's sarcophagus, Nov. 29, 1922; Feb. 12, 1924.

Tutankhamen's sepulchral chamber, Feb. 16, 1923.

Tweed, William Marcy, Apr. 3, 1823.

Twelfth Night (England), Jan. 5.

Twelve Brothers, Sep. 1.

Twentieth Amendment (U.S. Constitution), Feb. 6, 1933.

Twentieth Summer Olympics: open in Munich, Aug. 26, 1972.

Twenty-fifth Amendment (U.S. Constitution): ratified, Feb. 10, 1967.

Twenty-first Amendment: revokes Prohibition (18th Amendment), Dec. 5, 1933.

Twenty-fourth Amendment (U.S. Constitution), Feb. 4, 1964.

Twenty-fourth Infantry Regiment: disbanded, Jul. 26, 1951.

Twenty-second Amendment: ratified, Feb. 25, 1951.

Twenty-sixth Amendment (U.S. Constitution): ratified, Jun. 30, 1971.

Twenty-third Amendment: ratified, Mar. 29, 1961.

Twiggy (Leslie Hornby), Sep. 19, 1949.

Twining, Nathan Farragut, Oct. 11, 1897.

Twitty, Conway, Sep. 1, 1933.

Two Ewalds, Oct. 3.

Tydings-McDuffie Act, Mar. 24, 1934.

Tyler, John, Mar. 29, 1790; Mar. 4, 1841; Apr. 4, 1841.

Tynan, Kenneth, Apr. 2, 1927.

Tyndall, John, Aug. 2, 1820.

typewriter: first patent, Jan. 7, 1714.

Tyrol, Apr. 24, 1921.

Tyson, Cicely, Dec. 19, 1939.

Tyus, Wyomia, Aug. 29, 1945.

Tyutchev, Fyodor, Dec. 5, 1803.

Tyvendedagen (Norway), Jan. 13.

U

U-2 reconnaissance plane: shot down, May 1, 1960.

U9: German submarine, Sep. 22, 1914.

Udall, Morris (King), Jun. 15, 1922.

Udall, Stewart Lee, Jan. 31, 1920.

Uganda, Apr. 11, 1894; Mar. 10, 1900; independence, Oct. 9, 1962; admitted to UN, Oct. 25, 1962; businesses nationalized, May 1, 1970.

Uganda, Second Republic of, Jan. 25, 1971.

Ugarte, Augusto Pinochet, Nov. 11, 1915; Nov. 25, 1915.

Ugly Duckling, The: premiere, Dec. 10, 1916.

Ukraine, Jan. 28, 1918; Feb. 18, 1918; Jan. 2, 1922.

Ukranian Soviet Socialist Republic: independence, Dec. 27, 1917.

ukulele: patented, Sep. 18, 1917.

Ulanova, Galina Sergeyevna, Jan. 8, 1910.

Ullmann, Liv, Dec. 16, 1939.

Ulm, Mar. 14, 1647.

Ulmanis, Karlis, May 15, 1934.

Ulrica Eleanor (Sweden), Nov. 30, 1718; Feb. 29, 1720.

Ulrika Eleonora (Sweden), Jan. 23, 1688.

ultimus annus confusionis, p. xi.

Ululu, p. x.

Ulysses: published, Feb. 2, 1922.

Umberto II (Italy), Sep. 15, 1904.

Unamuno y Jugo, Miguel de, Sep. 2, 1864.

Understanding and Peace Day, World, Feb. intro.

Undset, Sigrid, May 20, 1882.

Unemployment Relief Act, Mar. 31, 1933.

U Ne Win, Mar. 2, 1974.

UNESCO, Nov. 4, 1946; to end membership, Dec. 29, 1983.

UN General Assembly: Rockefeller gift accepted, Dec. 14, 1946.

UN Headquarters: site chosen, Dec. 14, 1946.

UNICEF: established, Dec. 11, 1946.

UNICEF Anniversary Day, Dec. 11.

Unification of Italy, May 27, 1860.

Uniformity Act, Jan. 15, 1549.

Union Act: passed, Jul. 23, 1840.

Union Day (Burma), Feb. 12.

Union Day (Somali Democratic Republic), Jul. 1.

Union Day (Tanzania), Apr. 26.

Union of Central American Republics: formed, Mar. 21, 1847.

Union of Soviet Socialist Republics, Jan. 1, 1923, name adopted, Nov. 2, 1923.

Union of Sweden and Norway: ended, Oct. 26, 1905.

United African National Council (Rhodesia), Apr. 21, 1979.

United Arab Emirates: formation, Dec. 2, 1971.

United Arab Republic, formation, Feb. 1, 1958; Jun. 19, 1967.

United Automobile Workers, May 4, 1950.

United Front (Cambodia), Jan. 7, 1979.

United Kingdom, Jan. 1, 1801; capital punishment abolished, Dec. 18, 1969; Jan. 20, 1971; Mar. 13, 1972; Mar. 8, 1973.

United Kingdom of England and Ireland: first parliament, Feb. 2, 1801.

United Kingdom of the Serbs, Croats, and Slovenes: proclaimed, Nov. 24, 1918.

United Methodist Church, Nov. 11, 1966.

United Mine Workers, Mar. 6, 1947; Jan. 5, 1970; strike ends, Jun. 8, 1981.

United Nations, Jan. 1, 1942; Apr. 18, 1945; charter signed, Jun. 26, 1945; May 11, 1949; Apr. 27, 1960; Jan. 27, 1967.

United Nations Charter Day, Jun. 26.

United Nations Day, Oct. 23.

United Nations' Day (Barbados), Oct. intro.

United Nations Disarmament Commission, Feb. 4, 1952.

United Nations Educational, Scientific, and Cultural Organization (UNESCO):formed, Nov. 4, 1946.

United Nations Food and Agriculture Organization, Apr. 2, 1951.

United Nations General Assembly: first, Jan. 10, 1946.

United Nations Relief and Rehabilitation Administration: formed, Nov. 9, 1943.

United Provinces (Netherlands), Apr. 9, 1609.

United Service Organization: founded, Feb. 4, 1941.

United States: declares neutrality, Nov. 6, 1914.

United States, U.S.S., Oct. 25, 1812.

United States Navy: established, Mar. 27, 1794.

Unity Day (Egypt), Feb. 22.

Unity Day (Syria), Feb. 22.

Unity Day (Vanuatu), Nov. 29.

Unity Day (Zambia), Jul. intro.; Jul. 6.

Universal Children's Day, Oct. 6.

Universal Church, patron of, Mar. 19.

Universal Exhibition (Paris), May 6, 1889.

Universal Postal Union Day, Oct. 9.

universal suffrage: Portugal, Mar. 11, 1918.

Universal Vote Day (San Marino), Mar. 25.

universities, colleges and schools, patron of, Jan. 28.

University of Budapest: opens, Nov. 15, 1635.

University of Heidelberg: founded, Oct. 23, 1385.

Unlearned Parliment (England), Oct. 6, 1404.

Unser, Bobby, Feb. 20, 1934.

Untermeyer, Louis, Oct. 1, 1885.

U Nu, Mar. 2, 1962.

Unyamwize, Mar. 14, 1872.

Updike, John, Mar. 18, 1932.

Upjohn, Richard, Jan. 22, 1802.

Upper Volta, Mar. 1, 1919; independence, Aug. 5, 1960; Nov. 27, 1977.

Uranus, Mar. 13, 1781.

Urban VI (pope), Oct. 23, 1385.

Urban VII (pope), Aug. 4, 1521.

Urey, Harold Clayton, Apr. 29, 1893.

Uris, Leon (Marcus), Aug. 13, 1924.

Urrutia Lleo, Manuel, Dec. 8, 1901.

Ursuline Martyrs of Valenciennes, Oct. 17.

Uruguay: independence, Aug. 25, 1825.

U.S. and U.S.S.R.: first direct air service between, Jul. 15, 1968.

U.S. census: first, Mar. 1, 1790.

U.S. Civil War, Dec. 20, 1860; Jul. 1, 1863; Jul. 4, 1863; Nov. 25, 1863; Jun. 27, 1864; Aug. 5, 1864; Nov. 15, 1864; Nov. 30, 1864; Dec. 16, 1864.

U.S. copyright law: amended, Feb. 3, 1831.

U.S. First Army: begin operations in Germany, Oct. 2, 1944.

U.S. Golfers Association Open: first, Oct. 4, 1895.

U.S. Marine Corps headquarters: suicide attack in Beirut (Lebanon), Oct. 23, 1983.

U.S. Naval Academy: **see** U.S. Naval School, Oct. 10, 1845.

U.S. Naval School: opens, Oct. 10, 1845.

U.S. Naval War College: established, Oct. 6, 1884.

USO Anniversary (U.S.), Feb. intro.; Feb. 4.

U.S. Open tennis tournament, Sep. 9, 1968.

Ussher, James, Jan. 4, 1581.

U.S. Supreme Court: first meeting, Feb. 1, 1790.

U.S.S.R., Jan. 21, 1929; joins League of Nations, Sep. 18, 1934; new constitution, Dec. 5, 1936; invades Poland, Sep. 17, 1939; Jan. 27, 1962; Jan. 27, 1967; cultural exchange ban lifted by U.S., Dec. 20, 1968; Jan. 24, 1972; trade with Spain, Sep. 15, 1972. *See also* Russia.

U.S.S.R. and Canada: first direct air service between, Jul. 11, 1966.

U.S.S.R. and U.S.: first direct air service between, Jul. 15, 1968.

Ustinov, Peter, Apr. 16, 1921.

Utah, May 30, 1848; admitted to Union, Jan. 4, 1896.

Utah Medical Center, Dec. 2, 1982.

Utah State Prison, Jan. 17, 1977.

U Thant, Mar. 5, 1967.

Utrecht, Peace of, Feb. 28, 1474; Apr. 11, 1713.

V

V-1 rocket: first used, Jun. 12, 1944.

V-2 rocket: first fired on London, Sep. 7, 1944; first launch from ship, Sep. 6, 1947.

Vaccaro, Brenda, Nov. 18, 1939.

vaccination: development of, May 14, 1796.

Vadim, Roger, Jan. 26, 1928.

Vail, Theodore Newton, Jul. 16, 1845.

Valdez (Alaska), Jul. 28, 1977.

Val d'Isere: avalanche, Feb. 9, 1970.

Valence, patron of, Oct. 5.

Valens (Roman Emperor): killed, Aug. 9, 378.

Valentino, Rudolph, May 6, 1895.

Valera y Alcalá Galiano, Juan, Oct. 18, 1824.

Valery, Paul Ambroise Toussaint Jules, Oct. 30, 1871.

Vallandigham, Clement Laird, Jul. 29, 1820.

Vallee, Rudy, Jul. 28, 1901.

Valle-Riestra, José Maria, Dec. 26, 1900.

Valletta, Carnival in (Malta), May intro.

Valley Forge, Dec. 19, 1777.

Valois (Edris Stannus), Ninette de, Jun. 6, 1898.

Valromey, Jan. 17, 1601.

Valse Triste: premiere, Apr. 25, 1905.

Van Allen, James Alfred, Sep. 7, 1914.

Van Brocklin, Norm, Mar. 15, 1926.

Van Buren, Abigail, Jul. 4, 1918.

Van Buren, Martin, Dec. 5, 1782; inaugurated, Mar. 4, 1837.

Van (Caucasus), Apr. 20, 1915.

Vance, Cyrus, Mar. 27, 1917; Jan. 6, 1978.

Vancouver, George, Jun. 22, 1757.

Vandegrift, Alexander Archer, Mar. 13, 1887.

Vandenberg, Arthur Hendrick, Mar. 22, 1884.

Vanderbilt, Amy, Jul. 22, 1908.

Vanderbilt, Cornelius, May 27, 1794.

Vanderbilt, William Henry, May 8, 1821.

Vanderbilt, William Kissam, Dec. 12, 1849.

van der Rohe, Mies, Mar. 27, 1886.

Van Doren, Carl, Sep. 10, 1885.

Van Doren, Mark, Jun. 13, 1894.

Van Dyke, Sir Anthony, Mar. 22, 1599.

van Gogh, Vincent, Mar. 30, 1853.

Vanguard I, Mar. 17, 1958.

Van Heusen, Jimmy, Jan. 26, 1913.

Van Loon, Hendrik, Jan. 14, 1882.

Van Riebeeck Day (Republic of South Africa), Apr. 6.

Van't Hoff, Jacobus H., Aug. 30, 1852.

Vanuatu, Republic of: independence, Jul. 30, 1980.

Van Vleck, John Hasbrouck, Mar. 13, 1899.

Van Zeeland, Paul (Belgium), Mar. 25, 1935.

Vanzetti, Bartolomeo, Jul. 11, 1888.

Vardon, Harry, May 7, 1870.

Varennes: French royal family arrested, Jun. 21, 1791.

Varennes, Pierre Gaultier de, Nov. 17, 1685.

Vargas, Getulio Dorneles, Apr. 19, 1883.

Variag, Feb. 9, 1904.

Varna, Battle of, Nov. 10, 1444.

Vasa, Gustavus, Jun. 7, 1523.

Vasari, Giorgio, Jul. 30, 1511.

Vassy, Mar. 1, 1562.

Vatican, Jan. 8, 1966; abolition of book censure, Feb. 8, 1966; Jan. 29, 1967; Jan. 25, 1970; May 18, 1978.

Vatican City, Feb. 11, 1929.

Vatican Council, Second: opens, Oct. 11, 1962.

Vauban, Sebastien le Prestre de, May 15, 1633.

Vaucanson, Jacques de, Feb. 24, 1709.

Vaucelles, Truce of, Feb. 5, 1556.

Vaughan, Henry, Apr. 17, 1622.

Vaughan, Sarah, Mar. 27, 1924.

Veadar, p. x.

Veblen, Thorstein (Bunde), Jul. 30, 1857.

V-E Day, May 8.

Vedrines, J., Feb. 22, 1912.

Vega, Lope (Felix) de, Nov. 25, 1562.

Vega Day (Sweden), Apr. 24.

Veil, Simone, Jul. 13, 1927.

Veit, Philipp, Feb. 13, 1793.

Velasco Alvarado, Juan (Peru), Feb. 6, 1969.

Velázquez, Diego Rodriguez de Silva y, Jun. 6, 1599.

Velikovsky, Immanuel, Jun. 10, 1895.

vendredi, p. ix.

Venera 7, Dec. 15, 1970.

Venetia, Jul. 3, 1866.

Venetian Republic, Mar. 22, 1848.

Veneto, Vittorio, Nov. 3, 1918.

Venezuela: independence, Jul. 5, 1821; Jan. 23, 1961; Jan. 6, 1967.

Venice, patron of, Apr. 25.

Venice (Italy), Jan. 26, 1699; Apr. 25, 1903.

Venizelos, Eleutherios, Aug. 23, 1864.

Venus: information from *Mariner II,* Dec. 14, 1962; temperature, Feb. 26, 1963; Soviet spacecraft lands, Dec. 15, 1970.

Venus 3, Mar. 1, 1966.

Venus with the Mirror, Mar. 10, 1914.

Vera Cruz, Mar. 29, 1847.

Veracruz (Mexico), Apr. 21, 1914.

Vera-Ellen, Feb. 16, 1926.

Verdaguer, Jacinto, May 17, 1845.

Verdi, Giuseppe, Oct. 10, 1813.

Verdon, Gwen, Jan. 13, 1925.

Verdun, Jan. 15, 1552.

Verdun, Battle of, Feb. 20, 1916; Mar. 6, 1916; Apr. 20, 1916; ends, Dec. 18, 1916.

Vereeniging, Treaty of, May 31, 1902.

Verga, Giovanni, Sep. 2, 1840.

Verger, Jan. 3, 1857.

Vergil, Oct. 15, B.C..

Verlaine, Paul, Mar. 30, 1844.

Vermeer, Jan, Oct. 30, 1632.

Vermont, Jan. 15, 1777; admitted to Union, Mar. 4, 1791.

vernacular languages: authorized use in all Roman Catholic churches, Nov. 21, 1963.

Vernal Equinox Day (Japan), Mar. intro.

Verne, Jules, Feb. 8, 1828.

Verrazano Day (New York), Apr. 7.

Verrazano-Narrows Bridge: opens, Nov. 21, 1964.

Versailles, May 16, 1770.

Versailles, Treaty of, signed, Jun. 28, 1919; ratified by Germany, Jul. 7, 1919; ratified by France, Oct. 13, 1919; ratified by Britain and Italy, Oct. 15, 1919; Japan ratifies Oct. 30, 1919; U.S. rejects Mar. 19, 1920.

Vertieres Day (Haiti), Nov. 18.

Vesalius, Andreas, Dec. 31, 1514.

Vestmannaeyjax (Iceland), Jan. 23, 1973.

Veterans Administration Act, Jul. 3, 1930.

Veterans Administration, U.S.: created, Jul. 3, 1930.

Veterans Day (France), Nov. 11.

Veterans Day (U.S., Guam, Puerto Rico, Virgin Islands), Nov. 11.

Vetsera, Marie, Jan. 30, 1889.

Veuster Joseph Damie de (Father Damien), Jan. 3, 1840.

Vickers, Jon, Oct. 29, 1926.

Vicksburg: surrenders, Jul. 4, 1863.

Vico, Giovanni Battista, Jun. 23, 1668.

Victims' Rights Week, National, Apr. intro.

Victor, Alfred, Mar. 27, 1797.

Victor Emmanuel (Italy), Mar. 23, 1849; Nov. 7, 1860; Mar. 17, 1861; dies Jan. 9, 1878.

Victor Emmanuel II, Mar. 31, 1861; Sep. 21, 1870.

Victor Emmanuel III (Italy), Nov. 11, 1869.

Victoria (Australia), Jul. 1, 1851.

Victoria Cross, Order of, Jan. 29, 1857.

Victoria Day (Poland), May 9.

Victoria Day (Scotland, Canada), May intro.

Victoria (England), May 24, 1819; Jun. 20, 1837; Feb. 10, 1840; May 1, 1876; Jan. 1, 1877; Jan. 14, 1878; golden jubilee, Jun. 21, 1887; dies, Jan. 22, 1901.

Victoria Falls: discovered, Nov. 17, 1855.

Victoria Falls Bridge, Apr. 11, 1905.

Victory Day, Nov. 11.

Victory Day (Bangladesh), Dec. 16.

Victory Day (Rhode Island), Aug. intro.

Victory Day (Tunisia), Jun. 2.

Victory Day (Turkey), Aug. 30.

Victory Day (U.S.S.R.), May 9.

Victory of Aduwa Day (Ethiopia), Mar. 2.

Victory of Uprona (Burundi), Sep. 18.

Vidal, Gore, Oct. 3, 1925.

Videla, Jorge Rafaél, Mar. 24, 1976; Mar. 29, 1976.

Vienna: Turkish siege of, Sep. 12, 1683.

Vienna, Mar. 13, 1938.

Vienna, Peace of: signed, Oct. 14, 1809; Oct. 30, 1864.

Vienna, Treaty of, Oct. 5, 1735.

Viet Cong, Jan. 6, 1967.

Viet-Minh, Jan. 19, 1951; Mar. 13, 1954.

Vietnam: Japanese attack French, Sep. 22, 1940; Jan. 29, 1950; Jan. 31, 1964; U.S. P.O.W.'s released, Mar. 29, 1973; end of U.S. presence, Apr. 29, 1975; unification, Apr. 25, 1976; last U.S. personnel are withdrawn, Jul. 20, 1976; admitted to U.N., Sep. 20, 1977; Chinese invasion, Feb. 17, 1979; Chinese troop withdrawal, Mar. 5, 1979.

Vietnam, Democratic Republic of, Sep. 2, 1945.

Vietnam, North, Jan. 10, 1969; Jan. 21, 1970; Jul. 2, 1976.

Vietnam, South, Jan. 26, 1965; U.S. combat activity first acknowledged, Jun. 5, 1965; Jan. 6, 1967; Sep. 3, 1967; Jul. 2, 1976.

Vietnam Veterans' Day (U.S.), Mar. 29.

Vietnam War, first U.S.-Viet Cong skirmish, Mar. 12, 1965; Jun. 23, 1966; Nov. 26, 1966; Jan. 6, 1967; Feb. 22, 1967; May 13, 1967; Jul. 29, 1967; U.S. casualties exceed those of Korean War, Mar. 14, 1968; Mar. 16, 1968; peace negotiations begin, May 13, 1968; Jul. 18, 1968; May 20, 1969; Sep. 27, 1969; Jan. 15, 1973; Cease Fire, Jan. 27, 1973; deserters clemency, Sep. 16, 1974; Mar. 26, 1975.

Vietnam War Memorial: groundbreaking, Mar. 26, 1982.

Vietnam War protest (N.Y), Apr. 15, 1967; Berkeley (California), May 15, 1969.

Vigil of the Nativity of Jesus Christ, Dec. 23.

Vigneaud, Vincent Du, May 18, 1901.

Viking 1, Jul. 20, 1976.

Viking 1, Jul. 26, 1976.

Viking 2, Sep. 3, 1976.

Vilas, Guillermo, Aug. 17, 1952.

V.I. Lenin Memorial Day (U.S.S.R.), Apr. 22.

Vilijoen, Marais, Dec. 2, 1915.

Villa, Celso Torrelio, Jun. 3, 1931.

Villa, Francisco (*Pancho*), Jun. 5, 1878; Mar. 15, 1916.

Villa-Lobos, Hector, Mar. 5, 1887.

Villard, Henry, Apr. 10, 1835.

Villard, Oswald Garrison, Mar. 13, 1872.

Villa Viciosa, Dec. 10, 1710.

Villella, Edward, Oct. 1, 1936.

Villiers, George (1st Duke of Buckingham), Aug. 28, 1592; assassinated, Aug. 23, 1628.

Villmergen, Battle of, Jul. 25, 1712.

Vilna (Poland), Jan. 5, 1919; Apr. 19, 1919; Apr. 18, 1922.

Vimiera, Battle of, Aug. 21, 1808.

Vimy Ridge, Apr. 9, 1917.

Vinaroz, Apr. 15, 1938.

Vincent, John Heyl, Feb. 23, 1832.

vine growers, patron of, Jun. 16.

Vinje, Aasmund Olavssen, Apr. 6, 1818.

Vinland Map: existence disclosed, Oct. 10, 1965.

Vinson, Carl, Nov. 18, 1883.

Vinson, Frederick Moore, Jan. 22, 1890.

vintners, patron of, Aug. 10.

violet, Feb. intro.

violinists, patron of, Feb. 12.

Virchow, Rudolph, Oct. 13, 1821.

Virgin Mary, Birthday of the Blessed Feast of, Sep. 8.

Virgin Islands: ceded to U.S., Aug. 4, 1916, Jan. 17, 1917.

Virginia, Charter of, Apr. 10, 1606.

Virginia, West: admitted to the Union, Jun. 20, 1863.

Virginia schools: desegregation, Feb. 2, 1959.

virginity, patron of, Jan. 21.

virgins, patron of, Nov. 3, Dec. 6.

Virgo, Aug. intro.; Sep. intro.

Virtanen, Artturi I., Jan. 15, 1895.

Visconti, Luchino, Nov. 2, 1906.

Visitation of the Virgin Mary, Feast of the, May 31.

Viticulturists Day (Bulgaria), Feb. 14.

Vitoria: French defeated by British, Jun. 21, 1813.

Vittorio Veneto, Oct. 28, 1871.

Vittorio Veneto, Battle of: begins, Oct. 25, 1918.

Vivaldi, Antonio, Mar. 4, 1678.

Vives, Juan Luis, Mar. 6, 1492.

V-J Day, Aug. 14, 1945.

Vladislav II (Poland), Jan. 9, 1493.

Vocation Awareness Week, National, Oct. intro.

Vocational Service Month, Oct. intro.

Voight, Jon, Dec. 29, 1938.

Volcker, Paul A., Sep. 5, 1927.

Volgograd (U.S.S.R), Nov. 11, 1961.

Volkov, Victor I., Jun. 30, 1971.

Volstead, Andrew Joseph, Oct. 31, 1860.

Volta, Conte Alessandro Giuseppe, Feb. 18, 1745.

Voltaire, François Marie Arouet de, Nov. 21, 1694.

Volunteers of America Week, Mar. intro.

Vonnegut, Kurt, Jr., Nov. 11, 1922.

Von Zell, Harry, Jul. 11, 1906.

Voroshilov, Kliment Efremovich, Feb. 4, 1881; Jan. 27, 1962.

Vorster, Balthazar Johannes, Dec. 13, 1915.

Voskhod: first multi-seat spacecraft, Oct. 13, 1964.

Voskhod 2, Mar. 18, 1965.

Vostok I, Apr. 12, 1961.

Vostok VI, Jun. 16, 1963.

voting age: lowered to 18 in U.S., Mar. 12, 1970.

Vow Day of the (South Africa), Dec. 16.

Voyager I, Mar. 1, 1979; Mar. 5, 1979.

Voyager 2: passes Saturn, Aug. 25, 1981; Feb. 2, 1982.

Vries, Hugo Marie De, Feb. 16, 1848.

Vuillard, (Jean) Edouard, Nov. 11, 1868.

W

Waals, Johannes D. van der, Nov. 23, 1837.

Works Progress Administration, Apr. 8, 1934.

World Council of Churches, Feb. 13, 1970.

World Development Information Day, Oct. 23.

World Environment Day, Jun. 5.

World Food Day, Oct. 16.

World Health Day, Apr. 7.

World Health Organization, Apr. 7, 1948.

World Maritime Day (UN Member Countries), Mar. 17.

World Meteorological Day (UN Member Countries), Mar. 23.

World Meteorological Organization: established, Mar. 23, 1950.

World Poetry Day, Oct. 15.

World Telecommunications Day, May 17.

World Understanding Month, Feb. intro.

World Youth Day (U.S.S.R.), Nov. 10.

Worms, City of, Jan. 18, 1074.

Worms, Concordat of, Sep. 23, 1122.

Worms, Diet of, Apr. 17, 1541.

Worms, Edict of, May 26, 1521.

Worms, Synod of, Jan. 24, 1076.

Worship and Doctrine Measure (Church of England), Dec. 4, 1974.

Worshipful Company of Parish Clerks of the City of London, patron of, Dec. 6.

Wouk, Herman, May 27, 1915.

Wounded Knee, Battle of, Dec. 29, 1890.

Wounded Knee (South Dakota), Feb. 27, 1973; Apr. 5, 1973; siege of May 8, 1973.

W particles, Jan. 26, 1983; Jun. 1, 1983.

Wrangel, Baron Petr Nikolayevich, Aug. 27, 1878.

Wrangel, Baron von, Dec. 29, 1796.

Wren, Sir Christopher, Oct. 20, 1632.

Wreyford, Ronald George, Nov. 9, 1897.

Wright, Frances (Fanny), Sep. 6, 1795.

Wright, Orville, Aug. 19, 1871.

Wright, Richard, Sep. 4, 1908.

Wright, Robert, Dec. 3, 1953.

Wright, Sir Almroth E., Aug. 10, 1861.

Wright, Wilbur, Apr. 16, 1867.

Wright Brothers, Dec. 17, 1903.

Wright Brothers Day (U.S.), Dec. 17.

Wrigley, P(hilip) K(night), Dec. 5, 1894.

Wrigley, William, Jr., Sep. 30, 1861.

Wriston, Walter Bigelow, Aug. 3, 1919.

Wundt, Wilhelm, Aug. 16, 1832.

Wurlitzer, Rudolph, Jan. 31, 1831.

Wyatt, James, Aug. 3, 1746.

Wycliffe, John, Nov. 5, 1414; Feb. 22, 1418.

Wyeth, Andrew, Jul. 12, 1917.

Wyler, William, Jul. 1, 1902.

Wylie, Philip, May 12, 1902.

Wynn, Ed, Nov. 9, 1886.

Wynn, Keenan, Jul. 27, 1916.

Wyoming, May 30, 1848; admitted to Union, Jul. 11, 1890.

Wyoming, Territory of: women's suffrage, Dec. 10, 1869.

Wyoming Day (Wyoming), Dec. 10.

Wyss, Johann Rudolf, Mar. 4, 1782.

Wyszynski, Stephen (Cardinal), Aug. 3, 1901; Jan. 8, 1966.

X

X, Malcolm, May 19, 1925.

X-15 rocket plane, Oct. 11, 1961.

Xavier, Saint Francis, Apr. 7, 1506.

xerographic image: first, Oct. 22, 1938.

X-ray treatment: breast cancer, Jan. 29, 1896.

Y

Yablonski, Joseph A., Jan. 5, 1970.

Yahya Khan, Agha Muhammad, Feb. 4, 1917.

Yale, Linus, Apr. 5, 1821.

Yale University, Dec. 10, 1896.

Yalow, Rosalyn, Jul. 19, 1921.

Yalta Conference: begins, Feb. 4, 1945; ends, Feb. 11, 1945.

Yamagata Aritomo, Jun. 14, 1838.

Yamamoto, Isoroku, Apr. 4, 1884.

Yamashita, Tomoyuki, Nov. 8, 1885; Dec. 7, 1945.

Yamato: sunk, Apr. 7, 1945.

Yang, Chen Ning, Sep. 22, 1922.

Yangtze, War Lord of, Apr. 21, 1922.

Yankee Clipper, Jun. 28, 1939.

Yankee Stadium: opens, Apr. 18, 1923.

Yarmouth, Jan. 19, 1915.

Yarmuk, Battle of, Aug. 20, 636.

Yarrow, Peter, May 31, 1938.

Yastrzemski, Carl, Aug. 22, 1939.

Yazykov, Nikolay, Mar. 16, 1803.

year, beginning of the, Jan. intro.; Mar. intro.

Yeats, William Butler, Jun. 13, 1865.

Yeh, George K(ung) C(hao), Sep. 12, 1904.

Yellowstone National Park: established, Mar. 1, 1872.

Yemen, Apr. 28, 1964.

Yemen, People's Republic of, Nov. 30, 1970.

Yerba Buena, Jan. 3, 1847.

Yerby, Frank (Garvin), Sep. 5, 1916.

yereah, p. ix.

Yerkes, Robert Merans, May 26, 1876.

Yevtushenko, Yevgeny Aleksandrovich, Jul. 18, 1933.

Yip, Yip, Yaphank: premiere, Aug. 19, 1918.

YMCA: organized, Jun. 6, 1844.

Yokohama (Japan), Sep. 1, 1923; Apr. 18, 1942.

Yokoi, Shoichi, Jan. 24, 1972.

Yom Ha' Azma'ut, p. xii; Apr. intro.; May intro.

Yom Kippur, p. x, xii; Sept. intro.; Oct. intro.

Yongchong (Korea), Sep. 6, 1950.

York, Alvin Cullum, Dec. 13, 1887.

York, Michael, Mar. 27, 1942.

York, Parliament of, May 2, 1322.

Yorktown, Oct. 19, 1781.

Yoshihito (Emperor of Japan): dies, Dec. 25, 1926.

Yost, Charles W(oodruff), Nov. 6, 1907.

Youman Nabi (Guyana), Jan. 19.

Youmans, Vincent (Millie), Sep. 27, 1898; Mar. 11, 1925.

Young, Andrew, Mar. 12, 1932; resigns, Aug. 15, 1979.

Young, Brigham, Jun. 1, 1801; Apr. 6, 1868.

Young, Cy, Mar. 29, 1867; May 5, 1904.

Young, Ella Flagg, Jan. 15, 1845.

Young, Gig, Nov. 4, 1917.

Young, John, Mar. 23, 1965; Jul. 21, 1966; Apr. 27, 1972.

Young, John (Watts), Sep. 24, 1930; Apr. 21, 1972.

Young, Lester, Aug. 27, 1909.

Young, Milton R., Dec. 6, 1897.

Young, Neil, Nov. 12, 1945.

Young, Robert, Feb. 22, 1907.

Young, Sheila, Oct. 14, 1950.

Young, Thomas, Jun. 13, 1773.

Young, Whitney Moore, Jr., Jul. 31, 1921.

Young Child, Week of the, Apr. intro.

young children, patron of, Mar. 7.

young girls, patron of, Jan. 21.

Young Men's Hebrew Association: first meeting, Mar. 22, 1847.

Young Turks, Jan. 23, 1913.

Youth Activities Month, Sep. intro.

Youth and Martyrs' Day (Nationalist China (Taiwan)), Mar. 29.

Youth and Sports Day (Turkey), May 19.

Youth Art Month, National, Mar. intro.

Youth Day (Cameroon), Feb. 11.

Youth Day (Oklahoma), Mar. intro.

Youth Day (Popular Republic of Benin), Apr. 1.

Youth Day (Taiwan), Mar. intro.

Youth Day (Upper Volta), Nov. 30.

Youth Day (Zambia), Mar. intro.; Mar. 14.

Ypres, First Battle of: opens, Oct. 19, 1914.

Ypres, Second Battle of, Apr. 22, 1915; May 25, 1915.

Yüan Shih-K'ai, Feb. 15, 1912; Mar. 10, 1912.

Yugoslavia: formation, Jul. 20, 1917; Apr. 20, 1920; Oct. 3, 1929; Mar. 24, 1941; German invasion, Apr. 6, 1941; National Front wins elections, Nov. 11, 1945; constitution, Jan. 31, 1946; expelled from Cominform, Jun. 28, 1948; Jan. 31, 1968; Feb. 6, 1970.

Yugoslavia, Federal People's Republic of, Nov. 29, 1945.

Yugoslavia, Socialist Federal Republic of, Apr. 7, 1963.

Yugoslav Republic Day (Yugoslavia), Apr. 7.

Yukawa, Hideki, Jan. 23, 1907.

Yukon Territory: formed, Jun. 13, 1898.

Yule, Dec. intro.

Yusef, Pasha of Tripoli, May 14, 1801.

YWCA Day, World, Apr. intro.

YWCA Teen Week, National, Oct. intro.

YWCA Week, National, Apr. intro.

Z

Zaharias, Babe Didrickson, Jun. 26, 1914.